America
Votes™ 30

America Votes™ 30

ELECTION RETURNS BY STATE

RHODES COOK

2011–2012

Los Angeles | London | New Delhi
Singapore | Washington DC

Los Angeles | London | New Delhi
Singapore | Washington DC

FOR INFORMATION:

CQ Press
An Imprint of SAGE Publications, Inc.
2455 Teller Road
Thousand Oaks, California 91320
E-mail: order@sagepub.com

SAGE Publications Ltd.
1 Oliver's Yard
55 City Road
London, EC1Y 1SP
United Kingdom

SAGE Publications India Pvt. Ltd.
B 1/I 1 Mohan Cooperative Industrial Area
Mathura Road, New Delhi 110 044
India

SAGE Publications Asia-Pacific Pte. Ltd.
3 Church Street
#10–04 Samsung Hub
Singapore 049483

Developmental Editor: John Martino
Editorial Assistant: Josh Benjamin
Production Editor: David C. Felts
Typesetter: Hurix Systems Pvt. Ltd., India
Proofreader: Sally Jaskold
Cover Designer: Michael Dubowe
Marketing Manager: Carmel Schrire

Printed in the United States of America.

ISSN: 0065-678X
ISBN: 978-1-45228-328-9

13 14 15 16 17 10 9 8 7 6 5 4 3 2 1

This book is printed on acid-free paper.

Contents

List of Maps

Introduction

If there is one word that might describe the electoral results in 2012, it is "reelected." President Barack Obama was reelected. So in a sense were the Democratic Senate and Republican House. At the state level, the GOP maintained its grip on the lion's share of the nation's governorships, while in state after state the parties already in control won even firmer legislative majorities.

Yet not all victories were of equal import. If the 2012 elections were the Academy Awards, Democrats walked off with Oscars for Best Picture, Best Director, and the major acting prizes, while the Republicans won in categories such as cinematography and costume design.

In short, it was an election of both triumph and relief for the Democrats, and one of frustration and disappointment for the GOP. As late as Election Day, many Republican leaders believed the party was well positioned to score a Washington trifecta by winning the White House and both houses of Congress. The fact that they fell short led the Republicans into a period of introspection and soul searching.

Exit polls showed Republicans winning the white vote as usual. But Democrats prevailed by mining the growing minority vote of Hispanics, African Americans, and Asians, and by constructing an effective outreach effort to get them to the polls.

The struggling economy, which had been an ongoing albatross for Obama during his first term, showed signs of improvement as 2012 unfolded. The favorable trend helped to mute what many figured was the Republicans' best issue.

And the incumbent once again proved to be an effective campaigner. After a poor performance in the first presidential debate with Republican rival Mitt Romney in early October, Obama fared well in the last two.

In the final week of the campaign, he was also able to demonstrate presidential leadership as Hurricane Sandy plowed a path of destruction through much of New Jersey and the New York City area. The disaster provided Obama an opportunity to show his ability to work with Republicans, as he conspicuously visited damage sites with the Garden State's prominent GOP governor, Chris Christie.

In the end, Obama needed all of these assets to register a victory that was far more modest in size than his initial triumph in 2008.

2012: Reelected

Democrats dominated the highest-profile races in 2012, reelecting President Barack H. Obama and retaining control of the Senate. Republicans did better in balloting for other parts of government where they enjoyed the advantage, holding the House of Representatives and expanding their already solid majority of governorships.

The chart below reflects partisan seat totals immediately before and after the 2012 general election. The preelection House totals include Democratic vacancies in California, New Jersey, and Washington, which are credited to the Democrats, and Republican vacancies in Kentucky and Michigan, which are credited to the GOP. Two Independent senators who caucused with the Democrats are listed in the "Other" column. Before the 2012 election, they were Joseph I. Lieberman of Connecticut and Bernard Sanders of Vermont. After the election, they were Angus King of Maine and Sanders. There was one Independent governor both before and after the 2012 election, Lincoln Chafee of Rhode Island (although he has since become a Democrat).

	Preelection			Postelection		
	Rep.	Dem.	Other	Rep.	Dem.	Other
Governor	29	20	1	30	19	1
Senate	47	51	2	45	53	2
House	242	193	0	234	201	0

The president's share of the total popular vote dropped from 53 percent in 2008 to 51 percent four years later. His margin of victory declined from 9.5 million votes to just under 5 million. And his electoral vote fell from 365 to 332. Obama's 2012 victory margin in percentage points over Republican nominee W. Mitt Romney—3.9—was the third-smallest for any reelected president. The only other presidents with closer second-term wins were Republican George W. Bush (2.4 percent) in 2004 and Democrat Woodrow Wilson (3.1 percent) in 1916.

Romney, like most other recent Republican presidential candidates, won the lion's share of the nation's more

Counting the 2012 Vote

Democrats experienced success in federal elections in 2012, especially in Senate races where they had an 11-million-vote advantage. Democrat Barack Obama was reelected by a margin of nearly 5 million votes; it was not as large as his 2008 victory, but still substantial. Even in the House, where the Republicans won a majority of seats, the Democrats opened up a 1.3-million-vote advantage, which was even larger in contested House races. The lone Republican bright spot was in gubernatorial elections, where they enjoyed an 700,000+ advantage.

No blank or void ballots are included in the totals below. They are based on official returns from 14 gubernatorial contests (11 held in 2012, 3 held in 2011) and 33 Senate races, as well as two versions of the House vote. "All Races" features the results from the districts in which a vote was taken in 2012, including those in which only one major party ran a candidate. "Contested Races" are those in which both the Democrats and Republicans fielded candidates. There were 310 contested House races in 2012, of which the Republicans won 209 compared to 181 for the Democrats.

| Office | Total Vote | Republican | Democratic | Other | Rep.-Dem. Plurality | | Percentage of Total Vote | | |
							Rep.	Dem.	Other
President	129,085,474	60,933,500	65,915,796	2,236,178	4,982,296	D	47.2%	51.1%	1.7%
Governor	19,453,775	9,817,812	9,093,589	542,374	724,223	R	50.5%	46.7%	2.8%
Senate	93,061,498	39,418,955	50,424,353	3,218,190	11,005,398	D	42.4%	54.2%	3.4%
House									
All Races	121,351,579	58,285,212	59,653,081	3,413,286	1,367,869	D	48.0%	49.2%	5.9%
Contested Races	111,762,702	53,581,539	56,026,044	2,155,119	2,444,505	D	47.9%	50.1%	4.0%

2012: Close House Races

The volume of highly competitive House races in 2012 dropped significantly from two years earlier, as the number of winners with less than 52 percent of the total vote fell from 55 in 2010 to 33 in 2012. This was in spite of the decennial round of congressional redistricting before the latter election that changed district lines at least to some degree throughout the country. An asterisk (*) indicates an incumbent.

Republicans (14)	2012 Winning Percentage	Democrats (19)	2012 Winning Percentage
Rodney Davis, Ill. 13	46.5%	John F. Tierney, Mass. 6*	48.3%
Mike Coffman, Colo. 6*	47.8%	Kyrsten Sinema, Ariz. 9	48.7%
Dan Benishek, Mich. 1*	48.1%	Ann Kirkpatrick, Ariz. 1	48.8%
Jackie Walorski, Ind. 2	49.0%	Daniel B. Maffei, N.Y. 24	48.8%
Joe Heck, Nev. 3*	50.4%	Jim Matheson, Utah 4*	48.8%
Michele Bachmann, Minn. 6*	50.5%	Carol Shea-Porter, N.H. 1	49.8%
Garland "Andy" Barr, Ky. 6	50.6%	Mike McIntyre, N.C. 7*	50.1%
Kerry Bentivolio, Mich. 11	50.8%	Steven A. Horsford, Nev. 4	50.1%
Chris Collins, N.Y. 27	50.8%	William L. Owens, N.Y. 21*	50.1%
Lee Terry, Neb. 2*	50.8%	Ann McLane Kuster, N.H. 2	50.2%
Daniel Webster, Fla. 10*	51.7%	Patrick Murphy, Fla. 18	50.3%
Keith Rothfus, Pa. 12	51.7%	Pete P. Gallego, Texas 23	50.3%
Robert Pittenger, N.C. 9	51.8%	Ron Barber, Ariz. 2*	50.4%
Thomas W. Reed II, N.Y. 23*	51.9%	Brad Schneider, Ill. 10	50.6%
		Scott Peters, Calif. 52	51.2%
		Elizabeth Esty, Conn. 5	51.3%
		William Enyart, Ill. 12	51.7%
		Ami Bera, Calif. 7	51.7%
		Sean Patrick Maloney, N.Y. 18	51.9%

than 3,100 counties (and similar jurisdictions, such as independent cities). His total of roughly 2,450 counties was more than three times the number carried by the incumbent.

But Obama, like other recent Democratic nominees, won where it counted. Of the 39 counties with a population in excess of 1 million, the president took 35. They provided him with a margin of nearly 8 million votes, trumping Romney's edge of roughly 3 million votes in the rest of the country.

After a century in which presidential landslides were frequent, the 2012 contest was the third in the last four to be decided in the popular vote by less than 5 percentage points. Yet only four states were decided by a margin so small.

Florida was the closest, going to Obama by nine-tenths of a percentage point. Romney won North Carolina by 2.0 points, while Obama prevailed in Ohio by 3.0 points and Virginia by 3.9.

That's it. As presidential elections have grown closer of late, the number of competitive states has shrunk dramatically. It is a far cry from how it used to be, when much more of the electoral map was in play. In the tightly contested race in 1960 between Democrat John F. Kennedy and Republican Richard Nixon, 20 states were decided by less than 5 percentage points. By 2000, the number of such competitive states was down to a dozen, even though the election was a closely fought "split decision." Republican George W. Bush narrowly won the electoral vote while Democrat Al Gore took the popular vote.

The House Since 1990: A Political Weathervane

Control of the House of Representatives has swung back and forth over the last two decades. It went from the Democrats to the Republicans in 1994, back to the Democrats in 2006, before the House reverted to the GOP in 2010. It stayed in Republican hands in 2012. The cornerstone of the GOP congressional majority is the South, where they hold nearly three-quarters of all House seats. Republicans also have a decided advantage in the Midwest. Democrats control a majority of House seats in the East and the West. Regions are defined below. An "I" indicates Independent.

	South				West			Midwest			East				Total House			
	R	D	I		R	D		R	D		R	D	I		R	D	I	
1990	44	85	0	D	37	48	D	45	68	D	41	66	1	D	167	267	1	D
1992	52	85	0	D	38	55	D	44	61	D	42	57	1	D	176	258	1	D
1994	73	64	0	R	53	40	R	59	46	R	45	54	1	D	230	204	1	R
1996	82	55	0	R	51	42	R	55	50	R	39	60	1	D	227	207	1	R
1998	82	55	0	R	49	44	R	54	51	R	38	61	1	D	223	211	1	R
2000	81	55	1	R	43	50	D	57	48	R	40	59	1	D	221	212	2	R
2002	85	57	0	R	46	52	D	61	39	R	37	57	1	D	229	205	1	R
2004	91	51	0	R	45	53	D	60	40	R	36	58	1	D	232	202	1	R
2006	85	57	0	R	41	57	D	51	49	R	25	70	0	D	202	233	0	D
2008	80	62	0	R	35	63	D	45	55	D	18	77	0	D	178	257	0	D
2010	102	40	0	R	43	55	D	65	35	R	32	63	0	D	242	193	0	R
2012	108	41	0	R	39	63	D	59	35	R	28	62	0	D	234	201	0	R
Net Change in GOP Seats, 1994-2012	+ 35				− 14			0			− 17				+ 4			

EAST - Connecticut, Delaware, Maine, Maryland, Massachusetts, New Hampshire, New Jersey, New York, Pennsylvania, Rhode Island, Vermont, West Virginia.

MIDWEST - Illinois, Indiana, Iowa, Kansas, Michigan, Minnesota, Missouri, Nebraska, North Dakota, Ohio, South Dakota, Wisconsin.

SOUTH - Alabama, Arkansas, Florida, Georgia, Kentucky, Louisiana, Mississippi, North Carolina, Oklahoma, South Carolina, Tennessee, Texas, Virginia.

WEST - Alaska, Arizona, California, Colorado, Hawaii, Idaho, Montana, Nevada, New Mexico, Oregon, Utah, Washington, Wyoming.

Since then, the total number of states decided by less than 5 points has plummeted further—to 11 in 2004, six in 2008, and four in 2012.

Why the decline? An obvious reason is the increased polarization in the nation's voting. States do not swing back and forth *en masse* as they used to. Presidential election maps over the last two decades have largely featured the states of the Northeast and Pacific West shaded Democratic blue, and those of the heartland colored Republican red. Not surprisingly, nearly four times as many states were won in 2012 by supermajorities of at least 60 percent of the total vote—15—than were decided by less than 5 points. In the end, after the expenditure of hundreds of millions of dollars, just two states switched party hands. Indiana and North Carolina returned to the GOP electoral vote column after a brief flirtation with Obama in 2008.

It was definitely a "status quo" election at the gubernatorial and congressional levels as well. Republicans gained one of the 11 governorships at stake in 2012 to increase their nationwide total to 30. Meanwhile, both Senate Democrats and House Republicans maintained their solid majorities on Capitol Hill, with the former showing a net gain of two seats while the latter easily weathered modest Democratic inroads.

In a year that they had to defend 21 of 33 seats, Senate Democrats not only survived, but thrived. Meanwhile, House Republicans retained their advantage, primarily by dominating the redistricting process in many states where they had taken control of the levers of power in 2010. The GOP was so effective in their line drawing that they won 33 more House seats than the Democrats in 2012, even though the latter won more than one and a third million more votes in the aggregate nationwide tally of House elections.

On the Senate side, there was no such disparity. Democratic candidates for the upper chamber won roughly 11 million more votes than their GOP counterparts. It was a sizable advantage that was reflected in the Senate results, which culminated with the Democrats holding 53 seats, the Republicans 45, and two independents who caucus with the Democrats.

2012: Defeated Incumbents

The conventional wisdom of late is that members of Congress are more vulnerable in ideologically driven primaries than in the relatively safe confines of general elections, where in many districts one party or the other frequently boasts a decided advantage. But in recent elections, that has not been the case. In 2010 and 2012 combined, 81 House members were defeated in general elections compared to 17 who lost their seats through primary losses. In 2012 alone, 27 House incumbents lost in the fall, compared to 13 who were ousted in their party's primary. In 2010, the losses were almost exclusively on the Democratic side. In 2012, House incumbents of both parties were defeated, in large part a mixture of freshmen Republicans and longer-serving Democrats. The latest round of congressional redistricting fueled the volatility in 2012, with a number of House incumbents paired against a congressional colleague in either the primary or general election.

The chart below lists the Senate and House incumbents defeated in the 2012 primaries and general election, the number of full terms in office they were completing at the time of their loss in 2012, the percentage of the total vote they had received in the previous general election (2006 for senators and 2010 for House members), and their percentage of the total vote in the 2012 general election (for those who were not sidelined by the primaries). No sitting governors were defeated for renomination or reelection in 2012. Only two incumbent senators lost, veteran Republican Richard G. Lugar of Indiana in the primaries and a relative newcomer, Scott P. Brown of Massachusetts, in the general election. The "Previous Election Percentage" listed for Brown reflects the result of a January 2010 special election.

	Number of Terms	Previous Election Percentage	2012 Election Percentage
GOVERNORS (0)			
SENATORS (2)			
Primaries (1)			
(1 Republican)			
Richard G. Lugar, R-Ind.	6	87.4%	—
General Election (1)			
(1 Republican)			
Scott P. Brown, R-Mass.	@	51.9%	46.2%
REPRESENTATIVES (40)			
Primaries (13)			
(7 Democrats, 6 Republicans)			
Sandra "Sandy" Adams, R-Fla. 7#	1	59.6%	—
Jason Altmire, D-Pa. 12#	3	50.8%	—
Russ Carnahan, D-Mo. 1#	4	48.9%	—
Hansen Clarke, D-Mich. 14#	1	79.4%	—
Tim Holden, D-Pa. 17	10	55.5%	—
Dennis J. Kucinich, D-Ohio 9#	8	53.1%	—
Donald Manzullo, R-Ill. 16#	10	65.0%	—

	Number of Terms	Previous Election Percentage	2012 Election Percentage
Ben Quayle, R-Ariz. 6#	1	52.2%	—
Silvestre Reyes, D-Texas 16	8	58.1%	—
Steven R. Rothman, D-N.J. 9#	8	60.7%	—
Jean Schmidt, R-Ohio 2	3	58.5%	—
Clifford B. "Cliff" Stearns, R-Fla. 3	12	71.5%	—
John Sullivan, R-Okla. 1	5	76.8%	—
General Election (27)			
(17 Republicans, 10 Democrats)			
Joe Baca, D-Calif.35	6	65.5%	44.1%
Roscoe G. Bartlett, R-Md. 6	10	61.4%	37.9%
Charles Bass, R-N.H. 2	7	48.3%	45.3%
Howard L. Berman, D-Calif. 30#	15	69.5%	39.7%
Judy Biggert, R-Ill. 11	7	63.8%	41.4%
Brian P. Bilbray, R-Calif. 52	6	56.7%	48.8%
Leonard L. Boswell, D-Iowa 3#	8	50.7%	43.6%
Ann Marie Buerkle, R-N.Y. 24	1	50.1%	43.4%
Francisco "Quico" Canseco, R-Texas 23	1	49.4%	45.6%
Ben Chandler, D-Ky. 6	4	50.1%	46.7%
Chip Cravaack, R-Minn. 8	1	48.2%	45.4%
Mark S. Critz, D-Pa. 12	1	50.8%	48.3%
Robert Dold, R-Ill. 10	1	51.1%	49.4%
Frank C. Guinta, R-N.H. 1	1	54.0%	46.0%
Nan Hayworth, R-N.Y. 18	1	52.6%	48.0%
Kathy Courtney Hochul, D-N.Y. 27	@	47.3%**	49.2%
Larry Kissell, D-N.C. 8	2	53.0%	45.4%
Jeff Landry, R-La. 3#	1	63.8%	39.1%*
Dan Lungren, R-Calif. 7	9	50.1%	48.3%
Mary Bono Mack, R-Calif. 36	7	51.5%	47.1%
Laura Richardson, D-Calif. 44#	2	68.4%	39.8%
David Rivera, R-Fla. 26	1	52.1%	43.0%
Bobby Schilling, R-Ill. 17	1	52.6%	46.7%
Fortney Pete Stark, D-Calif. 15	20	72.0%	47.9%
Betty Sutton, D-Ohio 16#	3	55.7%	48.0%
Joe Walsh, R-Ill. 8	1	48.5%	45.3%
Allen West, R-Fla. 18	1	54.4%	49.7%

Note: A pound sign (#) indicates that the losing House member was paired against another incumbent in 2012 due to redistricting. An asterisk (*) denotes that the 2012 percentage for Rep. Jeff Landry (R-La. 3) was based on a December 2012 runoff election. @ indicates that the member was elected in a special election and had not served a full term at the time they were defeated. The double asterisk (**) denotes that the previous percentage for Kathy Hochul (D-NY 27) was the 2011 special election she won.

Democrats won all but one of the 21 Senate seats they were defending, losing only the open Nebraska seat being vacated by Ben Nelson.

Meanwhile, Republicans dropped three of the 10 seats that they sought to hold. GOP incumbent Scott P. Brown lost to Democrat Elizabeth Warren in "deep blue" Massachusetts. In Maine, Republicans could not retain the seat being vacated by Olympia Snowe, as the state's popular former governor, Angus King, won handily running as an independent. And in Indiana, the Senate seat opened by the primary defeat of veteran Republican incumbent Richard G. Lugar fell to Democrat Joseph S. Donnelly.

For much of the year, the Indiana race looked as though it was Republican Richard Mourdock's to lose. And he did, after making controversial comments about rape that sent his candidacy into free fall. Mourdock's demise mirrored that of Republican Todd Akin in Missouri, whose similar comments on the subject undermined what appeared to be a winnable challenge to embattled Democratic Sen. Claire McCaskill.

All in all, what began as a very promising year for Senate Republicans ended up as a major source of frustration.

On the House side, the Republican victory was based on two basic factors: their success in states where they controlled the congressional redistricting process and their dominance in the South. Republicans won 67 more House seats in the South than Democrats (108 to 41). In the rest of the country, Democrats had an edge of 34 seats (160 to 126).

The GOP's ace in the hole was their control of the post-2010 redistricting process in a number of states, especially in the industrial Frost Belt. Democratic House candidates drew more aggregate votes than their Republican counterparts in Michigan, Pennsylvania, and Wisconsin, and ran close to even with the GOP in Ohio.

All were states carried by Obama both times he ran, but Republicans controlled the redistricting in all of them, and drew new lines that helped the GOP win the bulk of the House seats in each in 2012. Republicans captured 13 of 18 seats in Pennsylvania, 12 of 16 in Ohio, nine of 14 in Michigan, and five of eight in Wisconsin. Added together, that was 39 seats for the Republicans and 17 seats for the Democrats in the four pro-Obama states.

The key to GOP congressional success was to cluster the Democratic vote into a handful of districts, while spreading out the Republican vote elsewhere. In Pennsylvania, for example, Republicans won nine of their 13 House seats with less than 60 percent of the vote, while Democrats carried three of their five with more than 75 percent.

As it was, Democrats scored a moral victory of sorts by winning the aggregate nationwide House vote. Normally, that does not have much currency, a matter of interest only to academics and political mavens. But in 2012, the Democrats' "popular vote" victory in the House balloting helped to undermine the contention of congressional Republicans that their majority was as much a popular mandate as President Obama's nearly 5-million-vote, 26-state, 332-electoral-vote reelection victory.

The Methodology

The thirtieth volume of *America Votes* follows the same general pattern of recent editions in this series. An introduction with text and tables ties together various aspects of the 2012 election cycle. The section that follows presents national tables with voter turnout and votes for presidential, gubernatorial, Senate, and House elections by state in the 2012 election cycle. Also featured are a summary of special elections held between the general elections of 2010 and 2012 to fill vacancies in the 112th Congress and a list of changes in congressional membership in the 113th Congress that occurred between the 2012 general election and August 15, 2013. The heart of the volume, 51 chapters—one for each state and the District of Columbia—follows this introductory material.

Each state chapter begins with a profile listing the current governor, senators, and representatives, followed by tables of the statewide vote for president, governor, and senator from 1946 or 1948 (in essence, the end of World War II) to the present. A map of the state shows its counties, major population centers, and congressional districts for members of the House in the 113th Congress. County-by-county tables of presidential, gubernatorial, and Senate elections follow the maps. All these tables are from the 2012 general election with the exception of the governorships in Kentucky, Louisiana, and Mississippi, where voting took place in 2011.

The county tables for presidential, gubernatorial, and Senate elections feature a three-column format of candidates (Republican, Democratic, Other). Exceptions occur where another candidate has received at least 10 percent of the statewide vote, in which case a column for his or her votes is also included. All the county tables include 2010 population figures from the Census Bureau.

A listing of votes cast for candidates for the House of Representatives is arranged by congressional district. The implementation of the 2010 Census for redistricting purposes led to changes in all states with more than one House member before the 2012 election. House results for elections before 2012 are not included for any state except those with a single member in the House.

The conclusion of each state chapter consists of two parts. The first part is a notes section containing a breakdown of votes cast in the general election for third party, independent, and write-in candidates who had their vote tabulated. The total of scattered write-in votes is also listed in states where they were included in the official returns. For those major party candidates who also ran on a third party ballot line, votes are aggregated as Democratic or Republican. Blank space in a column indicates that no votes were cast. The second part provides official results for the primary elections for president, governor, Senate, and House held in the 2012 election cycle.

In the chapters for New England states, tables list the vote for president, governor, and senator by larger cities and towns as well as by counties. In Rhode Island, the results are listed for all cities and towns.

The America Votes series is compiled from official results obtained from election authorities in each state. Although complete accuracy is always the goal, it can sometimes prove elusive in a work such as this. On occasion, states may belatedly report changes in their vote totals that occur after publication of this volume, and human nature being what it is, there is always an example or two (or three) of self-inflicted errors. The goal is always to keep these to a minimum. In light of the desire to make these reference volumes as useful as possible to readers and researchers, corrections of data are always welcome as are suggestions for new material.

The creation of each edition in this series has always taken the proverbial village. This time, though, more like a small city was required. John Martino, the Development Editor at CQ Press, deserves special thanks. He worked with a talented staff of colleagues (Violaine Iglesias, Joshua Benjamin, Matt Herb, Sal Hewavita, Andre Messier, Ed Moore, Luke Maury, and Lorna Notsch) who played a pivotal role in keeping this edition of *America Votes* on course toward publication. That was particularly necessary this summer when the author was sidelined for nearly two months as he recovered from surgery.

John also worked effectively with the book's compositors and David C. Felts, the Project Editor at CQ Press's parent company, SAGE Publications, to produce a volume that is both clean in presentation and as accurate as possible in its plethora of data.

As in the preparation of other recent editions of *America Votes* thanks are also in order to Eileen J. Leamon, the Deputy Assistant Staff Director for Disclosure at the Federal Election Commission (FEC). She oversees the FEC's biennial compilation of primary and general election results for federal races, which over the years has provided an important safety net in the compilation of data for *America Votes*.

As a final note, the author would like to dedicate this edition to Dr. Roland Radloff, a long-time friend with whom he has shared an interest in electoral politics for the last third of a century. Rollin's suggestions, guidance, and ongoing support have been greatly treasured.

Rhodes Cook
October 2013

UNITED STATES
VOTER TURNOUT 2012

State	2012 Voting Age Population	Registration– 2012 General Election	Percent Voting Age Registered	Presidential Vote	Presidential Vote as Percentage of Voting Age Population	Presidential Vote as Percentage of Registered Voters	House Vote	Senate Vote	Governor Vote
Alabama	3,600,000	3,162,135	87.8%	2,074,338	57.6%	65.6%	1,933,630	—	—
Alaska	517,000	506,434	98.0%	300,495	58.1%	59.3%	289,804	—	—
Arizona	4,472,000	3,725,362	83.3%	2,299,254	51.4%	61.7%	2,173,317	2,243,422	—
Arkansas	2,160,000	1,618,548	74.9%	1,069,468	49.5%	66.1%	1,038,054	—	—
California	23,572,000	18,245,970	77.4%	13,038,547	55.3%	71.5%	12,204,357	12,578,511	—
Colorado	3,635,000	3,645,274	100.3%	2,569,522	70.7%	70.5%	2,450,839	—	—
Connecticut	2,547,000	2,218,662	87.1%	1,558,960	61.2%	70.3%	1,466,511	1,511,764	—
Delaware	678,000	626,349	92.4%	413,921	61.1%	66.1%	388,059	399,607	398,033
Florida	13,542,000	11,934,446	88.1%	8,474,179	62.6%	71.0%	7,513,539	8,189,946	—
Georgia	6,865,000	5,428,980	79.1%	3,900,050	56.8%	71.8%	3,553,587	—	—
Hawaii	986,000	705,668	71.6%	434,697	44.1%	61.6%	422,539	430,483	—
Idaho	1,133,000	895,834	79.1%	652,346	57.6%	72.8%	635,218	—	—
Illinois	8,887,000	8,586,521	96.6%	5,242,014	59.0%	61.0%	5,058,133	—	—
Indiana	4,775,000	4,555,257	95.4%	2,624,534	55.0%	57.6%	2,553,746	2,560,102	2,577,329
Iowa	2,264,000	2,166,539	95.7%	1,582,180	69.9%	73.0%	1,536,849	—	—
Kansas	2,038,000	1,771,252	86.9%	1,159,971	56.9%	65.5%	1,057,739	—	—
Kentucky	3,286,000	3,037,153	92.4%	1,797,212	54.7%	59.2%	1,745,377	—	833,139
Louisiana	3,343,000	2,962,999	88.6%	1,994,065	59.6%	67.3%	1,705,617	—	1,023,163
Maine	1,054,000	963,152	91.4%	713,180	67.7%	74.0%	693,801	700,599	—
Maryland	4,096,000	3,694,527	90.2%	2,707,327	66.1%	73.3%	2,585,514	2,633,234	—
Massachussetts	4,700,000	4,342,841	92.4%	3,167,767	67.4%	72.9%	2,891,434	3,156,553	—
Michigan	7,317,000	7,454,553	101.9%	4,730,961	64.7%	63.5%	4,574,632	4,652,918	—
Minnesota	3,915,000	3,084,344	78.8%	2,936,561	75.0%	95.2%	2,813,383	2,843,207	—
Mississippi	2,203,000	1,905,605	86.5%	1,285,584	58.4%	67.5%	1,208,175	1,241,568	893,468
Missouri	4,525,000	4,180,659	92.4%	2,757,323	60.9%	66.0%	2,675,900	2,725,793	2,727,883
Montana	779,000	681,608	87.5%	484,048	62.1%	71.0%	479,740	486,066	483,489
Nebraska	1,330,000	1,163,871	87.5%	794,379	59.7%	68.3%	772,515	788,572	—
Nevada	1,869,000	1,257,621	67.3%	1,014,918	54.3%	80.7%	973,742	997,805	—
New Hampshire	1,022,000	791,434	77.4%	710,972	69.6%	89.8%	682,416	—	693,877
New Jersey	5,944,000	5,497,322	92.5%	3,640,292	61.2%	66.2%	3,281,954	3,374,668	—
New Mexico	1,463,000	1,255,273	85.8%	783,757	53.6%	62.4%	766,090	775,792	—
New York	13,302,000	11,969,192	90.0%	7,081,159	53.2%	59.2%	6,469,725	6,679,678	—
North Carolina	7,030,000	6,706,592	95.4%	4,505,372	64.1%	67.2%	4,384,112	—	4,468,295
North Dakota	523,000	See Notes	See Notes	322,627	See Notes	See Notes	316,071	320,851	317,812
Ohio	8,658,000	7,987,697	92.3%	5,580,840	64.5%	69.9%	5,140,574	5,449,114	—
Oklahoma	2,748,000	2,114,713	77.0%	1,334,872	48.6%	63.1%	1,325,935	—	—
Oregon	2,832,000	2,212,592	78.1%	1,789,270	63.2%	80.9%	1,708,168	—	—
Pennsylvania	9,677,000	8,503,377	87.9%	5,753,670	59.5%	67.7%	5,556,330	5,629,491	—
Rhode Island	768,000	725,309	94.4%	446,049	58.1%	61.5%	427,775	418,189	—
South Carolina	3,512,000	2,820,774	80.3%	1,964,118	55.9%	69.6%	1,802,734	—	—
South Dakota	613,000	531,664	86.7%	363,815	59.3%	68.4%	361,429	—	—
Tennessee	4,787,000	3,905,974	81.6%	2,458,577	51.4%	62.9%	2,283,727	2,321,477	—
Texas	16,302,000	13,646,226	83.7%	7,993,851	49.0%	58.6%	7,664,208	7,864,822	—
Utah	1,840,000	1,513,241	82.2%	1,017,440	55.3%	67.2%	998,897	1,006,901	1,006,524
Vermont	496,000	461,237	93.0%	299,290	60.3%	64.9%	289,931	294,267	295,261
Virginia	5,844,000	5,428,833	92.9%	3,854,489	66.0%	71.0%	3,740,455	3,802,196	—
Washington	4,861,000	4,335,775	89.2%	3,125,516	64.3%	72.1%	3,006,266	3,069,417	3,071,047
West Virginia	1,467,000	1,234,367	84.1%	670,438	45.7%	54.3%	641,354	660,212	664,455
Wisconsin	4,283,000	3,501,045	81.7%	3,068,434	71.6%	87.6%	2,866,050	3,009,411	—
Wyoming	435,000	240,438	55.3%	249,061	57.3%	103.6%	241,621	244,862	—
District of Columbia	464,000	501,535	108.1%	293,764	63.3%	58.6%	See Notes	—	—
Total	218,959,000	190,406,774	87.2%	129,085,474	58.9%	67.6%	121,351,573	93,061,498	19,453,775

Source: Registration and voting age population (VAP) figures were provided by the Center for the Study of the American Electorate. VAP figures are based on estimated numbers of citizens of voting age in each state (and nationally) at the time of the November 2012 general election. Figures do not account for felony or other forms of disenfranchisement. They also do not account for those living outside of the United States and those naturalized in 2012, both of which are enfranchised but not counted in the Census enumeration of age-eligible citizens. Registration figures must be viewed with significant caution. Some states give only "active" registration figures, while others include inactive voters as well, and both types of states include invalid registrations. These inaccuracies as well as estimations mean that some states have a registration number that is more than 100% of the VAP. North Dakota does not require voter registration. For more details on registration, consult the Election Assistance Commission's Election Administration and Voting Survey.

Notes: Does not include special elections or elections for non-voting delegates (such as the 278,563 votes for House delegate in the District of Columbia). The gubernatorial vote includes 2011 elections in Kentucky, Louisiana, and Mississippi. Includes vote totals for general election House races in Louisiana; does not include runoff votes in 3rd district. Because North Dakota does not conduct voter registration, the percentage of voting-age population registered and the presidential vote as percentage of registered voters exclude North Dakota.

GUBERNATORIAL ELECTIONS 2011 AND 2012

State	Total Vote	Republican		Democratic		Other Vote	Rep.-Dem. Plurality	Percentage Total Vote Rep.	Dem.	Major Vote Rep.	Dem.
		Vote	Candidate	Vote	Candidate						
Delaware	398,033	113,793	Cragg, Jeffrey	275,993	Markell, Jack	8,247	162,200 D	28.6%	69.3%	29.2%	70.8%
Indiana	2,577,329	1,275,424	Pence, Mike	1,200,016	Gregg, John R.	101,889	75,408 R	49.5%	46.6%	51.5%	48.5%
Kentucky (2011)	833,139	294,034	Williams, David Lynn	464,245	Beshear, Steven L.	74,860	170,211 D	35.3%	55.7%	38.8%	61.2%
Louisiana (2011)	1,023,163	673,239	Jindal, Bobby	288,161	Hollis, Tara (+ 3 others)	61,763	385,078 R	65.8%	28.2%	70.0%	30.0%
Mississippi (2011)	893,468	544,851	Bryant, Phil	348,617	Dupree, Johnny L.		196,234 R	61.0%	39.0%	61.0%	39.0%
Missouri	2,727,883	1,160,265	Spence, David "Dave"	1,494,056	Nixon, Jeremiah W. "Jay"	73,562	331,791 D	42.5%	54.8%	43.7%	56.3%
Montana	483,489	228,879	Hill, Rick	236,450	Bullock, Steve	18,160	7,571 D	47.3%	48.9%	49.2%	50.8%
New Hampshire	693,877	295,026	Lamontagne, Ovide M.	378,934	Hassan, Maggie	19,917	83,908 D	42.5%	54.6%	43.8%	56.2%
North Carolina	4,468,295	2,440,707	McCrory, Pat	1,931,580	Dalton, Walter H.	96,008	509,127 R	54.6%	43.2%	55.8%	44.2%
North Dakota	317,812	200,526	Dalrymple, Jack	109,047	Taylor, Ryan M.	8,239	91,479 R	63.1%	34.3%	64.8%	35.2%
Utah	1,006,524	688,592	Herbert, Gary R.	277,622	Cooke, Peter S.	40,310	410,970 R	68.4%	27.6%	71.3%	28.7%
Vermont	295,261	110,940	Brock, Randy	170,598	Shumlin, Peter	13,723	59,658 D	37.6%	57.8%	39.4%	60.6%
Washington	3,071,047	1,488,245	McKenna, Rob	1,582,802	Inslee, Jay		94,557 D	48.5%	51.5%	48.5%	51.5%
West Virginia	664,455	303,291	Maloney, Bill	335,468	Tomblin, Earl Ray	25,696	32,177 D	45.6%	50.5%	47.5%	52.5%
Total	19,453,775	9,817,812		9,093,589		542,374	724,223 R	50.5%	46.7%	51.9%	48.1%

Notes: Does not include special elections. The gubernatorial vote includes 2011 elections in Kentucky, Louisiana, and Mississippi; it does not include special gubernatorial elections in West Virginia (2011) or Wisconsin (2012). No independent or third-party candidate finished first or second or garnered more than 5% in any gubernatorial race nationwide. Louisiana has a unique election system for many offices, including governor. All candidates, regardless of party, appeared together on the October 22, 2011, ballot. If the highest vote-getter, Bobby Jindal, had not won a majority of the votes, there would have been a run-off between the top two vote-getters. In fact, Jindal, the only Republican on the ballot, received 673,239 votes, good for 65.8% of the vote. There were four Democratic candidates, garnering a combined 288,161 votes (28.2% of the total). Jindal's plurality is measured over the four Democratic candidates combined; the runner-up, Tara Hollis, received 182,925 votes, good for 17% of the total vote. No other candidate in the race received more than 5% of the vote. The nationwide Democratic gubernatorial vote includes the combined vote for the four Democratic gubernatorial candidates in Louisiana.

SENATE ELECTIONS 2012

State	Total Vote	Republican Vote	Candidate	Democratic Vote	Candidate	Other Vote	Plurality	Total Vote Rep.	Total Vote Dem.	Major Vote Rep.	Major Vote Dem.
Arizona	2,243,422	1,104,457	Flake, Jeff	1,036,542	Carmona, Richard	102,423	67,915 R	49.2%	46.2%	51.6%	48.4%
California	12,578,511	4,713,887	Emken, Elizabeth	7,864,624	Feinstein, Dianne		3,150,737 D	37.5%	62.5%	37.5%	62.5%
Connecticut	1,511,764	651,089	McMahon, Linda E.	828,761	Murphy, Christopher S.	31,914	177,672 D	43.1%	54.8%	44.0%	56.0%
Delaware	399,607	115,700	Wade, Kevin	265,415	Carper, Thomas R.	18,492	149,715 D	29.0%	66.4%	30.4%	69.6%
Florida	8,189,946	3,458,267	Mack, Connie IV	4,523,451	Nelson, Bill	208,228	1,065,184 D	42.2%	55.2%	43.3%	56.7%
Hawaii	430,483	160,994	Lingle, Linda	269,489	Hirono, Mazie K.		108,495 D	37.4%	62.6%	37.4%	62.6%
Indiana	2,560,102	1,133,621	Mourdock, Richard E.	1,281,181	Donnelly, Joseph S.	145,300	147,560 D	44.3%	50.0%	46.9%	53.1%
Maine	700,599	215,399	Summers, Charles E.	92,900	Dill, Cynthia Ann	392,300	155,181 I	30.7%	13.3%	69.9%	30.1%
Maryland	2,633,234	693,291	Bongino, Daniel John	1,474,028	Cardin, Benjamin L.	465,915	780,737 D	26.3%	56.0%	32.0%	68.0%
Massachusetts	3,156,553	1,458,048	Brown, Scott P.	1,696,346	Warren, Elizabeth	2,159	238,298 D	46.2%	53.7%	46.2%	53.8%
Michigan	4,652,918	1,767,386	Hoekstra, Peter	2,735,826	Stabenow, Debbie	149,706	968,440 D	38.0%	58.8%	39.2%	60.8%
Minnesota	2,843,207	867,974	Bills, Kurt	1,854,595	Klobuchar, Amy	120,638	986,621 D	30.5%	65.2%	31.9%	68.1%
Mississippi	1,241,568	709,626	Wicker, Roger F.	503,467	Gore, Albert N. Jr.	28,475	206,159 R	57.2%	40.6%	58.5%	41.5%
Missouri	2,725,793	1,066,159	Akin, Todd	1,494,125	McCaskill, Claire	165,509	427,966 D	39.1%	54.8%	41.6%	58.4%
Montana	486,066	218,051	Rehberg, Dennis "Denny"	236,123	Tester, Jon	31,892	18,072 D	44.9%	48.6%	48.0%	52.0%
Nebraska	788,572	455,593	Fischer, Deb	332,979	Kerrey, Bob		122,614 R	57.8%	42.2%	57.8%	42.2%
Nevada	997,805	457,656	Heller, Dean	446,080	Berkley, Shelley	94,069	11,576 R	45.9%	44.7%	50.6%	49.4%
New Jersey	3,374,668	1,329,405	Kyrillos, Joe	1,985,783	Menendez, Robert	59,480	656,378 D	39.4%	58.8%	40.1%	59.9%
New Mexico	775,792	351,259	Wilson, Heather A.	395,717	Heinrich, Martin T.	28,816	44,458 D	45.3%	51.0%	47.0%	53.0%
New York	6,679,678	1,758,702	Long, Wendy	4,822,330	Gillibrand, Kirsten E.	98,646	3,063,628 D	26.3%	72.2%	26.7%	73.3%
North Dakota	320,851	158,282	Berg, Rick	161,163	Heitkamp, Heidi	1,406	2,881 D	49.3%	50.2%	49.5%	50.5%
Ohio	5,449,114	2,435,740	Mandel, Josh	2,762,757	Brown, Sherrod	250,617	327,017 D	44.7%	50.7%	46.9%	53.1%
Pennsylvania	5,629,491	2,509,132	Smith, Tom	3,021,364	Casey, Bob Jr.	98,995	512,232 D	44.6%	53.7%	45.4%	54.6%
Rhode Island	418,189	146,222	Hinckley, Barry	271,034	Whitehouse, Sheldon	933	124,812 D	35.0%	64.8%	35.0%	65.0%
Tennessee	2,321,477	1,506,443	Corker, Bob	705,882	Clayton, Mark E.	109,152	800,561 R	64.9%	30.4%	68.1%	31.9%
Texas	7,864,822	4,440,137	Cruz, Ted	3,194,927	Sadler, Paul	229,758	1,245,210 R	56.5%	40.6%	58.2%	41.8%
Utah	1,006,901	657,608	Hatch, Orrin G.	301,873	Howell, Scott N.	47,420	355,735 R	65.3%	30.0%	68.5%	31.5%
Vermont	294,267	73,198	MacGovern, John			221,069	135,855 I	24.9%	0.0%	100.0%	0.0%
Virginia	3,802,196	1,785,542	Allen, George F.	2,010,067	Kaine, Timothy M.	6,587	224,525 D	47.0%	52.9%	47.0%	53.0%
Washington	3,069,417	1,213,924	Baumgartner, Michael	1,855,493	Cantwell, Maria		641,569 D	39.5%	60.5%	39.5%	60.5%
West Virginia	660,212	240,787	Raese, John R.	399,908	Manchin, Joe III	19,517	159,121 D	36.5%	60.6%	37.6%	62.4%
Wisconsin	3,009,411	1,380,126	Thompson, Tommy G.	1,547,104	Baldwin, Tammy	82,181	166,978 D	45.9%	51.4%	47.1%	52.9%
Wyoming	244,862	185,250	Barrasso, John	53,019	Chestnut, Tim	6,593	132,231 R	75.7%	21.7%	77.7%	22.3%
Total	93,061,498	39,418,955		50,424,353		3,218,190	11,005,398 D	42.4%	54.2%	43.9%	56.1%

Notes: All Senate elections were for full six-year terms and held in November 2012. The plurality is the difference between the top two vote-getters, regardless of party or independent status. In Maine, Independent Angus King garnered 370,580 votes and carried the state. In Vermont, Independent Bernie Sanders garnered 209,053 votes and won the state (there was a slight discrepancy in the official results from Vermont between the summary statewide vote totals and the detailed vote totals—this total uses the official detailed vote totals). The Democrats did not run a candidate in Vermont. Independent S. Rob Sobhani garnered 430,934 votes in Maryland, but finished third. No other third party candidate received more than 5% of the vote nationwide.

HOUSE OF REPRESENTATIVES ELECTIONS 2012

State	Seats Won Republican	Seats Won Democratic	Total Vote	Republican	Democratic	Other	Rep.-Dem. Plurality	Total Vote Rep.	Total Vote Dem.	Major Vote Rep.	Major Vote Dem.
Alabama	6	1	1,933,630	1,233,624	693,498	6,508	540,126 R	63.8%	35.9%	64.0%	36.0%
Alaska	1		289,804	185,296	82,927	21,581	102,369 R	63.9%	28.6%	69.1%	30.9%
Arizona	4	5	2,173,317	1,131,663	946,994	94,660	184,669 R	52.1%	43.6%	54.4%	45.6%
Arkansas	4		1,038,054	637,591	304,770	95,693	332,821 R	61.4%	29.4%	67.7%	32.3%
California	15	38	12,204,357	4,530,012	7,392,703	281,642	2,862,691 D	37.1%	60.6%	38.0%	62.0%
Colorado	4	3	2,450,839	1,143,796	1,080,454	226,589	63,342 R	46.7%	44.1%	51.4%	48.6%
Connecticut		5	1,466,511	500,290	951,281	14,940	450,991 D	34.1%	64.9%	34.5%	65.5%
Delaware		1	388,059	129,757	249,933	8,369	120,176 D	33.4%	64.4%	34.2%	65.8%
Florida	17	10	7,513,539	3,826,522	3,392,402	294,615	434,120 R	50.9%	45.2%	53.0%	47.0%
Georgia	9	5	3,553,587	2,104,098	1,448,869	620	655,229 R	59.2%	40.8%	59.2%	40.8%
Hawaii		2	422,539	137,531	285,008		147,477 D	32.5%	67.5%	32.5%	67.5%
Idaho	2		635,218	406,814	208,297	20,107	198,517 R	64.0%	32.8%	66.1%	33.9%
Illinois	6	12	5,058,133	2,207,818	2,743,702	106,613	535,884 D	43.6%	54.2%	44.6%	55.4%
Indiana	7	2	2,553,746	1,351,760	1,142,554	59,432	209,206 R	52.9%	44.7%	54.2%	45.8%
Iowa	2	2	1,536,849	726,505	772,387	37,957	45,882 D	47.3%	50.3%	48.5%	51.5%
Kansas	4		1,057,739	740,981	195,505	121,253	545,476 R	70.1%	18.5%	79.1%	20.9%
Kentucky	5	1	1,745,377	1,027,582	684,744	33,051	342,838 R	58.9%	39.2%	60.0%	40.0%
Louisiana	5	1	1,705,617	1,143,027	359,190	203,400	783,837 R	67.0%	21.1%	76.1%	23.9%
Maine		2	693,801	265,982	427,819		161,837 D	38.3%	61.7%	38.3%	61.7%
Maryland	1	7	2,585,514	858,406	1,626,872	100,236	768,466 D	33.2%	62.9%	34.5%	65.5%
Massachusetts		9	2,891,434	697,637	2,080,594	113,203	1,382,957 D	24.1%	72.0%	25.1%	74.9%
Michigan	9	5	4,574,632	2,086,804	2,327,985	159,843	241,181 D	45.6%	50.9%	47.3%	52.7%
Minnesota	3	5	2,813,383	1,210,409	1,560,984	41,990	350,575 D	43.0%	55.5%	43.7%	56.3%
Mississippi	3	1	1,208,175	703,635	411,398	93,142	292,237 R	58.2%	34.1%	63.1%	36.9%
Missouri	6	2	2,675,900	1,463,586	1,119,554	92,760	344,032 R	54.7%	41.8%	56.7%	43.3%
Montana	1		479,740	255,468	204,939	19,333	50,529 R	53.3%	42.7%	55.5%	44.5%
Nebraska	3		772,515	496,276	276,239		220,037 R	64.2%	35.8%	64.2%	35.8%
Nevada	2	2	973,742	457,239	453,310	63,193	3,929 R	47.0%	46.6%	50.2%	49.8%
New Hampshire		2	682,416	311,636	340,925	29,855	29,289 D	45.7%	50.0%	47.8%	52.2%
New Jersey	6	6	3,281,954	1,430,386	1,794,407	57,161	364,021 D	43.6%	54.7%	44.4%	55.6%
New Mexico	1	2	766,090	343,269	422,189	632	78,920 D	44.8%	55.1%	44.8%	55.2%
New York	6	21	6,469,725	2,245,236	4,143,414	81,075	1,898,178 D	34.7%	64.0%	35.1%	64.9%
North Carolina	9	4	4,384,112	2,137,167	2,218,357	28,588	81,190 D	48.7%	50.6%	49.1%	50.9%
North Dakota	1		316,071	173,433	131,869	10,769	41,564 R	54.9%	41.7%	56.8%	43.2%
Ohio	12	4	5,140,580	2,620,251	2,412,451	107,876	207,800 R	51.0%	46.9%	52.1%	47.9%
Oklahoma	5		1,325,935	856,872	410,324	58,739	446,548 R	64.6%	30.9%	67.6%	32.4%
Oregon	1	4	1,708,168	687,839	949,660	70,669	261,821 D	40.3%	55.6%	42.0%	58.0%
Pennsylvania	13	5	5,556,330	2,710,070	2,793,538	52,722	83,468 D	48.8%	50.3%	49.2%	50.8%
Rhode Island		2	427,775	161,926	232,679	33,170	70,753 D	37.9%	54.4%	41.0%	59.0%
South Carolina	6	1	1,802,734	1,026,129	742,805	33,800	283,324 R	56.9%	41.2%	58.0%	42.0%
South Dakota	1		361,429	207,640	153,789		53,851 R	57.4%	42.6%	57.4%	42.6%
Tennessee	7	2	2,283,727	1,369,562	796,513	117,652	573,049 R	60.0%	34.9%	63.2%	36.8%
Texas	24	12	7,664,208	4,429,270	2,949,900	285,038	1,479,370 R	57.8%	38.5%	60.0%	40.0%
Utah	3	1	998,897	647,873	324,309	26,715	323,564 R	64.9%	32.5%	66.6%	33.4%
Vermont		1	289,931	67,543	208,600	13,788	141,057 D	23.3%	71.9%	24.5%	75.5%
Virginia	8	3	3,740,455	1,876,761	1,806,025	57,669	70,736 R	50.2%	48.3%	51.0%	49.0%
Washington	4	6	3,006,266	1,369,540	1,636,726		267,186 D	45.6%	54.4%	45.6%	54.4%
West Virginia	2	1	641,354	384,253	257,101		127,152 R	59.9%	40.1%	59.9%	40.1%
Wisconsin	5	3	2,866,050	1,401,995	1,445,015	19,040	43,020 D	48.9%	50.4%	49.2%	50.8%
Wyoming	1		241,621	166,452	57,573	17,596	108,879 R	68.9%	23.8%	74.3%	25.7%
Total	*234*	*201*	*121,351,579*	*58,285,212*	*59,653,081*	*3,413,286*	*1,367,869 D*	*48.0%*	*49.2%*	*49.4%*	*50.6%*

Notes: Does not include special elections. In states such as Connecticut, New York, and South Carolina where third parties could endorse candidates of the major parties, all such votes are credited to the major party with which the candidates identified. Louisiana has a unique election system for many offices, including the U.S. House of Representatives. All candidates, regardless of party, appeared together on the November ballot. The vote totals for all Republicans and all Democrats are included in the state total for each party. If the highest vote-getter does not win a majority of the votes, there is a runoff between the top two vote-getters in December. In the 3rd district in Louisiana, there was a run-off on December 8, 2012, between Charles Boustany Jr. and Jeff Landry, both Republicans. This general election is included in the state vote totals, not the runoff.

UNITED STATES
SPECIAL ELECTIONS AND POSTELECTION CHANGES, 2011–2012

SUMMARY OF HOUSE SPECIAL ELECTIONS TO THE 112th CONGRESS

REPRESENTATIVES

District	Former Member	New Member	Date Elected	Winning Percentage	Voter Turnout
New York 26th	**Christopher Lee (R)**	**Kathy Hochul (D)**	**May 24, 2011**	47%	**111,338**
California 36th	Jane Harman (D)	Janice Hahn (D)	July 12, 2011	55%	85,624
Nevada 2nd	Dean Heller (R)	Mark Amodei (R)	September 13, 2011	58%	129,414
New York 9th	**Anthony Weiner (D)**	**Bob Turner (R)**	**September 13, 2011**	**52%**	**71,226**
Oregon 1st	David Wu (D)	Suzanne Bonamici (D)	January 31, 2012	54%	210,763
Arizona 8th	Gabrielle Giffords (D)	Ron Barber (D)	June 12, 2012	52%	213,344
Kentucky 4th	Geoff Davis (R)	Thomas Massie (R)	November 6, 2012	60%	290,677
Michigan 11th	**Thaddeus McCotter (R)**	**David Curson (D)**	**November 6, 2012**	**48%**	**329,137**
New Jersey 10th	Donald Payne (D)	Donald Payne Jr. (D)	November 6, 2012	97%	170,913
Washington 1st	Jay Inslee (D)	Suzan DelBene (D)	November 6, 2012	60%	357,735

SPECIAL ELECTIONS TO THE 112th CONGRESS

From the beginning of 2011 through the general election of 2012, 10 special elections were held in the House to fill unexpired terms in the 112th Congress. One vacancy, left by the resignation of Rep. Dennis Cardoza (D-Calif. 18), was not filled. There were no special elections in the Senate in this timeframe. In addition, an appointment was made to fill one vacant Senate seat. There were no party switches during the 112th Congress.

SENATORS

NEVADA

John Ensign (R) resigned May 3, 2011, in the midst of a Senate Ethics Committee investigation into conduct relating to a female aide. Dean Heller (R) was appointed to fill the vacancy and was sworn in May 9, 2011. Heller completed Ensign's term for the 112th Congress.

REPRESENTATIVES

ARIZONA 8th CD

Gabrielle Giffords (D) resigned January 25, 2012, to focus on her recovery from an assassination attempt a year earlier. Ron Barber (D), previously Giffords's chief of staff, was elected June 12, 2012, to fill the remainder of the term of the 112th Congress.

April 17, 2012 Special Democratic Primary
44,185 Ron Barber.

April 17, 2012 Special Republican Primary
27,101 Jesse Kelly; 19,413 Martha McSally; 17,497 Frank Antenori; 13,299 Dave Sitton.

June 12, 2012 Special General Election
111,204 Ron Barber (D); 96,465 Jesse Kelly (R); 4,869 Charlie Manolakis (Green); 806 Scattered Write-In.

CALIFORNIA 18th CD

Dennis Cardoza (D) resigned August 15, 2012, citing "increasing parenting challenges." This vacancy was not filled.

CALIFORNIA 36th CD

Jane Harman (D) resigned February 28, 2011, to become president of the Woodrow Wilson International Center for Scholars in Washington, D.C. The two top vote-getters in the May 17, 2011, special all-party open primary advanced to the July 12, 2011, special general election. Janice Hahn (D) was elected July 12, 2011, to fill the remainder of the term of the 112th Congress.

UNITED STATES
SPECIAL ELECTIONS AND POSTELECTION CHANGES, 2011–2012

May 17, 2011 Special Primary Election

15,647 Janice Hahn (D); **14,116 Craig Huey (R)**; 13,407 Debra Bowen (D); 5,905 Marcy Winograd (D); 4,997 Mike Gin (R); 3,895 Mike Webb (R); 2,296 Patricia Bobko (R); 896 Steve Collett (Libertarian); 788 Stephen Eisele (R); 361 Daniel H. Adler (D); 325 Loraine Goodwin (D); 324 Maria E. Montano (Peace and Freedom); 234 George Newberry (R); 157 Matthew Roozee (No Party); 126 Katherine Pilot (No Party); 108 Michael T. Chamness (No Party); 2 Vince Flaherty (Write-in).

July 12, 2011 Special General Election

47,000 Janice Hahn (D); 38,624 Craig Huey (R).

KENTUCKY 4th CD

Geoff Davis (R) resigned July 31, 2012, citing a family health issue. Each party chose a nominee for the November 6, 2012, special general election to serve for the remainder of the 112th Congress. This election was distinct from the November 6, 2012, general election to the 113th Congress, although the same candidate—Thomas Massie (R)—won both.

November 6, 2012 Special General Election

174,092 Thomas Massie (R); 106,598 William R. Adkins (D); 9,987 David Lewis (Independent).

MICHIGAN 11th CD

Thaddeus McCotter (R-Mich. 11) resigned July 6, 2012, after failing to get on his district's GOP primary ballot for the 113th Congress. Each party chose a nominee for the November 6, 2012, special general election to serve for the remainder of the 112th Congress. This election was distinct from the November 6, 2012, general election to the 113th Congress. The winner of the seat for the 112th Congress, David Curson (D), did not run for the 113th Congress.

September 5, 2012 Special Democratic Primary

11,450 David Curson.

September 5, 2012 Special Republican Primary

10,280 Kerry Bentivolio; 8,803 Nancy Cassis; 2,653 Carolyn Kavanagh; 1,715 Steve King; 1,208 Kenneth Crider.

November 6, 2012 Special General Election

159,258 David Curson (D); 151,736 Kerry Bentivolio (R); 11,606 John Tatar (Libertarian); 6,529 Marc Sosnowski (U.S. Taxpayers); 8 James Van Gilder (Write-in).

NEVADA 2nd CD

Dean Heller (R) resigned May 9, 2011, after his appointment to the Senate. Each party chose a nominee for the September 13, 2011, special general election. Mark Amodei (D) was elected September 13, 2011, to fill the remainder of the term of the 112th Congress.

September 13, 2011 Special General Election

74,976 Mark Amodei (R); 46,669 Kate Marshall (D); 5,354 Helmuth Lehmann (Independent); 2,415 Timothy Fasano (Independent American).

NEW JERSEY 10th CD

Donald Payne (D) died March 6, 2012, at age 77 of colon cancer. The Democratic Party held a special primary election on June 5, 2012, with the winner to appear in the November 6, 2012, special general election to serve for the remainder of the 112th Congress. This election was distinct from the November 6, 2012, general election to the 113th Congress, although the same candidate—David Payne Jr. (D), the son of the late Donald Payne—won both. The Republican Party did not run a candidate for the opening.

June 5, 2012 Special Democratic Primary

34,358 Donald M. Payne Jr.; 11,935 Ronald C. Rice; 2,318 Wayne Smith.

November 6, 2012 Special General Election

166,413 Donald M. Payne Jr. (D); 4,500 Joanne Miller (Change, Change, Change).

UNITED STATES
SPECIAL ELECTIONS AND POSTELECTION CHANGES, 2011–2012

NEW YORK 9th CD

Anthony Weiner (D) resigned June 21, 2011, due to a "sexting" scandal. Each party chose a nominee for the September 13, 2011, special general election. Bob Turner (R) was elected September 13, 2011, to fill the remainder of the term of the 112th Congress.

September 13, 2011 Special General Election

37,342 Bob Turner (R); 33,656 David I. Weprin (D); 143 Christopher P. Hoeppner (Socialist Workers Party); 85 Scattered Write-In.

NEW YORK 26th CD

Christopher Lee (R) resigned February 9, 2011, due to an Internet-related scandal. Each party chose a nominee for the May 24, 2011, special general election. Kathy Courtney Hochul (D), was elected May 24, 2011, to fill the remainder of the term of the 112th Congress.

May 24, 2011 Special General Election

52,713 Kathy Courtney Hochul (D); 47,187 Jane L. Corwin (R); 10,029 Jack Davis (Tea Party); 1,177 Ian L. Murphy (Green); 232 Scattered Write-In (Write-in).

OREGON 1st CD

David Wu (D) resigned August 3, 2011, following accusations of sexual misconduct by a female teenager. The winners of the Democratic and Republican primaries November 8, 2011, advanced to the January, 31, 2012, special general election. Suzanne Bonamici (D) was elected January 31, 2012, to serve for the remainder of the 112th Congress.

November 8, 2011 Special Democratic Primary

49,721 Suzanne Bonamici; 16,963 Brad Avakian; 6,003 Brad Witt; 1,212 Dan Strite; 923 Dominic Hammon; 651 Todd Lee Ritter; 250 Ahmed Saba; 91 Robert E. Lettin; 469 Scattered Write-In.

November 8, 2011 Special Republican Primary

40,227 Rob Cornilles; 6,360 Jim Greenfield; 5,739 Lisa Michaels; 1,657 Pavel Goberman; 847 D.R. Delgado-Morgan; 519 Scattered Write-In.

January 31, 2012 Special General Election

113,404 Suzanne Bonamici (D); 83,396 Rob Cornilles (R); 6,798 Steve Reynolds (Progressive); 6,618 James Foster (Libertarian); 547 Scattered Write-In.

WASHINGTON 1st CD

Jay Inslee (D) resigned March 20, 2012, to focus on his campaign for governor of Washington. The two top vote-getters in the August 7, 2012, special all-party open primary advanced to the November 6, 2012, special general election to serve for the remainder of the 112th Congress. This special general election was distinct from the November 6, 2012, general election to the 113th Congress, although the same candidate—Suzan DelBene (D)—won both.

August 7, 2012 Special Primary Election

56,631 John Koster (R); 39,620 Suzan DelBene (D); 23,902 Darcy Burner (D); 15,463 Laura Ruderman (D); 5,143 Darshan Rauniyar (D); 4,861 Brian Sullivan (D); 4,066 Steven J. Gerdes (R); 2,796 Brian Berry (D); 2,542 Bob Champion (Independent Party); 1,939 Ruth Morrison (D).

November 6, 2012 Special General Election

216,144 Suzan DelBene (D); 141,591 John Koster (R).

UNITED STATES
SPECIAL ELECTIONS TO THE 113TH CONGRESS

CHANGES FOLLOWING THE 2012 ELECTION

Following the 2012 general election, and through August 15, 2013, the following changes took place in the membership of the 113th Congress.

SENATORS

Hawaii – Daniel Inouye (D) died December 17, 2012, at age 88. Brian Schatz (D) was sworn in to fill the vacancy on an interim basis on December 27, 2012. A special election was scheduled for November 4, 2014.

Massachusetts – John Kerry (D) resigned February 1, 2013, to become secretary of state. William "Mo" Cowan (D) was sworn in February 7, 2013, on an interim basis to fill the Senate vacancy created by Kerry's resignation. Edward J. Markey (D) was elected June 25, 2013, to complete Kerry's term.

New Jersey – Frank Lautenberg (D) died June 3, 2013, at age 89. Jeffrey S. Chiesa (R) was sworn in June 10, 2013, on an interim basis to fill the Senate vacancy created by Lautenberg's death. A special election was scheduled for October 16, 2013.

South Carolina – Jim DeMint (R) resigned January 1, 2013, to become president of the Heritage Foundation. Tim Scott (R) was sworn in January 3, 2013, on an interim basis to replace him. A special election was scheduled for November 4, 2014.

REPRESENTATIVES

Alabama 1st District – Jo Bonner (R) resigned August 2, 2013, to become vice chancellor of government relations and economic development at the University of Alabama. A special election was scheduled for November 5, 2013, or December 17, 2013, depending on whether a primary runoff in either party was needed.

Illinois 2nd District – Jesse Jackson Jr. (D) resigned November 21, 2012, citing the need to focus on his health. Robin Kelly (D) was elected April 9, 2013, to replace him.

Massachusetts 5th District – Edward J. Markey (D) resigned on June 25, 2013, to fill John Kerry's Senate seat. A special election was scheduled for December 10, 2013.

Missouri 8th District – Jo Ann Emerson (R) resigned on January 22, 2013, to become president and chief executive officer of the National Rural Electric Cooperative Association. Jason Smith (R) won a special election on June 4, 2013, to replace her.

South Carolina 1st District – Tim Scott (R) resigned January 2, 2013, to fill the remainder of Jim DeMint's Senate term. Former South Carolina governor Mark Sanford (R) was elected May 7, 2013, to replace Scott.

UNITED STATES
PRESIDENT 2012

The presidential candidates listed below include all who appeared on the ballot in at least one state. Write-in votes for independent and third-party candidates are credited to their total below. See the minor parties table on page 11 for details. There, the state totals for all independent and third party candidates who received at least 100,000 votes in the 2012 presidential election are listed.

In New York the Democratic total includes Working Families votes and the Republican figures include Conservative and Independence votes.

In Minnesota the Democratic candidate appears on the ballot as Democratic-Farmer-Labor; in North Dakota as Democratic-Nonpartisan League. In many states various non-major party candidates appeared on the ballot with variations of the party designations (for instance, in Massachusetts, the Green Party affiliate is the Green-Rainbow Party), were carried with entirely different party labels, or were listed as "Independent."

65,915,796	Barack Obama and Joseph R. Biden Jr.	Democratic
60,933,500	W. Mitt Romney and Paul Ryan	Republican
1,275,970	Gary Johnson and James P. Gray	Libertarian
469,034	Jill Stein and Cheri Honkala/Ben Manski	Green
122,375	Virgil H. Goode Jr. and Jim Clymer	Constitution
67,037	Roseanne Barr and Cindy Sheehan	Peace and Freedom
39,997	Thomas Hoefling and J.D. Ellis/Robert Ornelas	American Independent
40,257	Ross C. "Rocky" Anderson and Luis J. Rodriguez	Justice
13,090	Randall Terry and Missy Smith	Independent
12,502	Richard Duncan and Rickey Johnson Sr.	Independent
7,791	Peta Lindsay and Yari Osorio	Socialism and Liberation
5,017	Chuck Baldwin and Joseph Martin	Reform
4,432	Will Christensen and Kenneth Gibbs	Constitution
4,091	Thomas Robert Stevens and Alden Link	Objectivist
4,051	Stewart Alexander and Alejandro "Alex" Mendoza	Socialist
3,992	James Harris and Alyson Kennedy/Maura DeLuca	Socialist Workers Party
3,149	Jim Carlson and George McMahon	Grassroots
2,669	Merlin Miller and Harry V. Bertram/Virginia Abernethy	American Third Position
2,589	Jill Reed and Tom Cary	Unaffiliated
2,559	Sheila Tittle and Matthew A. Turner	We the People
1,608	Gloria La Riva and Filberto Ramirez/Stefanie Beacham	Socialism and Liberation
1,097	Jerry White and Phyllis Scherrer	Socialist Equality
1,092	Dean Morstad and Josh Franke-Hyland	Constitutional Government
1,027	Jerry Litzel and Jim Litzel	Nominated by Petition
1,016	Barbara Dale Washer and Cathy L. Toole	Reform
1,007	Jeff Boss and Bob Pasternak	NSA Did 911
820	Andre Barnett and Ken Cross	Reform
518	Jack Fellure and Toby Davis	Prohibition

Note: In addition to the votes listed above, 116,751 scattered write-in votes were reported from various states, and 5,770 votes were cast for "None of These Candidates" in Nevada. Scattered write-ins may include some votes for the candidates listed above in states in which they were not on the ballot; however, all write-in votes for Gary Johnson, Jill Stein, and Virgil H. Goode Jr. should be included in their totals. The scattered write-in total does not include the votes received by Republican Ron Paul; Paul received 24,870 votes as a write-in candidate in California and Maine, although he did not appear on the ballot in either state.

UNITED STATES
PRESIDENT 2012

State	Electoral Vote Rep.	Electoral Vote Dem.	Total Vote	Republican	Democratic	Other	Rep.-Dem. Plurality	Percentage Total Vote Rep.	Percentage Total Vote Dem.	Percentage Major Vote Rep.	Percentage Major Vote Dem.
Alabama	9		2,074,338	1,255,925	795,696	22,717	460,229 R	60.5%	38.4%	61.2%	38.8%
Alaska	3		300,495	164,676	122,640	13,179	42,036 R	54.8%	40.8%	57.3%	42.7%
Arizona	11		2,299,254	1,233,654	1,025,232	40,368	208,422 R	53.7%	44.6%	54.6%	45.4%
Arkansas	6		1,069,468	647,744	394,409	27,315	253,335 R	60.6%	36.9%	62.2%	37.8%
California		55	13,038,547	4,839,958	7,854,285	344,304	3,014,327 D	37.1%	60.2%	38.1%	61.9%
Colorado		9	2,569,522	1,185,243	1,323,102	61,177	137,859 D	46.1%	51.5%	47.3%	52.7%
Connecticut		7	1,558,960	634,892	905,083	18,985	270,191 D	40.7%	58.1%	41.2%	58.8%
Delaware		3	413,921	165,484	242,584	5,853	77,100 D	40.0%	58.6%	40.6%	59.4%
Florida		29	8,474,179	4,163,447	4,237,756	72,976	74,309 D	49.1%	50.0%	49.6%	50.4%
Georgia	16		3,900,050	2,078,688	1,773,827	47,535	304,861 R	53.3%	45.5%	54.0%	46.0%
Hawaii		4	434,697	121,015	306,658	7,024	185,643 D	27.8%	70.5%	28.3%	71.7%
Idaho	4		652,346	420,911	212,787	18,648	208,124 R	64.5%	32.6%	66.4%	33.6%
Illinois		20	5,242,014	2,135,216	3,019,512	87,286	884,296 D	40.7%	57.6%	41.4%	58.6%
Indiana	11		2,624,534	1,420,543	1,152,887	51,104	267,656 R	54.1%	43.9%	55.2%	44.8%
Iowa		6	1,582,180	730,617	822,544	29,019	91,927 D	46.2%	52.0%	47.0%	53.0%
Kansas	6		1,159,971	692,634	440,726	26,611	251,908 R	59.7%	38.0%	61.1%	38.9%
Kentucky	8		1,797,212	1,087,190	679,370	30,652	407,820 R	60.5%	37.8%	61.5%	38.5%
Louisiana	8		1,994,065	1,152,262	809,141	32,662	343,121 R	57.8%	40.6%	58.7%	41.3%
Maine		4	713,180	292,276	401,306	19,598	109,030 D	41.0%	56.3%	42.1%	57.9%
Maryland		10	2,707,327	971,869	1,677,844	57,614	705,975 D	35.9%	62.0%	36.7%	63.3%
Massachusetts		11	3,167,767	1,188,314	1,921,290	58,163	732,976 D	37.5%	60.7%	38.2%	61.8%
Michigan		16	4,730,961	2,115,256	2,564,569	51,136	449,313 D	44.7%	54.2%	45.2%	54.8%
Minnesota		10	2,936,561	1,320,225	1,546,167	70,169	225,942 D	45.0%	52.7%	46.1%	53.9%
Mississippi	6		1,285,584	710,746	562,949	11,889	147,797 R	55.3%	43.8%	55.8%	44.2%
Missouri	10		2,757,323	1,482,440	1,223,796	51,087	258,644 R	53.8%	44.4%	54.8%	45.2%
Montana	3		484,048	267,928	201,839	14,281	66,089 R	55.4%	41.7%	57.0%	43.0%
Nebraska	5		794,379	475,064	302,081	17,234	172,983 R	59.8%	38.0%	61.1%	38.9%
Nevada		6	1,014,918	463,567	531,373	19,978	67,806 D	45.7%	52.4%	46.6%	53.4%
New Hampshire		4	710,972	329,918	369,561	11,493	39,643 D	46.4%	52.0%	47.2%	52.8%
New Jersey		14	3,640,292	1,477,568	2,125,101	37,623	647,533 D	40.6%	58.4%	41.0%	59.0%
New Mexico		5	783,757	335,788	415,335	32,634	79,547 D	42.8%	53.0%	44.7%	55.3%
New York		29	7,081,159	2,490,431	4,485,741	104,987	1,995,310 D	35.2%	63.3%	35.7%	64.3%
North Carolina	15		4,505,372	2,270,395	2,178,391	56,586	92,004 R	50.4%	48.4%	51.0%	49.0%
North Dakota	3		322,627	188,163	124,827	9,637	63,336 R	58.3%	38.7%	60.1%	39.9%
Ohio		18	5,580,840	2,661,433	2,827,710	91,697	166,277 D	47.7%	50.7%	48.5%	51.5%
Oklahoma	7		1,334,872	891,325	443,547		447,778 R	66.8%	33.2%	66.8%	33.2%
Oregon		7	1,789,270	754,175	970,488	64,607	216,313 D	42.1%	54.2%	43.7%	56.3%
Pennsylvania		20	5,753,670	2,680,434	2,990,274	82,962	309,840 D	46.6%	52.0%	47.3%	52.7%
Rhode Island		4	446,049	157,204	279,677	9,168	122,473 D	35.2%	62.7%	36.0%	64.0%
South Carolina	9		1,964,118	1,071,645	865,941	26,532	205,704 R	54.6%	44.1%	55.3%	44.7%
South Dakota	3		363,815	210,610	145,039	8,166	65,571 R	57.9%	39.9%	59.2%	40.8%
Tennessee	11		2,458,577	1,462,330	960,709	35,538	501,621 R	59.5%	39.1%	60.4%	39.6%
Texas	38		7,993,851	4,569,843	3,308,124	115,884	1,261,719 R	57.2%	41.4%	58.0%	42.0%
Utah	6		1,017,440	740,600	251,813	25,027	488,787 R	72.8%	24.7%	74.6%	25.4%
Vermont		3	299,290	92,698	199,239	7,353	106,541 D	31.0%	66.6%	31.8%	68.2%
Virginia		13	3,854,489	1,822,522	1,971,820	60,147	149,298 D	47.3%	51.2%	48.0%	52.0%
Washington		12	3,125,516	1,290,670	1,755,396	79,450	464,726 D	41.3%	56.2%	42.4%	57.6%
West Virginia	5		670,438	417,655	238,269	14,514	179,386 R	62.3%	35.5%	63.7%	36.3%
Wisconsin		10	3,068,434	1,407,966	1,620,985	39,483	213,019 D	45.9%	52.8%	46.5%	53.5%
Wyoming	3		249,061	170,962	69,286	8,813	101,676 R	68.6%	27.8%	71.2%	28.8%
District of Columbia		3	293,764	21,381	267,070	5,313	245,689 D	7.3%	90.9%	7.4%	92.6%
Total	206	332	129,085,474	60,933,500	65,915,796	2,236,178	4,982,296 D	47.2%	51.1%	48.0%	52.0%

UNITED STATES
PRESIDENT 2012 MINOR PARTIES

State	Total	Other Vote Total	Johnson (Libertarian)	Stein (Green)	Goode (Constitution)	Additional Candidates and Write-ins	Johnson (Lib.)	Stein (Green)	Goode (Con.)
Alabama	2,074,338	22,717	12,328	3,397	2,981	4,011	0.6%	0.2%	0.1%
Alaska	300,495	13,179	7,392	2,917		2,870	2.5%	1.0%	0.0%
Arizona	2,299,254	40,368	32,100	7,816	289*	163	1.4%	0.3%	0.0%
Arkansas	1,069,468	27,315	16,276	9,305		1,734	1.5%	0.9%	0.0%
California	13,038,547	344,304	143,221	85,638	503*	114,942	1.1%	0.7%	0.0%
Colorado	2,569,522	61,177	35,545	7,508	6,234	11,890	1.4%	0.3%	0.2%
Connecticut	1,558,960	18,985	12,580	863*		5,542	0.8%	0.0%	0.0%
Delaware	413,921	5,853	3,882	1,940	23*	8	0.9%	0.5%	0.0%
Florida	8,474,179	72,976	44,726	8,947	2,607	16,696	0.5%	0.1%	0.0%
Georgia	3,900,050	47,535	45,324	1,516*	432*	263	1.2%	0.0%	0.0%
Hawaii	434,697	7,024	3,840	3,184			0.9%	0.7%	0.0%
Idaho	652,346	18,648	9,453	4,402	2,222	2,571	1.4%	0.7%	0.3%
Illinois	5,242,014	87,286	56,229	30,222	415*	420	1.1%	0.6%	0.0%
Indiana	2,624,534	51,104	50,111	625*	290*	78	1.9%	0.0%	0.0%
Iowa	1,582,180	29,019	12,926	3,769	3,038	9,286	0.8%	0.2%	0.2%
Kansas	1,159,971	26,611	20,456	714*	187*	5,254	1.8%	0.1%	0.0%
Kentucky	1,797,212	30,652	17,063	6,337	245*	7,007	0.9%	0.4%	0.0%
Louisiana	1,994,065	32,662	18,157	6,978	2,508	5,019	0.9%	0.3%	0.1%
Maine	713,180	19,598	9,352	8,119		2,127	1.3%	1.1%	0.0%
Maryland	2,707,327	57,614	30,195	17,110	418*	9,891	1.1%	0.6%	0.0%
Massachusetts	3,167,767	58,163	30,920	20,691		6,552	1.0%	0.7%	0.0%
Michigan	4,730,961	51,136	7,774*	21,897	16,119	5,346	0.2%	0.5%	0.3%
Minnesota	2,936,561	70,169	35,098	13,023	3,722	18,326	1.2%	0.4%	0.1%
Mississippi	1,285,584	11,889	6,676	1,588	2,609	1,016	0.5%	0.1%	0.2%
Missouri	2,757,323	51,087	43,151		7,936		1.6%	0.0%	0.3%
Montana	484,048	14,281	14,165		39*	77	2.9%	0.0%	0.0%
Nebraska	794,379	17,234	11,109			6,125	1.4%	0.0%	0.0%
Nevada	1,014,918	19,978	10,968		3,240	5,770	1.1%	0.0%	0.3%
New Hampshire	710,972	11,493	8,212	324*	708	2,249	1.2%	0.0%	0.1%
New Jersey	3,640,292	37,623	21,045	9,888	2,064	4,626	0.6%	0.3%	0.1%
New Mexico	783,757	32,634	27,787	2,691	982	1,174	3.5%	0.3%	0.1%
New York	7,081,159	104,987	47,256	39,982	6,274	11,475	0.7%	0.6%	0.1%
North Carolina	4,505,372	56,586	44,515		534*	11,537	1.0%	0.0%	0.0%
North Dakota	322,627	9,637	5,231	1,361	1,185	1,860	1.6%	0.4%	0.4%
Ohio	5,580,840	91,697	49,493	18,574	8,151	15,479	0.9%	0.3%	0.1%
Oklahoma	1,334,872						0.0%	0.0%	0.0%
Oregon	1,789,270	64,607	24,089	19,427		21,091	1.3%	1.1%	0.0%
Pennsylvania	5,753,670	82,962	49,991	21,341	383*	11,247	0.9%	0.4%	0.0%
Rhode Island	446,049	9,168	4,388	2,421	430	1,929	1.0%	0.5%	0.1%
South Carolina	1,964,118	26,532	16,321	5,446	4,765		0.8%	0.3%	0.2%
South Dakota	363,815	8,166	5,795		2,371		1.6%	0.0%	0.7%
Tennessee	2,458,577	35,538	18,623	6,515	6,022	4,378	0.8%	0.3%	0.2%
Texas	7,993,851	115,884	88,580	24,657	1,287*	1,360	1.1%	0.3%	0.0%
Utah	1,017,440	25,027	12,572	3,817	2,871	5,767	1.2%	0.4%	0.3%
Vermont	299,290	7,353	3,487			3,866	1.2%	0.0%	0.0%
Virginia	3,854,489	60,147	31,216	8,627	13,058	7,246	0.8%	0.2%	0.3%
Washington	3,125,516	79,450	42,202	20,928	8,851	7,469	1.4%	0.7%	0.3%
West Virginia	670,438	14,514	6,302	4,406		3,806	0.9%	0.7%	0.0%
Wisconsin	3,068,434	39,483	20,439	7,665	4,930	6,449	0.7%	0.2%	0.2%
Wyoming	249,061	8,813	5,326		1,452	2,035	2.1%	0.0%	0.6%
District of Columbia	293,764	5,313	2,083	2,458		772	0.7%	0.8%	0.0%
Total	129,085,474	2,236,178	1,275,970	469,034	122,375	368,799	1.0%	0.4%	0.1%

Note: An asterisk (*) indicates write-in votes.

UNITED STATES

POPULAR VOTE FOR PRESIDENT 1920 TO 2012

Year	Total Vote	Republican Vote	Republican Candidate	Democratic Vote	Democratic Candidate	Other Vote	Rep.-Dem. Plurality	Percentage Total Vote Rep.	Dem.	Major Vote Rep.	Dem.
2012	129,085,474	60,933,500	Romney, W. Mitt	65,915,796	Obama, Barack	2,236,178	4,982,296 D	47.2%	51.1%	48.0%	52.0%
2008	131,313,820	59,948,323	McCain, John S. III	69,498,516	Obama, Barack	1,866,981	9,550,193 D	45.7%	52.9%	46.3%	53.7%
2004	122,295,345	62,040,610	Bush, George W.	59,028,439	Kerry, John	1,226,296	3,012,171 R	50.7%	48.3%	51.2%	48.8%
2000	105,396,627	50,455,156	Bush, George W.	50,992,335	Gore, Albert Jr.	3,949,136	537,179 D	47.9%	48.4%	49.7%	50.3%
1996	96,277,872	39,198,755	Dole, Bob	47,402,357	Clinton, Bill	9,676,760	8,203,602 D	40.7%	49.2%	45.3%	54.7%
1992	104,425,014	39,103,882	Bush, George H.	44,909,326	Clinton, Bill	20,411,806	5,805,444 D	37.4%	43.0%	46.5%	53.5%
1988	91,597,809	48,886,097	Bush, George H.	41,812,075	Dukakis, Michael S.	899,637	7,074,022 R	53.4%	45.6%	53.9%	46.1%
1984	92,652,842	54,455,075	Reagan, Ronald	37,577,185	Mondale, Walter F.	620,582	16,877,890 R	58.8%	40.6%	59.2%	40.8%
1980	86,515,221	43,904,153	Reagan, Ronald	35,483,883	Carter, Jimmy	7,127,185	8,420,270 R	50.7%	41.0%	55.3%	44.7%
1976	81,554,989	39,141,091	Ford, Gerald R.	40,829,763	Carter, Jimmy	1,584,135	1,688,672 D	48.0%	50.1%	48.9%	51.1%
1972	77,718,554	47,169,911	Nixon, Richard M.	29,170,383	McGovern, George S.	1,378,260	17,999,528 R	60.7%	37.5%	61.8%	38.2%
1968	73,211,875	31,785,480	Nixon, Richard M.	31,275,166	Humphrey, Hubert H.	10,151,229	510,314 R	43.4%	42.7%	50.4%	49.6%
1964	70,644,592	27,178,188	Goldwater, Barry M.	43,129,566	Johnson, Lyndon B.	336,838	15,951,378 D	38.5%	61.1%	38.7%	61.3%
1960	68,838,219	34,108,157	Nixon, Richard M.	34,226,731	Kennedy, John F.	503,331	118,574 D	49.5%	49.7%	49.9%	50.1%
1956	62,026,908	35,590,472	Eisenhower, Dwight D.	26,022,752	Stevenson, Adlai E.	413,684	9,567,720 R	57.4%	42.0%	57.8%	42.2%
1952	61,550,918	33,936,234	Eisenhower, Dwight D.	27,314,992	Stevenson, Adlai E.	299,692	6,621,242 R	55.1%	44.4%	55.4%	44.6%
1948	48,793,826	21,991,291	Dewey, Thomas E.	24,179,345	Truman, Harry S.	2,623,190	2,188,054 D	45.1%	49.6%	47.6%	52.4%
1944	47,976,670	22,017,617	Dewey, Thomas E.	25,612,610	Roosevelt, Franklin D.	346,443	3,594,993 D	45.9%	53.4%	46.2%	53.8%
1940	49,900,774	22,348,836	Willkie, Wendell	27,313,041	Roosevelt, Franklin D.	238,897	4,964,205 D	44.8%	54.7%	45.0%	55.0%
1936	45,654,763	16,684,231	Landon, Alfred M.	27,757,333	Roosevelt, Franklin D.	1,213,199	11,073,102 D	36.5%	60.8%	37.5%	62.5%
1932	39,761,034	15,760,684	Hoover, Herbert C.	22,829,501	Roosevelt, Franklin D.	1,170,849	7,068,817 D	39.6%	57.4%	40.8%	59.2%
1928	36,805,951	21,437,277	Hoover, Herbert C.	15,007,698	Smith, Alfred E.	360,976	6,429,579 R	58.2%	40.8%	58.8%	41.2%
1924	29,095,023	15,719,921	Coolidge, Calvin	8,386,704	Davis, John W.	4,988,398	7,333,217 R	54.0%	28.8%	65.2%	34.8%
1920	26,768,150	16,153,115	Harding, Warren G.	9,133,092	Cox, James M.	1,481,943	7,020,023 R	60.3%	34.1%	63.9%	36.1%

Republican George W. Bush lost the popular vote in 2000, but won the electoral vote and was elected president. In past elections, the other vote included: 2000 - 2,882,738 Green (Ralph Nader); 1996 - 8,085,402 Reform (Ross Perot); 1992 - 19,741,657 Independent (Ross Perot); 1980 - 5,720,060 Independent (John Anderson); 1968 - 9,906,473 American Independent (George Wallace); 1948 - 1,176,125 States Rights (Strom Thurmond); 1948 - 1,157,326 Progressive (Henry Wallace); 1924 - 4,832,532 Progressive (Robert LaFollette).

ELECTORAL COLLEGE VOTE 1920 TO 2012

Year	Total	Republican	Democratic	Other	Other Candidate	Other Party
2012	538	206	332	0		
2008	538	173	365	0		
2004	538	286	251	1	John Edwards*	Democrat
2000	538	271	266	1	Abstained*	
1996	538	159	379	0		
1992	538	168	370	0		
1988	538	426	111	1	Lloyd Bentsen*	Democrat
1984	538	525	13	0		
1980	538	489	49	0		
1976	538	240	297	1	Ronald Reagan*	Republican
1972	538	520	17	1	John Hospers*	Libertarian
1968	538	301	191	46	George Wallace	American Independent
1964	538	52	486	0		
1960	537	219	303	15	Harry Byrd	Democrat
1956	531	457	73	1	Walter Jones*	Democrat
1952	531	442	89	0		
1948	531	189	303	39	Strom Thurmond	States' Rights
1944	531	99	432	0		
1940	531	82	449	0		
1936	531	8	523	0		
1932	531	59	472	0		
1928	531	444	87	0		
1924	531	382	136	13	Robert M. La Follette	Progressive
1920	531	404	127	0		

Asterisks indicate "faithless" electors who did not vote for the presidential candidates to which they were pledged. One of the electoral votes for Strom Thurmond in 1948, Harry Byrd in 1960, and George Wallace in 1968 was cast by a faithless elector. The rest of Byrd's support in 1960 came from unpledged electors.

UNITED STATES
PRESIDENT 2008

The presidential candidates listed below include all who appeared on the ballot in at least one state. Write-in votes for independent and third party candidates are credited to their total below. See the minor parties table on page 11 for details. There, the state totals for all independent and third party candidates who received at least 100,000 votes in the 2008 presidential election are listed.

In New York the Democratic total includes Working Families votes and the Republican figures include Conservative and Independence votes.

In Minnesota the Democratic candidate appears on the ballot as Democratic-Farmer-Labor; in North Dakota as Democratic-Nonpartisan League. In many states various non-major party candidates appeared on the ballot with variations of the party designations, were carried with entirely different party labels, or were listed as "Independent."

69,498,516	Barack Obama and Joseph R. Biden Jr.	Democratic
59,948,323	John McCain and Sarah Palin	Republican
739,034	Ralph Nader and Matt Gonzalez	Independent
523,715	Bob Barr and Wayne A. Root	Libertarian
199,750	Chuck Baldwin and Darrell L. Castle	Constitution
161,797	Cynthia A. McKinney and Rosa A. Clemente	Green
47,746	Alan Keyes and Brian Rohrbough	America's Independent
42,426	Ron Paul and Barry Goldwater Jr./Michael Peroutka	Constitution/Louisiana Taxpayers
6,818	Gloria La Riva and Eugene Puryear/Robert Moses	Socialism and Liberation
6,538	Brian Moore and Stewart A. Alexander	Socialist
5,151	Roger Calero and Alyson Kennedy	Socialist Workers
3,905	Richard Duncan and Ricky Johnson	Independent
2,424	James Harris and Alyson Kennedy	Socialist Workers
2,422	Charles Jay and Dan Sallis Jr.	Boston Tea
1,149	John Polachek and "no candidate"	New
829	Frank McEnulty and David Mangan	New American Independent
764	Jeffrey Wamboldt and David J. Klimisch	Independent
755	Thomas Stevens and Alden Link	Objectivist
653	Gene Amondson and Leroy J. Pletten	Prohibition
639	Jeffrey Boss and Andrea Marie Psoras	Vote Here
531	George Phillies and Christopher Bennett	Libertarian
481	Ted Weill and Frank McEnulty	Reform
480	Jonathan Allen and Jeffrey D. Stath	HeartQuake '08
110	Bradford Lyttle and Abraham Bassford	U.S. Pacifist

Notes: In addition to the votes listed above, 112,597 scattered write-in votes were reported from various states, and 6,267 votes were cast for "None of These Candidates" in Nevada. In addition to Ron Paul and Gloria La Riva, Chuck Baldwin, Charles Jay, and Alan Keyes had a different vice-presidential candidate in at least one state.

UNITED STATES
PRESIDENT 2008

State	Electoral Vote Rep.	Electoral Vote Dem.	Total Vote	Republican	Democratic	Other	Rep.-Dem. Plurality	Percentage Total Vote Rep.	Percentage Total Vote Dem.	Percentage Major Vote Rep.	Percentage Major Vote Dem.
Alabama	9		2,099,819	1,266,546	813,479	19,794	453,067 R	60.3%	38.7%	60.9%	39.1%
Alaska	3		326,197	193,841	123,594	8,762	70,247 R	59.4%	37.9%	61.1%	38.9%
Arizona	10		2,293,475	1,230,111	1,034,707	28,657	195,404 R	53.6%	45.1%	54.3%	45.7%
Arkansas	6		1,086,617	638,017	422,310	26,290	215,707 R	58.7%	38.9%	60.2%	39.8%
California		55	13,561,900	5,011,781	8,274,473	275,646	3,262,692 D	37.0%	61.0%	37.7%	62.3%
Colorado		9	2,401,462	1,073,629	1,288,633	39,200	215,004 D	44.7%	53.7%	45.4%	54.6%
Connecticut		7	1,646,797	629,428	997,772	19,597	368,344 D	38.2%	60.6%	38.7%	61.3%
Delaware		3	412,412	152,374	255,459	4,579	103,085 D	36.9%	61.9%	37.4%	62.6%
Florida		27	8,390,744	4,045,624	4,282,074	63,046	236,450 D	48.2%	51.0%	48.6%	51.4%
Georgia	15		3,924,486	2,048,759	1,844,123	31,604	204,636 R	52.2%	47.0%	52.6%	47.4%
Hawaii		4	453,568	120,566	325,871	7,131	205,305 D	26.6%	71.8%	27.0%	73.0%
Idaho	4		655,122	403,012	236,440	15,670	166,572 R	61.5%	36.1%	63.0%	37.0%
Illinois		21	5,522,371	2,031,179	3,419,348	71,844	1,388,169 D	36.8%	61.9%	37.3%	62.7%
Indiana		11	2,751,054	1,345,648	1,374,039	31,367	28,391 D	48.9%	49.9%	49.5%	50.5%
Iowa		7	1,537,123	682,379	828,940	25,804	146,561 D	44.4%	53.9%	45.2%	54.8%
Kansas	6		1,235,872	699,655	514,765	21,452	184,890 R	56.6%	41.7%	57.6%	42.4%
Kentucky	8		1,826,620	1,048,462	751,985	26,173	296,477 R	57.4%	41.2%	58.2%	41.8%
Louisiana	9		1,960,761	1,148,275	782,989	29,497	365,286 R	58.6%	39.9%	59.5%	40.5%
Maine		4	731,163	295,273	421,923	13,967	126,650 D	40.4%	57.7%	41.2%	58.8%
Maryland		10	2,631,596	959,862	1,629,467	42,267	669,605 D	36.5%	61.9%	37.1%	62.9%
Massachusetts		12	3,080,985	1,108,854	1,904,097	68,034	795,243 D	36.0%	61.8%	36.8%	63.2%
Michigan		17	5,001,766	2,048,639	2,872,579	80,548	823,940 D	41.0%	57.4%	41.6%	58.4%
Minnesota		10	2,910,369	1,275,409	1,573,354	61,606	297,945 D	43.8%	54.1%	44.8%	55.2%
Mississippi	6		1,289,865	724,597	554,662	10,606	169,935 R	56.2%	43.0%	56.6%	43.4%
Missouri	11		2,925,205	1,445,814	1,441,911	37,480	3,903 R	49.4%	49.3%	50.1%	49.9%
Montana	3		490,302	242,763	231,667	15,872	11,096 R	49.5%	47.2%	51.2%	48.8%
Nebraska	4	1	801,281	452,979	333,319	14,983	119,660 R	56.5%	41.6%	57.6%	42.4%
Nevada		5	967,848	412,827	533,736	21,285	120,909 D	42.7%	55.1%	43.6%	56.4%
New Hampshire		4	710,970	316,534	384,826	9,610	68,292 D	44.5%	54.1%	45.1%	54.9%
New Jersey		15	3,868,237	1,613,207	2,215,422	39,608	602,215 D	41.7%	57.3%	42.1%	57.9%
New Mexico		5	830,158	346,832	472,422	10,904	125,590 D	41.8%	56.9%	42.3%	57.7%
New York		31	7,640,931	2,752,771	4,804,945	83,215	2,052,174 D	36.0%	62.9%	36.4%	63.6%
North Carolina		15	4,310,789	2,128,474	2,142,651	39,664	14,177 D	49.4%	49.7%	49.8%	50.2%
North Dakota	3		316,621	168,601	141,278	6,742	27,323 R	53.3%	44.6%	54.4%	45.6%
Ohio		20	5,708,350	2,677,820	2,940,044	90,486	262,224 D	46.9%	51.5%	47.7%	52.3%
Oklahoma	7		1,462,661	960,165	502,496		457,669 R	65.6%	34.4%	65.6%	34.4%
Oregon		7	1,827,864	738,475	1,037,291	52,098	298,816 D	40.4%	56.7%	41.6%	58.4%
Pennsylvania		21	6,013,272	2,655,885	3,276,363	81,024	620,478 D	44.2%	54.5%	44.8%	55.2%
Rhode Island		4	471,766	165,391	296,571	9,804	131,180 D	35.1%	62.9%	35.8%	64.2%
South Carolina	8		1,920,969	1,034,896	862,449	23,624	172,447 R	53.9%	44.9%	54.5%	45.5%
South Dakota	3		381,975	203,054	170,924	7,997	32,130 R	53.2%	44.7%	54.3%	45.7%
Tennessee	11		2,599,749	1,479,178	1,087,437	33,134	391,741 R	56.9%	41.8%	57.6%	42.4%
Texas	34		8,077,795	4,479,328	3,528,633	69,834	950,695 R	55.5%	43.7%	55.9%	44.1%
Utah	5		952,370	596,030	327,670	28,670	268,360 R	62.6%	34.4%	64.5%	35.5%
Vermont		3	325,046	98,974	219,262	6,810	120,288 D	30.4%	67.5%	31.1%	68.9%
Virginia		13	3,723,260	1,725,005	1,959,532	38,723	234,527 D	46.3%	52.6%	46.8%	53.2%
Washington		11	3,036,878	1,229,216	1,750,848	56,814	521,632 D	40.5%	57.7%	41.2%	58.8%
West Virginia	5		713,451	397,466	303,857	12,128	93,609 R	55.7%	42.6%	56.7%	43.3%
Wisconsin		10	2,983,417	1,262,393	1,677,211	43,813	414,818 D	42.3%	56.2%	42.9%	57.1%
Wyoming	3		254,658	164,958	82,868	6,832	82,090 R	64.8%	32.5%	66.6%	33.4%
District of Columbia		3	265,853	17,367	245,800	2,686	228,433 D	6.5%	92.5%	6.6%	93.4%
Total	173	365	131,313,820	59,948,323	69,498,516	1,866,981	9,550,193 D	45.7%	52.9%	46.3%	53.7%

UNITED STATES
PRESIDENT 2008 MINOR PARTIES

State	Total	Nader (Independent)	Barr (Libertarian)	Baldwin (Constitution)	McKinney (Green)	Other Candidates and Scattered Write-ins	Nader (Ind.)	Barr (Libert.)	Baldwin (Const.)	McKinney (Green)
Alabama	19,794	6,788	4,991	4,310		3,705	0.3%	0.2%	0.2%	
Alaska	8,762	3,783	1,589	1,660		1,730	1.2%	0.5%	0.5%	
Arizona	28,657	11,301	12,555	1,371*	3,406	24	0.5%	0.5%	0.1%	0.1%
Arkansas	26,290	12,882	4,776	4,023	3,470	1,139	1.2%	0.4%	0.4%	0.3%
California	275,646	108,381	67,582	3,145*	38,774	57,764	0.8%	0.5%		0.3%
Colorado	39,200	13,352	10,898	6,233	2,822	5,895	0.6%	0.5%	0.3%	0.1%
Connecticut	19,597	19,162		311*	90*	34	1.2%			
Delaware	4,579	2,401	1,109	626	385	58	0.6%	0.3%	0.2%	0.1%
Florida	63,046	28,124	17,218	7,915	2,887	6,902	0.3%	0.2%	0.1%	0.0%
Georgia	31,604	1,158*	28,731	1,402*	250*	63	0.0%	0.7%		
Hawaii	7,131	3,825	1,314	1,013	979		0.8%	0.3%	0.2%	0.2%
Idaho	15,670	7,175	3,658	4,747	39*	51	1.1%	0.6%	0.7%	
Illinois	71,844	30,948	19,642	8,256	11,838	1,160	0.6%	0.4%	0.1%	0.2%
Indiana	31,367	909*	29,257	1,024*	87*	90		1.1%		
Iowa	25,804	8,014	4,590	4,445	1,423	7,332	0.5%	0.3%	0.3%	0.1%
Kansas	21,452	10,527	6,706	4,148	35*	36	0.9%	0.5%	0.3%	
Kentucky	26,173	15,378	5,989	4,694		112	0.8%	0.3%	0.3%	
Louisiana	29,497	6,997		2,581	9,187	10,732	0.4%		0.1%	0.5%
Maine	13,967	10,636	251*	177*	2,900	3	1.5%			0.4%
Maryland	42,267	14,713	9,842	3,760	4,747	9,205	0.6%	0.4%	0.1%	0.2%
Massachusetts	68,034	28,841	13,189	4,971	6,550	14,483	0.9%	0.4%	0.2%	0.2%
Michigan	80,548	33,085	23,716	14,685	8,892	170	0.7%	0.5%	0.3%	0.2%
Minnesota	61,606	30,152	9,174	6,787	5,174	10,319	1.0%	0.3%	0.2%	0.2%
Mississippi	10,606	4,011	2,529	2,551	1,034	481	0.3%	0.2%	0.2%	0.1%
Missouri	37,480	17,813	11,386	8,201	80*		0.6%	0.4%	0.3%	
Montana	15,872	3,686	1,355	143*	23*	10,665	0.8%	0.3%		
Nebraska	14,983	5,406	2,740	2,972	1,028	2,837	0.7%	0.3%	0.4%	0.1%
Nevada	21,285	6,150	4,263	3,194	1,411	6,267	0.6%	0.4%	0.3%	0.1%
New Hampshire	9,610	3,503	2,217	226*	40*	3,624	0.5%	0.3%		
New Jersey	39,608	21,298	8,441	3,956	3,636	2,277	0.6%	0.2%	0.1%	0.1%
New Mexico	10,904	5,327	2,428	1,597	1,552		0.6%	0.3%	0.2%	0.2%
New York	83,215	41,249	19,596	634*	12,801	8,935	0.5%	0.3%		0.2%
North Carolina	39,664	1,448*	25,722		158*	12,336		0.6%		
North Dakota	6,742	4,189	1,354	1,199			1.3%	0.4%	0.4%	
Ohio	90,486	42,337	19,917	12,565	8,518	7,149	0.7%	0.3%	0.2%	0.1%
Oklahoma										
Oregon	52,098	18,614	7,635	7,693	4,543	13,613	1.0%	0.4%	0.4%	0.2%
Pennsylvania	81,024	42,977	19,912	1,092*		17,043	0.7%	0.3%		
Rhode Island	9,804	4,829	1,382	675	797	2,121	1.0%	0.3%	0.1%	0.2%
South Carolina	23,624	5,053	7,283	6,827	4,461		0.3%	0.4%	0.4%	0.2%
South Dakota	7,997	4,267	1,835	1,895			1.1%	0.5%	0.5%	
Tennessee	33,134	11,560	8,547	8,191	2,499	2,337	0.4%	0.3%	0.3%	0.1%
Texas	69,834	5,751*	56,116	5,708*	909*	1,350	0.1%	0.7%	0.1%	
Utah	28,670	8,416	6,966	12,012	982	294	0.9%	0.7%	1.3%	0.1%
Vermont	6,810	3,339	1,067	500	66*	1,838	1.0%	0.3%	0.2%	
Virginia	38,723	11,483	11,067	7,474	2,344	6,355	0.3%	0.3%	0.2%	0.1%
Washington	56,814	29,489	12,728	9,432	3,819	1,346	1.0%	0.4%	0.3%	0.1%
West Virginia	12,128	7,219		2,465	2,355	89	1.0%		0.3%	0.3%
Wisconsin	43,813	17,605	8,858	5,072	4,216	8,062	0.6%	0.3%	0.2%	0.1%
Wyoming	6,832	2,525	1,594	1,192		1,521	1.0%	0.6%	0.5%	
District of Columbia	2,686	958			590	1,138	0.4%			0.2%
Total	1,866,981	739,034	523,715	199,750	161,797	242,685	0.6%	0.4%	0.2%	0.1%

Note: An asterisk (*) indicates write-in votes.

PRESIDENT 2004

In New York the Republican total includes votes for their candidate on the Conservative line and the Democratic total includes votes for their candidate on the Working Families line.

In Minnesota the Democratic candidate appears on the ballot as Democratic-Farmer-Labor; in North Dakota as Democratic-Nonpartisan League. In many states various third party candidates appeared on the ballot with variations of the party designations, were carried with entirely different party labels, or were listed as "Independent."

The candidates listed below include all who appeared on the ballot in at least one state. Write-in votes for third party candidates are credited to their total below. See the third party chart on page 15 for details.

62,040,610	George W. Bush and Richard B. Cheney	Republican
59,028,439	John Kerry and John Edwards	Democratic
465,650	Ralph Nader and Peter Miguel Camejo	Independent
397,265	Michael Badnarik and Richard V. Campagna	Libertarian
143,630	Michael Peroutka and Chuck Baldwin	Constitution
119,859	David Cobb and Patricia LaMarche	Green
27,607	Leonard Peltier and Janice Jordan	Peace and Freedom
10,837	Walter F. Brown and Mary Alice Herbert	Socialist
7,102	James Harris and Margaret Trowe	Socialist Workers
3,689	Roger Calero and Arrin Hawkins	Socialist Workers
2,387	Thomas J. Harens and Jennifer A. Ryan	Christian Freedom
1,944	Gene Amondson and Leroy Pletten	Concerns of People
1,861	Bill Van Auken and Jim Lawrence	Socialist Equality
1,646	John Parker and Teresa Gutierrez	Workers World
946	Charles Jay and Marilyn Chambers Taylor	Personal Choice
804	Stanford E. "Andy" Andress and Irene M. Deasy	Unaffiliated
140	Earl F. Dodge and Howard F. Lydick	Prohibition

Notes: In addition to the votes listed above, 37,241 scattered write-in votes were reported from various states, and 3,688 votes were cast for "None of these Candidates" in Nevada.

UNITED STATES
PRESIDENT 2004

State	Electoral Vote Rep.	Electoral Vote Dem.	Electoral Vote Other	Total Vote	Republican	Democratic	Other	Rep.-Dem. Plurality	Percentage Total Vote Rep.	Total Vote Dem.	Major Vote Rep.	Major Vote Dem.
Alabama	9			1,883,449	1,176,394	693,933	13,122	482,461 R	62.5%	36.8%	62.9%	37.1%
Alaska	3			312,598	190,889	111,025	10,684	79,864 R	61.1%	35.5%	63.2%	36.8%
Arizona	10			2,012,585	1,104,294	893,524	14,767	210,770 R	54.9%	44.4%	55.3%	44.7%
Arkansas	6			1,054,945	572,898	469,953	12,094	102,945 R	54.3%	44.5%	54.9%	45.1%
California		55		12,421,852	5,509,826	6,745,485	166,541	1,235,659 D	44.4%	54.3%	45.0%	55.0%
Colorado	9			2,130,330	1,101,255	1,001,732	27,343	99,523 R	51.7%	47.0%	52.4%	47.6%
Connecticut		7		1,578,769	693,826	857,488	27,455	163,662 D	43.9%	54.3%	44.7%	55.3%
Delaware		3		375,190	171,660	200,152	3,378	28,492 D	45.8%	53.3%	46.2%	53.8%
Florida	27			7,609,810	3,964,522	3,583,544	61,744	380,978 R	52.1%	47.1%	52.5%	47.5%
Georgia	15			3,301,875	1,914,254	1,366,149	21,472	548,105 R	58.0%	41.4%	58.4%	41.6%
Hawaii		4		429,013	194,191	231,708	3,114	37,517 D	45.3%	54.0%	45.6%	54.4%
Idaho	4			598,447	409,235	181,098	8,114	228,137 R	68.4%	30.3%	69.3%	30.7%
Illinois		21		5,274,322	2,345,946	2,891,550	36,826	545,604 D	44.5%	54.8%	44.8%	55.2%
Indiana	11			2,468,002	1,479,438	969,011	19,553	510,427 R	59.9%	39.3%	60.4%	39.6%
Iowa	7			1,506,908	751,957	741,898	13,053	10,059 R	49.9%	49.2%	50.3%	49.7%
Kansas	6			1,187,756	736,456	434,993	16,307	301,463 R	62.0%	36.6%	62.9%	37.1%
Kentucky	8			1,795,882	1,069,439	712,733	13,710	356,706 R	59.5%	39.7%	60.0%	40.0%
Louisiana	9			1,943,106	1,102,169	820,299	20,638	281,870 R	56.7%	42.2%	57.3%	42.7%
Maine		4		740,752	330,201	396,842	13,709	66,641 D	44.6%	53.6%	45.4%	54.6%
Maryland		10		2,386,678	1,024,703	1,334,493	27,482	309,790 D	42.9%	55.9%	43.4%	56.6%
Massachusetts		12		2,912,388	1,071,109	1,803,800	37,479	732,691 D	36.8%	61.9%	37.3%	62.7%
Michigan		17		4,839,252	2,313,746	2,479,183	46,323	165,437 D	47.8%	51.2%	48.3%	51.7%
Minnesota		9	1	2,828,387	1,346,695	1,445,014	36,678	98,319 D	47.6%	51.1%	48.2%	51.8%
Mississippi	6			1,152,145	684,981	458,094	9,070	226,887 R	59.5%	39.8%	59.9%	40.1%
Missouri	11			2,731,364	1,455,713	1,259,171	16,480	196,542 R	53.3%	46.1%	53.6%	46.4%
Montana	3			450,445	266,063	173,710	10,672	92,353 R	59.1%	38.6%	60.5%	39.5%
Nebraska	5			778,186	512,814	254,328	11,044	258,486 R	65.9%	32.7%	66.8%	33.2%
Nevada	5			829,587	418,690	397,190	13,707	21,500 R	50.5%	47.9%	51.3%	48.7%
New Hampshire		4		677,738	331,237	340,511	5,990	9,274 D	48.9%	50.2%	49.3%	50.7%
New Jersey		15		3,611,691	1,670,003	1,911,430	30,258	241,427 D	46.2%	52.9%	46.6%	53.4%
New Mexico	5			756,304	376,930	370,942	8,432	5,988 R	49.8%	49.0%	50.4%	49.6%
New York		31		7,391,036	2,962,567	4,314,280	114,189	1,351,713 D	40.1%	58.4%	40.7%	59.3%
North Carolina	15			3,501,007	1,961,166	1,525,849	13,992	435,317 R	56.0%	43.6%	56.2%	43.8%
North Dakota	3			312,833	196,651	111,052	5,130	85,599 R	62.9%	35.5%	63.9%	36.1%
Ohio	20			5,627,908	2,859,768	2,741,167	26,973	118,601 R	50.8%	48.7%	51.1%	48.9%
Oklahoma	7			1,463,758	959,792	503,966		455,826 R	65.6%	34.4%	65.6%	34.4%
Oregon		7		1,836,782	866,831	943,163	26,788	76,332 D	47.2%	51.3%	47.9%	52.1%
Pennsylvania		21		5,769,590	2,793,847	2,938,095	37,648	144,248 D	48.4%	50.9%	48.7%	51.3%
Rhode Island		4		437,134	169,046	259,760	8,328	90,714 D	38.7%	59.4%	39.4%	60.6%
South Carolina	8			1,617,730	937,974	661,699	18,057	276,275 R	58.0%	40.9%	58.6%	41.4%
South Dakota	3			388,215	232,584	149,244	6,387	83,340 R	59.9%	38.4%	60.9%	39.1%
Tennessee	11			2,437,319	1,384,375	1,036,477	16,467	347,898 R	56.8%	42.5%	57.2%	42.8%
Texas	34			7,410,765	4,526,917	2,832,704	51,144	1,694,213 R	61.1%	38.2%	61.5%	38.5%
Utah	5			927,844	663,742	241,199	22,903	422,543 R	71.5%	26.0%	73.3%	26.7%
Vermont		3		312,309	121,180	184,067	7,062	62,887 D	38.8%	58.9%	39.7%	60.3%
Virginia	13			3,198,367	1,716,959	1,454,742	26,666	262,217 R	53.7%	45.5%	54.1%	45.9%
Washington		11		2,859,084	1,304,894	1,510,201	43,989	205,307 D	45.6%	52.8%	46.4%	53.6%
West Virginia	5			755,887	423,778	326,541	5,568	97,237 R	56.1%	43.2%	56.5%	43.5%
Wisconsin		10		2,997,007	1,478,120	1,489,504	29,383	11,384 D	49.3%	49.7%	49.8%	50.2%
Wyoming	3			243,428	167,629	70,776	5,023	96,853 R	68.9%	29.1%	70.3%	29.7%
District of Columbia		3		227,586	21,256	202,970	3,360	181,714 D	9.3%	89.2%	9.5%	90.5%
Total	286	251	1	122,295,345	62,040,610	59,028,439	1,226,296	3,012,171 R	50.7%	48.3%	51.2%	48.8%

Note: A Democratic elector in Minnesota cast a vote for Edwards rather than Kerry.

UNITED STATES
PRESIDENT 2004 MINOR PARTIES

State	Total	Nader	Badnarik	Peroutka	Cobb	Other Candidates and Scattered Write-ins
Alabama	13,122	6,701	3,529	1,994		898
Alaska	10,684	5,069	1,675	2,092	1,058	790
Arizona	14,767	2,773*	11,856		138*	
Arkansas	12,094	6,171	2,352	2,083	1,488	
California	166,541	21,213*	50,165	26,645	40,771	27,747
Colorado	27,343	12,718	7,664	2,562	1,591	2,808
Connecticut	27,455	12,969	3,367	1,543	9,564	12
Delaware	3,378	2,153	586	289	250	100
Florida	61,744	32,971	11,996	6,626	3,917	6,234
Georgia	21,472	2,231*	18,387	580*	228*	46
Hawaii	3,114		1,377		1,737	
Idaho	8,114	1,115*	3,844	3,084	58*	13
Illinois	36,826	3,571*	32,442	440*	241*	132
Indiana	19,553	1,328*	18,058		102*	65
Iowa	13,053	5,973	2,992	1,304	1,141	1,643
Kansas	16,307	9,348	4,013	2,899	33*	14
Kentucky	13,710	8,856	2,619	2,213		22
Louisiana	20,638	7,032	2,781	5,203	1,276	4,346
Maine	13,709	8,069	1,965	735	2,936	4
Maryland	27,482	11,854	6,094	3,421	3,632	2,481
Massachusetts	37,479	4,806*	15,022		10,623	7,028
Michigan	46,323	24,035	10,552	4,980	5,325	1,431
Minnesota	36,678	18,683	4,639	3,074	4,408	5,874
Mississippi	9,070	3,177	1,793	1,759	1,073	1,268
Missouri	16,480	1,294*	9,831	5,355		
Montana	10,672	6,168	1,733	1,764	996	11
Nebraska	11,044	5,698	2,041	1,314	978	1,013
Nevada	13,707	4,838	3,176	1,152	853	3,688
New Hampshire	5,990	4,479	372*	161*		978
New Jersey	30,258	19,418	4,514	2,750	1,807	1,769
New Mexico	8,432	4,053	2,382	771	1,226	
New York	114,189	99,873	11,607	207*	87*	2,415
North Carolina	13,992	1,805*	11,731		108*	348
North Dakota	5,130	3,756	851	514		9
Ohio	26,973		14,676	11,939	192*	166
Oklahoma						
Oregon	26,788		7,260	5,257	5,315	8,956
Pennsylvania	37,648	2,656*	21,185	6,318	6,319	1,170
Rhode Island	8,328	4,651	907	339	1,333	1,098
South Carolina	18,057	5,520	3,608	5,317	1,488	2,124
South Dakota	6,387	4,320	964	1,103		
Tennessee	16,467	8,992	4,866	2,570	33*	6
Texas	51,144	9,159*	38,787	1,636*	1,014*	548
Utah	22,903	11,305	3,375	6,841	39*	1,343
Vermont	7,062	4,494	1,102			1,466
Virginia	26,666	2,393*	11,032	10,161	104*	2,976
Washington	43,989	23,283	11,955	3,922	2,974	1,855
West Virginia	5,568	4,063	1,405	82*	5*	13
Wisconsin	29,383	16,390	6,464		2,661	3,868
Wyoming	5,023	2,741	1,171	631		480
District of Columbia	3,360	1,485	502		737	636
Total	1,226,296	465,650	397,265	143,630	119,859	99,892

Note: An asterisk (*) indicates write-in votes.

UNITED STATES
VOTER TURNOUT 2004

State	2004 Voting Age Population	Registration: 2004 General Election	Percentage Voting Age Registered	Presidential Vote	Presidential Vote as Percentage of — Voting Age Population	Presidential Vote as Percentage of — Registered Voters	U.S. House Vote	Senate Vote	Governor Vote
Alabama	3,419,000	2,842,985	83.2%	1,883,449	55.1%	66.2%	1,792,759	1,839,066	—
Alaska	447,000	473,927	106.0%	312,598	69.9%	66.0%	299,996	308,315	—
Arizona	3,768,000	2,643,331	70.2%	2,012,585	53.4%	76.1%	1,871,445	1,961,677	—
Arkansas	2,057,000	1,684,684	81.9%	1,054,945	51.3%	62.6%	791,240	1,039,349	—
California	20,754,000	16,557,273	79.8%	12,421,852	59.9%	75.0%	11,623,753	12,053,295	8,657,915
Colorado	3,275,000	3,114,566	95.1%	2,130,330	65.0%	68.4%	2,039,011	2,107,554	—
Connecticut	2,390,000	2,044,181	85.5%	1,578,769	66.1%	77.2%	1,428,738	1,424,726	—
Delaware	601,000	553,885	92.2%	375,190	62.4%	67.7%	356,045	—	365,008
Florida	11,904,000	10,301,290	86.5%	7,609,810	63.9%	73.9%	5,627,494	7,429,894	—
Georgia	6,135,000	4,951,955	80.7%	3,301,875	53.8%	66.7%	2,960,763	3,220,981	—
Hawaii	877,000	647,238	73.8%	429,013	48.9%	66.3%	416,570	415,347	—
Idaho	985,000	798,015	81.0%	598,447	60.8%	75.0%	572,426	503,932	—
Illinois	8,544,000	7,499,488	87.8%	5,274,322	61.7%	70.3%	4,988,665	5,141,520	—
Indiana	4,572,000	4,296,602	94.0%	2,468,002	54.0%	57.4%	2,416,251	2,428,233	2,448,498
Iowa	2,190,000	2,106,658	96.2%	1,506,908	68.8%	71.5%	1,458,161	1,479,228	—
Kansas	1,954,000	1,591,428	81.4%	1,187,756	60.8%	74.6%	1,156,383	1,129,022	—
Kentucky	3,134,000	2,794,286	89.2%	1,795,882	57.3%	64.3%	1,635,243	1,724,362	1,083,443
Louisiana	3,310,000	2,923,395	88.3%	1,943,106	58.7%	66.5%	1,545,982	1,848,056	1,407,842
Maine	984,000	1,023,956	104.1%	740,752	75.3%	72.3%	710,176	—	—
Maryland	3,804,000	3,074,889	80.8%	2,386,678	62.7%	77.6%	2,255,955	2,323,183	—
Massachusetts	4,501,000	4,098,634	91.1%	2,912,388	64.7%	71.1%	2,580,955	—	—
Michigan	7,289,000	7,164,047	98.3%	4,839,252	66.4%	67.5%	4,631,058	—	—
Minnesota	3,658,000	3,559,400	97.3%	2,828,387	77.3%	79.5%	2,721,681	—	—
Mississippi	2,155,000	1,791,666	83.1%	1,152,145	53.5%	64.3%	1,116,203	—	894,487
Missouri	4,242,000	4,194,146	98.9%	2,731,364	64.4%	65.1%	2,667,023	2,706,402	2,719,599
Montana	709,000	638,474	90.1%	450,445	63.5%	70.6%	444,230	—	446,146
Nebraska	1,256,000	1,160,199	92.4%	778,186	62.0%	67.1%	764,972	—	—
Nevada	1,528,000	1,071,101	70.1%	829,587	54.3%	77.5%	791,433	810,068	—
New Hampshire	942,000	855,861	90.9%	677,738	71.9%	79.2%	651,566	657,086	667,020
New Jersey	5,702,000	5,005,959	87.8%	3,611,691	63.3%	72.1%	3,284,595	—	—
New Mexico	1,322,000	1,105,372	83.6%	756,304	57.2%	68.4%	742,899	—	—
New York	12,496,000	11,837,068	94.7%	7,391,036	59.1%	62.4%	6,222,418	6,702,875	—
North Carolina	6,208,000	5,519,992	88.9%	3,501,007	56.4%	63.4%	3,413,071	3,472,082	3,486,688
North Dakota	483,000	—		312,833	64.8%	—	310,814	310,696	309,873
Ohio	8,486,000	7,972,826	94.0%	5,627,908	66.3%	70.6%	5,183,508	5,426,196	—
Oklahoma	2,581,000	2,143,978	83.1%	1,463,758	56.7%	68.3%	1,374,610	1,446,846	—
Oregon	2,581,000	2,141,243	83.0%	1,836,782	71.2%	85.8%	1,772,306	1,780,550	—
Pennsylvania	9,230,000	8,366,663	90.6%	5,769,590	62.5%	69.0%	5,152,274	5,559,105	—
Rhode Island	752,000	651,950	86.7%	437,134	58.1%	67.1%	402,175	—	—
South Carolina	3,120,000	2,315,462	74.2%	1,617,730	51.9%	69.9%	1,439,118	1,597,221	—
South Dakota	569,000	552,441	97.1%	388,215	68.2%	70.3%	389,468	391,188	—
Tennessee	4,462,000	3,742,829	83.9%	2,437,319	54.6%	65.1%	2,218,738	—	—
Texas	14,197,000	13,098,329	92.3%	7,410,765	52.2%	56.6%	6,958,603	—	—
Utah	1,587,000	1,278,251	80.5%	927,844	58.5%	72.6%	908,857	911,726	919,960
Vermont	470,000	444,077	94.5%	312,309	66.4%	70.3%	305,008	307,208	309,285
Virginia	5,290,000	4,517,980	85.4%	3,198,367	60.5%	70.8%	3,004,007	—	—
Washington	4,370,000	3,508,208	80.3%	2,859,084	65.4%	81.5%	2,729,995	2,818,651	2,810,058
West Virginia	1,423,000	1,168,694	82.1%	755,887	53.1%	64.7%	721,656	—	744,433
Wisconsin	4,057,000	—		2,997,007	73.9%	—	2,821,613	2,949,743	—
Wyoming	380,000	232,396	61.2%	243,428	64.1%	104.7%	239,034	—	—
District of Columbia	391,000	383,919	98.2%	227,586	58.2%	59.3%	—	—	—
Total	201,541,000	172,445,197	85.6%	122,295,345	60.7%	70.9%	111,910,944	86,225,383	27,270,255

Sources: Voting age population figures were compiled by the Committee for the Study of the American Electorate (CSAE) and represent the estimated citizen voting age population in each state (and nationally) at the time of the November 2004 general election. CSAE employs a more conservative methodology than does the Census Bureau, which no longer provides election-year voting age population estimates. Registration figures are as of the November 2004 general election and were obtained from state election officials. In some cases, the registration totals are suspect as a number of states include inactive voters in their totals. In Alaska and Wyoming, for instance, the number of registered voters was more than 100 percent of the voting age population. The Minnesota total includes election-day registrations. The Mississippi total was as of April 2004. North Dakota and Wisconsin did not compile statewide registration figures.

Notes: Votes are from the November 2004 general election, with the exception of gubernatorial elections in California, Kentucky, Louisiana, and Mississippi, which were held in 2003. The California gubernatorial contest was a special recall election.

PRESIDENT 2000

In New York the Republican figures include Conservative votes and the Democratic figures include Liberal and Working Families votes.

In Minnesota the Democratic candidate appears on the ballot as Democratic-Farmer-Labor. In many states various non-major party candidates appeared on the ballot with variations of the party designations, were carried with entirely different party labels, or were listed as "Independent."

The candidates listed below include all those who appeared on the ballot in at least one state. Write-in votes for minor party candidates are credited to their total below. See the minor parties table on page 19 for details.

50,455,156	George W. Bush and Richard B. Cheney	Republican
50,992,335	Al Gore and Joseph I. Lieberman	Democratic
2,882,738	Ralph Nader and Winona LaDuke	Green
449,077	Pat Buchanan and Ezola Foster	Reform
384,429	Harry Browne and Art Olivier	Libertarian
98,020	Howard Phillips and J. Curtis Frazier	Constitution
83,525	John Hagelin and Nat Goldhaber	Natural Law
7,378	James E. Harris Jr. and Margaret Trowe	Socialist Worker
5,775	L. Neil Smith and Vin Suprynowicz	Arizona Libertarian
5,602	David McReynolds and Mary Cal Hollis	Socialist
4,795	Monica Moorehead and Gloria La Riva	Workers World
1,606	Cathy Gordon Brown and Sabrina R. Allen	Independent
1,044	Denny Lane and Dale Wilkinson	Vermont Grassroots
535	Randall Venson and Gene Kelly	Independent
208	Earl F. Dodge and W. Dean Watkins	Prohibition
161	Louie G. Youngkeit and Robert Leo Beck	Unaffiliated

Notes: In addition to the votes listed above, 20,928 scattered write-in votes were reported from various states, and 3,315 votes were cast for "None of These Candidates" in Nevada.

UNITED STATES
PRESIDENT 2000

State	Electoral Vote Rep.	Electoral Vote Dem.	Electoral Vote Other	Total Vote	Republican	Democratic	Green (Nader)	Other	Rep.-Dem. Plurality		Rep.	Dem.	Green
Alabama	9			1,666,272	941,173	692,611	18,323	14,165	248,562	R	56.5%	41.6%	1.1%
Alaska	3			285,560	167,398	79,004	28,747	10,411	88,394	R	58.6%	27.7%	10.1%
Arizona	8			1,532,016	781,652	685,341	45,645	19,378	96,311	R	51.0%	44.7%	3.0%
Arkansas	6			921,781	472,940	422,768	13,421	12,652	50,172	R	51.3%	45.9%	1.5%
California		54		10,965,856	4,567,429	5,861,203	418,707	118,517	1,293,774	D	41.7%	53.4%	3.8%
Colorado	8			1,741,368	883,748	738,227	91,434	27,959	145,521	R	50.8%	42.4%	5.3%
Connecticut		8		1,459,525	561,094	816,015	64,452	17,964	254,921	D	38.4%	55.9%	4.4%
Delaware		3		327,622	137,288	180,068	8,307	1,959	42,780	D	41.9%	55.0%	2.5%
Florida	25			5,963,110	2,912,790	2,912,253	97,488	40,579	537	R	48.8%	48.8%	1.6%
Georgia	13			2,596,645	1,419,720	1,116,230	13,273	47,422	303,490	R	54.7%	43.0%	0.5%
Hawaii		4		367,951	137,845	205,286	21,623	3,197	67,441	D	37.5%	55.8%	5.9%
Idaho	4			501,621	336,937	138,637	12,292	13,755	198,300	R	67.2%	27.6%	2.5%
Illinois		22		4,742,123	2,019,421	2,589,026	103,759	29,917	569,605	D	42.6%	54.6%	2.2%
Indiana	12			2,199,302	1,245,836	901,980	18,531	32,955	343,856	R	56.6%	41.0%	0.8%
Iowa		7		1,315,563	634,373	638,517	29,374	13,299	4,144	D	48.2%	48.5%	2.2%
Kansas	6			1,072,218	622,332	399,276	36,086	14,524	223,056	R	58.0%	37.2%	3.4%
Kentucky	8			1,544,187	872,492	638,898	23,192	9,605	233,594	R	56.5%	41.4%	1.5%
Louisiana	9			1,765,656	927,871	792,344	20,473	24,968	135,527	R	52.6%	44.9%	1.2%
Maine		4		651,817	286,616	319,951	37,127	8,123	33,335	D	44.0%	49.1%	5.7%
Maryland		10		2,020,480	813,797	1,140,782	53,768	12,133	326,985	D	40.3%	56.5%	2.7%
Massachusetts		12		2,702,984	878,502	1,616,487	173,564	34,431	737,985	D	32.5%	59.8%	6.4%
Michigan		18		4,232,711	1,953,139	2,170,418	84,165	24,989	217,279	D	46.1%	51.3%	2.0%
Minnesota		10		2,438,685	1,109,659	1,168,266	126,696	34,064	58,607	D	45.5%	47.9%	5.2%
Mississippi	7			994,184	572,844	404,614	8,122	8,604	168,230	R	57.6%	40.7%	0.8%
Missouri	11			2,359,892	1,189,924	1,111,138	38,515	20,315	78,786	R	50.4%	47.1%	1.6%
Montana	3			410,997	240,178	137,126	24,437	9,256	103,052	R	58.4%	33.4%	5.9%
Nebraska	5			697,019	433,862	231,780	24,540	6,837	202,082	R	62.2%	33.3%	3.5%
Nevada	4			608,970	301,575	279,978	15,008	12,409	21,597	R	49.5%	46.0%	2.5%
New Hampshire	4			569,081	273,559	266,348	22,198	6,976	7,211	R	48.1%	46.8%	3.9%
New Jersey		15		3,187,226	1,284,173	1,788,850	94,554	19,649	504,677	D	40.3%	56.1%	3.0%
New Mexico		5		598,605	286,417	286,783	21,251	4,154	366	D	47.8%	47.9%	3.6%
New York		33		6,821,999	2,403,374	4,107,697	244,030	66,898	1,704,323	D	35.2%	60.2%	3.6%
North Carolina	14			2,911,262	1,631,163	1,257,692	—	22,407	373,471	R	56.0%	43.2%	—
North Dakota	3			288,256	174,852	95,284	9,486	8,634	79,568	R	60.7%	33.1%	3.3%
Ohio	21			4,701,998	2,350,363	2,183,628	117,799	50,208	166,735	R	50.0%	46.4%	2.5%
Oklahoma	8			1,234,229	744,337	474,276		15,616	270,061	R	60.3%	38.4%	—
Oregon		7		1,533,968	713,577	720,342	77,357	22,692	6,765	D	46.5%	47.0%	5.0%
Pennsylvania		23		4,913,119	2,281,127	2,485,967	103,392	42,633	204,840	D	46.4%	50.6%	2.1%
Rhode Island		4		409,047	130,555	249,508	25,052	3,932	118,953	D	31.9%	61.0%	6.1%
South Carolina	8			1,382,717	785,937	565,561	20,200	11,019	220,376	R	56.8%	40.9%	1.5%
South Dakota	3			316,269	190,700	118,804	—	6,765	71,896	R	60.3%	37.6%	—
Tennessee	11			2,076,181	1,061,949	981,720	19,781	12,731	80,229	R	51.1%	47.3%	1.0%
Texas	32			6,407,637	3,799,639	2,433,746	137,994	36,258	1,365,893	R	59.3%	38.0%	2.2%
Utah	5			770,754	515,096	203,053	35,850	16,755	312,043	R	66.8%	26.3%	4.7%
Vermont		3		294,308	119,775	149,022	20,374	5,137	29,247	D	40.7%	50.6%	6.9%
Virginia	13			2,739,447	1,437,490	1,217,290	59,398	25,269	220,200	R	52.5%	44.4%	2.2%
Washington		11		2,487,433	1,108,864	1,247,652	103,002	27,915	138,788	D	44.6%	50.2%	4.1%
West Virginia	5			648,124	336,475	295,497	10,680	5,472	40,978	R	51.9%	45.6%	1.6%
Wisconsin		11		2,598,607	1,237,279	1,242,987	94,070	24,271	5,708	D	47.6%	47.8%	3.6%
Wyoming	3			218,351	147,947	60,481	4,625	5,298	87,466	R	67.8%	27.7%	2.1%
District of Columbia		2	1	201,894	18,073	171,923	10,576	1,322	153,850	D	9.0%	85.2%	5.2%
Total	271	266	1	105,396,627	50,455,156	50,992,335	2,882,738	1,066,398	537,179	D	47.9%	48.4%	2.7%

UNITED STATES
PRESIDENT 2000 MINOR PARTIES

State	Total	Buchanan	Browne	Phillips	Hagelin	Other Candidates and Scattered Write-ins
Alabama	14,165	6,351	5,893	775	447	699
Alaska	10,411	5,192	2,636	596	919	1,068
Arizona	19,378	12,373		110	1,120	5,775
Arkansas	12,652	7,358	2,781	1,415	1,098	—
California	118,517	44,987	45,520	17,042	10,934	34
Colorado	27,959	10,465	12,799	1,319	2,240	1,136
Connecticut	17,964	4,731	3,484	9,695	40	14
Delaware	1,959	777	774	208	107	93
Florida	40,579	17,484	16,415	1,371	2,281	3,028
Georgia	47,422	10,926	36,332	140		24
Hawaii	3,197	1,071	1,477	343	306	—
Idaho	13,755	7,615	3,488	1,469	1,177	6
Illinois	29,917	16,106	11,623	57	2,127	4
Indiana	32,955	16,959	15,530	200	167	99
Iowa	13,299	5,731	3,209	613	2,281	1,465
Kansas	14,524	7,370	4,525	1,254	1,375	—
Kentucky	9,605	4,173	2,896	923	1,533	80
Louisiana	24,968	14,356	2,951	5,483	1,075	1,103
Maine	8,123	4,443	3,074	579		27
Maryland	12,133	4,248	5,310	919	176	1,480
Massachusetts	34,431	11,149	16,366		2,884	4,032
Michigan	24,989	2061	16,711	3,791	2,426	—
Minnesota	34,064	22,166	5,282	3,272	2,294	1,050
Mississippi	8,604	2,265	2,009	3,267	450	613
Missouri	20,315	9,818	7,436	1,957	1,104	—
Montana	9,256	5,697	1,718	1,155	675	11
Nebraska	6,837	3,646	2,245	468	478	—
Nevada	12,409	4,747	3,311	621	415	3,315
New Hampshire	6,976	2,615	2,757	328		1,276
New Jersey	19,649	6,989	6,312	1,409	2,215	2,724
New Mexico	4,154	1,392	2,058	343	361	—
New York	66,898	31,599	7,649	1,498	24,361	1,791
North Carolina	22,407	8,874	12,307			1,226
North Dakota	8,634	7,288	660	373	313	—
Ohio	50,208	26,721	13,473	3,823	6,181	10
Oklahoma	15,616	9,014	6,602			—
Oregon	22,692	7,063	7,447	2,189	2,574	3,419
Pennsylvania	42,633	16,023	11,248	14,428		934
Rhode Island	3,932	2,273	742	97	271	549
South Carolina	11,019	3,519	4,876	1,682	942	—
South Dakota	6,765	3,322	1,662	1,781		—
Tennessee	12,731	4,250	4,284	1,015	613	2,569
Texas	36,258	12,394	23,160	567		137
Utah	16,755	9,319	3,616	2,709	763	348
Vermont	5,137	2,192	784	153	219	1,789
Virginia	25,269	5,455	15,198	1,809		2,807
Washington	27,915	7,171	13,135	1,989	2,927	2,693
West Virginia	5,472	3,169	1,912	23	367	1
Wisconsin	24,271	11,446	6,640	2,042	878	3,265
Wyoming	5,298	2,724	1,443	720	411	—
District of Columbia	1,322		669			653
Total	*1,066,398*	*449,077*	*384,429*	*98,020*	*83,525*	*51,347*

UNITED STATES
VOTER TURNOUT 2000

State	2000 Voting Age Population Est.	November 2000 Registration	Percentage Voting Age Registered	Presidential Vote	Presidential Vote as Percentage of		House Vote	Senate Vote	Governor Vote
					Voting Age Population	Registered Voters			
Alabama	3,333,000	2,528,963	75.9%	1,666,272	50.0%	65.9%	1,438,994		
Alaska	430,000	473,648	110.2%	285,560	66.4%	60.3%	274,393		
Arizona	3,625,000	2,654,700	73.2%	1,532,016	42.3%	57.7%	1,465,656	1,397,076	
Arkansas	1,929,000	1,555,809	80.7%	921,781	47.8%	59.2%	632,765		
California	24,873,000	15,707,307	63.2%	10,965,856	44.1%	69.8%	10,437,665	10,623,614	
Colorado	3,067,000	2,858,239	93.2%	1,741,368	56.8%	60.9%	1,623,882		
Connecticut	2,499,000	2,031,626	81.3%	1,459,525	58.4%	71.8%	1,313,490	1,311,261	
Delaware	582,000	503,672	86.5%	327,622	56.3%	65.0%	313,171	327,017	323,688
Florida	11,774,000	8,752,717	74.3%	5,963,110	50.6%	68.1%	5,011,372	5,856,731	
Georgia	5,893,000	4,648,205	78.9%	2,596,645	44.1%	55.9%	2,416,622	2,428,510	
Hawaii	909,000	637,349	70.1%	367,951	40.5%	57.7%	340,424	345,623	
Idaho	921,000	728,085	79.1%	501,621	54.5%	68.9%	492,835		
Illinois	8,983,000	7,117,449	79.2%	4,742,123	52.8%	66.6%	4,393,352		
Indiana	4,448,000	4,000,809	89.9%	2,199,302	49.4%	55.0%	2,156,744	2,145,209	2,179,413
Iowa	2,165,000	1,969,199	91.0%	1,315,563	60.8%	66.8%	1,275,934		
Kansas	1,983,000	1,623,623	81.9%	1,072,218	54.1%	66.0%	1,038,379		
Kentucky	2,993,000	2,556,815	85.4%	1,544,187	51.6%	60.4%	1,435,409		580,074
Louisiana	3,255,000	2,782,929	85.5%	1,765,656	54.2%	63.4%	1,202,171		1,295,205
Maine	968,000	947,189	97.9%	651,817	67.3%	68.8%	638,399	634,872	
Maryland	3,925,000	2,715,366	69.2%	2,020,480	51.5%	74.4%	1,926,764	1,946,898	
Massachusetts	4,749,000	4,000,218	84.2%	2,702,984	56.9%	67.6%	2,347,375	2,599,420	
Michigan	7,358,000	6,861,342	93.3%	4,232,711	56.6%	60.7%	4,069,736	4,167,685	
Minnesota	3,547,000	2,801,077	79.0%	2,438,685	68.8%	87.1%	2,363,738	2,419,520	
Mississippi	2,047,000			994,184	48.6%		986,139	994,144	763,938
Missouri	4,105,000	3,676,664	89.6%	2,359,892	57.5%	64.2%	2,325,788	2,361,586	2,346,830
Montana	668,000	698,260	104.5%	410,997	61.5%	58.9%	410,523	411,601	410,192
Nebraska	1,234,000	1,085,272	87.9%	697,019	56.5%	64.2%	683,071	692,344	
Nevada	1,390,000	878,970	63.2%	608,970	43.8%	69.3%	585,204	600,250	
New Hampshire	911,000	856,519	94.0%	569,081	62.5%	66.4%	556,417		564,953
New Jersey	6,245,000	4,710,768	75.4%	3,187,226	51.0%	67.7%	2,988,233	3,015,662	
New Mexico	1,263,000	928,931	73.5%	598,605	47.4%	64.4%	587,514	589,526	
New York	13,805,000	11,262,816	81.6%	6,821,999	49.4%	60.6%	5,823,850	6,779,839	
North Carolina	5,797,000	5,186,094	89.5%	2,911,262	50.2%	56.1%	2,779,800		2,942,062
North Dakota	477,000			288,256	60.4%		285,658	287,539	289,412
Ohio	8,433,000	7,537,822	89.4%	4,701,998	55.8%	62.4%	4,517,838	4,448,801	
Oklahoma	2,531,000	2,233,602	88.2%	1,234,229	48.8%	55.3%	1,087,515		
Oregon	2,530,000	1,950,902	77.1%	1,533,968	60.6%	78.6%	1,440,002		
Pennsylvania	9,155,000	7,781,997	85.0%	4,913,119	53.7%	63.1%	4,554,347	4,735,504	
Rhode Island	753,000	655,107	87.0%	409,047	54.3%	62.4%	384,127	391,537	
South Carolina	2,977,000	2,266,200	76.1%	1,382,717	46.4%	61.0%	1,321,312		
South Dakota	542,000	520,881	96.1%	316,269	58.4%	60.7%	314,761		
Tennessee	4,221,000	3,400,487	80.6%	2,076,181	49.2%	61.1%	1,854,378	1,928,613	
Texas	14,850,000	12,365,235	83.3%	6,407,637	43.1%	51.8%	5,985,763	6,276,652	
Utah	1,465,000	1,120,129	76.5%	770,754	52.6%	68.8%	758,754	769,704	761,806
Vermont	460,000	427,354	92.9%	294,308	64.0%	68.9%	283,366	288,500	293,473
Virginia	5,263,000	4,071,471	77.4%	2,739,447	52.1%	67.3%	2,421,729	2,718,301	
Washington	4,368,000	3,335,714	76.4%	2,487,433	56.9%	74.6%	2,382,411	2,461,379	2,469,852
West Virginia	1,416,000	1,067,822	75.4%	648,124	45.8%	60.7%	579,872	603,477	648,047
Wisconsin	3,930,000			2,598,607	66.1%		2,506,314	2,540,083	
Wyoming	358,000	220,012	61.5%	218,351	61.0%	99.2%	212,312	213,659	
District of Columbia	411,000	354,410		201,894	49.1%	57.0%			
Total	205,814,000	159,049,775	77.3%	105,396,627	51.2%	66.3%	97,226,268	79,312,137	15,868,945

Sources: Registration figures—Committee for the Study of the American Electorate; voting age population—U.S. Census Bureau

Notes: Voting age population excluding states without registration: 199,360,000. Wisconsin and North Dakota do not maintain registration systems. Figures for Mississippi were unavailable. Excluding these states, the percentage of the voting age population that was registered was 79.8 percent. The presidential vote as a percentage of the voting age population was 50.9 percent and as a percentage of registered voters was 63.8 percent.

PRESIDENT 1996

In New York the Republican figures include Conservative, Freedom, and Right to Life votes and the Democratic figures include Liberal votes.

In Minnesota the Democratic candidate appears on the ballot as Democratic-Farmer-Labor. In many states various non-major party candidates appeared on the ballot with variations of the party designations, were carried with entirely different party labels, or were listed as "Independent."

The candidates listed below include all those who appeared on the ballot in at least one state. Write-in votes for minor party candidates are credited to their total below. See the minor parties table on page 23 for details.

47,402,357	Bill Clinton and Al Gore	Democratic
39,198,755	Bob Dole and Jack Kemp	Republican
8,085,402	Ross Perot and Pat Choate	Reform
685,040	Ralph Nader and Winona LaDuke	Green
485,798	Harry Browne and Jo Jorgensen	Libertarian
184,658	Howard Phillips and Herbert W. Titus	U.S. Taxpayers
113,668	John Hagelin and Mike Tompkins	Natural Law
29,083	Monica Moorehead and Gloria La Riva	Workers World
25,332	Marsha Feinland and Kate McClatchy	Peace and Freedom
8,930	Charles Collins and Rosemary Giumarra	Independent
8,476	James Harris and Laura Garza	Socialist Workers
5,378	Dennis Peron and Arlin D. Troutt Jr.	Grassroots
4,706	Mary Cal Hollis and Eric Chester	Socialist
2,438	Jerome White and Fred Mazelis	Socialist Equality
1,847	Diane Beall Templin and Gary Van Horn	American
1,298	Earl F. Dodge and Rachel B. Kelly	Prohibition
1,101	A. Peter Crane and Connie Chandler	Independent
932	Ralph Forbes and "Pro-Life" Anderson	America First
787	John Birrenbach and George McMahon	Independent Grassroots
752	Isabell Masters and Shirley Jean Masters	Looking Back
408	Steve Michael and Ann Northrop	Independent

Notes: In addition to the votes listed above, 25,118 scattered write-in votes were reported from various states, and 5,608 votes were cast for "None of These Candidates" in Nevada.

UNITED STATES
PRESIDENT 1996

State	Electoral Vote Rep.	Dem.	Other	Total Vote	Republican	Democratic	Reform	Other	Plurality		Percentage Rep.	Dem.	Reform
Alabama	9			1,534,349	769,044	662,165	92,149	10,991	106,879	R	50.1%	43.2%	6.0%
Alaska	3			241,620	122,746	80,380	26,333	12,161	42,366	R	50.8%	33.3%	10.9%
Arizona		8		1,404,405	622,073	653,288	112,072	16,972	31,215	D	44.3%	46.5%	8.0%
Arkansas		6		884,262	325,416	475,171	69,884	13,791	149,755	D	36.8%	53.7%	7.9%
California		54		10,019,484	3,828,380	5,119,835	697,847	373,422	1,291,455	D	38.2%	51.1%	7.0%
Colorado	8			1,510,704	691,848	671,152	99,629	48,075	20,696	R	45.8%	44.4%	6.6%
Connecticut		8		1,392,614	483,109	735,740	139,523	34,242	252,631	D	34.7%	52.8%	10.0%
Delaware		3		271,084	99,062	140,355	28,719	2,948	41,293	D	36.5%	51.8%	10.6%
Florida		25		5,303,794	2,244,536	2,546,870	483,870	28,518	302,334	D	42.3%	48.0%	9.1%
Georgia	13			2,299,071	1,080,843	1,053,849	146,337	18,042	26,994	R	47.0%	45.8%	6.4%
Hawaii		4		360,120	113,943	205,012	27,358	13,807	91,069	D	31.6%	56.9%	7.6%
Idaho	4			491,719	256,595	165,443	62,518	7,163	91,152	R	52.2%	33.6%	12.7%
Illinois		22		4,311,391	1,587,021	2,341,744	346,408	36,218	754,723	D	36.8%	54.3%	8.0%
Indiana	12			2,135,842	1,006,693	887,424	224,299	17,426	119,269	R	47.1%	41.5%	10.5%
Iowa		7		1,234,075	492,644	620,258	105,159	16,014	127,614	D	39.9%	50.3%	8.5%
Kansas	6			1,074,300	583,245	387,659	92,639	10,757	195,586	R	54.3%	36.1%	8.6%
Kentucky		8		1,388,708	623,283	636,614	120,396	8,415	13,331	D	44.9%	45.8%	8.7%
Louisiana		9		1,783,959	712,586	927,837	123,293	20,243	215,251	D	39.9%	52.0%	6.9%
Maine		4		605,897	186,378	312,788	85,970	20,761	126,410	D	30.8%	51.6%	14.2%
Maryland		10		1,780,870	681,530	966,207	115,812	17,321	284,677	D	38.3%	54.3%	6.5%
Massachusetts		12		2,556,785	718,107	1,571,763	227,217	39,698	853,656	D	28.1%	61.5%	8.9%
Michigan		18		3,848,844	1,481,212	1,989,653	336,670	41,309	508,441	D	38.5%	51.7%	8.7%
Minnesota		10		2,192,640	766,476	1,120,438	257,704	48,022	353,962	D	35.0%	51.1%	11.8%
Mississippi	7			893,857	439,838	394,022	52,222	7,775	45,816	R	49.2%	44.1%	5.8%
Missouri		11		2,158,065	890,016	1,025,935	217,188	24,926	135,919	D	41.2%	47.5%	10.1%
Montana	3			407,261	179,652	167,922	55,229	4,458	11,730	R	44.1%	41.2%	13.6%
Nebraska	5			677,415	363,467	236,761	71,278	5,909	126,706	R	53.7%	35.0%	10.5%
Nevada		4		464,279	199,244	203,974	43,986	17,075	4,730	D	42.9%	43.9%	9.5%
New Hampshire		4		499,175	196,532	246,214	48,390	8,039	49,682	D	39.4%	49.3%	9.7%
New Jersey		15		3,075,807	1,103,078	1,652,329	262,134	58,266	549,251	D	35.9%	53.7%	8.5%
New Mexico		5		556,074	232,751	273,495	32,257	17,571	40,744	D	41.9%	49.2%	5.8%
New York		33		6,316,129	1,933,492	3,756,177	503,458	123,002	1,822,685	D	30.6%	59.5%	8.0%
North Carolina	14			2,515,807	1,225,938	1,107,849	168,059	13,961	118,089	R	48.7%	44.0%	6.7%
North Dakota	3			266,411	125,050	106,905	32,515	1,941	18,145	R	46.9%	40.1%	12.2%
Ohio		21		4,534,434	1,859,883	2,148,222	483,207	43,122	288,339	D	41.0%	47.4%	10.7%
Oklahoma	8			1,206,713	582,315	488,105	130,788	5,505	94,210	R	48.3%	40.4%	10.8%
Oregon		7		1,377,760	538,152	649,641	121,221	68,746	111,489	D	39.1%	47.2%	8.8%
Pennsylvania		23		4,506,118	1,801,169	2,215,819	430,984	58,146	414,650	D	40.0%	49.2%	9.6%
Rhode Island		4		390,284	104,683	233,050	43,723	8,828	128,367	D	26.8%	59.7%	11.2%
South Carolina	8			1,151,689	573,458	506,283	64,386	7,562	67,175	R	49.8%	44.0%	5.6%
South Dakota	3			323,826	150,543	139,333	31,250	2,700	11,210	R	46.5%	43.0%	9.7%
Tennessee		11		1,894,105	863,530	909,146	105,918	15,511	45,616	D	45.6%	48.0%	5.6%
Texas	32			5,611,644	2,736,167	2,459,683	378,537	37,257	276,484	R	48.8%	43.8%	6.7%
Utah	5			665,629	361,911	221,633	66,461	15,624	140,278	R	54.4%	33.3%	10.0%
Vermont		3		258,449	80,352	137,894	31,024	9,179	57,542	D	31.1%	53.4%	12.0%
Virginia	13			2,416,642	1,138,350	1,091,060	159,861	27,371	47,290	R	47.1%	45.1%	6.6%
Washington		11		2,253,837	840,712	1,123,323	201,003	88,799	282,611	D	37.3%	49.8%	8.9%
West Virginia		5		636,459	233,946	327,812	71,639	3,062	93,866	D	36.8%	51.5%	11.3%
Wisconsin		11		2,196,169	845,029	1,071,971	227,339	51,830	226,942	D	38.5%	48.8%	10.4%
Wyoming	3			211,571	105,388	77,934	25,928	2,321	27,454	R	49.8%	36.8%	12.3%
District of Columbia		3		185,726	17,339	158,220	3,611	6,556	140,881	D	9.3%	85.2%	1.9%
Total	*159*	*379*		*96,277,872*	*39,198,755*	*47,402,357*	*8,085,402*	*1,591,358*	*8,203,602*	*D*	*40.7%*	*49.2%*	*8.4%*

UNITED STATES
PRESIDENT 1996 MINOR PARTIES

State	Total	Nader	Browne	Phillips	Hagelin	Moorehead	Feinland	Other Candidates and Scattered Write-ins
Alabama	10,991		5,290	2,365	1,697			1,639
Alaska	12,161	7,597	2,276	925	729			634
Arizona	16,972	2,062*	14,358	347*	153*			52
Arkansas	13,791	3,649	3,076	2,065	729	747		3,525
California	373,422	237,016	73,600	21,202	15,403		25,332	869
Colorado	48,075	25,070	12,392	2,813	2,547	599		4,654
Connecticut	34,242	24,321	5,788	2,425	1,703			5
Delaware	2,948	156*	2,052	348	274			118
Florida	28,518	4,101*	23,965		418*			34
Georgia	18,042		17,870	145*				27
Hawaii	13,807	10,386	2,493	358	570			
Idaho	7,163		3,325	2,230	1,600			8
Illinois	36,218	1,447*	22,548	7,606	4,606			11
Indiana	17,426	895*	15,632	291*	118*			490
Iowa	16,014	6,550	2,315	2,229	3,349			1,571
Kansas	10,757	914*	4,557	3,519	1,655			112
Kentucky	8,415	701*	4,009	2,204	1,493			8
Louisiana	20,243	4,719	7,499	3,366	2,981	1,678		
Maine	20,761	15,279	2,996	1,517	825			144
Maryland	17,321	2,606*	8,765	3,402	2,517			31
Massachusetts	39,698	4,565*	20,426		5,184	3,277		6,246
Michigan	41,309	2,322*	27,670	539*	4,254	3,153		3,371
Minnesota	48,022	24,908	8,271	3,416	1,808			9,619
Mississippi	7,775		2,809	2,314	1,447			1,205
Missouri	24,926	534*	10,522	11,521	2,287			62
Montana	4,458		2,526	152*	1,754			26
Nebraska	5,909		2,792	1,928	1,189			
Nevada	17,075	4,730	4,460	1,732	545			5,608
New Hampshire	8,039		4,237	1,346				2,456
New Jersey	58,266	32,465	14,763	3,440	3,887	1,337		2,374
New Mexico	17,571	13,218	2,996	713	644			
New York	123,002	75,956	12,220	23,580	5,011	3,473		2,762
North Carolina	13,961	2,108*	8,740	258*	2,771			84
North Dakota	1,941		847	745	349			
Ohio	43,122	2,962*	12,851	7,361	9,120	10,813		15
Oklahoma	5,505		5,505					
Oregon	68,746	49,415	8,903	3,379	2,798			4,251
Pennsylvania	58,146	3,086*	28,000	19,552	5,783			1,725
Rhode Island	8,828	6,040	1,109	1,021	435	186		37
South Carolina	7,562		4,271	2,043	1,248			
South Dakota	2,700		1,472	912	316			
Tennessee	15,511	6,427	5,020	1,818	636			1,610
Texas	37,257	4,810*	20,256	7,472	4,422			297
Utah	15,624	4,615	4,129	2,601	1,085	298		2,896
Vermont	9,179	5,585	1,183	382	498			1,531
Virginia	27,371		9,174	13,687	4,510			
Washington	88,799	60,322	12,522	4,578	6,076	2,189		3,112
West Virginia	3,062		3,062					
Wisconsin	51,830	28,723	7,929	8,811	1,379	1,333		3,655
Wyoming	2,321		1,739		582			
District of Columbia	6,556	4,780	588		283			905
Total	1,591,358	685,040	485,798	184,658	113,668	29,083	25,332	67,779

Notes: An asterisk (*) indicates write-in votes. The vote, including write-ins, for other minor party candidates who were listed on the ballot in at least one state: 8,930 Collins (Arizona, Arkansas, California, Colorado, Georgia, Idaho, Kansas, Maryland, Mississippi, Missouri, Montana, Tennessee, Utah, Washington); 8,476 Harris (Alabama, California, Colorado, Connecticut, Florida, Georgia, Iowa, Minnesota, New Jersey, New York, North Carolina, Utah, Vermont, Washington, Wisconsin, District of Columbia); 5,378 Peron (Minnesota, Vermont); 4,706 Holllis (Arkansas, Colorado, Florida, Maryland, Massachusetts, Montana, Oregon, Texas, Utah, Vermont, Wisconsin); 2,438 White (Michigan, Minnesota, New Jersey); 1,847 Templin (Colorado, Utah); 1,298 Dodge (Arkansas, Colorado, Illinois, Massachusetts, Tennessee, Utah); 1,101 Crane (Utah); 932 Forbes (Arkansas); 787 Birrenbach (Minnesota); 752 Masters (Arkansas, California, Maryland); 408 Michael (Tennessee). The Other Candidates and Scattered Write-ins column includes 5,608 votes cast in Nevada for "None of These Candidates" and 25,118 scattered write-ins.

UNITED STATES
VOTER TURNOUT 1996

State	1996 Census Voting Age Pop. Est.	November 1996 Registration	Percentage Voting Age Registered	Total Valid Vote President	Percentage Voting Age Voted	Percentage Registered Voted
Alabama	3,218,000	2,470,766	76.8%	1,534,349	47.7%	62.1%
Alaska	425,000	414,817	97.6%	241,620	56.9%	58.2%
Arizona	3,094,000	2,244,672	72.5%	1,404,405	45.4%	62.6%
Arkansas	1,860,000	1,396,459	75.1%	884,262	47.5%	63.3%
California	23,133,000	15,662,075	67.7%	10,019,484	43.3%	64.0%
Colorado	2,843,000	2,285,503	80.4%	1,510,704	53.1%	66.1%
Connecticut	2,468,000	1,975,000	80.0%	1,392,614	56.4%	70.5%
Delaware	547,000	419,695	76.7%	271,084	49.6%	64.6%
Florida	11,043,000	8,077,877	73.1%	5,303,794	48.0%	65.7%
Georgia	5,396,000	3,811,284	70.6%	2,299,071	42.6%	60.3%
Hawaii	882,000	544,916	61.8%	360,120	40.8%	66.1%
Idaho	845,000	700,430	82.9%	491,719	58.2%	70.2%
Illinois	8,764,000	6,663,301	76.0%	4,311,391	49.2%	64.7%
Indiana	4,369,000	3,484,033	79.7%	2,135,842	48.9%	61.3%
Iowa	2,138,000	1,776,433	83.1%	1,234,075	57.7%	69.5%
Kansas	1,898,000	1,436,418	75.7%	1,074,300	56.6%	74.8%
Kentucky	2,924,000	2,396,086	81.9%	1,388,708	47.5%	58.0%
Louisiana	3,137,000	2,539,240	80.9%	1,783,959	56.9%	70.3%
Maine	939,000	1,001,292	106.6%	605,897	64.5%	60.5%
Maryland	3,811,000	2,587,977	67.9%	1,780,870	46.7%	68.8%
Massachusetts	4,623,000	3,459,193	74.8%	2,556,785	55.3%	73.9%
Michigan	7,067,000	6,688,893	94.6%	3,848,844	54.5%	57.5%
Minnesota	3,412,000	2,730,505	80.0%	2,192,640	64.3%	80.3%
Mississippi	1,961,000			893,857	45.6%	
Missouri	3,980,000	3,339,852	83.9%	2,158,065	54.2%	64.6%
Montana	647,000	590,749	91.3%	407,261	62.9%	68.9%
Nebraska	1,208,000	1,015,056	84.0%	677,415	56.1%	66.7%
Nevada	1,180,000	778,298	66.0%	464,279	39.3%	59.7%
New Hampshire	860,000	713,236	82.9%	499,175	58.0%	70.0%
New Jersey	6,005,000	4,320,866	72.0%	3,075,807	51.2%	71.2%
New Mexico	1,210,000	837,794	69.2%	556,074	46.0%	66.4%
New York	13,579,000	10,162,156	74.8%	6,316,129	46.5%	62.2%
North Carolina	5,499,000	4,315,723	78.5%	2,515,807	45.8%	58.3%
North Dakota	473,000			266,411	56.3%	
Ohio	8,358,000	6,879,687	82.3%	4,534,434	54.3%	65.9%
Oklahoma	2,419,000	1,979,017	81.8%	1,206,713	49.9%	61.0%
Oregon	2,396,000	1,962,155	81.9%	1,377,760	57.5%	70.2%
Pennsylvania	9,196,000	6,799,637	73.9%	4,506,118	49.0%	66.3%
Rhode Island	750,000	602,692	80.4%	390,284	52.0%	64.8%
South Carolina	2,777,000	1,814,777	65.4%	1,151,689	41.5%	63.5%
South Dakota	530,000	476,422	89.9%	323,826	61.1%	68.0%
Tennessee	4,021,000	3,097,336	77.0%	1,894,105	47.1%	61.2%
Texas	13,622,000	10,520,379	77.2%	5,611,644	41.2%	53.3%
Utah	1,323,000	1,050,452	79.4%	665,629	50.3%	63.4%
Vermont	441,000	385,328	87.4%	258,449	58.6%	67.1%
Virginia	5,089,000	3,322,740	65.3%	2,416,642	47.5%	72.7%
Washington	4,122,000	3,081,971	74.8%	2,253,837	54.7%	73.1%
West Virginia	1,414,000	970,745	68.7%	636,459	45.0%	65.6%
Wisconsin	3,824,000			2,196,169	57.4%	
Wyoming	352,000			211,571	60.1%	
District of Columbia	435,000	361,419	83.1%	185,726	42.7%	51.4%
Total	196,507,000	144,145,352	73.4%	96,277,872	49.0%	66.8%

Source: Registration figures—Committee for the Study of the American Electorate.

Notes: Mississippi, North Dakota, Wisconsin, and Wyoming do not maintain formal voter registration systems or had no figures readily available. Excluding these four states, the percentage of the voting age population registered in the remaining states was 75.9 percent, and the percentage of registered that voted was 64.3 percent.

PRESIDENT 1992

In New York the Republican figures include Conservative and Right to Life votes and the Democratic figures include Liberal votes.

In Minnesota the Republican candidates appear on the ballot as Independent-Republican, the Democratic as Democratic-Farmer-Labor. In many states various non-major party candidates appeared on the ballot with variations of the party designations, were carried with entirely different party labels, or were listed as "Independent." In several states minor party vice-presidential candidates were different from those listed below.

The candidates listed below include all those who appeared on the ballot in at least one state. Write-in votes for minor party candidates are credited to their total below.

44,909,326	Bill Clinton and Al Gore	Democratic
39,103,882	George Bush and J. Danforth Quayle	Republican
19,741,657	Ross Perot and James Stockdale	Independent
291,627	Andre V. Marrou and Nancy Lord	Libertarian
107,014	James Gritz and Cyril Minett	America First
73,714	Lenora B. Fulani and Maria E. Munoz	New Alliance
43,434	Howard Phillips and Albion W. Knight	Taxpayers
39,179	John Hagelin and Mike Tompkins	Natural Law
27,961	Ron Daniels and Asiba Tupahache	Peace and Freedom
26,333	Lyndon H. LaRouche Jr. and James L. Bevel	Economic Recovery
23,096	James Warren and Willie Mae Reid	Socialist Workers
4,749	Drew Bradford and no vice-presidential candidate	Independent
3,875	Jack Herer and Derrick P. Grimmer	Grassroots
3,057	J. Quinn Brisben and Barbara Garson	Socialist
3,050	Helen Halyard and Fred Mazelis	Workers League
2,199	John Yiamouyiannis and Allen C. McCone	Take Back America
1,149	Delbert L. Ehlers and Rick Wendt	Independent
961	Earl F. Dodge and George Ormsby	Prohibition
956	Jim Boren and Will Weidman	Apathy
405	Eugene A. Hem and Joanne Roland	Third Party
339	Isabell Masters and Walter Masters	Looking Back
292	Robert J. Smith and Doris Feimer	American
181	Gloria La Riva and Larry Holmes	Workers World

Notes: In addition to the votes listed above, 14,041 scattered write-in votes were reported from various states, and 2,537 votes were cast for "None of These Candidates" in Nevada.

UNITED STATES
PRESIDENT 1992

State	Electoral Vote Rep.	Dem.	Other	Total Vote	Republican	Democratic	Independent	Other	Plurality		Percentage Rep.	Dem.	Ind.
Alabama	9			1,688,060	804,283	690,080	183,109	10,588	114,203	R	47.6%	40.9%	10.8%
Alaska	3			258,506	102,000	78,294	73,481	4,731	23,706	R	39.5%	30.3%	28.4%
Arizona	8			1,486,975	572,086	543,050	353,741	18,098	29,036	R	38.5%	36.5%	23.8%
Arkansas		6		950,653	337,324	505,823	99,132	8,374	168,499	D	35.5%	53.2%	10.4%
California		54		11,131,721	3,630,574	5,121,325	2,296,006	83,816	1,490,751	D	32.6%	46.0%	20.6%
Colorado		8		1,569,180	562,850	629,681	366,010	10,639	66,831	D	35.9%	40.1%	23.3%
Connecticut		8		1,616,332	578,313	682,318	348,771	6,930	104,005	D	35.8%	42.2%	21.6%
Delaware		3		289,735	102,313	126,054	59,213	2,155	23,741	D	35.3%	43.5%	20.4%
Florida	25			5,314,392	2,173,310	2,072,698	1,053,067	15,317	100,612	R	40.9%	39.0%	19.8%
Georgia		13		2,321,125	995,252	1,008,966	309,657	7,250	13,714	D	42.9%	43.5%	13.3%
Hawaii		4		372,842	136,822	179,310	53,003	3,707	42,488	D	36.7%	48.1%	14.2%
Idaho	4			482,142	202,645	137,013	130,395	12,089	65,632	R	42.0%	28.4%	27.0%
Illinois		22		5,050,157	1,734,096	2,453,350	840,515	22,196	719,254	D	34.3%	48.6%	16.6%
Indiana	12			2,305,871	989,375	848,420	455,934	12,142	140,955	R	42.9%	36.8%	19.8%
Iowa		7		1,354,607	504,891	586,353	253,468	9,895	81,462	D	37.3%	43.3%	18.7%
Kansas	6			1,157,335	449,951	390,434	312,358	4,592	59,517	R	38.9%	33.7%	27.0%
Kentucky		8		1,492,900	617,178	665,104	203,944	6,674	47,926	D	41.3%	44.6%	13.7%
Louisiana		9		1,790,017	733,386	815,971	211,478	29,182	82,585	D	41.0%	45.6%	11.8%
Maine		4		679,499	206,504	263,420	206,820	2,755	56,600	D	30.4%	38.8%	30.4%
Maryland		10		1,985,046	707,094	988,571	281,414	7,967	281,477	D	35.6%	49.8%	14.2%
Massachusetts		12		2,773,700	805,049	1,318,662	630,731	19,258	513,613	D	29.0%	47.5%	22.7%
Michigan		18		4,274,673	1,554,940	1,871,182	824,813	23,738	316,242	D	36.4%	43.8%	19.3%
Minnesota		10		2,347,948	747,841	1,020,997	562,506	16,604	273,156	D	31.9%	43.5%	24.0%
Mississippi	7			981,793	487,793	400,258	85,626	8,116	87,535	R	49.7%	40.8%	8.7%
Missouri		11		2,391,565	811,159	1,053,873	518,741	7,792	242,714	D	33.9%	44.1%	21.7%
Montana		3		410,611	144,207	154,507	107,225	4,672	10,300	D	35.1%	37.6%	26.1%
Nebraska	5			737,546	343,678	216,864	174,104	2,900	126,814	R	46.6%	29.4%	23.6%
Nevada		4		506,318	175,828	189,148	132,580	8,762	13,320	D	34.7%	37.4%	26.2%
New Hampshire		4		537,943	202,484	209,040	121,337	5,082	6,556	D	37.6%	38.9%	22.6%
New Jersey		15		3,343,594	1,356,865	1,436,206	521,829	28,694	79,341	D	40.6%	43.0%	15.6%
New Mexico		5		569,986	212,824	261,617	91,895	3,650	48,793	D	37.3%	45.9%	16.1%
New York		33		6,926,925	2,346,649	3,444,450	1,090,721	45,105	1,097,801	D	33.9%	49.7%	15.7%
North Carolina	14			2,611,850	1,134,661	1,114,042	357,864	5,283	20,619	R	43.4%	42.7%	13.7%
North Dakota	3			308,133	136,244	99,168	71,084	1,637	37,076	R	44.2%	32.2%	23.1%
Ohio		21		4,939,967	1,894,310	1,984,942	1,036,426	24,289	90,632	D	38.3%	40.2%	21.0%
Oklahoma	8			1,390,359	592,929	473,066	319,878	4,486	119,863	R	42.6%	34.0%	23.0%
Oregon		7		1,462,643	475,757	621,314	354,091	11,481	145,557	D	32.5%	42.5%	24.2%
Pennsylvania		23		4,959,810	1,791,841	2,239,164	902,667	26,138	447,323	D	36.1%	45.1%	18.2%
Rhode Island	*	4		453,477	131,601	213,299	105,045	3,532	81,698	D	29.0%	47.0%	23.2%
South Carolina	8			1,202,527	577,507	479,514	138,872	6,634	97,993	R	48.0%	39.9%	11.5%
South Dakota	3			336,254	136,718	124,888	73,295	1,353	11,830	R	40.7%	37.1%	21.8%
Tennessee		11		1,982,638	841,300	933,521	199,968	7,849	92,221	D	42.4%	47.1%	10.1%
Texas	32			6,154,018	2,496,071	2,281,815	1,354,781	21,351	214,256	R	40.6%	37.1%	22.0%
Utah	5			743,999	322,632	183,429	203,400	34,538	119,232	R	43.4%	24.7%	27.3%
Vermont		3		289,701	88,122	133,592	65,991	1,996	45,470	D	30.4%	46.1%	22.8%
Virginia	13			2,558,665	1,150,517	1,038,650	348,639	20,859	111,867	R	45.0%	40.6%	13.6%
Washington		11		2,288,230	731,234	993,037	541,780	22,179	261,803	D	32.0%	43.4%	23.7%
West Virginia		5		683,762	241,974	331,001	108,829	1,958	89,027	D	35.4%	48.4%	15.9%
Wisconsin		11		2,531,114	930,855	1,041,066	544,479	14,714	110,211	D	36.8%	41.1%	21.5%
Wyoming	3			200,598	79,347	68,160	51,263	1,828	11,187	R	39.6%	34.0%	25.6%
District of Columbia		3		227,572	20,698	192,619	9,681	4,574	171,921	D	9.1%	84.6%	4.3%
Total	168	370		104,425,014	39,103,882	44,909,326	19,741,657	670,149	5,805,444	D	37.4%	43.0%	18.9%

PRESIDENT 1988

In West Virginia one Democratic elector voted in the electoral college for Lloyd Bentsen for president and Michael S. Dukakis for vice president.

In New York the Republican figures include Conservative votes and the Democratic figures include Liberal votes.

In Minnesota the Republican candidates appear on the ballot as Independent-Republican, the Democratic as Democratic-Farmer-Labor. In many states various non-major party candidates appeared on the ballot with variations of the party designations, were listed as "Independent," or were carried with entirely different party labels.

In several states minor party vice-presidential candidates were different from those listed below. The full list of candidates for president and vice president was:

48,886,097	George Bush and J. Danforth Quayle	Republican
41,809,074	Michael S. Dukakis and Lloyd Bentsen	Democratic
432,179	Ron Paul and Andre V. Marrou	Libertarian
217,219	Lenora B. Fulani and Joyce Dattner	New Alliance
47,047	David E. Duke and Floyd C. Parker	Populist
30,905	Eugene J. McCarthy and Florence Rice	Consumer
27,818	James C. Griffin and Charles J. Morsa	American Independent
25,562	Lyndon H. LaRouche and Debra H. Freeman	National Economic Recovery
20,504	William A. Matra and Joan Andrews	Right to Life
18,693	Ed Winn and Barry Porster	Workers League
15,604	James Warren and Kathleen Mickells	Socialist Workers
10,370	Herbert Lewin and Vikki Murdock	Peace and Freedom
8,002	Earl F. Dodge and George Ormsby	Prohibition
7,846	Larry Holmes and Gloria LaRiva	Workers World
3,882	Willa Kenoyer and Ron Ehrenreich	Socialist
3,475	Delmar Dennis and Earl Jeppson	American
1,949	Jack Herer and Dana Beal	Grassroots
372	Louie G. Youngkeit with no vice presidential candidate	Independent
236	John G. Martin and Cleveland Sparrow	Third World Assembly

Notes: The candidates listed above are those who appeared on the ballot in at least one state. Republican, Democratic, and New Alliance candidates appeared on the ballot in all fifty-one jurisdictions. The Libertarian nominees were on the ballot in 47 jurisdictions. Where identified by state authorities, write-in votes for minor party candidates were credited to their total above. In addition to the votes listed, 21,041 scattered write-in votes were reported from various states, and 6,934 votes were cast for "None of These Candidates" in Nevada.

UNITED STATES
PRESIDENT 1988

State	Electoral Vote Rep.	Dem.	Other	Total Vote	Republican	Democratic	Other	Plurality		Percentage Total Vote Rep.	Dem.	Major Vote Rep.	Dem.
Alabama	9			1,378,476	815,576	549,506	13,394	266,070	R	59.2%	39.9%	59.7%	40.3%
Alaska	3			200,116	119,251	72,584	8,281	46,667	R	59.6%	36.3%	62.2%	37.8%
Arizona	7			1,171,873	702,541	454,029	15,303	248,512	R	60.0%	38.7%	60.7%	39.3%
Arkansas	6			827,738	466,578	349,237	11,923	117,341	R	56.4%	42.2%	57.2%	42.8%
California	47			9,887,065	5,054,917	4,702,233	129,915	352,684	R	51.1%	47.6%	51.8%	48.2%
Colorado	8			1,372,394	728,177	621,453	22,764	106,724	R	53.1%	45.3%	54.0%	46.0%
Connecticut	8			1,443,394	750,241	676,584	16,569	73,657	R	52.0%	46.9%	52.6%	47.4%
Delaware	3			249,891	139,639	108,647	1,605	30,992	R	55.9%	43.5%	56.2%	43.8%
Florida	21			4,302,313	2,618,885	1,656,701	26,727	962,184	R	60.9%	38.5%	61.3%	38.7%
Georgia	12			1,809,672	1,081,331	714,792	13,549	366,539	R	59.8%	39.5%	60.2%	39.8%
Hawaii		4		354,461	158,625	192,364	3,472	33,739	D	44.8%	54.3%	45.2%	54.8%
Idaho	4			408,968	253,881	147,272	7,815	106,609	R	62.1%	36.0%	63.3%	36.7%
Illinois	24			4,559,120	2,310,939	2,215,940	32,241	94,999	R	50.7%	48.6%	51.0%	49.0%
Indiana	12			2,168,621	1,297,763	860,643	10,215	437,120	R	59.8%	39.7%	60.1%	39.9%
Iowa		8		1,225,614	545,355	670,557	9,702	125,202	D	44.5%	54.7%	44.9%	55.1%
Kansas	7			993,044	554,049	422,636	16,359	131,413	R	55.8%	42.6%	56.7%	43.3%
Kentucky	9			1,322,517	734,281	580,368	7,868	153,913	R	55.5%	43.9%	55.9%	44.1%
Louisiana	10			1,628,202	883,702	717,460	27,040	166,242	R	54.3%	44.1%	55.2%	44.8%
Maine	4			555,035	307,131	243,569	4,335	63,562	R	55.3%	43.9%	55.8%	44.2%
Maryland	10			1,714,358	876,167	826,304	11,887	49,863	R	51.1%	48.2%	51.5%	48.5%
Massachusetts		13		2,632,805	1,194,635	1,401,415	36,755	206,780	D	45.4%	53.2%	46.0%	54.0%
Michigan	20			3,669,163	1,965,486	1,675,783	27,894	289,703	R	53.6%	45.7%	54.0%	46.0%
Minnesota		10		2,096,790	962,337	1,109,471	24,982	147,134	D	45.9%	52.9%	46.4%	53.6%
Mississippi	7			931,527	557,890	363,921	9,716	193,969	R	59.9%	39.1%	60.5%	39.5%
Missouri	11			2,093,713	1,084,953	1,001,619	7,141	83,334	R	51.8%	47.8%	52.0%	48.0%
Montana	4			365,674	190,412	168,936	6,326	21,476	R	52.1%	46.2%	53.0%	47.0%
Nebraska	5			661,465	397,956	259,235	4,274	138,721	R	60.2%	39.2%	60.6%	39.4%
Nevada	4			350,067	206,040	132,738	11,289	73,302	R	58.9%	37.9%	60.8%	39.2%
New Hampshire	4			451,074	281,537	163,696	5,841	117,841	R	62.4%	36.3%	63.2%	36.8%
New Jersey	16			3,099,553	1,743,192	1,320,352	36,009	422,840	R	56.2%	42.6%	56.9%	43.1%
New Mexico	5			521,287	270,341	244,497	6,449	25,844	R	51.9%	46.9%	52.5%	47.5%
New York		36		6,485,683	3,081,871	3,347,882	55,930	266,011	D	47.5%	51.6%	47.9%	52.1%
North Carolina	13			2,134,370	1,237,258	890,167	6,945	347,091	R	58.0%	41.7%	58.2%	41.8%
North Dakota	3			297,261	166,559	127,739	2,963	38,820	R	56.0%	43.0%	56.6%	43.4%
Ohio	23			4,393,699	2,416,549	1,939,629	37,521	476,920	R	55.0%	44.1%	55.5%	44.5%
Oklahoma	8			1,171,036	678,367	483,423	9,246	194,944	R	57.9%	41.3%	58.4%	41.6%
Oregon		7		1,201,694	560,126	616,206	25,362	56,080	D	46.6%	51.3%	47.6%	52.4%
Pennsylvania	25			4,536,251	2,300,087	2,194,944	41,220	105,143	R	50.7%	48.4%	51.2%	48.8%
Rhode Island		4		404,620	177,761	225,123	1,736	47,362	D	43.9%	55.6%	44.1%	55.9%
South Carolina	8			986,009	606,443	370,554	9,012	235,889	R	61.5%	37.6%	62.1%	37.9%
South Dakota	3			312,991	165,415	145,560	2,016	19,855	R	52.8%	46.5%	53.2%	46.8%
Tennessee	11			1,636,250	947,233	679,794	9,223	267,439	R	57.9%	41.5%	58.2%	41.8%
Texas	29			5,427,410	3,036,829	2,352,748	37,833	684,081	R	56.0%	43.3%	56.3%	43.7%
Utah	5			647,008	428,442	207,343	11,223	221,099	R	66.2%	32.0%	67.4%	32.6%
Vermont	3			243,328	124,331	115,775	3,222	8,556	R	51.1%	47.6%	51.8%	48.2%
Virginia	12			2,191,609	1,309,162	859,799	22,648	449,363	R	59.7%	39.2%	60.4%	39.6%
Washington		10		1,865,253	903,835	933,516	27,902	29,681	D	48.5%	50.0%	49.2%	50.8%
West Virginia		5	1	653,311	310,065	341,016	2,230	30,951	D	47.5%	52.2%	47.6%	52.4%
Wisconsin		11		2,191,608	1,047,499	1,126,794	17,315	79,295	D	47.8%	51.4%	48.2%	51.8%
Wyoming	3			176,551	106,867	67,113	2,571	39,754	R	60.5%	38.0%	61.4%	38.6%
District of Columbia		3		192,877	27,590	159,407	5,880	131,817	D	14.3%	82.6%	14.8%	85.2%
Total	426	111	1	91,594,809	48,886,097	41,809,074	899,638	7,077,023	R	53.4%	45.6%	53.9%	46.1%

PRESIDENT 1984

In New York the Republican figures include Conservative votes and the Democratic figures include Liberal votes.

In Minnesota the Republican candidates appear on the ballot as Independent-Republican, the Democratic as Democratic-Farmer-Labor. In many states various non-major party candidates appeared on the ballot with variations of the party designations, were listed as "Independent" or "Non-Party," or were carried with entirely different party labels.

The Workers World candidate for president was Gavrielle Holmes in Ohio and Rhode Island; in several states minor party vice-presidential candidates were different from those listed below.

The full list of candidates for president and vice president was:

54,455,075	Ronald Reagan and George Bush	Republican
37,577,185	Walter F. Mondale and Geraldine A. Ferraro	Democratic
228,314	David Bergland and James A. Lewis	Libertarian
78,807	Lyndon H. LaRouche Jr. and Billy M. Davis	Independent
72,200	Sonia Johnson and Richard Walton	Citizens
66,336	Bob Richards and Maureen Salaman	Populist
46,868	Dennis L. Serrette and Nancy Ross	Alliance
36,386	Gus Hall and Angela Davis	Communist
24,706	Mel Mason and Matilde Zimmermann	Socialist Workers
17,985	Larry Holmes and Gloria La Riva	Workers World
13,161	Delmar Dennis and Traves Brownlee	American
10,801	Ed Winn and Helen Halyard	Workers League
4,242	Earl F. Dodge and Warren C. Martin	Prohibition
1,486	John B. Anderson and Grace Pierce	National Unity
892	Gerald Baker and Ferris Alger	Big Deal
825	Arthur J. Lowery and Raymond L. Garland	United Sovereign Citizens

Notes: The candidates listed above are those who appeared on the ballot in at least one state. Where identified by state authorities, write-in votes for minor party candidates are credited to their total above. In addition to the votes listed above, 13,623 scattered write-in votes were reported from various states, and 3,950 votes were cast for "None of These Candidates" in Nevada.

UNITED STATES
PRESIDENT 1984

State	Electoral Vote Rep.	Electoral Vote Dem.	Electoral Vote Other	Total Vote	Republican	Democratic	Other	Plurality		Percentage Total Vote Rep.	Percentage Total Vote Dem.	Percentage Major Vote Rep.	Percentage Major Vote Dem.
Alabama	9			1,441,713	872,849	551,899	16,965	320,950	R	60.5%	38.3%	61.3%	38.7%
Alaska	3			207,605	138,377	62,007	7,221	76,370	R	66.7%	29.9%	69.1%	30.9%
Arizona	7			1,025,897	681,416	333,854	10,627	347,562	R	66.4%	32.5%	67.1%	32.9%
Arkansas	6			884,406	534,774	338,646	10,986	196,128	R	60.5%	38.3%	61.2%	38.8%
California	47			9,505,423	5,467,009	3,922,519	115,895	1,544,490	R	57.5%	41.3%	58.2%	41.8%
Colorado	8			1,295,380	821,817	454,975	18,588	366,842	R	63.4%	35.1%	64.4%	35.6%
Connecticut	8			1,466,900	890,877	569,597	6,426	321,280	R	60.7%	38.8%	61.0%	39.0%
Delaware	3			254,572	152,190	101,656	726	50,534	R	59.8%	39.9%	60.0%	40.0%
Florida	21			4,180,051	2,730,350	1,448,816	885	1,281,534	R	65.3%	34.7%	65.3%	34.7%
Georgia	12			1,776,120	1,068,722	706,628	770	362,094	R	60.2%	39.8%	60.2%	39.8%
Hawaii	4			335,846	185,050	147,154	3,642	37,896	R	55.1%	43.8%	55.7%	44.3%
Idaho	4			411,144	297,523	108,510	5,111	189,013	R	72.4%	26.4%	73.3%	26.7%
Illinois	24			4,819,088	2,707,103	2,086,499	25,486	620,604	R	56.2%	43.3%	56.5%	43.5%
Indiana	12			2,233,069	1,377,230	841,481	14,358	535,749	R	61.7%	37.7%	62.1%	37.9%
Iowa	8			1,319,805	703,088	605,620	11,097	97,468	R	53.3%	45.9%	53.7%	46.3%
Kansas	7			1,021,991	677,296	333,149	11,546	344,147	R	66.3%	32.6%	67.0%	33.0%
Kentucky	9			1,369,345	821,702	539,539	8,104	282,163	R	60.0%	39.4%	60.4%	39.6%
Louisiana	10			1,706,822	1,037,299	651,586	17,937	385,713	R	60.8%	38.2%	61.4%	38.6%
Maine	4			553,144	336,500	214,515	2,129	121,985	R	60.8%	38.8%	61.1%	38.9%
Maryland	10			1,675,873	879,918	787,935	8,020	91,983	R	52.5%	47.0%	52.8%	47.2%
Massachusetts	13			2,559,453	1,310,936	1,239,606	8,911	71,330	R	51.2%	48.4%	51.4%	48.6%
Michigan	20			3,801,658	2,251,571	1,529,638	20,449	721,933	R	59.2%	40.2%	59.5%	40.5%
Minnesota		10		2,084,449	1,032,603	1,036,364	15,482	3,761	D	49.5%	49.7%	49.9%	50.1%
Mississippi	7			941,104	582,377	352,192	6,535	230,185	R	61.9%	37.4%	62.3%	37.7%
Missouri	11			2,122,783	1,274,188	848,583	12	425,605	R	60.0%	40.0%	60.0%	40.0%
Montana	4			384,377	232,450	146,742	5,185	85,708	R	60.5%	38.2%	61.3%	38.7%
Nebraska	5			652,090	460,054	187,866	4,170	272,188	R	70.6%	28.8%	71.0%	29.0%
Nevada	4			286,667	188,770	91,655	6,242	97,115	R	65.8%	32.0%	67.3%	32.7%
New Hampshire	4			389,066	267,051	120,395	1,620	146,656	R	68.6%	30.9%	68.9%	31.1%
New Jersey	16			3,217,862	1,933,630	1,261,323	22,909	672,307	R	60.1%	39.2%	60.5%	39.5%
New Mexico	5			514,370	307,101	201,769	5,500	105,332	R	59.7%	39.2%	60.3%	39.7%
New York	36			6,806,810	3,664,763	3,119,609	22,438	545,154	R	53.8%	45.8%	54.0%	46.0%
North Carolina	13			2,175,361	1,346,481	824,287	4,593	522,194	R	61.9%	37.9%	62.0%	38.0%
North Dakota	3			308,971	200,336	104,429	4,206	95,907	R	64.8%	33.8%	65.7%	34.3%
Ohio	23			4,547,619	2,678,560	1,825,440	43,619	853,120	R	58.9%	40.1%	59.5%	40.5%
Oklahoma	8			1,255,676	861,530	385,080	9,066	476,450	R	68.6%	30.7%	69.1%	30.9%
Oregon	7			1,226,527	685,700	536,479	4,348	149,221	R	55.9%	43.7%	56.1%	43.9%
Pennsylvania	25			4,844,903	2,584,323	2,228,131	32,449	356,192	R	53.3%	46.0%	53.7%	46.3%
Rhode Island	4			410,492	212,080	197,106	1,306	14,974	R	51.7%	48.0%	51.8%	48.2%
South Carolina	8			968,529	615,539	344,459	8,531	271,080	R	63.6%	35.6%	64.1%	35.9%
South Dakota	3			317,867	200,267	116,113	1,487	84,154	R	63.0%	36.5%	63.3%	36.7%
Tennessee	11			1,711,994	990,212	711,714	10,068	278,498	R	57.8%	41.6%	58.2%	41.8%
Texas	29			5,397,571	3,433,428	1,949,276	14,867	1,484,152	R	63.6%	36.1%	63.8%	36.2%
Utah	5			629,656	469,105	155,369	5,182	313,736	R	74.5%	24.7%	75.1%	24.9%
Vermont	3			234,561	135,865	95,730	2,966	40,135	R	57.9%	40.8%	58.7%	41.3%
Virginia	12			2,146,635	1,337,078	796,250	13,307	540,828	R	62.3%	37.1%	62.7%	37.3%
Washington	10			1,883,910	1,051,670	807,352	24,888	244,318	R	55.8%	42.9%	56.6%	43.4%
West Virginia	6			735,742	405,483	328,125	2,134	77,358	R	55.1%	44.6%	55.3%	44.7%
Wisconsin	11			2,211,689	1,198,584	995,740	17,365	202,844	R	54.2%	45.0%	54.6%	45.4%
Wyoming	3			188,968	133,241	53,370	2,357	79,871	R	70.5%	28.2%	71.4%	28.6%
District of Columbia		3		211,288	29,009	180,408	1,871	151,399	D	13.7%	85.4%	13.9%	86.1%
Total	525	13		92,652,842	54,455,075	37,577,185	620,582	16,877,890	R	58.8%	40.6%	59.2%	40.8%

PRESIDENT 1980

In New York the Republican figures include Conservative votes. In many states various non-major party candidates appeared on the ballot with variations of the party designations, without any party designation, or with entirely different party names.

In several cases vice presidential nominees were different from those listed for most states. The Socialist Workers Party nominee for president varied from state to state.

43,904,153	Ronald Reagan and George Bush	Republican
35,483,883	Jimmy Carter and Walter F. Mondale	Democratic
5,720,060	John B. Anderson and Patrick J. Lucey	Independent
921,299	Edward E. Clark and David Koch	Libertarian
234,294	Barry Commoner and LaDonna Harris	Citizens
45,023	Gus Hall and Angela Davis	Communist
41,268	John R. Rarick and Eileen M. Shearer	American Independent
38,737	Clifton DeBerry and Matilde Zimmermann	Socialist Workers
32,327	Ellen McCormack and Carroll Driscoll	Right to Life
18,116	Maureen Smith and Elizabeth Barron	Peace and Freedom
13,300	Deirdre Griswold and Larry Holmes	Workers World
7,212	Benjamin C. Bubar and Earl F. Dodge	Statesman
6,898	David McReynolds and Diane Drufenbrock	Socialist
6,647	Percy L. Greaves and Frank L. Varnum	American
6,272	Andrew Pulley and Matilde Zimmermann	Socialist Workers
4,029	Richard Congress and Matilde Zimmermann	Socialist Workers
3,694	Kurt Lynen and Harry Kieve	Middle Class
1,718	Bill Gahres and J. F. Loughlin	Down With Lawyers
1,555	Frank W. Shelton and George E. Jackson	American
923	Martin E. Wendelken with no vice-presidential candidate	Independent
296	Harley McLain and Jewelie Goeller	Natural Peoples

Notes: In addition to the votes listed above, 13,185 scattered write-in votes were reported from various states, 6,139 votes were cast in Minnesota for American Party electors without designated national nominees, and 4,193 votes were cast for "None of These Candidates" in Nevada.

UNITED STATES
PRESIDENT 1980

State	Electoral Vote Rep.	Electoral Vote Dem.	Electoral Vote Other	Total Vote	Republican	Democratic	Other	Plurality		Percentage Total Vote Rep.	Percentage Total Vote Dem.	Percentage Major Vote Rep.	Percentage Major Vote Dem.
Alabama	9			1,341,929	654,192	636,730	51,007	17,462	R	48.8%	47.4%	50.7%	49.3%
Alaska	3			158,445	86,112	41,842	30,491	44,270	R	54.3%	26.4%	67.3%	32.7%
Arizona	6			873,945	529,688	246,843	97,414	282,845	R	60.6%	28.2%	68.2%	31.8%
Arkansas	6			837,582	403,164	398,041	36,377	5,123	R	48.1%	47.5%	50.3%	49.7%
California	45			8,587,063	4,524,858	3,083,661	978,544	1,441,197	R	52.7%	35.9%	59.5%	40.5%
Colorado	7			1,184,415	652,264	367,973	164,178	284,291	R	55.1%	31.1%	63.9%	36.1%
Connecticut	8			1,406,285	677,210	541,732	187,343	135,478	R	48.2%	38.5%	55.6%	44.4%
Delaware	3			235,900	111,252	105,754	18,894	5,498	R	47.2%	44.8%	51.3%	48.7%
Florida	17			3,686,930	2,046,951	1,419,475	220,504	627,476	R	55.5%	38.5%	59.1%	40.9%
Georgia		12		1,596,695	654,168	890,733	51,794	236,565	D	41.0%	55.8%	42.3%	57.7%
Hawaii		4		303,287	130,112	135,879	37,296	5,767	D	42.9%	44.8%	48.9%	51.1%
Idaho	4			437,431	290,699	110,192	36,540	180,507	R	66.5%	25.2%	72.5%	27.5%
Illinois	26			4,749,721	2,358,049	1,981,413	410,259	376,636	R	49.6%	41.7%	54.3%	45.7%
Indiana	13			2,242,033	1,255,656	844,197	142,180	411,459	R	56.0%	37.7%	59.8%	40.2%
Iowa	8			1,317,661	676,026	508,672	132,963	167,354	R	51.3%	38.6%	57.1%	42.9%
Kansas	7			979,795	566,812	326,150	86,833	240,662	R	57.9%	33.3%	63.5%	36.5%
Kentucky	9			1,294,627	635,274	616,417	42,936	18,857	R	49.1%	47.6%	50.8%	49.2%
Louisiana	10			1,548,591	792,853	708,453	47,285	84,400	R	51.2%	45.7%	52.8%	47.2%
Maine	4			523,011	238,522	220,974	63,515	17,548	R	45.6%	42.3%	51.9%	48.1%
Maryland		10		1,540,496	680,606	726,161	133,729	45,555	D	44.2%	47.1%	48.4%	51.6%
Massachusetts	14			2,524,298	1,057,631	1,053,802	412,865	3,829	R	41.9%	41.7%	50.1%	49.9%
Michigan	21			3,909,725	1,915,225	1,661,532	332,968	253,693	R	49.0%	42.5%	53.5%	46.5%
Minnesota		10		2,051,980	873,268	954,174	224,538	80,906	D	42.6%	46.5%	47.8%	52.2%
Mississippi	7			892,620	441,089	429,281	22,250	11,808	R	49.4%	48.1%	50.7%	49.3%
Missouri	12			2,099,824	1,074,181	931,182	94,461	142,999	R	51.2%	44.3%	53.6%	46.4%
Montana	4			363,952	206,814	118,032	39,106	88,782	R	56.8%	32.4%	63.7%	36.3%
Nebraska	5			640,854	419,937	166,851	54,066	253,086	R	65.5%	26.0%	71.6%	28.4%
Nevada	3			247,885	155,017	66,666	26,202	88,351	R	62.5%	26.9%	69.9%	30.1%
New Hampshire	4			383,990	221,705	108,864	53,421	112,841	R	57.7%	28.4%	67.1%	32.9%
New Jersey	17			2,975,684	1,546,557	1,147,364	281,763	399,193	R	52.0%	38.6%	57.4%	42.6%
New Mexico	4			456,971	250,779	167,826	38,366	82,953	R	54.9%	36.7%	59.9%	40.1%
New York	41			6,201,959	2,893,831	2,728,372	579,756	165,459	R	46.7%	44.0%	51.5%	48.5%
North Carolina	13			1,855,833	915,018	875,635	65,180	39,383	R	49.3%	47.2%	51.1%	48.9%
North Dakota	3			301,545	193,695	79,189	28,661	114,506	R	64.2%	26.3%	71.0%	29.0%
Ohio	25			4,283,603	2,206,545	1,752,414	324,644	454,131	R	51.5%	40.9%	55.7%	44.3%
Oklahoma	8			1,149,708	695,570	402,026	52,112	293,544	R	60.5%	35.0%	63.4%	36.6%
Oregon	6			1,181,516	571,044	456,890	153,582	114,154	R	48.3%	38.7%	55.6%	44.4%
Pennsylvania	27			4,561,501	2,261,872	1,937,540	362,089	324,332	R	49.6%	42.5%	53.9%	46.1%
Rhode Island		4		416,072	154,793	198,342	62,937	43,549	D	37.2%	47.7%	43.8%	56.2%
South Carolina	8			894,071	441,841	430,385	21,845	11,456	R	49.4%	48.1%	50.7%	49.3%
South Dakota	4			327,703	198,343	103,855	25,505	94,488	R	60.5%	31.7%	65.6%	34.4%
Tennessee	10			1,617,616	787,761	783,051	46,804	4,710	R	48.7%	48.4%	50.1%	49.9%
Texas	26			4,541,636	2,510,705	1,881,147	149,784	629,558	R	55.3%	41.4%	57.2%	42.8%
Utah	4			604,222	439,687	124,266	40,269	315,421	R	72.8%	20.6%	78.0%	22.0%
Vermont	3			213,299	94,628	81,952	36,719	12,676	R	44.4%	38.4%	53.6%	46.4%
Virginia	12			1,866,032	989,609	752,174	124,249	237,435	R	53.0%	40.3%	56.8%	43.2%
Washington	9			1,742,394	865,244	650,193	226,957	215,051	R	49.7%	37.3%	57.1%	42.9%
West Virginia		6		737,715	334,206	367,462	36,047	33,256	D	45.3%	49.8%	47.6%	52.4%
Wisconsin	11			2,273,221	1,088,845	981,584	202,792	107,261	R	47.9%	43.2%	52.6%	47.4%
Wyoming	3			176,713	110,700	49,427	16,586	61,273	R	62.6%	28.0%	69.1%	30.9%
District of Columbia		3		175,237	23,545	131,113	20,579	107,568	D	13.4%	74.8%	15.2%	84.8%
Total	*489*	*49*		*86,515,221*	*43,904,153*	*35,483,883*	*7,127,185*	*8,420,270*	*R*	*50.7%*	*41.0%*	*55.3%*	*44.7%*

PRESIDENT 1976

In Washington one Republican elector voted in the electoral college for Ronald Reagan for president and Robert Dole for vice president.

In New York the Republican figures include Conservative votes, and the Democratic figures include Liberal votes; in Vermont the Democratic figures include votes cast on the Independent Vermonters Party ticket.

In many states various non-major party candidates appeared on the ballot with variations of the party designations and in several states with entirely different party names.

The ballot designations for electors for Eugene J. McCarthy for president varied from state to state, as did the names of vice-presidential candidates running with him. In New Jersey the Maddox vice-presidential candidate was Edmund O. Matzal.

The full list of candidates for president and vice president was:

40,830,763	Jimmy Carter and Walter F. Mondale	Democratic
39,147,793	Gerald R. Ford and Robert Dole	Republican
756,691	Eugene J. McCarthy with various vice-presidential candidates	Independent
173,011	Roger L. MacBride and David D. Bergland	Libertarian
170,531	Lester G. Maddox and William D. Dyke	American Independent
160,773	Thomas J. Anderson and Rufus Shackelford	American
91,314	Peter Camejo and Willie Mae Reid	Socialist Workers
58,992	Gus Hall and Jarvis Tyner	Communist
49,024	Margaret Wright and Benjamin Spock	People's
40,043	Lyndon H. LaRouche Jr. and R. W. Evans	United States Labor
15,934	Benjamin C. Bubar and Earl F. Dodge	Prohibition
9,616	Julius Levin and Constance Blomen	Socialist Labor
6,038	Frank P. Zeidler and J. Q. Brisben	Socialist
361	Ernest L. Miller and Roy N. Eddy	Restoration
36	Frank Taylor and Henry Swan	United American

Notes: In addition to the votes listed above, 39,861 scattered write-in votes were reported from various states, and 5,108 votes were cast for "None of These Candidates" in Nevada.

UNITED STATES
PRESIDENT 1976

State	Electoral Vote Rep.	Electoral Vote Dem.	Electoral Vote Other	Total Vote	Republican	Democratic	Other	Plurality		Percentage Total Vote Rep.	Percentage Total Vote Dem.	Percentage Major Vote Rep.	Percentage Major Vote Dem.
Alabama		9		1,182,850	504,070	659,170	19,610	155,100	D	42.6%	55.7%	43.3%	56.7%
Alaska	3			123,574	71,555	44,058	7,961	27,497	R	57.9%	35.7%	61.9%	38.1%
Arizona	6			742,719	418,642	295,602	28,475	123,040	R	56.4%	39.8%	58.6%	41.4%
Arkansas		6		767,535	267,903	498,604	1,028	230,701	D	34.9%	65.0%	35.0%	65.0%
California	45			7,867,117	3,882,244	3,742,284	242,589	139,960	R	49.3%	47.6%	50.9%	49.1%
Colorado	7			1,081,554	584,367	460,353	36,834	124,014	R	54.0%	42.6%	55.9%	44.1%
Connecticut	8			1,381,526	719,261	647,895	14,370	71,366	R	52.1%	46.9%	52.6%	47.4%
Delaware		3		235,834	109,831	122,596	3,407	12,765	D	46.6%	52.0%	47.3%	52.7%
Florida		17		3,150,631	1,469,531	1,636,000	45,100	166,469	D	46.6%	51.9%	47.3%	52.7%
Georgia		12		1,467,458	483,743	979,409	4,306	495,666	D	33.0%	66.7%	33.1%	66.9%
Hawaii		4		291,301	140,003	147,375	3,923	7,372	D	48.1%	50.6%	48.7%	51.3%
Idaho	4			344,071	204,151	126,549	13,371	77,602	R	59.3%	36.8%	61.7%	38.3%
Illinois	26			4,718,914	2,364,269	2,271,295	83,350	92,974	R	50.1%	48.1%	51.0%	49.0%
Indiana	13			2,220,362	1,183,958	1,014,714	21,690	169,244	R	53.3%	45.7%	53.8%	46.2%
Iowa	8			1,279,306	632,863	619,931	26,512	12,932	R	49.5%	48.5%	50.5%	49.5%
Kansas	7			957,845	502,752	430,421	24,672	72,331	R	52.5%	44.9%	53.9%	46.1%
Kentucky		9		1,167,142	531,852	615,717	19,573	83,865	D	45.6%	52.8%	46.3%	53.7%
Louisiana		10		1,278,439	587,446	661,365	29,628	73,919	D	46.0%	51.7%	47.0%	53.0%
Maine	4			483,216	236,320	232,279	14,617	4,041	R	48.9%	48.1%	50.4%	49.6%
Maryland		10		1,439,897	672,661	759,612	7,624	86,951	D	46.7%	52.8%	47.0%	53.0%
Massachusetts		14		2,547,558	1,030,276	1,429,475	87,807	399,199	D	40.4%	56.1%	41.9%	58.1%
Michigan	21			3,653,749	1,893,742	1,696,714	63,293	197,028	R	51.8%	46.4%	52.7%	47.3%
Minnesota		10		1,949,931	819,395	1,070,440	60,096	251,045	D	42.0%	54.9%	43.4%	56.6%
Mississippi		7		769,361	366,846	381,309	21,206	14,463	D	47.7%	49.6%	49.0%	51.0%
Missouri		12		1,953,600	927,443	998,387	27,770	70,944	D	47.5%	51.1%	48.2%	51.8%
Montana	4			328,734	173,703	149,259	5,772	24,444	R	52.8%	45.4%	53.8%	46.2%
Nebraska	5			607,668	359,705	233,692	14,271	126,013	R	59.2%	38.5%	60.6%	39.4%
Nevada	3			201,876	101,273	92,479	8,124	8,794	R	50.2%	45.8%	52.3%	47.7%
New Hampshire	4			339,618	185,935	147,635	6,048	38,300	R	54.7%	43.5%	55.7%	44.3%
New Jersey	17			3,014,472	1,509,688	1,444,653	60,131	65,035	R	50.1%	47.9%	51.1%	48.9%
New Mexico	4			418,409	211,419	201,148	5,842	10,271	R	50.5%	48.1%	51.2%	48.8%
New York		41		6,534,170	3,100,791	3,389,558	43,821	288,767	D	47.5%	51.9%	47.8%	52.2%
North Carolina		13		1,678,914	741,960	927,365	9,589	185,405	D	44.2%	55.2%	44.4%	55.6%
North Dakota	3			297,188	153,470	136,078	7,640	17,392	R	51.6%	45.8%	53.0%	47.0%
Ohio		25		4,111,873	2,000,505	2,011,621	99,747	11,116	D	48.7%	48.9%	49.9%	50.1%
Oklahoma	8			1,092,251	545,708	532,442	14,101	13,266	R	50.0%	48.7%	50.6%	49.4%
Oregon	6			1,029,876	492,120	490,407	47,349	1,713	R	47.8%	47.6%	50.1%	49.9%
Pennsylvania		27		4,620,787	2,205,604	2,328,677	86,506	123,073	D	47.7%	50.4%	48.6%	51.4%
Rhode Island		4		411,170	181,249	227,636	2,285	46,387	D	44.1%	55.4%	44.3%	55.7%
South Carolina		8		802,583	346,149	450,807	5,627	104,658	D	43.1%	56.2%	43.4%	56.6%
South Dakota	4			300,678	151,505	147,068	2,105	4,437	R	50.4%	48.9%	50.7%	49.3%
Tennessee		10		1,476,345	633,969	825,879	16,497	191,910	D	42.9%	55.9%	43.4%	56.6%
Texas		26		4,071,884	1,953,300	2,082,319	36,265	129,019	D	48.0%	51.1%	48.4%	51.6%
Utah	4			541,198	337,908	182,110	21,180	155,798	R	62.4%	33.6%	65.0%	35.0%
Vermont	3			187,765	102,085	80,954	4,726	21,131	R	54.4%	43.1%	55.8%	44.2%
Virginia	12			1,697,094	836,554	813,896	46,644	22,658	R	49.3%	48.0%	50.7%	49.3%
Washington	8		1	1,555,534	777,732	717,323	60,479	60,409	R	50.0%	46.1%	52.0%	48.0%
West Virginia		6		750,964	314,760	435,914	290	121,154	D	41.9%	58.0%	41.9%	58.1%
Wisconsin		11		2,104,175	1,004,987	1,040,232	58,956	35,245	D	47.8%	49.4%	49.1%	50.9%
Wyoming	3			156,343	92,717	62,239	1,387	30,478	R	59.3%	39.8%	59.8%	40.2%
District of Columbia		3		168,830	27,873	137,818	3,139	109,945	D	16.5%	81.6%	16.8%	83.2%
Total	240	297	1	81,555,889	39,147,793	40,830,763	1,577,333	1,682,970	D	48.0%	50.1%	48.9%	51.1%

PRESIDENT 1972

In Virginia one Republican elector voted in the electoral college for the Libertarian candidates for president and vice president.

In New York the Republican figures include Conservative votes, and the Democratic figures include Liberal votes. In Alabama the Democratic figures include votes cast on the National Democratic Party of Alabama ticket, and in South Carolina they include United Citizens Party votes.

In many states various non-major party candidates appeared on the ballot under party names other than those used below; for the Socialist Workers Party the votes listed for Jenness and Pulley were actually cast for substitute candidates (Reed and DeBerry) or without named candidates in several states.

The Democratic vice-presidential candidate originally was Sen. Thomas F. Eagleton; upon his withdrawal shortly after the party convention, R. Sargent Shriver was named by the Democratic National Committee as the candidate.

The full list of candidates for president and vice president was:

47,169,911	Richard M. Nixon and Spiro T. Agnew	Republican
29,170,383	George S. McGovern and R. Sargent Shriver	Democratic
1,099,482	John G. Schmitz and Thomas J. Anderson	American
78,756	Benjamin Spock and Julius Hobson	People's
66,677	Linda Jenness and Andrew Pulley	Socialist Workers
53,814	Louis Fisher and Genevieve Gunderson	Socialist Labor
25,595	Gus Hail and Jarvis Tyner	Communist
13,505	E. Harold Munn and Marshall E. Uncapher	Prohibition
3,673	John Hospers and Theodora Nathan	Libertarian
1,743	John V. Mahalchik and Irving Homer	America First
220	Gabriel Green and Daniel Fry	Universal

Notes: In addition to the votes listed above, 34,795 scattered write-in votes were reported from various states. Vice President Agnew resigned in October 1973 and Rep. Gerald R. Ford of Michigan was nominated by President Nixon to fill the vacancy. In November (Senate) and December (House of Representatives) this action was approved by Congress. In August 1974 President Nixon resigned and was succeeded by Vice President Ford. In the same month Nelson A. Rockefeller, former governor of New York, was nominated to be vice president and was confirmed by Congress in December 1974.

UNITED STATES
PRESIDENT 1972

State	Electoral Vote Rep.	Electoral Vote Dem.	Electoral Vote Other	Total Vote	Republican	Democratic	Other	Plurality		Percentage Total Vote Rep.	Percentage Total Vote Dem.	Major Vote Rep.	Major Vote Dem.
Alabama	9			1,006,111	728,701	256,923	20,487	471,778	R	72.4%	25.5%	73.9%	26.1%
Alaska	3			95,219	55,349	32,967	6,903	22,382	R	58.1%	34.6%	62.7%	37.3%
Arizona	6			622,926	402,812	198,540	21,574	204,272	R	64.7%	31.9%	67.0%	33.0%
Arkansas	6			651,320	448,541	199,892	2,887	248,649	R	68.9%	30.7%	69.2%	30.8%
California	45			8,367,862	4,602,096	3,475,847	289,919	1,126,249	R	55.0%	41.5%	57.0%	43.0%
Colorado	7			953,884	597,189	329,980	26,715	267,209	R	62.6%	34.6%	64.4%	35.6%
Connecticut	8			1,384,277	810,763	555,498	18,016	255,265	R	58.6%	40.1%	59.3%	40.7%
Delaware	3			235,516	140,357	92,283	2,876	48,074	R	59.6%	39.2%	60.3%	39.7%
Florida	17			2,583,283	1,857,759	718,117	7,407	1,139,642	R	71.9%	27.8%	72.1%	27.9%
Georgia	12			1,174,772	881,496	289,529	3,747	591,967	R	75.0%	24.6%	75.3%	24.7%
Hawaii	4			270,274	168,865	101,409		67,456	R	62.5%	37.5%	62.5%	37.5%
Idaho	4			310,379	199,384	80,826	30,169	118,558	R	64.2%	26.0%	71.2%	28.8%
Illinois	26			4,723,236	2,788,179	1,913,472	21,585	874,707	R	59.0%	40.5%	59.3%	40.7%
Indiana	13			2,125,529	1,405,154	708,568	11,807	696,586	R	66.1%	33.3%	66.5%	33.5%
Iowa	8			1,225,944	706,207	496,206	23,531	210,001	R	57.6%	40.5%	58.7%	41.3%
Kansas	7			916,095	619,812	270,287	25,996	349,525	R	67.7%	29.5%	69.6%	30.4%
Kentucky	9			1,067,499	676,446	371,159	19,894	305,287	R	63.4%	34.8%	64.6%	35.4%
Louisiana	10			1,051,491	686,852	298,142	66,497	388,710	R	65.3%	28.4%	69.7%	30.3%
Maine	4			417,042	256,458	160,584		95,874	R	61.5%	38.5%	61.5%	38.5%
Maryland	10			1,353,812	829,305	505,781	18,726	323,524	R	61.3%	37.4%	62.1%	37.9%
Massachusetts		14		2,458,756	1,112,078	1,332,540	14,138	220,462	D	45.2%	54.2%	45.5%	54.5%
Michigan	21			3,489,727	1,961,721	1,459,435	68,571	502,286	R	56.2%	41.8%	57.3%	42.7%
Minnesota	10			1,741,652	898,269	802,346	41,037	95,923	R	51.6%	46.1%	52.8%	47.2%
Mississippi	7			645,963	505,125	126,782	14,056	378,343	R	78.2%	19.6%	79.9%	20.1%
Missouri	12			1,855,803	1,153,852	697,147	4,804	456,705	R	62.2%	37.6%	62.3%	37.7%
Montana	4			317,603	183,976	120,197	13,430	63,779	R	57.9%	37.8%	60.5%	39.5%
Nebraska	5			576,289	406,298	169,991		236,307	R	70.5%	29.5%	70.5%	29.5%
Nevada	3			181,766	115,750	66,016		49,734	R	63.7%	36.3%	63.7%	36.3%
New Hampshire	4			334,055	213,724	116,435	3,896	97,289	R	64.0%	34.9%	64.7%	35.3%
New Jersey	17			2,997,229	1,845,502	1,102,211	49,516	743,291	R	61.6%	36.8%	62.6%	37.4%
New Mexico	4			386,241	235,606	141,084	9,551	94,522	R	61.0%	36.5%	62.5%	37.5%
New York	41			7,165,919	4,192,778	2,951,084	22,057	1,241,694	R	58.5%	41.2%	58.7%	41.3%
North Carolina	13			1,518,612	1,054,889	438,705	25,018	616,184	R	69.5%	28.9%	70.6%	29.4%
North Dakota	3			280,514	174,109	100,384	6,021	73,725	R	62.1%	35.8%	63.4%	36.6%
Ohio	25			4,094,787	2,441,827	1,558,889	94,071	882,938	R	59.6%	38.1%	61.0%	39.0%
Oklahoma	8			1,029,900	759,025	247,147	23,728	511,878	R	73.7%	24.0%	75.4%	24.6%
Oregon	6			927,946	486,686	392,760	48,500	93,926	R	52.4%	42.3%	55.3%	44.7%
Pennsylvania	27			4,592,106	2,714,521	1,796,951	80,634	917,570	R	59.1%	39.1%	60.2%	39.8%
Rhode Island	4			415,808	220,383	194,645	780	25,738	R	53.0%	46.8%	53.1%	46.9%
South Carolina	8			673,960	477,044	186,824	10,092	290,220	R	70.8%	27.7%	71.9%	28.1%
South Dakota	4			307,415	166,476	139,945	994	26,531	R	54.2%	45.5%	54.3%	45.7%
Tennessee	10			1,201,182	813,147	357,293	30,742	455,854	R	67.7%	29.7%	69.5%	30.5%
Texas	26			3,471,281	2,298,896	1,154,289	18,096	1,144,607	R	66.2%	33.3%	66.6%	33.4%
Utah	4			478,476	323,643	126,284	28,549	197,359	R	67.6%	26.4%	71.9%	28.1%
Vermont	3			186,947	117,149	68,174	1,624	48,975	R	62.7%	36.5%	63.2%	36.8%
Virginia	11		1	1,457,019	988,493	438,887	29,639	549,606	R	67.8%	30.1%	69.3%	30.7%
Washington	9			1,470,847	837,135	568,334	65,378	268,801	R	56.9%	38.6%	59.6%	40.4%
West Virginia	6			762,399	484,964	277,435		207,529	R	63.6%	36.4%	63.6%	36.4%
Wisconsin	11			1,852,890	989,430	810,174	53,286	179,256	R	53.4%	43.7%	55.0%	45.0%
Wyoming	3			145,570	100,464	44,358	748	56,106	R	69.0%	30.5%	69.4%	30.6%
District of Columbia		3		163,421	35,226	127,627	568	92,401	D	21.6%	78.1%	21.6%	78.4%
Total	520	17	1	77,718,554	47,169,911	29,170,383	1,378,260	17,999,528	R	60.7%	37.5%	61.8%	38.2%

PRESIDENT 1968

In North Carolina one Republican elector voted in the electoral college for the American Independent candidates for president and vice president.

In New York the Democratic figure includes Liberal votes, and in Alabama the Democratic vote is the total of the Alabama Independent Democratic and National Democratic Party of Alabama vote. In many states various non-major party candidates appeared on the ballot with variations of the party designations, and in most states the vice-presidential candidate of the American Independent party was listed as Marvin Griffin rather than Curtis E. LeMay.

The full list of candidates for president and vice president was:

31,785,480	Richard M. Nixon and Spiro T. Agnew	Republican
31,275,166	Hubert H. Humphrey and Edmund S. Muskie	Democratic
9,906,473	George C. Wallace and Curtis E. LeMay	American Independent
52,588	Henning A. Blomen and George S. Taylor	Socialist Labor
47,133	Dick Gregory	Peace and Freedom, with various vice-presidential candidates
41,388	Fred Halstead and Paul Boutelle	Socialist Workers
36,563	Eldridge Cleaver	Peace and Freedom, with various vice-presidential candidates
25,552	Eugene J. McCarthy	Under various titles and written-in, but without indication of vice-presidential candidates
15,123	E. Harold Munn and Rolland E. Fisher	Prohibition
1,519	Ventura Chavez and Adelicio Moya	People's Constitutional
1,075	Charlene Mitchell and Michael Zagarell	Communist
142	James Hensley and Roscoe B. MacKenna	Universal
34	Richard K. Troxell and Merle Thayer	Constitution
7	Kent M. Soeters and James P. Powers	Berkeley Defense Group

Notes: In addition to the votes listed above, 11,192 scattered write-in votes were reported from various states, and 12,430 were cast for elector tickets for which there were no formal presidential or vice-presidential candidates. In the vote listed above for Eldridge Cleaver, two states are included (California and Utah) in which only the party vice-presidential candidate appeared on the ballot.

UNITED STATES
PRESIDENT 1968

State	Electoral Vote Rep.	Electoral Vote Dem.	Electoral Vote Other	Total Vote	Republican	Democratic	American Independent	Other	Plurality		Percentage Rep.	Percentage Dem.	Percentage Amer. Ind.
Alabama			10	1,049,922	146,923	196,579	691,425	14,995	494,846	A	14.0%	18.7%	65.9%
Alaska	3			83,035	37,600	35,411	10,024		2,189	R	45.3%	42.6%	12.1%
Arizona	5			486,936	266,721	170,514	46,573	3,128	96,207	R	54.8%	35.0%	9.6%
Arkansas			6	619,969	190,759	188,228	240,982		50,223	A	30.8%	30.4%	38.9%
California	40			7,251,587	3,467,664	3,244,318	487,270	52,335	223,346	R	47.8%	44.7%	6.7%
Colorado	6			811,199	409,345	335,174	60,813	5,867	74,171	R	50.5%	41.3%	7.5%
Connecticut		8		1,256,232	556,721	621,561	76,650	1,300	64,840	D	44.3%	49.5%	6.1%
Delaware	3			214,367	96,714	89,194	28,459		7,520	R	45.1%	41.6%	13.3%
Florida	14			2,187,805	886,804	676,794	624,207		210,010	R	40.5%	30.9%	28.5%
Georgia			12	1,250,266	380,111	334,440	535,550	165	155,439	A	30.4%	26.7%	42.8%
Hawaii				236,218	91,425	141,324	3,469		49,899	D	38.7%	59.8%	1.5%
Idaho	4	4		291,183	165,369	89,273	36,541		76,096	R	56.8%	30.7%	12.5%
Illinois	26			4,619,749	2,174,774	2,039,814	390,958	14,203	134,960	R	47.1%	44.2%	8.5%
Indiana	13			2,123,597	1,067,885	806,659	243,108	5,945	261,226	R	50.3%	38.0%	11.4%
Iowa	9			1,167,931	619,106	476,699	66,422	5,704	142,407	R	53.0%	40.8%	5.7%
Kansas	7			872,783	478,674	302,996	88,921	2,192	175,678	R	54.8%	34.7%	10.2%
Kentucky	9			1,055,893	462,411	397,541	193,098	2,843	64,870	R	43.8%	37.6%	18.3%
Louisiana			10	1,097,450	257,535	309,615	530,300		220,685	A	23.5%	28.2%	48.3%
Maine		4		392,936	169,254	217,312	6,370		48,058	D	43.1%	55.3%	1.6%
Maryland		10		1,235,039	517,995	538,310	178,734		20,315	D	41.9%	43.6%	14.5%
Massachusetts		14		2,331,752	766,844	1,469,218	87,088	8,602	702,374	D	32.9%	63.0%	3.7%
Michigan		21		3,306,250	1,370,665	1,593,082	331,968	10,535	222,417	D	41.5%	48.2%	10.0%
Minnesota		10		1,588,506	658,643	857,738	68,931	3,194	199,095	D	41.5%	54.0%	4.3%
Mississippi			7	654,509	88,516	150,644	415,349		264,705	A	13.5%	23.0%	63.5%
Missouri	12			1,809,502	811,932	791,444	206,126		20,488	R	44.9%	43.7%	11.4%
Montana	4			274,404	138,835	114,117	20,015	1,437	24,718	R	50.6%	41.6%	7.3%
Nebraska	5			536,851	321,163	170,784	44,904		150,379	R	59.8%	31.8%	8.4%
Nevada	3			154,218	73,188	60,598	20,432		12,590	R	47.5%	39.3%	13.2%
New Hampshire	4			297,298	154,903	130,589	11,173	633	24,314	R	52.1%	43.9%	3.8%
New Jersey	17			2,875,395	1,325,467	1,264,206	262,187	23,535	61,261	R	46.1%	44.0%	9.1%
New Mexico	4			327,350	169,692	130,081	25,737	1,840	39,611	R	51.8%	39.7%	7.9%
New York		43		6,791,688	3,007,932	3,378,470	358,864	46,422	370,538	D	44.3%	49.7%	5.3%
North Carolina	12		1	1,587,493	627,192	464,113	496,188		131,004	R	39.5%	29.2%	31.3%
North Dakota	4			247,882	138,669	94,769	14,244	200	43,900	R	55.9%	38.2%	5.7%
Ohio	26			3,959,698	1,791,014	1,700,586	467,495	603	90,428	R	45.2%	42.9%	11.8%
Oklahoma	8			943,086	449,697	301,658	191,731		148,039	R	47.7%	32.0%	20.3%
Oregon	6			819,622	408,433	358,866	49,683	2,640	49,567	R	49.8%	43.8%	6.1%
Pennsylvania		29		4,747,928	2,090,017	2,259,405	378,582	19,924	169,388	D	44.0%	47.6%	8.0%
Rhode Island		4		385,000	122,359	246,518	15,678	445	124,159	D	31.8%	64.0%	4.1%
South Carolina	8			666,978	254,062	197,486	215,430		38,632	R	38.1%	29.6%	32.3%
South Dakota	4			281,264	149,841	118,023	13,400		31,818	R	53.3%	42.0%	4.8%
Tennessee	11			1,248,617	472,592	351,233	424,792		47,800	R	37.8%	28.1%	34.0%
Texas		25		3,079,216	1,227,844	1,266,804	584,269	299	38,960	D	39.9%	41.1%	19.0%
Utah	4			422,568	238,728	156,665	26,906	269	82,063	R	56.5%	37.1%	6.4%
Vermont	3			161,404	85,142	70,255	5,104	903	14,887	R	52.8%	43.5%	3.2%
Virginia	12			1,361,491	590,319	442,387	321,833	6,952	147,932	R	43.4%	32.5%	23.6%
Washington		9		1,304,281	588,510	616,037	96,990	2,744	27,527	D	45.1%	47.2%	7.4%
West Virginia		7		754,206	307,555	374,091	72,560		66,536	D	40.8%	49.6%	9.6%
Wisconsin	12			1,691,538	809,997	748,804	127,835	4,902	61,193	R	47.9%	44.3%	7.6%
Wyoming	3			127,205	70,927	45,173	11,105		25,754	R	55.8%	35.5%	8.7%
District of Columbia		3		170,578	31,012	139,566			108,554	D	18.2%	81.8%	
Total	301	191	46	73,211,875	31,785,480	31,275,166	9,906,473	244,756	510,314	R	43.4%	42.7%	13.5%

PRESIDENT 1964

In New York the Democratic figure includes Liberal votes.

The full list of candidates for president and vice president was:

43,129,566	Lyndon B. Johnson and Hubert H. Humphrey	Democratic
27,178,188	Barry M. Goldwater and William E. Miller	Republican
45,219	Eric Hass and Henning A. Blomen	Socialist Labor
32,720	Clifton DeBerry and Edward Shaw	Socialist Workers
23,267	E. Harold Munn and Mark R. Shaw	Prohibition
6,953	John Kasper and J. B. Stoner	National States Rights
5,060	Joseph B. Lightburn and T. C. Billings	Constitution
19	James Hensley and John O. Hopkins	Universal

Notes: In addition to the votes listed above, 12,868 scattered write-in votes were reported from various states, and 210,732 votes were cast in Alabama for an unpledged Democratic elector ticket.

UNITED STATES
PRESIDENT 1964

State	Electoral Vote Rep.	Electoral Vote Dem.	Electoral Vote Other	Total Vote	Republican	Democratic	Other	Plurality		Percentage Total Vote Rep.	Dem.	Percentage Major Vote Rep.	Dem.
Alabama	10			689,818	479,085		210,733	479,085	R	69.5%		100.0%	
Alaska		3		67,259	22,930	44,329		21,399	D	34.1%	65.9%	34.1%	65.9%
Arizona	5			480,770	242,535	237,753	482	4,782	R	50.4%	49.5%	50.5%	49.5%
Arkansas		6		560,426	243,264	314,197	2,965	70,933	D	43.4%	56.1%	43.6%	56.4%
California		40		7,057,586	2,879,108	4,171,877	6,601	1,292,769	D	40.8%	59.1%	40.8%	59.2%
Colorado		6		776,986	296,767	476,024	4,195	179,257	D	38.2%	61.3%	38.4%	61.6%
Connecticut		8		1,218,578	390,996	826,269	1,313	435,273	D	32.1%	67.8%	32.1%	67.9%
Delaware		3		201,320	78,078	122,704	538	44,626	D	38.8%	60.9%	38.9%	61.1%
Florida		14		1,854,481	905,941	948,540		42,599	D	48.9%	51.1%	48.9%	51.1%
Georgia	12			1,139,335	616,584	522,556	195	94,028	R	54.1%	45.9%	54.1%	45.9%
Hawaii		4		207,271	44,022	163,249		119,227	D	21.2%	78.8%	21.2%	78.8%
Idaho		4		292,477	143,557	148,920		5,363	D	49.1%	50.9%	49.1%	50.9%
Illinois		26		4,702,841	1,905,946	2,796,833	62	890,887	D	40.5%	59.5%	40.5%	59.5%
Indiana		13		2,091,606	911,118	1,170,848	9,640	259,730	D	43.6%	56.0%	43.8%	56.2%
Iowa		9		1,184,539	449,148	733,030	2,361	283,882	D	37.9%	61.9%	38.0%	62.0%
Kansas		7		857,901	386,579	464,028	7,294	77,449	D	45.1%	54.1%	45.4%	54.6%
Kentucky		9		1,046,105	372,977	669,659	3,469	296,682	D	35.7%	64.0%	35.8%	64.2%
Louisiana	10			896,293	509,225	387,068		122,157	R	56.8%	43.2%	56.8%	43.2%
Maine		4		380,965	118,701	262,264		143,563	D	31.2%	68.8%	31.2%	68.8%
Maryland		10		1,116,457	385,495	730,912	50	345,417	D	34.5%	65.5%	34.5%	65.5%
Massachusetts		14		2,344,798	549,727	1,786,422	8,649	1,236,695	D	23.4%	76.2%	23.5%	76.5%
Michigan		21		3,203,102	1,060,152	2,136,615	6,335	1,076,463	D	33.1%	66.7%	33.2%	66.8%
Minnesota		10		1,554,462	559,624	991,117	3,721	431,493	D	36.0%	63.8%	36.1%	63.9%
Mississippi	7			409,146	356,528	52,618		303,910	R	87.1%	12.9%	87.1%	12.9%
Missouri		12		1,817,879	653,535	1,164,344		510,809	D	36.0%	64.0%	36.0%	64.0%
Montana		4		278,628	113,032	164,246	1,350	51,214	D	40.6%	58.9%	40.8%	59.2%
Nebraska		5		584,154	276,847	307,307		30,460	D	47.4%	52.6%	47.4%	52.6%
Nevada		3		135,433	56,094	79,339		23,245	D	41.4%	58.6%	41.4%	58.6%
New Hampshire		4		288,093	104,029	184,064		80,035	D	36.1%	63.9%	36.1%	63.9%
New Jersey		17		2,847,663	964,174	1,868,231	15,258	904,057	D	33.9%	65.6%	34.0%	66.0%
New Mexico		4		328,645	132,838	194,015	1,792	61,177	D	40.4%	59.0%	40.6%	59.4%
New York		43		7,166,275	2,243,559	4,913,102	9,614	2,669,543	D	31.3%	68.6%	31.3%	68.7%
North Carolina		13		1,424,983	624,844	800,139		175,295	D	43.8%	56.2%	43.8%	56.2%
North Dakota		4		258,389	108,207	149,784	398	41,577	D	41.9%	58.0%	41.9%	58.1%
Ohio		26		3,969,196	1,470,865	2,498,331		1,027,466	D	37.1%	62.9%	37.1%	62.9%
Oklahoma		8		932,499	412,665	519,834		107,169	D	44.3%	55.7%	44.3%	55.7%
Oregon		6		786,305	282,779	501,017	2,509	218,238	D	36.0%	63.7%	36.1%	63.9%
Pennsylvania		29		4,822,690	1,673,657	3,130,954	18,079	1,457,297	D	34.7%	64.9%	34.8%	65.2%
Rhode Island		4		390,091	74,615	315,463	13	240,848	D	19.1%	80.9%	19.1%	80.9%
South Carolina	8			524,779	309,048	215,723	8	93,325	R	58.9%	41.1%	58.9%	41.1%
South Dakota		4		293,118	130,108	163,010		32,902	D	44.4%	55.6%	44.4%	55.6%
Tennessee		11		1,143,946	508,965	634,947	34	125,982	D	44.5%	55.5%	44.5%	55.5%
Texas		25		2,626,811	958,566	1,663,185	5,060	704,619	D	36.5%	63.3%	36.6%	63.4%
Utah		4		401,413	181,785	219,628		37,843	D	45.3%	54.7%	45.3%	54.7%
Vermont		3		163,089	54,942	108,127	20	53,185	D	33.7%	66.3%	33.7%	66.3%
Virginia		12		1,042,267	481,334	558,038	2,895	76,704	D	46.2%	53.5%	46.3%	53.7%
Washington		9		1,258,556	470,366	779,881	8,309	309,515	D	37.4%	62.0%	37.6%	62.4%
West Virginia		7		792,040	253,953	538,087		284,134	D	32.1%	67.9%	32.1%	67.9%
Wisconsin		12		1,691,815	638,495	1,050,424	2,896	411,929	D	37.7%	62.1%	37.8%	62.2%
Wyoming		3		142,716	61,998	80,718		18,720	D	43.4%	56.6%	43.4%	56.6%
District of Columbia		3		198,597	28,801	169,796		140,995	D	14.5%	85.5%	14.5%	85.5%
Total	52	486		70,644,592	27,178,188	43,129,566	336,838	15,951,378	D	38.5%	61.1%	38.7%	61.3%

PRESIDENT 1960

Sen. Harry Flood Byrd received 15 votes for president in the electoral college; these were the votes of 6 of the 11 Democratic electors in Alabama, all 8 unpledged Democratic electors in Mississippi, and 1 of the 8 Republican electors in Oklahoma. The Alabama and Mississippi electors also cast 14 votes for Sen. Strom Thurmond for vice president; the single Oklahoma elector voted for Sen. Barry M. Goldwater for vice president.

In New York the Democratic figure includes Liberal votes.

The full list of candidates for president and vice president was:

34,226,731	John F. Kennedy and Lyndon B. Johnson	Democratic
34,108,157	Richard M. Nixon and Henry Cabot Lodge	Republican
47,522	Eric Hass and Georgia Cozzini	Socialist Labor
46,203	Rutherford L. Decker and E. Harold Munn	Prohibition
44,977	Orval E. Faubus and John G. Crommelin	National States Rights
40,165	Farrell Dobbs and Myra Tanner Weiss	Socialist Workers
18,162	Charles L. Sullivan and Merritt B. Curtis	Constitution
8,708	J. Bracken Lee and Kent H. Courtney	Conservative
4,204	C. Benton Coiner and Edward J. Silverman	Conservative
1,767	Lar Daly and B. M. Miller	Tax Cut
1,485	Clennon King and Reginald Carter	Independent Afro-American
1,401	Merritt B. Curtis and B. M. Miller	Constitution

Notes: In addition to the votes listed above, 2,378 scattered write-in votes were reported from various states, 169,572 votes were cast in Louisiana for Independent electors, and 116,248 votes were cast in Mississippi for an unpledged Democratic elector ticket. Another 539 votes were cast in Michigan for an Independent American ticket.

UNITED STATES
PRESIDENT 1960

State	Electoral Vote Rep.	Electoral Vote Dem.	Electoral Vote Other	Total Vote	Republican	Democratic	Other	Plurality		Percentage Total Vote Rep.	Percentage Total Vote Dem.	Percentage Major Vote Rep.	Percentage Major Vote Dem.
Alabama		5	6	570,225	237,981	324,050	8,194	86,069	D	41.7%	56.8%	42.3%	57.7%
Alaska	3			60,762	30,953	29,809		1,144	R	50.9%	49.1%	50.9%	49.1%
Arizona	4			398,491	221,241	176,781	469	44,460	R	55.5%	44.4%	55.6%	44.4%
Arkansas		8		428,509	184,508	215,049	28,952	30,541	D	43.1%	50.2%	46.2%	53.8%
California	32			6,506,578	3,259,722	3,224,099	22,757	35,623	R	50.1%	49.6%	50.3%	49.7%
Colorado	6			736,236	402,242	330,629	3,365	71,613	R	54.6%	44.9%	54.9%	45.1%
Connecticut		8		1,222,883	565,813	657,055	15	91,242	D	46.3%	53.7%	46.3%	53.7%
Delaware		3		196,683	96,373	99,590	720	3,217	D	49.0%	50.6%	49.2%	50.8%
Florida	10			1,544,176	795,476	748,700		46,776	R	51.5%	48.5%	51.5%	48.5%
Georgia		12		733,349	274,472	458,638	239	184,166	D	37.4%	62.5%	37.4%	62.6%
Hawaii		3		184,705	92,295	92,410		115	D	50.0%	50.0%	50.0%	50.0%
Idaho	4			300,450	161,597	138,853		22,744	R	53.8%	46.2%	53.8%	46.2%
Illinois	27			4,757,409	2,368,988	2,377,846	10,575	8,858	D	49.8%	50.0%	49.9%	50.1%
Indiana	13			2,135,360	1,175,120	952,358	7,882	222,762	R	55.0%	44.6%	55.2%	44.8%
Iowa	10			1,273,810	722,381	550,565	864	171,816	R	56.7%	43.2%	56.7%	43.3%
Kansas	8			928,825	561,474	363,213	4,138	198,261	R	60.4%	39.1%	60.7%	39.3%
Kentucky	10			1,124,462	602,607	521,855		80,752	R	53.6%	46.4%	53.6%	46.4%
Louisiana		10		807,891	230,980	407,339	169,572	176,359	D	28.6%	50.4%	36.2%	63.8%
Maine	5			421,767	240,608	181,159		59,449	R	57.0%	43.0%	57.0%	43.0%
Maryland		9		1,055,349	489,538	565,808	3	76,270	D	46.4%	53.6%	46.4%	53.6%
Massachusetts		16		2,469,480	976,750	1,487,174	5,556	510,424	D	39.6%	60.2%	39.6%	60.4%
Michigan		20		3,318,097	1,620,428	1,687,269	10,400	66,841	D	48.8%	50.9%	49.0%	51.0%
Minnesota		11		1,541,887	757,915	779,933	4,039	22,018	D	49.2%	50.6%	49.3%	50.7%
Mississippi			8	298,171	73,561	108,362	116,248	34,801	D	24.7%	36.3%	40.4%	59.6%
Missouri		13		1,934,422	962,221	972,201		9,980	D	49.7%	50.3%	49.7%	50.3%
Montana	4			277,579	141,841	134,891	847	6,950	R	51.1%	48.6%	51.3%	48.7%
Nebraska	6			613,095	380,553	232,542		148,011	R	62.1%	37.9%	62.1%	37.9%
Nevada		3		107,267	52,387	54,880		2,493	D	48.8%	51.2%	48.8%	51.2%
New Hampshire	4			295,761	157,989	137,772		20,217	R	53.4%	46.6%	53.4%	46.6%
New Jersey		16		2,773,111	1,363,324	1,385,415	24,372	22,091	D	49.2%	50.0%	49.6%	50.4%
New Mexico		4		311,107	153,733	156,027	1,347	2,294	D	49.4%	50.2%	49.6%	50.4%
New York		45		7,291,079	3,446,419	3,830,085	14,575	383,666	D	47.3%	52.5%	47.4%	52.6%
North Carolina		14		1,368,556	655,420	713,136		57,716	D	47.9%	52.1%	47.9%	52.1%
North Dakota	4			278,431	154,310	123,963	158	30,347	R	55.4%	44.5%	55.5%	44.5%
Ohio	25			4,161,859	2,217,611	1,944,248		273,363	R	53.3%	46.7%	53.3%	46.7%
Oklahoma	7		1	903,150	533,039	370,111		162,928	R	59.0%	41.0%	59.0%	41.0%
Oregon	6			776,421	408,060	367,402	959	40,658	R	52.6%	47.3%	52.6%	47.4%
Pennsylvania		32		5,006,541	2,439,956	2,556,282	10,303	116,326	D	48.7%	51.1%	48.8%	51.2%
Rhode Island		4		405,535	147,502	258,032	1	110,530	D	36.4%	63.6%	36.4%	63.6%
South Carolina		8		386,688	188,558	198,129	1	9,571	D	48.8%	51.2%	48.8%	51.2%
South Dakota	4			306,487	178,417	128,070		50,347	R	58.2%	41.8%	58.2%	41.8%
Tennessee	11			1,051,792	556,577	481,453	13,762	75,124	R	52.9%	45.8%	53.6%	46.4%
Texas		24		2,311,084	1,121,310	1,167,567	22,207	46,257	D	48.5%	50.5%	49.0%	51.0%
Utah	4			374,709	205,361	169,248	100	36,113	R	54.8%	45.2%	54.8%	45.2%
Vermont	3			167,324	98,131	69,186	7	28,945	R	58.6%	41.3%	58.6%	41.4%
Virginia	12			771,449	404,521	362,327	4,601	42,194	R	52.4%	47.0%	52.8%	47.2%
Washington	9			1,241,572	629,273	599,298	13,001	29,975	R	50.7%	48.3%	51.2%	48.8%
West Virginia		8		837,781	395,995	441,786		45,791	D	47.3%	52.7%	47.3%	52.7%
Wisconsin	12			1,729,082	895,175	830,805	3,102	64,370	R	51.8%	48.0%	51.9%	48.1%
Wyoming	3			140,782	77,451	63,331		14,120	R	55.0%	45.0%	55.0%	45.0%
Total	219	303	15	68,838,219	34,108,157	34,226,731	503,331	118,574	D	49.5%	49.7%	49.9%	50.1%

PRESIDENTIAL PRIMARIES 2012

In 2012, 38 states and the District of Columbia held presidential primaries, in which at least one of the parties held contests where voters balloted directly for candidates or for a statewide slate of delegates that was pledged to a candidate. States not listed in this listing held a caucus (with participation limited to a small number of party members); in some states the Democratic Party did not hold a primary or did not record votes because Obama was unopposed. Jurisdictions without electoral votes are not included in this listing.

The list below, alphabetical by state, gives primary vote totals for all candidates who were listed on the ballot or received write-in votes that were counted (excludes write-in votes for Republicans in the New Hampshire Democratic primary, and vice versa). The tables on pages 51–54 give a chronological summary of the primary votes for those candidates in the Democratic and Republican parties who received at least 200,000 votes nationwide, with the vote totals for minor candidates in the footnotes.

Republican candidates on the ballot in at least one primary were: Wayne Charles Arnett, Michele Bachmann, Donald Benjamin, Bear Betzler, Peter "Simon" Bollander, Timothy Brewer, Herman Cain, Mark Callahan, Cesar Cisneros, Hugh Cort, Randy Crow, John Davis, L. John Davis Jr., Kip Dean, Keith Drummond, Newt Gingrich, Sarah Gonzales, Stewart J. Greenleaf, Christopher Hill, Jon Huntsman Jr., Gary E. Johnson, Fred Karger, Jeff Lawman, Michael Levinson, Benjamin Linn, Frank Lynch, Andy Martin, Michael J. Meehan, Ron Paul, Raymond Scott Perkins, Al "Dick" Perry, Rick Perry, Joe Robinson, Charles "Buddy" Roemer, W. Mitt Romney, Kevin Rubash, Rick Santorum, Paul Sims, Charles Skelley, Joe Story, Linden Swift, Jim Terr, James A. Vestermark, Matt Welch, Vern Wuensche, Ronald Zack

Democratic candidates on the ballot in at least one primary were: Ed Cowan, Bob Ely, Craig "Tax Freeze" Freis, Bob Greene, John Haywood, Robert B. Jordan, Keith Judd, Barack H. Obama, Cornelius E. O'Connor, Edward T. O'Donnell Jr., Darcy Richardson, Jim Rogers, Vermin Supreme, Randall Terry, Aldous C. Tyler Jr.

ALABAMA   March 13

Republican   214,628 Santorum; 182,292 Gingrich; 180,336 Romney; 30,950 Paul; 9,259 Uncommitted; 1,869 Perry; 1,701 Bachmann; 1,049 Huntsman

Democrat   241,276 Obama; 45,615 Uncommitted

ARIZONA   February 28

Republican   239,167 Romney; 138,031 Santorum; 81,748 Gingrich; 43,952 Paul; 2,023 Perry; 1,544 Gonzales; 692 Roemer; 530 Sims; 418 Cisneros; 358 Callahan; 310 Perry; 223 Benjamin; 217 Levinson; 198 Dean; 156 Zack; 139 Hill; 110 Lynch; 96 Arnett; 90 Perkins; 86 Welch; 59 Terr; 57 Skelley; 54 Bollander

ARKANSAS   May 22

Republican   104,200 Romney; 20,399 Paul; 20,308 Santorum; 7,453 Gingrich

Democrat   94,936 Obama; 67,711 Wolfe

CALIFORNIA   June 5

Republican   1,530,513 Romney; 199,246 Paul; 102,258 Santorum; 72,022 Gingrich; 12,520 Roemer; 8,393 Karger; 11 Hannon; 5 Gonzales; 2 Howard

Democrat   2,075,905 Obama; 221 Richardson; 129 Meyer; 54 Ramos

CONNECTICUT   April 24

Republican   40,171 Romney; 8,032 Paul; 6,135 Gingrich; 4,072 Santorum; 1,168 Uncommitted

DELAWARE   April 24

Republican   16,143 Romney; 7,742 Gingrich; 3,017 Paul; 1,690 Santorum

PRESIDENTIAL PRIMARIES 2012

DISTRICT OF COLUMBIA   April 3

Republican   3,577 Romney; 621 Paul; 558 Gingrich; 348 Huntsman

Democrat   56,503 Obama; 1,100 Uncommitted; 386 Scattered Write-In

FLORIDA   January 31

Republican   776,159 Romney; 534,121 Gingrich; 223,249 Santorum; 117,461 Paul; 6,775 Perry; 6,204 Huntsman; 3,967 Bachmann; 3,503 Cain; 1,195 Johnson

GEORGIA   March 6

Republican   425,395 Gingrich; 233,611 Romney; 176,259 Santorum; 59,100 Paul; 1,813 Huntsman; 1,714 Bachmann; 1,696 Perry; 1,142 Roemer; 740 Johnson

Democrat   139,273 Obama

ILLINOIS   March 20

Republican   435,859 Romney; 326,778 Santorum; 87,044 Paul; 74,482 Gingrich; 5,568 Perry; 3,723 Roemer

Democrat   652,583 Obama; 134 Terry

INDIANA   May 8

Republican   410,635 Romney; 98,487 Paul; 85,332 Santorum; 41,135 Gingrich

Democrat   221,466 Obama

KENTUCKY   May 22

Republican   117,621 Romney; 22,074 Paul; 15,629 Santorum; 10,479 Gingrich; 10,357 Uncommitted

Democrat   119,293 Obama; 86,925 Uncommitted

LOUISIANA   March 24

Republican   91,321 Santorum; 49,758 Romney; 29,656 Gingrich; 11,467 Paul; 2,203 Roemer; 955 Perry; 622 Bachmann; 242 Huntsman; 186 Crow

Democrat   115,150 Obama; 17,804 Wolfe; 9,897 Ely; 7,750 Richardson

MARYLAND   April 3

Republican   122,400 Romney; 71,349 Santorum; 27,240 Gingrich; 23,609 Paul; 1,484 Huntsman; 1,108 Perry; 901 Roemer; 377 Karger

Democrat   288,766 Obama; 37,704 Uncommitted

MASSACHUSETTS   March 6

Republican   266,313 Romney; 44,564 Santorum; 35,219 Paul; 16,991 Gingrich; 2,268 Huntsman; 1,793 No Preference; 991 Perry; 865 Bachmann; 613 Scattered Write-In

Democrat   127,909 Obama; 16,075 No Preference; 3,889 Scattered Write-In

PRESIDENTIAL PRIMARIES 2012

MICHIGAN   February 28

Republican   409,522 Romney; 377,372 Santorum; 115,911 Paul; 65,027 Gingrich; 18,809 Uncommitted; 1,816 Perry; 1,784 Roemer; 1,735 Bachmann; 1,674 Huntsman; 1,211 Cain; 1,180 Karger; 458 Johnson

Democrat   174,054 Obama; 20,833 Uncommitted

MISSISSIPPI   March 13

Republican   96,258 Santorum; 91,612 Gingrich; 90,161 Romney; 12,955 Paul; 1,350 Perry; 971 Bachmann; 413 Huntsman; 392 Johnson

Democrat   97,304 Obama

MISSOURI   February 7

Republican   139,272 Santorum; 63,882 Romney; 30,647 Paul; 9,853 Uncommitted; 2,456 Perry; 2,306 Cain; 1,680 Bachmann; 1,044 Huntsman; 536 Johnson; 356 Meehan; 153 Drummond

Democrat   64,435 Obama; 4,582 Uncommitted; 1,998 Terry; 1,000 Wolfe; 873 Richardson

MONTANA   June 5

Republican   96,121 Romney; 20,227 Paul; 12,546 Santorum; 6,107 Gingrich; 5,456 No Preference

Democrat   79,932 Obama; 8,270 No Preference; 10 Wolfe

NEBRASKA   May 15

Republican   131,436 Romney; 25,830 Santorum; 18,508 Paul; 9,628 Gingrich

Democrat   63,881 Obama

NEW HAMPSHIRE   January 10

Republican   97,591 Romney; 56,872 Paul; 41,964 Huntsman; 23,432 Santorum; 23,421 Gingrich; 1,764 Perry; 950 Roemer; 549 Scattered Write-In; 350 Bachmann; 345 Karger; 250 Rubash; 181 Johnson; 161 Cain; 119 Lawman; 108 Hill; 83 Linn; 54 Meehan; 42 Drummond; 42 Story; 29 Betzler; 25 Robinson; 24 Greenleaf; 20 Callahan; 19 Martin; 18 Swift; 15 Brewer; 15 Wuensche; 14 Davis; 12 Crow; 3 Cort; 3 Vestermark

Democrat   49,080 Obama; 6,778 Scattered Write-In; 945 Cowan; 833 Supreme; 442 Terry; 423 Haywood; 400 Freis; 287 Ely; 266 O'Connor; 264 Richardson; 245 Wolfe; 222 O'Donnell; 213 Greene; 155 Jordan; 106 Tyler

NEW JERSEY   June 5

Republican   188,121 Romney; 24,017 Paul; 12,115 Santorum; 7,212 Gingrich

Democrat   283,673 Obama

NEW MEXICO   June 5

Republican   65,935 Romney; 9,517 Santorum; 9,363 Paul; 5,298 Gingrich

Democrat   122,958 Obama

PRESIDENTIAL PRIMARIES 2012

NEW YORK   April 24

Republican   118,912 Romney; 27,699 Paul; 23,990 Gingrich; 18,997 Santorum; 1 Scattered Write-In

NORTH CAROLINA   May 8

Republican   638,601 Romney; 108,217 Paul; 101,093 Santorum; 74,367 Gingrich; 50,928 No Preference

Democrat   766,077 Obama; 200,810 No Preference

OHIO   March 6

Republican   460,831 Romney; 448,580 Santorum; 177,183 Gingrich; 113,256 Paul; 7,539 Perry; 6,490 Huntsman

Democrat   542,086 Obama

OKLAHOMA   March 6

Republican   96,849 Santorum; 80,356 Romney; 78,730 Gingrich; 27,596 Paul; 1,291 Perry; 951 Bachmann; 750 Huntsman

Democrat   64,389 Obama; 20,312 Terry; 15,546 Rogers; 7,201 Richardson; 5,323 Ely

OREGON   May 15

Republican   204,176 Romney; 36,810 Paul; 27,042 Santorum; 15,451 Gingrich; 4,476 Scattered Write-In

Democrat   309,358 Obama; 16,998 Scattered Write-In

PENNSYLVANIA   April 24

Republican   468,374 Romney; 149,056 Santorum; 106,148 Paul; 84,537 Gingrich; 2,819 Scattered Write-In

Democrat   616,102 Obama; 19,082 Scattered Write-In

RHODE ISLAND   April 24

Republican   9,178 Romney; 3,473 Paul; 880 Gingrich; 825 Santorum; 131 Uncommitted; 40 Roemer; 37 Scattered Write-In

Democrat   6,759 Obama; 1,133 Uncommitted; 214 Scattered Write-In

SOUTH CAROLINA   January 21

Republican   244,065 Gingrich; 168,123 Romney; 102,475 Santorum; 78,360 Paul; 6,338 Cain; 2,534 Perry; 1,173 Huntsman; 491 Bachmann; 211 Johnson

SOUTH DAKOTA   June 5

Republican   33,872 Romney; 6,657 Paul; 5,844 Santorum; 2,771 Uncommitted; 2,001 Gingrich

TENNESSEE   March 6

Republican   205,809 Santorum; 155,630 Romney; 132,889 Gingrich; 50,156 Paul; 3,536 Uncommitted; 1,966 Perry; 1,895 Bachmann; 1,239 Huntsman; 881 Roemer; 572 Johnson

Democrat   80,705 Obama; 10,497 Uncommitted; 7 Wolfe

PRESIDENTIAL PRIMARIES 2012

TEXAS   May 29

Republican   1,001,387 Romney; 174,207 Paul; 115,584 Santorum; 68,247 Gingrich; 60,659 Uncommitted; 12,097 Bachmann; 8,695 Huntsman; 4,714 Roemer; 3,887 Davis

Democrat   520,410 Obama; 29,879 Wolfe; 25,430 Richardson; 14,445 Ely

UTAH   June 26

Republican   225,428 Romney; 11,520 Paul; 3,594 Santorum; 1,146 Gingrich; 584 Karger

VERMONT   March 6

Republican   24,008 Romney; 15,391 Paul; 14,368 Santorum; 4,949 Gingrich; 1,198 Huntsman; 544 Perry; 392 Scattered Write-In

Democrat   40,247 Obama; 675 Scattered Write-In

VIRGINIA   March 6

Republican   158,119 Romney; 107,451 Paul

WEST VIRGINIA   May 8

Republican   78,197 Romney; 13,590 Santorum; 12,412 Paul; 7,076 Gingrich; 1,141 Roemer

Democrat   106,770 Obama; 73,138 Judd

WISCONSIN   April 3

Republican   346,876 Romney; 290,139 Santorum; 87,858 Paul; 45,978 Gingrich; 6,045 Bachmann; 5,083 Huntsman; 4,200 Uninstructed Delegation; 1,668 Scattered Write-In

Democrat   293,914 Obama; 5,492 Uninstructed Delegation; 849 Scattered Write-In

DEMOCRATIC PRESIDENTIAL PRIMARIES 2012

Date	State	Total vote	Obama	Uncommitted	Other
January 10	New Hampshire	60,659	49,080 **80.9%**		11,579 **19.1%**
February 7	Missouri	72,888	64,435 **88.4%**	4,582 **6.3%**	3,871 **5.3%**
February 28	Michigan	194,887	174,054 **89.3%**	20,833 **10.7%**	
March 6	Georgia	139,273	139,273 **100.0%**		
March 6	Massachusetts	147,873	127,909 **86.5%**		19,964 **13.5%**
March 6	Ohio	542,086	542,086 **100.0%**		
March 6	Oklahoma	112,771	64,389 **57.1%**		48,382 **42.9%**
March 6	Tennessee	91,209	80,705 **88.5%**	10,497 **11.5%**	7 **0.0%**
March 6	Vermont	40,922	40,247 **98.4%**		675 **1.6%**
March 13	Alabama	286,891	241,276 **84.1%**	45,615 **15.9%**	
March 13	Mississippi	97,304	97,304 **100.0%**		
March 20	Illinois	652,717	652,583 **100.0%**		134 **0.0%**
March 24	Louisiana	150,601	115,150 **76.5%**		35,451 **23.5%**
April 3	District of Columbia	57,989	56,503 **97.4%**	1,100 **1.9%**	386 **0.7%**
April 3	Maryland	326,470	288,766 **88.5%**	37,704 **11.5%**	
April 3	Wisconsin	300,255	293,914 **97.9%**		6,341 **2.1%**
April 24	Pennsylvania	635,184	616,102 **97.0%**		19,082 **3.0%**
April 24	Rhode Island	8,106	6,759 **83.4%**	1,133 **14.0%**	214 **2.6%**
May 8	Indiana	221,466	221,466 **100.0%**		
May 8	North Carolina	966,887	766,077 **79.2%**		200,810 **20.8%**
May 8	West Virginia	179,908	106,770 **59.3%**		73,138 **40.7%**
May 15	Nebraska	63,881	63,881 **100.0%**		
May 15	Oregon	326,356	309,358 **94.8%**		16,998 **5.2%**
May 22	Arkansas	162,647	94,936 **58.4%**		67,711 **41.6%**
May 22	Kentucky	206,218	119,293 **57.8%**	86,925 **42.2%**	
May 29	Texas	590,164	520,410 **88.2%**		69,754 **11.8%**
June 5	California	2,076,309	2,075,905 **100.0%**		404 **0.0%**

DEMOCRATIC PRESIDENTIAL PRIMARIES 2012

Date	State	Total vote	Obama	Uncommitted	Other
June 5	Montana	88,212	79,932 **90.6%**		8,280 **9.4%**
June 5	New Jersey	283,673	283,673 **100.0%**		
June 5	New Mexico	122,958	122,958 **100.0%**		
	Total	*9,206,764*	*8,415,194* **91.4%**	*208,389* **2.3%**	*583,181* **6.3%**

Notes: Table is limited to jurisdictions that vote for president in November—namely, the 50 states and District of Columbia. States not listed in the primary table held caucuses (Alaska, Colorado, Hawaii, Idaho, Iowa, Kansas, Maine, Minnesota, Nevada, North Dakota, Utah, Wyoming) or cancelled their primary/did not record votes because Obama was unopposed (Arizona, Connecticut, Delaware, Florida, New York, South Carolina, South Dakota, Virginia, Washington).

Candidates who received at least 200,000 votes in the Democratic primaries are included in the table above. Other vote for names on the ballot in at least one primary: 116,646 John Wolfe; 73,138 Keith Judd; 41,518 Darcy Richardson; 29,952 Bob Ely; 22,752 Randall Terry; 15,546 Jim Rogers; 945 Ed Cowan; 833 Vermin Supreme; 423 John Haywood; 400 Craig "Tax Freeze" Freis; 266 Cornelius E. O'Connor; 222 Edward T. O'Donnell Jr.; 213 Bob Greene; 155 Robert B. Jordan; 106 Aldous C. Tyler Jr. In addition, 5,492 voters in Wisconsin opted for an "Uninstructed Delegation," and there were 29,789 scattered write-In votes.

REPUBLICAN PRESIDENTIAL PRIMARIES 2012

Date	State	Total vote	Romney	Gingrich	Paul	Santorum	Uncommitted	Other
January 10	New Hampshire	248,475	97,591 39.3%	23,421 9.4%	56,872 22.9%	23,432 9.4%		47,159 19.0%
January 21	South Carolina	603,770	168,123 27.8%	244,065 40.4%	78,360 13.0%	102,475 17.0%		10,747 1.8%
January 31	Florida	1,672,634	776,159 46.4%	534,121 31.9%	117,461 7.0%	223,249 13.3%		21,644 1.3%
February 7	Missouri	252,185	63,882 25.3%		30,647 12.2%	139,272 55.2%	9,853 3.9%	8,531 3.4%
February 28	Arizona	510,258	239,167 46.9%	81,748 16.0%	43,952 8.6%	138,031 27.1%		7,360 1.4%
February 28	Michigan	996,499	409,522 41.1%	65,027 6.5%	115,911 11.6%	377,372 37.9%	18,809 1.9%	9,858 1.0%
March 6	Georgia	901,470	233,611 25.9%	425,395 47.2%	59,100 6.6%	176,259 19.6%		7,105 0.8%
March 6	Massachusetts	369,617	266,313 72.1%	16,991 4.6%	35,219 9.5%	44,564 12.1%		6,530 1.8%
March 6	Ohio	1,213,879	460,831 38.0%	177,183 14.6%	113,256 9.3%	448,580 37.0%		14,029 1.2%
March 6	Oklahoma	286,523	80,356 28.0%	78,730 27.5%	27,596 9.6%	96,849 33.8%		2,992 1.0%
March 6	Tennessee	554,573	155,630 28.1%	132,889 24.0%	50,156 9.0%	205,809 37.1%	3,536 0.6%	6,553 1.2%
March 6	Vermont	60,850	24,008 39.5%	4,949 8.1%	15,391 25.3%	14,368 23.6%		2,134 3.5%
March 6	Virginia	265,570	158,119 59.5%		107,451 40.5%			
March 13	Alabama	622,084	180,336 29.0%	182,292 29.3%	30,950 5.0%	214,628 34.5%	9,259 1.5%	4,619 0.7%
March 13	Mississippi	294,112	90,161 30.7%	91,612 31.1%	12,955 4.4%	96,258 32.7%		3,126 1.1%
March 20	Illinois	933,454	435,859 46.7%	74,482 8.0%	87,044 9.3%	326,778 35.0%		9,291 1.0%
March 24	Louisiana	186,410	49,758 26.7%	29,656 15.9%	11,467 6.2%	91,321 49.0%		4,208 2.3%
April 3	District of Columbia	5,104	3,577 70.1%	558 10.9%	621 12.2%			348 6.8%
April 3	Maryland	248,468	122,400 49.3%	27,240 11.0%	23,609 9.5%	71,349 28.7%		3,870 1.6%
April 3	Wisconsin	787,847	346,876 44.0%	45,978 5.8%	87,858 11.2%	290,139 36.8%		16,996 2.2%
April 24	Connecticut	59,578	40,171 67.4%	6,135 10.3%	8,032 13.5%	4,072 6.8%	1,168 2.0%	
April 24	Delaware	28,592	16,143 56.5%	7,742 27.1%	3,017 10.6%	1,690 5.9%		
April 24	New York	189,599	118,912 62.7%	23,990 12.7%	27,699 14.6%	18,997 10.0%		1 0.0%
April 24	Pennsylvania	810,934	468,374 57.8%	84,537 10.4%	106,148 13.1%	149,056 18.4%		2,819 0.3%
April 24	Rhode Island	14,564	9,178 63.0%	880 6.0%	3,473 23.8%	825 5.7%	131 0.9%	77 0.5%
May 8	Indiana	635,589	410,635 64.6%	41,135 6.5%	98,487 15.5%	85,332 13.4%		
May 8	North Carolina	973,206	638,601 65.6%	74,367 7.6%	108,217 11.1%	101,093 10.4%		50,928 5.2%

REPUBLICAN PRESIDENTIAL PRIMARIES 2012

Date	State	Total vote	Romney	Gingrich	Paul	Santorum	Uncommitted	Other
May 8	West Virginia	112,416	78,197 **69.6%**	7,076 **6.3%**	12,412 **11.0%**	13,590 **12.1%**		1,141 **1.0%**
May 15	Nebraska	185,402	131,436 **70.9%**	9,628 **5.2%**	18,508 **10.0%**	25,830 **13.9%**		
May 15	Oregon	287,955	204,176 **70.9%**	15,451 **5.4%**	36,810 **12.8%**	27,042 **9.4%**		4,476 **1.6%**
May 22	Arkansas	152,360	104,200 **68.4%**	7,453 **4.9%**	20,399 **13.4%**	20,308 **13.3%**		
May 22	Kentucky	176,160	117,621 **66.8%**	10,479 **5.9%**	22,074 **12.5%**	15,629 **8.9%**	10,357 **5.9%**	
May 29	Texas	1,449,477	1,001,387 **69.1%**	68,247 **4.7%**	174,207 **12.0%**	115,584 **8.0%**	60,659 **4.2%**	29,393 **2.0%**
June 5	California	1,924,970	1,530,513 **79.5%**	72,022 **3.7%**	199,246 **10.4%**	102,258 **5.3%**		20,931 **1.1%**
June 5	Montana	140,457	96,121 **68.4%**	6,107 **4.3%**	20,227 **14.4%**	12,546 **8.9%**		5,456 **3.9%**
June 5	New Jersey	231,465	188,121 **81.3%**	7,212 **3.1%**	24,017 **10.4%**	12,115 **5.2%**		
June 5	New Mexico	90,113	65,935 **73.2%**	5,298 **5.9%**	9,363 **10.4%**	9,517 **10.6%**		
June 5	South Dakota	51,145	33,872 **66.2%**	2,001 **3.9%**	6,657 **13.0%**	5,844 **11.4%**	2,771 **5.4%**	
June 26	Utah	242,272	225,428 **93.0%**	1,146 **0.5%**	11,520 **4.8%**	3,594 **1.5%**		584 **0.2%**
	Total	*18,770,036*	*9,841,300* **52.4%**	*2,687,243* **14.3%**	*2,016,389* **10.7%**	*3,805,655* **20.3%**	*116,543* **0.6%**	*302,906* **1.6%**

Notes: Table is limited to jurisdictions that vote for president in November—namely, the 50 states and District of Columbia. States not listed in the primary table held caucuses (Alaska, Colorado, Hawaii, Idaho, Iowa, Kansas, Maine, Minnesota, Nevada, North Dakota, Washington, Wyoming) limited to a handful of party members.

Candidates who received at least 200,000 votes in the Republican primaries are included in the table above. Other vote for names on the ballot in at least one primary: 83,131 Jon Huntsman Jr.; 42,245 Rick Perry; 35,084 Michele Bachmann; 30,691 Charles Roemer; 13,519 Herman Cain; 10,879 Fred Karger; 4,285 Gary E. Johnson; 3,887 John Davis; 1,544 Sarah Gonzales; 530 Paul Sims; 418 Cesar Cisneros; 410 Michael J. Meehan; 378 Mark Callahan; 310 Al "Dick" Perry; 250 Kevin Rubash; 247 Christopher Hill; 223 Donald Benjamin; 217 Michael Levinson; 198 Randy Crow; 198 Kip Dean; 195 Keith Drummond; 156 Ronald Zack; 119 Jeff Lawman; 110 Frank Lynch; 96 Wayne Charles Arnett; 90 Raymond Scott Perkins; 86 Matt Welch; 83 Benjamin Linn; 59 Jim Terr; 57 Charles Skelley; 54 Peter "Simon" Bollander; 42 Joe Story; 29 Bear Betzler; 25 Joe Robinson; 24 Stewart J. Greenleaf; 19 Andy Martin; 18 Linden Swift; 15 Vern Wuensche; 15 Timothy Brewer; 14 L. John Davis Jr.; 3 Hugh Cort; 3 James A. Vestermark. In addition, 116,543 voters voted for "Uncommitted," 58,177 in Massachussetts, Montana, and North Carolina indicated "No Preference," 4,200 voters in Wisconsin opted for an "Uninstructed Delegation," and there were 7,736 scattered write-In votes.

ALABAMA

Congressional districts first established for elections held in 2012

7 members

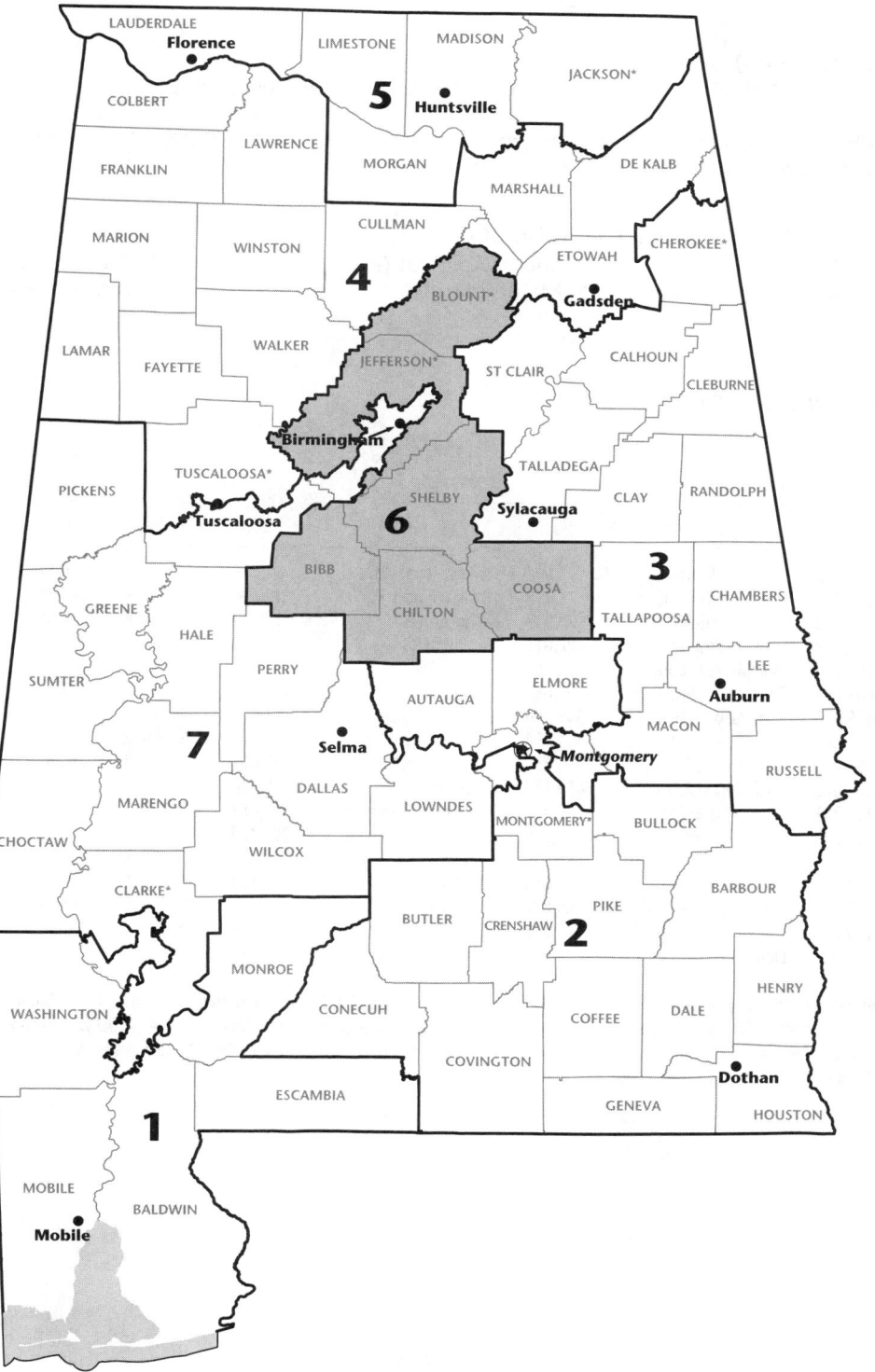

* Asterisk indicates a county whose boundaries include parts of two or more Congressional districts.

ALABAMA

GOVERNOR
Robert Bentley (R). Elected 2010 to a four-year term.

SENATORS (2 Republicans)
Jeff Sessions (R). Reelected 2008 to a six-year term. Previously elected 2002, 1996.

Richard C. Shelby (R). Reelected 2010 to a six-year term. Previously elected 2004, 1998, 1992, 1986. Changed party affiliation from Democratic to Republican in November 1994.

REPRESENTATIVES (6 Republicans, 1 Democrat)
1. Josiah Robins "Jo" Bonner Jr. (R)
2. Martha Roby (R)
3. Mike D. Rogers (R)
4. Robert Aderholt (R)
5. Mo Brooks (R)
6. Spencer Bachus (R)
7. Terri A. Sewell (D)

POSTWAR VOTE FOR PRESIDENT

Year	Total Vote	Republican Vote	Republican Candidate	Democratic Vote	Democratic Candidate	Other Vote	Rep.-Dem. Plurality	Total Vote Rep.	Total Vote Dem.	Major Vote Rep.	Major Vote Dem.
2012	2,074,338	1,255,925	Romney, W. Mitt	795,696	Obama, Barack H.*	22,717	460,229 R	60.5%	38.4%	61.2%	38.8%
2008	2,099,819	1,266,546	McCain, John S. III	813,479	Obama, Barack H.	19,794	453,067 R	60.3%	38.7%	60.9%	39.1%
2004	1,883,449	1,176,394	Bush, George W.*	693,933	Kerry, John F.	13,122	482,461 R	62.5%	36.8%	62.9%	37.1%
2000**	1,666,272	941,173	Bush, George W.	692,611	Gore, Albert Jr.	32,488	248,562 R	56.5%	41.6%	57.6%	42.4%
1996**	1,534,349	769,044	Dole, Robert "Bob"	662,165	Clinton, Bill*	103,140	106,879 R	50.1%	43.2%	53.7%	46.3%
1992**	1,688,060	804,283	Bush, George H.*	690,080	Clinton, Bill	193,697	114,203 R	47.6%	40.9%	53.8%	46.2%
1988	1,378,476	815,576	Bush, George H.	549,506	Dukakis, Michael S.	13,394	266,070 R	59.2%	39.9%	59.7%	40.3%
1984	1,441,713	872,849	Reagan, Ronald*	551,899	Mondale, Walter F.	16,965	320,950 R	60.5%	38.3%	61.3%	38.7%
1980**	1,341,929	654,192	Reagan, Ronald	636,730	Carter, Jimmy*	51,007	17,462 R	48.8%	47.4%	50.7%	49.3%
1976	1,182,850	504,070	Ford, Gerald R.*	659,170	Carter, Jimmy	19,610	155,100 D	42.6%	55.7%	43.3%	56.7%
1972	1,006,111	728,701	Nixon, Richard M.*	256,923	McGovern, George S.	20,487	471,778 R	72.4%	25.5%	73.9%	26.1%
1968**	1,049,922	146,923	Nixon, Richard M.	196,579	Humphrey, Hubert H. Jr.	706,420	49,656 D**	14.0%	18.7%	42.8%	57.2%
1964**	689,818	479,085	Goldwater, Barry M. Sr.		Johnson, Lyndon B.*	210,733	479,085 R	69.5%		100.0%	
1960	570,225	237,981	Nixon, Richard M.	324,050	Kennedy, John F.	8,194	86,069 D	41.7%	56.8%	42.3%	57.7%
1956	496,861	195,694	Eisenhower, Dwight D.*	280,844	Stevenson, Adlai E. II	20,323	85,150 D	39.4%	56.5%	41.1%	58.9%
1952	426,120	149,231	Eisenhower, Dwight D.	275,075	Stevenson, Adlai E. II	1,814	125,844 D	35.0%	64.6%	35.2%	64.8%
1948**	214,980	40,930	Dewey, Thomas E.		Truman, Harry S.*	174,050	40,930 R	19.0%		100.0%	

Note: An asterisk (*) denotes incumbent. **In past elections, the other vote included: 2000 - 18,323 Green (Ralph Nader); 1996 - 92,149 Reform (Ross Perot); 1992 - 183,109 Independent (Perot); 1980 - 16,481 Independent (John Anderson); 1968 - 691,425 American Independent (George Wallace); 1964 - 210,732 Unpledged Democratic; 1948 - 171,443 States' Rights (Strom Thurmond). In 1964 and 1948, the Democratic presidential candidates were not listed on the ballot. Wallace carried Alabama in 1968 with 65.9 percent of the total vote. Thurmond won the state in 1948 with 79.7 percent.

ALABAMA

POSTWAR VOTE FOR GOVERNOR

Year	Total Vote	Republican Vote	Republican Candidate	Democratic Vote	Democratic Candidate	Other Vote	Rep.-Dem. Plurality	Total Vote Rep.	Total Vote Dem.	Major Vote Rep.	Major Vote Dem.
2010	1,494,273	860,472	Bentley, Robert	625,710	Sparks, Ron	8,091	234,762 R	57.6%	41.9%	57.9%	42.1%
2006	1,250,401	718,327	Riley, Robert*	519,827	Baxley, Lucy	12,247	198,500 R	57.4%	41.6%	58.0%	42.0%
2002	1,367,053	672,225	Riley, Robert	669,105	Siegelman, Don*	25,723	3,120 R	49.2%	48.9%	50.1%	49.9%
1998	1,317,842	554,746	James, Forrest H.*	760,155	Siegelman, Don	2,941	205,409 D	42.1%	57.7%	42.2%	57.8%
1994	1,201,969	604,926	James, Forrest H.	594,169	Folsom, James E. Jr.*	2,874	10,757 R	50.3%	49.4%	50.4%	49.6%
1990	1,216,250	633,519	Hunt, Guy*	582,106	Hubbert, Paul R.	625	51,413 R	52.1%	47.9%	52.1%	47.9%
1986	1,236,230	696,203	Hunt, Guy	537,163	Baxley, Bill	2,864	159,040 R	56.3%	43.5%	56.4%	43.6%
1982	1,128,725	440,815	Folmar, Emory	650,538	Wallace, George C.	37,372	209,723 D	39.1%	57.6%	40.4%	59.6%
1978	760,474	196,963	Hunt, Guy	551,886	James, Forrest H.	11,625	354,923 D	25.9%	72.6%	26.3%	73.7%
1974	598,305	88,381	McCary, Elvin	497,574	Wallace, George C.*	12,350	409,193 D	14.8%	83.2%	15.1%	84.9%
1970**	854,952			637,046	Wallace, George C.	217,906	637,046 D		74.5%		100.0%
1966	848,101	262,943	Martin, James D.	537,505	Wallace, Lurleen B.	47,653	274,562 D	31.0%	63.4%	32.8%	67.2%
1962	315,776			303,987	Wallace, George C.	11,789	303,987 D		96.3%		100.0%
1958	270,952	30,415	Longshore, William L. Jr.	239,633	Patterson, John	904	209,218 D	11.2%	88.4%	11.3%	88.7%
1954	333,090	88,688	Abernethy, Tom	244,401	Folsom, James E.	1	155,713 D	26.6%	73.4%	26.6%	73.4%
1950	170,591	15,177	Crowder, John S.	155,414	Persons, Gordon		140,237 D	8.9%	91.1%	8.9%	91.1%
1946	197,321	22,362	Ward, Lyman	174,959	Folsom, James E.		152,597 D	11.3%	88.7%	11.3%	88.7%

Note: An asterisk (*) denotes incumbent. **In past elections, the other vote included: 1970 - 125,491 National Democratic Party of Alabama (John Logan Cashin), who finished second. The Republican Party did not run a candidate in the 1962 and 1970 gubernatorial elections.

POSTWAR VOTE FOR SENATOR

Year	Total Vote	Republican Vote	Republican Candidate	Democratic Vote	Democratic Candidate	Other Vote	Rep.-Dem. Plurality	Total Vote Rep.	Total Vote Dem.	Major Vote Rep.	Major Vote Dem.
2010	1,485,499	968,181	Shelby, Richard C.*	515,619	Barnes, William G.	1,699	452,562 R	65.2%	34.7%	65.3%	34.7%
2008	2,060,191	1,305,383	Sessions, Jeff*	752,391	Figures, Vivian Davis	2,417	552,992 R	63.4%	36.5%	63.4%	36.6%
2004	1,839,066	1,242,200	Shelby, Richard C.*	595,018	Sowell, Wayne	1,848	647,182 R	67.5%	32.4%	67.6%	32.4%
2002	1,353,023	792,561	Sessions, Jeff*	538,878	Parker, Susan	21,584	253,683 R	58.6%	39.8%	59.5%	40.5%
1998	1,293,405	817,973	Shelby, Richard C.*	474,568	Suddith, Clayton	864	343,405 R	63.2%	36.7%	63.3%	36.7%
1996	1,499,393	786,436	Sessions, Jeff	681,651	Bedford, Roger	31,306	104,785 R	52.5%	45.5%	53.6%	46.4%
1992	1,577,899	522,015	Sellers, Richard*	1,022,698	Shelby, Richard C.*	33,186	500,683 D	33.1%	64.8%	33.8%	66.2%
1990	1,185,563	467,190	Cabaniss, Bill	717,814	Heflin, Howell*	559	250,624 D	39.4%	60.5%	39.4%	60.6%
1986	1,211,953	602,537	Denton, Jeremiah*	609,360	Shelby, Richard C.	56	6,823 D	49.7%	50.3%	49.7%	50.3%
1984	1,371,238	498,508	Smith, Albert Lee Jr.	860,535	Heflin, Howell*	12,195	362,027 D	36.4%	62.8%	36.7%	63.3%
1980	1,296,757	650,362	Denton, Jeremiah	610,175	Folsom, James E. Jr.	36,220	40,187 R	50.2%	47.1%	51.6%	48.4%
1978	582,025			547,054	Heflin, Howell	34,971	547,054 D		94.0%		100.0%
1978S	731,610	316,170	Martin, James D.	401,852	Stewart, Donald W.	13,588	85,682 D	43.2%	54.9%	44.0%	56.0%
1974	523,290			501,541	Allen, James B.*	21,749	501,541 D		95.8%		100.0%
1972	1,051,099	347,523	Blount, Winton M.	654,491	Sparkman, John J.*	49,085	306,968 D	33.1%	62.3%	34.7%	65.3%
1968	912,708	201,227	Hooper, Perry	638,774	Allen, James B.	72,707	437,547 D	22.0%	70.0%	24.0%	76.0%
1966	802,608	313,018	Grenier, John	482,138	Sparkman, John J.*	7,452	169,120 D	39.0%	60.1%	39.4%	60.6%
1962	397,079	195,134	Martin, James D.	201,937	Hill, Lister*	8	6,803 D	49.1%	50.9%	49.1%	50.9%
1960	554,081	164,868	Elgin, Julian	389,196	Sparkman, John J.*	17	224,328 D	29.8%	70.2%	29.8%	70.2%
1956	330,191			330,182	Hill, Lister*	9	330,182 D		100.0%		100.0%
1954	314,459	55,110	Guin, J. Foy Jr.	259,348	Sparkman, John J.*	1	204,238 D	17.5%	82.5%	17.5%	82.5%
1950	164,011			125,534	Hill, Lister*	38,477	125,534 D		76.5%		100.0%
1948	220,875	35,341	Parsons, Paul G.	185,534	Sparkman, John J.*		150,193 D	16.0%	84.0%	16.0%	84.0%
1946S	163,217			163,217	Sparkman, John J.*		163,217 D		100.0%		100.0%

Note: An asterisk (*) denotes incumbent. **The 1946 election and one of the 1978 elections were for short terms to fill vacancies. The Republican Party did not run a candidate in Senate elections in 1946, 1950, 1956, 1974 and 1978.

ALABAMA

PRESIDENT 2012

2010 Census Population	County	Total Vote	Republican (Romney)	Democratic (Obama)	Other	Rep.-Dem. Plurality	Percentage Total Vote Rep.	Dem.	Major Vote Rep.	Dem.
54,571	AUTAUGA	23,973	17,379	6,363	231	11,016 R	72.5%	26.5%	73.2%	26.8%
182,265	BALDWIN	85,491	66,016	18,424	1,051	47,592 R	77.2%	21.6%	78.2%	21.8%
27,457	BARBOUR	11,517	5,550	5,912	55	362 D	48.2%	51.3%	48.4%	51.6%
22,915	BIBB	8,420	6,132	2,202	86	3,930 R	72.8%	26.2%	73.6%	26.4%
57,322	BLOUNT	24,060	20,757	2,970	333	17,787 R	86.3%	12.3%	87.5%	12.5%
10,914	BULLOCK	5,322	1,251	4,061	10	2,810 D	23.5%	76.3%	23.6%	76.4%
20,947	BUTLER	9,502	5,087	4,374	41	713 R	53.5%	46.0%	53.8%	46.2%
118,572	CALHOUN	46,364	30,278	15,511	575	14,767 R	65.3%	33.5%	66.1%	33.9%
34,215	CHAMBERS	14,629	7,626	6,871	132	755 R	52.1%	47.0%	52.6%	47.4%
25,989	CHEROKEE	9,792	7,506	2,132	154	5,374 R	76.7%	21.8%	77.9%	22.1%
43,643	CHILTON	17,485	13,932	3,397	156	10,535 R	79.7%	19.4%	80.4%	19.6%
13,859	CHOCTAW	7,976	4,152	3,786	38	366 R	52.1%	47.5%	52.3%	47.7%
25,833	CLARKE	13,860	7,470	6,334	56	1,136 R	53.9%	45.7%	54.1%	45.9%
13,932	CLAY	6,679	4,817	1,777	85	3,040 R	72.1%	26.6%	73.1%	26.9%
14,972	CLEBURNE	6,319	5,272	971	76	4,301 R	83.4%	15.4%	84.4%	15.6%
49,948	COFFEE	19,821	14,666	4,925	230	9,741 R	74.0%	24.8%	74.9%	25.1%
54,428	COLBERT	23,444	13,936	9,166	342	4,770 R	59.4%	39.1%	60.3%	39.7%
13,228	CONECUH	7,025	3,439	3,555	31	116 D	49.0%	50.6%	49.2%	50.8%
11,539	COOSA	5,282	3,049	2,191	42	858 R	57.7%	41.5%	58.2%	41.8%
37,765	COVINGTON	15,439	12,153	3,158	128	8,995 R	78.7%	20.5%	79.4%	20.6%
13,906	CRENSHAW	6,424	4,331	2,050	43	2,281 R	67.4%	31.9%	67.9%	32.1%
80,406	CULLMAN	34,555	28,999	5,052	504	23,947 R	83.9%	14.6%	85.2%	14.8%
50,251	DALE	18,601	13,108	5,286	207	7,822 R	70.5%	28.4%	71.3%	28.7%
43,820	DALLAS	20,964	6,288	14,612	64	8,324 D	30.0%	69.7%	30.1%	69.9%
71,109	DEKALB	23,950	18,331	5,239	380	13,092 R	76.5%	21.9%	77.8%	22.2%
79,303	ELMORE	35,546	26,253	8,954	339	17,299 R	73.9%	25.2%	74.6%	25.4%
38,319	ESCAMBIA	14,894	9,287	5,489	118	3,798 R	62.4%	36.9%	62.9%	37.1%
104,430	ETOWAH	42,624	29,130	12,803	691	16,327 R	68.3%	30.0%	69.5%	30.5%
17,241	FAYETTE	7,958	6,054	1,817	87	4,237 R	76.1%	22.8%	76.9%	23.1%
31,704	FRANKLIN	10,881	7,567	3,171	143	4,396 R	69.5%	29.1%	70.5%	29.5%
26,790	GENEVA	11,331	9,175	2,039	117	7,136 R	81.0%	18.0%	81.8%	18.2%
9,045	GREENE	5,343	804	4,521	18	3,717 D	15.0%	84.6%	15.1%	84.9%
15,760	HALE	8,647	3,210	5,411	26	2,201 D	37.1%	62.6%	37.2%	62.8%
17,302	HENRY	8,766	5,628	3,083	55	2,545 R	64.2%	35.2%	64.6%	35.4%
101,547	HOUSTON	41,984	29,270	12,367	347	16,903 R	69.7%	29.5%	70.3%	29.7%
53,227	JACKSON	20,632	14,439	5,822	371	8,617 R	70.0%	28.2%	71.3%	28.7%
658,466	JEFFERSON	304,523	141,683	159,876	2,964	18,193 D	46.5%	52.5%	47.0%	53.0%
14,564	LAMAR	7,176	5,457	1,646	73	3,811 R	76.0%	22.9%	76.8%	23.2%
92,709	LAUDERDALE	37,032	23,911	12,511	610	11,400 R	64.6%	33.8%	65.6%	34.4%
34,339	LAWRENCE	14,148	8,874	5,069	205	3,805 R	62.7%	35.8%	63.6%	36.4%
140,247	LEE	54,496	32,194	21,381	921	10,813 R	59.1%	39.2%	60.1%	39.9%
82,782	LIMESTONE	35,540	25,295	9,829	416	15,466 R	71.2%	27.7%	72.0%	28.0%
11,299	LOWNDES	7,523	1,756	5,747	20	3,991 D	23.3%	76.4%	23.4%	76.6%
21,452	MACON	10,396	1,331	9,045	20	7,714 D	12.8%	87.0%	12.8%	87.2%
334,811	MADISON	155,428	90,884	62,015	2,529	28,869 R	58.5%	39.9%	59.4%	40.6%
21,027	MARENGO	11,543	5,336	6,167	40	831 D	46.2%	53.4%	46.4%	53.6%
30,776	MARION	12,129	9,697	2,249	183	7,448 R	79.9%	18.5%	81.2%	18.8%
93,019	MARSHALL	32,644	25,867	6,299	478	19,568 R	79.2%	19.3%	80.4%	19.6%
412,992	MOBILE	175,140	94,893	78,760	1,487	16,133 R	54.2%	45.0%	54.6%	45.4%
23,068	MONROE	10,717	5,741	4,914	62	827 R	53.6%	45.9%	53.9%	46.1%
229,363	MONTGOMERY	102,067	38,332	63,085	650	24,753 D	37.6%	61.8%	37.8%	62.2%
119,490	MORGAN	49,459	35,391	13,439	629	21,952 R	71.6%	27.2%	72.5%	27.5%
10,591	PERRY	6,101	1,506	4,568	27	3,062 D	24.7%	74.9%	24.8%	75.2%
19,746	PICKENS	9,621	5,124	4,455	42	669 R	53.3%	46.3%	53.5%	46.5%
32,899	PIKE	14,123	7,963	6,035	125	1,928 R	56.4%	42.7%	56.9%	43.1%
22,913	RANDOLPH	10,421	7,224	3,078	119	4,146 R	69.3%	29.5%	70.1%	29.9%
52,947	RUSSELL	18,910	8,278	10,500	132	2,222 D	43.8%	55.5%	44.1%	55.9%
195,085	SHELBY	92,742	71,436	20,051	1,255	51,385 R	77.0%	21.6%	78.1%	21.9%
83,593	ST. CLAIR	35,235	29,031	5,801	403	23,230 R	82.4%	16.5%	83.3%	16.7%
13,763	SUMTER	7,030	1,586	5,421	23	3,835 D	22.6%	77.1%	22.6%	77.4%

ALABAMA

PRESIDENT 2012

2010 Census Population	County	Total Vote	Republican (Romney)	Democratic (Obama)	Other	Rep.-Dem. Plurality	Total Vote Rep.	Total Vote Dem.	Major Vote Rep.	Major Vote Dem.
82,291	TALLADEGA	33,416	19,246	13,905	265	5,341 R	57.6%	41.6%	58.1%	41.9%
41,616	TALLAPOOSA	18,851	12,396	6,319	136	6,077 R	65.8%	33.5%	66.2%	33.8%
194,656	TUSCALOOSA	78,772	45,748	32,048	976	13,700 R	58.1%	40.7%	58.8%	41.2%
67,023	WALKER	28,585	21,651	6,557	377	15,094 R	75.7%	22.9%	76.8%	23.2%
17,581	WASHINGTON	8,787	5,761	2,976	50	2,785 R	65.6%	33.9%	65.9%	34.1%
11,670	WILCOX	6,555	1,679	4,868	8	3,189 D	25.6%	74.3%	25.6%	74.4%
24,484	WINSTON	9,728	8,312	1,286	130	7,026 R	85.4%	13.2%	86.6%	13.4%
4,779,736	TOTAL	2,074,338	1,255,925	795,696	22,717	460,229 R	60.5%	38.4%	61.2%	38.8%

ALABAMA

HOUSE OF REPRESENTATIVES

CD	Year	Total Vote	Republican Vote	Republican Candidate	Democratic Vote	Democratic Candidate	Other Vote	Rep.-Dem. Plurality	Total Vote Rep.	Total Vote Dem.	Major Vote Rep.	Major Vote Dem.
1	2012	200,676	196,374	BONNER, JOSIAH ROBINS "JO" JR.*			4,302	196,374 R	97.9%		100.0%	
2	2012	283,953	180,591	ROBY, MARTHA*	103,092	FORD, THERESE	270	77,499 R	63.6%	36.3%	63.7%	36.3%
3	2012	273,930	175,306	ROGERS, MIKE D.*	98,141	HARRIS, JOHN ANDREW	483	77,165 R	64.0%	35.8%	64.1%	35.9%
4	2012	269,118	199,071	ADERHOLT, ROBERT*	69,706	BOMAN, DANIEL H.	341	129,365 R	74.0%	25.9%	74.1%	25.9%
5	2012	291,293	189,185	BROOKS, MO*	101,772	HOLLEY, CHARLIE L.	336	87,413 R	64.9%	34.9%	65.0%	35.0%
6	2012	308,102	219,262	BACHUS, SPENCER*	88,267	BAILEY, PENNY "COLONEL"	573	130,995 R	71.2%	28.6%	71.3%	28.7%
7	2012	306,558	73,835	CHAMBERLAIN, DON	232,520	SEWELL, TERRI A.*	203	158,685 D	24.1%	75.8%	24.1%	75.9%
TOTAL	2012	1,933,630	1,233,624		693,498		6,508	540,126 R	63.8%	35.9%	64.0%	36.0%

Note: An asterisk (*) denotes incumbent.

ALABAMA

GENERAL AND PRIMARY ELECTIONS

2012 GENERAL ELECTIONS: OTHER VOTE

President Other vote was 12,328 Libertarian (Gary E. Johnson), 4,011 Write-in (Scattered Write-In), 3,397 Green (Jill Stein), 2,981 Constitution (Virgil H. Goode).

House Other vote was:

CD 1 4,302 Write-in (Scattered Write-In)
CD 2 270 Write-in (Scattered Write-In)
CD 3 483 Write-in (Scattered Write-In)
CD 4 341 Write-in (Scattered Write-In)
CD 5 336 Write-in (Scattered Write-In)
CD 6 573 Write-in (Scattered Write-In)
CD 7 203 Write-in (Scattered Write-In)

ALABAMA

GENERAL AND PRIMARY ELECTIONS

2012 PRIMARY ELECTIONS: SUPPLEMENTARY INFORMATION

Primary	March 13, 2012	**Registration** (as of February 28, 2012 – includes 349,880 inactive registrants)	2,971,575	No Party Registration

Primary Type   Open—Any registered voter could vote in either the Democratic or Republican primary, although any voter that participated in the Republican primary could not vote in the Democratic runoff. There was no such restriction on participation in the Republican runoff.

	REPUBLICAN PRIMARIES			DEMOCRATIC PRIMARIES		
President	Santorum, Rick	214,628	34.5%	Obama, Barack H.*	241,276	84.1%
	Gingrich, Newt	182,292	29.3%	Uncommitted	45,615	15.9%
	Romney, W. Mitt	180,336	29.0%			
	Paul, Ron	30,950	5.0%			
	Uncommitted	9,259	1.5%			
	Perry, Rick	1,869	0.3%			
	Bachmann, Michele	1,701	0.3%			
	Huntsman, Jon Jr.	1,049	0.2%			
	TOTAL	622,084		TOTAL	286,891	
Congressional District 1	Bonner, Josiah Robins "Jo" Jr.*	48,702	55.5%			
	Young, Dean	21,308	24.3%			
	Riehm, Pete	13,809	15.8%			
	Gounares, Peter	3,854	4.4%			
	TOTAL	87,673				
Congressional District 2	Roby, Martha*	Unopposed		Ford, Therese	Unopposed	
Congressional District 3	Rogers, Mike D.*	Unopposed		Harris, John Andrew	Unopposed	
Congressional District 4	Aderholt, Robert*	Unopposed		Boman, Daniel H.	10,971	51.4%
				Neighbors, Rick	10,353	48.6%
				TOTAL	21,324	
Congressional District 5	Brooks, Mo*	65,163	70.9%	Holley, Charlie L.	Unopposed	
	Griffith, Parker	26,694	29.1%			
	TOTAL	91,857				
Congressional District 6	Bachus, Spencer*	63,360	61.4%	Bailey, Penny "Colonel"	5,061	61.0%
	Beason, Scott	28,673	27.8%	Barnes, William G.	3,229	39.0%
	Standridge, David	8,120	7.9%			
	Mickle, Al	2,930	2.8%			
	Pate, Stan	33				
	TOTAL	103,116		TOTAL	8,290	
Congressional District 7	Chamberlain, Don*	11,537	66.1%	Sewell, Terri A.*	Unopposed	
	Norris, Phillip	5,918	33.9%			
	TOTAL	17,455				

Notes: An asterisk (*) denotes incumbent. Names of unopposed candidates did not appear on the primary ballot; therefore, no votes were cast for these candidates. Stan Pate withdrew from the Republican primary election in the 6th district, but his name appeared on some absentee ballots.

ALASKA

One member At Large

Alaska reports election results by legislative district. The districts indicated were first effective for the 2012 elections.

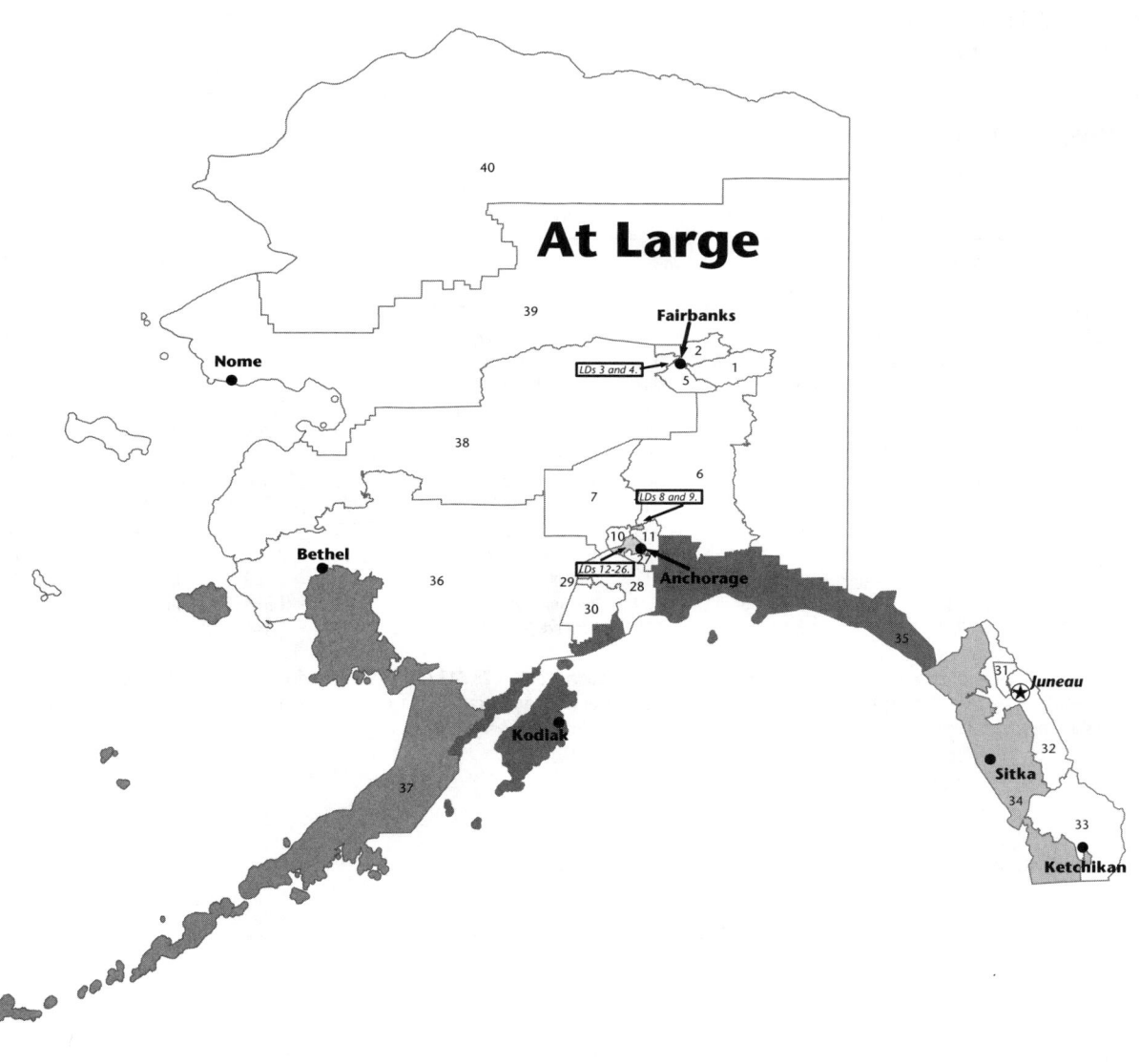

40

At Large

39

Nome

Fairbanks

LDs 3 and 4. 2

5 1

38

6

7

LDs 8 and 9.

10 11

Bethel

LDs 12-26.

36

29 28 Anchorage

30

35

31 Juneau

Kodiak

32

Sitka

34

37

33

Ketchikan

Alaska includes more islands to the west of those that are illustrated on this map.

ALASKA

GOVERNOR

Sean R. Parnell (R). Elected 2010 to a four-year term. Assumed office July 26, 2009, upon the resignation of Sarah H. Palin (R).

SENATORS (1 Democrat, 1 Republican)

Mark Begich (D). Elected 2008 to a six-year term.

Lisa Murkowski (R). Reelected 2010 to a six-year term as a write-in candidate. Previously elected 2004. Had been appointed December 20, 2002, to fill the vacancy created by the resignation of her father, Frank H. Murkowski (R), to become governor of Alaska.

REPRESENTATIVE (1 Republican)

At Large. Don Young (R)

POSTWAR VOTE FOR PRESIDENT

		Republican		Democratic		Other	Rep.-Dem.	Total Vote (Percentage)		Major Vote (Percentage)	
Year	Total Vote	Vote	Candidate	Vote	Candidate	Vote	Plurality	Rep.	Dem.	Rep.	Dem.
2012	300,495	164,676	Romney, W. Mitt	122,640	Obama, Barack H.*	13,179	42,036 R	54.8%	40.8%	57.3%	42.7%
2008	326,197	193,841	McCain, John S. III	123,594	Obama, Barack H.	8,762	70,247 R	59.4%	37.9%	61.1%	38.9%
2004	312,598	190,889	Bush, George W.*	111,025	Kerry, John F.	10,684	79,864 R	61.1%	35.5%	63.2%	36.8%
2000**	285,560	167,398	Bush, George W.	79,004	Gore, Albert Jr.	39,158	88,394 R	58.6%	27.7%	67.9%	32.1%
1996**	241,620	122,746	Dole, Robert "Bob"	80,380	Clinton, Bill*	38,494	42,366 R	50.8%	33.3%	60.4%	39.6%
1992**	258,506	102,000	Bush, George H.*	78,294	Clinton, Bill	78,212	23,706 R	39.5%	30.3%	56.6%	43.4%
1988	200,116	119,251	Bush, George H.	72,584	Dukakis, Michael S.	8,281	46,667 R	59.6%	36.3%	62.2%	37.8%
1984	207,605	138,377	Reagan, Ronald*	62,007	Mondale, Walter F.	7,221	76,370 R	66.7%	29.9%	69.1%	30.9%
1980**	158,445	86,112	Reagan, Ronald	41,842	Carter, Jimmy*	30,491	44,270 R	54.3%	26.4%	67.3%	32.7%
1976	123,574	71,555	Ford, Gerald R.*	44,058	Carter, Jimmy	7,961	27,497 R	57.9%	35.7%	61.9%	38.1%
1972	95,219	55,349	Nixon, Richard M.*	32,967	McGovern, George S.	6,903	22,382 R	58.1%	34.6%	62.7%	37.3%
1968**	83,035	37,600	Nixon, Richard M.	35,411	Humphrey, Hubert H. Jr.	10,024	2,189 R	45.3%	42.6%	51.5%	48.5%
1964	67,259	22,930	Goldwater, Barry M. Sr.	44,329	Johnson, Lyndon B.*		21,399 D	34.1%	65.9%	34.1%	65.9%
1960	60,762	30,953	Nixon, Richard M.	29,809	Kennedy, John F.		1,144 R	50.9%	49.1%	50.9%	49.1%

Note: An asterisk (*) denotes incumbent. **In past elections, the other vote included: 2000 - 28,747 Green (Ralph Nader); 1996 - 26,333 Reform (Ross Perot); 1992 - 73,481 Independent (Perot); 1980 - 18,479 Libertarian (Ed Clark) and 11,155 Independent (John Anderson); 1968 - 10,024 American Independent (George Wallace). Alaska was formally admitted as a state in January 1959.

ALASKA

POSTWAR VOTE FOR GOVERNOR

Year	Total Vote	Republican Vote	Republican Candidate	Democratic Vote	Democratic Candidate	Other Vote	Rep.-Dem. Plurality	Total Vote Rep.	Total Vote Dem.	Major Vote Rep.	Major Vote Dem.
2010	256,192	151,318	Parnell, Sean R.*	96,519	Berkowitz, Ethan A.	8,355	54,799 R	59.1%	37.7%	61.1%	38.9%
2006	237,322	114,697	Palin, Sarah H.	97,238	Knowles, Tony	25,387	17,459 R	48.3%	41.0%	54.1%	45.9%
2002	231,484	129,279	Murkowski, Frank H.	94,216	Ulmer, Fran	7,989	35,063 R	55.8%	40.7%	57.8%	42.2%
1998**	220,177	39,331	Lindauer, John	112,879	Knowles, Tony*	67,967	73,548 D	17.9%	51.3%	25.8%	74.2%
1994**	213,435	87,157	Campbell, James O.	87,693	Knowles, Tony*	38,585	536 D	40.8%	41.1%	49.8%	50.2%
1990**	194,750	50,991	Sturgulewski, Arliss	60,201	Knowles, Tony	83,558	9,210 D**	26.2%	30.9%	45.9%	54.1%
1986	179,555	76,515	Sturgulewski, Arliss	84,943	Cowper, Steve	18,097	8,428 D	42.6%	47.3%	47.4%	52.6%
1982**	194,885	72,291	Fink, Tom	89,918	Sheffield, Bill	32,676	17,627 D	37.1%	46.1%	44.6%	55.4%
1978**	126,910	49,580	Hammond, Jay S.*	25,656	Croft, Chancy	51,674	23,924 R	39.1%	20.2%	65.9%	34.1%
1974	96,163	45,840	Hammond, Jay S.	45,553	Egan, William A.*	4,770	287 R	47.7%	47.4%	50.2%	49.8%
1970	80,779	37,264	Miller, Keith	42,309	Egan, William A.	1,206	5,045 D	46.1%	52.4%	46.8%	53.2%
1966	66,294	33,145	Hickel, Walter J.	32,065	Egan, William A.*	1,084	1,080 R	50.0%	48.4%	50.8%	49.2%
1962	56,681	27,054	Stepovich, Mike	29,627	Egan, William A.*		2,573 D	47.7%	52.3%	47.7%	52.3%
1958	48,968	19,299	Butrovich, John Jr.	29,189	Egan, William A.	480	9,890 D	39.4%	59.6%	39.8%	60.2%

Note: An asterisk (*) denotes incumbent. **In past elections, the other vote included: 1998 - 40,209 write-in (Robin Taylor), who finished second; 1994 - 27,838 Alaskan Independence (John B. "Jack" Coghill); 1990 - 75,721 Alaskan Independence (Walter J. Hickel); 1982 - 29,067 Libertarian (Richard L. Randolph); 1978 - 33,555 write-in (Hickel) and 15,656 Alaskans for Kelly (Tom Kelly). Hickel won the 1990 election with 38.9 percent of the total vote and finished second in 1978.

POSTWAR VOTE FOR SENATOR

Year	Total Vote	Republican Vote	Republican Candidate	Democratic Vote	Democratic Candidate	Other Vote	Rep.-Dem. Plurality	Total Vote Rep.	Total Vote Dem.	Major Vote Rep.	Major Vote Dem.
2010**	255,474	90,839	Miller, Joe	60,045	McAdams, Scott T.	104,590	30,794 R**	35.6%	23.5%	60.2%	39.8%
2008	317,723	147,814	Stevens, Ted*	151,767	Begich, Mark	18,142	3,953 D	46.5%	47.8%	49.3%	50.7%
2004	308,315	149,773	Murkowski, Lisa A.*	140,424	Knowles, Tony	18,118	9,349 R	48.6%	45.5%	51.6%	48.4%
2002	229,548	179,438	Stevens, Ted*	24,133	Vondersaar, Frank	25,977	155,305 R	78.2%	10.5%	88.1%	11.9%
1998	221,807	165,227	Murkowski, Frank H.*	43,743	Sonneman, Joseph	12,837	121,484 R	74.5%	19.7%	79.1%	20.9%
1996**	231,916	177,893	Stevens, Ted*	23,977	Obermeyer, Theresa N.	30,046	153,916 R	76.7%	10.3%	88.1%	11.9%
1992	239,714	127,163	Murkowski, Frank H.*	92,065	Smith, Tony	20,486	35,098 R	53.0%	38.4%	58.0%	42.0%
1990	189,957	125,806	Stevens, Ted*	61,152	Beasley, Michael	2,999	64,654 R	66.2%	32.2%	67.3%	32.7%
1986	180,801	97,674	Murkowski, Frank H.*	79,727	Olds, Glenn	3,400	17,947 R	54.0%	44.1%	55.1%	44.9%
1984	206,438	146,919	Stevens, Ted*	58,804	Havelock, John E.	715	88,115 R	71.2%	28.5%	71.4%	28.6%
1980	156,762	84,159	Murkowski, Frank H.	72,007	Gruening, Clark S.	596	12,152 R	53.7%	45.9%	53.9%	46.1%
1978	122,741	92,783	Stevens, Ted*	29,574	Hobbs, Donald W.	384	63,209 R	75.6%	24.1%	75.8%	24.2%
1974	93,275	38,914	Lewis, C. R.	54,361	Gravel, Mike*		15,447 D	41.7%	58.3%	41.7%	58.3%
1972	96,007	74,216	Stevens, Ted*	21,791	Guess, Gene		52,425 R	77.3%	22.7%	77.3%	22.7%
1970S	80,364	47,908	Stevens, Ted*	32,456	Kay, Wendell P.		15,452 R	59.6%	40.4%	59.6%	40.4%
1968	80,931	30,286	Rasmuson, Elmer	36,527	Gravel, Mike	14,118	6,241 D	37.4%	45.1%	45.3%	54.7%
1966	65,250	15,961	McKinley, Lee L.	49,289	Bartlett, E. L.*		33,328 D	24.5%	75.5%	24.5%	75.5%
1962	58,181	24,354	Stevens, Ted	33,827	Gruening, Ernest*		9,473 D	41.9%	58.1%	41.9%	58.1%
1960	59,978	21,937	McKinley, Lee L.	38,041	Bartlett, E. L.*		16,104 D	36.6%	63.4%	36.6%	63.4%
1958	48,837	7,299	Robertson, R. E.	40,939	Bartlett, E. L.	599	33,640 D	14.9%	83.8%	15.1%	84.9%
1958	49,525	23,462	Stepovich, Mike	26,063	Gruening, Ernest		2,601 D	47.4%	52.6%	47.4%	52.6%

Note: An asterisk (*) denotes incumbent. **In past elections, the other vote included: 2010 - 101,091 Republican write-in (Lisa Murkowski), who won reelection with 39.6 percent of the vote; 1996 - 29,037 Green (Jed Whittaker), who finished second. The 1970 election was for a short term to fill a vacancy. The two 1958 elections were held to indeterminate terms and the Senate later determined by lot that Senator Gruening would serve four years, Senator Bartlett two. The plurality for 2010 shows the difference between the official Republican and Democratic candidates.

ALASKA

PRESIDENT 2012

2010 Census Population	Election District	Total Vote	Republican (Romney)	Democratic (Obama)	Other	Rep.-Dem. Plurality	Percentage Total Vote Rep.	Dem.	Major Vote Rep.	Dem.
18,563	Election District 1	7,722	5,899	1,518	305	4,381 R	76.4%	19.7%	79.5%	20.5%
17,131	Election District 2	9,058	5,509	3,096	453	2,413 R	60.8%	34.2%	64.0%	36.0%
18,133	Election District 3	6,069	3,769	2,034	266	1,735 R	62.1%	33.5%	64.9%	35.1%
17,837	Election District 4	6,787	3,586	2,864	337	722 R	52.8%	42.2%	55.6%	44.4%
17,182	Election District 5	8,143	4,027	3,644	472	383 R	49.5%	44.8%	52.5%	47.5%
18,398	Election District 6	7,793	5,254	2,145	394	3,109 R	67.4%	27.5%	71.0%	29.0%
18,150	Election District 7	7,575	5,247	1,962	366	3,285 R	69.3%	25.9%	72.8%	27.2%
18,071	Election District 8	8,242	5,826	2,083	333	3,743 R	70.7%	25.3%	73.7%	26.3%
17,958	Election District 9	7,408	5,432	1,667	309	3,765 R	73.3%	22.5%	76.5%	23.5%
17,220	Election District 10	6,570	4,928	1,344	298	3,584 R	75.0%	20.5%	78.6%	21.4%
17,594	Election District 11	8,631	6,057	2,222	352	3,835 R	70.2%	25.7%	73.2%	26.8%
18,026	Election District 12	6,482	4,300	1,901	281	2,399 R	66.3%	29.3%	69.3%	30.7%
17,723	Election District 13	5,707	3,078	2,425	204	653 R	53.9%	42.5%	55.9%	44.1%
17,635	Election District 14	7,068	3,453	3,340	275	113 R	48.9%	47.3%	50.8%	49.2%
17,789	Election District 15	6,451	2,875	3,283	293	408 D	44.6%	50.9%	46.7%	53.3%
17,799	Election District 16	7,181	2,876	4,013	292	1,137 D	40.1%	55.9%	41.7%	58.3%
17,683	Election District 17	4,589	1,542	2,853	194	1,311 D	33.6%	62.2%	35.1%	64.9%
17,921	Election District 18	6,930	2,369	4,247	314	1,878 D	34.2%	61.3%	35.8%	64.2%
17,672	Election District 19	8,286	3,855	4,126	305	271 D	46.5%	49.8%	48.3%	51.7%
17,678	Election District 20	7,964	4,544	3,081	339	1,463 R	57.1%	38.7%	59.6%	40.4%
17,924	Election District 21	8,866	5,262	3,316	288	1,946 R	59.4%	37.4%	61.3%	38.7%
17,768	Election District 22	6,555	3,445	2,859	251	586 R	52.6%	43.6%	54.6%	45.4%
17,513	Election District 23	8,370	4,926	3,167	277	1,759 R	58.9%	37.8%	60.9%	39.1%
17,631	Election District 24	7,289	3,912	3,128	249	784 R	53.7%	42.9%	55.6%	44.4%
17,593	Election District 25	8,661	4,569	3,739	353	830 R	52.8%	43.2%	55.0%	45.0%
17,991	Election District 26	10,491	6,968	3,169	354	3,799 R	66.4%	30.2%	68.7%	31.3%
17,853	Election District 27	10,823	6,015	4,463	345	1,552 R	55.6%	41.2%	57.4%	42.6%
17,995	Election District 28	8,449	5,882	2,188	379	3,694 R	69.6%	25.9%	72.9%	27.1%
17,478	Election District 29	8,011	5,774	1,933	304	3,841 R	72.1%	24.1%	74.9%	25.1%
17,822	Election District 30	9,505	5,492	3,578	435	1,914 R	57.8%	37.6%	60.6%	39.4%
17,929	Election District 31	9,335	4,219	4,679	437	460 D	45.2%	50.1%	47.4%	52.6%
17,744	Election District 32	9,528	3,095	5,930	503	2,835 D	32.5%	62.2%	34.3%	65.7%
18,493	Election District 33	7,471	4,289	2,716	466	1,573 R	57.4%	36.4%	61.2%	38.8%
18,159	Election District 34	8,637	3,523	4,662	452	1,139 D	40.8%	54.0%	43.0%	57.0%
17,413	Election District 35	6,932	3,804	2,830	298	974 R	54.9%	40.8%	57.3%	42.7%
17,219	Election District 36	4,972	1,386	3,341	245	1,955 D	27.9%	67.2%	29.3%	70.7%
18,670	Election District 37	4,335	1,517	2,631	187	1,114 D	35.0%	60.7%	36.6%	63.4%
16,969	Election District 38	6,814	2,259	4,101	454	1,842 D	33.2%	60.2%	35.5%	64.5%
16,951	Election District 39	6,560	2,566	3,645	349	1,079 D	39.1%	55.6%	41.3%	58.7%
16,953	Election District 40	4,235	1,347	2,717	171	1,370 D	31.8%	64.2%	33.1%	66.9%
710,231	TOTAL	300,495	164,676	122,640	13,179	42,036 R	54.8%	40.8%	57.3%	42.7%

ALASKA

HOUSE OF REPRESENTATIVES

CD	Year	Total Vote	Republican Vote	Candidate	Democratic Vote	Candidate	Other Vote	Rep.-Dem. Plurality	Percentage Total Vote Rep.	Dem.	Major Vote Rep.	Dem.
At Large	2012	289,804	185,296	YOUNG, DON*	82,927	CISSNA, SHARON M.	21,581	102,369 R	63.9%	28.6%	69.1%	30.9%
At Large	2010	254,335	175,384	YOUNG, DON*	77,606	CRAWFORD, HARRY T.	1,345	97,778 R	69.0%	30.5%	69.3%	30.7%
At Large	2008	316,978	158,939	YOUNG, DON*	142,560	BERKOWITZ, ETHAN A.	15,479	16,379 R	50.1%	45.0%	52.7%	47.3%
At Large	2006	234,645	132,743	YOUNG, DON*	93,879	BENSON, DIANE E.	8,023	38,864 R	56.6%	40.0%	58.6%	41.4%
At Large	2004	299,996	213,216	YOUNG, DON*	67,074	HIGGINS, THOMAS M.	19,706	146,142 R	71.1%	22.4%	76.1%	23.9%
At Large	2002	227,725	169,685	YOUNG, DON*	39,357	GREENE, CLIFFORD	18,683	130,328 R	74.5%	17.3%	81.2%	18.8%
At Large	2000	274,393	190,862	YOUNG, DON*	45,372	GREENE, CLIFFORD	38,159	145,490 R	69.6%	16.5%	80.8%	19.2%
At Large	1998	223,300	139,676	YOUNG, DON*	77,232	DUNCAN, JIM	6,392	62,444 R	62.6%	34.6%	64.4%	35.6%

ALASKA

HOUSE OF REPRESENTATIVES

CD	Year	Total Vote	Republican		Democratic		Other Vote	Rep.-Dem. Plurality	Percentage			
									Total Vote		Major Vote	
			Vote	Candidate	Vote	Candidate			Rep.	Dem.	Rep.	Dem.
At Large	1996	233,700	138,834	YOUNG, DON*	85,114	LINCOLN, GEORGIANNA	9,752	53,720 R	59.4%	36.4%	62.0%	38.0%
At Large	1994	208,240	118,537	YOUNG, DON*	68,172	SMITH, TONY	21,531	50,365 R	56.9%	32.7%	63.5%	36.5%
At Large	1992	239,116	111,849	YOUNG, DON*	102,378	DEVENS, JOHN S.	24,889	9,471 R	46.8%	42.8%	52.2%	47.8%
At Large	1990	191,647	99,003	YOUNG, DON*	91,677	DEVENS, JOHN S.	967	7,326 R	51.7%	47.8%	51.9%	48.1%
At Large	1988	192,955	120,595	YOUNG, DON*	71,881	GRUENSTEIN, PETER	479	48,714 R	62.5%	37.3%	62.7%	37.3%
At Large	1986	180,277	101,799	YOUNG, DON*	74,053	BEGICH, PEGGE	4,425	27,746 R	56.5%	41.1%	57.9%	42.1%
At Large	1984	206,437	113,582	YOUNG, DON*	86,052	BEGICH, PEGGE	6,803	27,530 R	55.0%	41.7%	56.9%	43.1%
At Large	1982	181,084	128,274	YOUNG, DON*	52,011	CARLSON, DAVE	799	76,263 R	70.8%	28.7%	71.2%	28.8%
At Large	1980	154,618	114,089	YOUNG, DON*	39,922	PARNELL, KEVIN	607	74,167 R	73.8%	25.8%	74.1%	25.9%
At Large	1978	124,187	68,811	YOUNG, DON*	55,176	RODEY, PATRICK	200	13,635 R	55.4%	44.4%	55.5%	44.5%
At Large	1976	118,208	83,722	YOUNG, DON*	34,194	HOPSON, EBEN	292	49,528 R	70.8%	28.9%	71.0%	29.0%
At Large	1974	95,921	51,641	YOUNG, DON*	44,280	HENSLEY, WILLIAM L.		7,361 R	53.8%	46.2%	53.8%	46.2%
At Large	1972	95,401	41,750	YOUNG, DON	53,651	BEGICH, NICHOLAS J.*		11,901 D	43.8%	56.2%	43.8%	56.2%
At Large	1970	80,084	35,947	MURKOWSKI, FRANK H.	44,137	BEGICH, NICHOLAS J.		8,190 D	44.9%	55.1%	44.9%	55.1%
At Large	1968	80,362	43,577	POLLOCK, HOWARD W.*	36,785	BEGICH, NICHOLAS J.		6,792 R	54.2%	45.8%	54.2%	45.8%
At Large	1966	65,907	34,040	POLLOCK, HOWARD W.	31,867	RIVERS, RALPH J.*		2,173 R	51.6%	48.4%	51.6%	48.4%
At Large	1964	67,156	32,566	THOMAS, LOWELL	34,590	RIVERS, RALPH J.*		2,024 D	48.5%	51.5%	48.5%	51.5%
At Large	1962	58,591	26,638	THOMAS, LOWELL	31,953	RIVERS, RALPH J.*		5,315 D	45.5%	54.5%	45.5%	54.5%
At Large	1960	59,063	25,517	RETTIG, R. L.	33,546	RIVERS, RALPH J.*		8,029 D	43.2%	56.8%	43.2%	56.8%
At Large	1958	48,644	20,699	BENSON, HENRY A.	27,945	RIVERS, RALPH J.		7,246 D	42.6%	57.4%	42.6%	57.4%

Notes: An asterisk (*) denotes incumbent. Alaska became a state in 1959; the 1958 House election was in anticipation of statehood.

ALASKA

GENERAL AND PRIMARY ELECTIONS

2012 GENERAL ELECTIONS: OTHER VOTE

President   Other vote was 7,392 Libertarian (Gary E. Johnson), 2,917 Green (Jill Stein), 2,870 Write-in (Scattered Write-In)

House   Other vote was:

At Large   15,028 Libertarian (Jim C. McDermott), 5,589 Non Affiliated (Ted Gianoutsos), 964 Write-in (Scattered Write-In)

2012 PRIMARY ELECTIONS: SUPPLEMENTARY INFORMATION

Primary	August 28, 2012	**Registration** (as of August 3, 2012)	496,952	Republican	134,601
				Democratic	72,124
				Alaskan Independence	15,466
				Libertarian	7,715
				Green	2,016
				Veterans	1,306
				Constitution	65
				Nonpartisan	80,990
				Undeclared	182,669

Primary Type   Any registered voter could participate in the Democratic primary. The Republican primary was restricted to registered Republican, Undeclared, and Nonpartisan voters. (Undeclared voters may be associated with a party, but do not wish to declare which one. Nonpartisan voters are not associated with any party.) Democratic candidates were listed on the primary ballot together with candidates of the Alaskan Independence and Libertarian parties. The high vote-getter of each party went onto the general election ballot. Republican candidates were listed on a primary ballot of their own.

ALASKA

GENERAL AND PRIMARY ELECTIONS

	REPUBLICAN PRIMARIES			DEMOCRATIC PRIMARIES		
House	Young, Don*	58,789	78.6%	Cissna, Sharon M.	16,329	42.8%
At Large	Cox, John R.	11,179	14.9%	Moore, Matt	7,374	19.3%
	Gales, Terre L.	4,841	6.5%	McDermott, Jim C.	5,741	15.0%
				Chesnut, Debra	5,626	14.7%
				Vondersaar, Frank	2,085	5.5%
				Urquidi, Doug	1,034	2.7%
	TOTAL	74,809		TOTAL	38,189	

Note: An asterisk (*) denotes incumbent.

ARIZONA

Congressional districts first established for elections held in 2012

9 members

COCONINO

MOHAVE*

NAVAJO

APACHE

● Flagstaff

● Sedona

YAVAPAI*

● Prescott

4

LA PAZ

GILA*

Scottsdale

8

Sun City ●

6

● *Phoenix* Mesa

Mesa

7

5

Tempe ●

GREENLEE

9

PINAL*

MARICOPA*

GRAHAM

YUMA*

Casa Grande ●

1

3

● Yuma

Tucson ●

PIMA*

2

COCHISE

SANTA CRUZ

Sierra Vista ●

* Asterisk indicates a county whose boundaries include parts of two or more Congressional districts.

ARIZONA
Greater Phoenix Area

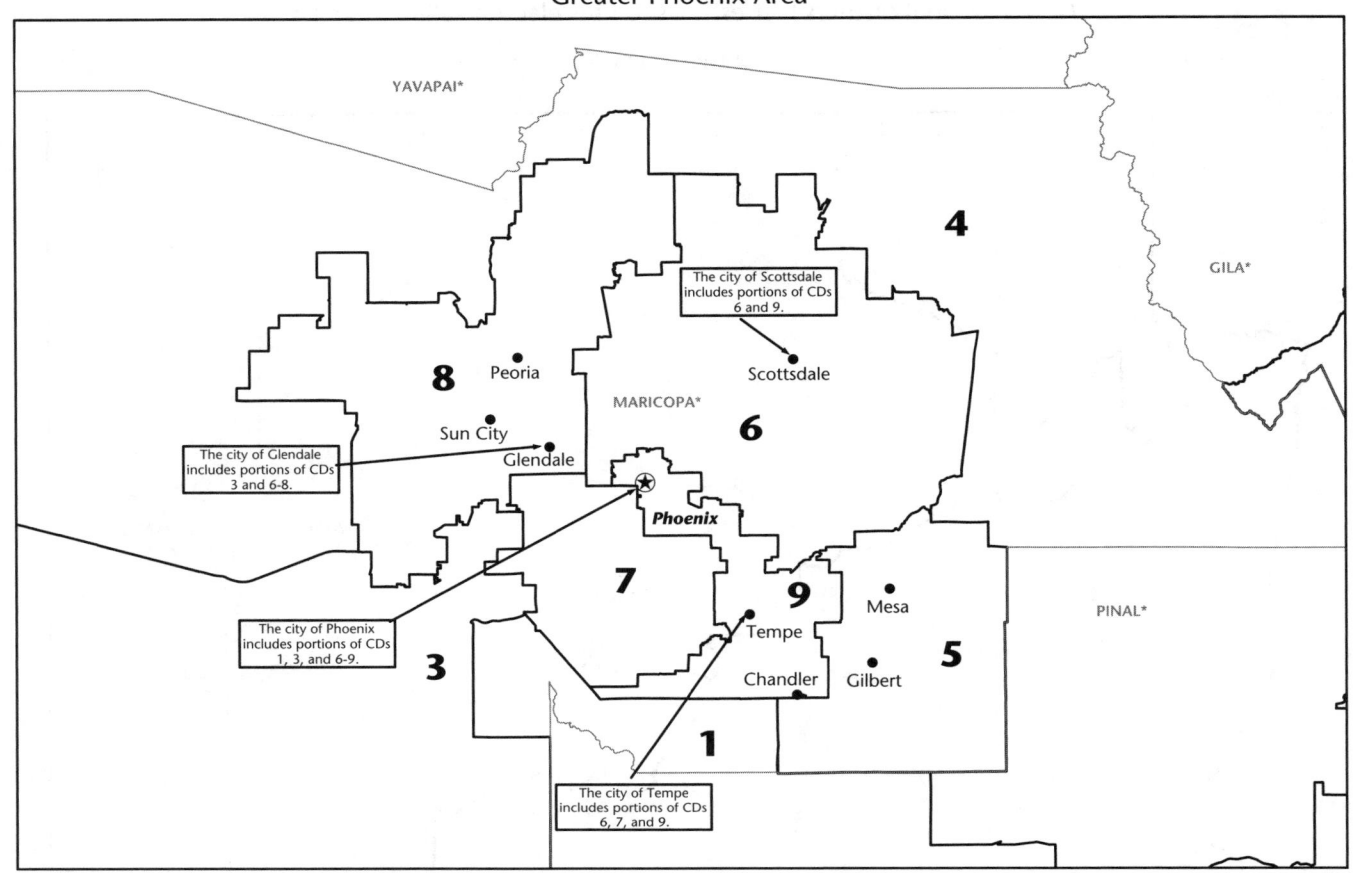

ARIZONA

GOVERNOR

Jan Brewer (R). Elected 2010 to a four-year term. Sworn in as governor January 21, 2009, to fill the vacancy created by the resignation of Janet Napolitano (D) to become U.S. Secretary of Homeland Security.

SENATORS (2 Republicans)

John McCain (R). Reelected 2010 to a six-year term. Previously elected 2004, 1998, 1992, 1986.

Jeff Flake (R). Elected 2012 to a six-year term.

REPRESENTATIVES (4 Republicans, 5 Democrats)

1. Ann Kirkpatrick (D)
2. Ron Barber (D)
3. Raúl M. Grijalva (D)
4. Paul Gosar (R)
5. Matt Salmon (R)
6. David Schweikert (R)
7. Ed Pastor (D)
8. Trent Franks (R)
9. Kyrsten Sinema (D)

POSTWAR VOTE FOR PRESIDENT

		Republican		Democratic		Other	Rep.-Dem.	Total Vote		Major Vote	
Year	Total Vote	Vote	Candidate	Vote	Candidate	Vote	Plurality	Rep.	Dem.	Rep.	Dem.
2012	2,299,254	1,233,654	Romney, W. Mitt	1,025,232	Obama, Barack H.*	40,368	208,422 R	53.7%	44.6%	54.6%	45.4%
2008	2,293,475	1,230,111	McCain, John S. III	1,034,707	Obama, Barack H.	28,657	195,404 R	53.6%	45.1%	54.3%	45.7%
2004	2,012,585	1,104,294	Bush, George W.*	893,524	Kerry, John F.	14,767	210,770 R	54.9%	44.4%	55.3%	44.7%
2000**	1,532,016	781,652	Bush, George W.	685,341	Gore, Albert Jr.	65,023	96,311 R	51.0%	44.7%	53.3%	46.7%
1996**	1,404,405	622,073	Dole, Robert "Bob"	653,288	Clinton, Bill*	129,044	31,215 D	44.3%	46.5%	48.8%	51.2%
1992**	1,486,975	572,086	Bush, George H.*	543,050	Clinton, Bill	371,839	29,036 R	38.5%	36.5%	51.3%	48.7%
1988	1,171,873	702,541	Bush, George H.	454,029	Dukakis, Michael S.	15,303	248,512 R	60.0%	38.7%	60.7%	39.3%
1984	1,025,897	681,416	Reagan, Ronald*	333,854	Mondale, Walter F.	10,627	347,562 R	66.4%	32.5%	67.1%	32.9%
1980**	873,945	529,688	Reagan, Ronald	246,843	Carter, Jimmy*	97,414	282,845 R	60.6%	28.2%	68.2%	31.8%
1976	742,719	418,642	Ford, Gerald R.*	295,602	Carter, Jimmy	28,475	123,040 R	56.4%	39.8%	58.6%	41.4%
1972	622,926	402,812	Nixon, Richard M.*	198,540	McGovern, George S.	21,574	204,272 R	64.7%	31.9%	67.0%	33.0%
1968**	486,936	266,721	Nixon, Richard M.	170,514	Humphrey, Hubert H. Jr.	49,701	96,207 R	54.8%	35.0%	61.0%	39.0%
1964	480,770	242,535	Goldwater, Barry M. Sr.	237,753	Johnson, Lyndon B.*	482	4,782 R	50.4%	49.5%	50.5%	49.5%
1960	398,491	221,241	Nixon, Richard M.	176,781	Kennedy, John F.	469	44,460 R	55.5%	44.4%	55.6%	44.4%
1956	290,173	176,990	Eisenhower, Dwight D.*	112,880	Stevenson, Adlai E. II	303	64,110 R	61.0%	38.9%	61.1%	38.9%
1952	260,570	152,042	Eisenhower, Dwight D.	108,528	Stevenson, Adlai E. II		43,514 R	58.3%	41.7%	58.3%	41.7%
1948	177,065	77,597	Dewey, Thomas E.	95,251	Truman, Harry S.*	4,217	17,654 D	43.8%	53.8%	44.9%	55.1%

Note: An asterisk (*) denotes incumbent. **In past elections, the other vote included: 2000 - 45,645 Green (Ralph Nader); 1996 - 112,072 Reform (Ross Perot); 1992 - 353,741 Independent (Perot); 1980 - 76,952 Independent (John Anderson); 1968 - 46,573 American Independent (George Wallace).

ARIZONA

POSTWAR VOTE FOR GOVERNOR

Year	Total Vote	Republican Vote	Republican Candidate	Democratic Vote	Democratic Candidate	Other Vote	Rep.-Dem. Plurality	Total Vote Rep.	Total Vote Dem.	Major Vote Rep.	Major Vote Dem.
2010	1,728,081	938,934	Brewer, Jan*	733,935	Goddard, Terry	55,212	204,999 R	54.3%	42.5%	56.1%	43.9%
2006	1,533,645	543,528	Munsil, Len	959,830	Napolitano, Janet*	30,287	416,302 D	35.4%	62.6%	36.2%	63.8%
2002	1,226,111	554,465	Salmon, Matt	566,284	Napolitano, Janet	105,362	11,819 D	45.2%	46.2%	49.5%	50.5%
1998	1,017,616	620,188	Hull, Jane Dee*	361,552	Johnson, Paul	35,876	258,636 R	60.9%	35.5%	63.2%	36.8%
1994	1,129,607	593,492	Symington, Fife*	500,702	Basha, Eddie	35,413	92,790 R	52.5%	44.3%	54.2%	45.8%
1991S	940,737	492,569	Symington, Fife	448,168	Goddard, Terry		44,401 R	52.4%	47.6%	52.4%	47.6%
1986**	866,984	343,913	Mecham, Evan	298,986	Warner, Carolyn	224,085	44,927 R	39.7%	34.5%	53.5%	46.5%
1982	726,364	235,877	Corbet, Leo	453,795	Babbitt, Bruce*	36,692	217,918 D	32.5%	62.5%	34.2%	65.8%
1978	538,556	241,093	Mecham, Evan	282,605	Babbitt, Bruce*	14,858	41,512 D	44.8%	52.5%	46.0%	54.0%
1974	552,202	273,674	Williams, Jack R.*	278,375	Castro, Raul H.	153	4,701 D	49.6%	50.4%	49.6%	50.4%
1970**	411,409	209,522	Williams, Jack R.*	201,887	Castro, Raul H.		7,635 R	50.9%	49.1%	50.9%	49.1%
1968	483,998	279,923	Williams, Jack R.*	204,075	Goddard, Sam		75,848 R	57.8%	42.2%	57.8%	42.2%
1966	378,342	203,438	Williams, Jack R.	174,904	Goddard, Sam*		28,534 R	53.8%	46.2%	53.8%	46.2%
1964	473,502	221,404	Kleindienst, Richard	252,098	Goddard, Sam		30,694 D	46.8%	53.2%	46.8%	53.2%
1962	365,841	200,578	Fannin, Paul*	165,263	Goddard, Sam		35,315 R	54.8%	45.2%	54.8%	45.2%
1960	397,107	235,502	Fannin, Paul*	161,605	Ackerman, Lee		73,897 R	59.3%	40.7%	59.3%	40.7%
1958	290,465	160,136	Fannin, Paul	130,329	Morrison, Robert		29,807 R	55.1%	44.9%	55.1%	44.9%
1956	288,592	116,744	Griffen, Horace B.	171,848	McFarland, Ernest W.*		55,104 D	40.5%	59.5%	40.5%	59.5%
1954	243,970	115,866	Pyle, Howard*	128,104	McFarland, Ernest W.		12,238 D	47.5%	52.5%	47.5%	52.5%
1952	260,285	156,592	Pyle, Howard*	103,693	Haldiman, Joe C.		52,899 R	60.2%	39.8%	60.2%	39.8%
1950	195,227	99,109	Pyle, Howard	96,118	Frohmiller, Ana		2,991 R	50.8%	49.2%	50.8%	49.2%
1948	175,767	70,419	Brockett, Bruce D.	104,008	Garvey, Dan E.	1,340	33,589 D	40.1%	59.2%	40.4%	59.6%
1946	122,462	48,867	Brockett, Bruce D.	73,595	Osborn, Sidney P.*		24,728 D	39.9%	60.1%	39.9%	60.1%

Note: An asterisk (*) denotes incumbent. **In 1990 neither major party candidate won an absolute majority, therefore a runoff election was held February 26, 1991; the vote above is for the February runoff. In the November 1990 election, a total of 1,055,406 votes were cast as follows: 523,984 (49.6%) Republican (Fife Symington); 519,691 (49.2%) Democratic (Terry Goddard); 11,731 (1.1%) Other. In past elections, the other vote included: 1986 - 224,085 Independent (Bill Schulz). The term of office for Arizona's Governor was increased from two to four years effective with the 1970 election.

POSTWAR VOTE FOR SENATOR

Year	Total Vote	Republican Vote	Republican Candidate	Democratic Vote	Democratic Candidate	Other Vote	Rep.-Dem. Plurality	Total Vote Rep.	Total Vote Dem.	Major Vote Rep.	Major Vote Dem.
2012	2,243,422	1,104,457	Flake, Jeff	1,036,542	Carmona, Richard	102,423	67,915 R	49.2%	46.2%	51.6%	48.4%
2010	1,708,484	1,005,615	McCain, John S. III*	592,011	Glassman, Rodney	110,858	413,604 R	58.9%	34.7%	62.9%	37.1%
2006	1,526,782	814,398	Kyl, Jon*	664,141	Pederson, Jim	48,243	150,257 R	53.3%	43.5%	55.1%	44.9%
2004	1,961,677	1,505,372	McCain, John S. III*	404,507	Starky, Stuart Marc	51,798	1,100,865 R	76.7%	20.6%	78.8%	21.2%
2000	1,397,076	1,108,196	Kyl, Jon*			288,880	1,108,196 R	79.3%		100.0%	
1998	1,013,280	696,577	McCain, John S. III*	275,224	Ranger, Ed	41,479	421,353 R	68.7%	27.2%	71.7%	28.3%
1994	1,119,060	600,999	Kyl, Jon	442,510	Coopersmith, Sam	75,551	158,489 R	53.7%	39.5%	57.6%	42.4%
1992**	1,382,051	771,395	McCain, John S. III*	436,321	Sargent, Claire	174,335	335,074 R	55.8%	31.6%	63.9%	36.1%
1988	1,164,539	478,060	DeGreen, Keith	660,403	DeConcini, Dennis*	26,076	182,343 D	41.1%	56.7%	42.0%	58.0%
1986	862,921	521,850	McCain, John S. III	340,965	Kimball, Richard	106	180,885 R	60.5%	39.5%	60.5%	39.5%
1982	723,885	291,749	Dunn, Pete	411,970	DeConcini, Dennis*	20,166	120,221 D	40.3%	56.9%	41.5%	58.5%
1980	874,178	432,371	Goldwater, Barry M. Sr.*	422,972	Schulz, Bill	18,835	9,399 R	49.5%	48.4%	50.5%	49.5%
1976	741,210	321,236	Steiger, Sam	400,334	DeConcini, Dennis	19,640	79,098 D	43.3%	54.0%	44.5%	55.5%
1974	549,919	320,396	Goldwater, Barry M. Sr.*	229,523	Marshall, Jonathan		90,873 R	58.3%	41.7%	58.3%	41.7%
1970	407,796	228,284	Fannin, Paul*	179,512	Grossman, Sam		48,772 R	56.0%	44.0%	56.0%	44.0%
1968	479,945	274,607	Goldwater, Barry M. Sr.	205,338	Elson, Roy L.		69,269 R	57.2%	42.8%	57.2%	42.8%
1964	468,788	241,084	Fannin, Paul	227,704	Elson, Roy L.		13,380 R	51.4%	48.6%	51.4%	48.6%
1962	362,605	163,388	Mecham, Evan	199,217	Hayden, Carl*		35,829 D	45.1%	54.9%	45.1%	54.9%
1958	293,623	164,593	Goldwater, Barry M. Sr.*	129,030	McFarland, Ernest W.		35,563 R	56.1%	43.9%	56.1%	43.9%
1956	278,263	107,447	Jones, Ross F.	170,816	Hayden, Carl*		63,369 D	38.6%	61.4%	38.6%	61.4%
1952	257,401	132,063	Goldwater, Barry M. Sr.	125,338	McFarland, Ernest W.*		6,725 R	51.3%	48.7%	51.3%	48.7%
1950	185,092	68,846	Brockett, Bruce	116,246	Hayden, Carl*		47,400 D	37.2%	62.8%	37.2%	62.8%
1946	116,239	35,022	Powers, Ward S.	80,415	McFarland, Ernest W.*	802	45,393 D	30.1%	69.2%	30.3%	69.7%

Note: An asterisk (*) denotes incumbent. **In past elections, the other vote included: 1992 - 145,361 Independent (Evan Mecham). The Democratic Party did not run a candidate in the 2000 Senate election.

ARIZONA

PRESIDENT 2012

2010 Census Population	County	Total Vote	Republican (Romney)	Democratic (Obama)	Other	Rep.-Dem. Plurality	Percentage			
							Total Vote		Major Vote	
							Rep.	Dem.	Rep.	Dem.
71,518	APACHE	25,848	8,250	17,147	451	8,897 D	31.9%	66.3%	32.5%	67.5%
131,346	COCHISE	49,003	29,497	18,546	960	10,951 R	60.2%	37.8%	61.4%	38.6%
134,421	COCONINO	51,731	21,220	29,257	1,254	8,037 D	41.0%	56.6%	42.0%	58.0%
53,597	GILA	21,528	13,455	7,697	376	5,758 R	62.5%	35.8%	63.6%	36.4%
37,220	GRAHAM	11,855	8,076	3,609	170	4,467 R	68.1%	30.4%	69.1%	30.9%
8,437	GREENLEE	2,974	1,592	1,310	72	282 R	53.5%	44.0%	54.9%	45.1%
20,489	LA PAZ	5,717	3,714	1,880	123	1,834 R	65.0%	32.9%	66.4%	33.6%
3,817,117	MARICOPA	1,376,558	749,885	602,288	24,385	147,597 R	54.5%	43.8%	55.5%	44.5%
200,186	MOHAVE	70,010	49,168	19,533	1,309	29,635 R	70.2%	27.9%	71.6%	28.4%
107,449	NAVAJO	37,335	19,884	16,945	506	2,939 R	53.3%	45.4%	54.0%	46.0%
980,263	PIMA	382,250	174,779	201,251	6,220	26,472 D	45.7%	52.6%	46.5%	53.5%
375,770	PINAL	108,315	62,079	44,306	1,930	17,773 R	57.3%	40.9%	58.4%	41.6%
47,420	SANTA CRUZ	13,894	4,235	9,486	173	5,251 D	30.5%	68.3%	30.9%	69.1%
211,033	YAVAPAI	100,283	64,468	33,918	1,897	30,550 R	64.3%	33.8%	65.5%	34.5%
195,751	YUMA	41,953	23,352	18,059	542	5,293 R	55.7%	43.0%	56.4%	43.6%
6,392,017	TOTAL	2,299,254	1,233,654	1,025,232	40,368	208,422 R	53.7%	44.6%	54.6%	45.4%

ARIZONA

SENATOR 2012

2010 Census Population	County	Total Vote	Republican (Flake)	Democratic (Carmona)	Other	Rep.-Dem. Plurality	Percentage			
							Total Vote		Major Vote	
							Rep.	Dem.	Rep.	Dem.
71,518	APACHE	25,232	7,680	16,455	1,097	8,775 D	30.4%	65.2%	31.8%	68.2%
131,346	COCHISE	48,221	26,208	19,736	2,277	6,472 R	54.3%	40.9%	57.0%	43.0%
134,421	COCONINO	50,647	19,334	28,723	2,590	9,389 D	38.2%	56.7%	40.2%	59.8%
53,597	GILA	21,193	11,954	8,099	1,140	3,855 R	56.4%	38.2%	59.6%	40.4%
37,220	GRAHAM	11,697	7,352	3,771	574	3,581 R	62.9%	32.2%	66.1%	33.9%
8,437	GREENLEE	2,912	1,365	1,342	205	23 R	46.9%	46.1%	50.4%	49.6%
20,489	LA PAZ	5,507	3,120	1,961	426	1,159 R	56.7%	35.6%	61.4%	38.6%
3,817,117	MARICOPA	1,341,066	675,500	602,809	62,757	72,691 R	50.4%	44.9%	52.8%	47.2%
200,186	MOHAVE	68,107	42,410	20,865	4,832	21,545 R	62.3%	30.6%	67.0%	33.0%
107,449	NAVAJO	36,743	18,228	16,881	1,634	1,347 R	49.6%	45.9%	51.9%	48.1%
980,263	PIMA	373,762	153,846	207,578	12,338	53,732 D	41.2%	55.5%	42.6%	57.4%
375,770	PINAL	106,459	55,008	45,558	5,893	9,450 R	51.7%	42.8%	54.7%	45.3%
47,420	SANTA CRUZ	13,508	3,617	9,454	437	5,837 D	26.8%	70.0%	27.7%	72.3%
211,033	YAVAPAI	97,871	57,838	34,902	5,131	22,936 R	59.1%	35.7%	62.4%	37.6%
195,751	YUMA	40,497	20,997	18,408	1,092	2,589 R	51.8%	45.5%	53.3%	46.7%
6,392,017	TOTAL	2,243,422	1,104,457	1,036,542	102,423	67,915 R	49.2%	46.2%	51.6%	48.4%

ARIZONA

HOUSE OF REPRESENTATIVES

CD	Year	Total Vote	Republican Vote	Republican Candidate	Democratic Vote	Democratic Candidate	Other Vote	Rep.-Dem. Plurality	Total Vote Rep.	Total Vote Dem.	Major Vote Rep.	Major Vote Dem.
1	2012	251,595	113,594	PATON, JONATHAN	122,774	KIRKPATRICK, ANN	15,227	9,180 D	45.1%	48.8%	48.1%	51.9%
2	2012	292,279	144,884	MCSALLY, MARTHA	147,338	BARBER, RON*	57	2,454 D	49.6%	50.4%	49.6%	50.4%
3	2012	168,698	62,663	SAUCEDO MERCER, GABRIELLA	98,468	GRIJALVA, RAUL M.*	7,567	35,805 D	37.1%	58.4%	38.9%	61.1%
4	2012	243,760	162,907	GOSAR, PAUL*	69,154	ROBINSON, JOHNNIE	11,699	93,753 R	66.8%	28.4%	70.2%	29.8%
5	2012	273,059	183,470	SALMON, MATT	89,589	MORGAN, SPENCER		93,881 R	67.2%	32.8%	67.2%	32.8%
6	2012	293,177	179,706	SCHWEIKERT, DAVID*	97,666	JETTE, MATTHEW	15,805	82,040 R	61.3%	33.3%	64.8%	35.2%
7	2012	127,827			104,489	PASTOR, ED*	23,338	104,489 D		81.7%		100.0%
8	2012	272,791	172,809	FRANKS, TRENT*	95,635	SCHARER, GENE	4,347	77,174 R	63.3%	35.1%	64.4%	35.6%
9	2012	250,131	111,630	PARKER, VERNON B.	121,881	SINEMA, KYRSTEN	16,620	10,251 D	44.6%	48.7%	47.8%	52.2%
TOTAL	2012	2,173,317	1,131,663		946,994		94,660	184,669 R	52.1%	43.6%	54.4%	45.6%

Note: An asterisk (*) denotes incumbent.

ARIZONA

GENERAL AND PRIMARY ELECTIONS

2012 GENERAL ELECTIONS: OTHER VOTE

President   Other vote was 32,100 Libertarian (Gary E. Johnson), 7,816 Green (Jill Stein), 289 Constitution (Virgil H. Goode), 163 Write-in (Scattered Write-In)

Senator   Other vote was 102,109 Libertarian (Marc Victor), 314 Write-in (Scattered Write-In)

House   Other vote was:

CD 1   15,227 Libertarian (Kim Allen)
CD 2   57 Write-in (Anthony Prowell)
CD 3   7,567 Libertarian (Blanca Guerra)
CD 4   9,306 Libertarian (Joe Pamelia), 2,393 Americans Elect (Richard Grayson)
CD 6   10,167 Libertarian (Jack Anderson), 5,637 Green (Mark Salazar), 1 Write-in (James Ketover)
CD 7   23,338 Libertarian (Joe Cobb)
CD 8   4,347 Americans Elect (Stephen Dolgos)
CD 9   16,620 Libertarian (Powell E. Gammill)

2012 PRIMARY ELECTIONS: SUPPLEMENTARY INFORMATION

Primary   February 28, 2012 (President) August 28, 2012 (Congress)   **Registration** (as of August 28, 2012)   3,100,575

Republican	1,113,123
Democratic	935,098
Libertarian	21,770
Green	4,773
Other	1,025,811

Primary Type   Semi-open—Registered Democrats and Republicans could vote only in their party's primary. But voters not registered with any political party could participate in either the Democratic or Republican primary.

ARIZONA

GENERAL AND PRIMARY ELECTIONS

	REPUBLICAN PRIMARIES			DEMOCRATIC PRIMARIES		
President	Romney, W. Mitt	239,167	46.9%			
	Santorum, Rick	138,031	27.1%			
	Gingrich, Newt	81,748	16.0%			
	Paul, Ron	43,952	8.6%			
	Perry, Rick	2,023	0.4%			
	Gonzales, Sarah	1,544	0.3%			
	Roemer, Charles	692	0.1%			
	Sims, Paul	530	0.1%			
	Cisneros, Cesar	418	0.1%			
	Callahan, Mark	358	0.1%			
	Perry, Al "Dick"	310	0.1%			
	Benjamin, Donald	223				
	Levinson, Michael	217				
	Dean, Kip	198				
	Zack, Ronald	156				
	Hill, Christopher	139				
	Lynch, Frank	110				
	Arnett, Wayne Charles	96				
	Perkins, Raymond Scott	90				
	Welch, Matt	86				
	Terr, Jim	59				
	Skelley, Charles	57				
	Bollander, Peter "Simon"	54				
	TOTAL	*510,258*				
Senator	Flake, Jeff	357,360	69.3%	Carmona, Richard	289,881	100.0%
	Cardon, Wil	110,150	21.3%			
	Van Steenwyk, Clair	29,159	5.7%			
	Hackbarth, Bryan	19,174	3.7%			
	Lyon, John	126				
	Acle, Luis	56				
	TOTAL	*516,025*		*TOTAL*	*289,881*	
Congressional District 1	Paton, Jonathan	28,644	60.9%	Kirkpatrick, Ann	33,831	63.7%
	Martin, Gaither	8,958	19.0%	Benally Baldenegro, Wenona	19,247	36.3%
	Wade, Douglas	6,758	14.4%			
	Gatti, Patrick	2,707	5.8%			
	TOTAL	*47,067*		*TOTAL*	*53,078*	
Congressional District 2	McSally, Martha	52,809	81.7%	Barber, Ron*	51,206	82.0%
	Koskiniemi, Mark	11,828	18.3%	Heinz, Matt	11,213	18.0%
				Manolakis, Charlie	4	
	TOTAL	*64,637*		*TOTAL*	*62,423*	
Congressional District 3	Saucedo Mercer, Gabriella	12,474	65.3%	Grijalva, Raúl M.*	24,044	65.6%
	Vasquez, Jaime	6,622	34.7%	Aguirre, Amanda	9,484	25.9%
				Arreguin, Manny	3,105	8.5%
	TOTAL	*19,096*		*TOTAL*	*36,633*	
Congressional District 4	Gosar, Paul*	40,033	51.3%	Robinson, Johnnie	10,183	50.0%
	Gould, Ron	24,617	31.6%	Weisser, Mikel	10,164	50.0%
	Murphy, Rick L.	13,315	17.1%			
	TOTAL	*77,965*		*TOTAL*	*20,347*	
Congressional District 5	Salmon, Matt	41,078	51.8%	Morgan, Spencer	19,659	100.0%
	Adams, Kirk	38,152	48.2%			
	TOTAL	*79,230*		*TOTAL*	*19,659*	
Congressional District 6	Schweikert, David*	41,821	51.5%	Jette, Matthew	12,383	51.9%
	Quayle, Ben	39,414	48.5%	Williamson, W. John	11,471	48.1%
	TOTAL	*81,235*		*TOTAL*	*23,854*	
Congressional District 7	Fistler, Scott	116	100.0%	Pastor, Ed*	22,664	79.0%
				DeWitt, Rebecca	6,013	21.0%
	TOTAL	*116*		*TOTAL*	*28,677*	

ARIZONA

GENERAL AND PRIMARY ELECTIONS

		REPUBLICAN PRIMARIES			DEMOCRATIC PRIMARIES		
Congressional	Franks, Trent*	57,257	83.2%	Scharer, Gene	24,510	100.0%
District 8	Passalacqua, Tony	11,572	16.8%			
	Hack, Helmuth	18				
	TOTAL	68,847		TOTAL	24,510	
Congressional	Parker, Vernon B.	11,184	22.5%	Sinema, Kyrsten	15,536	40.8%
District 9	Rogers, Wendy	10,479	21.0%	Schapira, David	11,419	30.0%
	Sepulveda, Martin	10,165	20.4%	Cherny, Andrei	11,146	29.3%
	Grantham, Travis	9,179	18.4%			
	Thompson, Jeff	3,358	6.7%			
	Borowsky, Lisa	3,281	6.6%			
	Campos Schandlbauer, Leah	2,139	4.3%			
	TOTAL	49,785		TOTAL	38,101	

Notes: An asterisk (*) denotes incumbent. Due to redistricting, the 6th district Republican primary pitted two incumbents against each other (Quayle, former 3rd district, and Schweikert, former 5th district).

ARKANSAS

Congressional districts first established for elections held in 2012

4 members

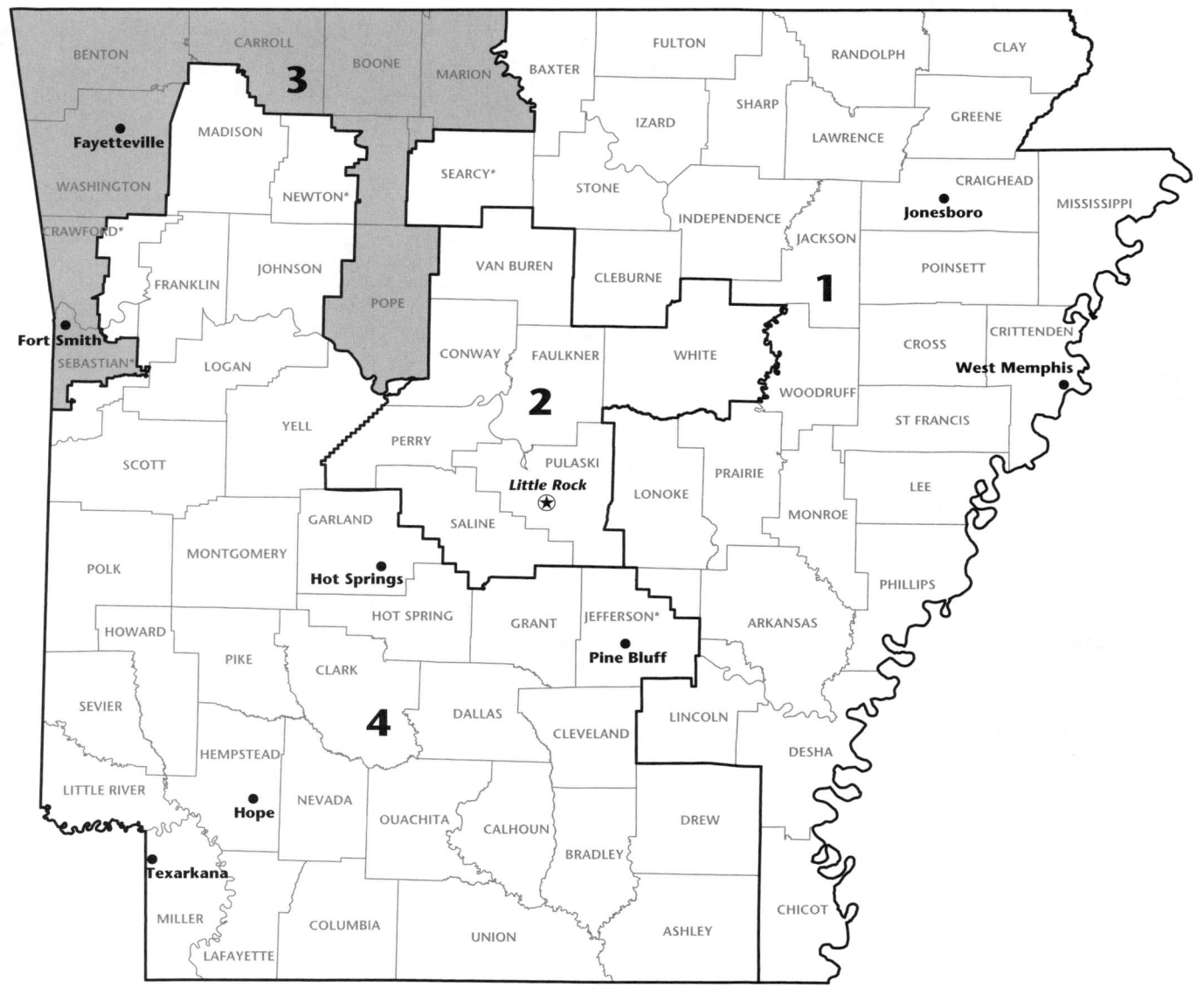

* Asterisk indicates a county whose boundaries include parts of two or more Congressional districts.

ARKANSAS

GOVERNOR

Mike D. Beebe (D). Reelected 2010 to a four-year term. Previously elected 2006.

SENATORS (1 Republican, 1 Democrat)

Mark Pryor (D). Reelected 2008 to a six-year term. Previously elected 2002.

John Boozman (R). Elected 2010 to a six-year term.

REPRESENTATIVES (4 Republicans)

1. Rick Crawford (R)
2. Tim Griffin (R)

3. Steve Womack (R)
4. Tom Cotton (R)

POSTWAR VOTE FOR PRESIDENT

| | | Republican | | Democratic | | Other | Rep.-Dem. | Percentage | | | |
| | | | | | | | | Total Vote | | Major Vote | |
Year	Total Vote	Vote	Candidate	Vote	Candidate	Vote	Plurality	Rep.	Dem.	Rep.	Dem.
2012	1,069,468	647,744	Romney, W. Mitt	394,409	Obama, Barack H.*	27,315	253,335 R	60.6%	36.9%	62.2%	37.8%
2008	1,086,617	638,017	McCain, John S. III	422,310	Obama, Barack H.	26,290	215,707 R	58.7%	38.9%	60.2%	39.8%
2004	1,054,945	572,898	Bush, George W.*	469,953	Kerry, John F.	12,094	102,945 R	54.3%	44.5%	54.9%	45.1%
2000**	921,781	472,940	Bush, George W.	422,768	Gore, Albert Jr.	26,073	50,172 R	51.3%	45.9%	52.8%	47.2%
1996**	884,262	325,416	Dole, Robert "Bob"	475,171	Clinton, Bill*	83,675	149,755 D	36.8%	53.7%	40.6%	59.4%
1992**	950,653	337,324	Bush, George H.*	505,823	Clinton, Bill	107,506	168,499 D	35.5%	53.2%	40.0%	60.0%
1988	827,738	466,578	Bush, George H.	349,237	Dukakis, Michael S.	11,923	117,341 R	56.4%	42.2%	57.2%	42.8%
1984	884,406	534,774	Reagan, Ronald*	338,646	Mondale, Walter F.	10,986	196,128 R	60.5%	38.3%	61.2%	38.8%
1980**	837,582	403,164	Reagan, Ronald	398,041	Carter, Jimmy*	36,377	5,123 R	48.1%	47.5%	50.3%	49.7%
1976	767,535	267,903	Ford, Gerald R.*	498,604	Carter, Jimmy	1,028	230,701 D	34.9%	65.0%	35.0%	65.0%
1972	651,320	448,541	Nixon, Richard M.*	199,892	McGovern, George S.	2,887	248,649 R	68.9%	30.7%	69.2%	30.8%
1968**	619,969	190,759	Nixon, Richard M.	188,228	Humphrey, Hubert H. Jr.	240,982	2,531 R**	30.8%	30.4%	50.3%	49.7%
1964	560,426	243,264	Goldwater, Barry M. Sr.	314,197	Johnson, Lyndon B.*	2,965	70,933 D	43.4%	56.1%	43.6%	56.4%
1960	428,509	184,508	Nixon, Richard M.	215,049	Kennedy, John F.	28,952	30,541 D	43.1%	50.2%	46.2%	53.8%
1956	406,572	186,287	Eisenhower, Dwight D.*	213,277	Stevenson, Adlai E. II	7,008	26,990 D	45.8%	52.5%	46.6%	53.4%
1952	404,800	177,155	Eisenhower, Dwight D.	226,300	Stevenson, Adlai E. II	1,345	49,145 D	43.8%	55.9%	43.9%	56.1%
1948**	242,475	50,959	Dewey, Thomas E.	149,659	Truman, Harry S.*	41,857	98,700 D	21.0%	61.7%	25.4%	74.6%

Note: An asterisk (*) denotes incumbent. **In past elections, the other vote included: 2000 - 13,421 Green (Ralph Nader); 1996 - 69,884 Reform (Ross Perot); 1992 - 99,132 Independent (Perot); 1980 - 22,468 Independent (John Anderson); 1968 - 240,982 American Independent (Wallace); 1948 - 40,068 States' Rights (Strom Thurmond). Wallace carried Arkansas in 1968 with 38.9 percent of the vote.

ARKANSAS

POSTWAR VOTE FOR GOVERNOR

Year	Total Vote	Republican Vote	Republican Candidate	Democratic Vote	Democratic Candidate	Other Vote	Rep.-Dem. Plurality	Total Vote Rep.	Total Vote Dem.	Major Vote Rep.	Major Vote Dem.
2010	781,333	262,784	Keet, Jim	503,336	Beebe, Mike D.*	15,213	240,552 D	33.6%	64.4%	34.3%	65.7%
2006	774,680	315,040	Hutchinson, Asa	430,765	Beebe, Mike D.	28,875	115,725 D	40.7%	55.6%	42.2%	57.8%
2002	805,696	427,082	Huckabee, Mike*	378,250	Fisher, Jimmie Lou	364	48,832 R	53.0%	46.9%	53.0%	47.0%
1998	728,619	430,919	Huckabee, Mike*	278,155	King, James H.	19,545	152,764 R	59.1%	38.2%	60.8%	39.2%
1994	716,840	287,904	Nelson, Sheffield	428,936	Tucker, Jim Guy*		141,032 D	40.2%	59.8%	40.2%	59.8%
1990	696,412	295,925	Nelson, Sheffield	400,386	Clinton, Bill*	101	104,461 D	42.5%	57.5%	42.5%	57.5%
1986**	688,851	248,727	White, Frank D.	439,882	Clinton, Bill*	242	191,155 D	36.1%	63.9%	36.1%	63.9%
1984	886,548	331,987	Freeman, Woody	554,561	Clinton, Bill*		222,574 D	37.4%	62.6%	37.4%	62.6%
1982	789,351	357,496	White, Frank D.*	431,855	Clinton, Bill		74,359 D	45.3%	54.7%	45.3%	54.7%
1980	838,925	435,684	White, Frank D.	403,241	Clinton, Bill*		32,443 R	51.9%	48.1%	51.9%	48.1%
1978	528,912	193,746	Lowe, A. Lynn	335,101	Clinton, Bill	65	141,355 D	36.6%	63.4%	36.6%	63.4%
1976	726,949	121,716	Griffith, Leon	605,083	Pryor, David H.*	150	483,367 D	16.7%	83.2%	16.7%	83.3%
1974	545,974	187,872	Coon, Ken	358,018	Pryor, David H.	84	170,146 D	34.4%	65.6%	34.4%	65.6%
1972	648,069	159,177	Blaylock, Len E.	488,892	Bumpers, Dale*		329,715 D	24.6%	75.4%	24.6%	75.4%
1970	608,198	196,418	Rockefeller, Winthrop*	375,648	Bumpers, Dale	36,132	179,230 D	32.3%	61.8%	34.3%	65.7%
1968	615,590	322,777	Rockefeller, Winthrop*	292,813	Crank, Marion		29,964 R	52.4%	47.6%	52.4%	47.6%
1966	563,527	306,324	Rockefeller, Winthrop	257,203	Johnson, James		49,121 R	54.4%	45.6%	54.4%	45.6%
1964	592,113	254,561	Rockefeller, Winthrop	337,489	Faubus, Orval E.*	63	82,928 D	43.0%	57.0%	43.0%	57.0%
1962	308,092	82,349	Ricketts, Willis	225,743	Faubus, Orval E.*		143,394 D	26.7%	73.3%	26.7%	73.3%
1960	421,985	129,921	Britt, Henry M.	292,064	Faubus, Orval E.*		162,143 D	30.8%	69.2%	30.8%	69.2%
1958	286,886	50,288	Johnson, George W.	236,598	Faubus, Orval E.*		186,310 D	17.5%	82.5%	17.5%	82.5%
1956	399,012	77,215	Mitchell, Roy	321,797	Faubus, Orval E.*		244,582 D	19.4%	80.6%	19.4%	80.6%
1954	335,176	127,004	Remmel, Pratt C.	208,121	Faubus, Orval E.	51	81,117 D	37.9%	62.1%	37.9%	62.1%
1952	391,592	49,292	Speck, Jefferson W.	342,292	Cherry, Francis	8	293,000 D	12.6%	87.4%	12.6%	87.4%
1950	317,081	50,303	Speck, Jefferson W.	266,778	McMath, Sidney S.*		216,475 D	15.9%	84.1%	15.9%	84.1%
1948	244,271	26,500	Black, Charles R.	217,771	McMath, Sidney S.		191,271 D	10.8%	89.2%	10.8%	89.2%
1946	152,162	24,133	Mills, W. T.	128,029	Laney, Ben*		103,896 D	15.9%	84.1%	15.9%	84.1%

Note: An asterisk (*) denotes incumbent. **The term of office for Arkansas Governor was increased from two to four years effective with the 1986 election.

POSTWAR VOTE FOR SENATOR

Year	Total Vote	Republican Vote	Republican Candidate	Democratic Vote	Democratic Candidate	Other Vote	Rep.-Dem. Plurality	Total Vote Rep.	Total Vote Dem.	Major Vote Rep.	Major Vote Dem.
2010	779,957	451,618	Boozman, John	288,156	Lincoln, Blanche L.*	40,183	163,462 R	57.9%	36.9%	61.0%	39.0%
2008**	1,011,754			804,678	Pryor, Mark*	207,076	804,678 D		79.5%		100.0%
2004	1,039,349	458,036	Holt, Jim L.	580,973	Lincoln, Blanche L.*	340	122,937 D	44.1%	55.9%	44.1%	55.9%
2002	803,959	370,653	Hutchinson, Tim*	433,306	Pryor, Mark		62,653 D	46.1%	53.9%	46.1%	53.9%
1998	700,644	295,870	Boozman, Fay	385,878	Lincoln, Blanche L.	18,896	90,008 D	42.2%	55.1%	43.4%	56.6%
1996	846,183	445,942	Hutchinson, Tim	400,241	Bryant, Winston		45,701 R	52.7%	47.3%	52.7%	47.3%
1992	920,008	366,373	Huckabee, Mike	553,635	Bumpers, Dale*		187,262 D	39.8%	60.2%	39.8%	60.2%
1990**	494,735			493,910	Pryor, David H.*	825	493,910 D		99.8%		100.0%
1986	695,487	262,313	Hutchinson, Asa	433,122	Bumpers, Dale*	52	170,809 D	37.7%	62.3%	37.7%	62.3%
1984	875,956	373,615	Bethune, Ed	502,341	Pryor, David H.*		128,726 D	42.7%	57.3%	42.7%	57.3%
1980	808,812	330,576	Clark, Bill	477,905	Bumpers, Dale*	331	147,329 D	40.9%	59.1%	40.9%	59.1%
1978	522,239	84,722	Kelly, Tom	399,916	Pryor, David H.	37,601	315,194 D	16.2%	76.6%	17.5%	82.5%
1974	543,082	82,026	Jones, John H.	461,056	Bumpers, Dale		379,030 D	15.1%	84.9%	15.1%	84.9%
1972	634,636	248,238	Babbitt, Wayne H.	386,398	McClellan, John L.*		138,160 D	39.1%	60.9%	39.1%	60.9%
1968	591,704	241,739	Bernard, Charles T.	349,965	Fulbright, J. William*		108,226 D	40.9%	59.1%	40.9%	59.1%
1966**					McClellan, John L.*						
1962	312,880	98,013	Jones, Kenneth	214,867	Fulbright, J. William*		116,854 D	31.3%	68.7%	31.3%	68.7%
1960**					McClellan, John L.*						
1956	399,695	68,016	Henley, Ben C.	331,679	Fulbright, J. William*		263,663 D	17.0%	83.0%	17.0%	83.0%
1954	291,058			291,058	McClellan, John L.*		291,058 D		100.0%		100.0%
1950	302,582			302,582	Fulbright, J. William*		302,582 D		100.0%		100.0%
1948	216,401			216,401	McClellan, John L.*		216,401 D		100.0%		100.0%

Note: An asterisk (*) denotes incumbent. **In past elections, the other vote included: 2008 - 207,076 Green (Rebekah Kennedy), who finished second. In 1990 the vote for Senator David H. Pryor was not canvassed in seven counties because he was unopposed. Senator John L. McClellan was reelected in 1960 and in 1966, but his vote was not canvassed in many counties. The Republican Party did not run a candidate in the 1948, 1950, 1954, 1960, 1966, 1990, and 2008 Senate elections.

ARKANSAS

PRESIDENT 2012

2010 Census Population	County	Total Vote	Republican (Romney)	Democratic (Obama)	Other	Rep.-Dem. Plurality	Percentage			
							Total Vote		Major Vote	
							Rep.	Dem.	Rep.	Dem.
19,019	ARKANSAS	6,494	3,897	2,455	142	1,442 R	60.0%	37.8%	61.4%	38.6%
21,853	ASHLEY	7,921	4,867	2,859	195	2,008 R	61.4%	36.1%	63.0%	37.0%
41,513	BAXTER	19,339	13,688	5,172	479	8,516 R	70.8%	26.7%	72.6%	27.4%
221,339	BENTON	79,257	54,646	22,636	1,975	32,010 R	68.9%	28.6%	70.7%	29.3%
36,903	BOONE	15,391	11,159	3,772	460	7,387 R	72.5%	24.5%	74.7%	25.3%
11,508	BRADLEY	3,652	2,134	1,449	69	685 R	58.4%	39.7%	59.6%	40.4%
5,368	CALHOUN	2,174	1,458	660	56	798 R	67.1%	30.4%	68.8%	31.2%
27,446	CARROLL	10,183	6,125	3,696	362	2,429 R	60.1%	36.3%	62.4%	37.6%
11,800	CHICOT	4,361	1,670	2,649	42	979 D	38.3%	60.7%	38.7%	61.3%
22,995	CLARK	8,409	4,343	3,811	255	532 R	51.6%	45.3%	53.3%	46.7%
16,083	CLAY	5,110	3,225	1,738	147	1,487 R	63.1%	34.0%	65.0%	35.0%
25,970	CLEBURNE	11,647	8,693	2,620	334	6,073 R	74.6%	22.5%	76.8%	23.2%
8,689	CLEVELAND	3,266	2,313	845	108	1,468 R	70.8%	25.9%	73.2%	26.8%
24,552	COLUMBIA	9,455	5,790	3,557	108	2,233 R	61.2%	37.6%	61.9%	38.1%
21,273	CONWAY	7,730	4,514	3,005	211	1,509 R	58.4%	38.9%	60.0%	40.0%
96,443	CRAIGHEAD	31,700	20,350	10,527	823	9,823 R	64.2%	33.2%	65.9%	34.1%
61,948	CRAWFORD	20,591	15,145	4,881	565	10,264 R	73.6%	23.7%	75.6%	24.4%
50,902	CRITTENDEN	16,716	6,998	9,487	231	2,489 D	41.9%	56.8%	42.5%	57.5%
17,870	CROSS	6,681	4,269	2,279	133	1,990 R	63.9%	34.1%	65.2%	34.8%
8,116	DALLAS	3,084	1,665	1,337	82	328 R	54.0%	43.4%	55.5%	44.5%
13,008	DESHA	4,420	1,896	2,443	81	547 D	42.9%	55.3%	43.7%	56.3%
18,509	DREW	6,633	3,887	2,630	116	1,257 R	58.6%	39.7%	59.6%	40.4%
113,237	FAULKNER	41,460	26,722	13,621	1,117	13,101 R	64.5%	32.9%	66.2%	33.8%
18,125	FRANKLIN	6,540	4,631	1,726	183	2,905 R	70.8%	26.4%	72.8%	27.2%
12,245	FULTON	4,522	2,949	1,452	121	1,497 R	65.2%	32.1%	67.0%	33.0%
96,024	GARLAND	40,728	26,014	13,804	910	12,210 R	63.9%	33.9%	65.3%	34.7%
17,853	GRANT	6,479	4,829	1,468	182	3,361 R	74.5%	22.7%	76.7%	23.3%
42,090	GREENE	13,761	9,071	4,000	690	5,071 R	65.9%	29.1%	69.4%	30.6%
22,609	HEMPSTEAD	6,921	4,284	2,468	169	1,816 R	61.9%	35.7%	63.4%	36.6%
32,923	HOT SPRING	11,260	7,097	3,830	333	3,267 R	63.0%	34.0%	64.9%	35.1%
13,789	HOWARD	4,462	2,892	1,471	99	1,421 R	64.8%	33.0%	66.3%	33.7%
36,647	INDEPENDENCE	12,397	8,728	3,281	388	5,447 R	70.4%	26.5%	72.7%	27.3%
13,696	IZARD	5,278	3,575	1,524	179	2,051 R	67.7%	28.9%	70.1%	29.9%
17,997	JACKSON	5,347	3,072	2,095	180	977 R	57.5%	39.2%	59.5%	40.5%
77,435	JEFFERSON	27,383	9,520	17,470	393	7,950 D	34.8%	63.8%	35.3%	64.7%
25,540	JOHNSON	8,098	5,064	2,799	235	2,265 R	62.5%	34.6%	64.4%	35.6%
7,645	LAFAYETTE	2,929	1,713	1,173	43	540 R	58.5%	40.0%	59.4%	40.6%
17,415	LAWRENCE	5,540	3,536	1,788	216	1,748 R	63.8%	32.3%	66.4%	33.6%
10,424	LEE	3,424	1,280	2,107	37	827 D	37.4%	61.5%	37.8%	62.2%
14,134	LINCOLN	3,726	2,199	1,425	102	774 R	59.0%	38.2%	60.7%	39.3%
13,171	LITTLE RIVER	5,051	3,385	1,552	114	1,833 R	67.0%	30.7%	68.6%	31.4%
22,353	LOGAN	7,331	5,079	2,009	243	3,070 R	69.3%	27.4%	71.7%	28.3%
68,356	LONOKE	24,114	17,880	5,625	609	12,255 R	74.1%	23.3%	76.1%	23.9%
15,717	MADISON	6,568	4,263	2,099	206	2,164 R	64.9%	32.0%	67.0%	33.0%
16,653	MARION	7,051	4,774	2,037	240	2,737 R	67.7%	28.9%	70.1%	29.9%
43,462	MILLER	15,329	10,622	4,518	189	6,104 R	69.3%	29.5%	70.2%	29.8%
46,480	MISSISSIPPI	13,375	6,603	6,467	305	136 R	49.4%	48.4%	50.5%	49.5%
8,149	MONROE	3,230	1,585	1,583	62	2 R	49.1%	49.0%	50.0%	50.0%
9,487	MONTGOMERY	3,404	2,369	920	115	1,449 R	69.6%	27.0%	72.0%	28.0%
8,997	NEVADA	3,384	1,996	1,314	74	682 R	59.0%	38.8%	60.3%	39.7%
8,330	NEWTON	3,661	2,508	993	160	1,515 R	68.5%	27.1%	71.6%	28.4%
26,120	OUACHITA	10,315	5,521	4,633	161	888 R	53.5%	44.9%	54.4%	45.6%
10,445	PERRY	3,938	2,581	1,187	170	1,394 R	65.5%	30.1%	68.5%	31.5%
21,757	PHILLIPS	7,930	2,598	5,202	130	2,604 D	32.8%	65.6%	33.3%	66.7%
11,291	PIKE	3,788	2,847	851	90	1,996 R	75.2%	22.5%	77.0%	23.0%
24,583	POINSETT	7,560	4,974	2,390	196	2,584 R	65.8%	31.6%	67.5%	32.5%
20,662	POLK	7,726	5,955	1,556	215	4,399 R	77.1%	20.1%	79.3%	20.7%
61,754	POPE	20,439	14,763	5,126	550	9,637 R	72.2%	25.1%	74.2%	25.8%
8,715	PRAIRIE	3,141	2,153	880	108	1,273 R	68.5%	28.0%	71.0%	29.0%
382,748	PULASKI	159,381	68,984	87,248	3,149	18,264 D	43.3%	54.7%	44.2%	55.8%

ARKANSAS

PRESIDENT 2012

2010 Census Population	County	Total Vote	Republican (Romney)	Democratic (Obama)	Other	Rep.-Dem. Plurality	Percentage			
							Total Vote		Major Vote	
							Rep.	Dem.	Rep.	Dem.
17,969	RANDOLPH	5,956	3,701	2,046	209	1,655 R	62.1%	34.4%	64.4%	35.6%
107,118	SALINE	47,062	32,963	12,869	1,230	20,094 R	70.0%	27.3%	71.9%	28.1%
11,233	SCOTT	3,640	2,631	897	112	1,734 R	72.3%	24.6%	74.6%	25.4%
8,195	SEARCY	3,694	2,699	814	181	1,885 R	73.1%	22.0%	76.8%	23.2%
125,744	SEBASTIAN	43,362	29,169	13,092	1,101	16,077 R	67.3%	30.2%	69.0%	31.0%
17,058	SEVIER	4,330	3,136	1,042	152	2,094 R	72.4%	24.1%	75.1%	24.9%
17,264	SHARP	7,283	4,921	2,092	270	2,829 R	67.6%	28.7%	70.2%	29.8%
28,258	ST. FRANCIS	8,362	3,368	4,910	84	1,542 D	40.3%	58.7%	40.7%	59.3%
12,394	STONE	5,354	3,776	1,356	222	2,420 R	70.5%	25.3%	73.6%	26.4%
41,639	UNION	17,177	10,699	6,196	282	4,503 R	62.3%	36.1%	63.3%	36.7%
17,295	VAN BUREN	6,430	4,365	1,832	233	2,533 R	67.9%	28.5%	70.4%	29.6%
203,065	WASHINGTON	70,460	39,688	28,236	2,536	11,452 R	56.3%	40.1%	58.4%	41.6%
77,076	WHITE	26,514	20,011	5,765	738	14,246 R	75.5%	21.7%	77.6%	22.4%
7,260	WOODRUFF	2,685	1,227	1,340	118	113 D	45.7%	49.9%	47.8%	52.2%
22,185	YELL	5,974	4,042	1,722	210	2,320 R	67.7%	28.8%	70.1%	29.9%
2,915,918	TOTAL	1,069,468	647,744	394,409	27,315	253,335 R	60.6%	36.9%	62.2%	37.8%

ARKANSAS

HOUSE OF REPRESENTATIVES

CD	Year	Total Vote	Republican		Democratic		Other Vote	Rep.-Dem. Plurality	Percentage			
			Vote	Candidate	Vote	Candidate			Total Vote		Major Vote	
									Rep.	Dem.	Rep.	Dem.
1	2012	246,843	138,800	CRAWFORD, RICK*	96,601	ELLINGTON, SCOTT	11,442	42,199 R	56.2%	39.1%	59.0%	41.0%
2	2012	286,598	158,175	GRIFFIN, TIM*	113,156	RULE, HERB	15,267	45,019 R	55.2%	39.5%	58.3%	41.7%
3	2012	245,660	186,467	WOMACK, STEVE*			59,193	186,467 R	75.9%		100.0%	
4	2012	258,953	154,149	COTTON, TOM	95,013	JEFFRESS, GENE	9,791	59,136 R	59.5%	36.7%	61.9%	38.1%
TOTAL	2012	1,038,054	637,591		304,770		95,693	332,821 R	61.4%	29.4%	67.7%	32.3%

Note: An asterisk (*) denotes incumbent.

ARKANSAS

GENERAL AND PRIMARY ELECTIONS

2012 GENERAL ELECTIONS: OTHER VOTE

President Other vote was 16,276 Libertarian (Gary E. Johnson), 9,305 Green (Jill Stein), 1,734 Independent (Peta Lindsay)

House Other vote was:

CD 1 6,427 Libertarian (Jessica Paxton), 5,015 Green (Jacob Holloway)
CD 2 8,566 Green (Barbara Ward), 6,701 Libertarian (Chris Hayes)
CD 3 39,318 Green (Rebekah Kennedy), 19,875 Libertarian (David Pangrac)
CD 4 4,984 Libertarian (Bobby Tullis), 4,807 Green (Josh Drake)

ARKANSAS

GENERAL AND PRIMARY ELECTIONS

2012 GENERAL ELECTIONS: OTHER VOTE

President Other vote was 16,276 Libertarian (Gary E. Johnson), 9,305 Green (Jill Stein), 1,734 Independent (Peta Lindsay)

House Other vote was:

CD 1 6,427 Libertarian (Jessica Paxton), 5,015 Green (Jacob Holloway)
CD 2 8,566 Green (Barbara Ward), 6,701 Libertarian (Chris Hayes)
CD 3 39,318 Green (Rebekah Kennedy), 19,875 Libertarian (David Pangrac)
CD 4 4,984 Libertarian (Bobby Tullis), 4,807 Green (Josh Drake)

2012 PRIMARY ELECTIONS: SUPPLEMENTARY INFORMATION

Primary May 22, 2012 **Registration** 1,538,619 No Party Registration
(as of May 5, 2012)

Primary Runoff June 12, 2012

Primary Type Any registered voter could participate in either the Democratic or Republican primary. However, if they participated in one party's primary they could not vote in the runoff of the other party.

	REPUBLICAN PRIMARIES			DEMOCRATIC PRIMARIES		
President	Romney, W. Mitt	104,200	68.4%	Obama, Barack H.*	94,936	58.4%
	Paul, Ron	20,399	13.4%	Wolfe, John	67,711	41.6%
	Santorum, Rick	20,308	13.3%			
	Gingrich, Newt	7,453	4.9%			
	TOTAL	152,360		TOTAL	162,647	
Congressional District 1	Crawford, Rick*	Unopposed		Ellington, Scott	27,936	49.5%
				Hall, Clark M.	21,861	38.8%
				Latanich, Gary	6,605	11.7%
				TOTAL	56,402	
				PRIMARY RUNOFF		
				Ellington, Scott	10,028	50.7%
				Hall, Clark M.	9,737	49.3%
				TOTAL	19,765	
Congressional District 2	Griffin, Tim*	Unopposed		Rule, Herb	Unopposed	
Congressional District 3	Womack, Steve*	Unopposed		Aden, Ken	Unopposed	
				Ken Aden ran unopposed in the Democratic primary but subsequently withdrew from the race after accusations that he mischaracterized himself as a Green Beret. The Democrats did not run a candidate in the general election.		
Congressional District 4	Cotton, Tom	20,899	57.6%	Jeffress, Gene	23,848	43.0%
	Rankin, Beth Anne	13,460	37.1%	Hurst, Q. Byrum	19,812	35.7%
	Cowart, John	1,953	5.4%	Morrison, D.C.	11,771	21.2%
	TOTAL	36,312		TOTAL	55,431	
				PRIMARY RUNOFF		
				Jeffress, Gene	15,266	60.7%
				Hurst, Q. Byrum	9,895	39.3%
				TOTAL	25,161	

Notes: An asterisk (*) denotes incumbent. No votes were tallied district- or statewide in contests where a candidate ran unopposed. If no candidate received a majority of the primary vote, a runoff was held between the top two finishers.

CALIFORNIA

Congressional districts first established for elections held in 2012

53 members

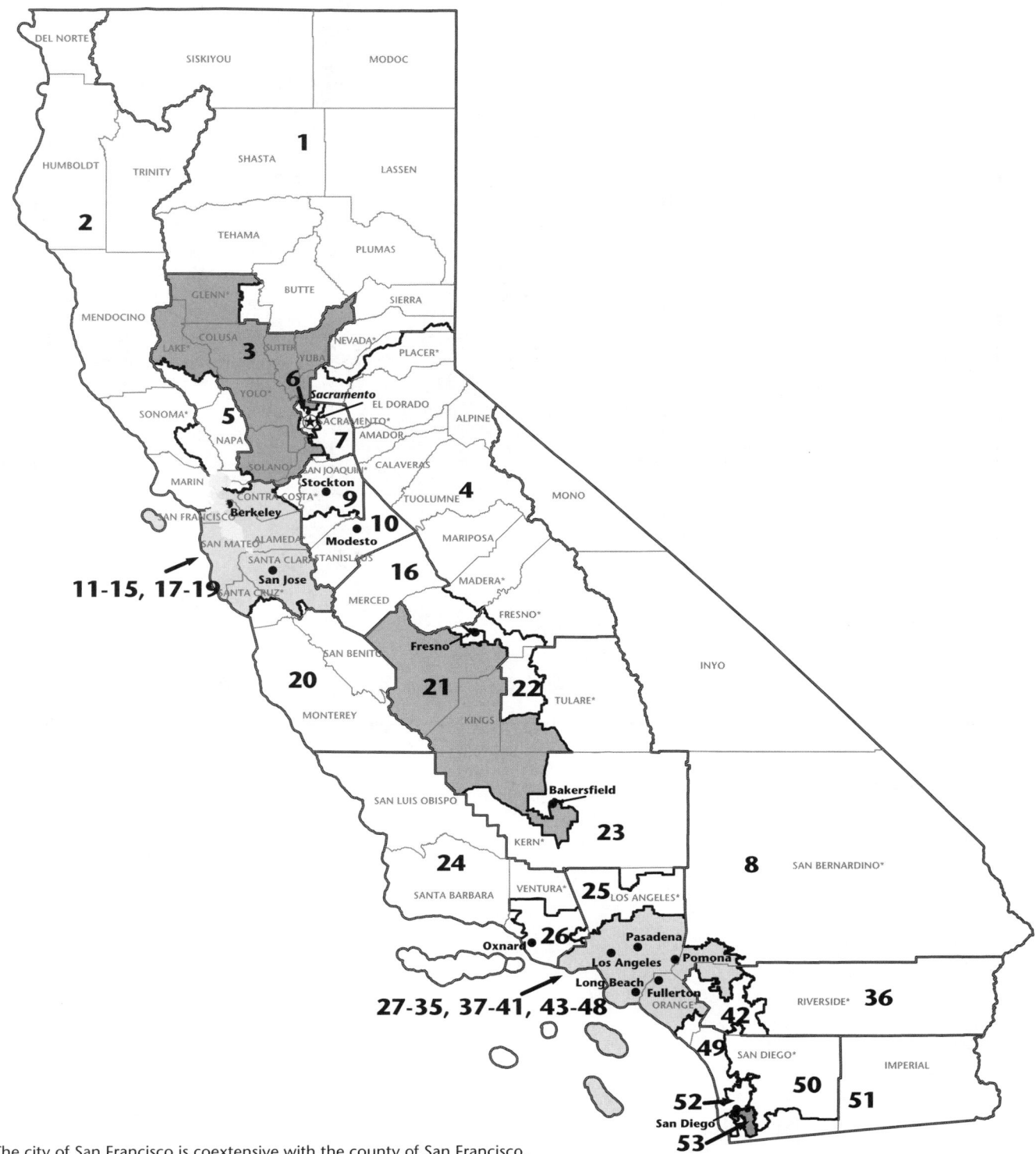

The city of San Francisco is coextensive with the county of San Francisco.

* Asterisk indicates a county whose boundaries include parts of two or more Congressional districts.

CALIFORNIA

Greater San Francisco Bay Area

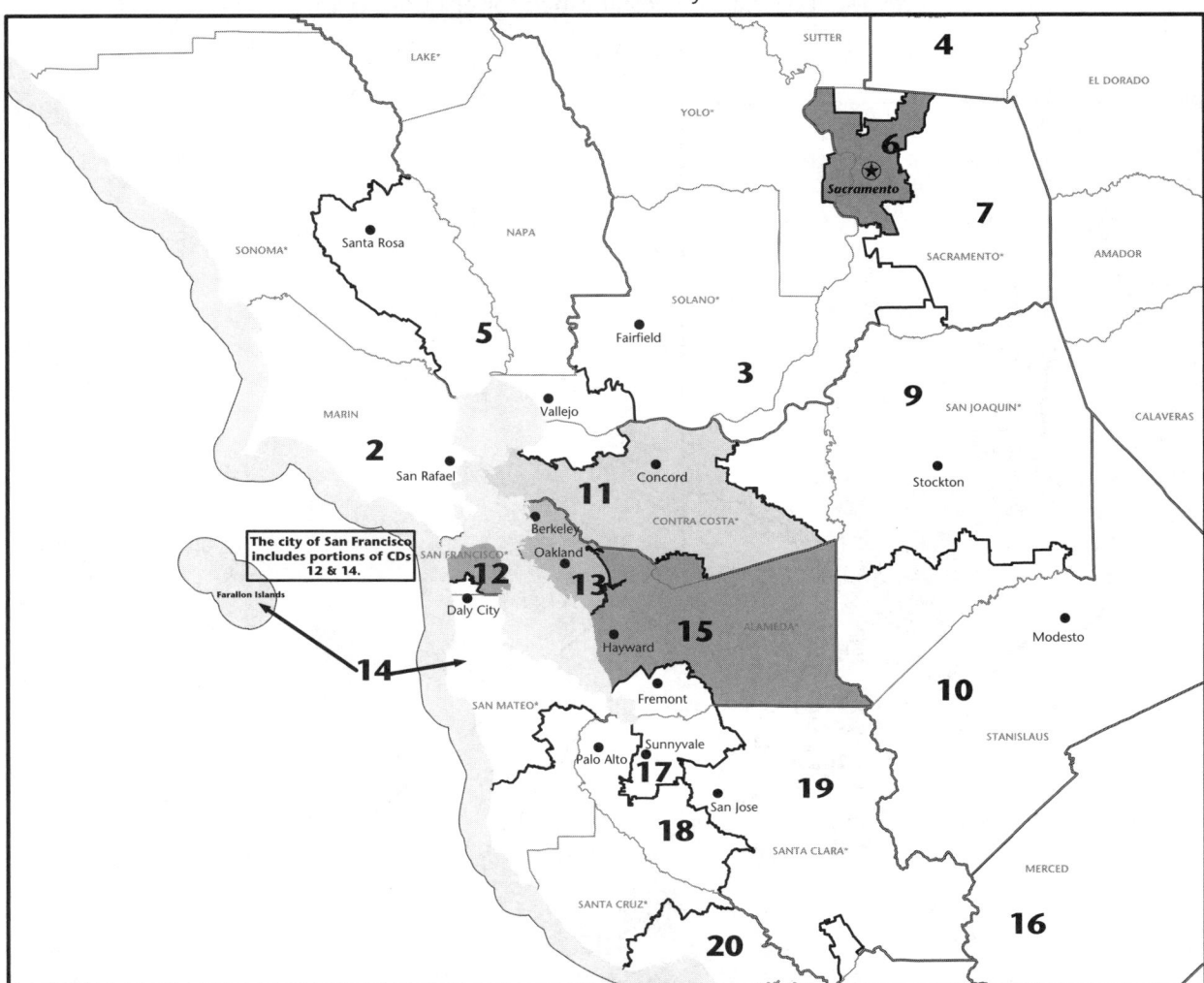

* Asterisk indicates a county whose boundaries include parts of two or more Congressional districts.

CALIFORNIA

Greater Los Angeles, San Diego Areas

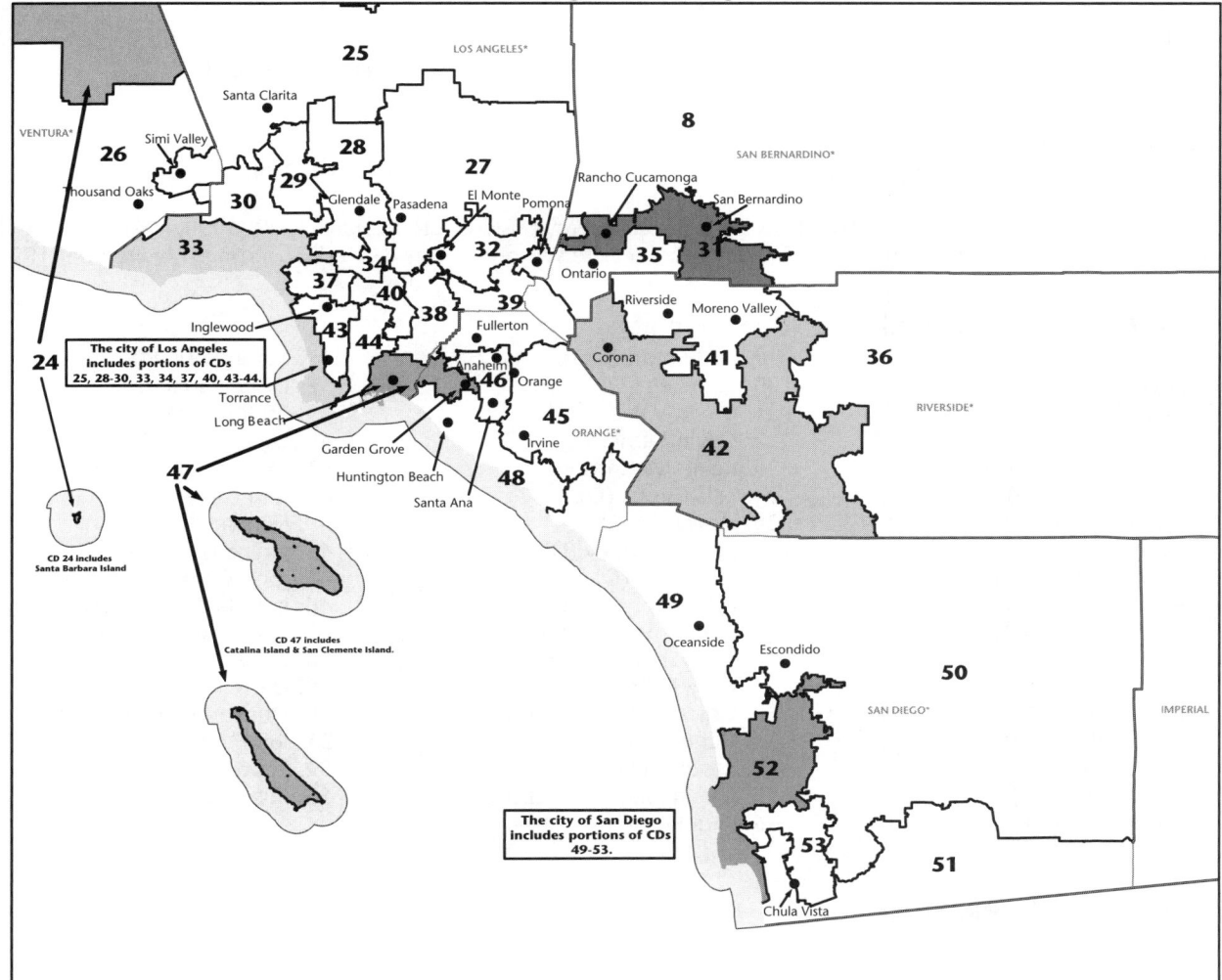

The city of Los Angeles includes portions of CDs 25, 28-30, 33, 34, 37, 40, 43-44.

CD 24 includes Santa Barbara Island

CD 47 includes Catalina Island & San Clemente Island.

The city of San Diego includes portions of CDs 49-53.

* Asterisk indicates a county whose boundaries include parts of two or more Congressional districts.

CALIFORNIA

GOVERNOR
Edmund G. "Jerry" Brown Jr. (D). Elected 2010 to a four-year term. Previously elected 1978, 1974.

SENATORS (2 Democrats)
Barbara Boxer (D). Reelected 2010 to a six-year term. Previously elected 2004, 1998, 1992.

Dianne Feinstein (D). Reelected 2012 to a six-year term. Previously elected 2006, 2000, 1994, and 1992 to fill the remaining two years of the term vacated when Senator Pete Wilson (R) was elected Governor in November 1990.

REPRESENTATIVES (15 Republicans, 38 Democrats)

1. Doug LaMalfa (R)
2. Jared Huffman (D)
3. John Garamendi (D)
4. Tom McClintock (R)
5. Mike Thompson (D)
6. Doris Matsui (D)
7. Ami Bera (D)
8. Paul Cook (R)
9. Jerry McNerney (D)
10. Jeff Denham (R)
11. George Miller (D)
12. Nancy Pelosi (D)
13. Barbara Lee (D)
14. Jackie Speier (D)
15. Eric Swalwell (D)
16. Jim Costa (D)
17. Mike Honda (D)
18. Anna G. Eshoo (D)
19. Zoe Lofgren (D)
20. Sam Farr (D)
21. David Valadao (R)
22. Devin Nunes (R)
23. Kevin McCarthy (R)
24. Lois Capps (D)
25. Howard P. "Buck" McKeon (R)
26. Julia Brownley (D)
27. Judy Chu (D)
28. Adam Schiff (D)
29. Tony Cárdenas (D)
30. Brad Sherman (D)
31. Gary Miller (R)
32. Grace F. Napolitano (D)
33. Henry A. Waxman (D)
34. Xavier Becerra (D)
35. Gloria Negrete McLeod (D)
36. Raul Ruiz (D)
37. Karen Bass (D)
38. Linda Sánchez (D)
39. Ed Royce (R)
40. Lucille Roybal-Allard (D)
41. Mark Takano (D)
42. Ken Calvert (R)
43. Maxine Waters (D)
44. Janice Hahn (D)
45. John Campbell (R)
46. Loretta Sanchez (D)
47. Alan Lowenthal (D)
48. Dana Rohrabacher (R)
49. Darrell Issa (R)
50. Duncan D. Hunter (R)
51. Juan Vargas (D)
52. Scott Peters (D)
53. Susan Davis (D)

POSTWAR VOTE FOR PRESIDENT

Year	Total Vote	Republican Vote	Republican Candidate	Democratic Vote	Democratic Candidate	Other Vote	Rep.-Dem. Plurality	Total Vote Rep.	Total Vote Dem.	Major Vote Rep.	Major Vote Dem.
2012	13,038,547	4,839,958	Romney, W. Mitt	7,854,285	Obama, Barack H.*	344,304	3,014,327 D	37.1%	60.2%	38.1%	61.9%
2008	13,561,900	5,011,781	McCain, John S. III	8,274,473	Obama, Barack H.	275,646	3,262,692 D	37.0%	61.0%	37.7%	62.3%
2004	12,421,852	5,509,826	Bush, George W.*	6,745,485	Kerry, John F.	166,541	1,235,659 D	44.4%	54.3%	45.0%	55.0%
2000**	10,965,856	4,567,429	Bush, George W.	5,861,203	Gore, Albert Jr.	537,224	1,293,774 D	41.7%	53.4%	43.8%	56.2%
1996**	10,019,484	3,828,380	Dole, Robert "Bob"	5,119,835	Clinton, Bill*	1,071,269	1,291,455 D	38.2%	51.1%	42.8%	57.2%
1992**	11,131,721	3,630,574	Bush, George H.*	5,121,325	Clinton, Bill	2,379,822	1,490,751 D	32.6%	46.0%	41.5%	58.5%
1988	9,887,065	5,054,917	Bush, George H.	4,702,233	Dukakis, Michael S.	129,915	352,684 R	51.1%	47.6%	51.8%	48.2%
1984	9,505,423	5,467,009	Reagan, Ronald*	3,922,519	Mondale, Walter F.	115,895	1,544,490 R	57.5%	41.3%	58.2%	41.8%
1980**	8,587,063	4,524,858	Reagan, Ronald	3,083,661	Carter, Jimmy*	978,544	1,441,197 R	52.7%	35.9%	59.5%	40.5%
1976	7,867,117	3,882,244	Ford, Gerald R.*	3,742,284	Carter, Jimmy	242,589	139,960 R	49.3%	47.6%	50.9%	49.1%
1972	8,367,862	4,602,096	Nixon, Richard M.*	3,475,847	McGovern, George S.	289,919	1,126,249 R	55.0%	41.5%	57.0%	43.0%
1968**	7,251,587	3,467,664	Nixon, Richard M.	3,244,318	Humphrey, Hubert H. Jr.	539,605	223,346 R	47.8%	44.7%	51.7%	48.3%
1964	7,057,586	2,879,108	Goldwater, Barry M. Sr.	4,171,877	Johnson, Lyndon B.*	6,601	1,292,769 D	40.8%	59.1%	40.8%	59.2%
1960	6,506,578	3,259,722	Nixon, Richard M.	3,224,099	Kennedy, John F.	22,757	35,623 R	50.1%	49.6%	50.3%	49.7%
1956	5,466,355	3,027,668	Eisenhower, Dwight D.*	2,420,135	Stevenson, Adlai E. II	18,552	607,533 R	55.4%	44.3%	55.6%	44.4%
1952	5,141,849	2,897,310	Eisenhower, Dwight D.	2,197,548	Stevenson, Adlai E. II	46,991	699,762 R	56.3%	42.7%	56.9%	43.1%
1948	4,021,538	1,895,269	Dewey, Thomas E.	1,913,134	Truman, Harry S.*	213,135	17,865 D	47.1%	47.6%	49.8%	50.2%

Note: An asterisk (*) denotes incumbent. **In past elections, the other vote included: 2000 - 418,707 Green (Ralph Nader); 1996 - 697,847 Reform (Ross Perot); 1992 - 2,296,006 Independent (Perot); 1980 - 739,833 Independent (John Anderson); 1968 - 487,270 American Independent (George Wallace).

CALIFORNIA

POSTWAR VOTE FOR GOVERNOR

Year	Total Vote	Republican		Democratic		Other Vote	Rep.-Dem. Plurality	Percentage			
								Total Vote		Major Vote	
		Vote	Candidate	Vote	Candidate			Rep.	Dem.	Rep.	Dem.
2010	10,095,185	4,127,391	Whitman, Meg	5,428,149	Brown, Edmund G. Jr.	539,645	1,300,758 D	40.9%	53.8%	43.2%	56.8%
2006	8,679,416	4,850,157	Schwarzenegger, Arnold*	3,376,732	Angelides, Phil	452,527	1,473,425 R	55.9%	38.9%	59.0%	41.0%
2003S	8,657,915	4,206,284	Schwarzenegger, Arnold	2,724,874	Bustamante, Cruz	1,726,757	1,481,410 R	48.6%	31.5%	60.7%	39.3%
2002	7,476,311	3,169,801	Simon, Bill	3,533,490	Davis, Gray*	773,020	363,689 D	42.4%	47.3%	47.3%	52.7%
1998	8,385,196	3,218,030	Lungren, Dan	4,860,702	Davis, Gray	306,464	1,642,672 D	38.4%	58.0%	39.8%	60.2%
1994	8,665,375	4,781,766	Wilson, Pete*	3,519,799	Brown, Kathleen	363,810	1,261,967 R	55.2%	40.6%	57.6%	42.4%
1990	7,699,467	3,791,904	Wilson, Pete	3,525,197	Feinstein, Dianne	382,366	266,707 R	49.2%	45.8%	51.8%	48.2%
1986	7,443,551	4,506,601	Deukmejian, George*	2,781,714	Bradley, Tom	155,236	1,724,887 R	60.5%	37.4%	61.8%	38.2%
1982	7,876,698	3,881,014	Deukmejian, George	3,787,669	Bradley, Tom	208,015	93,345 R	49.3%	48.1%	50.6%	49.4%
1978	6,922,378	2,526,534	Younger, Evelle J.	3,878,812	Brown, Edmund G. Jr.*	517,032	1,352,278 D	36.5%	56.0%	39.4%	60.6%
1974	6,248,070	2,952,954	Flournoy, Houston I.	3,131,648	Brown, Edmund G. Jr.	163,468	178,694 D	47.3%	50.1%	48.5%	51.5%
1970	6,510,272	3,439,664	Reagan, Ronald*	2,938,807	Unruh, Jess	131,801	500,857 R	52.8%	45.1%	53.9%	46.1%
1966	6,503,445	3,742,913	Reagan, Ronald	2,749,174	Brown, Edmund G.*	11,358	993,739 R	57.6%	42.3%	57.7%	42.3%
1962	5,853,270	2,740,351	Nixon, Richard M.	3,037,109	Brown, Edmund G.*	75,810	296,758 D	46.8%	51.9%	47.4%	52.6%
1958	5,255,777	2,110,911	Knowland, William F.	3,140,076	Brown, Edmund G.	4,790	1,029,165 D	40.2%	59.7%	40.2%	59.8%
1954	4,030,368	2,290,519	Knight, Goodwin J.*	1,739,368	Graves, Richard Perrin	481	551,151 R	56.8%	43.2%	56.8%	43.2%
1950	3,796,090	2,461,754	Warren, Earl*	1,333,856	Roosevelt, James	480	1,127,898 R	64.8%	35.1%	64.9%	35.1%
1946**	2,558,399	2,344,542	Warren, Earl*			213,857	2,344,542 R	91.6%		100.0%	

Note: An asterisk (*) denotes incumbent. **The 2003 election was for a short term to fill a vacancy created by voter approval of a measure to remove Governor Gray Davis (D) from office. The measure passed by a vote of 4,976,274 votes (55.4 percent) for recall to 4,007,783 (44.6 percent) against recall. In the same election, more than 100 candidates ran for the right to succeed Davis. No primary election was held to cull the field. All candidates, regardless of party, ran together on the same ballot. The winner, Arnold Schwarzenegger, is listed as the Republican candidate. The leading Democratic vote-getter, Cruz Bustamante, is listed as the Democratic candidate. The percentages given are for Schwarzenegger and Bustamante. The leading "Other" candidate was Republican Tom McClintock, who received 1,161,287 votes (13.4 percent of the total). The percentage columns are for Schwarzenegger and Bustamante and do not include additional candidates. In 1946 the Republican candidate won both major party nominations.

POSTWAR VOTE FOR SENATOR

Year	Total Vote	Republican		Democratic		Other Vote	Rep.-Dem. Plurality	Percentage			
								Total Vote		Major Vote	
		Vote	Candidate	Vote	Candidate			Rep.	Dem.	Rep.	Dem.
2012	12,578,511	4,713,887	Emken, Elizabeth	7,864,624	Feinstein, Dianne*		3,150,737 D	37.5%	62.5%	37.5%	62.5%
2010	9,999,860	4,217,386	Fiorina, Carly	5,218,137	Boxer, Barbara*	564,337	1,000,751 D	42.2%	52.2%	44.7%	55.3%
2006	8,541,476	2,990,822	Mountjoy, Dick	5,076,289	Feinstein, Dianne*	474,365	2,085,467 D	35.0%	59.4%	37.1%	62.9%
2004	12,053,295	4,555,922	Jones, Bill	6,955,728	Boxer, Barbara*	541,645	2,399,806 D	37.8%	57.7%	39.6%	60.4%
2000	10,623,614	3,886,853	Campbell, Tom	5,932,522	Feinstein, Dianne*	804,239	2,045,669 D	36.6%	55.8%	39.6%	60.4%
1998	8,314,953	3,576,351	Fong, Matt	4,411,705	Boxer, Barbara*	326,897	835,354 D	43.0%	53.1%	44.8%	55.2%
1994	8,514,089	3,817,025	Huffington, Michael	3,979,152	Feinstein, Dianne*	717,912	162,127 D	44.8%	46.7%	49.0%	51.0%
1992	10,799,703	4,644,182	Sargent, Claire	5,173,467	Boxer, Barbara	982,054	529,285 D	43.0%	47.9%	47.3%	52.7%
1992S	10,782,743	4,093,501	Seymour, John*	5,853,651	Feinstein, Dianne	835,591	1,760,150 D	38.0%	54.3%	41.2%	58.8%
1988	9,743,598	5,143,409	Wilson, Pete*	4,287,253	McCarthy, Leo	312,936	856,156 R	52.8%	44.0%	54.5%	45.5%
1986	7,398,522	3,541,804	Zschau, Ed	3,646,672	Cranston, Alan*	210,046	104,868 D	47.9%	49.3%	49.3%	50.7%
1982	7,805,538	4,022,565	Wilson, Pete	3,494,968	Brown, Edmund G. Jr.	288,005	527,597 R	51.5%	44.8%	53.5%	46.5%
1980	8,327,481	3,093,426	Gann, Paul	4,705,399	Cranston, Alan*	528,656	1,611,973 D	37.1%	56.5%	39.7%	60.3%
1976	7,472,268	3,748,973	Hayakawa, S. I.	3,502,862	Tunney, John V.*	220,433	246,111 R	50.2%	46.9%	51.7%	48.3%
1974	6,102,432	2,210,267	Richardson, H. L.	3,693,160	Cranston, Alan*	199,005	1,482,893 D	36.2%	60.5%	37.4%	62.6%
1970	6,492,157	2,877,617	Murphy, George*	3,496,558	Tunney, John V.	117,982	618,941 D	44.3%	53.9%	45.1%	54.9%
1968	7,102,465	3,329,148	Rafferty, Max	3,680,352	Cranston, Alan	92,965	351,204 D	46.9%	51.8%	47.5%	52.5%
1964	7,041,821	3,628,555	Murphy, George	3,411,912	Salinger, Pierre*	1,354	216,643 R	51.5%	48.5%	51.5%	48.5%
1962	5,647,952	3,180,483	Kuchel, Thomas H.*	2,452,839	Richards, Richard	14,630	727,644 R	56.3%	43.4%	56.5%	43.5%
1958	5,135,221	2,204,337	Knight, Goodwin J.	2,927,693	Engle, Clair	3,191	723,356 D	42.9%	57.0%	43.0%	57.0%
1956	5,361,467	2,892,918	Kuchel, Thomas H.*	2,445,816	Richards, Richard	22,733	447,102 R	54.0%	45.6%	54.2%	45.8%
1954S	3,929,668	2,090,836	Kuchel, Thomas H.*	1,788,071	Yorty, Samuel William	50,761	302,765 R	53.2%	45.5%	53.9%	46.1%
1952**	4,542,548	3,982,448	Knowland, William F.*			560,100	3,982,448 R	87.7%		100.0%	
1950	3,686,315	2,183,454	Nixon, Richard M.	1,502,507	Douglas, Helen Gahagan	354	680,947 R	59.2%	40.8%	59.2%	40.8%
1946	2,639,465	1,428,067	Knowland, William F.*	1,167,161	Rogers, Will Jr.	44,237	260,906 R	54.1%	44.2%	55.0%	45.0%

Note: An asterisk (*) denotes incumbent. **In past elections, the other vote included: 1952 - 542,270 Progressive (Reuben W. Borough), who finished second. The Republican candidate that year (William F. Knowland) won both major party nominations. The 1954 election was for a short term to fill a vacancy, as was one of the 1992 elections.

CALIFORNIA
PRESIDENT 2012

2010 Census Population	County	Total Vote	Republican (Romney)	Democratic (Obama)	Other	Rep.-Dem. Plurality	Percentage Total Vote Rep.	Dem.	Major Vote Rep.	Dem.
1,510,271	ALAMEDA	595,642	108,182	469,684	17,776	361,502 D	18.2%	78.9%	18.7%	81.3%
1,175	ALPINE	653	236	389	28	153 D	36.1%	59.6%	37.8%	62.2%
38,091	AMADOR	17,649	10,281	6,830	538	3,451 R	58.3%	38.7%	60.1%	39.9%
220,000	BUTTE	90,752	44,479	42,669	3,604	1,810 R	49.0%	47.0%	51.0%	49.0%
45,578	CALAVERAS	21,786	12,365	8,670	751	3,695 R	56.8%	39.8%	58.8%	41.2%
21,419	COLUSA	6,034	3,601	2,314	119	1,287 R	59.7%	38.3%	60.9%	39.1%
1,049,025	CONTRA COSTA	438,226	136,517	290,824	10,885	154,307 D	31.2%	66.4%	31.9%	68.1%
28,610	DEL NORTE	8,770	4,614	3,791	365	823 R	52.6%	43.2%	54.9%	45.1%
181,058	EL DORADO	88,774	50,973	35,166	2,635	15,807 R	57.4%	39.6%	59.2%	40.8%
930,450	FRESNO	258,827	124,490	129,129	5,208	4,639 D	48.1%	49.9%	49.1%	50.9%
28,122	GLENN	9,211	5,632	3,301	278	2,331 R	61.1%	35.8%	63.0%	37.0%
134,623	HUMBOLDT	57,470	18,825	34,457	4,188	15,632 D	32.8%	60.0%	35.3%	64.7%
174,528	IMPERIAL	38,565	12,777	25,136	652	12,359 D	33.1%	65.2%	33.7%	66.3%
18,546	INYO	8,036	4,340	3,422	274	918 R	54.0%	42.6%	55.9%	44.1%
839,631	KERN	221,472	126,618	89,495	5,359	37,123 R	57.2%	40.4%	58.6%	41.4%
152,982	KINGS	31,418	17,671	12,979	768	4,692 R	56.2%	41.3%	57.7%	42.3%
64,665	LAKE	23,391	9,200	13,163	1,028	3,963 D	39.3%	56.3%	41.1%	58.9%
34,895	LASSEN	10,683	7,296	3,053	334	4,243 R	68.3%	28.6%	70.5%	29.5%
9,818,605	LOS ANGELES	3,181,067	885,333	2,216,903	78,831	1,331,570 D	27.8%	69.7%	28.5%	71.5%
150,865	MADERA	39,866	22,852	16,018	996	6,834 R	57.3%	40.2%	58.8%	41.2%
252,409	MARIN	134,516	30,880	99,896	3,740	69,016 D	23.0%	74.3%	23.6%	76.4%
18,251	MARIPOSA	9,000	5,140	3,498	362	1,642 R	57.1%	38.9%	59.5%	40.5%
87,841	MENDOCINO	35,017	9,658	23,193	2,166	13,535 D	27.6%	66.2%	29.4%	70.6%
255,793	MERCED	62,057	27,581	33,005	1,471	5,424 D	44.4%	53.2%	45.5%	54.5%
9,686	MODOC	3,986	2,777	1,111	98	1,666 R	69.7%	27.9%	71.4%	28.6%
14,202	MONO	5,181	2,285	2,733	163	448 D	44.1%	52.8%	45.5%	54.5%
415,057	MONTEREY	123,518	37,390	82,920	3,208	45,530 D	30.3%	67.1%	31.1%	68.9%
136,484	NAPA	56,968	19,526	35,870	1,572	16,344 D	34.3%	63.0%	35.2%	64.8%
98,764	NEVADA	51,676	24,986	24,663	2,027	323 R	48.4%	47.7%	50.3%	49.7%
3,010,232	ORANGE	1,122,664	582,332	512,440	27,892	69,892 R	51.9%	45.6%	53.2%	46.8%
348,432	PLACER	171,322	99,921	66,818	4,583	33,103 R	58.3%	39.0%	59.9%	40.1%
20,007	PLUMAS	10,047	5,721	4,026	300	1,695 R	56.9%	40.1%	58.7%	41.3%
2,189,641	RIVERSIDE	661,907	318,127	329,063	14,717	10,936 D	48.1%	49.7%	49.2%	50.8%
1,418,788	SACRAMENTO	516,809	202,514	300,503	13,792	97,989 D	39.2%	58.1%	40.3%	59.7%
55,269	SAN BENITO	19,044	7,343	11,276	425	3,933 D	38.6%	59.2%	39.4%	60.6%
2,035,210	SAN BERNARDINO	581,517	262,358	305,109	14,050	42,751 D	45.1%	52.5%	46.2%	53.8%
3,095,313	SAN DIEGO	1,192,282	536,726	626,957	28,599	90,231 D	45.0%	52.6%	46.1%	53.9%
805,235	SAN FRANCISCO	361,209	47,076	301,723	12,410	254,647 D	13.0%	83.5%	13.5%	86.5%
685,306	SAN JOAQUIN	204,697	86,071	114,121	4,505	28,050 D	42.0%	55.8%	43.0%	57.0%
269,637	SAN LUIS OBISPO	125,638	59,967	61,258	4,413	1,291 D	47.7%	48.8%	49.5%	50.5%
718,451	SAN MATEO	285,720	72,756	206,085	6,879	133,329 D	25.5%	72.1%	26.1%	73.9%
423,895	SANTA BARBARA	163,320	64,606	94,129	4,585	29,523 D	39.6%	57.6%	40.7%	59.3%
1,781,642	SANTA CLARA	643,091	174,843	450,818	17,430	275,975 D	27.2%	70.1%	27.9%	72.1%
262,382	SANTA CRUZ	120,095	24,047	90,805	5,243	66,758 D	20.0%	75.6%	20.9%	79.1%
177,223	SHASTA	76,335	48,067	25,819	2,449	22,248 R	63.0%	33.8%	65.1%	34.9%
3,240	SIERRA	1,795	1,056	653	86	403 R	58.8%	36.4%	61.8%	38.2%
44,900	SISKIYOU	19,910	11,077	8,046	787	3,031 R	55.6%	40.4%	57.9%	42.1%
413,344	SOLANO	152,444	52,092	96,783	3,569	44,691 D	34.2%	63.5%	35.0%	65.0%
483,878	SONOMA	216,508	54,784	153,942	7,782	99,158 D	25.3%	71.1%	26.2%	73.8%
514,453	STANISLAUS	155,369	73,459	77,724	4,186	4,265 D	47.3%	50.0%	48.6%	51.4%
94,737	SUTTER	31,026	18,122	12,192	712	5,930 R	58.4%	39.3%	59.8%	40.2%
63,463	TEHAMA	22,977	14,235	7,934	808	6,301 R	62.0%	34.5%	64.2%	35.8%
13,786	TRINITY	5,674	2,716	2,674	284	42 R	47.9%	47.1%	50.4%	49.6%
442,179	TULARE	101,100	56,956	41,752	2,392	15,204 R	56.3%	41.3%	57.7%	42.3%
55,365	TUOLUMNE	24,687	13,880	9,998	809	3,882 R	56.2%	40.5%	58.1%	41.9%
823,318	VENTURA	326,974	147,958	170,929	8,087	22,971 D	45.3%	52.3%	46.4%	53.6%
200,849	YOLO	74,475	23,368	48,715	2,392	25,347 D	31.4%	65.4%	32.4%	67.6%
72,155	YUBA	19,700	11,275	7,711	714	3,564 R	57.2%	39.1%	59.4%	40.6%
37,253,956	TOTAL	13,038,547	4,839,958	7,854,285	344,304	3,014,327 D	37.1%	60.2%	38.1%	61.9%

CALIFORNIA
SENATOR 2012

2010 Census Population	County	Total Vote	Republican (Emken)	Democratic (Feinstein)	Other	Rep.-Dem. Plurality		Percentage Total Vote Rep.	Dem.	Major Vote Rep.	Dem.
1,510,271	ALAMEDA	571,769	103,313	468,456		365,143	D	18.1%	81.9%	18.1%	81.9%
1,175	ALPINE	638	229	409		180	D	35.9%	64.1%	35.9%	64.1%
38,091	AMADOR	17,283	10,232	7,051		3,181	R	59.2%	40.8%	59.2%	40.8%
220,000	BUTTE	88,662	44,981	43,681		1,300	R	50.7%	49.3%	50.7%	49.3%
45,578	CALAVERAS	21,357	12,479	8,878		3,601	R	58.4%	41.6%	58.4%	41.6%
21,419	COLUSA	5,735	3,253	2,482		771	R	56.7%	43.3%	56.7%	43.3%
1,049,025	CONTRA COSTA	428,504	128,310	300,194		171,884	D	29.9%	70.1%	29.9%	70.1%
28,610	DEL NORTE	8,567	4,502	4,065		437	R	52.6%	47.4%	52.6%	47.4%
181,058	EL DORADO	86,596	50,820	35,776		15,044	R	58.7%	41.3%	58.7%	41.3%
930,450	FRESNO	252,766	123,499	129,267		5,768	D	48.9%	51.1%	48.9%	51.1%
28,122	GLENN	9,035	5,515	3,520		1,995	R	61.0%	39.0%	61.0%	39.0%
134,623	HUMBOLDT	55,599	19,437	36,162		16,725	D	35.0%	65.0%	35.0%	65.0%
174,528	IMPERIAL	37,688	12,346	25,342		12,996	D	32.8%	67.2%	32.8%	67.2%
18,546	INYO	7,827	4,494	3,333		1,161	R	57.4%	42.6%	57.4%	42.6%
839,631	KERN	218,158	125,906	92,252		33,654	R	57.7%	42.3%	57.7%	42.3%
152,982	KINGS	31,220	17,916	13,304		4,612	R	57.4%	42.6%	57.4%	42.6%
64,665	LAKE	22,967	9,424	13,543		4,119	D	41.0%	59.0%	41.0%	59.0%
34,895	LASSEN	10,540	7,390	3,150		4,240	R	70.1%	29.9%	70.1%	29.9%
9,818,605	LOS ANGELES	3,052,578	868,924	2,183,654		1,314,730	D	28.5%	71.5%	28.5%	71.5%
150,865	MADERA	38,939	22,942	15,997		6,945	R	58.9%	41.1%	58.9%	41.1%
252,409	MARIN	131,258	26,105	105,153		79,048	D	19.9%	80.1%	19.9%	80.1%
18,251	MARIPOSA	8,819	5,268	3,551		1,717	R	59.7%	40.3%	59.7%	40.3%
87,841	MENDOCINO	34,478	10,224	24,254		14,030	D	29.7%	70.3%	29.7%	70.3%
255,793	MERCED	59,955	27,000	32,955		5,955	D	45.0%	55.0%	45.0%	55.0%
9,686	MODOC	3,949	2,761	1,188		1,573	R	69.9%	30.1%	69.9%	30.1%
14,202	MONO	5,004	2,404	2,600		196	D	48.0%	52.0%	48.0%	52.0%
415,057	MONTEREY	121,515	36,930	84,585		47,655	D	30.4%	69.6%	30.4%	69.6%
136,484	NAPA	55,804	18,682	37,122		18,440	D	33.5%	66.5%	33.5%	66.5%
98,764	NEVADA	50,573	25,078	25,495		417	D	49.6%	50.4%	49.6%	50.4%
3,010,232	ORANGE	1,086,476	570,574	515,902		54,672	R	52.5%	47.5%	52.5%	47.5%
348,432	PLACER	165,738	97,139	68,599		28,540	R	58.6%	41.4%	58.6%	41.4%
20,007	PLUMAS	9,722	5,560	4,162		1,398	R	57.2%	42.8%	57.2%	42.8%
2,189,641	RIVERSIDE	631,349	303,651	327,698		24,047	D	48.1%	51.9%	48.1%	51.9%
1,418,788	SACRAMENTO	497,490	195,412	302,078		106,666	D	39.3%	60.7%	39.3%	60.7%
55,269	SAN BENITO	18,644	7,255	11,389		4,134	D	38.9%	61.1%	38.9%	61.1%
2,035,210	SAN BERNARDINO	551,500	253,433	298,067		44,634	D	46.0%	54.0%	46.0%	54.0%
3,095,313	SAN DIEGO	1,144,665	521,884	622,781		100,897	D	45.6%	54.4%	45.6%	54.4%
805,235	SAN FRANCISCO	344,715	39,589	305,126		265,537	D	11.5%	88.5%	11.5%	88.5%
685,306	SAN JOAQUIN	199,493	85,787	113,706		27,919	D	43.0%	57.0%	43.0%	57.0%
269,637	SAN LUIS OBISPO	122,478	60,262	62,216		1,954	D	49.2%	50.8%	49.2%	50.8%
718,451	SAN MATEO	276,482	62,979	213,503		150,524	D	22.8%	77.2%	22.8%	77.2%
423,895	SANTA BARBARA	157,520	63,599	93,921		30,322	D	40.4%	59.6%	40.4%	59.6%
1,781,642	SANTA CLARA	623,369	168,722	454,647		285,925	D	27.1%	72.9%	27.1%	72.9%
262,382	SANTA CRUZ	116,572	25,463	91,109		65,646	D	21.8%	78.2%	21.8%	78.2%
177,223	SHASTA	74,339	47,184	27,155		20,029	R	63.5%	36.5%	63.5%	36.5%
3,240	SIERRA	1,755	1,078	677		401	R	61.4%	38.6%	61.4%	38.6%
44,900	SISKIYOU	19,530	11,334	8,196		3,138	R	58.0%	42.0%	58.0%	42.0%
413,344	SOLANO	148,885	50,634	98,251		47,617	D	34.0%	66.0%	34.0%	66.0%
483,878	SONOMA	210,148	55,256	154,892		99,636	D	26.3%	73.7%	26.3%	73.7%
514,453	STANISLAUS	151,530	73,060	78,470		5,410	D	48.2%	51.8%	48.2%	51.8%
94,737	SUTTER	30,110	17,715	12,395		5,320	R	58.8%	41.2%	58.8%	41.2%
63,463	TEHAMA	22,590	14,241	8,349		5,892	R	63.0%	37.0%	63.0%	37.0%
13,786	TRINITY	5,601	2,943	2,658		285	R	52.5%	47.5%	52.5%	47.5%
442,179	TULARE	98,894	56,499	42,395		14,104	R	57.1%	42.9%	57.1%	42.9%
55,365	TUOLUMNE	24,159	13,823	10,336		3,487	R	57.2%	42.8%	57.2%	42.8%
823,318	VENTURA	315,086	143,603	171,483		27,880	D	45.6%	54.4%	45.6%	54.4%
200,849	YOLO	72,616	23,468	49,148		25,680	D	32.3%	67.7%	32.3%	67.7%
72,155	YUBA	19,272	11,376	7,896		3,480	R	59.0%	41.0%	59.0%	41.0%
37,253,956	TOTAL	12,578,511	4,713,887	7,864,624		3,150,737	D	37.5%	62.5%	37.5%	62.5%

CALIFORNIA

HOUSE OF REPRESENTATIVES

CD	Year	Total Vote	Republican Vote	Republican Candidate	Democratic Vote	Democratic Candidate	Other Vote	Rep.-Dem. Plurality	Total Vote Rep.	Total Vote Dem.	Major Vote Rep.	Major Vote Dem.
1	2012	294,213	168,827	LAMALFA, DOUG	125,386	REED, JIM		43,441 R	57.4%	42.6%	57.4%	42.6%
2	2012	317,526	91,310	ROBERTS, DANIEL W.	226,216	HUFFMAN, JARED		134,906 D	28.8%	71.2%	28.8%	71.2%
3	2012	233,968	107,086	VANN, KIM	126,882	GARAMENDI, JOHN*		19,796 D	45.8%	54.2%	45.8%	54.2%
4	2012	323,688	197,803	MCCLINTOCK, TOM*	125,885	UPPAL, JACK		71,918 R	61.1%	38.9%	61.1%	38.9%
5	2012	272,417	69,545	LOFTIN, RANDY	202,872	THOMPSON, MIKE*		133,327 D	25.5%	74.5%	25.5%	74.5%
6	2012	214,073	53,406	MCCRAY, JOSEPH SR.	160,667	MATSUI, DORIS*		107,261 D	24.9%	75.1%	24.9%	75.1%
7	2012	273,291	132,050	LUNGREN, DAN*	141,241	BERA, AMI		9,191 D	48.3%	51.7%	48.3%	51.7%
8	2012	179,644	103,093	COOK, PAUL			76,551	103,093 R	57.4%		100.0%	
9	2012	213,077	94,704	GILL, RICKY	118,373	MCNERNEY, JERRY*		23,669 D	44.4%	55.6%	44.4%	55.6%
10	2012	209,199	110,265	DENHAM, JEFF*	98,934	HERNANDEZ, JOSE		11,331 R	52.7%	47.3%	52.7%	47.3%
11	2012	287,879	87,136	FULLER, VIRGINIA	200,743	MILLER, GEORGE*		113,607 D	30.3%	69.7%	30.3%	69.7%
12	2012	298,187	44,478	DENNIS, JOHN	253,709	PELOSI, NANCY*		209,231 D	14.9%	85.1%	14.9%	85.1%
13	2012	288,582			250,436	LEE, BARBARA*	38,146	250,436 D		86.8%		100.0%
14	2012	258,283	54,455	BACIGALUPI, DEBORAH "DEBBIE"	203,828	SPEIER, JACKIE*		149,373 D	21.1%	78.9%	21.1%	78.9%
15	2012	231,034			120,388	SWALWELL, ERIC	110,646	120,388 D		52.1%		100.0%
16	2012	147,450	62,801	WHELAN, BRIAN DANIEL	84,649	COSTA, JIM*		21,848 D	42.6%	57.4%	42.6%	57.4%
17	2012	216,728	57,336	LI, EVELYN	159,392	HONDA, MIKE*		102,056 D	26.5%	73.5%	26.5%	73.5%
18	2012	301,934	89,103	CHAPMAN, DAVE	212,831	ESHOO, ANNA G.*		123,728 D	29.5%	70.5%	29.5%	70.5%
19	2012	221,613	59,313	MURRAY, ROBERT	162,300	LOFGREN, ZOE*		102,987 D	26.8%	73.2%	26.8%	73.2%
20	2012	233,562	60,566	TAYLOR, JEFF	172,996	FARR, SAM*		112,430 D	25.9%	74.1%	25.9%	74.1%
21	2012	116,283	67,164	VALADAO, DAVID	49,119	HERNANDEZ, JOHN		18,045 R	57.8%	42.2%	57.8%	42.2%
22	2012	213,941	132,386	NUNES, DEVIN*	81,555	LEE, OTTO		50,831 R	61.9%	38.1%	61.9%	38.1%
23	2012	216,003	158,161	MCCARTHY, KEVIN*			57,842	132,386 R	73.2%		100.0%	
24	2012	284,495	127,746	MALDONADO, ABEL	156,749	CAPPS, LOIS*		29,003 D	44.9%	55.1%	44.9%	55.1%
25	2012	236,575	129,593	MCKEON, HOWARD P. "BUCK"*	106,982	ROGERS, LEE C.		22,611 R	54.8%	45.2%	54.8%	45.2%
26	2012	263,935	124,863	STRICKLAND, TONY	139,072	BROWNLEY, JULIA		14,209 D	47.3%	52.7%	47.3%	52.7%
27	2012	241,008	86,817	ORSWELL, JACK	154,191	CHU, JUDY*		67,374 D	36.0%	64.0%	36.0%	64.0%
28	2012	246,711	58,008	JENNERJAHN, PHIL	188,703	SCHIFF, ADAM B.*		130,695 D	23.5%	76.5%	23.5%	76.5%
29	2012	150,281			111,287	CARDENAS, TONY	38,994	111,287 D		74.1%		100.0%
30	2012	247,851			149,456	SHERMAN, BRAD	98,395	149,456 D		60.3%		100.0%
31	2012	161,219	88,964	MILLER, GARY*			72,255	88,964 R	55.2%		100.0%	
32	2012	190,111	65,208	MILLER, DAVID L.	124,903	NAPOLITANO, GRACE FLORES*		59,695 D	34.3%	65.7%	34.3%	65.7%
33	2012	318,520			171,860	WAXMAN, HENRY A.*	146,660	171,860 D		54.0%		100.0%
34	2012	140,590	20,223	SMITH, STEPHEN	120,367	BECERRA, XAVIER*		100,144 D	14.4%	85.6%	14.4%	85.6%
35	2012	142,680			79,698	MCLEOD, GLORIA NEGRETE	62,982	79,698 D		55.9%		100.0%
36	2012	208,142	97,953	BONO MACK, MARY*	110,189	RUIZ, RAUL		12,236 D	47.1%	52.9%	47.1%	52.9%
37	2012	239,580	32,541	OSBORNE, MORGAN	207,039	BASS, KAREN*		174,498 D	13.6%	86.4%	13.6%	86.4%
38	2012	215,087	69,807	CAMPOS, BENJAMIN	145,280	SÁNCHEZ, LINDA T.*		75,473 D	32.5%	67.5%	32.5%	67.5%
39	2012	251,967	145,607	ROYCE, ED*	106,360	CHEN, JAY		39,247 R	57.8%	42.2%	57.8%	42.2%
40	2012	125,553			73,940	ROYBAL-ALLARD, LUCILLE*	51,613	73,940 D		58.9%		100.0%
41	2012	175,652	72,074	TAVAGLIONE, JOHN	103,578	TAKANO, MARK		31,504 D	41.0%	59.0%	41.0%	59.0%
42	2012	214,947	130,245	CALVERT, KEN*	84,702	WILLIAMSON, MICHAEL		45,543 R	60.6%	39.4%	60.6%	39.4%
43	2012	200,894			143,123	WATERS, MAXINE*	57,771	143,123 D		71.2%		100.0%
44	2012	165,898			99,909	HAHN, JANICE	65,989	99,909 D		60.2%		100.0%
45	2012	293,231	171,417	CAMPBELL, JOHN*	121,814	KANG, SUKHEE		49,603 R	58.5%	41.5%	58.5%	41.5%
46	2012	149,815	54,121	HAYDEN, JERRY	95,694	SANCHEZ, LORETTA*		41,573 D	36.1%	63.9%	36.1%	63.9%
47	2012	230,012	99,919	DELONG, GARY	130,093	LOWENTHAL, ALAN		30,174 D	43.4%	56.6%	43.4%	56.6%
48	2012	290,502	177,144	ROHRABACHER, DANA*	113,358	VARASTEH, RON		63,786 R	61.0%	39.0%	61.0%	39.0%
49	2012	274,618	159,725	ISSA, DARRELL*	114,893	TETALMAN, JERRY		44,832 R	58.2%	41.8%	58.2%	41.8%
50	2012	258,293	174,838	HUNTER, DUNCAN D.*	83,455	SECOR, DAVID B.		91,383 R	67.7%	32.3%	67.7%	32.3%
51	2012	159,398	45,464	CRIMMINS, MICHAEL	113,934	VARGAS, JUAN		68,470 D	28.5%	71.5%	28.5%	71.5%
52	2012	295,910	144,459	BILBRAY, BRIAN P.*	151,451	PETERS, SCOTT		6,992 D	48.8%	51.2%	48.8%	51.2%
53	2012	268,307	103,482	POPADITCH, NICK	164,825	DAVIS, SUSAN*		61,343 D	38.6%	61.4%	38.6%	61.4%
TOTAL	2012	12,204,357	4,381,206		6,945,307		877,844	2,564,101 D	35.9%	56.9%	38.7%	61.3%

Notes: An asterisk (*) denotes incumbent. Due to California's all-party primary, which qualifies the top two vote-getters for the general election, the general election in many districts pitted two Democrats or two Republicans. Two Republicans in two districts: 8th district, second place was Gregg Imus. Two Democrats: 15th district, second place was Fortney Pete Stark; 30th district, second place was Howard L. Berman; 35th district, second place was Joe Baca; 40th district, second place was David Sanchez; 43rd district, second place was Bob Flores; 44th district, second place was Laura Richardson. When this happened, the second place same-party candidate is included in the Other Vote in the table above; only the top vote-getter from either party is used to calculate the plurality, total vote, and major vote. Because there are two candidates only in the general election, the other vote is exactly the total of the second place finisher. The second place vote-getter in the following districts was a third party candidate: 13th, 23rd, 29th, 33rd. See General Elections: Other Votes for their names and vote totals. In addition, due to redistricting, some of these races pitted two incumbents: the 30th district (Berman v. Sherman) and 44th district (Hahn v. Richardson). The aggregate vote total for all Democratic candidates on the 2012 general election ballot was 7,392,703; for all Republican candidates, 4,530,012; for all Other candidates, 281,642. These totals are listed in the 2012 national vote table for the House of Representatives on page 4.

CALIFORNIA

GENERAL AND PRIMARY ELECTIONS

2012 GENERAL ELECTIONS: OTHER VOTE

President Other vote was 143,221 Libertarian (Gary E. Johnson), 85,638 Green (Jill Stein), 53,824 Peace and Freedom (Roseanne Barr), 38,372 American Independent (Thomas Hoefling), 21,461 Write-in (Ron Paul), 1,285 Write-in (Scattered Write-In), 503 Constitution (Virgil H. Goode)

Senator Due to California's primary system, only two candidates were in the Senate race.

House Other vote was:

CD 13 38,146 No Party Affiliation (Marilyn Singleton)
CD 23 57,842 No Party Affiliation (Terry Phillips)
CD 29 38,994 No Party Affiliation (David R. Hernandez)
CD 33 146,660 No Party Affiliation (Bill Bloomfield)

2012 PRIMARY ELECTIONS: SUPPLEMENTARY INFORMATION

Primary June 5, 2012 **Registration** (as of May 21, 2012) 12,153,699 No Party Registration

Primary Type Open—Any registered voter could participate in the primary.

REPUBLICAN PRIMARIES

President			
Romney, W. Mitt	1,530,513	79.5%
Paul, Ron	199,246	10.4%
Santorum, Rick	102,258	5.3%
Gingrich, Newt	72,022	3.7%
Roemer, Charles	12,520	0.7%
Karger, Fred	8,393	0.4%
Hannon, Jeremy	11	
Gonzales, Donald James	5	
Howard, Sheldon Yeu	2	
TOTAL	1,924,970	

DEMOCRATIC PRIMARIES

President		
Obama, Barack H.*	2,075,905	100.0%
Richardson, Darcy	221	
Meyer, Michael W.R. Jr.	129	
Ramos, Luis Alberto Jr.	54	
TOTAL	2,076,309	

ALL-PARTY PRIMARIES

Senator		
Feinstein, Dianne* (Democrat)	2,392,822	49.3%
Emken, Elizabeth (Republican)	613,613	12.6%
Hughes, Dan (Republican)	323,840	6.7%
Williams, Rick (Republican)	157,946	3.3%
Taitz, Orly (Democrat)	154,781	3.2%
Jackson, Dennis (Republican)	137,120	2.8%
Conlon, Greg (Republican)	135,421	2.8%
Ramirez, Al (Republican)	109,399	2.3%
Lightfoot, Gail K. (Libertarian)	101,648	2.1%
Stewart, Diane (Democrat)	97,782	2.0%
Strimling, Michael (Democrat)	97,024	2.0%
Levitt, David Alex (Democrat)	76,482	1.6%
Braun, Oscar Alejandro (Republican)	75,842	1.6%
Feinland, Marsha (Peace and Freedom)	57,720	1.2%
Lauten, Robert (Republican)	56,524	1.2%
Fernald, Colleen (Democrat)	51,623	1.1%
Krampe, Donald (Republican)	39,035	0.8%
Grundmann, Don J. (American Independent)	33,037	0.7%
Konopik, Dirk Allen (Republican)	29,997	0.6%
Boruff, John (Republican)	29,357	0.6%
Shah, Nak (Democrat)	27,203	0.6%
Gloria, Rogelio T. (Republican)	22,529	0.5%
Shifren, Nachum (Republican)	21,762	0.4%
Ali, Kabiruddin Karim (Peace and Freedom)	12,269	0.3%
Price, Linda R. (Write-in)	25	
TOTAL	4,854,801	

CALIFORNIA

GENERAL AND PRIMARY ELECTIONS

ALL-PARTY PRIMARIES

Congressional District 1	LaMalfa, Doug (Republican)	66,527	37.9%
	Reed, Jim (Democrat)	43,409	24.8%
	Aanestad, Sam (Republican)	25,224	14.4%
	Dacquisto, Michael (Republican)	10,530	6.0%
	Stiglich, Pete (Republican)	10,258	5.8%
	Arrowsmith, Nathan L. (Democrat)	8,598	4.9%
	Oxley, Gary Allen (No Party)	5,901	3.4%
	Cheadle, Gregory (Republican)	4,939	2.8%
	TOTAL	*175,386*	
Congressional District 2	Huffman, Jared (Democrat)	63,922	37.5%
	Roberts, Daniel W. (Republican)	25,635	15.0%
	Solomon, Norman (Democrat)	25,462	14.9%
	Lawson, Stacey (Democrat)	16,946	9.9%
	Adams, Susan L. (Democrat)	14,041	8.2%
	Halliwell, Michael (Republican)	10,008	5.9%
	Clarke, Brooke (No Party)	3,715	2.2%
	Renée, Tiffany (Democrat)	3,033	1.8%
	Lewallen, John (No Party)	2,488	1.5%
	Courtney, William L. (Democrat)	2,385	1.4%
	Caffrey, Andy (Democrat)	1,737	1.0%
	Fritzlan, Larry (Democrat)	1,151	0.7%
	TOTAL	*170,523*	
Congressional District 3	Garamendi, John* (Democrat)	59,546	51.5%
	Vann, Kim (Republican)	30,254	26.2%
	Tubbs, Rick (Republican)	17,902	15.5%
	Carlos, Tony (Republican)	5,541	4.8%
	Ray, Eugene (Republican)	2,438	2.1%
	TOTAL	*115,681*	
Congressional District 4	McClintock, Tom* (Republican)	114,311	64.8%
	Uppal, Jack (Democrat)	62,130	35.2%
	TOTAL	*176,441*	
Congressional District 5	Thompson, Mike* (Democrat)	95,748	72.2%
	Loftin, Randy (Republican)	22,137	16.7%
	Cilley, Stewart John (Republican)	14,734	11.1%
	TOTAL	*132,619*	
Congressional District 6	Matsui, Doris* (Democrat)	67,174	71.4%
	McCray, Joseph Sr. (Republican)	15,647	16.6%
	Smitt, Erik (Republican)	11,254	12.0%
	TOTAL	*94,075*	
Congressional District 7	Lungren, Dan* (Republican)	63,586	52.7%
	Bera, Ami (Democrat)	49,433	41.0%
	Taras, Curt (No Party)	3,854	3.2%
	Tuma, Douglas Arthur (Libertarian)	3,707	3.1%
	TOTAL	*120,580*	
Congressional District 8	Imus, Gregg (Republican)	12,754	15.6%
	Cook, Paul (Republican)	12,517	15.3%
	Liberatore, Phil (Republican)	12,277	15.0%
	Conaway, Jackie (Democrat)	11,674	14.3%
	Mitzelfelt, Brad (Republican)	8,801	10.8%
	Pinkerton, John (Democrat)	7,941	9.7%
	Valles, Angela (Republican)	4,924	6.0%
	McEachron, Ryan (Republican)	3,181	3.9%
	Adams, Anthony (No Party)	2,750	3.4%
	Jensen, Bill (Republican)	1,850	2.3%
	Craig, George (Republican)	1,376	1.7%
	Napolitano, Joseph D. (Republican)	1,050	1.3%
	Albertsen, Dennis L. (Republican)	761	0.9%
	TOTAL	*81,856*	

CALIFORNIA

GENERAL AND PRIMARY ELECTIONS

ALL-PARTY PRIMARIES

Congressional District 9	McNerney, Jerry* (Democrat)	45,696	47.8%
	Gill, Ricky (Republican)	38,488	40.2%
	McDonald, John (Republican)	11,458	12.0%
	TOTAL	95,642	
Congressional District 10	Denham, Jeff* (Republican)	45,779	49.2%
	Hernandez, Jose (Democrat)	26,072	28.0%
	Condit, Chad M. (No Party)	13,983	15.0%
	Barkley, Michael "Mike" (Democrat)	5,028	5.4%
	McComak, Troy Wayne (No Party)	2,114	2.3%
	TOTAL	92,976	
Congressional District 11	Miller, George* (Democrat)	76,163	58.5%
	Fuller, Virginia (Republican)	40,333	31.0%
	Fitzgerald, John (Democrat)	9,092	7.0%
	Sudduth, Cheryl (Democrat)	4,635	3.6%
	TOTAL	130,223	
Congressional District 12	Pelosi, Nancy* (Democrat)	89,446	74.9%
	Dennis, John (Republican)	16,206	13.6%
	Hermanson, Barry (Green)	6,398	5.4%
	Peterson, David (Democrat)	3,756	3.1%
	Shields, Summer Justice (Democrat)	2,146	1.8%
	Diaz, Américo Arturo (Democrat)	1,499	1.3%
	TOTAL	119,451	
Congressional District 13	Lee, Barbara* (Democrat)	94,709	83.1%
	Singleton, Marilyn (No Party Affiliation)	13,502	11.8%
	Jelincic, Justin (Democrat)	5,741	5.0%
	TOTAL	113,952	
Congressional District 14	Speier, Jackie* (Democrat)	80,850	74.3%
	Bacigalupi, Deborah "Debbie" (Republican)	23,299	21.4%
	Moloney, Mike (Democrat)	4,607	4.2%
	TOTAL	108,756	
Congressional District 15	Stark, Fortney Pete* (Democrat)	39,943	42.1%
	Swalwell, Eric (Democrat)	34,347	36.2%
	Pareja, Christopher J. "Chris" (No Party)	20,618	21.7%
	TOTAL	94,908	
Congressional District 16	Costa, Jim* (Democrat)	25,355	42.7%
	Whelan, Brian Daniel (Republican)	15,053	25.3%
	Tacherra, Johnny M. (Republican)	6,776	11.4%
	Garcia, Mark (Republican)	6,529	11.0%
	Goodwin, Loraine (Democrat)	5,703	9.6%
	TOTAL	59,416	
Congressional District 17	Honda, Mike* (Democrat)	60,252	66.7%
	Li, Evelyn (Republican)	24,916	27.6%
	Richardson, Charles (No Party)	5,163	5.7%
	TOTAL	90,331	
Congressional District 18	Eshoo, Anna G.* (Democrat)	86,851	61.5%
	Chapman, Dave (Republican)	42,174	29.8%
	Parks, William (Democrat)	6,504	4.6%
	Brouillet, Carol (Green)	5,777	4.1%
	TOTAL	141,306	
Congressional District 19	Lofgren, Zoe* (Democrat)	60,726	65.2%
	Murray, Robert (Republican)	21,421	23.0%
	Nguyen, Phat (Republican)	7,192	7.7%
	Cabrera, Jay Blas Jacob (No Party)	3,829	4.1%
	TOTAL	93,168	

CALIFORNIA

GENERAL AND PRIMARY ELECTIONS

ALL-PARTY PRIMARIES

Congressional District 20	Farr, Sam* (Democrat)	68,895	64.4%
	Taylor, Jeff (Republican)	23,905	22.3%
	LeBarre, Mike (Republican)	5,487	5.1%
	Dunn, Art (Democrat)	4,095	3.8%
	Petersen, Eric (Green)	2,211	2.1%
	Kabat, Ronald Paul (No Party)	1,733	1.6%
	Caudle, Dan (No Party)	703	0.7%
	TOTAL	107,029	
Congressional District 21	Valadao, David (Republican)	27,251	57.0%
	Hernandez, John (Democrat)	10,575	22.1%
	Xiong, Blong (Democrat)	9,990	20.9%
	TOTAL	47,816	
Congressional District 22	Nunes, Devin* (Republican)	67,386	70.6%
	Lee, Otto (Democrat)	28,091	29.4%
	TOTAL	95,477	
Congressional District 23	McCarthy, Kevin* (Republican)	71,109	72.2%
	Phillips, Terry (No Party Affiliation)	17,018	17.3%
	Parker, Eric (Republican)	10,414	10.6%
	TOTAL	98,541	
Congressional District 24	Capps, Lois* (Democrat)	72,356	46.4%
	Maldonado, Abel (Republican)	46,295	29.7%
	Mitchum, Chris (Republican)	33,604	21.5%
	Boutté, Matt (No Party)	3,832	2.5%
	TOTAL	156,087	
Congressional District 25	McKeon, Howard P. "Buck"* (Republican)	39,997	50.5%
	Rogers, Lee C. (Democrat)	23,542	29.7%
	Acosta, Dante (Republican)	10,387	13.1%
	Wright, Cathie (Republican)	5,215	6.6%
	TOTAL	79,141	
Congressional District 26	Strickland, Tony (Republican)	49,043	44.1%
	Brownley, Julia (Democrat)	29,892	26.9%
	Parks, Linda (No Party)	20,301	18.3%
	Herrera, Jess (Democrat)	7,244	6.5%
	Thayne, David Cruz (Democrat)	2,809	2.5%
	Goldberg, Albert Maxwell (Democrat)	1,880	1.7%
	TOTAL	111,169	
Congressional District 27	Chu, Judy* (Democrat)	50,203	57.8%
	Orswell, Jack (Republican)	20,868	24.0%
	Duran, Bob (Republican)	15,819	18.2%
	TOTAL	86,890	
Congressional District 28	Schiff, Adam B.* (Democrat)	42,797	59.0%
	Jennerjahn, Phil (Republican)	12,633	17.4%
	Worman, Jenny (Republican)	5,978	8.2%
	Mailyan, Garen (Republican)	3,749	5.2%
	Genovese, Sal (Democrat)	2,829	3.9%
	Munroe, Massie (Democrat)	2,437	3.4%
	Kalbfeld, Jonathan Ryan (Democrat)	2,119	2.9%
	TOTAL	72,542	
Congressional District 29	Cárdenas, Tony (Democrat)	24,882	64.4%
	Hernandez, David R. Jr. (No Party Affiliation)	8,382	21.7%
	Valdez, Richard A. (Democrat)	5,379	13.9%
	TOTAL	38,643	

CALIFORNIA

GENERAL AND PRIMARY ELECTIONS

ALL-PARTY PRIMARIES

Congressional District 30	Sherman, Brad* (Democrat)	40,589	42.4%
	Berman, Howard L.* (Democrat)	31,086	32.4%
	Reed, Mark (Republican)	11,991	12.5%
	Singh, Navraj (Republican)	5,521	5.8%
	Shelley, Susan (Republican)	3,878	4.0%
	Powelson, Michael W. (Green)	1,976	2.1%
	Gilmore, Vince (Democrat)	792	0.8%
	TOTAL	95,833	
Congressional District 31	Miller, Gary* (Republican)	16,708	26.7%
	Dutton, Robert (Republican)	15,557	24.8%
	Aguilar, Pete (Democrat)	14,181	22.6%
	Kim, Justin (Democrat)	8,487	13.5%
	Wickman, Renea (Democrat)	4,188	6.7%
	Ramirez-Dean, Rita (Democrat)	3,546	5.7%
	TOTAL	62,667	
Congressional District 32	Napolitano, Grace Flores* (Democrat)	24,094	46.1%
	Miller, David L. (Republican)	21,843	41.8%
	Gonzalez, G. Bill (Democrat)	6,322	12.1%
	TOTAL	52,259	
Congressional District 33	Waxman, Henry A.* (Democrat)	51,235	45.3%
	Bloomfield, Bill (No Party Affiliation)	27,850	24.6%
	David, Christopher (Republican)	17,264	15.3%
	Margolin, Bruce (Democrat)	5,020	4.4%
	Collet, Steve (Libertarian)	4,916	4.3%
	Steinman, David William (Green)	3,940	3.5%
	Obagi, Zein E. (Democrat)	1,988	1.8%
	Pape, Tim (Democrat)	847	0.7%
	TOTAL	113,060	
Congressional District 34	Becerra, Xavier* (Democrat)	27,939	77.3%
	Smith, Stephen (Republican)	5,793	16.0%
	Johnson, Howard (Other)	2,407	6.7%
	TOTAL	36,139	
Congressional District 35	Baca, Joe* (Democrat)	15,388	45.0%
	McLeod, Gloria Negrete (Democrat)	12,425	36.3%
	Vieyra, Anthony W. (Green)	6,372	18.6%
	TOTAL	34,185	
Congressional District 36	Bono Mack, Mary* (Republican)	52,474	58.1%
	Ruiz, Raul (Democrat)	37,847	41.9%
	TOTAL	90,321	
Congressional District 37	Bass, Karen* (Democrat)	54,345	99.9%
	Osborne, Morgan (Write-in)	36	0.1%
	Shbeita, Adam (Write-in)	8	
	McGary, Sean P. (Write-in)	4	
	TOTAL	54,393	
Congressional District 38	Sánchez, Linda T.* (Democrat)	33,223	56.0%
	Campos, Benjamin (Republican)	13,363	22.5%
	Robles, Jorge (Republican)	12,713	21.4%
	TOTAL	59,299	
Congressional District 39	Royce, Ed* (Republican)	62,874	66.3%
	Chen, Jay (Democrat)	28,457	30.0%
	Mulattieri, D'Marie (No Party)	3,561	3.8%
	TOTAL	94,892	
Congressional District 40	Roybal-Allard, Lucille* (Democrat)	16,596	65.4%
	Sanchez, David (Democrat)	8,777	34.6%
	TOTAL	25,373	

CALIFORNIA

GENERAL AND PRIMARY ELECTIONS

ALL-PARTY PRIMARIES

Congressional District 41	Tavaglione, John (Republican)	25,379	44.6%
	Takano, Mark (Democrat)	20,860	36.7%
	Nevenic, Anna (Democrat)	4,991	8.8%
	Sawyer, Vince (Republican)	4,723	8.3%
	Pearne, George (Republican)	956	1.7%
	TOTAL	56,909	
Congressional District 42	Calvert, Ken* (Republican)	35,392	51.3%
	Williamson, Michael (Democrat)	9,860	14.3%
	Smith, Cliff (Democrat)	7,377	10.7%
	Thibodeau, Clayton (Republican)	6,374	9.2%
	Johnson, Eva (Republican)	5,678	8.2%
	Novak, Curt (No Party)	4,254	6.2%
	TOTAL	68,935	
Congressional District 43	Waters, Maxine* (Democrat)	36,062	65.4%
	Flores, Bob (Democrat)	19,061	34.6%
	TOTAL	55,123	
Congressional District 44	Hahn, Janice* (Democrat)	24,843	60.1%
	Richardson, Laura* (Democrat)	16,523	39.9%
	TOTAL	41,366	
Congressional District 45	Campbell, John* (Republican)	54,346	51.0%
	Kang, Sukhee (Democrat)	35,182	33.0%
	Webb, John (Republican)	17,014	16.0%
	TOTAL	106,542	
Congressional District 46	Sanchez, Loretta* (Democrat)	25,706	52.1%
	Hayden, Jerry (Republican)	14,571	29.5%
	Cullum, John J. (Republican)	5,251	10.6%
	Rocha, Jorge (No Party)	1,969	4.0%
	Garcia, Pat (Republican)	1,852	3.8%
	TOTAL	49,349	
Congressional District 47	Lowenthal, Alan (Democrat)	27,356	33.8%
	DeLong, Gary (Republican)	23,831	29.4%
	Kuykendall, Steven (Republican)	8,769	10.8%
	Mathews, Peter (Democrat)	7,951	9.8%
	Foley, Steve (Republican)	5,848	7.2%
	Kahn, Sanford W. (Republican)	2,563	3.2%
	Shah, Usha (Democrat)	2,350	2.9%
	Shah, Jay A. (Democrat)	2,273	2.8%
	TOTAL	80,941	
Congressional District 48	Rohrabacher, Dana* (Republican)	73,302	66.3%
	Varasteh, Ron (Democrat)	31,912	28.9%
	Schlar, Alan (No Party)	5,355	4.8%
	TOTAL	110,569	
Congressional District 49	Issa, Darrell* (Republican)	71,329	61.1%
	Tetalman, Jerry (Democrat)	35,816	30.7%
	Eiden, Dick (No Party)	7,988	6.8%
	Novinec, Albin (No Party)	1,626	1.4%
	TOTAL	116,759	
Congressional District 50	Hunter, Duncan D.* (Republican)	76,818	67.4%
	Secor, David B. (Democrat)	19,142	16.8%
	Frankowiak, Connie (Democrat)	8,553	7.5%
	Benoit, Michael (Libertarian)	6,160	5.4%
	Linnell, Terri R. (Republican)	3,275	2.9%
	TOTAL	113,948	

CALIFORNIA

GENERAL AND PRIMARY ELECTIONS

ALL-PARTY PRIMARIES

Congressional District 51	Vargas, Juan (Democrat)	30,143	46.0%
	Crimmins, Michael (Republican)	13,016	19.9%
	Ducheny, Denise Moreno (Democrat)	10,107	15.4%
	Gionis, Xanthi (Republican)	4,487	6.8%
	Brooks, John (Democrat)	3,290	5.0%
	Ramirez, Daniel C. "Danny" (Democrat)	2,794	4.3%
	Portley, Bernard (Republican)	1,667	2.5%
	TOTAL	*65,504*	
Congressional District 52	Bilbray, Brian P.* (Republican)	61,930	41.0%
	Peters, Scott (Democrat)	34,106	22.6%
	Saldaña, Lori (Democrat)	33,387	22.1%
	Doyle, Jack (No Party)	6,138	4.1%
	Stahl, John K. (Republican)	5,502	3.6%
	Iverson, Wayne (Republican)	4,476	3.0%
	Decourt-Park, Shirley (Democrat)	2,368	1.6%
	Shehata, Ehab T. (No Party)	1,156	0.8%
	Subka, John L. (Republican)	1,091	0.7%
	Carswell, Gene Hamilton (Republican)	828	0.5%
	TOTAL	*150,982*	
Congressional District 53	Davis, Susan* (Democrat)	70,462	57.8%
	Popaditch, Nick (Republican)	51,423	42.2%
	Marchese, Joel A. (Write-in)	7	
	Edwards, John R. (Write-in)	3	
	TOTAL	*121,895*	

Notes: An asterisk (*) denotes incumbent. California held an all-party primary, in which candidates of all parties ran together on a single ballot. The top two vote-getters, regardless of party, advanced to the November general election. Candidates identified themselves on the ballot as "preferring" a particular party (or independent, non-party status), whether or not they were a member of that party or were supported by that party.

COLORADO

Congressional districts first established for elections held in 2012

7 members

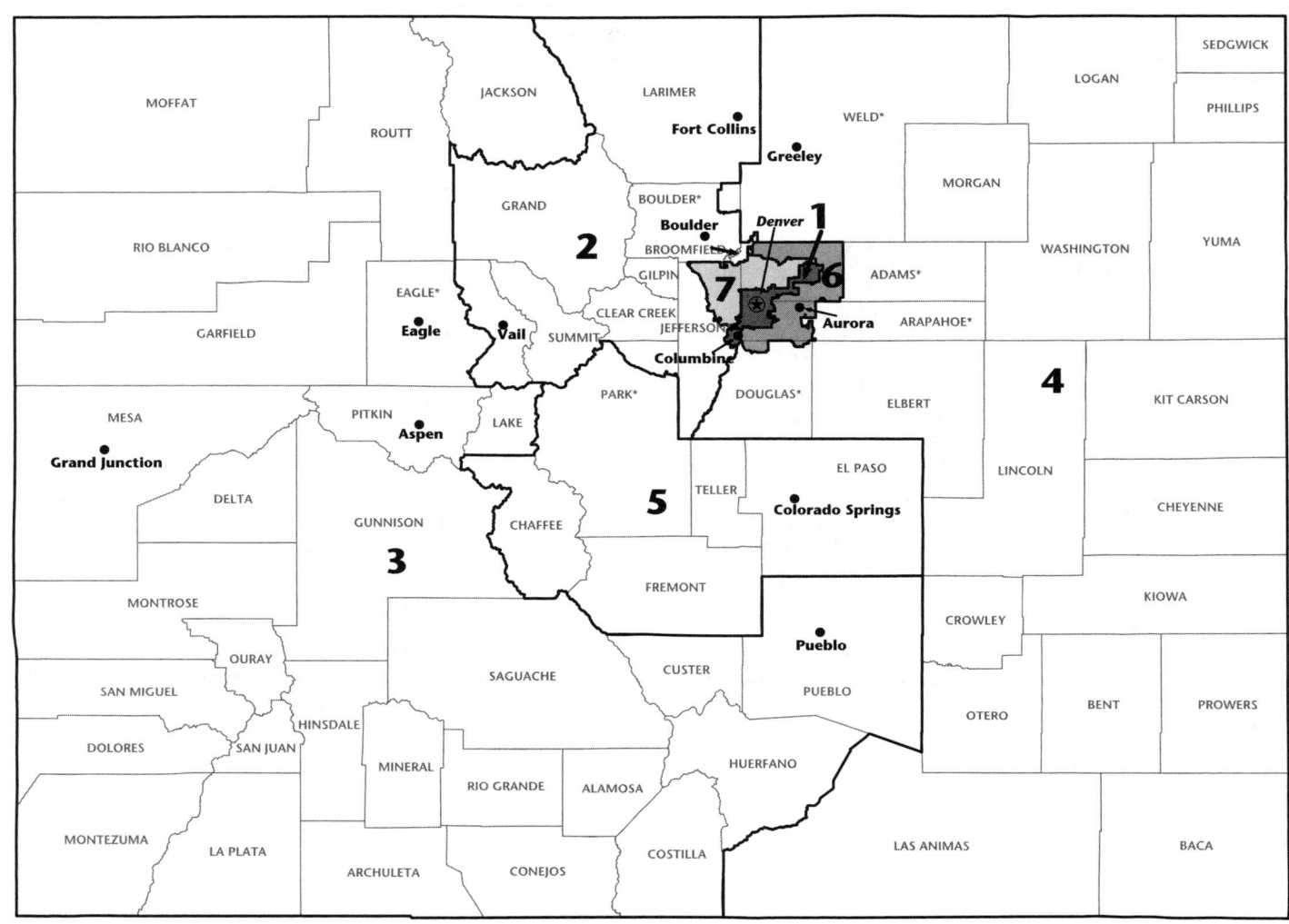

* Asterisk indicates a county whose boundaries include parts of two or more Congressional districts.

COLORADO
Denver Area

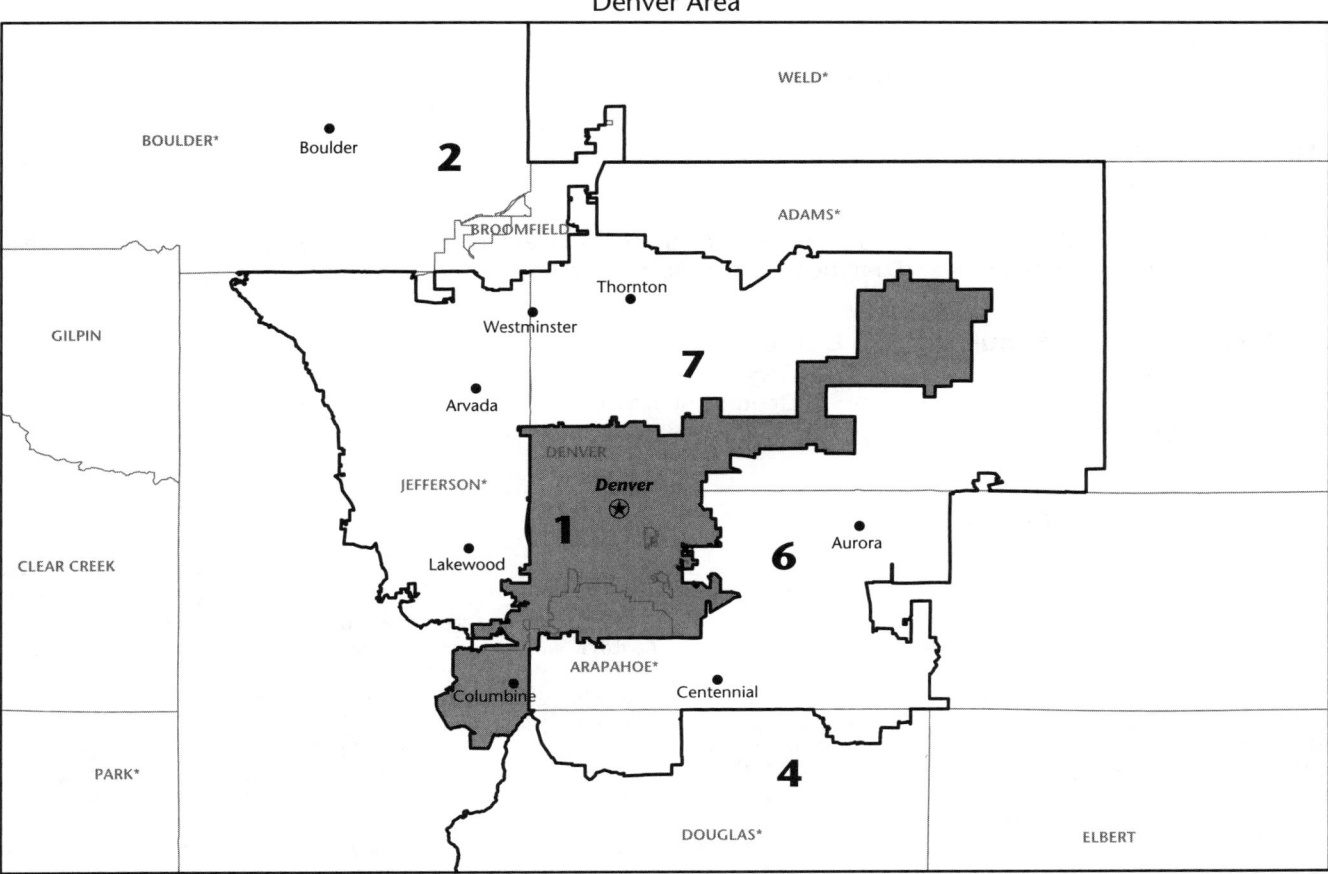

* Asterisk indicates a county whose boundaries include parts of two or more Congressional districts.

COLORADO

GOVERNOR
John Hickenlooper (D). Elected 2010 to a four-year term.

SENATORS (2 Democrats)
Mark Udall (D). Elected 2008 to a six-year term.

Michael F. Bennet (D). Elected 2010 to a six-year term. Sworn in as senator January 22, 2009, to fill the vacancy created by the resignation of Ken Salazar (D) to become U.S. Secretary of Interior.

REPRESENTATIVES (4 Republicans, 3 Democrats)
1. Diana DeGette (D)
2. Jared Polis (D)
3. Scott Tipton (R)
4. Cory Gardner (R)
5. Doug Lamborn (R)
6. Mike Coffman (R)
7. Ed Perlmutter (D)

POSTWAR VOTE FOR PRESIDENT

		Republican		Democratic				Total Vote		Major Vote	
Year	Total Vote	Vote	Candidate	Vote	Candidate	Other Vote	Rep.-Dem. Plurality	Rep.	Dem.	Rep.	Dem.
2012	2,569,522	1,185,243	Romney, W. Mitt	1,323,102	Obama, Barack H.*	61,177	137,859 D	46.1%	51.5%	47.3%	52.7%
2008	2,401,462	1,073,629	McCain, John S. III	1,288,633	Obama, Barack H.	39,200	215,004 D	44.7%	53.7%	45.4%	54.6%
2004	2,130,330	1,101,255	Bush, George W.*	1,001,732	Kerry, John F.	27,343	99,523 R	51.7%	47.0%	52.4%	47.6%
2000**	1,741,368	883,748	Bush, George W.	738,227	Gore, Albert Jr.	119,393	145,521 R	50.8%	42.4%	54.5%	45.5%
1996**	1,510,704	691,848	Dole, Robert "Bob"	671,152	Clinton, Bill*	147,704	20,696 R	45.8%	44.4%	50.8%	49.2%
1992**	1,569,180	562,850	Bush, George H.*	629,681	Clinton, Bill	376,649	66,831 D	35.9%	40.1%	47.2%	52.8%
1988	1,372,394	728,177	Bush, George H.	621,453	Dukakis, Michael S.	22,764	106,724 R	53.1%	45.3%	54.0%	46.0%
1984	1,295,380	821,817	Reagan, Ronald*	454,975	Mondale, Walter F.	18,588	366,842 R	63.4%	35.1%	64.4%	35.6%
1980**	1,184,415	652,264	Reagan, Ronald	367,973	Carter, Jimmy*	164,178	284,291 R	55.1%	31.1%	63.9%	36.1%
1976	1,081,554	584,367	Ford, Gerald R.*	460,353	Carter, Jimmy	36,834	124,014 R	54.0%	42.6%	55.9%	44.1%
1972	953,884	597,189	Nixon, Richard M.*	329,980	McGovern, George S.	26,715	267,209 R	62.6%	34.6%	64.4%	35.6%
1968**	811,199	409,345	Nixon, Richard M.	335,174	Humphrey, Hubert H. Jr.	66,680	74,171 R	50.5%	41.3%	55.0%	45.0%
1964	776,986	296,767	Goldwater, Barry M. Sr.	476,024	Johnson, Lyndon B.*	4,195	179,257 D	38.2%	61.3%	38.4%	61.6%
1960	736,236	402,242	Nixon, Richard M.	330,629	Kennedy, John F.	3,365	71,613 R	54.6%	44.9%	54.9%	45.1%
1956	657,074	394,479	Eisenhower, Dwight D.*	257,997	Stevenson, Adlai E. II	4,598	136,482 R	60.0%	39.3%	60.5%	39.5%
1952	630,103	379,782	Eisenhower, Dwight D.	245,504	Stevenson, Adlai E. II	4,817	134,278 R	60.3%	39.0%	60.7%	39.3%
1948	515,237	239,714	Dewey, Thomas E.	267,288	Truman, Harry S.*	8,235	27,574 D	46.5%	51.9%	47.3%	52.7%

Note: An asterisk (*) denotes incumbent. **In past elections, the other vote included: 2000 - 91,434 Green (Ralph Nader); 1996 - 99,629 Reform (Ross Perot); 1992 - 366,010 Independent (Perot); 1980 - 130,633 Independent (John Anderson); 1968 - 60,813 American Independent (George Wallace).

COLORADO

POSTWAR VOTE FOR GOVERNOR

| Year | Total Vote | Republican | | Democratic | | Other Vote | Rep.-Dem. Plurality | Percentage | | | |
| | | Vote | Candidate | Vote | Candidate | | | Total Vote | | Major Vote | |
								Rep.	Dem.	Rep.	Dem.
2010**	1,788,001	199,062	Maes, Dan	912,189	Hickenlooper, John	676,750	713,127 D	11.1%	51.0%	17.9%	82.1%
2006	1,558,387	625,886	Beauprez, Bob	888,096	Ritter, Bill Jr.	44,405	262,210 D	40.2%	57.0%	41.3%	58.7%
2002	1,412,602	884,583	Owens, Bill*	475,373	Heath, Rollie	52,646	409,210 R	62.6%	33.7%	65.0%	35.0%
1998	1,323,530	649,688	Owens, Bill	639,358	Schoettler, Gail	34,484	10,330 R	49.1%	48.3%	50.4%	49.6%
1994	1,116,307	432,042	Benson, Bruce	619,205	Romer, Roy*	65,060	187,163 D	38.7%	55.5%	41.1%	58.9%
1990	1,011,272	358,403	Andrews, John	626,032	Romer, Roy*	26,837	267,629 D	35.4%	61.9%	36.4%	63.6%
1986	1,058,928	434,420	Strickland, Ted	616,325	Romer, Roy	8,183	181,905 D	41.0%	58.2%	41.3%	58.7%
1982	956,021	302,740	Fuhr, John D.	627,960	Lamm, Richard D.*	25,321	325,220 D	31.7%	65.7%	32.5%	67.5%
1978	823,807	317,292	Strickland, Ted	483,985	Lamm, Richard D.*	22,530	166,693 D	38.5%	58.7%	39.6%	60.4%
1974	828,968	378,907	Vanderhoof, John D.*	441,199	Lamm, Richard D.	8,862	62,292 D	45.7%	53.2%	46.2%	53.8%
1970	668,496	350,690	Love, John A.*	302,432	Hogan, Mark	15,374	48,258 R	52.5%	45.2%	53.7%	46.3%
1966	660,063	356,730	Love, John A.*	287,132	Knous, Robert L.	16,201	69,598 R	54.0%	43.5%	55.4%	44.6%
1962	616,481	349,342	Love, John A.	262,890	McNichols, Stephen L.R.*	4,249	86,452 R	56.7%	42.6%	57.1%	42.9%
1958**	549,808	228,643	Burch, Palmer L.	321,165	McNichols, Stephen L.R.*		92,522 D	41.6%	58.4%	41.6%	58.4%
1956	645,233	313,950	Brotzman, Donald G.	331,283	McNichols, Stephen L.R.		17,333 D	48.7%	51.3%	48.7%	51.3%
1954	489,540	227,335	Brotzman, Donald G.	262,205	Johnson, Edwin C.		34,870 D	46.4%	53.6%	46.4%	53.6%
1952	613,034	349,924	Thornton, Dan*	260,044	Metzger, John W.	3,066	89,880 R	57.1%	42.4%	57.4%	42.6%
1950	450,994	236,472	Thornton, Dan	212,976	Johnson, Walter W.	1,546	23,496 R	52.4%	47.2%	52.6%	47.4%
1948	501,680	168,928	Hamil, David A.	332,752	Knous, William Lee*		163,824 D	33.7%	66.3%	33.7%	66.3%
1946	335,087	160,483	Lavington, Leon E.	174,604	Knous, William Lee		14,121 D	47.9%	52.1%	47.9%	52.1%

Note: An asterisk (*) denotes incumbent. **In past elections, the other vote included: 2010 - 651,232 American Constitution (Tom Tancredo), who finished second. The term of office of Colorado's governor was increased from two to four years effective with the 1958 election.

POSTWAR VOTE FOR SENATOR

| Year | Total Vote | Republican | | Democratic | | Other Vote | Rep.-Dem. Plurality | Percentage | | | |
| | | Vote | Candidate | Vote | Candidate | | | Total Vote | | Major Vote | |
								Rep.	Dem.	Rep.	Dem.
2010	1,772,570	822,802	Buck, Ken	851,778	Bennet, Michael F.*	97,990	28,976 D	46.4%	48.1%	49.1%	50.9%
2008	2,331,712	990,784	Schaffer, Bob	1,231,049	Udall, Mark	109,879	240,265 D	42.5%	52.8%	44.6%	55.4%
2004	2,107,554	980,668	Coors, Pete	1,081,188	Salazar, Ken	45,698	100,520 D	46.5%	51.3%	47.6%	52.4%
2002	1,416,082	717,893	Allard, Wayne*	648,130	Strickland, Tom	50,059	69,763 R	50.7%	45.8%	52.6%	47.4%
1998	1,327,235	829,370	Campbell, Ben Nighthorse*	464,754	Lamm, Dottie	33,111	364,616 R	62.5%	35.0%	64.1%	35.9%
1996	1,469,611	750,325	Allard, Wayne	677,600	Strickland, Tom	41,686	72,725 R	51.1%	46.1%	52.5%	47.5%
1992	1,552,289	662,893	Considine, Terry	803,725	Campbell, Ben Nighthorse	85,671	140,832 D	42.7%	51.8%	45.2%	54.8%
1990	1,022,027	569,048	Brown, Hank	425,746	Heath, Josie	27,233	143,302 R	55.7%	41.7%	57.2%	42.8%
1986	1,060,765	512,994	Kramer, Ken	529,449	Wirth, Timothy E.	18,322	16,455 D	48.4%	49.9%	49.2%	50.8%
1984	1,297,809	833,821	Armstrong, William L.*	449,327	Dick, Nancy	14,661	384,494 R	64.2%	34.6%	65.0%	35.0%
1980	1,173,646	571,295	Buchanan, Mary E.	590,501	Hart, Gary W.*	11,850	19,206 D	48.7%	50.3%	49.2%	50.8%
1978	819,150	480,596	Armstrong, William L.	330,247	Haskell, Floyd K.*	8,307	150,349 R	58.7%	40.3%	59.3%	40.7%
1974	824,166	325,508	Dominick, Peter H.*	471,691	Hart, Gary W.	26,967	146,183 D	39.5%	57.2%	40.8%	59.2%
1972	926,093	447,957	Alott, Gordon Llewellyn*	457,545	Haskell, Floyd K.	20,591	9,588 D	48.4%	49.4%	49.5%	50.5%
1968	785,536	459,952	Dominick, Peter H.*	325,584	McNichols, Stephen		134,368 R	58.6%	41.4%	58.6%	41.4%
1966	634,837	368,307	Alott, Gordon Llewellyn*	266,198	Romer, Roy	332	102,109 R	58.0%	41.9%	58.0%	42.0%
1962	613,444	328,655	Dominick, Peter H.	279,586	Carroll, John*	5,203	49,069 R	53.6%	45.6%	54.0%	46.0%
1960	727,633	389,428	Alott, Gordon Llewellyn*	334,854	Knous, Robert L.	3,351	54,574 R	53.5%	46.0%	53.8%	46.2%
1956	636,974	317,102	Thornton, Dan	319,872	Carroll, John		2,770 D	49.8%	50.2%	49.8%	50.2%
1954	484,188	248,502	Alott, Gordon Llewellyn	235,686	Carroll, John		12,816 R	51.3%	48.7%	51.3%	48.7%
1950	450,176	239,734	Millikin, Eugene D.*	210,442	Carroll, John		29,292 R	53.3%	46.7%	53.3%	46.7%
1948	510,121	165,069	Nicholson, Will F.	340,719	Johnson, Edwin C.*	4,333	175,650 D	32.4%	66.8%	32.6%	67.4%

Note: An asterisk (*) denotes incumbent.

COLORADO
PRESIDENT 2012

2010 Census Population	County	Total Vote	Republican (Romney)	Democratic (Obama)	Other	Rep.-Dem. Plurality	Percentage			
							Total Vote		Major Vote	
							Rep.	Dem.	Rep.	Dem.
441,603	ADAMS	176,230	70,972	100,649	4,609	29,677 D	40.3%	57.1%	41.4%	58.6%
15,445	ALAMOSA	6,715	2,705	3,811	199	1,106 D	40.3%	56.8%	41.5%	58.5%
572,003	ARAPAHOE	285,516	125,588	153,905	6,023	28,317 D	44.0%	53.9%	44.9%	55.1%
12,084	ARCHULETA	6,734	3,872	2,679	183	1,193 R	57.5%	39.8%	59.1%	40.9%
3,788	BACA	2,106	1,559	467	80	1,092 R	74.0%	22.2%	76.9%	23.1%
6,499	BENT	1,942	1,075	815	52	260 R	55.4%	42.0%	56.9%	43.1%
294,567	BOULDER	179,499	49,981	125,091	4,427	75,110 D	27.8%	69.7%	28.5%	71.5%
55,889	BROOMFIELD	32,777	15,008	16,966	803	1,958 D	45.8%	51.8%	46.9%	53.1%
17,809	CHAFFEE	10,462	5,070	5,086	306	16 D	48.5%	48.6%	49.9%	50.1%
1,836	CHEYENNE	1,093	889	172	32	717 R	81.3%	15.7%	83.8%	16.2%
9,088	CLEAR CREEK	5,743	2,430	3,119	194	689 D	42.3%	54.3%	43.8%	56.2%
8,256	CONEJOS	4,101	1,835	2,213	53	378 D	44.7%	54.0%	45.3%	54.7%
3,524	COSTILLA	1,837	446	1,340	51	894 D	24.3%	72.9%	25.0%	75.0%
5,823	CROWLEY	1,502	924	535	43	389 R	61.5%	35.6%	63.3%	36.7%
4,255	CUSTER	2,715	1,788	868	59	920 R	65.9%	32.0%	67.3%	32.7%
30,952	DELTA	15,925	10,915	4,622	388	6,293 R	68.5%	29.0%	70.3%	29.7%
600,158	DENVER	301,694	73,111	222,018	6,565	148,907 D	24.2%	73.6%	24.8%	75.2%
2,064	DOLORES	1,245	859	334	52	525 R	69.0%	26.8%	72.0%	28.0%
285,465	DOUGLAS	168,084	104,397	61,094	2,593	43,303 R	62.1%	36.3%	63.1%	36.9%
52,197	EAGLE	22,668	9,411	12,792	465	3,381 D	41.5%	56.4%	42.4%	57.6%
622,263	EL PASO	290,175	170,952	111,819	7,404	59,133 R	58.9%	38.5%	60.5%	39.5%
23,086	ELBERT	14,178	10,266	3,603	309	6,663 R	72.4%	25.4%	74.0%	26.0%
46,824	FREMONT	20,416	13,174	6,704	538	6,470 R	64.5%	32.8%	66.3%	33.7%
56,389	GARFIELD	24,408	12,535	11,305	568	1,230 R	51.4%	46.3%	52.6%	47.4%
5,441	GILPIN	3,338	1,346	1,892	100	546 D	40.3%	56.7%	41.6%	58.4%
14,843	GRAND	8,187	4,253	3,684	250	569 R	51.9%	45.0%	53.6%	46.4%
15,324	GUNNISON	8,667	3,341	5,044	282	1,703 D	38.5%	58.2%	39.8%	60.2%
843	HINSDALE	600	353	229	18	124 R	58.8%	38.2%	60.7%	39.3%
6,711	HUERFANO	3,714	1,646	1,953	115	307 D	44.3%	52.6%	45.7%	54.3%
1,394	JACKSON	848	600	216	32	384 R	70.8%	25.5%	73.5%	26.5%
534,543	JEFFERSON	311,052	144,197	159,296	7,559	15,099 D	46.4%	51.2%	47.5%	52.5%
1,398	KIOWA	821	677	118	26	559 R	82.5%	14.4%	85.2%	14.8%
8,270	KIT CARSON	3,702	2,785	838	79	1,947 R	75.2%	22.6%	76.9%	23.1%
51,334	LA PLATA	29,184	12,794	15,489	901	2,695 D	43.8%	53.1%	45.2%	54.8%
7,310	LAKE	3,040	1,098	1,839	103	741 D	36.1%	60.5%	37.4%	62.6%
299,630	LARIMER	180,180	82,376	92,747	5,057	10,371 D	45.7%	51.5%	47.0%	53.0%
15,507	LAS ANIMAS	6,862	3,263	3,445	154	182 D	47.6%	50.2%	48.6%	51.4%
5,467	LINCOLN	2,287	1,687	552	48	1,135 R	73.8%	24.1%	75.3%	24.7%
22,709	LOGAN	9,124	6,179	2,712	233	3,467 R	67.7%	29.7%	69.5%	30.5%
146,723	MESA	72,947	47,472	23,846	1,629	23,626 R	65.1%	32.7%	66.6%	33.4%
712	MINERAL	650	344	291	15	53 R	52.9%	44.8%	54.2%	45.8%
13,795	MOFFAT	6,168	4,695	1,330	143	3,365 R	76.1%	21.6%	77.9%	22.1%
25,535	MONTEZUMA	12,318	7,401	4,542	375	2,859 R	60.1%	36.9%	62.0%	38.0%
41,276	MONTROSE	20,130	13,552	6,138	440	7,414 R	67.3%	30.5%	68.8%	31.2%
28,159	MORGAN	10,777	6,602	3,912	263	2,690 R	61.3%	36.3%	62.8%	37.2%
18,831	OTERO	8,192	4,382	3,647	163	735 R	53.5%	44.5%	54.6%	45.4%
4,436	OURAY	3,202	1,481	1,646	75	165 D	46.3%	51.4%	47.4%	52.6%
16,206	PARK	9,366	5,236	3,862	268	1,374 R	55.9%	41.2%	57.6%	42.4%
4,442	PHILLIPS	2,265	1,637	588	40	1,049 R	72.3%	26.0%	73.6%	26.4%
17,148	PITKIN	10,075	3,024	6,849	202	3,825 D	30.0%	68.0%	30.6%	69.4%
12,551	PROWERS	4,863	3,230	1,519	114	1,711 R	66.4%	31.2%	68.0%	32.0%
159,063	PUEBLO	76,194	31,894	42,551	1,749	10,657 D	41.9%	55.8%	42.8%	57.2%
6,666	RIO BLANCO	3,369	2,724	568	77	2,156 R	80.9%	16.9%	82.7%	17.3%
11,982	RIO GRANDE	5,533	2,918	2,478	137	440 R	52.7%	44.8%	54.1%	45.9%
23,509	ROUTT	13,317	5,469	7,547	301	2,078 D	41.1%	56.7%	42.0%	58.0%
6,108	SAGUACHE	2,932	964	1,865	103	901 D	32.9%	63.6%	34.1%	65.9%
699	SAN JUAN	506	212	266	28	54 D	41.9%	52.6%	44.4%	55.6%
7,359	SAN MIGUEL	4,256	1,154	2,992	110	1,838 D	27.1%	70.3%	27.8%	72.2%
2,379	SEDGWICK	1,338	881	419	38	462 R	65.8%	31.3%	67.8%	32.2%
27,994	SUMMIT	15,312	5,571	9,347	394	3,776 D	36.4%	61.0%	37.3%	62.7%

COLORADO
PRESIDENT 2012

2010 Census Population	County	Total Vote	Republican (Romney)	Democratic (Obama)	Other	Rep.-Dem. Plurality	Percentage			
							Total Vote		Major Vote	
							Rep.	Dem.	Rep.	Dem.
23,350	TELLER	13,407	8,702	4,333	372	4,369 R	64.9%	32.3%	66.8%	33.2%
4,814	WASHINGTON	2,591	2,076	468	47	1,608 R	80.1%	18.1%	81.6%	18.4%
252,825	WELD	115,866	63,775	49,050	3,041	14,725 R	55.0%	42.3%	56.5%	43.5%
10,043	YUMA	4,577	3,490	987	100	2,503 R	76.3%	21.6%	78.0%	22.0%
5,029,196	TOTAL	2,569,522	1,185,243	1,323,102	61,177	137,859 D	46.1%	51.5%	47.3%	52.7%

COLORADO
HOUSE OF REPRESENTATIVES

CD	Year	Total Vote	Republican		Democratic		Other Vote	Rep.-Dem. Plurality	Percentage			
			Vote	Candidate	Vote	Candidate			Total Vote		Major Vote	
									Rep.	Dem.	Rep.	Dem.
1	2012	348,228	93,217	STROUD, DANNY	237,579	DEGETTE, DIANA*	17,432	144,362 D	26.8%	68.2%	28.2%	71.8%
2	2012	421,580	162,639	LUNDBERG, KEVIN	234,758	POLIS, JARED*	24,183	72,119 D	38.6%	55.7%	40.9%	59.1%
3	2012	347,574	185,291	TIPTON, SCOTT*	142,920	PACE, SAL	19,363	42,371 R	53.3%	41.1%	56.5%	43.5%
4	2012	342,336	200,006	GARDNER, CORY*	125,800	SHAFFER, BRANDON	16,530	74,206 R	58.4%	36.7%	61.4%	38.6%
5	2012	307,237	199,639	LAMBORN, DOUG*			107,598	199,639 R	65.0%		100.0%	
6	2012	342,914	163,938	COFFMAN, MIKE*	156,937	MIKLOSI, JOE	22,039	7,001 R	47.8%	45.8%	51.1%	48.9%
7	2012	340,970	139,066	COORS, JOE	182,460	PERLMUTTER, ED*	19,444	43,394 D	40.8%	53.5%	43.3%	56.7%
TOTAL	2012	2,450,839	1,143,796		1,080,454		226,589	63,342 R	46.7%	44.1%	51.4%	48.6%

Note: An asterisk (*) denotes incumbent.

COLORADO
GENERAL AND PRIMARY ELECTIONS

2012 GENERAL ELECTIONS: OTHER VOTE

President   Other vote was 35,545 Libertarian (Gary E. Johnson), 7,508 Green (Jill Stein), 6,234 Constitution (Virgil H. Goode), 5,059 Peace and Freedom (Roseanne Barr), 2,589 Unaffiliated (Jill Reed), 1,260 Justice (Ross C. "Rocky" Anderson), 792 We the People (Sheila "Samm" Tittle), 679 American Independent (Thomas Hoefling), 317 Socialism and Liberation (Gloria La Riva), 308 Socialist (Stewart Alexander), 266 American Third Position (Merlin Miller), 235 Objectivist (Thomas Robert Stevens), 192 Socialist Workers Party (James Harris), 189 Socialist Equality (Jerry White), 4 Write-in (Randall Terry)

House   Other vote was:

CD 1   12,585 Libertarian (Frank Atwood), 4,829 Green (Gary Swing), 18 Write-in (Thomas Henry Juniel)

CD 2   13,770 Libertarian (Randy Luallin), 10,413 Green (Susan P. Hall)

CD 3   11,125 Unaffiliated (Tisha Casida), 8,212 Libertarian (Gregory Gilman), 26 Write-in (Jaime McMillan)

CD 4   10,682 Libertarian (Josh Gilliland), 5,848 American Constitution (Doug Aden)

CD 5   53,318 Unaffiliated (Dave Anderson), 22,778 Libertarian (Jim Pirtle), 18,284 Green (Misha Luzov), 13,212 Constitution (Kenneth R. Harvell), 6 Write-in (George Allen Cantrell)

CD 6   13,442 Unaffiliated (Kathy Polhemus), 8,597 Libertarian (Patrick E. Provost)

CD 7   10,296 American Constitution (Douglas "Dayhorse" Campbell), 9,148 Libertarian (Buck Bailey)

COLORADO
GENERAL AND PRIMARY ELECTIONS

2012 PRIMARY ELECTIONS: SUPPLEMENTARY INFORMATION

Primary	June 26, 2012	**Registration** (as of June 1, 2012 – includes 832,686 inactive registrants)	3,530,485	Republican Democratic Libertarian Green American Constitution Americans Elect Unaffiliated	1,121,727 1,107,630 24,978 9,807 7,108 3,734 1,255,501

Primary Type   Semi-open—Registered Democrats and Republicans could vote only in their party's primary. "Unaffiliated" voters could participate in either the Democratic or Republican primary but in the process had to declare their affiliation with that party.

	REPUBLICAN PRIMARIES			DEMOCRATIC PRIMARIES		
Congressional District 1	Stroud, Danny Murphy, Richard W. *TOTAL*	11,936 6,407 *18,343*	65.1% 34.9%	DeGette, Diana* *TOTAL*	37,072 *37,072*	100.0%
Congressional District 2	Lundberg, Kevin Weissmann, Eric *TOTAL*	21,547 18,890 *40,437*	53.3% 46.7%	Polis, Jared* *TOTAL*	36,097 *36,097*	100.0%
Congressional District 3	Tipton, Scott* *TOTAL*	48,465 *48,465*	100.0%	Pace, Sal *TOTAL*	33,970 *33,970*	100.0%
Congressional District 4	Gardner, Cory* *TOTAL*	49,340 *49,340*	100.0%	Shaffer, Brandon *TOTAL*	20,671 *20,671*	100.0%
Congressional District 5	Lamborn, Doug* Blaha, Robert *TOTAL*	43,929 27,245 *71,174*	61.7% 38.3%			
Congressional District 6	Coffman, Mike* *TOTAL*	35,721 *35,721*	100.0%	Miklosi, Joe *TOTAL*	22,938 *22,938*	100.0%
Congressional District 7	Coors, Joe *TOTAL*	31,254 *31,254*	100.0%	Perlmutter, Ed* *TOTAL*	29,987 *29,987*	100.0%

Note: An asterisk (*) denotes incumbent.

CONNECTICUT

Congressional districts first established for elections held in 2012

5 members

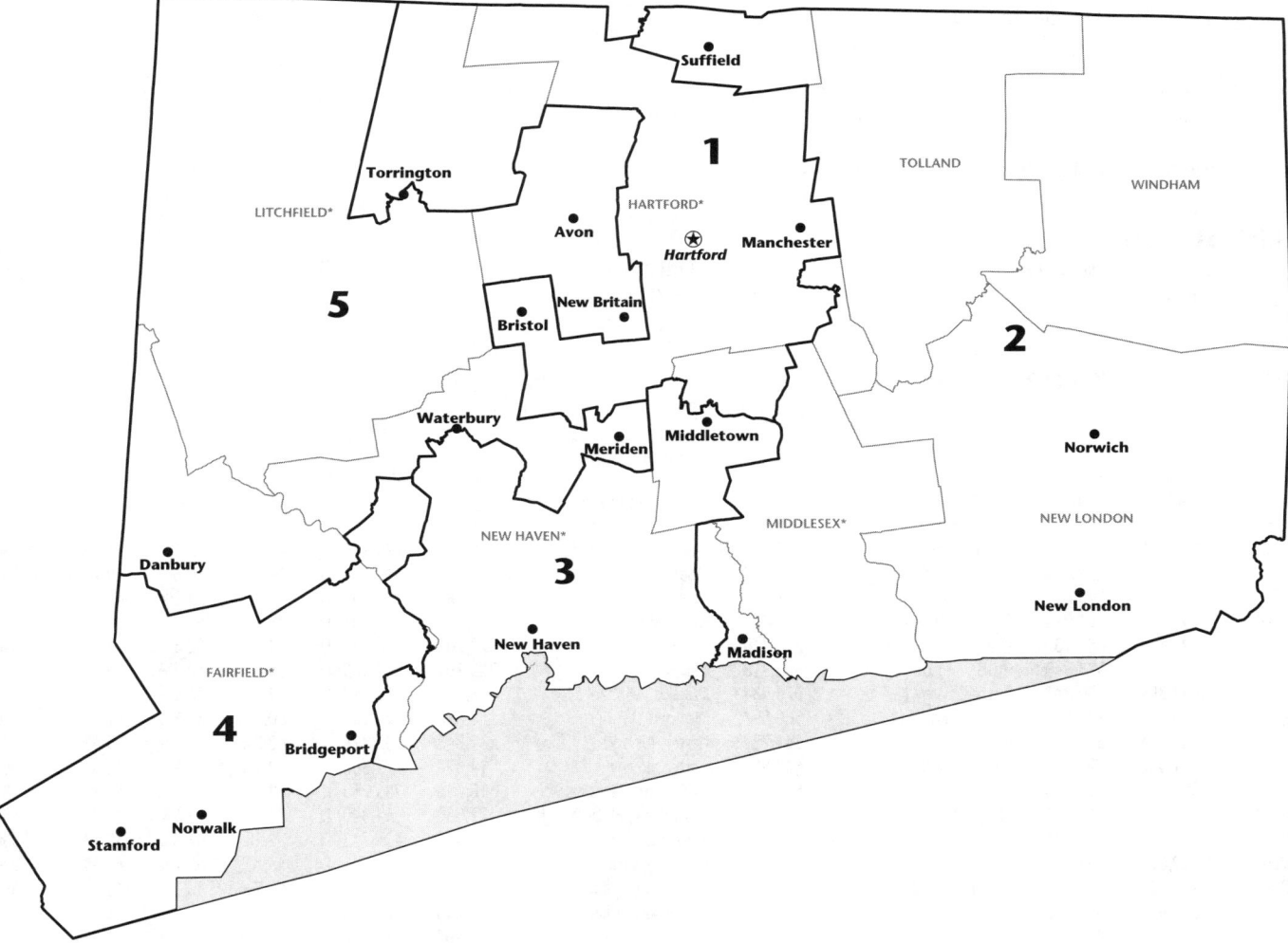

* Asterisk indicates a county whose boundaries include parts of two or more Congressional districts.

CONNECTICUT

GOVERNOR

Dan Malloy (D). Elected 2010 to a four-year term.

SENATORS (2 Democrats)

Richard Blumenthal (D). Elected 2010 to a six-year term.

Chris Murphy (D). Elected 2012 to a six-year term.

REPRESENTATIVES (5 Democrats)

1. John B. Larson (D)
2. Joe Courtney (D)
3. Rosa L. DeLauro (D)
4. Jim Himes (D)
5. Elizabeth Esty (D)

POSTWAR VOTE FOR PRESIDENT

| | | Republican | | Democratic | | Other Vote | Rep.-Dem. Plurality | Percentage | | | |
| | | | | | | | | Total Vote | | Major Vote | |
Year	Total Vote	Vote	Candidate	Vote	Candidate			Rep.	Dem.	Rep.	Dem.
2012	1,558,960	634,892	Romney, W. Mitt	905,083	Obama, Barack H.*	18,985	270,191 D	40.7%	58.1%	41.2%	58.8%
2008	1,646,792	629,428	McCain, John S. III	997,772	Obama, Barack H.	19,592	368,344 D	38.2%	60.6%	38.7%	61.3%
2004	1,578,769	693,826	Bush, George W.*	857,488	Kerry, John F.	27,455	163,662 D	43.9%	54.3%	44.7%	55.3%
2000**	1,459,525	561,094	Bush, George W.	816,015	Gore, Albert Jr.	82,416	254,921 D	38.4%	55.9%	40.7%	59.3%
1996**	1,392,614	483,109	Dole, Robert "Bob"	735,740	Clinton, Bill*	173,765	252,631 D	34.7%	52.8%	39.6%	60.4%
1992**	1,616,332	578,313	Bush, George H.*	682,318	Clinton, Bill	355,701	104,005 D	35.8%	42.2%	45.9%	54.1%
1988	1,443,394	750,241	Bush, George H.	676,584	Dukakis, Michael S.	16,569	73,657 R	52.0%	46.9%	52.6%	47.4%
1984	1,466,900	890,877	Reagan, Ronald*	569,597	Mondale, Walter F.	6,426	321,280 R	60.7%	38.8%	61.0%	39.0%
1980**	1,406,285	677,210	Reagan, Ronald	541,732	Carter, Jimmy*	187,343	135,478 R	48.2%	38.5%	55.6%	44.4%
1976	1,381,526	719,261	Ford, Gerald R.*	647,895	Carter, Jimmy	14,370	71,366 R	52.1%	46.9%	52.6%	47.4%
1972	1,384,277	810,763	Nixon, Richard M.*	555,498	McGovern, George S.	18,016	255,265 R	58.6%	40.1%	59.3%	40.7%
1968**	1,256,232	556,721	Nixon, Richard M.	621,561	Humphrey, Hubert H. Jr.	77,950	64,840 D	44.3%	49.5%	47.2%	52.8%
1964	1,218,578	390,996	Goldwater, Barry M. Sr.	826,269	Johnson, Lyndon B.*	1,313	435,273 D	32.1%	67.8%	32.1%	67.9%
1960	1,222,883	565,813	Nixon, Richard M.	657,055	Kennedy, John F.	15	91,242 D	46.3%	53.7%	46.3%	53.7%
1956	1,117,121	711,837	Eisenhower, Dwight D.*	405,079	Stevenson, Adlai E. II	205	306,758 R	63.7%	36.3%	63.7%	36.3%
1952	1,096,911	611,012	Eisenhower, Dwight D.	481,649	Stevenson, Adlai E. II	4,250	129,363 R	55.7%	43.9%	55.9%	44.1%
1948	883,518	437,754	Dewey, Thomas E.	423,297	Truman, Harry S.*	22,467	14,457 R	49.5%	47.9%	50.8%	49.2%

Note: An asterisk (*) denotes incumbent. **In past elections, the other vote included: 2000 - 64,452 Green (Ralph Nader); 1996 - 139,523 Reform (Ross Perot); 1992 - 348,771 Independent (Perot); 1980 - 171,807 Independent (John Anderson); 1968 - 76,650 American Independent (George Wallace).

CONNECTICUT

POSTWAR VOTE FOR GOVERNOR

		Republican		Democratic		Other	Rep.-Dem.	Percentage Total Vote		Major Vote	
Year	Total Vote	Vote	Candidate	Vote	Candidate	Vote	Plurality	Rep.	Dem.	Rep.	Dem.
2010	1,145,799	560,874	Foley, Tom C.	567,278	Malloy, Dan	17,647	6,404 D	49.0%	49.5%	49.7%	50.3%
2006	1,123,466	710,048	Rell, M. Jodi*	398,220	DeStefano, John Jr.	15,198	311,828 R	63.2%	35.4%	64.1%	35.9%
2002	1,022,998	573,958	Rowland, John G.*	448,984	Curry, Bill	56	124,974 R	56.1%	43.9%	56.1%	43.9%
1998	999,537	628,707	Rowland, John G.*	354,187	Kennelly, Barbara B.	16,643	274,520 R	62.9%	35.4%	64.0%	36.0%
1994**	1,147,084	415,201	Rowland, John G.	375,133	Curry, Bill	356,750	40,068 R	36.2%	32.7%	52.5%	47.5%
1990**	1,142,101	427,840	Rowland, John G.	237,641	Morrison, Bruce A.	476,620	190,199 R**	37.5%	20.8%	64.3%	35.7%
1986	993,692	408,489	Belaga, Julie D.	575,638	O'Neill, William A.*	9,565	167,149 D	41.1%	57.9%	41.5%	58.5%
1982	1,083,876	497,773	Rome, Lewis B.	578,264	O'Neill, William A.*	7,839	80,491 D	45.9%	53.4%	46.3%	53.7%
1978	1,036,608	422,316	Sarasin, Ronald A.	613,109	Grasso, Ella T.*	1,183	190,793 D	40.7%	59.1%	40.8%	59.2%
1974	1,102,773	440,169	Steele, Robert H.	643,490	Grasso, Ella T.	19,114	203,321 D	39.9%	58.4%	40.6%	59.4%
1970	1,082,797	582,160	Meskill, Thomas J.	500,561	Daddario, Emilio	76	81,599 R	53.8%	46.2%	53.8%	46.2%
1966	1,008,557	446,536	Gengras, E. Clayton	561,599	Dempsey, John N.*	422	115,063 D	44.3%	55.7%	44.3%	55.7%
1962	1,031,902	482,852	Alsop, John	549,027	Dempsey, John N.*	23	66,175 D	46.8%	53.2%	46.8%	53.2%
1958	974,509	360,644	Zeller, Fred R.	607,012	Ribicoff, Abraham A.*	6,853	246,368 D	37.0%	62.3%	37.3%	62.7%
1954	936,753	460,528	Lodge, John D.*	463,643	Ribicoff, Abraham A.	12,582	3,115 D	49.2%	49.5%	49.8%	50.2%
1950**	878,735	436,418	Lodge, John D.	419,404	Bowles, Chester*	22,913	17,014 R	49.7%	47.7%	51.0%	49.0%
1948	875,620	429,071	Shannon, James C.*	431,746	Bowles, Chester	14,803	2,675 D	49.0%	49.3%	49.8%	50.2%
1946	683,831	371,852	McConaughy, James L.	276,335	Snow, Wilbert*	35,644	95,517 R	54.4%	40.4%	57.4%	42.6%

Note: An asterisk (*) denotes incumbent. **In past elections, the other vote included: 1994 - 216,585 A Connecticut Party (Elaine Strong Groark); 130,128 Independent (Tom Scott); 1990 - 460,576 A Connecticut Party (Lowell P. Weicker Jr.). Weicker won the 1990 election with 40.4 percent of the total vote. The term of office for Connecticut's governor was increased from two to four years effective with the 1950 election.

POSTWAR VOTE FOR SENATOR

		Republican		Democratic		Other	Rep.-Dem.	Percentage Total Vote		Major Vote	
Year	Total Vote	Vote	Candidate	Vote	Candidate	Vote	Plurality	Rep.	Dem.	Rep.	Dem.
2012	1,511,764	651,089	McMahon, Linda E.	828,761	Murphy, Chris	31,914	177,672 D	43.1%	54.8%	44.0%	56.0%
2010	1,153,115	498,341	McMahon, Linda E.	636,040	Blumenthal, Richard	18,734	137,699 D	43.2%	55.2%	43.9%	56.1%
2006**	1,134,780	109,198	Achlesinger, Alan	450,844	Lamont, Ned	574,738	341,646 D**	9.6%	39.7%	19.5%	80.5%
2004	1,424,726	457,749	Orchulli, Jack	945,347	Dodd, Christopher J.*	21,630	487,598 D	32.1%	66.4%	32.6%	67.4%
2000	1,311,261	448,077	Giordano, Phil	828,902	Lieberman, Joseph I.*	34,282	380,825 D	34.2%	63.2%	35.1%	64.9%
1998	964,457	312,177	Franks, Gary A.	628,306	Dodd, Christopher J.*	23,974	316,129 D	32.4%	65.1%	33.2%	66.8%
1994	1,079,767	334,833	Labriola, Jerry Jr.	723,842	Lieberman, Joseph I.*	21,092	389,009 D	31.0%	67.0%	31.6%	68.4%
1992	1,500,709	572,036	Johnson, Brook	882,569	Dodd, Christopher J.*	46,104	310,533 D	38.1%	58.8%	39.3%	60.7%
1988	1,383,526	678,454	Weicker, Lowell P. Jr.*	688,499	Lieberman, Joseph I.	16,573	10,045 D	49.0%	49.8%	49.6%	50.4%
1986	976,933	340,438	Eddy, Roger W.	632,695	Dodd, Christopher J.*	3,800	292,257 D	34.8%	64.8%	35.0%	65.0%
1982	1,083,613	545,987	Weicker, Lowell P. Jr.*	499,146	Moffett, Anthony T.	38,480	46,841 R	50.4%	46.1%	52.2%	47.8%
1980	1,356,075	581,884	Buckley, James L.	763,969	Dodd, Christopher J.	10,222	182,085 D	42.9%	56.3%	43.2%	56.8%
1976	1,361,666	785,683	Weicker, Lowell P. Jr.*	561,018	Schaffer, Gloria	14,965	224,665 R	57.7%	41.2%	58.3%	41.7%
1974	1,084,918	372,055	Brannen, James H.	690,820	Ribicoff, Abraham A.*	22,043	318,765 D	34.3%	63.7%	35.0%	65.0%
1970**	1,089,353	454,721	Weicker, Lowell P. Jr.	368,111	Duffey, Joseph D.	266,521	86,610 R	41.7%	33.8%	55.3%	44.7%
1968	1,206,537	551,455	May, Edwin H.	655,043	Ribicoff, Abraham A.*	39	103,588 D	45.7%	54.3%	45.7%	54.3%
1964	1,208,163	426,939	Lodge, John	781,008	Dodd, Thomas J.*	216	354,069 D	35.3%	64.6%	35.3%	64.7%
1962	1,029,301	501,694	Seely-Brown, Horace	527,522	Ribicoff, Abraham A.	85	25,828 D	48.7%	51.3%	48.7%	51.3%
1958	965,463	410,622	Purtell, William A.*	554,841	Dodd, Thomas J.		144,219 D	42.5%	57.5%	42.5%	57.5%
1956	1,113,819	610,829	Bush, Prescott S.*	479,460	Dodd, Thomas J.	23,530	131,369 R	54.8%	43.0%	56.0%	44.0%
1952	1,093,467	573,854	Purtell, William A.	485,066	Benton, William*	34,547	88,788 R	52.5%	44.4%	54.2%	45.8%
1952S	1,093,268	559,465	Bush, Prescott S.	530,505	Ribicoff, Abraham A.	3,298	28,960 R	51.2%	48.5%	51.3%	48.7%
1950	877,827	409,053	Talbot, Joseph E.	453,646	McMahon, Brien*	15,128	44,593 D	46.6%	51.7%	47.4%	52.6%
1950S	877,135	430,311	Bush, Prescott S.	431,413	Benton, William	15,411	1,102 D	49.1%	49.2%	49.9%	50.1%
1946	682,921	381,328	Baldwin, Raymond E.*	276,424	Tone, Joseph M.	25,169	104,904 R	55.8%	40.5%	58.0%	42.0%

Note: An asterisk (*) denotes incumbent. **In past elections, the other vote included: 2006 - 564,095 Connecticut For Lieberman (Joseph I. Lieberman); 1970 - 266,497 Independent (Thomas J. Dodd). Lieberman won the 2006 election with 49.7 percent of the vote. One each of the 1950 and 1952 elections were for short terms to fill a vacancy.

CONNECTICUT

PRESIDENT 2012

2010 Census Population	County	Total Vote	Republican (Romney)	Democratic (Obama)	Other	Rep.-Dem. Plurality	Percentage			
							Total Vote		Major Vote	
							Rep.	Dem.	Rep.	Dem.
916,829	FAIRFIELD	396,116	175,168	217,294	3,654	42,126 D	44.2%	54.9%	44.6%	55.4%
894,014	HARTFORD	392,019	143,238	244,639	4,142	101,401 D	36.5%	62.4%	36.9%	63.1%
189,927	LITCHFIELD	92,312	47,201	43,856	1,255	3,345 R	51.1%	47.5%	51.8%	48.2%
165,676	MIDDLESEX	83,492	34,591	47,855	1,046	13,264 D	41.4%	57.3%	42.0%	58.0%
862,477	NEW HAVEN	360,832	138,357	218,972	3,503	80,615 D	38.3%	60.7%	38.7%	61.3%
274,055	NEW LONDON	115,093	46,119	67,144	1,830	21,025 D	40.1%	58.3%	40.7%	59.3%
152,691	TOLLAND	70,928	30,450	39,366	1,112	8,916 D	42.9%	55.5%	43.6%	56.4%
118,428	WINDHAM	46,494	19,768	25,957	769	6,189 D	42.5%	55.8%	43.2%	56.8%
	Votes Not Reported by County	1,674			1,674					
3,574,097	TOTAL	1,558,960	634,892	905,083	18,985	270,191 D	40.7%	58.1%	41.2%	58.8%

2010 Census Population	City/Town	Total Vote	Republican (Romney)	Democratic (Obama)	Other	Rep.-Dem. Plurality	Percentage			
							Total Vote		Major Vote	
							Rep.	Dem.	Rep.	Dem.
19,249	ANSONIA	6,967	2,596	4,273	98	1,677 D	37.3%	61.3%	37.8%	62.2%
20,486	BLOOMFIELD	11,895	1,925	9,921	49	7,996 D	16.2%	83.4%	16.3%	83.7%
28,026	BRANFORD	14,262	5,817	8,301	144	2,484 D	40.8%	58.2%	41.2%	58.8%
144,229	BRIDGEPORT	37,476	5,168	32,135	173	26,967 D	13.8%	85.7%	13.9%	86.1%
60,477	BRISTOL	24,429	10,004	14,146	279	4,142 D	41.0%	57.9%	41.4%	58.6%
29,261	CHESHIRE	14,894	7,311	7,397	186	86 D	49.1%	49.7%	49.7%	50.3%
80,893	DANBURY	26,161	10,590	15,290	281	4,700 D	40.5%	58.4%	40.9%	59.1%
20,732	DARIEN	10,973	7,175	3,777	21	3,398 R	65.4%	34.4%	65.5%	34.5%
51,252	EAST HARTFORD	18,855	4,556	14,149	150	9,593 D	24.2%	75.0%	24.4%	75.6%
29,257	EAST HAVEN	11,302	4,650	6,533	119	1,883 D	41.1%	57.8%	41.6%	58.4%
44,654	ENFIELD	18,156	7,709	10,152	295	2,443 D	42.5%	55.9%	43.2%	56.8%
59,404	FAIRFIELD	29,940	14,357	15,283	300	926 D	48.0%	51.0%	48.4%	51.6%
25,340	FARMINGTON	13,782	6,611	7,013	158	402 D	48.0%	50.9%	48.5%	51.5%
34,427	GLASTONBURY	19,166	8,809	10,135	222	1,326 D	46.0%	52.9%	46.5%	53.5%
61,171	GREENWICH	29,790	16,456	13,079	255	3,377 R	55.2%	43.9%	55.7%	44.3%
40,115	GROTON	13,964	5,367	8,384	213	3,017 D	38.4%	60.0%	39.0%	61.0%
22,375	GUILFORD	12,693	5,170	7,411	112	2,241 D	40.7%	58.4%	41.1%	58.9%
60,960	HAMDEN	26,900	7,482	19,181	237	11,699 D	27.8%	71.3%	28.1%	71.9%
124,775	HARTFORD	34,037	2,138	31,735	164	29,597 D	6.3%	93.2%	6.3%	93.7%
58,241	MANCHESTER	23,869	7,961	15,565	343	7,604 D	33.4%	65.2%	33.8%	66.2%
26,543	MANSFIELD	9,363	2,193	6,941	229	4,748 D	23.4%	74.1%	24.0%	76.0%
60,868	MERIDEN	22,006	6,880	14,886	240	8,006 D	31.3%	67.6%	31.6%	68.4%
47,648	MIDDLETOWN	20,223	6,105	13,834	284	7,729 D	30.2%	68.4%	30.6%	69.4%
52,759	MILFORD	25,477	11,462	13,668	347	2,206 D	45.0%	53.6%	45.6%	54.4%
31,862	NAUGATUCK	11,918	5,807	5,923	188	116 D	48.7%	49.7%	49.5%	50.5%
73,206	NEW BRITAIN	21,032	4,783	16,052	197	11,269 D	22.7%	76.3%	23.0%	77.0%
129,779	NEW HAVEN	44,643	4,430	39,865	348	35,435 D	9.9%	89.3%	10.0%	90.0%
27,620	NEW LONDON	8,500	1,654	6,710	136	5,056 D	19.5%	78.9%	19.8%	80.2%
28,142	NEW MILFORD	13,160	6,330	6,640	190	310 D	48.1%	50.5%	48.8%	51.2%
30,562	NEWINGTON	14,739	5,752	8,792	195	3,040 D	39.0%	59.7%	39.5%	60.5%
27,560	NEWTOWN	14,398	7,451	6,784	163	667 R	51.8%	47.1%	52.3%	47.7%
24,093	NORTH HAVEN	12,502	5,990	6,376	136	386 D	47.9%	51.0%	48.4%	51.6%
85,603	NORWALK	35,499	12,773	22,369	357	9,596 D	36.0%	63.0%	36.3%	63.7%
40,493	NORWICH	12,923	4,144	8,541	238	4,397 D	32.1%	66.1%	32.7%	67.3%
24,638	RIDGEFIELD	13,955	7,360	6,461	134	899 R	52.7%	46.3%	53.3%	46.7%
39,559	SHELTON	18,904	10,327	8,362	215	1,965 R	54.6%	44.2%	55.3%	44.7%
23,511	SIMSBURY	13,742	6,710	6,853	179	143 D	48.8%	49.9%	49.5%	50.5%
25,709	SOUTH WINDSOR	13,660	5,775	7,708	177	1,933 D	42.3%	56.4%	42.8%	57.2%
43,069	SOUTHINGTON	21,462	10,452	10,727	283	275 D	48.7%	50.0%	49.4%	50.6%
122,643	STAMFORD	47,529	17,473	29,623	433	12,150 D	36.8%	62.3%	37.1%	62.9%

CONNECTICUT

PRESIDENT 2012

2010 Census Population	City/Town	Total Vote	Republican (Romney)	Democratic (Obama)	Other	Rep.-Dem. Plurality		Total Vote		Major Vote	
								Rep.	Dem.	Rep.	Dem.
51,384	STRATFORD	23,034	9,324	13,483	227	4,159 D		40.5%	58.5%	40.9%	59.1%
36,383	TORRINGTON	14,419	7,320	6,843	256	477 R		50.8%	47.5%	51.7%	48.3%
36,018	TRUMBULL	18,869	9,986	8,703	180	1,283 R		52.9%	46.1%	53.4%	46.6%
29,179	VERNON	12,832	5,085	7,556	191	2,471 D		39.6%	58.9%	40.2%	59.8%
45,135	WALLINGFORD	21,084	9,259	11,560	265	2,301 D		43.9%	54.8%	44.5%	55.5%
110,366	WATERBURY	32,240	11,043	20,931	266	9,888 D		34.3%	64.9%	34.5%	65.5%
22,514	WATERTOWN	10,960	6,644	4,181	135	2,463 R		60.6%	38.1%	61.4%	38.6%
63,268	WEST HARTFORD	31,928	10,511	21,069	348	10,558 D		32.9%	66.0%	33.3%	66.7%
55,564	WEST HAVEN	20,278	5,789	14,286	203	8,497 D		28.5%	70.5%	28.8%	71.2%
26,391	WESTPORT	15,048	6,439	8,495	114	2,056 D		42.8%	56.5%	43.1%	56.9%
26,668	WETHERSFIELD	13,936	6,015	7,753	168	1,738 D		43.2%	55.6%	43.7%	56.3%
25,268	WINDHAM	7,875	1,944	5,818	113	3,874 D		24.7%	73.9%	25.0%	75.0%
29,044	WINDSOR	15,940	4,305	11,463	172	7,158 D		27.0%	71.9%	27.3%	72.7%

CONNECTICUT

SENATOR 2012

2010 Census Population	County	Total Vote	Republican (McMahon)	Democratic (Murphy)	Other	Rep.-Dem. Plurality		Total Vote		Major Vote	
								Rep.	Dem.	Rep.	Dem.
916,829	FAIRFIELD	386,963	179,440	202,539	4,984	23,099 D		46.4%	52.3%	47.0%	53.0%
894,014	HARTFORD	378,894	148,754	224,187	5,953	75,433 D		39.3%	59.2%	39.9%	60.1%
189,927	LITCHFIELD	89,385	48,316	39,577	1,492	8,739 R		54.1%	44.3%	55.0%	45.0%
165,676	MIDDLESEX	80,781	35,474	43,591	1,716	8,117 D		43.9%	54.0%	44.9%	55.1%
862,477	NEW HAVEN	346,717	141,408	199,779	5,530	58,371 D		40.8%	57.6%	41.4%	58.6%
274,055	NEW LONDON	109,318	46,056	60,595	2,667	14,539 D		42.1%	55.4%	43.2%	56.8%
152,691	TOLLAND	68,279	30,877	35,781	1,621	4,904 D		45.2%	52.4%	46.3%	53.7%
118,428	WINDHAM	44,558	20,764	22,712	1,082	1,948 D		46.6%	51.0%	47.8%	52.2%
	Votes Not Reported by County	6,869			6,869						
3,574,097	TOTAL	1,511,764	651,089	828,761	31,914	177,672 D		43.1%	54.8%	44.0%	56.0%

Note: Candidates in Connecticut can appear on the ballot line of more than one party. In the 2012 Senate election, the candidates received the following votes per party: Christopher S. Murphy - 792,983 (Democrat), 35,778 (Working Families); Linda E. McMahon - 604,569 (Republican), 46,520 (Independent Party).

2010 Census Population	City/Town	Total Vote	Republican (McMahon)	Democratic (Murphy)	Other	Rep.-Dem. Plurality		Total Vote		Major Vote	
								Rep.	Dem.	Rep.	Dem.
19,249	ANSONIA	6,536	2,783	3,637	116	854 D		42.6%	55.6%	43.3%	56.7%
20,486	BLOOMFIELD	11,360	2,101	9,144	115	7,043 D		18.5%	80.5%	18.7%	81.3%
28,026	BRANFORD	13,884	5,794	7,838	252	2,044 D		41.7%	56.5%	42.5%	57.5%
144,229	BRIDGEPORT	41,233	11,956	29,055	222	17,099 D		29.0%	70.5%	29.2%	70.8%
60,477	BRISTOL	23,753	10,625	12,733	395	2,108 D		44.7%	53.6%	45.5%	54.5%
29,261	CHESHIRE	14,595	7,269	7,081	245	188 R		49.8%	48.5%	50.7%	49.3%
80,893	DANBURY	25,353	10,924	14,046	383	3,122 D		43.1%	55.4%	43.7%	56.3%
20,732	DARIEN	10,603	6,776	3,706	121	3,070 R		63.9%	35.0%	64.6%	35.4%
51,252	EAST HARTFORD	17,578	5,195	12,157	226	6,962 D		29.6%	69.2%	29.9%	70.1%
29,257	EAST HAVEN	10,688	4,721	5,759	208	1,038 D		44.2%	53.9%	45.0%	55.0%

CONNECTICUT

SENATOR 2012

2010 Census Population	City/Town	Total Vote	Republican (McMahon)	Democratic (Murphy)	Other	Rep.-Dem. Plurality	Percentage Total Vote Rep.	Dem.	Major Vote Rep.	Dem.
44,654	ENFIELD	17,454	7,716	9,302	436	1,586 D	44.2%	53.3%	45.3%	54.7%
59,404	FAIRFIELD	28,995	14,050	14,508	437	458 D	48.5%	50.0%	49.2%	50.8%
25,340	FARMINGTON	13,444	6,516	6,720	208	204 D	48.5%	50.0%	49.2%	50.8%
34,427	GLASTONBURY	18,621	8,972	9,341	308	369 D	48.2%	50.2%	49.0%	51.0%
61,171	GREENWICH	28,476	15,682	12,481	313	3,201 R	55.1%	43.8%	55.7%	44.3%
40,115	GROTON	13,186	5,261	7,644	281	2,383 D	39.9%	58.0%	40.8%	59.2%
22,375	GUILFORD	12,355	5,053	7,082	220	2,029 D	40.9%	57.3%	41.6%	58.4%
60,960	HAMDEN	25,784	7,505	17,926	353	10,421 D	29.1%	69.5%	29.5%	70.5%
124,775	HARTFORD	33,123	3,373	29,557	193	26,184 D	10.2%	89.2%	10.2%	89.8%
58,241	MANCHESTER	22,700	8,393	13,924	383	5,531 D	37.0%	61.3%	37.6%	62.4%
26,543	MANSFIELD	8,979	2,404	6,381	194	3,977 D	26.8%	71.1%	27.4%	72.6%
60,868	MERIDEN	20,901	7,500	13,094	307	5,594 D	35.9%	62.6%	36.4%	63.6%
47,648	MIDDLETOWN	19,357	6,470	12,491	396	6,021 D	33.4%	64.5%	34.1%	65.9%
52,759	MILFORD	24,373	11,265	12,562	546	1,297 D	46.2%	51.5%	47.3%	52.7%
31,862	NAUGATUCK	11,398	6,242	4,924	232	1,318 R	54.8%	43.2%	55.9%	44.1%
73,206	NEW BRITAIN	19,936	5,526	14,139	271	8,613 D	27.7%	70.9%	28.1%	71.9%
129,779	NEW HAVEN	42,508	5,289	36,892	327	31,603 D	12.4%	86.8%	12.5%	87.5%
27,620	NEW LONDON	7,659	1,843	5,648	168	3,805 D	24.1%	73.7%	24.6%	75.4%
28,142	NEW MILFORD	12,378	6,271	5,883	224	388 R	50.7%	47.5%	51.6%	48.4%
30,562	NEWINGTON	14,176	5,909	8,035	232	2,126 D	41.7%	56.7%	42.4%	57.6%
27,560	NEWTOWN	14,117	7,411	6,504	202	907 R	52.5%	46.1%	53.3%	46.7%
24,093	NORTH HAVEN	12,158	5,911	6,021	226	110 D	48.6%	49.5%	49.5%	50.5%
85,603	NORWALK	34,032	13,008	20,540	484	7,532 D	38.2%	60.4%	38.8%	61.2%
40,493	NORWICH	11,721	4,211	7,191	319	2,980 D	35.9%	61.4%	36.9%	63.1%
24,638	RIDGEFIELD	13,532	7,259	6,082	191	1,177 R	53.6%	44.9%	54.4%	45.6%
39,559	SHELTON	18,231	10,168	7,726	337	2,442 R	55.8%	42.4%	56.8%	43.2%
23,511	SIMSBURY	13,412	6,635	6,563	214	72 R	49.5%	48.9%	50.3%	49.7%
25,709	SOUTH WINDSOR	13,181	5,782	7,120	279	1,338 D	43.9%	54.0%	44.8%	55.2%
43,069	SOUTHINGTON	20,994	10,901	9,707	386	1,194 R	51.9%	46.2%	52.9%	47.1%
122,643	STAMFORD	45,084	17,273	27,280	531	10,007 D	38.3%	60.5%	38.8%	61.2%
51,384	STRATFORD	22,237	9,526	12,347	364	2,821 D	42.8%	55.5%	43.6%	56.4%
36,383	TORRINGTON	13,796	7,659	5,832	305	1,827 R	55.5%	42.3%	56.8%	43.2%
36,018	TRUMBULL	17,979	9,700	8,022	257	1,678 R	54.0%	44.6%	54.7%	45.3%
29,179	VERNON	12,237	5,181	6,751	305	1,570 D	42.3%	55.2%	43.4%	56.6%
45,135	WALLINGFORD	20,397	9,572	10,437	388	865 D	46.9%	51.2%	47.8%	52.2%
110,366	WATERBURY	30,453	11,909	18,177	367	6,268 D	39.1%	59.7%	39.6%	60.4%
22,514	WATERTOWN	10,702	6,674	3,858	170	2,816 R	62.4%	36.0%	63.4%	36.6%
63,268	WEST HARTFORD	31,325	10,483	20,402	440	9,919 D	33.5%	65.1%	33.9%	66.1%
55,564	WEST HAVEN	18,985	6,103	12,524	358	6,421 D	32.1%	66.0%	32.8%	67.2%
26,391	WESTPORT	14,583	6,106	8,342	135	2,236 D	41.9%	57.2%	42.3%	57.7%
26,668	WETHERSFIELD	13,167	5,979	6,966	222	987 D	45.4%	52.9%	46.2%	53.8%
25,268	WINDHAM	7,389	2,253	4,992	144	2,739 D	30.5%	67.6%	31.1%	68.9%
29,044	WINDSOR	15,356	4,724	10,396	236	5,672 D	30.8%	67.7%	31.2%	68.8%

CONNECTICUT

HOUSE OF REPRESENTATIVES

| | | | Republican | | Democratic | | Other | Rep.-Dem. | Percentage | | | |
| | | | | | | | | | Total Vote | | Major Vote | |
CD	Year	Total Vote	Vote	Candidate	Vote	Candidate	Vote	Plurality	Rep.	Dem.	Rep.	Dem.
1	2012	297,061	82,321	DECKER, JOHN HENRY	206,973	LARSON, JOHN B.*	7,767	124,652 D	27.7%	69.7%	28.5%	71.5%
2	2012	299,960	88,103	FORMICA, PAUL	204,708	COURTNEY, JOE*	7,149	116,605 D	29.4%	68.2%	30.1%	69.9%
3	2012	291,301	73,726	WINSLEY, WAYNE	217,573	DELAURO, ROSA L.*	2	143,847 D	25.3%	74.7%	25.3%	74.7%
4	2012	293,432	117,503	OBSITNIK, STEVE	175,929	HIMES, JIM*		58,426 D	40.0%	60.0%	40.0%	60.0%
5	2012	284,757	138,637	RORABACK, ANDREW	146,098	ESTY, ELIZABETH	22	7,461 D	48.7%	51.3%	48.7%	51.3%
TOTAL	2012	1,466,511	500,290		951,281		14,940	450,991 D	34.1%	64.9%	34.5%	65.5%

Notes: An asterisk (*) denotes incumbent. Votes received by each Democratic and Republican candidate on the ballot lines of other parties are included in their totals above. All Democratic Party candidates in Connecticut received Working Party votes in 2012. Roraback (5th district) received Independent Party votes.

CONNECTICUT

GENERAL AND PRIMARY ELECTIONS

2012 GENERAL ELECTIONS: OTHER VOTE

President Other vote was 12,580 Libertarian (Gary E. Johnson), 5,487 Justice (Ross C. "Rocky" Anderson), 918 Write-in (Scattered Write-In)

Senator Other vote was 25,045 Libertarian (Paul Passarelli), 6,869 Write-in (Scattered Write-In)

House Other vote was:

CD 1 5,477 Green (S. Michael DeRosa), 2,290 Unaffiliated (Matthew M. Corey)
CD 2 3,638 Green (Colin D. Bennett), 3,511 Libertarian (Daniel J. Reale)
CD 3 2 Write-in (Scattered Write-In)
CD 5 22 Write-in (Scattered Write-In)

2012 PRIMARY ELECTIONS: SUPPLEMENTARY INFORMATION

Primary	April 24, 2012 (President) August 14, 2012 (Congress)	**Registration** (as of October 25, 2011 – includes 131,980 inactive registrants)	2,121,442	Republican Democratic Other Unaffiliated	431,721 784,280 14,524 890,917

Primary Type Closed—Only registered Democrats and Republicans could vote in their party's primary.

	REPUBLICAN PRIMARIES			**DEMOCRATIC PRIMARIES**		
President	Romney, W. Mitt	40,171	67.4%			
	Paul, Ron	8,032	13.5%			
	Gingrich, Newt	6,135	10.3%			
	Santorum, Rick	4,072	6.8%			
	Uncommitted	1,168	2.0%			
	TOTAL	59,578				
Senator	McMahon, Linda E.	82,646	72.8%	Murphy, Christopher S.	94,424	66.7%
	Shays, Christopher	30,802	27.2%	Bysiewicz, Susan	47,109	33.3%
	TOTAL	113,448		TOTAL	141,533	

CONNECTICUT

GENERAL AND PRIMARY ELECTIONS

	REPUBLICAN PRIMARIES			DEMOCRATIC PRIMARIES		
Congressional District 1	Decker, John Henry	Unopposed		Larson, John B.*	Unopposed	
Congressional District 2	Formica, Paul	14,256	66.9%	Courtney, Joe*	Unopposed	
	Novak, Daria	7,050	33.1%			
	TOTAL	21,306				
Congressional District 3	Winsley, Wayne	Unopposed		DeLauro, Rosa L.*	Unopposed	
Congressional District 4	Obsitnik, Steve	Unopposed		Himes, Jim*	Unopposed	
Congressional District 5	Roraback, Andrew	9,536	32.1%	Esty, Elizabeth	12,717	44.6%
	Greenberg, Mark	8,033	27.0%	Donovan, Chris	9,216	32.3%
	Bernier, Justin	6,167	20.8%	Roberti, Dan	6,582	23.1%
	Foley, Lisa Wilson	5,966	20.1%			
	TOTAL	29,702		TOTAL	28,515	

Notes: An asterisk (*) denotes incumbent. A Senate or House candidate either had to receive at least 15 percent of the vote in a pre-primary convention to force a primary or had to petition to appear on the primary ballot.

DELAWARE

One member At Large

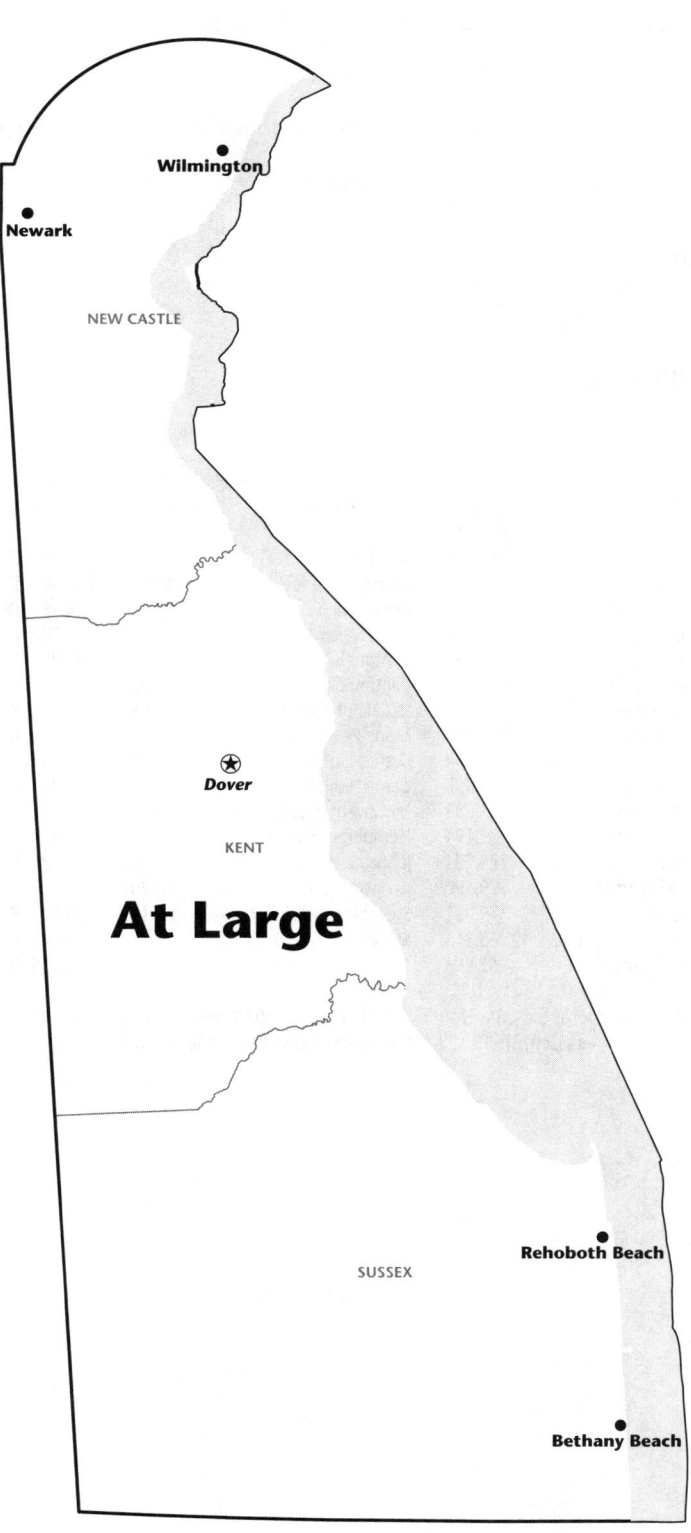

DELAWARE

GOVERNOR
Jack Markell (D). Reelected 2012 to a four-year term. Previously elected 2008.

SENATORS (2 Democrats)
Thomas R. Carper (D). Reelected 2012 to a six-year term. Previously elected 2006, 2000.

Christopher A. Coons (D). Elected 2010 to a six-year term.

REPRESENTATIVE (1 Democrat)
At Large. John C. Carney, Jr. (D)

POSTWAR VOTE FOR PRESIDENT

Year	Total Vote	Republican		Democratic		Other Vote	Rep.-Dem. Plurality	Percentage			
								Total Vote		Major Vote	
		Vote	Candidate	Vote	Candidate			Rep.	Dem.	Rep.	Dem.
2012	413,921	165,484	Romney, W. Mitt	242,584	Obama, Barack H.*	5,853	77,100 D	40.0%	58.6%	40.6%	59.4%
2008	412,412	152,374	McCain, John S. III	255,459	Obama, Barack H.	4,579	103,085 D	36.9%	61.9%	37.4%	62.6%
2004	375,190	171,660	Bush, George W.*	200,152	Kerry, John F.	3,378	28,492 D	45.8%	53.3%	46.2%	53.8%
2000**	327,622	137,288	Bush, George W.	180,068	Gore, Albert Jr.	10,266	42,780 D	41.9%	55.0%	43.3%	56.7%
1996**	271,084	99,062	Dole, Robert "Bob"	140,355	Clinton, Bill*	31,667	41,293 D	36.5%	51.8%	41.4%	58.6%
1992**	289,735	102,313	Bush, George H.*	126,054	Clinton, Bill	61,368	23,741 D	35.3%	43.5%	44.8%	55.2%
1988	249,891	139,639	Bush, George H.	108,647	Dukakis, Michael S.	1,605	30,992 R	55.9%	43.5%	56.2%	43.8%
1984	254,572	152,190	Reagan, Ronald*	101,656	Mondale, Walter F.	726	50,534 R	59.8%	39.9%	60.0%	40.0%
1980**	235,900	111,252	Reagan, Ronald	105,754	Carter, Jimmy*	18,894	5,498 R	47.2%	44.8%	51.3%	48.7%
1976	235,834	109,831	Ford, Gerald R.*	122,596	Carter, Jimmy	3,407	12,765 D	46.6%	52.0%	47.3%	52.7%
1972	235,516	140,357	Nixon, Richard M.*	92,283	McGovern, George S.	2,876	48,074 R	59.6%	39.2%	60.3%	39.7%
1968**	214,367	96,714	Nixon, Richard M.	89,194	Humphrey, Hubert H. Jr.	28,459	7,520 R	45.1%	41.6%	52.0%	48.0%
1964	201,320	78,078	Goldwater, Barry M. Sr.	122,704	Johnson, Lyndon B.*	538	44,626 D	38.8%	60.9%	38.9%	61.1%
1960	196,683	96,373	Nixon, Richard M.	99,590	Kennedy, John F.	720	3,217 D	49.0%	50.6%	49.2%	50.8%
1956	177,988	98,057	Eisenhower, Dwight D.*	79,421	Stevenson, Adlai E. II	510	18,636 R	55.1%	44.6%	55.3%	44.7%
1952	174,025	90,059	Eisenhower, Dwight D.	83,315	Stevenson, Adlai E. II	651	6,744 R	51.8%	47.9%	51.9%	48.1%
1948	139,073	69,588	Dewey, Thomas E.	67,813	Truman, Harry S.*	1,672	1,775 R	50.0%	48.8%	50.6%	49.4%

Note: An asterisk (*) denotes incumbent. **In past elections, the other vote included: 2000 - 8,307 Green (Ralph Nader); 1996 - 28,719 Reform (Ross Perot); 1992 - 59,213 Independent (Perot); 1980 - 16,288 Independent (John Anderson); 1968 - 28,459 American Independent (George Wallace).

DELAWARE

POSTWAR VOTE FOR GOVERNOR

Year	Total Vote	Republican		Democratic		Other Vote	Rep.-Dem. Plurality	Percentage			
								Total Vote		Major Vote	
		Vote	Candidate	Vote	Candidate			Rep.	Dem.	Rep.	Dem.
2012	398,033	113,793	Cragg, Jeffrey	275,993	Markell, Jack*	8,247	162,200 D	28.6%	69.3%	29.2%	70.8%
2008	395,204	126,662	Lee, William Swain	266,861	Markell, Jack	1,681	140,199 D	32.0%	67.5%	32.2%	67.8%
2004	365,008	167,115	Lee, William Swain	185,687	Minner, Ruth Ann*	12,206	18,572 D	45.8%	50.9%	47.4%	52.6%
2000	323,688	128,603	Burris, John M.	191,695	Minner, Ruth Ann	3,390	63,092 D	39.7%	59.2%	40.2%	59.8%
1996	271,122	82,654	Rzewnicki, Janet C.	188,300	Carper, Thomas R.*	168	105,646 D	30.5%	69.5%	30.5%	69.5%
1992	277,058	90,725	Scott, B. Gary	179,365	Carper, Thomas R.	6,968	88,640 D	32.7%	64.7%	33.6%	66.4%
1988	239,969	169,733	Castle, Michael N.*	70,236	Kreshtoll, Jacob		99,497 R	70.7%	29.3%	70.7%	29.3%
1984	243,565	135,250	Castle, Michael N.	108,315	Quillen, William T.		26,935 R	55.5%	44.5%	55.5%	44.5%
1980	225,081	159,004	du Pont, Pierre S. IV*	64,217	Gordy, William J.	1,860	94,787 R	70.6%	28.5%	71.2%	28.8%
1976	229,563	130,531	du Pont, Pierre S. IV	97,480	Tribbitt, Sherman W.*	1,552	33,051 R	56.9%	42.5%	57.2%	42.8%
1972	228,722	109,583	Peterson, Russell W.*	117,274	Tribbitt, Sherman W.	1,865	7,691 D	47.9%	51.3%	48.3%	51.7%
1968	206,834	104,474	Peterson, Russell W.	102,360	Terry, Charles L. Jr.*		2,114 R	50.5%	49.5%	50.5%	49.5%
1964	200,171	97,374	Buckson, David P.	102,797	Terry, Charles L. Jr.		5,423 D	48.6%	51.4%	48.6%	51.4%
1960	194,835	94,043	Rollins, John W.	100,792	Carvel, Elbert N.		6,749 D	48.3%	51.7%	48.3%	51.7%
1956	177,012	91,965	Boggs, James Caleb*	85,047	McConnell, J. H. Tyler		6,918 R	52.0%	48.0%	52.0%	48.0%
1952	170,749	88,977	Boggs, James Caleb	81,772	Carvel, Elbert N.*		7,205 R	52.1%	47.9%	52.1%	47.9%
1948	140,335	64,996	George, Hyland P.	75,339	Carvel, Elbert N.		10,343 D	46.3%	53.7%	46.3%	53.7%

Note: An asterisk (*) denotes incumbent.

POSTWAR VOTE FOR SENATOR

Year	Total Vote	Republican		Democratic		Other Vote	Rep.-Dem. Plurality	Percentage			
								Total Vote		Major Vote	
		Vote	Candidate	Vote	Candidate			Rep.	Dem.	Rep.	Dem.
2012	399,607	115,700	Wade, Kevin	265,415	Carper, Thomas R.*	18,492	149,715 D	29.0%	66.4%	30.4%	69.6%
2010S	307,402	123,053	O'Donnell, Christine	174,012	Coons, Christopher A.	10,337	50,959 D	40.0%	56.6%	41.4%	58.6%
2008	398,134	140,595	O'Donnell, Christine	257,539	Biden, Joseph R. Jr.*		116,944 D	35.3%	64.7%	35.3%	64.7%
2006	254,099	69,734	Ting, Jan	170,567	Carper, Thomas R.*	13,798	100,833 D	27.4%	67.1%	29.0%	71.0%
2002	232,314	94,793	Clatworthy, Raymond J.	135,253	Biden, Joseph R. Jr.*	2,268	40,460 D	40.8%	58.2%	41.2%	58.8%
2000	327,017	142,891	Roth, William V.*	181,566	Carper, Thomas R.	2,560	38,675 D	43.7%	55.5%	44.0%	56.0%
1996	275,591	105,088	Clatworthy, Raymond J.	165,465	Biden, Joseph R. Jr.*	5,038	60,377 D	38.1%	60.0%	38.8%	61.2%
1994	199,029	111,088	Roth, William V.*	84,554	Oberly, Charles M.	3,387	26,534 R	55.8%	42.5%	56.8%	43.2%
1990	180,152	64,554	Brady, M. Jane	112,918	Biden, Joseph R. Jr.*	2,680	48,364 D	35.8%	62.7%	36.4%	63.6%
1988	243,493	151,115	Roth, William V.*	92,378	Woo, S. B.		58,737 R	62.1%	37.9%	62.1%	37.9%
1984	245,932	98,101	Burris, John M.	147,831	Biden, Joseph R. Jr.*		49,730 D	39.9%	60.1%	39.9%	60.1%
1982	190,960	105,357	Roth, William V.*	84,413	Levinson, David N.	1,190	20,944 R	55.2%	44.2%	55.5%	44.5%
1978	162,072	66,479	Baxter, James H.	93,930	Biden, Joseph R. Jr.*	1,663	27,451 D	41.0%	58.0%	41.4%	58.6%
1976	224,859	125,502	Roth, William V.*	98,055	Maloney, Thomas C.	1,302	27,447 R	55.8%	43.6%	56.1%	43.9%
1972	229,828	112,844	Boggs, James Caleb*	116,006	Biden, Joseph R. Jr.	978	3,162 D	49.1%	50.5%	49.3%	50.7%
1970	161,439	94,979	Roth, William V.	64,740	Zimmerman, Jacob	1,720	30,239 R	58.8%	40.1%	59.5%	40.5%
1966	164,531	97,268	Boggs, James Caleb*	67,263	Tunnell, James M. Jr.		30,005 R	59.1%	40.9%	59.1%	40.9%
1964	200,703	103,782	Williams, John J.*	96,850	Carvel, Elbert N.	71	6,932 R	51.7%	48.3%	51.7%	48.3%
1960	194,964	98,874	Boggs, James Caleb	96,090	Frear, J. Allen Jr.*		2,784 R	50.7%	49.3%	50.7%	49.3%
1958	154,432	82,280	Williams, John J.*	72,152	Carvel, Elbert N.		10,128 R	53.3%	46.7%	53.3%	46.7%
1954	144,900	62,389	Warburton, Herbert B.	82,511	Frear, J. Allen Jr.*		20,122 D	43.1%	56.9%	43.1%	56.9%
1952	170,705	93,020	Williams, John J.*	77,685	du Pont Bayard, Alexis I.		15,335 R	54.5%	45.5%	54.5%	45.5%
1948	141,362	68,246	Buck, Clayton Douglass*	71,888	Frear, J. Allen Jr.	1,228	3,642 D	48.3%	50.9%	48.7%	51.3%
1946	113,513	62,603	Williams, John J.	50,910	Tunnell, James M.*		11,693 R	55.2%	44.8%	55.2%	44.8%

Note: An asterisk (*) denotes incumbent.

DELAWARE

PRESIDENT 2012

2010 Census Population	County	Total Vote	Republican (Romney)	Democratic (Obama)	Other	Rep.-Dem. Plurality	Total Vote Rep.	Total Vote Dem.	Major Vote Rep.	Major Vote Dem.
162,310	KENT	68,680	32,135	35,527	1,018	3,392 D	46.8%	51.7%	47.5%	52.5%
538,479	NEW CASTLE	252,012	81,230	167,082	3,700	85,852 D	32.2%	66.3%	32.7%	67.3%
197,145	SUSSEX	93,229	52,119	39,975	1,135	12,144 R	55.9%	42.9%	56.6%	43.4%
897,934	TOTAL	413,921	165,484	242,584	5,853	77,100 D	40.0%	58.6%	40.6%	59.4%

DELAWARE

GOVERNOR 2012

2010 Census Population	County	Total Vote	Republican (Cragg)	Democratic (Markell)	Other	Rep.-Dem. Plurality	Total Vote Rep.	Total Vote Dem.	Major Vote Rep.	Major Vote Dem.
162,310	KENT	66,170	23,846	40,696	1,628	16,850 D	36.0%	61.5%	36.9%	63.1%
538,479	NEW CASTLE	242,139	53,510	183,858	4,771	130,348 D	22.1%	75.9%	22.5%	77.5%
197,145	SUSSEX	89,724	36,437	51,439	1,848	15,002 D	40.6%	57.3%	41.5%	58.5%
897,934	TOTAL	398,033	113,793	275,993	8,247	162,200 D	28.6%	69.3%	29.2%	70.8%

DELAWARE

SENATOR 2012

2010 Census Population	County	Total Vote	Republican (Wade)	Democratic (Carper)	Other	Rep.-Dem. Plurality	Total Vote Rep.	Total Vote Dem.	Major Vote Rep.	Major Vote Dem.
162,310	KENT	66,290	22,561	40,750	2,979	18,189 D	34.0%	61.5%	35.6%	64.4%
538,479	NEW CASTLE	242,836	56,666	177,244	8,926	120,578 D	23.3%	73.0%	24.2%	75.8%
197,145	SUSSEX	90,481	36,473	47,421	6,587	10,948 D	40.3%	52.4%	43.5%	56.5%
897,934	TOTAL	399,607	115,700	265,415	18,492	149,715 D	29.0%	66.4%	30.4%	69.6%

DELAWARE

HOUSE OF REPRESENTATIVES

CD	Year	Total Vote	Republican Vote	Republican Candidate	Democratic Vote	Democratic Candidate	Other Vote	Rep.-Dem. Plurality	Total Vote Rep.	Total Vote Dem.	Major Vote Rep.	Major Vote Dem.
At Large	2012	388,059	129,757	KOVACH, THOMAS H.	249,933	CARNEY, JOHN C. JR.*	8,369	120,176 D	33.4%	64.4%	34.2%	65.8%
At Large	2010	305,636	125,442	URQUHART, GLEN	173,543	CARNEY, JOHN C. JR.	6,651	48,101 D	41.0%	56.8%	42.0%	58.0%
At Large	2008	385,457	235,437	CASTLE, MICHAEL N.*	146,434	HARTLEY-NAGLE, KAREN	3,586	89,003 R	61.1%	38.0%	61.7%	38.3%
At Large	2006	251,694	143,897	CASTLE, MICHAEL N.*	97,565	SPIVACK, DENNIS	10,232	46,332 R	57.2%	38.8%	59.6%	40.4%
At Large	2004	356,045	245,978	CASTLE, MICHAEL N.*	105,716	DONNELLY, PAUL	4,351	140,262 R	69.1%	29.7%	69.9%	30.1%
At Large	2002	228,405	164,605	CASTLE, MICHAEL N.*	61,011	MILLER, MICHEAL C.	2,789	103,594 R	72.1%	26.7%	73.0%	27.0%
At Large	2000	313,171	211,797	CASTLE, MICHAEL N.*	96,488	MILLER, MICHEAL C.	4,886	115,309 R	67.6%	30.8%	68.7%	31.3%
At Large	1998	180,527	119,811	CASTLE, MICHAEL N.*	57,446	WILLIAMS, DENNIS E.	3,270	62,365 R	66.4%	31.8%	67.6%	32.4%
At Large	1996	266,836	185,576	CASTLE, MICHAEL N.*	73,253	WILLIAMS, DENNIS E.	8,007	112,323 R	69.5%	27.5%	71.7%	28.3%
At Large	1994	195,037	137,960	CASTLE, MICHAEL N.*	51,803	DESANTIS, CAROL ANN	5,274	86,157 R	70.7%	26.6%	72.7%	27.3%
At Large	1992	276,157	153,037	CASTLE, MICHAEL N.	117,426	WOO, S. B.	5,694	35,611 R	55.4%	42.5%	56.6%	43.4%
At Large	1990	177,432	58,037	WILLIAMS, RALPH O.	116,274	CARPER, THOMAS R.*	3,121	58,237 D	32.7%	65.5%	33.3%	66.7%

DELAWARE

HOUSE OF REPRESENTATIVES

CD	Year	Total Vote	Republican		Democratic		Other Vote	Rep.-Dem. Plurality	Percentage			
									Total Vote		Major Vote	
			Vote	Candidate	Vote	Candidate			Rep.	Dem.	Rep.	Dem.
At Large	1988	234,517	76,179	KRAPF, JAMES P.	158,338	CARPER, THOMAS R.*		82,159 D	32.5%	67.5%	32.5%	67.5%
At Large	1986	160,757	53,767	NEUBERGER, THOMAS S.	106,351	CARPER, THOMAS R.*	639	52,584 D	33.4%	66.2%	33.6%	66.4%
At Large	1984	243,014	100,650	DUPONT, ELISE	142,070	CARPER, THOMAS R.*	294	41,420 D	41.4%	58.5%	41.5%	58.5%
At Large	1982	188,064	87,153	EVANS, THOMAS B.*	98,533	CARPER, THOMAS R.	2,378	11,380 D	46.3%	52.4%	46.9%	53.1%
At Large	1980	216,629	133,842	EVANS, THOMAS B.*	81,227	MAXWELL, ROBERT L.	1,560	52,615 R	61.8%	37.5%	62.2%	37.8%
At Large	1978	157,566	91,689	EVANS, THOMAS B.*	64,863	HINDES, GARY E.	1,014	26,826 R	58.2%	41.2%	58.6%	41.4%
At Large	1976	214,799	110,677	EVANS, THOMAS B.	102,431	SHIPLEY, SAMUEL L.	1,691	8,246 R	51.5%	47.7%	51.9%	48.1%
At Large	1974	160,328	93,826	DU PONT, PIERRE S. IV*	63,490	SOLES, JAMES	3,012	30,336 R	58.5%	39.6%	59.6%	40.4%
At Large	1972	225,851	141,237	DU PONT, PIERRE S. IV*	83,230	HANDLOFF, NORMA	1,384	58,007 R	62.5%	36.9%	62.9%	37.1%
At Large	1970	160,313	86,125	DU PONT, PIERRE S. IV	71,429	DANIELLO, JOHN D.	2,759	14,696 R	53.7%	44.6%	54.7%	45.3%
At Large	1968	200,820	117,827	ROTH, WILLIAM V.*	82,993	MCDOWELL, HARRIS B. JR.		34,834 R	58.7%	41.3%	58.7%	41.3%
At Large	1966	163,093	90,961	ROTH, WILLIAM V.	72,132	MCDOWELL, HARRIS B. JR.*		18,829 R	55.8%	44.2%	55.8%	44.2%
At Large	1964	198,691	86,254	SNOWDEN, JAMES H.	112,361	MCDOWELL, HARRIS B. JR.*	76	26,107 D	43.4%	56.6%	43.4%	56.6%
At Large	1962	153,356	71,934	WILLIAMS, WILMER F.	81,166	MCDOWELL, HARRIS B. JR.*	256	9,232 D	46.9%	52.9%	47.0%	53.0%
At Large	1960	194,564	96,337	MCKINSTRY, JAMES T.	98,227	MCDOWELL, HARRIS B. JR.*		1,890 D	49.5%	50.5%	49.5%	50.5%
At Large	1958	152,896	76,099	HASKELL, HARRY G. JR.*	76,797	MCDOWELL, HARRIS B. JR.*		698 D	49.8%	50.2%	49.8%	50.2%
At Large	1956	176,182	91,538	HASKELL, HARRY G. JR.	84,644	MCDOWELL, HARRIS B. JR.*		6,894 R	52.0%	48.0%	52.0%	48.0%
At Large	1954	144,236	65,035	MARTIN, LILLIAN I.	79,201	MCDOWELL, HARRIS B. JR.		14,166 D	45.1%	54.9%	45.1%	54.9%
At Large	1952	170,015	88,285	WARBURTON, H. B.	81,730	SCANNELL, JOSEPH S.		6,555 R	51.9%	48.1%	51.9%	48.1%
At Large	1950	129,404	73,313	BOGGS, JAMES CALEB*	56,091	WINCHESTER, H. M.		17,222 R	56.7%	43.3%	56.7%	43.3%
At Large	1948	140,535	71,127	BOGGS, JAMES CALEB*	68,909	MCGUIGAN, J. CARL	499	2,218 R	50.6%	49.0%	50.8%	49.2%
At Large	1946	112,621	63,516	BOGGS, JAMES CALEB	49,105	TRAYNOR, PHILIP A.*		14,411 R	56.4%	43.6%	56.4%	43.6%

Note: An asterisk (*) denotes incumbent.

DELAWARE

GENERAL AND PRIMARY ELECTIONS

2012 GENERAL ELECTIONS: OTHER VOTE

President   Other vote was 3,882 Libertarian (Gary E. Johnson), 1,940 Green (Jill Stein), 23 Write-in (Virgil H. Goode), 8 Write-in (Scattered Write-In)

Governor   Other vote was 4,575 Green (Mark Perri), 3,668 Libertarian (Jesse McVay), 4 Write-in (David Charles Graham)

Senator   Other vote was 15,300 Independent Party (Alexander Pires), 3,191 Green (Andrew Richard Groff), 1 Write-in (Richard Thomas Ruzicka)

House   Other vote was:

At Large   4,273 Green (Bernard August), 4,096 Libertarian (Scott Gesty)

2012 PRIMARY ELECTIONS: SUPPLEMENTARY INFORMATION

Primary	April 24, 2012 (President) September 11, 2012 (Congress)	**Registration** (as of September 11, 2012)	623,292	Democratic	290,944	
				Republican	178,402	
				Other	145,025	

Primary Type   Closed—Only registered Democrats and Republicans could vote in their party's primary.

DELAWARE

GENERAL AND PRIMARY ELECTIONS

	REPUBLICAN PRIMARIES			DEMOCRATIC PRIMARIES		
President	Romney, W. Mitt	16,143	56.5%			
	Gingrich, Newt	7,742	27.1%			
	Paul, Ron	3,017	10.6%			
	Santorum, Rick	1,690	5.9%			
	TOTAL	28,592				
Senator	Wade, Kevin	Unopposed		Carper, Thomas R.*	43,587	87.9%
				Spanarelli, Keith	6,028	12.1%
				TOTAL	49,615	
Governor	Cragg, Jeffrey	Unopposed		Markell, Jack*	Unopposed	
House At Large	Kovach, Thomas H.	15,018	65.6%	Carney, John C. Jr.*	Unopposed	
	Izzo, Rose	7,888	34.4%			
	TOTAL	22,906				

Notes: An asterisk (*) denotes incumbent. The names of unopposed candidates did not appear on the primary ballot; therefore, no votes were cast for these candidates.

FLORIDA

Congressional districts first established for elections held in 2012

27 members

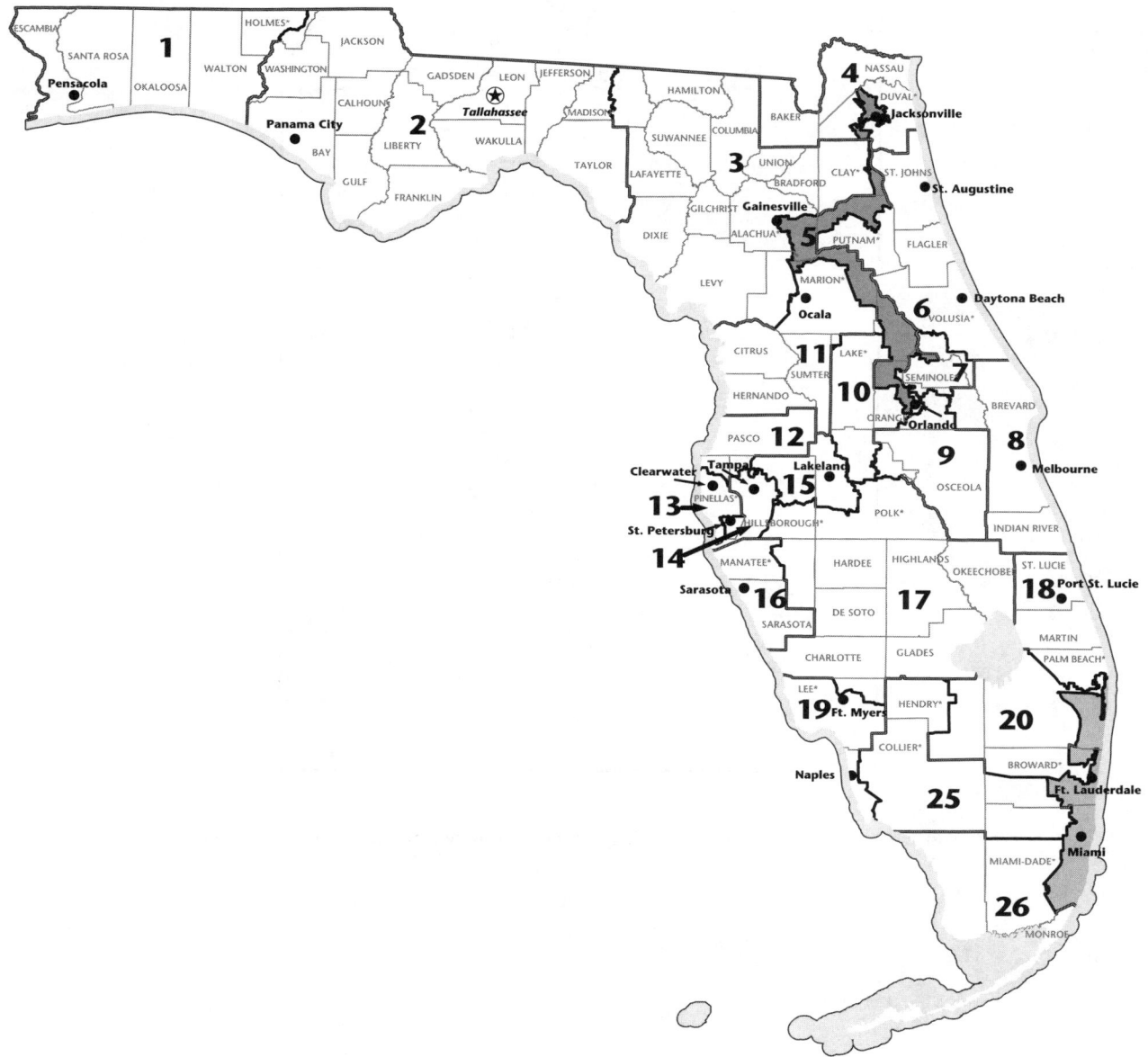

* Asterisk indicates a county whose boundaries include parts of two or more Congressional districts.

FLORIDA

St.Petersburg, Tampa, Fort Myers Areas

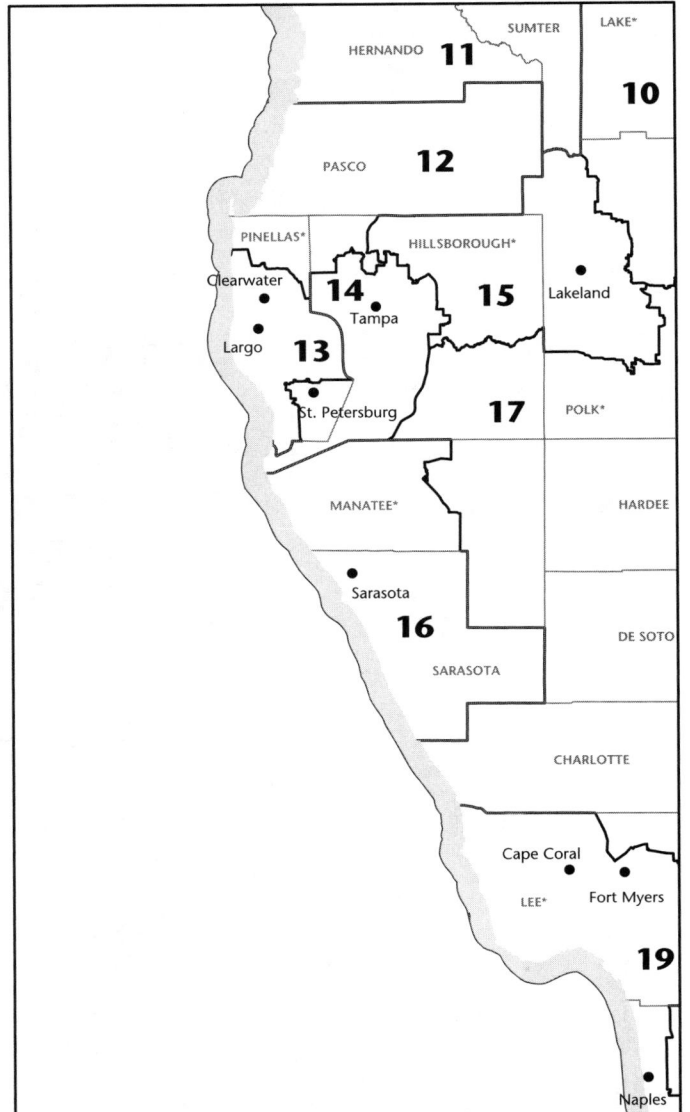

* Asterisk indicates a county whose boundaries include parts of two or more Congressional districts.

FLORIDA

Greater Miami, Fort Lauderdale Areas

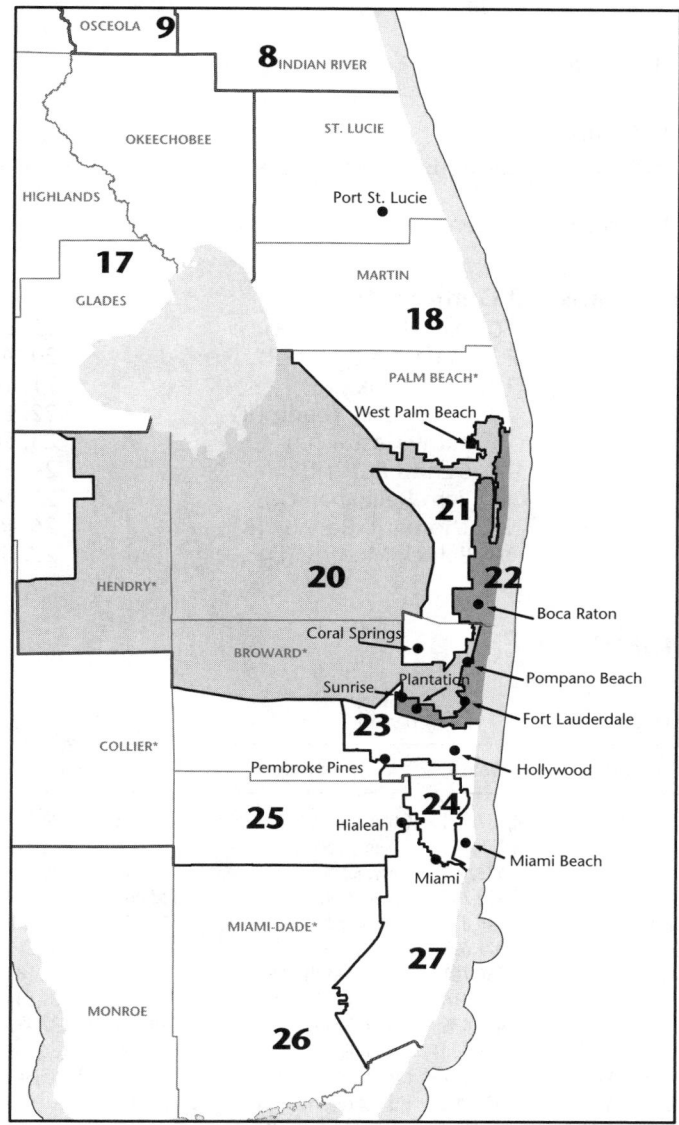

* Asterisk indicates a county whose boundaries include parts of two or more Congressional districts.

FLORIDA

GOVERNOR

Rick Scott (R). Elected 2010 to a four-year term.

SENATORS (1 Republican, 1 Democrat)

Bill Nelson (D). Reelected 2012 to a six-year term. Previously elected 2006, 2000.

Marco Rubio (R). Elected 2010 to a six-year term.

REPRESENTATIVES (17 Republicans, 10 Democrats)

1. Jeff Miller (R)
2. Steve Southerland (R)
3. Ted Yoho (R)
4. Ander Crenshaw (R)
5. Corrine Brown (D)
6. Ron DeSantis (R)
7. John Mica (R)
8. Bill Posey (R)
9. Alan Grayson (D)
10. Daniel Webster (R)
11. Richard Nugent (R)
12. Gus Bilirakis (R)
13. C. W. (Bill) Young (R)
14. Kathy Castor (D)
15. Dennis Ross (R)
16. Vern Buchanan (R)
17. Thomas J. Rooney (R)
18. Patrick Murphy (D)
19. Trey Radel (R)
20. Alcee L. Hastings (D)
21. Ted Deutch (D)
22. Lois Frankel (D)
23. Debbie Wasserman Schultz (D)
24. Frederica Wilson (D)
25. Mario Diaz-Balart (R)
26. Joe Garcia (D)
27. Ileana Ros-Lehtinen (R)

POSTWAR VOTE FOR PRESIDENT

		Republican		Democratic		Other	Rep.-Dem.	Total Vote		Major Vote	
Year	Total Vote	Vote	Candidate	Vote	Candidate	Vote	Plurality	Rep.	Dem.	Rep.	Dem.
2012	8,474,179	4,163,447	Romney, W. Mitt	4,237,756	Obama, Barack H.*	72,976	74,309 D	49.1%	50.0%	49.6%	50.4%
2008	8,390,744	4,045,624	McCain, John S. III	4,282,074	Obama, Barack H.	63,046	236,450 D	48.2%	51.0%	48.6%	51.4%
2004	7,609,810	3,964,522	Bush, George W.*	3,583,544	Kerry, John F.	61,744	380,978 R	52.1%	47.1%	52.5%	47.5%
2000**	5,963,110	2,912,790	Bush, George W.	2,912,253	Gore, Albert Jr.	138,067	537 R	48.8%	48.8%	50.0%	50.0%
1996**	5,303,794	2,244,536	Dole, Robert "Bob"	2,546,870	Clinton, Bill*	512,388	302,334 D	42.3%	48.0%	46.8%	53.2%
1992**	5,314,392	2,173,310	Bush, George H.*	2,072,698	Clinton, Bill	1,068,384	100,612 R	40.9%	39.0%	51.2%	48.8%
1988	4,302,313	2,618,885	Bush, George H.	1,656,701	Dukakis, Michael S.	26,727	962,184 R	60.9%	38.5%	61.3%	38.7%
1984	4,180,051	2,730,350	Reagan, Ronald*	1,448,816	Mondale, Walter F.	885	1,281,534 R	65.3%	34.7%	65.3%	34.7%
1980**	3,686,930	2,046,951	Reagan, Ronald	1,419,475	Carter, Jimmy*	220,504	627,476 R	55.5%	38.5%	59.1%	40.9%
1976	3,150,631	1,469,531	Ford, Gerald R.*	1,636,000	Carter, Jimmy	45,100	166,469 D	46.6%	51.9%	47.3%	52.7%
1972	2,583,283	1,857,759	Nixon, Richard M.*	718,117	McGovern, George S.	7,407	1,139,642 R	71.9%	27.8%	72.1%	27.9%
1968**	2,187,805	886,804	Nixon, Richard M.	676,794	Humphrey, Hubert H. Jr.	624,207	210,010 R	40.5%	30.9%	56.7%	43.3%
1964	1,854,481	905,941	Goldwater, Barry M. Sr.	948,540	Johnson, Lyndon B.*		42,599 D	48.9%	51.1%	48.9%	51.1%
1960	1,544,176	795,476	Nixon, Richard M.	748,700	Kennedy, John F.		46,776 R	51.5%	48.5%	51.5%	48.5%
1956	1,125,762	643,849	Eisenhower, Dwight D.*	480,371	Stevenson, Adlai E. II	1,542	163,478 R	57.2%	42.7%	57.3%	42.7%
1952	989,337	544,036	Eisenhower, Dwight D.	444,950	Stevenson, Adlai E. II	351	99,086 R	55.0%	45.0%	55.0%	45.0%
1948**	577,643	194,280	Dewey, Thomas E.	281,988	Truman, Harry S.*	101,375	87,708 D	33.6%	48.8%	40.8%	59.2%

Note: An asterisk (*) denotes incumbent. **In past elections, the other vote included: 2000 - 97,488 Green (Ralph Nader); 1996 - 483,870 Reform (Ross Perot); 1992 - 1,053,067 Independent (Perot); 1980 - 189,692 Independent (John Anderson); 1968 - 624,207 American Independent (George Wallace); 1948 - 89,755 States' Rights (Strom Thurmond).

FLORIDA

POSTWAR VOTE FOR GOVERNOR

Year	Total Vote	Republican		Democratic		Other Vote	Rep.-Dem. Plurality	Percentage			
								Total Vote		Major Vote	
		Vote	Candidate	Vote	Candidate			Rep.	Dem.	Rep.	Dem.
2010	5,359,735	2,619,335	Scott, Rick	2,557,785	Sink, Alex	182,615	61,550 R	48.9%	47.7%	50.6%	49.4%
2006	4,829,270	2,519,845	Crist, Charlie	2,178,289	Davis, Jim	131,136	341,556 R	52.2%	45.1%	53.6%	46.4%
2002	5,100,581	2,856,845	Bush, Jeb*	2,201,427	McBride, Bill	42,309	655,418 R	56.0%	43.2%	56.5%	43.5%
1998	3,964,441	2,191,105	Bush, Jeb	1,773,054	MacKay, Kenneth H. "Buddy"*	282	418,051 R	55.3%	44.7%	55.3%	44.7%
1994	4,206,659	2,071,068	Bush, Jeb	2,135,008	Chiles, Lawton*	583	63,940 D	49.2%	50.8%	49.2%	50.8%
1990	3,530,871	1,535,068	Martinez, Bob*	1,995,206	Chiles, Lawton	597	460,138 D	43.5%	56.5%	43.5%	56.5%
1986	3,386,171	1,847,525	Martinez, Bob	1,538,620	Pajcic, Steve	26	308,905 R	54.6%	45.4%	54.6%	45.4%
1982	2,688,566	949,013	Bafalis, L. A.	1,739,553	Graham, Bob*		790,540 D	35.3%	64.7%	35.3%	64.7%
1978	2,530,468	1,123,888	Eckerd, Jack M.	1,406,580	Graham, Bob		282,692 D	44.4%	55.6%	44.4%	55.6%
1974	1,828,392	709,438	Thomas, Jerry	1,118,954	Askew, Reubin*		409,516 D	38.8%	61.2%	38.8%	61.2%
1970	1,730,813	746,243	Kirk, Claude R. Jr.*	984,305	Askew, Reubin	265	238,062 D	43.1%	56.9%	43.1%	56.9%
1966	1,489,661	821,190	Kirk, Claude R. Jr.	668,233	High, Robert King	238	152,957 R	55.1%	44.9%	55.1%	44.9%
1964**	1,663,481	686,297	Holley, Charles R.	933,554	Burns, Haydon	43,630	247,257 D	41.3%	56.1%	42.4%	57.6%
1960	1,419,343	569,936	Petersen, George C.	849,407	Bryant, Farris		279,471 D	40.2%	59.8%	40.2%	59.8%
1956	1,014,733	266,980	Washburn, William A. Jr.	747,753	Collins, Leroy*		480,773 D	26.3%	73.7%	26.3%	73.7%
1954S	357,783	69,852	Watson, J. Tom	287,769	Collins, Leroy	162	217,917 D	19.5%	80.4%	19.5%	80.5%
1952	834,518	210,009	Swan, Harry S.	624,463	McCarty, Daniel T.	46	414,454 D	25.2%	74.8%	25.2%	74.8%
1948	457,638	76,153	Acker, Bert Lee	381,459	Warren, Fuller	26	305,306 D	16.6%	83.4%	16.6%	83.4%

Note: An asterisk (*) denotes incumbent. **The 1964 election was for a two-year term to permit shifting the vote for governor to non-presidential years. The 1954 election was for a short term to fill a vacancy.

POSTWAR VOTE FOR SENATOR

Year	Total Vote	Republican		Democratic		Other Vote	Rep.-Dem. Plurality	Percentage			
								Total Vote		Major Vote	
		Vote	Candidate	Vote	Candidate			Rep.	Dem.	Rep.	Dem.
2012	8,189,946	3,458,267	Mack, Connie IV	4,523,451	Nelson, Bill*	208,228	1,065,184 D	42.2%	55.2%	43.3%	56.7%
2010**	5,411,106	2,645,743	Rubio, Marco	1,092,936	Meek, Kendrick B.	1,672,427	1,552,807 R	48.9%	20.2%	70.8%	29.2%
2006	4,793,534	1,826,127	Harris, Katherine	2,890,548	Nelson, Bill*	76,859	1,064,421 D	38.1%	60.3%	38.7%	61.3%
2004	7,429,894	3,672,864	Martinez, Mel	3,590,201	Castor, Betty	166,829	82,663 R	49.4%	48.3%	50.6%	49.4%
2000	5,856,731	2,705,348	McCollum, Bill	2,989,487	Nelson, Bill	161,896	284,139 D	46.2%	51.0%	47.5%	52.5%
1998	3,900,162	1,463,755	Crist, Charlie	2,436,407	Graham, Bob*		972,652 D	37.5%	62.5%	37.5%	62.5%
1994	4,106,176	2,894,726	Mack, Connie III*	1,210,412	Rodham, Hugh E.	1,038	1,684,314 R	70.5%	29.5%	70.5%	29.5%
1992	4,962,290	1,716,505	Grant, Bill	3,245,565	Graham, Bob*	220	1,529,060 D	34.6%	65.4%	34.6%	65.4%
1988	4,068,209	2,051,071	Mack, Connie III	2,016,553	MacKay, Buddy	585	34,518 R	50.4%	49.6%	50.4%	49.6%
1986	3,429,996	1,552,376	Hawkins, Paula*	1,877,543	Graham, Bob	77	325,167 D	45.3%	54.7%	45.3%	54.7%
1982	2,653,419	1,015,330	Poole, Van B.	1,637,667	Chiles, Lawton*	422	622,337 D	38.3%	61.7%	38.3%	61.7%
1980	3,528,028	1,822,460	Hawkins, Paula	1,705,409	Gunter, Bill	159	117,051 R	51.7%	48.3%	51.7%	48.3%
1976	2,857,534	1,057,886	Grady, John	1,799,518	Chiles, Lawton*	130	741,632 D	37.0%	63.0%	37.0%	63.0%
1974**	1,800,539	736,674	Eckerd, Jack M.	781,031	Stone, Richard	282,834	44,357 D	40.9%	43.4%	48.5%	51.5%
1970	1,675,378	772,817	Cramer, William C.	902,438	Chiles, Lawton	123	129,621 D	46.1%	53.9%	46.1%	53.9%
1968	2,024,136	1,131,499	Gurney, Edward J.	892,637	Collins, Leroy		238,862 R	55.9%	44.1%	55.9%	44.1%
1964	1,560,337	562,212	Kirk, Claude R. Jr.	997,585	Holland, Spessard L.*	540	435,373 D	36.0%	63.9%	36.0%	64.0%
1962	939,207	281,381	Rupert, Emerson	657,633	Smathers, George A.*	193	376,252 D	30.0%	70.0%	30.0%	70.0%
1958	542,069	155,956	Hyzer, Leland	386,113	Holland, Spessard L.*		230,157 D	28.8%	71.2%	28.8%	71.2%
1956	655,418			655,418	Smathers, George A.*		655,418 D		100.0%		100.0%
1952	617,800			616,665	Holland, Spessard L.*	1,135	616,665 D		99.8%		100.0%
1950	313,487	74,228	Booth, John P.	238,987	Smathers, George A.	272	164,759 D	23.7%	76.2%	23.7%	76.3%
1946	198,645	42,413	Schad, J. Harry	156,232	Holland, Spessard L.		113,819 D	21.4%	78.6%	21.4%	78.6%

Note: An asterisk (*) denotes incumbent. **In past elections, the other vote included: 2010 - 1,607,549 Independent (Charlie Crist), who placed second; 1974 - 282,659 American (John Grady). The Republican Party did not run a candidate in the 1952 and 1956 Senate elections.

FLORIDA

PRESIDENT 2012

2010 Census Population	County	Total Vote	Republican (Romney)	Democratic (Obama)	Other	Rep.-Dem. Plurality	Total Vote Rep.	Total Vote Dem.	Major Vote Rep.	Major Vote Dem.
247,336	ALACHUA	120,418	48,797	69,699	1,922	20,902 D	40.5%	57.9%	41.2%	58.8%
27,115	BAKER	11,368	8,975	2,311	82	6,664 R	78.9%	20.3%	79.5%	20.5%
168,852	BAY	79,861	56,876	22,051	934	34,825 R	71.2%	27.6%	72.1%	27.9%
28,520	BRADFORD	11,635	8,219	3,325	91	4,894 R	70.6%	28.6%	71.2%	28.8%
543,376	BREVARD	285,559	159,300	122,993	3,266	36,307 R	55.8%	43.1%	56.4%	43.6%
1,748,066	BROWARD	756,422	244,101	508,312	4,009	264,211 D	32.3%	67.2%	32.4%	67.6%
14,625	CALHOUN	6,152	4,366	1,664	122	2,702 R	71.0%	27.0%	72.4%	27.6%
159,978	CHARLOTTE	84,682	47,996	35,906	780	12,090 R	56.7%	42.4%	57.2%	42.8%
141,236	CITRUS	73,935	44,662	28,460	813	16,202 R	60.4%	38.5%	61.1%	38.9%
190,865	CLAY	96,589	70,022	25,759	808	44,263 R	72.5%	26.7%	73.1%	26.9%
321,520	COLLIER	149,112	96,520	51,698	894	44,822 R	64.7%	34.7%	65.1%	34.9%
67,531	COLUMBIA	27,163	18,429	8,462	272	9,967 R	67.8%	31.2%	68.5%	31.5%
34,862	DESOTO	9,865	5,587	4,174	104	1,413 R	56.6%	42.3%	57.2%	42.8%
16,422	DIXIE	6,941	5,052	1,798	91	3,254 R	72.8%	25.9%	73.8%	26.2%
864,263	DUVAL	411,848	211,615	196,737	3,496	14,878 R	51.4%	47.8%	51.8%	48.2%
297,619	ESCAMBIA	148,502	88,711	58,185	1,606	30,526 R	59.7%	39.2%	60.4%	39.6%
95,696	FLAGLER	50,595	26,969	23,207	419	3,762 R	53.3%	45.9%	53.7%	46.3%
11,549	FRANKLIN	5,474	3,570	1,845	59	1,725 R	65.2%	33.7%	65.9%	34.1%
46,389	GADSDEN	22,499	6,630	15,770	99	9,140 D	29.5%	70.1%	29.6%	70.4%
16,939	GILCHRIST	7,909	5,917	1,885	107	4,032 R	74.8%	23.8%	75.8%	24.2%
12,884	GLADES	3,989	2,344	1,603	42	741 R	58.8%	40.2%	59.4%	40.6%
15,863	GULF	7,108	4,995	2,014	99	2,981 R	70.3%	28.3%	71.3%	28.7%
14,799	HAMILTON	5,407	3,138	2,228	41	910 R	58.0%	41.2%	58.5%	41.5%
27,731	HARDEE	7,226	4,696	2,463	67	2,233 R	65.0%	34.1%	65.6%	34.4%
39,140	HENDRY	10,185	5,355	4,751	79	604 R	52.6%	46.6%	53.0%	47.0%
172,778	HERNANDO	83,667	44,938	37,830	899	7,108 R	53.7%	45.2%	54.3%	45.7%
98,786	HIGHLANDS	42,444	25,915	16,148	381	9,767 R	61.1%	38.0%	61.6%	38.4%
1,229,226	HILLSBOROUGH	542,102	250,186	286,467	5,449	36,281 D	46.2%	52.8%	46.6%	53.4%
19,927	HOLMES	8,274	6,919	1,264	91	5,655 R	83.6%	15.3%	84.6%	15.4%
138,028	INDIAN RIVER	71,464	43,450	27,492	522	15,958 R	60.8%	38.5%	61.2%	38.8%
49,746	JACKSON	20,941	13,418	7,342	181	6,076 R	64.1%	35.1%	64.6%	35.4%
14,761	JEFFERSON	7,808	3,808	3,945	55	137 D	48.8%	50.5%	49.1%	50.9%
8,870	LAFAYETTE	3,399	2,668	687	44	1,981 R	78.5%	20.2%	79.5%	20.5%
297,052	LAKE	150,811	87,643	61,799	1,369	25,844 R	58.1%	41.0%	58.6%	41.4%
618,754	LEE	266,166	154,163	110,157	1,846	44,006 R	57.9%	41.4%	58.3%	41.7%
275,487	LEON	148,353	55,805	90,881	1,667	35,076 D	37.6%	61.3%	38.0%	62.0%
40,801	LEVY	18,399	12,054	6,119	226	5,935 R	65.5%	33.3%	66.3%	33.7%
8,365	LIBERTY	3,284	2,301	942	41	1,359 R	70.1%	28.7%	71.0%	29.0%
19,224	MADISON	8,715	4,474	4,176	65	298 R	51.3%	47.9%	51.7%	48.3%
322,833	MANATEE	153,491	85,627	66,503	1,361	19,124 R	55.8%	43.3%	56.3%	43.7%
331,298	MARION	161,385	93,043	66,831	1,511	26,212 R	57.7%	41.4%	58.2%	41.8%
146,318	MARTIN	78,873	48,183	30,107	583	18,076 R	61.1%	38.2%	61.5%	38.5%
2,496,435	MIAMI-DADE	878,314	332,981	541,440	3,893	208,459 D	37.9%	61.6%	38.1%	61.9%
73,090	MONROE	39,057	19,234	19,404	419	170 D	49.2%	49.7%	49.8%	50.2%
73,314	NASSAU	40,528	29,929	10,251	348	19,678 R	73.8%	25.3%	74.5%	25.5%
180,822	OKALOOSA	94,798	70,168	23,421	1,209	46,747 R	74.0%	24.7%	75.0%	25.0%
39,996	OKEECHOBEE	12,324	7,328	4,856	140	2,472 R	59.5%	39.4%	60.1%	39.9%
1,145,956	ORANGE	466,359	188,589	273,665	4,105	85,076 D	40.4%	58.7%	40.8%	59.2%
268,685	OSCEOLA	108,698	40,592	67,239	867	26,647 D	37.3%	61.9%	37.6%	62.4%
1,320,134	PALM BEACH	600,721	247,398	349,651	3,672	102,253 D	41.2%	58.2%	41.4%	58.6%
464,697	PASCO	213,573	112,427	98,263	2,883	14,164 R	52.6%	46.0%	53.4%	46.6%
916,542	PINELLAS	457,702	213,258	239,104	5,340	25,846 D	46.6%	52.2%	47.1%	52.9%
602,095	POLK	248,683	131,577	114,622	2,484	16,955 R	52.9%	46.1%	53.4%	46.6%
74,364	PUTNAM	31,324	19,326	11,667	331	7,659 R	61.7%	37.2%	62.4%	37.6%
151,372	SANTA ROSA	76,846	58,186	17,768	892	40,418 R	75.7%	23.1%	76.6%	23.4%
379,448	SARASOTA	207,480	110,504	95,119	1,857	15,385 R	53.3%	45.8%	53.7%	46.3%
422,718	SEMINOLE	208,620	109,943	96,445	2,232	13,498 R	52.7%	46.2%	53.3%	46.7%
190,039	ST. JOHNS	114,795	78,513	35,190	1,092	43,323 R	68.4%	30.7%	69.1%	30.9%
277,789	ST. LUCIE	123,027	56,202	65,869	956	9,667 D	45.7%	53.5%	46.0%	54.0%
93,420	SUMTER	60,479	40,646	19,524	309	21,122 R	67.2%	32.3%	67.6%	32.4%

FLORIDA

PRESIDENT 2012

2010 Census Population	County	Total Vote	Republican (Romney)	Democratic (Obama)	Other	Rep.-Dem. Plurality	Percentage			
							Total Vote		Major Vote	
							Rep.	Dem.	Rep.	Dem.
41,551	SUWANNEE	17,629	12,672	4,751	206	7,921 R	71.9%	26.9%	72.7%	27.3%
22,570	TAYLOR	9,120	6,249	2,764	107	3,485 R	68.5%	30.3%	69.3%	30.7%
15,535	UNION	5,393	3,980	1,339	74	2,641 R	73.8%	24.8%	74.8%	25.2%
494,593	VOLUSIA	234,536	117,490	114,748	2,298	2,742 R	50.1%	48.9%	50.6%	49.4%
30,776	WAKULLA	14,660	9,290	5,175	195	4,115 R	63.4%	35.3%	64.2%	35.8%
55,043	WALTON	28,494	21,490	6,671	333	14,819 R	75.4%	23.4%	76.3%	23.7%
24,896	WASHINGTON	10,999	8,038	2,820	141	5,218 R	73.1%	25.6%	74.0%	26.0%
18,801,310	TOTAL	8,474,179	4,163,447	4,237,756	72,976	74,309 D	49.1%	50.0%	49.6%	50.4%

FLORIDA

SENATOR 2012

2010 Census Population	County	Total Vote	Republican (Mack)	Democratic (Nelson)	Other	Rep.-Dem. Plurality	Percentage			
							Total Vote		Major Vote	
							Rep.	Dem.	Rep.	Dem.
247,336	ALACHUA	116,728	41,834	72,439	2,455	30,605 D	35.8%	62.1%	36.6%	63.4%
27,115	BAKER	11,139	6,940	3,884	315	3,056 R	62.3%	34.9%	64.1%	35.9%
168,852	BAY	78,495	47,530	28,480	2,485	19,050 R	60.6%	36.3%	62.5%	37.5%
28,520	BRADFORD	11,460	6,605	4,529	326	2,076 R	57.6%	39.5%	59.3%	40.7%
543,376	BREVARD	278,873	127,177	142,072	9,624	14,895 D	45.6%	50.9%	47.2%	52.8%
1,748,066	BROWARD	733,961	212,803	510,987	10,171	298,184 D	29.0%	69.6%	29.4%	70.6%
14,625	CALHOUN	6,032	3,035	2,737	260	298 R	50.3%	45.4%	52.6%	47.4%
159,978	CHARLOTTE	82,993	42,168	37,617	3,208	4,551 R	50.8%	45.3%	52.9%	47.1%
141,236	CITRUS	72,631	35,112	34,574	2,945	538 R	48.3%	47.6%	50.4%	49.6%
190,865	CLAY	93,725	59,584	30,999	3,142	28,585 R	63.6%	33.1%	65.8%	34.2%
321,520	COLLIER	143,514	85,194	54,784	3,536	30,410 R	59.4%	38.2%	60.9%	39.1%
67,531	COLUMBIA	26,599	15,055	10,725	819	4,330 R	56.6%	40.3%	58.4%	41.6%
34,862	DESOTO	9,646	4,661	4,637	348	24 R	48.3%	48.1%	50.1%	49.9%
16,422	DIXIE	6,737	3,755	2,724	258	1,031 R	55.7%	40.4%	58.0%	42.0%
864,263	DUVAL	401,233	177,958	211,493	11,782	33,535 D	44.4%	52.7%	45.7%	54.3%
297,619	ESCAMBIA	144,852	76,893	64,793	3,166	12,100 R	53.1%	44.7%	54.3%	45.7%
95,696	FLAGLER	48,918	22,029	25,430	1,459	3,401 D	45.0%	52.0%	46.4%	53.6%
11,549	FRANKLIN	5,376	2,621	2,622	133	1 D	48.8%	48.8%	50.0%	50.0%
46,389	GADSDEN	22,185	5,429	16,442	314	11,013 D	24.5%	74.1%	24.8%	75.2%
16,939	GILCHRIST	7,713	4,692	2,783	238	1,909 R	60.8%	36.1%	62.8%	37.2%
12,884	GLADES	3,866	1,903	1,823	140	80 R	49.2%	47.2%	51.1%	48.9%
15,863	GULF	7,027	3,675	3,123	229	552 R	52.3%	44.4%	54.1%	45.9%
14,799	HAMILTON	5,260	2,554	2,561	145	7 D	48.6%	48.7%	49.9%	50.1%
27,731	HARDEE	7,037	3,611	3,101	325	510 R	51.3%	44.1%	53.8%	46.2%
39,140	HENDRY	9,967	4,632	5,002	333	370 D	46.5%	50.2%	48.1%	51.9%
172,778	HERNANDO	81,764	34,902	43,691	3,171	8,789 D	42.7%	53.4%	44.4%	55.6%
98,786	HIGHLANDS	40,972	20,354	19,110	1,508	1,244 R	49.7%	46.6%	51.6%	48.4%
1,229,226	HILLSBOROUGH	525,862	203,595	308,910	13,357	105,315 D	38.7%	58.7%	39.7%	60.3%
19,927	HOLMES	8,140	5,589	2,236	315	3,353 R	68.7%	27.5%	71.4%	28.6%
138,028	INDIAN RIVER	68,259	36,551	29,563	2,145	6,988 R	53.5%	43.3%	55.3%	44.7%
49,746	JACKSON	20,682	10,624	9,574	484	1,050 R	51.4%	46.3%	52.6%	47.4%
14,761	JEFFERSON	7,641	2,941	4,549	151	1,608 D	38.5%	59.5%	39.3%	60.7%
8,870	LAFAYETTE	3,345	2,130	1,119	96	1,011 R	63.7%	33.5%	65.6%	34.4%
297,052	LAKE	146,275	71,463	69,791	5,021	1,672 R	48.9%	47.7%	50.6%	49.4%
618,754	LEE	259,792	133,746	117,773	8,273	15,973 R	51.5%	45.3%	53.2%	46.8%

FLORIDA

SENATOR 2012

2010 Census Population	County	Total Vote	Republican (Mack)	Democratic (Nelson)	Other	Rep.-Dem. Plurality		Total Vote Rep.	Dem.	Major Vote Rep.	Dem.
275,487	LEON	143,543	46,379	94,323	2,841	47,944	D	32.3%	65.7%	33.0%	67.0%
40,801	LEVY	17,999	9,557	7,833	609	1,724	R	53.1%	43.5%	55.0%	45.0%
8,365	LIBERTY	3,237	1,539	1,587	111	48	D	47.5%	49.0%	49.2%	50.8%
19,224	MADISON	8,520	3,545	4,763	212	1,218	D	41.6%	55.9%	42.7%	57.3%
322,833	MANATEE	149,652	70,721	73,985	4,946	3,264	D	47.3%	49.4%	48.9%	51.1%
331,298	MARION	158,123	75,967	76,930	5,226	963	D	48.0%	48.7%	49.7%	50.3%
146,318	MARTIN	76,220	40,901	33,767	1,552	7,134	R	53.7%	44.3%	54.8%	45.2%
2,496,435	MIAMI-DADE	827,969	292,757	523,461	11,751	230,704	D	35.4%	63.2%	35.9%	64.1%
73,090	MONROE	37,286	17,013	19,506	767	2,493	D	45.6%	52.3%	46.6%	53.4%
73,314	NASSAU	39,341	24,773	13,313	1,255	11,460	R	63.0%	33.8%	65.0%	35.0%
180,822	OKALOOSA	92,177	61,796	27,098	3,283	34,698	R	67.0%	29.4%	69.5%	30.5%
39,996	OKEECHOBEE	11,941	5,554	5,972	415	418	D	46.5%	50.0%	48.2%	51.8%
1,145,956	ORANGE	444,293	153,241	282,090	8,962	128,849	D	34.5%	63.5%	35.2%	64.8%
268,685	OSCEOLA	104,886	32,331	69,690	2,865	37,359	D	30.8%	66.4%	31.7%	68.3%
1,320,134	PALM BEACH	569,067	198,238	362,499	8,330	164,261	D	34.8%	63.7%	35.4%	64.6%
464,697	PASCO	207,786	87,620	111,764	8,402	24,144	D	42.2%	53.8%	43.9%	56.1%
916,542	PINELLAS	445,436	167,380	263,427	14,629	96,047	D	37.6%	59.1%	38.9%	61.1%
602,095	POLK	241,667	107,393	126,722	7,552	19,329	D	44.4%	52.4%	45.9%	54.1%
74,364	PUTNAM	30,729	14,942	14,560	1,227	382	R	48.6%	47.4%	50.6%	49.4%
151,372	SANTA ROSA	75,065	50,772	21,893	2,400	28,879	R	67.6%	29.2%	69.9%	30.1%
379,448	SARASOTA	201,365	93,502	102,569	5,294	9,067	D	46.4%	50.9%	47.7%	52.3%
422,718	SEMINOLE	201,645	90,179	106,371	5,095	16,192	D	44.7%	52.8%	45.9%	54.1%
190,039	ST. JOHNS	111,515	66,626	41,171	3,718	25,455	R	59.7%	36.9%	61.8%	38.2%
277,789	ST. LUCIE	118,943	45,989	70,179	2,775	24,190	D	38.7%	59.0%	39.6%	60.4%
93,420	SUMTER	59,210	34,058	23,410	1,742	10,648	R	57.5%	39.5%	59.3%	40.7%
41,551	SUWANNEE	17,356	10,480	6,277	599	4,203	R	60.4%	36.2%	62.5%	37.5%
22,570	TAYLOR	8,972	4,802	3,914	256	888	R	53.5%	43.6%	55.1%	44.9%
15,535	UNION	5,272	3,070	2,057	145	1,013	R	58.2%	39.0%	59.9%	40.1%
494,593	VOLUSIA	228,992	95,927	126,302	6,763	30,375	D	41.9%	55.2%	43.2%	56.8%
30,776	WAKULLA	14,337	7,098	6,700	539	398	R	49.5%	46.7%	51.4%	48.6%
55,043	WALTON	27,829	18,433	8,480	916	9,953	R	66.2%	30.5%	68.5%	31.5%
24,896	WASHINGTON	10,874	6,339	4,161	374	2,178	R	58.3%	38.3%	60.4%	39.6%
18,801,310	TOTAL	8,189,946	3,458,267	4,523,451	208,228	1,065,184	D	42.2%	55.2%	43.3%	56.7%

FLORIDA

HOUSE OF REPRESENTATIVES

CD	Year	Total Vote	Republican Vote	Candidate	Democratic Vote	Candidate	Other Vote	Rep.-Dem. Plurality		Total Vote Rep.	Dem.	Major Vote Rep.	Dem.
1	2012	342,594	238,440	MILLER, JEFF*	92,961	BRYAN, JIM	11,193	145,479	R	69.6%	27.1%	71.9%	28.1%
2	2012	333,718	175,856	SOUTHERLAND, STEVE*	157,634	LAWSON, AL	228	18,222	R	52.7%	47.2%	52.7%	47.3%
3	2012	315,669	204,331	YOHO, TED	102,468	GAILLOT, J.R.	8,870	101,863	R	64.7%	32.5%	66.6%	33.4%
4	2012	315,470	239,988	CRENSHAW, ANDER*			75,482	239,988	R	76.1%		100.0%	
5	2012	269,153	70,700	KOLB, LEANNE	190,472	BROWN, CORRINE*	7,981	119,772	D	26.3%	70.8%	27.1%	72.9%
6	2012	342,451	195,962	DESANTIS, RON	146,489	BEAVEN, HEATHER		49,473	R	57.2%	42.8%	57.2%	42.8%
7	2012	316,010	185,518	MICA, JOHN*	130,479	KENDALL, JASON H.	13	55,039	R	58.7%	41.3%	58.7%	41.3%
8	2012	348,909	205,432	POSEY, BILL*	130,870	ROBERTS, SHANNON	12,607	74,562	R	58.9%	37.5%	61.1%	38.9%
9	2012	263,747	98,856	LONG, TODD	164,891	GRAYSON, ALAN		66,035	D	37.5%	62.5%	37.5%	62.5%
10	2012	318,269	164,649	WEBSTER, DANIEL*	153,574	DEMINGS, VAL B.	46	11,075	R	51.7%	48.3%	51.7%	48.3%
11	2012	338,663	218,360	NUGENT, RICHARD*	120,303	WERDER, H. DAVID		98,057	R	64.5%	35.5%	64.5%	35.5%
12	2012	330,167	209,604	BILIRAKIS, GUS*	108,770	SNOW, JONATHAN MICHAEL	11,793	100,834	R	63.5%	32.9%	65.8%	34.2%
13	2012	329,347	189,605	YOUNG, C.W. BILL*	139,742	EHRLICH, JESSICA		49,863	R	57.6%	42.4%	57.6%	42.4%
14	2012	280,601	83,480	OTERO, EVELIO "EJ"	197,121	CASTOR, KATHY*		113,641	D	29.8%	70.2%	29.8%	70.2%
15	2012			ROSS, DENNIS									
16	2012	349,076	187,147	BUCHANAN, VERN*	161,929	FITZGERALD, KEITH		25,218	R	53.6%	46.4%	53.6%	46.4%

FLORIDA

HOUSE OF REPRESENTATIVES

| | | | Republican | | Democratic | | | | Percentage | | | |
| | | | | | | | | | Total Vote | | Major Vote | |
CD	Year	Total Vote	Vote	Candidate	Vote	Candidate	Other Vote	Rep.-Dem. Plurality	Rep.	Dem.	Rep.	Dem.
17	2012	282,271	165,488	ROONEY, THOMAS J.*	116,766	BRONSON, WILLIAM	17	48,722 R	58.6%	41.4%	58.6%	41.4%
18	2012	330,665	164,353	WEST, ALLEN*	166,257	MURPHY, PATRICK	55	1,904 D	49.7%	50.3%	49.7%	50.3%
19	2012	306,216	189,833	RADEL, TREY	109,746	ROACH, JIM	6,637	80,087 R	62.0%	35.8%	63.4%	36.6%
20	2012	244,285			214,727	HASTINGS, ALCEE L.*	29,558	214,727 D		87.9%		100.0%
21	2012	284,400			221,263	DEUTCH, TED*	63,137	221,263 D		77.8%		100.0%
22	2012	313,071	142,050	HASNER, ADAM	171,021	FRANKEL, LOIS		28,971 D	45.4%	54.6%	45.4%	54.6%
23	2012	275,430	98,096	HARRINGTON, KAREN	174,205	WASSERMAN-SCHULTZ, DEBBIE*	3,129	76,109 D	35.6%	63.2%	36.0%	64.0%
24	2012					WILSON, FREDERICA						
25	2012	200,229	151,466	DIAZ-BALART, MARIO*			48,763	151,466 R	75.6%		100.0%	
26	2012	252,957	108,820	RIVERA, DAVID*	135,694	GARCIA, JOE	8,443	26,874 D	43.0%	53.6%	44.5%	55.5%
27	2012	230,171	138,488	ROS-LEHTINEN, ILEANA*	85,020	YEVANCEY, MANNY	6,663	53,468 R	60.2%	36.9%	62.0%	38.0%
TOTAL	2012	7,513,539	3,826,522		3,392,402		294,615	434,120 R	50.9%	45.2%	53.0%	47.0%

Note: An asterisk (*) denotes incumbent.

FLORIDA

GENERAL AND PRIMARY ELECTIONS

GENERAL ELECTIONS: OTHER VOTE

President Other vote was 44,726 Libertarian (Gary E. Johnson), 8,947 Green (Jill Stein), 8,154 Peace and Freedom (Roseanne Barr), 3,856 Objectivist (Thomas Robert Stevens), 2,607 Constitution (Virgil H. Goode), 1,754 Justice (Ross C. "Rocky" Anderson), 946 American Independent (Thomas Hoefling), 820 Reform (Andre Barnett), 799 Socialist (Stewart Alexander), 322 Socialism and Liberation (Peta Lindsay), 45 Write-in (Scattered Write-In)

Senator Other vote was 126,079 Independent (Bill Gaylor), 82,089 Independent (Chris Borgia), 60 Write-in (Scattered Write-In)

House Other vote was:

CD 1 11,176 Libertarian (Calen Fretts), 17 Write-in (William Cleave Drummond)

CD 2 228 Write-in (Floyd Miller)

CD 3 8,870 Unaffiliated (Philip Dodds)

CD 4 75,236 Unaffiliated (Jim Klauder), 246 Write-in (Gary Koniz)

CD 5 7,978 No Party Affiliation (Eileen Fleming), 3 Write-in (Bruce Ray Riggs)

CD 7 13 Write-in (Fred Marra)

CD 8 12,607 No Party Affiliation (Richard Gillmor)

CD 10 46 Write-in (Naipaul Seegolam)

CD 12 6,878 No Party Affiliation (John Russell), 4,915 No Party Affiliation (Paul Sidney Elliott)

CD 17 17 Write-in (Tom Baumann)

CD 18 55 Write-in (Marilyn Davis Holloman)

CD 19 6,637 No Party Affiliation (Brandon M. Smith)

CD 20 29,553 Write-in (Randall Terry), 5 Write-in (Anthony M. Dutrow)

CD 21 37,776 No Party Affiliation (W. Michael "Mike" Trout), 25,361 No Party Affiliation (Cesar Henao)

CD 23 3,129 No Party Affiliation (Ilya Katz)

CD 25 31,664 No Party Affiliation (Stanley Blumenthal), 17,099 No Party Affiliation (Voteforeddie.com)

CD 26 5,726 No Party Affiliation (Angel Fernandez), 2,717 No Party Affiliation (Jose Peixoto)

CD 27 6,663 No Party Affiliation (Thomas Joe Cruz-Wiggins)

FLORIDA

GENERAL AND PRIMARY ELECTIONS

PRIMARY ELECTIONS: SUPPLEMENTARY INFORMATION

Primary	January 31, 2012 (President) August 14, 2012 (Congress)	**Registration** (as of July 16, 2012)	11,446,540	Democratic Republican Independent Party of Florida Independence Party of Florida Libertarian Green Other Parties No Party Affiliation	4,581,056 4,137,890 258,968 55,945 17,708 5,622 4,028 2,385,323

Primary Type Closed—Only registered Democrats and Republicans could vote in their party's primary, with the exception of races where there were to be no other candidates (including write-ins) on the general election ballot. Then, the contested primary would be open to all voters.

	REPUBLICAN PRIMARIES			DEMOCRATIC PRIMARIES		
President	Romney, W. Mitt	776,159	46.4%			
	Gingrich, Newt	534,121	31.9%			
	Santorum, Rick	223,249	13.3%			
	Paul, Ron	117,461	7.0%			
	Perry, Rick	6,775	0.4%			
	Huntsman, Jon Jr.	6,204	0.4%			
	Bachmann, Michele	3,967	0.2%			
	Cain, Herman	3,503	0.2%			
	Johnson, Gary E.	1,195	0.1%			
	TOTAL	1,672,634				
Senator	Mack, Connie IV	661,570	58.7%	Nelson, Bill*	690,112	78.8%
	Weldon, Dave	226,901	20.1%	Burkett, Glenn	185,629	21.2%
	McCalister, Mike	156,158	13.9%			
	Stuart, Marielena	82,390	7.3%			
	TOTAL	1,127,019		TOTAL	875,741	
Congressional District 1	Miller, Jeff*	Unopposed		Bryan, Jim	Unopposed	
Congressional District 2	Southerland, Steve*	Unopposed		Lawson, Al	46,900	54.6%
				Bembry, Leonard	22,357	26.0%
				Peters, Alvin L.	11,919	13.9%
				Schlakman, Mark	4,653	5.4%
				TOTAL	85,829	
Congressional District 3	Yoho, Ted	22,273	34.4%	Gaillot, J.R.	Unopposed	
	Stearns, Clifford B. "Cliff"*	21,398	33.0%			
	Oelrich, Steve	12,329	19.0%			
	Jett, James	8,769	13.5%			
	TOTAL	64,769				
Congressional District 4	Crenshaw, Ander*	46,788	71.9%			
	Black, Bob	11,816	18.1%			
	Pueschel, Deborah Katz	6,505	10.0%			
	TOTAL	65,109				
Congressional District 5	Kolb, LeAnne	Unopposed		Brown, Corrine*	Unopposed	

FLORIDA

GENERAL AND PRIMARY ELECTIONS

	REPUBLICAN PRIMARIES			DEMOCRATIC PRIMARIES		
Congressional District 6	DeSantis, Ron	24,132	38.8%	Beaven, Heather	29,009	80.0%
	Costello, Fred	14,189	22.8%	Verma, Vipin	7,253	20.0%
	Slough, Beverly	8,229	13.2%			
	Miller, Craig S.	8,113	13.1%			
	Clark, Richard	6,090	9.8%			
	Pueschel, Alec	739	1.2%			
	Kogut, William Billy	628	1.0%			
	TOTAL	*62,120*		*TOTAL*	*36,262*	
Congressional District 7	Mica, John*	32,119	61.2%	Kendall, Jason H.	12,816	61.3%
	Adams, Sandra "Sandy"*	20,404	38.8%	Ruiz, Nicholas	8,088	38.7%
	TOTAL	*52,523*		*TOTAL*	*20,904*	
Congressional District 8	Posey, Bill*	Unopposed		Roberts, Shannon	Unopposed	
Congressional District 9	Long, Todd	12,585	47.3%	Grayson, Alan	Unopposed	
	Quinones, John "Q"	7,514	28.3%			
	Melendez, Julius Anthony	3,983	15.0%			
	Oxner, Mark	2,510	9.4%			
	TOTAL	*26,592*				
Congressional District 10	Webster, Daniel*	Unopposed		Demings, Val B.	Unopposed	
Congressional District 11	Nugent, Richard*	Unopposed		Werder, H. David	Unopposed	
Congressional District 12	Bilirakis, Gus*	Unopposed		Snow, Jonathan Michael	Unopposed	
Congressional District 13	Young, C.W. Bill*	39,395	69.1%	Ehrlich, Jessica	Unopposed	
	Ayres, Darren	10,548	18.5%			
	Vance, Madeline	7,049	12.4%			
	TOTAL	*56,992*				
Congressional District 14	Otero, Evelio "EJ"	12,084	60.3%	Castor, Kathy*	Unopposed	
	Adams, Eddie Jr.	7,953	39.7%			
	TOTAL	*20,037*				
Congressional District 15	Ross, Dennis*	Unopposed				
Congressional District 16	Buchanan, Vern*	Unopposed		Fitzgerald, Keith	Unopposed	
Congressional District 17	Rooney, Thomas J.*	37,881	73.2%	Bronson, William	Unopposed	
	Arnold, Joe	13,871	26.8%			
	TOTAL	*51,752*				
Congressional District 18	West, Allen*	45,790	74.4%	Murphy, Patrick	26,791	79.7%
	Crowder, Robert L.	15,758	25.6%	Horn, Jim	3,843	11.4%
				Buechler, Jerry Lee	2,984	8.9%
	TOTAL	*61,548*		*TOTAL*	*33,618*	
Congressional District 19	Radel, Trey	22,304	30.0%	Roach, James Lloyd	Unopposed	
	Goss, Chauncey Porter	16,005	21.5%			
	Kreegel, Paige	13,167	17.7%			
	Aubuchon, Gary	11,498	15.5%			
	Donalds, Byron	10,389	14.0%			
	Davidow, Joe	1,028	1.4%			
	TOTAL	*74,391*				

FLORIDA

GENERAL AND PRIMARY ELECTIONS

	REPUBLICAN PRIMARIES			DEMOCRATIC PRIMARIES		
Congressional District 20				Hastings, Alcee L.*	Unopposed	
Congressional District 21				Deutch, Ted*	Unopposed	
Congressional District 22	Hasner, Adam	Unopposed		Frankel, Lois	18,483	61.4%
				Jacobs, Kristin	11,644	38.6%
				TOTAL	30,127	
Congressional District 23	Harrington, Karen	8,043	47.8%	Wasserman-Schultz, Debbie*	Unopposed	
	Kaufman, Joseph "Joe"	3,383	20.1%			
	deFaria, Ozzie	2,356	14.0%			
	Garcia, Juan Eliel	1,674	9.9%			
	Bresso, Gineen	1,380	8.2%			
	TOTAL	16,836				
Congressional District 24				Wilson, Frederica*	42,807	66.4%
				Moise, Rudolph	21,680	33.6%
				TOTAL	64,487	
Congressional District 25	Diaz-Balart, Mario*	Unopposed				
Congressional District 26	Rivera, David*	Unopposed		Garcia, Joe	13,927	53.4%
				Roses, Gloria Romero	8,027	30.8%
				Sternad, Lamar	2,856	10.9%
				Marin, Gustavo	1,286	4.9%
				TOTAL	26,096	
Congressional District 27	Ros-Lehtinen, Ileana*	Unopposed		Yevancey, Manny	Unopposed	

Notes: An asterisk (*) denotes incumbent. The names of unopposed candidates did not appear on the primary ballot; therefore, no votes were cast for these candidates. Due to redistricting, the 7th district Republican primary pitted two incumbents against each other (Mica, former 7th district and Adams, former 24th district).

GEORGIA

Congressional districts first established for elections held in 2012

14 members

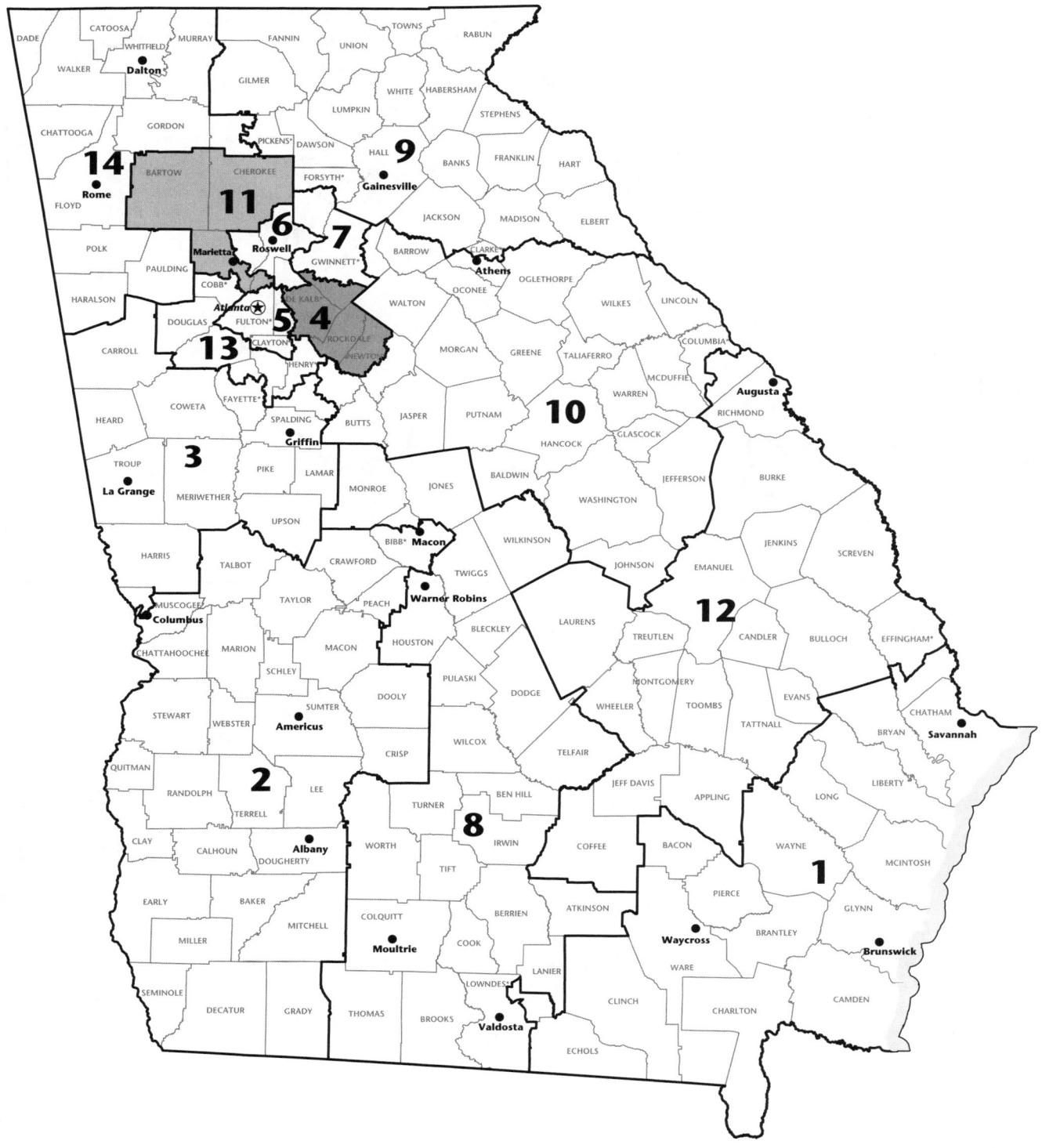

* Asterisk indicates a county whose boundaries include parts of two or more Congressional districts.

GEORGIA
Atlanta Area

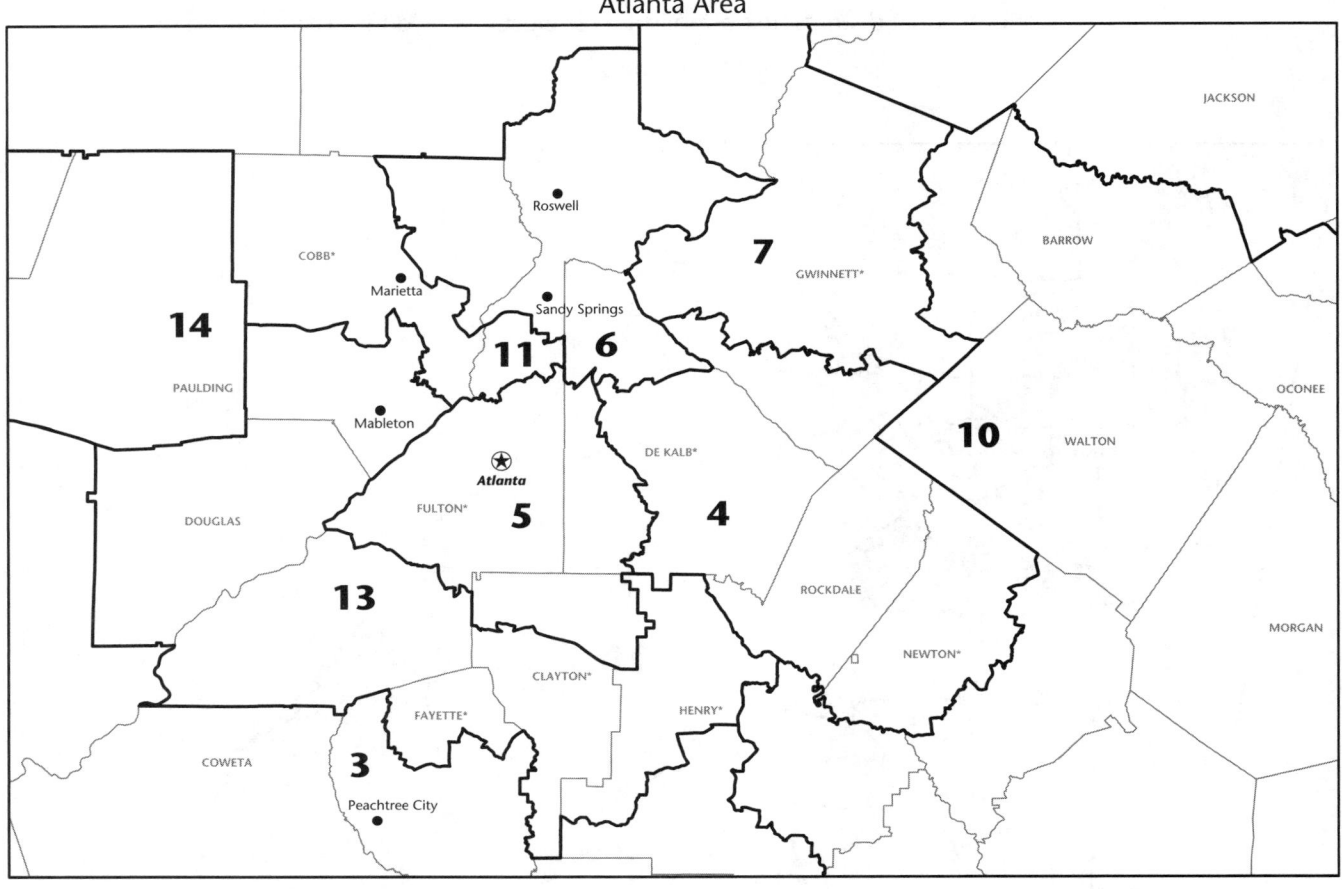

* Asterisk indicates a county whose boundaries include parts of two or more Congressional districts.

GEORGIA

GOVERNOR
Nathan Deal (R). Elected 2010 to a four-year term.

SENATORS (2 Republicans)
Saxby Chambliss (R). Reelected 2008 to a six-year term. Previously elected 2002.

Johnny Isakson (R). Reelected 2010 to a six-year term. Previously elected 2004.

REPRESENTATIVES (9 Republicans, 5 Democrats)

1. Jack Kingston (R)
2. Sanford D. Bishop Jr. (D)
3. Lynn A. Westmoreland (R)
4. Hank Johnson (D)
5. John Lewis (D)
6. Tom Price (R)
7. Rob Woodall (R)
8. Austin Scott (R)
9. Doug Collins (R)
10. Paul C. Broun (R)
11. Phil Gingrey (R)
12. John Barrow (D)
13. David Scott (D)
14. Tom Graves (R)

POSTWAR VOTE FOR PRESIDENT

		Republican		Democratic		Other	Rep.-Dem.	Total Vote		Major Vote	
Year	Total Vote	Vote	Candidate	Vote	Candidate	Vote	Plurality	Rep.	Dem.	Rep.	Dem.
2012	3,900,050	2,078,688	Romney, W. Mitt	1,773,827	Obama, Barack H.*	47,535	304,861 R	53.3%	45.5%	54.0%	46.0%
2008	3,924,486	2,048,759	McCain, John S. III	1,844,123	Obama, Barack H.	31,604	204,636 R	52.2%	47.0%	52.6%	47.4%
2004	3,301,875	1,914,254	Bush, George W.*	1,366,149	Kerry, John F.	21,472	548,105 R	58.0%	41.4%	58.4%	41.6%
2000**	2,596,645	1,419,720	Bush, George W.	1,116,230	Gore, Albert Jr.	60,695	303,490 R	54.7%	43.0%	56.0%	44.0%
1996**	2,299,071	1,080,843	Dole, Robert "Bob"	1,053,849	Clinton, Bill*	164,379	26,994 R	47.0%	45.8%	50.6%	49.4%
1992**	2,321,125	995,252	Bush, George H.*	1,008,966	Clinton, Bill	316,907	13,714 D	42.9%	43.5%	49.7%	50.3%
1988	1,812,672	1,081,331	Bush, George H.	717,792	Dukakis, Michael S.	13,549	363,539 R	59.7%	39.6%	60.1%	39.9%
1984	1,776,120	1,068,722	Reagan, Ronald*	706,628	Mondale, Walter F.	770	362,094 R	60.2%	39.8%	60.2%	39.8%
1980**	1,596,695	654,168	Reagan, Ronald	890,733	Carter, Jimmy*	51,794	236,565 D	41.0%	55.8%	42.3%	57.7%
1976	1,467,458	483,743	Ford, Gerald R.*	979,409	Carter, Jimmy	4,306	495,666 D	33.0%	66.7%	33.1%	66.9%
1972	1,174,772	881,496	Nixon, Richard M.*	289,529	McGovern, George S.	3,747	591,967 R	75.0%	24.6%	75.3%	24.7%
1968**	1,250,266	380,111	Nixon, Richard M.	334,440	Humphrey, Hubert H. Jr.	535,715	45,671 R**	30.4%	26.7%	53.2%	46.8%
1964	1,139,335	616,584	Goldwater, Barry M. Sr.	522,556	Johnson, Lyndon B.*	195	94,028 R	54.1%	45.9%	54.1%	45.9%
1960	733,349	274,472	Nixon, Richard M.	458,638	Kennedy, John F.	239	184,166 D	37.4%	62.5%	37.4%	62.6%
1956	669,655	222,778	Eisenhower, Dwight D.*	444,688	Stevenson, Adlai E. II	2,189	221,910 D	33.3%	66.4%	33.4%	66.6%
1952	655,785	198,961	Eisenhower, Dwight D.	456,823	Stevenson, Adlai E. II	1	257,862 D	30.3%	69.7%	30.3%	69.7%
1948**	418,844	76,691	Dewey, Thomas E.	254,646	Truman, Harry S.*	87,507	177,955 D	18.3%	60.8%	23.1%	76.9%

Note: An asterisk (*) denotes incumbent. **In past elections, the other vote included: 2000 - 13,273 Green (Ralph Nader); 1996 - 146,337 Reform (Ross Perot); 1992 - 309,657 Independent (Perot); 1980 - 36,055 Independent (John Anderson); 1968 - 535,550 American Independent (George Wallace); 1948 - 85,135 States' Rights (Strom Thurmond, who placed second statewide). Wallace carried Georgia in 1968 with 42.8 percent of the vote.

GEORGIA

POSTWAR VOTE FOR GOVERNOR

| Year | Total Vote | Republican | | Democratic | | Other Vote | Rep.-Dem. Plurality | Percentage | | | |
| | | Vote | Candidate | Vote | Candidate | | | Total Vote | | Major Vote | |
								Rep.	Dem.	Rep.	Dem.
2010	2,576,161	1,365,832	Deal, Nathan	1,107,011	Barnes, Roy E.	103,318	258,821 R	53.0%	43.0%	55.2%	44.8%
2006	2,122,258	1,229,724	Perdue, Sonny*	811,049	Taylor, Mark	81,485	418,675 R	57.9%	38.2%	60.3%	39.7%
2002	2,027,177	1,041,700	Perdue, Sonny	937,070	Barnes, Roy E.*	48,407	104,630 R	51.4%	46.2%	52.6%	47.4%
1998	1,792,808	790,201	Millner, Guy	941,076	Barnes, Roy E.	61,531	150,875 D	44.1%	52.5%	45.6%	54.4%
1994	1,545,328	756,371	Millner, Guy	788,926	Miller, Zell*	31	32,555 D	48.9%	51.1%	48.9%	51.1%
1990	1,449,682	645,625	Isakson, Johnny	766,662	Miller, Zell	37,395	121,037 D	44.5%	52.9%	45.7%	54.3%
1986	1,175,114	346,512	Davis, Guy	828,465	Harris, Joe Frank*	137	481,953 D	29.5%	70.5%	29.5%	70.5%
1982	1,169,043	434,496	Bell, Robert H.	734,092	Harris, Joe Frank	455	299,596 D	37.2%	62.8%	37.2%	62.8%
1978	662,862	128,139	Cook, Rodney M.	534,572	Busbee, George*	151	406,433 D	19.3%	80.6%	19.3%	80.7%
1974	936,438	289,113	Thompson, Ronnie	646,777	Busbee, George	548	357,664 D	30.9%	69.1%	30.9%	69.1%
1970	1,046,663	424,983	Suit, Hal	620,419	Carter, Jimmy	1,261	195,436 D	40.6%	59.3%	40.7%	59.3%
1966**	975,019	453,665	Callaway, Howard H.	450,626	Maddox, Lester	70,728	3,039 R	46.5%	46.2%	50.2%	49.8%
1962	311,691			311,524	Sanders, Carl E.	167	311,524 D		99.9%		100.0%
1958	168,497			168,414	Vandiver, S. Ernest	83	168,414 D		100.0%		100.0%
1954	331,966			331,899	Griffin, S. Marvin	67	331,899 D		100.0%		100.0%
1950	234,430			230,771	Talmadge, Herman E.*	3,659	230,771 D		98.4%		100.0%
1948S	363,764			354,712	Talmadge, Herman E.	9,052	354,712 D		97.5%		100.0%
1946	146,191			144,067	Talmadge, Eugene	2,124	144,067 D		98.5%		100.0%

Note: An asterisk (*) denotes incumbent. **In 1966 in the absence of a majority for any candidate, the State Legislature elected Democrat Lester Maddox to a four-year term. The 1948 election was for a short term to fill a vacancy. The Republican Party did not run a candidate in the 1946, 1948, 1950, 1954, 1958, and 1962 gubernatorial elections.

POSTWAR VOTE FOR SENATOR

| Year | Total Vote | Republican | | Democratic | | Other Vote | Rep.-Dem. Plurality | Percentage | | | |
| | | Vote | Candidate | Vote | Candidate | | | Total Vote | | Major Vote | |
								Rep.	Dem.	Rep.	Dem.
2010	2,555,258	1,489,904	Isakson, Johnny*	996,516	Thurmond, Michael	68,838	493,388 R	58.3%	39.0%	59.9%	40.1%
2008**	3,752,485	1,867,097	Chambliss, Saxby*	1,757,393	Martin, Jim	127,995	109,704 R	49.8%	46.8%	51.5%	48.5%
2008S	2,137,956	1,228,033	Chambliss, Saxby*	909,923	Martin, Jim		318,110 R	57.4%	42.6%	57.4%	42.6%
2004	3,220,981	1,864,202	Isakson, Johnny	1,287,690	Majette, Denise L.	69,089	576,512 R	57.9%	40.0%	59.1%	40.9%
2002	2,030,608	1,071,464	Chambliss, Saxby	932,156	Cleland, Max*	26,988	139,308 R	52.8%	45.9%	53.5%	46.5%
2000S	2,428,510	920,478	Mattingly, Mack F.	1,413,224	Miller, Zell*	94,808	492,746 D	37.9%	58.2%	39.4%	60.6%
1998	1,753,911	918,540	Coverdell, Paul*	791,904	Coles, Michael	43,467	126,636 R	52.4%	45.2%	53.7%	46.3%
1996	2,259,232	1,073,969	Millner, Guy	1,103,993	Cleland, Max	81,270	30,024 D	47.5%	48.9%	49.3%	50.7%
1992**	2,251,587	1,073,282	Coverdell, Paul	1,108,416	Fowler, Wyche*	69,889	35,134 D	47.7%	49.2%	49.2%	50.8%
1992S	1,253,991	635,114	Coverdell, Paul	618,877	Fowler, Wyche*		16,237 R	50.6%	49.4%	50.6%	49.4%
1990	1,033,517			1,033,439	Nunn, Sam*	78	1,033,439 D		100.0%		100.0%
1986	1,225,008	601,241	Mattingly, Mack F.*	623,707	Fowler, Wyche	60	22,466 D	49.1%	50.9%	49.1%	50.9%
1984	1,681,344	337,196	Hicks, John Michael	1,344,104	Nunn, Sam*	44	1,006,908 D	20.1%	79.9%	20.1%	79.9%
1980	1,580,340	803,686	Mattingly, Mack F.	776,143	Talmadge, Herman E.*	511	27,543 R	50.9%	49.1%	50.9%	49.1%
1978	645,164	108,808	Stokes, John W.	536,320	Nunn, Sam*	36	427,512 D	16.9%	83.1%	16.9%	83.1%
1974	874,555	246,866	Johnson, Jerry R.	627,376	Talmadge, Herman E.*	313	380,510 D	28.2%	71.7%	28.2%	71.8%
1972	1,178,708	542,331	Thompson, S. Fletcher	635,970	Nunn, Sam	407	93,639 D	46.0%	54.0%	46.0%	54.0%
1968	1,141,889	256,796	Patton, E. Earl	885,093	Talmadge, Herman E.*		628,297 D	22.5%	77.5%	22.5%	77.5%
1966	631,330			631,002	Russell, Richard B.*	328	631,002 D		99.9%		100.0%
1962	306,250			306,250	Talmadge, Herman E.*		306,250 D		100.0%		100.0%
1960	576,495			576,140	Russell, Richard B.*	355	576,140 D		99.9%		100.0%
1956	541,267			541,094	Talmadge, Herman E.	173	541,094 D		100.0%		100.0%
1954	333,936			333,917	Russell, Richard B.*	19	333,917 D		100.0%		100.0%
1950	261,293			261,290	George, Walter F.*	3	261,290 D		100.0%		100.0%
1948	362,504			362,104	Russell, Richard B.*	400	362,104 D		99.9%		100.0%

Note: An asterisk (*) denotes incumbent. **The 2000 election was for a short term to fill a vacancy. In 1992 and 2008, no candidate drew a majority of the general election vote required by state law, forcing runoff elections whose results are listed above for each year. In 2008 the November general election vote was 1,867,097 (49.8%) Republican (Saxby Chambliss); 1,757,393 (46.8%) Democratic (Jim Martin); and 127,995 (3.4%) Other. In 1992 the November general election vote was 1,073,282 (47.7%) Republican (Paul Coverdell); 1,108,416 (49.2%) Democratic (Wyche Fowler); and 69,889 (3.1%) Other. The 2008 runoff was held December 2; the 1992 runoff took place on November 24. The Republican Party did not run a candidate in the 1948, 1950, 1954, 1956, 1960, 1962, 1966, and 1990 Senate elections.

GEORGIA

PRESIDENT 2012

2010 Census Population	County	Total Vote	Republican (Romney)	Democratic (Obama)	Other	Rep.-Dem. Plurality	Percentage			
							Total Vote		Major Vote	
							Rep.	Dem.	Rep.	Dem.
18,236	APPLING	7,086	5,233	1,758	95	3,475 R	73.8%	24.8%	74.9%	25.1%
8,375	ATKINSON	2,902	1,938	930	34	1,008 R	66.8%	32.0%	67.6%	32.4%
11,096	BACON	3,931	3,093	791	47	2,302 R	78.7%	20.1%	79.6%	20.4%
3,451	BAKER	1,589	785	794	10	9 D	49.4%	50.0%	49.7%	50.3%
45,720	BALDWIN	16,238	7,589	8,483	166	894 D	46.7%	52.2%	47.2%	52.8%
18,395	BANKS	6,195	5,354	780	61	4,574 R	86.4%	12.6%	87.3%	12.7%
69,367	BARROW	25,199	18,725	6,028	446	12,697 R	74.3%	23.9%	75.6%	24.4%
100,157	BARTOW	35,802	26,876	8,396	530	18,480 R	75.1%	23.5%	76.2%	23.8%
17,634	BEN HILL	5,956	3,396	2,512	48	884 R	57.0%	42.2%	57.5%	42.5%
19,286	BERRIEN	6,201	4,843	1,273	85	3,570 R	78.1%	20.5%	79.2%	20.8%
155,547	BIBB	64,718	25,623	38,585	510	12,962 D	39.6%	59.6%	39.9%	60.1%
13,063	BLECKLEY	4,907	3,587	1,269	51	2,318 R	73.1%	25.9%	73.9%	26.1%
18,411	BRANTLEY	6,002	4,964	939	99	4,025 R	82.7%	15.6%	84.1%	15.9%
16,243	BROOKS	6,742	3,554	3,138	50	416 R	52.7%	46.5%	53.1%	46.9%
30,233	BRYAN	13,453	9,560	3,707	186	5,853 R	71.1%	27.6%	72.1%	27.9%
70,217	BULLOCH	24,085	14,174	9,593	318	4,581 R	58.8%	39.8%	59.6%	40.4%
23,316	BURKE	9,779	4,301	5,405	73	1,104 D	44.0%	55.3%	44.3%	55.7%
23,655	BUTTS	9,381	6,306	2,968	107	3,338 R	67.2%	31.6%	68.0%	32.0%
6,694	CALHOUN	2,188	883	1,298	7	415 D	40.4%	59.3%	40.5%	59.5%
50,513	CAMDEN	17,983	11,343	6,377	263	4,966 R	63.1%	35.5%	64.0%	36.0%
10,998	CANDLER	3,528	2,344	1,157	27	1,187 R	66.4%	32.8%	67.0%	33.0%
110,527	CARROLL	41,549	28,280	12,688	581	15,592 R	68.1%	30.5%	69.0%	31.0%
63,942	CATOOSA	23,678	17,858	5,365	455	12,493 R	75.4%	22.7%	76.9%	23.1%
12,171	CHARLTON	3,764	2,527	1,197	40	1,330 R	67.1%	31.8%	67.9%	32.1%
265,128	CHATHAM	108,628	47,204	60,246	1,178	13,042 D	43.5%	55.5%	43.9%	56.1%
11,267	CHATTAHOOCHEE	1,490	735	729	26	6 R	49.3%	48.9%	50.2%	49.8%
26,015	CHATTOOGA	7,822	5,452	2,232	138	3,220 R	69.7%	28.5%	71.0%	29.0%
214,346	CHEROKEE	98,220	76,514	19,841	1,865	56,673 R	77.9%	20.2%	79.4%	20.6%
116,714	CLARKE	40,368	13,815	25,431	1,122	11,616 D	34.2%	63.0%	35.2%	64.8%
3,183	CLAY	1,402	537	862	3	325 D	38.3%	61.5%	38.4%	61.6%
259,424	CLAYTON	96,067	14,164	81,479	424	67,315 D	14.7%	84.8%	14.8%	85.2%
6,798	CLINCH	2,472	1,598	852	22	746 R	64.6%	34.5%	65.2%	34.8%
688,078	COBB	310,116	171,722	133,124	5,270	38,598 R	55.4%	42.9%	56.3%	43.7%
42,356	COFFEE	14,454	9,248	5,057	149	4,191 R	64.0%	35.0%	64.6%	35.4%
45,498	COLQUITT	13,328	9,243	3,973	112	5,270 R	69.4%	29.8%	69.9%	30.1%
124,053	COLUMBIA	58,924	41,765	16,451	708	25,314 R	70.9%	27.9%	71.7%	28.3%
17,212	COOK	6,033	3,935	2,042	56	1,893 R	65.2%	33.8%	65.8%	34.2%
127,317	COWETA	55,555	39,653	15,168	734	24,485 R	71.4%	27.3%	72.3%	27.7%
12,630	CRAWFORD	5,133	3,368	1,706	59	1,662 R	65.6%	33.2%	66.4%	33.6%
23,439	CRISP	7,396	4,182	3,167	47	1,015 R	56.5%	42.8%	56.9%	43.1%
16,633	DADE	6,020	4,471	1,411	138	3,060 R	74.3%	23.4%	76.0%	24.0%
22,330	DAWSON	10,244	8,847	1,241	156	7,606 R	86.4%	12.1%	87.7%	12.3%
27,842	DECATUR	10,485	5,824	4,591	70	1,233 R	55.5%	43.8%	55.9%	44.1%
691,893	DEKALB	306,263	64,392	238,224	3,647	173,832 D	21.0%	77.8%	21.3%	78.7%
21,796	DODGE	7,733	5,214	2,442	77	2,772 R	67.4%	31.6%	68.1%	31.9%
14,918	DOOLY	4,298	1,985	2,285	28	300 D	46.2%	53.2%	46.5%	53.5%
94,565	DOUGHERTY	37,919	11,449	26,295	175	14,846 D	30.2%	69.3%	30.3%	69.7%
132,403	DOUGLAS	55,268	26,241	28,441	586	2,200 D	47.5%	51.5%	48.0%	52.0%
11,008	EARLY	5,353	2,557	2,765	31	208 D	47.8%	51.7%	48.0%	52.0%
4,034	ECHOLS	1,102	917	173	12	744 R	83.2%	15.7%	84.1%	15.9%
52,250	EFFINGHAM	20,813	15,596	4,947	270	10,649 R	74.9%	23.8%	75.9%	24.1%
20,166	ELBERT	8,143	4,859	3,181	103	1,678 R	59.7%	39.1%	60.4%	39.6%
22,598	EMANUEL	8,083	5,100	2,927	56	2,173 R	63.1%	36.2%	63.5%	36.5%
11,000	EVANS	3,563	2,268	1,268	27	1,000 R	63.7%	35.6%	64.1%	35.9%
23,682	FANNIN	10,017	7,857	2,028	132	5,829 R	78.4%	20.2%	79.5%	20.5%
106,567	FAYETTE	58,568	38,075	19,736	757	18,339 R	65.0%	33.7%	65.9%	34.1%
96,317	FLOYD	32,829	22,733	9,640	456	13,093 R	69.2%	29.4%	70.2%	29.8%
175,511	FORSYTH	81,731	65,908	14,571	1,252	51,337 R	80.6%	17.8%	81.9%	18.1%
22,084	FRANKLIN	7,762	6,114	1,499	149	4,615 R	78.8%	19.3%	80.3%	19.7%
920,581	FULTON	397,410	137,124	255,470	4,816	118,346 D	34.5%	64.3%	34.9%	65.1%

GEORGIA

PRESIDENT 2012

2010 Census Population	County	Total Vote	Republican (Romney)	Democratic (Obama)	Other	Rep.-Dem. Plurality	Percentage Total Vote Rep.	Dem.	Major Vote Rep.	Dem.
28,292	GILMER	11,018	8,926	1,958	134	6,968 R	81.0%	17.8%	82.0%	18.0%
3,082	GLASCOCK	1,333	1,135	176	22	959 R	85.1%	13.2%	86.6%	13.4%
79,626	GLYNN	33,133	20,893	11,950	290	8,943 R	63.1%	36.1%	63.6%	36.4%
55,186	GORDON	16,897	13,197	3,440	260	9,757 R	78.1%	20.4%	79.3%	20.7%
25,011	GRADY	9,396	5,924	3,419	53	2,505 R	63.0%	36.4%	63.4%	36.6%
15,994	GREENE	8,323	5,071	3,201	51	1,870 R	60.9%	38.5%	61.3%	38.7%
805,321	GWINNETT	296,727	159,855	132,509	4,363	27,346 R	53.9%	44.7%	54.7%	45.3%
43,041	HABERSHAM	14,642	12,166	2,301	175	9,865 R	83.1%	15.7%	84.1%	15.9%
179,684	HALL	61,364	47,481	12,999	884	34,482 R	77.4%	21.2%	78.5%	21.5%
9,429	HANCOCK	4,088	769	3,308	11	2,539 D	18.8%	80.9%	18.9%	81.1%
28,780	HARALSON	10,376	8,446	1,789	141	6,657 R	81.4%	17.2%	82.5%	17.5%
32,024	HARRIS	15,490	11,197	4,145	148	7,052 R	72.3%	26.8%	73.0%	27.0%
25,213	HART	9,511	6,517	2,870	124	3,647 R	68.5%	30.2%	69.4%	30.6%
11,834	HEARD	4,172	3,160	948	64	2,212 R	75.7%	22.7%	76.9%	23.1%
203,922	HENRY	91,377	46,774	43,761	842	3,013 R	51.2%	47.9%	51.7%	48.3%
139,900	HOUSTON	58,054	34,662	22,702	690	11,960 R	59.7%	39.1%	60.4%	39.6%
9,538	IRWIN	3,709	2,538	1,141	30	1,397 R	68.4%	30.8%	69.0%	31.0%
60,485	JACKSON	23,704	19,135	4,238	331	14,897 R	80.7%	17.9%	81.9%	18.1%
13,900	JASPER	6,031	4,136	1,845	50	2,291 R	68.6%	30.6%	69.2%	30.8%
15,068	JEFF DAVIS	5,336	3,996	1,275	65	2,721 R	74.9%	23.9%	75.8%	24.2%
16,930	JEFFERSON	7,298	2,999	4,261	38	1,262 D	41.1%	58.4%	41.3%	58.7%
8,340	JENKINS	3,390	1,887	1,488	15	399 R	55.7%	43.9%	55.9%	44.1%
9,980	JOHNSON	3,774	2,440	1,305	29	1,135 R	64.7%	34.6%	65.2%	34.8%
28,669	JONES	12,105	7,744	4,274	87	3,470 R	64.0%	35.3%	64.4%	35.6%
18,317	LAMAR	7,592	4,899	2,602	91	2,297 R	64.5%	34.3%	65.3%	34.7%
10,078	LANIER	2,972	1,820	1,114	38	706 R	61.2%	37.5%	62.0%	38.0%
48,434	LAURENS	19,603	11,950	7,513	140	4,437 R	61.0%	38.3%	61.4%	38.6%
28,298	LEE	13,628	10,314	3,196	118	7,118 R	75.7%	23.5%	76.3%	23.7%
63,453	LIBERTY	16,170	5,565	10,457	148	4,892 D	34.4%	64.7%	34.7%	65.3%
7,996	LINCOLN	4,429	2,807	1,586	36	1,221 R	63.4%	35.8%	63.9%	36.1%
14,464	LONG	3,802	2,306	1,442	54	864 R	60.7%	37.9%	61.5%	38.5%
109,233	LOWNDES	39,137	21,327	17,470	340	3,857 R	54.5%	44.6%	55.0%	45.0%
29,966	LUMPKIN	10,905	8,647	2,055	203	6,592 R	79.3%	18.8%	80.8%	19.2%
14,740	MACON	4,781	1,545	3,211	25	1,666 D	32.3%	67.2%	32.5%	67.5%
28,120	MADISON	11,104	8,443	2,494	167	5,949 R	76.0%	22.5%	77.2%	22.8%
8,742	MARION	3,170	1,733	1,412	25	321 R	54.7%	44.5%	55.1%	44.9%
21,875	MCDUFFIE	9,592	5,475	4,044	73	1,431 R	57.1%	42.2%	57.5%	42.5%
14,333	MCINTOSH	6,341	3,409	2,864	68	545 R	53.8%	45.2%	54.3%	45.7%
21,992	MERIWETHER	9,267	4,856	4,331	80	525 R	52.4%	46.7%	52.9%	47.1%
6,125	MILLER	2,775	1,905	852	18	1,053 R	68.6%	30.7%	69.1%	30.9%
23,498	MITCHELL	8,275	4,155	4,081	39	74 R	50.2%	49.3%	50.4%	49.6%
26,424	MONROE	12,277	8,361	3,785	131	4,576 R	68.1%	30.8%	68.8%	31.2%
9,123	MONTGOMERY	3,832	2,662	1,135	35	1,527 R	69.5%	29.6%	70.1%	29.9%
17,868	MORGAN	9,027	6,186	2,753	88	3,433 R	68.5%	30.5%	69.2%	30.8%
39,628	MURRAY	11,217	8,443	2,542	232	5,901 R	75.3%	22.7%	76.9%	23.1%
189,885	MUSCOGEE	70,604	27,510	42,573	521	15,063 D	39.0%	60.3%	39.3%	60.7%
99,958	NEWTON	43,233	20,982	21,851	400	869 D	48.5%	50.5%	49.0%	51.0%
32,808	OCONEE	17,817	13,098	4,421	298	8,677 R	73.5%	24.8%	74.8%	25.2%
14,899	OGLETHORPE	6,273	4,251	1,914	108	2,337 R	67.8%	30.5%	69.0%	31.0%
142,324	PAULDING	57,399	40,846	15,825	728	25,021 R	71.2%	27.6%	72.1%	27.9%
27,695	PEACH	11,514	5,287	6,148	79	861 D	45.9%	53.4%	46.2%	53.8%
29,431	PICKENS	12,680	10,547	1,975	158	8,572 R	83.2%	15.6%	84.2%	15.8%
18,758	PIERCE	6,846	5,667	1,124	55	4,543 R	82.8%	16.4%	83.4%	16.6%
17,869	PIKE	8,109	6,668	1,356	85	5,312 R	82.2%	16.7%	83.1%	16.9%
41,475	POLK	13,608	9,811	3,615	182	6,196 R	72.1%	26.6%	73.1%	26.9%
12,010	PULASKI	3,682	2,444	1,219	19	1,225 R	66.4%	33.1%	66.7%	33.3%
21,218	PUTNAM	9,222	6,215	2,926	81	3,289 R	67.4%	31.7%	68.0%	32.0%
2,513	QUITMAN	1,128	510	612	6	102 D	45.2%	54.3%	45.5%	54.5%
16,276	RABUN	7,463	5,754	1,559	150	4,195 R	77.1%	20.9%	78.7%	21.3%
7,719	RANDOLPH	3,058	1,271	1,770	17	499 D	41.6%	57.9%	41.8%	58.2%

GEORGIA

PRESIDENT 2012

2010 Census Population	County	Total Vote	Republican (Romney)	Democratic (Obama)	Other	Rep.-Dem. Plurality	Percentage Total Vote Rep.	Total Vote Dem.	Major Vote Rep.	Major Vote Dem.
200,549	RICHMOND	79,020	25,845	52,560	615	26,715 D	32.7%	66.5%	33.0%	67.0%
85,215	ROCKDALE	38,085	15,716	22,023	346	6,307 D	41.3%	57.8%	41.6%	58.4%
5,010	SCHLEY	1,748	1,286	448	14	838 R	73.6%	25.6%	74.2%	25.8%
14,593	SCREVEN	6,100	3,287	2,774	39	513 R	53.9%	45.5%	54.2%	45.8%
8,729	SEMINOLE	3,769	2,245	1,478	46	767 R	59.6%	39.2%	60.3%	39.7%
64,073	SPALDING	25,088	14,911	9,898	279	5,013 R	59.4%	39.5%	60.1%	39.9%
26,175	STEPHENS	9,498	7,221	2,131	146	5,090 R	76.0%	22.4%	77.2%	22.8%
6,058	STEWART	2,076	745	1,323	8	578 D	35.9%	63.7%	36.0%	64.0%
32,819	SUMTER	11,831	5,378	6,375	78	997 D	45.5%	53.9%	45.8%	54.2%
6,865	TALBOT	3,491	1,202	2,265	24	1,063 D	34.4%	64.9%	34.7%	65.3%
1,717	TALIAFERRO	963	323	636	4	313 D	33.5%	66.0%	33.7%	66.3%
25,520	TATTNALL	6,667	4,706	1,897	64	2,809 R	70.6%	28.5%	71.3%	28.7%
8,906	TAYLOR	3,538	1,948	1,572	18	376 R	55.1%	44.4%	55.3%	44.7%
16,500	TELFAIR	4,336	2,480	1,805	51	675 R	57.2%	41.6%	57.9%	42.1%
9,315	TERRELL	4,398	1,834	2,544	20	710 D	41.7%	57.8%	41.9%	58.1%
44,720	THOMAS	18,953	11,156	7,653	144	3,503 R	58.9%	40.4%	59.3%	40.7%
40,118	TIFT	13,927	9,185	4,660	82	4,525 R	66.0%	33.5%	66.3%	33.7%
27,223	TOOMBS	9,344	6,524	2,746	74	3,778 R	69.8%	29.4%	70.4%	29.6%
10,471	TOWNS	6,211	4,876	1,273	62	3,603 R	78.5%	20.5%	79.3%	20.7%
6,885	TREUTLEN	2,750	1,652	1,074	24	578 R	60.1%	39.1%	60.6%	39.4%
67,044	TROUP	25,986	15,179	10,547	260	4,632 R	58.4%	40.6%	59.0%	41.0%
8,930	TURNER	3,559	2,028	1,510	21	518 R	57.0%	42.4%	57.3%	42.7%
9,023	TWIGGS	4,202	1,907	2,270	25	363 D	45.4%	54.0%	45.7%	54.3%
21,356	UNION	11,079	8,773	2,139	167	6,634 R	79.2%	19.3%	80.4%	19.6%
27,153	UPSON	11,263	7,230	3,959	74	3,271 R	64.2%	35.2%	64.6%	35.4%
68,756	WALKER	21,896	16,247	5,274	375	10,973 R	74.2%	24.1%	75.5%	24.5%
83,768	WALTON	37,612	29,036	8,148	428	20,888 R	77.2%	21.7%	78.1%	21.9%
36,312	WARE	11,939	7,941	3,900	98	4,041 R	66.5%	32.7%	67.1%	32.9%
5,834	WARREN	2,526	990	1,529	7	539 D	39.2%	60.5%	39.3%	60.7%
21,187	WASHINGTON	8,808	4,035	4,714	59	679 D	45.8%	53.5%	46.1%	53.9%
30,099	WAYNE	10,269	7,557	2,596	116	4,961 R	73.6%	25.3%	74.4%	25.6%
2,799	WEBSTER	1,187	601	582	4	19 R	50.6%	49.0%	50.8%	49.2%
7,421	WHEELER	2,160	1,366	772	22	594 R	63.2%	35.7%	63.9%	36.1%
27,144	WHITE	10,488	8,651	1,671	166	6,980 R	82.5%	15.9%	83.8%	16.2%
102,599	WHITFIELD	26,876	19,305	7,210	361	12,095 R	71.8%	26.8%	72.8%	27.2%
9,255	WILCOX	3,129	2,053	1,060	16	993 R	65.6%	33.9%	65.9%	34.1%
10,593	WILKES	4,761	2,635	2,087	39	548 R	55.3%	43.8%	55.8%	44.2%
9,563	WILKINSON	4,450	2,246	2,181	23	65 R	50.5%	49.0%	50.7%	49.3%
21,679	WORTH	8,419	5,869	2,487	63	3,382 R	69.7%	29.5%	70.2%	29.8%
9,687,653	TOTAL	3,900,050	2,078,688	1,773,827	47,535	304,861 R	53.3%	45.5%	54.0%	46.0%

GEORGIA

HOUSE OF REPRESENTATIVES

CD	Year	Total Vote	Republican Vote	Republican Candidate	Democratic Vote	Democratic Candidate	Other Vote	Rep.-Dem. Plurality	Percentage Total Vote Rep.	Total Vote Dem.	Major Vote Rep.	Major Vote Dem.
1	2012	249,580	157,181	KINGSTON, JACK*	92,399	MESSINGER, LESLI		64,782 R	63.0%	37.0%	63.0%	37.0%
2	2012	255,161	92,410	HOUSE, JOHN	162,751	BISHOP, SANFORD D. JR.*		70,341 D	36.2%	63.8%	36.2%	63.8%
3	2012	232,485	232,380	WESTMORELAND, LYNN A.*			105	232,380 R	100%		100.0%	
4	2012	283,962	75,041	VAUGHN, J. CHRIS	208,861	JOHNSON, HANK*	60	133,820 D	26.4%	73.6%	26.4%	73.6%
5	2012	277,689	43,335	STOPECK, HOWARD	234,330	LEWIS, JOHN*	24	190,995 D	15.6%	84.4%	15.6%	84.4%
6	2012	294,034	189,669	PRICE, TOM*	104,365	KAZANOW, JEFF		85,304 R	64.5%	35.5%	64.5%	35.5%
7	2012	252,066	156,689	WOODALL, ROB*	95,377	REILLY, STEVE		61,312 R	62.2%	37.8%	62.2%	37.8%
8	2012	197,789	197,789	SCOTT, AUSTIN*				197,789 R	100.0%		100.0%	

GEORGIA

HOUSE OF REPRESENTATIVES

CD	Year	Total Vote	Republican Vote	Republican Candidate	Democratic Vote	Democratic Candidate	Other Vote	Rep.-Dem. Plurality	Total Vote Rep.	Total Vote Dem.	Major Vote Rep.	Major Vote Dem.
9	2012	252,153	192,101	COLLINS, DOUG	60,052	COOLEY, JODY		132,049 R	76.2%	23.8%	76.2%	23.8%
10	2012	211,466	211,065	BROUN, PAUL C.*			401	211,065 R	99.8%		100.0%	
11	2012	287,351	196,968	GINGREY, PHIL*	90,353	THOMPSON, PATRICK	30	106,615 R	68.5%	31.4%	68.6%	31.4%
12	2012	259,121	119,973	ANDERSON, LEE	139,148	BARROW, JOHN*		19,175 D	46.3%	53.7%	46.3%	53.7%
13	2012	281,538	79,550	MALIK, S.	201,988	SCOTT, DAVID*		122,438 D	28.3%	71.7%	28.3%	71.7%
14	2012	219,192	159,947	GRAVES, TOM*	59,245	GRANT, DANIEL "DANNY"		100,702 R	73.0%	27.0%	73.0%	27.0%
TOTAL	2012	3,553,587	2,104,098		1,448,869		620	655,229 R	59.2%	40.8%	59.2%	40.8%

Note: An asterisk (*) denotes incumbent.

GEORGIA

GENERAL AND PRIMARY ELECTIONS

2012 GENERAL ELECTIONS: OTHER VOTE

President   Other vote was 45,324 Libertarian (Gary E. Johnson), 1,516 Write-in (Jill Stein), 432 Write-in (Virgil H. Goode), 263 Write-in (Scattered Write-In)

House   Other vote was:

CD 3   105 Write-in (David Ferguson)
CD 4   58 Write-in (Cynthia McKinney), 2 Write-in (Rachele Fruit)
CD 5   24 Write-in (Scattered Write-In)
CD 10   401 Write-in (Brian Russell Brown)
CD 11   30 Write-in (Allan Levene)

2012 PRIMARY ELECTIONS: SUPPLEMENTARY INFORMATION

Primary   March 6, 2012 (President)   **Registration**   5,905,825   No Party Registration
July 31, 2012 (Congress)   (as of June 1, 2012
– includes 752,067 inactive voters)

Primary Runoff   August 21, 2012

Primary Type   Open—Any registered voter could participate in either the Democratic or Republican primary, although if they voted in one party's primary they could not participate in a primary runoff of the other party. Voters who did not participate in the primary could vote in either party's runoff.

	REPUBLICAN PRIMARIES			DEMOCRATIC PRIMARIES		
President	Gingrich, Newt	425,395	47.2%	Obama, Barack H.*	139,273	100.0%
	Romney, W. Mitt	233,611	25.9%			
	Santorum, Rick	176,259	19.6%			
	Paul, Ron	59,100	6.6%			
	Huntsman, Jon Jr.	1,813	0.2%			
	Bachmann, Michele	1,714	0.2%			
	Perry, Rick	1,696	0.2%			
	Roemer, Charles	1,142	0.1%			
	Johnson, Gary E.	740	0.1%			
	TOTAL	901,470		TOTAL	139,273	

GEORGIA

GENERAL AND PRIMARY ELECTIONS

	REPUBLICAN PRIMARIES			DEMOCRATIC PRIMARIES		
Congressional District 1	Kingston, Jack*	61,353	100.0%	Messinger, Lesli	15,390	54.3%
				Russo, Nathan C.	12,952	45.7%
	TOTAL	61,353		TOTAL	28,342	
Congressional District 2	Allen, Rick	11,312	41.9%	Bishop, Sanford B. Jr.*	68,981	100.0%
	House, John	8,614	31.9%			
	DeLoach, Ken	7,043	26.1%			
	TOTAL	26,969		TOTAL	68,981	
	PRIMARY RUNOFF					
	House, John	2,705	55.0%			
	Allen, Rick	2,217	45.0%			
	TOTAL	4,922				
Congressional District 3	Westmoreland, Lynn A.*	64,765	71.6%			
	Flanegan	13,139	14.5%			
	Kingsley, Kent	12,517	13.8%			
	TOTAL	90,421				
Congressional District 4	Vaughn, J. Chris	17,261	54.5%	Johnson, Hank*	52,982	77.0%
	Pallen, Greg	14,422	45.5%	Dillard, Courtney L.	13,130	19.1%
				Nunally, Lincoln	2,728	4.0%
	TOTAL	31,683		TOTAL	68,840	
Congressional District 5	Stopeck, Howard	11,426	100.0%	Lewis, John*	69,985	80.8%
				Johnson, Michael	16,666	19.2%
	TOTAL	11,426		TOTAL	86,651	
Congressional District 6	Price, Tom*	71,032	100.0%	Kazanow, Jeff	10,313	51.1%
				Montigel, Robert	9,881	48.9%
	TOTAL	71,032		TOTAL	20,194	
Congressional District 7	Woodall, Rob*	45,157	71.8%	Reilly, Steve	12,394	100.0%
	Hancock, David	17,730	28.2%			
	TOTAL	62,887		TOTAL	12,394	
Congressional District 8	Scott, Austin*	59,300	100.0%			
	TOTAL	59,300				
Congressional District 9	Collins, Doug	45,894	41.8%	Cooley, Jody	8,963	100.0%
	Zoller, Martha	45,160	41.1%			
	Fitzpatrick, Roger D.	18,730	17.1%			
	TOTAL	109,784		TOTAL	8,963	
	PRIMARY RUNOFF					
	Collins, Doug	39,016	54.6%			
	Zoller, Martha	32,417	45.4%			
	TOTAL	71,433				
Congressional District 10	Broun, Paul C.*	58,405	69.0%			
	Simpson, Stephen K.	26,256	31.0%			
	TOTAL	84,661				
Congressional District 11	Gingrey, Phil*	75,697	80.9%	Thompson, Patrick	14,162	100.0%
	Opitz, Michael S.	9,231	9.9%			
	Llop, William	8,604	9.2%			
	TOTAL	93,532		TOTAL	14,162	

GEORGIA

GENERAL AND PRIMARY ELECTIONS

	REPUBLICAN PRIMARIES			DEMOCRATIC PRIMARIES		
Congressional District 12	Anderson, Lee	20,551	34.2%	Barrow, John*	41,587	100.0%
	Allen, Rick W.	15,436	25.7%			
	Mcleod, Wright	14,856	24.7%			
	Sheffield, Maria	9,207	15.3%			
	TOTAL	60,050		TOTAL	41,587	
	PRIMARY RUNOFF					
	Anderson, Lee	13,785	50.3%			
	Allen, Rick W.	13,626	49.7%			
	TOTAL	27,411				
Congressional District 13	Malik, S.	28,693	100.0%	Scott, David*	55,214	100.0%
	TOTAL	28,693		TOTAL	55,214	
Congressional District 14	Graves, Tom*	65,873	100.0%	Grant, Daniel "Danny"	10,228	100.0%
	TOTAL	65,873		TOTAL	10,228	

Note: An asterisk (*) denotes incumbent.

HAWAII

Congressional districts first established for elections held in 2012

2 members

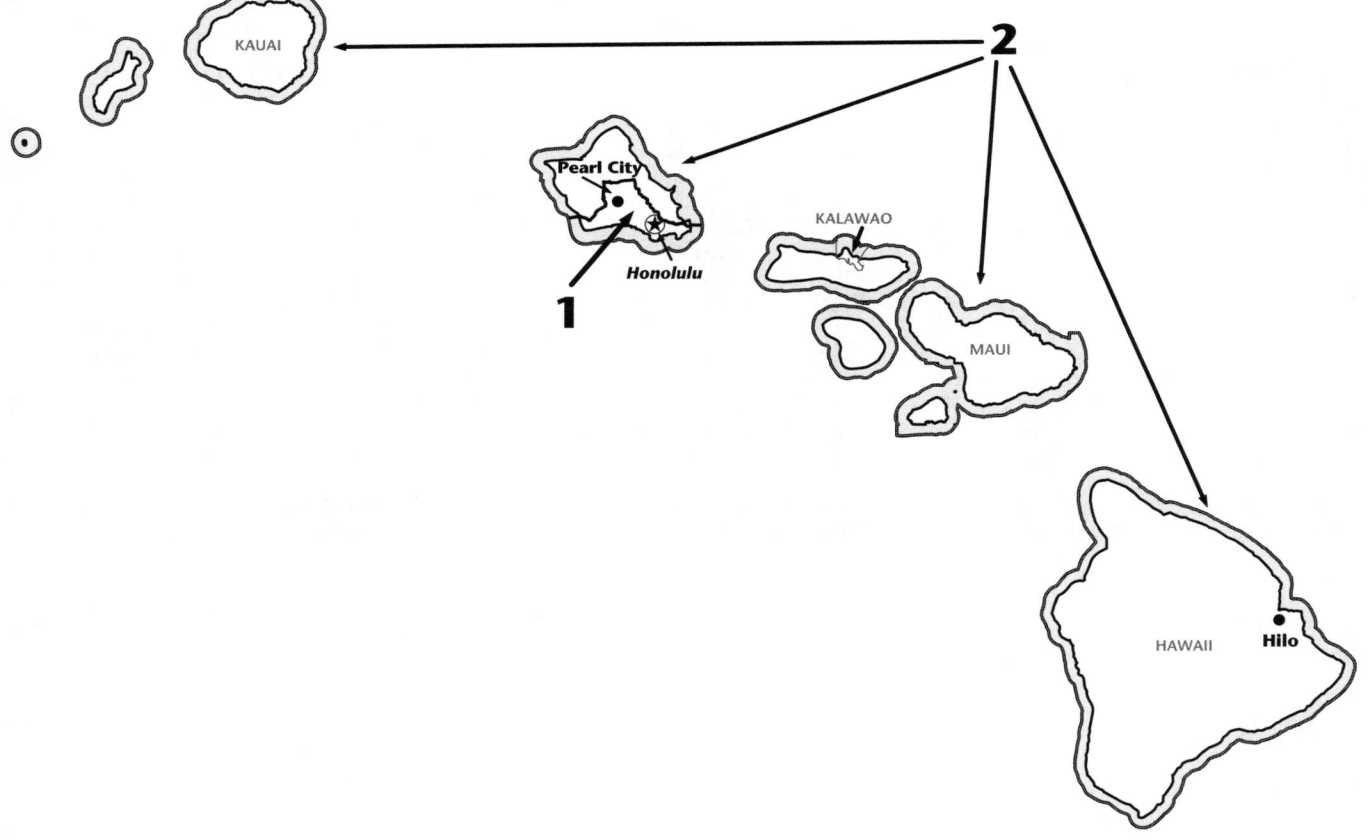

Hawaii includes more islands to the west of those that are illustrated on this map.

HAWAII

GOVERNOR
Neil Abercrombie (D). Elected 2010 to a four-year term.

SENATORS (2 Democrats)
Brian Schatz (D). Appointed December 27, 2012, to fill the seat vacated by the death of Senator Daniel K. Inouye until a special election to be held on November 4, 2014.

Mazie K. Hirono (D). Elected 2012 to a six-year term.

REPRESENTATIVES (2 Democrats)
1. Colleen Hanabusa (D)   2. Tulsi Gabbard (D)

POSTWAR VOTE FOR PRESIDENT

| | | Republican | | Democratic | | | | Percentage | | | |
| | | | | | | | | Total Vote | | Major Vote | |
Year	Total Vote	Vote	Candidate	Vote	Candidate	Other Vote	Rep.-Dem. Plurality	Rep.	Dem.	Rep.	Dem.
2012	434,697	121,015	Romney, W. Mitt	306,658	Obama, Barack H.*	7,024	185,643 D	27.8%	70.5%	28.3%	71.7%
2008	453,568	120,566	McCain, John S. III	325,871	Obama, Barack H.	7,131	205,305 D	26.6%	71.8%	27.0%	73.0%
2004	429,013	194,191	Bush, George W.*	231,708	Kerry, John F.	3,114	37,517 D	45.3%	54.0%	45.6%	54.4%
2000**	367,951	137,845	Bush, George W.	205,286	Gore, Albert Jr.	24,820	67,441 D	37.5%	55.8%	40.2%	59.8%
1996**	360,120	113,943	Dole, Robert "Bob"	205,012	Clinton, Bill*	41,165	91,069 D	31.6%	56.9%	35.7%	64.3%
1992**	372,842	136,822	Bush, George H.*	179,310	Clinton, Bill	56,710	42,488 D	36.7%	48.1%	43.3%	56.7%
1988	354,461	158,625	Bush, George H.	192,364	Dukakis, Michael S.	3,472	33,739 D	44.8%	54.3%	45.2%	54.8%
1984	335,846	185,050	Reagan, Ronald*	147,154	Mondale, Walter F.	3,642	37,896 R	55.1%	43.8%	55.7%	44.3%
1980**	303,287	130,112	Reagan, Ronald	135,879	Carter, Jimmy*	37,296	5,767 D	42.9%	44.8%	48.9%	51.1%
1976	291,301	140,003	Ford, Gerald R.*	147,375	Carter, Jimmy	3,923	7,372 D	48.1%	50.6%	48.7%	51.3%
1972	270,274	168,865	Nixon, Richard M.*	101,409	McGovern, George S.		67,456 R	62.5%	37.5%	62.5%	37.5%
1968**	236,218	91,425	Nixon, Richard M.	141,324	Humphrey, Hubert H. Jr.	3,469	49,899 D	38.7%	59.8%	39.3%	60.7%
1964	207,271	44,022	Goldwater, Barry M. Sr.	163,249	Johnson, Lyndon B.*		119,227 D	21.2%	78.8%	21.2%	78.8%
1960	184,705	92,295	Nixon, Richard M.	92,410	Kennedy, John F.		115 D	50.0%	50.0%	50.0%	50.0%

Note: An asterisk (*) denotes incumbent. **In past elections, the other vote included: 2000 - 21,623 Green (Ralph Nader); 1996 - 27,358 Reform (Ross Perot); 1992 - 53,003 Independent (Perot); 1980 - 32,021 Independent (John Anderson); 1968 - 3,469 American Independent (George Wallace). Hawaii was formally admitted as a state in August 1959.

HAWAII

POSTWAR VOTE FOR GOVERNOR

		Republican		Democratic				Percentage			
								Total Vote		Major Vote	
Year	Total Vote	Vote	Candidate	Vote	Candidate	Other Vote	Rep.-Dem. Plurality	Rep.	Dem.	Rep.	Dem.
2010	382,563	157,311	Aiona, Duke	222,724	Abercrombie, Neil	2,528	65,413 D	41.1%	58.2%	41.4%	58.6%
2006	344,315	215,313	Lingle, Linda*	121,717	Iwase, Randy	7,285	93,596 R	62.5%	35.4%	63.9%	36.1%
2002	382,110	197,009	Lingle, Linda	179,647	Hirono, Mazie K.	5,454	17,362 R	51.6%	47.0%	52.3%	47.7%
1998	407,556	198,952	Lingle, Linda	204,206	Cayetano, Benjamin J.*	4,398	5,254 D	48.8%	50.1%	49.3%	50.7%
1994**	369,013	107,908	Saiki, Patricia	134,978	Cayetano, Benjamin J.	126,127	27,070 D	29.2%	36.6%	44.4%	55.6%
1990	340,132	131,310	Hemmings, Fred	203,491	Waihee, John*	5,331	72,181 D	38.6%	59.8%	39.2%	60.8%
1986	334,115	160,460	Anderson, D. G.	173,655	Waihee, John		13,195 D	48.0%	52.0%	48.0%	52.0%
1982**	311,853	81,507	Anderson, D. G.	141,043	Ariyoshi, George R.*	89,303	59,536 D	26.1%	45.2%	36.6%	63.4%
1978	281,587	124,610	Leopold, John	153,394	Ariyoshi, George R.*	3,583	28,784 D	44.3%	54.5%	44.8%	55.2%
1974	249,650	113,388	Crossley, Randolph	136,262	Ariyoshi, George R.		22,874 D	45.4%	54.6%	45.4%	54.6%
1970	239,061	101,249	King, Samuel P.	137,812	Burns, John A.*		36,563 D	42.4%	57.6%	42.4%	57.6%
1966	213,164	104,324	Crossley, Randolph	108,840	Burns, John A.*		4,516 D	48.9%	51.1%	48.9%	51.1%
1962	196,015	81,707	Quinn, Willam F.*	114,308	Burns, John A.		32,601 D	41.7%	58.3%	41.7%	58.3%
1959S	168,662	86,213	Quinn, Willam F.	82,074	Burns, John A.	375	4,139 R	51.1%	48.7%	51.2%	48.8%

Note: An asterisk (*) denotes incumbent. **In past elections, the other vote included: 1994 - 113,158 Best Party (Frank F. Fasi); 1982 - 89,303 Independent Democrat (Fasi). In both 1982 and 1994, Fasi finished second. The 1959 election was for a short term pending the regular vote in 1962.

POSTWAR VOTE FOR SENATOR

		Republican		Democratic				Percentage			
								Total Vote		Major Vote	
Year	Total Vote	Vote	Candidate	Vote	Candidate	Other Vote	Rep.-Dem. Plurality	Rep.	Dem.	Rep.	Dem.
2012	430,483	160,994	Lingle, Linda	269,489	Hirono, Mazie K.		108,495 D	37.4%	62.6%	37.4%	62.6%
2010	370,583	79,939	Cavasso, Cam	277,228	Inouye, Daniel K.*	13,416	197,289 D	21.6%	74.8%	22.4%	77.6%
2006	342,842	126,097	Thielen, Cynthia	210,330	Akaka, Daniel K.*	6,415	84,233 D	36.8%	61.3%	37.5%	62.5%
2004	415,347	87,172	Cavasso, Cam	313,629	Inouye, Daniel K.*	14,546	226,457 D	21.0%	75.5%	21.7%	78.3%
2000	345,623	84,701	Carroll, John	251,215	Akaka, Daniel K.*	9,707	166,514 D	24.5%	72.7%	25.2%	74.8%
1998	398,124	70,964	Young, Crystal	315,252	Inouye, Daniel K.*	11,908	244,288 D	17.8%	79.2%	18.4%	81.6%
1994	356,902	86,320	Hustace, Maria M.	256,189	Akaka, Daniel K.*	14,393	169,869 D	24.2%	71.8%	25.2%	74.8%
1992**	363,662	97,928	Reed, Rick	208,266	Inouye, Daniel K.*	57,468	110,338 D	26.9%	57.3%	32.0%	68.0%
1990S	349,666	155,978	Saiki, Patricia	188,901	Akaka, Daniel K.	4,787	32,923 D	44.6%	54.0%	45.2%	54.8%
1988	323,876	66,987	Hustace, Maria M.	247,941	Matsunaga, Spark M.*	8,948	180,954 D	20.7%	76.6%	21.3%	78.7%
1986	328,797	86,910	Hutchinson, Frank	241,887	Inouye, Daniel K.*		154,977 D	26.4%	73.6%	26.4%	73.6%
1982	306,410	52,071	Brown, Clarence J.	245,386	Matsunaga, Spark M.*	8,953	193,315 D	17.0%	80.1%	17.5%	82.5%
1980	288,006	53,068	Brown, Cooper	224,485	Inouye, Daniel K.*	10,453	171,417 D	18.4%	77.9%	19.1%	80.9%
1976	302,092	122,724	Quinn, Willam F.	162,305	Matsunaga, Spark M.	17,063	39,581 D	40.6%	53.7%	43.1%	56.9%
1974**	250,221			207,454	Inouye, Daniel K.*	42,767	207,454 D		82.9%		100.0%
1970	240,760	124,163	Fong, Hiram L.*	116,597	Heftel, Cecil		7,566 R	51.6%	48.4%	51.6%	48.4%
1968	226,927	34,008	Thiessen, Wayne C.	189,248	Inouye, Daniel K.*	3,671	155,240 D	15.0%	83.4%	15.2%	84.8%
1964	208,814	110,747	Fong, Hiram L.*	96,789	Gill, Thomas P.	1,278	13,958 R	53.0%	46.4%	53.4%	46.6%
1962	196,361	60,067	Dillingham, Ben	136,294	Inouye, Daniel K.		76,227 D	30.6%	69.4%	30.6%	69.4%
1959S*	163,875	79,123	Tsukiyama, Wilfred C.	83,700	Long, Oren E.	1,052	4,577 D	48.3%	51.1%	48.6%	51.4%
1959S	164,808	87,161	Fong, Hiram L.	77,647	Fasi, Frank F.		9,514 R	52.9%	47.1%	52.9%	47.1%

Note: An asterisk (*) denotes incumbent. **In past elections, the other vote was: 1992 - 49,921 Green (Linda B. Martin); 1974 - 42,767 Peoples (James D. Kimmel), who finished second. The 1990 election was for a short term to fill a vacancy. The two 1959 elections were held to indeterminate terms and the Senate later determined by lot that Senator Long would serve a short term, Senator Fong a long term. The Republican Party did not run a Senate candidate in the 1974 election.

HAWAII

PRESIDENT 2012

2010 Census Population	County Absentee	Total Vote	Republican (Romney)	Democratic (Obama)	Other	Rep.-Dem. Plurality	Percentage			
							Total Vote		Major Vote	
							Rep.	Dem.	Rep.	Dem.
185,079	HAWAII	63,454	14,753	47,224	1,477	32,471 D	23.2%	74.4%	23.8%	76.2%
953,207	HONOLULU	296,742	88,461	204,349	3,932	115,888 D	29.8%	68.9%	30.2%	69.8%
67,091	KAUAI	25,372	6,121	18,641	610	12,520 D	24.1%	73.5%	24.7%	75.3%
154,834	MAUI	48,653	11,602	36,052	999	24,450 D	23.8%	74.1%	24.3%	75.7%
	OVERSEAS VOTE	476	78	392	6	314 D	16.4%	82.4%	16.6%	83.4%
1,360,211	TOTAL	434,697	121,015	306,658	7,024	185,643 D	27.8%	70.5%	28.3%	71.7%

HAWAII

SENATOR 2012

2010 Census Population	County Absentee	Total Vote	Republican (Lingle)	Democratic (Hirono)	Other	Rep.-Dem. Plurality	Percentage			
							Total Vote		Major Vote	
							Rep.	Dem.	Rep.	Dem.
185,079	HAWAII	62,874	19,491	43,383		23,892 D	31.0%	69.0%	31.0%	69.0%
953,207	HONOLULU	293,810	119,176	174,634		55,458 D	40.6%	59.4%	40.6%	59.4%
67,091	KAUAI	25,107	7,134	17,973		10,839 D	28.4%	71.6%	28.4%	71.6%
154,834	MAUI	48,265	15,096	33,169		18,073 D	31.3%	68.7%	31.3%	68.7%
	OVERSEAS VOTE	427	97	330		233 D	22.7%	77.3%	22.7%	77.3%
1,360,211	TOTAL	430,483	160,994	269,489		108,495 D	37.4%	62.6%	37.4%	62.6%

HAWAII

HOUSE OF REPRESENTATIVES

CD	Year	Total Vote	Republican		Democratic		Other Vote	Rep.-Dem. Plurality	Percentage			
			Vote	Candidate	Vote	Candidate			Total Vote		Major Vote	
									Rep.	Dem.	Rep.	Dem.
1	2012	213,329	96,824	DJOU, CHARLES	116,505	HANABUSA, COLLEEN*		19,681 D	45.4%	54.6%	45.4%	54.6%
2	2012	209,210	40,707	CROWLEY, KAWIKA	168,503	GABBARD, TULSI		127,796 D	19.5%	80.5%	19.5%	80.5%
TOTAL	2012	422,539	137,531		285,008			147,477 D	32.5%	67.5%	32.5%	67.5%

Note: An asterisk (*) denotes incumbent.

HAWAII

GENERAL AND PRIMARY ELECTIONS

2012 GENERAL ELECTIONS: OTHER VOTE

President   Other vote was 3,840 Libertarian (Gary E. Johnson), 3,184 Green (Jill Stein)

2012 PRIMARY ELECTIONS: SUPPLEMENTARY INFORMATION

Primary   August 11, 2012   **Registration**   687,500   No Party Registration
(as of August 11, 2012)

Primary Type   Open—Any registered voter could participate in the party primary of their choice.

	REPUBLICAN PRIMARIES			DEMOCRATIC PRIMARIES		
Senator	Lingle, Linda	44,252	91.6%	Hirono, Mazie K.	134,745	57.7%
	Carroll, John	2,900	6.0%	Case, Edward E.	95,553	40.9%
	Roco, John	545	1.1%	Reyes, Arturo P. "Art"	1,720	0.7%
	Collins, Charles Augustine	366	0.8%	Gillespie, Michael D.	1,104	0.5%
	Pirkowski, Eddie	232	0.5%	Gimbernat, Antonio	517	0.2%
	TOTAL	48,295		TOTAL	233,639	
Congressional District 1	Djou, Charles	25,984	95.7%	Hanabusa, Colleen*	92,136	84.1%
	Amsterdam, C. Kaui Jochanan	799	2.9%	Wyttenbach, Roy	17,369	15.9%
	Giuffre, John	376	1.4%			
	TOTAL	27,159		TOTAL	109,505	
Congressional District 2	Crowley, Kawika	9,056	60.8%	Gabbard, Tulsi	62,882	55.1%
	DiGeronimo, Matthew	5,843	39.2%	Hannemann, Mufi	39,176	34.3%
				Kia'Aina, Esther	6,681	5.9%
				Marx, Bob	4,327	3.8%
				Shiratori, Miles	573	0.5%
				Del Castillo, Rafael	520	0.5%
	TOTAL	14,899		TOTAL	114,159	

Note: An asterisk (*) denotes incumbent.

144

IDAHO

Congressional districts first established for elections held in 2012

2 members

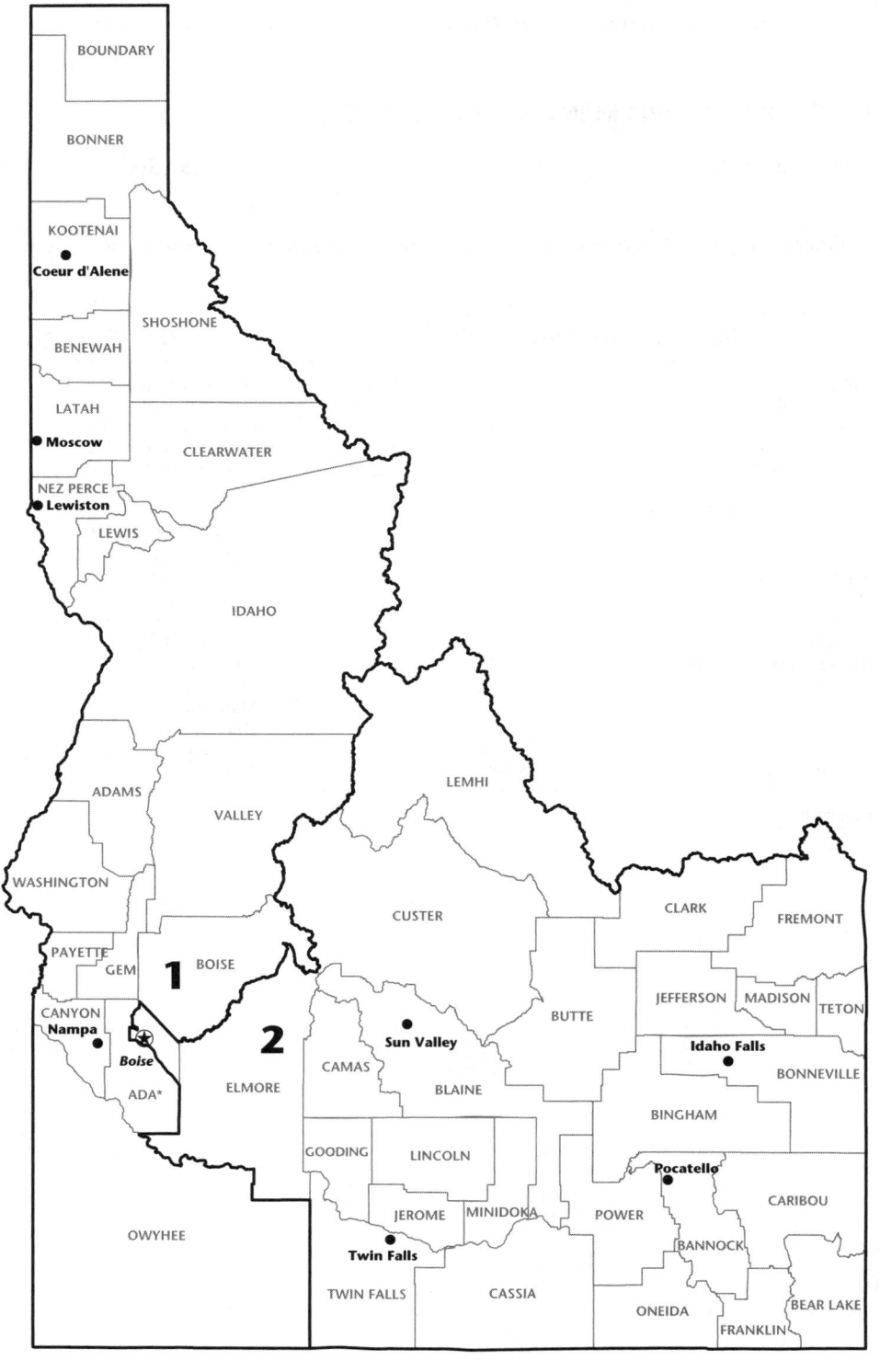

* Asterisk indicates a county whose boundaries include parts of two or more Congressional districts.

IDAHO

GOVERNOR
C.L. "Butch" Otter (R). Reelected 2010 to a four-year term. Previously elected 2006.

SENATORS (2 Republicans)
Michael D. Crapo (R). Reelected 2010 to a six-year term. Previously elected 2004, 1998.

Jim Risch (R). Elected 2008 to a six-year term.

REPRESENTATIVES (2 Republicans)
1. Raúl Labrador (R)   2. Mike Simpson (R)

POSTWAR VOTE FOR PRESIDENT

		Republican		Democratic		Other	Rep.-Dem.	Total Vote		Major Vote	
Year	Total Vote	Vote	Candidate	Vote	Candidate	Vote	Plurality	Rep.	Dem.	Rep.	Dem.
2012	652,346	420,911	Romney, W. Mitt	212,787	Obama, Barack H.*	18,648	208,124 R	64.5%	32.6%	66.4%	33.6%
2008	655,122	403,012	McCain, John S. III	236,440	Obama, Barack H.	15,670	166,572 R	61.5%	36.1%	63.0%	37.0%
2004	598,447	409,235	Bush, George W.*	181,098	Kerry, John F.	8,114	228,137 R	68.4%	30.3%	69.3%	30.7%
2000**	501,621	336,937	Bush, George W.	138,637	Gore, Albert Jr.	26,047	198,300 R	67.2%	27.6%	70.8%	29.2%
1996**	491,719	256,595	Dole, Robert "Bob"	165,443	Clinton, Bill*	69,681	91,152 R	52.2%	33.6%	60.8%	39.2%
1992**	482,142	202,645	Bush, George H.*	137,013	Clinton, Bill	142,484	65,632 R	42.0%	28.4%	59.7%	40.3%
1988	408,968	253,881	Bush, George H.	147,272	Dukakis, Michael S.	7,815	106,609 R	62.1%	36.0%	63.3%	36.7%
1984	411,144	297,523	Reagan, Ronald*	108,510	Mondale, Walter F.	5,111	189,013 R	72.4%	26.4%	73.3%	26.7%
1980**	437,431	290,699	Reagan, Ronald	110,192	Carter, Jimmy*	36,540	180,507 R	66.5%	25.2%	72.5%	27.5%
1976	344,071	204,151	Ford, Gerald R.*	126,549	Carter, Jimmy	13,371	77,602 R	59.3%	36.8%	61.7%	38.3%
1972	310,379	199,384	Nixon, Richard M.*	80,826	McGovern, George S.	30,169	118,558 R	64.2%	26.0%	71.2%	28.8%
1968**	291,183	165,369	Nixon, Richard M.	89,273	Humphrey, Hubert H. Jr.	36,541	76,096 R	56.8%	30.7%	64.9%	35.1%
1964	292,477	143,557	Goldwater, Barry M. Sr.	148,920	Johnson, Lyndon B.*		5,363 D	49.1%	50.9%	49.1%	50.9%
1960	300,450	161,597	Nixon, Richard M.	138,853	Kennedy, John F.		22,744 R	53.8%	46.2%	53.8%	46.2%
1956	272,989	166,979	Eisenhower, Dwight D.*	105,868	Stevenson, Adlai E. II	142	61,111 R	61.2%	38.8%	61.2%	38.8%
1952	276,254	180,707	Eisenhower, Dwight D.	95,081	Stevenson, Adlai E. II	466	85,626 R	65.4%	34.4%	65.5%	34.5%
1948	214,816	101,514	Dewey, Thomas E.	107,370	Truman, Harry S.*	5,932	5,856 D	47.3%	50.0%	48.6%	51.4%

Note: An asterisk (*) denotes incumbent. **In past elections, the other vote included: 2000 - 12,292 Green (Ralph Nader); 1996 - 62,518 Reform (Ross Perot); 1992 - 130,395 Independent (Perot); 1980 - 27,058 Independent (John Anderson); 1968 - 36,541 American Independent (George Wallace).

IDAHO

POSTWAR VOTE FOR GOVERNOR

Year	Total Vote	Republican		Democratic		Other Vote	Rep.-Dem. Plurality	Percentage			
								Total Vote		Major Vote	
		Vote	Candidate	Vote	Candidate			Rep.	Dem.	Rep.	Dem.
2010	452,535	267,483	Otter, C. L. "Butch"*	148,680	Allred, Keith	36,372	118,803 R	59.1%	32.9%	64.3%	35.7%
2006	450,850	237,437	Otter, C. L. "Butch"	198,845	Brady, Jerry M.	14,568	38,592 R	52.7%	44.1%	54.4%	45.6%
2002	411,477	231,566	Kempthorne, Dirk*	171,711	Brady, Jerry M.	8,200	59,855 R	56.3%	41.7%	57.4%	42.6%
1998	381,248	258,095	Kempthorne, Dirk	110,815	Huntley, Robert C.	12,338	147,280 R	67.7%	29.1%	70.0%	30.0%
1994	413,346	216,123	Batt, Phil	181,363	Echohawk, Larry	15,860	34,760 R	52.3%	43.9%	54.4%	45.6%
1990	320,610	101,937	Fairchild, Roger	218,673	Andrus, Cecil D.*		116,736 D	31.8%	68.2%	31.8%	68.2%
1986	387,426	189,794	Leroy, David H.	193,429	Andrus, Cecil D.	4,203	3,635 D	49.0%	49.9%	49.5%	50.5%
1982	326,522	161,157	Batt, Phil	165,365	Evans, John V.*		4,208 D	49.4%	50.6%	49.4%	50.6%
1978	288,566	114,149	Larsen, Allan	169,540	Evans, John V.*	4,877	55,391 D	39.6%	58.8%	40.2%	59.8%
1974	259,632	68,731	Murphy, Jack M.	184,142	Andrus, Cecil D.*	6,759	115,411 D	26.5%	70.9%	27.2%	72.8%
1970	245,112	117,108	Samuelson, Don*	128,004	Andrus, Cecil D.		10,896 D	47.8%	52.2%	47.8%	52.2%
1966**	252,593	104,586	Samuelson, Don	93,744	Andrus, Cecil D.	54,263	10,842 R	41.4%	37.1%	52.7%	47.3%
1962	255,454	139,578	Smylie, Robert E.*	115,876	Smith, Vernon K.		23,702 R	54.6%	45.4%	54.6%	45.4%
1958	239,046	121,810	Smylie, Robert E.*	117,236	Derr, A. M.		4,574 R	51.0%	49.0%	51.0%	49.0%
1954	228,685	124,038	Smylie, Robert E.	104,647	Hamilton, Clark		19,391 R	54.2%	45.8%	54.2%	45.8%
1950	204,792	107,642	Jordan, Len B.	97,150	Wright, Calvin E.		10,492 R	52.6%	47.4%	52.6%	47.4%
1946	181,364	102,233	Robins, Charles A.	79,131	Williams, Arnold*		23,102 R	56.4%	43.6%	56.4%	43.6%

Note: An asterisk (*) denotes incumbent. **In past elections, the other vote included: 1966 - 30,913 Independent (Perry Swisher).

POSTWAR VOTE FOR SENATOR

Year	Total Vote	Republican		Democratic		Other Vote	Rep.-Dem. Plurality	Percentage			
								Total Vote		Major Vote	
		Vote	Candidate	Vote	Candidate			Rep.	Dem.	Rep.	Dem.
2010	449,530	319,953	Crapo, Michael D.*	112,057	Sullivan, P. Tom	17,520	207,896 R	71.2%	24.9%	74.1%	25.9%
2008	644,780	371,744	Risch, Jim	219,903	Larocco, Larry	53,133	151,841 R	57.7%	34.1%	62.8%	37.2%
2004**	503,932	499,796	Crapo, Michael D.*			4,136	499,796 R	99.2%		100.0%	
2002	408,544	266,215	Craig, Larry E.*	132,975	Blinken, Alan	9,354	133,240 R	65.2%	32.5%	66.7%	33.3%
1998	378,174	262,966	Crapo, Michael D.	107,375	Mauk, Bill	7,833	155,591 R	69.5%	28.4%	71.0%	29.0%
1996	497,233	283,532	Craig, Larry E.*	198,422	Minnick, Walt	15,279	85,110 R	57.0%	39.9%	58.8%	41.2%
1992	478,504	270,468	Kempthorne, Dirk	208,036	Stallings, Richard		62,432 R	56.5%	43.5%	56.5%	43.5%
1990	315,936	193,641	Craig, Larry E.	122,295	Twilegar, Ron J.		71,346 R	61.3%	38.7%	61.3%	38.7%
1986	382,024	196,958	Symms, Steven D.*	185,066	Evans, John V.		11,892 R	51.6%	48.4%	51.6%	48.4%
1984	406,168	293,193	McClure, James A.*	105,591	Busch, Peter M.	7,384	187,602 R	72.2%	26.0%	73.5%	26.5%
1980	439,647	218,701	Symms, Steven D.	214,439	Church, Frank*	6,507	4,262 R	49.7%	48.8%	50.5%	49.5%
1978	284,047	194,412	McClure, James A.*	89,635	Jensen, Dwight		104,777 R	68.4%	31.6%	68.4%	31.6%
1974	258,847	109,072	Smith, Robert L.	145,140	Church, Frank*	4,635	36,068 D	42.1%	56.1%	42.9%	57.1%
1972	309,602	161,804	McClure, James A.	140,913	Davis, William E.	6,885	20,891 R	52.3%	45.5%	53.5%	46.5%
1968	287,876	114,394	Hansen, George V.	173,482	Church, Frank*		59,088 D	39.7%	60.3%	39.7%	60.3%
1966	252,456	139,819	Jordan, Len B.*	112,637	Harding, Ralph R.		27,182 R	55.4%	44.6%	55.4%	44.6%
1962	258,786	117,129	Hawley, Jack	141,657	Church, Frank*		24,528 D	45.3%	54.7%	45.3%	54.7%
1962S	257,677	131,279	Jordan, Len B.*	126,398	Pfost, Gracie		4,881 R	50.9%	49.1%	50.9%	49.1%
1960	292,096	152,648	Dworshak, Henry C.*	139,448	McLaughlin, R. F.		13,200 R	52.3%	47.7%	52.3%	47.7%
1956	265,292	102,781	Welker, Herman*	149,096	Church, Frank	13,415	46,315 D	38.7%	56.2%	40.8%	59.2%
1954	226,408	142,269	Dworshak, Henry C.*	84,139	Taylor, Glen H.		58,130 R	62.8%	37.2%	62.8%	37.2%
1950	201,417	124,237	Welker, Herman	77,180	Clark, D. Worth		47,057 R	61.7%	38.3%	61.7%	38.3%
1950S	201,700	104,608	Dworshak, Henry C.	97,092	Burtenshaw, Claude J.		7,516 R	51.9%	48.1%	51.9%	48.1%
1948	214,188	103,868	Dworshak, Henry C.*	107,000	Miller, Bert C.	3,320	3,132 D	48.5%	50.0%	49.3%	50.7%
1946S	180,152	105,523	Dworshak, Henry C.	74,629	Donart, George E.		30,894 R	58.6%	41.4%	58.6%	41.4%

Note: An asterisk (*) denotes incumbent. **In 2004 there was no candidate on the Democratic line. A write-in candidate, who was a Democrat, received 4,136 votes, which are listed in the Other Vote column. The 1946 election and one each of the 1950 and 1962 elections were for short terms to fill vacancies.

IDAHO

PRESIDENT 2012

2010 Census Population	County	Total Vote	Republican (Romney)	Democratic (Obama)	Other	Rep.-Dem. Plurality	Percentage			
							Total Vote		Major Vote	
							Rep.	Dem.	Rep.	Dem.
392,365	ADA	180,562	97,554	77,137	5,871	20,417 R	54.0%	42.7%	55.8%	44.2%
3,976	ADAMS	2,061	1,413	577	71	836 R	68.6%	28.0%	71.0%	29.0%
82,839	BANNOCK	35,264	21,010	13,214	1,040	7,796 R	59.6%	37.5%	61.4%	38.6%
5,986	BEAR LAKE	2,822	2,489	302	31	2,187 R	88.2%	10.7%	89.2%	10.8%
9,285	BENEWAH	3,885	2,596	1,164	125	1,432 R	66.8%	30.0%	69.0%	31.0%
45,607	BINGHAM	17,606	13,440	3,822	344	9,618 R	76.3%	21.7%	77.9%	22.1%
21,376	BLAINE	10,194	3,939	5,992	263	2,053 D	38.6%	58.8%	39.7%	60.3%
7,028	BOISE	3,446	2,284	1,053	109	1,231 R	66.3%	30.6%	68.4%	31.6%
40,877	BONNER	18,536	11,367	6,500	669	4,867 R	61.3%	35.1%	63.6%	36.4%
104,234	BONNEVILLE	43,217	32,276	9,903	1,038	22,373 R	74.7%	22.9%	76.5%	23.5%
10,972	BOUNDARY	4,544	3,138	1,225	181	1,913 R	69.1%	27.0%	71.9%	28.1%
2,891	BUTTE	1,286	1,001	258	27	743 R	77.8%	20.1%	79.5%	20.5%
1,117	CAMAS	578	402	159	17	243 R	69.6%	27.5%	71.7%	28.3%
188,923	CANYON	66,101	44,369	19,866	1,866	24,503 R	67.1%	30.1%	69.1%	30.9%
6,963	CARIBOU	3,052	2,608	386	58	2,222 R	85.5%	12.6%	87.1%	12.9%
22,952	CASSIA	8,396	7,154	1,098	144	6,056 R	85.2%	13.1%	86.7%	13.3%
982	CLARK	328	235	66	27	169 R	71.6%	20.1%	78.1%	21.9%
8,761	CLEARWATER	3,696	2,541	1,032	123	1,509 R	68.8%	27.9%	71.1%	28.9%
4,368	CUSTER	2,355	1,744	530	81	1,214 R	74.1%	22.5%	76.7%	23.3%
27,038	ELMORE	8,003	5,227	2,513	263	2,714 R	65.3%	31.4%	67.5%	32.5%
12,786	FRANKLIN	5,600	5,195	325	80	4,870 R	92.8%	5.8%	94.1%	5.9%
13,242	FREMONT	5,802	4,907	810	85	4,097 R	84.6%	14.0%	85.8%	14.2%
16,719	GEM	7,491	5,311	1,957	223	3,354 R	70.9%	26.1%	73.1%	26.9%
15,464	GOODING	5,118	3,696	1,287	135	2,409 R	72.2%	25.1%	74.2%	25.8%
16,267	IDAHO	7,840	5,921	1,708	211	4,213 R	75.5%	21.8%	77.6%	22.4%
26,140	JEFFERSON	11,381	9,895	1,303	183	8,592 R	86.9%	11.4%	88.4%	11.6%
22,374	JEROME	6,681	4,804	1,699	178	3,105 R	71.9%	25.4%	73.9%	26.1%
138,494	KOOTENAI	59,833	39,381	18,851	1,601	20,530 R	65.8%	31.5%	67.6%	32.4%
37,244	LATAH	16,767	7,589	8,306	872	717 D	45.3%	49.5%	47.7%	52.3%
7,936	LEMHI	4,110	3,029	960	121	2,069 R	73.7%	23.4%	75.9%	24.1%
3,821	LEWIS	1,615	1,173	396	46	777 R	72.6%	24.5%	74.8%	25.2%
5,208	LINCOLN	1,663	1,141	469	53	672 R	68.6%	28.2%	70.9%	29.1%
37,536	MADISON	14,412	13,445	832	135	12,613 R	93.3%	5.8%	94.2%	5.8%
20,069	MINIDOKA	6,973	5,442	1,390	141	4,052 R	78.0%	19.9%	79.7%	20.3%
39,265	NEZ PERCE	16,850	9,967	6,451	432	3,516 R	59.2%	38.3%	60.7%	39.3%
4,286	ONEIDA	2,089	1,838	217	34	1,621 R	88.0%	10.4%	89.4%	10.6%
11,526	OWYHEE	3,724	2,794	833	97	1,961 R	75.0%	22.4%	77.0%	23.0%
22,623	PAYETTE	8,495	6,004	2,271	220	3,733 R	70.7%	26.7%	72.6%	27.4%
7,817	POWER	2,904	1,870	982	52	888 R	64.4%	33.8%	65.6%	34.4%
12,765	SHOSHONE	5,148	2,699	2,277	172	422 R	52.4%	44.2%	54.2%	45.8%
10,170	TETON	4,523	2,458	1,926	139	532 R	54.3%	42.6%	56.1%	43.9%
77,230	TWIN FALLS	28,145	19,773	7,541	831	12,232 R	70.3%	26.8%	72.4%	27.6%
9,862	VALLEY	4,919	2,664	2,095	160	569 R	54.2%	42.6%	56.0%	44.0%
10,198	WASHINGTON	4,331	3,128	1,104	99	2,024 R	72.2%	25.5%	73.9%	26.1%
1,567,582	TOTAL	652,346	420,911	212,787	18,648	208,124 R	64.5%	32.6%	66.4%	33.6%

IDAHO

HOUSE OF REPRESENTATIVES

CD	Year	Total Vote	Republican		Democratic		Other Vote	Rep.-Dem. Plurality	Percentage			
									Total Vote		Major Vote	
			Vote	Candidate	Vote	Candidate			Rep.	Dem.	Rep.	Dem.
1	2012	316,724	199,402	LABRADOR, RAÚL R.*	97,450	FARRIS, JIMMY	19,872	101,952 R	63.0%	30.8%	67.2%	32.8%
2	2012	318,494	207,412	SIMPSON, MIKE*	110,847	LEFAVOUR, NICOLE	235	96,565 R	65.1%	34.8%	65.2%	34.8%
TOTAL	2012	635,218	406,814		208,297		20,107	198,517 R	64.0%	32.8%	66.1%	33.9%

Note: An asterisk (*) denotes incumbent.

IDAHO

GENERAL AND PRIMARY ELECTIONS

2012 GENERAL ELECTIONS: OTHER VOTE

President   Other vote was 9,453 Libertarian (Gary E. Johnson), 4,402 Green (Jill Stein), 2,499 Justice (Ross C. "Rocky" Anderson), 2,222 Constitution (Virgil H. Goode), 72 Write-in (Scattered Write-In)

House   Other vote was:

CD 1   12,265 Libertarian (Rob Oates), 7,607 Independent (Pro-Life)
CD 2   235 Write-in (Jack Wayne Chappell)

2012 PRIMARY ELECTIONS: SUPPLEMENTARY INFORMATION

Primary   May 15, 2012   **Registration** (as of May 15, 2012)   753,880   No Party Registration

Primary Type   Open—Any registered voter could participate in either the Democratic or Republican primary.

	REPUBLICAN PRIMARIES			DEMOCRATIC PRIMARIES		
Congressional District 1	Labrador, Raúl R.*	58,003	80.6%	Farris, Jimmy	5,362	53.2%
	McCandless, Reed C.	13,917	19.4%	Clinkingbeard, Cynthia	4,723	46.8%
	TOTAL	71,920		TOTAL	10,085	
Congressional District 2	Simpson, Mike*	50,799	69.6%	LeFavour, Nicole	10,528	84.1%
	Heileson, M.C. "Chick"	22,240	30.4%	Chappell, Jack Wayne	1,997	15.9%
	TOTAL	73,039		TOTAL	12,525	

Note: An asterisk (*) denotes incumbent.

ILLINOIS

Congressional districts first established for elections held in 2012

18 members

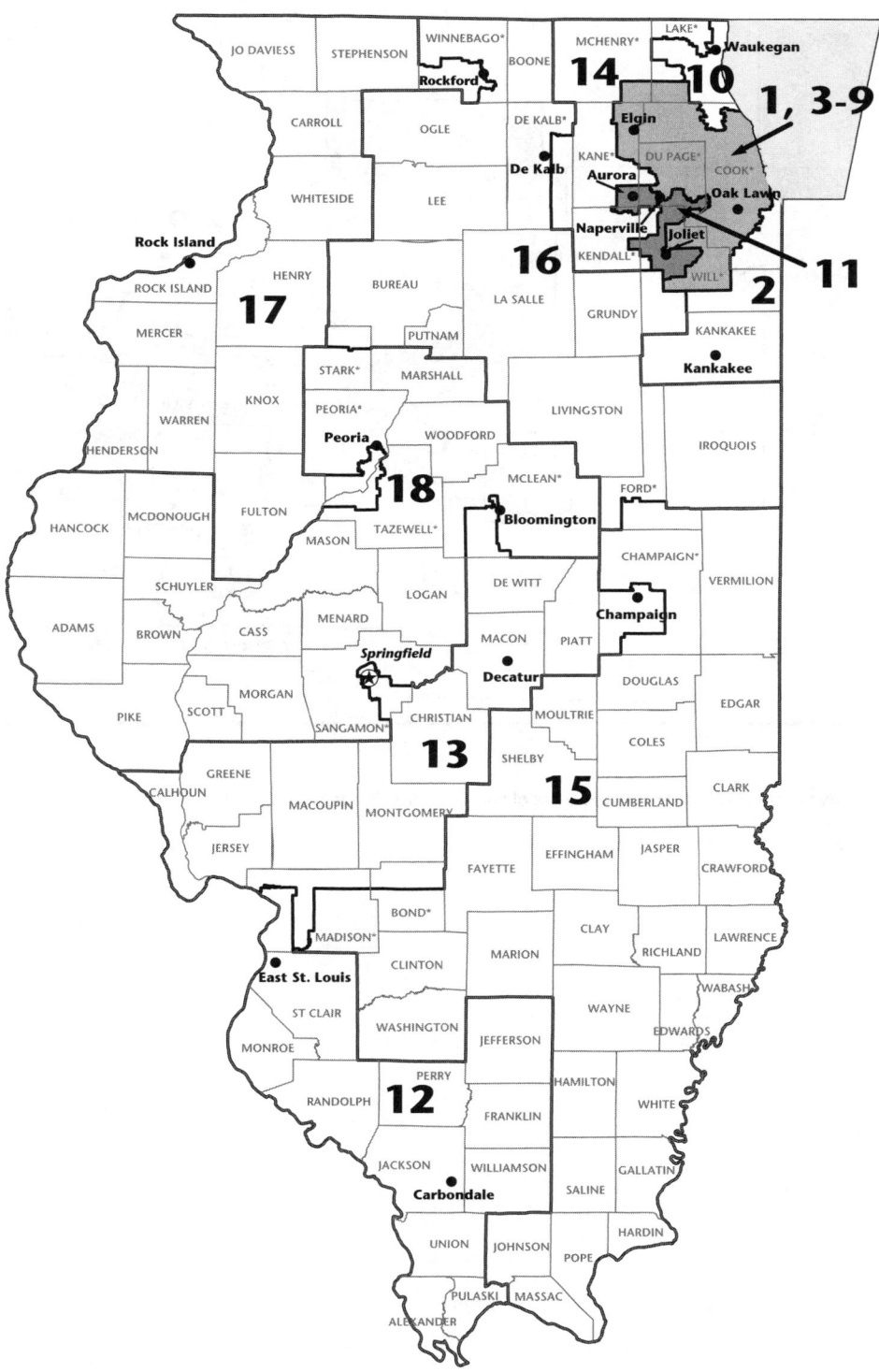

* Asterisk indicates a county whose boundaries include parts of two or more Congressional districts.

ILLINOIS
Chicago Area

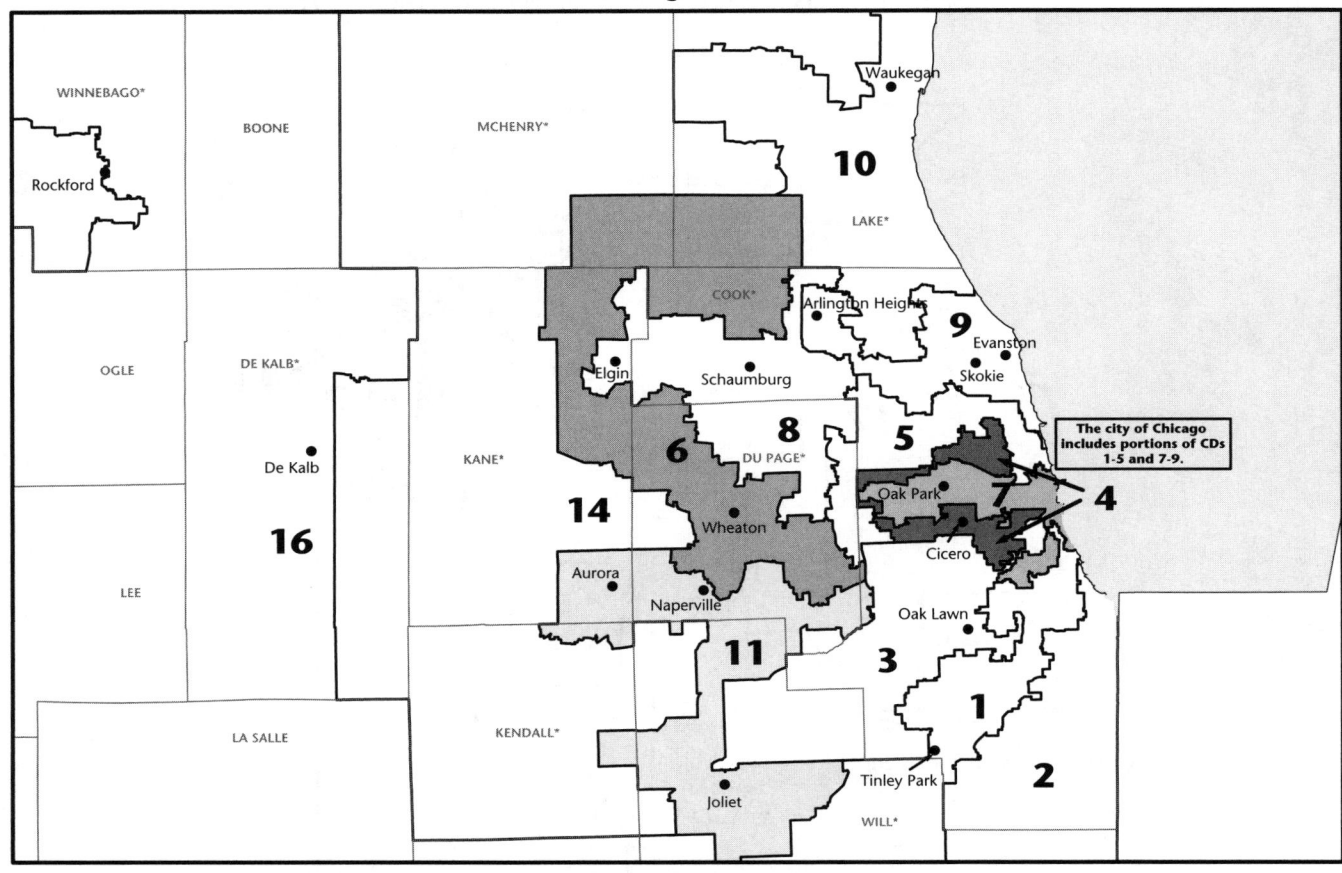

The city of Chicago includes portions of CDs 1-5 and 7-9.

* Asterisk indicates a county whose boundaries include parts of two or more Congressional districts.

ILLINOIS

GOVERNOR

Pat Quinn (D). Elected 2010 to a four-year term. Assumed office January 29, 2009, upon the impeachment and expulsion from office of Rod R. Blagojevich (D).

SENATORS (1 Republican, 1 Democrat)

Richard J. "Dick" Durbin (D). Reelected 2008 to a six-year term. Previously elected 2002, 1996.

Mark Steven Kirk (R). Elected 2010 to a six-year term. Also won special election held in conjunction with the 2010 general election to replace the appointed senator, Roland Burris (D).

REPRESENTATIVES (6 Republicans, 12 Democrats)

1. Bobby L. Rush (D)
2. Robin Kelly (D)
3. Daniel Lipinski (D)
4. Luis V. Gutierrez (D)
5. Mike Quigley (D)
6. Peter Roskam (R)
7. Danny K. Davis (D)
8. Tammy Duckworth (D)
9. Jan Schakowsky (D)
10. Brad Schneider (D)
11. Bill Foster (D)
12. William Enyart (D)
13. Rodney L. Davis (R)
14. Randy Hultgren (R)
15. John Shimkus (R)
16. Adam Kinzinger (R)
17. Cheri Bustos (D)
18. Aaron Schock (R)

POSTWAR VOTE FOR PRESIDENT

| | | Republican | | Democratic | | Other | Rep.-Dem. | Percentage | | | |
| | | | | | | | | Total Vote | | Major Vote | |
Year	Total Vote	Vote	Candidate	Vote	Candidate	Vote	Plurality	Rep.	Dem.	Rep.	Dem.
2012	5,242,014	2,135,216	Romney, W. Mitt	3,019,512	Obama, Barack H.*	87,286	884,296 D	40.7%	57.6%	41.4%	58.6%
2008	5,522,371	2,031,179	McCain, John S. III	3,419,348	Obama, Barack H.	71,844	1,388,169 D	36.8%	61.9%	37.3%	62.7%
2004	5,274,322	2,345,946	Bush, George W.*	2,891,550	Kerry, John F.	36,826	545,604 D	44.5%	54.8%	44.8%	55.2%
2000**	4,742,123	2,019,421	Bush, George W.	2,589,026	Gore, Albert Jr.	133,676	569,605 D	42.6%	54.6%	43.8%	56.2%
1996**	4,311,391	1,587,021	Dole, Robert "Bob"	2,341,744	Clinton, Bill*	382,626	754,723 D	36.8%	54.3%	40.4%	59.6%
1992**	5,050,157	1,734,096	Bush, George H.*	2,453,350	Clinton, Bill	862,711	719,254 D	34.3%	48.6%	41.4%	58.6%
1988	4,559,120	2,310,939	Bush, George H.	2,215,940	Dukakis, Michael S.	32,241	94,999 R	50.7%	48.6%	51.0%	49.0%
1984	4,819,088	2,707,103	Reagan, Ronald*	2,086,499	Mondale, Walter F.	25,486	620,604 R	56.2%	43.3%	56.5%	43.5%
1980**	4,749,721	2,358,049	Reagan, Ronald	1,981,413	Carter, Jimmy*	410,259	376,636 R	49.6%	41.7%	54.3%	45.7%
1976	4,718,914	2,364,269	Ford, Gerald R.*	2,271,295	Carter, Jimmy	83,350	92,974 R	50.1%	48.1%	51.0%	49.0%
1972	4,723,236	2,788,179	Nixon, Richard M.*	1,913,472	McGovern, George S.	21,585	874,707 R	59.0%	40.5%	59.3%	40.7%
1968**	4,619,749	2,174,774	Nixon, Richard M.	2,039,814	Humphrey, Hubert H. Jr.	405,161	134,960 R	47.1%	44.2%	51.6%	48.4%
1964	4,702,841	1,905,946	Goldwater, Barry M. Sr.	2,796,833	Johnson, Lyndon B.*	62	890,887 D	40.5%	59.5%	40.5%	59.5%
1960	4,757,409	2,368,988	Nixon, Richard M.	2,377,846	Kennedy, John F.	10,575	8,858 D	49.8%	50.0%	49.9%	50.1%
1956	4,407,407	2,623,327	Eisenhower, Dwight D.*	1,775,682	Stevenson, Adlai E. II	8,398	847,645 R	59.5%	40.3%	59.6%	40.4%
1952	4,481,058	2,457,327	Eisenhower, Dwight D.	2,013,920	Stevenson, Adlai E. II	9,811	443,407 R	54.8%	44.9%	55.0%	45.0%
1948	3,984,046	1,961,103	Dewey, Thomas E.	1,994,715	Truman, Harry S.*	28,228	33,612 D	49.2%	50.1%	49.6%	50.4%

Note: An asterisk (*) denotes incumbent. **In past elections, the other vote included: 2000 - 103,759 Green (Ralph Nader); 1996 - 346,408 Reform (Ross Perot); 1992 - 840,515 Independent (Perot); 1980 - 346,754 Independent (John Anderson); 1968 - 390,958 American Independent (George Wallace).

ILLINOIS

POSTWAR VOTE FOR GOVERNOR

Year	Total Vote	Republican		Democratic		Other Vote	Rep.-Dem. Plurality	Percentage			
								Total Vote		Major Vote	
		Vote	Candidate	Vote	Candidate			Rep.	Dem.	Rep.	Dem.
2010	3,729,989	1,713,385	Brady, Bill	1,745,219	Quinn, Pat*	271,385	31,834 D	45.9%	46.8%	49.5%	50.5%
2006**	3,487,989	1,369,315	Topinka, Judy Baar	1,736,731	Blagojevich, Rod R.*	381,943	367,416 D	39.3%	49.8%	44.1%	55.9%
2002	3,538,891	1,594,960	Ryan, Jim	1,847,040	Blagojevich, Rod R.	96,891	252,080 D	45.1%	52.2%	46.3%	53.7%
1998	3,358,705	1,714,094	Ryan, George H.	1,594,191	Poshard, Glenn	50,420	119,903 R	51.0%	47.5%	51.8%	48.2%
1994	3,106,566	1,984,318	Edgar, Jim*	1,069,850	Netsch, Dawn C.	52,398	914,468 R	63.9%	34.4%	65.0%	35.0%
1990	3,257,410	1,653,126	Edgar, Jim	1,569,217	Hartigan, Neil F.	35,067	83,909 R	50.7%	48.2%	51.3%	48.7%
1986**	3,143,978	1,655,849	Thompson, James R.*	208,830	Fairchild, Mark	1,279,299	1,447,019 R	52.7%	6.6%	88.8%	11.2%
1982	3,673,681	1,816,101	Thompson, James R.*	1,811,027	Stevenson, Adlai E. III	46,553	5,074 R	49.4%	49.3%	50.1%	49.9%
1978	3,150,095	1,859,684	Thompson, James R.*	1,263,134	Bakalis, Michael	27,277	596,550 R	59.0%	40.1%	59.6%	40.4%
1976**	4,635,728	3,000,395	Thompson, James R.	1,606,989	Howlett, Michael J.	28,344	1,393,406 R	64.7%	34.7%	65.1%	34.9%
1972	4,678,802	2,293,809	Ogilvie, Richard B.*	2,371,301	Walker, Daniel	13,692	77,492 D	49.0%	50.7%	49.2%	50.8%
1968	4,506,000	2,307,295	Ogilvie, Richard B.	2,179,501	Shapiro, Samuel H.	19,204	127,794 R	51.2%	48.4%	51.4%	48.6%
1964	4,657,500	2,239,095	Percy, Charles H.	2,418,394	Kerner, Otto*	11	179,299 D	48.1%	51.9%	48.1%	51.9%
1960	4,674,187	2,070,479	Stratton, William G.*	2,594,731	Kerner, Otto	8,977	524,252 D	44.3%	55.5%	44.4%	55.6%
1956	4,314,611	2,171,786	Stratton, William G.*	2,134,909	Austin, Richard B.	7,916	36,877 R	50.3%	49.5%	50.4%	49.6%
1952	4,415,864	2,317,363	Stratton, William G.	2,089,721	Dixon, Sherwood	8,780	227,642 R	52.5%	47.3%	52.6%	47.4%
1948	3,940,257	1,678,007	Green, Dwight H.*	2,250,074	Stevenson, Adlai E. II	12,176	572,067 D	42.6%	57.1%	42.7%	57.3%

Note: An asterisk (*) denotes incumbent. **In past elections, the other vote included: 2006 - 361,336 Green (Rich Whitney); 1986 - 1,256,626 Illinois Solidarity (Adlai E. Stevenson III). In 1986 there was no Democratic candidate for Governor on the ballot. Mark Fairchild, a supporter of Lyndon H. LaRouche Jr., was the "paired" Democratic candidate for Lt. Governor and the Democratic vote was cast for this ticket of "no name" and Fairchild. Running on the Illinois Solidarity line, Stevenson finished second with 40.0 percent of the vote. The 1976 vote was for a two-year term to permit shifting the election for governor to non-presidential years.

POSTWAR VOTE FOR SENATOR

Year	Total Vote	Republican		Democratic		Other Vote	Rep.-Dem. Plurality	Percentage			
								Total Vote		Major Vote	
		Vote	Candidate	Vote	Candidate			Rep.	Dem.	Rep.	Dem.
2010	3,704,473	1,778,698	Kirk, Mark Steven	1,719,478	Giannoulias, Alexander	206,297	59,220 R	48.0%	46.4%	50.8%	49.2%
2008	5,329,884	1,520,621	Sauerberg, Steve	3,615,844	Durbin, Richard J.*	193,419	2,095,223 D	28.5%	67.8%	29.6%	70.4%
2004	5,141,520	1,390,690	Keyes, Alan L.	3,597,456	Obama, Barack H.	153,374	2,206,766 D	27.0%	70.0%	27.9%	72.1%
2002	3,486,851	1,325,703	Durkin, Jim	2,103,766	Durbin, Richard J.*	57,382	778,063 D	38.0%	60.3%	38.7%	61.3%
1998	3,392,845	1,709,041	Fitzgerald, Peter G.	1,610,496	Moseley-Braun, Carol*	73,308	98,545 R	50.4%	47.5%	51.5%	48.5%
1996	4,250,722	1,728,824	Salvi, Al	2,384,028	Durbin, Richard J.	137,870	655,204 D	40.7%	56.1%	42.0%	58.0%
1992	4,939,558	2,126,833	Williamson, Richard S.	2,631,229	Moseley-Braun, Carol	181,496	504,396 D	43.1%	53.3%	44.7%	55.3%
1990	3,251,005	1,135,628	Martin, Lynn	2,115,377	Simon, Paul*		979,749 D	34.9%	65.1%	34.9%	65.1%
1986	3,122,883	1,053,734	Koehler, Judy	2,033,783	Dixon, Alan J.*	35,366	980,049 D	33.7%	65.1%	34.1%	65.9%
1984	4,787,473	2,308,039	Percy, Charles H.*	2,397,303	Simon, Paul	82,131	89,264 D	48.2%	50.1%	49.1%	50.9%
1980	4,580,029	1,946,296	O'Neal, David C.	2,565,302	Dixon, Alan J.	68,431	619,006 D	42.5%	56.0%	43.1%	56.9%
1978	3,184,764	1,698,711	Percy, Charles H.*	1,448,187	Seith, Alex	37,866	250,524 R	53.3%	45.5%	54.0%	46.0%
1974	2,914,666	1,084,884	Burditt, George M.	1,811,496	Stevenson, Adlai E. III*	18,286	726,612 D	37.2%	62.2%	37.5%	62.5%
1972	4,608,380	2,867,078	Percy, Charles H.*	1,721,031	Pucinski, Roman C.	20,271	1,146,047 R	62.2%	37.3%	62.5%	37.5%
1970S	3,599,272	1,519,718	Smith, Ralph T.*	2,065,054	Stevenson, Adlai E. III	14,500	545,336 D	42.2%	57.4%	42.4%	57.6%
1968	4,449,757	2,358,947	Dirksen, Everett M.*	2,073,242	Clark, William G.	17,568	285,705 R	53.0%	46.6%	53.2%	46.8%
1966	3,822,725	2,100,449	Percy, Charles H.	1,678,147	Douglas, Paul H.*	44,129	422,302 R	54.9%	43.9%	55.6%	44.4%
1962	3,709,216	1,961,202	Dirksen, Everett M.*	1,748,007	Yates, Sidney R.	7	213,195 R	52.9%	47.1%	52.9%	47.1%
1960	4,632,796	2,093,846	Witwer, Samuel W.	2,530,943	Douglas, Paul H.*	8,007	437,097 D	45.2%	54.6%	45.3%	54.7%
1956	4,264,830	2,307,352	Dirksen, Everett M.*	1,949,883	Stengel, Richard	7,595	357,469 R	54.1%	45.7%	54.2%	45.8%
1954	3,368,025	1,563,683	Meek, Joseph T.	1,804,338	Douglas, Paul H.*	4	240,655 D	46.4%	53.6%	46.4%	53.6%
1950	3,622,673	1,951,984	Dirksen, Everett M.	1,657,630	Lucas, Scott W.*	13,059	294,354 R	53.9%	45.8%	54.1%	45.9%
1948	3,900,285	1,740,026	Brooks, C. Wayland*	2,147,754	Douglas, Paul H.	12,505	407,728 D	44.6%	55.1%	44.8%	55.2%

Note: An asterisk (*) denotes incumbent. **The 1970 election was for a short term to fill a vacancy.

ILLINOIS

PRESIDENT 2012

2010 Census Population	County	Total Vote	Republican (Romney)	Democratic (Obama)	Other	Rep.-Dem. Plurality	Percentage Total Vote Rep.	Dem.	Major Vote Rep.	Dem.
67,103	ADAMS	30,607	20,416	9,648	543	10,768 R	66.7%	31.5%	67.9%	32.1%
8,238	ALEXANDER	3,501	1,487	1,965	49	478 D	42.5%	56.1%	43.1%	56.9%
17,768	BOND	7,336	4,095	3,020	221	1,075 R	55.8%	41.2%	57.6%	42.4%
54,165	BOONE	21,365	11,096	9,883	386	1,213 R	51.9%	46.3%	52.9%	47.1%
6,937	BROWN	2,364	1,513	787	64	726 R	64.0%	33.3%	65.8%	34.2%
34,978	BUREAU	16,631	8,164	8,134	333	30 R	49.1%	48.9%	50.1%	49.9%
5,089	CALHOUN	2,576	1,440	1,080	56	360 R	55.9%	41.9%	57.1%	42.9%
15,387	CARROLL	7,386	3,555	3,665	166	110 D	48.1%	49.6%	49.2%	50.8%
13,642	CASS	4,862	2,707	2,053	102	654 R	55.7%	42.2%	56.9%	43.1%
201,081	CHAMPAIGN	78,359	35,312	40,831	2,216	5,519 D	45.1%	52.1%	46.4%	53.6%
34,800	CHRISTIAN	14,701	8,885	5,494	322	3,391 R	60.4%	37.4%	61.8%	38.2%
16,335	CLARK	7,860	5,144	2,591	125	2,553 R	65.4%	33.0%	66.5%	33.5%
13,815	CLAY	5,908	4,190	1,584	134	2,606 R	70.9%	26.8%	72.6%	27.4%
37,762	CLINTON	16,450	10,524	5,596	330	4,928 R	64.0%	34.0%	65.3%	34.7%
53,873	COLES	21,358	11,631	9,262	465	2,369 R	54.5%	43.4%	55.7%	44.3%
5,194,675	COOK	2,011,598	495,542	1,488,537	27,519	992,995 D	24.6%	74.0%	25.0%	75.0%
19,817	CRAWFORD	8,609	5,585	2,858	166	2,727 R	64.9%	33.2%	66.1%	33.9%
11,048	CUMBERLAND	5,295	3,509	1,641	145	1,868 R	66.3%	31.0%	68.1%	31.9%
16,561	DE WITT	7,345	4,579	2,601	165	1,978 R	62.3%	35.4%	63.8%	36.2%
105,160	DEKALB	41,092	18,934	21,207	951	2,273 D	46.1%	51.6%	47.2%	52.8%
19,980	DOUGLAS	7,897	5,334	2,430	133	2,904 R	67.5%	30.8%	68.7%	31.3%
916,924	DU PAGE	401,081	195,046	199,460	6,575	4,414 D	48.6%	49.7%	49.4%	50.6%
18,576	EDGAR	7,819	5,132	2,565	122	2,567 R	65.6%	32.8%	66.7%	33.3%
6,721	EDWARDS	3,228	2,405	754	69	1,651 R	74.5%	23.4%	76.1%	23.9%
34,242	EFFINGHAM	16,613	12,501	3,861	251	8,640 R	75.2%	23.2%	76.4%	23.6%
22,140	FAYETTE	8,971	5,951	2,853	167	3,098 R	66.3%	31.8%	67.6%	32.4%
14,081	FORD	6,006	4,229	1,656	121	2,573 R	70.4%	27.6%	71.9%	28.1%
39,561	FRANKLIN	17,914	10,267	7,254	393	3,013 R	57.3%	40.5%	58.6%	41.4%
37,069	FULTON	15,356	6,632	8,328	396	1,696 D	43.2%	54.2%	44.3%	55.7%
5,589	GALLATIN	2,573	1,492	1,029	52	463 R	58.0%	40.0%	59.2%	40.8%
13,886	GREENE	5,622	3,451	2,023	148	1,428 R	61.4%	36.0%	63.0%	37.0%
50,063	GRUNDY	21,244	11,343	9,451	450	1,892 R	53.4%	44.5%	54.5%	45.5%
8,457	HAMILTON	3,941	2,566	1,269	106	1,297 R	65.1%	32.2%	66.9%	33.1%
19,104	HANCOCK	9,111	5,271	3,650	190	1,621 R	57.9%	40.1%	59.1%	40.9%
4,320	HARDIN	2,330	1,535	742	53	793 R	65.9%	31.8%	67.4%	32.6%
7,331	HENDERSON	3,568	1,541	1,978	49	437 D	43.2%	55.4%	43.8%	56.2%
50,486	HENRY	24,322	11,583	12,332	407	749 D	47.6%	50.7%	48.4%	51.6%
29,718	IROQUOIS	12,784	9,120	3,413	251	5,707 R	71.3%	26.7%	72.8%	27.2%
60,218	JACKSON	24,012	9,864	13,319	829	3,455 D	41.1%	55.5%	42.5%	57.5%
9,698	JASPER	5,043	3,514	1,436	93	2,078 R	69.7%	28.5%	71.0%	29.0%
38,827	JEFFERSON	16,320	9,811	6,089	420	3,722 R	60.1%	37.3%	61.7%	38.3%
22,985	JERSEY	9,959	6,039	3,667	253	2,372 R	60.6%	36.8%	62.2%	37.8%
22,678	JO DAVIESS	11,429	5,534	5,667	228	133 D	48.4%	49.6%	49.4%	50.6%
12,582	JOHNSON	5,672	3,963	1,572	137	2,391 R	69.9%	27.7%	71.6%	28.4%
515,269	KANE	181,648	88,335	90,332	2,981	1,997 D	48.6%	49.7%	49.4%	50.6%
113,449	KANKAKEE	45,509	23,136	21,595	778	1,541 R	50.8%	47.5%	51.7%	48.3%
114,736	KENDALL	47,295	24,047	22,471	777	1,576 R	50.8%	47.5%	51.7%	48.3%
52,919	KNOX	23,278	9,408	13,451	419	4,043 D	40.4%	57.8%	41.2%	58.8%
113,924	LA SALLE	47,259	23,256	23,073	930	183 R	49.2%	48.8%	50.2%	49.8%
703,462	LAKE	287,493	129,764	153,757	3,972	23,993 D	45.1%	53.5%	45.8%	54.2%
16,833	LAWRENCE	5,989	3,857	2,011	121	1,846 R	64.4%	33.6%	65.7%	34.3%
36,031	LEE	15,301	8,059	6,937	305	1,122 R	52.7%	45.3%	53.7%	46.3%
38,950	LIVINGSTON	15,039	9,753	5,020	266	4,733 R	64.9%	33.4%	66.0%	34.0%
30,305	LOGAN	12,053	7,844	3,978	231	3,866 R	65.1%	33.0%	66.4%	33.6%
110,768	MACON	48,899	25,309	22,780	810	2,529 R	51.8%	46.6%	52.6%	47.4%
47,765	MACOUPIN	21,010	10,946	9,464	600	1,482 R	52.1%	45.0%	53.6%	46.4%
269,282	MADISON	122,473	60,608	58,922	2,943	1,686 R	49.5%	48.1%	50.7%	49.3%
39,437	MARION	15,764	9,248	6,225	291	3,023 R	58.7%	39.5%	59.8%	40.2%
12,640	MARSHALL	5,850	3,290	2,455	105	835 R	56.2%	42.0%	57.3%	42.7%
14,666	MASON	6,272	3,265	2,867	140	398 R	52.1%	45.7%	53.2%	46.8%

ILLINOIS

PRESIDENT 2012

2010 Census Population	County	Total Vote	Republican (Romney)	Democratic (Obama)	Other	Rep.-Dem. Plurality	Percentage			
							Total Vote		Major Vote	
							Rep.	Dem.	Rep.	Dem.
15,429	MASSAC	6,495	4,278	2,092	125	2,186 R	65.9%	32.2%	67.2%	32.8%
32,612	MCDONOUGH	12,454	6,147	5,967	340	180 R	49.4%	47.9%	50.7%	49.3%
308,760	MCHENRY	133,844	71,598	59,797	2,449	11,801 R	53.5%	44.7%	54.5%	45.5%
169,572	MCLEAN	73,382	39,947	31,883	1,552	8,064 R	54.4%	43.4%	55.6%	44.4%
12,705	MENARD	6,151	3,948	2,100	103	1,848 R	64.2%	34.1%	65.3%	34.7%
16,434	MERCER	8,534	3,876	4,507	151	631 D	45.4%	52.8%	46.2%	53.8%
32,957	MONROE	17,432	10,888	6,215	329	4,673 R	62.5%	35.7%	63.7%	36.3%
30,104	MONTGOMERY	12,133	6,776	5,058	299	1,718 R	55.8%	41.7%	57.3%	42.7%
35,547	MORGAN	14,096	7,972	5,806	318	2,166 R	56.6%	41.2%	57.9%	42.1%
14,846	MOULTRIE	6,057	3,784	2,144	129	1,640 R	62.5%	35.4%	63.8%	36.2%
53,497	OGLE	23,367	13,422	9,514	431	3,908 R	57.4%	40.7%	58.5%	41.5%
186,494	PEORIA	78,411	36,774	40,209	1,428	3,435 D	46.9%	51.3%	47.8%	52.2%
22,350	PERRY	9,549	5,507	3,819	223	1,688 R	57.7%	40.0%	59.0%	41.0%
16,729	PIATT	8,707	5,413	3,090	204	2,323 R	62.2%	35.5%	63.7%	36.3%
16,430	PIKE	7,286	4,860	2,278	148	2,582 R	66.7%	31.3%	68.1%	31.9%
4,470	POPE	2,222	1,512	650	60	862 R	68.0%	29.3%	69.9%	30.1%
6,161	PULASKI	3,003	1,564	1,389	50	175 R	52.1%	46.3%	53.0%	47.0%
6,006	PUTNAM	3,135	1,502	1,559	74	57 D	47.9%	49.7%	49.1%	50.9%
33,476	RANDOLPH	14,392	8,290	5,759	343	2,531 R	57.6%	40.0%	59.0%	41.0%
16,233	RICHLAND	7,282	4,756	2,362	164	2,394 R	65.3%	32.4%	66.8%	33.2%
147,546	ROCK ISLAND	65,016	24,934	39,157	925	14,223 D	38.4%	60.2%	38.9%	61.1%
24,913	SALINE	10,720	6,806	3,701	213	3,105 R	63.5%	34.5%	64.8%	35.2%
197,465	SANGAMON	94,297	50,225	42,107	1,965	8,118 R	53.3%	44.7%	54.4%	45.6%
7,544	SCHUYLER	3,890	2,069	1,727	94	342 R	53.2%	44.4%	54.5%	45.5%
5,355	SCOTT	2,555	1,587	910	58	677 R	62.1%	35.6%	63.6%	36.4%
22,363	SHELBY	10,395	6,843	3,342	210	3,501 R	65.8%	32.2%	67.2%	32.8%
270,056	ST. CLAIR	119,466	50,125	67,285	2,056	17,160 D	42.0%	56.3%	42.7%	57.3%
5,994	STARK	2,662	1,528	1,095	39	433 R	57.4%	41.1%	58.3%	41.7%
47,711	STEPHENSON	21,055	10,512	10,165	378	347 R	49.9%	48.3%	50.8%	49.2%
135,394	TAZEWELL	61,048	35,335	24,438	1,275	10,897 R	57.9%	40.0%	59.1%	40.9%
17,808	UNION	8,282	4,957	3,137	188	1,820 R	59.9%	37.9%	61.2%	38.8%
81,625	VERMILION	30,314	16,892	12,878	544	4,014 R	55.7%	42.5%	56.7%	43.3%
11,947	WABASH	5,134	3,478	1,590	66	1,888 R	67.7%	31.0%	68.6%	31.4%
17,707	WARREN	7,793	3,618	4,044	131	426 D	46.4%	51.9%	47.2%	52.8%
14,716	WASHINGTON	7,405	4,792	2,450	163	2,342 R	64.7%	33.1%	66.2%	33.8%
16,760	WAYNE	7,680	5,988	1,514	178	4,474 R	78.0%	19.7%	79.8%	20.2%
14,665	WHITE	7,064	4,731	2,188	145	2,543 R	67.0%	31.0%	68.4%	31.6%
58,498	WHITESIDE	25,768	10,448	14,833	487	4,385 D	40.5%	57.6%	41.3%	58.7%
677,560	WILL	277,387	128,969	144,229	4,189	15,260 D	46.5%	52.0%	47.2%	52.8%
66,357	WILLIAMSON	29,143	17,909	10,647	587	7,262 R	61.5%	36.5%	62.7%	37.3%
295,266	WINNEBAGO	118,984	55,138	61,732	2,114	6,594 D	46.3%	51.9%	47.2%	52.8%
38,664	WOODFORD	18,874	12,961	5,572	341	7,389 R	68.7%	29.5%	69.9%	30.1%
12,830,632	TOTAL	5,242,014	2,135,216	3,019,512	87,286	884,296 D	40.7%	57.6%	41.4%	58.6%

ILLINOIS

HOUSE OF REPRESENTATIVES

CD	Year	Total Vote	Republican		Democratic		Other Vote	Rep.-Dem. Plurality	Percentage			
									Total Vote		Major Vote	
			Vote	Candidate	Vote	Candidate			Rep.	Dem.	Rep.	Dem.
1	2012	320,844	83,989	PELOQUIN, DONALD E.	236,854	RUSH, BOBBY L.*	1	152,865 D	26.2%	73.8%	26.2%	73.8%
2	2012	297,712	69,115	WOODWORTH, BRIAN	188,303	JACKSON, JESSE L. JR.*	40,294	119,188 D	23.2%	63.3%	26.8%	73.2%
3	2012	246,398	77,653	GRABOWSKI, RICHARD	168,738	LIPINSKI, DANIEL*	7	91,085 D	31.5%	68.5%	31.5%	68.5%
4	2012	160,509	27,279	CONCEPCION, HECTOR	133,226	GUTIERREZ, LUIS V.*	4	105,947 D	17.0%	83.0%	17.0%	83.0%
5	2012	270,377	77,289	SCHMITT, DAN	177,729	QUIGLEY, MIKE*	15,359	100,440 D	28.6%	65.7%	30.3%	69.7%
6	2012	326,129	193,138	ROSKAM, PETER*	132,991	COOLIDGE, LESLIE		60,147 R	59.2%	40.8%	59.2%	40.8%
7	2012	286,435	31,466	ZAK, RITA	242,439	DAVIS, DANNY K.*	12,530	210,973 D	11.0%	84.6%	11.5%	88.5%
8	2012	225,066	101,860	WALSH, JOE*	123,206	DUCKWORTH, TAMMY		21,346 D	45.3%	54.7%	45.3%	54.7%
9	2012	293,807	98,924	WOLFE, TIMOTHY	194,869	SCHAKOWSKY, JAN*	14	95,945 D	33.7%	66.3%	33.7%	66.3%
10	2012	264,454	130,564	DOLD, ROBERT*	133,890	SCHNEIDER, BRAD		3,326 D	49.4%	50.6%	49.4%	50.6%
11	2012	254,295	105,348	BIGGERT, JUDY*	148,928	FOSTER, BILL	19	43,580 D	41.4%	58.6%	41.4%	58.6%
12	2012	303,949	129,902	PLUMMER, JASON	157,000	ENYART, WILLIAM	17,047	27,098 D	42.7%	51.7%	45.3%	54.7%
13	2012	294,385	137,034	DAVIS, RODNEY L.	136,032	GILL, DAVID*	21,319	1,002 R	46.5%	46.2%	50.2%	49.8%
14	2012	301,954	177,603	HULTGREN, RANDY*	124,351	ANDERSON, DENNIS		53,252 R	58.8%	41.2%	58.8%	41.2%
15	2012	299,937	205,775	SHIMKUS, JOHN*	94,162	MICHAEL, ANGELA		111,613 R	68.6%	31.4%	68.6%	31.4%
16	2012	294,090	181,789	KINZINGER, ADAM*	112,301	ROHL, WANDA		69,488 R	61.8%	38.2%	61.8%	38.2%
17	2012	288,161	134,623	SCHILLING, BOBBY*	153,519	BUSTOS, CHERI	19	18,896 D	46.7%	53.3%	46.7%	53.3%
18	2012	329,631	244,467	SCHOCK, AARON*	85,164	WATERWORTH, STEVE		159,303 R	74.2%	25.8%	74.2%	25.8%
TOTAL	2012	5,058,133	2,207,818		2,743,702		106,613	535,884 D	43.6%	54.2%	44.6%	55.4%

Notes: An asterisk (*) denotes incumbent. Brad Harriman withdrew after the primary election and William Enyart was selected by the Democratic Party to fill the vacancy on the general election ballot for the 12th district. Timothy V. Johnson withdrew after the primary election and Rodney L. Davis was selected by the Republican Party to fill the vacancy on the general election ballot in the 13th District.

ILLINOIS

GENERAL AND PRIMARY ELECTIONS

2012 GENERAL ELECTIONS: OTHER VOTE

President   Other vote was 56,229 Libertarian (Gary E. Johnson), 30,222 Green (Jill Stein), 420 Write-in (Scattered Write-In), 415 Write-in (Virgil H. Goode).

House   Other vote was:

CD 1   1 Write-in (John Hawkins)
CD 2   40,006 Independent (Marcus Lewis), 288 Write-in (Anthony W. Williams)
CD 3   7 Write-in (Laura Anderson)
CD 4   4 Write-in (Ymelda Viramontes)
CD 5   15,359 Green (Nancy Wade)
CD 7   12,523 Independent (John Monaghan), 5 Write-in (Phil Collins), 2 Write-in (Dennis Richter)
CD 9   8 Write-in (Hilaire Fuji Shioura), 6 Write-in (Susanne Atanus)
CD 11   19 Write-in (Chris Michel)
CD 12   17,045 Green (Paula Bradshaw), 2 Write-in (Shon-Tiyon Horton)
CD 13   21,319 Independent (John Hartman)
CD 17   10 Write-in (Eric Reyes), 9 Write-in (Joe Faber)

2012 PRIMARY ELECTIONS: SUPPLEMENTARY INFORMATION

Primary   March 20, 2012   **Registration**   7,304,333   No Party Registration
(as of March 20, 2012)

Primary Type   Open—Any registered voter could participate in the primary of either party.

ILLINOIS

GENERAL AND PRIMARY ELECTIONS

	REPUBLICAN PRIMARIES			DEMOCRATIC PRIMARIES		
President	Romney, W. Mitt	435,859	46.7%	Obama, Barack H.*	652,583	100%
	Santorum, Rick	326,778	35.0%	Terry, Randall	134	
	Paul, Ron	87,044	9.3%			
	Gingrich, Newt	74,482	8.0%			
	Perry, Rick	5,568	0.6%			
	Roemer, Charles	3,723	0.4%			
	TOTAL	*933,454*		*TOTAL*	*652,717*	
Congressional District 1	Peloquin, Donald E.	16,355	69.2%	Rush, Bobby L.*	64,533	83.8%
	Collins, Frederick	5,773	24.4%	Lodato, Raymond M.	3,210	4.2%
	Tillman, Jimmy Lee II	1,501	6.4%	Bailey, Harold L.	2,598	3.4%
				Russell, Clifford M. Jr.	2,412	3.1%
				Smith, Fred	2,232	2.9%
				Sims, Jordan	1,980	2.6%
	TOTAL	*23,629*		*TOTAL*	*76,965*	
Congressional District 2	Woodworth, Brian	11,123	63.7%	Jackson, Jesse L. Jr.*	56,109	71.2%
	Taylor, James	6,347	36.3%	Halvorson, Deborah L.	22,672	28.8%
	TOTAL	*17,470*		*TOTAL*	*78,781*	
Congressional District 3	Grabowski, Richard	20,895	59.4%	Lipinski, Daniel*	44,532	87.3%
	Falvey, Jim	10,449	29.7%	Baqai, Farah	6,463	12.7%
	Jones, Arthur J.	3,861	11.0%			
	TOTAL	*35,205*		*TOTAL*	*50,995*	
Congressional District 4	Concepcion, Hector	10	100.0%	Gutierrez, Luis V.*	30,908	100.0%
				Zavala, Jorge	6	
	TOTAL	*10*		*TOTAL*	*30,914*	
Congressional District 5	Schmitt, Dan	23,940	100.0%	Quigley, Mike*	37,967	100.0%
	TOTAL	*23,940*		*TOTAL*	*37,967*	
Congressional District 6	Roskam, Peter*	76,146	100.0%	Coolidge, Leslie	9,919	54.5%
				Yates, Maureen E.	5,934	32.6%
				Petzel, Geoffrey	2,343	12.9%
	TOTAL	*76,146*		*TOTAL*	*18,196*	
Congressional District 7	Zak, Rita			Davis, Danny K.*	57,896	84.5%
	Rita Zak was nominated as an alternate for the 7th district and became the Republican nominee when no one ran in the Republican primary.			Conway, Jacques A.	10,638	15.5%
				TOTAL	*68,534*	
Congressional District 8	Walsh, Joe*	35,102	99.8%	Duckworth, Tammy	17,097	66.2%
	Canfield, Robert "Bob"	54	0.2%	Krishnamoorthi, Raja	8,736	33.8%
	TOTAL	*35,156*		*TOTAL*	*25,833*	
Congressional District 9	Wolfe, Timothy	32,043	100.0%	Schakowsky Jan*	48,124	91.9%
				Ribeiro, Simon M.	4,270	8.1%
	TOTAL	*32,043*		*TOTAL*	*52,394*	
Congressional District 10	Dold, Robert*	36,647	100.0%	Schneider, Brad	15,530	46.9%
				Sheyman, Ilya	12,767	38.5%
				Tree, John	2,938	8.9%
				Bavda, Vivek	1,881	5.7%
				Rutagwibira, Aloys	8	
	TOTAL	*36,647*		*TOTAL*	*33,124*	
Congressional District 11	Biggert, Judy*	31,471	99.9%	Foster, Bill	12,126	58.5%
	Harris, Diane M.	37	0.1%	Thomas, Juan	5,212	25.1%
				Hickey, Jim	3,399	16.4%
	TOTAL	*31,508*		*TOTAL*	*20,737*	

ILLINOIS

GENERAL AND PRIMARY ELECTIONS

REPUBLICAN PRIMARIES				DEMOCRATIC PRIMARIES		
Congressional District 12	Plummer, Jason	25,280	55.7%	Harriman, Brad	27,409	69.8%
	Cook, Rodger	16,313	35.9%			
	Kormos, Theresa	3,811	8.4%	*Brad Harriman withdrew after the primary. Democratic officials replaced him on the general election ballot with William Enyart.*		
				Miller, Christopher	8,874	22.6%
				Wiezer, Kenneth Charles "Bud"	2,967	7.6%
	TOTAL	45,404		TOTAL	39,250	
Congressional District 13	Johnson, Timothy V.*	35,655	68.7%	Gill, David M.	15,536	50.3%
	Timothy V. Johnson withdrew after the primary. Republican officials replaced him on the ballot with Rodney L. Davis.			Goetten, Matthew J.	15,373	49.7%
	Metzger, Frank L.	9,571	18.4%			
	Firsching, Michael	6,706	12.9%			
	TOTAL	51,932		TOTAL	30,909	
Congressional District 14	Hultgren, Randy*	64,419	100.0%	Anderson, Dennis	9,344	74.1%
	Mastrogiovanni, Mark Alan	1		Farnick, Jonathan	3,258	25.9%
	TOTAL	64,420		TOTAL	12,602	
Congressional District 15	Shimkus, John*	66,709	100.0%	Michael, Angela	16,831	100.0%
	TOTAL	66,709		TOTAL	16,831	
Congressional District 16	Kinzinger, Adam*	45,546	53.9%	Rohl, Wanda	Unopposed	
	Manzullo, Donald*	38,889	46.1%			
	TOTAL	84,435				
Congressional District 17	Schilling, Bobby*	46,263	100.0%	Bustos, Cheri	18,652	54.4%
				Gaulrapp, George W.	8,838	25.8%
				Aguilar, Greg	6,798	19.8%
	TOTAL	46,263		TOTAL	34,288	
Congressional District 18	Schock, Aaron*	87,441	100.0%	Waterworth, Steve	10,211	69.6%
				Woodmancy, Matthew A.	4,465	30.4%
	TOTAL	87,441		TOTAL	14,676	

Notes: An asterisk (*) denotes incumbent. Due to redistricting, the 16th district Republican primary pitted two incumbents against each other (Kinzinger, former 11th district and Manzullo, former 16th district).

INDIANA

Congressional districts first established for elections held in 2012

9 members

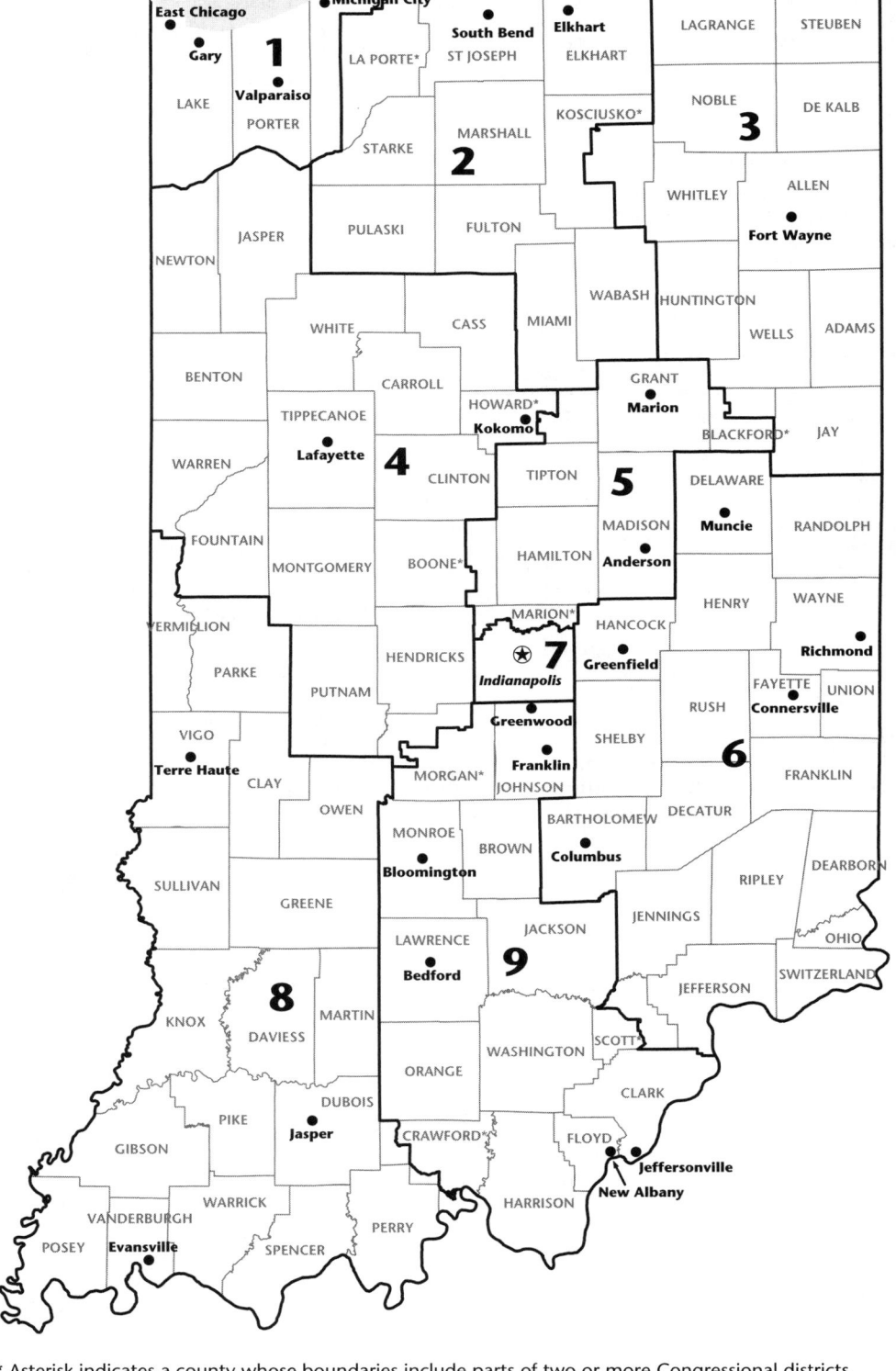

* Asterisk indicates a county whose boundaries include parts of two or more Congressional districts.

INDIANA

GOVERNOR

Mike Pence (R). Elected 2012 to a four-year term.

SENATORS (2 Republicans)

Dan Coats (R). Elected 2010 to a six-year term. Previously elected 1992, 1990.

Joe Donnelly (D). Elected 2012 to a six-year term.

REPRESENTATIVES (7 Republicans, 2 Democrats)

1. Pete Visclosky (D)
2. Jackie Walorski (R)
3. Marlin Stutzman (R)
4. Todd Rokita (R)
5. Susan Brooks (R)
6. Luke Messer (R)
7. André Carson (D)
8. Larry Bucshon (R)
9. Todd Young (R)

POSTWAR VOTE FOR PRESIDENT

| | | Republican | | Democratic | | | | Percentage | | | |
| | | | | | | Other | Rep.-Dem. | Total Vote | | Major Vote | |
Year	Total Vote	Vote	Candidate	Vote	Candidate	Vote	Plurality	Rep.	Dem.	Rep.	Dem.
2012	2,624,534	1,420,543	Romney, W. Mitt	1,152,887	Obama, Barack H.*	51,104	267,656 R	54.1%	43.9%	55.2%	44.8%
2008	2,751,054	1,345,648	McCain, John S. III	1,374,039	Obama, Barack H.	31,367	28,391 D	48.9%	49.9%	49.5%	50.5%
2004	2,468,002	1,479,438	Bush, George W.*	969,011	Kerry, John F.	19,553	510,427 R	59.9%	39.3%	60.4%	39.6%
2000**	2,199,305	1,245,836	Bush, George W.	901,980	Gore, Albert Jr.	51,489	343,856 R	56.6%	41.0%	58.0%	42.0%
1996**	2,135,842	1,006,693	Dole, Robert "Bob"	887,424	Clinton, Bill*	241,725	119,269 R	47.1%	41.5%	53.1%	46.9%
1992**	2,305,871	989,375	Bush, George H.*	848,420	Clinton, Bill	468,076	140,955 R	42.9%	36.8%	53.8%	46.2%
1988	2,168,621	1,297,763	Bush, George H.	860,643	Dukakis, Michael S.	10,215	437,120 R	59.8%	39.7%	60.1%	39.9%
1984	2,233,069	1,377,230	Reagan, Ronald*	841,481	Mondale, Walter F.	14,358	535,749 R	61.7%	37.7%	62.1%	37.9%
1980**	2,242,033	1,255,656	Reagan, Ronald	844,197	Carter, Jimmy*	142,180	411,459 R	56.0%	37.7%	59.8%	40.2%
1976	2,220,362	1,183,958	Ford, Gerald R.*	1,014,714	Carter, Jimmy	21,690	169,244 R	53.3%	45.7%	53.8%	46.2%
1972	2,125,529	1,405,154	Nixon, Richard M.*	708,568	McGovern, George S.	11,807	696,586 R	66.1%	33.3%	66.5%	33.5%
1968**	2,123,597	1,067,885	Nixon, Richard M.	806,659	Humphrey, Hubert H. Jr.	249,053	261,226 R	50.3%	38.0%	57.0%	43.0%
1964	2,091,606	911,118	Goldwater, Barry M. Sr.	1,170,848	Johnson, Lyndon B.*	9,640	259,730 D	43.6%	56.0%	43.8%	56.2%
1960	2,135,360	1,175,120	Nixon, Richard M.	952,358	Kennedy, John F.	7,882	222,762 R	55.0%	44.6%	55.2%	44.8%
1956	1,974,607	1,182,811	Eisenhower, Dwight D.*	783,908	Stevenson, Adlai E. II	7,888	398,903 R	59.9%	39.7%	60.1%	39.9%
1952	1,955,049	1,136,259	Eisenhower, Dwight D.	801,530	Stevenson, Adlai E. II	17,260	334,729 R	58.1%	41.0%	58.6%	41.4%
1948	1,656,212	821,079	Dewey, Thomas E.	807,831	Truman, Harry S.*	27,302	13,248 R	49.6%	48.8%	50.4%	49.6%

Note: An asterisk (*) denotes incumbent. **In past elections, the other vote included: 2000 - 18,531 Green (Ralph Nader); 1996 - 224,299 Reform (Ross Perot); 1992 - 455,934 Independent (Perot); 1980 - 111,639 Independent (John Anderson); 1968 - 243,108 American Independent (George Wallace).

INDIANA

POSTWAR VOTE FOR GOVERNOR

Year	Total Vote	Republican		Democratic		Other Vote	Rep.-Dem. Plurality	Percentage			
								Total Vote		Major Vote	
		Vote	Candidate	Vote	Candidate			Rep.	Dem.	Rep.	Dem.
2012	2,577,329	1,275,424	Pence, Mike	1,200,016	Gregg, John R.	101,889	75,408 R	49.5%	46.6%	51.5%	48.5%
2008	2,703,752	1,563,885	Daniels, Mitch*	1,082,463	Thompson, Jill Long	57,404	481,422 R	57.8%	40.0%	59.1%	40.9%
2004	2,448,498	1,302,912	Daniels, Mitch	1,113,900	Kernan, Joseph E.	31,686	189,012 R	53.2%	45.5%	53.9%	46.1%
2000	2,179,413	908,285	McIntosh, David M.	1,232,525	O'Bannon, Frank*	38,603	324,240 D	41.7%	56.6%	42.4%	57.6%
1996	2,110,047	986,982	Goldsmith, Stephen	1,087,128	O'Bannon, Frank	35,937	100,146 D	46.8%	51.5%	47.6%	52.4%
1992	2,229,116	822,533	Pearson, Linley E.	1,382,151	Bayh, Evan*	24,432	559,618 D	36.9%	62.0%	37.3%	62.7%
1988	2,140,781	1,002,207	Mutz, John M.	1,138,574	Bayh, Evan		136,367 D	46.8%	53.2%	46.8%	53.2%
1984	2,197,988	1,146,497	Orr, Robert D.*	1,036,922	Townsend, W. Wayne	14,569	109,575 R	52.2%	47.2%	52.5%	47.5%
1980	2,178,403	1,257,383	Orr, Robert D.	913,116	Hillenbrand, John A.	7,904	344,267 R	57.7%	41.9%	57.9%	42.1%
1976	2,175,324	1,236,555	Bowen, Otis R.*	927,243	Conrad, Larry A.	11,526	309,312 R	56.8%	42.6%	57.1%	42.9%
1972	2,120,847	1,203,903	Bowen, Otis R.	900,489	Welsh, Matthew E.	16,455	303,414 R	56.8%	42.5%	57.2%	42.8%
1968	2,049,063	1,080,262	Whitcomb, Edgar D.	965,816	Rock, Robert L.	2,985	114,446 R	52.7%	47.1%	52.8%	47.2%
1964	2,073,058	901,342	Ristine, Richard O.	1,164,763	Branigin, Roger D.	6,953	263,421 D	43.5%	56.2%	43.6%	56.4%
1960	2,128,965	1,049,540	Parker, Crawford F.	1,072,717	Welsh, Matthew E.	6,708	23,177 D	49.3%	50.4%	49.5%	50.5%
1956	1,954,290	1,086,868	Handley, Harold W.	859,393	Tucker, Ralph	8,029	227,475 R	55.6%	44.0%	55.8%	44.2%
1952	1,931,869	1,075,685	Craig, George N.	841,984	Watkins, John A.	14,200	233,701 R	55.7%	43.6%	56.1%	43.9%
1948	1,652,321	745,892	Creighton, Hobart	884,995	Schricker, Henry F.	21,434	139,103 D	45.1%	53.6%	45.7%	54.3%

Note: An asterisk (*) denotes incumbent.

POSTWAR VOTE FOR SENATOR

Year	Total Vote	Republican		Democratic		Other Vote	Rep.-Dem. Plurality	Percentage			
								Total Vote		Major Vote	
		Vote	Candidate	Vote	Candidate			Rep.	Dem.	Rep.	Dem.
2012	2,560,102	1,133,621	Mourdock, Richard E.	1,281,181	Donnelly, Joseph	145,300	147,560 D	44.3%	50.0%	46.9%	53.1%
2010	1,744,481	952,116	Coats, Dan	697,775	Ellsworth, Brad	94,590	254,341 R	54.6%	40.0%	57.7%	42.3%
2006**	1,341,111	1,171,553	Lugar, Richard G.*			169,558	1,171,553 R	87.4%		100.0%	
2004	2,428,233	903,913	Scott, Marvin B.	1,496,976	Bayh, Evan*	27,344	593,063 D	37.2%	61.6%	37.6%	62.4%
2000	2,145,209	1,427,944	Lugar, Richard G.*	683,273	Johnson, David L.	33,992	744,671 R	66.6%	31.9%	67.6%	32.4%
1998	1,588,617	552,732	Helmke, Paul	1,012,244	Bayh, Evan	23,641	459,512 D	34.8%	63.7%	35.3%	64.7%
1994	1,543,568	1,039,625	Lugar, Richard G.*	470,799	Jontz, Jim	33,144	568,826 R	67.4%	30.5%	68.8%	31.2%
1992	2,211,426	1,267,972	Coats, Dan*	900,148	Hogsett, Joseph H.	43,306	367,824 R	57.3%	40.7%	58.5%	41.5%
1990S	1,504,302	806,048	Coats, Dan*	696,639	Hill, Baron P.	1,615	109,409 R	53.6%	46.3%	53.6%	46.4%
1988	2,099,303	1,430,525	Lugar, Richard G.*	668,778	Wickes, Jack		761,747 R	68.1%	31.9%	68.1%	31.9%
1986	1,545,563	936,143	Quayle, John Danforth*	595,192	Long, Jill L.	14,228	340,951 R	60.6%	38.5%	61.1%	38.9%
1982	1,817,287	978,301	Lugar, Richard G.*	828,400	Fithian, Floyd	10,586	149,901 R	53.8%	45.6%	54.1%	45.9%
1980	2,198,376	1,182,414	Quayle, John Danforth	1,015,962	Bayh, Birch Evan*		166,452 R	53.8%	46.2%	53.8%	46.2%
1976	2,171,187	1,275,833	Lugar, Richard G.	878,522	Hartke, R. Vance*	16,832	397,311 R	58.8%	40.5%	59.2%	40.8%
1974	1,752,978	814,117	Lugar, Richard G.	889,269	Bayh, Birch Evan*	49,592	75,152 D	46.4%	50.7%	47.8%	52.2%
1970	1,737,697	866,707	Roudebush, Richard	870,990	Hartke, R. Vance*		4,283 D	49.9%	50.1%	49.9%	50.1%
1968	2,053,118	988,571	Ruckelshaus, William	1,060,456	Bayh, Birch Evan*	4,091	71,885 D	48.1%	51.7%	48.2%	51.8%
1964	2,076,963	941,519	Bontrager, D. Russell	1,128,505	Hartke, R. Vance*	6,939	186,986 D	45.3%	54.3%	45.5%	54.5%
1962	1,800,038	894,547	Capehart, Homer E.*	905,491	Bayh, Birch Evan		10,944 D	49.7%	50.3%	49.7%	50.3%
1958	1,724,598	731,635	Handley, Harold W.	973,636	Hartke, R. Vance	19,327	242,001 D	42.4%	56.5%	42.9%	57.1%
1956	1,963,986	1,084,262	Capehart, Homer E.*	871,781	Wickard, Claude R.	7,943	212,481 R	55.2%	44.4%	55.4%	44.6%
1952	1,946,118	1,020,605	Jenner, William E.*	911,169	Schricker, Henry F.	14,344	109,436 R	52.4%	46.8%	52.8%	47.2%
1950	1,598,724	844,303	Capehart, Homer E.*	741,025	Campbell, Alex M.	13,396	103,278 R	52.8%	46.4%	53.3%	46.7%
1946	1,347,434	739,809	Jenner, William E.	584,288	Townsend, M. Clifford	23,337	155,521 R	54.9%	43.4%	55.9%	44.1%

Note: An asterisk (*) denotes incumbent. **In past elections, the other vote included: 2006 - 168,820 Libertarian (Steve Osborn), who finished second. The 1990 election was for a short term to fill a vacancy. The Democratic Party did not run a candidate in the 2006 Senate election.

INDIANA

PRESIDENT 2012

2010 Census Population	County	Total Vote	Republican (Romney)	Democratic (Obama)	Other	Rep.-Dem. Plurality	Percentage			
							Total Vote		Major Vote	
							Rep.	Dem.	Rep.	Dem.
34,387	ADAMS	13,011	8,937	3,806	268	5,131 R	68.7%	29.3%	70.1%	29.9%
355,329	ALLEN	146,939	84,613	60,036	2,290	24,577 R	57.6%	40.9%	58.5%	41.5%
76,794	BARTHOLOMEW	29,326	18,083	10,625	618	7,458 R	61.7%	36.2%	63.0%	37.0%
8,854	BENTON	3,578	2,329	1,159	90	1,170 R	65.1%	32.4%	66.8%	33.2%
12,766	BLACKFORD	4,743	2,711	1,927	105	784 R	57.2%	40.6%	58.5%	41.5%
56,640	BOONE	27,737	18,808	8,328	601	10,480 R	67.8%	30.0%	69.3%	30.7%
15,242	BROWN	7,604	4,332	3,060	212	1,272 R	57.0%	40.2%	58.6%	41.4%
20,155	CARROLL	7,810	4,999	2,635	176	2,364 R	64.0%	33.7%	65.5%	34.5%
38,966	CASS	14,161	8,443	5,371	347	3,072 R	59.6%	37.9%	61.1%	38.9%
110,232	CLARK	47,146	25,450	20,807	889	4,643 R	54.0%	44.1%	55.0%	45.0%
26,890	CLAY	10,784	7,096	3,460	228	3,636 R	65.8%	32.1%	67.2%	32.8%
33,224	CLINTON	9,883	6,338	3,308	237	3,030 R	64.1%	33.5%	65.7%	34.3%
10,713	CRAWFORD	4,590	2,421	2,041	128	380 R	52.7%	44.5%	54.3%	45.7%
31,648	DAVIESS	10,250	7,638	2,437	175	5,201 R	74.5%	23.8%	75.8%	24.2%
50,047	DEARBORN	22,356	15,394	6,528	434	8,866 R	68.9%	29.2%	70.2%	29.8%
25,740	DECATUR	10,308	7,119	2,941	248	4,178 R	69.1%	28.5%	70.8%	29.2%
42,223	DEKALB	16,328	10,587	5,419	322	5,168 R	64.8%	33.2%	66.1%	33.9%
117,671	DELAWARE	44,968	21,251	22,654	1,063	1,403 D	47.3%	50.4%	48.4%	51.6%
41,889	DUBOIS	18,542	11,654	6,522	366	5,132 R	62.9%	35.2%	64.1%	35.9%
197,559	ELKHART	67,852	42,378	24,399	1,075	17,979 R	62.5%	36.0%	63.5%	36.5%
24,277	FAYETTE	8,837	5,045	3,555	237	1,490 R	57.1%	40.2%	58.7%	41.3%
74,578	FLOYD	35,305	19,878	14,812	615	5,066 R	56.3%	42.0%	57.3%	42.7%
17,240	FOUNTAIN	7,111	4,664	2,237	210	2,427 R	65.6%	31.5%	67.6%	32.4%
23,087	FRANKLIN	10,560	7,424	2,909	227	4,515 R	70.3%	27.5%	71.8%	28.2%
20,836	FULTON	8,126	5,317	2,621	188	2,696 R	65.4%	32.3%	67.0%	33.0%
33,503	GIBSON	14,721	9,487	4,928	306	4,559 R	64.4%	33.5%	65.8%	34.2%
70,061	GRANT	25,285	15,151	9,589	545	5,562 R	59.9%	37.9%	61.2%	38.8%
33,165	GREENE	13,111	8,457	4,350	304	4,107 R	64.5%	33.2%	66.0%	34.0%
274,569	HAMILTON	136,863	90,747	43,796	2,320	46,951 R	66.3%	32.0%	67.4%	32.6%
70,002	HANCOCK	32,843	22,796	9,319	728	13,477 R	69.4%	28.4%	71.0%	29.0%
39,364	HARRISON	17,671	10,640	6,607	424	4,033 R	60.2%	37.4%	61.7%	38.3%
145,448	HENDRICKS	66,644	44,312	21,112	1,220	23,200 R	66.5%	31.7%	67.7%	32.3%
49,462	HENRY	19,007	10,838	7,613	556	3,225 R	57.0%	40.1%	58.7%	41.3%
82,752	HOWARD	36,290	20,327	15,135	828	5,192 R	56.0%	41.7%	57.3%	42.7%
37,124	HUNTINGTON	15,765	10,862	4,596	307	6,266 R	68.9%	29.2%	70.3%	29.7%
42,376	JACKSON	16,712	10,419	5,838	455	4,581 R	62.3%	34.9%	64.1%	35.9%
33,478	JASPER	12,896	7,955	4,672	269	3,283 R	61.7%	36.2%	63.0%	37.0%
21,253	JAY	7,901	4,645	3,063	193	1,582 R	58.8%	38.8%	60.3%	39.7%
32,428	JEFFERSON	13,126	7,096	5,728	302	1,368 R	54.1%	43.6%	55.3%	44.7%
28,525	JENNINGS	10,250	6,120	3,821	309	2,299 R	59.7%	37.3%	61.6%	38.4%
139,654	JOHNSON	57,964	39,513	17,260	1,191	22,253 R	68.2%	29.8%	69.6%	30.4%
38,440	KNOX	15,145	9,612	5,228	305	4,384 R	63.5%	34.5%	64.8%	35.2%
77,358	KOSCIUSKO	30,060	22,558	6,862	640	15,696 R	75.0%	22.8%	76.7%	23.3%
111,467	LA PORTE	43,681	18,615	24,107	959	5,492 D	42.6%	55.2%	43.6%	56.4%
37,128	LAGRANGE	9,316	6,231	2,898	187	3,333 R	66.9%	31.1%	68.3%	31.7%
496,005	LAKE	201,758	68,431	130,897	2,430	62,466 D	33.9%	64.9%	34.3%	65.7%
46,134	LAWRENCE	17,822	11,622	5,779	421	5,843 R	65.2%	32.4%	66.8%	33.2%
131,636	MADISON	52,370	26,769	24,407	1,194	2,362 R	51.1%	46.6%	52.3%	47.7%
903,393	MARION	359,009	136,509	216,336	6,164	79,827 D	38.0%	60.3%	38.7%	61.3%
47,051	MARSHALL	17,765	11,260	6,137	368	5,123 R	63.4%	34.5%	64.7%	35.3%
10,334	MARTIN	4,743	3,262	1,351	130	1,911 R	68.8%	28.5%	70.7%	29.3%
36,903	MIAMI	12,781	8,174	4,222	385	3,952 R	64.0%	33.0%	65.9%	34.1%
137,974	MONROE	57,223	22,481	33,436	1,306	10,955 D	39.3%	58.4%	40.2%	59.8%
38,124	MONTGOMERY	14,440	9,824	4,271	345	5,553 R	68.0%	29.6%	69.7%	30.3%
68,894	MORGAN	28,266	19,591	7,969	706	11,622 R	69.3%	28.2%	71.1%	28.9%
14,244	NEWTON	5,654	3,291	2,212	151	1,079 R	58.2%	39.1%	59.8%	40.2%
47,536	NOBLE	16,244	10,680	5,229	335	5,451 R	65.7%	32.2%	67.1%	32.9%
6,128	OHIO	2,819	1,759	994	66	765 R	62.4%	35.3%	63.9%	36.1%
19,840	ORANGE	7,776	4,617	2,939	220	1,678 R	59.4%	37.8%	61.1%	38.9%
21,575	OWEN	8,113	5,062	2,823	228	2,239 R	62.4%	34.8%	64.2%	35.8%

INDIANA

PRESIDENT 2012

2010 Census Population	County	Total Vote	Republican (Romney)	Democratic (Obama)	Other	Rep.-Dem. Plurality		Percentage			
								Total Vote		Major Vote	
								Rep.	Dem.	Rep.	Dem.
17,339	PARKE	6,515	4,234	2,110	171	2,124	R	65.0%	32.4%	66.7%	33.3%
19,338	PERRY	7,875	3,403	4,316	156	913	D	43.2%	54.8%	44.1%	55.9%
12,845	PIKE	5,926	3,627	2,125	174	1,502	R	61.2%	35.9%	63.1%	36.9%
164,343	PORTER	73,039	34,406	37,252	1,381	2,846	D	47.1%	51.0%	48.0%	52.0%
25,910	POSEY	12,226	7,430	4,533	263	2,897	R	60.8%	37.1%	62.1%	37.9%
13,402	PULASKI	5,399	3,366	1,899	134	1,467	R	62.3%	35.2%	63.9%	36.1%
37,963	PUTNAM	13,829	9,005	4,507	317	4,498	R	65.1%	32.6%	66.6%	33.4%
26,171	RANDOLPH	10,189	6,218	3,769	202	2,449	R	61.0%	37.0%	62.3%	37.7%
28,818	RIPLEY	10,983	7,484	3,241	258	4,243	R	68.1%	29.5%	69.8%	30.2%
17,392	RUSH	7,026	4,633	2,221	172	2,412	R	65.9%	31.6%	67.6%	32.4%
24,181	SCOTT	8,720	4,539	3,998	183	541	R	52.1%	45.8%	53.2%	46.8%
44,436	SHELBY	16,760	10,978	5,359	423	5,619	R	65.5%	32.0%	67.2%	32.8%
20,952	SPENCER	9,728	5,515	4,026	187	1,489	R	56.7%	41.4%	57.8%	42.2%
266,931	ST. JOSEPH	110,704	52,578	56,460	1,666	3,882	D	47.5%	51.0%	48.2%	51.8%
23,363	STARKE	8,754	4,738	3,809	207	929	R	54.1%	43.5%	55.4%	44.6%
34,185	STEUBEN	13,695	8,547	4,853	295	3,694	R	62.4%	35.4%	63.8%	36.2%
21,475	SULLIVAN	8,290	4,902	3,191	197	1,711	R	59.1%	38.5%	60.6%	39.4%
10,613	SWITZERLAND	3,397	1,872	1,437	88	435	R	55.1%	42.3%	56.6%	43.4%
172,780	TIPPECANOE	56,896	28,757	26,711	1,428	2,046	R	50.5%	46.9%	51.8%	48.2%
15,936	TIPTON	7,365	4,773	2,432	160	2,341	R	64.8%	33.0%	66.2%	33.8%
7,516	UNION	3,100	2,022	1,018	60	1,004	R	65.2%	32.8%	66.5%	33.5%
179,703	VANDERBURGH	72,404	39,389	31,725	1,290	7,664	R	54.4%	43.8%	55.4%	44.6%
16,212	VERMILLION	6,581	3,426	2,979	176	447	R	52.1%	45.3%	53.5%	46.5%
107,848	VIGO	39,877	19,369	19,712	796	343	D	48.6%	49.4%	49.6%	50.4%
32,888	WABASH	12,874	8,644	3,973	257	4,671	R	67.1%	30.9%	68.5%	31.5%
8,508	WARREN	3,800	2,377	1,324	99	1,053	R	62.6%	34.8%	64.2%	35.8%
59,689	WARRICK	24,630	15,351	8,793	486	6,558	R	62.3%	35.7%	63.6%	36.4%
28,262	WASHINGTON	10,737	6,533	3,909	295	2,624	R	60.8%	36.4%	62.6%	37.4%
68,917	WAYNE	25,477	14,321	10,591	565	3,730	R	56.2%	41.6%	57.5%	42.5%
27,636	WELLS	12,935	9,256	3,436	243	5,820	R	71.6%	26.6%	72.9%	27.1%
24,643	WHITE	9,903	5,970	3,637	296	2,333	R	60.3%	36.7%	62.1%	37.9%
33,292	WHITLEY	15,011	10,258	4,420	333	5,838	R	68.3%	29.4%	69.9%	30.1%
6,483,802	TOTAL	2,624,534	1,420,543	1,152,887	51,104	267,656	R	54.1%	43.9%	55.2%	44.8%

INDIANA

GOVERNOR 2012

2010 Census Population	County	Total Vote	Republican (Pence)	Democratic (Gregg)	Other	Rep.-Dem. Plurality		Percentage			
								Total Vote		Major Vote	
								Rep.	Dem.	Rep.	Dem.
34,387	ADAMS	12,959	8,109	4,521	329	3,588	R	62.6%	34.9%	64.2%	35.8%
355,329	ALLEN	144,172	78,869	61,491	3,812	17,378	R	54.7%	42.7%	56.2%	43.8%
76,794	BARTHOLOMEW	29,155	17,417	10,608	1,130	6,809	R	59.7%	36.4%	62.1%	37.9%
8,854	BENTON	3,547	1,944	1,374	229	570	R	54.8%	38.7%	58.6%	41.4%
12,766	BLACKFORD	4,657	2,433	2,012	212	421	R	52.2%	43.2%	54.7%	45.3%
56,640	BOONE	27,569	17,416	8,711	1,442	8,705	R	63.2%	31.6%	66.7%	33.3%
15,242	BROWN	7,639	3,774	3,409	456	365	R	49.4%	44.6%	52.5%	47.5%
20,155	CARROLL	7,776	4,169	3,136	471	1,033	R	53.6%	40.3%	57.1%	42.9%
38,966	CASS	14,172	7,114	6,253	805	861	R	50.2%	44.1%	53.2%	46.8%
110,232	CLARK	46,026	24,343	20,134	1,549	4,209	R	52.9%	43.7%	54.7%	45.3%

INDIANA

GOVERNOR 2012

2010 Census Population	County	Total Vote	Republican (Pence)	Democratic (Gregg)	Other	Rep.-Dem. Plurality		Percentage			
								Total Vote		Major Vote	
								Rep.	Dem.	Rep.	Dem.
26,890	CLAY	10,878	5,547	4,765	566	782	R	51.0%	43.8%	53.8%	46.2%
33,224	CLINTON	9,853	5,412	3,876	565	1,536	R	54.9%	39.3%	58.3%	41.7%
10,713	CRAWFORD	4,499	2,099	2,267	133	168	D	46.7%	50.4%	48.1%	51.9%
31,648	DAVIESS	10,063	5,386	4,396	281	990	R	53.5%	43.7%	55.1%	44.9%
50,047	DEARBORN	21,540	14,354	6,211	975	8,143	R	66.6%	28.8%	69.8%	30.2%
25,740	DECATUR	10,277	6,479	3,182	616	3,297	R	63.0%	31.0%	67.1%	32.9%
42,223	DEKALB	16,002	9,583	5,848	571	3,735	R	59.9%	36.5%	62.1%	37.9%
117,671	DELAWARE	43,884	19,996	21,920	1,968	1,924	D	45.6%	49.9%	47.7%	52.3%
41,889	DUBOIS	18,327	10,931	6,958	438	3,973	R	59.6%	38.0%	61.1%	38.9%
197,559	ELKHART	67,334	38,997	26,358	1,979	12,639	R	57.9%	39.1%	59.7%	40.3%
24,277	FAYETTE	8,690	4,574	3,664	452	910	R	52.6%	42.2%	55.5%	44.5%
74,578	FLOYD	34,690	18,990	14,746	954	4,244	R	54.7%	42.5%	56.3%	43.7%
17,240	FOUNTAIN	7,066	3,762	2,890	414	872	R	53.2%	40.9%	56.6%	43.4%
23,087	FRANKLIN	10,268	6,970	2,859	439	4,111	R	67.9%	27.8%	70.9%	29.1%
20,836	FULTON	8,090	4,534	3,194	362	1,340	R	56.0%	39.5%	58.7%	41.3%
33,503	GIBSON	14,626	7,731	6,508	387	1,223	R	52.9%	44.5%	54.3%	45.7%
70,061	GRANT	25,072	13,827	10,313	932	3,514	R	55.1%	41.1%	57.3%	42.7%
33,165	GREENE	13,143	5,486	7,307	350	1,821	D	41.7%	55.6%	42.9%	57.1%
274,569	HAMILTON	135,097	88,070	41,762	5,265	46,308	R	65.2%	30.9%	67.8%	32.2%
70,002	HANCOCK	32,695	20,331	10,483	1,881	9,848	R	62.2%	32.1%	66.0%	34.0%
39,364	HARRISON	17,515	9,997	6,964	554	3,033	R	57.1%	39.8%	58.9%	41.1%
145,448	HENDRICKS	65,627	40,245	22,125	3,257	18,120	R	61.3%	33.7%	64.5%	35.5%
49,462	HENRY	19,017	9,439	8,277	1,301	1,162	R	49.6%	43.5%	53.3%	46.7%
82,752	HOWARD	36,167	17,811	16,550	1,806	1,261	R	49.2%	45.8%	51.8%	48.2%
37,124	HUNTINGTON	15,352	9,623	5,212	517	4,411	R	62.7%	33.9%	64.9%	35.1%
42,376	JACKSON	16,638	9,613	6,377	648	3,236	R	57.8%	38.3%	60.1%	39.9%
33,478	JASPER	12,454	6,987	5,055	412	1,932	R	56.1%	40.6%	58.0%	42.0%
21,253	JAY	7,857	4,326	3,183	348	1,143	R	55.1%	40.5%	57.6%	42.4%
32,428	JEFFERSON	12,728	6,715	5,610	403	1,105	R	52.8%	44.1%	54.5%	45.5%
28,525	JENNINGS	10,139	5,653	4,028	458	1,625	R	55.8%	39.7%	58.4%	41.6%
139,654	JOHNSON	57,694	36,168	18,271	3,255	17,897	R	62.7%	31.7%	66.4%	33.6%
38,440	KNOX	15,195	5,031	9,911	253	4,880	D	33.1%	65.2%	33.7%	66.3%
77,358	KOSCIUSKO	29,752	20,530	8,303	919	12,227	R	69.0%	27.9%	71.2%	28.8%
111,467	LA PORTE	42,009	16,164	24,190	1,655	8,026	D	38.5%	57.6%	40.1%	59.9%
37,128	LAGRANGE	9,266	5,654	3,257	355	2,397	R	61.0%	35.2%	63.4%	36.6%
496,005	LAKE	181,685	55,776	122,324	3,585	66,548	D	30.7%	67.3%	31.3%	68.7%
46,134	LAWRENCE	17,664	10,094	6,830	740	3,264	R	57.1%	38.7%	59.6%	40.4%
131,636	MADISON	52,217	24,052	25,393	2,772	1,341	D	46.1%	48.6%	48.6%	51.4%
903,393	MARION	357,193	129,501	210,119	17,573	80,618	D	36.3%	58.8%	38.1%	61.9%
47,051	MARSHALL	17,611	9,901	7,112	598	2,789	R	56.2%	40.4%	58.2%	41.8%
10,334	MARTIN	4,719	2,471	2,050	198	421	R	52.4%	43.4%	54.7%	45.3%
36,903	MIAMI	12,644	6,892	4,985	767	1,907	R	54.5%	39.4%	58.0%	42.0%
137,974	MONROE	56,220	20,176	33,628	2,416	13,452	D	35.9%	59.8%	37.5%	62.5%
38,124	MONTGOMERY	14,454	8,147	5,522	785	2,625	R	56.4%	38.2%	59.6%	40.4%
68,894	MORGAN	28,090	17,082	9,297	1,711	7,785	R	60.8%	33.1%	64.8%	35.2%
14,244	NEWTON	5,555	3,015	2,287	253	728	R	54.3%	41.2%	56.9%	43.1%
47,536	NOBLE	16,000	9,405	6,047	548	3,358	R	58.8%	37.8%	60.9%	39.1%
6,128	OHIO	2,752	1,556	1,086	110	470	R	56.5%	39.5%	58.9%	41.1%
19,840	ORANGE	7,638	4,114	3,273	251	841	R	53.9%	42.9%	55.7%	44.3%
21,575	OWEN	8,097	4,164	3,456	477	708	R	51.4%	42.7%	54.6%	45.4%
17,339	PARKE	6,510	3,372	2,821	317	551	R	51.8%	43.3%	54.4%	45.6%
19,338	PERRY	7,824	3,132	4,524	168	1,392	D	40.0%	57.8%	40.9%	59.1%
12,845	PIKE	5,890	2,661	3,066	163	405	D	45.2%	52.1%	46.5%	53.5%
164,343	PORTER	71,866	29,503	40,154	2,209	10,651	D	41.1%	55.9%	42.4%	57.6%
25,910	POSEY	12,117	6,457	5,344	316	1,113	R	53.3%	44.1%	54.7%	45.3%
13,402	PULASKI	5,213	2,809	2,189	215	620	R	53.9%	42.0%	56.2%	43.8%
37,963	PUTNAM	13,732	7,558	5,309	865	2,249	R	55.0%	38.7%	58.7%	41.3%
26,171	RANDOLPH	10,102	5,709	3,939	454	1,770	R	56.5%	39.0%	59.2%	40.8%
28,818	RIPLEY	10,800	7,018	3,224	558	3,794	R	65.0%	29.9%	68.5%	31.5%
17,392	RUSH	6,960	4,120	2,370	470	1,750	R	59.2%	34.1%	63.5%	36.5%

INDIANA

GOVERNOR 2012

2010 Census Population	County	Total Vote	Republican (Pence)	Democratic (Gregg)	Other	Rep.-Dem. Plurality	Percentage Total Vote Rep.	Dem.	Major Vote Rep.	Dem.
24,181	SCOTT	8,610	4,069	4,287	254	218 D	47.3%	49.8%	48.7%	51.3%
44,436	SHELBY	16,729	9,650	5,995	1,084	3,655 R	57.7%	35.8%	61.7%	38.3%
20,952	SPENCER	9,659	5,059	4,385	215	674 R	52.4%	45.4%	53.6%	46.4%
266,931	ST. JOSEPH	109,491	47,182	59,411	2,898	12,229 D	43.1%	54.3%	44.3%	55.7%
23,363	STARKE	8,456	3,828	4,291	337	463 D	45.3%	50.7%	47.1%	52.9%
34,185	STEUBEN	13,601	7,777	5,314	510	2,463 R	57.2%	39.1%	59.4%	40.6%
21,475	SULLIVAN	8,345	2,948	5,179	218	2,231 D	35.3%	62.1%	36.3%	63.7%
10,613	SWITZERLAND	3,284	1,666	1,489	129	177 R	50.7%	45.3%	52.8%	47.2%
172,780	TIPPECANOE	56,349	25,749	27,669	2,931	1,920 D	45.7%	49.1%	48.2%	51.8%
15,936	TIPTON	7,289	4,136	2,752	401	1,384 R	56.7%	37.8%	60.0%	40.0%
7,516	UNION	3,048	1,963	940	145	1,023 R	64.4%	30.8%	67.6%	32.4%
179,703	VANDERBURGH	71,369	36,529	32,869	1,971	3,660 R	51.2%	46.1%	52.6%	47.4%
16,212	VERMILLION	6,582	2,617	3,639	326	1,022 D	39.8%	55.3%	41.8%	58.2%
107,848	VIGO	39,533	15,013	22,992	1,528	7,979 D	38.0%	58.2%	39.5%	60.5%
32,888	WABASH	12,612	7,622	4,512	478	3,110 R	60.4%	35.8%	62.8%	37.2%
8,508	WARREN	3,780	2,013	1,579	188	434 R	53.3%	41.8%	56.0%	44.0%
59,689	WARRICK	24,275	13,655	10,031	589	3,624 R	56.3%	41.3%	57.7%	42.3%
28,262	WASHINGTON	10,621	6,130	4,108	383	2,022 R	57.7%	38.7%	59.9%	40.1%
68,917	WAYNE	25,425	13,895	10,267	1,263	3,628 R	54.7%	40.4%	57.5%	42.5%
27,636	WELLS	12,872	8,518	3,999	355	4,519 R	66.2%	31.1%	68.1%	31.9%
24,643	WHITE	9,883	5,032	4,281	570	751 R	50.9%	43.3%	54.0%	46.0%
33,292	WHITLEY	14,787	9,085	5,209	493	3,876 R	61.4%	35.2%	63.6%	36.4%
6,483,802	TOTAL	2,577,329	1,275,424	1,200,016	101,889	75,408 R	49.5%	46.6%	51.5%	48.5%

INDIANA

SENATOR 2012

2010 Census Population	County	Total Vote	Republican (Mourdock)	Democratic (Donnelly)	Other	Rep.-Dem. Plurality	Percentage Total Vote Rep.	Dem.	Major Vote Rep.	Dem.
34,387	ADAMS	12,823	7,426	4,613	784	2,813 R	57.9%	36.0%	61.7%	38.3%
355,329	ALLEN	143,726	71,734	65,053	6,939	6,681 R	49.9%	45.3%	52.4%	47.6%
76,794	BARTHOLOMEW	28,719	14,430	12,214	2,075	2,216 R	50.2%	42.5%	54.2%	45.8%
8,854	BENTON	3,517	1,798	1,416	303	382 R	51.1%	40.3%	55.9%	44.1%
12,766	BLACKFORD	4,666	2,059	2,228	379	169 D	44.1%	47.7%	48.0%	52.0%
56,640	BOONE	27,324	15,007	10,251	2,066	4,756 R	54.9%	37.5%	59.4%	40.6%
15,242	BROWN	7,569	3,544	3,476	549	68 R	46.8%	45.9%	50.5%	49.5%
20,155	CARROLL	7,747	3,916	3,194	637	722 R	50.5%	41.2%	55.1%	44.9%
38,966	CASS	14,080	6,622	6,323	1,135	299 R	47.0%	44.9%	51.2%	48.8%
110,232	CLARK	46,158	21,120	22,776	2,262	1,656 D	45.8%	49.3%	48.1%	51.9%
26,890	CLAY	10,285	5,192	4,359	734	833 R	50.5%	42.4%	54.4%	45.6%
33,224	CLINTON	9,701	4,938	3,931	832	1,007 R	50.9%	40.5%	55.7%	44.3%
10,713	CRAWFORD	4,468	2,000	2,256	212	256 D	44.8%	50.5%	47.0%	53.0%
31,648	DAVIESS	9,846	6,088	3,295	463	2,793 R	61.8%	33.5%	64.9%	35.1%
50,047	DEARBORN	21,691	13,422	7,313	956	6,109 R	61.9%	33.7%	64.7%	35.3%
25,740	DECATUR	9,620	5,302	3,478	840	1,824 R	55.1%	36.2%	60.4%	39.6%
42,223	DEKALB	15,885	8,793	6,059	1,033	2,734 R	55.4%	38.1%	59.2%	40.8%
117,671	DELAWARE	43,374	15,797	24,525	3,052	8,728 D	36.4%	56.5%	39.2%	60.8%
41,889	DUBOIS	18,058	9,143	8,054	861	1,089 R	50.6%	44.6%	53.2%	46.8%
197,559	ELKHART	67,188	35,858	28,230	3,100	7,628 R	53.4%	42.0%	56.0%	44.0%

INDIANA
SENATOR 2012

2010 Census Population	County	Total Vote	Republican (Mourdock)	Democratic (Donnelly)	Other	Rep.-Dem. Plurality		Percentage			
								Total Vote		Major Vote	
								Rep.	Dem.	Rep.	Dem.
24,277	FAYETTE	8,053	3,498	3,856	699	358	D	43.4%	47.9%	47.6%	52.4%
74,578	FLOYD	34,724	16,568	16,602	1,554	34	D	47.7%	47.8%	49.9%	50.1%
17,240	FOUNTAIN	6,951	3,541	2,738	672	803	R	50.9%	39.4%	56.4%	43.6%
23,087	FRANKLIN	10,213	6,192	3,512	509	2,680	R	60.6%	34.4%	63.8%	36.2%
20,836	FULTON	8,108	4,123	3,555	430	568	R	50.9%	43.8%	53.7%	46.3%
33,503	GIBSON	14,629	7,562	6,339	728	1,223	R	51.7%	43.3%	54.4%	45.6%
70,061	GRANT	24,883	12,549	10,789	1,545	1,760	R	50.4%	43.4%	53.8%	46.2%
33,165	GREENE	12,819	6,494	5,480	845	1,014	R	50.7%	42.7%	54.2%	45.8%
274,569	HAMILTON	134,092	72,587	52,925	8,580	19,662	R	54.1%	39.5%	57.8%	42.2%
70,002	HANCOCK	32,373	17,635	11,677	3,061	5,958	R	54.5%	36.1%	60.2%	39.8%
39,364	HARRISON	17,532	9,005	7,768	759	1,237	R	51.4%	44.3%	53.7%	46.3%
145,448	HENDRICKS	65,128	35,541	25,208	4,379	10,333	R	54.6%	38.7%	58.5%	41.5%
49,462	HENRY	18,730	8,000	8,914	1,816	914	D	42.7%	47.6%	47.3%	52.7%
82,752	HOWARD	34,083	15,739	17,660	684	1,921	D	46.2%	51.8%	47.1%	52.9%
37,124	HUNTINGTON	15,206	9,077	5,166	963	3,911	R	59.7%	34.0%	63.7%	36.3%
42,376	JACKSON	16,445	8,292	7,045	1,108	1,247	R	50.4%	42.8%	54.1%	45.9%
33,478	JASPER	12,488	6,673	5,335	480	1,338	R	53.4%	42.7%	55.6%	44.4%
21,253	JAY	7,368	3,533	3,295	540	238	R	48.0%	44.7%	51.7%	48.3%
32,428	JEFFERSON	12,338	5,624	6,104	610	480	D	45.6%	49.5%	48.0%	52.0%
28,525	JENNINGS	10,075	4,937	4,441	697	496	R	49.0%	44.1%	52.6%	47.4%
139,654	JOHNSON	57,067	31,529	21,256	4,282	10,273	R	55.2%	37.2%	59.7%	40.3%
38,440	KNOX	14,661	6,959	6,873	829	86	R	47.5%	46.9%	50.3%	49.7%
77,358	KOSCIUSKO	29,745	19,908	8,239	1,598	11,669	R	66.9%	27.7%	70.7%	29.3%
111,467	LA PORTE	42,627	14,033	26,764	1,830	12,731	D	32.9%	62.8%	34.4%	65.6%
37,128	LAGRANGE	9,219	5,293	3,300	626	1,993	R	57.4%	35.8%	61.6%	38.4%
496,005	LAKE	182,916	52,072	126,736	4,108	74,664	D	28.5%	69.3%	29.1%	70.9%
46,134	LAWRENCE	17,525	9,365	7,008	1,152	2,357	R	53.4%	40.0%	57.2%	42.8%
131,636	MADISON	51,767	20,422	27,183	4,162	6,761	D	39.4%	52.5%	42.9%	57.1%
903,393	MARION	355,579	106,919	227,858	20,802	120,939	D	30.1%	64.1%	31.9%	68.1%
47,051	MARSHALL	17,633	8,930	7,867	836	1,063	R	50.6%	44.6%	53.2%	46.8%
10,334	MARTIN	4,662	2,606	1,796	260	810	R	55.9%	38.5%	59.2%	40.8%
36,903	MIAMI	12,497	6,363	4,925	1,209	1,438	R	50.9%	39.4%	56.4%	43.6%
137,974	MONROE	56,384	17,633	35,421	3,330	17,788	D	31.3%	62.8%	33.2%	66.8%
38,124	MONTGOMERY	14,314	7,622	5,291	1,401	2,331	R	53.2%	37.0%	59.0%	41.0%
68,894	MORGAN	27,898	15,867	9,777	2,254	6,090	R	56.9%	35.0%	61.9%	38.1%
14,244	NEWTON	5,571	2,719	2,588	264	131	R	48.8%	46.5%	51.2%	48.8%
47,536	NOBLE	15,891	8,946	5,939	1,006	3,007	R	56.3%	37.4%	60.1%	39.9%
6,128	OHIO	2,761	1,536	1,116	109	420	R	55.6%	40.4%	57.9%	42.1%
19,840	ORANGE	7,587	3,959	3,242	386	717	R	52.2%	42.7%	55.0%	45.0%
21,575	OWEN	7,981	4,033	3,270	678	763	R	50.5%	41.0%	55.2%	44.8%
17,339	PARKE	6,395	3,168	2,672	555	496	R	49.5%	41.8%	54.2%	45.8%
19,338	PERRY	7,724	2,660	4,722	342	2,062	D	34.4%	61.1%	36.0%	64.0%
12,845	PIKE	5,803	2,781	2,676	346	105	R	47.9%	46.1%	51.0%	49.0%
164,343	PORTER	72,065	27,481	42,062	2,522	14,581	D	38.1%	58.4%	39.5%	60.5%
25,910	POSEY	12,115	5,897	5,605	613	292	R	48.7%	46.3%	51.3%	48.7%
13,402	PULASKI	5,237	2,640	2,284	313	356	R	50.4%	43.6%	53.6%	46.4%
37,963	PUTNAM	13,043	6,839	5,196	1,008	1,643	R	52.4%	39.8%	56.8%	43.2%
26,171	RANDOLPH	9,445	4,650	4,073	722	577	R	49.2%	43.1%	53.3%	46.7%
28,818	RIPLEY	10,742	6,394	3,818	530	2,576	R	59.5%	35.5%	62.6%	37.4%
17,392	RUSH	6,857	3,392	2,729	736	663	R	49.5%	39.8%	55.4%	44.6%
24,181	SCOTT	8,563	3,589	4,552	422	963	D	41.9%	53.2%	44.1%	55.9%
44,436	SHELBY	15,823	8,083	6,282	1,458	1,801	R	51.1%	39.7%	56.3%	43.7%
20,952	SPENCER	9,546	4,451	4,650	445	199	D	46.6%	48.7%	48.9%	51.1%
266,931	ST. JOSEPH	110,115	40,418	65,689	4,008	25,271	D	36.7%	59.7%	38.1%	61.9%
23,363	STARKE	8,539	3,607	4,484	448	877	D	42.2%	52.5%	44.6%	55.4%
34,185	STEUBEN	13,476	7,056	5,443	977	1,613	R	52.4%	40.4%	56.5%	43.5%
21,475	SULLIVAN	8,106	3,491	4,134	481	643	D	43.1%	51.0%	45.8%	54.2%
10,613	SWITZERLAND	3,293	1,581	1,536	176	45	R	48.0%	46.6%	50.7%	49.3%
172,780	TIPPECANOE	56,159	23,130	29,181	3,848	6,051	D	41.2%	52.0%	44.2%	55.8%
15,936	TIPTON	7,198	3,533	3,001	664	532	R	49.1%	41.7%	54.1%	45.9%

INDIANA

SENATOR 2012

2010 Census Population	County	Total Vote	Republican (Mourdock)	Democratic (Donnelly)	Other	Rep.-Dem. Plurality	Percentage Total Vote Rep.	Dem.	Major Vote Rep.	Dem.
7,516	UNION	3,015	1,732	1,098	185	634 R	57.4%	36.4%	61.2%	38.8%
179,703	VANDERBURGH	71,542	32,947	35,430	3,165	2,483 D	46.1%	49.5%	48.2%	51.8%
16,212	VERMILLION	6,501	2,490	3,543	468	1,053 D	38.3%	54.5%	41.3%	58.7%
107,848	VIGO	39,077	14,233	22,342	2,502	8,109 D	36.4%	57.2%	38.9%	61.1%
32,888	WABASH	12,516	7,287	4,454	775	2,833 R	58.2%	35.6%	62.1%	37.9%
8,508	WARREN	3,754	1,887	1,615	252	272 R	50.3%	43.0%	53.9%	46.1%
59,689	WARRICK	24,291	12,524	10,569	1,198	1,955 R	51.6%	43.5%	54.2%	45.8%
28,262	WASHINGTON	10,646	5,512	4,571	563	941 R	51.8%	42.9%	54.7%	45.3%
68,917	WAYNE	25,280	11,529	11,752	1,999	223 D	45.6%	46.5%	49.5%	50.5%
27,636	WELLS	11,787	7,456	3,668	663	3,788 R	63.3%	31.1%	67.0%	33.0%
24,643	WHITE	9,785	4,526	4,291	968	235 R	46.3%	43.9%	51.3%	48.7%
33,292	WHITLEY	14,696	8,584	5,157	955	3,427 R	58.4%	35.1%	62.5%	37.5%
6,483,802	TOTAL	2,560,102	1,133,621	1,281,181	145,300	147,560 D	44.3%	50.0%	46.9%	53.1%

INDIANA

HOUSE OF REPRESENTATIVES

CD	Year	Total Vote	Republican Vote	Candidate	Democratic Vote	Candidate	Other Vote	Rep.-Dem. Plurality	Total Vote Rep.	Dem.	Major Vote Rep.	Dem.
1	2012	279,034	91,291	PHELPS, JOEL	187,743	VISCLOSKY, PETE*		96,452 D	32.7%	67.3%	32.7%	67.3%
2	2012	273,475	134,033	WALORSKI, JACKIE	130,113	MULLEN, BRENDAN	9,329	3,920 R	49.0%	47.6%	50.7%	49.3%
3	2012	280,235	187,872	STUTZMAN, MARLIN A.*	92,363	BOYD, KEVIN		95,509 R	67.0%	33.0%	67.0%	33.0%
4	2012	272,268	168,688	ROKITA, TODD*	93,015	NELSON, TARA E.	10,565	75,673 R	62.0%	34.2%	64.5%	35.5%
5	2012	333,359	194,570	BROOKS, SUSAN	125,347	RESKE, SCOTT	13,442	69,223 R	58.4%	37.6%	60.8%	39.2%
6	2012	275,253	162,613	MESSER, LUKE	96,678	BOOKOUT, BRAD	15,962	65,935 R	59.1%	35.1%	62.7%	37.3%
7	2012	257,950	95,828	MAY, CARLOS	162,122	CARSON, ANDRE*		66,294 D	37.1%	62.9%	37.1%	62.9%
8	2012	283,992	151,533	BUCSHON, LARRY*	122,325	CROOKS, DAVE	10,134	29,208 R	53.4%	43.1%	55.3%	44.7%
9	2012	298,180	165,332	YOUNG, TODD*	132,848	YODER, SHELLI		32,484 R	55.4%	44.6%	55.4%	44.6%
TOTAL	2012	2,553,746	1,351,760		1,142,554		59,432	209,206 R	52.9%	44.7%	54.2%	45.8%

Note: An asterisk (*) denotes incumbent.

INDIANA

GENERAL AND PRIMARY ELECTIONS

2012 GENERAL ELECTIONS: OTHER VOTE

President Other vote was 50,111 Libertarian (Gary E. Johnson), 625 Write-in (Jill Stein), 290 Write-in (Virgil H. Goode), 78 Write-in (Scattered Write-In)

Governor Other vote was 101,868 Libertarian (Rupert Boneham), 21 Write-in (Scattered Write-In)

Senator Other vote was 145,282 Libertarian (Andrew M. "Andy" Horning), 18 Write-in (Scattered Write-In)

House Other vote was:

CD 2 9,326 Libertarian (Joe Ruiz), 3 Write-in (Kenneth R. Lunce)
CD 4 10,565 Libertarian (Benjamin Gehlhausen)
CD 5 13,442 Libertarian (Chard Reid)
CD 6 15,962 Libertarian (Rex Bell)
CD 8 10,134 Libertarian (Bart Gadau)

INDIANA

GENERAL AND PRIMARY ELECTIONS

2012 PRIMARY ELECTIONS: SUPPLEMENTARY INFORMATION

Primary	May 8, 2012	**Registration** (as of May 8, 2012)	4,409,890	No Party Registration

Primary Type   Open—Any registered voter could participate in the primary of either party, although they could be challenged based on party affiliation. When a voter is challenged, they must execute a statement saying that they voted for a majority of the party's candidates in the previous general election. If they did not vote in the previous general election, they must indicate that they will vote for a majority of the party's candidates in the next general election.

	REPUBLICAN PRIMARIES			DEMOCRATIC PRIMARIES		
President	Romney, W. Mitt	410,635	64.6%	Obama, Barack H.*	221,466	100.0%
	Paul, Ron	98,487	15.5%			
	Santorum, Rick	85,332	13.4%			
	Gingrich, Newt	41,135	6.5%			
	TOTAL	*635,589*		*TOTAL*	*221,466*	
Senator	Mourdock, Richard E.	400,321	60.5%	Donnelly, Joseph	207,715	100.0%
	Lugar, Richard G.*	261,285	39.5%			
	TOTAL	*661,606*		*TOTAL*	*207,715*	
Governor	Pence, Mike	554,412	100.0%	Gregg, John R.	207,365	100.0%
	TOTAL	*554,412*		*TOTAL*	*207,365*	
Congressional District 1	Phelps, Joel	17,164	59.0%	Visclosky, Pete*	42,219	100.0%
	Wenger, Dave	11,952	41.0%			
	TOTAL	*29,116*		*TOTAL*	*42,219*	
Congressional District 2	Walorski, Jackie	46,873	72.8%	Mullen, Brendan	11,218	54.1%
	Andrews, Greg	17,522	27.2%	Morrison, Dan	9,519	45.9%
	TOTAL	*64,395*		*TOTAL*	*20,737*	
Congressional District 3	Stutzman, Marlin A.*	74,812	100.0%	Boyd, Kevin	5,985	47.8%
				Schrader, Thomas Allen	1,694	13.5%
				Hope, Stephen G.	1,441	11.5%
				Kuhnle, Justin	1,265	10.1%
				Sowards, David	1,172	9.4%
				Roberson, John Forrest	966	7.7%
	TOTAL	*74,812*		*TOTAL*	*12,523*	
Congressional District 4	Rokita, Todd*	73,089	100.0%	Nelson, Tara E.	7,018	58.3%
				Moore, Lester Terry	5,010	41.7%
	TOTAL	*73,089*		*TOTAL*	*12,028*	
Congressional District 5	Brooks, Susan	31,185	30.0%	Reske, Scott	13,175	63.1%
	McIntosh, David M.	30,175	29.0%	Long, Tony	7,692	36.9%
	McGoff, John	23,773	22.8%			
	Seybold, Wayne	11,874	11.4%			
	Lugar, John R. "Jack"	4,758	4.6%			
	Anderson, Jason	1,036	1.0%			
	Salin, William "Bill"	869	0.8%			
	Mount, Matthew	453	0.4%			
	TOTAL	*104,123*		*TOTAL*	*20,867*	

INDIANA

GENERAL AND PRIMARY ELECTIONS

	REPUBLICAN PRIMARIES			DEMOCRATIC PRIMARIES		
Congressional District 6	Messer, Luke	32,859	40.4%	Bookout, Brad	8,278	31.0%
	Hankins, Travis	23,276	28.6%	Heitzman, Susan Hall	7,077	26.5%
	Bates, Don Jr.	10,913	13.4%	Crone, Jim	5,611	21.0%
	Frazier, Bill	8,446	10.4%	Bolling, Dan	3,719	13.9%
	Sizemore, Joe	2,346	2.9%	Holland, George Thomas	2,059	7.7%
	Smith, Allen K. II	1,679	2.1%			
	Van Wye, Joseph S. Sr.	989	1.2%			
	Hatter, John	917	1.1%			
	TOTAL	*81,425*		*TOTAL*	*26,744*	
Congressional District 7	May, Carlos	10,783	26.8%	Carson, André*	34,782	90.3%
	Ping, Catherine "Cat"	9,771	24.3%	Kern, Bob	2,048	5.3%
	Davis, Steven	7,727	19.2%	Wilcox, Woodrow	1,082	2.8%
	Harmon, Wayne E.	4,252	10.6%	Pullins, Pierre Quincy	586	1.5%
	Duncan, Anthony W. "Tony"	4,079	10.1%			
	Miniear, JD	2,227	5.5%			
	Shouse, Lawrence B. "Larry"	1,412	3.5%			
	TOTAL	*40,251*		*TOTAL*	*38,498*	
Congressional District 8	Bucshon, Larry*	34,511	58.0%	Crooks, Dave	18,634	57.7%
	Risk, Kristi	24,960	42.0%	Barnett, Thomas	10,638	32.9%
				Bryk, William	3,023	9.4%
	TOTAL	*59,471*		*TOTAL*	*32,295*	
Congressional District 9	Young, Todd*	59,327	100.0%	Yoder, Shelli	13,186	47.7%
				Winningham, Robert	5,590	20.2%
				George, Jonathan	4,591	16.6%
				Tilford, John W.	2,233	8.1%
				Miller, John Griffin	2,062	7.5%
	TOTAL	*59,327*		*TOTAL*	*27,662*	

Note: An asterisk (*) denotes incumbent.

IOWA

Congressional districts first established for elections held in 2012

4 members

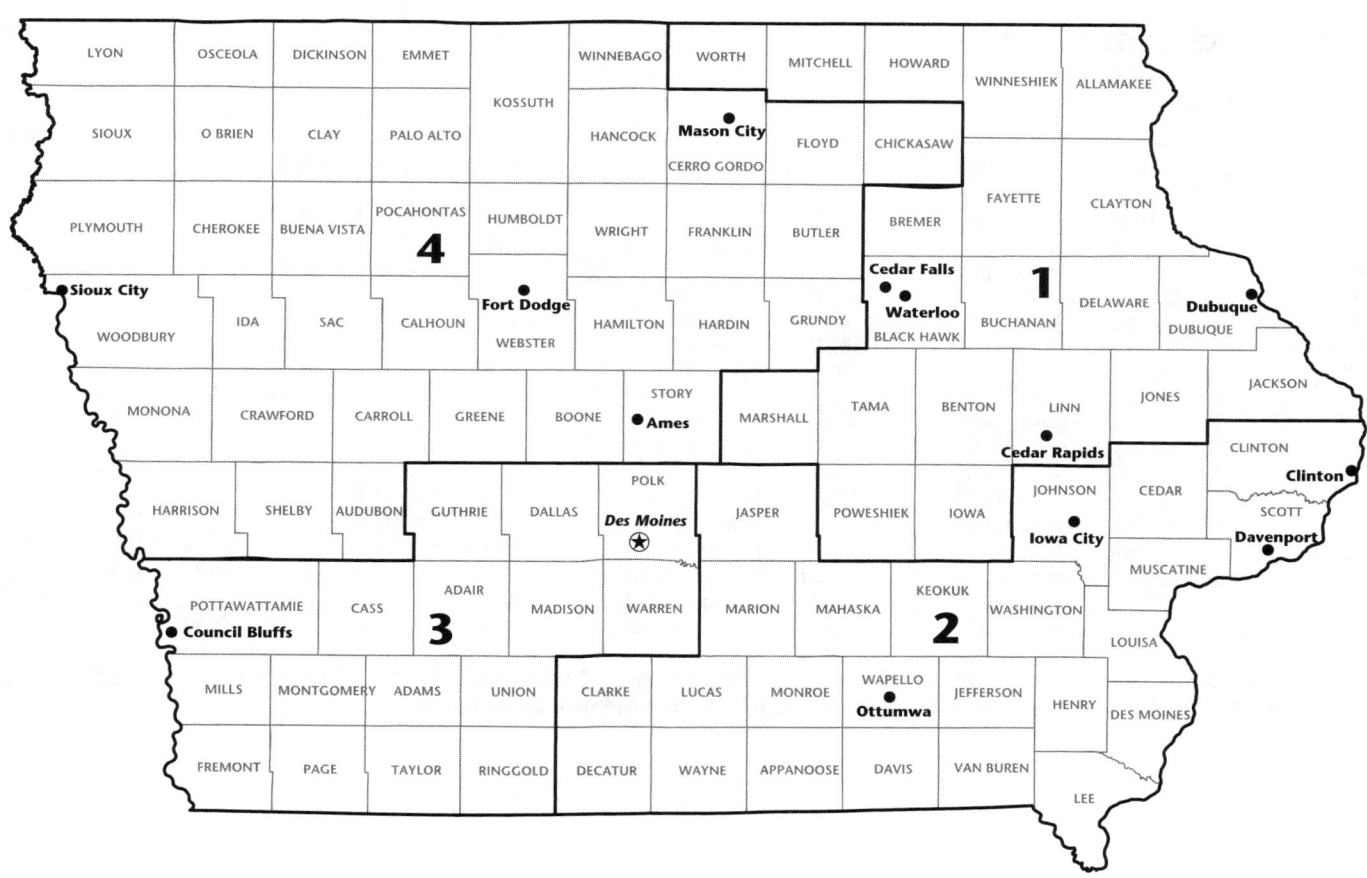

IOWA

GOVERNOR

Terry E. Branstad (R). Elected 2010 to a four-year term. Previously elected 1994, 1990, 1986, 1982.

SENATORS (1 Republican, 1 Democrat)

Chuck Grassley (R). Reelected 2010 to a six-year term. Previously elected 2004, 1998, 1992, 1986, 1980.

Tom Harkin (D). Reelected 2008 to a six-year term. Previously elected 2002, 1996, 1990, 1984.

REPRESENTATIVES (2 Republicans, 2 Democrats)

1. Bruce Braley (D)
2. Dave Loebsack (D)
3. Tom Latham (R)
4. Steve King (R)

POSTWAR VOTE FOR PRESIDENT

| | | Republican | | Democratic | | Other Vote | Rep.-Dem. Plurality | Percentage | | | |
| | | | | | | | | Total Vote | | Major Vote | |
Year	Total Vote	Vote	Candidate	Vote	Candidate			Rep.	Dem.	Rep.	Dem.
2012	1,582,180	730,617	Romney, W. Mitt	822,544	Obama, Barack H.*	29,019	91,927 D	46.2%	52.0%	47.0%	53.0%
2008	1,537,123	682,379	McCain, John S. III	828,940	Obama, Barack H.	25,804	146,561 D	44.4%	53.9%	45.2%	54.8%
2004	1,506,908	751,957	Bush, George W.*	741,898	Kerry, John F.	13,053	10,059 R	49.9%	49.2%	50.3%	49.7%
2000**	1,315,563	634,373	Bush, George W.	638,517	Gore, Albert Jr.	42,673	4,144 D	48.2%	48.5%	49.8%	50.2%
1996**	1,234,075	492,644	Dole, Robert "Bob"	620,258	Clinton, Bill*	121,173	127,614 D	39.9%	50.3%	44.3%	55.7%
1992**	1,354,607	504,891	Bush, George H.*	586,353	Clinton, Bill	263,363	81,462 D	37.3%	43.3%	46.3%	53.7%
1988	1,225,614	545,355	Bush, George H.	670,557	Dukakis, Michael S.	9,702	125,202 D	44.5%	54.7%	44.9%	55.1%
1984	1,319,805	703,088	Reagan, Ronald*	605,620	Mondale, Walter F.	11,097	97,468 R	53.3%	45.9%	53.7%	46.3%
1980**	1,317,661	676,026	Reagan, Ronald	508,672	Carter, Jimmy*	132,963	167,354 R	51.3%	38.6%	57.1%	42.9%
1976	1,279,306	632,863	Ford, Gerald R.*	619,931	Carter, Jimmy	26,512	12,932 R	49.5%	48.5%	50.5%	49.5%
1972	1,225,944	706,207	Nixon, Richard M.*	496,206	McGovern, George S.	23,531	210,001 R	57.6%	40.5%	58.7%	41.3%
1968**	1,167,931	619,106	Nixon, Richard M.	476,699	Humphrey, Hubert H. Jr.	72,126	142,407 R	53.0%	40.8%	56.5%	43.5%
1964	1,184,539	449,148	Goldwater, Barry M. Sr.	733,030	Johnson, Lyndon B.*	2,361	283,882 D	37.9%	61.9%	38.0%	62.0%
1960	1,273,810	722,381	Nixon, Richard M.	550,565	Kennedy, John F.	864	171,816 R	56.7%	43.2%	56.7%	43.3%
1956	1,234,564	729,187	Eisenhower, Dwight D.*	501,858	Stevenson, Adlai E. II	3,519	227,329 R	59.1%	40.7%	59.2%	40.8%
1952	1,268,773	808,906	Eisenhower, Dwight D.	451,513	Stevenson, Adlai E. II	8,354	357,393 R	63.8%	35.6%	64.2%	35.8%
1948	1,038,264	494,018	Dewey, Thomas E.	522,380	Truman, Harry S.*	21,866	28,362 D	47.6%	50.3%	48.6%	51.4%

Note: An asterisk (*) denotes incumbent. **In past elections, the other vote included: 2000 - 29,374 Green (Ralph Nader); 1996 - 105,159 Reform (Ross Perot); 1992 - 253,468 Independent (Perot); 1980 - 115,633 Independent (John Anderson); 1968 - 66,422 American Independent (George Wallace).

IOWA

POSTWAR VOTE FOR GOVERNOR

Year	Total Vote	Republican Vote	Republican Candidate	Democratic Vote	Democratic Candidate	Other Vote	Rep.-Dem. Plurality	Total Vote Rep.	Total Vote Dem.	Major Vote Rep.	Major Vote Dem.
2010	1,122,013	592,494	Branstad, Terry E.	484,798	Culver, Chet*	44,721	107,696 R	52.8%	43.2%	55.0%	45.0%
2006	1,053,255	467,425	Nussle, Jim	569,021	Culver, Chet	16,809	101,596 D	44.4%	54.0%	45.1%	54.9%
2002	1,025,802	456,612	Gross, Doug	540,449	Vilsack, Tom*	28,741	83,837 D	44.5%	52.7%	45.8%	54.2%
1998	956,418	444,787	Lightfoot, Jim Ross	500,231	Vilsack, Tom	11,400	55,444 D	46.5%	52.3%	47.1%	52.9%
1994	997,248	566,395	Branstad, Terry E.*	414,453	Campbell, Bonnie J.	16,400	151,942 R	56.8%	41.6%	57.7%	42.3%
1990	976,483	591,852	Branstad, Terry E.*	379,372	Avenson, Donald D.	5,259	212,480 R	60.6%	38.9%	60.9%	39.1%
1986	910,623	472,712	Branstad, Terry E.*	436,987	Junkins, Lowell L.	924	35,725 R	51.9%	48.0%	52.0%	48.0%
1982	1,038,229	548,313	Branstad, Terry E.	483,291	Conlin, Roxanne	6,625	65,022 R	52.8%	46.5%	53.2%	46.8%
1978	843,190	491,713	Ray, Robert E.*	345,519	Fitzgerald, Jerome D.	5,958	146,194 R	58.3%	41.0%	58.7%	41.3%
1974**	920,458	534,518	Ray, Robert E.*	377,553	Schaben, James F.	8,387	156,965 R	58.1%	41.0%	58.6%	41.4%
1972	1,210,222	707,177	Ray, Robert E.*	487,282	Franzenburg, Paul	15,763	219,895 R	58.4%	40.3%	59.2%	40.8%
1970	791,241	403,394	Ray, Robert E.*	368,911	Fulton, Robert	18,936	34,483 R	51.0%	46.6%	52.2%	47.8%
1968	1,135,988	613,827	Ray, Robert E.	521,216	Franzenburg, Paul	945	92,611 R	54.0%	45.9%	54.1%	45.9%
1966	893,175	394,518	Murray, William G.	494,259	Hughes, Harold E.*	4,398	99,741 D	44.2%	55.3%	44.4%	55.6%
1964	1,167,734	365,131	Hultman, Evan	794,610	Hughes, Harold E.*	7,993	429,479 D	31.3%	68.0%	31.5%	68.5%
1962	819,854	388,955	Erbe, Norman A.*	430,899	Hughes, Harold E.		41,944 D	47.4%	52.6%	47.4%	52.6%
1960	1,237,089	645,026	Erbe, Norman A.	592,063	McManus, E. J.		52,963 R	52.1%	47.9%	52.1%	47.9%
1958	859,095	394,071	Murray, William G.	465,024	Loveless, Herschel C.*		70,953 D	45.9%	54.1%	45.9%	54.1%
1956	1,204,235	587,383	Hoegh, Leo A.*	616,852	Loveless, Herschel C.		29,469 D	48.8%	51.2%	48.8%	51.2%
1954	848,592	435,944	Hoegh, Leo A.	410,255	Herring, Clyde E.	2,393	25,689 R	51.4%	48.3%	51.5%	48.5%
1952	1,230,045	638,388	Beardsley, William*	587,671	Loveless, Herschel C.	3,986	50,717 R	51.9%	47.8%	52.1%	47.9%
1950	857,213	506,642	Beardsley, William*	347,176	Gillette, Lester S.	3,395	159,466 R	59.1%	40.5%	59.3%	40.7%
1948	994,833	553,900	Beardsley, William	434,432	Switzer, Carroll O.	6,501	119,468 R	55.7%	43.7%	56.0%	44.0%
1946	631,681	362,592	Blue, Robert D.	266,190	Miles, Frank	2,899	96,402 R	57.4%	42.1%	57.7%	42.3%

Note: An asterisk (*) denotes incumbent. **The term of office of Iowa's governor was increased from two to four years effective with the 1974 election.

POSTWAR VOTE FOR SENATOR

Year	Total Vote	Republican Vote	Republican Candidate	Democratic Vote	Democratic Candidate	Other Vote	Rep.-Dem. Plurality	Total Vote Rep.	Total Vote Dem.	Major Vote Rep.	Major Vote Dem.
2010	1,116,063	718,215	Grassley, Chuck*	371,686	Conlin, Roxanne	26,162	346,529 R	64.4%	33.3%	65.9%	34.1%
2008	1,502,918	560,006	Reed, Christopher	941,665	Harkin, Tom*	1,247	381,659 D	37.3%	62.7%	37.3%	62.7%
2004	1,479,228	1,038,175	Grassley, Chuck*	412,365	Small, Arthur A.	28,688	625,810 R	70.2%	27.9%	71.6%	28.4%
2002	1,023,075	447,892	Ganske, Greg	554,278	Harkin, Tom*	20,905	106,386 D	43.8%	54.2%	44.7%	55.3%
1998	947,907	648,480	Grassley, Chuck*	289,049	Osterberg, David	10,378	359,431 R	68.4%	30.5%	69.2%	30.8%
1996	1,224,054	571,807	Lightfoot, Jim Ross	634,166	Harkin, Tom*	18,081	62,359 D	46.7%	51.8%	47.4%	52.6%
1992	1,292,494	899,761	Grassley, Chuck*	351,561	Lloyd-Jones, Jean	41,172	548,200 R	69.6%	27.2%	71.9%	28.1%
1990	983,933	446,869	Tauke, Tom	535,975	Harkin, Tom*	1,089	89,106 D	45.4%	54.5%	45.5%	54.5%
1986	891,762	588,880	Grassley, Chuck*	299,406	Roehrick, John P.	3,476	289,474 R	66.0%	33.6%	66.3%	33.7%
1984	1,292,700	564,381	Jepsen, Roger W.*	716,883	Harkin, Tom	11,436	152,502 D	43.7%	55.5%	44.0%	56.0%
1980	1,277,034	683,014	Grassley, Chuck	581,545	Culver, John C.*	12,475	101,469 R	53.5%	45.5%	54.0%	46.0%
1978	824,654	421,598	Jepsen, Roger W.	395,066	Clark, Richard*	7,990	26,532 R	51.1%	47.9%	51.6%	48.4%
1974	889,561	420,546	Stanley, David M.	462,947	Culver, John C.	6,068	42,401 D	47.3%	52.0%	47.6%	52.4%
1972	1,203,333	530,525	Miller, Jack*	662,637	Clark, Richard	10,171	132,112 D	44.1%	55.1%	44.5%	55.5%
1968	1,144,086	568,469	Stanley, David M.	574,884	Hughes, Harold E.	733	6,415 D	49.7%	50.2%	49.7%	50.3%
1966	857,496	522,339	Miller, Jack*	324,114	Smith, E. B.	11,043	198,225 R	60.9%	37.8%	61.7%	38.3%
1962	807,972	431,364	Hickenlooper, Bourke B.*	376,602	Smith, E. B.	6	54,762 R	53.4%	46.6%	53.4%	46.6%
1960	1,237,582	642,463	Miller, Jack	595,119	Loveless, Herschel C.		47,344 R	51.9%	48.1%	51.9%	48.1%
1956	1,178,655	635,499	Hickenlooper, Bourke B.*	543,156	Evans, R. M.		92,343 R	53.9%	46.1%	53.9%	46.1%
1954	847,355	442,409	Martin, Thomas E.	402,712	Gillette, Guy M.*	2,234	39,697 R	52.2%	47.5%	52.3%	47.7%
1950	858,523	470,613	Hickenlooper, Bourke B.*	383,766	Loveland, Albert J.	4,144	86,847 R	54.8%	44.7%	55.1%	44.9%
1948	1,000,412	415,778	Wilson, George*	578,226	Gillette, Guy M.	6,408	162,448 D	41.6%	57.8%	41.8%	58.2%

Note: An asterisk (*) denotes incumbent.

IOWA

PRESIDENT 2012

2010 Census Population	County	Total Vote	Republican (Romney)	Democratic (Obama)	Other	Rep.-Dem. Plurality	Percentage			
							Total Vote		Major Vote	
							Rep.	Dem.	Rep.	Dem.
7,682	ADAIR	3,996	2,114	1,790	92	324 R	52.9%	44.8%	54.1%	45.9%
4,029	ADAMS	2,185	1,108	1,028	49	80 R	50.7%	47.0%	51.9%	48.1%
14,330	ALLAMAKEE	6,934	3,264	3,553	117	289 D	47.1%	51.2%	47.9%	52.1%
12,887	APPANOOSE	6,245	3,161	2,951	133	210 R	50.6%	47.3%	51.7%	48.3%
6,119	AUDUBON	3,457	1,802	1,611	44	191 R	52.1%	46.6%	52.8%	47.2%
26,076	BENTON	14,023	6,940	6,862	221	78 R	49.5%	48.9%	50.3%	49.7%
131,090	BLACK HAWK	67,141	26,235	39,821	1,085	13,586 D	39.1%	59.3%	39.7%	60.3%
26,306	BOONE	14,388	6,556	7,512	320	956 D	45.6%	52.2%	46.6%	53.4%
24,276	BREMER	13,346	6,405	6,763	178	358 D	48.0%	50.7%	48.6%	51.4%
20,958	BUCHANAN	10,535	4,450	5,911	174	1,461 D	42.2%	56.1%	42.9%	57.1%
20,260	BUENA VISTA	8,383	4,554	3,700	129	854 R	54.3%	44.1%	55.2%	44.8%
14,867	BUTLER	7,545	4,106	3,329	110	777 R	54.4%	44.1%	55.2%	44.8%
9,670	CALHOUN	5,230	2,891	2,238	101	653 R	55.3%	42.8%	56.4%	43.6%
20,816	CARROLL	10,674	5,601	4,947	126	654 R	52.5%	46.3%	53.1%	46.9%
13,956	CASS	7,205	4,217	2,858	130	1,359 R	58.5%	39.7%	59.6%	40.4%
18,499	CEDAR	9,649	4,529	4,972	148	443 D	46.9%	51.5%	47.7%	52.3%
44,151	CERRO GORDO	23,824	10,128	13,316	380	3,188 D	42.5%	55.9%	43.2%	56.8%
12,072	CHEROKEE	6,415	3,662	2,634	119	1,028 R	57.1%	41.1%	58.2%	41.8%
12,439	CHICKASAW	6,484	2,836	3,554	94	718 D	43.7%	54.8%	44.4%	55.6%
9,286	CLARKE	4,430	2,124	2,189	117	65 D	47.9%	49.4%	49.2%	50.8%
16,667	CLAY	8,502	4,951	3,385	166	1,566 R	58.2%	39.8%	59.4%	40.6%
18,129	CLAYTON	9,138	4,164	4,806	168	642 D	45.6%	52.6%	46.4%	53.6%
49,116	CLINTON	25,000	9,432	15,141	427	5,709 D	37.7%	60.6%	38.4%	61.6%
17,096	CRAWFORD	6,752	3,595	3,066	91	529 R	53.2%	45.4%	54.0%	46.0%
66,135	DALLAS	38,116	20,988	16,576	552	4,412 R	55.1%	43.5%	55.9%	44.1%
8,753	DAVIS	3,773	2,138	1,520	115	618 R	56.7%	40.3%	58.4%	41.6%
8,457	DECATUR	3,833	1,947	1,791	95	156 R	50.8%	46.7%	52.1%	47.9%
17,764	DELAWARE	9,378	4,636	4,616	126	20 R	49.4%	49.2%	50.1%	49.9%
40,325	DES MOINES	20,385	8,136	11,888	361	3,752 D	39.9%	58.3%	40.6%	59.4%
16,667	DICKINSON	10,159	5,912	4,095	152	1,817 R	58.2%	40.3%	59.1%	40.9%
93,653	DUBUQUE	50,894	21,280	28,768	846	7,488 D	41.8%	56.5%	42.5%	57.5%
10,302	EMMET	4,687	2,507	2,099	81	408 R	53.5%	44.8%	54.4%	45.6%
20,880	FAYETTE	10,366	4,492	5,732	142	1,240 D	43.3%	55.3%	43.9%	56.1%
16,303	FLOYD	8,257	3,472	4,680	105	1,208 D	42.0%	56.7%	42.6%	57.4%
10,680	FRANKLIN	5,186	2,823	2,266	97	557 R	54.4%	43.7%	55.5%	44.5%
7,441	FREMONT	3,668	1,972	1,637	59	335 R	53.8%	44.6%	54.6%	45.4%
9,336	GREENE	4,846	2,380	2,375	91	5 R	49.1%	49.0%	50.1%	49.9%
12,453	GRUNDY	6,962	4,215	2,635	112	1,580 R	60.5%	37.8%	61.5%	38.5%
10,954	GUTHRIE	5,888	3,171	2,569	148	602 R	53.9%	43.6%	55.2%	44.8%
15,673	HAMILTON	7,927	3,991	3,782	154	209 R	50.3%	47.7%	51.3%	48.7%
11,341	HANCOCK	5,925	3,317	2,521	87	796 R	56.0%	42.5%	56.8%	43.2%
17,534	HARDIN	8,898	4,670	4,075	153	595 R	52.5%	45.8%	53.4%	46.6%
14,928	HARRISON	7,322	4,065	3,136	121	929 R	55.5%	42.8%	56.5%	43.5%
20,145	HENRY	9,697	5,035	4,460	202	575 R	51.9%	46.0%	53.0%	47.0%
9,566	HOWARD	4,645	1,795	2,768	82	973 D	38.6%	59.6%	39.3%	60.7%
9,815	HUMBOLDT	5,158	3,099	1,972	87	1,127 R	60.1%	38.2%	61.1%	38.9%
7,089	IDA	3,663	2,286	1,321	56	965 R	62.4%	36.1%	63.4%	36.6%
16,355	IOWA	8,866	4,569	4,144	153	425 R	51.5%	46.7%	52.4%	47.6%
19,848	JACKSON	10,242	4,177	5,907	158	1,730 D	40.8%	57.7%	41.4%	58.6%
36,842	JASPER	19,515	8,877	10,257	381	1,380 D	45.5%	52.6%	46.4%	53.6%
16,843	JEFFERSON	8,530	3,436	4,798	296	1,362 D	40.3%	56.2%	41.7%	58.3%
130,882	JOHNSON	75,977	23,698	50,666	1,613	26,968 D	31.2%	66.7%	31.9%	68.1%
20,638	JONES	10,449	4,721	5,534	194	813 D	45.2%	53.0%	46.0%	54.0%
10,511	KEOKUK	5,266	2,843	2,303	120	540 R	54.0%	43.7%	55.2%	44.8%
15,543	KOSSUTH	8,923	4,937	3,850	136	1,087 R	55.3%	43.1%	56.2%	43.8%
35,862	LEE	18,911	7,785	10,714	412	2,929 D	41.2%	56.7%	42.1%	57.9%
211,226	LINN	118,453	47,622	68,581	2,250	20,959 D	40.2%	57.9%	41.0%	59.0%
11,387	LOUISA	4,968	2,420	2,452	96	32 D	48.7%	49.4%	49.7%	50.3%
8,898	LUCAS	4,323	2,254	1,987	82	267 R	52.1%	46.0%	53.1%	46.9%
11,581	LYON	6,509	4,978	1,423	108	3,555 R	76.5%	21.9%	77.8%	22.2%

IOWA

PRESIDENT 2012

2010 Census Population	County	Total Vote	Republican (Romney)	Democratic (Obama)	Other	Rep.-Dem. Plurality	Percentage			
							Total Vote		Major Vote	
							Rep.	Dem.	Rep.	Dem.
15,679	MADISON	8,458	4,638	3,630	190	1,008 R	54.8%	42.9%	56.1%	43.9%
22,381	MAHASKA	10,883	6,448	4,213	222	2,235 R	59.2%	38.7%	60.5%	39.5%
33,309	MARION	17,687	9,828	7,507	352	2,321 R	55.6%	42.4%	56.7%	43.3%
40,648	MARSHALL	19,064	8,472	10,257	335	1,785 D	44.4%	53.8%	45.2%	54.8%
15,059	MILLS	7,212	4,216	2,848	148	1,368 R	58.5%	39.5%	59.7%	40.3%
10,776	MITCHELL	5,586	2,643	2,831	112	188 D	47.3%	50.7%	48.3%	51.7%
9,243	MONONA	4,742	2,557	2,101	84	456 R	53.9%	44.3%	54.9%	45.1%
7,970	MONROE	3,830	2,026	1,731	73	295 R	52.9%	45.2%	53.9%	46.1%
10,740	MONTGOMERY	5,025	3,001	1,922	102	1,079 R	59.7%	38.2%	61.0%	39.0%
42,745	MUSCATINE	19,865	8,168	11,323	374	3,155 D	41.1%	57.0%	41.9%	58.1%
14,398	O'BRIEN	7,341	5,266	1,969	106	3,297 R	71.7%	26.8%	72.8%	27.2%
6,462	OSCEOLA	3,194	2,230	912	52	1,318 R	69.8%	28.6%	71.0%	29.0%
15,932	PAGE	7,079	4,348	2,613	118	1,735 R	61.4%	36.9%	62.5%	37.5%
9,421	PALO ALTO	4,887	2,660	2,139	88	521 R	54.4%	43.8%	55.4%	44.6%
24,986	PLYMOUTH	12,950	8,597	4,164	189	4,433 R	66.4%	32.2%	67.4%	32.6%
7,310	POCAHONTAS	4,032	2,396	1,523	113	873 R	59.4%	37.8%	61.1%	38.9%
430,640	POLK	228,882	96,096	128,465	4,321	32,369 D	42.0%	56.1%	42.8%	57.2%
93,158	POTTAWATTAMIE	42,301	21,860	19,644	797	2,216 R	51.7%	46.4%	52.7%	47.3%
18,914	POWESHIEK	9,975	4,424	5,357	194	933 D	44.4%	53.7%	45.2%	54.8%
5,131	RINGGOLD	2,599	1,368	1,186	45	182 R	52.6%	45.6%	53.6%	46.4%
10,350	SAC	5,291	3,094	2,122	75	972 R	58.5%	40.1%	59.3%	40.7%
165,224	SCOTT	90,263	38,251	50,652	1,360	12,401 D	42.4%	56.1%	43.0%	57.0%
12,167	SHELBY	6,483	3,911	2,469	103	1,442 R	60.3%	38.1%	61.3%	38.7%
33,704	SIOUX	17,308	14,407	2,700	201	11,707 R	83.2%	15.6%	84.2%	15.8%
89,542	STORY	47,150	19,668	26,192	1,290	6,524 D	41.7%	55.6%	42.9%	57.1%
17,767	TAMA	9,017	4,098	4,768	151	670 D	45.4%	52.9%	46.2%	53.8%
6,317	TAYLOR	2,995	1,683	1,262	50	421 R	56.2%	42.1%	57.1%	42.9%
12,534	UNION	5,957	2,813	3,043	101	230 D	47.2%	51.1%	48.0%	52.0%
7,570	VAN BUREN	3,569	2,064	1,402	103	662 R	57.8%	39.3%	59.5%	40.5%
35,625	WAPELLO	15,770	6,789	8,663	318	1,874 D	43.1%	54.9%	43.9%	56.1%
46,225	WARREN	26,072	13,052	12,551	469	501 R	50.1%	48.1%	51.0%	49.0%
21,704	WASHINGTON	11,004	5,562	5,115	327	447 R	50.5%	46.5%	52.1%	47.9%
6,403	WAYNE	2,900	1,583	1,251	66	332 R	54.6%	43.1%	55.9%	44.1%
38,013	WEBSTER	18,292	8,469	9,537	286	1,068 D	46.3%	52.1%	47.0%	53.0%
10,866	WINNEBAGO	5,918	2,906	2,903	109	3 R	49.1%	49.1%	50.0%	50.0%
21,056	WINNESHIEK	11,084	4,622	6,256	206	1,634 D	41.7%	56.4%	42.5%	57.5%
102,172	WOODBURY	45,019	21,841	22,302	876	461 D	48.5%	49.5%	49.5%	50.5%
7,598	WORTH	4,172	1,744	2,350	78	606 D	41.8%	56.3%	42.6%	57.4%
13,229	WRIGHT	6,278	3,349	2,836	93	513 R	53.3%	45.2%	54.1%	45.9%
3,046,355	TOTAL	1,582,180	730,617	822,544	29,019	91,927 D	46.2%	52.0%	47.0%	53.0%

IOWA

HOUSE OF REPRESENTATIVES

CD	Year	Total Vote	Republican		Democratic		Other Vote	Rep.-Dem. Plurality	Percentage			
			Vote	Candidate	Vote	Candidate			Total Vote		Major Vote	
									Rep.	Dem.	Rep.	Dem.
1	2012	390,849	162,465	LANGE, BENJAMIN M.	222,422	BRALEY, BRUCE*	5,962	59,957 D	41.6%	56.9%	42.2%	57.8%
2	2012	381,275	161,977	ARCHER, JOHN	211,863	LOEBSACK, DAVE*	7,435	49,886 D	42.5%	55.6%	43.3%	56.7%
3	2012	386,842	202,000	LATHAM, TOM*	168,632	BOSWELL, LEONARD*	16,210	33,368 R	52.2%	43.6%	54.5%	45.5%
4	2012	377,883	200,063	KING, STEVE*	169,470	VILSACK, CHRISTIE	8,350	30,593 R	52.9%	44.8%	54.1%	45.9%
TOTAL	2012	1,536,849	726,505		772,387		37,957	45,882 D	47.3%	50.3%	48.5%	51.5%

Notes: An asterisk (*) denotes incumbent. Due to redistricting, the 3rd district general election pitted two incumbents against each other (Latham, former 4th district, and Boswell, former 3rd district).

IOWA

GENERAL AND PRIMARY ELECTIONS

2012 GENERAL ELECTIONS: OTHER VOTE

President Other vote was 12,926 Libertarian (Gary E. Johnson), 7,442 Write-in (Scattered Write-In), 3,769 Green (Jill Stein), 3,038 Constitution (Virgil H. Goode), 1,027 Nominated by Petition (Jerry Litzel), 445 Socialist Workers Party (James Harris), 372 Socialism and Liberation (Gloria La Riva)

House Other vote was:

CD 1 4,772 Nominated by Petition (Gregory James Hughes), 931 Nominated by Petition (George Todd Krail), 259 Write-in (Scattered Write-In)

CD 2 7,112 Nominated by Petition (Alan Aversa), 323 Write-in (Scattered Write-In)

CD 3 9,352 Nominated by Petition (Scott G. Batcher), 6,286 Socialist Workers Party (David Rosenfeld), 572 Write-in (Scattered Write-In)

CD 4 8,124 Nominated by Petition (Martin James Monroe), 226 Write-in (Scattered Write-In)

2012 PRIMARY ELECTIONS: SUPPLEMENTARY INFORMATION

Primary Precinct Caucus: January 3, 2012. (President) June 5, 2012 (Congress)

Registration (as of June 1, 2012 – includes 238,053 inactive registrants)

2,107,093

Republican	607,936
Democratic	595,423
No Party	663,969
Other	1,712

Primary Type Semi-open—Registered Democrats and Republicans could vote only in their party's primary, although any registered voter (including those not affiliated with either party) could participate in either party's primary by changing their registration to that party on primary day.

	REPUBLICAN PRIMARIES			DEMOCRATIC PRIMARIES		
Congressional District 1	Lange, Benjamin M.	13,217	53.1%	Braley, Bruce*	11,912	99.2%
	Blum, Rod	11,551	46.4%	Scattered Write-In	92	0.8%
	Scattered Write-In	143	0.6%			
	TOTAL	24,911		TOTAL	12,004	
Congressional District 2	Archer, John	16,604	60.5%	Loebsack, Dave*	17,467	81.5%
	Dolan, Dan	10,775	39.3%	Seng, Joe M.	3,913	18.3%
	Scattered Write-In	57	0.2%	Scattered Write-In	39	0.2%
	TOTAL	27,436		TOTAL	21,419	
Congressional District 3	Latham, Tom*	27,757	99.2%	Boswell, Leonard*	8,382	98.3%
	Scattered Write-In	218	0.8%	Scattered Write-In	145	1.7%
	TOTAL	27,975		TOTAL	8,527	
Congressional District 4	King, Steve*	38,238	98.9%	Vilsack, Christie	10,765	99.2%
	Scattered Write-In	420	1.1%	Scattered Write-In	88	0.8%
	TOTAL	38,658		TOTAL	10,853	

Notes: An asterisk (*) denotes incumbent. Iowa held a Republican precinct caucus on January 3, 2012, which is not a primary, but is highly reported and influential. However, the Iowa GOP declared no winner in 2012. W. Mitt Romney was ahead by 8 votes at the end of caucus night, but when results were finalized several weeks later, Rick Santorum had a lead of 34 votes. But results from all precincts could not be retrieved, leading the state party to extend congratulations to both candidates.

KANSAS

Congressional districts first established for elections held in 2012

4 members

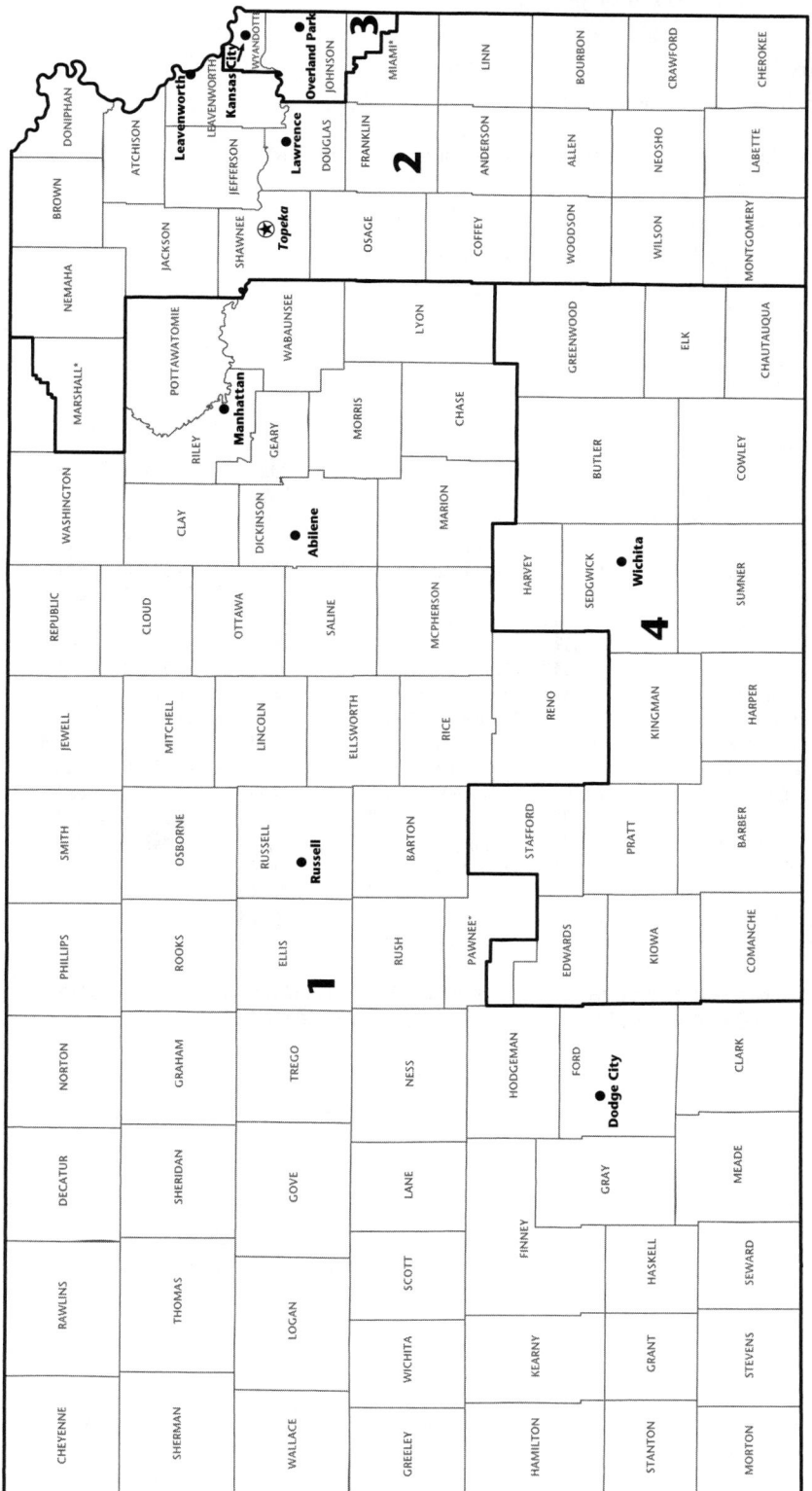

KANSAS

GOVERNOR
Sam Brownback (R). Elected 2010 to a four-year term.

SENATORS (2 Republicans)
Jerry Moran (R). Elected 2010 to a six-year term.

Pat Roberts (R). Reelected 2008 to a six-year term. Previously elected 2002, 1996.

REPRESENTATIVES (4 Republicans)
1. Tim Huelskamp (R)
2. Lynn Jenkins (R)
3. Kevin Yoder (R)
4. Mike Pompeo (R)

POSTWAR VOTE FOR PRESIDENT

| | | Republican | | Democratic | | Other | Rep.-Dem. | Percentage | | | |
| | | | | | | | | Total Vote | | Major Vote | |
Year	Total Vote	Vote	Candidate	Vote	Candidate	Vote	Plurality	Rep.	Dem.	Rep.	Dem.
2012	1,159,971	692,634	Romney, W. Mitt	440,726	Obama, Barack H.*	26,611	251,908 R	59.7%	38.0%	61.1%	38.9%
2008	1,235,872	699,655	McCain, John S. III	514,765	Obama, Barack H.	21,452	184,890 R	56.6%	41.7%	57.6%	42.4%
2004	1,187,756	736,456	Bush, George W.*	434,993	Kerry, John F.	16,307	301,463 R	62.0%	36.6%	62.9%	37.1%
2000**	1,072,218	622,332	Bush, George W.	399,276	Gore, Albert Jr.	50,610	223,056 R	58.0%	37.2%	60.9%	39.1%
1996**	1,074,300	583,245	Dole, Robert "Bob"	387,659	Clinton, Bill*	103,396	195,586 R	54.3%	36.1%	60.1%	39.9%
1992**	1,157,335	449,951	Bush, George H.*	390,434	Clinton, Bill	316,950	59,517 R	38.9%	33.7%	53.5%	46.5%
1988	993,044	554,049	Bush, George H.	422,636	Dukakis, Michael S.	16,359	131,413 R	55.8%	42.6%	56.7%	43.3%
1984	1,021,991	677,296	Reagan, Ronald*	333,149	Mondale, Walter F.	11,546	344,147 R	66.3%	32.6%	67.0%	33.0%
1980**	979,795	566,812	Reagan, Ronald	326,150	Carter, Jimmy*	86,833	240,662 R	57.9%	33.3%	63.5%	36.5%
1976	957,845	502,752	Ford, Gerald R.*	430,421	Carter, Jimmy	24,672	72,331 R	52.5%	44.9%	53.9%	46.1%
1972	916,095	619,812	Nixon, Richard M.*	270,287	McGovern, George S.	25,996	349,525 R	67.7%	29.5%	69.6%	30.4%
1968**	872,783	478,674	Nixon, Richard M.	302,996	Humphrey, Hubert H. Jr.	91,113	175,678 R	54.8%	34.7%	61.2%	38.8%
1964	857,901	386,579	Goldwater, Barry M. Sr.	464,028	Johnson, Lyndon B.*	7,294	77,449 D	45.1%	54.1%	45.4%	54.6%
1960	928,825	561,474	Nixon, Richard M.	363,213	Kennedy, John F.	4,138	198,261 R	60.4%	39.1%	60.7%	39.3%
1956	866,243	566,878	Eisenhower, Dwight D.*	296,317	Stevenson, Adlai E. II	3,048	270,561 R	65.4%	34.2%	65.7%	34.3%
1952	896,166	616,302	Eisenhower, Dwight D.	273,296	Stevenson, Adlai E. II	6,568	343,006 R	68.8%	30.5%	69.3%	30.7%
1948	788,819	423,039	Dewey, Thomas E.	351,902	Truman, Harry S.*	13,878	71,137 R	53.6%	44.6%	54.6%	45.4%

Note: An asterisk (*) denotes incumbent. **In past elections, the other vote included: 2000 - 36,086 Green (Ralph Nader); 1996 - 92,639 Reform (Ross Perot); 1992 - 312,358 Independent (Perot); 1980 - 68,231 Independent (John Anderson); 1968 - 88,921 American Independent (George Wallace).

KANSAS

POSTWAR VOTE FOR GOVERNOR

Year	Total Vote	Republican Vote	Republican Candidate	Democratic Vote	Democratic Candidate	Other Vote	Rep.-Dem. Plurality	Total Vote Rep.	Total Vote Dem.	Major Vote Rep.	Major Vote Dem.
2010	838,790	530,760	Brownback, Sam	270,166	Holland, Tom	37,864	260,594 R	63.3%	32.2%	66.3%	33.7%
2006	849,700	343,586	Barnett, Jim	491,993	Sebelius, Kathleen*	14,121	148,407 D	40.4%	57.9%	41.1%	58.9%
2002	835,692	376,830	Shallenburger, Tim	441,858	Sebelius, Kathleen	17,004	65,028 D	45.1%	52.9%	46.0%	54.0%
1998	742,665	544,882	Graves, Bill*	168,243	Sawyer, Tom	29,540	376,639 R	73.4%	22.7%	76.4%	23.6%
1994	821,030	526,113	Graves, Bill	294,733	Slattery, Jim	184	231,380 R	64.1%	35.9%	64.1%	35.9%
1990	783,325	333,589	Hayden, Mike*	380,609	Finney, Joan	69,127	47,020 D	42.6%	48.6%	46.7%	53.3%
1986	840,605	436,267	Hayden, Mike	404,338	Docking, Thomas R.		31,929 R	51.9%	48.1%	51.9%	48.1%
1982	763,263	339,356	Hardage, Sam	405,772	Carlin, John*	18,135	66,416 D	44.5%	53.2%	45.5%	54.5%
1978	736,246	348,015	Bennett, Robert F.*	363,835	Carlin, John	24,396	15,820 D	47.3%	49.4%	48.9%	51.1%
1974**	783,875	387,792	Bennett, Robert F.	384,115	Miller, Vern	11,968	3,677 R	49.5%	49.0%	50.2%	49.8%
1972	921,550	341,438	Kay, Morris	571,256	Docking, Robert*	8,856	229,818 D	37.1%	62.0%	37.4%	62.6%
1970	745,196	333,227	Frizzell, Kent	404,611	Docking, Robert*	7,358	71,384 D	44.7%	54.3%	45.2%	54.8%
1968	862,473	410,673	Harman, Rick	447,269	Docking, Robert*	4,531	36,596 D	47.6%	51.9%	47.9%	52.1%
1966	692,955	304,325	Avery, William H.*	380,030	Docking, Robert	8,600	75,705 D	43.9%	54.8%	44.5%	55.5%
1964	850,414	432,667	Avery, William H.	400,264	Wiles, Harry G.	17,483	32,403 R	50.9%	47.1%	51.9%	48.1%
1962	638,798	341,257	Anderson, John Jr.*	291,285	Saffels, Dale E.	6,256	49,972 R	53.4%	45.6%	54.0%	46.0%
1960	922,522	511,534	Anderson, John Jr.	402,261	Docking, George*	8,727	109,273 R	55.4%	43.6%	56.0%	44.0%
1958	735,939	313,036	Reed, Clyde M.	415,506	Docking, George*	7,397	102,470 D	42.5%	56.5%	43.0%	57.0%
1956	864,935	364,340	Shaw, Warren W.	479,701	Docking, George	20,894	115,361 D	42.1%	55.5%	43.2%	56.8%
1954	622,633	329,868	Hall, Fred	286,218	Docking, George	6,547	43,650 R	53.0%	46.0%	53.5%	46.5%
1952	872,139	491,338	Arn, Edward F.*	363,482	Rooney, Charles	17,319	127,856 R	56.3%	41.7%	57.5%	42.5%
1950	619,310	333,001	Arn, Edward F.	275,494	Anderson, Kenneth T.	10,815	57,507 R	53.8%	44.5%	54.7%	45.3%
1948	760,407	433,396	Carlson, Frank*	307,485	Carpenter, Randolph	19,526	125,911 R	57.0%	40.4%	58.5%	41.5%
1946	577,694	309,064	Carlson, Frank	254,283	Woodring, Harry H.	14,347	54,781 R	53.5%	44.0%	54.9%	45.1%

Note: An asterisk (*) denotes incumbent. **The term of office of Kansas's governor was increased from two to four years effective with the 1974 election.

POSTWAR VOTE FOR SENATOR

Year	Total Vote	Republican Vote	Republican Candidate	Democratic Vote	Democratic Candidate	Other Vote	Rep.-Dem. Plurality	Total Vote Rep.	Total Vote Dem.	Major Vote Rep.	Major Vote Dem.
2010	837,692	587,175	Moran, Jerry	220,971	Johnston, Lisa	29,546	366,204 R	70.1%	26.4%	72.7%	27.3%
2008	1,210,690	727,121	Roberts, Pat*	441,399	Slattery, Jim	42,170	285,722 R	60.1%	36.5%	62.2%	37.8%
2004	1,129,022	780,863	Brownback, Sam*	310,337	Jones, Lee	37,822	470,526 R	69.2%	27.5%	71.6%	28.4%
2002	776,850	641,075	Roberts, Pat*			135,775	641,075 R	82.5%		100.0%	
1998	727,236	474,639	Brownback, Sam*	229,718	Feleciano, Paul Jr.	22,879	244,921 R	65.3%	31.6%	67.4%	32.6%
1996	1,052,300	652,677	Roberts, Pat	362,380	Thompson, Sally	37,243	290,297 R	62.0%	34.4%	64.3%	35.7%
1996S	1,064,716	574,021	Brownback, Sam	461,344	Docking, Jill	29,351	112,677 R	53.9%	43.3%	55.4%	44.6%
1992	1,126,447	706,246	Dole, Robert "Bob"*	349,525	O'Dell, Gloria	70,676	356,721 R	62.7%	31.0%	66.9%	33.1%
1990	786,235	578,605	Kassebaum, Nancy Landon*	207,491	Williams, Dick	139	371,114 R	73.6%	26.4%	73.6%	26.4%
1986	823,566	576,902	Dole, Robert "Bob"*	246,664	MacDonald, Guy		330,238 R	70.0%	30.0%	70.0%	30.0%
1984	996,729	757,402	Kassebaum, Nancy Landon*	211,664	Maher, James	27,663	545,738 R	76.0%	21.2%	78.2%	21.8%
1980	938,957	598,686	Dole, Robert "Bob"*	340,271	Simpson, John		258,415 R	63.8%	36.2%	63.8%	36.2%
1978	748,839	403,354	Kassebaum, Nancy Landon	317,602	Roy, William R.	27,883	85,752 R	53.9%	42.4%	55.9%	44.1%
1974	794,437	403,983	Dole, Robert "Bob"*	390,451	Roy, William R.	3	13,532 R	50.9%	49.1%	50.9%	49.1%
1972	871,702	622,591	Pearson, James B.*	200,764	Tetzlaff, Arch O.	48,347	421,827 R	71.4%	23.0%	75.6%	24.4%
1968	817,096	490,911	Dole, Robert "Bob"	315,911	Robinson, William I.	10,274	175,000 R	60.1%	38.7%	60.8%	39.2%
1966	671,345	350,077	Pearson, James B.*	303,223	Breeding, J. Floyd	18,045	46,854 R	52.1%	45.2%	53.6%	46.4%
1962	622,232	388,500	Carlson, Frank*	223,630	Smith, K. L.	10,102	164,870 R	62.4%	35.9%	63.5%	36.5%
1962S	613,250	344,689	Pearson, James B.*	260,756	Aylward, Paul L.	7,805	83,933 R	56.2%	42.5%	56.9%	43.1%
1960	888,592	485,499	Schoeppel, Andrew F.*	388,895	Theis, Frank	14,198	96,604 R	54.6%	43.8%	55.5%	44.5%
1956	825,280	477,822	Carlson, Frank*	333,939	Hart, George	13,519	143,883 R	57.9%	40.5%	58.9%	41.1%
1954	618,063	348,144	Schoeppel, Andrew F.*	258,575	McGill, George	11,344	89,569 R	56.3%	41.8%	57.4%	42.6%
1950	619,104	335,880	Carlson, Frank*	271,365	Aiken, Paul	11,859	64,515 R	54.3%	43.8%	55.3%	44.7%
1948	716,342	393,412	Schoeppel, Andrew F.	305,987	McGill, George	16,943	87,425 R	54.9%	42.7%	56.3%	43.7%

Note: An asterisk (*) denotes incumbent. **One of the 1996 and 1962 elections was for a short term to fill a vacancy. The Democratic Party did not run a candidate in the 2002 Senate election.

KANSAS

PRESIDENT 2012

2010 Census Population	County	Total Vote	Republican (Romney)	Democratic (Obama)	Other	Rep.-Dem. Plurality	Percentage Total Vote Rep.	Dem.	Percentage Major Vote Rep.	Dem.
13,371	ALLEN	5,310	3,316	1,869	125	1,447 R	62.4%	35.2%	64.0%	36.0%
8,102	ANDERSON	3,315	2,276	944	95	1,332 R	68.7%	28.5%	70.7%	29.3%
16,924	ATCHISON	6,674	3,917	2,567	190	1,350 R	58.7%	38.5%	60.4%	39.6%
4,861	BARBER	2,314	1,772	482	60	1,290 R	76.6%	20.8%	78.6%	21.4%
27,674	BARTON	10,341	7,874	2,297	170	5,577 R	76.1%	22.2%	77.4%	22.6%
15,173	BOURBON	6,254	4,102	1,996	156	2,106 R	65.6%	31.9%	67.3%	32.7%
9,984	BROWN	3,993	2,829	1,076	88	1,753 R	70.8%	26.9%	72.4%	27.6%
65,880	BUTLER	26,085	18,157	7,282	646	10,875 R	69.6%	27.9%	71.4%	28.6%
2,790	CHASE	1,271	875	358	38	517 R	68.8%	28.2%	71.0%	29.0%
3,669	CHAUTAUQUA	1,630	1,304	280	46	1,024 R	80.0%	17.2%	82.3%	17.7%
21,603	CHEROKEE	8,571	5,456	2,930	185	2,526 R	63.7%	34.2%	65.1%	34.9%
2,726	CHEYENNE	1,426	1,159	233	34	926 R	81.3%	16.3%	83.3%	16.7%
2,215	CLARK	1,017	805	174	38	631 R	79.2%	17.1%	82.2%	17.8%
8,535	CLAY	3,686	2,788	834	64	1,954 R	75.6%	22.6%	77.0%	23.0%
9,533	CLOUD	4,058	2,954	974	130	1,980 R	72.8%	24.0%	75.2%	24.8%
8,601	COFFEY	3,906	2,903	898	105	2,005 R	74.3%	23.0%	76.4%	23.6%
1,891	COMANCHE	928	767	143	18	624 R	82.7%	15.4%	84.3%	15.7%
36,311	COWLEY	12,710	8,081	4,319	310	3,762 R	63.6%	34.0%	65.2%	34.8%
39,134	CRAWFORD	14,945	7,708	6,826	411	882 R	51.6%	45.7%	53.0%	47.0%
2,961	DECATUR	1,532	1,218	266	48	952 R	79.5%	17.4%	82.1%	17.9%
19,754	DICKINSON	8,042	5,832	2,020	190	3,812 R	72.5%	25.1%	74.3%	25.7%
7,945	DONIPHAN	3,403	2,414	902	87	1,512 R	70.9%	26.5%	72.8%	27.2%
110,826	DOUGLAS	48,145	17,401	29,267	1,477	11,866 D	36.1%	60.8%	37.3%	62.7%
3,037	EDWARDS	1,385	1,059	298	28	761 R	76.5%	21.5%	78.0%	22.0%
2,882	ELK	1,369	1,049	281	39	768 R	76.6%	20.5%	78.9%	21.1%
28,452	ELLIS	11,714	8,399	3,057	258	5,342 R	71.7%	26.1%	73.3%	26.7%
6,497	ELLSWORTH	2,712	1,930	702	80	1,228 R	71.2%	25.9%	73.3%	26.7%
36,776	FINNEY	9,084	6,219	2,682	183	3,537 R	68.5%	29.5%	69.9%	30.1%
33,848	FORD	8,362	5,602	2,600	160	3,002 R	67.0%	31.1%	68.3%	31.7%
25,992	FRANKLIN	10,990	6,984	3,694	312	3,290 R	63.5%	33.6%	65.4%	34.6%
34,362	GEARY	7,845	4,372	3,332	141	1,040 R	55.7%	42.5%	56.7%	43.3%
2,695	GOVE	1,383	1,168	176	39	992 R	84.5%	12.7%	86.9%	13.1%
2,597	GRAHAM	1,340	1,056	256	28	800 R	78.8%	19.1%	80.5%	19.5%
7,829	GRANT	2,306	1,811	456	39	1,355 R	78.5%	19.8%	79.9%	20.1%
6,006	GRAY	1,958	1,603	324	31	1,279 R	81.9%	16.5%	83.2%	16.8%
1,247	GREELEY	670	543	113	14	430 R	81.0%	16.9%	82.8%	17.2%
6,689	GREENWOOD	2,123	1,590	478	55	1,112 R	74.9%	22.5%	76.9%	23.1%
2,690	HAMILTON	877	693	163	21	530 R	79.0%	18.6%	81.0%	19.0%
6,034	HARPER	2,389	1,759	550	80	1,209 R	73.6%	23.0%	76.2%	23.8%
34,684	HARVEY	14,294	8,588	5,373	333	3,215 R	60.1%	37.6%	61.5%	38.5%
4,256	HASKELL	1,396	1,159	215	22	944 R	83.0%	15.4%	84.4%	15.6%
1,916	HODGEMAN	1,060	868	179	13	689 R	81.9%	16.9%	82.9%	17.1%
13,462	JACKSON	5,561	3,527	1,901	133	1,626 R	63.4%	34.2%	65.0%	35.0%
19,126	JEFFERSON	8,013	4,827	2,977	209	1,850 R	60.2%	37.2%	61.9%	38.1%
3,077	JEWELL	1,497	1,235	229	33	1,006 R	82.5%	15.3%	84.4%	15.6%
544,179	JOHNSON	274,365	158,401	110,526	5,438	47,875 R	57.7%	40.3%	58.9%	41.1%
3,977	KEARNY	1,386	1,097	268	21	829 R	79.1%	19.3%	80.4%	19.6%
7,858	KINGMAN	3,231	2,397	733	101	1,664 R	74.2%	22.7%	76.6%	23.4%
2,553	KIOWA	1,144	976	163	5	813 R	85.3%	14.2%	85.7%	14.3%
21,607	LABETTE	8,037	4,742	3,117	178	1,625 R	59.0%	38.8%	60.3%	39.7%
1,750	LANE	928	739	172	17	567 R	79.6%	18.5%	81.1%	18.9%
76,227	LEAVENWORTH	29,085	17,059	11,357	669	5,702 R	58.7%	39.0%	60.0%	40.0%
3,241	LINCOLN	1,483	1,165	289	29	876 R	78.6%	19.5%	80.1%	19.9%
9,656	LINN	4,467	3,177	1,170	120	2,007 R	71.1%	26.2%	73.1%	26.9%
2,756	LOGAN	1,350	1,126	197	27	929 R	83.4%	14.6%	85.1%	14.9%
33,690	LYON	11,875	6,470	5,111	294	1,359 R	54.5%	43.0%	55.9%	44.1%
12,660	MARION	5,409	3,889	1,385	135	2,504 R	71.9%	25.6%	73.7%	26.3%
10,117	MARSHALL	4,773	3,195	1,469	109	1,726 R	66.9%	30.8%	68.5%	31.5%
29,180	MCPHERSON	12,297	8,545	3,449	303	5,096 R	69.5%	28.0%	71.2%	28.8%
4,575	MEADE	1,709	1,428	258	23	1,170 R	83.6%	15.1%	84.7%	15.3%

KANSAS

PRESIDENT 2012

2010 Census Population	County	Total Vote	Republican (Romney)	Democratic (Obama)	Other	Rep.-Dem. Plurality	Percentage Total Vote Rep.	Dem.	Major Vote Rep.	Dem.
32,787	MIAMI	14,856	9,858	4,712	286	5,146 R	66.4%	31.7%	67.7%	32.3%
6,373	MITCHELL	2,965	2,327	584	54	1,743 R	78.5%	19.7%	79.9%	20.1%
35,471	MONTGOMERY	12,417	8,630	3,501	286	5,129 R	69.5%	28.2%	71.1%	28.9%
5,923	MORRIS	2,562	1,773	718	71	1,055 R	69.2%	28.0%	71.2%	28.8%
3,233	MORTON	1,278	1,072	189	17	883 R	83.9%	14.8%	85.0%	15.0%
10,178	NEMAHA	5,026	3,930	1,000	96	2,930 R	78.2%	19.9%	79.7%	20.3%
16,512	NEOSHO	6,480	4,272	2,050	158	2,222 R	65.9%	31.6%	67.6%	32.4%
3,107	NESS	1,444	1,209	218	17	991 R	83.7%	15.1%	84.7%	15.3%
5,671	NORTON	2,325	1,878	398	49	1,480 R	80.8%	17.1%	82.5%	17.5%
16,295	OSAGE	6,906	4,427	2,268	211	2,159 R	64.1%	32.8%	66.1%	33.9%
3,858	OSBORNE	1,838	1,479	324	35	1,155 R	80.5%	17.6%	82.0%	18.0%
6,091	OTTAWA	2,933	2,295	558	80	1,737 R	78.2%	19.0%	80.4%	19.6%
6,973	PAWNEE	2,608	1,836	718	54	1,118 R	70.4%	27.5%	71.9%	28.1%
5,642	PHILLIPS	2,565	2,135	382	48	1,753 R	83.2%	14.9%	84.8%	15.2%
21,604	POTTAWATOMIE	9,479	6,804	2,335	340	4,469 R	71.8%	24.6%	74.5%	25.5%
9,656	PRATT	3,801	2,771	980	50	1,791 R	72.9%	25.8%	73.9%	26.1%
2,519	RAWLINS	1,444	1,223	190	31	1,033 R	84.7%	13.2%	86.6%	13.4%
64,511	RENO	24,422	15,718	8,085	619	7,633 R	64.4%	33.1%	66.0%	34.0%
4,980	REPUBLIC	2,686	2,134	477	75	1,657 R	79.4%	17.8%	81.7%	18.3%
10,083	RICE	3,681	2,676	911	94	1,765 R	72.7%	24.7%	74.6%	25.4%
71,115	RILEY	21,101	11,507	8,977	617	2,530 R	54.5%	42.5%	56.2%	43.8%
5,181	ROOKS	2,460	2,038	361	61	1,677 R	82.8%	14.7%	85.0%	15.0%
3,307	RUSH	1,570	1,166	367	37	799 R	74.3%	23.4%	76.1%	23.9%
6,970	RUSSELL	3,200	2,553	593	54	1,960 R	79.8%	18.5%	81.2%	18.8%
55,606	SALINE	21,496	13,840	7,040	616	6,800 R	64.4%	32.8%	66.3%	33.7%
4,936	SCOTT	2,052	1,728	277	47	1,451 R	84.2%	13.5%	86.2%	13.8%
498,365	SEDGWICK	182,895	106,506	71,977	4,412	34,529 R	58.2%	39.4%	59.7%	40.3%
22,952	SEWARD	5,176	3,617	1,490	69	2,127 R	69.9%	28.8%	70.8%	29.2%
177,934	SHAWNEE	76,508	37,782	36,975	1,751	807 R	49.4%	48.3%	50.5%	49.5%
2,556	SHERIDAN	1,342	1,154	168	20	986 R	86.0%	12.5%	87.3%	12.7%
6,010	SHERMAN	2,623	1,976	577	70	1,399 R	75.3%	22.0%	77.4%	22.6%
3,853	SMITH	2,023	1,624	358	41	1,266 R	80.3%	17.7%	81.9%	18.1%
4,437	STAFFORD	1,839	1,385	404	50	981 R	75.3%	22.0%	77.4%	22.6%
2,235	STANTON	759	605	143	11	462 R	79.7%	18.8%	80.9%	19.1%
5,724	STEVENS	2,034	1,749	252	33	1,497 R	86.0%	12.4%	87.4%	12.6%
24,132	SUMNER	9,141	6,260	2,658	223	3,602 R	68.5%	29.1%	70.2%	29.8%
7,900	THOMAS	3,474	2,788	598	88	2,190 R	80.3%	17.2%	82.3%	17.7%
3,001	TREGO	1,579	1,261	291	27	970 R	79.9%	18.4%	81.2%	18.8%
7,053	WABAUNSEE	3,267	2,256	918	93	1,338 R	69.1%	28.1%	71.1%	28.9%
1,485	WALLACE	798	719	68	11	651 R	90.1%	8.5%	91.4%	8.6%
5,799	WASHINGTON	2,889	2,316	524	49	1,792 R	80.2%	18.1%	81.5%	18.5%
2,234	WICHITA	987	821	157	9	664 R	83.2%	15.9%	83.9%	16.1%
9,409	WILSON	7,434	5,650	1,636	148	4,014 R	76.0%	22.0%	77.5%	22.5%
3,309	WOODSON	1,447	1,035	380	32	655 R	71.5%	26.3%	73.1%	26.9%
157,505	WYANDOTTE	50,738	15,496	34,302	940	18,806 D	30.5%	67.6%	31.1%	68.9%
2,853,118	TOTAL	1,159,971	692,634	440,726	26,611	251,908 R	59.7%	38.0%	61.1%	38.9%

KANSAS

HOUSE OF REPRESENTATIVES

CD	Year	Total Vote	Republican Vote	Republican Candidate	Democratic Vote	Democratic Candidate	Other Vote	Rep.-Dem. Plurality	Total Vote Rep.	Total Vote Dem.	Major Vote Rep.	Major Vote Dem.
1	2012	211,337	211,337	HUELSKAMP, TIM*				211,337 R	100.0%		100.0%	
2	2012	293,718	167,463	JENKINS, LYNN*	113,735	SCHLINGENSIEPEN, TOBIAS	12,520	53,728 R	57.0%	38.7%	59.6%	40.4%
3	2012	293,762	201,087	YODER, KEVIN*			92,675	201,087 R	68.5%		100.0%	
4	2012	258,922	161,094	POMPEO, MIKE*	81,770	TILLMAN, ROBERT	16,058	79,324 R	62.2%	31.6%	66.3%	33.7%
TOTAL	2012	1,057,739	740,981		195,505		121,253	545,476 R	70.1%	18.5%	79.1%	20.9%

Note: An asterisk (*) denotes incumbent.

KANSAS

GENERAL AND PRIMARY ELECTIONS

GENERAL ELECTIONS: OTHER VOTE

President   Other vote was 20,456 Libertarian (Gary E. Johnson), 5,017 Reform (Chuck Baldwin), 714 Write-in (Jill Stein), 237 Write-in (Scattered Write-In), 187 Write-in (Virgil H. Goode)

House   Other vote was:

CD 2   12,520 Libertarian (Dennis Hawver)
CD 3   92,675 Libertarian (Joel Balam)
CD 4   16,058 Libertarian (Thomas Jefferson)

PRIMARY ELECTIONS: SUPPLEMENTARY INFORMATION

Primary	August 7, 2012	**Registration** (as of October 2012)	1,719,469	Republican	790,345
				Democratic	446,237
				Libertarian	11,373
				Reform	978
				Americans Elect	223
				Unaffiliated	522,096

Primary Type   Semi-open—Registered Democrats and Republicans could vote only in their party's primary. "Unaffiliated" voters could participate in either primary, although if they voted in the Republican primary they had to change their registration to Republican on primary day.

	REPUBLICAN PRIMARIES			DEMOCRATIC PRIMARIES		
Congressional District 1	Huelskamp, Tim*	79,633	100.0%			
Congressional District 2	Jenkins, Lynn*	64,008	100.0%	Schlingensiepen, Tobias	11,747	39.5%
				Eye, Robert V.	10,353	34.8%
				Barnhart, Scott	7,627	25.7%
	TOTAL	64,008		TOTAL	29,727	
Congressional District 3	Yoder, Kevin*	50,270	100.0%			
Congressional District 4	Pompeo, Mike*	60,195	100.0%	Tillman, Robert	11,224	70.8%
				Freeman, Esau A.	4,618	29.2%
	TOTAL	60,195		TOTAL	15,842	

Note: An asterisk (*) denotes incumbent.

KENTUCKY

Congressional districts first established for elections held in 2012

6 members

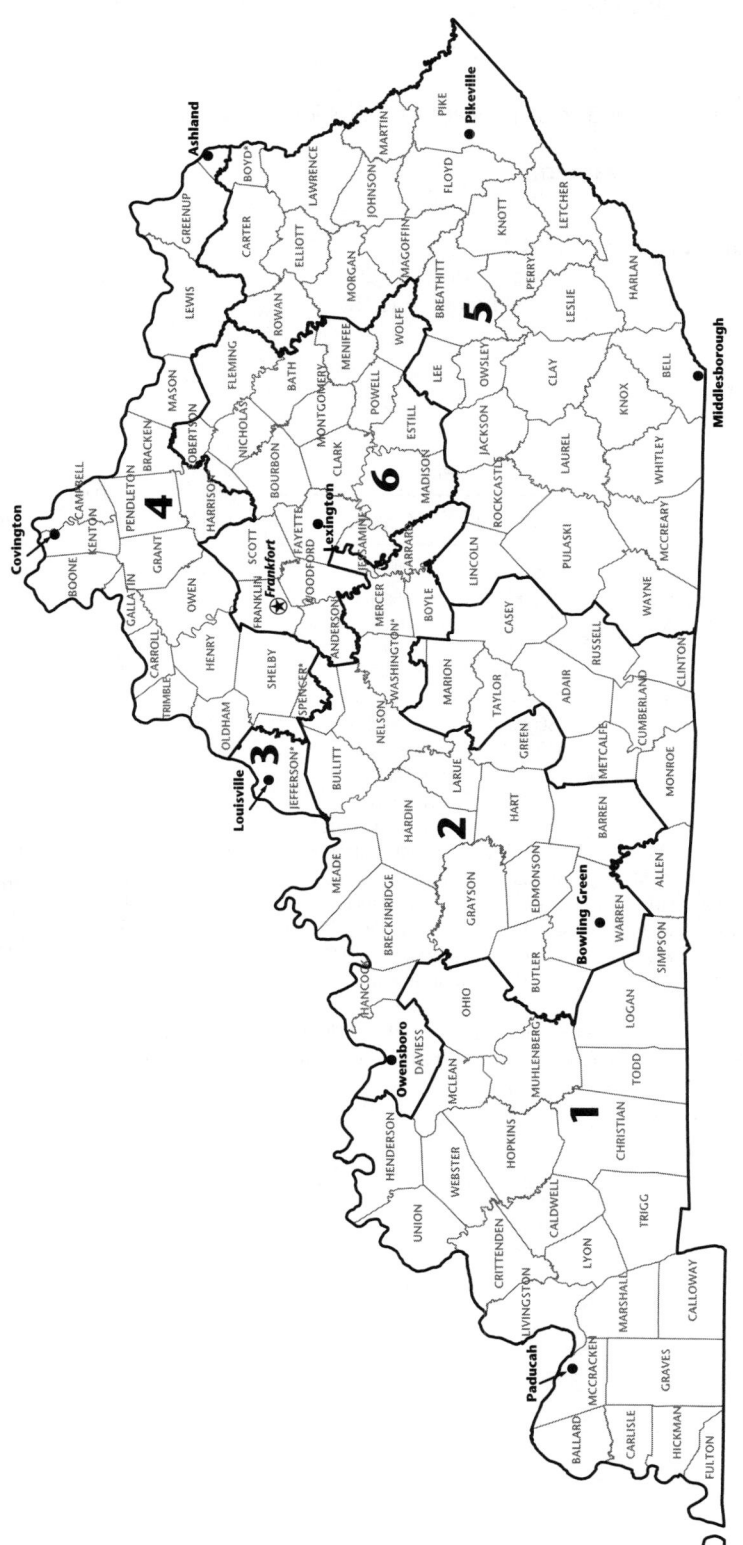

* Asterisk indicates a county whose boundaries include parts of two or more Congressional districts.

KENTUCKY

GOVERNOR
Steven L. Beshear (D). Reelected 2011 to a four-year term. Previously elected 2007.

SENATORS (2 Republicans)
A. Mitch McConnell (R). Reelected 2008 to a six-year term. Previously elected 2002, 1996, 1990, 1984.

Rand Paul (R). Elected 2010 to a six-year term.

REPRESENTATIVES (5 Republicans, 1 Democrat)
1. Ed Whitfield (R)
2. Brett Guthrie (R)
3. John Yarmuth (D)
4. Thomas Massie (R)
5. Hal Rogers (R)
6. Andy Barr (R)

POSTWAR VOTE FOR PRESIDENT

| | | Republican | | Democratic | | Other Vote | Rep.-Dem. Plurality | Percentage | | | |
| | | | | | | | | Total Vote | | Major Vote | |
Year	Total Vote	Vote	Candidate	Vote	Candidate			Rep.	Dem.	Rep.	Dem.
2012	1,797,212	1,087,190	Romney, W. Mitt	679,370	Obama, Barack H.*	30,652	407,820 R	60.5%	37.8%	61.5%	38.5%
2008	1,826,620	1,048,462	McCain, John S. III	751,985	Obama, Barack H.	26,173	296,477 R	57.4%	41.2%	58.2%	41.8%
2004	1,795,882	1,069,439	Bush, George W.*	712,733	Kerry, John F.	13,710	356,706 R	59.5%	39.7%	60.0%	40.0%
2000**	1,544,187	872,492	Bush, George W.	638,898	Gore, Albert Jr.	32,797	233,594 R	56.5%	41.4%	57.7%	42.3%
1996**	1,388,708	623,283	Dole, Robert "Bob"	636,614	Clinton, Bill*	128,811	13,331 D	44.9%	45.8%	49.5%	50.5%
1992**	1,492,900	617,178	Bush, George H.*	665,104	Clinton, Bill	210,618	47,926 D	41.3%	44.6%	48.1%	51.9%
1988	1,322,517	734,281	Bush, George H.	580,368	Dukakis, Michael S.	7,868	153,913 R	55.5%	43.9%	55.9%	44.1%
1984	1,369,345	821,702	Reagan, Ronald*	539,539	Mondale, Walter F.	8,104	282,163 R	60.0%	39.4%	60.4%	39.6%
1980**	1,294,627	635,274	Reagan, Ronald	616,417	Carter, Jimmy*	42,936	18,857 R	49.1%	47.6%	50.8%	49.2%
1976	1,167,142	531,852	Ford, Gerald R.*	615,717	Carter, Jimmy	19,573	83,865 D	45.6%	52.8%	46.3%	53.7%
1972	1,067,499	676,446	Nixon, Richard M.*	371,159	McGovern, George S.	19,894	305,287 R	63.4%	34.8%	64.6%	35.4%
1968**	1,055,893	462,411	Nixon, Richard M.	397,541	Humphrey, Hubert H. Jr.	195,941	64,870 R	43.8%	37.6%	53.8%	46.2%
1964	1,046,105	372,977	Goldwater, Barry M. Sr.	669,659	Johnson, Lyndon B.*	3,469	296,682 D	35.7%	64.0%	35.8%	64.2%
1960	1,124,462	602,607	Nixon, Richard M.	521,855	Kennedy, John F.		80,752 R	53.6%	46.4%	53.6%	46.4%
1956	1,053,805	572,192	Eisenhower, Dwight D.*	476,453	Stevenson, Adlai E. II	5,160	95,739 R	54.3%	45.2%	54.6%	45.4%
1952	993,148	495,029	Eisenhower, Dwight D.	495,729	Stevenson, Adlai E. II	2,390	700 D	49.8%	49.9%	50.0%	50.0%
1948	822,658	341,210	Dewey, Thomas E.	466,756	Truman, Harry S.*	14,692	125,546 D	41.5%	56.7%	42.2%	57.8%

Note: An asterisk (*) denotes incumbent. **In past elections, the other vote included: 2000 - 23,192 Green (Ralph Nader); 1996 - 120,396 Reform (Ross Perot); 1992 - 203,944 Independent (Perot); 1980 - 31,127 Independent (John Anderson); 1968 - 193,098 American Independent (George Wallace).

KENTUCKY

POSTWAR VOTE FOR GOVERNOR

Year	Total Vote	Republican Vote	Republican Candidate	Democratic Vote	Democratic Candidate	Other Vote	Rep.-Dem. Plurality	Total Vote Rep.	Total Vote Dem.	Major Vote Rep.	Major Vote Dem.
2011	833,139	294,034	Williams, David Lynn	464,245	Beshear, Steven L.*	74,860	170,211 D	35.3%	55.7%	38.8%	61.2%
2007	1,055,325	435,773	Fletcher, Ernest*	619,552	Beshear, Steven L.		183,779 D	41.3%	58.7%	41.3%	58.7%
2003	1,083,443	596,284	Fletcher, Ernest	487,159	Chandler, Ben		109,125 R	55.0%	45.0%	55.0%	45.0%
1999**	580,074	128,788	Martin, Peppy	352,099	Patton, Paul E.*	99,187	223,311 D	22.2%	60.7%	26.8%	73.2%
1995	983,979	479,227	Forgy, Larry	500,787	Patton, Paul E.	3,965	21,560 D	48.7%	50.9%	48.9%	51.1%
1991	834,920	294,452	Harper, John	540,468	Jones, Brereton C.		246,016 D	35.3%	64.7%	35.3%	64.7%
1987	777,815	273,141	Harper, John	504,674	Wilkinson, Wallace G.		231,533 D	35.1%	64.9%	35.1%	64.9%
1983	1,030,628	454,650	Bunning, Jim	561,674	Collins, Martha Layne	14,304	107,024 D	44.1%	54.5%	44.7%	55.3%
1979	939,366	381,278	Nunn, Louie B.	558,088	Brown, J. Y. Jr.		176,810 D	40.6%	59.4%	40.6%	59.4%
1975	748,157	277,998	Gable, Robert E.	470,159	Carroll, Julian*		192,161 D	37.2%	62.8%	37.2%	62.8%
1971	930,792	412,653	Emberton, Thomas	470,722	Ford, Wendell H.	47,417	58,069 D	44.3%	50.6%	46.7%	53.3%
1967	886,146	453,323	Nunn, Louie B.	425,674	Ward, Henry	7,149	27,649 R	51.2%	48.0%	51.6%	48.4%
1963	886,047	436,496	Nunn, Louie B.	449,551	Breathitt, Edward T.		13,055 D	49.3%	50.7%	49.3%	50.7%
1959	853,005	336,456	Robsion, John M. Jr.	516,549	Combs, Bert T.		180,093 D	39.4%	60.6%	39.4%	60.6%
1955	778,488	322,671	Denney, Edwin R.	451,647	Chandler, Happy	4,170	128,976 D	41.4%	58.0%	41.7%	58.3%
1951	634,359	288,014	Siler, Eugene	346,345	Wetherby, Lawrence W.		58,331 D	45.4%	54.6%	45.4%	54.6%
1947	675,551	287,756	Dummit, Eldon S.	387,795	Clements, Earle C.		100,039 D	42.6%	57.4%	42.6%	57.4%

Note: An asterisk (*) denotes incumbent. **In past elections, the other vote included: 1999 - 88,930 Reform (Gatewood Galbraith).

POSTWAR VOTE FOR SENATOR

Year	Total Vote	Republican Vote	Republican Candidate	Democratic Vote	Democratic Candidate	Other Vote	Rep.-Dem. Plurality	Total Vote Rep.	Total Vote Dem.	Major Vote Rep.	Major Vote Dem.
2010	1,356,468	755,411	Paul, Rand	599,843	Conway, Jack	1,214	155,568 R	55.7%	44.2%	55.7%	44.3%
2008	1,800,821	953,816	McConnell, A. Mitch*	847,005	Lunsford, Bruce		106,811 R	53.0%	47.0%	53.0%	47.0%
2004	1,724,362	873,507	Bunning, Jim*	850,855	Mongiardo, Frank Daniel		22,652 R	50.7%	49.3%	50.7%	49.3%
2002	1,131,475	731,679	McConnell, A. Mitch*	399,634	Weinberg, Lois Combs	162	332,045 R	64.7%	35.3%	64.7%	35.3%
1998	1,145,414	569,817	Bunning, Jim	563,051	Baesler, Scott	12,546	6,766 R	49.7%	49.2%	50.3%	49.7%
1996	1,307,046	724,794	McConnell, A. Mitch*	560,012	Beshear, Steven L.	22,240	164,782 R	55.5%	42.8%	56.4%	43.6%
1992	1,330,858	476,604	Williams, David Lynn	836,888	Ford, Wendell H.*	17,366	360,284 D	35.8%	62.9%	36.3%	63.7%
1990	916,010	478,034	McConnell, A. Mitch*	437,976	Sloane, Harvey		40,058 R	52.2%	47.8%	52.2%	47.8%
1986	677,280	173,330	Andrews, Jackson M.	503,775	Ford, Wendell H.*	175	330,445 D	25.6%	74.4%	25.6%	74.4%
1984	1,292,407	644,990	McConnell, A. Mitch	639,721	Huddleston, Walter*	7,696	5,269 R	49.9%	49.5%	50.2%	49.8%
1980	1,106,890	386,029	Foust, Mary Louise	720,861	Ford, Wendell H.*		334,832 D	34.9%	65.1%	34.9%	65.1%
1978	476,783	175,766	Guenthner, Louie	290,730	Huddleston, Walter*	10,287	114,964 D	36.9%	61.0%	37.7%	62.3%
1974	745,994	328,982	Cook, Marlow W.*	399,406	Ford, Wendell H.	17,606	70,424 D	44.1%	53.5%	45.2%	54.8%
1972	1,037,861	494,337	Nunn, Louie B.	528,550	Huddleston, Walter	14,974	34,213 D	47.6%	50.9%	48.3%	51.7%
1968	942,865	484,260	Cook, Marlow W.	448,960	Peden, Katherine	9,645	35,300 R	51.4%	47.6%	51.9%	48.1%
1966	749,884	483,805	Cooper, John Sherman*	266,079	Brown, John Young		217,726 R	64.5%	35.5%	64.5%	35.5%
1962	820,088	432,648	Morton, Thruston B.*	387,440	Wyatt, Wilson W.		45,208 R	52.8%	47.2%	52.8%	47.2%
1960	1,088,377	644,087	Cooper, John Sherman*	444,290	Johnson, Keen		199,797 R	59.2%	40.8%	59.2%	40.8%
1956	1,006,825	506,903	Morton, Thruston B.	499,922	Clements, Earle C.*		6,981 R	50.3%	49.7%	50.3%	49.7%
1956S	1,011,645	538,505	Cooper, John Sherman	473,140	Wetherby, Lawrence W.		65,365 R	53.2%	46.8%	53.2%	46.8%
1954	797,057	362,948	Cooper, John Sherman*	434,109	Barkley, Alben W.		71,161 D	45.5%	54.5%	45.5%	54.5%
1952S	960,228	494,576	Cooper, John Sherman	465,652	Underwood, Thomas R.		28,924 R	51.5%	48.5%	51.5%	48.5%
1950	612,617	278,368	Dawson, Charles I.	334,249	Clements, Earle C.*		55,881 D	45.4%	54.6%	45.4%	54.6%
1948	794,469	383,776	Cooper, John Sherman*	408,256	Chapman, Virgil	2,437	24,480 D	48.3%	51.4%	48.5%	51.5%
1946S	615,119	327,652	Cooper, John Sherman	285,829	Brown, John Young	1,638	41,823 R	53.3%	46.5%	53.4%	46.6%

Note: An asterisk (*) denotes incumbent. The elections in 1946 and 1952 as well as one in 1956 were for short terms to fill vacancies.

KENTUCKY

PRESIDENT 2012

2010 Census Population	County	Total Vote	Republican (Romney)	Democratic (Obama)	Other	Rep.-Dem. Plurality		Percentage			
								Total Vote		Major Vote	
								Rep.	Dem.	Rep.	Dem.
18,656	ADAIR	7,600	5,841	1,660	99	4,181 R		76.9%	21.8%	77.9%	22.1%
19,956	ALLEN	7,100	5,184	1,808	108	3,376 R		73.0%	25.5%	74.1%	25.9%
21,421	ANDERSON	10,320	6,822	3,315	183	3,507 R		66.1%	32.1%	67.3%	32.7%
8,249	BALLARD	3,895	2,647	1,189	59	1,458 R		68.0%	30.5%	69.0%	31.0%
42,173	BARREN	16,568	10,922	5,400	246	5,522 R		65.9%	32.6%	66.9%	33.1%
11,591	BATH	4,122	2,275	1,770	77	505 R		55.2%	42.9%	56.2%	43.8%
28,691	BELL	9,482	7,127	2,224	131	4,903 R		75.2%	23.5%	76.2%	23.8%
118,811	BOONE	52,511	35,922	15,629	960	20,293 R		68.4%	29.8%	69.7%	30.3%
19,985	BOURBON	7,923	4,692	3,075	156	1,617 R		59.2%	38.8%	60.4%	39.6%
49,542	BOYD	19,049	10,884	7,776	389	3,108 R		57.1%	40.8%	58.3%	41.7%
28,432	BOYLE	12,373	7,703	4,471	199	3,232 R		62.3%	36.1%	63.3%	36.7%
8,488	BRACKEN	3,232	2,029	1,147	56	882 R		62.8%	35.5%	63.9%	36.1%
13,878	BREATHITT	5,008	3,318	1,562	128	1,756 R		66.3%	31.2%	68.0%	32.0%
20,059	BRECKINRIDGE	7,969	5,025	2,825	119	2,200 R		63.1%	35.4%	64.0%	36.0%
74,319	BULLITT	31,779	21,306	9,971	502	11,335 R		67.0%	31.4%	68.1%	31.9%
12,690	BUTLER	5,060	3,716	1,293	51	2,423 R		73.4%	25.6%	74.2%	25.8%
12,984	CALDWELL	5,860	3,904	1,852	104	2,052 R		66.6%	31.6%	67.8%	32.2%
37,191	CALLOWAY	15,072	9,440	5,317	315	4,123 R		62.6%	35.3%	64.0%	36.0%
90,336	CAMPBELL	40,177	24,240	15,080	857	9,160 R		60.3%	37.5%	61.6%	38.4%
5,104	CARLISLE	2,619	1,835	750	34	1,085 R		70.1%	28.6%	71.0%	29.0%
10,811	CARROLL	3,680	1,999	1,629	52	370 R		54.3%	44.3%	55.1%	44.9%
27,720	CARTER	8,908	5,279	3,383	246	1,896 R		59.3%	38.0%	60.9%	39.1%
15,955	CASEY	6,091	4,904	1,086	101	3,818 R		80.5%	17.8%	81.9%	18.1%
73,955	CHRISTIAN	21,955	13,475	8,252	228	5,223 R		61.4%	37.6%	62.0%	38.0%
35,613	CLARK	15,416	9,931	5,228	257	4,703 R		64.4%	33.9%	65.5%	34.5%
21,730	CLAY	7,383	6,176	1,111	96	5,065 R		83.7%	15.0%	84.8%	15.2%
10,272	CLINTON	4,393	3,569	752	72	2,817 R		81.2%	17.1%	82.6%	17.4%
9,315	CRITTENDEN	3,854	2,839	960	55	1,879 R		73.7%	24.9%	74.7%	25.3%
6,856	CUMBERLAND	2,854	2,216	599	39	1,617 R		77.6%	21.0%	78.7%	21.3%
96,656	DAVIESS	42,087	25,092	16,208	787	8,884 R		59.6%	38.5%	60.8%	39.2%
12,161	EDMONSON	4,668	3,232	1,374	62	1,858 R		69.2%	29.4%	70.2%	29.8%
7,852	ELLIOTT	2,399	1,126	1,186	87	60 D		46.9%	49.4%	48.7%	51.3%
14,672	ESTILL	5,184	3,749	1,356	79	2,393 R		72.3%	26.2%	73.4%	26.6%
295,803	FAYETTE	125,866	60,795	62,080	2,991	1,285 D		48.3%	49.3%	49.5%	50.5%
14,348	FLEMING	5,782	3,780	1,911	91	1,869 R		65.4%	33.1%	66.4%	33.6%
39,451	FLOYD	14,890	9,784	4,733	373	5,051 R		65.7%	31.8%	67.4%	32.6%
49,285	FRANKLIN	23,337	11,345	11,535	457	190 D		48.6%	49.4%	49.6%	50.4%
6,813	FULTON	2,481	1,425	1,022	34	403 R		57.4%	41.2%	58.2%	41.8%
8,589	GALLATIN	3,061	1,758	1,238	65	520 R		57.4%	40.4%	58.7%	41.3%
16,912	GARRARD	7,077	5,310	1,661	106	3,649 R		75.0%	23.5%	76.2%	23.8%
24,662	GRANT	8,608	5,664	2,810	134	2,854 R		65.8%	32.6%	66.8%	33.2%
37,121	GRAVES	15,503	10,699	4,547	257	6,152 R		69.0%	29.3%	70.2%	29.8%
25,746	GRAYSON	9,271	6,404	2,744	123	3,660 R		69.1%	29.6%	70.0%	30.0%
11,258	GREEN	4,856	3,634	1,165	57	2,469 R		74.8%	24.0%	75.7%	24.3%
36,910	GREENUP	15,168	8,855	6,027	286	2,828 R		58.4%	39.7%	59.5%	40.5%
8,565	HANCOCK	4,134	2,212	1,833	89	379 R		53.5%	44.3%	54.7%	45.3%
105,543	HARDIN	39,218	23,357	15,214	647	8,143 R		59.6%	38.8%	60.6%	39.4%
29,278	HARLAN	10,657	8,652	1,830	175	6,822 R		81.2%	17.2%	82.5%	17.5%
18,846	HARRISON	7,163	4,556	2,471	136	2,085 R		63.6%	34.5%	64.8%	35.2%
18,199	HART	6,622	4,257	2,283	82	1,974 R		64.3%	34.5%	65.1%	34.9%
46,250	HENDERSON	18,622	10,296	8,091	235	2,205 R		55.3%	43.4%	56.0%	44.0%
15,416	HENRY	6,590	3,940	2,530	120	1,410 R		59.8%	38.4%	60.9%	39.1%
4,902	HICKMAN	2,139	1,431	686	22	745 R		66.9%	32.1%	67.6%	32.4%
46,920	HOPKINS	19,767	13,681	5,789	297	7,892 R		69.2%	29.3%	70.3%	29.7%
13,494	JACKSON	5,061	4,365	612	84	3,753 R		86.2%	12.1%	87.7%	12.3%
741,096	JEFFERSON	339,579	148,423	186,181	4,975	37,758 D		43.7%	54.8%	44.4%	55.6%
48,586	JESSAMINE	20,633	14,233	6,001	399	8,232 R		69.0%	29.1%	70.3%	29.7%
23,356	JOHNSON	9,035	7,095	1,723	217	5,372 R		78.5%	19.1%	80.5%	19.5%
159,720	KENTON	67,704	41,389	24,920	1,395	16,469 R		61.1%	36.8%	62.4%	37.6%
16,346	KNOTT	5,693	4,130	1,420	143	2,710 R		72.5%	24.9%	74.4%	25.6%

KENTUCKY
PRESIDENT 2012

2010 Census Population	County	Total Vote	Republican (Romney)	Democratic (Obama)	Other	Rep.-Dem. Plurality	Percentage Total Vote Rep.	Dem.	Major Vote Rep.	Dem.
31,883	KNOX	11,100	8,467	2,484	149	5,983 R	76.3%	22.4%	77.3%	22.7%
14,193	LARUE	5,764	3,911	1,733	120	2,178 R	67.9%	30.1%	69.3%	30.7%
58,849	LAUREL	22,408	18,151	3,905	352	14,246 R	81.0%	17.4%	82.3%	17.7%
15,860	LAWRENCE	5,592	3,995	1,520	77	2,475 R	71.4%	27.2%	72.4%	27.6%
7,887	LEE	2,623	1,977	595	51	1,382 R	75.4%	22.7%	76.9%	23.1%
11,310	LESLIE	4,950	4,439	433	78	4,006 R	89.7%	8.7%	91.1%	8.9%
24,519	LETCHER	8,758	6,811	1,702	245	5,109 R	77.8%	19.4%	80.0%	20.0%
13,870	LEWIS	4,769	3,326	1,342	101	1,984 R	69.7%	28.1%	71.3%	28.7%
24,742	LINCOLN	9,152	6,416	2,582	154	3,834 R	70.1%	28.2%	71.3%	28.7%
9,519	LIVINGSTON	4,511	3,089	1,346	76	1,743 R	68.5%	29.8%	69.7%	30.3%
26,835	LOGAN	10,510	6,899	3,469	142	3,430 R	65.6%	33.0%	66.5%	33.5%
8,314	LYON	3,839	2,412	1,373	54	1,039 R	62.8%	35.8%	63.7%	36.3%
82,916	MADISON	33,322	21,128	11,512	682	9,616 R	63.4%	34.5%	64.7%	35.3%
13,333	MAGOFFIN	4,906	3,391	1,433	82	1,958 R	69.1%	29.2%	70.3%	29.7%
19,820	MARION	7,318	3,800	3,418	100	382 R	51.9%	46.7%	52.6%	47.4%
31,448	MARSHALL	15,719	10,402	5,022	295	5,380 R	66.2%	31.9%	67.4%	32.6%
12,929	MARTIN	3,824	3,180	574	70	2,606 R	83.2%	15.0%	84.7%	15.3%
17,490	MASON	6,881	4,197	2,592	92	1,605 R	61.0%	37.7%	61.8%	38.2%
65,565	MCCRACKEN	30,551	19,979	10,062	510	9,917 R	65.4%	32.9%	66.5%	33.5%
18,306	MCCREARY	5,707	4,564	1,069	74	3,495 R	80.0%	18.7%	81.0%	19.0%
9,531	MCLEAN	4,200	2,705	1,432	63	1,273 R	64.4%	34.1%	65.4%	34.6%
28,602	MEADE	10,916	6,606	4,122	188	2,484 R	60.5%	37.8%	61.6%	38.4%
6,306	MENIFEE	2,598	1,484	1,048	66	436 R	57.1%	40.3%	58.6%	41.4%
21,331	MERCER	9,939	6,820	2,966	153	3,854 R	68.6%	29.8%	69.7%	30.3%
10,099	METCALFE	4,184	2,676	1,425	83	1,251 R	64.0%	34.1%	65.3%	34.7%
10,963	MONROE	4,746	3,762	936	48	2,826 R	79.3%	19.7%	80.1%	19.9%
26,499	MONTGOMERY	10,248	6,398	3,701	149	2,697 R	62.4%	36.1%	63.4%	36.6%
13,923	MORGAN	4,472	3,021	1,369	82	1,652 R	67.6%	30.6%	68.8%	31.2%
31,499	MUHLENBERG	12,739	7,762	4,771	206	2,991 R	60.9%	37.5%	61.9%	38.1%
43,437	NELSON	18,533	10,673	7,611	249	3,062 R	57.6%	41.1%	58.4%	41.6%
7,135	NICHOLAS	2,581	1,583	948	50	635 R	61.3%	36.7%	62.5%	37.5%
23,842	OHIO	9,646	6,470	2,987	189	3,483 R	67.1%	31.0%	68.4%	31.6%
60,316	OLDHAM	29,884	20,179	9,240	465	10,939 R	67.5%	30.9%	68.6%	31.4%
10,841	OWEN	4,557	2,971	1,501	85	1,470 R	65.2%	32.9%	66.4%	33.6%
4,755	OWSLEY	1,580	1,279	283	18	996 R	80.9%	17.9%	81.9%	18.1%
14,877	PENDLETON	5,534	3,556	1,859	119	1,697 R	64.3%	33.6%	65.7%	34.3%
28,712	PERRY	10,241	8,040	2,047	154	5,993 R	78.5%	20.0%	79.7%	20.3%
65,024	PIKE	23,636	17,590	5,646	400	11,944 R	74.4%	23.9%	75.7%	24.3%
12,613	POWELL	4,481	2,766	1,620	95	1,146 R	61.7%	36.2%	63.1%	36.9%
63,063	PULASKI	26,003	20,714	4,976	313	15,738 R	79.7%	19.1%	80.6%	19.4%
2,282	ROBERTSON	935	579	340	16	239 R	61.9%	36.4%	63.0%	37.0%
17,056	ROCKCASTLE	6,216	5,028	1,097	91	3,931 R	80.9%	17.6%	82.1%	17.9%
23,333	ROWAN	7,665	4,035	3,438	192	597 R	52.6%	44.9%	54.0%	46.0%
17,565	RUSSELL	7,909	6,346	1,445	118	4,901 R	80.2%	18.3%	81.5%	18.5%
47,173	SCOTT	20,573	12,679	7,532	362	5,147 R	61.6%	36.6%	62.7%	37.3%
42,074	SHELBY	18,663	11,790	6,634	239	5,156 R	63.2%	35.5%	64.0%	36.0%
17,327	SIMPSON	7,093	4,355	2,650	88	1,705 R	61.4%	37.4%	62.2%	37.8%
17,061	SPENCER	8,431	5,726	2,549	156	3,177 R	67.9%	30.2%	69.2%	30.8%
24,512	TAYLOR	10,950	7,551	3,285	114	4,266 R	69.0%	30.0%	69.7%	30.3%
12,460	TODD	4,718	3,247	1,403	68	1,844 R	68.8%	29.7%	69.8%	30.2%
14,339	TRIGG	6,742	4,520	2,115	107	2,405 R	67.0%	31.4%	68.1%	31.9%
8,809	TRIMBLE	3,543	2,133	1,355	55	778 R	60.2%	38.2%	61.2%	38.8%
15,007	UNION	5,979	3,955	1,942	82	2,013 R	66.1%	32.5%	67.1%	32.9%
113,792	WARREN	43,903	26,384	16,805	714	9,579 R	60.1%	38.3%	61.1%	38.9%
11,717	WASHINGTON	5,219	3,495	1,669	55	1,826 R	67.0%	32.0%	67.7%	32.3%
20,813	WAYNE	7,210	5,289	1,855	66	3,434 R	73.4%	25.7%	74.0%	26.0%
13,621	WEBSTER	5,470	3,607	1,765	98	1,842 R	65.9%	32.3%	67.1%	32.9%
35,637	WHITLEY	13,072	10,232	2,683	157	7,549 R	78.3%	20.5%	79.2%	20.8%
7,355	WOLFE	2,559	1,542	976	41	566 R	60.3%	38.1%	61.2%	38.8%
24,939	WOODFORD	12,332	7,219	4,883	230	2,336 R	58.5%	39.6%	59.7%	40.3%
4,339,367	TOTAL	1,797,212	1,087,190	679,370	30,652	407,820 R	60.5%	37.8%	61.5%	38.5%

KENTUCKY

GOVERNOR 2011

2010 Census Population	County	Total Vote	Republican (Williams)	Democratic (Beshear)	Other	Rep.-Dem. Plurality		Percentage			
								Total Vote		Major Vote	
								Rep.	Dem.	Rep.	Dem.
18,656	ADAIR	3,676	1,877	1,606	193	271	R	51.1%	43.7%	53.9%	46.1%
19,956	ALLEN	2,894	1,540	1,221	133	319	R	53.2%	42.2%	55.8%	44.2%
21,421	ANDERSON	6,068	1,577	3,048	1,443	1,471	D	26.0%	50.2%	34.1%	65.9%
8,249	BALLARD	2,159	773	1,274	112	501	D	35.8%	59.0%	37.8%	62.2%
42,173	BARREN	7,858	3,003	4,425	430	1,422	D	38.2%	56.3%	40.4%	59.6%
11,591	BATH	1,844	417	1,081	346	664	D	22.6%	58.6%	27.8%	72.2%
28,691	BELL	3,583	1,797	1,550	236	247	R	50.2%	43.3%	53.7%	46.3%
118,811	BOONE	18,107	9,160	8,292	655	868	R	50.6%	45.8%	52.5%	47.5%
19,985	BOURBON	4,057	906	2,223	928	1,317	D	22.3%	54.8%	29.0%	71.0%
49,542	BOYD	7,767	2,617	4,879	271	2,262	D	33.7%	62.8%	34.9%	65.1%
28,432	BOYLE	6,327	1,839	3,476	1,012	1,637	D	29.1%	54.9%	34.6%	65.4%
8,488	BRACKEN	1,372	510	758	104	248	D	37.2%	55.2%	40.2%	59.8%
13,878	BREATHITT	2,238	711	1,236	291	525	D	31.8%	55.2%	36.5%	63.5%
20,059	BRECKINRIDGE	4,058	1,495	2,376	187	881	D	36.8%	58.6%	38.6%	61.4%
74,319	BULLITT	13,807	5,656	7,370	781	1,714	D	41.0%	53.4%	43.4%	56.6%
12,690	BUTLER	2,172	1,140	938	94	202	R	52.5%	43.2%	54.9%	45.1%
12,984	CALDWELL	3,452	1,157	2,075	220	918	D	33.5%	60.1%	35.8%	64.2%
37,191	CALLOWAY	6,764	2,567	3,914	283	1,347	D	38.0%	57.9%	39.6%	60.4%
90,336	CAMPBELL	15,759	6,780	8,320	659	1,540	D	43.0%	52.8%	44.9%	55.1%
5,104	CARLISLE	1,398	575	758	65	183	D	41.1%	54.2%	43.1%	56.9%
10,811	CARROLL	1,767	480	1,176	111	696	D	27.2%	66.6%	29.0%	71.0%
27,720	CARTER	3,860	1,216	2,466	178	1,250	D	31.5%	63.9%	33.0%	67.0%
15,955	CASEY	2,814	1,522	1,038	254	484	R	54.1%	36.9%	59.5%	40.5%
73,955	CHRISTIAN	7,356	3,455	3,582	319	127	D	47.0%	48.7%	49.1%	50.9%
35,613	CLARK	7,685	2,255	3,966	1,464	1,711	D	29.3%	51.6%	36.2%	63.8%
21,730	CLAY	2,857	1,602	1,010	245	592	R	56.1%	35.4%	61.3%	38.7%
10,272	CLINTON	2,126	1,540	514	72	1,026	R	72.4%	24.2%	75.0%	25.0%
9,315	CRITTENDEN	2,067	1,020	942	105	78	R	49.3%	45.6%	52.0%	48.0%
6,856	CUMBERLAND	2,079	1,629	374	76	1,255	R	78.4%	18.0%	81.3%	18.7%
96,656	DAVIESS	19,639	7,302	11,579	758	4,277	D	37.2%	59.0%	38.7%	61.3%
12,161	EDMONSON	2,306	1,166	1,067	73	99	R	50.6%	46.3%	52.2%	47.8%
7,852	ELLIOTT	1,996	392	1,460	144	1,068	D	19.6%	73.1%	21.2%	78.8%
14,672	ESTILL	2,505	1,048	1,000	457	48	R	41.8%	39.9%	51.2%	48.8%
295,803	FAYETTE	60,202	14,123	32,948	13,131	18,825	D	23.5%	54.7%	30.0%	70.0%
14,348	FLEMING	3,070	979	1,653	438	674	D	31.9%	53.8%	37.2%	62.8%
39,451	FLOYD	6,621	1,790	4,208	623	2,418	D	27.0%	63.6%	29.8%	70.2%
49,285	FRANKLIN	16,602	2,686	9,896	4,020	7,210	D	16.2%	59.6%	21.3%	78.7%
6,813	FULTON	1,168	454	667	47	213	D	38.9%	57.1%	40.5%	59.5%
8,589	GALLATIN	1,067	403	607	57	204	D	37.8%	56.9%	39.9%	60.1%
16,912	GARRARD	3,276	1,252	1,373	651	121	D	38.2%	41.9%	47.7%	52.3%
24,662	GRANT	3,244	1,422	1,621	201	199	D	43.8%	50.0%	46.7%	53.3%
37,121	GRAVES	7,896	3,158	4,292	446	1,134	D	40.0%	54.4%	42.4%	57.6%
25,746	GRAYSON	4,431	1,891	2,306	234	415	D	42.7%	52.0%	45.1%	54.9%
11,258	GREEN	2,492	1,137	1,213	142	76	D	45.6%	48.7%	48.4%	51.6%
36,910	GREENUP	6,415	2,286	3,895	234	1,609	D	35.6%	60.7%	37.0%	63.0%
8,565	HANCOCK	1,856	600	1,164	92	564	D	32.3%	62.7%	34.0%	66.0%
105,543	HARDIN	18,544	6,885	10,722	937	3,837	D	37.1%	57.8%	39.1%	60.9%
29,278	HARLAN	3,629	1,621	1,712	296	91	D	44.7%	47.2%	48.6%	51.4%
18,846	HARRISON	3,876	1,158	1,982	736	824	D	29.9%	51.1%	36.9%	63.1%
18,199	HART	3,198	1,122	1,909	167	787	D	35.1%	59.7%	37.0%	63.0%
46,250	HENDERSON	8,141	2,326	5,593	222	3,267	D	28.6%	68.7%	29.4%	70.6%
15,416	HENRY	3,975	1,185	2,338	452	1,153	D	29.8%	58.8%	33.6%	66.4%
4,902	HICKMAN	1,183	450	682	51	232	D	38.0%	57.7%	39.8%	60.2%
46,920	HOPKINS	9,104	2,666	6,084	354	3,418	D	29.3%	66.8%	30.5%	69.5%
13,494	JACKSON	2,152	1,404	537	211	867	R	65.2%	25.0%	72.3%	27.7%
741,096	JEFFERSON	161,111	44,192	107,871	9,048	63,679	D	27.4%	67.0%	29.1%	70.9%
48,586	JESSAMINE	9,965	3,686	4,045	2,234	359	D	37.0%	40.6%	47.7%	52.3%
23,356	JOHNSON	3,477	1,560	1,668	249	108	D	44.9%	48.0%	48.3%	51.7%
159,720	KENTON	26,186	11,818	13,326	1,042	1,508	D	45.1%	50.9%	47.0%	53.0%
16,346	KNOTT	2,743	1,082	1,422	239	340	D	39.4%	51.8%	43.2%	56.8%

KENTUCKY
GOVERNOR 2011

2010 Census Population	County	Total Vote	Republican (Williams)	Democratic (Beshear)	Other	Rep.-Dem. Plurality	Total Vote Rep.	Total Vote Dem.	Major Vote Rep.	Major Vote Dem.
31,883	KNOX	4,740	2,048	2,368	324	320 D	43.2%	50.0%	46.4%	53.6%
14,193	LARUE	2,940	1,075	1,686	179	611 D	36.6%	57.3%	38.9%	61.1%
58,849	LAUREL	9,296	4,858	3,710	728	1,148 R	52.3%	39.9%	56.7%	43.3%
15,860	LAWRENCE	2,340	952	1,270	118	318 D	40.7%	54.3%	42.8%	57.2%
7,887	LEE	1,313	594	482	237	112 R	45.2%	36.7%	55.2%	44.8%
11,310	LESLIE	1,960	1,246	607	107	639 R	63.6%	31.0%	67.2%	32.8%
24,519	LETCHER	3,562	1,366	1,810	386	444 D	38.3%	50.8%	43.0%	57.0%
13,870	LEWIS	1,781	917	765	99	152 R	51.5%	43.0%	54.5%	45.5%
24,742	LINCOLN	4,227	1,633	2,018	576	385 D	38.6%	47.7%	44.7%	55.3%
9,519	LIVINGSTON	2,342	828	1,366	148	538 D	35.4%	58.3%	37.7%	62.3%
26,835	LOGAN	3,704	1,612	1,951	141	339 D	43.5%	52.7%	45.2%	54.8%
8,314	LYON	2,299	802	1,366	131	564 D	34.9%	59.4%	37.0%	63.0%
82,916	MADISON	15,653	5,090	7,804	2,759	2,714 D	32.5%	49.9%	39.5%	60.5%
13,333	MAGOFFIN	2,464	829	1,476	159	647 D	33.6%	59.9%	36.0%	64.0%
19,820	MARION	4,017	738	2,929	350	2,191 D	18.4%	72.9%	20.1%	79.9%
31,448	MARSHALL	8,270	3,183	4,639	448	1,456 D	38.5%	56.1%	40.7%	59.3%
12,929	MARTIN	1,177	700	414	63	286 R	59.5%	35.2%	62.8%	37.2%
17,490	MASON	3,144	1,054	1,862	228	808 D	33.5%	59.2%	36.1%	63.9%
65,565	MCCRACKEN	14,012	5,940	7,341	731	1,401 D	42.4%	52.4%	44.7%	55.3%
18,306	MCCREARY	1,949	1,206	639	104	567 R	61.9%	32.8%	65.4%	34.6%
9,531	MCLEAN	2,056	625	1,372	59	747 D	30.4%	66.7%	31.3%	68.7%
28,602	MEADE	5,446	1,901	3,228	317	1,327 D	34.9%	59.3%	37.1%	62.9%
6,306	MENIFEE	1,214	346	703	165	357 D	28.5%	57.9%	33.0%	67.0%
21,331	MERCER	5,420	1,664	2,745	1,011	1,081 D	30.7%	50.6%	37.7%	62.3%
10,099	METCALFE	2,166	851	1,187	128	336 D	39.3%	54.8%	41.8%	58.2%
10,963	MONROE	2,895	1,925	883	87	1,042 R	66.5%	30.5%	68.6%	31.4%
26,499	MONTGOMERY	4,900	1,393	2,612	895	1,219 D	28.4%	53.3%	34.8%	65.2%
13,923	MORGAN	2,117	629	1,220	268	591 D	29.7%	57.6%	34.0%	66.0%
31,499	MUHLENBERG	5,557	1,528	3,859	170	2,331 D	27.5%	69.4%	28.4%	71.6%
43,437	NELSON	8,969	2,809	5,575	585	2,766 D	31.3%	62.2%	33.5%	66.5%
7,135	NICHOLAS	1,407	280	661	466	381 D	19.9%	47.0%	29.8%	70.2%
23,842	OHIO	4,211	1,773	2,266	172	493 D	42.1%	53.8%	43.9%	56.1%
60,316	OLDHAM	14,083	6,082	7,079	922	997 D	43.2%	50.3%	46.2%	53.8%
10,841	OWEN	2,499	807	1,279	413	472 D	32.3%	51.2%	38.7%	61.3%
4,755	OWSLEY	762	388	286	88	102 R	50.9%	37.5%	57.6%	42.4%
14,877	PENDLETON	2,160	881	1,159	120	278 D	40.8%	53.7%	43.2%	56.8%
28,712	PERRY	4,480	2,006	2,092	382	86 D	44.8%	46.7%	49.0%	51.0%
65,024	PIKE	9,091	3,217	5,261	613	2,044 D	35.4%	57.9%	37.9%	62.1%
12,613	POWELL	3,062	792	1,712	558	920 D	25.9%	55.9%	31.6%	68.4%
63,063	PULASKI	12,118	6,274	4,825	1,019	1,449 R	51.8%	39.8%	56.5%	43.5%
2,282	ROBERTSON	432	135	229	68	94 D	31.2%	53.0%	37.1%	62.9%
17,056	ROCKCASTLE	2,820	1,506	948	366	558 R	53.4%	33.6%	61.4%	38.6%
23,333	ROWAN	3,782	1,028	2,308	446	1,280 D	27.2%	61.0%	30.8%	69.2%
17,565	RUSSELL	4,332	2,240	1,783	309	457 R	51.7%	41.2%	55.7%	44.3%
47,173	SCOTT	9,925	2,843	5,241	1,841	2,398 D	28.6%	52.8%	35.2%	64.8%
42,074	SHELBY	10,281	3,744	5,516	1,021	1,772 D	36.4%	53.7%	40.4%	59.6%
17,327	SIMPSON	2,393	994	1,325	74	331 D	41.5%	55.4%	42.9%	57.1%
17,061	SPENCER	4,060	1,646	2,093	321	447 D	40.5%	51.6%	44.0%	56.0%
24,512	TAYLOR	5,813	2,292	3,139	382	847 D	39.4%	54.0%	42.2%	57.8%
12,460	TODD	1,726	841	814	71	27 R	48.7%	47.2%	50.8%	49.2%
14,339	TRIGG	3,061	1,500	1,422	139	78 R	49.0%	46.5%	51.3%	48.7%
8,809	TRIMBLE	1,691	587	1,008	96	421 D	34.7%	59.6%	36.8%	63.2%
15,007	UNION	2,725	676	1,973	76	1,297 D	24.8%	72.4%	25.5%	74.5%
113,792	WARREN	19,725	8,107	10,676	942	2,569 D	41.1%	54.1%	43.2%	56.8%
11,717	WASHINGTON	2,856	965	1,607	284	642 D	33.8%	56.3%	37.5%	62.5%
20,813	WAYNE	3,634	1,740	1,710	184	30 R	47.9%	47.1%	50.4%	49.6%
13,621	WEBSTER	2,708	731	1,885	92	1,154 D	27.0%	69.6%	27.9%	72.1%
35,637	WHITLEY	6,930	3,535	2,921	474	614 R	51.0%	42.2%	54.8%	45.2%
7,355	WOLFE	1,324	348	780	196	432 D	26.3%	58.9%	30.9%	69.1%
24,939	WOODFORD	7,077	1,674	3,632	1,771	1,958 D	23.7%	51.3%	31.5%	68.5%
4,339,367	TOTAL	833,139	294,034	464,245	74,860	170,211 D	35.3%	55.7%	38.8%	61.2%

KENTUCKY

HOUSE OF REPRESENTATIVES

CD	Year	Total Vote	Republican Vote	Republican Candidate	Democratic Vote	Democratic Candidate	Other Vote	Rep.-Dem. Plurality	Total Vote Rep.	Total Vote Dem.	Major Vote Rep.	Major Vote Dem.
1	2012	287,155	199,956	WHITFIELD, ED*	87,199	HATCHETT, CHARLES KENDALL		112,757 R	69.6%	30.4%	69.6%	30.4%
2	2012	282,267	181,508	GUTHRIE, BRETT*	89,541	WILLIAMS, DAVID LYNN	11,218	91,967 R	64.3%	31.7%	67.0%	33.0%
3	2012	322,656	111,452	WICKER, BROOKS	206,385	YARMUTH, JOHN*	4,819	94,933 D	34.5%	64.0%	35.1%	64.9%
4	2012	299,444	186,036	MASSIE, THOMAS	104,734	ADKINS, WILLIAM R. "BILL"	8,674	81,302 R	62.1%	35.0%	64.0%	36.0%
5	2012	250,855	195,408	ROGERS, HAL*	55,447	STEPP, KENNETH		139,961 R	77.9%	22.1%	77.9%	22.1%
6	2012	303,000	153,222	BARR, ANDY	141,438	CHANDLER, ALBERT BENJAMIN "BEN"*	8,340	11,784 R	50.6%	46.7%	52.0%	48.0%
TOTAL	2012	1,745,377	1,027,582		684,744		33,051	342,838 R	58.9%	39.2%	60.0%	40.0%

Note: An asterisk (*) denotes incumbent.

KENTUCKY

GENERAL AND PRIMARY ELECTIONS

GENERAL ELECTIONS: OTHER VOTE

President Other vote was 17,063 Libertarian (Gary E. Johnson), 6,872 Independent (Randall Terry), 6,337 Green (Jill Stein), 245 Write-in (Virgil H. Goode), 135 Write-in (Scattered Write-In)

Governor (2011) 74,860 Independent (Gatewood Galbraith)

House Other vote was:

CD 2 6,304 Independent (Andrew R. Beacham), 4,914 Libertarian (Craig R. Astor)
CD 3 4,819 Independent (Bob DeVore)
CD 4 8,674 Independent (David Lewis)
CD 6 8,340 Independent (Randolph Vance)

PRIMARY ELECTIONS: SUPPLEMENTARY INFORMATION

Primary May 22, 2012 **Registration** 2,980,008 Democratic 1,646,927
May 17, 2011 (Governor) (as of May 22, 2012) Republican 1,122,447
Other 210,634

Primary Type Closed—Only registered Democrats and Republicans could vote in their party's primary.

REPUBLICAN PRIMARIES			DEMOCRATIC PRIMARIES		
President	Romney, W. Mitt	117,621	66.8%	Obama, Barack H.*	119,293	57.8%
	Paul, Ron	22,074	12.5%	Uncommitted	86,925	42.2%
	Santorum, Rick	15,629	8.9%			
	Gingrich, Newt	10,479	5.9%			
	Uncommitted	10,357	5.9%			
	TOTAL	176,160		TOTAL	206,218	
Governor (2011)	Williams, David L.	68,528	48.2%	Beshear, Steven L.*	Unopposed	
	Moffett, Phil	53,966	38.0%			
	Holsclaw, Barbara "Bobbie"	19,614	13.8%			
	TOTAL	142,108				
Congressional District 1	Whitfield, Ed*	Unopposed		Hatchett, Charles Kendall	19,127	59.1%
				Buckmaster, James	13,239	40.9%
				TOTAL	32,366	

KENTUCKY

GENERAL AND PRIMARY ELECTIONS

	REPUBLICAN PRIMARIES			DEMOCRATIC PRIMARIES		
Congressional District 2	Guthrie, Brett*	Unopposed		Williams, David Lynn	Unopposed	
Congressional District 3	Wicker, Brooks	Unopposed		Yarmuth, John*	43,635	86.7%
				Farnsley, Burrel Charles	6,716	13.3%
				TOTAL	*50,351*	
Congressional District 4	Massie, Thomas	19,689	44.8%	Adkins, William R. "Bill"	17,209	68.6%
	Webb-Edgington, Alecia	12,557	28.6%	Frank, Greg	7,869	31.4%
	Moore, Gary	6,521	14.8%			
	Schumm, Walter Christian	3,514	8.0%			
	Carey, Marc	783	1.8%			
	Wurtz, Tom	598	1.4%			
	Oerther, Brian D.	257	0.6%			
	TOTAL	*43,919*		*TOTAL*	*25,078*	
Congressional District 5	Rogers, Hal*	Unopposed		Stepp, Kenneth	12,275	52.7%
				Ackerman, Michael	11,016	47.3%
				TOTAL	*23,291*	
Congressional District 6	Barr, Andy	20,104	82.8%	Chandler, Albert Benjamin "Ben"*	Unopposed	
	Kelly, Patrick J. II	2,823	11.6%			
	Kenimer, Curtis	1,354	5.6%			
	TOTAL	*24,281*				

Notes: An asterisk (*) denotes incumbent. The names of unopposed candidates did not appear on the primary ballot; therefore, no votes were cast for these candidates.

LOUISIANA

Congressional districts first established for elections held in 2012

6 members

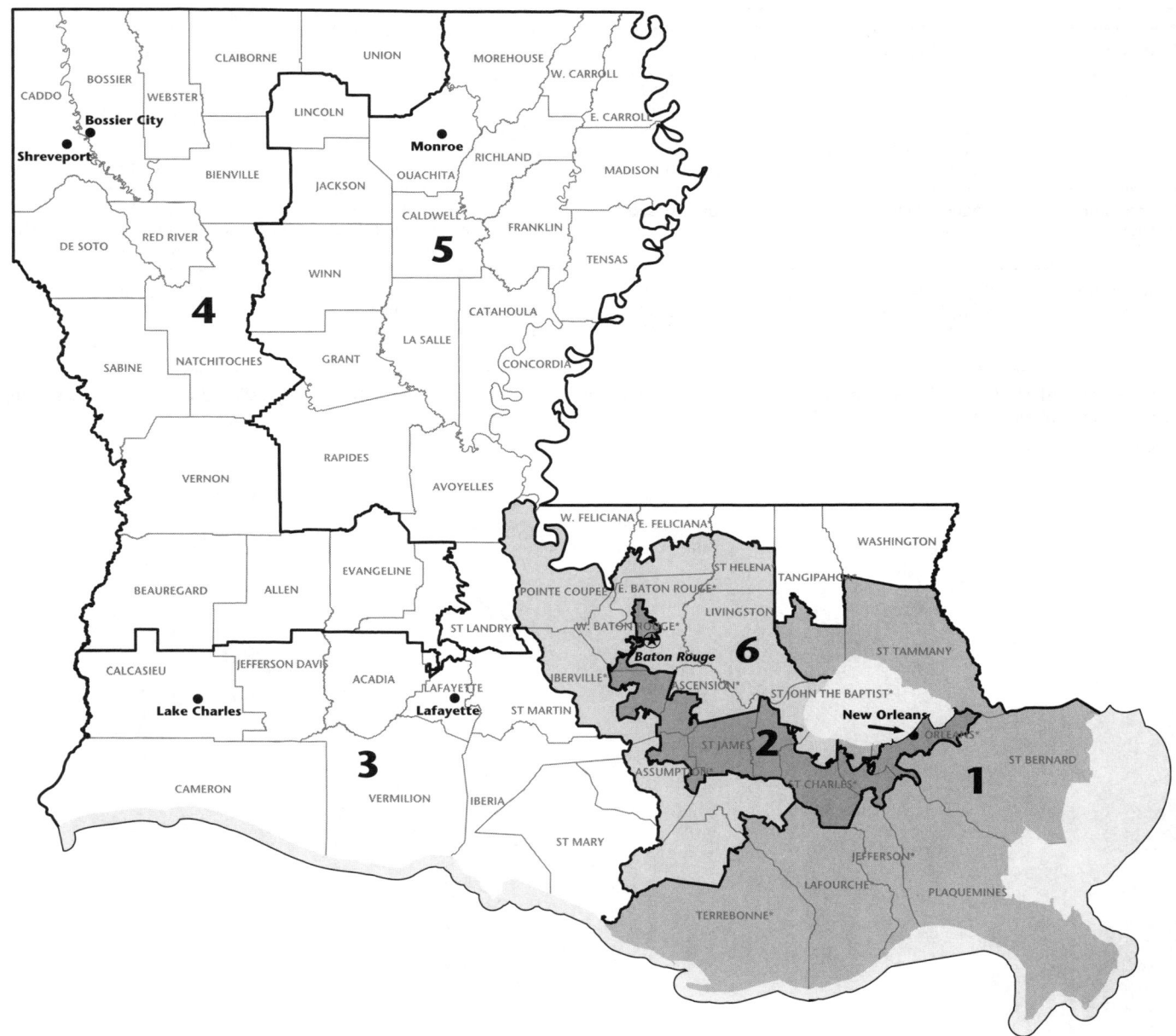

* Asterisk indicates a county whose boundaries include parts of two or more Congressional districts.

LOUISIANA

GOVERNOR
Bobby Jindal (R). Reelected 2011 to a four-year term. Previously elected 2007.

SENATORS (1 Republican, 1 Democrat)
Mary L. Landrieu (D). Reelected 2008 to a six-year term. Previously elected 2002, 1996.

David Vitter (R). Reelected 2010 to a six-year term. Previously elected 2004.

REPRESENTATIVES (5 Republicans, 1 Democrat)
1. Steve Scalise (R)
2. Cedric Richmond (D)
3. Charles W. Boustany Jr. (R)
4. John Fleming (R)
5. Rodney Alexander (R)
6. Bill Cassidy (R)

POSTWAR VOTE FOR PRESIDENT

| Year | Total Vote | Republican | | Democratic | | Other Vote | Rep.-Dem. Plurality | Percentage | | | |
| | | Vote | Candidate | Vote | Candidate | | | Total Vote | | Major Vote | |
								Rep.	Dem.	Rep.	Dem.
2012	1,994,065	1,152,262	Romney, W. Mitt	809,141	Obama, Barack H.*	32,662	343,121 R	57.8%	40.6%	58.7%	41.3%
2008	1,960,761	1,148,275	McCain, John S. III	782,989	Obama, Barack H.	29,497	365,286 R	58.6%	39.9%	59.5%	40.5%
2004	1,943,106	1,102,169	Bush, George W.*	820,299	Kerry, John F.	20,638	281,870 R	56.7%	42.2%	57.3%	42.7%
2000**	1,765,656	927,871	Bush, George W.	792,344	Gore, Albert Jr.	45,441	135,527 R	52.6%	44.9%	53.9%	46.1%
1996**	1,783,959	712,586	Dole, Robert "Bob"	927,837	Clinton, Bill*	143,536	215,251 D	39.9%	52.0%	43.4%	56.6%
1992**	1,790,017	733,386	Bush, George H.*	815,971	Clinton, Bill	240,660	82,585 D	41.0%	45.6%	47.3%	52.7%
1988	1,628,202	883,702	Bush, George H.	717,460	Dukakis, Michael S.	27,040	166,242 R	54.3%	44.1%	55.2%	44.8%
1984	1,706,822	1,037,299	Reagan, Ronald*	651,586	Mondale, Walter F.	17,937	385,713 R	60.8%	38.2%	61.4%	38.6%
1980**	1,548,591	792,853	Reagan, Ronald	708,453	Carter, Jimmy*	47,285	84,400 R	51.2%	45.7%	52.8%	47.2%
1976	1,278,539	587,446	Ford, Gerald R.*	661,365	Carter, Jimmy	29,728	73,919 D	45.9%	51.7%	47.0%	53.0%
1972	1,051,491	686,852	Nixon, Richard M.*	298,142	McGovern, George S.	66,497	388,710 R	65.3%	28.4%	69.7%	30.3%
1968**	1,097,450	257,535	Nixon, Richard M.	309,615	Humphrey, Hubert H. Jr.	530,300	52,080 D**	23.5%	28.2%	45.4%	54.6%
1964	896,293	509,225	Goldwater, Barry M. Sr.	387,068	Johnson, Lyndon B.*		122,157 R	56.8%	43.2%	56.8%	43.2%
1960**	807,891	230,980	Nixon, Richard M.	407,339	Kennedy, John F.	169,572	176,359 D	28.6%	50.4%	36.2%	63.8%
1956	617,544	329,047	Eisenhower, Dwight D.*	243,977	Stevenson, Adlai E. II	44,520	85,070 R	53.3%	39.5%	57.4%	42.6%
1952	651,952	306,925	Eisenhower, Dwight D.	345,027	Stevenson, Adlai E. II		38,102 D	47.1%	52.9%	47.1%	52.9%
1948**	416,336	72,657	Dewey, Thomas E.	136,344	Truman, Harry S.*	207,335	63,687 D**	17.5%	32.7%	34.8%	65.2%

Note: An asterisk (*) denotes incumbent. **In past elections, the other vote included: 2000 - 20,473 Green (Ralph Nader); 1996 - 123,293 Reform (Ross Perot); 1992 - 211,478 Independent (Perot); 1980 - 26,345 Independent (John Anderson); 1968 - 530,300 American Independent (George Wallace); 1960 - 169,572 Unpledged Independent Electors; 1948 - 204,290 States' Rights (Strom Thurmond). Wallace carried Louisiana in 1968 with 48.3 percent of the vote. Thurmond won the state in 1948 with 49.1 percent.

LOUISIANA

POSTWAR VOTE FOR GOVERNOR

Year	Total Vote	Republican Vote	Republican Candidate	Democratic Vote	Democratic Candidate	Other Vote	Rep.-Dem. Plurality	Total Vote Rep.	Total Vote Dem.	Major Vote Rep.	Major Vote Dem.
2011	1,023,163	673,239	Jindal, Bobby*	182,925	Hollis, Tara	166,999	490,314 R	65.8%	17.9%	78.6%	21.4%
2007**	1,297,840	699,275	Jindal, Bobby	226,476	Boasso, Walter J.	372,089	472,799 R	53.9%	17.5%	75.5%	24.5%
2003**	1,407,842	676,484	Jindal, Bobby	731,358	Kathleen, Babineaux		54,874 D	48.1%	51.9%	48.1%	51.9%
1999	1,295,205	805,203	Foster, Mike*	382,445	Jefferson, William J.	107,557	422,758 R	62.2%	29.5%	67.8%	32.2%
1995**	1,550,360	984,499	Foster, Mike	565,861	Fields, Cleo		418,638 R	63.5%	36.5%	63.5%	36.5%
1991**	1,728,040	671,009	Duke, David E.	1,057,031	Edwards, Edwin W.		386,022 D	38.8%	61.2%	38.8%	61.2%
1987**	1,558,730	287,780	Livingston, Bob	516,078	Roemer, Charles	754,872	228,298 D	18.5%	33.1%	35.8%	64.2%
1983	1,615,905	588,508	Treen, David Conner*	1,006,561	Edwards, Edwin W.	20,836	418,053 D	36.4%	62.3%	36.9%	63.1%
1979**	1,371,825	690,691	Treen, David Conner	681,134	Lambert, Louis		9,557 R	50.3%	49.7%	50.3%	49.7%
1975	430,095			430,095	Edwards, Edwin W.*		430,095 D		100.0%		100.0%
1972	1,121,570	480,424	Treen, David Conner	641,146	Edwards, Edwin W.		160,722 D	42.8%	57.2%	42.8%	57.2%
1968	372,762			372,762	McKeithen, John J.*		372,762 D		100.0%		100.0%
1964	773,390	297,753	Lyons, Charlton H. Sr.	469,589	McKeithen, John J.	6,048	171,836 D	38.5%	60.7%	38.8%	61.2%
1960	506,562	86,135	Grevemberg, F. C.	407,907	Davis, Jimmie H.	12,520	321,772 D	17.0%	80.5%	17.4%	82.6%
1956	172,291			172,291	Long, Earl K.		172,291 D		100.0%		100.0%
1952	118,723			118,723	Kennon, Robert F.		118,723 D		100.0%		100.0%
1948	76,566			76,566	Long, Earl K.		76,566 D		100.0%		100.0%

Note: An asterisk (*) denotes incumbent. **Since the 1970s, Louisiana has had a two-tier election system for governor in which all candidates, regardless of party, run together in an open election. A candidate who wins a majority of the vote is elected. If no candidate receives 50 percent, a runoff is held between the top two finishers. The results of the runoff are listed in this chart for 1979, 1991, 1995, and 2003. In elections that did not require a runoff, the leading Democratic and Republican candidates are listed with their votes from the first-round, open election. The votes for other candidates are listed in the "Other Vote" column, regardless of whether they were Democratic, Republican, or independent. In past elections, the other vote included: 2007 - 186,682 No Party (John Georges), 161,665 Democrat (Foster Campbell); 1987 - 437,801 Democrat (Edwin W. Edwards). In 1987, Edwards withdrew after finishing second in the initial round of voting. Democrat Charles Roemer finished first with 33.1 percent and with Edwards's withdrawal, no runoff was held. The major party vote percentages are calculated for the top vote-getter for each party only; it does not include additional members of the same party. The Republican Party did not run a candidate in the 1948, 1952, 1956, 1968, and 1975 gubernatorial elections.

POSTWAR VOTE FOR SENATOR

Year	Total Vote	Republican Vote	Republican Candidate	Democratic Vote	Democratic Candidate	Other Vote	Rep.-Dem. Plurality	Total Vote Rep.	Total Vote Dem.	Major Vote Rep.	Major Vote Dem.
2010	1,264,994	715,415	Vitter, David*	476,572	Melancon, Charlie R.	73,007	238,843 R	56.6%	37.7%	60.0%	40.0%
2008	1,896,574	867,177	Kennedy, John	988,298	Landrieu, Mary L.*	41,099	121,121 D	45.7%	52.1%	46.7%	53.3%
2004**	1,848,056	943,014	Vitter, David	542,150	John, Chris	362,892	400,864 R	51.0%	29.3%	63.5%	36.5%
2002	1,235,296	596,642	Terrell, Suzanne Haik	638,654	Landrieu, Mary L.*		42,012 D	48.3%	51.7%	48.3%	51.7%
1998	969,165	306,616	Donelon, Jim	620,502	Breaux, John B.*	42,047	313,886 D	31.6%	64.0%	33.1%	66.9%
1996**	1,700,102	847,157	Jenkins, Louis	852,945	Landrieu, Mary L.		5,788 D	49.8%	50.2%	49.8%	50.2%
1992	843,037	69,986	Stockstill, Lyle	616,021	Breaux, John B.*	157,030	546,035 D	8.3%	73.1%	10.2%	89.8%
1990	1,396,113	607,391	Duke, David E.	752,902	Johnston, J. Bennett*	35,820	145,511 D	43.5%	53.9%	44.7%	55.3%
1986**	1,369,897	646,311	Moore, W. Henson	723,586	Breaux, John B.		77,275 D	47.2%	52.8%	47.2%	52.8%
1984	977,473	86,546	Ross, Robert M.	838,181	Johnston, J. Bennett*	52,746	751,635 D	8.9%	85.7%	9.4%	90.6%
1980**	843,362	13,739	Bardwell, Jerry C.	484,770	Long, Russell B.*	342,504	471,031 D		57.5%		100.0%
1978**	839,669			498,773	Johnston, J. Bennett*	340,896	498,773 D		59.4%		100.0%
1974	434,643			434,643	Long, Russell B.*		434,643 D	1.6%	57.6%	2.8%	97.2%
1972**	1,084,904	206,846	Toledano, Ben C.	598,987	Johnston, J. Bennett	279,071	392,141 D	19.1%	55.2%	25.7%	74.3%
1968	518,586			518,586	Long, Russell B.*		518,586 D		100.0%		100.0%
1966	437,695			437,695	Ellender, Allen J.*		437,695 D		100.0%		100.0%
1962	421,904	103,066	O'Hearn, Taylor Walters	318,838	Long, Russell B.*		215,772 D	24.4%	75.6%	24.4%	75.6%
1960	541,928	109,698	Reese, George W.	432,228	Ellender, Allen J.*	2	322,530 D	20.2%	79.8%	20.2%	79.8%
1956	335,564			335,564	Long, Russell B.*		335,564 D		100.0%		100.0%
1954	207,115			207,115	Ellender, Allen J.*		207,115 D		100.0%		100.0%
1950	251,838	30,931	Gerth, Charles S.	220,907	Long, Russell B.*		189,976 D	12.3%	87.7%	12.3%	87.7%
1948	330,324			330,315	Ellender, Allen J.	9	330,315 D		100.0%		100.0%
1948S	407,685	102,339	Clarke, Clem S.	305,346	Long, Russell B.		203,007 D	25.1%	74.9%	25.1%	74.9%

Note: An asterisk (*) denotes incumbent. **In 2008 and 2010, Louisiana used the more typical system of party primaries followed by a general election to fill seats in Congress. From 1978 through 2004, Senate seats were decided in open elections in which candidates of all parties ran together on the same ballot. If no candidate won a majority of the vote in the first round, a runoff was held between the top two vote-getters, regardless of party. The Senate elections in 1986, 1996, and 2002 were decided by a run-off, with the results of the runoff listed in this chart. In elections that did not require a runoff, the leading Democratic and Republican candidates are listed with their votes in the first-round, open election. The votes for other candidates are listed in the "Other Vote" column, regardless of whether they were Democratic, Republican, or independent. In past elections, the other vote included: 2004 - 275,821 Democrat (John Kennedy); 1980 - 325,922 Democrat (Louis Jenkins), who finished second; 1978 - 340,896 Democrat (Louis Jenkins), who finished second; 1972 - 250,161 Independent (John J. McKeithen), who finished second. One of the 1948 elections was for a short term to fill a vacancy. The major party vote percentages are calculated for the top vote-getter for each party only; it does not include additional members of the same party. The Republican Party did not run a candidate in Senate elections in 1948, 1954, 1956, 1966, 1968, 1974, and 1978.

LOUISIANA

PRESIDENT 2012

2010 Census Population	Parish	Total Vote	Republican (Romney)	Democratic (Obama)	Other	Rep.-Dem. Plurality	Percentage Total Vote Rep.	Dem.	Major Vote Rep.	Dem.
61,773	ACADIA	26,835	19,931	6,560	344	13,371 R	74.3%	24.4%	75.2%	24.8%
25,764	ALLEN	9,307	6,495	2,617	195	3,878 R	69.8%	28.1%	71.3%	28.7%
107,215	ASCENSION	51,073	33,856	16,349	868	17,507 R	66.3%	32.0%	67.4%	32.6%
23,421	ASSUMPTION	10,992	6,083	4,754	155	1,329 R	55.3%	43.2%	56.1%	43.9%
42,073	AVOYELLES	17,032	10,670	6,077	285	4,593 R	62.6%	35.7%	63.7%	36.3%
35,654	BEAUREGARD	14,225	11,112	2,828	285	8,284 R	78.1%	19.9%	79.7%	20.3%
14,353	BIENVILLE	7,203	3,641	3,490	72	151 R	50.5%	48.5%	51.1%	48.9%
116,979	BOSSIER	48,562	34,988	12,956	618	22,032 R	72.0%	26.7%	73.0%	27.0%
254,969	CADDO	111,765	52,459	58,042	1,264	5,583 D	46.9%	51.9%	47.5%	52.5%
192,768	CALCASIEU	81,726	51,850	28,359	1,517	23,491 R	63.4%	34.7%	64.6%	35.4%
10,132	CALDWELL	4,716	3,640	1,016	60	2,624 R	77.2%	21.5%	78.2%	21.8%
6,839	CAMERON	3,744	3,260	408	76	2,852 R	87.1%	10.9%	88.9%	11.1%
10,407	CATAHOULA	4,193	2,744	1,408	41	1,336 R	65.4%	33.6%	66.1%	33.9%
17,195	CLAIBORNE	6,732	3,649	3,014	69	635 R	54.2%	44.8%	54.8%	45.2%
20,822	CONCORDIA	9,380	5,450	3,833	97	1,617 R	58.1%	40.9%	58.7%	41.3%
26,656	DE SOTO	13,051	7,353	5,553	145	1,800 R	56.3%	42.5%	57.0%	43.0%
440,171	EAST BATON ROUGE	198,171	92,292	102,656	3,223	10,364 D	46.6%	51.8%	47.3%	52.7%
7,759	EAST CARROLL	4,008	1,508	2,478	22	970 D	37.6%	61.8%	37.8%	62.2%
20,267	EAST FELICIANA	10,209	5,397	4,648	164	749 R	52.9%	45.5%	53.7%	46.3%
33,984	EVANGELINE	15,770	10,181	5,330	259	4,851 R	64.6%	33.8%	65.6%	34.4%
20,767	FRANKLIN	9,336	6,294	2,921	121	3,373 R	67.4%	31.3%	68.3%	31.7%
22,309	GRANT	8,667	7,082	1,422	163	5,660 R	81.7%	16.4%	83.3%	16.7%
73,240	IBERIA	33,397	20,892	12,132	373	8,760 R	62.6%	36.3%	63.3%	36.7%
33,387	IBERVILLE	17,014	7,271	9,548	195	2,277 D	42.7%	56.1%	43.2%	56.8%
16,274	JACKSON	7,529	5,132	2,305	92	2,827 R	68.2%	30.6%	69.0%	31.0%
432,552	JEFFERSON	176,343	102,536	70,384	3,423	32,152 R	58.1%	39.9%	59.3%	40.7%
31,594	JEFFERSON DAVIS	13,734	10,014	3,484	236	6,530 R	72.9%	25.4%	74.2%	25.8%
14,890	LA SALLE	6,572	5,726	764	82	4,962 R	87.1%	11.6%	88.2%	11.8%
221,578	LAFAYETTE	98,642	64,992	31,768	1,882	33,224 R	65.9%	32.2%	67.2%	32.8%
96,318	LAFOURCHE	39,075	28,592	9,623	860	18,969 R	73.2%	24.6%	74.8%	25.2%
46,735	LINCOLN	18,993	10,739	7,956	298	2,783 R	56.5%	41.9%	57.4%	42.6%
128,026	LIVINGSTON	54,062	45,513	7,451	1,098	38,062 R	84.2%	13.8%	85.9%	14.1%
12,093	MADISON	5,187	2,000	3,154	33	1,154 D	38.6%	60.8%	38.8%	61.2%
27,979	MOREHOUSE	12,614	6,591	5,888	135	703 R	52.3%	46.7%	52.8%	47.2%
39,566	NATCHITOCHES	17,258	9,077	7,942	239	1,135 R	52.6%	46.0%	53.3%	46.7%
343,829	ORLEANS	157,813	28,003	126,722	3,088	98,719 D	17.7%	80.3%	18.1%	81.9%
153,720	OUACHITA	68,474	40,948	26,645	881	14,303 R	59.8%	38.9%	60.6%	39.4%
23,042	PLAQUEMINES	10,239	6,471	3,599	169	2,872 R	63.2%	35.1%	64.3%	35.7%
22,802	POINTE COUPEE	12,147	6,548	5,436	163	1,112 R	53.9%	44.8%	54.6%	45.4%
131,613	RAPIDES	58,019	37,193	20,045	781	17,148 R	64.1%	34.5%	65.0%	35.0%
9,091	RED RIVER	4,807	2,483	2,253	71	230 R	51.7%	46.9%	52.4%	47.6%
20,725	RICHLAND	9,329	5,846	3,387	96	2,459 R	62.7%	36.3%	63.3%	36.7%
24,233	SABINE	10,053	7,738	2,194	121	5,544 R	77.0%	21.8%	77.9%	22.1%
35,897	ST. BERNARD	13,955	8,501	5,059	395	3,442 R	60.9%	36.3%	62.7%	37.3%
52,780	ST. CHARLES	25,333	15,937	8,896	500	7,041 R	62.9%	35.1%	64.2%	35.8%
11,203	ST. HELENA	6,394	2,529	3,780	85	1,251 D	39.6%	59.1%	40.1%	59.9%
22,102	ST. JAMES	12,395	5,209	7,059	127	1,850 D	42.0%	57.0%	42.5%	57.5%
45,924	ST. JOHN THE BAPTIST	21,123	7,620	13,179	324	5,559 D	36.1%	62.4%	36.6%	63.4%
83,384	ST. LANDRY	41,647	21,475	19,668	504	1,807 R	51.6%	47.2%	52.2%	47.8%
52,160	ST. MARTIN	25,433	15,653	9,422	358	6,231 R	61.5%	37.0%	62.4%	37.6%
54,650	ST. MARY	23,640	13,885	9,450	305	4,435 R	58.7%	40.0%	59.5%	40.5%
233,740	ST. TAMMANY	112,902	84,723	25,728	2,451	58,995 R	75.0%	22.8%	76.7%	23.3%
121,097	TANGIPAHOA	50,099	31,590	17,722	787	13,868 R	63.1%	35.4%	64.1%	35.9%
5,252	TENSAS	2,812	1,230	1,564	18	334 D	43.7%	55.6%	44.0%	56.0%
111,860	TERREBONNE	42,341	29,503	12,074	764	17,429 R	69.7%	28.5%	71.0%	29.0%
22,721	UNION	10,766	7,561	3,075	130	4,486 R	70.2%	28.6%	71.1%	28.9%
57,999	VERMILION	24,987	18,910	5,720	357	13,190 R	75.7%	22.9%	76.8%	23.2%
52,334	VERNON	15,610	12,150	3,173	287	8,977 R	77.8%	20.3%	79.3%	20.7%
47,168	WASHINGTON	18,581	11,798	6,466	317	5,332 R	63.5%	34.8%	64.6%	35.4%
41,207	WEBSTER	18,416	11,400	6,802	214	4,598 R	61.9%	36.9%	62.6%	37.4%

LOUISIANA

PRESIDENT 2012

2010 Census Population	Parish	Total Vote	Republican (Romney)	Democratic (Obama)	Other	Rep.-Dem. Plurality	Percentage Total Vote Rep.	Dem.	Major Vote Rep.	Dem.
23,788	WEST BATON ROUGE	12,774	6,922	5,692	160	1,230 R	54.2%	44.6%	54.9%	45.1%
11,604	WEST CARROLL	4,548	3,628	853	67	2,775 R	79.8%	18.8%	81.0%	19.0%
15,625	WEST FELICIANA	5,777	3,257	2,441	79	816 R	56.4%	42.3%	57.2%	42.8%
15,313	WINN	6,534	4,541	1,919	74	2,622 R	69.5%	29.4%	70.3%	29.7%
4,533,372	TOTAL	1,994,065	1,152,262	809,141	32,662	343,121 R	57.8%	40.6%	58.7%	41.3%

LOUISIANA

GOVERNOR 2011

2010 Census Population	Parish	Total Vote	Republican (Jindal)	Democratic (Hollis)	Other	Rep.-Dem. Plurality	Percentage Total Vote Rep.	Dem.	Major Vote Rep.	Dem.
61,773	ACADIA	15,560	11,727	1,719	2,114	10,008 R	75.4%	11.0%	87.2%	12.8%
25,764	ALLEN	7,170	4,892	875	1,403	4,017 R	68.2%	12.2%	84.8%	15.2%
107,215	ASCENSION	24,052	16,431	4,256	3,365	12,175 R	68.3%	17.7%	79.4%	20.6%
23,421	ASSUMPTION	8,015	5,045	1,540	1,430	3,505 R	62.9%	19.2%	76.6%	23.4%
42,073	AVOYELLES	12,449	5,363	4,744	2,342	619 R	43.1%	38.1%	53.1%	46.9%
35,654	BEAUREGARD	8,449	6,403	895	1,151	5,508 R	75.8%	10.6%	87.7%	12.3%
14,353	BIENVILLE	3,717	1,983	809	925	1,174 R	53.3%	21.8%	71.0%	29.0%
116,979	BOSSIER	20,962	16,411	2,273	2,278	14,138 R	78.3%	10.8%	87.8%	12.2%
254,969	CADDO	48,639	26,296	13,207	9,136	13,089 R	54.1%	27.2%	66.6%	33.4%
192,768	CALCASIEU	34,980	24,367	4,371	6,242	19,996 R	69.7%	12.5%	84.8%	15.2%
10,132	CALDWELL	3,815	2,413	700	702	1,713 R	63.3%	18.3%	77.5%	22.5%
6,839	CAMERON	3,116	2,523	280	313	2,243 R	81.0%	9.0%	90.0%	10.0%
10,407	CATAHOULA	3,705	2,509	623	573	1,886 R	67.7%	16.8%	80.1%	19.9%
17,195	CLAIBORNE	4,225	2,346	1,270	609	1,076 R	55.5%	30.1%	64.9%	35.1%
20,822	CONCORDIA	6,380	4,565	760	1,055	3,805 R	71.6%	11.9%	85.7%	14.3%
26,656	DE SOTO	6,954	4,171	1,255	1,528	2,916 R	60.0%	18.0%	76.9%	23.1%
440,171	EAST BATON ROUGE	85,786	43,707	27,431	14,648	16,276 R	50.9%	32.0%	61.4%	38.6%
7,759	EAST CARROLL	3,215	1,433	635	1,147	798 R	44.6%	19.8%	69.3%	30.7%
20,267	EAST FELICIANA	6,832	3,361	2,162	1,309	1,199 R	49.2%	31.6%	60.9%	39.1%
33,984	EVANGELINE	10,903	7,056	1,519	2,328	5,537 R	64.7%	13.9%	82.3%	17.7%
20,767	FRANKLIN	7,051	5,068	900	1,083	4,168 R	71.9%	12.8%	84.9%	15.1%
22,309	GRANT	6,432	4,411	1,113	908	3,298 R	68.6%	17.3%	79.9%	20.1%
73,240	IBERIA	17,585	12,705	2,166	2,714	10,539 R	72.2%	12.3%	85.4%	14.6%
33,387	IBERVILLE	13,226	6,939	3,267	3,020	3,672 R	52.5%	24.7%	68.0%	32.0%
16,274	JACKSON	4,365	2,920	874	571	2,046 R	66.9%	20.0%	77.0%	23.0%
432,552	JEFFERSON	76,715	58,579	7,418	10,718	51,161 R	76.4%	9.7%	88.8%	11.2%
31,594	JEFFERSON DAVIS	9,515	7,274	1,017	1,224	6,257 R	76.4%	10.7%	87.7%	12.3%
14,890	LA SALLE	5,426	4,229	488	709	3,741 R	77.9%	9.0%	89.7%	10.3%
221,578	LAFAYETTE	46,064	32,507	7,967	5,590	24,540 R	70.6%	17.3%	80.3%	19.7%
96,318	LAFOURCHE	21,028	16,470	2,151	2,407	14,319 R	78.3%	10.2%	88.4%	11.6%
46,735	LINCOLN	8,931	5,665	1,895	1,371	3,770 R	63.4%	21.2%	74.9%	25.1%
128,026	LIVINGSTON	33,697	25,897	4,245	3,555	21,652 R	76.9%	12.6%	85.9%	14.1%
12,093	MADISON	3,158	1,630	575	953	1,055 R	51.6%	18.2%	73.9%	26.1%
27,979	MOREHOUSE	4,850	3,232	849	769	2,383 R	66.6%	17.5%	79.2%	20.8%
39,566	NATCHITOCHES	11,877	6,599	2,876	2,402	3,723 R	55.6%	24.2%	69.6%	30.4%
343,829	ORLEANS	49,987	18,794	15,525	15,668	3,269 R	37.6%	31.1%	54.8%	45.2%
153,720	OUACHITA	33,771	23,551	5,949	4,271	17,602 R	69.7%	17.6%	79.8%	20.2%
23,042	PLAQUEMINES	8,096	6,383	476	1,237	5,907 R	78.8%	5.9%	93.1%	6.9%
22,802	POINTE COUPEE	6,823	3,796	1,682	1,345	2,114 R	55.6%	24.7%	69.3%	30.7%
131,613	RAPIDES	37,481	22,871	9,126	5,484	13,745 R	61.0%	24.3%	71.5%	28.5%

LOUISIANA

GOVERNOR 2011

2010 Census Population	Parish	Total Vote	Republican (Jindal)	Democratic (Hollis)	Other	Rep.-Dem. Plurality	Percentage Total Vote Rep.	Dem.	Major Vote Rep.	Dem.
9,091	RED RIVER	4,004	2,396	649	959	1,747 R	59.8%	16.2%	78.7%	21.3%
20,725	RICHLAND	6,682	4,586	986	1,110	3,600 R	68.6%	14.8%	82.3%	17.7%
24,233	SABINE	6,778	4,941	761	1,076	4,180 R	72.9%	11.2%	86.7%	13.3%
35,897	ST. BERNARD	12,451	9,960	796	1,695	9,164 R	80.0%	6.4%	92.6%	7.4%
52,780	ST. CHARLES	15,435	11,313	1,789	2,333	9,524 R	73.3%	11.6%	86.3%	13.7%
11,203	ST. HELENA	4,903	1,976	1,478	1,449	498 R	40.3%	30.1%	57.2%	42.8%
22,102	ST. JAMES	9,184	4,983	2,091	2,110	2,892 R	54.3%	22.8%	70.4%	29.6%
45,924	ST. JOHN THE BAPTIST	14,237	7,702	2,611	3,924	5,091 R	54.1%	18.3%	74.7%	25.3%
83,384	ST. LANDRY	21,389	12,871	4,059	4,459	8,812 R	60.2%	19.0%	76.0%	24.0%
52,160	ST. MARTIN	14,159	10,032	1,952	2,175	8,080 R	70.9%	13.8%	83.7%	16.3%
54,650	ST. MARY	14,645	9,792	2,343	2,510	7,449 R	66.9%	16.0%	80.7%	19.3%
233,740	ST. TAMMANY	46,307	38,716	3,552	4,039	35,164 R	83.6%	7.7%	91.6%	8.4%
121,097	TANGIPAHOA	27,615	19,164	3,484	4,967	15,680 R	69.4%	12.6%	84.6%	15.4%
5,252	TENSAS	2,338	1,300	272	766	1,028 R	55.6%	11.6%	82.7%	17.3%
111,860	TERREBONNE	24,119	19,754	2,204	2,161	17,550 R	81.9%	9.1%	90.0%	10.0%
22,721	UNION	6,708	5,013	1,078	617	3,935 R	74.7%	16.1%	82.3%	17.7%
57,999	VERMILION	14,781	11,236	1,816	1,729	9,420 R	76.0%	12.3%	86.1%	13.9%
52,334	VERNON	9,525	7,298	1,123	1,104	6,175 R	76.6%	11.8%	86.7%	13.3%
47,168	WASHINGTON	12,651	8,706	1,578	2,367	7,128 R	68.8%	12.5%	84.7%	15.3%
41,207	WEBSTER	9,133	5,887	1,914	1,332	3,973 R	64.5%	21.0%	75.5%	24.5%
23,788	WEST BATON ROUGE	8,286	4,783	1,978	1,525	2,805 R	57.7%	23.9%	70.7%	29.3%
11,604	WEST CARROLL	3,571	2,842	400	329	2,442 R	79.6%	11.2%	87.7%	12.3%
15,625	WEST FELICIANA	4,167	2,084	1,412	671	672 R	50.0%	33.9%	59.6%	40.4%
15,313	WINN	5,093	3,382	716	995	2,666 R	66.4%	14.1%	82.5%	17.5%
4,533,372	TOTAL	1,023,163	673,239	182,925	166,999	490,314 R	65.8%	17.9%	78.6%	21.4%

Note: Parishes are equivalent to counties. Louisiana has a unique two-tier electoral system for governor that features candidates from all parties running together on the same ballot. A candidate who wins the majority of the vote in the first round is elected, which was the case in 2011; otherwise, the top two finishers would meet in a run-off. "Total Vote" refers to the percentage of total votes garnered by the top two vote-getters, Bobby Jindal (Rep.) and Tara Hollis (Dem.). "Major Vote" shows the percentage of votes between those two candidates only—it does not include other Democratic candidates.

LOUISIANA

HOUSE OF REPRESENTATIVES

CD	Year	Total Vote	Republican Vote	Candidate	Democratic Vote	Candidate	Other Vote	Rep.-Dem. Plurality	Percentage Total Vote Rep.	Dem.	Major Vote Rep.	Dem.
1	2012	290,410	193,496	SCALISE, STEVE*	61,703	MENDOZA, M.V. VINNY	35,211	131,793 R	66.6%	21.2%	75.8%	24.2%
2	2012	287,354	38,801	BAILEY, DWAYNE	158,501	RICHMOND, CEDRIC*	90,052	119,700 D	13.5%	55.2%	19.7%	80.3%
3	2012	311,393	139,123	BOUSTANY, CHARLES W. JR.*	67,070	RICHARD, RON	105,200	72,053 R	44.7%	21.5%	67.5%	32.5%
4	2012	249,531	187,894	FLEMING, JOHN*			61,637	187,894 R	75.3%		100.0%	
5	2012	260,216	202,536	ALEXANDER, RODNEY*			57,680	202,536 R	77.8%		100.0%	
6	2012	306,713	243,553	CASSIDY, BILL*			63,160	243,553 R	79.4%		100.0%	
TOTAL	2012	1,705,617	1,005,403		287,274		412,940	718,129 R	58.9%	16.8%	77.8%	22.2%

Note: An asterisk (*) denotes incumbent. Louisiana has a unique two-tier electoral system for House seats, with a first round of voting that featured candidates from all parties running together on the same ballot. A candidate who won a majority of the vote in the first round was elected. Otherwise, the top two finishers require a runoff. The 3rd district required a runoff on December 8, 2012. Republican Charles W. Boustany Jr. (58,820 votes) defeated Jeff Landry (37,767 votes), or 60.9 percent of the vote to 39.1 percent. In the first round, Landry received 93,527 votes (30.0 percent of the total vote). The votes shown in the table above are for the first round of voting, which did not produce a 50% majority for Boustany. Both candidates were incumbents (Boustany, former 7th district, and Landry, former 3rd district). The votes for other candidates are listed in the "Other Vote," column regardless of whether they were Democratic, Republican, or unaffiliated with either major party. The major vote and total vote percentages are calculated only for the top candidate for each party in the district.

LOUISIANA

GENERAL AND PRIMARY ELECTIONS

GENERAL ELECTIONS: OTHER VOTE

President	Other vote was 18,157 Libertarian (Gary E. Johnson), 6,978 Green (Jill Stein), 2,508 Constitution (Virgil H. Goode), 1,767 We the People (Sheila "Samm" Tittle), 1,368 Justice (Ross C. "Rocky" Anderson), 622 Socialism and Liberation (Peta Lindsay), 518 Prohibition (Jack Fellure), 389 Socialist Workers Party (James Harris), 355 Socialist Equality (Jerry White)
Governor (2011)	Other vote was 50,071 Democrat (Cary Deaton), 33,280 Democrat (Ivo Roberts), 26,705 No Party (David Blanchard), 21,885 Democrat (Niki Bird Papazoglakis), 12,528 Libertarian (Scott Lewis), 9,109 No Party (William Robert Lang Jr.), 8,179 No Party (Ron Caesar), 5,242 No Party (Leonard "Lenny" Bollingham)
House	Other vote was:
CD 1	24,844 Republican (Gary King), 6,079 No Party (David "Turk" Turknett), 4,288 No Party (Arden Wells)
CD 2	71,916 Democrat (Gary Landrieu), 11,345 Republican (Josue Larose), 6,791 Libertarian (Caleb Trotter)
CD 3	93,527 Republican (Jeff Landry), 7,908 Republican (Bryan Barrilleaux), 3,765 Libertarian (Jim Stark)
CD 4	61,637 Libertarian (Randall Lord)
CD 5	37,486 No Party (Ron Ceasar), 20,194 Libertarian (Clay Steven Grant)
CD 6	32,185 Libertarian (Rufus Holt Craig), 30,975 No Party (Richard Torregano)

PRIMARY ELECTIONS: SUPPLEMENTARY INFORMATION

Primary	March 24, 2012 (President) November 6, 2012 (Congress)	**Registration** (as of March 1, 2012)	2,862,351	Democratic Republican Other Parties	1,402,791 776,567 682,993

Primary Type For governor and other federal offices, Louisiana has a two-tier electoral system open to all voters, with a first round of voting (sometimes called an open or "jungle" primary) that features candidates from all parties running together on the same ballot. A candidate who wins a majority of the vote in the first round is elected. Otherwise, there is a runoff held several weeks later between the top two finishers. A runoff was necessary in the Louisiana 3rd District in 2012.

	REPUBLICAN PRIMARIES			DEMOCRATIC PRIMARIES		
President	Santorum, Rick	91,321	49.0%	Obama, Barack H.*	115,150	76.5%
	Romney, W. Mitt	49,758	26.7%	Wolfe, John	17,804	11.8%
	Gingrich, Newt	29,656	15.9%	Ely, Bob	9,897	6.6%
	Paul, Ron	11,467	6.2%	Richardson, Darcy	7,750	5.1%
	Roemer, Charles	2,203	1.2%			
	Perry, Rick	955	0.5%			
	Bachmann, Michele	622	0.3%			
	Huntsman, Jon Jr.	242	0.1%			
	Crow, Randy	186	0.1%			
	TOTAL	*186,410*		*TOTAL*	*150,601*	

Note: An asterisk (*) denotes incumbent. Louisiana has a unique primary system whose votes are not listed here; see the Note under the House of Representatives.

MAINE

Congressional districts first established for elections held in 2012

2 members

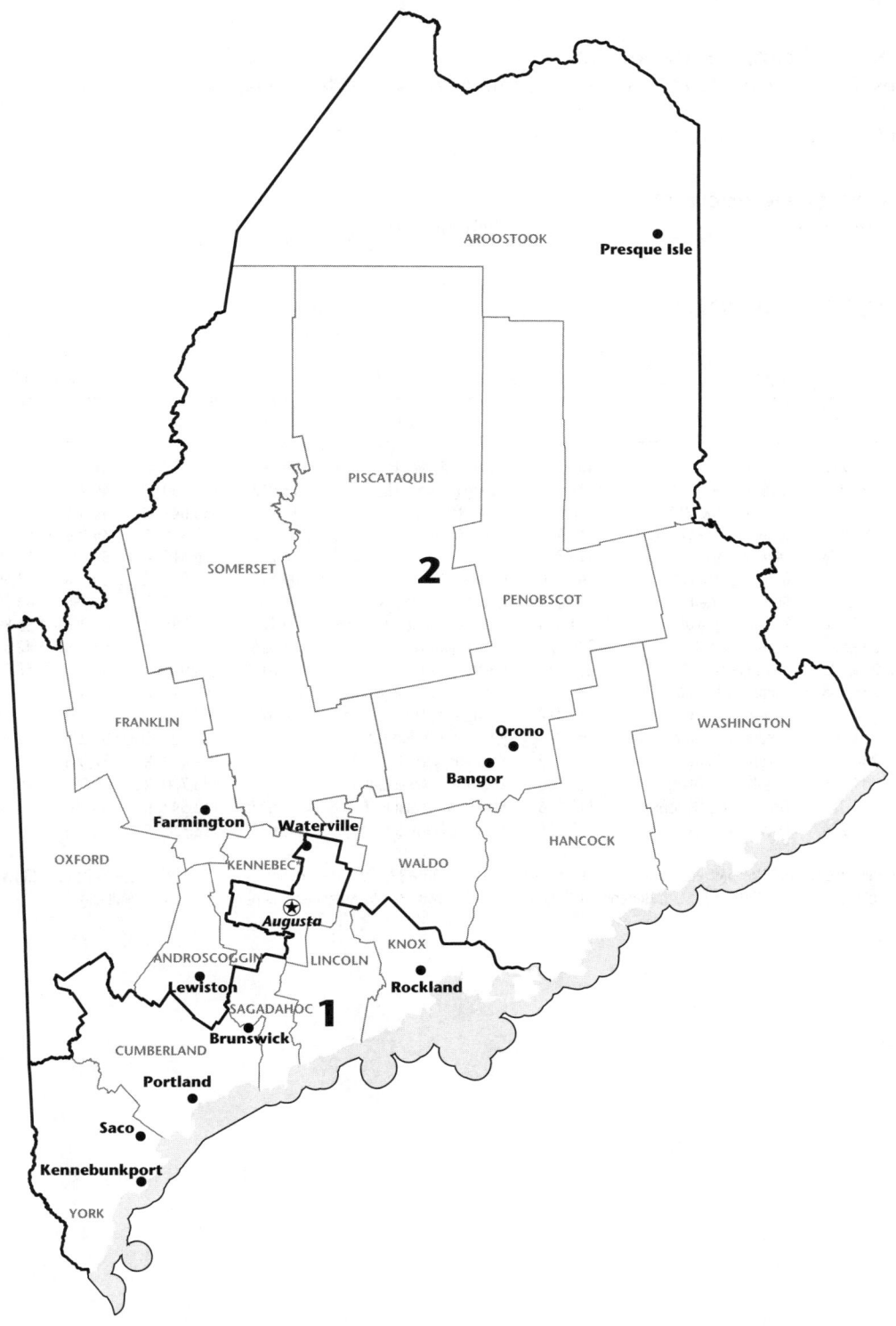

* Asterisk indicates a county whose boundaries include parts of two or more Congressional districts.

MAINE

GOVERNOR
Paul R. LePage (R). Elected 2010 to a four-year term.

SENATORS (1 Republican, 1 Independent)
Susan Collins (R). Reelected 2008 to a six-year term. Previously elected 2002, 1996.

Angus King (Ind.). Elected 2012 to a six-year term.

REPRESENTATIVES (2 Democrats)
1. Chellie Pingree (D)   2. Mike Michaud (D)

POSTWAR VOTE FOR PRESIDENT

Year	Total Vote	Republican Vote	Republican Candidate	Democratic Vote	Democratic Candidate	Other Vote	Rep.-Dem. Plurality	Total Vote Rep.	Total Vote Dem.	Major Vote Rep.	Major Vote Dem.
2012	713,180	292,276	Romney, W. Mitt	401,306	Obama, Barack H.*	19,598	109,030 D	41.0%	56.3%	42.1%	57.9%
2008	731,163	295,273	McCain, John S. III	421,923	Obama, Barack H.	13,967	126,650 D	40.4%	57.7%	41.2%	58.8%
2004	740,752	330,201	Bush, George W.*	396,842	Kerry, John F.	13,709	66,641 D	44.6%	53.6%	45.4%	54.6%
2000**	651,817	286,616	Bush, George W.	319,951	Gore, Albert Jr.	45,250	33,335 D	44.0%	49.1%	47.3%	52.7%
1996**	605,897	186,378	Dole, Robert "Bob"	312,788	Clinton, Bill*	106,731	126,410 D	30.8%	51.6%	37.3%	62.7%
1992**	679,499	206,504	Bush, George H.*	263,420	Clinton, Bill	209,575	56,916 D	30.4%	38.8%	43.9%	56.1%
1988	555,035	307,131	Bush, George H.	243,569	Dukakis, Michael S.	4,335	63,562 R	55.3%	43.9%	55.8%	44.2%
1984	553,144	336,500	Reagan, Ronald*	214,515	Mondale, Walter F.	2,129	121,985 R	60.8%	38.8%	61.1%	38.9%
1980**	523,011	238,522	Reagan, Ronald	220,974	Carter, Jimmy*	63,515	17,548 R	45.6%	42.3%	51.9%	48.1%
1976	483,216	236,320	Ford, Gerald R.*	232,279	Carter, Jimmy	14,617	4,041 R	48.9%	48.1%	50.4%	49.6%
1972	417,042	256,458	Nixon, Richard M.*	160,584	McGovern, George S.		95,874 R	61.5%	38.5%	61.5%	38.5%
1968**	392,936	169,254	Nixon, Richard M.	217,312	Humphrey, Hubert H. Jr.	6,370	48,058 D	43.1%	55.3%	43.8%	56.2%
1964	380,965	118,701	Goldwater, Barry M. Sr.	262,264	Johnson, Lyndon B.*		143,563 D	31.2%	68.8%	31.2%	68.8%
1960	421,767	240,608	Nixon, Richard M.	181,159	Kennedy, John F.		59,449 R	57.0%	43.0%	57.0%	43.0%
1956	351,706	249,238	Eisenhower, Dwight D.*	102,468	Stevenson, Adlai E. II		146,770 R	70.9%	29.1%	70.9%	29.1%
1952	351,786	232,353	Eisenhower, Dwight D.	118,806	Stevenson, Adlai E. II	627	113,547 R	66.0%	33.8%	66.2%	33.8%
1948	264,787	150,234	Dewey, Thomas E.	111,916	Truman, Harry S.*	2,637	38,318 R	56.7%	42.3%	57.3%	42.7%

Note: An asterisk (*) denotes incumbent. **In past elections, the other vote included: 2000 - 37,127 Green (Ralph Nader); 1996 - 85,970 Reform (Ross Perot); 1992 - 206,820 Independent (Perot), who placed second; 1980 - 53,327 Independent (John Anderson); 1968 - 6,370 American Independent (George Wallace).

MAINE

POSTWAR VOTE FOR GOVERNOR

Year	Total Vote	Republican Vote	Republican Candidate	Democratic Vote	Democratic Candidate	Other Vote	Rep.-Dem. Plurality	Total Vote Rep.	Total Vote Dem.	Major Vote Rep.	Major Vote Dem.
2010**	572,766	218,065	LePage, Paul R.	109,387	Mitchell, Elizabeth H. "Libby"	245,314	108,678 R	38.1%	19.1%	66.6%	33.4%
2006**	550,865	166,425	Woodcock, Chandler E.	209,927	Baldacci, John*	174,513	43,502 D	30.2%	38.1%	44.2%	55.8%
2002	505,190	209,496	Cianchette, Peter E.	238,179	Baldacci, John	57,515	28,683 D	41.5%	47.1%	46.8%	53.2%
1998**	421,009	79,716	Longley, James B. Jr.	50,506	Connolly, Thomas J.	290,787	29,210 R**	18.9%	12.0%	61.2%	38.8%
1994**	511,308	117,990	Collins, Susan	172,951	Brennan, Joseph E.	220,367	54,961 D	23.1%	33.8%	40.6%	59.4%
1990	522,492	243,766	McKernan, John R.*	230,038	Brennan, Joseph E.	48,688	13,728 R	46.7%	44.0%	51.4%	48.6%
1986**	426,861	170,312	McKernan, John R.	128,744	Tierney, James J.	127,805	41,568 R	39.9%	30.2%	56.9%	43.1%
1982	460,295	172,949	Cragin, Charles L.	281,066	Brennan, Joseph E.*	6,280	108,117 D	37.6%	61.1%	38.1%	61.9%
1978**	370,258	126,862	Palmer, Linwood E.	176,493	Brennan, Joseph E.	66,903	49,631 D**	34.3%	47.7%	41.8%	58.2%
1974**	363,945	84,176	Erwin, James S.	132,219	Mitchell, George J.	147,550	48,043 D**	23.1%	36.3%	38.9%	61.1%
1970	325,386	162,248	Erwin, James S.	163,138	Curtis, Kenneth M.*		890 D	49.9%	50.1%	49.9%	50.1%
1966	323,838	151,802	Reed, John H.*	172,036	Curtis, Kenneth M.		20,234 D	46.9%	53.1%	46.9%	53.1%
1962	292,725	146,604	Reed, John H.*	146,121	Dolloff, Maynard C.		483 R	50.1%	49.9%	50.1%	49.9%
1960S	417,215	219,768	Reed, John H.	197,447	Coffin, Frank M.		22,321 R	52.7%	47.3%	52.7%	47.3%
1958**	280,245	134,572	Hildreth, Horace A.	145,673	Clauson, Clinton A.		11,101 D	48.0%	52.0%	48.0%	52.0%
1956	304,649	124,395	Trafton, Willis A. Jr.	180,254	Muskie, Edmund S.*		55,859 D	40.8%	59.2%	40.8%	59.2%
1954	248,971	113,298	Cross, Burton M.*	135,673	Muskie, Edmund S.		22,375 D	45.5%	54.5%	45.5%	54.5%
1952	248,441	128,532	Cross, Burton M.	82,538	Oliver, James C.	37,371	45,994 R	51.7%	33.2%	60.9%	39.1%
1950	241,177	145,823	Payne, Frederick G.*	94,304	Grant, Earle S.	1,050	51,519 R	60.5%	39.1%	60.7%	39.3%
1948	222,500	145,956	Payne, Frederick G.	76,544	Lausier, Louis B.		69,412 R	65.6%	34.4%	65.6%	34.4%
1946	179,951	110,327	Hildreth, Horace A.	69,624	Clark, F. Davis		40,703 R	61.3%	38.7%	61.3%	38.7%

Note: An asterisk (*) denotes incumbent. **In past elections, the other vote included: 2010 - 208,270 Independent (Eliot R. Cutler), who placed second; 2006 - 118,715 Independent Maine Course (Barbara Merrill); 1998 - 246,772 Independent (Angus King), who was reelected with 58.6 percent of the total vote; 1994 - 180,829 Independent (King), who was elected with 35.4 percent of the total vote; 1986 - 64,317 Independent (Sherry F. Huber), 63,474 Independent (John E. Menario); 1978 - 65,889 Independent (Herman C. Frankland); 1974 - 142,464 Independent (James B. Longley), who was elected with 39.1 percent of the total vote. The 1960 election was for a short term to fill a vacancy. The term of office of Maine's governor was increased from two to four years effective with the 1958 election.

POSTWAR VOTE FOR SENATOR

Year	Total Vote	Republican Vote	Republican Candidate	Democratic Vote	Democratic Candidate	Other Vote	Rep.-Dem. Plurality	Total Vote Rep.	Total Vote Dem.	Major Vote Rep.	Major Vote Dem.
2012**	700,599	215,399	Summers, Charles E.	92,900	Dill, Cynthia Ann	392,300	122,499 R**	30.7%	13.3%	69.9%	30.1%
2008	724,430	444,300	Collins, Susan*	279,510	Allen, Tom	620	164,790 R	61.3%	38.6%	61.4%	38.6%
2006	543,981	402,598	Snowe, Olympia J.*	111,984	Bright, Jean Hay	29,399	290,614 R	74.0%	20.6%	78.2%	21.8%
2002	504,899	295,041	Collins, Susan*	209,858	Pingree, Chellie		85,183 R	58.4%	41.6%	58.4%	41.6%
2000	634,872	437,689	Snowe, Olympia J.*	197,183	Lawrence, Mark W.		240,506 R	68.9%	31.1%	68.9%	31.1%
1996	606,777	298,422	Collins, Susan	266,226	Brennan, Joseph E.	42,129	32,196 R	49.2%	43.9%	52.9%	47.1%
1994	511,733	308,244	Snowe, Olympia J.	186,042	Andrews, Thomas H.	17,447	122,202 R	60.2%	36.4%	62.4%	37.6%
1990	520,320	319,167	Cohen, William S.*	201,053	Rolde, Neil	100	118,114 R	61.3%	38.6%	61.4%	38.6%
1988	557,375	104,758	Wyman, Jasper S.	452,590	Mitchell, George J.*	27	347,832 D	18.8%	81.2%	18.8%	81.2%
1984	551,406	404,414	Cohen, William S.*	142,626	Mitchell, Elizabeth H. "Libby"	4,366	261,788 R	73.3%	25.9%	73.9%	26.1%
1982	459,715	179,882	Emery, David F.	279,819	Mitchell, George J.	14	99,937 D	39.1%	60.9%	39.1%	60.9%
1978	375,172	212,294	Cohen, William S.	127,327	Hathaway, William D.*	35,551	84,967 R	56.6%	33.9%	62.5%	37.5%
1976	486,254	193,489	Monks, Robert A.G.	292,704	Muskie, Edmund S.*	61	99,215 D	39.8%	60.2%	39.8%	60.2%
1972	421,310	197,040	Smith, Margaret Chase*	224,270	Hathaway, William D.		27,230 D	46.8%	53.2%	46.8%	53.2%
1970	323,860	123,906	Bishop, Neil S.	199,954	Muskie, Edmund S.*		76,048 D	38.3%	61.7%	38.3%	61.7%
1966	319,535	188,291	Smith, Margaret Chase*	131,136	Violette, Elmer H.	108	57,155 R	58.9%	41.0%	58.9%	41.1%
1964	380,551	127,040	McIntire, Clifford G.	253,511	Muskie, Edmund S.*		126,471 D	33.4%	66.6%	33.4%	66.6%
1960	416,699	256,890	Smith, Margaret Chase*	159,809	Cormier, Lucia M.		97,081 R	61.6%	38.4%	61.6%	38.4%
1958	284,364	111,522	Payne, Frederick G.*	172,842	Muskie, Edmund S.		61,320 D	39.2%	60.8%	39.2%	60.8%
1954	246,605	144,530	Smith, Margaret Chase*	102,075	Fullam, Paul A.		42,455 R	58.6%	41.4%	58.6%	41.4%
1952	237,164	139,205	Payne, Frederick G.	82,665	Dube, Roger P.	15,294	56,540 R	58.7%	34.9%	62.7%	37.3%
1948	223,256	159,182	Smith, Margaret Chase	64,074	Scolten, Adrian H.		95,108 R	71.3%	28.7%	71.3%	28.7%
1946	175,014	111,215	Brewster, Ralph O.*	63,799	MacDonald, Peter M.		47,416 R	63.5%	36.5%	63.5%	36.5%

Note: An asterisk (*) denotes incumbent. **In past elections, the other vote included: 2012 - 370,580 Independent (Angus King), who received 52.9 percent of the total vote and was elected.

MAINE

PRESIDENT 2012

| 2010 Census Population | County | Total Vote | Republican (Romney) | Democratic (Obama) | Other | Rep.-Dem. Plurality | Percentage | | | |
| | | | | | | | Total Vote | | Major Vote | |
							Rep.	Dem.	Rep.	Dem.
107,702	ANDROSCOGGIN	52,862	22,232	28,989	1,641	6,757 D	42.1%	54.8%	43.4%	56.6%
71,870	AROOSTOOK	33,860	15,196	17,777	887	2,581 D	44.9%	52.5%	46.1%	53.9%
281,674	CUMBERLAND	163,786	57,821	101,950	4,015	44,129 D	35.3%	62.2%	36.2%	63.8%
30,768	FRANKLIN	16,282	6,369	9,367	546	2,998 D	39.1%	57.5%	40.5%	59.5%
54,418	HANCOCK	30,799	12,324	17,569	906	5,245 D	40.0%	57.0%	41.2%	58.8%
122,151	KENNEBEC	63,497	26,519	35,068	1,910	8,549 D	41.8%	55.2%	43.1%	56.9%
39,736	KNOX	22,067	8,248	13,223	596	4,975 D	37.4%	59.9%	38.4%	61.6%
34,457	LINCOLN	20,757	8,899	11,315	543	2,416 D	42.9%	54.5%	44.0%	56.0%
57,833	OXFORD	29,420	11,996	16,330	1,094	4,334 D	40.8%	55.5%	42.3%	57.7%
153,923	PENOBSCOT	77,306	36,547	38,811	1,948	2,264 D	47.3%	50.2%	48.5%	51.5%
17,535	PISCATAQUIS	8,955	4,530	4,149	276	381 R	50.6%	46.3%	52.2%	47.8%
35,293	SAGADAHOC	20,794	8,429	11,821	544	3,392 D	40.5%	56.8%	41.6%	58.4%
52,228	SOMERSET	24,787	11,800	12,216	771	416 D	47.6%	49.3%	49.1%	50.9%
38,786	WALDO	21,061	9,058	11,296	707	2,238 D	43.0%	53.6%	44.5%	55.5%
32,856	WASHINGTON	15,836	7,550	7,803	483	253 D	47.7%	49.3%	49.2%	50.8%
197,131	YORK	108,057	43,900	61,551	2,606	17,651 D	40.6%	57.0%	41.6%	58.4%
	Votes Not Reported by County	3,054	858	2,071	125	1,213 D	28.1%	67.8%	29.3%	70.7%
1,328,361	TOTAL	713,180	292,276	401,306	19,598	109,030 D	41.0%	56.3%	42.1%	57.9%

MAINE

PRESIDENT 2012

| 2010 Census Population | City/Town | Total Vote | Republican (Romney) | Democratic (Obama) | Other | Rep.-Dem. Plurality | Percentage | | | |
| | | | | | | | Total Vote | | Major Vote | |
							Rep.	Dem.	Rep.	Dem.
23,055	AUBURN	11,332	4,462	6,503	367	2,041 D	39.4%	57.4%	40.7%	59.3%
19,136	AUGUSTA	8,851	3,351	5,220	280	1,869 D	37.9%	59.0%	39.1%	60.9%
33,039	BANGOR	14,946	5,788	8,781	377	2,993 D	38.7%	58.8%	39.7%	60.3%
8,514	BATH	4,549	1,512	2,895	142	1,383 D	33.2%	63.6%	34.3%	65.7%
6,668	BELFAST	3,620	1,240	2,274	106	1,034 D	34.3%	62.8%	35.3%	64.7%
7,246	BERWICK	3,642	1,812	1,733	97	79 R	49.8%	47.6%	51.1%	48.9%
21,277	BIDDEFORD	9,902	3,047	6,618	237	3,571 D	30.8%	66.8%	31.5%	68.5%
9,482	BREWER	5,081	2,542	2,450	89	92 R	50.0%	48.2%	50.9%	49.1%
20,278	BRUNSWICK	11,899	3,670	7,900	329	4,230 D	30.8%	66.4%	31.7%	68.3%
8,034	BUXTON	4,239	1,909	2,212	118	303 D	45.0%	52.2%	46.3%	53.7%
4,850	CAMDEN	3,176	914	2,201	61	1,287 D	28.8%	69.3%	29.3%	70.7%
9,015	CAPE ELIZABETH	6,370	2,261	4,018	91	1,757 D	35.5%	63.1%	36.0%	64.0%
8,189	CARIBOU	3,669	1,665	1,910	94	245 D	45.4%	52.1%	46.6%	53.4%
7,211	CUMBERLAND TOWN	4,917	2,221	2,619	77	398 D	45.2%	53.3%	45.9%	54.1%
6,204	ELIOT	3,931	1,644	2,210	77	566 D	41.8%	56.2%	42.7%	57.3%
7,741	ELLSWORTH	3,948	1,846	1,952	150	106 D	46.8%	49.4%	48.6%	51.4%
6,735	FAIRFIELD	3,203	1,359	1,719	125	360 D	42.4%	53.7%	44.2%	55.8%
11,185	FALMOUTH	7,590	3,319	4,150	121	831 D	43.7%	54.7%	44.4%	55.6%
7,760	FARMINGTON	3,897	1,288	2,441	168	1,153 D	33.1%	62.6%	34.5%	65.5%
7,879	FREEPORT	5,099	1,726	3,266	107	1,540 D	33.8%	64.1%	34.6%	65.4%
5,800	GARDINER	2,984	1,158	1,702	124	544 D	38.8%	57.0%	40.5%	59.5%
16,381	GORHAM	9,073	3,742	5,123	208	1,381 D	41.2%	56.5%	42.2%	57.8%
7,761	GRAY	4,530	2,144	2,260	126	116 D	47.3%	49.9%	48.7%	51.3%
7,257	HAMPDEN	4,191	2,099	2,013	79	86 R	50.1%	48.0%	51.0%	49.0%
4,740	HARPSWELL	3,376	1,371	1,940	65	569 D	40.6%	57.5%	41.4%	58.6%

MAINE

PRESIDENT 2012

2010 Census Population	City/Town	Total Vote	Republican (Romney)	Democratic (Obama)	Other	Rep.-Dem. Plurality	Total Vote Rep.	Total Vote Dem.	Major Vote Rep.	Major Vote Dem.
6,123	HOULTON	2,511	1,307	1,133	71	174 R	52.1%	45.1%	53.6%	46.4%
4,851	JAY	2,548	868	1,615	65	747 D	34.1%	63.4%	35.0%	65.0%
10,798	KENNEBUNK	6,842	2,784	3,927	131	1,143 D	40.7%	57.4%	41.5%	58.5%
9,490	KITTERY	5,377	1,814	3,443	120	1,629 D	33.7%	64.0%	34.5%	65.5%
36,592	LEWISTON	15,880	5,796	9,624	460	3,828 D	36.5%	60.6%	37.6%	62.4%
2,314	LIMESTONE	863	324	511	28	187 D	37.5%	59.2%	38.8%	61.2%
5,085	LINCOLN TOWN	2,389	1,338	977	74	361 R	56.0%	40.9%	57.8%	42.2%
9,009	LISBON	4,783	2,228	2,381	174	153 D	46.6%	49.8%	48.3%	51.7%
4,506	MILLINOCKET	2,311	937	1,317	57	380 D	40.5%	57.0%	41.6%	58.4%
6,240	OAKLAND	3,222	1,435	1,686	101	251 D	44.5%	52.3%	46.0%	54.0%
8,624	OLD ORCHARD BEACH	5,156	1,804	3,247	105	1,443 D	35.0%	63.0%	35.7%	64.3%
7,840	OLD TOWN	3,801	1,330	2,340	131	1,010 D	35.0%	61.6%	36.2%	63.8%
10,362	ORONO	5,386	1,396	3,761	229	2,365 D	25.9%	69.8%	27.1%	72.9%
66,194	PORTLAND	36,345	7,488	27,739	1,118	20,251 D	20.6%	76.3%	21.3%	78.7%
9,692	PRESQUE ISLE	4,231	1,885	2,231	115	346 D	44.6%	52.7%	45.8%	54.2%
7,297	ROCKLAND	3,360	1,065	2,198	97	1,133 D	31.7%	65.4%	32.6%	67.4%
5,841	RUMFORD	2,678	915	1,671	92	756 D	34.2%	62.4%	35.4%	64.6%
18,482	SACO	9,947	3,569	6,179	199	2,610 D	35.9%	62.1%	36.6%	63.4%
20,798	SANFORD	9,575	3,701	5,588	286	1,887 D	38.7%	58.4%	39.8%	60.2%
18,919	SCARBOROUGH	11,765	5,187	6,351	227	1,164 D	44.1%	54.0%	45.0%	55.0%
8,589	SKOWHEGAN	3,909	1,558	2,225	126	667 D	39.9%	56.9%	41.2%	58.8%
7,220	SOUTH BERWICK	4,006	1,626	2,276	104	650 D	40.6%	56.8%	41.7%	58.3%
25,002	SOUTH PORTLAND	14,383	4,104	9,958	321	5,854 D	28.5%	69.2%	29.2%	70.8%
9,874	STANDISH	5,067	2,400	2,554	113	154 D	47.4%	50.4%	48.4%	51.6%
8,784	TOPSHAM	5,532	2,259	3,153	120	894 D	40.8%	57.0%	41.7%	58.3%
15,722	WATERVILLE	6,998	2,107	4,693	198	2,586 D	30.1%	67.1%	31.0%	69.0%
9,589	WELLS	5,906	2,612	3,182	112	570 D	44.2%	53.9%	45.1%	54.9%
17,494	WESTBROOK	8,823	3,053	5,528	242	2,475 D	34.6%	62.7%	35.6%	64.4%
17,001	WINDHAM	9,041	4,107	4,704	230	597 D	45.4%	52.0%	46.6%	53.4%
7,794	WINSLOW	4,090	1,781	2,206	103	425 D	43.5%	53.9%	44.7%	55.3%
6,092	WINTHROP	3,466	1,496	1,877	93	381 D	43.2%	54.2%	44.4%	55.6%
8,349	YARMOUTH	5,576	2,128	3,358	90	1,230 D	38.2%	60.2%	38.8%	61.2%
12,529	YORK TOWN	8,569	3,594	4,888	87	1,294 D	41.9%	57.0%	42.4%	57.6%

MAINE

SENATOR 2012

2010 Census Population	County	Total Vote	Republican (Summers)	Democratic (Dill)	Independent (King)	Other	Plurality	Rep.	Dem.	Ind.
107,702	ANDROSCOGGIN	52,031	15,641	6,824	27,629	1,937	11,988 I	30.1%	13.1%	53.1%
71,870	AROOSTOOK	32,956	11,547	5,263	14,897	1,249	3,350 I	35.0%	16.0%	45.2%
281,674	CUMBERLAND	161,448	42,336	21,149	93,746	4,217	51,410 I	26.2%	13.1%	58.1%
30,768	FRANKLIN	16,055	4,819	2,096	8,552	588	3,733 I	30.0%	13.1%	53.3%
54,418	HANCOCK	30,239	9,698	4,177	15,456	908	5,758 I	32.1%	13.8%	51.1%
122,151	KENNEBEC	62,743	19,216	8,131	33,438	1,958	14,222 I	30.6%	13.0%	53.3%
39,736	KNOX	21,721	6,129	2,533	12,533	526	6,404 I	28.2%	11.7%	57.7%
34,457	LINCOLN	20,544	6,639	1,857	11,515	533	4,876 I	32.3%	9.0%	56.1%
57,833	OXFORD	28,928	8,688	3,886	15,283	1,071	6,595 I	30.0%	13.4%	52.8%
153,923	PENOBSCOT	75,429	27,913	9,633	35,517	2,366	7,604 I	37.0%	12.8%	47.1%

MAINE

SENATOR 2012

2010 Census Population	County	Total Vote	Republican (Summers)	Democratic (Dill)	Independent (King)	Other	Plurality	Percentage of Total Vote		
								Rep.	Dem.	Ind.
17,535	PISCATAQUIS	8,787	3,522	911	4,016	338	494 I	40.1%	10.4%	45.7%
35,293	SAGADAHOC	20,652	5,789	1,818	12,422	623	6,633 I	28.0%	8.8%	60.1%
52,228	SOMERSET	24,341	8,986	3,387	11,045	923	2,059 I	36.9%	13.9%	45.4%
38,786	WALDO	20,537	6,922	2,525	10,392	698	3,470 I	33.7%	12.3%	50.6%
32,856	WASHINGTON	15,269	5,739	2,249	6,662	619	923 I	37.6%	14.7%	43.6%
197,131	YORK	106,008	31,228	15,759	55,958	3,063	24,730 I	29.5%	14.9%	52.8%
	Votes Not Reported by County	2,911	587	702	1,519	103	817 I	20.2%	24.1%	52.2%
1,328,361	TOTAL	700,599	215,399	92,900	370,580	21,720	155,181 I	30.7%	13.3%	52.9%

Note: In each county, as well as statewide, the plurality is based on the winner's margin over the second-place finisher. The independent candidate, Angus King, finished first in all counties as well as the category labeled "Votes Not Reported by County."

MAINE

SENATOR 2012

2010 Census Population	City/Town	Total Vote	Republican (Summers)	Democratic (Dill)	Independent (King)	Other	Plurality	Percentage of Total Vote		
								Rep.	Dem.	Ind.
23,055	AUBURN	11,207	3,177	1,407	6,241	382	3,064 I	28.3%	12.6%	55.7%
19,136	AUGUSTA	8,768	2,357	1,233	4,918	260	2,561 I	26.9%	14.1%	56.1%
33,039	BANGOR	14,473	4,418	2,138	7,447	470	3,029 I	30.5%	14.8%	51.5%
8,514	BATH	4,504	953	544	2,853	154	1,900 I	21.2%	12.1%	63.3%
6,668	BELFAST	3,543	935	453	2,054	101	1,119 I	26.4%	12.8%	58.0%
7,246	BERWICK	3,516	1,220	559	1,591	146	371 I	34.7%	15.9%	45.3%
21,277	BIDDEFORD	9,650	2,343	1,878	5,088	341	2,745 I	24.3%	19.5%	52.7%
9,482	BREWER	5,010	1,886	580	2,409	135	523 I	37.6%	11.6%	48.1%
20,278	BRUNSWICK	11,727	2,399	1,103	7,935	290	5,536 I	20.5%	9.4%	67.7%
8,034	BUXTON	4,204	1,498	406	2,203	97	705 I	35.6%	9.7%	52.4%
4,850	CAMDEN	3,137	616	411	2,063	47	1,447 I	19.6%	13.1%	65.8%
9,015	CAPE ELIZABETH	6,314	1,539	1,006	3,717	52	2,178 I	24.4%	15.9%	58.9%
8,189	CARIBOU	3,622	1,331	568	1,598	125	267 I	36.7%	15.7%	44.1%
7,211	CUMBERLAND TOWN	4,881	1,602	321	2,853	105	1,251 I	32.8%	6.6%	58.5%
6,204	ELIOT	3,824	1,062	642	2,006	114	944 I	27.8%	16.8%	52.5%
7,741	ELLSWORTH	3,887	1,467	509	1,759	152	292 I	37.7%	13.1%	45.3%
6,735	FAIRFIELD	3,175	1,015	476	1,553	131	538 I	32.0%	15.0%	48.9%
11,185	FALMOUTH	7,510	2,314	624	4,428	144	2,114 I	30.8%	8.3%	59.0%
7,760	FARMINGTON	3,821	968	526	2,175	152	1,207 I	25.3%	13.8%	56.9%
7,879	FREEPORT	5,061	1,223	504	3,179	155	1,956 I	24.2%	10.0%	62.8%
5,800	GARDINER	2,977	875	362	1,639	101	764 I	29.4%	12.2%	55.1%
16,381	GORHAM	8,887	2,771	972	4,902	242	2,131 I	31.2%	10.9%	55.2%
7,761	GRAY	4,465	1,549	415	2,338	163	789 I	34.7%	9.3%	52.4%
7,257	HAMPDEN	4,091	1,552	349	2,092	98	540 I	37.9%	8.5%	51.1%
4,740	HARPSWELL	3,355	933	254	2,065	103	1,132 I	27.8%	7.6%	61.5%
6,123	HOULTON	2,450	962	294	1,098	96	136 I	39.3%	12.0%	44.8%
4,851	JAY	2,524	685	422	1,335	82	650 I	27.1%	16.7%	52.9%
10,798	KENNEBUNK	6,758	1,964	778	3,898	118	1,934 I	29.1%	11.5%	57.7%
9,490	KITTERY	5,187	1,183	949	2,913	142	1,730 I	22.8%	18.3%	56.2%
36,592	LEWISTON	15,499	4,017	2,676	8,235	571	4,218 I	25.9%	17.3%	53.1%
2,314	LIMESTONE	852	280	162	367	43	87 I	32.9%	19.0%	43.1%
5,085	LINCOLN TOWN	2,345	963	318	967	97	4 I	41.1%	13.6%	41.2%
9,009	LISBON	4,719	1,545	494	2,515	165	970 I	32.7%	10.5%	53.3%
4,506	MILLINOCKET	2,282	716	325	1,149	92	433 I	31.4%	14.2%	50.4%
6,240	OAKLAND	3,176	1,064	405	1,588	119	524 I	33.5%	12.8%	50.0%
8,624	OLD ORCHARD BEACH	5,105	1,387	846	2,717	155	1,330 I	27.2%	16.6%	53.2%
7,840	OLD TOWN	3,747	1,014	638	1,985	110	971 I	27.1%	17.0%	53.0%
10,362	ORONO	5,136	975	878	3,146	137	2,171 I	19.0%	17.1%	61.3%
66,194	PORTLAND	35,507	5,557	7,097	21,923	930	14,826 I	15.7%	20.0%	61.7%
9,692	PRESQUE ISLE	4,181	1,467	584	1,995	135	528 I	35.1%	14.0%	47.7%

MAINE

SENATOR 2012

2010 Census Population	City/Town	Total Vote	Republican (Summers)	Democratic (Dill)	Independent (King)	Other	Plurality	Percentage of Total Vote		
								Rep.	Dem.	Ind.
7,297	ROCKLAND	3,271	787	535	1,851	98	1,064 I	24.1%	16.4%	56.6%
5,841	RUMFORD	2,646	639	543	1,355	109	716 I	24.1%	20.5%	51.2%
18,482	SACO	9,820	2,757	1,452	5,379	232	2,622 I	28.1%	14.8%	54.8%
20,798	SANFORD	9,386	2,520	1,528	5,021	317	2,501 I	26.8%	16.3%	53.5%
18,919	SCARBOROUGH	11,630	4,321	1,214	5,912	183	1,591 I	37.2%	10.4%	50.8%
8,589	SKOWHEGAN	3,867	1,205	578	1,966	118	761 I	31.2%	14.9%	50.8%
7,220	SOUTH BERWICK	3,908	1,071	657	2,049	131	978 I	27.4%	16.8%	52.4%
25,002	SOUTH PORTLAND	14,182	3,073	2,465	8,305	339	5,232 I	21.7%	17.4%	58.6%
9,874	STANDISH	5,021	1,766	561	2,552	142	786 I	35.2%	11.2%	50.8%
8,784	TOPSHAM	5,490	1,561	446	3,353	130	1,792 I	28.4%	8.1%	61.1%
15,722	WATERVILLE	6,822	1,460	1,448	3,697	217	2,237 I	21.4%	21.2%	54.2%
9,589	WELLS	5,790	1,778	869	3,014	129	1,236 I	30.7%	15.0%	52.1%
17,494	WESTBROOK	8,696	2,235	1,352	4,844	265	2,609 I	25.7%	15.5%	55.7%
17,001	WINDHAM	8,866	3,088	956	4,595	227	1,507 I	34.8%	10.8%	51.8%
7,794	WINSLOW	4,038	1,272	579	2,066	121	794 I	31.5%	14.3%	51.2%
6,092	WINTHROP	3,460	1,074	364	1,919	103	845 I	31.0%	10.5%	55.5%
8,349	YARMOUTH	5,546	1,386	390	3,534	236	2,148 I	25.0%	7.0%	63.7%
12,529	YORK TOWN	8,384	2,501	1,384	4,311	188	1,810 I	29.8%	16.5%	51.4%

Note: In each city/town, as well as statewide, the plurality is based on the winner's margin over the second-place finisher. The Independent candidate, Angus King, finished first in all cities/towns included in this chart.

MAINE

HOUSE OF REPRESENTATIVES

CD	Year	Total Vote	Republican		Democratic		Other Vote	Rep.-Dem. Plurality	Percentage			
									Total Vote		Major Vote	
			Vote	Candidate	Vote	Candidate			Rep.	Dem.	Rep.	Dem.
1	2012	364,803	128,440	COURTNEY, JONATHAN T.E.	236,363	PINGREE, CHELLIE*		107,923 D	35.2%	64.8%	35.2%	64.8%
2	2012	328,998	137,542	RAYE, KEVIN L.	191,456	MICHAUD, MICHAEL*		53,914 D	41.8%	58.2%	41.8%	58.2%
TOTAL	2012	693,801	265,982		427,819			161,837 D	38.3%	61.7%	38.3%	61.7%

Note: An asterisk (*) denotes incumbent.

MAINE

GENERAL AND PRIMARY ELECTIONS

GENERAL ELECTIONS: OTHER VOTE

President Other vote was 9,352 Libertarian (Gary E. Johnson), 8,119 Green (Jill Stein), 2,035 Write-in (Ron Paul), 92 Write-in (Scattered Write-In)

Senator Other vote was 370,580 Independent (Angus King), 10,289 Independent (Stephen Woods), 5,807 Non-Party (Danny Dalton), 5,624 Independent (Andrew Dodge)

MAINE

GENERAL AND PRIMARY ELECTIONS

PRIMARY ELECTIONS: SUPPLEMENTARY INFORMATION

Primary	June 12, 2012	**Registration** (as of June 12, 2012 – includes 41,224 inactive registrants)	1,025,444	Democratic Republican Green Unenrolled	326,862 278,138 39,792 380,575

Primary Type   Semi-open—Registered voters in a political party could participate only in their party's primary. "Unenrolled" and new voters could vote in either party's primary by enrolling in that party on primary day.

	REPUBLICAN PRIMARIES			DEMOCRATIC PRIMARIES		
Senator	Summers, Charles E.	20,732	29.5%	Dill, Cynthia Ann	22,974	44.2%
	Poliquin, Bruce L.	16,064	22.8%	Dunlap, Matthew G.	18,546	35.7%
	Bennett, Richard A.	12,576	17.9%	Hinck, Jon	6,414	12.3%
	D'Amboise, L. Scott	7,722	11.0%	Pollard, Justin Benjamin	4,007	7.7%
	Schneider, William J.	6,875	9.8%			
	Plowman, Debra D.	6,309	9.0%			
	Scattered Write-In	68	0.1%			
	TOTAL	*70,346*		*TOTAL*	*51,941*	
Congressional District 1	Courtney, Jonathan T.E.	14,588	50.4%	Pingree, Chellie*	31,965	100.0%
	Calder, Patrick D.	14,330	49.6%			
	TOTAL	*28,918*		*TOTAL*	*31,965*	
Congressional District 2	Raye, Kevin L.	18,703	60.0%	Michaud, Michael*	21,895	100.0%
	Richardson, R. Blaine	12,465	40.0%			
	TOTAL	*31,168*		*TOTAL*	*21,895*	

Note: An asterisk (*) denotes incumbent.

MARYLAND

Congressional districts first established for elections held in 2012
8 members

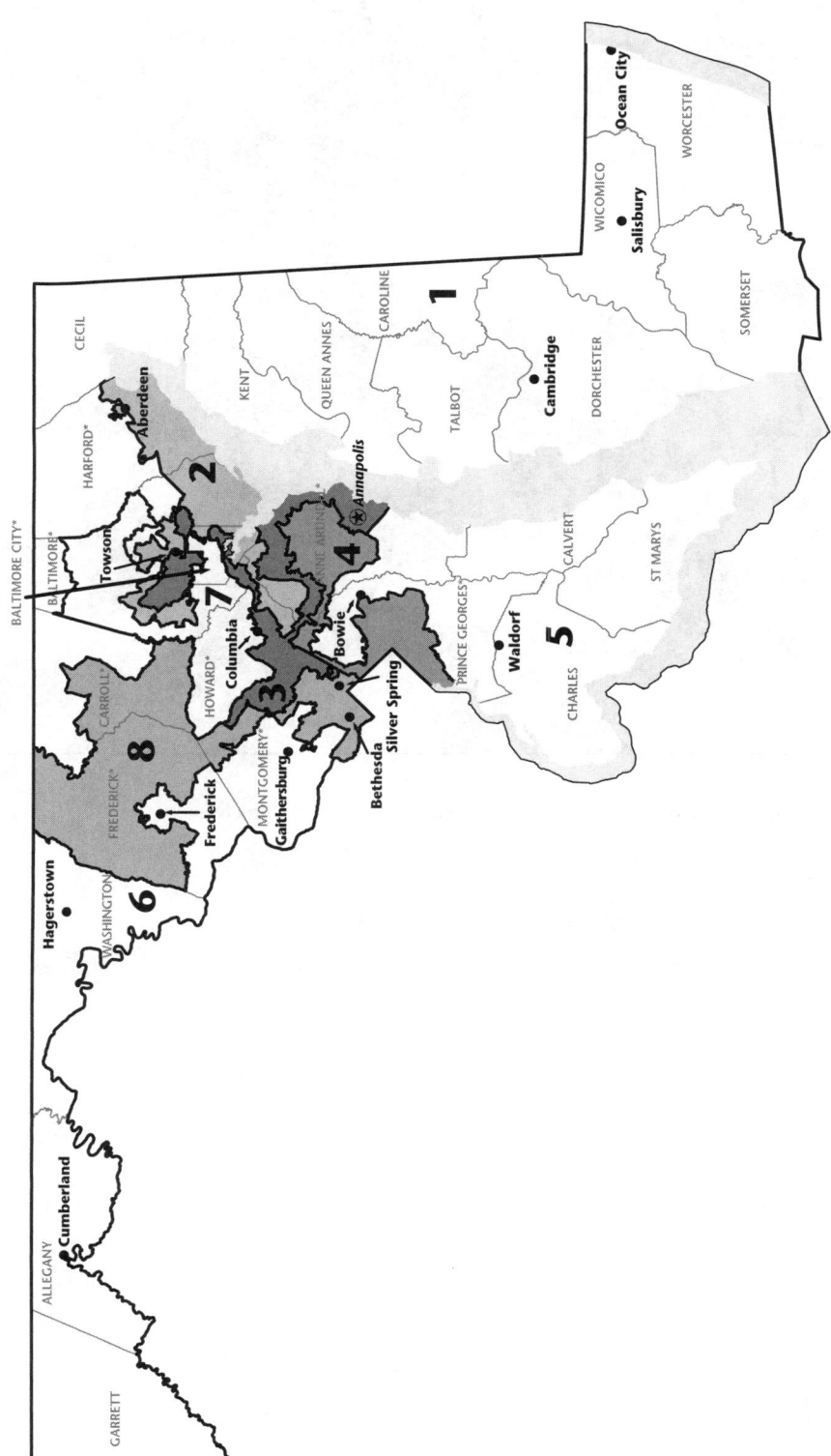

The city of Baltimore City is an independent city that is treated as a county equivalent.

* Asterisk indicates a county whose boundaries include parts of two or more Congressional districts.

MARYLAND
Baltimore, Washington, D.C., Areas

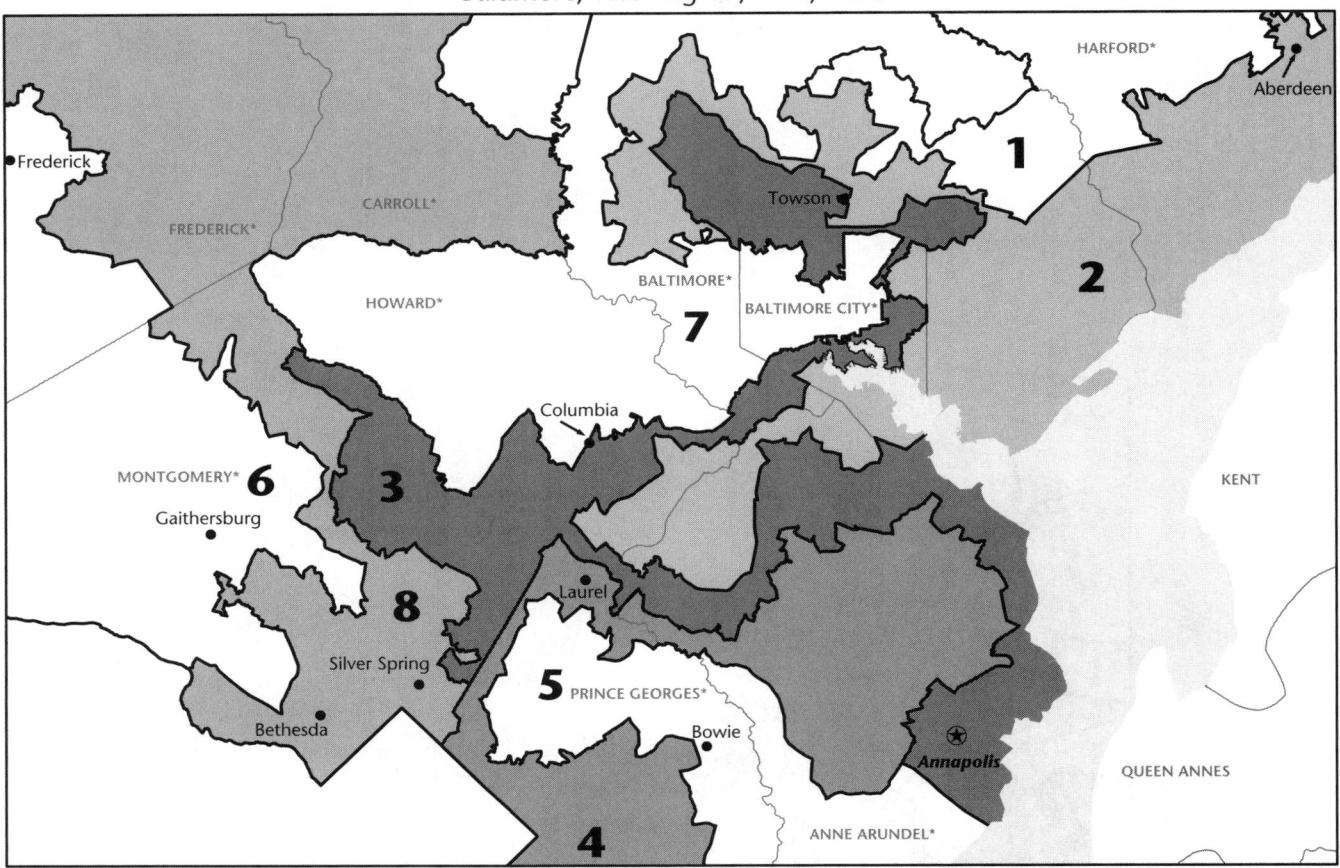

* Asterisk indicates a county whose boundaries include parts of two or more Congressional districts.

MARYLAND

GOVERNOR
Martin O'Malley (D). Reelected 2010 to a four-year term. Previously elected 2006.

SENATORS (2 Democrats)
Barbara A. Mikulski (D). Reelected 2010 to a six-year term. Previously elected 2004, 1998, 1992, 1986.

Benjamin L. Cardin (D). Reelected 2012 to a six-year term. Previously elected 2006.

REPRESENTATIVES (1 Republican, 7 Democrats)
1. Andy Harris (R)
2. C. A. (Dutch) Ruppersberger (D)
3. John Sarbanes (D)
4. Donna Edwards (D)
5. Steny Hoyer (D)
6. John Delaney (D)
7. Elijah E. Cummings (D)
8. Chris Van Hollen (D)

POSTWAR VOTE FOR PRESIDENT

Year	Total Vote	Republican Vote	Republican Candidate	Democratic Vote	Democratic Candidate	Other Vote	Rep.-Dem. Plurality	Total Vote Rep.	Total Vote Dem.	Major Vote Rep.	Major Vote Dem.
2012	2,707,327	971,869	Romney, W. Mitt	1,677,844	Obama, Barack H.*	57,614	705,975 D	35.9%	62.0%	36.7%	63.3%
2008	2,631,596	959,862	McCain, John S. III	1,629,467	Obama, Barack H.	42,267	669,605 D	36.5%	61.9%	37.1%	62.9%
2004	2,386,678	1,024,703	Bush, George W.*	1,334,493	Kerry, John F.	27,482	309,790 D	42.9%	55.9%	43.4%	56.6%
2000**	2,020,480	813,797	Bush, George W.	1,140,782	Gore, Albert Jr.	65,901	326,985 D	40.3%	56.5%	41.6%	58.4%
1996**	1,780,870	681,530	Dole, Robert "Bob"	966,207	Clinton, Bill*	133,133	284,677 D	38.3%	54.3%	41.4%	58.6%
1992**	1,985,046	707,094	Bush, George H.*	988,571	Clinton, Bill	289,381	281,477 D	35.6%	49.8%	41.7%	58.3%
1988	1,714,358	876,167	Bush, George H.	826,304	Dukakis, Michael S.	11,887	49,863 R	51.1%	48.2%	51.5%	48.5%
1984	1,675,873	879,918	Reagan, Ronald*	787,935	Mondale, Walter F.	8,020	91,983 R	52.5%	47.0%	52.8%	47.2%
1980**	1,540,496	680,606	Reagan, Ronald	726,161	Carter, Jimmy*	133,729	45,555 D	44.2%	47.1%	48.4%	51.6%
1976	1,439,897	672,661	Ford, Gerald R.*	759,612	Carter, Jimmy	7,624	86,951 D	46.7%	52.8%	47.0%	53.0%
1972	1,353,812	829,305	Nixon, Richard M.*	505,781	McGovern, George S.	18,726	323,524 R	61.3%	37.4%	62.1%	37.9%
1968**	1,235,039	517,995	Nixon, Richard M.	538,310	Humphrey, Hubert H. Jr.	178,734	20,315 D	41.9%	43.6%	49.0%	51.0%
1964	1,116,457	385,495	Goldwater, Barry M. Sr.	730,912	Johnson, Lyndon B.*	50	345,417 D	34.5%	65.5%	34.5%	65.5%
1960	1,055,349	489,538	Nixon, Richard M.	565,808	Kennedy, John F.	3	76,270 D	46.4%	53.6%	46.4%	53.6%
1956	932,827	559,738	Eisenhower, Dwight D.*	372,613	Stevenson, Adlai E. II	476	187,125 R	60.0%	39.9%	60.0%	40.0%
1952	902,074	499,424	Eisenhower, Dwight D.	395,337	Stevenson, Adlai E. II	7,313	104,087 R	55.4%	43.8%	55.8%	44.2%
1948	596,748	294,814	Dewey, Thomas E.	286,521	Truman, Harry S.*	15,413	8,293 R	49.4%	48.0%	50.7%	49.3%

Note: An asterisk (*) denotes incumbent. **In past elections, the other vote included: 2000 - 53,768 Green (Ralph Nader); 1996 - 115,812 Reform (Ross Perot); 1992 - 281,414 Independent (Perot); 1980 - 119,537 Independent (John Anderson); 1968 - 178,734 American Independent (George Wallace).

MARYLAND

POSTWAR VOTE FOR GOVERNOR

Year	Total Vote	Republican		Democratic		Other Vote	Rep.-Dem. Plurality	Percentage			
		Vote	Candidate	Vote	Candidate			Total Vote		Major Vote	
								Rep.	Dem.	Rep.	Dem.
2010	1,857,880	776,319	Ehrlich, Robert L. "Bob" Jr.	1,044,961	O'Malley, Martin*	36,600	268,642 D	41.8%	56.2%	42.6%	57.4%
2006	1,788,316	825,464	Ehrlich, Robert L. "Bob" Jr.*	942,279	O'Malley, Martin	20,573	116,815 D	46.2%	52.7%	46.7%	53.3%
2002	1,706,179	879,592	Ehrlich, Robert L. "Bob" Jr.	813,422	Townsend, Kathleen Kennedy	13,165	66,170 R	51.6%	47.7%	52.0%	48.0%
1998	1,535,978	688,357	Sauerbrey, Ellen R.	846,972	Glendening, Parris N.*	649	158,615 D	44.8%	55.1%	44.8%	55.2%
1994	1,410,300	702,101	Sauerbrey, Ellen R.	708,094	Glendening, Parris N.	105	5,993 D	49.8%	50.2%	49.8%	50.2%
1990	1,111,088	446,980	Shepard, William S.	664,015	Schaefer, William D.*	93	217,035 D	40.2%	59.8%	40.2%	59.8%
1986	1,101,476	194,185	Mooney, Thomas J.	907,291	Schaefer, William D.		713,106 D	17.6%	82.4%	17.6%	82.4%
1982	1,139,149	432,826	Pascal, Robert A.	705,910	Hughes, Harry*	413	273,084 D	38.0%	62.0%	38.0%	62.0%
1978	1,011,963	293,635	Beall, John Glenn Jr.	718,328	Hughes, Harry		424,693 D	29.0%	71.0%	29.0%	71.0%
1974	949,097	346,449	Gore, Louise	602,648	Mandel, Marvin*		256,199 D	36.5%	63.5%	36.5%	63.5%
1970	973,099	314,336	Blair, C. Stanley	639,579	Mandel, Marvin*	19,184	325,243 D	32.3%	65.7%	33.0%	67.0%
1966	919,760	455,318	Agnew, Spiro T.	373,543	Mahoney, George P.	90,899	81,775 R	49.5%	40.6%	54.9%	45.1%
1962	769,347	341,271	Small, Frank Jr.	428,071	Tawes, J. Millard*	5	86,800 D	44.4%	55.6%	44.4%	55.6%
1958	763,234	278,173	Devereux, James Patrick	485,061	Tawes, J. Millard		206,888 D	36.4%	63.6%	36.4%	63.6%
1954	700,484	381,451	McKeldin, Theodore R.*	319,033	Byrd, Harry Clifton		62,418 R	54.5%	45.5%	54.5%	45.5%
1950	645,631	369,807	McKeldin, Theodore R.	275,824	Lane, William Preston		93,983 R	57.3%	42.7%	57.3%	42.7%
1946	489,836	221,752	McKeldin, Theodore R.	268,084	Lane, William Preston*		46,332 D	45.3%	54.7%	45.3%	54.7%

Note: An asterisk (*) denotes incumbent.

POSTWAR VOTE FOR SENATOR

Year	Total Vote	Republican		Democratic		Other Vote	Rep.-Dem. Plurality	Percentage			
		Vote	Candidate	Vote	Candidate			Total Vote		Major Vote	
								Rep.	Dem.	Rep.	Dem.
2012**	2,633,234	693,291	Bongino, Daniel John	1,474,028	Cardin, Benjamin L.*	465,915	780,737 D	26.3%	56.0%	32.0%	68.0%
2010	1,833,858	655,666	Wartotz, Eric	1,140,531	Mikulski, Barbara A.*	37,661	484,865 D	35.8%	62.2%	36.5%	63.5%
2006	1,781,139	787,182	Steele, Michael	965,477	Cardin, Benjamin L.	28,480	178,295 D	44.2%	54.2%	44.9%	55.1%
2004	2,323,183	783,055	Pipkin, Edward J.	1,504,691	Mikulski, Barbara A.*	35,437	721,636 D	33.7%	64.8%	34.2%	65.8%
2000	1,946,898	715,178	Rappaport, Paul H.	1,230,013	Sarbanes, Paul S.*	1,707	514,835 D	36.7%	63.2%	36.8%	63.2%
1998	1,507,447	444,637	Pierpont, Ross Z.	1,062,810	Mikulski, Barbara A.*		618,173 D	29.5%	70.5%	29.5%	70.5%
1994	1,369,104	559,908	Brock, William E.	809,125	Sarbanes, Paul S.*	71	249,217 D	40.9%	59.1%	40.9%	59.1%
1992	1,841,735	533,688	Keyes, Alan	1,307,610	Mikulski, Barbara A.*	437	773,922 D	29.0%	71.0%	29.0%	71.0%
1988	1,617,065	617,537	Keyes, Alan	999,166	Sarbanes, Paul S.*	362	381,629 D	38.2%	61.8%	38.2%	61.8%
1986	1,112,637	437,411	Chavez, Linda	675,225	Mikulski, Barbara A.	1	237,814 D	39.3%	60.7%	39.3%	60.7%
1982	1,114,690	407,334	Hogan, Lawrence J.	707,356	Sarbanes, Paul S.*		300,022 D	36.5%	63.5%	36.5%	63.5%
1980	1,286,088	850,970	Mathias, Charles*	435,118	Conroy, Edward T.		415,852 R	66.2%	33.8%	66.2%	33.8%
1976	1,365,568	530,439	Beall, John Glenn Jr.*	772,101	Sarbanes, Paul S.	63,028	241,662 D	38.8%	56.5%	40.7%	59.3%
1974	877,786	503,223	Mathias, Charles*	374,563	Mikulski, Barbara A.		128,660 R	57.3%	42.7%	57.3%	42.7%
1970	956,370	484,960	Beall, John Glenn Jr.	460,422	Tydings, Joseph D.*	10,988	24,538 R	50.7%	48.1%	51.3%	48.7%
1968**	1,133,727	541,893	Mathias, Charles	443,367	Brewster, Daniel B.*	148,467	98,526 R	47.8%	39.1%	55.0%	45.0%
1964	1,081,049	402,393	Beall, James Glenn*	678,649	Tydings, Joseph D.	7	276,256 D	37.2%	62.8%	37.2%	62.8%
1962	708,855	269,131	Miller, Edward T.	439,723	Brewster, Daniel B.	1	170,592 D	38.0%	62.0%	38.0%	62.0%
1958	749,291	382,021	Beall, James Glenn*	367,270	D'Alesandro, Thomas Jr.		14,751 R	51.0%	49.0%	51.0%	49.0%
1956	892,167	473,059	Butler, John Marshall*	419,108	Mahoney, George P.		53,951 R	53.0%	47.0%	53.0%	47.0%
1952	856,193	449,823	Beall, James Glenn	406,370	Mahoney, George P.		43,453 R	52.5%	47.5%	52.5%	47.5%
1950	615,614	326,291	Butler, John Marshall	283,180	Tydings, Millard E.*	6,143	43,111 R	53.0%	46.0%	53.5%	46.5%
1946	472,232	235,000	Markey, David John	237,232	O'Conor, Herbert R.		2,232 D	49.8%	50.2%	49.8%	50.2%

Note: An asterisk (*) denotes incumbent. **In past elections, the other vote included: 2012 - 430,934 Independent (S. Rob Sobhani); 1968 - 148,467 Independent (George P. Mahoney).

MARYLAND

PRESIDENT 2012

2010 Census Population	County	Total Vote	Republican (Romney)	Democratic (Obama)	Other	Rep.-Dem. Plurality	Percentage			
							Total Vote		Major Vote	
							Rep.	Dem.	Rep.	Dem.
75,087	ALLEGANY	29,850	19,230	9,805	815	9,425 R	64.4%	32.8%	66.2%	33.8%
537,656	ANNE ARUNDEL	260,155	126,832	126,635	6,688	197 R	48.8%	48.7%	50.0%	50.0%
620,961	BALTIMORE CITY	254,005	28,171	221,478	4,356	193,307 D	11.1%	87.2%	11.3%	88.7%
805,029	BALTIMORE COUNTY	384,782	154,908	220,322	9,552	65,414 D	40.3%	57.3%	41.3%	58.7%
88,737	CALVERT	45,518	23,952	20,529	1,037	3,423 R	52.6%	45.1%	53.8%	46.2%
33,066	CAROLINE	13,357	8,098	4,970	289	3,128 R	60.6%	37.2%	62.0%	38.0%
167,134	CARROLL	87,536	56,761	27,939	2,836	28,822 R	64.8%	31.9%	67.0%	33.0%
101,108	CECIL	42,480	24,806	16,557	1,117	8,249 R	58.4%	39.0%	60.0%	40.0%
146,551	CHARLES	75,222	25,178	48,774	1,270	23,596 D	33.5%	64.8%	34.0%	66.0%
32,618	DORCHESTER	15,444	7,976	7,257	211	719 R	51.6%	47.0%	52.4%	47.6%
233,385	FREDERICK	117,115	58,798	55,146	3,171	3,652 R	50.2%	47.1%	51.6%	48.4%
30,097	GARRETT	13,157	9,743	3,124	290	6,619 R	74.1%	23.7%	75.7%	24.3%
244,826	HARFORD	125,954	72,911	49,729	3,314	23,182 R	57.9%	39.5%	59.5%	40.5%
287,085	HOWARD	153,108	57,758	91,393	3,957	33,635 D	37.7%	59.7%	38.7%	61.3%
20,197	KENT	9,904	4,870	4,842	192	28 R	49.2%	48.9%	50.1%	49.9%
971,777	MONTGOMERY	455,992	123,353	323,400	9,239	200,047 D	27.1%	70.9%	27.6%	72.4%
863,420	PRINCE GEORGES	387,744	35,734	347,938	4,072	312,204 D	9.2%	89.7%	9.3%	90.7%
47,798	QUEEN ANNES	24,888	15,823	8,556	509	7,267 R	63.6%	34.4%	64.9%	35.1%
26,470	SOMERSET	10,399	5,042	5,240	117	198 D	48.5%	50.4%	49.0%	51.0%
105,151	ST. MARYS	47,824	26,797	19,711	1,316	7,086 R	56.0%	41.2%	57.6%	42.4%
37,782	TALBOT	20,459	11,339	8,808	312	2,531 R	55.4%	43.1%	56.3%	43.7%
147,430	WASHINGTON	62,755	36,074	25,042	1,639	11,032 R	57.5%	39.9%	59.0%	41.0%
98,733	WICOMICO	42,259	21,764	19,635	860	2,129 R	51.5%	46.5%	52.6%	47.4%
51,454	WORCESTER	27,420	15,951	11,014	455	4,937 R	58.2%	40.2%	59.2%	40.8%
5,773,552	TOTAL	2,707,327	971,869	1,677,844	57,614	705,975 D	35.9%	62.0%	36.7%	63.3%

MARYLAND

SENATOR 2012

2010 Census Population	County	Total Vote	Republican (Bongino)	Democratic (Cardin)	Unaffiliated (Sobhani)	Other	Plurality	Percentage of Total Vote		
								Rep.	Dem.	Ind.
75,087	ALLEGANY	28,479	14,667	9,507	3,920	385	5,160 R	51.5%	33.4%	13.8%
537,656	ANNE ARUNDEL	254,196	93,804	108,328	48,503	3,561	14,524 D	36.9%	42.6%	19.1%
620,961	BALTIMORE CITY	245,003	16,931	189,128	35,724	3,220	153,404 D	6.9%	77.2%	14.6%
805,029	BALTIMORE COUNTY	377,347	95,297	198,290	78,887	4,873	102,993 D	25.3%	52.5%	20.9%
88,737	CALVERT	43,940	17,272	17,296	8,806	566	24 D	39.3%	39.4%	20.0%
33,066	CAROLINE	13,036	5,898	4,423	2,575	140	1,475 R	45.2%	33.9%	19.8%
167,134	CARROLL	85,549	41,795	22,837	19,733	1,184	18,958 R	48.9%	26.7%	23.1%
101,108	CECIL	41,179	18,452	14,994	7,137	596	3,458 R	44.8%	36.4%	17.3%
146,551	CHARLES	73,205	16,752	42,638	13,036	779	25,886 D	22.9%	58.2%	17.8%
32,618	DORCHESTER	14,793	5,526	6,552	2,567	148	1,026 D	37.4%	44.3%	17.4%
233,385	FREDERICK	113,469	48,563	45,161	17,913	1,832	3,402 R	42.8%	39.8%	15.8%
30,097	GARRETT	12,372	8,263	3,448	492	169	4,815 R	66.8%	27.9%	4.0%
244,826	HARFORD	123,487	45,404	43,274	33,148	1,661	2,130 R	36.8%	35.0%	26.8%
287,085	HOWARD	149,582	42,892	80,265	23,815	2,610	37,373 D	28.7%	53.7%	15.9%
20,197	KENT	9,700	3,608	4,312	1,660	120	704 D	37.2%	44.5%	17.1%
971,777	MONTGOMERY	443,581	94,010	293,715	49,611	6,245	199,705 D	21.2%	66.2%	11.2%
863,420	PRINCE GEORGES	375,648	25,080	305,771	40,937	3,860	264,834 D	6.7%	81.4%	10.9%
47,798	QUEEN ANNES	24,514	12,540	7,385	4,344	245	5,155 R	51.2%	30.1%	17.7%
26,470	SOMERSET	10,035	3,568	4,686	1,682	99	1,118 D	35.6%	46.7%	16.8%
105,151	ST. MARYS	45,876	19,480	17,566	8,065	765	1,914 R	42.5%	38.3%	17.6%

MARYLAND

SENATOR 2012

2010 Census Population	County	Total Vote	Republican (Bongino)	Democratic (Cardin)	Unaffiliated (Sobhani)	Other	Plurality	Percentage of Total Vote		
								Rep.	Dem.	Ind.
37,782	TALBOT	20,020	8,986	8,100	2,729	205	886 R	44.9%	40.5%	13.6%
147,430	WASHINGTON	60,516	28,161	19,702	11,788	865	8,459 R	46.5%	32.6%	19.5%
98,733	WICOMICO	40,987	15,072	16,974	8,426	515	1,902 D	36.8%	41.4%	20.6%
51,454	WORCESTER	26,720	11,270	9,676	5,436	338	1,594 R	42.2%	36.2%	20.3%
5,773,552	TOTAL	2,633,234	693,291	1,474,028	430,934	34,981	780,737 D	26.3%	56.0%	16.4%

Note: In each county, as well as statewide, the plurality is based on the winner's margin over the second-place finisher. The Independent candidate, S. Rob Sobhani, finished second in Baltimore city and Prince Georges County.

MARYLAND

HOUSE OF REPRESENTATIVES

CD	Year	Total Vote	Republican		Democratic		Other Vote	Rep.-Dem. Plurality	Percentage			
			Vote	Candidate	Vote	Candidate			Total Vote		Major Vote	
									Rep.	Dem.	Rep.	Dem.
1	2012	337,760	214,204	HARRIS, ANDY*	92,812	ROSEN, WENDY	30,744	121,392 R	63.4%	27.5%	69.8%	30.2%
2	2012	295,940	92,071	JACOBS, NANCY C.	194,088	RUPPERSBERGER, C.A. (DUTCH)*	9,781	102,017 D	31.1%	65.6%	32.2%	67.8%
3	2012	319,859	94,549	KNOWLES, ERIC DELANO	213,747	SARBANES, JOHN*	11,563	119,198 D	29.6%	66.8%	30.7%	69.3%
4	2012	311,512	64,560	LOUDON, FAITH M.	240,385	EDWARDS, DONNA*	6,567	175,825 D	20.7%	77.2%	21.2%	78.8%
5	2012	343,820	95,271	O'DONNELL, TONY	238,618	HOYER, STENY*	9,931	143,347 D	27.7%	69.4%	28.5%	71.5%
6	2012	309,549	117,313	BARTLETT, ROSCOE G.*	181,921	DELANEY, JOHN	10,315	64,608 D	37.9%	58.8%	39.2%	60.8%
7	2012	323,818	67,405	MIRABILE, FRANK C.	247,770	CUMMINGS, ELIJAH E.*	8,643	180,365 D	20.8%	76.5%	21.4%	78.6%
8	2012	343,256	113,033	TIMMERMAN, KENNETH R.	217,531	VAN HOLLEN, CHRIS*	12,692	104,498 D	32.9%	63.4%	34.2%	65.8%
TOTAL	2012	2,585,514	858,406		1,626,872		100,236	768,466 D	33.2%	62.9%	34.5%	65.5%

Note: An asterisk (*) denotes incumbent.

MARYLAND

GENERAL AND PRIMARY ELECTIONS

GENERAL ELECTIONS: OTHER VOTE

President Other vote was 30,195 Libertarian (Gary E. Johnson), 17,110 Green (Jill Stein), 9,891 Write-in (Scattered Write-In), 418 Write-in (Virgil H. Goode), Scattered write-in for president included 625 votes for Santa Claus.

Senator Other vote was 430,934 Unaffiliated (S. Rob Sobhani), 32,252 Libertarian (Dean Ahmad), 2,729 Write-in (Scattered Write-In)

House Other vote was:

CD 1 14,858 Write-in (John LaFerla), 12,857 Libertarian (Muir Wayne Boda), 2,932 Write-in (Scattered Write-In), 71 Write-in (Michael Calpino), 26 Write-in (Douglas Dryden Rae)

CD 2 9,344 Libertarian (Leo Wayne Dymowski), 415 Write-in (Scattered Write-In), 22 Write-in (Ray Bly)

CD 3 11,028 Libertarian (Paul W. Drgos), 535 Write-in (Scattered Write-In)

CD 4 6,204 Libertarian (Scott Soffen), 363 Write-in (Scattered Write-In)

CD 5 5,040 Green (Bob Shipley Auerbach), 4,503 Libertarian (Arvin Vohra), 388 Write-in (Scattered Write-In)

CD 6 9,916 Libertarian (Nickolaus Mueller), 399 Write-in (Scattered Write-In)

CD 7 8,211 Libertarian (Ronald M. Owens-Bey), 394 Write-in (Scattered Write-In), 28 Write-in (Charles U. Smith), 10 Write-in (Ty Glen Busch)

CD 8 7,235 Libertarian (Mark Grannis), 5,064 Green (George Gluck), 393 Write-in (Scattered Write-In)

MARYLAND

GENERAL AND PRIMARY ELECTIONS

PRIMARY ELECTIONS: SUPPLEMENTARY INFORMATION

Primary	April 3, 2012	**Registration** (as of April 3, 2012 – active registrants only)	3,177,817	Republican	1,964,655	
				Democratic	935,122	
				Green	3,111	
				Libertarian	3,801	
				Unaffiliated	254,538	
				Other	16,590	

Primary Type   Closed—Only registered Democrats and Republicans could vote in their party's primary.

	REPUBLICAN PRIMARIES			DEMOCRATIC PRIMARIES		
President	Romney, W. Mitt	122,400	49.3%	Obama, Barack H.*	288,766	88.5%
	Santorum, Rick	71,349	28.7%	Uncommitted	37,704	11.5%
	Gingrich, Newt	27,240	11.0%			
	Paul, Ron	23,609	9.5%			
	Huntsman, Jon Jr.	1,484	0.6%			
	Perry, Rick	1,108	0.4%			
	Roemer, Charles	901	0.4%			
	Karger, Fred	377	0.2%			
	TOTAL	248,468		TOTAL	326,470	
Senator	Bongino, Daniel John	68,597	33.6%	Cardin, Benjamin L.*	240,704	74.2%
	Douglas, Richard J.	57,776	28.3%	Muse, C. Anthony	50,807	15.7%
	Alexander, Joseph	18,171	8.9%	Garner, Chris	9,274	2.9%
	Broadus, Robert	11,020	5.4%	Blagmon, Raymond Levi	5,909	1.8%
	Hoover, Rick	10,787	5.3%	Cusick, James Patrick Sr.	4,778	1.5%
	Kimble, John B.	10,506	5.1%	Taylor, Blaine	4,376	1.3%
	Jones, David	8,380	4.1%	Young, Lih	3,993	1.2%
	Vaughn, Corrogan R.	8,158	4.0%	Jaffe, Ralph	3,313	1.0%
	Capps, William Thomas Jr.	7,092	3.5%	Tinus, Ed	1,064	0.3%
	Vaeth, Brian	3,781	1.9%			
	TOTAL	204,268		TOTAL	324,218	
Congressional District 1	Harris, Andy*	44,599	100%	Rosen, Wendy	10,907	43.1%
				LaFerla, John	10,850	42.8%
				Letke, Kim	3,564	14.1%
	TOTAL	44,599		TOTAL	25,321	
Congressional District 2	Jacobs, Nancy C.	12,372	58.9%	Ruppersberger, C.A. (Dutch)*	26,465	100%
	Impallaria, Rick	4,998	23.8%			
	Smith, Larry John	2,392	11.4%			
	Orton, Howard H.	500	2.4%			
	Bly, Raymond J.	415	2.0%			
	Degen, Vlad	324	1.5%			
	TOTAL	21,001		TOTAL	26,465	
Congressional District 3	Knowles, Eric Delano	6,845	33.5%	Sarbanes, John*	32,527	86.4%
	Harris, Thomas E. Pinkston	5,874	28.7%	Lockwood, David H.	5,111	13.6%
	Girard, Armand F.	4,809	23.5%			
	Phelps, Draper S.	2,935	14.3%			
	TOTAL	20,463		TOTAL	37,638	
Congressional District 4	Loudon, Faith M.	9,175	61.3%	Edwards, Donna*	42,815	91.8%
	Gearhart, Randy	2,977	19.9%	McDermott, George E.	2,359	5.1%
	Shepherd, Charles	1,443	9.6%	Garner, Ian	1,464	3.1%
	Holmes, Greg	1,370	9.2%			
	TOTAL	14,965		TOTAL	46,638	

MARYLAND

GENERAL AND PRIMARY ELECTIONS

	REPUBLICAN PRIMARIES			DEMOCRATIC PRIMARIES		
Congressional District 5	O'Donnell, Tony	17,329	73.7%	Hoyer, Steny*	36,961	84.7%
	Hill, David	3,289	14.0%	Pendleton, Cathy Johnson	6,688	15.3%
	Morton, Glenn	2,903	12.3%			
	TOTAL	23,521		TOTAL	43,649	
Congressional District 6	Bartlett, Roscoe G.*	17,600	43.6%	Delaney, John	20,414	54.2%
	Brinkley, David R.	7,987	19.8%	Garagiola, Rob	10,981	29.1%
	Afzali, Kathy	4,115	10.2%	Pooran, Milad	3,590	9.5%
	Krysztoforski, Joseph T.	3,073	7.6%	Bailey, Charles	1,572	4.2%
	Ficker, Robin	2,854	7.1%	Little, Ron	1,131	3.0%
	Rippeon, Brandon Orman	2,843	7.0%			
	Coblentz, Robert	970	2.4%			
	James, Peter	933	2.3%			
	TOTAL	40,375		TOTAL	37,688	
Congressional District 7	Mirabile, Frank C.	10,849	69.8%	Cummings, Elijah E.*	49,625	100%
	Kinsey, M. Justin	4,695	30.2%			
	TOTAL	15,544		TOTAL	49,625	
Congressional District 8	Timmerman, Kenneth R.	13,340	46.2%	Van Hollen, Chris*	35,989	92.2%
	Wallace, Dave	9,319	32.3%	English, George	3,041	7.8%
	Skolnick, Shelly	3,671	12.7%			
	Alzona, Gus	2,542	8.8%			
	TOTAL	28,872		TOTAL	39,030	

Note: An asterisk (*) denotes incumbent.

MASSACHUSETTS

Congressional districts first established for elections held in 2012

9 members

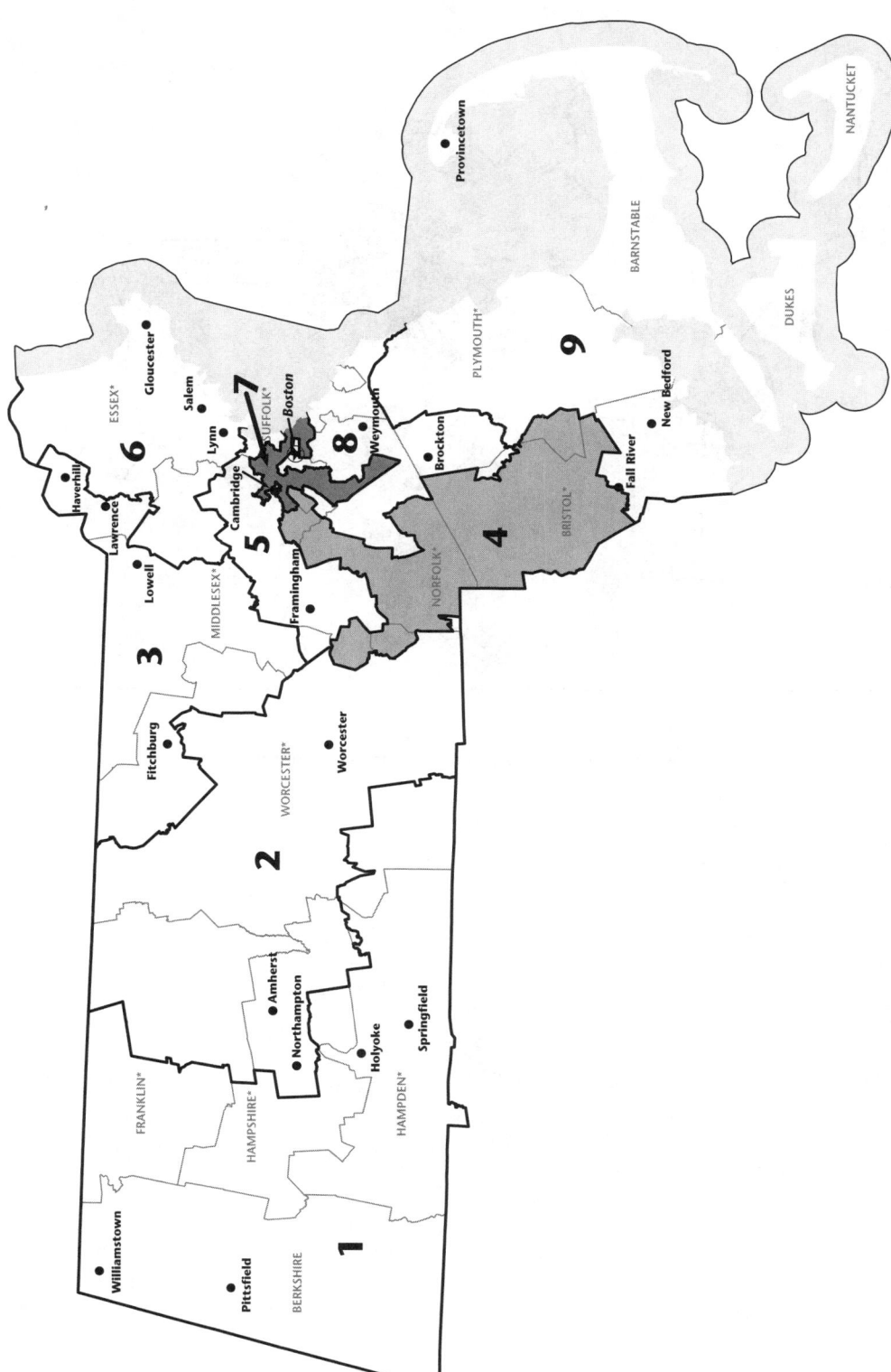

MASSACHUSETTS

Boston Area

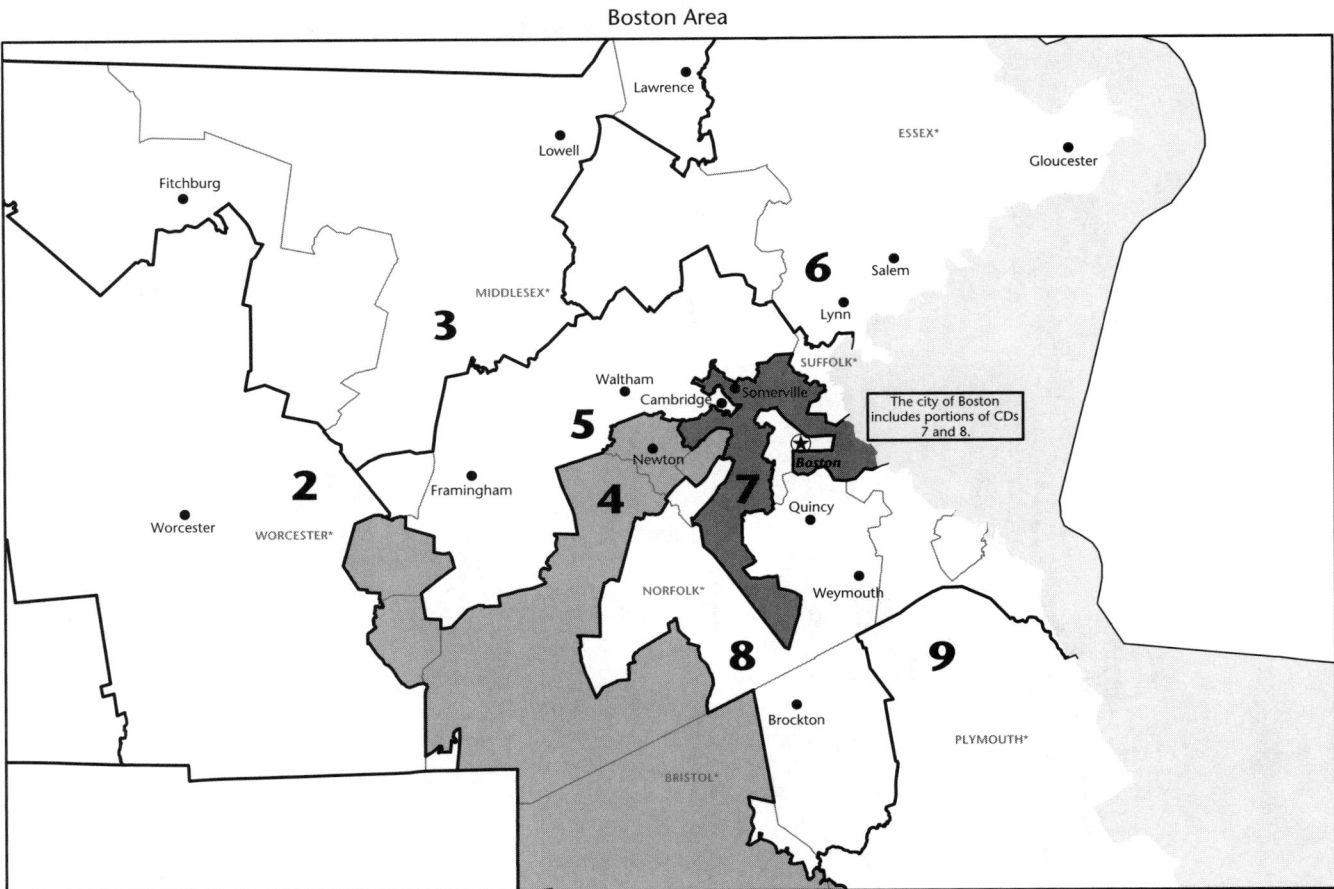

The city of Boston includes portions of CDs 7 and 8.

* Asterisk indicates a county whose boundaries include parts of two or more Congressional districts.

MASSACHUSETTS

GOVERNOR

Deval Patrick (D). Reelected 2010 to a four-year term. Previously elected 2006.

SENATORS (2 Democrats)

Elizabeth Warren (D). Elected 2012 to a six-year term.

Edward J. Markey (D). Elected June 25, 2013, to serve the remainder of the term vacated by the January 2013 resignation of John Kerry to become Secretary of State. William "Mo" Cowan (D) had been appointed on January 30, 2013, to fill the vacant seat until the June special election.

REPRESENTATIVES (8 Democrats, 1 Vacancy)

1. Richard Neal (D)
2. Jim McGovern (D)
3. Niki Tsongas (D)
4. Joe Kennedy (D)
5. Vacancy
6. John F. Tierney (D)
7. Michael E. Capuano (D)
8. Stephen F. Lynch (D)
9. William R. Keating (D)

POSTWAR VOTE FOR PRESIDENT

Year	Total Vote	Republican		Democratic		Other Vote	Rep.-Dem. Plurality	Percentage			
								Total Vote		Major Vote	
		Vote	Candidate	Vote	Candidate			Rep.	Dem.	Rep.	Dem.
2012	3,167,767	1,188,314	Romney, W. Mitt	1,921,290	Obama, Barack H.*	58,163	732,976 D	37.5%	60.7%	38.2%	61.8%
2008	3,080,985	1,108,854	McCain, John S. III	1,904,097	Obama, Barack H.	68,034	795,243 D	36.0%	61.8%	36.8%	63.2%
2004	2,912,388	1,071,109	Bush, George W.*	1,803,800	Kerry, John F.	37,479	732,691 D	36.8%	61.9%	37.3%	62.7%
2000**	2,702,984	878,502	Bush, George W.	1,616,487	Gore, Albert Jr.	207,995	737,985 D	32.5%	59.8%	35.2%	64.8%
1996**	2,556,785	718,107	Dole, Robert "Bob"	1,571,763	Clinton, Bill*	266,915	853,656 D	28.1%	61.5%	31.4%	68.6%
1992**	2,773,700	805,049	Bush, George H.*	1,318,662	Clinton, Bill	649,989	513,613 D	29.0%	47.5%	37.9%	62.1%
1988	2,632,805	1,194,635	Bush, George H.	1,401,415	Dukakis, Michael S.	36,755	206,780 D	45.4%	53.2%	46.0%	54.0%
1984	2,559,453	1,310,936	Reagan, Ronald*	1,239,606	Mondale, Walter F.	8,911	71,330 R	51.2%	48.4%	51.4%	48.6%
1980**	2,524,298	1,057,631	Reagan, Ronald	1,053,802	Carter, Jimmy*	412,865	3,829 R	41.9%	41.7%	50.1%	49.9%
1976	2,547,558	1,030,276	Ford, Gerald R.*	1,429,475	Carter, Jimmy	87,807	399,199 D	40.4%	56.1%	41.9%	58.1%
1972	2,458,756	1,112,078	Nixon, Richard M.*	1,332,540	McGovern, George S.	14,138	220,462 D	45.2%	54.2%	45.5%	54.5%
1968**	2,331,752	766,844	Nixon, Richard M.	1,469,218	Humphrey, Hubert H. Jr.	95,690	702,374 D	32.9%	63.0%	34.3%	65.7%
1964	2,344,798	549,727	Goldwater, Barry M. Sr.	1,786,422	Johnson, Lyndon B.*	8,649	1,236,695 D	23.4%	76.2%	23.5%	76.5%
1960	2,469,480	976,750	Nixon, Richard M.	1,487,174	Kennedy, John F.	5,556	510,424 D	39.6%	60.2%	39.6%	60.4%
1956	2,348,506	1,393,197	Eisenhower, Dwight D.*	948,190	Stevenson, Adlai E. II	7,119	445,007 R	59.3%	40.4%	59.5%	40.5%
1952	2,383,398	1,292,325	Eisenhower, Dwight D.	1,083,525	Stevenson, Adlai E. II	7,548	208,800 R	54.2%	45.5%	54.4%	45.6%
1948	2,107,146	909,370	Dewey, Thomas E.	1,151,788	Truman, Harry S.*	45,988	242,418 D	43.2%	54.7%	44.1%	55.9%

Note: An asterisk (*) denotes incumbent. **In past elections, the other vote included: 2000 - 173,564 Green (Ralph Nader); 1996 - 227,217 Reform (Ross Perot); 1992 - 630,731 Independent (Perot); 1980 - 382,539 Independent (John Anderson); 1968 - 87,088 American Independent (George Wallace).

MASSACHUSETTS

POSTWAR VOTE FOR GOVERNOR

Year	Total Vote	Republican Vote	Republican Candidate	Democratic Vote	Democratic Candidate	Other Vote	Rep.-Dem. Plurality	Total Vote Rep.	Total Vote Dem.	Major Vote Rep.	Major Vote Dem.
2010	2,297,039	964,866	Baker, Charles D.	1,112,283	Patrick, Deval*	219,890	147,417 D	42.0%	48.4%	46.5%	53.5%
2006	2,219,779	784,342	Healey, Kerry	1,234,984	Patrick, Deval	200,453	450,642 D	35.3%	55.6%	38.8%	61.2%
2002	2,194,179	1,091,988	Romney, W. Mitt	985,981	O'Brien, Shannon P.	116,210	106,007 R	49.8%	44.9%	52.6%	47.4%
1998	1,903,336	967,160	Cellucci, Argeo "Paul"*	901,843	Harshbarger, Scott	34,333	65,317 R	50.8%	47.4%	51.7%	48.3%
1994	2,164,318	1,533,430	Weld, William F.*	611,650	Roosevelt, Mark	19,238	921,780 R	70.9%	28.3%	71.5%	28.5%
1990	2,342,927	1,175,817	Weld, William F.	1,099,878	Silber, John	67,232	75,939 R	50.2%	46.9%	51.7%	48.3%
1986	1,684,079	525,364	Kariotis, George	1,157,786	Dukakis, Michael S.*	929	632,422 D	31.2%	68.7%	31.2%	68.8%
1982	2,050,254	749,679	Sears, John W.	1,219,109	Dukakis, Michael S.	81,466	469,430 D	36.6%	59.5%	38.1%	61.9%
1978	1,962,251	926,072	Hatch, Francis W.	1,030,294	King, Edward J.	5,885	104,222 D	47.2%	52.5%	47.3%	52.7%
1974	1,854,798	784,353	Sargent, Francis W.*	992,284	Dukakis, Michael S.	78,161	207,931 D	42.3%	53.5%	44.1%	55.9%
1970	1,867,906	1,058,623	Sargent, Francis W.*	799,269	White, Keith	10,014	259,354 R	56.7%	42.8%	57.0%	43.0%
1966**	2,041,177	1,277,358	Volpe, John A.*	752,720	McCormack, Edward J.	11,099	524,638 R	62.6%	36.9%	62.9%	37.1%
1964	2,340,130	1,176,462	Volpe, John A.*	1,153,416	Bellotti, Francis X.	10,252	23,046 R	50.3%	49.3%	50.5%	49.5%
1962	2,109,089	1,047,891	Volpe, John A.*	1,053,322	Peabody, Endicott	7,876	5,431 D	49.7%	49.9%	49.9%	50.1%
1960	2,417,133	1,269,295	Volpe, John A.	1,130,810	Ward, Joseph D.	17,028	138,485 R	52.5%	46.8%	52.9%	47.1%
1958	1,899,117	818,463	Gibbons, Charles	1,067,020	Furcolo, Foster*	13,634	248,557 D	43.1%	56.2%	43.4%	56.6%
1956	2,339,884	1,096,759	Whittier, Sumner G.	1,234,618	Furcolo, Foster	8,507	137,859 D	46.9%	52.8%	47.0%	53.0%
1954	1,903,774	985,339	Herter, Christian A.*	910,087	Murphy, Robert F.	8,348	75,252 R	51.8%	47.8%	52.0%	48.0%
1952	2,356,298	1,175,955	Herter, Christian A.	1,161,499	Dever, Paul A.*	18,844	14,456 R	49.9%	49.3%	50.3%	49.7%
1950	1,910,180	824,069	Coolidge, Arthur W.	1,074,570	Dever, Paul A.	11,541	250,501 D	43.1%	56.3%	43.4%	56.6%
1948	2,099,250	849,895	Bradford, Robert F.*	1,239,247	Dever, Paul A.	10,108	389,352 D	40.5%	59.0%	40.7%	59.3%
1946	1,683,452	911,152	Bradford, Robert F.	762,743	Tobin, Maurice J.*	9,557	148,409 R	54.1%	45.3%	54.4%	45.6%

Note: An asterisk (*) denotes incumbent. **The term of office of Massachusetts's governor was increased from two to four years effective with the 1966 election.

POSTWAR VOTE FOR SENATOR

Year	Total Vote	Republican Vote	Republican Candidate	Democratic Vote	Democratic Candidate	Other Vote	Rep.-Dem. Plurality	Total Vote Rep.	Total Vote Dem.	Major Vote Rep.	Major Vote Dem.
2012	3,156,553	1,458,048	Brown, Scott P.*	1,696,346	Warren, Elizabeth	2,159	238,298 D	46.2%	53.7%	46.2%	53.8%
2010S	2,252,582	1,168,178	Brown, Scott P.	1,060,861	Coakley, Martha	23,543	107,317 R	51.9%	47.1%	52.4%	47.6%
2008	2,994,247	926,044	Beatty, Jeffrey K.	1,971,974	Kerry, John F.*	96,229	1,045,930 D	30.9%	65.9%	32.0%	68.0%
2006	2,165,490	661,532	Chase, Kenneth G.	1,500,738	Kennedy, Edward M.*	3,220	839,206 D	30.5%	69.3%	30.6%	69.4%
2002**	2,006,758			1,605,976	Kerry, John F.*	400,782	1,605,976 D		80.0%		100.0%
2000**	2,599,420	334,341	Robinson, Jack E. III	1,889,494	Kennedy, Edward M.*	375,585	1,555,153 D	12.9%	72.7%	15.0%	85.0%
1996	2,555,886	1,142,837	Weld, William F.	1,334,345	Kerry, John F.*	78,704	191,508 D	44.7%	52.2%	46.1%	53.9%
1994	2,179,964	894,005	Romney, W. Mitt	1,266,011	Kennedy, Edward M.*	19,948	372,006 D	41.0%	58.1%	41.4%	58.6%
1990	2,316,212	992,917	Rappaport, Jim	1,321,712	Kerry, John F.*	1,583	328,795 D	42.9%	57.1%	42.9%	57.1%
1988	2,606,225	884,267	Malone, Joseph	1,693,344	Kennedy, Edward M.*	28,614	809,077 D	33.9%	65.0%	34.3%	65.7%
1984	2,530,195	1,136,806	Shamie, Raymond	1,392,981	Kerry, John F.	408	256,175 D	44.9%	55.1%	44.9%	55.1%
1982	2,050,769	784,602	Shamie, Raymond	1,247,084	Kennedy, Edward M.*	19,083	462,482 D	38.3%	60.8%	38.6%	61.4%
1978	1,985,700	890,584	Brooke, Edward W. III*	1,093,283	Tsongas, Paul E.	1,833	202,699 D	44.8%	55.1%	44.9%	55.1%
1976	2,491,255	722,641	Robertson, Michael	1,726,657	Kennedy, Edward M.*	41,957	1,004,016 D	29.0%	69.3%	29.5%	70.5%
1972	2,370,676	1,505,932	Brooke, Edward W. III*	823,278	Droney, John J.	41,466	682,654 R	63.5%	34.7%	64.7%	35.3%
1970	1,935,607	715,978	Spaulding, Josiah A.	1,202,856	Kennedy, Edward M.*	16,773	486,878 D	37.0%	62.1%	37.3%	62.7%
1966	1,999,949	1,213,473	Brooke, Edward W. III	774,761	Peabody, Endicott	11,715	438,712 R	60.7%	38.7%	61.0%	39.0%
1964	2,312,028	587,663	Whitmore, Howard Jr.	1,716,907	Kennedy, Edward M.*	7,458	1,129,244 D	25.4%	74.3%	25.5%	74.5%
1962S	2,097,085	877,669	Lodge, George C.	1,162,611	Kennedy, Edward M.	56,805	284,942 D	41.9%	55.4%	43.0%	57.0%
1960	2,417,813	1,358,556	Saltonstall, Leverett*	1,050,725	O'Connor, Thomas J. Jr.	8,532	307,831 R	56.2%	43.5%	56.4%	43.6%
1958	1,862,041	488,318	Celeste, Vincent J.	1,362,926	Kennedy, John F.*	10,797	874,608 D	26.2%	73.2%	26.4%	73.6%
1954	1,892,710	956,605	Saltonstall, Leverett*	927,899	Furcolo, Foster	8,206	28,706 R	50.5%	49.0%	50.8%	49.2%
1952	2,360,425	1,141,247	Lodge, Henry Cabot Jr.*	1,211,984	Kennedy, John F.	7,194	70,737 D	48.3%	51.3%	48.5%	51.5%
1948	2,055,798	1,088,475	Saltonstall, Leverett*	954,398	Fitzgerald, John I.	12,925	134,077 R	52.9%	46.4%	53.3%	46.7%
1946	1,662,063	989,736	Lodge, Henry Cabot Jr.	660,200	Walsh, David I.*	12,127	329,536 R	59.5%	39.7%	60.0%	40.0%

Note: An asterisk (*) denotes incumbent. **In past elections, the other vote included: 2002 - 369,807 Libertarian (Michael E. Cloud); 2000 - 308,748 Libertarian (Carla Howell). The Republican Party did not run a candidate in the 2002 Senate election. The 1962 and 2010 elections were for short terms to fill a vacancy; the latter election was held in January 2010.

MASSACHUSETTS

PRESIDENT 2012

2010 Census Population	County	Total Vote	Republican (Romney)	Democratic (Obama)	Other	Rep.-Dem. Plurality	Percentage			
							Total Vote		Major Vote	
							Rep.	Dem.	Rep.	Dem.
215,888	BARNSTABLE	133,115	60,446	70,822	1,847	10,376 D	45.4%	53.2%	46.0%	54.0%
131,219	BERKSHIRE	64,486	14,252	48,843	1,391	34,591 D	22.1%	75.7%	22.6%	77.4%
548,285	BRISTOL	241,509	93,752	142,962	4,795	49,210 D	38.8%	59.2%	39.6%	60.4%
16,535	DUKES	10,968	2,792	7,978	198	5,186 D	25.5%	72.7%	25.9%	74.1%
743,159	ESSEX	366,357	150,480	210,302	5,575	59,822 D	41.1%	57.4%	41.7%	58.3%
71,372	FRANKLIN	37,758	9,344	27,072	1,342	17,728 D	24.7%	71.7%	25.7%	74.3%
463,490	HAMPDEN	200,399	73,392	123,619	3,388	50,227 D	36.6%	61.7%	37.3%	62.7%
158,080	HAMPSHIRE	81,621	21,480	57,359	2,782	35,879 D	26.3%	70.3%	27.2%	72.8%
1,503,085	MIDDLESEX	754,170	267,321	471,804	15,045	204,483 D	35.4%	62.6%	36.2%	63.8%
10,172	NANTUCKET	6,120	2,187	3,830	103	1,643 D	35.7%	62.6%	36.3%	63.7%
670,850	NORFOLK	356,523	148,393	202,714	5,416	54,321 D	41.6%	56.9%	42.3%	57.7%
494,919	PLYMOUTH	256,531	121,086	131,845	3,600	10,759 D	47.2%	51.4%	47.9%	52.1%
722,023	SUFFOLK	289,098	59,999	223,896	5,203	163,897 D	20.8%	77.4%	21.1%	78.9%
798,552	WORCESTER	369,112	163,390	198,244	7,478	34,854 D	44.3%	53.7%	45.2%	54.8%
6,547,629	TOTAL	3,167,767	1,188,314	1,921,290	58,163	732,976 D	37.5%	60.7%	38.2%	61.8%

2010 Census Population	City/Town	Total Vote	Republican (Romney)	Democratic (Obama)	Other	Rep.-Dem. Plurality	Percentage			
							Total Vote		Major Vote	
							Rep.	Dem.	Rep.	Dem.
21,924	ACTON	11,983	3,875	7,872	236	3,997 D	32.3%	65.7%	33.0%	67.0%
28,438	AGAWAM	14,387	6,870	7,288	229	418 D	47.8%	50.7%	48.5%	51.5%
37,819	AMHERST	15,484	1,911	12,798	775	10,887 D	12.3%	82.7%	13.0%	87.0%
33,201	ANDOVER	18,760	9,096	9,401	263	305 D	48.5%	50.1%	49.2%	50.8%
42,844	ARLINGTON	26,159	6,694	18,850	615	12,156 D	25.6%	72.1%	26.2%	73.8%
43,593	ATTLEBORO	19,384	8,470	10,502	412	2,032 D	43.7%	54.2%	44.6%	55.4%
45,193	BARNSTABLE	25,611	12,355	12,947	309	592 D	48.2%	50.6%	48.8%	51.2%
24,729	BELMONT	14,341	4,752	9,313	276	4,561 D	33.1%	64.9%	33.8%	66.2%
39,502	BEVERLY	20,916	8,328	12,158	430	3,830 D	39.8%	58.1%	40.7%	59.3%
40,243	BILLERICA	20,164	9,959	9,839	366	120 R	49.4%	48.8%	50.3%	49.7%
617,594	BOSTON	253,889	48,985	200,190	4,714	151,205 D	19.3%	78.8%	19.7%	80.3%
35,744	BRAINTREE	19,574	9,232	10,059	283	827 D	47.2%	51.4%	47.9%	52.1%
93,810	BROCKTON	34,334	8,710	25,262	362	16,552 D	25.4%	73.6%	25.6%	74.4%
58,732	BROOKLINE	28,653	5,880	22,277	496	16,397 D	20.5%	77.7%	20.9%	79.1%
24,498	BURLINGTON	13,360	6,191	6,983	186	792 D	46.3%	52.3%	47.0%	53.0%
105,162	CAMBRIDGE	50,619	5,476	43,515	1,628	38,039 D	10.8%	86.0%	11.2%	88.8%
21,561	CANTON	12,419	5,779	6,488	152	709 D	46.5%	52.2%	47.1%	52.9%
33,802	CHELMSFORD	19,580	9,573	9,651	356	78 D	48.9%	49.3%	49.8%	50.2%
55,298	CHICOPEE	23,036	8,241	14,302	493	6,061 D	35.8%	62.1%	36.6%	63.4%
17,668	CONCORD	11,026	3,527	7,316	183	3,789 D	32.0%	66.4%	32.5%	67.5%
26,493	DANVERS	14,581	6,997	7,367	217	370 D	48.0%	50.5%	48.7%	51.3%
34,032	DARTMOUTH	16,142	5,985	9,880	277	3,895 D	37.1%	61.2%	37.7%	62.3%
24,729	DEDHAM	13,709	5,734	7,757	218	2,023 D	41.8%	56.6%	42.5%	57.5%
29,457	DRACUT	15,207	8,042	6,941	224	1,101 R	52.9%	45.6%	53.7%	46.3%
23,112	EASTON	12,107	6,060	5,262	785	798 R	50.1%	43.5%	53.5%	46.5%
41,667	EVERETT	13,175	3,589	9,409	177	5,820 D	27.2%	71.4%	27.6%	72.4%
88,857	FALL RIVER	29,746	7,390	21,878	478	14,488 D	24.8%	73.5%	25.2%	74.8%
31,531	FALMOUTH	19,589	8,163	11,127	299	2,964 D	41.7%	56.8%	42.3%	57.7%
40,318	FITCHBURG	14,390	5,602	8,547	241	2,945 D	38.9%	59.4%	39.6%	60.4%
68,318	FRAMINGHAM	27,971	8,978	18,499	494	9,521 D	32.1%	66.1%	32.7%	67.3%
31,635	FRANKLIN	17,489	8,566	8,616	307	50 D	49.0%	49.3%	49.9%	50.1%
28,789	GLOUCESTER	15,616	5,535	9,780	301	4,245 D	35.4%	62.6%	36.1%	63.9%
60,879	HAVERHILL	27,979	11,894	15,592	493	3,698 D	42.5%	55.7%	43.3%	56.7%
22,157	HINGHAM	14,222	7,249	6,803	170	446 R	51.0%	47.8%	51.6%	48.4%
39,880	HOLYOKE	16,449	3,656	12,536	257	8,880 D	22.2%	76.2%	22.6%	77.4%

MASSACHUSETTS
PRESIDENT 2012

2010 Census Population	City/Town	Total Vote	Republican (Romney)	Democratic (Obama)	Other	Rep.-Dem. Plurality	Percentage			
							Total Vote		Major Vote	
							Rep.	Dem.	Rep.	Dem.
76,377	LAWRENCE	21,962	3,462	18,278	222	14,816 D	15.8%	83.2%	15.9%	84.1%
40,759	LEOMINSTER	18,694	8,552	9,792	350	1,240 D	45.7%	52.4%	46.6%	53.4%
31,394	LEXINGTON	18,365	5,293	12,750	322	7,457 D	28.8%	69.4%	29.3%	70.7%
106,519	LOWELL	34,081	10,643	22,771	667	12,128 D	31.2%	66.8%	31.9%	68.1%
90,329	LYNN	32,076	8,512	23,124	440	14,612 D	26.5%	72.1%	26.9%	73.1%
59,450	MALDEN	21,105	5,730	15,010	365	9,280 D	27.1%	71.1%	27.6%	72.4%
19,808	MARBLEHEAD	12,660	5,510	6,991	159	1,481 D	43.5%	55.2%	44.1%	55.9%
38,499	MARLBOROUGH	16,761	6,870	9,587	304	2,717 D	41.0%	57.2%	41.7%	58.3%
25,132	MARSHFIELD	15,112	7,874	7,046	192	828 R	52.1%	46.6%	52.8%	47.2%
56,173	MEDFORD	27,811	8,359	18,874	578	10,515 D	30.1%	67.9%	30.7%	69.3%
26,983	MELROSE	15,584	5,971	9,368	245	3,397 D	38.3%	60.1%	38.9%	61.1%
47,255	METHUEN	21,572	10,198	11,092	282	894 D	47.3%	51.4%	47.9%	52.1%
27,999	MILFORD	12,898	5,519	7,159	220	1,640 D	42.8%	55.5%	43.5%	56.5%
27,003	MILTON	15,917	6,133	9,569	215	3,436 D	38.5%	60.1%	39.1%	60.9%
33,006	NATICK	18,775	6,792	11,685	298	4,893 D	36.2%	62.2%	36.8%	63.2%
28,886	NEEDHAM	17,275	6,614	10,452	209	3,838 D	38.3%	60.5%	38.8%	61.2%
95,072	NEW BEDFORD	33,383	7,550	25,253	580	17,703 D	22.6%	75.6%	23.0%	77.0%
85,146	NEWTON	45,039	12,154	32,099	786	19,945 D	27.0%	71.3%	27.5%	72.5%
28,352	NORTH ANDOVER	15,278	8,045	7,073	160	972 R	52.7%	46.3%	53.2%	46.8%
28,712	NORTH ATTLEBOROUGH	14,253	7,359	6,651	243	708 R	51.6%	46.7%	52.5%	47.5%
28,549	NORTHAMPTON	16,106	2,182	13,259	665	11,077 D	13.5%	82.3%	14.1%	85.9%
28,602	NORWOOD	14,871	6,389	8,235	247	1,846 D	43.0%	55.4%	43.7%	56.3%
51,251	PEABODY	26,999	11,622	15,027	350	3,405 D	43.0%	55.7%	43.6%	56.4%
44,737	PITTSFIELD	20,065	4,057	15,648	360	11,591 D	20.2%	78.0%	20.6%	79.4%
56,468	PLYMOUTH	30,032	14,347	15,233	452	886 D	47.8%	50.7%	48.5%	51.5%
92,271	QUINCY	40,456	14,850	24,849	757	9,999 D	36.7%	61.4%	37.4%	62.6%
32,112	RANDOLPH	15,149	3,552	11,441	156	7,889 D	23.4%	75.5%	23.7%	76.3%
24,747	READING	14,411	6,683	7,515	213	832 D	46.4%	52.1%	47.1%	52.9%
51,755	REVERE	17,832	5,921	11,665	246	5,744 D	33.2%	65.4%	33.7%	66.3%
41,340	SALEM	19,738	5,725	13,605	408	7,880 D	29.0%	68.9%	29.6%	70.4%
26,628	SAUGUS	13,740	6,590	6,990	160	400 D	48.0%	50.9%	48.5%	51.5%
18,133	SCITUATE	11,425	5,697	5,582	146	115 R	49.9%	48.9%	50.5%	49.5%
35,608	SHREWSBURY	18,197	8,180	9,754	263	1,574 D	45.0%	53.6%	45.6%	54.4%
75,754	SOMERVILLE	35,156	4,885	28,853	1,418	23,968 D	13.9%	82.1%	14.5%	85.5%
153,060	SPRINGFIELD	55,069	10,515	43,869	685	33,354 D	19.1%	79.7%	19.3%	80.7%
21,437	STONEHAM	12,471	5,609	6,696	166	1,087 D	45.0%	53.7%	45.6%	54.4%
26,962	STOUGHTON	13,921	5,594	8,119	208	2,525 D	40.2%	58.3%	40.8%	59.2%
55,874	TAUNTON	23,112	8,925	13,769	418	4,844 D	38.6%	59.6%	39.3%	60.7%
28,961	TEWKSBURY	16,205	8,360	7,578	267	782 R	51.6%	46.8%	52.5%	47.5%
24,932	WAKEFIELD	14,559	6,820	7,515	224	695 D	46.8%	51.6%	47.6%	52.4%
24,070	WALPOLE	14,047	7,466	6,385	196	1,081 R	53.2%	45.5%	53.9%	46.1%
60,632	WALTHAM	25,316	8,856	15,906	554	7,050 D	35.0%	62.8%	35.8%	64.2%
31,915	WATERTOWN	16,800	4,526	11,912	362	7,386 D	26.9%	70.9%	27.5%	72.5%
27,982	WELLESLEY	14,961	6,264	8,530	167	2,266 D	41.9%	57.0%	42.3%	57.7%
28,391	WEST SPRINGFIELD	11,543	5,172	6,175	196	1,003 D	44.8%	53.5%	45.6%	54.4%
41,094	WESTFIELD	17,882	8,218	9,281	383	1,063 D	46.0%	51.9%	47.0%	53.0%
53,743	WEYMOUTH	27,985	12,362	15,166	457	2,804 D	44.2%	54.2%	44.9%	55.1%
21,374	WINCHESTER	12,937	5,635	7,107	195	1,472 D	43.6%	54.9%	44.2%	55.8%
38,120	WOBURN	19,386	8,730	10,385	271	1,655 D	45.0%	53.6%	45.7%	54.3%
181,045	WORCESTER	61,393	17,949	42,210	1,234	24,261 D	29.2%	68.8%	29.8%	70.2%
23,793	YARMOUTH	13,917	6,541	7,198	178	657 D	47.0%	51.7%	47.6%	52.4%

MASSACHUSETTS

SENATOR 2012

2010 Census Population	County	Total Vote	Republican (Brown)	Democratic (Warren)	Other	Rep.-Dem. Plurality		Total Vote Rep.	Total Vote Dem.	Major Vote Rep.	Major Vote Dem.
215,888	BARNSTABLE	132,916	69,597	63,277	42	6,320	R	52.4%	47.6%	52.4%	47.6%
131,219	BERKSHIRE	63,971	18,683	45,256	32	26,573	D	29.2%	70.7%	29.2%	70.8%
548,285	BRISTOL	240,291	114,277	125,906	108	11,629	D	47.6%	52.4%	47.6%	52.4%
16,535	DUKES	10,912	3,520	7,387	5	3,867	D	32.3%	67.7%	32.3%	67.7%
743,159	ESSEX	365,275	184,225	180,861	189	3,364	R	50.4%	49.5%	50.5%	49.5%
71,372	FRANKLIN	37,636	12,495	25,114	27	12,619	D	33.2%	66.7%	33.2%	66.8%
463,490	HAMPDEN	199,168	90,538	108,414	216	17,876	D	45.5%	54.4%	45.5%	54.5%
158,080	HAMPSHIRE	81,319	27,827	53,417	75	25,590	D	34.2%	65.7%	34.3%	65.7%
1,503,085	MIDDLESEX	751,691	331,004	420,142	545	89,138	D	44.0%	55.9%	44.1%	55.9%
10,172	NANTUCKET	6,091	2,653	3,435	3	782	D	43.6%	56.4%	43.6%	56.4%
670,850	NORFOLK	355,679	181,187	174,269	223	6,918	R	50.9%	49.0%	51.0%	49.0%
494,919	PLYMOUTH	255,952	144,172	111,643	137	32,529	R	56.3%	43.6%	56.4%	43.6%
722,023	SUFFOLK	287,541	78,469	208,779	293	130,310	D	27.3%	72.6%	27.3%	72.7%
798,552	WORCESTER	368,111	199,401	168,446	264	30,955	R	54.2%	45.8%	54.2%	45.8%
6,547,629	TOTAL	3,156,553	1,458,048	1,696,346	2,159	238,298	D	46.2%	53.7%	46.2%	53.8%

2010 Census Population	City/Town	Total Vote	Republican (Brown)	Democratic (Warren)	Other	Rep.-Dem. Plurality		Total Vote Rep.	Total Vote Dem.	Major Vote Rep.	Major Vote Dem.
21,924	ACTON	11,957	4,965	6,977	15	2,012	D	41.5%	58.4%	41.6%	58.4%
28,438	AGAWAM	14,327	8,207	6,109	11	2,098	R	57.3%	42.6%	57.3%	42.7%
37,819	AMHERST	15,363	3,002	12,330	31	9,328	D	19.5%	80.3%	19.6%	80.4%
33,201	ANDOVER	18,705	10,591	8,106	8	2,485	R	56.6%	43.3%	56.6%	43.4%
42,844	ARLINGTON	26,084	8,314	17,748	22	9,434	D	31.9%	68.0%	31.9%	68.1%
43,593	ATTLEBORO	19,305	10,492	8,807	6	1,685	R	54.3%	45.6%	54.4%	45.6%
45,193	BARNSTABLE	25,573	14,116	11,457		2,659	R	55.2%	44.8%	55.2%	44.8%
24,729	BELMONT	14,291	5,612	8,668	11	3,056	D	39.3%	60.7%	39.3%	60.7%
39,502	BEVERLY	20,864	10,547	10,305	12	242	R	50.6%	49.4%	50.6%	49.4%
40,243	BILLERICA	20,151	12,049	8,084	18	3,965	R	59.8%	40.1%	59.8%	40.2%
617,594	BOSTON	252,523	64,827	187,432	264	122,605	D	25.7%	74.2%	25.7%	74.3%
35,744	BRAINTREE	19,544	11,050	8,478	16	2,572	R	56.5%	43.4%	56.6%	43.4%
93,810	BROCKTON	34,188	11,022	23,155	11	12,133	D	32.2%	67.7%	32.2%	67.8%
58,732	BROOKLINE	28,573	7,496	21,068	9	13,572	D	26.2%	73.7%	26.2%	73.8%
24,498	BURLINGTON	13,335	7,464	5,858	13	1,606	R	56.0%	43.9%	56.0%	44.0%
105,162	CAMBRIDGE	50,312	7,637	42,622	53	34,985	D	15.2%	84.7%	15.2%	84.8%
21,561	CANTON	12,391	6,763	5,624	4	1,139	R	54.6%	45.4%	54.6%	45.4%
33,802	CHELMSFORD	19,526	11,580	7,939	7	3,641	R	59.3%	40.7%	59.3%	40.7%
55,298	CHICOPEE	22,915	10,678	12,180	57	1,502	D	46.6%	53.2%	46.7%	53.3%
17,668	CONCORD	10,998	4,232	6,764	2	2,532	D	38.5%	61.5%	38.5%	61.5%
26,493	DANVERS	14,561	8,605	5,952	4	2,653	R	59.1%	40.9%	59.1%	40.9%
34,032	DARTMOUTH	16,077	7,318	8,751	8	1,433	D	45.5%	54.4%	45.5%	54.5%
24,729	DEDHAM	13,678	6,951	6,715	12	236	R	50.8%	49.1%	50.9%	49.1%
29,457	DRACUT	15,193	9,694	5,499		4,195	R	63.8%	36.2%	63.8%	36.2%
23,112	EASTON	12,074	7,212	4,858	4	2,354	R	59.7%	40.2%	59.8%	40.2%
41,667	EVERETT	13,095	4,664	8,416	15	3,752	D	35.6%	64.3%	35.7%	64.3%
88,857	FALL RIVER	29,405	9,501	19,898	6	10,397	D	32.3%	67.7%	32.3%	67.7%
31,531	FALMOUTH	19,528	9,543	9,973	12	430	D	48.9%	51.1%	48.9%	51.1%
40,318	FITCHBURG	14,431	7,087	7,339	5	252	D	49.1%	50.9%	49.1%	50.9%
68,318	FRAMINGHAM	27,883	11,399	16,460	24	5,061	D	40.9%	59.0%	40.9%	59.1%
31,635	FRANKLIN	17,461	10,737	6,709	15	4,028	R	61.5%	38.4%	61.5%	38.5%
28,789	GLOUCESTER	15,548	7,417	8,119	12	702	D	47.7%	52.2%	47.7%	52.3%
60,879	HAVERHILL	27,896	14,648	13,241	7	1,407	R	52.5%	47.5%	52.5%	47.5%
22,157	HINGHAM	14,171	8,339	5,824	8	2,515	R	58.8%	41.1%	58.9%	41.1%
39,880	HOLYOKE	16,353	4,921	11,432		6,511	D	30.1%	69.9%	30.1%	69.9%

MASSACHUSETTS

SENATOR 2012

2010 Census Population	City/Town	Total Vote	Republican (Brown)	Democratic (Warren)	Other	Rep.-Dem. Plurality	Percentage			
							Total Vote		Major Vote	
							Rep.	Dem.	Rep.	Dem.
76,377	LAWRENCE	21,773	4,517	17,235	21	12,718 D	20.7%	79.2%	20.8%	79.2%
40,759	LEOMINSTER	18,668	10,200	8,459	9	1,741 R	54.6%	45.3%	54.7%	45.3%
31,394	LEXINGTON	18,322	6,397	11,922	3	5,525 D	34.9%	65.1%	34.9%	65.1%
106,519	LOWELL	33,839	13,989	19,825	25	5,836 D	41.3%	58.6%	41.4%	58.6%
90,329	LYNN	31,949	11,097	20,811	41	9,714 D	34.7%	65.1%	34.8%	65.2%
59,450	MALDEN	20,962	7,353	13,582	27	6,229 D	35.1%	64.8%	35.1%	64.9%
19,808	MARBLEHEAD	12,650	6,573	6,076	1	497 R	52.0%	48.0%	52.0%	48.0%
38,499	MARLBOROUGH	16,715	8,648	8,055	12	593 R	51.7%	48.2%	51.8%	48.2%
25,132	MARSHFIELD	15,094	9,284	5,804	6	3,480 R	61.5%	38.5%	61.5%	38.5%
56,173	MEDFORD	27,696	10,686	16,984	26	6,298 D	38.6%	61.3%	38.6%	61.4%
26,983	MELROSE	15,549	7,465	8,076	8	611 D	48.0%	51.9%	48.0%	52.0%
47,255	METHUEN	21,504	12,173	9,325	6	2,848 R	56.6%	43.4%	56.6%	43.4%
27,999	MILFORD	12,858	6,835	6,011	12	824 R	53.2%	46.7%	53.2%	46.8%
27,003	MILTON	15,878	7,381	8,491	6	1,110 D	46.5%	53.5%	46.5%	53.5%
33,006	NATICK	18,742	8,624	10,113	5	1,489 D	46.0%	54.0%	46.0%	54.0%
28,886	NEEDHAM	17,247	8,187	9,054	6	867 D	47.5%	52.5%	47.5%	52.5%
95,072	NEW BEDFORD	33,083	9,866	23,178	39	13,312 D	29.8%	70.1%	29.9%	70.1%
85,146	NEWTON	44,939	15,034	29,868	37	14,834 D	33.5%	66.5%	33.5%	66.5%
28,352	NORTH ANDOVER	15,244	9,384	5,860		3,524 R	61.6%	38.4%	61.6%	38.4%
28,712	NORTH ATTLEBOROUGH	14,241	9,064	5,177		3,887 R	63.6%	36.4%	63.6%	36.4%
28,549	NORTHAMPTON	16,028	2,965	13,052	11	10,087 D	18.5%	81.4%	18.5%	81.5%
28,602	NORWOOD	14,843	7,922	6,911	10	1,011 R	53.4%	46.6%	53.4%	46.6%
51,251	PEABODY	26,920	14,389	12,510	21	1,879 R	53.5%	46.5%	53.5%	46.5%
44,737	PITTSFIELD	19,899	5,413	14,486		9,073 D	27.2%	72.8%	27.2%	72.8%
56,468	PLYMOUTH	29,967	17,264	12,689	14	4,575 R	57.6%	42.3%	57.6%	42.4%
92,271	QUINCY	40,240	18,619	21,580	41	2,961 D	46.3%	53.6%	46.3%	53.7%
32,112	RANDOLPH	15,084	4,496	10,580	8	6,084 D	29.8%	70.1%	29.8%	70.2%
24,747	READING	14,367	8,017	6,342	8	1,675 R	55.8%	44.1%	55.8%	44.2%
51,755	REVERE	17,739	7,235	10,486	18	3,251 D	40.8%	59.1%	40.8%	59.2%
41,340	SALEM	19,680	7,717	11,953	10	4,236 D	39.2%	60.7%	39.2%	60.8%
26,628	SAUGUS	13,711	7,808	5,899	4	1,909 R	56.9%	43.0%	57.0%	43.0%
18,133	SCITUATE	11,420	6,723	4,693	4	2,030 R	58.9%	41.1%	58.9%	41.1%
35,608	SHREWSBURY	18,136	10,025	8,103	8	1,922 R	55.3%	44.7%	55.3%	44.7%
75,754	SOMERVILLE	34,898	7,071	27,782	45	20,711 D	20.3%	79.6%	20.3%	79.7%
153,060	SPRINGFIELD	54,498	14,088	40,341	69	26,253 D	25.9%	74.0%	25.9%	74.1%
21,437	STONEHAM	12,451	6,841	5,610		1,231 R	54.9%	45.1%	54.9%	45.1%
26,962	STOUGHTON	13,882	6,810	7,066	6	256 D	49.1%	50.9%	49.1%	50.9%
55,874	TAUNTON	23,002	11,116	11,874	12	758 D	48.3%	51.6%	48.4%	51.6%
28,961	TEWKSBURY	16,173	9,975	6,173	25	3,802 R	61.7%	38.2%	61.8%	38.2%
24,932	WAKEFIELD	14,531	8,445	6,066	20	2,379 R	58.1%	41.7%	58.2%	41.8%
24,070	WALPOLE	14,055	9,002	5,047	6	3,955 R	64.0%	35.9%	64.1%	35.9%
60,632	WALTHAM	25,216	11,147	14,051	18	2,904 D	44.2%	55.7%	44.2%	55.8%
31,915	WATERTOWN	16,764	5,952	10,802	10	4,850 D	35.5%	64.4%	35.5%	64.5%
27,982	WELLESLEY	14,885	7,415	7,470		55 D	49.8%	50.2%	49.8%	50.2%
28,391	WEST SPRINGFIELD	11,480	6,305	5,167	8	1,138 R	54.9%	45.0%	55.0%	45.0%
41,094	WESTFIELD	17,822	10,083	7,722	17	2,361 R	56.6%	43.3%	56.6%	43.4%
53,743	WEYMOUTH	27,922	15,143	12,755	24	2,388 R	54.2%	45.7%	54.3%	45.7%
21,374	WINCHESTER	12,897	6,623	6,268	6	355 R	51.4%	48.6%	51.4%	48.6%
38,120	WOBURN	19,354	10,646	8,702	6	1,944 R	55.0%	45.0%	55.0%	45.0%
181,045	WORCESTER	61,154	23,037	38,051	66	15,014 D	37.7%	62.2%	37.7%	62.3%
23,793	YARMOUTH	13,904	7,486	6,412	6	1,074 R	53.8%	46.1%	53.9%	46.1%

MASSACHUSETTS

HOUSE OF REPRESENTATIVES

CD	Year	Total Vote	Republican Vote	Republican Candidate	Democratic Vote	Democratic Candidate	Other Vote	Rep.-Dem. Plurality	Percentage Total Vote Rep.	Dem.	Major Vote Rep.	Dem.
1	2012	266,133			261,936	NEAL, RICHARD*	4,197	261,936 D		98.4%		100.0%
2	2012	263,335			259,257	MCGOVERN, JIM*	4,078	259,257 D		98.5%		100.0%
3	2012	321,753	109,372	GOLNIK, JONATHAN A.	212,119	TSONGAS, NIKI*	262	102,747 D	34.0%	65.9%	34.0%	66.0%
4	2012	362,245	129,936	BIELAT, SEAN	221,303	KENNEDY, JOE	11,006	91,367 D	35.9%	61.1%	37.0%	63.0%
5	2012	341,109	82,944	TIERNEY, TOM	257,490	MARKEY, EDWARD J.*	675	174,546 D	24.3%	75.5%	24.4%	75.6%
6	2012	374,807	176,612	TISEI, RICHARD	180,942	TIERNEY, JOHN F.*	17,253	4,330 D	47.1%	48.3%	49.4%	50.6%
7	2012	252,836			210,794	CAPUANO, MICHAEL E.*	42,042	210,794 D		83.4%		100.0%
8	2012	346,811	82,242	SELVAGGI, JOE	263,999	LYNCH, STEPHEN F.*	570	181,757 D	23.7%	76.1%	23.8%	76.2%
9	2012	362,405	116,531	SHELDON, CHRISTOPHER	212,754	KEATING, WILLIAM R.*	33,120	96,223 D	32.2%	58.7%	35.4%	64.6%
TOTAL	2012	2,891,434	697,637		2,080,594		113,203	1,382,957 D	24.1%	72.0%	25.1%	74.9%

Note: An asterisk (*) denotes incumbent.

MASSACHUSETTS

GENERAL AND PRIMARY ELECTIONS

GENERAL ELECTIONS: OTHER VOTE

President Other vote was 30,920 Libertarian (Gary E. Johnson), 20,691 Green (Jill Stein), 6,552 Write-in (Scattered Write-In)

Senator Other vote was 2,159 Write-in (Scattered Write-In)

House Other vote was:

CD 1 4,197 Write-in (Scattered Write-In)
CD 2 4,078 Write-in (Scattered Write-In)
CD 3 262 Write-in (Scattered Write-In)
CD 4 10,741 Independent (David A. Rosa), 265 Write-in (Scattered Write-In)
CD 5 675 Write-in (Scattered Write-In)
CD 6 16,739 Libertarian (Daniel Fishman), 514 Write-in (Scattered Write-In)
CD 7 41,199 Independent (Karla Romero), 843 Write-in (Scattered Write-In)
CD 8 570 Write-in (Scattered Write-In)
CD 9 32,655 Independent (Daniel Botelho), 465 Write-in (Scattered Write-In)

PRIMARY ELECTIONS: SUPPLEMENTARY INFORMATION

Primary	March 6, 2012 (President) September 6, 2012 (Congress)	**Registration** (as of September 6, 2012)	4,163,243	Democratic Republican Green Unenrolled	1,486,648 471,829 5,727 2,199,039

Primary Type Semi-open—Registered Democrats and Republicans could vote only in their party's primary. "Unenrolled" voters could participate in either party's primary.

MASSACHUSETTS

GENERAL AND PRIMARY ELECTIONS

	REPUBLICAN PRIMARIES			DEMOCRATIC PRIMARIES		
President	Romney, W. Mitt	266,313	72.1%	Obama, Barack H.*	127,909	86.5%
	Santorum, Rick	44,564	12.1%	No Preference	16,075	10.9%
	Paul, Ron	35,219	9.5%	Scattered Write-In	3,889	2.6%
	Gingrich, Newt	16,991	4.6%			
	Huntsman, Jon Jr.	2,268	0.6%			
	No Preference	1,793	0.5%			
	Perry, Rick	991	0.3%			
	Bachmann, Michele	865	0.2%			
	Scattered Write-In	613	0.2%			
	TOTAL	369,617		TOTAL	147,873	
Senator	Brown, Scott P.*	133,860	99.5%	Warren, Elizabeth	308,979	97.6%
	Scattered Write-In	733	0.5%	Scattered Write-In	7,638	2.4%
	TOTAL	134,593		TOTAL	316,617	
Congressional District 1	Scattered Write-In	1,021	100.0%	Neal, Richard*	40,295	65.5%
				Nuciforo, Andrea F. Jr.	15,159	24.6%
				Shein, Bill	6,059	9.8%
				Scattered Write-In	33	0.1%
	TOTAL	1,021		TOTAL	61,546	
Congressional District 2	Scattered Write-In	569	100.0%	McGovern, Jim*	24,375	91.3%
				Feegbeh, William	2,265	8.5%
				Scattered Write-In	44	0.2%
	TOTAL	569		TOTAL	26,684	
Congressional District 3	Golnik, Jonathan A.	12,928	66.3%	Tsongas, Niki*	24,105	99.2%
	Weaver, Thomas J.M.	6,527	33.5%	Scattered Write-In	196	0.8%
	Scattered Write-In	38	0.2%			
	TOTAL	19,493		TOTAL	24,301	
Congressional District 4	Bielat, Sean	14,834	73.2%	Kennedy, Joe	36,557	90.0%
	Childs, Elizabeth	2,735	13.5%	Brown, Rachel E.	2,635	6.5%
	Steinhof, David L.	2,669	13.2%	Robinson, Herb	1,373	3.4%
	Scattered Write-In	25	0.1%	Scattered Write-In	73	0.2%
	TOTAL	20,263		TOTAL	40,638	
Congressional District 5	Tierney, Tom	4,789	41.2%	Markey, Edward J.*	38,196	99.2%
	Addivinola, Frank John Jr.	3,531	30.3%	Scattered Write-In	316	0.8%
	Semon, Jeffrey M.	3,250	27.9%			
	Scattered Write-In	65	0.6%			
	TOTAL	11,635		TOTAL	38,512	
Congressional District 6	Tisei, Richard	18,331	99.0%	Tierney, John F.*	28,395	98.2%
	Scattered Write-In	186	1.0%	Scattered Write-In	517	1.8%
	TOTAL	18,517		TOTAL	28,912	
Congressional District 7	Scattered Write-In	466	100.0%	Capuano, Michael E.*	32,445	98.6%
				Scattered Write-In	446	1.4%
	TOTAL	466		TOTAL	32,891	
Congressional District 8	Selvaggi, Joe	5,968	59.1%	Lynch, Stephen F.*	29,352	98.8%
	Temperley, Matias	4,081	40.4%	Scattered Write-In	369	1.2%
	Scattered Write-In	47	0.5%			
	TOTAL	10,096		TOTAL	29,721	
Congressional District 9	Sheldon, Christopher	11,046	50.6%	Keating, William R.*	31,366	59.1%
	Chaprales, Adam G.	10,697	49.0%	Sutter, C. Samuel	21,675	40.8%
	Scattered Write-In	94	0.4%	Scattered Write-In	47	0.1%
	TOTAL	21,837		TOTAL	53,088	

Note: An asterisk (*) denotes incumbent.

MICHIGAN

Congressional districts first established for elections held in 2012

14 members

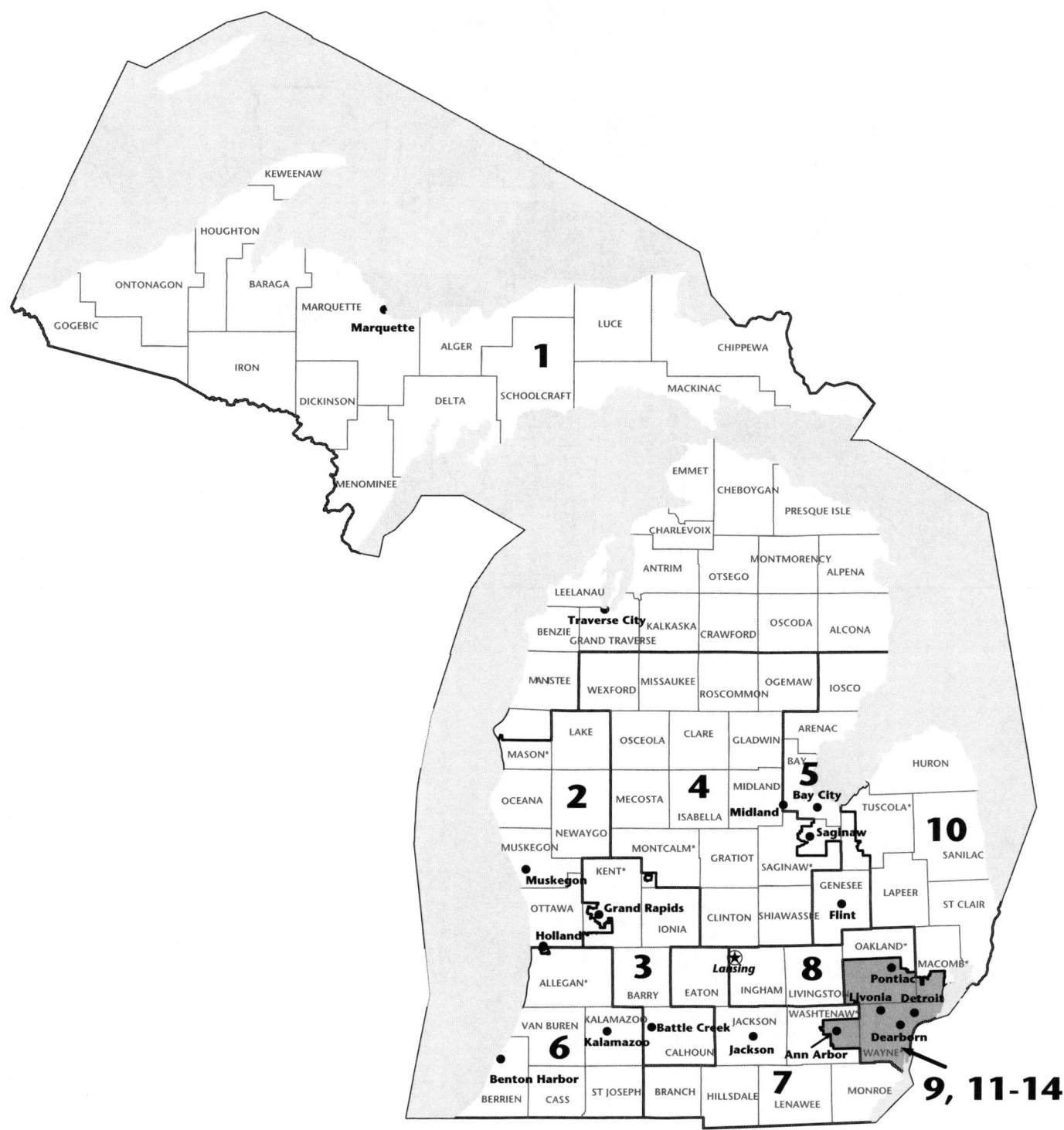

* Asterisk indicates a county whose boundaries include parts of two or more Congressional districts.

MICHIGAN
Detroit Area

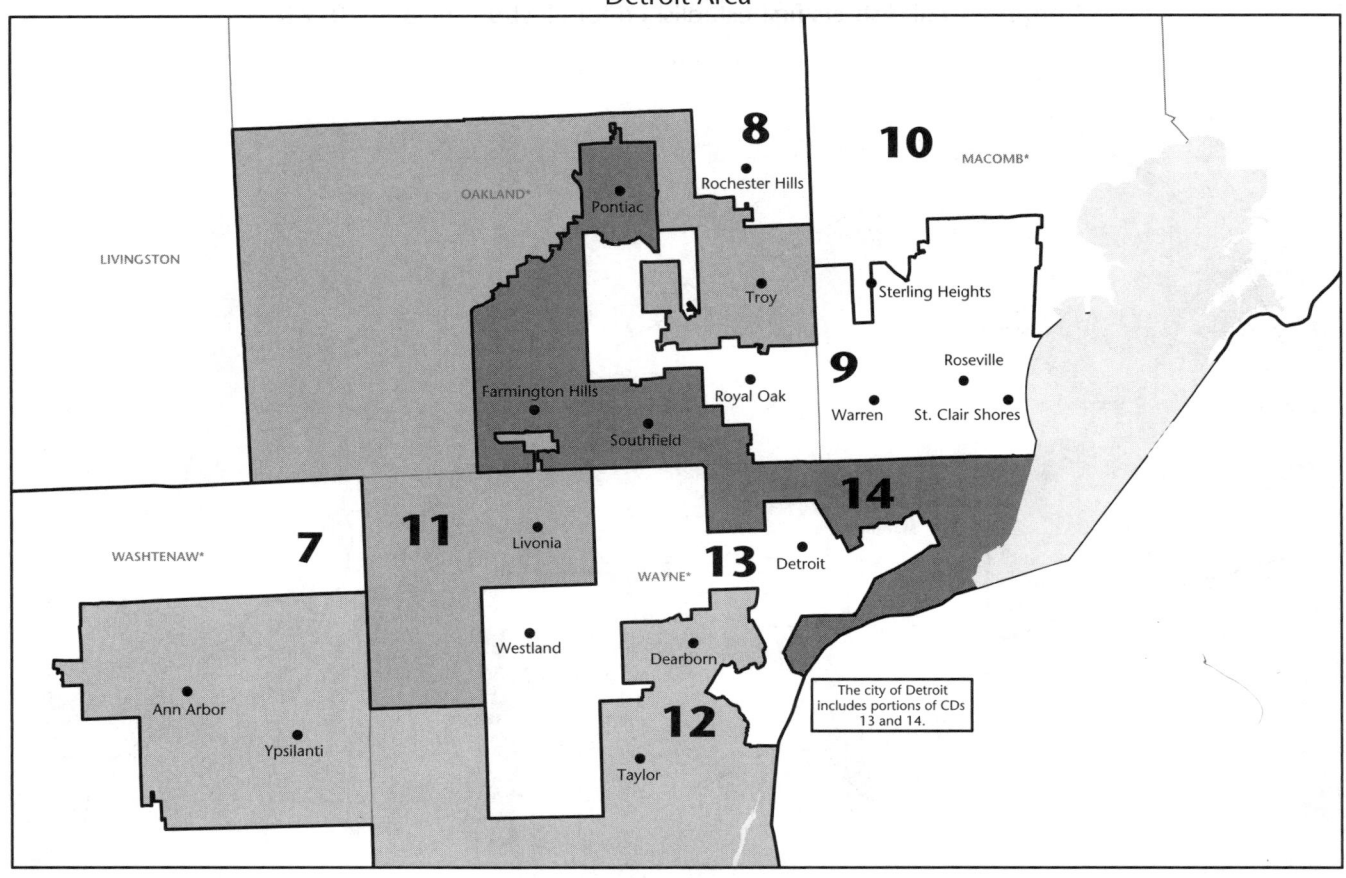

* Asterisk indicates a county whose boundaries include parts of two or more Congressional districts.

MICHIGAN

GOVERNOR
Rick Snyder (R). Elected 2010 to a four-year term.

SENATORS (2 Democrats)
Carl Levin (D). Reelected 2008 to a six-year term. Previously elected 2002, 1996, 1990, 1984, 1978.

Debbie Stabenow (D). Reelected 2012 to a six-year term. Previously elected 2006, 2000.

REPRESENTATIVES (9 Republicans, 5 Democrats)
1. Dan Benishek (R)
2. Bill Huizenga (R)
3. Justin Amash (R)
4. Dave Camp (R)
5. Dan Kildee (D)
6. Fred Upton (R)
7. Tim Walberg (R)
8. Mike Rogers (R)
9. Sander Levin (D)
10. Candice S. Miller (R)
11. Kerry Bentivolio (R)
12. John D. Dingell (D)
13. John Conyers Jr. (D)
14. Gary Peters (D)

POSTWAR VOTE FOR PRESIDENT

		Republican		Democratic		Other	Rep.-Dem.	Total Vote		Major Vote	
Year	Total Vote	Vote	Candidate	Vote	Candidate	Vote	Plurality	Rep.	Dem.	Rep.	Dem.
2012	4,730,961	2,115,256	Romney, W. Mitt	2,564,569	Obama, Barack H.*	51,136	449,313 D	44.7%	54.2%	45.2%	54.8%
2008	5,001,766	2,048,639	McCain, John S. III	2,872,579	Obama, Barack H.	80,548	823,940 D	41.0%	57.4%	41.6%	58.4%
2004	4,839,252	2,313,746	Bush, George W.*	2,479,183	Kerry, John F.	46,323	165,437 D	47.8%	51.2%	48.3%	51.7%
2000**	4,232,711	1,953,139	Bush, George W.	2,170,418	Gore, Albert Jr.	109,154	217,279 D	46.1%	51.3%	47.4%	52.6%
1996**	3,848,844	1,481,212	Dole, Robert "Bob"	1,989,653	Clinton, Bill*	377,979	508,441 D	38.5%	51.7%	42.7%	57.3%
1992**	4,274,673	1,554,940	Bush, George H.*	1,871,182	Clinton, Bill	848,551	316,242 D	36.4%	43.8%	45.4%	54.6%
1988	3,669,163	1,965,486	Bush, George H.	1,675,783	Dukakis, Michael S.	27,894	289,703 R	53.6%	45.7%	54.0%	46.0%
1984	3,801,658	2,251,571	Reagan, Ronald*	1,529,638	Mondale, Walter F.	20,449	721,933 R	59.2%	40.2%	59.5%	40.5%
1980**	3,909,725	1,915,225	Reagan, Ronald	1,661,532	Carter, Jimmy*	332,968	253,693 R	49.0%	42.5%	53.5%	46.5%
1976	3,653,749	1,893,742	Ford, Gerald R.*	1,696,714	Carter, Jimmy	63,293	197,028 R	51.8%	46.4%	52.7%	47.3%
1972	3,489,727	1,961,721	Nixon, Richard M.*	1,459,435	McGovern, George S.	68,571	502,286 R	56.2%	41.8%	57.3%	42.7%
1968**	3,306,250	1,370,665	Nixon, Richard M.	1,593,082	Humphrey, Hubert H. Jr.	342,503	222,417 D	41.5%	48.2%	46.2%	53.8%
1964	3,203,102	1,060,152	Goldwater, Barry M. Sr.	2,136,615	Johnson, Lyndon B.*	6,335	1,076,463 D	33.1%	66.7%	33.2%	66.8%
1960	3,318,097	1,620,428	Nixon, Richard M.	1,687,269	Kennedy, John F.	10,400	66,841 D	48.8%	50.9%	49.0%	51.0%
1956	3,080,468	1,713,647	Eisenhower, Dwight D.*	1,359,898	Stevenson, Adlai E. II	6,923	353,749 R	55.6%	44.1%	55.8%	44.2%
1952	2,798,592	1,551,529	Eisenhower, Dwight D.	1,230,657	Stevenson, Adlai E. II	16,406	320,872 R	55.4%	44.0%	55.8%	44.2%
1948	2,109,609	1,038,595	Dewey, Thomas E.	1,003,448	Truman, Harry S.*	67,566	35,147 R	49.2%	47.6%	50.9%	49.1%

Note: An asterisk (*) denotes incumbent. **In past elections, the other vote included: 2000 - 84,165 Green (Ralph Nader); 1996 - 336,670 Reform (Ross Perot); 1992 - 824,813 Independent (Perot); 1980 - 275,223 Independent (John Anderson); 1968 - 331,968 American Independent (George Wallace).

MICHIGAN

POSTWAR VOTE FOR GOVERNOR

Year	Total Vote	Republican		Democratic		Other Vote	Rep.-Dem. Plurality	Percentage			
								Total Vote		Major Vote	
		Vote	Candidate	Vote	Candidate			Rep.	Dem.	Rep.	Dem.
2010	3,226,088	1,874,834	Snyder, Rick	1,287,320	Bernero, Virg	63,934	587,514 R	58.1%	39.9%	59.3%	40.7%
2006	3,801,256	1,608,086	DeVos, Dick	2,142,513	Granholm, Jennifer M.*	50,657	534,427 D	42.3%	56.4%	42.9%	57.1%
2002	3,177,565	1,506,104	Posthumus, Dick	1,633,796	Granholm, Jennifer M.	37,665	127,692 D	47.4%	51.4%	48.0%	52.0%
1998	3,027,104	1,883,005	Engler, John*	1,143,574	Fieger, Geoffrey	525	739,431 R	62.2%	37.8%	62.2%	37.8%
1994	3,089,077	1,899,101	Engler, John*	1,188,438	Wolpe, Howard	1,538	710,663 R	61.5%	38.5%	61.5%	38.5%
1990	2,564,563	1,276,134	Engler, John	1,258,539	Blanchard, James J.*	29,890	17,595 R	49.8%	49.1%	50.3%	49.7%
1986	2,396,564	753,647	Lucas, William	1,632,138	Blanchard, James J.*	10,779	878,491 D	31.4%	68.1%	31.6%	68.4%
1982	3,040,008	1,369,582	Headlee, Richard H.	1,561,291	Blanchard, James J.	109,135	191,709 D	45.1%	51.4%	46.7%	53.3%
1978	2,867,212	1,628,485	Milliken, William G.*	1,237,256	Fitzgerald, William	1,471	391,229 R	56.8%	43.2%	56.8%	43.2%
1974	2,657,020	1,356,865	Milliken, William G.*	1,242,250	Levin, Sander	57,905	114,615 R	51.1%	46.8%	52.2%	47.8%
1970	2,656,093	1,338,711	Milliken, William G.*	1,294,600	Levin, Sander	22,782	44,111 R	50.4%	48.7%	50.8%	49.2%
1966**	2,461,909	1,490,430	Romney, George W.*	963,383	Ferency, Zoltan A.	8,096	527,047 R	60.5%	39.1%	60.7%	39.3%
1964	3,158,102	1,764,355	Romney, George W.*	1,381,442	Staebler, Neil	12,305	382,913 R	55.9%	43.7%	56.1%	43.9%
1962	2,764,839	1,420,086	Romney, George W.	1,339,513	Swainson, John B.*	5,240	80,573 R	51.4%	48.4%	51.5%	48.5%
1960	3,255,991	1,602,022	Bagwell, Paul D.	1,643,634	Swainson, John B.	10,335	41,612 D	49.2%	50.5%	49.4%	50.6%
1958	2,312,184	1,078,089	Bagwell, Paul D.	1,225,533	Williams, G. Mennen*	8,562	147,444 D	46.6%	53.0%	46.8%	53.2%
1956	3,049,651	1,376,376	Cobo, Albert E.	1,666,689	Williams, G. Mennen*	6,586	290,313 D	45.1%	54.7%	45.2%	54.8%
1954	2,187,027	963,300	Leonard, Donald S.	1,216,308	Williams, G. Mennen*	7,419	253,008 D	44.0%	55.6%	44.2%	55.8%
1952	2,865,980	1,423,275	Alger, Fred M. Jr.	1,431,893	Williams, G. Mennen*	10,812	8,618 D	49.7%	50.0%	49.8%	50.2%
1950	1,879,382	933,998	Kelly, Harry F.	935,152	Williams, G. Mennen*	10,232	1,154 D	49.7%	49.8%	50.0%	50.0%
1948	2,113,122	964,810	Sigler, Kim*	1,128,664	Williams, G. Mennen	19,648	163,854 D	45.7%	53.4%	46.1%	53.9%
1946	1,665,475	1,003,878	Sigler, Kim	644,540	Van Wagoner, Murray D.	17,057	359,338 R	60.3%	38.7%	60.9%	39.1%

Note: An asterisk (*) denotes incumbent. **The term of office of Michigan's governor was increased from two to four years effective with the 1966 election.

POSTWAR VOTE FOR SENATOR

Year	Total Vote	Republican		Democratic		Other Vote	Rep.-Dem. Plurality	Percentage			
								Total Vote		Major Vote	
		Vote	Candidate	Vote	Candidate			Rep.	Dem.	Rep.	Dem.
2012	4,652,918	1,767,386	Hoekstra, Peter	2,735,826	Stabenow, Debbie*	149,706	968,440 D	38.0%	58.8%	39.2%	60.8%
2008	4,848,620	1,641,070	Hoogendyk, Jack Jr.	3,038,386	Levin, Carl*	169,164	1,397,316 D	33.8%	62.7%	35.1%	64.9%
2006	3,780,142	1,559,597	Bouchard, Michael	2,151,278	Stabenow, Debbie*	69,267	591,681 D	41.3%	56.9%	42.0%	58.0%
2002	3,129,287	1,185,545	Raczkowski, Andrew	1,896,614	Levin, Carl*	47,128	711,069 D	37.9%	60.6%	38.5%	61.5%
2000	4,167,685	1,994,693	Abraham, Spencer*	2,061,952	Stabenow, Debbie	111,040	67,259 D	47.9%	49.5%	49.2%	50.8%
1996	3,762,575	1,500,106	Romney, Ronna	2,195,738	Levin, Carl*	66,731	695,632 D	39.9%	58.4%	40.6%	59.4%
1994	3,043,385	1,578,770	Abraham, Spencer	1,300,960	Carr, M. Robert	163,655	277,810 R	51.9%	42.7%	54.8%	45.2%
1990	2,560,494	1,055,695	Schuette, Bill	1,471,753	Levin, Carl*	33,046	416,058 D	41.2%	57.5%	41.8%	58.2%
1988	3,505,985	1,348,219	Dunn, Jim	2,116,865	Riegle, Donald W.*	40,901	768,646 D	38.5%	60.4%	38.9%	61.1%
1984	3,700,938	1,745,302	Lousma, Jack	1,915,831	Levin, Carl*	39,805	170,529 D	47.2%	51.8%	47.7%	52.3%
1982	2,994,334	1,223,288	Ruppe, Philip E.	1,728,793	Riegle, Donald W.*	42,253	505,505 D	40.9%	57.7%	41.4%	58.6%
1978	2,846,630	1,362,165	Griffin, Robert P.*	1,484,193	Levin, Carl	272	122,028 D	47.9%	52.1%	47.9%	52.1%
1976	3,484,664	1,635,087	Esch, Marvin L.	1,831,031	Riegle, Donald W.	18,546	195,944 D	46.9%	52.5%	47.2%	52.8%
1972	3,406,906	1,781,065	Griffin, Robert P.*	1,577,178	Kelley, Frank J.	48,663	203,887 R	52.3%	46.3%	53.0%	47.0%
1970	2,610,763	858,438	Romney, Lenore	1,744,672	Hart, Philip A.*	7,653	886,234 D	32.9%	66.8%	33.0%	67.0%
1966	2,439,365	1,363,530	Griffin, Robert P.*	1,069,484	Williams, G. Mennen	6,351	294,046 R	55.9%	43.8%	56.0%	44.0%
1964	3,101,667	1,096,272	Peterson, Elly M.	1,996,912	Hart, Philip A.*	8,483	900,640 D	35.3%	64.4%	35.4%	64.6%
1960	3,226,647	1,548,873	Bentley, Alvin M.	1,669,179	McNamara, Patrick V.*	8,595	120,306 D	48.0%	51.7%	48.1%	51.9%
1958	2,271,644	1,046,963	Potter, Charles E.*	1,216,966	Hart, Philip A.	7,715	170,003 D	46.1%	53.6%	46.2%	53.8%
1954	2,144,840	1,049,420	Ferguson, Homer*	1,088,550	McNamara, Patrick V.	6,870	39,130 D	48.9%	50.8%	49.1%	50.9%
1952	2,821,133	1,428,352	Potter, Charles E.	1,383,416	Moody, Blair	9,365	44,936 R	50.6%	49.0%	50.8%	49.2%
1948	2,062,097	1,045,156	Ferguson, Homer*	1,000,329	Hook, Frank E.	16,612	44,827 R	50.7%	48.5%	51.1%	48.9%
1946	1,618,720	1,085,570	Vandenberg, Arthur H.*	517,923	Lee, James H.	15,227	567,647 R	67.1%	32.0%	67.7%	32.3%

Note: An asterisk (*) denotes incumbent.

MICHIGAN
PRESIDENT 2012

2010 Census Population	County	Total Vote	Republican (Romney)	Democratic (Obama)	Other	Rep.-Dem. Plurality	Percentage			
							Total Vote		Major Vote	
							Rep.	Dem.	Rep.	Dem.
10,942	ALCONA	6,104	3,571	2,472	61	1,099 R	58.5%	40.5%	59.1%	40.9%
9,601	ALGER	4,618	2,330	2,212	76	118 R	50.5%	47.9%	51.3%	48.7%
111,408	ALLEGAN	52,619	31,123	20,806	690	10,317 R	59.1%	39.5%	59.9%	40.1%
29,598	ALPENA	14,014	7,298	6,549	167	749 R	52.1%	46.7%	52.7%	47.3%
23,580	ANTRIM	13,195	7,917	5,107	171	2,810 R	60.0%	38.7%	60.8%	39.2%
15,899	ARENAC	7,841	4,057	3,669	115	388 R	51.7%	46.8%	52.5%	47.5%
8,860	BARAGA	3,490	1,866	1,574	50	292 R	53.5%	45.1%	54.2%	45.8%
59,173	BARRY	28,512	16,655	11,491	366	5,164 R	58.4%	40.3%	59.2%	40.8%
107,771	BAY	53,381	24,911	27,877	593	2,966 D	46.7%	52.2%	47.2%	52.8%
17,525	BENZIE	9,901	5,075	4,685	141	390 R	51.3%	47.3%	52.0%	48.0%
156,813	BERRIEN	72,498	38,209	33,465	824	4,744 R	52.7%	46.2%	53.3%	46.7%
45,248	BRANCH	17,147	10,035	6,913	199	3,122 R	58.5%	40.3%	59.2%	40.8%
136,146	CALHOUN	58,326	28,333	29,267	726	934 D	48.6%	50.2%	49.2%	50.8%
52,293	CASS	22,490	12,659	9,591	240	3,068 R	56.3%	42.6%	56.9%	43.1%
25,949	CHARLEVOIX	14,090	8,000	5,939	151	2,061 R	56.8%	42.2%	57.4%	42.6%
26,152	CHEBOYGAN	13,311	7,286	5,831	194	1,455 R	54.7%	43.8%	55.5%	44.5%
38,520	CHIPPEWA	15,564	8,278	7,100	186	1,178 R	53.2%	45.6%	53.8%	46.2%
30,926	CLARE	13,504	6,988	6,338	178	650 R	51.7%	46.9%	52.4%	47.6%
75,382	CLINTON	39,235	20,650	18,191	394	2,459 R	52.6%	46.4%	53.2%	46.8%
14,074	CRAWFORD	6,814	3,744	2,994	76	750 R	54.9%	43.9%	55.6%	44.4%
37,069	DELTA	18,050	9,534	8,330	186	1,204 R	52.8%	46.1%	53.4%	46.6%
26,168	DICKINSON	12,810	7,688	4,952	170	2,736 R	60.0%	38.7%	60.8%	39.2%
107,759	EATON	54,788	26,197	27,913	678	1,716 D	47.8%	50.9%	48.4%	51.6%
32,694	EMMET	17,709	10,253	7,225	231	3,028 R	57.9%	40.8%	58.7%	41.3%
425,790	GENESEE	202,933	71,808	128,978	2,147	57,170 D	35.4%	63.6%	35.8%	64.2%
25,692	GLADWIN	12,583	6,661	5,760	162	901 R	52.9%	45.8%	53.6%	46.4%
16,427	GOGEBIC	7,576	3,444	4,058	74	614 D	45.5%	53.6%	45.9%	54.1%
86,986	GRAND TRAVERSE	47,999	26,534	20,875	590	5,659 R	55.3%	43.5%	56.0%	44.0%
42,476	GRATIOT	16,035	8,241	7,610	184	631 R	51.4%	47.5%	52.0%	48.0%
46,688	HILLSDALE	19,100	11,727	7,106	267	4,621 R	61.4%	37.2%	62.3%	37.7%
36,628	HOUGHTON	15,282	8,196	6,801	285	1,395 R	53.6%	44.5%	54.7%	45.3%
33,118	HURON	15,484	8,806	6,518	160	2,288 R	56.9%	42.1%	57.5%	42.5%
280,895	INGHAM	127,910	45,306	80,847	1,757	35,541 D	35.4%	63.2%	35.9%	64.1%
63,905	IONIA	25,761	14,315	11,018	428	3,297 R	55.6%	42.8%	56.5%	43.5%
25,887	IOSCO	13,344	6,909	6,242	193	667 R	51.8%	46.8%	52.5%	47.5%
11,817	IRON	5,988	3,224	2,687	77	537 R	53.8%	44.9%	54.5%	45.5%
70,311	ISABELLA	24,119	10,800	13,038	281	2,238 D	44.8%	54.1%	45.3%	54.7%
160,248	JACKSON	69,446	36,298	32,301	847	3,997 R	52.3%	46.5%	52.9%	47.1%
250,331	KALAMAZOO	123,178	52,662	69,051	1,465	16,389 D	42.8%	56.1%	43.3%	56.7%
17,153	KALKASKA	8,299	4,901	3,272	126	1,629 R	59.1%	39.4%	60.0%	40.0%
602,622	KENT	292,985	155,925	133,408	3,652	22,517 R	53.2%	45.5%	53.9%	46.1%
2,156	KEWEENAW	1,392	774	582	36	192 R	55.6%	41.8%	57.1%	42.9%
11,539	LAKE	5,287	2,487	2,752	48	265 D	47.0%	52.1%	47.5%	52.5%
88,319	LAPEER	43,115	23,734	18,796	585	4,938 R	55.0%	43.6%	55.8%	44.2%
21,708	LEELANAU	14,176	7,483	6,576	117	907 R	52.8%	46.4%	53.2%	46.8%
99,892	LENAWEE	44,724	22,351	21,776	597	575 R	50.0%	48.7%	50.7%	49.3%
180,967	LIVINGSTON	98,337	60,083	37,216	1,038	22,867 R	61.1%	37.8%	61.8%	38.2%
6,631	LUCE	2,596	1,580	991	25	589 R	60.9%	38.2%	61.5%	38.5%
11,113	MACKINAC	6,099	3,397	2,652	50	745 R	55.7%	43.5%	56.2%	43.8%
840,978	MACOMB	404,086	191,913	208,016	4,157	16,103 D	47.5%	51.5%	48.0%	52.0%
24,733	MANISTEE	12,402	5,737	6,473	192	736 D	46.3%	52.2%	47.0%	53.0%
67,077	MARQUETTE	32,194	13,606	18,115	473	4,509 D	42.3%	56.3%	42.9%	57.1%
28,705	MASON	14,604	7,580	6,856	168	724 R	51.9%	46.9%	52.5%	47.5%
42,798	MECOSTA	16,913	9,176	7,515	222	1,661 R	54.3%	44.4%	55.0%	45.0%
24,029	MENOMINEE	10,923	5,564	5,242	117	322 R	50.9%	48.0%	51.5%	48.5%
83,629	MIDLAND	41,754	23,919	17,450	385	6,469 R	57.3%	41.8%	57.8%	42.2%
14,849	MISSAUKEE	7,027	4,665	2,274	88	2,391 R	66.4%	32.4%	67.2%	32.8%
152,021	MONROE	72,853	35,593	36,310	950	717 D	48.9%	49.8%	49.5%	50.5%
63,342	MONTCALM	25,431	13,621	11,430	380	2,191 R	53.6%	44.9%	54.4%	45.6%
9,765	MONTMORENCY	5,051	2,928	2,049	74	879 R	58.0%	40.6%	58.8%	41.2%

MICHIGAN

PRESIDENT 2012

2010 Census Population	County	Total Vote	Republican (Romney)	Democratic (Obama)	Other	Rep.-Dem. Plurality	Total Vote Rep.	Dem.	Major Vote Rep.	Dem.
172,188	MUSKEGON	76,163	30,884	44,436	843	13,552 D	40.5%	58.3%	41.0%	59.0%
48,460	NEWAYGO	21,478	12,457	8,728	293	3,729 R	58.0%	40.6%	58.8%	41.2%
1,202,362	OAKLAND	651,607	296,514	349,002	6,091	52,488 D	45.5%	53.6%	45.9%	54.1%
26,570	OCEANA	11,450	6,239	5,063	148	1,176 R	54.5%	44.2%	55.2%	44.8%
21,699	OGEMAW	10,361	5,437	4,791	133	646 R	52.5%	46.2%	53.2%	46.8%
6,780	ONTONAGON	3,539	1,906	1,586	47	320 R	53.9%	44.8%	54.6%	45.4%
23,528	OSCEOLA	10,278	6,141	3,981	156	2,160 R	59.7%	38.7%	60.7%	39.3%
8,640	OSCODA	4,042	2,308	1,657	77	651 R	57.1%	41.0%	58.2%	41.8%
24,164	OTSEGO	11,832	7,011	4,681	140	2,330 R	59.3%	39.6%	60.0%	40.0%
263,801	OTTAWA	132,312	88,166	42,737	1,409	45,429 R	66.6%	32.3%	67.4%	32.6%
13,376	PRESQUE ISLE	7,080	3,794	3,192	94	602 R	53.6%	45.1%	54.3%	45.7%
24,449	ROSCOMMON	13,032	6,701	6,198	133	503 R	51.4%	47.6%	51.9%	48.1%
200,169	SAGINAW	98,062	42,720	54,381	961	11,661 D	43.6%	55.5%	44.0%	56.0%
43,114	SANILAC	18,369	10,963	7,212	194	3,751 R	59.7%	39.3%	60.3%	39.7%
8,485	SCHOOLCRAFT	4,048	2,142	1,865	41	277 R	52.9%	46.1%	53.5%	46.5%
70,648	SHIAWASSEE	33,679	15,962	17,197	520	1,235 D	47.4%	51.1%	48.1%	51.9%
163,040	ST. CLAIR	74,181	39,271	33,983	927	5,288 R	52.9%	45.8%	53.6%	46.4%
61,295	ST. JOSEPH	23,341	12,978	10,112	251	2,866 R	55.6%	43.3%	56.2%	43.8%
55,729	TUSCOLA	26,003	14,240	11,425	338	2,815 R	54.8%	43.9%	55.5%	44.5%
76,258	VAN BUREN	32,837	16,141	16,290	406	149 D	49.2%	49.6%	49.8%	50.2%
344,791	WASHTENAW	179,592	56,412	120,890	2,290	64,478 D	31.4%	67.3%	31.8%	68.2%
1,820,584	WAYNE	815,825	213,814	595,846	6,165	382,032 D	26.2%	73.0%	26.4%	73.6%
32,735	WEXFORD	14,853	8,450	6,184	219	2,266 R	56.9%	41.6%	57.7%	42.3%
9,883,640	TOTAL	4,730,961	2,115,256	2,564,569	51,136	449,313 D	44.7%	54.2%	45.2%	54.8%

MICHIGAN

SENATOR 2012

2010 Census Population	County	Total Vote	Republican (Hoekstra)	Democratic (Stabenow)	Other	Rep.-Dem. Plurality	Total Vote Rep.	Dem.	Major Vote Rep.	Dem.
10,942	ALCONA	6,035	2,812	3,047	176	235 D	46.6%	50.5%	48.0%	52.0%
9,601	ALGER	4,549	1,809	2,575	165	766 D	39.8%	56.6%	41.3%	58.7%
111,408	ALLEGAN	52,105	28,350	21,842	1,913	6,508 R	54.4%	41.9%	56.5%	43.5%
29,598	ALPENA	13,905	5,561	7,910	434	2,349 D	40.0%	56.9%	41.3%	58.7%
23,580	ANTRIM	13,068	6,834	5,785	449	1,049 R	52.3%	44.3%	54.2%	45.8%
15,899	ARENAC	7,662	2,940	4,411	311	1,471 D	38.4%	57.6%	40.0%	60.0%
8,860	BARAGA	3,429	1,392	1,929	108	537 D	40.6%	56.3%	41.9%	58.1%
59,173	BARRY	28,239	14,581	12,614	1,044	1,967 R	51.6%	44.7%	53.6%	46.4%
107,771	BAY	52,537	18,940	31,840	1,757	12,900 D	36.1%	60.6%	37.3%	62.7%
17,525	BENZIE	9,736	4,331	5,096	309	765 D	44.5%	52.3%	45.9%	54.1%
156,813	BERRIEN	70,975	35,610	32,855	2,510	2,755 R	50.2%	46.3%	52.0%	48.0%
45,248	BRANCH	16,856	8,470	7,775	611	695 R	50.2%	46.1%	52.1%	47.9%
136,146	CALHOUN	57,416	24,204	31,237	1,975	7,033 D	42.2%	54.4%	43.7%	56.3%
52,293	CASS	21,942	11,673	9,426	843	2,247 R	53.2%	43.0%	55.3%	44.7%
25,949	CHARLEVOIX	13,898	6,830	6,591	477	239 R	49.1%	47.4%	50.9%	49.1%
26,152	CHEBOYGAN	13,141	5,825	6,872	444	1,047 D	44.3%	52.3%	45.9%	54.1%
38,520	CHIPPEWA	15,394	6,231	8,581	582	2,350 D	40.5%	55.7%	42.1%	57.9%
30,926	CLARE	13,282	5,015	7,749	518	2,734 D	37.8%	58.3%	39.3%	60.7%
75,382	CLINTON	38,594	17,272	20,286	1,036	3,014 D	44.8%	52.6%	46.0%	54.0%
14,074	CRAWFORD	6,712	2,902	3,555	255	653 D	43.2%	53.0%	44.9%	55.1%
37,069	DELTA	17,737	7,333	9,875	529	2,542 D	41.3%	55.7%	42.6%	57.4%
26,168	DICKINSON	12,511	5,928	6,180	403	252 D	47.4%	49.4%	49.0%	51.0%
107,759	EATON	54,004	21,762	30,403	1,839	8,641 D	40.3%	56.3%	41.7%	58.3%
32,694	EMMET	17,524	8,912	8,028	584	884 R	50.9%	45.8%	52.6%	47.4%
425,790	GENESEE	200,682	56,502	137,711	6,469	81,209 D	28.2%	68.6%	29.1%	70.9%

MICHIGAN

SENATOR 2012

2010 Census Population	County	Total Vote	Republican (Hoekstra)	Democratic (Stabenow)	Other	Rep.-Dem. Plurality	Percentage			
							Total Vote		Major Vote	
							Rep.	Dem.	Rep.	Dem.
25,692	GLADWIN	12,355	4,909	7,046	400	2,137 D	39.7%	57.0%	41.1%	58.9%
16,427	GOGEBIC	7,442	2,724	4,477	241	1,753 D	36.6%	60.2%	37.8%	62.2%
86,986	GRAND TRAVERSE	47,289	23,487	22,158	1,644	1,329 R	49.7%	46.9%	51.5%	48.5%
42,476	GRATIOT	15,799	6,341	8,978	480	2,637 D	40.1%	56.8%	41.4%	58.6%
46,688	HILLSDALE	18,773	9,724	8,287	762	1,437 R	51.8%	44.1%	54.0%	46.0%
36,628	HOUGHTON	15,113	6,815	7,750	548	935 D	45.1%	51.3%	46.8%	53.2%
33,118	HURON	15,252	5,702	9,174	376	3,472 D	37.4%	60.1%	38.3%	61.7%
280,895	INGHAM	126,033	37,503	84,547	3,983	47,044 D	29.8%	67.1%	30.7%	69.3%
63,905	IONIA	25,363	12,006	12,365	992	359 D	47.3%	48.8%	49.3%	50.7%
25,887	IOSCO	13,148	5,120	7,566	462	2,446 D	38.9%	57.5%	40.4%	59.6%
11,817	IRON	5,884	2,448	3,211	225	763 D	41.6%	54.6%	43.3%	56.7%
70,311	ISABELLA	23,672	8,489	14,340	843	5,851 D	35.9%	60.6%	37.2%	62.8%
160,248	JACKSON	68,241	30,157	35,730	2,354	5,573 D	44.2%	52.4%	45.8%	54.2%
250,331	KALAMAZOO	120,970	47,608	69,072	4,290	21,464 D	39.4%	57.1%	40.8%	59.2%
17,153	KALKASKA	8,170	3,940	3,859	371	81 R	48.2%	47.2%	50.5%	49.5%
602,622	KENT	289,597	145,033	135,093	9,471	9,940 R	50.1%	46.6%	51.8%	48.2%
2,156	KEWEENAW	1,369	628	694	47	66 D	45.9%	50.7%	47.5%	52.5%
11,539	LAKE	5,223	2,028	2,997	198	969 D	38.8%	57.4%	40.4%	59.6%
88,319	LAPEER	42,432	18,798	22,070	1,564	3,272 D	44.3%	52.0%	46.0%	54.0%
21,708	LEELANAU	14,071	6,609	7,089	373	480 D	47.0%	50.4%	48.2%	51.8%
99,892	LENAWEE	43,654	19,081	22,803	1,770	3,722 D	43.7%	52.2%	45.6%	54.4%
180,967	LIVINGSTON	96,448	51,329	41,738	3,381	9,591 R	53.2%	43.3%	55.2%	44.8%
6,631	LUCE	2,557	1,174	1,307	76	133 D	45.9%	51.1%	47.3%	52.7%
11,113	MACKINAC	6,021	2,696	3,174	151	478 D	44.8%	52.7%	45.9%	54.1%
840,978	MACOMB	395,070	146,108	236,071	12,891	89,963 D	37.0%	59.8%	38.2%	61.8%
24,733	MANISTEE	12,310	4,906	6,998	406	2,092 D	39.9%	56.8%	41.2%	58.8%
67,077	MARQUETTE	31,792	10,511	20,280	1,001	9,769 D	33.1%	63.8%	34.1%	65.9%
28,705	MASON	14,451	6,689	7,356	406	667 D	46.3%	50.9%	47.6%	52.4%
42,798	MECOSTA	16,728	7,670	8,469	589	799 D	45.9%	50.6%	47.5%	52.5%
24,029	MENOMINEE	10,466	4,492	5,639	335	1,147 D	42.9%	53.9%	44.3%	55.7%
83,629	MIDLAND	41,209	20,040	19,826	1,343	214 R	48.6%	48.1%	50.3%	49.7%
14,849	MISSAUKEE	6,944	3,991	2,748	205	1,243 R	57.5%	39.6%	59.2%	40.8%
152,021	MONROE	70,179	28,089	39,700	2,390	11,611 D	40.0%	56.6%	41.4%	58.6%
63,342	MONTCALM	25,150	11,391	12,836	923	1,445 D	45.3%	51.0%	47.0%	53.0%
9,765	MONTMORENCY	4,994	2,284	2,510	200	226 D	45.7%	50.3%	47.6%	52.4%
172,188	MUSKEGON	75,147	27,253	45,417	2,477	18,164 D	36.3%	60.4%	37.5%	62.5%
48,460	NEWAYGO	21,313	10,941	9,632	740	1,309 R	51.3%	45.2%	53.2%	46.8%
1,202,362	OAKLAND	638,848	251,995	367,034	19,819	115,039 D	39.4%	57.5%	40.7%	59.3%
26,570	OCEANA	11,342	5,520	5,469	353	51 R	48.7%	48.2%	50.2%	49.8%
21,699	OGEMAW	10,135	3,877	5,875	383	1,998 D	38.3%	58.0%	39.8%	60.2%
6,780	ONTONAGON	3,457	1,399	1,956	102	557 D	40.5%	56.6%	41.7%	58.3%
23,528	OSCEOLA	10,184	5,002	4,809	373	193 R	49.1%	47.2%	51.0%	49.0%
8,640	OSCODA	3,980	1,848	1,938	194	90 D	46.4%	48.7%	48.8%	51.2%
24,164	OTSEGO	11,702	5,846	5,421	435	425 R	50.0%	46.3%	51.9%	48.1%
263,801	OTTAWA	131,177	83,853	43,807	3,517	40,046 R	63.9%	33.4%	65.7%	34.3%
13,376	PRESQUE ISLE	7,006	2,946	3,818	242	872 D	42.0%	54.5%	43.6%	56.4%
24,449	ROSCOMMON	12,829	5,071	7,357	401	2,286 D	39.5%	57.3%	40.8%	59.2%
200,169	SAGINAW	96,337	33,915	59,918	2,504	26,003 D	35.2%	62.2%	36.1%	63.9%
43,114	SANILAC	18,180	7,959	9,665	556	1,706 D	43.8%	53.2%	45.2%	54.8%
8,485	SCHOOLCRAFT	3,945	1,627	2,201	117	574 D	41.2%	55.8%	42.5%	57.5%
70,648	SHIAWASSEE	33,195	12,796	19,103	1,296	6,307 D	38.5%	57.5%	40.1%	59.9%
163,040	ST. CLAIR	72,815	29,079	41,107	2,629	12,028 D	39.9%	56.5%	41.4%	58.6%
61,295	ST. JOSEPH	22,919	11,311	10,767	841	544 R	49.4%	47.0%	51.2%	48.8%
55,729	TUSCOLA	25,609	10,666	13,922	1,021	3,256 D	41.6%	54.4%	43.4%	56.6%
76,258	VAN BUREN	32,301	14,024	17,166	1,111	3,142 D	43.4%	53.1%	45.0%	55.0%
344,791	WASHTENAW	176,563	48,514	122,094	5,955	73,580 D	27.5%	69.2%	28.4%	71.6%
1,820,584	WAYNE	803,115	172,365	608,169	22,581	435,804 D	21.5%	75.7%	22.1%	77.9%
32,735	WEXFORD	14,717	7,040	7,050	627	10 D	47.8%	47.9%	50.0%	50.0%
9,883,640	*TOTAL*	*4,652,918*	*1,767,386*	*2,735,826*	*149,706*	*968,440 D*	*38.0%*	*58.8%*	*39.2%*	*60.8%*

MICHIGAN

HOUSE OF REPRESENTATIVES

CD	Year	Total Vote	Republican Vote	Candidate	Democratic Vote	Candidate	Other Vote	Rep.-Dem. Plurality	Total Vote Rep.	Total Vote Dem.	Major Vote Rep.	Major Vote Dem.
1	2012	347,037	167,060	BENISHEK, DAN*	165,179	MCDOWELL, GARY	14,798	1,881 R	48.1%	47.6%	50.3%	49.7%
2	2012	318,267	194,653	HUIZENGA, BILL*	108,973	GERMAN, WILLIE JR.	14,641	85,680 R	61.2%	34.2%	64.1%	35.9%
3	2012	326,283	171,675	AMASH, JUSTIN*	144,108	PESTKA, STEVE	10,500	27,567 R	52.6%	44.2%	54.4%	45.6%
4	2012	312,949	197,386	CAMP, DAVE*	104,996	WIRTH, DEBRA FREIDELL	10,567	92,390 R	63.1%	33.6%	65.3%	34.7%
5	2012	330,146	103,931	SLEZAK, JIM	214,531	KILDEE, DAN	11,684	110,600 D	31.5%	65.0%	32.6%	67.4%
6	2012	320,475	174,955	UPTON, FRED*	136,563	O'BRIEN, MIKE	8,957	38,392 R	54.6%	42.6%	56.2%	43.8%
7	2012	318,069	169,668	WALBERG, TIM*	136,849	HASKELL, KURT R.	11,552	32,819 R	53.3%	43.0%	55.4%	44.6%
8	2012	345,054	202,217	ROGERS, MIKE*	128,657	ENDERLE, LANCE	14,180	73,560 R	58.6%	37.3%	61.1%	38.9%
9	2012	337,316	114,760	VOLARIC, DON	208,846	LEVIN, SANDER*	13,710	94,086 D	34.0%	61.9%	35.5%	64.5%
10	2012	328,612	226,075	MILLER, CANDICE S.*	97,734	STADLER, CHUCK	4,803	128,341 R	68.8%	29.7%	69.8%	30.2%
11	2012	358,139	181,788	BENTIVOLIO, KERRY	158,879	TAJ, SYED	17,472	22,909 R	50.8%	44.4%	53.4%	46.6%
12	2012	319,223	92,472	KALLGREN, CYNTHIA	216,884	DINGELL, JOHN D.*	9,867	124,412 D	29.0%	67.9%	29.9%	70.1%
13	2012	284,270	38,769	SAWICKI, HARRY	235,336	CONYERS, JOHN JR.*	10,165	196,567 D	13.6%	82.8%	14.1%	85.9%
14	2012	328,792	51,395	HAULER, JOHN	270,450	PETERS, GARY*	6,947	219,055 D	15.6%	82.3%	16.0%	84.0%
TOTAL	2012	4,574,632	2,086,804		2,327,985		159,843	241,181 D	45.6%	50.9%	47.3%	52.7%

Note: An asterisk (*) denotes incumbent.

MICHIGAN

GENERAL AND PRIMARY ELECTIONS

GENERAL ELECTIONS: OTHER VOTE

President Other vote was 21,897 Green (Jill Stein), 16,119 Constitution (Virgil H. Goode), 7,774 Write-in (Gary E. Johnson), 5,147 Natural Law (Ross C. "Rocky" Anderson), 199 Write-in (Scattered Write-In)

Senator Other vote was 84,480 Libertarian (Scotty Boman), 27,890 Green (Harley G. Mikkelson), 26,038 U.S. Taxpayers (Richard Matkin), 11,229 Natural Law (John Litle), 69 Write-in (Scattered Write-In)

House Other vote was:

CD 1 10,630 Libertarian (Emily Salvette), 4,168 Green (Ellis Boal)

CD 2 8,750 Libertarian (Mary Buzuma), 3,176 U.S. Taxpayers (Ronald E. Graeser), 2,715 Green (William Opalicky)

CD 3 10,498 Libertarian (Bill Gelineau), 2 Write-in (Steven Butler)

CD 4 4,285 Libertarian (John Gelineau), 3,506 U.S. Taxpayers (George Zimmer), 2,776 Green (Pat Timmons)

CD 5 6,694 No Party Affiliation (David Davenport), 4,990 Libertarian (Gregory Creswell)

CD 6 6,366 Libertarian (Christie Gelineau), 2,591 U.S. Taxpayers (Jason Gatties)

CD 7 8,088 Libertarian (Ken Procter), 3,464 Green (Richard Wunsch)

CD 8 8,083 Libertarian (Daniel Goebel), 6,097 No Party Affiliation (Preston Brooks)

CD 9 6,100 Libertarian (Jim Fulner), 4,708 Green (Julia Williams), 2,902 U.S. Taxpayers (Les Townsend)

CD 10 4,803 Libertarian (Bhagwan Dashairya)

CD 11 9,637 Libertarian (John Tatar), 4,569 Green (Steven Duke), 3,251 Natural Law (Daniel Johnson), 14 Write-in (James Van Gilder), 1 Write-in (Ralph Sherman)

CD 12 9,867 Libertarian (Richard Secula)

CD 13 6,076 Libertarian (Chris Sharer), 4,089 U.S. Taxpayers (Martin Gray)

CD 14 3,968 Libertarian (Leonard Schwartz), 2,979 Green (Douglas Campbell)

PRIMARY ELECTIONS: SUPPLEMENTARY INFORMATION

Primary February 28, 2012 (President) August 7, 2012 (Congress) **Registration** (as of July 1, 2012) 7,334,233 No Party Registration

Primary Type Open—Any registered voter could participate in the primary of either party.

MICHIGAN

GENERAL AND PRIMARY ELECTIONS

	REPUBLICAN PRIMARIES			DEMOCRATIC PRIMARIES		
President	Romney, W. Mitt	409,522	41.1%	Obama, Barack H.*	174,054	89.3%
	Santorum, Rick	377,372	37.9%	Uncommitted	20,833	10.7%
	Paul, Ron	115,911	11.6%			
	Gingrich, Newt	65,027	6.5%			
	Uncommitted	18,809	1.9%			
	Perry, Rick	1,816	0.2%			
	Roemer, Charles	1,784	0.2%			
	Bachmann, Michele	1,735	0.2%			
	Huntsman, Jon Jr.	1,674	0.2%			
	Cain, Herman	1,211	0.1%			
	Karger, Fred	1,180	0.1%			
	Johnson, Gary E.	458				
	TOTAL	996,499		TOTAL	194,887	
Senator	Hoekstra, Peter	398,873	54.3%	Stabenow, Debbie*	555,719	100.0%
	Durant, Clark	246,685	33.6%			
	Hekman, Randy	48,761	6.6%			
	Glenn, Gary	40,600	5.5%			
	TOTAL	734,919		TOTAL	555,719	
Congressional District 1	Benishek, Dan*	64,411	100.0%	McDowell, Gary	36,339	100.0%
	TOTAL	64,411		TOTAL	36,339	
Congressional District 2	Huizenga, Bill*	58,170	100.0%	German, Willie Jr.	1,813	100.0%
	TOTAL	58,170		TOTAL	1,813	
Congressional District 3	Amash, Justin*	51,113	100.0%	Pestka, Steve	13,414	59.0%
	Butler, Steven	16		Thomas, Trevor	9,321	41.0%
	TOTAL	51,129		TOTAL	22,735	
Congressional District 4	Camp, Dave*	67,028	100.0%	Wirth, Debra Freidell	20,519	100.0%
	TOTAL	67,028		TOTAL	20,519	
Congressional District 5	Slezak, Jim	16,951	72.0%	Kildee, Dan	51,840	100.0%
	Wassa, Tom	6,583	28.0%			
	TOTAL	23,534		TOTAL	51,840	
Congressional District 6	Upton, Fred*	45,919	66.6%	O'Brien, Mike	14,224	100.0%
	Hoogendyk, Jack Jr.	23,072	33.4%			
	TOTAL	68,991		TOTAL	14,224	
Congressional District 7	Walberg, Tim*	45,592	76.0%	Haskell, Kurt R.	18,812	66.7%
	Davis, Dan	14,386	24.0%	Marquez, Ruben	9,371	33.3%
	TOTAL	59,978		TOTAL	28,183	
Congressional District 8	Rogers, Mike*	56,208	85.7%	Enderle, Lance	29,322	100.0%
	Hetrick, Brian	6,098	9.3%			
	Molnar, Vernon	3,257	5.0%			
	TOTAL	65,563		TOTAL	29,322	
Congressional District 9	Volaric, Don	24,521	61.6%	Levin, Sander*	55,198	100.0%
	Dildilian, Gregory	15,283	38.4%			
	TOTAL	39,804		TOTAL	55,198	
Congressional District 10	Miller, Candice S.*	68,063	100.0%	Stadler, Chuck	13,480	58.1%
				Quinn, Jerome	9,705	41.9%
	TOTAL	68,063		TOTAL	23,185	

MICHIGAN

GENERAL AND PRIMARY ELECTIONS

	REPUBLICAN PRIMARIES			DEMOCRATIC PRIMARIES		
Congressional District 11	Bentivolio, Kerry	42,470	66.3%	Taj, Syed	21,953	58.9%
	Cassis, Nancy	21,436	33.5%	Roberts, William	15,338	41.1%
	Morton, Drexel	161	0.3%			
	Bennett, Loren	14				
	TOTAL	*64,081*		*TOTAL*	*37,291*	
Congressional District 12	Kallgren, Cynthia	12,028	50.7%	Dingell, John D.*	41,116	78.6%
	Jacobsen, Karen	11,670	49.2%	Marcin, Daniel	11,226	21.4%
	Kachinski, Timothy	10				
	TOTAL	*23,708*		*TOTAL*	*52,342*	
Congressional District 13	Sawicki, Harry	8,462	100.0%	Conyers, John Jr.*	38,371	55.4%
				Anderson, Glenn	12,586	18.2%
				Jackson, Shanelle	8,708	12.6%
				Johnson, Bert	6,928	10.0%
				Goci, John	2,664	3.8%
	TOTAL	*8,462*		*TOTAL*	*69,257*	
Congressional District 14	Hauler, John	17,691	100.0%	Peters, Gary*	41,230	47.0%
				Clarke, Hansen*	30,847	35.2%
				Lawrence, Brenda	11,644	13.3%
				Waters, Mary	2,919	3.3%
				Costello, Bob	1,027	1.2%
	TOTAL	*17,691*		*TOTAL*	*87,667*	

Note: An asterisk (*) denotes incumbent. Due to redistricting, the 14th district Democratic primary pitted two incumbents against each other (Peters, former 9th district, and Clarke, former 13th district).

MINNESOTA

Congressional districts first established for elections held in 2012

8 members

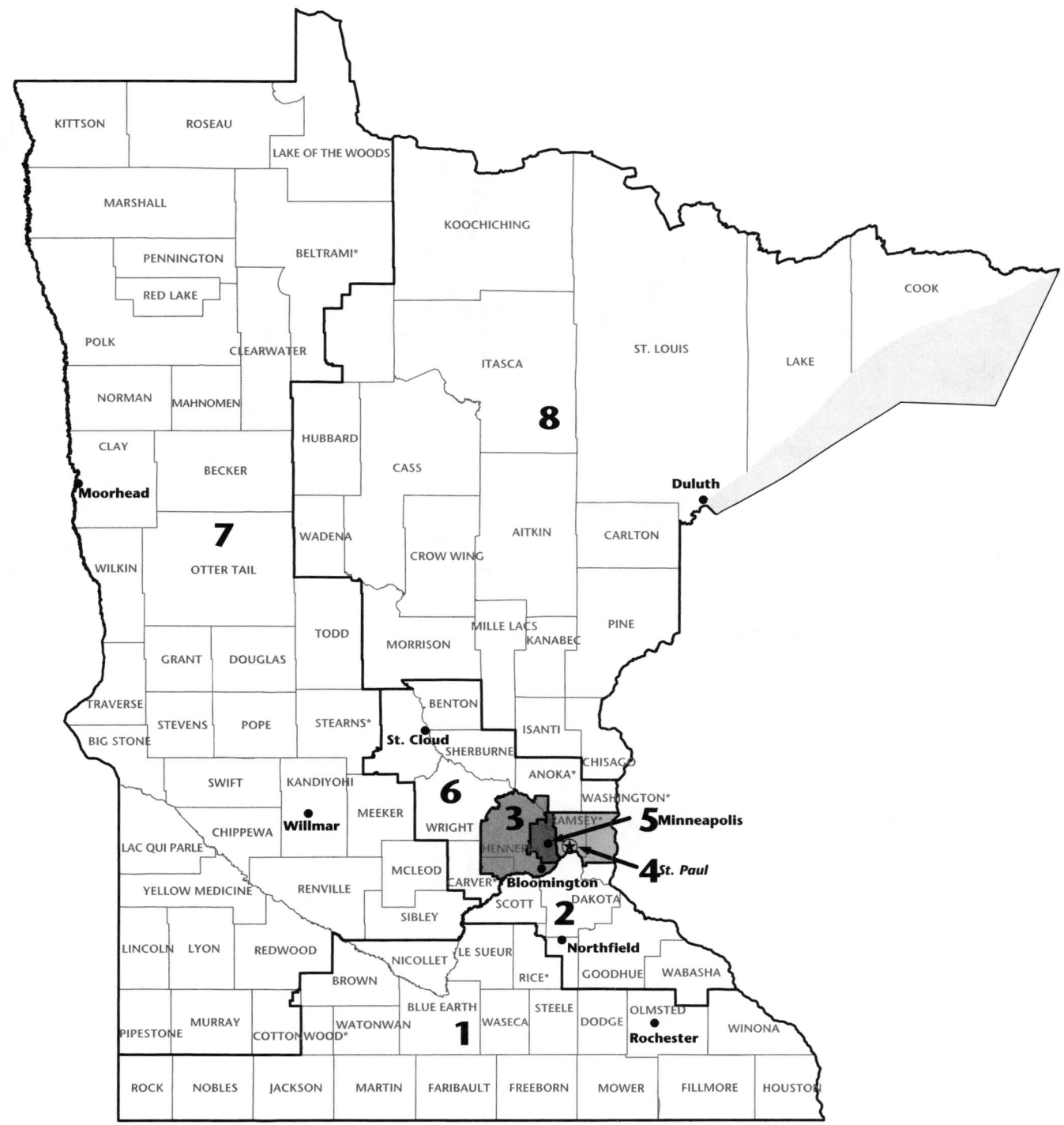

KITTSON

ROSEAU

LAKE OF THE WOODS

MARSHALL

KOOCHICHING

PENNINGTON

BELTRAMI*

COOK

RED LAKE

POLK

CLEARWATER

ST. LOUIS

LAKE

NORMAN

MAHNOMEN

ITASCA

CLAY

HUBBARD

8

BECKER

CASS

Moorhead

Duluth

WADENA

7

AITKIN

CARLTON

WILKIN

OTTER TAIL

CROW WING

TRAVERSE

GRANT

DOUGLAS

TODD

MILLE LACS

PINE

MORRISON

KANABEC

STEVENS

POPE

BENTON

BIG STONE

STEARNS*

ISANTI

St. Cloud

SHERBURNE

SWIFT

KANDIYOHI

ANOKA*

CHISAGO

MEEKER

6

WASHINGTON*

CHIPPEWA

Willmar

WRIGHT

3

RAMSEY*

5 Minneapolis

LAC QUI PARLE

MCLEOD

HENNEP

4 St. Paul

YELLOW MEDICINE

RENVILLE

CARVER*

Bloomington

SCOTT

DAKOTA

SIBLEY

2

LINCOLN

LYON

REDWOOD

NICOLLET

LE SUEUR

Northfield

BROWN

RICE*

GOODHUE

WABASHA

PIPESTONE

MURRAY

WATONWAN

BLUE EARTH

WASECA

STEELE

DODGE

OLMSTED

WINONA

COTTONWOOD*

1

MURRAY

Rochester

ROCK

NOBLES

JACKSON

MARTIN

FARIBAULT

FREEBORN

MOWER

FILLMORE

HOUSTON

* Asterisk indicates a county whose boundaries include parts of two or more Congressional districts.

MINNESOTA
Minneapolis–St. Paul Area

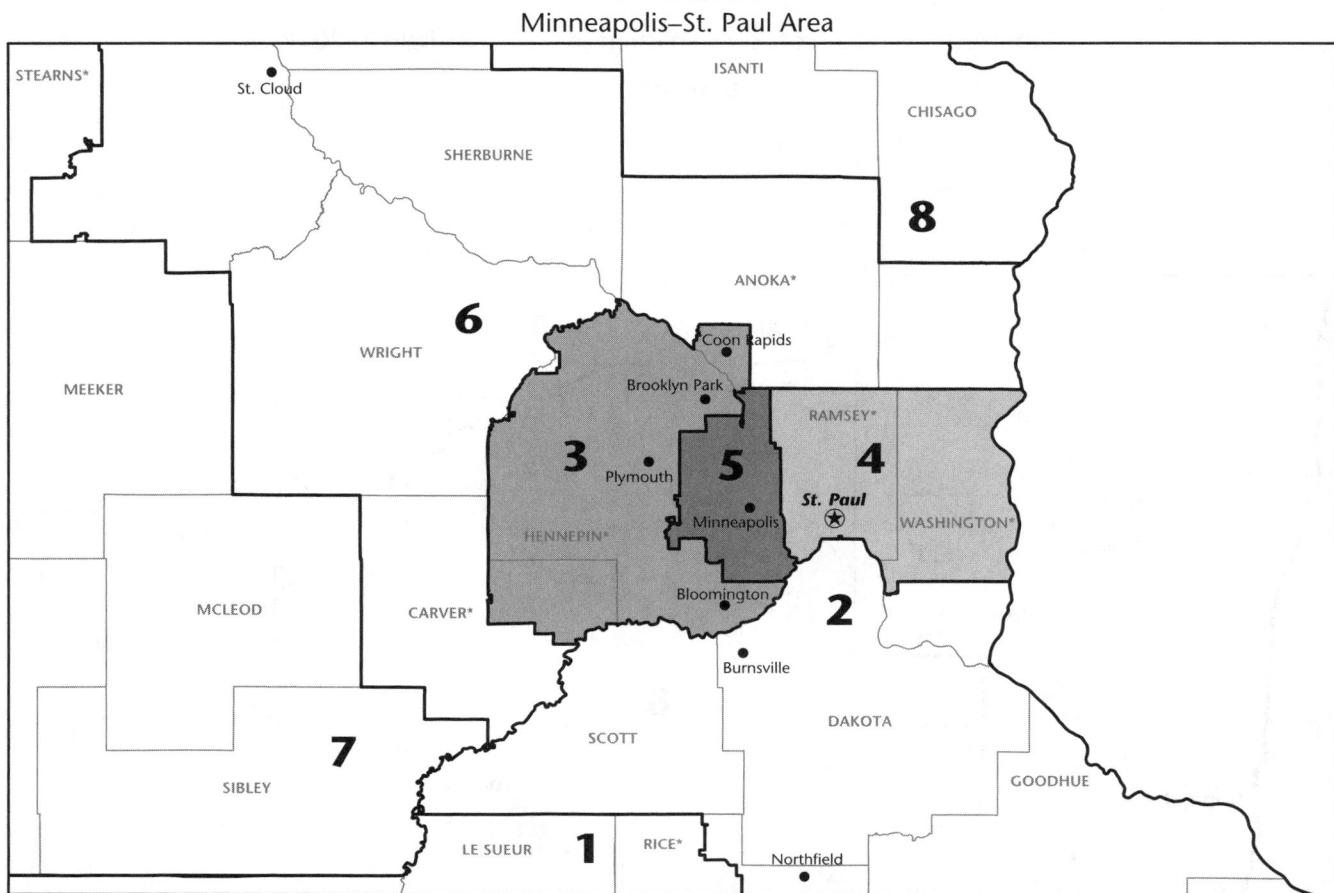

STEARNS*

St. Cloud

SHERBURNE

ISANTI

CHISAGO

8

ANOKA*

6

WRIGHT

Coon Rapids

Brooklyn Park

MEEKER

RAMSEY*

3

Plymouth

5

4

St. Paul

HENNEPIN*

Minneapolis

WASHINGTON*

MCLEOD

CARVER*

Bloomington

2

Burnsville

DAKOTA

7

SCOTT

GOODHUE

SIBLEY

LE SUEUR

1

RICE*

Northfield

* Asterisk indicates a county whose boundaries include parts of two or more Congressional districts.

MINNESOTA

GOVERNOR
Mark Dayton (D). Elected 2010 to a four-year term.

SENATORS (2 Democrats)
Amy Klobuchar (D). Reelected 2012 to a six-year term. Previously elected 2006.

Al Franken (D). Elected 2008 to a six-year term.

REPRESENTATIVES (3 Republicans, 5 Democrats)
1. Tim Walz (D)
2. John Kline (R)
3. Erik Paulsen (R)
4. Betty McCollum (D)
5. Keith Ellison (D)
6. Michele Bachmann (R)
7. Collin C. Peterson (D)
8. Rick Nolan (D)

POSTWAR VOTE FOR PRESIDENT

		Republican		Democratic		Other	Rep.-Dem.	Total Vote		Major Vote	
Year	Total Vote	Vote	Candidate	Vote	Candidate	Vote	Plurality	Rep.	Dem.	Rep.	Dem.
2012	2,936,561	1,320,225	Romney, W. Mitt	1,546,167	Obama, Barack H.*	70,169	225,942 D	45.0%	52.7%	46.1%	53.9%
2008	2,910,369	1,275,409	McCain, John S. III	1,573,354	Obama, Barack H.	61,606	297,945 D	43.8%	54.1%	44.8%	55.2%
2004	2,828,387	1,346,695	Bush, George W.*	1,445,014	Kerry, John F.	36,678	98,319 D	47.6%	51.1%	48.2%	51.8%
2000**	2,438,685	1,109,659	Bush, George W.	1,168,266	Gore, Albert Jr.	160,760	58,607 D	45.5%	47.9%	48.7%	51.3%
1996**	2,192,640	766,476	Dole, Robert "Bob"	1,120,438	Clinton, Bill*	305,726	353,962 D	35.0%	51.1%	40.6%	59.4%
1992**	2,347,948	747,841	Bush, George H.*	1,020,997	Clinton, Bill	579,110	273,156 D	31.9%	43.5%	42.3%	57.7%
1988	2,096,790	962,337	Bush, George H.	1,109,471	Dukakis, Michael S.	24,982	147,134 D	45.9%	52.9%	46.4%	53.6%
1984	2,084,449	1,032,603	Reagan, Ronald*	1,036,364	Mondale, Walter F.	15,482	3,761 D	49.5%	49.7%	49.9%	50.1%
1980**	2,051,980	873,268	Reagan, Ronald	954,174	Carter, Jimmy*	224,538	80,906 D	42.6%	46.5%	47.8%	52.2%
1976	1,949,931	819,395	Ford, Gerald R.*	1,070,440	Carter, Jimmy	60,096	251,045 D	42.0%	54.9%	43.4%	56.6%
1972	1,741,652	898,269	Nixon, Richard M.*	802,346	McGovern, George S.	41,037	95,923 R	51.6%	46.1%	52.8%	47.2%
1968**	1,588,506	658,643	Nixon, Richard M.	857,738	Humphrey, Hubert H. Jr.	72,125	199,095 D	41.5%	54.0%	43.4%	56.6%
1964	1,554,462	559,624	Goldwater, Barry M. Sr.	991,117	Johnson, Lyndon B.*	3,721	431,493 D	36.0%	63.8%	36.1%	63.9%
1960	1,541,887	757,915	Nixon, Richard M.	779,933	Kennedy, John F.	4,039	22,018 D	49.2%	50.6%	49.3%	50.7%
1956	1,340,005	719,302	Eisenhower, Dwight D.*	617,525	Stevenson, Adlai E. II	3,178	101,777 R	53.7%	46.1%	53.8%	46.2%
1952	1,379,483	763,211	Eisenhower, Dwight D.	608,458	Stevenson, Adlai E. II	7,814	154,753 R	55.3%	44.1%	55.6%	44.4%
1948	1,212,226	483,617	Dewey, Thomas E.	692,966	Truman, Harry S.*	35,643	209,349 D	39.9%	57.2%	41.1%	58.9%

Note: An asterisk (*) denotes incumbent. **In past elections, the other vote included: 2000 - 126,696 Green (Nader); 1996 - 257,704 Reform (Ross Perot); 1992 - 562,506 Independent (Perot); 1980 - 174,990 Independent (John Anderson); 1968 - 68,931 American Independent (George Wallace).

MINNESOTA

POSTWAR VOTE FOR GOVERNOR

Year	Total Vote	Republican Vote	Republican Candidate	Democratic Vote	Democratic Candidate	Other Vote	Rep.-Dem. Plurality	Total Vote Rep.	Total Vote Dem.	Major Vote Rep.	Major Vote Dem.
2010**	2,107,021	910,462	Emmer, Tom	919,232	Dayton, Mark	277,327	8,770 D	43.2%	43.6%	49.8%	50.2%
2006	2,202,937	1,028,568	Pawlenty, Tim*	1,007,460	Hatch, Mike	166,909	21,108 R	46.7%	45.7%	50.5%	49.5%
2002**	2,252,473	999,473	Pawlenty, Tim	821,268	Moe, Roger D.	431,732	178,205 R	44.4%	36.5%	54.9%	45.1%
1998**	2,090,518	716,880	Coleman, Norm	587,060	Humphrey, Hubert H. III	786,578	129,820 R**	34.3%	28.1%	55.0%	45.0%
1994	1,765,590	1,094,165	Carlson, Arne*	589,344	Marty, John	82,081	504,821 R	62.0%	33.4%	65.0%	35.0%
1990	1,806,777	895,988	Carlson, Arne	836,218	Perpich, Rudy*	74,571	59,770 R	49.6%	46.3%	51.7%	48.3%
1986	1,415,989	606,755	Ludeman, Cal R.	790,138	Perpich, Rudy*	19,096	183,383 D	42.9%	55.8%	43.4%	56.6%
1982	1,789,539	715,796	Whitney, Wheelock	1,049,104	Perpich, Rudy*	24,639	333,308 D	40.0%	58.6%	40.6%	59.4%
1978	1,585,702	830,019	Quie, Albert H.	718,244	Perpich, Rudy*	37,439	111,775 R	52.3%	45.3%	53.6%	46.4%
1974	1,252,898	367,722	Johnson, John W.	786,787	Anderson, Wendell R.*	98,389	419,065 D	29.3%	62.8%	31.9%	68.1%
1970	1,365,443	621,780	Head, Douglas M.	737,921	Anderson, Wendell R.	5,742	116,141 D	45.5%	54.0%	45.7%	54.3%
1966	1,295,058	680,593	Levander, Harold	607,943	Rolvaag, Karl F.*	6,522	72,650 R	52.6%	46.9%	52.8%	47.2%
1962**	1,246,904	619,751	Andersen, Elmer L.*	619,842	Rolvaag, Karl F.	7,311	91 D	49.7%	49.7%	50.0%	50.0%
1960	1,550,265	783,813	Andersen, Elmer L.	760,934	Freeman, Orville L.	5,518	22,879 R	50.6%	49.1%	50.7%	49.3%
1958	1,159,915	490,731	MacKinnon, George	658,326	Freeman, Orville L.*	10,858	167,595 D	42.3%	56.8%	42.7%	57.3%
1956	1,422,161	685,196	Nelsen, Ancher	731,180	Freeman, Orville L.*	5,785	45,984 D	48.2%	51.4%	48.4%	51.6%
1954	1,151,417	538,865	Anderson, C. Elmer*	607,099	Freeman, Orville L.	5,453	68,234 D	46.8%	52.7%	47.0%	53.0%
1952	1,418,869	785,125	Anderson, C. Elmer	624,480	Freeman, Orville L.	9,264	160,645 R	55.3%	44.0%	55.7%	44.3%
1950	1,046,632	635,800	Youngdahl, Luther W.*	400,637	Peterson, Harry H.	10,195	235,163 R	60.7%	38.3%	61.3%	38.7%
1948	1,210,874	643,572	Youngdahl, Luther W.*	545,746	Halsted, Charles L.	21,556	97,826 R	53.1%	45.1%	54.1%	45.9%
1946	880,348	519,067	Youngdahl, Luther W.	349,565	Barker, Harold H.	11,716	169,502 R	59.0%	39.7%	59.8%	40.2%

Note: An asterisk (*) denotes incumbent. **In past elections, the other vote included: 2010 - 251,487 Independence (Tom Horner); 2002 - 364,534 Independence (Timothy J. Penny); 1998 - 773,403 Reform (Jesse Ventura), who was elected with 37.0 percent of the total vote. The term of office of Minnesota's governor was increased from two to four years effective with the 1962 election.

POSTWAR VOTE FOR SENATOR

Year	Total Vote	Republican Vote	Republican Candidate	Democratic Vote	Democratic Candidate	Other Vote	Rep.-Dem. Plurality	Total Vote Rep.	Total Vote Dem.	Major Vote Rep.	Major Vote Dem.
2012	2,843,207	867,974	Bills, Kurt	1,854,595	Klobuchar, Amy*	120,638	986,621 D	30.5%	65.2%	31.9%	68.1%
2008**	2,862,142	1,212,206	Coleman, Norm*	1,212,431	Franken, Al	437,505	225 D	42.4%	42.4%	50.0%	50.0%
2006	2,202,772	835,653	Kennedy, Mark	1,278,849	Klobuchar, Amy	88,270	443,196 D	37.9%	58.1%	39.5%	60.5%
2002**	2,254,639	1,116,697	Coleman, Norm	1,067,246	Mondale, Walter F.	70,696	49,451 R	49.5%	47.3%	51.1%	48.9%
2000	2,419,520	1,047,474	Grams, Rod*	1,181,553	Dayton, Mark	190,493	134,079 D	43.3%	48.8%	47.0%	53.0%
1996	2,183,062	901,282	Boschwitz, Rudy	1,098,493	Wellstone, Paul D.*	183,287	197,211 D	41.3%	50.3%	45.1%	54.9%
1994	1,772,929	869,653	Grams, Rod	781,860	Wynia, Ann	121,416	87,793 R	49.1%	44.1%	52.7%	47.3%
1990	1,808,045	864,375	Boschwitz, Rudy*	911,999	Wellstone, Paul D.	31,671	47,624 D	47.8%	50.4%	48.7%	51.3%
1988	2,093,953	1,176,210	Durenberger, David*	856,694	Humphrey, Hubert H. III	61,049	319,516 R	56.2%	40.9%	57.9%	42.1%
1984	2,066,143	1,199,926	Boschwitz, Rudy*	852,844	Growe, Joan Anderson	13,373	347,082 R	58.1%	41.3%	58.5%	41.5%
1982	1,804,676	949,207	Durenberger, David*	840,401	Dayton, Mark	15,068	108,806 R	52.6%	46.6%	53.0%	47.0%
1978	1,580,778	894,092	Boschwitz, Rudy	638,375	Anderson, Wendell R.*	48,311	255,717 R	56.6%	40.4%	58.3%	41.7%
1978S	1,560,724	957,908	Durenberger, David	538,675	Short, Robert E.	64,141	419,233 R	61.4%	34.5%	64.0%	36.0%
1976	1,912,068	478,611	Brekke, Gerald W.	1,290,736	Humphrey, Hubert H. Jr.*	142,721	812,125 D	25.0%	67.5%	27.1%	72.9%
1972	1,731,653	742,121	Hansen, Philip	981,340	Mondale, Walter F.*	8,192	239,219 D	42.9%	56.7%	43.1%	56.9%
1970	1,364,887	568,025	MacGregor, Clark	788,256	Humphrey, Hubert H. Jr.*	8,606	220,231 D	41.6%	57.8%	41.9%	58.1%
1966	1,271,426	574,868	Forsythe, Robert A.	685,840	Mondale, Walter F.	10,718	110,972 D	45.2%	53.9%	45.6%	54.4%
1964	1,543,600	605,933	Whitney, Wheelock	931,363	McCarthy, Eugene J.*	6,304	325,430 D	39.3%	60.3%	39.4%	60.6%
1960	1,536,839	648,586	Peterson, P. Kenneth	884,168	Humphrey, Hubert H. Jr.*	4,085	235,582 D	42.2%	57.5%	42.3%	57.7%
1958	1,150,883	536,629	Thye, Edward J.	608,847	McCarthy, Eugene J.	5,407	72,218 D	46.6%	52.9%	46.8%	53.2%
1954	1,138,952	479,619	Bjornson, Val	642,193	Humphrey, Hubert H. Jr.*	17,140	162,574 D	42.1%	56.4%	42.8%	57.2%
1952	1,387,419	785,649	Thye, Edward J.*	590,011	Carlson, William E.	11,759	195,638 R	56.6%	42.5%	57.1%	42.9%
1948	1,217,250	482,801	Ball, Joseph H.*	729,494	Humphrey, Hubert H. Jr.	4,955	246,693 D	39.7%	59.9%	39.8%	60.2%
1946	878,731	517,775	Thye, Edward J.	349,520	Jorgenson, Theodore	11,436	168,255 R	58.9%	39.8%	59.7%	40.3%

Note: An asterisk (*) denotes incumbent. **In past elections, the other vote included: 2008 - 437,505 Independence (Dean Barkley). In October 2002 the Democratic incumbent, Paul Wellstone, was killed in an airplane crash. Walter F. Mondale was named to replace him on the general election ballot. One of the 1978 elections was for a short term to fill a vacancy.

MINNESOTA

PRESIDENT 2012

2010 Census Population	County	Total Vote	Republican (Romney)	Democratic (Obama)	Other	Rep.-Dem. Plurality		Percentage			
								Total Vote		Major Vote	
								Rep.	Dem.	Rep.	Dem.
16,202	AITKIN	9,142	4,533	4,412	197	121	R	49.6%	48.3%	50.7%	49.3%
330,844	ANOKA	186,465	93,430	88,614	4,421	4,816	R	50.1%	47.5%	51.3%	48.7%
32,504	BECKER	16,382	9,204	6,829	349	2,375	R	56.2%	41.7%	57.4%	42.6%
44,442	BELTRAMI	22,051	9,637	11,818	596	2,181	D	43.7%	53.6%	44.9%	55.1%
38,451	BENTON	19,619	10,849	8,173	597	2,676	R	55.3%	41.7%	57.0%	43.0%
5,269	BIG STONE	2,789	1,385	1,345	59	40	R	49.7%	48.2%	50.7%	49.3%
64,013	BLUE EARTH	34,274	14,916	18,164	1,194	3,248	D	43.5%	53.0%	45.1%	54.9%
25,893	BROWN	13,929	7,938	5,630	361	2,308	R	57.0%	40.4%	58.5%	41.5%
35,386	CARLTON	18,436	6,586	11,389	461	4,803	D	35.7%	61.8%	36.6%	63.4%
91,042	CARVER	52,899	31,155	20,745	999	10,410	R	58.9%	39.2%	60.0%	40.0%
28,567	CASS	16,141	8,957	6,858	326	2,099	R	55.5%	42.5%	56.6%	43.4%
12,441	CHIPPEWA	6,201	2,967	3,083	151	116	D	47.8%	49.7%	49.0%	51.0%
53,887	CHISAGO	29,441	16,227	12,524	690	3,703	R	55.1%	42.5%	56.4%	43.6%
58,999	CLAY	28,886	12,920	15,208	758	2,288	D	44.7%	52.6%	45.9%	54.1%
8,695	CLEARWATER	4,197	2,359	1,753	85	606	R	56.2%	41.8%	57.4%	42.6%
5,176	COOK	3,322	1,221	1,993	108	772	D	36.8%	60.0%	38.0%	62.0%
11,687	COTTONWOOD	5,862	3,316	2,433	113	883	R	56.6%	41.5%	57.7%	42.3%
62,500	CROW WING	34,920	19,415	14,760	745	4,655	R	55.6%	42.3%	56.8%	43.2%
398,552	DAKOTA	230,821	109,516	116,255	5,050	6,739	D	47.4%	50.4%	48.5%	51.5%
20,087	DODGE	10,327	5,522	4,487	318	1,035	R	53.5%	43.4%	55.2%	44.8%
36,009	DOUGLAS	20,953	11,884	8,653	416	3,231	R	56.7%	41.3%	57.9%	42.1%
14,553	FARIBAULT	7,713	4,104	3,407	202	697	R	53.2%	44.2%	54.6%	45.4%
20,866	FILLMORE	10,892	4,913	5,713	266	800	D	45.1%	52.5%	46.2%	53.8%
31,255	FREEBORN	16,706	6,969	9,326	411	2,357	D	41.7%	55.8%	42.8%	57.2%
46,183	GOODHUE	25,801	12,986	12,212	603	774	R	50.3%	47.3%	51.5%	48.5%
6,018	GRANT	3,487	1,748	1,647	92	101	R	50.1%	47.2%	51.5%	48.5%
1,152,425	HENNEPIN	680,065	240,073	423,982	16,010	183,909	D	35.3%	62.3%	36.2%	63.8%
19,027	HOUSTON	10,446	4,951	5,281	214	330	D	47.4%	50.6%	48.4%	51.6%
20,428	HUBBARD	11,520	6,622	4,676	222	1,946	R	57.5%	40.6%	58.6%	41.4%
37,816	ISANTI	20,217	11,675	8,024	518	3,651	R	57.7%	39.7%	59.3%	40.7%
45,058	ITASCA	23,919	10,501	12,852	566	2,351	D	43.9%	53.7%	45.0%	55.0%
10,266	JACKSON	5,430	3,044	2,268	118	776	R	56.1%	41.8%	57.3%	42.7%
16,239	KANABEC	8,150	4,328	3,593	229	735	R	53.1%	44.1%	54.6%	45.4%
42,239	KANDIYOHI	21,465	11,240	9,805	420	1,435	R	52.4%	45.7%	53.4%	46.6%
4,552	KITTSON	2,420	1,095	1,241	84	146	D	45.2%	51.3%	46.9%	53.1%
13,311	KOOCHICHING	6,458	2,841	3,451	166	610	D	44.0%	53.4%	45.2%	54.8%
7,259	LAC QUI PARLE	3,984	1,938	1,974	72	36	D	48.6%	49.5%	49.5%	50.5%
10,866	LAKE	6,820	2,610	4,043	167	1,433	D	38.3%	59.3%	39.2%	60.8%
4,045	LAKE OF THE WOODS	2,234	1,306	859	69	447	R	58.5%	38.5%	60.3%	39.7%
27,703	LE SUEUR	14,795	7,715	6,753	327	962	R	52.1%	45.6%	53.3%	46.7%
5,896	LINCOLN	3,120	1,595	1,429	96	166	R	51.1%	45.8%	52.7%	47.3%
25,857	LYON	12,388	6,594	5,465	329	1,129	R	53.2%	44.1%	54.7%	45.3%
5,413	MAHNOMEN	2,182	871	1,276	35	405	D	39.9%	58.5%	40.6%	59.4%
9,439	MARSHALL	4,698	2,569	1,998	131	571	R	54.7%	42.5%	56.3%	43.7%
20,840	MARTIN	10,968	6,657	4,054	257	2,603	R	60.7%	37.0%	62.2%	37.8%
36,651	MCLEOD	18,553	11,069	6,968	516	4,101	R	59.7%	37.6%	61.4%	38.6%
23,300	MEEKER	12,214	6,913	4,969	332	1,944	R	56.6%	40.7%	58.2%	41.8%
26,097	MILLE LACS	13,091	6,951	5,829	311	1,122	R	53.1%	44.5%	54.4%	45.6%
33,198	MORRISON	16,714	10,159	6,153	402	4,006	R	60.8%	36.8%	62.3%	37.7%
39,163	MOWER	18,539	6,938	11,129	472	4,191	D	37.4%	60.0%	38.4%	61.6%
8,725	MURRAY	4,767	2,504	2,160	103	344	R	52.5%	45.3%	53.7%	46.3%
32,727	NICOLLET	18,357	8,214	9,652	491	1,438	D	44.7%	52.6%	46.0%	54.0%
21,378	NOBLES	8,520	4,581	3,793	146	788	R	53.8%	44.5%	54.7%	45.3%
6,852	NORMAN	3,207	1,384	1,730	93	346	D	43.2%	53.9%	44.4%	55.6%
144,248	OLMSTED	78,316	36,832	39,338	2,146	2,506	D	47.0%	50.2%	48.4%	51.6%
57,303	OTTER TAIL	31,670	18,860	12,165	645	6,695	R	59.6%	38.4%	60.8%	39.2%
13,930	PENNINGTON	6,517	3,305	3,024	188	281	R	50.7%	46.4%	52.2%	47.8%
29,750	PINE	13,965	6,845	6,750	370	95	R	49.0%	48.3%	50.3%	49.7%
9,596	PIPESTONE	4,646	2,826	1,725	95	1,101	R	60.8%	37.1%	62.1%	37.9%
31,600	POLK	14,693	7,615	6,773	305	842	R	51.8%	46.1%	52.9%	47.1%

MINNESOTA

PRESIDENT 2012

2010 Census Population	County	Total Vote	Republican (Romney)	Democratic (Obama)	Other	Rep.-Dem. Plurality	Percentage Total Vote Rep.	Dem.	Major Vote Rep.	Dem.
10,995	POPE	6,246	3,142	2,981	123	161 R	50.3%	47.7%	51.3%	48.7%
508,640	RAMSEY	278,822	86,800	184,938	7,084	98,138 D	31.1%	66.3%	31.9%	68.1%
4,089	RED LAKE	1,975	978	928	69	50 R	49.5%	47.0%	51.3%	48.7%
16,059	REDWOOD	7,790	4,570	3,008	212	1,562 R	58.7%	38.6%	60.3%	39.7%
15,730	RENVILLE	7,710	4,149	3,394	167	755 R	53.8%	44.0%	55.0%	45.0%
64,142	RICE	32,267	14,384	17,054	829	2,670 D	44.6%	52.9%	45.8%	54.2%
9,687	ROCK	4,846	2,810	1,946	90	864 R	58.0%	40.2%	59.1%	40.9%
15,629	ROSEAU	7,352	4,409	2,772	171	1,637 R	60.0%	37.7%	61.4%	38.6%
129,928	SCOTT	71,647	40,323	29,712	1,612	10,611 R	56.3%	41.5%	57.6%	42.4%
88,499	SHERBURNE	46,509	27,848	17,597	1,064	10,251 R	59.9%	37.8%	61.3%	38.7%
15,226	SIBLEY	7,815	4,693	2,916	206	1,777 R	60.1%	37.3%	61.7%	38.3%
200,226	ST. LOUIS	115,594	39,131	73,378	3,085	34,247 D	33.9%	63.5%	34.8%	65.2%
150,642	STEARNS	78,477	43,015	33,551	1,911	9,464 R	54.8%	42.8%	56.2%	43.8%
36,576	STEELE	19,124	9,903	8,706	515	1,197 R	51.8%	45.5%	53.2%	46.8%
9,726	STEVENS	5,652	2,766	2,742	144	24 R	48.9%	48.5%	50.2%	49.8%
9,783	SWIFT	5,119	2,248	2,751	120	503 D	43.9%	53.7%	45.0%	55.0%
24,895	TODD	11,803	6,719	4,819	265	1,900 R	56.9%	40.8%	58.2%	41.8%
3,558	TRAVERSE	1,847	861	943	43	82 D	46.6%	51.1%	47.7%	52.3%
21,676	WABASHA	11,763	6,049	5,415	299	634 R	51.4%	46.0%	52.8%	47.2%
13,843	WADENA	6,791	4,143	2,492	156	1,651 R	61.0%	36.7%	62.4%	37.6%
19,136	WASECA	9,747	5,116	4,370	261	746 R	52.5%	44.8%	53.9%	46.1%
238,136	WASHINGTON	142,133	69,137	70,203	2,793	1,066 D	48.6%	49.4%	49.6%	50.4%
11,211	WATONWAN	5,144	2,517	2,494	133	23 R	48.9%	48.5%	50.2%	49.8%
6,576	WILKIN	3,222	1,884	1,258	80	626 R	58.5%	39.0%	60.0%	40.0%
51,461	WINONA	27,232	11,480	14,980	772	3,500 D	42.2%	55.0%	43.4%	56.6%
124,700	WRIGHT	67,816	40,466	25,741	1,609	14,725 R	59.7%	38.0%	61.1%	38.9%
10,438	YELLOW MEDICINE	5,414	2,806	2,465	143	341 R	51.8%	45.5%	53.2%	46.8%
5,303,925	TOTAL	2,936,561	1,320,225	1,546,167	70,169	225,942 D	45.0%	52.7%	46.1%	53.9%

Note: Democratic candidates, including Barack Obama in 2012, appear on the ballot in Minnesota for the Democratic-Farmer-Labor (DFL) party.

MINNESOTA

SENATOR 2012

2010 Census Population	County	Total Vote	Republican (Bills)	Democratic (Klobuchar)	Other	Rep.-Dem. Plurality	Percentage Total Vote Rep.	Dem.	Major Vote Rep.	Dem.
16,202	AITKIN	8,831	2,810	5,628	393	2,818 D	31.8%	63.7%	33.3%	66.7%
330,844	ANOKA	181,359	59,991	113,611	7,757	53,620 D	33.1%	62.6%	34.6%	65.4%
32,504	BECKER	15,891	6,095	8,998	798	2,903 D	38.4%	56.6%	40.4%	59.6%
44,442	BELTRAMI	21,310	6,710	13,604	996	6,894 D	31.5%	63.8%	33.0%	67.0%
38,451	BENTON	18,827	6,267	11,542	1,018	5,275 D	33.3%	61.3%	35.2%	64.8%
5,269	BIG STONE	2,731	788	1,818	125	1,030 D	28.9%	66.6%	30.2%	69.8%
64,013	BLUE EARTH	32,626	9,338	21,289	1,999	11,951 D	28.6%	65.3%	30.5%	69.5%
25,893	BROWN	13,584	4,803	8,149	632	3,346 D	35.4%	60.0%	37.1%	62.9%
35,386	CARLTON	17,980	4,290	13,054	636	8,764 D	23.9%	72.6%	24.7%	75.3%
91,042	CARVER	51,294	21,378	28,205	1,711	6,827 D	41.7%	55.0%	43.1%	56.9%
28,567	CASS	15,653	5,930	8,996	727	3,066 D	37.9%	57.5%	39.7%	60.3%
12,441	CHIPPEWA	6,054	1,592	4,176	286	2,584 D	26.3%	69.0%	27.6%	72.4%
53,887	CHISAGO	28,333	10,371	16,758	1,204	6,387 D	36.6%	59.1%	38.2%	61.8%
58,999	CLAY	27,774	8,064	18,607	1,103	10,543 D	29.0%	67.0%	30.2%	69.8%
8,695	CLEARWATER	4,081	1,709	2,172	200	463 D	41.9%	53.2%	44.0%	56.0%

MINNESOTA
SENATOR 2012

2010 Census Population	County	Total Vote	Republican (Bills)	Democratic (Klobuchar)	Other	Rep.-Dem. Plurality	Percentage Total Vote Rep.	Total Vote Dem.	Major Vote Rep.	Major Vote Dem.
5,176	COOK	3,198	820	2,263	115	1,443 D	25.6%	70.8%	26.6%	73.4%
11,687	COTTONWOOD	5,740	1,985	3,457	298	1,472 D	34.6%	60.2%	36.5%	63.5%
62,500	CROW WING	33,753	12,467	19,568	1,718	7,101 D	36.9%	58.0%	38.9%	61.1%
398,552	DAKOTA	224,529	77,031	139,161	8,337	62,130 D	34.3%	62.0%	35.6%	64.4%
20,087	DODGE	10,044	3,627	5,926	491	2,299 D	36.1%	59.0%	38.0%	62.0%
36,009	DOUGLAS	20,357	7,233	12,199	925	4,966 D	35.5%	59.9%	37.2%	62.8%
14,553	FARIBAULT	7,519	2,377	4,788	354	2,411 D	31.6%	63.7%	33.2%	66.8%
20,866	FILLMORE	10,522	3,100	6,810	612	3,710 D	29.5%	64.7%	31.3%	68.7%
31,255	FREEBORN	16,237	4,406	11,107	724	6,701 D	27.1%	68.4%	28.4%	71.6%
46,183	GOODHUE	25,226	8,277	15,777	1,172	7,500 D	32.8%	62.5%	34.4%	65.6%
6,018	GRANT	3,422	1,036	2,222	164	1,186 D	30.3%	64.9%	31.8%	68.2%
1,152,425	HENNEPIN	658,864	165,612	469,119	24,133	303,507 D	25.1%	71.2%	26.1%	73.9%
19,027	HOUSTON	9,989	3,909	5,174	906	1,265 D	39.1%	51.8%	43.0%	57.0%
20,428	HUBBARD	11,182	4,311	6,353	518	2,042 D	38.6%	56.8%	40.4%	59.6%
37,816	ISANTI	19,506	7,438	11,131	937	3,693 D	38.1%	57.1%	40.1%	59.9%
45,058	ITASCA	23,181	6,967	15,382	832	8,415 D	30.1%	66.4%	31.2%	68.8%
10,266	JACKSON	5,285	1,802	3,157	326	1,355 D	34.1%	59.7%	36.3%	63.7%
16,239	KANABEC	7,872	2,697	4,819	356	2,122 D	34.3%	61.2%	35.9%	64.1%
42,239	KANDIYOHI	20,861	6,990	13,033	838	6,043 D	33.5%	62.5%	34.9%	65.1%
4,552	KITTSON	2,374	625	1,674	75	1,049 D	26.3%	70.5%	27.2%	72.8%
13,311	KOOCHICHING	6,255	1,704	4,315	236	2,611 D	27.2%	69.0%	28.3%	71.7%
7,259	LAC QUI PARLE	3,893	1,035	2,674	184	1,639 D	26.6%	68.7%	27.9%	72.1%
10,866	LAKE	6,618	1,702	4,678	238	2,976 D	25.7%	70.7%	26.7%	73.3%
4,045	LAKE OF THE WOODS	2,163	839	1,218	106	379 D	38.8%	56.3%	40.8%	59.2%
27,703	LE SUEUR	14,347	4,489	9,144	714	4,655 D	31.3%	63.7%	32.9%	67.1%
5,896	LINCOLN	3,013	1,112	1,712	189	600 D	36.9%	56.8%	39.4%	60.6%
25,857	LYON	12,043	4,085	7,320	638	3,235 D	33.9%	60.8%	35.8%	64.2%
5,413	MAHNOMEN	2,125	531	1,483	111	952 D	25.0%	69.8%	26.4%	73.6%
9,439	MARSHALL	4,586	1,448	2,973	165	1,525 D	31.6%	64.8%	32.8%	67.2%
20,840	MARTIN	10,663	3,924	6,167	572	2,243 D	36.8%	57.8%	38.9%	61.1%
36,651	MCLEOD	18,113	6,617	10,553	943	3,936 D	36.5%	58.3%	38.5%	61.5%
23,300	MEEKER	11,969	4,224	7,111	634	2,887 D	35.3%	59.4%	37.3%	62.7%
26,097	MILLE LACS	12,652	4,234	7,737	681	3,503 D	33.5%	61.2%	35.4%	64.6%
33,198	MORRISON	16,113	6,027	9,233	853	3,206 D	37.4%	57.3%	39.5%	60.5%
39,163	MOWER	17,954	4,443	12,475	1,036	8,032 D	24.7%	69.5%	26.3%	73.7%
8,725	MURRAY	4,653	1,715	2,674	264	959 D	36.9%	57.5%	39.1%	60.9%
32,727	NICOLLET	17,726	4,912	11,968	846	7,056 D	27.7%	67.5%	29.1%	70.9%
21,378	NOBLES	8,179	3,024	4,587	568	1,563 D	37.0%	56.1%	39.7%	60.3%
6,852	NORMAN	3,126	749	2,262	115	1,513 D	24.0%	72.4%	24.9%	75.1%
144,248	OLMSTED	75,226	25,721	46,067	3,438	20,346 D	34.2%	61.2%	35.8%	64.2%
57,303	OTTER TAIL	30,906	12,931	16,542	1,433	3,611 D	41.8%	53.5%	43.9%	56.1%
13,930	PENNINGTON	6,343	1,956	4,098	289	2,142 D	30.8%	64.6%	32.3%	67.7%
29,750	PINE	13,459	4,269	8,449	741	4,180 D	31.7%	62.8%	33.6%	66.4%
9,596	PIPESTONE	4,480	2,228	1,981	271	247 R	49.7%	44.2%	52.9%	47.1%
31,600	POLK	14,150	4,555	8,975	620	4,420 D	32.2%	63.4%	33.7%	66.3%
10,995	POPE	6,105	1,831	4,005	269	2,174 D	30.0%	65.6%	31.4%	68.6%
508,640	RAMSEY	267,912	58,824	196,972	12,116	138,148 D	22.0%	73.5%	23.0%	77.0%
4,089	RED LAKE	1,925	527	1,306	92	779 D	27.4%	67.8%	28.8%	71.2%
16,059	REDWOOD	7,604	2,741	4,494	369	1,753 D	36.0%	59.1%	37.9%	62.1%
15,730	RENVILLE	7,573	2,215	4,996	362	2,781 D	29.2%	66.0%	30.7%	69.3%
64,142	RICE	30,969	8,943	20,657	1,369	11,714 D	28.9%	66.7%	30.2%	69.8%
9,687	ROCK	4,691	2,245	2,148	298	97 R	47.9%	45.8%	51.1%	48.9%
15,629	ROSEAU	7,180	2,835	4,009	336	1,174 D	39.5%	55.8%	41.4%	58.6%
129,928	SCOTT	68,938	26,941	39,072	2,925	12,131 D	39.1%	56.7%	40.8%	59.2%
88,499	SHERBURNE	45,233	18,290	25,020	1,923	6,730 D	40.4%	55.3%	42.2%	57.8%
15,226	SIBLEY	7,642	2,667	4,603	372	1,936 D	34.9%	60.2%	36.7%	63.3%
200,226	ST. LOUIS	111,856	25,684	82,504	3,668	56,820 D	23.0%	73.8%	23.7%	76.3%
150,642	STEARNS	75,431	25,373	46,312	3,746	20,939 D	33.6%	61.4%	35.4%	64.6%
36,576	STEELE	18,525	5,716	11,781	1,028	6,065 D	30.9%	63.6%	32.7%	67.3%
9,726	STEVENS	5,497	1,820	3,456	221	1,636 D	33.1%	62.9%	34.5%	65.5%

MINNESOTA

SENATOR 2012

2010 Census Population	County	Total Vote	Republican (Bills)	Democratic (Klobuchar)	Other	Rep.-Dem. Plurality	Percentage			
							Total Vote		Major Vote	
							Rep.	Dem.	Rep.	Dem.
9,783	SWIFT	5,006	1,285	3,497	224	2,212 D	25.7%	69.9%	26.9%	73.1%
24,895	TODD	11,480	4,139	6,796	545	2,657 D	36.1%	59.2%	37.9%	62.1%
3,558	TRAVERSE	1,803	505	1,222	76	717 D	28.0%	67.8%	29.2%	70.8%
21,676	WABASHA	11,400	3,705	7,142	553	3,437 D	32.5%	62.6%	34.2%	65.8%
13,843	WADENA	6,585	2,753	3,541	291	788 D	41.8%	53.8%	43.7%	56.3%
19,136	WASECA	9,541	2,988	6,063	490	3,075 D	31.3%	63.5%	33.0%	67.0%
238,136	WASHINGTON	138,462	45,135	88,581	4,746	43,446 D	32.6%	64.0%	33.8%	66.2%
11,211	WATONWAN	4,989	1,388	3,373	228	1,985 D	27.8%	67.6%	29.2%	70.8%
6,576	WILKIN	3,129	1,114	1,881	134	767 D	35.6%	60.1%	37.2%	62.8%
51,461	WINONA	25,624	8,360	15,463	1,801	7,103 D	32.6%	60.3%	35.1%	64.9%
124,700	WRIGHT	66,030	27,072	36,038	2,920	8,966 D	41.0%	54.6%	42.9%	57.1%
10,438	YELLOW MEDICINE	5,333	1,558	3,540	235	1,982 D	29.2%	66.4%	30.6%	69.4%
5,303,925	TOTAL	2,843,207	867,974	1,854,595	120,638	986,621 D	30.5%	65.2%	31.9%	68.1%

Note: Democratic candidates in Minnesota appear on the ballot for the Democratic–Farmer–Labor (DFL) Party.

MINNESOTA

HOUSE OF REPRESENTATIVES

CD	Year	Total Vote	Republican		Democratic		Other Vote	Rep.-Dem. Plurality	Percentage			
			Vote	Candidate	Vote	Candidate			Total Vote		Major Vote	
									Rep.	Dem.	Rep.	Dem.
1	2012	335,880	142,164	QUIST, ALLEN	193,211	WALZ, TIM*	505	51,047 D	42.3%	57.5%	42.4%	57.6%
2	2012	358,446	193,587	KLINE, JOHN*	164,338	OBERMUELLER, MIKE	521	29,249 R	54.0%	45.8%	54.1%	45.9%
3	2012	382,705	222,335	PAULSEN, ERIK*	159,937	BARNES, BRIAN	433	62,398 R	58.1%	41.8%	58.2%	41.8%
4	2012	347,991	109,659	HERNANDEZ, TONY	216,685	MCCOLLUM, BETTY*	21,647	107,026 D	31.5%	62.3%	33.6%	66.4%
5	2012	351,969	88,753	FIELDS, CHRIS	262,102	ELLISON, KEITH*	1,114	173,349 D	25.2%	74.5%	25.3%	74.7%
6	2012	355,153	179,240	BACHMANN, MICHELE*	174,944	GRAVES, JIM	969	4,296 R	50.5%	49.3%	50.6%	49.4%
7	2012	327,576	114,151	BYBERG, LEE	197,791	PETERSON, COLLIN C.*	15,634	83,640 D	34.8%	60.4%	36.6%	63.4%
8	2012	353,663	160,520	CRAVAACK, CHIP*	191,976	NOLAN, RICK	1,167	31,456 D	45.4%	54.3%	45.5%	54.5%
TOTAL	2012	2,813,383	1,210,409		1,560,984		41,990	350,575 D	43.0%	55.5%	43.7%	56.3%

Note: An asterisk (*) denotes incumbent. Democratic candidates in Minnesota appear on the ballot for the Democratic-Farmer-Labor (DFL) party.

MINNESOTA

GENERAL AND PRIMARY ELECTIONS

GENERAL ELECTIONS: OTHER VOTE

President   Other vote was 35,098 Libertarian (Gary E. Johnson), 13,023 Green (Jill Stein), 10,641 Write-in (Scattered Write-In), 3,722 Constitution (Virgil H. Goode), 3,149 Grassroots (Jim Carlson), 1,996 Justice (Ross C. "Rocky" Anderson), 1,092 Constitutional Government (Dean Morstad), 1,051 Socialist Workers Party (James Harris), 397 Socialism and Liberation (Peta Lindsay)

Senator   Other vote was 73,539 Independence (Stephen Williams), 30,531 Grassroots (Tim Davis), 13,986 Minnesota Open Progressives (Michael Cavlan), 2,582 Write-in (Scattered Write-In)

MINNESOTA

GENERAL AND PRIMARY ELECTIONS

House	Other vote was:
CD 1	505 Write-in (Scattered Write-In)
CD 2	521 Write-in (Scattered Write-In)
CD 3	433 Write-in (Scattered Write-In)
CD 4	21,135 Independent (Steve Carlson), 512 Write-in (Scattered Write-In)
CD 5	1,114 Write-in (Scattered Write-In)
CD 6	969 Write-in (Scattered Write-In)
CD 7	15,298 Independent (Adam Steele), 336 Write-in (Scattered Write-In)
CD 8	1,167 Write-in (Scattered Write-In)

PRIMARY ELECTIONS: SUPPLEMENTARY INFORMATION

Primary	August 14, 2012	Registration (as of August 6, 2012)	3,059,234	No Party Registration

Primary Type Open—Any registered voter could participate in the party primary of their choice.

	REPUBLICAN PRIMARIES			DEMOCRATIC PRIMARIES		
Senator	Bills, Kurt	63,383	51.1%	Klobuchar, Amy*	183,766	90.8%
	Carlson, David	43,852	35.4%	Franson, Dick	6,837	3.4%
	Carney, Bob Jr.	16,759	13.5%	Shepard, Jack	6,632	3.3%
				Stanton, Darryl	5,155	2.5%
	TOTAL	*123,994*		*TOTAL*	*202,390*	
Congressional District 1	Quist, Allen	12,540	54.1%	Walz, Tim*	15,697	100.0%
	Parry, Mike	10,622	45.9%			
	TOTAL	*23,162*		*TOTAL*	*15,697*	
Congressional District 2	Kline, John*	15,859	85.1%	Obermueller, Mike	11,628	100.0%
	Gerson, David	2,772	14.9%			
	TOTAL	*18,631*		*TOTAL*	*11,628*	
Congressional District 3	Paulsen, Erik*	18,672	90.2%	Barnes, Brian	11,786	100.0%
	Howard, John W. III	2,032	9.8%			
	TOTAL	*20,704*		*TOTAL*	*11,786*	
Congressional District 4	Hernandez, Tony	6,876	64.1%	McCollum, Betty*	27,291	84.2%
	Seiford, Ron	3,856	35.9%	Longrie, Diana	3,212	9.9%
				Stalboerger, Brian	1,913	5.9%
	TOTAL	*10,732*		*TOTAL*	*32,416*	
Congressional District 5	Fields, Chris	5,966	100.0%	Ellison, Keith*	30,609	89.6%
				Iverson, Gregg A.	2,143	6.3%
				Boisclair, Gary	1,397	4.1%
	TOTAL	*5,966*		*TOTAL*	*34,149*	
Congressional District 6	Bachmann, Michele*	14,569	80.3%	Graves, Jim	8,600	100.0%
	Thompson, Stephen	2,322	12.8%			
	Immelman, Aubrey	1,242	6.8%			
	TOTAL	*18,133*		*TOTAL*	*8,600*	
Congressional District 7	Byberg, Lee	Unopposed		Peterson, Collin C.*	Unopposed	
Congressional District 8	Cravaack, Chip*	20,471	100.0%	Nolan, Rick	20,840	38.3%
				Clark, Tarryl	17,554	32.3%
				Anderson, Jeff	16,035	29.5%
	TOTAL	*20,471*		*TOTAL*	*54,429*	

Note: An asterisk (*) denotes incumbent. No votes were tallied for unopposed candidates in districts where none of the parties had a contested primary.

MISSISSIPPI

Congressional districts first established for elections held in 2012

4 members

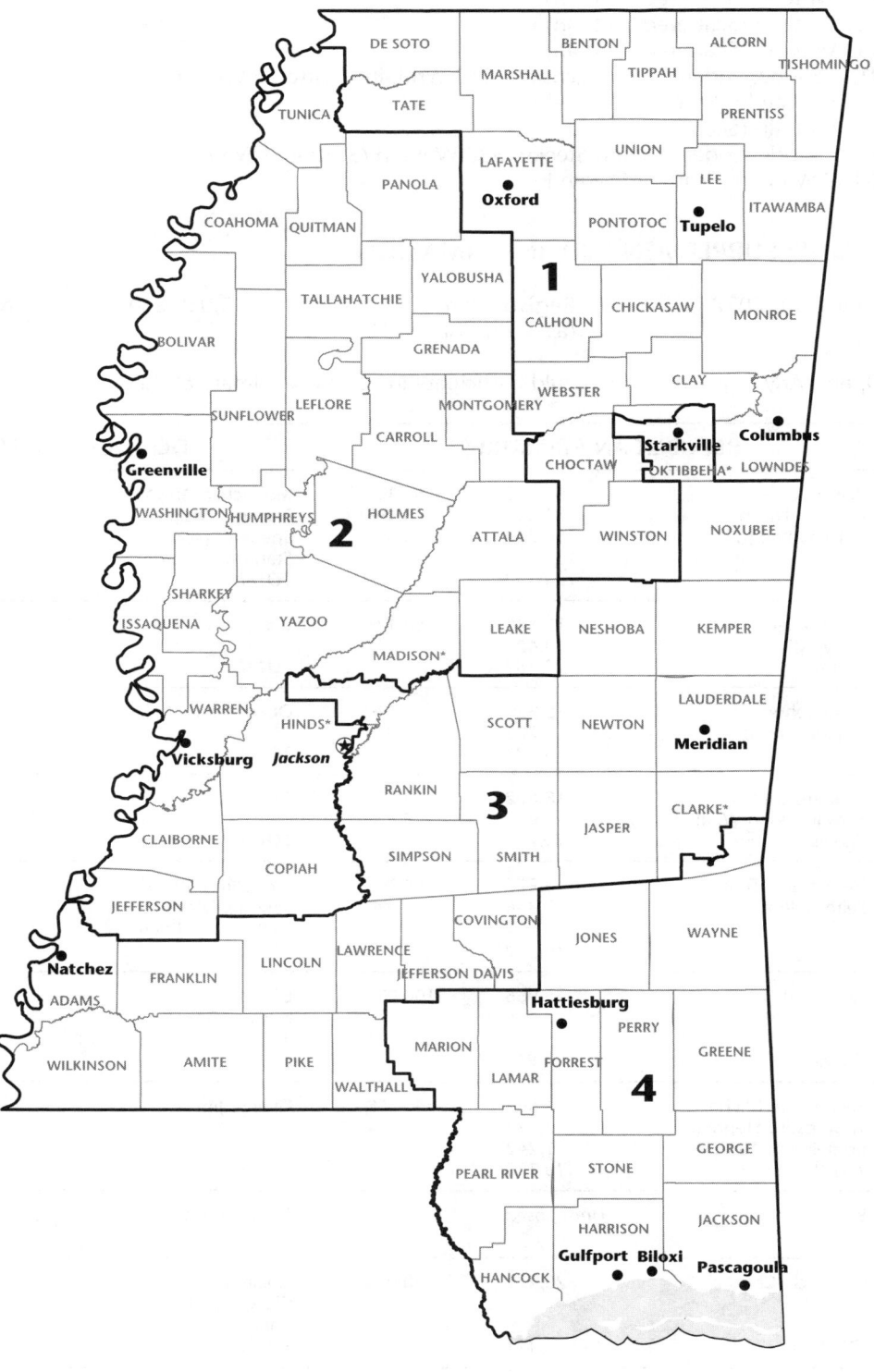

* Asterisk indicates a county whose boundaries include parts of two or more Congressional districts.

MISSISSIPPI

GOVERNOR
Phil Bryant (R). Elected 2011 to a four-year term.

SENATORS (2 Republicans)
Thad Cochran (R). Reelected 2008 to a six-year term. Previously elected 2002, 1996, 1990, 1984, 1978.

Roger Wicker (R). Reelected 2012 to a six-year term. Previously elected 2008 to fill the final four years of the term vacated by the December 2007 resignation of Senator C. Trent Lott. Wicker had earlier been appointed to fill the vacancy and was sworn in as senator on December 31, 2007.

REPRESENTATIVES (3 Republicans, 1 Democrat)
1. Alan Nunnelee (R)
2. Bennie Thompson (D)
3. Gregg Harper (R)
4. Steven Palazzo (R)

POSTWAR VOTE FOR PRESIDENT

| | | Republican | | Democratic | | Other | Rep.-Dem. | Percentage | | | |
| | | | | | | | | Total Vote | | Major Vote | |
Year	Total Vote	Vote	Candidate	Vote	Candidate	Vote	Plurality	Rep.	Dem.	Rep.	Dem.
2012	1,285,584	710,746	Romney, W. Mitt	562,949	Obama, Barack H.*	11,889	147,797 R	55.3%	43.8%	55.8%	44.2%
2008	1,289,865	724,597	McCain, John S. III	554,662	Obama, Barack H.	10,606	169,935 R	56.2%	43.0%	56.6%	43.4%
2004	1,152,145	684,981	Bush, George W.*	458,094	Kerry, John F.	9,070	226,887 R	59.5%	39.8%	59.9%	40.1%
2000**	994,184	572,844	Bush, George W.	404,614	Gore, Albert Jr.	16,726	168,230 R	57.6%	40.7%	58.6%	41.4%
1996**	893,857	439,838	Dole, Robert "Bob"	394,022	Clinton, Bill*	59,997	45,816 R	49.2%	44.1%	52.7%	47.3%
1992**	981,793	487,793	Bush, George H.*	400,258	Clinton, Bill	93,742	87,535 R	49.7%	40.8%	54.9%	45.1%
1988	931,527	557,890	Bush, George H.	363,921	Dukakis, Michael S.	9,716	193,969 R	59.9%	39.1%	60.5%	39.5%
1984	941,104	582,377	Reagan, Ronald*	352,192	Mondale, Walter F.	6,535	230,185 R	61.9%	37.4%	62.3%	37.7%
1980**	892,620	441,089	Reagan, Ronald	429,281	Carter, Jimmy*	22,250	11,808 R	49.4%	48.1%	50.7%	49.3%
1976	769,361	366,846	Ford, Gerald R.*	381,309	Carter, Jimmy	21,206	14,463 D	47.7%	49.6%	49.0%	51.0%
1972	645,963	505,125	Nixon, Richard M.*	126,782	McGovern, George S.	14,056	378,343 R	78.2%	19.6%	79.9%	20.1%
1968**	654,509	88,516	Nixon, Richard M.	150,644	Humphrey, Hubert H. Jr.	415,349	62,128 D**	13.5%	23.0%	37.0%	63.0%
1964	409,146	356,528	Goldwater, Barry M. Sr.	52,618	Johnson, Lyndon B.*		303,910 R	87.1%	12.9%	87.1%	12.9%
1960**	298,171	73,561	Nixon, Richard M.	108,362	Kennedy, John F.	116,248	34,801 D**	24.7%	36.3%	40.4%	59.6%
1956	248,104	60,685	Eisenhower, Dwight D.*	144,453	Stevenson, Adlai E. II	42,966	83,768 D	24.5%	58.2%	29.6%	70.4%
1952	285,532	112,966	Eisenhower, Dwight D.	172,566	Stevenson, Adlai E. II		59,600 D	39.6%	60.4%	39.6%	60.4%
1948**	192,190	5,043	Dewey, Thomas E.	19,384	Truman, Harry S.*	167,763	14,341 D**	2.6%	10.1%	20.6%	79.4%

Note: An asterisk (*) denotes incumbent. **In past elections, the other vote included: 2000 - 8,122 Green (Ralph Nader); 1996 - 52,222 Reform (Ross Perot); 1992 - 85,626 Independent (Perot); 1980 - 12,036 Independent (John Anderson); 1968 - 415,349 American Independent (George Wallace); 1960 - 116,248 Unpledged Independent Democratic electors; 1948 - 167,538 States' Rights (Strom Thurmond). Thurmond won Mississippi in 1948 with 87.2 percent of the vote. The slate of Unpledged Independent Democratic electors carried the state in 1960 with 39.0 percent. Wallace won Mississippi in 1968 with 63.5 percent of the vote.

MISSISSIPPI

POSTWAR VOTE FOR GOVERNOR

Year	Total Vote	Republican		Democratic		Other Vote	Rep.-Dem. Plurality	Percentage			
								Total Vote		Major Vote	
		Vote	Candidate	Vote	Candidate			Rep.	Dem.	Rep.	Dem.
2011	893,468	544,851	Bryant, Phil	348,617	DuPree, Johnny L.		196,234 R	61.0%	39.0%	61.0%	39.0%
2007	744,039	430,807	Barbour, Haley*	313,232	Eaves, John A.		117,575 R	57.9%	42.1%	57.9%	42.1%
2003	894,487	470,404	Barbour, Haley	409,787	Musgrove, Ronnie*	14,296	60,617 R	52.6%	45.8%	53.4%	46.6%
1999**	763,938	370,691	Parker, Mike	379,034	Musgrove, Ronnie	14,213	8,343 D	48.5%	49.6%	49.4%	50.6%
1995	819,471	455,261	Fordice, Kirk*	364,210	Molpus, Dick		91,051 R	55.6%	44.4%	55.6%	44.4%
1991	711,188	361,500	Fordice, Kirk	338,435	Mabus, Ray*	11,253	23,065 R	50.8%	47.6%	51.6%	48.4%
1987	721,695	336,006	Reed, Jack R.	385,689	Mabus, Ray		49,683 D	46.6%	53.4%	46.6%	53.4%
1983	742,737	288,764	Bramlett, Leon	409,209	Allain, William A.	44,764	120,445 D	38.9%	55.1%	41.4%	58.6%
1979	677,322	263,702	Carmichael, Gil	413,620	Winter, William F.		149,918 D	38.9%	61.1%	38.9%	61.1%
1975	708,033	319,632	Carmichael, Gil	369,568	Finch, Cliff	18,833	49,936 D	45.1%	52.2%	46.4%	53.6%
1971**	780,537			601,122	Waller, William L.	179,415	601,122 D		77.0%		100%
1967	448,696	133,378	Phillips, Rubel L.	315,318	Williams, John Bell		181,940 D	29.7%	70.3%	29.7%	70.3%
1963	363,971	138,515	Phillips, Rubel L.	225,456	Johnson, Paul B. Jr.		86,941 D	38.1%	61.9%	38.1%	61.9%
1959	57,671			57,671	Barnett, Ross R.		57,671 D		100%		100%
1955	40,707			40,707	Coleman, James P.		40,707 D		100%		100%
1951	43,422			43,422	White, Hugh L.		43,422 D		100%		100%
1947	166,095			161,993	Wright, Fielding L.	4,102	161,993 D		97.5%		100%

Note: An asterisk (*) denotes incumbent. **In past elections, the other vote included: 1971 - 172,762 Independent (Charles Evers), who finished second. In 1999 no candidate received a majority of the vote. Democrat Ronnie Musgrove was elected in January 2000 by the Mississippi House of Representatives. The Republican Party did not run a gubernatorial candidate in 1947, 1951, 1955, 1959, and 1971.

POSTWAR VOTE FOR SENATOR

Year	Total Vote	Republican		Democratic		Other Vote	Rep.-Dem. Plurality	Percentage			
								Total Vote		Major Vote	
		Vote	Candidate	Vote	Candidate			Rep.	Dem.	Rep.	Dem.
2012	1,241,568	709,626	Wicker, Roger*	503,467	Gore, Albert N. Jr.	28,475	206,159 R	57.2%	40.6%	58.5%	41.5%
2008S	1,243,473	683,409	Wicker, Roger*	560,064	Musgrove, Ronnie		123,345 R	55.0%	45.0%	55.0%	45.0%
2008	1,247,026	766,111	Cochran, Thad*	480,915	Fleming, Erik R.		285,196 R	61.4%	38.6%	61.4%	38.6%
2006	610,921	388,399	Lott, C. Trent*	213,000	Fleming, Erik R.	9,522	175,399 R	63.6%	34.9%	64.6%	35.4%
2002**	630,495	533,269	Cochran, Thad*			97,226	533,269 R	84.6%		100.0%	
2000	994,144	654,941	Lott, C. Trent*	314,090	Brown, Troy	25,113	340,851 R	65.9%	31.6%	67.6%	32.4%
1996	878,662	624,154	Cochran, Thad*	240,647	Hunt, James W.	13,861	383,507 R	71.0%	27.4%	72.2%	27.8%
1994	608,085	418,333	Lott, C. Trent*	189,752	Harper, Ken		228,581 R	68.8%	31.2%	68.8%	31.2%
1990	274,244	274,244	Cochran, Thad*				274,244 R	100.0%		100.0%	
1988	946,719	510,380	Lott, C. Trent	436,339	Dowdy, Wayne		74,041 R	53.9%	46.1%	53.9%	46.1%
1984	952,240	580,314	Cochran, W. Thad*	371,926	Winter, William F.		208,388 R	60.9%	39.1%	60.9%	39.1%
1982	645,026	230,927	Barbour, Haley	414,099	Stennis, John*		183,172 D	35.8%	64.2%	35.8%	64.2%
1978**	583,936	263,089	Cochran, Thad	185,454	Dantin, Maurice	135,393	77,635 R	45.1%	31.8%	58.7%	41.3%
1976	554,433			554,433	Stennis, John*		554,433 D		100.0%		100.0%
1972	645,746	249,779	Carmichael, Gil	375,102	Eastland, James O.*	20,865	125,323 D	38.7%	58.1%	40.0%	60.0%
1970**	324,215			286,622	Stennis, John*	37,593	286,622 D		88.4%		100.0%
1966	394,541	105,652	Walker, Prentiss	258,248	Eastland, James O.*	30,641	152,596 D	26.8%	65.5%	29.0%	71.0%
1964	343,364			343,364	Stennis, John*		343,364 D		100.0%		100.0%
1960	266,148	21,807	Moore, Joe A.	244,341	Eastland, James O.*		222,534 D	8.2%	91.8%	8.2%	91.8%
1958	61,039			61,039	Stennis, John*		61,039 D		100.0%		100.0%
1954	105,526	4,678	White, James A.	100,848	Eastland, James O.*		96,170 D	4.4%	95.6%	4.4%	95.6%
1952	233,919			233,919	Stennis, John*		233,919 D		100.0%		100.0%
1948	151,478			151,478	Eastland, James O.*		151,478 D		100.0%		100.0%
1947S**	193,086				Stennis, John	193,086					
1946	46,747			46,747	Bilbo, Theodore G.*		46,747 D		100.0%		100.0%

Note: An asterisk (*) denotes incumbent. **In past elections, the other vote included: 2002 - 97,226 Reform (Shawn O'Hara), who finished second; 1978 - 133,646 Independent (Charles Evers). The 1947 election and one of the 2008 elections were for short terms to fill a vacancy. Both special elections were held without party designation or nomination. In 1947 John Stennis received 52,068 votes (26.9 percent of the total vote) and won the election with a plurality of 6,343 votes. Other candidates that year included: 45,725 W. M. Colmer; 43,642 Forrest B. Jackson; 27,159 Paul B. Johnson; 24,492 John E. Rankin. The Republican Party did not run a candidate in Senate elections in 1946, 1948, 1952, 1958, 1964, 1970, and 1976. The Democratic Party did not run a candidate in Senate elections in 1990 and 2002.

MISSISSIPPI

PRESIDENT 2012

2010 Census Population	County	Total Vote	Republican (Romney)	Democratic (Obama)	Other	Rep.-Dem. Plurality	Total Vote Rep.	Total Vote Dem.	Major Vote Rep.	Major Vote Dem.
32,297	ADAMS	15,447	6,293	9,061	93	2,768 D	40.7%	58.7%	41.0%	59.0%
37,057	ALCORN	14,830	11,111	3,511	208	7,600 R	74.9%	23.7%	76.0%	24.0%
13,131	AMITE	7,706	4,414	3,242	50	1,172 R	57.3%	42.1%	57.7%	42.3%
19,564	ATTALA	9,092	5,126	3,927	39	1,199 R	56.4%	43.2%	56.6%	43.4%
8,729	BENTON	4,116	2,041	2,051	24	10 D	49.6%	49.8%	49.9%	50.1%
34,145	BOLIVAR	15,428	4,701	10,582	145	5,881 D	30.5%	68.6%	30.8%	69.2%
14,962	CALHOUN	7,068	4,412	2,586	70	1,826 R	62.4%	36.6%	63.0%	37.0%
10,597	CARROLL	5,992	3,960	2,007	25	1,953 R	66.1%	33.5%	66.4%	33.6%
17,392	CHICKASAW	8,503	3,994	4,378	131	384 D	47.0%	51.5%	47.7%	52.3%
8,547	CHOCTAW	4,273	2,812	1,428	33	1,384 R	65.8%	33.4%	66.3%	33.7%
9,604	CLAIBORNE	5,484	625	4,838	21	4,213 D	11.4%	88.2%	11.4%	88.6%
16,732	CLARKE	8,253	5,049	3,111	93	1,938 R	61.2%	37.7%	61.9%	38.1%
20,634	CLAY	11,072	4,291	6,712	69	2,421 D	38.8%	60.6%	39.0%	61.0%
26,151	COAHOMA	10,549	2,712	7,792	45	5,080 D	25.7%	73.9%	25.8%	74.2%
29,449	COPIAH	14,123	6,282	7,749	92	1,467 D	44.5%	54.9%	44.8%	55.2%
19,568	COVINGTON	9,348	5,405	3,878	65	1,527 R	57.8%	41.5%	58.2%	41.8%
161,252	DE SOTO	65,794	43,559	21,575	660	21,984 R	66.2%	32.8%	66.9%	33.1%
74,934	FORREST	30,236	16,574	13,272	390	3,302 R	54.8%	43.9%	55.5%	44.5%
8,118	FRANKLIN	4,493	2,735	1,726	32	1,009 R	60.9%	38.4%	61.3%	38.7%
22,578	GEORGE	9,856	8,376	1,359	121	7,017 R	85.0%	13.8%	86.0%	14.0%
14,400	GREENE	5,922	4,531	1,325	66	3,206 R	76.5%	22.4%	77.4%	22.6%
21,906	GRENADA	11,335	5,986	5,288	61	698 R	52.8%	46.7%	53.1%	46.9%
43,929	HANCOCK	17,167	12,964	3,917	286	9,047 R	75.5%	22.8%	76.8%	23.2%
187,105	HARRISON	63,328	39,470	23,119	739	16,351 R	62.3%	36.5%	63.1%	36.9%
245,285	HINDS	106,491	29,664	76,112	715	46,448 D	27.9%	71.5%	28.0%	72.0%
19,198	HOLMES	9,288	1,435	7,812	41	6,377 D	15.5%	84.1%	15.5%	84.5%
9,375	HUMPHREYS	5,212	1,293	3,903	16	2,610 D	24.8%	74.9%	24.9%	75.1%
1,406	ISSAQUENA	787	302	479	6	177 D	38.4%	60.9%	38.7%	61.3%
23,401	ITAWAMBA	9,318	7,393	1,706	219	5,687 R	79.3%	18.3%	81.3%	18.7%
139,668	JACKSON	53,655	35,747	17,299	609	18,448 R	66.6%	32.2%	67.4%	32.6%
17,062	JASPER	9,340	4,193	5,097	50	904 D	44.9%	54.6%	45.1%	54.9%
7,726	JEFFERSON	4,433	468	3,951	14	3,483 D	10.6%	89.1%	10.6%	89.4%
12,487	JEFFERSON DAVIS	6,864	2,507	4,267	90	1,760 D	36.5%	62.2%	37.0%	63.0%
67,761	JONES	30,159	20,687	9,211	261	11,476 R	68.6%	30.5%	69.2%	30.8%
10,456	KEMPER	5,052	1,789	3,239	24	1,450 D	35.4%	64.1%	35.6%	64.4%
47,351	LAFAYETTE	19,505	11,075	8,091	339	2,984 R	56.8%	41.5%	57.8%	42.2%
55,658	LAMAR	24,889	19,101	5,494	294	13,607 R	76.7%	22.1%	77.7%	22.3%
80,261	LAUDERDALE	32,777	18,700	13,814	263	4,886 R	57.1%	42.1%	57.5%	42.5%
12,929	LAWRENCE	6,698	4,192	2,468	38	1,724 R	62.6%	36.8%	62.9%	37.1%
23,805	LEAKE	8,983	4,863	4,079	41	784 R	54.1%	45.4%	54.4%	45.6%
82,910	LEE	35,306	22,415	12,563	328	9,852 R	63.5%	35.6%	64.1%	35.9%
32,317	LEFLORE	12,773	3,587	9,119	67	5,532 D	28.1%	71.4%	28.2%	71.8%
34,869	LINCOLN	16,414	10,839	5,471	104	5,368 R	66.0%	33.3%	66.5%	33.5%
59,779	LOWNDES	27,158	13,518	13,388	252	130 R	49.8%	49.3%	50.2%	49.8%
95,203	MADISON	49,571	28,507	20,722	342	7,785 R	57.5%	41.8%	57.9%	42.1%
27,088	MARION	12,729	8,237	4,393	99	3,844 R	64.7%	34.5%	65.2%	34.8%
37,144	MARSHALL	16,240	6,473	9,650	117	3,177 D	39.9%	59.4%	40.1%	59.9%
36,989	MONROE	16,918	9,723	7,056	139	2,667 R	57.5%	41.7%	57.9%	42.1%
10,925	MONTGOMERY	5,645	2,947	2,675	23	272 R	52.2%	47.4%	52.4%	47.6%
29,676	NESHOBA	11,015	7,837	3,089	89	4,748 R	71.1%	28.0%	71.7%	28.3%
21,720	NEWTON	9,777	6,394	3,319	64	3,075 R	65.4%	33.9%	65.8%	34.2%
11,545	NOXUBEE	6,264	1,325	4,920	19	3,595 D	21.2%	78.5%	21.2%	78.8%
47,671	OKTIBBEHA	18,117	8,761	9,095	261	334 D	48.4%	50.2%	49.1%	50.9%
34,707	PANOLA	16,826	7,629	9,079	118	1,450 D	45.3%	54.0%	45.7%	54.3%
55,834	PEARL RIVER	22,224	17,549	4,366	309	13,183 R	79.0%	19.6%	80.1%	19.9%
12,250	PERRY	5,722	4,137	1,527	58	2,610 R	72.3%	26.7%	73.0%	27.0%
40,404	PIKE	17,974	8,181	9,650	143	1,469 D	45.5%	53.7%	45.9%	54.1%
29,957	PONTOTOC	12,411	9,448	2,804	159	6,644 R	76.1%	22.6%	77.1%	22.9%
25,276	PRENTISS	10,033	7,075	2,817	141	4,258 R	70.5%	28.1%	71.5%	28.5%
8,223	QUITMAN	3,979	1,116	2,837	26	1,721 D	28.0%	71.3%	28.2%	71.8%

MISSISSIPPI

PRESIDENT 2012

2010 Census Population	County	Total Vote	Republican (Romney)	Democratic (Obama)	Other	Rep.-Dem. Plurality	Percentage			
							Total Vote		Major Vote	
							Rep.	Dem.	Rep.	Dem.
141,617	RANKIN	64,145	48,444	14,988	713	33,456 R	75.5%	23.4%	76.4%	23.6%
28,264	SCOTT	11,202	6,089	5,031	82	1,058 R	54.4%	44.9%	54.8%	45.2%
4,916	SHARKEY	2,532	737	1,782	13	1,045 D	29.1%	70.4%	29.3%	70.7%
27,503	SIMPSON	12,249	7,424	4,723	102	2,701 R	60.6%	38.6%	61.1%	38.9%
16,491	SMITH	8,099	6,049	1,979	71	4,070 R	74.7%	24.4%	75.3%	24.7%
17,786	STONE	7,532	5,420	2,003	109	3,417 R	72.0%	26.6%	73.0%	27.0%
29,450	SUNFLOWER	11,228	2,929	8,199	100	5,270 D	26.1%	73.0%	26.3%	73.7%
15,378	TALLAHATCHIE	6,503	2,499	3,959	45	1,460 D	38.4%	60.9%	38.7%	61.3%
28,886	TATE	12,406	7,332	4,933	141	2,399 R	59.1%	39.8%	59.8%	40.2%
22,232	TIPPAH	9,164	6,717	2,317	130	4,400 R	73.3%	25.3%	74.4%	25.6%
19,593	TISHOMINGO	7,936	6,133	1,643	160	4,490 R	77.3%	20.7%	78.9%	21.1%
10,778	TUNICA	4,382	883	3,475	24	2,592 D	20.2%	79.3%	20.3%	79.7%
27,134	UNION	11,365	8,498	2,742	125	5,756 R	74.8%	24.1%	75.6%	24.4%
15,443	WALTHALL	7,551	4,051	3,422	78	629 R	53.6%	45.3%	54.2%	45.8%
48,773	WARREN	21,391	10,457	10,786	148	329 D	48.9%	50.4%	49.2%	50.8%
51,137	WASHINGTON	19,715	5,651	13,981	83	8,330 D	28.7%	70.9%	28.8%	71.2%
20,747	WAYNE	10,332	6,111	4,148	73	1,963 R	59.1%	40.1%	59.6%	40.4%
10,253	WEBSTER	5,234	3,992	1,190	52	2,802 R	76.3%	22.7%	77.0%	23.0%
9,878	WILKINSON	4,853	1,415	3,412	26	1,997 D	29.2%	70.3%	29.3%	70.7%
19,198	WINSTON	9,829	5,168	4,607	54	561 R	52.6%	46.9%	52.9%	47.1%
12,678	YALOBUSHA	6,354	3,276	3,030	48	246 R	51.6%	47.7%	52.0%	48.0%
28,065	YAZOO	11,620	4,941	6,603	76	1,662 D	42.5%	56.8%	42.8%	57.2%
2,967,297	TOTAL	1,285,584	710,746	562,949	11,889	147,797 R	55.3%	43.8%	55.8%	44.2%

MISSISSIPPI

GOVERNOR 2011

2010 Census Population	County	Total Vote	Republican (Bryant)	Democratic (DuPree)	Other	Rep.-Dem. Plurality	Percentage			
							Total Vote		Major Vote	
							Rep.	Dem.	Rep.	Dem.
32,297	ADAMS	10,459	5,056	5,403		347 D	48.3%	51.7%	48.3%	51.7%
37,057	ALCORN	11,320	8,210	3,110		5,100 R	72.5%	27.5%	72.5%	27.5%
13,131	AMITE	6,285	3,637	2,648		989 R	57.9%	42.1%	57.9%	42.1%
19,564	ATTALA	6,006	3,771	2,235		1,536 R	62.8%	37.2%	62.8%	37.2%
8,729	BENTON	3,429	1,924	1,505		419 R	56.1%	43.9%	56.1%	43.9%
34,145	BOLIVAR	10,565	4,083	6,482		2,399 D	38.6%	61.4%	38.6%	61.4%
14,962	CALHOUN	5,945	4,123	1,822		2,301 R	69.4%	30.6%	69.4%	30.6%
10,597	CARROLL	4,715	3,358	1,357		2,001 R	71.2%	28.8%	71.2%	28.8%
17,392	CHICKASAW	6,668	3,626	3,042		584 R	54.4%	45.6%	54.4%	45.6%
8,547	CHOCTAW	3,093	2,225	868		1,357 R	71.9%	28.1%	71.9%	28.1%
9,604	CLAIBORNE	3,765	627	3,138		2,511 D	16.7%	83.3%	16.7%	83.3%
16,732	CLARKE	6,593	4,322	2,271		2,051 R	65.6%	34.4%	65.6%	34.4%
20,634	CLAY	7,447	3,552	3,895		343 D	47.7%	52.3%	47.7%	52.3%
26,151	COAHOMA	5,149	2,022	3,127		1,105 D	39.3%	60.7%	39.3%	60.7%
29,449	COPIAH	9,582	5,073	4,509		564 R	52.9%	47.1%	52.9%	47.1%
19,568	COVINGTON	7,723	4,567	3,156		1,411 R	59.1%	40.9%	59.1%	40.9%
161,252	DE SOTO	36,944	28,257	8,687		19,570 R	76.5%	23.5%	76.5%	23.5%
74,934	FORREST	21,842	12,574	9,268		3,306 R	57.6%	42.4%	57.6%	42.4%
8,118	FRANKLIN	3,339	2,228	1,111		1,117 R	66.7%	33.3%	66.7%	33.3%
22,578	GEORGE	6,701	5,360	1,341		4,019 R	80.0%	20.0%	80.0%	20.0%
14,400	GREENE	4,412	3,239	1,173		2,066 R	73.4%	26.6%	73.4%	26.6%
21,906	GRENADA	7,666	4,495	3,171		1,324 R	58.6%	41.4%	58.6%	41.4%
43,929	HANCOCK	12,167	8,837	3,330		5,507 R	72.6%	27.4%	72.6%	27.4%
187,105	HARRISON	40,028	25,488	14,540		10,948 R	63.7%	36.3%	63.7%	36.3%
245,285	HINDS	69,943	24,092	45,851		21,759 D	34.4%	65.6%	34.4%	65.6%

MISSISSIPPI

GOVERNOR 2011

2010 Census Population	County	Total Vote	Republican (Bryant)	Democratic (DuPree)	Other	Rep.-Dem. Plurality		Percentage			
								Total Vote		Major Vote	
								Rep.	Dem.	Rep.	Dem.
19,198	HOLMES	6,024	1,421	4,603		3,182	D	23.6%	76.4%	23.6%	76.4%
9,375	HUMPHREYS	3,869	1,367	2,502		1,135	D	35.3%	64.7%	35.3%	64.7%
1,406	ISSAQUENA	499	253	246		7	R	50.7%	49.3%	50.7%	49.3%
23,401	ITAWAMBA	7,584	5,893	1,691		4,202	R	77.7%	22.3%	77.7%	22.3%
139,668	JACKSON	33,920	23,444	10,476		12,968	R	69.1%	30.9%	69.1%	30.9%
17,062	JASPER	6,813	3,124	3,689		565	D	45.9%	54.1%	45.9%	54.1%
7,726	JEFFERSON	3,197	503	2,694		2,191	D	15.7%	84.3%	15.7%	84.3%
12,487	JEFFERSON DAVIS	5,426	2,313	3,113		800	D	42.6%	57.4%	42.6%	57.4%
67,761	JONES	23,544	16,696	6,848		9,848	R	70.9%	29.1%	70.9%	29.1%
10,456	KEMPER	4,465	1,864	2,601		737	D	41.7%	58.3%	41.7%	58.3%
47,351	LAFAYETTE	12,811	7,827	4,984		2,843	R	61.1%	38.9%	61.1%	38.9%
55,658	LAMAR	18,307	14,468	3,839		10,629	R	79.0%	21.0%	79.0%	21.0%
80,261	LAUDERDALE	21,073	13,838	7,235		6,603	R	65.7%	34.3%	65.7%	34.3%
12,929	LAWRENCE	5,736	3,756	1,980		1,776	R	65.5%	34.5%	65.5%	34.5%
23,805	LEAKE	6,520	3,983	2,537		1,446	R	61.1%	38.9%	61.1%	38.9%
82,910	LEE	24,827	17,087	7,740		9,347	R	68.8%	31.2%	68.8%	31.2%
32,317	LEFLORE	8,834	3,413	5,421		2,008	D	38.6%	61.4%	38.6%	61.4%
34,869	LINCOLN	12,525	8,761	3,764		4,997	R	69.9%	30.1%	69.9%	30.1%
59,779	LOWNDES	17,485	10,272	7,213		3,059	R	58.7%	41.3%	58.7%	41.3%
95,203	MADISON	33,525	21,176	12,349		8,827	R	63.2%	36.8%	63.2%	36.8%
27,088	MARION	10,481	7,012	3,469		3,543	R	66.9%	33.1%	66.9%	33.1%
37,144	MARSHALL	9,167	4,529	4,638		109	D	49.4%	50.6%	49.4%	50.6%
36,989	MONROE	12,238	7,721	4,517		3,204	R	63.1%	36.9%	63.1%	36.9%
10,925	MONTGOMERY	4,135	2,518	1,617		901	R	60.9%	39.1%	60.9%	39.1%
29,676	NESHOBA	8,314	6,390	1,924		4,466	R	76.9%	23.1%	76.9%	23.1%
21,720	NEWTON	7,222	5,169	2,053		3,116	R	71.6%	28.4%	71.6%	28.4%
11,545	NOXUBEE	3,935	1,099	2,836		1,737	D	27.9%	72.1%	27.9%	72.1%
47,671	OKTIBBEHA	12,601	7,087	5,514		1,573	R	56.2%	43.8%	56.2%	43.8%
34,707	PANOLA	13,398	7,258	6,140		1,118	R	54.2%	45.8%	54.2%	45.8%
55,834	PEARL RIVER	13,879	11,080	2,799		8,281	R	79.8%	20.2%	79.8%	20.2%
12,250	PERRY	4,806	3,514	1,292		2,222	R	73.1%	26.9%	73.1%	26.9%
40,404	PIKE	13,121	6,663	6,458		205	R	50.8%	49.2%	50.8%	49.2%
29,957	PONTOTOC	10,364	7,947	2,417		5,530	R	76.7%	23.3%	76.7%	23.3%
25,276	PRENTISS	7,708	5,423	2,285		3,138	R	70.4%	29.6%	70.4%	29.6%
8,223	QUITMAN	2,316	1,009	1,307		298	D	43.6%	56.4%	43.6%	56.4%
141,617	RANKIN	44,329	35,399	8,930		26,469	R	79.9%	20.1%	79.9%	20.1%
28,264	SCOTT	8,166	5,166	3,000		2,166	R	63.3%	36.7%	63.3%	36.7%
4,916	SHARKEY	2,068	788	1,280		492	D	38.1%	61.9%	38.1%	61.9%
27,503	SIMPSON	9,467	6,208	3,259		2,949	R	65.6%	34.4%	65.6%	34.4%
16,491	SMITH	7,028	5,377	1,651		3,726	R	76.5%	23.5%	76.5%	23.5%
17,786	STONE	5,921	4,207	1,714		2,493	R	71.1%	28.9%	71.1%	28.9%
29,450	SUNFLOWER	5,946	2,389	3,557		1,168	D	40.2%	59.8%	40.2%	59.8%
15,378	TALLAHATCHIE	4,336	2,112	2,224		112	D	48.7%	51.3%	48.7%	51.3%
28,886	TATE	8,233	5,612	2,621		2,991	R	68.2%	31.8%	68.2%	31.8%
22,232	TIPPAH	7,821	5,895	1,926		3,969	R	75.4%	24.6%	75.4%	24.6%
19,593	TISHOMINGO	6,256	4,718	1,538		3,180	R	75.4%	24.6%	75.4%	24.6%
10,778	TUNICA	3,246	949	2,297		1,348	D	29.2%	70.8%	29.2%	70.8%
27,134	UNION	8,926	6,997	1,929		5,068	R	78.4%	21.6%	78.4%	21.6%
15,443	WALTHALL	5,329	3,261	2,068		1,193	R	61.2%	38.8%	61.2%	38.8%
48,773	WARREN	15,399	9,019	6,380		2,639	R	58.6%	41.4%	58.6%	41.4%
51,137	WASHINGTON	10,887	4,456	6,431		1,975	D	40.9%	59.1%	40.9%	59.1%
20,747	WAYNE	8,659	5,110	3,549		1,561	R	59.0%	41.0%	59.0%	41.0%
10,253	WEBSTER	4,405	3,459	946		2,513	R	78.5%	21.5%	78.5%	21.5%
9,878	WILKINSON	3,134	1,067	2,067		1,000	D	34.0%	66.0%	34.0%	66.0%
19,198	WINSTON	8,220	4,797	3,423		1,374	R	58.4%	41.6%	58.4%	41.6%
12,678	YALOBUSHA	4,774	2,749	2,025		724	R	57.6%	42.4%	57.6%	42.4%
28,065	YAZOO	8,463	4,492	3,971		521	R	53.1%	46.9%	53.1%	46.9%
2,967,297	TOTAL	893,468	544,851	348,617		196,234	R	61.0%	39.0%	61.0%	39.0%

MISSISSIPPI

SENATOR 2012

2010 Census Population	County	Total Vote	Republican (Wicker)	Democratic (Gore)	Other	Rep.-Dem. Plurality	Percentage			
							Total Vote		Major Vote	
							Rep.	Dem.	Rep.	Dem.
32,297	ADAMS	14,517	6,052	8,207	258	2,155 D	41.7%	56.5%	42.4%	57.6%
37,057	ALCORN	14,442	10,417	3,722	303	6,695 R	72.1%	25.8%	73.7%	26.3%
13,131	AMITE	7,461	4,315	2,959	187	1,356 R	57.8%	39.7%	59.3%	40.7%
19,564	ATTALA	8,687	5,037	3,492	158	1,545 R	58.0%	40.2%	59.1%	40.9%
8,729	BENTON	3,969	2,010	1,866	93	144 R	50.6%	47.0%	51.9%	48.1%
34,145	BOLIVAR	13,688	4,939	8,277	472	3,338 D	36.1%	60.5%	37.4%	62.6%
14,962	CALHOUN	6,956	4,626	2,216	114	2,410 R	66.5%	31.9%	67.6%	32.4%
10,597	CARROLL	5,728	3,881	1,738	109	2,143 R	67.8%	30.3%	69.1%	30.9%
17,392	CHICKASAW	8,304	4,223	3,935	146	288 R	50.9%	47.4%	51.8%	48.2%
8,547	CHOCTAW	4,152	2,835	1,237	80	1,598 R	68.3%	29.8%	69.6%	30.4%
9,604	CLAIBORNE	5,115	843	4,129	143	3,286 D	16.5%	80.7%	17.0%	83.0%
16,732	CLARKE	8,008	4,996	2,727	285	2,269 R	62.4%	34.1%	64.7%	35.3%
20,634	CLAY	10,814	4,579	6,067	168	1,488 D	42.3%	56.1%	43.0%	57.0%
26,151	COAHOMA	9,766	2,769	6,807	190	4,038 D	28.4%	69.7%	28.9%	71.1%
29,449	COPIAH	13,412	6,446	6,672	294	226 D	48.1%	49.7%	49.1%	50.9%
19,568	COVINGTON	9,090	5,440	3,382	268	2,058 R	59.8%	37.2%	61.7%	38.3%
161,252	DE SOTO	64,430	41,912	21,255	1,263	20,657 R	65.1%	33.0%	66.4%	33.6%
74,934	FORREST	29,532	16,659	12,053	820	4,606 R	56.4%	40.8%	58.0%	42.0%
8,118	FRANKLIN	4,362	2,686	1,579	97	1,107 R	61.6%	36.2%	63.0%	37.0%
22,578	GEORGE	9,540	7,434	1,751	355	5,683 R	77.9%	18.4%	80.9%	19.1%
14,400	GREENE	5,650	3,884	1,462	304	2,422 R	68.7%	25.9%	72.7%	27.3%
21,906	GRENADA	10,942	5,857	4,963	122	894 R	53.5%	45.4%	54.1%	45.9%
43,929	HANCOCK	16,709	11,980	4,037	692	7,943 R	71.7%	24.2%	74.8%	25.2%
187,105	HARRISON	62,297	40,061	20,452	1,784	19,609 R	64.3%	32.8%	66.2%	33.8%
245,285	HINDS	100,113	31,183	67,329	1,601	36,146 D	31.1%	67.3%	31.7%	68.3%
19,198	HOLMES	8,378	1,731	6,389	258	4,658 D	20.7%	76.3%	21.3%	78.7%
9,375	HUMPHREYS	4,772	1,460	3,169	143	1,709 D	30.6%	66.4%	31.5%	68.5%
1,406	ISSAQUENA	709	306	382	21	76 D	43.2%	53.9%	44.5%	55.5%
23,401	ITAWAMBA	9,215	7,379	1,593	243	5,786 R	80.1%	17.3%	82.2%	17.8%
139,668	JACKSON	52,417	34,863	16,043	1,511	18,820 R	66.5%	30.6%	68.5%	31.5%
17,062	JASPER	9,097	4,232	4,596	269	364 D	46.5%	50.5%	47.9%	52.1%
7,726	JEFFERSON	4,110	673	3,302	135	2,629 D	16.4%	80.3%	16.9%	83.1%
12,487	JEFFERSON DAVIS	6,622	2,631	3,712	279	1,081 D	39.7%	56.1%	41.5%	58.5%
67,761	JONES	29,511	20,083	8,633	795	11,450 R	68.1%	29.3%	69.9%	30.1%
10,456	KEMPER	4,888	1,989	2,708	191	719 D	40.7%	55.4%	42.3%	57.7%
47,351	LAFAYETTE	19,113	11,302	7,481	330	3,821 R	59.1%	39.1%	60.2%	39.8%
55,658	LAMAR	24,453	18,679	5,085	689	13,594 R	76.4%	20.8%	78.6%	21.4%
80,261	LAUDERDALE	31,655	19,119	12,011	525	7,108 R	60.4%	37.9%	61.4%	38.6%
12,929	LAWRENCE	6,574	4,089	2,336	149	1,753 R	62.2%	35.5%	63.6%	36.4%
23,805	LEAKE	8,566	4,861	3,531	174	1,330 R	56.7%	41.2%	57.9%	42.1%
82,910	LEE	34,806	23,043	11,227	536	11,816 R	66.2%	32.3%	67.2%	32.8%
32,317	LEFLORE	11,577	3,892	7,462	223	3,570 D	33.6%	64.5%	34.3%	65.7%
34,869	LINCOLN	16,221	10,697	5,185	339	5,512 R	65.9%	32.0%	67.4%	32.6%
59,779	LOWNDES	26,627	14,063	12,171	393	1,892 R	52.8%	45.7%	53.6%	46.4%
95,203	MADISON	47,898	29,188	17,937	773	11,251 R	60.9%	37.4%	61.9%	38.1%
27,088	MARION	12,462	7,919	4,247	296	3,672 R	63.5%	34.1%	65.1%	34.9%
37,144	MARSHALL	15,637	6,409	8,894	334	2,485 D	41.0%	56.9%	41.9%	58.1%
36,989	MONROE	16,604	10,020	6,325	259	3,695 R	60.3%	38.1%	61.3%	38.7%
10,925	MONTGOMERY	5,337	2,938	2,289	110	649 R	55.0%	42.9%	56.2%	43.8%
29,676	NESHOBA	10,846	7,728	2,916	202	4,812 R	71.3%	26.9%	72.6%	27.4%
21,720	NEWTON	9,572	6,367	3,056	149	3,311 R	66.5%	31.9%	67.6%	32.4%
11,545	NOXUBEE	5,676	1,648	3,946	82	2,298 D	29.0%	69.5%	29.5%	70.5%
47,671	OKTIBBEHA	17,671	9,184	8,163	324	1,021 R	52.0%	46.2%	52.9%	47.1%
34,707	PANOLA	16,104	7,471	8,243	390	772 D	46.4%	51.2%	47.5%	52.5%
55,834	PEARL RIVER	21,440	15,732	4,702	1,006	11,030 R	73.4%	21.9%	77.0%	23.0%
12,250	PERRY	5,560	3,935	1,403	222	2,532 R	70.8%	25.2%	73.7%	26.3%
40,404	PIKE	17,475	8,464	8,653	358	189 D	48.4%	49.5%	49.4%	50.6%
29,957	PONTOTOC	12,264	9,637	2,391	236	7,246 R	78.6%	19.5%	80.1%	19.9%
25,276	PRENTISS	9,877	7,024	2,665	188	4,359 R	71.1%	27.0%	72.5%	27.5%
8,223	QUITMAN	3,602	1,109	2,368	125	1,259 D	30.8%	65.7%	31.9%	68.1%

MISSISSIPPI

SENATOR 2012

2010 Census Population	County	Total Vote	Republican (Wicker)	Democratic (Gore)	Other	Rep.-Dem. Plurality	Percentage			
							Total Vote		Major Vote	
							Rep.	Dem.	Rep.	Dem.
141,617	RANKIN	63,394	48,641	13,542	1,211	35,099 R	76.7%	21.4%	78.2%	21.8%
28,264	SCOTT	10,926	6,211	4,474	241	1,737 R	56.8%	40.9%	58.1%	41.9%
4,916	SHARKEY	2,237	830	1,356	51	526 D	37.1%	60.6%	38.0%	62.0%
27,503	SIMPSON	12,021	7,492	4,289	240	3,203 R	62.3%	35.7%	63.6%	36.4%
16,491	SMITH	8,015	5,930	1,881	204	4,049 R	74.0%	23.5%	75.9%	24.1%
17,786	STONE	7,379	5,308	1,826	245	3,482 R	71.9%	24.7%	74.4%	25.6%
29,450	SUNFLOWER	10,502	3,228	6,945	329	3,717 D	30.7%	66.1%	31.7%	68.3%
15,378	TALLAHATCHIE	5,985	2,629	3,202	154	573 D	43.9%	53.5%	45.1%	54.9%
28,886	TATE	12,075	7,069	4,723	283	2,346 R	58.5%	39.1%	59.9%	40.1%
22,232	TIPPAH	8,971	6,418	2,367	186	4,051 R	71.5%	26.4%	73.1%	26.9%
19,593	TISHOMINGO	7,790	5,899	1,733	158	4,166 R	75.7%	22.2%	77.3%	22.7%
10,778	TUNICA	4,034	923	2,947	164	2,024 D	22.9%	73.1%	23.9%	76.1%
27,134	UNION	11,237	8,669	2,394	174	6,275 R	77.1%	21.3%	78.4%	21.6%
15,443	WALTHALL	7,106	3,948	2,852	306	1,096 R	55.6%	40.1%	58.1%	41.9%
48,773	WARREN	20,462	10,610	9,409	443	1,201 R	51.9%	46.0%	53.0%	47.0%
51,137	WASHINGTON	18,044	6,117	11,578	349	5,461 D	33.9%	64.2%	34.6%	65.4%
20,747	WAYNE	10,109	5,802	3,961	346	1,841 R	57.4%	39.2%	59.4%	40.6%
10,253	WEBSTER	5,144	3,937	1,133	74	2,804 R	76.5%	22.0%	77.7%	22.3%
9,878	WILKINSON	4,440	1,363	2,908	169	1,545 D	30.7%	65.5%	31.9%	68.1%
19,198	WINSTON	9,747	5,244	4,351	152	893 R	53.8%	44.6%	54.7%	45.3%
12,678	YALOBUSHA	6,274	3,392	2,751	131	641 R	54.1%	43.8%	55.2%	44.8%
28,065	YAZOO	10,656	5,037	5,317	302	280 D	47.3%	49.9%	48.6%	51.4%
2,967,297	TOTAL	1,241,568	709,626	503,467	28,475	206,159 R	57.2%	40.6%	58.5%	41.5%

MISSISSIPPI

HOUSE OF REPRESENTATIVES

CD	Year	Total Vote	Republican		Democratic		Other Vote	Rep.-Dem. Plurality	Percentage			
			Vote	Candidate	Vote	Candidate			Total Vote		Major Vote	
									Rep.	Dem.	Rep.	Dem.
1	2012	309,177	186,760	NUNNELEE, ALAN*	114,076	MORRIS, BRAD	8,341	72,684 R	60.4%	36.9%	62.1%	37.9%
2	2012	320,244	99,160	MARCY, BILL	214,978	THOMPSON, BENNIE*	6,106	115,818 D	31.0%	67.1%	31.6%	68.4%
3	2012	293,322	234,717	HARPER, GREGG*			58,605	234,717 R	80.0%		100.0%	
4	2012	285,432	182,998	PALAZZO, STEVEN*	82,344	MOORE, MATT	20,090	100,654 R	64.1%	28.8%	69.0%	31.0%
TOTAL	2012	1,208,175	703,635		411,398		93,142	292,237 R	58.2%	34.1%	63.1%	36.9%

Note: An asterisk (*) denotes incumbent.

MISSISSIPPI

GENERAL AND PRIMARY ELECTIONS

GENERAL ELECTIONS: OTHER VOTE

President   Other vote was 6,676 Libertarian (Gary E. Johnson), 2,609 Constitution (Virgil H. Goode), 1,588 Green (Jill Stein), 1,016 Reform (Barbara Dale Washer)

Senator   Other vote was 15,281 Constitution (Thomas Cramer), 13,194 Reform (Shawn O'Hara)

MISSISSIPPI

GENERAL AND PRIMARY ELECTIONS

House	Other vote was:
CD 1	3,584 Libertarian (Danny Bedwell), 2,390 Constitution (Jim R. Bourland), 2,367 Reform (Chris Potts)
CD 2	4,605 Independent (Cobby Mondale Williams), 1,501 Reform (Lajena Williams)
CD 3	58,605 Reform (John Luke Pannell)
CD 4	17,982 Libertarian (Ron Williams), 2,108 Reform (Robert Claunch)

PRIMARY ELECTIONS: SUPPLEMENTARY INFORMATION

Primary	March 13, 2012 August 8, 2011 (Governor)	Registration	Unknown	No Party Registration

Primary Type Open—Any registered voter could participate in the party primary of their choice. But traditionally, any voter who cast a ballot in the primary of one party could not vote in the runoff of the other party.

	REPUBLICAN PRIMARIES			DEMOCRATIC PRIMARIES		
President	Santorum, Rick	96,258	32.7%	Obama, Barack H.*	97,304	100.0%
	Gingrich, Newt	91,612	31.1%			
	Romney, W. Mitt	90,161	30.7%			
	Paul, Ron	12,955	4.4%			
	Perry, Rick	1,350	0.5%			
	Bachmann, Michele	971	0.3%			
	Huntsman, Jon Jr.	413	0.1%			
	Johnson, Gary E.	392	0.1%			
	TOTAL	*294,112*		*TOTAL*	*97,304*	
Senator	Wicker, Roger*	254,936	89.2%	Gore, Albert N. Jr.	49,157	56.8%
	Maloney, Robert	18,857	6.6%	Weiner, Roger	21,131	24.4%
	Hathcock, E. Allen	12,106	4.2%	Oatis, Will	16,300	18.8%
	TOTAL	*285,899*		*TOTAL*	*86,588*	
Governor (2011)	Bryant, Phil	172,300	59.5%	Dupree, Johnny L.	179,748	43.6%
	Dennis, Dave	74,546	25.7%	Luckett, Bill	161,833	39.2%
	Williams, Ron	25,555	8.8%	Compton, William Bond Jr.	40,452	9.8%
	Holiday, Hudson	13,761	4.7%	Shaw, Gay Dale	30,497	7.4%
	Broadwater, James	3,626	1.3%			
	TOTAL	*289,788*		*TOTAL*	*412,530*	
Congressional District 1	Nunnelee, Alan*	43,518	57.3%	Morris, Brad	11,120	100.0%
	Ross, Henry	22,067	29.0%			
	Estes, Robert	10,394	13.7%			
	TOTAL	*75,979*		*TOTAL*	*11,120*	
Congressional District 2	Marcy, Bill	26,041	100.0%	Thompson, Bennie*	49,083	87.5%
				McTeer, Heather	7,040	12.5%
	TOTAL	*26,041*		*TOTAL*	*56,123*	
Congressional District 3	Harper, Gregg*	78,735	91.8%	Biggs, Crystal	15,291	100.0%
	Allen, Robert	7,027	8.2%	*Crystal Biggs withdrew after the Democratic primary election in the 3rd district.*		
	TOTAL	*85,762*		*TOTAL*	*15,291*	
Congressional District 4	Palazzo, Steven*	60,897	73.9%	Herrington, Michael	8,988	83.8%
	Vincent, Ron	15,391	18.7%	*Michael Herrington withdrew after the Democratic primary election, and Matt Moore was selected by the party to fill the vacancy on the general election ballot in the 4th district.*		
	Burleson, Cindy	6,100	7.4%			
				Vitosky, Jason	1,743	16.2%
	TOTAL	*82,388*		*TOTAL*	*10,731*	

Note: An asterisk (*) denotes incumbent. If no candidate received a majority of the primary vote, a runoff was held between the top two finishers. The names of unopposed candidates did not have to appear on the primary ballot; therefore, in some races no votes were cast for these candidates.

MISSOURI

Congressional districts first established for elections held in 2012

8 members

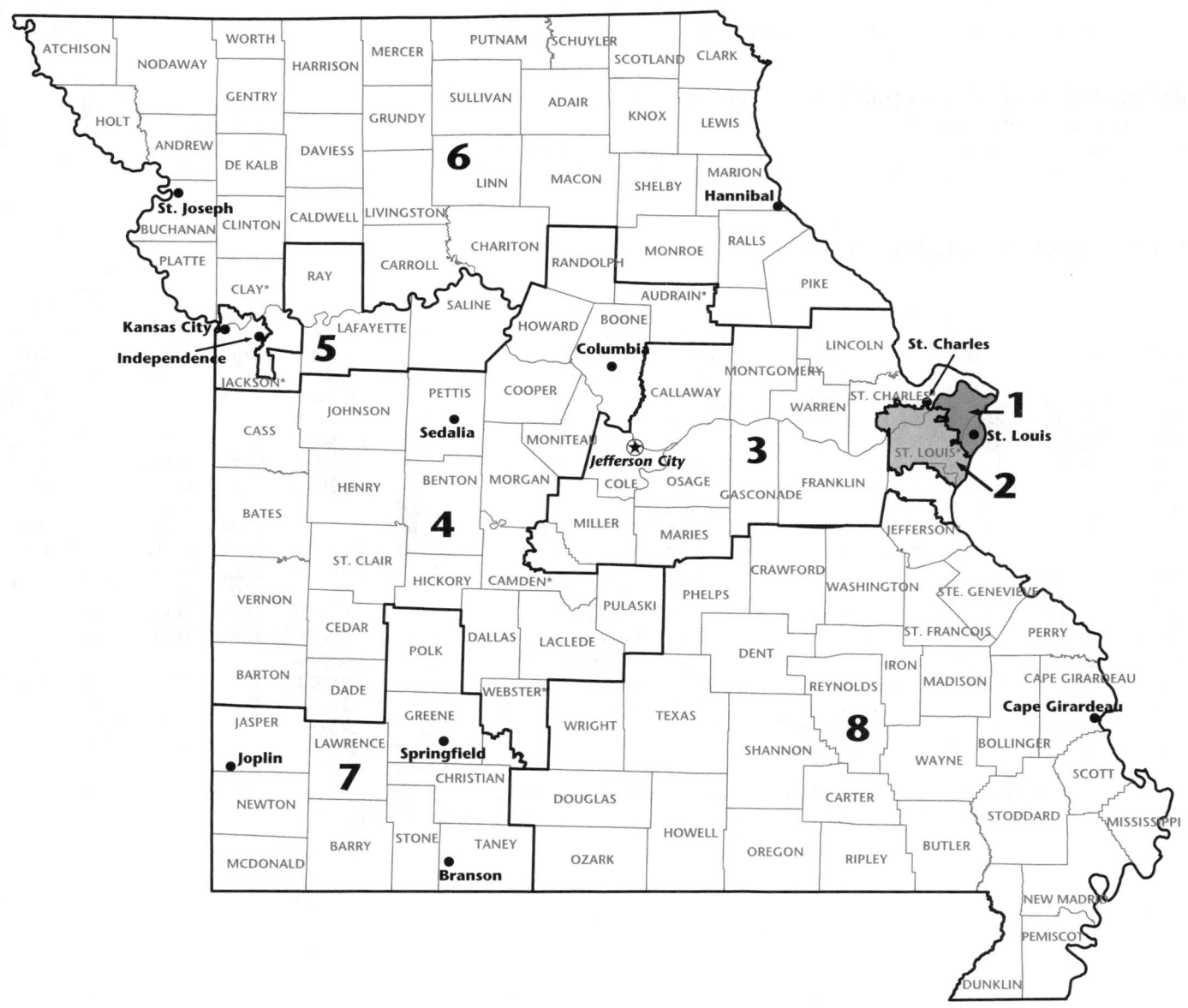

The city of St. Louis is an independent city that is treated as a county equivalent; so is Kansas City for voting purposes.

* Asterisk indicates a county whose boundaries include parts of two or more Congressional districts.

MISSOURI

GOVERNOR
Jeremiah W. "Jay" Nixon (D). Reelected 2012 to a four-year term. Previously elected 2008.

SENATORS (1 Republican, 1 Democrat)
Claire McCaskill (D). Reelected 2012 to a six-year term. Previously elected 2006.

Roy Blunt (R). Elected 2010 to a six-year term.

REPRESENTATIVES (6 Republicans, 2 Democrats)

1. William Lacy Clay (D)
2. Ann Wagner (R)
3. Blaine Luetkemeyer (R)
4. Vicky Hartzler (R)
5. Emanuel Cleaver II (D)
6. Sam Graves (R)
7. Billy Long (R)
8. Jason Smith (R)

POSTWAR VOTE FOR PRESIDENT

| Year | Total Vote | Republican | | Democratic | | Other Vote | Rep.-Dem. Plurality | Percentage | | | |
| | | Vote | Candidate | Vote | Candidate | | | Total Vote | | Major Vote | |
								Rep.	Dem.	Rep.	Dem.
2012	2,757,323	1,482,440	Romney, W. Mitt	1,223,796	Obama, Barack H.*	51,087	258,644 R	53.8%	44.4%	54.8%	45.2%
2008	2,925,205	1,445,814	McCain, John S. III	1,441,911	Obama, Barack H.	37,480	3,903 R	49.4%	49.3%	50.1%	49.9%
2004	2,731,364	1,455,713	Bush, George W.*	1,259,171	Kerry, John F.	16,480	196,542 R	53.3%	46.1%	53.6%	46.4%
2000**	2,359,892	1,189,924	Bush, George W.	1,111,138	Gore, Albert Jr.	58,830	78,786 R	50.4%	47.1%	51.7%	48.3%
1996**	2,158,065	890,016	Dole, Robert "Bob"	1,025,935	Clinton, Bill*	242,114	135,919 D	41.2%	47.5%	46.5%	53.5%
1992**	2,391,565	811,159	Bush, George H.*	1,053,873	Clinton, Bill	526,533	242,714 D	33.9%	44.1%	43.5%	56.5%
1988	2,093,713	1,084,953	Bush, George H.	1,001,619	Dukakis, Michael S.	7,141	83,334 R	51.8%	47.8%	52.0%	48.0%
1984	2,122,783	1,274,188	Reagan, Ronald*	848,583	Mondale, Walter F.	12	425,605 R	60.0%	40.0%	60.0%	40.0%
1980**	2,099,824	1,074,181	Reagan, Ronald	931,182	Carter, Jimmy*	94,461	142,999 R	51.2%	44.3%	53.6%	46.4%
1976	1,953,600	927,443	Ford, Gerald R.*	998,387	Carter, Jimmy	27,770	70,944 D	47.5%	51.1%	48.2%	51.8%
1972	1,855,803	1,153,852	Nixon, Richard M.*	697,147	McGovern, George S.	4,804	456,705 R	62.2%	37.6%	62.3%	37.7%
1968**	1,809,502	811,932	Nixon, Richard M.	791,444	Humphrey, Hubert H. Jr.	206,126	20,488 R	44.9%	43.7%	50.6%	49.4%
1964	1,817,879	653,535	Goldwater, Barry M. Sr.	1,164,344	Johnson, Lyndon B.*		510,809 D	36.0%	64.0%	36.0%	64.0%
1960	1,934,422	962,221	Nixon, Richard M.	972,201	Kennedy, John F.		9,980 D	49.7%	50.3%	49.7%	50.3%
1956	1,832,562	914,289	Eisenhower, Dwight D.*	918,273	Stevenson, Adlai E. II		3,984 D	49.9%	50.1%	49.9%	50.1%
1952	1,892,062	959,429	Eisenhower, Dwight D.	929,830	Stevenson, Adlai E. II	2,803	29,599 R	50.7%	49.1%	50.8%	49.2%
1948	1,578,628	655,039	Dewey, Thomas E.	917,315	Truman, Harry S.*	6,274	262,276 D	41.5%	58.1%	41.7%	58.3%

Note: An asterisk (*) denotes incumbent. **In past elections, the other vote included: 2000 - 38,515 Green (Ralph Nader); 1996 - 217,188 Reform (Ross Perot); 1992 - 518,741 Independent (Perot); 1980 - 77,920 Independent (John Anderson); 1968 - 206,126 American Independent (George Wallace).

MISSOURI

POSTWAR VOTE FOR GOVERNOR

Year	Total Vote	Republican		Democratic		Other Vote	Rep.-Dem. Plurality	Percentage			
		Vote	Candidate	Vote	Candidate			Total Vote		Major Vote	
								Rep.	Dem.	Rep.	Dem.
2012	2,727,883	1,160,265	Spence, David "Dave"	1,494,056	Nixon, Jeremiah W. "Jay"*	73,562	333,791 D	42.5%	54.8%	43.7%	56.3%
2008	2,877,778	1,136,364	Hulshof, Kenny	1,680,611	Nixon, Jeremiah W. "Jay"	60,803	544,247 D	39.5%	58.4%	40.3%	59.7%
2004	2,719,599	1,382,419	Blunt, Matt	1,301,442	McCaskill, Claire	35,738	80,977 R	50.8%	47.9%	51.5%	48.5%
2000	2,346,830	1,131,307	Talent, James M.	1,152,752	Holden, Bob	62,771	21,445 D	48.2%	49.1%	49.5%	50.5%
1996	2,142,518	866,268	Kelly, Margaret	1,224,801	Carnahan, Mel*	51,449	358,533 D	40.4%	57.2%	41.4%	58.6%
1992	2,343,999	968,574	Webster, William L.	1,375,425	Carnahan, Mel		406,851 D	41.3%	58.7%	41.3%	58.7%
1988	2,085,928	1,339,531	Ashcroft, John*	724,919	Hearnes, Betty C.	21,478	614,612 R	64.2%	34.8%	64.9%	35.1%
1984	2,108,210	1,194,506	Ashcroft, John	913,700	Rothman, Kenneth J.	4	280,806 R	56.7%	43.3%	56.7%	43.3%
1980	2,088,028	1,098,950	Bond, Kit	981,884	Teasdale, Joseph P.*	7,194	117,066 R	52.6%	47.0%	52.8%	47.2%
1976	1,933,575	958,110	Bond, Kit*	971,184	Teasdale, Joseph P.	4,281	13,074 D	49.6%	50.2%	49.7%	50.3%
1972	1,865,683	1,029,451	Bond, Kit	832,751	Dowd, Edward L.	3,481	196,700 R	55.2%	44.6%	55.3%	44.7%
1968	1,764,602	691,797	Roos, Lawrence K.	1,072,805	Hearnes, Warren E.*		381,008 D	39.2%	60.8%	39.2%	60.8%
1964	1,789,600	678,949	Shepley, Ethan A.H.	1,110,651	Hearnes, Warren E.		431,702 D	37.9%	62.1%	37.9%	62.1%
1960	1,887,326	792,131	Farmer, Edward G.	1,095,195	Dalton, John M.		303,064 D	42.0%	58.0%	42.0%	58.0%
1956	1,808,338	866,810	Hocker, Lon	941,528	Blair, James T. Jr.		74,718 D	47.9%	52.1%	47.9%	52.1%
1952	1,870,998	886,270	Elliott, Howard	983,169	Donnelly, Phil M.	1,559	96,899 D	47.4%	52.5%	47.4%	52.6%
1948	1,567,338	670,064	Thompson, Murray E.	893,092	Smith, Forrest	4,182	223,028 D	42.8%	57.0%	42.9%	57.1%

Note: An asterisk (*) denotes incumbent.

POSTWAR VOTE FOR SENATOR

Year	Total Vote	Republican		Democratic		Other Vote	Rep.-Dem. Plurality	Percentage			
		Vote	Candidate	Vote	Candidate			Total Vote		Major Vote	
								Rep.	Dem.	Rep.	Dem.
2012	2,725,793	1,066,159	Akin, Todd	1,494,125	McCaskill, Claire*	165,509	427,966 D	39.1%	54.8%	41.6%	58.4%
2010	1,943,899	1,054,160	Blunt, Roy	789,736	Carnahan, Robin	100,003	264,424 R	54.2%	40.6%	57.2%	42.8%
2006	2,128,459	1,006,941	Talent, James M.*	1,055,255	McCaskill, Claire	66,263	48,314 D	47.3%	49.6%	48.8%	51.2%
2004	2,706,402	1,518,089	Bond, Kit*	1,158,261	Farmer, Nancy	30,052	359,828 R	56.1%	42.8%	56.7%	43.3%
2002S	1,877,620	935,032	Talent, James M.	913,778	Carnahan, Jean*	28,810	21,254 R	49.8%	48.7%	50.6%	49.4%
2000**	2,361,586	1,142,852	Ashcroft, John*	1,191,812	Carnahan, Mel	26,922	48,960 D	48.4%	50.5%	49.0%	51.0%
1998	1,576,857	830,625	Bond, Kit*	690,208	Nixon, Jay W.	56,024	140,417 R	52.7%	43.8%	54.6%	45.4%
1994	1,775,116	1,060,149	Ashcroft, John	633,697	Wheat, Alan	81,270	426,452 R	59.7%	35.7%	62.6%	37.4%
1992	2,354,925	1,221,901	Bond, Kit*	1,057,967	Rothman-Serot, Geri	75,057	163,934 R	51.9%	44.9%	53.6%	46.4%
1988	2,078,875	1,407,416	Danforth, John C.*	660,045	Nixon, Jay W.	11,414	747,371 R	67.7%	31.8%	68.1%	31.9%
1986	1,477,327	777,612	Bond, Kit	699,624	Woods, Harriett	91	77,988 R	52.6%	47.4%	52.6%	47.4%
1982	1,543,521	784,876	Danforth, John C.*	758,629	Woods, Harriett	16	26,247 R	50.8%	49.1%	50.9%	49.1%
1980	2,066,965	985,399	McNary, Gene	1,074,859	Eagleton, Thomas F.*	6,707	89,460 D	47.7%	52.0%	47.8%	52.2%
1976	1,914,777	1,090,061	Danforth, John C.*	813,571	Hearnes, Warren E.	11,139	276,496 R	56.9%	42.5%	57.3%	42.7%
1974	1,224,303	480,900	Curtis, Thomas B.	735,433	Eagleton, Thomas F.*	7,970	254,533 D	39.3%	60.1%	39.5%	60.5%
1970	1,283,912	617,903	Danforth, John C.	655,431	Symington, Stuart*	10,578	37,528 D	48.1%	51.0%	48.5%	51.5%
1968	1,737,958	850,544	Curtis, Thomas B.	887,414	Eagleton, Thomas F.		36,870 D	48.9%	51.1%	48.9%	51.1%
1964	1,783,043	596,377	Bradshaw, Jean Paul	1,186,666	Symington, Stuart*		590,289 D	33.4%	66.6%	33.4%	66.6%
1962	1,222,259	555,330	Kemper, Crosby	666,929	Long, Edward V.*		111,599 D	45.4%	54.6%	45.4%	54.6%
1960S	1,880,232	880,576	Hocker, Lon	999,656	Long, Edward V.*		119,080 D	46.8%	53.2%	46.8%	53.2%
1958	1,173,930	393,847	Palmer, Hazel	780,083	Symington, Stuart*		386,236 D	33.5%	66.5%	33.5%	66.5%
1956	1,800,984	785,048	Douglas, Herbert	1,015,936	Hennings, Thomas C. Jr.*		230,888 D	43.6%	56.4%	43.6%	56.4%
1952	1,868,083	858,170	Kem, James P.*	1,008,523	Symington, Stuart	1,390	150,353 D	45.9%	54.0%	46.0%	54.0%
1950	1,279,631	593,139	Donnell, Forrest C.*	685,732	Hennings, Thomas C. Jr.	760	92,593 D	46.4%	53.6%	46.4%	53.6%
1946	1,084,100	572,556	Kem, James P.	511,544	Briggs, Frank		61,012 R	52.8%	47.2%	52.8%	47.2%

Note: An asterisk (*) denotes incumbent. **In 2000 the Democratic candidate, Mel Carnahan, was killed in an airplane crash in October but his name remained on the ballot and he won the election in November. Subsequently, his widow, Jean Carnahan, was appointed to fill the seat until an election could be held in 2002 for the remaining four years of the term. The 1960 and 2002 elections were for short terms to fill a vacancy.

MISSOURI

PRESIDENT 2012

2010 Census Population	County/City	Total Vote	Republican (Romney)	Democratic (Obama)	Other	Rep.-Dem. Plurality	Percentage			
							Total Vote		Major Vote	
							Rep.	Dem.	Rep.	Dem.
25,607	ADAIR	10,126	5,651	4,219	256	1,432 R	55.8%	41.7%	57.3%	42.7%
17,291	ANDREW	8,306	5,457	2,649	200	2,808 R	65.7%	31.9%	67.3%	32.7%
5,685	ATCHISON	2,709	1,902	756	51	1,146 R	70.2%	27.9%	71.6%	28.4%
25,529	AUDRAIN	9,952	6,186	3,539	227	2,647 R	62.2%	35.6%	63.6%	36.4%
35,597	BARRY	13,806	9,832	3,667	307	6,165 R	71.2%	26.6%	72.8%	27.2%
12,402	BARTON	5,746	4,418	1,230	98	3,188 R	76.9%	21.4%	78.2%	21.8%
17,049	BATES	7,771	5,020	2,557	194	2,463 R	64.6%	32.9%	66.3%	33.7%
19,056	BENTON	9,157	6,069	2,925	163	3,144 R	66.3%	31.9%	67.5%	32.5%
12,363	BOLLINGER	5,456	4,095	1,213	148	2,882 R	75.1%	22.2%	77.1%	22.9%
162,642	BOONE	79,422	37,404	39,847	2,171	2,443 D	47.1%	50.2%	48.4%	51.6%
89,201	BUCHANAN	35,106	18,660	15,594	852	3,066 R	53.2%	44.4%	54.5%	45.5%
42,794	BUTLER	16,889	12,248	4,363	278	7,885 R	72.5%	25.8%	73.7%	26.3%
9,424	CALDWELL	4,167	2,721	1,312	134	1,409 R	65.3%	31.5%	67.5%	32.5%
44,332	CALLAWAY	18,232	11,745	6,071	416	5,674 R	64.4%	33.3%	65.9%	34.1%
44,002	CAMDEN	21,945	15,092	6,458	395	8,634 R	68.8%	29.4%	70.0%	30.0%
75,674	CAPE GIRARDEAU	35,716	25,370	9,728	618	15,642 R	71.0%	27.2%	72.3%	27.7%
9,295	CARROLL	4,304	3,072	1,154	78	1,918 R	71.4%	26.8%	72.7%	27.3%
6,265	CARTER	2,799	1,978	754	67	1,224 R	70.7%	26.9%	72.4%	27.6%
99,478	CASS	48,913	30,912	17,044	957	13,868 R	63.2%	34.8%	64.5%	35.5%
13,982	CEDAR	6,045	4,376	1,537	132	2,839 R	72.4%	25.4%	74.0%	26.0%
7,831	CHARITON	3,821	2,402	1,339	80	1,063 R	62.9%	35.0%	64.2%	35.8%
77,422	CHRISTIAN	37,964	27,473	9,813	678	17,660 R	72.4%	25.8%	73.7%	26.3%
7,139	CLARK	3,225	1,730	1,398	97	332 R	53.6%	43.3%	55.3%	44.7%
221,939	CLAY	105,589	56,191	47,310	2,088	8,881 R	53.2%	44.8%	54.3%	45.7%
20,743	CLINTON	9,861	5,931	3,688	242	2,243 R	60.1%	37.4%	61.7%	38.3%
75,990	COLE	37,062	24,490	12,005	567	12,485 R	66.1%	32.4%	67.1%	32.9%
17,601	COOPER	7,511	4,887	2,474	150	2,413 R	65.1%	32.9%	66.4%	33.6%
24,696	CRAWFORD	9,579	6,434	2,951	194	3,483 R	67.2%	30.8%	68.6%	31.4%
7,883	DADE	3,896	2,895	939	62	1,956 R	74.3%	24.1%	75.5%	24.5%
16,777	DALLAS	7,279	4,992	2,122	165	2,870 R	68.6%	29.2%	70.2%	29.8%
8,433	DAVIESS	3,521	2,290	1,125	106	1,165 R	65.0%	32.0%	67.1%	32.9%
12,892	DEKALB	4,350	3,056	1,194	100	1,862 R	70.3%	27.4%	71.9%	28.1%
15,657	DENT	6,643	4,883	1,585	175	3,298 R	73.5%	23.9%	75.5%	24.5%
13,684	DOUGLAS	6,557	4,649	1,710	198	2,939 R	70.9%	26.1%	73.1%	26.9%
31,953	DUNKLIN	10,651	6,850	3,636	165	3,214 R	64.3%	34.1%	65.3%	34.7%
101,492	FRANKLIN	46,755	29,396	16,347	1,012	13,049 R	62.9%	35.0%	64.3%	35.7%
15,222	GASCONADE	7,134	4,895	2,099	140	2,796 R	68.6%	29.4%	70.0%	30.0%
6,738	GENTRY	2,999	1,988	937	74	1,051 R	66.3%	31.2%	68.0%	32.0%
275,174	GREENE	125,848	76,900	46,219	2,729	30,681 R	61.1%	36.7%	62.5%	37.5%
10,261	GRUNDY	4,374	3,030	1,212	132	1,818 R	69.3%	27.7%	71.4%	28.6%
8,957	HARRISON	3,695	2,624	984	87	1,640 R	71.0%	26.6%	72.7%	27.3%
22,272	HENRY	10,123	6,229	3,606	288	2,623 R	61.5%	35.6%	63.3%	36.7%
9,627	HICKORY	4,680	2,835	1,733	112	1,102 R	60.6%	37.0%	62.1%	37.9%
4,912	HOLT	2,310	1,725	551	34	1,174 R	74.7%	23.9%	75.8%	24.2%
10,144	HOWARD	4,867	3,017	1,723	127	1,294 R	62.0%	35.4%	63.6%	36.4%
40,400	HOWELL	16,346	11,544	4,395	407	7,149 R	70.6%	26.9%	72.4%	27.6%
10,630	IRON	4,031	2,252	1,669	110	583 R	55.9%	41.4%	57.4%	42.6%
674,158	JACKSON	174,764	93,199	78,283	3,282	14,916 R	53.3%	44.8%	54.3%	45.7%
117,404	JASPER	45,218	31,349	12,809	1,060	18,540 R	69.3%	28.3%	71.0%	29.0%
218,733	JEFFERSON	97,611	53,978	41,564	2,069	12,414 R	55.3%	42.6%	56.5%	43.5%
52,595	JOHNSON	21,021	12,763	7,667	591	5,096 R	60.7%	36.5%	62.5%	37.5%
(See Note)	KANSAS CITY	136,813	29,509	105,670	1,634	76,161 D	21.6%	77.2%	21.8%	78.2%
4,131	KNOX	1,957	1,205	698	54	507 R	61.6%	35.7%	63.3%	36.7%
35,571	LACLEDE	15,362	10,934	4,093	335	6,841 R	71.2%	26.6%	72.8%	27.2%
33,381	LAFAYETTE	15,795	9,803	5,655	337	4,148 R	62.1%	35.8%	63.4%	36.6%
38,634	LAWRENCE	15,755	11,421	4,017	317	7,404 R	72.5%	25.5%	74.0%	26.0%
10,211	LEWIS	4,279	2,677	1,508	94	1,169 R	62.6%	35.2%	64.0%	36.0%
52,566	LINCOLN	22,652	14,332	7,734	586	6,598 R	63.3%	34.1%	65.0%	35.0%
12,761	LINN	5,550	3,344	2,041	165	1,303 R	60.3%	36.8%	62.1%	37.9%
15,195	LIVINGSTON	6,054	4,006	1,906	142	2,100 R	66.2%	31.5%	67.8%	32.2%

MISSOURI
PRESIDENT 2012

2010 Census Population	County/City	Total Vote	Republican (Romney)	Democratic (Obama)	Other	Rep.-Dem. Plurality	Percentage Total Vote Rep.	Total Vote Dem.	Major Vote Rep.	Major Vote Dem.
15,566	MACON	7,160	4,701	2,309	150	2,392 R	65.7%	32.2%	67.1%	32.9%
12,226	MADISON	4,930	3,227	1,588	115	1,639 R	65.5%	32.2%	67.0%	33.0%
9,176	MARIES	4,538	3,165	1,299	74	1,866 R	69.7%	28.6%	70.9%	29.1%
28,781	MARION	12,158	7,923	4,031	204	3,892 R	65.2%	33.2%	66.3%	33.7%
23,083	MCDONALD	7,817	5,694	1,920	203	3,774 R	72.8%	24.6%	74.8%	25.2%
3,785	MERCER	1,655	1,255	353	47	902 R	75.8%	21.3%	78.0%	22.0%
24,748	MILLER	11,019	8,099	2,651	269	5,448 R	73.5%	24.1%	75.3%	24.7%
14,358	MISSISSIPPI	4,920	2,997	1,858	65	1,139 R	60.9%	37.8%	61.7%	38.3%
15,607	MONITEAU	6,443	4,704	1,608	131	3,096 R	73.0%	25.0%	74.5%	25.5%
8,840	MONROE	4,057	2,564	1,398	95	1,166 R	63.2%	34.5%	64.7%	35.3%
12,236	MONTGOMERY	5,327	3,490	1,740	97	1,750 R	65.5%	32.7%	66.7%	33.3%
20,565	MORGAN	8,688	5,733	2,773	182	2,960 R	66.0%	31.9%	67.4%	32.6%
18,956	NEW MADRID	7,250	4,284	2,814	152	1,470 R	59.1%	38.8%	60.4%	39.6%
58,114	NEWTON	25,083	18,181	6,425	477	11,756 R	72.5%	25.6%	73.9%	26.1%
23,370	NODAWAY	8,976	5,593	3,172	211	2,421 R	62.3%	35.3%	63.8%	36.2%
10,881	OREGON	4,421	2,886	1,419	116	1,467 R	65.3%	32.1%	67.0%	33.0%
13,878	OSAGE	6,919	5,329	1,473	117	3,856 R	77.0%	21.3%	78.3%	21.7%
9,723	OZARK	4,453	3,080	1,261	112	1,819 R	69.2%	28.3%	71.0%	29.0%
18,296	PEMISCOT	6,335	3,598	2,671	66	927 R	56.8%	42.2%	57.4%	42.6%
18,971	PERRY	7,987	5,669	2,184	134	3,485 R	71.0%	27.3%	72.2%	27.8%
42,201	PETTIS	17,175	10,842	5,904	429	4,938 R	63.1%	34.4%	64.7%	35.3%
45,156	PHELPS	18,190	11,895	5,798	497	6,097 R	65.4%	31.9%	67.2%	32.8%
18,516	PIKE	7,321	4,577	2,582	162	1,995 R	62.5%	35.3%	63.9%	36.1%
89,322	PLATTE	45,552	25,618	19,175	759	6,443 R	56.2%	42.1%	57.2%	42.8%
31,137	POLK	13,119	9,252	3,580	287	5,672 R	70.5%	27.3%	72.1%	27.9%
52,274	PULASKI	13,571	9,092	4,199	280	4,893 R	67.0%	30.9%	68.4%	31.6%
4,979	PUTNAM	2,309	1,673	587	49	1,086 R	72.5%	25.4%	74.0%	26.0%
10,167	RALLS	5,036	3,231	1,736	69	1,495 R	64.2%	34.5%	65.0%	35.0%
25,414	RANDOLPH	9,944	6,667	3,031	246	3,636 R	67.0%	30.5%	68.7%	31.3%
23,494	RAY	10,367	5,815	4,275	277	1,540 R	56.1%	41.2%	57.6%	42.4%
6,696	REYNOLDS	3,202	1,931	1,157	114	774 R	60.3%	36.1%	62.5%	37.5%
14,100	RIPLEY	5,263	3,743	1,396	124	2,347 R	71.1%	26.5%	72.8%	27.2%
23,370	SALINE	9,108	5,104	3,790	214	1,314 R	56.0%	41.6%	57.4%	42.6%
4,431	SCHUYLER	1,939	1,174	697	68	477 R	60.5%	35.9%	62.7%	37.3%
4,843	SCOTLAND	1,936	1,246	643	47	603 R	64.4%	33.2%	66.0%	34.0%
39,191	SCOTT	16,999	11,623	5,122	254	6,501 R	68.4%	30.1%	69.4%	30.6%
8,441	SHANNON	3,692	2,262	1,302	128	960 R	61.3%	35.3%	63.5%	36.5%
6,373	SHELBY	3,232	2,188	966	78	1,222 R	67.7%	29.9%	69.4%	30.6%
360,485	ST. CHARLES	185,690	110,784	71,838	3,068	38,946 R	59.7%	38.7%	60.7%	39.3%
9,805	ST. CLAIR	4,626	3,019	1,460	147	1,559 R	65.3%	31.6%	67.4%	32.6%
65,359	ST. FRANCOIS	22,582	13,248	8,829	505	4,419 R	58.7%	39.1%	60.0%	40.0%
319,294	ST. LOUIS CITY	143,607	22,943	118,780	1,884	95,837 D	16.0%	82.7%	16.2%	83.8%
998,954	ST. LOUIS COUNTY	528,676	224,742	297,097	6,837	72,355 D	42.5%	56.2%	43.1%	56.9%
18,145	STE. GENEVIEVE	8,070	4,055	3,813	202	242 R	50.2%	47.2%	51.5%	48.5%
29,968	STODDARD	12,866	9,496	3,153	217	6,343 R	73.8%	24.5%	75.1%	24.9%
32,202	STONE	15,984	11,787	3,923	274	7,864 R	73.7%	24.5%	75.0%	25.0%
6,714	SULLIVAN	2,595	1,610	908	77	702 R	62.0%	35.0%	63.9%	36.1%
51,675	TANEY	21,659	15,746	5,479	434	10,267 R	72.7%	25.3%	74.2%	25.8%
26,008	TEXAS	10,764	7,618	2,871	275	4,747 R	70.8%	26.7%	72.6%	27.4%
21,159	VERNON	8,521	5,758	2,580	183	3,178 R	67.6%	30.3%	69.1%	30.9%
32,513	WARREN	14,676	9,150	5,219	307	3,931 R	62.3%	35.6%	63.7%	36.3%
25,195	WASHINGTON	8,695	5,071	3,417	207	1,654 R	58.3%	39.3%	59.7%	40.3%
13,521	WAYNE	5,720	3,790	1,813	117	1,977 R	66.3%	31.7%	67.6%	32.4%
36,202	WEBSTER	15,429	10,708	4,409	312	6,299 R	69.4%	28.6%	70.8%	29.2%
2,171	WORTH	1,048	664	341	43	323 R	63.4%	32.5%	66.1%	33.9%
18,815	WRIGHT	7,955	5,830	1,953	172	3,877 R	73.3%	24.6%	74.9%	25.1%
5,988,927	TOTAL	2,757,323	1,482,440	1,223,796	51,087	258,644 R	53.8%	44.4%	54.8%	45.2%

Note: Although Kansas City is part of Jackson County, its results are listed separately.

MISSOURI
GOVERNOR 2012

2010 Census Population	County	Total Vote	Republican (Spence)	Democratic (Nixon)	Other	Rep.-Dem. Plurality	Percentage Total Vote Rep.	Percentage Total Vote Dem.	Percentage Major Vote Rep.	Percentage Major Vote Dem.
25,607	ADAIR	10,003	4,656	5,066	281	410 D	46.5%	50.6%	47.9%	52.1%
17,291	ANDREW	8,273	4,301	3,692	280	609 R	52.0%	44.6%	53.8%	46.2%
5,685	ATCHISON	2,647	1,319	1,240	88	79 R	49.8%	46.8%	51.5%	48.5%
25,529	AUDRAIN	9,890	4,633	4,922	335	289 D	46.8%	49.8%	48.5%	51.5%
35,597	BARRY	13,706	7,769	5,491	446	2,278 R	56.7%	40.1%	58.6%	41.4%
12,402	BARTON	5,713	3,644	1,900	169	1,744 R	63.8%	33.3%	65.7%	34.3%
17,049	BATES	7,728	3,513	3,972	243	459 D	45.5%	51.4%	46.9%	53.1%
19,056	BENTON	9,110	4,641	4,213	256	428 R	50.9%	46.2%	52.4%	47.6%
12,363	BOLLINGER	5,419	3,115	2,142	162	973 R	57.5%	39.5%	59.3%	40.7%
162,642	BOONE	77,598	29,171	45,302	3,125	16,131 D	37.6%	58.4%	39.2%	60.8%
89,201	BUCHANAN	34,863	13,810	19,685	1,368	5,875 D	39.6%	56.5%	41.2%	58.8%
42,794	BUTLER	16,680	9,251	7,036	393	2,215 R	55.5%	42.2%	56.8%	43.2%
9,424	CALDWELL	4,152	2,092	1,882	178	210 R	50.4%	45.3%	52.6%	47.4%
44,332	CALLAWAY	18,143	9,489	8,012	642	1,477 R	52.3%	44.2%	54.2%	45.8%
44,002	CAMDEN	21,828	11,986	9,210	632	2,776 R	54.9%	42.2%	56.5%	43.5%
75,674	CAPE GIRARDEAU	35,340	19,797	14,686	857	5,111 R	56.0%	41.6%	57.4%	42.6%
9,295	CARROLL	4,264	2,256	1,902	106	354 R	52.9%	44.6%	54.3%	45.7%
6,265	CARTER	2,746	1,414	1,235	97	179 R	51.5%	45.0%	53.4%	46.6%
99,478	CASS	48,459	23,837	23,168	1,454	669 R	49.2%	47.8%	50.7%	49.3%
13,982	CEDAR	5,995	3,383	2,453	159	930 R	56.4%	40.9%	58.0%	42.0%
7,831	CHARITON	3,799	1,770	1,937	92	167 D	46.6%	51.0%	47.7%	52.3%
77,422	CHRISTIAN	37,754	21,902	15,000	852	6,902 R	58.0%	39.7%	59.4%	40.6%
7,139	CLARK	3,217	1,312	1,822	83	510 D	40.8%	56.6%	41.9%	58.1%
221,939	CLAY	104,498	43,398	57,962	3,138	14,564 D	41.5%	55.5%	42.8%	57.2%
20,743	CLINTON	9,815	4,461	5,003	351	542 D	45.5%	51.0%	47.1%	52.9%
75,990	COLE	36,869	19,099	16,810	960	2,289 R	51.8%	45.6%	53.2%	46.8%
17,601	COOPER	7,481	3,837	3,418	226	419 R	51.3%	45.7%	52.9%	47.1%
24,696	CRAWFORD	9,531	4,978	4,275	278	703 R	52.2%	44.9%	53.8%	46.2%
7,883	DADE	3,884	2,237	1,557	90	680 R	57.6%	40.1%	59.0%	41.0%
16,777	DALLAS	7,267	3,882	3,148	237	734 R	53.4%	43.3%	55.2%	44.8%
8,433	DAVIESS	3,515	1,697	1,691	127	6 R	48.3%	48.1%	50.1%	49.9%
12,892	DEKALB	4,348	2,394	1,815	139	579 R	55.1%	41.7%	56.9%	43.1%
15,657	DENT	6,633	3,595	2,823	215	772 R	54.2%	42.6%	56.0%	44.0%
13,684	DOUGLAS	6,510	3,869	2,407	234	1,462 R	59.4%	37.0%	61.6%	38.4%
31,953	DUNKLIN	10,471	4,560	5,657	254	1,097 D	43.5%	54.0%	44.6%	55.4%
101,492	FRANKLIN	46,456	22,335	22,869	1,252	534 D	48.1%	49.2%	49.4%	50.6%
15,222	GASCONADE	7,098	3,775	3,162	161	613 R	53.2%	44.5%	54.4%	45.6%
6,738	GENTRY	2,982	1,458	1,429	95	29 R	48.9%	47.9%	50.5%	49.5%
275,174	GREENE	125,289	59,660	61,970	3,659	2,310 D	47.6%	49.5%	49.1%	50.9%
10,261	GRUNDY	4,367	2,352	1,852	163	500 R	53.9%	42.4%	55.9%	44.1%
8,957	HARRISON	3,649	2,072	1,453	124	619 R	56.8%	39.8%	58.8%	41.2%
22,272	HENRY	10,084	4,277	5,430	377	1,153 D	42.4%	53.8%	44.1%	55.9%
9,627	HICKORY	4,667	2,177	2,334	156	157 D	46.6%	50.0%	48.3%	51.7%
4,912	HOLT	2,298	1,296	956	46	340 R	56.4%	41.6%	57.5%	42.5%
10,144	HOWARD	4,807	2,302	2,350	155	48 D	47.9%	48.9%	49.5%	50.5%
40,400	HOWELL	16,319	8,849	6,950	520	1,899 R	54.2%	42.6%	56.0%	44.0%
10,630	IRON	4,003	1,596	2,278	129	682 D	39.9%	56.9%	41.2%	58.8%
674,158	JACKSON	172,661	73,518	94,008	5,135	20,490 D	42.6%	54.4%	43.9%	56.1%
117,404	JASPER	45,031	24,218	19,457	1,356	4,761 R	53.8%	43.2%	55.5%	44.5%
218,733	JEFFERSON	96,925	40,470	53,971	2,484	13,501 D	41.8%	55.7%	42.9%	57.1%
52,595	JOHNSON	20,765	9,484	10,428	853	944 D	45.7%	50.2%	47.6%	52.4%
(See Note)	KANSAS CITY	134,336	23,806	107,474	3,056	83,668 D	17.7%	80.0%	18.1%	81.9%
4,131	KNOX	1,926	912	966	48	54 D	47.4%	50.2%	48.6%	51.4%
35,571	LACLEDE	15,354	8,751	6,128	475	2,623 R	57.0%	39.9%	58.8%	41.2%
33,381	LAFAYETTE	15,733	7,537	7,758	438	221 D	47.9%	49.3%	49.3%	50.7%
38,634	LAWRENCE	15,688	9,022	6,261	405	2,761 R	57.5%	39.9%	59.0%	41.0%
10,211	LEWIS	4,241	2,046	2,101	94	55 D	48.2%	49.5%	49.3%	50.7%
52,566	LINCOLN	22,525	11,092	10,730	703	362 R	49.2%	47.6%	50.8%	49.2%
12,761	LINN	5,528	2,456	2,888	184	432 D	44.4%	52.2%	46.0%	54.0%
15,195	LIVINGSTON	5,997	2,922	2,906	169	16 R	48.7%	48.5%	50.1%	49.9%

MISSOURI
GOVERNOR 2012

2010 Census Population	County	Total Vote	Republican (Spence)	Democratic (Nixon)	Other	Rep.-Dem. Plurality		Percentage			
								Total Vote		Major Vote	
								Rep.	Dem.	Rep.	Dem.
15,566	MACON	7,104	3,868	3,086	150	782	R	54.4%	43.4%	55.6%	44.4%
12,226	MADISON	4,895	2,298	2,455	142	157	D	46.9%	50.2%	48.3%	51.7%
9,176	MARIES	4,537	2,337	2,068	132	269	R	51.5%	45.6%	53.1%	46.9%
28,781	MARION	12,031	6,380	5,394	257	986	R	53.0%	44.8%	54.2%	45.8%
23,083	MCDONALD	7,746	4,823	2,564	359	2,259	R	62.3%	33.1%	65.3%	34.7%
3,785	MERCER	1,645	1,090	503	52	587	R	66.3%	30.6%	68.4%	31.6%
24,748	MILLER	10,940	6,547	4,012	381	2,535	R	59.8%	36.7%	62.0%	38.0%
14,358	MISSISSIPPI	4,858	1,822	2,938	98	1,116	D	37.5%	60.5%	38.3%	61.7%
15,607	MONITEAU	6,412	3,568	2,649	195	919	R	55.6%	41.3%	57.4%	42.6%
8,840	MONROE	4,012	1,948	1,953	111	5	D	48.6%	48.7%	49.9%	50.1%
12,236	MONTGOMERY	5,313	2,842	2,338	133	504	R	53.5%	44.0%	54.9%	45.1%
20,565	MORGAN	8,868	4,575	3,983	310	592	R	51.6%	44.9%	53.5%	46.5%
18,956	NEW MADRID	7,153	2,732	4,270	151	1,538	D	38.2%	59.7%	39.0%	61.0%
58,114	NEWTON	25,024	14,483	9,880	661	4,603	R	57.9%	39.5%	59.4%	40.6%
23,370	NODAWAY	8,906	4,118	4,522	266	404	D	46.2%	50.8%	47.7%	52.3%
10,881	OREGON	4,399	2,200	2,061	138	139	R	50.0%	46.9%	51.6%	48.4%
13,878	OSAGE	6,880	4,016	2,712	152	1,304	R	58.4%	39.4%	59.7%	40.3%
9,723	OZARK	4,435	2,334	1,948	153	386	R	52.6%	43.9%	54.5%	45.5%
18,296	PEMISCOT	6,050	2,338	3,559	153	1,221	D	38.6%	58.8%	39.6%	60.4%
18,971	PERRY	7,867	4,057	3,647	163	410	R	51.6%	46.4%	52.7%	47.3%
42,201	PETTIS	17,059	8,073	8,490	496	417	D	47.3%	49.8%	48.7%	51.3%
45,156	PHELPS	18,118	9,282	8,271	565	1,011	R	51.2%	45.7%	52.9%	47.1%
18,516	PIKE	7,306	3,482	3,655	169	173	D	47.7%	50.0%	48.8%	51.2%
89,322	PLATTE	45,147	20,154	23,654	1,339	3,500	D	44.6%	52.4%	46.0%	54.0%
31,137	POLK	13,087	7,052	5,647	388	1,405	R	53.9%	43.1%	55.5%	44.5%
52,274	PULASKI	12,679	6,454	5,829	396	625	R	50.9%	46.0%	52.5%	47.5%
4,979	PUTNAM	2,266	1,485	726	55	759	R	65.5%	32.0%	67.2%	32.8%
10,167	RALLS	4,984	2,595	2,279	110	316	R	52.1%	45.7%	53.2%	46.8%
25,414	RANDOLPH	9,895	5,055	4,491	349	564	R	51.1%	45.4%	53.0%	47.0%
23,494	RAY	10,305	4,252	5,722	331	1,470	D	41.3%	55.5%	42.6%	57.4%
6,696	REYNOLDS	3,142	1,239	1,795	108	556	D	39.4%	57.1%	40.8%	59.2%
14,100	RIPLEY	5,198	2,822	2,216	160	606	R	54.3%	42.6%	56.0%	44.0%
23,370	SALINE	9,071	3,489	5,275	307	1,786	D	38.5%	58.2%	39.8%	60.2%
4,431	SCHUYLER	1,902	961	867	74	94	R	50.5%	45.6%	52.6%	47.4%
4,843	SCOTLAND	1,913	930	921	62	9	R	48.6%	48.1%	50.2%	49.8%
39,191	SCOTT	16,846	8,421	8,092	333	329	R	50.0%	48.0%	51.0%	49.0%
8,441	SHANNON	3,698	1,601	1,978	119	377	D	43.3%	53.5%	44.7%	55.3%
6,373	SHELBY	3,212	1,721	1,426	65	295	R	53.6%	44.4%	54.7%	45.3%
360,485	ST. CHARLES	183,491	89,144	89,860	4,487	716	D	48.6%	49.0%	49.8%	50.2%
9,805	ST. CLAIR	4,639	2,335	2,121	183	214	R	50.3%	45.7%	52.4%	47.6%
65,359	ST. FRANCOIS	22,543	9,965	11,930	648	1,965	D	44.2%	52.9%	45.5%	54.5%
319,294	ST. LOUIS CITY	141,123	19,478	117,979	3,666	98,501	D	13.8%	83.6%	14.2%	85.8%
998,954	ST. LOUIS COUNTY	520,998	185,704	324,748	10,546	139,044	D	35.6%	62.3%	36.4%	63.6%
18,145	STE. GENEVIEVE	7,961	2,878	4,884	199	2,006	D	36.2%	61.3%	37.1%	62.9%
29,968	STODDARD	12,774	6,514	5,980	280	534	R	51.0%	46.8%	52.1%	47.9%
32,202	STONE	15,912	9,434	6,025	453	3,409	R	59.3%	37.9%	61.0%	39.0%
6,714	SULLIVAN	2,603	1,429	1,104	70	325	R	54.9%	42.4%	56.4%	43.6%
51,675	TANEY	21,425	12,761	8,071	593	4,690	R	59.6%	37.7%	61.3%	38.7%
26,008	TEXAS	10,787	5,831	4,635	321	1,196	R	54.1%	43.0%	55.7%	44.3%
21,159	VERNON	8,466	4,424	3,759	283	665	R	52.3%	44.4%	54.1%	45.9%
32,513	WARREN	14,576	7,338	6,819	419	519	R	50.3%	46.8%	51.8%	48.2%
25,195	WASHINGTON	8,750	3,697	4,823	230	1,126	D	42.3%	55.1%	43.4%	56.6%
13,521	WAYNE	5,643	2,642	2,865	136	223	D	46.8%	50.8%	48.0%	52.0%
36,202	WEBSTER	15,406	8,406	6,570	430	1,836	R	54.6%	42.6%	56.1%	43.9%
2,171	WORTH	1,045	524	486	35	38	R	50.1%	46.5%	51.9%	48.1%
18,815	WRIGHT	7,960	4,866	2,878	216	1,988	R	61.1%	36.2%	62.8%	37.2%
5,988,927	TOTAL	2,727,883	1,160,265	1,494,056	73,562	333,791	D	42.5%	54.8%	43.7%	56.3%

Note: Although Kansas City is part of Jackson County, its results are listed separately.

MISSOURI

SENATOR 2012

2010 Census Population	County	Total Vote	Republican (Akin)	Democratic (McCaskill)	Other	Rep.-Dem. Plurality	Percentage			
							Total Vote		Major Vote	
							Rep.	Dem.	Rep.	Dem.
25,607	ADAIR	10,021	4,018	5,457	546	1,439 D	40.1%	54.5%	42.4%	57.6%
17,291	ANDREW	8,224	3,664	3,952	608	288 D	44.6%	48.1%	48.1%	51.9%
5,685	ATCHISON	2,664	1,340	1,155	169	185 R	50.3%	43.4%	53.7%	46.3%
25,529	AUDRAIN	9,825	4,420	4,640	765	220 D	45.0%	47.2%	48.8%	51.2%
35,597	BARRY	13,604	7,319	5,115	1,170	2,204 R	53.8%	37.6%	58.9%	41.1%
12,402	BARTON	5,699	3,551	1,802	346	1,749 R	62.3%	31.6%	66.3%	33.7%
17,049	BATES	7,698	3,345	3,716	637	371 D	43.5%	48.3%	47.4%	52.6%
19,056	BENTON	9,059	4,277	4,083	699	194 R	47.2%	45.1%	51.2%	48.8%
12,363	BOLLINGER	5,425	3,035	2,098	292	937 R	55.9%	38.7%	59.1%	40.9%
162,642	BOONE	77,982	25,431	46,332	6,219	20,901 D	32.6%	59.4%	35.4%	64.6%
89,201	BUCHANAN	34,796	11,913	20,437	2,446	8,524 D	34.2%	58.7%	36.8%	63.2%
42,794	BUTLER	16,710	9,079	6,783	848	2,296 R	54.3%	40.6%	57.2%	42.8%
9,424	CALDWELL	4,134	1,880	1,832	422	48 R	45.5%	44.3%	50.6%	49.4%
44,332	CALLAWAY	18,031	8,664	7,968	1,399	696 R	48.1%	44.2%	52.1%	47.9%
44,002	CAMDEN	21,857	10,883	9,391	1,583	1,492 R	49.8%	43.0%	53.7%	46.3%
75,674	CAPE GIRARDEAU	35,242	18,913	14,390	1,939	4,523 R	53.7%	40.8%	56.8%	43.2%
9,295	CARROLL	4,209	1,926	1,906	377	20 R	45.8%	45.3%	50.3%	49.7%
6,265	CARTER	2,771	1,400	1,211	160	189 R	50.5%	43.7%	53.6%	46.4%
99,478	CASS	48,362	21,557	22,626	4,179	1,069 D	44.6%	46.8%	48.8%	51.2%
13,982	CEDAR	5,969	3,205	2,332	432	873 R	53.7%	39.1%	57.9%	42.1%
7,831	CHARITON	3,780	1,690	1,856	234	166 D	44.7%	49.1%	47.7%	52.3%
77,422	CHRISTIAN	37,469	20,383	14,312	2,774	6,071 R	54.4%	38.2%	58.7%	41.3%
7,139	CLARK	3,221	1,288	1,811	122	523 D	40.0%	56.2%	41.6%	58.4%
221,939	CLAY	104,254	37,967	57,654	8,633	19,687 D	36.4%	55.3%	39.7%	60.3%
20,743	CLINTON	9,789	4,142	4,777	870	635 D	42.3%	48.8%	46.4%	53.6%
75,990	COLE	36,545	18,918	15,394	2,233	3,524 R	51.8%	42.1%	55.1%	44.9%
17,601	COOPER	7,420	3,494	3,335	591	159 R	47.1%	44.9%	51.2%	48.8%
24,696	CRAWFORD	9,517	4,654	4,240	623	414 R	48.9%	44.6%	52.3%	47.7%
7,883	DADE	3,856	2,128	1,472	256	656 R	55.2%	38.2%	59.1%	40.9%
16,777	DALLAS	7,196	3,514	3,072	610	442 R	48.8%	42.7%	53.4%	46.6%
8,433	DAVIESS	3,513	1,532	1,654	327	122 D	43.6%	47.1%	48.1%	51.9%
12,892	DEKALB	4,329	2,015	1,950	364	65 R	46.5%	45.0%	50.8%	49.2%
15,657	DENT	6,575	3,499	2,558	518	941 R	53.2%	38.9%	57.8%	42.2%
13,684	DOUGLAS	6,532	3,498	2,486	548	1,012 R	53.6%	38.1%	58.5%	41.5%
31,953	DUNKLIN	10,548	4,806	5,347	395	541 D	45.6%	50.7%	47.3%	52.7%
101,492	FRANKLIN	46,285	21,281	21,826	3,178	545 D	46.0%	47.2%	49.4%	50.6%
15,222	GASCONADE	7,023	3,603	2,927	493	676 R	51.3%	41.7%	55.2%	44.8%
6,738	GENTRY	2,970	1,235	1,463	272	228 D	41.6%	49.3%	45.8%	54.2%
275,174	GREENE	124,480	55,304	59,979	9,197	4,675 D	44.4%	48.2%	48.0%	52.0%
10,261	GRUNDY	4,343	1,912	2,032	399	120 D	44.0%	46.8%	48.5%	51.5%
8,957	HARRISON	3,618	1,744	1,558	316	186 R	48.2%	43.1%	52.8%	47.2%
22,272	HENRY	10,030	4,066	5,119	845	1,053 D	40.5%	51.0%	44.3%	55.7%
9,627	HICKORY	4,643	1,982	2,292	369	310 D	42.7%	49.4%	46.4%	53.6%
4,912	HOLT	2,277	1,169	959	149	210 R	51.3%	42.1%	54.9%	45.1%
10,144	HOWARD	4,810	2,101	2,298	411	197 D	43.7%	47.8%	47.8%	52.2%
40,400	HOWELL	16,242	8,340	6,692	1,210	1,648 R	51.3%	41.2%	55.5%	44.5%
10,630	IRON	4,002	1,461	2,252	289	791 D	36.5%	56.3%	39.3%	60.7%
674,158	JACKSON	172,486	65,714	94,193	12,579	28,479 D	38.1%	54.6%	41.1%	58.9%
117,404	JASPER	44,761	24,563	17,485	2,713	7,078 R	54.9%	39.1%	58.4%	41.6%
218,733	JEFFERSON	96,923	38,745	51,862	6,316	13,117 D	40.0%	53.5%	42.8%	57.2%
52,595	JOHNSON	20,769	8,613	10,197	1,959	1,584 D	41.5%	49.1%	45.8%	54.2%
(See Note)	KANSAS CITY	135,573	20,660	110,098	4,815	89,438 D	15.2%	81.2%	15.8%	84.2%
4,131	KNOX	1,942	905	965	72	60 D	46.6%	49.7%	48.4%	51.6%
35,571	LACLEDE	15,213	7,721	6,273	1,219	1,448 R	50.8%	41.2%	55.2%	44.8%
33,381	LAFAYETTE	15,620	6,663	7,695	1,262	1,032 D	42.7%	49.3%	46.4%	53.6%
38,634	LAWRENCE	15,592	8,510	5,830	1,252	2,680 R	54.6%	37.4%	59.3%	40.7%
10,211	LEWIS	4,222	1,982	2,093	147	111 D	46.9%	49.6%	48.6%	51.4%
52,566	LINCOLN	22,564	10,860	10,225	1,479	635 R	48.1%	45.3%	51.5%	48.5%
12,761	LINN	5,512	2,170	2,911	431	741 D	39.4%	52.8%	42.7%	57.3%
15,195	LIVINGSTON	5,954	2,592	2,877	485	285 D	43.5%	48.3%	47.4%	52.6%

MISSOURI

SENATOR 2012

2010 Census Population	County	Total Vote	Republican (Akin)	Democratic (McCaskill)	Other	Rep.-Dem. Plurality	Percentage			
							Total Vote		Major Vote	
							Rep.	Dem.	Rep.	Dem.
15,566	MACON	7,067	3,444	3,256	367	188 R	48.7%	46.1%	51.4%	48.6%
12,226	MADISON	4,910	2,242	2,360	308	118 D	45.7%	48.1%	48.7%	51.3%
9,176	MARIES	4,509	2,312	1,870	327	442 R	51.3%	41.5%	55.3%	44.7%
28,781	MARION	12,060	6,350	5,281	429	1,069 R	52.7%	43.8%	54.6%	45.4%
23,083	MCDONALD	7,781	4,667	2,644	470	2,023 R	60.0%	34.0%	63.8%	36.2%
3,785	MERCER	1,625	813	664	148	149 R	50.0%	40.9%	55.0%	45.0%
24,748	MILLER	10,862	6,084	3,912	866	2,172 R	56.0%	36.0%	60.9%	39.1%
14,358	MISSISSIPPI	4,869	2,098	2,618	153	520 D	43.1%	53.8%	44.5%	55.5%
15,607	MONITEAU	6,356	3,483	2,394	479	1,089 R	54.8%	37.7%	59.3%	40.7%
8,840	MONROE	4,003	1,917	1,888	198	29 R	47.9%	47.2%	50.4%	49.6%
12,236	MONTGOMERY	5,268	2,554	2,331	383	223 R	48.5%	44.2%	52.3%	47.7%
20,565	MORGAN	8,614	4,190	3,773	651	417 R	48.6%	43.8%	52.6%	47.4%
18,956	NEW MADRID	7,144	2,908	3,966	270	1,058 D	40.7%	55.5%	42.3%	57.7%
58,114	NEWTON	24,881	14,574	8,933	1,374	5,641 R	58.6%	35.9%	62.0%	38.0%
23,370	NODAWAY	8,897	3,543	4,656	698	1,113 D	39.8%	52.3%	43.2%	56.8%
10,881	OREGON	4,404	2,095	2,048	261	47 R	47.6%	46.5%	50.6%	49.4%
13,878	OSAGE	6,815	3,986	2,359	470	1,627 R	58.5%	34.6%	62.8%	37.2%
9,723	OZARK	4,406	2,202	1,866	338	336 R	50.0%	42.4%	54.1%	45.9%
18,296	PEMISCOT	6,145	2,487	3,498	160	1,011 D	40.5%	56.9%	41.6%	58.4%
18,971	PERRY	7,843	4,012	3,439	392	573 R	51.2%	43.8%	53.8%	46.2%
42,201	PETTIS	16,942	7,196	8,246	1,500	1,050 D	42.5%	48.7%	46.6%	53.4%
45,156	PHELPS	17,964	8,579	8,133	1,252	446 R	47.8%	45.3%	51.3%	48.7%
18,516	PIKE	7,296	3,381	3,449	466	68 D	46.3%	47.3%	49.5%	50.5%
89,322	PLATTE	44,941	17,870	23,578	3,493	5,708 D	39.8%	52.5%	43.1%	56.9%
31,137	POLK	12,948	6,789	5,226	933	1,563 R	52.4%	40.4%	56.5%	43.5%
52,274	PULASKI	13,352	6,094	6,278	980	184 D	45.6%	47.0%	49.3%	50.7%
4,979	PUTNAM	2,283	1,296	895	92	401 R	56.8%	39.2%	59.2%	40.8%
10,167	RALLS	5,015	2,596	2,248	171	348 R	51.8%	44.8%	53.6%	46.4%
25,414	RANDOLPH	9,863	4,750	4,286	827	464 R	48.2%	43.5%	52.6%	47.4%
23,494	RAY	10,287	3,960	5,439	888	1,479 D	38.5%	52.9%	42.1%	57.9%
6,696	REYNOLDS	3,166	1,247	1,700	219	453 D	39.4%	53.7%	42.3%	57.7%
14,100	RIPLEY	5,198	2,771	2,147	280	624 R	53.3%	41.3%	56.3%	43.7%
23,370	SALINE	9,012	3,121	5,143	748	2,022 D	34.6%	57.1%	37.8%	62.2%
4,431	SCHUYLER	1,903	793	985	125	192 D	41.7%	51.8%	44.6%	55.4%
4,843	SCOTLAND	1,915	900	941	74	41 D	47.0%	49.1%	48.9%	51.1%
39,191	SCOTT	16,850	8,514	7,627	709	887 R	50.5%	45.3%	52.7%	47.3%
8,441	SHANNON	3,704	1,536	1,935	233	399 D	41.5%	52.2%	44.3%	55.7%
6,373	SHELBY	3,220	1,667	1,424	129	243 R	51.8%	44.2%	53.9%	46.1%
360,485	ST. CHARLES	183,291	82,319	90,040	10,932	7,721 D	44.9%	49.1%	47.8%	52.2%
9,805	ST. CLAIR	4,623	2,132	2,101	390	31 R	46.1%	45.4%	50.4%	49.6%
65,359	ST. FRANCOIS	22,433	9,142	11,751	1,540	2,609 D	40.8%	52.4%	43.8%	56.2%
319,294	ST. LOUIS CITY	142,468	15,385	123,000	4,083	107,615 D	10.8%	86.3%	11.1%	88.9%
998,954	ST. LOUIS COUNTY	521,339	164,267	335,573	21,499	171,306 D	31.5%	64.4%	32.9%	67.1%
18,145	STE. GENEVIEVE	7,956	2,735	4,758	463	2,023 D	34.4%	59.8%	36.5%	63.5%
29,968	STODDARD	12,753	6,757	5,328	668	1,429 R	53.0%	41.8%	55.9%	44.1%
32,202	STONE	15,749	8,769	5,699	1,281	3,070 R	55.7%	36.2%	60.6%	39.4%
6,714	SULLIVAN	2,600	1,128	1,309	163	181 D	43.4%	50.3%	46.3%	53.7%
51,675	TANEY	21,294	11,940	7,834	1,520	4,106 R	56.1%	36.8%	60.4%	39.6%
26,008	TEXAS	10,700	5,340	4,544	816	796 R	49.9%	42.5%	54.0%	46.0%
21,159	VERNON	8,473	4,171	3,810	492	361 R	49.2%	45.0%	52.3%	47.7%
32,513	WARREN	14,530	7,040	6,591	899	449 R	48.5%	45.4%	51.6%	48.4%
25,195	WASHINGTON	8,695	3,486	4,648	561	1,162 D	40.1%	53.5%	42.9%	57.1%
13,521	WAYNE	5,672	2,693	2,697	282	4 D	47.5%	47.5%	50.0%	50.0%
36,202	WEBSTER	15,302	7,739	6,363	1,200	1,376 R	50.6%	41.6%	54.9%	45.1%
2,171	WORTH	1,042	449	515	78	66 D	43.1%	49.4%	46.6%	53.4%
18,815	WRIGHT	7,875	4,402	2,883	590	1,519 R	55.9%	36.6%	60.4%	39.6%
5,988,927	TOTAL	2,725,793	1,066,159	1,494,125	165,509	427,966 D	39.1%	54.8%	41.6%	58.4%

Note: Although Kansas City is part of Jackson County, its results are listed separately.

MISSOURI

HOUSE OF REPRESENTATIVES

CD	Year	Total Vote	Republican		Democratic		Other Vote	Rep.-Dem. Plurality	Percentage			
									Total Vote		Major Vote	
			Vote	Candidate	Vote	Candidate			Rep.	Dem.	Rep.	Dem.
1	2012	340,583	60,832	HAMLIN, ROBYN	267,927	CLAY, WILLIAM LACY*	11,824	207,095 D	17.9%	78.7%	18.5%	81.5%
2	2012	394,448	236,971	WAGNER, ANN	146,272	KOENEN, GLENN	11,205	90,699 R	60.1%	37.1%	61.8%	38.2%
3	2012	338,385	214,843	LUETKEMEYER, BLAINE*	111,189	MAYER, ERIC C.	12,353	103,654 R	63.5%	32.9%	65.9%	34.1%
4	2012	318,723	192,237	HARTZLER, VICKY*	113,120	HENSLEY, TERESA	13,366	79,117 R	60.3%	35.5%	63.0%	37.0%
5	2012	330,942	122,149	TURK, JACOB	200,290	CLEAVER, EMANUEL II*	8,503	78,141 D	36.9%	60.5%	37.9%	62.1%
6	2012	333,688	216,906	GRAVES, SAM*	108,503	YARBER, KYLE	8,279	108,403 R	65.0%	32.5%	66.7%	33.3%
7	2012	318,740	203,565	LONG, BILLY*	98,498	EVANS, JIM	16,677	105,067 R	63.9%	30.9%	67.4%	32.6%
8	2012	300,391	216,083	EMERSON, JO ANN*	73,755	RUSHIN, JACK	10,553	142,328 R	71.9%	24.6%	74.6%	25.4%
TOTAL	2012	2,675,900	1,463,586		1,119,554		92,760	344,032 R	54.7%	41.8%	56.7%	43.3%

Note: An asterisk (*) denotes incumbent.

MISSOURI

GENERAL AND PRIMARY ELECTIONS

GENERAL ELECTIONS: OTHER VOTE

President Other vote was 43,151 Libertarian (Gary E. Johnson), 7,936 Constitution (Virgil H. Goode)

Governor Other vote was 73,509 Libertarian (Jim Higgins), 53 Write-in (Scattered Write-In)

Senator Other vote was 165,468 Libertarian (Jonathan Dine), 41 Write-in (Scattered Write-In)

House Other vote was:

CD 1 11,824 Libertarian (Robb E. Cunningham)
CD 2 9,193 Libertarian (Bill Slantz), 2,012 Constitution (Anatol Zorikova)
CD 3 12,353 Libertarian (Steven Wilson)
CD 4 10,407 Libertarian (Thomas Holbrook), 2,959 Constitution (Greg Cowan)
CD 5 8,497 Libertarian (Randall D. "Randy" Langkraehr), 6 Write-in (Andrew Feagle)
CD 6 8,279 Libertarian (Russ Lee Monchil)
CD 7 16,668 Libertarian (Kevin Craig), 9 Write-in (Kenneth Joe Brown)
CD 8 10,553 Libertarian (Rick Vandeven)

PRIMARY ELECTIONS: SUPPLEMENTARY INFORMATION

Primary February 7, 2012 (President) **Registration** 4,102,977 No Party
August 7, 2012 (Congress) (as of August 1, 2012 Registration
– includes inactive registrants)

Primary Type Open—Any registered voter could participate in the party primary of their choice.

	REPUBLICAN PRIMARIES			DEMOCRATIC PRIMARIES		
President	Santorum, Rick	139,272	55.2%	Obama, Barack H.*	64,435	88.4%
	Romney, W. Mitt	63,882	25.3%	Uncommitted	4,582	6.3%
	Paul, Ron	30,647	12.2%	Terry, Randall	1,998	2.7%
	Uncommitted	9,853	3.9%	Wolfe, John	1,000	1.4%
	Perry, Rick	2,456	1.0%	Richardson, Darcy	873	1.2%
	Cain, Herman	2,306	0.9%			
	Bachmann, Michele	1,680	0.7%			
	Huntsman, Jon Jr.	1,044	0.4%			
	Johnson, Gary E.	536	0.2%			
	Meehan, Michael J.	356	0.1%			
	Drummond, Keith	153	0.1%			
	TOTAL	252,185		TOTAL	72,888	

MISSOURI

GENERAL AND PRIMARY ELECTIONS

	REPUBLICAN PRIMARIES			DEMOCRATIC PRIMARIES		
Senator	Akin, Todd	217,468	36.0%	McCaskill, Claire*	289,481	100.0%
	Brunner, John G.	180,821	30.0%			
	Steelman, Sarah	176,189	29.2%			
	Beck, Jerry	9,791	1.6%			
	Maldonado, Hector	7,412	1.2%			
	Poole, Robert "Bob"	6,097	1.0%			
	Memoly, Mark	3,200	0.5%			
	Lodes, Mark Patrick	2,282	0.4%			
	TOTAL	603,260		TOTAL	289,481	
Governor	Spence, David "Dave"	333,682	59.9%	Nixon, Jeremiah W. "Jay"*	270,140	86.0%
	Randles, Bill	90,686	16.3%	Campbell, William B.	25,775	8.2%
	Sauer, Fred	84,019	15.1%	Thunderhawk, Clay	18,243	5.8%
	Weiler, John D.	49,019	8.8%			
	TOTAL	557,406		TOTAL	314,158	
Congressional District 1	Hamlin, Robyn	9,737	57.9%	Clay, William Lacy*	57,791	63.3%
	Baker, Martin D.	7,085	42.1%	Carnahan, Russ*	30,943	33.9%
				Britton, Candice "Britt"	2,570	2.8%
	TOTAL	16,822		TOTAL	91,304	
Congressional District 2	Wagner, Ann	53,583	65.8%	Koenen, Glenn	7,894	28.4%
	Jotte, Randy	18,644	22.9%	Whitfield, Harold	7,848	28.2%
	Morris, John	6,041	7.4%	Weber, George D.	7,541	27.1%
	Baker, James O.	3,185	3.9%	Works, Marshall	4,532	16.3%
	TOTAL	81,453		TOTAL	27,815	
Congressional District 3	Luetkemeyer, Blaine*	79,661	100.0%	Mayer, Eric C.	22,478	100.0%
Congressional District 4	Hartzler, Vicky*	71,615	84.0%	Hensley, Teresa	24,631	100.0%
	Mowinski, Bernie	13,645	16.0%			
	TOTAL	85,260		TOTAL	24,631	
Congressional District 5	Turk, Jacob	24,814	58.9%	Cleaver, Emanuel II*	43,712	100.0%
	Nolte, Jerry	10,734	25.5%			
	Greene, Jason	5,067	12.0%			
	Shawd, Ron	1,542	3.7%			
	TOTAL	42,157		TOTAL	43,712	
Congressional District 6	Graves, Sam*	59,388	80.3%	Yarber, Kyle	10,242	32.6%
	Ryan, Christopher	9,945	13.5%	Hedge, W.A. "Bill"	8,620	27.4%
	Gough, Bob	4,598	6.2%	Harris, Ronald	7,483	23.8%
				Rights, Ted	5,118	16.3%
	TOTAL	73,931		TOTAL	31,463	
Congressional District 7	Long, Billy*	62,917	59.7%	Evans, Jim	14,446	100.0%
	Moon, Mike	22,860	21.7%			
	Stilson, Tom	19,666	18.7%			
	TOTAL	105,443		TOTAL	14,446	
Congressional District 8	Emerson, Jo Ann*	61,975	67.1%	Rushin, Jack	27,839	100.0%
	Parker, Bob	30,429	32.9%			
	TOTAL	92,404		TOTAL	27,839	

Note: An asterisk (*) denotes incumbent. Due to redistricting, the 1st district Democratic primary pitted two incumbents against each other (Clay, former 1st district, and Carnahan, former 3rd district).

MONTANA

One member At Large

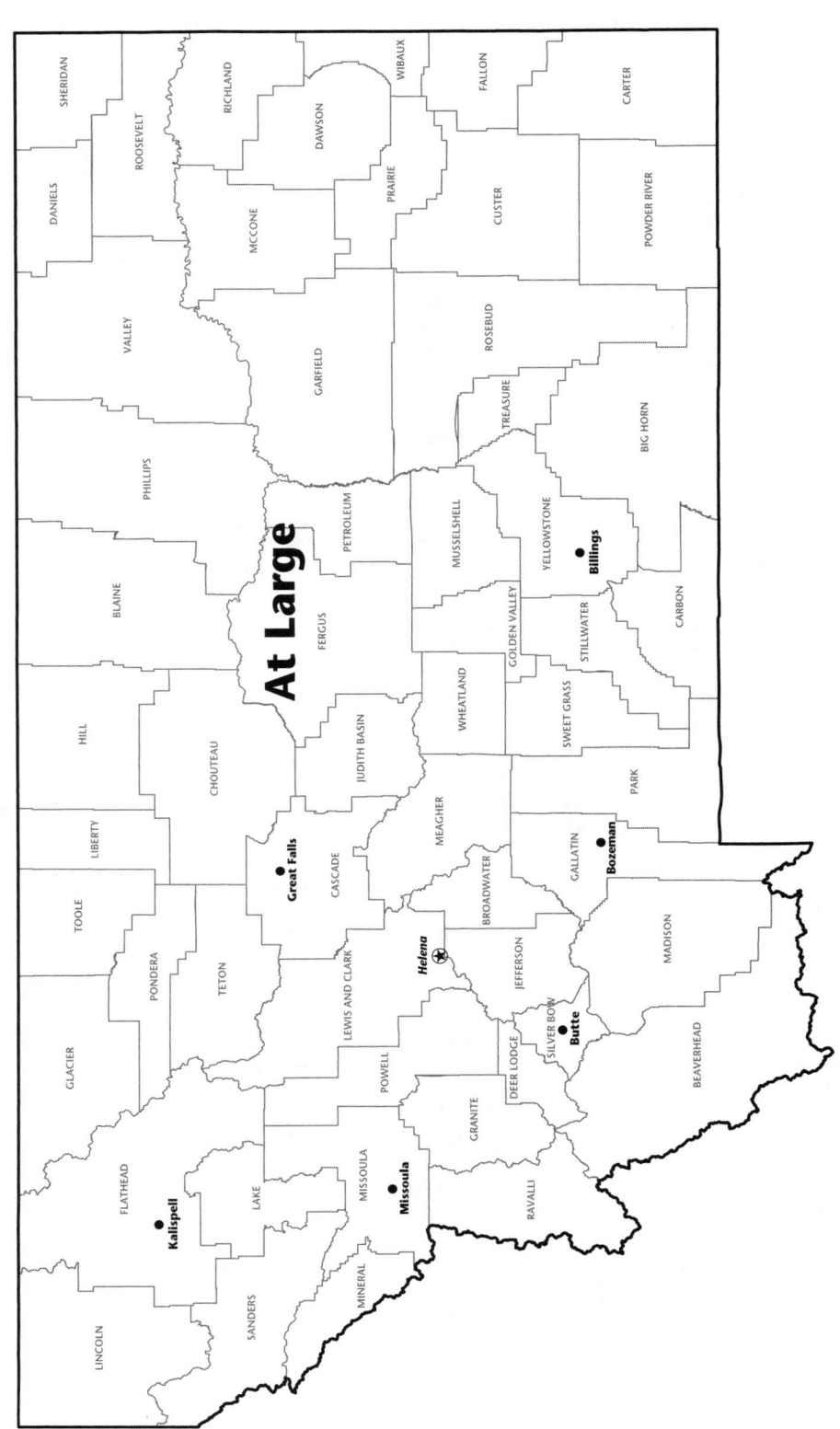

MONTANA

GOVERNOR
Steve Bullock (D). Elected 2012 to a four-year term.

SENATORS (2 Democrats)
Max Baucus (D). Reelected 2008 to a six-year term. Previously elected 2002, 1996, 1990, 1984, 1978.

Jon Tester (D). Reelected 2012 to a six-year term. Previously elected 2006.

REPRESENTATIVE (1 Republican)
At Large. Steve Daines (R)

POSTWAR VOTE FOR PRESIDENT

| | | Republican | | Democratic | | Other | Rep.-Dem. | Percentage | | | |
| | | | | | | | | Total Vote | | Major Vote | |
Year	Total Vote	Vote	Candidate	Vote	Candidate	Vote	Plurality	Rep.	Dem.	Rep.	Dem.
2012	484,048	267,928	Romney, W. Mitt	201,839	Obama, Barack H.*	14,281	66,089 R	55.4%	41.7%	57.0%	43.0%
2008	490,302	242,763	McCain, John S. III	231,667	Obama, Barack H.	15,872	11,096 R	49.5%	47.2%	51.2%	48.8%
2004	450,445	266,063	Bush, George W.*	173,710	Kerry, John F.	10,672	92,353 R	59.1%	38.6%	60.5%	39.5%
2000**	410,997	240,178	Bush, George W.	137,126	Gore, Albert Jr.	33,693	103,052 R	58.4%	33.4%	63.7%	36.3%
1996**	407,261	179,652	Dole, Robert "Bob"	167,922	Clinton, Bill*	59,687	11,730 R	44.1%	41.2%	51.7%	48.3%
1992**	410,611	144,207	Bush, George H.*	154,507	Clinton, Bill	111,897	10,300 D	35.1%	37.6%	48.3%	51.7%
1988	365,674	190,412	Bush, George H.	168,936	Dukakis, Michael S.	6,326	21,476 R	52.1%	46.2%	53.0%	47.0%
1984	384,377	232,450	Reagan, Ronald*	146,742	Mondale, Walter F.	5,185	85,708 R	60.5%	38.2%	61.3%	38.7%
1980**	363,952	206,814	Reagan, Ronald	118,032	Carter, Jimmy*	39,106	88,782 R	56.8%	32.4%	63.7%	36.3%
1976	328,734	173,703	Ford, Gerald R.*	149,259	Carter, Jimmy	5,772	24,444 R	52.8%	45.4%	53.8%	46.2%
1972	317,603	183,976	Nixon, Richard M.*	120,197	McGovern, George S.	13,430	63,779 R	57.9%	37.8%	60.5%	39.5%
1968**	274,404	138,835	Nixon, Richard M.	114,117	Humphrey, Hubert H. Jr.	21,452	24,718 R	50.6%	41.6%	54.9%	45.1%
1964	278,628	113,032	Goldwater, Barry M. Sr.	164,246	Johnson, Lyndon B.*	1,350	51,214 D	40.6%	58.9%	40.8%	59.2%
1960	277,579	141,841	Nixon, Richard M.	134,891	Kennedy, John F.	847	6,950 R	51.1%	48.6%	51.3%	48.7%
1956	271,171	154,933	Eisenhower, Dwight D.*	116,238	Stevenson, Adlai E. II		38,695 R	57.1%	42.9%	57.1%	42.9%
1952	265,037	157,394	Eisenhower, Dwight D.	106,213	Stevenson, Adlai E. II	1,430	51,181 R	59.4%	40.1%	59.7%	40.3%
1948	224,278	96,770	Dewey, Thomas E.	119,071	Truman, Harry S.*	8,437	22,301 D	43.1%	53.1%	44.8%	55.2%

Note: An asterisk (*) denotes incumbent. **In past elections, the other vote included: 2000 - 24,437 Green (Ralph Nader); 1996 - 55,229 Reform (Ross Perot); 1992 - 107,225 Independent (Perot); 1980 - 29,281 Independent (John Anderson); 1968 - 20,015 American Independent (George Wallace).

MONTANA

POSTWAR VOTE FOR GOVERNOR

Year	Total Vote	Republican		Democratic		Other Vote	Rep.-Dem. Plurality	Percentage			
		Vote	Candidate	Vote	Candidate			Total Vote		Major Vote	
								Rep.	Dem.	Rep.	Dem.
2012	483,489	228,879	Hill, Rick	236,450	Bullock, Steve	18,160	7,571 D	47.3%	48.9%	49.2%	50.8%
2008	486,734	158,268	Brown, Roy	318,670	Schweitzer, Brian*	9,796	160,402 D	32.5%	65.5%	33.2%	66.8%
2004	446,146	205,313	Brown, Bob	225,016	Schweitzer, Brian	15,817	19,703 D	46.0%	50.4%	47.7%	52.3%
2000	410,192	209,135	Martz, Judy	193,131	O'Keefe, Mark	7,926	16,004 R	51.0%	47.1%	52.0%	48.0%
1996**	405,175	320,768	Racicot, Marc*	84,407	Jacobson, Judy		236,361 R	79.2%	20.8%	79.2%	20.8%
1992	407,842	209,401	Racicot, Marc	198,421	Bradley, Dorothy	20	10,980 R	51.3%	48.7%	51.3%	48.7%
1988	367,021	190,604	Stephens, Stan	169,313	Judge, Thomas L.	7,104	21,291 R	51.9%	46.1%	53.0%	47.0%
1984	378,970	100,070	Goodover, Pat M.	266,578	Schwinden, Ted*	12,322	166,508 D	26.4%	70.3%	27.3%	72.7%
1980	360,470	160,896	Ramirez, Jack	199,574	Schwinden, Ted		38,678 D	44.6%	55.4%	44.6%	55.4%
1976	316,720	115,848	Woodahl, Robert	195,420	Judge, Thomas L.*	5,452	79,572 D	36.6%	61.7%	37.2%	62.8%
1972	318,754	146,231	Smith, Ed	172,523	Judge, Thomas L.		26,292 D	45.9%	54.1%	45.9%	54.1%
1968	278,112	116,432	Babcock, Tim M.*	150,481	Anderson, Forrest H.	11,199	34,049 D	41.9%	54.1%	43.6%	56.4%
1964	280,975	144,113	Babcock, Tim M.	136,862	Renne, Roland		7,251 R	51.3%	48.7%	51.3%	48.7%
1960	279,881	154,230	Nutter, Donald G.	125,651	Cannon, Paul		28,579 R	55.1%	44.9%	55.1%	44.9%
1956	270,366	138,878	Aronson, John Hugo*	131,488	Olsen, Arnold H.		7,390 R	51.4%	48.6%	51.4%	48.6%
1952	263,792	134,423	Aronson, John Hugo	129,369	Bonner, John W.*		5,054 R	51.0%	49.0%	51.0%	49.0%
1948	222,964	97,792	Ford, Samuel C.*	124,267	Bonner, John W.	905	26,475 D	43.9%	55.7%	44.0%	56.0%

Note: An asterisk (*) denotes incumbent. **In 1996 the Democratic vote total included 7,936 absentee ballots cast for the party's initial gubernatorial candidate, Chet Blaylock, who died that October.

POSTWAR VOTE FOR SENATOR

Year	Total Vote	Republican		Democratic		Other Vote	Rep.-Dem. Plurality	Percentage			
		Vote	Candidate	Vote	Candidate			Total Vote		Major Vote	
								Rep.	Dem.	Rep.	Dem.
2012	486,066	218,051	Rehberg, Dennis "Denny"	236,123	Tester, Jon*	31,892	18,072 D	44.9%	48.6%	48.0%	52.0%
2008	477,658	129,369	Kelleher, Bob	348,289	Baucus, Max*		218,920 D	27.1%	72.9%	27.1%	72.9%
2006	406,505	196,283	Burns, Conrad*	199,845	Tester, Jon	10,377	3,562 D	48.3%	49.2%	49.6%	50.4%
2002	326,537	103,611	Taylor, Mike	204,853	Baucus, Max*	18,073	101,242 D	31.7%	62.7%	33.6%	66.4%
2000	411,601	208,082	Burns, Conrad*	194,430	Schweitzer, Brian	9,089	13,652 R	50.6%	47.2%	51.7%	48.3%
1996	407,490	182,111	Rehberg, Dennis "Denny"	201,935	Baucus, Max*	23,444	19,824 D	44.7%	49.6%	47.4%	52.6%
1994	350,409	218,542	Burns, Conrad*	131,845	Mudd, Jack	22	86,697 R	62.4%	37.6%	62.4%	37.6%
1990	319,336	93,836	Kolstad, Allen C.	217,563	Baucus, Max*	7,937	123,727 D	29.4%	68.1%	30.1%	69.9%
1988	365,254	189,445	Burns, Conrad	175,809	Melcher, John*		13,636 R	51.9%	48.1%	51.9%	48.1%
1984	379,155	154,308	Cozzens, Chuck	215,704	Baucus, Max*	9,143	61,396 D	40.7%	56.9%	41.7%	58.3%
1982	321,062	133,789	Williams, Larry	174,861	Melcher, John*	12,412	41,072 D	41.7%	54.5%	43.3%	56.7%
1978	287,942	127,589	Williams, Larry	160,353	Baucus, Max		32,764 D	44.3%	55.7%	44.3%	55.7%
1976	321,445	115,213	Burger, Stanley C.	206,232	Melcher, John		91,019 D	35.8%	64.2%	35.8%	64.2%
1972	314,925	151,316	Hibbard, Henry S.	163,609	Metcalf, Lee		12,293 D	48.0%	52.0%	48.0%	52.0%
1970	247,869	97,809	Wallace, Harold E.	150,060	Mansfield, Mike*		52,251 D	39.5%	60.5%	39.5%	60.5%
1966	259,863	121,697	Babcock, Tim M.	138,166	Metcalf, Lee*		16,469 D	46.8%	53.2%	46.8%	53.2%
1964	280,010	99,367	Blewett, Alex	180,643	Mansfield, Mike*		81,276 D	35.5%	64.5%	35.5%	64.5%
1960	276,612	136,281	Fjare, Orvin B.	140,331	Metcalf, Lee		4,050 D	49.3%	50.7%	49.3%	50.7%
1958	229,483	54,573	Welch, Lou W.	174,910	Mansfield, Mike*		120,337 D	23.8%	76.2%	23.8%	76.2%
1954	227,454	112,863	D'Ewart, Wesley A.	114,591	Murray, James E.*		1,728 D	49.6%	50.4%	49.6%	50.4%
1952	262,297	127,360	Ecton, Zales N.*	133,109	Mansfield, Mike	1,828	5,749 D	48.6%	50.7%	48.9%	51.1%
1948	221,003	94,458	Davis, Tom J.	125,193	Murray, James E.*	1,352	30,735 D	42.7%	56.6%	43.0%	57.0%
1946	190,566	101,901	Ecton, Zales N.	86,476	Erickson, Leif	2,189	15,425 R	53.5%	45.4%	54.1%	45.9%

Note: An asterisk (*) denotes incumbent.

MONTANA
PRESIDENT 2012

2010 Census Population	County	Total Vote	Republican (Romney)	Democratic (Obama)	Other	Rep.-Dem. Plurality		Percentage			
								Total Vote		Major Vote	
								Rep.	Dem.	Rep.	Dem.
9,246	BEAVERHEAD	4,812	3,289	1,371	152	1,918 R		68.3%	28.5%	70.6%	29.4%
12,865	BIG HORN	4,626	1,667	2,882	77	1,215 D		36.0%	62.3%	36.6%	63.4%
6,491	BLAINE	2,859	1,178	1,616	65	438 D		41.2%	56.5%	42.2%	57.8%
5,612	BROADWATER	3,011	2,152	764	95	1,388 R		71.5%	25.4%	73.8%	26.2%
10,078	CARBON	5,847	3,533	2,146	168	1,387 R		60.4%	36.7%	62.2%	37.8%
1,160	CARTER	796	678	96	22	582 R		85.2%	12.1%	87.6%	12.4%
81,327	CASCADE	34,576	18,345	15,232	999	3,113 R		53.1%	44.1%	54.6%	45.4%
5,813	CHOUTEAU	2,821	1,758	978	85	780 R		62.3%	34.7%	64.3%	35.7%
11,699	CUSTER	5,365	3,373	1,833	159	1,540 R		62.9%	34.2%	64.8%	35.2%
1,751	DANIELS	1,007	740	237	30	503 R		73.5%	23.5%	75.7%	24.3%
8,966	DAWSON	4,423	3,029	1,219	175	1,810 R		68.5%	27.6%	71.3%	28.7%
9,298	DEER LODGE	4,460	1,448	2,860	152	1,412 D		32.5%	64.1%	33.6%	66.4%
2,890	FALLON	1,406	1,128	237	41	891 R		80.2%	16.9%	82.6%	17.4%
11,586	FERGUS	6,071	4,257	1,640	174	2,617 R		70.1%	27.0%	72.2%	27.8%
90,928	FLATHEAD	43,476	28,309	13,892	1,275	14,417 R		65.1%	32.0%	67.1%	32.9%
89,513	GALLATIN	47,908	24,358	21,961	1,589	2,397 R		50.8%	45.8%	52.6%	47.4%
1,206	GARFIELD	701	622	66	13	556 R		88.7%	9.4%	90.4%	9.6%
13,399	GLACIER	4,452	1,415	2,924	113	1,509 D		31.8%	65.7%	32.6%	67.4%
884	GOLDEN VALLEY	479	351	110	18	241 R		73.3%	23.0%	76.1%	23.9%
3,079	GRANITE	1,705	1,107	533	65	574 R		64.9%	31.3%	67.5%	32.5%
16,096	HILL	6,825	3,164	3,403	258	239 D		46.4%	49.9%	48.2%	51.8%
11,406	JEFFERSON	6,521	4,055	2,272	194	1,783 R		62.2%	34.8%	64.1%	35.9%
2,072	JUDITH BASIN	1,215	854	337	24	517 R		70.3%	27.7%	71.7%	28.3%
28,746	LAKE	13,304	7,135	5,805	364	1,330 R		53.6%	43.6%	55.1%	44.9%
63,395	LEWIS AND CLARK	33,318	16,803	15,620	895	1,183 R		50.4%	46.9%	51.8%	48.2%
2,339	LIBERTY	998	702	257	39	445 R		70.3%	25.8%	73.2%	26.8%
19,687	LINCOLN	8,890	6,057	2,552	281	3,505 R		68.1%	28.7%	70.4%	29.6%
7,691	MADISON	4,532	3,130	1,289	113	1,841 R		69.1%	28.4%	70.8%	29.2%
1,734	MCCONE	993	745	223	25	522 R		75.0%	22.5%	77.0%	23.0%
1,891	MEAGHER	972	670	269	33	401 R		68.9%	27.7%	71.4%	28.6%
4,223	MINERAL	2,021	1,216	700	105	516 R		60.2%	34.6%	63.5%	36.5%
109,299	MISSOULA	57,232	22,652	32,824	1,756	10,172 D		39.6%	57.4%	40.8%	59.2%
4,538	MUSSELSHELL	2,407	1,833	492	82	1,341 R		76.2%	20.4%	78.8%	21.2%
15,636	PARK	8,768	4,709	3,783	276	926 R		53.7%	43.1%	55.5%	44.5%
494	PETROLEUM	298	240	49	9	191 R		80.5%	16.4%	83.0%	17.0%
4,253	PHILLIPS	2,228	1,688	471	69	1,217 R		75.8%	21.1%	78.2%	21.8%
6,153	PONDERA	2,719	1,673	975	71	698 R		61.5%	35.9%	63.2%	36.8%
1,743	POWDER RIVER	1,027	833	170	24	663 R		81.1%	16.6%	83.1%	16.9%
7,027	POWELL	2,777	1,806	888	83	918 R		65.0%	32.0%	67.0%	33.0%
1,179	PRAIRIE	703	520	167	16	353 R		74.0%	23.8%	75.7%	24.3%
40,212	RAVALLI	22,212	14,307	7,285	620	7,022 R		64.4%	32.8%	66.3%	33.7%
9,746	RICHLAND	4,648	3,510	1,002	136	2,508 R		75.5%	21.6%	77.8%	22.2%
10,425	ROOSEVELT	3,672	1,514	2,086	72	572 D		41.2%	56.8%	42.1%	57.9%
9,233	ROSEBUD	3,523	2,004	1,422	97	582 R		56.9%	40.4%	58.5%	41.5%
11,413	SANDERS	5,901	3,980	1,720	201	2,260 R		67.4%	29.1%	69.8%	30.2%
3,384	SHERIDAN	1,928	1,207	665	56	542 R		62.6%	34.5%	64.5%	35.5%
34,200	SILVER BOW	16,756	5,430	10,857	469	5,427 D		32.4%	64.8%	33.3%	66.7%
9,117	STILLWATER	4,702	3,337	1,248	117	2,089 R		71.0%	26.5%	72.8%	27.2%
3,651	SWEET GRASS	2,117	1,594	475	48	1,119 R		75.3%	22.4%	77.0%	23.0%
6,073	TETON	3,281	2,113	1,082	86	1,031 R		64.4%	33.0%	66.1%	33.9%
5,324	TOOLE	2,102	1,440	582	80	858 R		68.5%	27.7%	71.2%	28.8%
718	TREASURE	455	319	114	22	205 R		70.1%	25.1%	73.7%	26.3%
7,369	VALLEY	3,859	2,337	1,385	137	952 R		60.6%	35.9%	62.8%	37.2%
2,168	WHEATLAND	992	693	272	27	421 R		69.9%	27.4%	71.8%	28.2%
1,017	WIBAUX	544	421	98	25	323 R		77.4%	18.0%	81.1%	18.9%
147,972	YELLOWSTONE	68,807	40,500	26,403	1,904	14,097 R		58.9%	38.4%	60.5%	39.5%
989,415	TOTAL	484,048	267,928	201,839	14,281	66,089 R		55.4%	41.7%	57.0%	43.0%

MONTANA

GOVERNOR 2012

2010 Census Population	County	Total Vote	Republican (Hill)	Democratic (Bullock)	Other	Rep.-Dem. Plurality	Percentage			
							Total Vote		Major Vote	
							Rep.	Dem.	Rep.	Dem.
9,246	BEAVERHEAD	4,824	2,945	1,689	190	1,256 R	61.0%	35.0%	63.6%	36.4%
12,865	BIG HORN	4,619	1,445	3,051	123	1,606 D	31.3%	66.1%	32.1%	67.9%
6,491	BLAINE	2,857	989	1,788	80	799 D	34.6%	62.6%	35.6%	64.4%
5,612	BROADWATER	3,014	1,800	1,104	110	696 R	59.7%	36.6%	62.0%	38.0%
10,078	CARBON	5,834	3,046	2,576	212	470 R	52.2%	44.2%	54.2%	45.8%
1,160	CARTER	781	646	103	32	543 R	82.7%	13.2%	86.2%	13.8%
81,327	CASCADE	34,564	14,164	19,138	1,262	4,974 D	41.0%	55.4%	42.5%	57.5%
5,813	CHOUTEAU	2,830	1,470	1,266	94	204 R	51.9%	44.7%	53.7%	46.3%
11,699	CUSTER	5,383	2,926	2,246	211	680 R	54.4%	41.7%	56.6%	43.4%
1,751	DANIELS	988	638	310	40	328 R	64.6%	31.4%	67.3%	32.7%
8,966	DAWSON	4,411	2,712	1,537	162	1,175 R	61.5%	34.8%	63.8%	36.2%
9,298	DEER LODGE	4,478	1,119	3,188	171	2,069 D	25.0%	71.2%	26.0%	74.0%
2,890	FALLON	1,381	1,010	325	46	685 R	73.1%	23.5%	75.7%	24.3%
11,586	FERGUS	6,042	3,726	2,084	232	1,642 R	61.7%	34.5%	64.1%	35.9%
90,928	FLATHEAD	43,382	25,286	16,348	1,748	8,938 R	58.3%	37.7%	60.7%	39.3%
89,513	GALLATIN	47,509	21,576	24,091	1,842	2,515 D	45.4%	50.7%	47.2%	52.8%
1,206	GARFIELD	702	573	107	22	466 R	81.6%	15.2%	84.3%	15.7%
13,399	GLACIER	4,445	1,200	3,071	174	1,871 D	27.0%	69.1%	28.1%	71.9%
884	GOLDEN VALLEY	483	309	156	18	153 R	64.0%	32.3%	66.5%	33.5%
3,079	GRANITE	1,696	988	628	80	360 R	58.3%	37.0%	61.1%	38.9%
16,096	HILL	6,830	2,583	3,969	278	1,386 D	37.8%	58.1%	39.4%	60.6%
11,406	JEFFERSON	6,538	3,502	2,796	240	706 R	53.6%	42.8%	55.6%	44.4%
2,072	JUDITH BASIN	1,225	743	450	32	293 R	60.7%	36.7%	62.3%	37.7%
28,746	LAKE	13,272	6,317	6,364	591	47 D	47.6%	48.0%	49.8%	50.2%
63,395	LEWIS AND CLARK	33,501	12,826	19,775	900	6,949 D	38.3%	59.0%	39.3%	60.7%
2,339	LIBERTY	1,002	573	395	34	178 R	57.2%	39.4%	59.2%	40.8%
19,687	LINCOLN	8,849	5,487	2,920	442	2,567 R	62.0%	33.0%	65.3%	34.7%
7,691	MADISON	4,531	2,846	1,509	176	1,337 R	62.8%	33.3%	65.4%	34.6%
1,734	MCCONE	1,001	676	286	39	390 R	67.5%	28.6%	70.3%	29.7%
1,891	MEAGHER	974	612	324	38	288 R	62.8%	33.3%	65.4%	34.6%
4,223	MINERAL	2,017	1,026	856	135	170 R	50.9%	42.4%	54.5%	45.5%
109,299	MISSOULA	57,118	19,454	35,557	2,107	16,103 D	34.1%	62.3%	35.4%	64.6%
4,538	MUSSELSHELL	2,394	1,577	671	146	906 R	65.9%	28.0%	70.2%	29.8%
15,636	PARK	8,766	4,198	4,197	371	1 R	47.9%	47.9%	50.0%	50.0%
494	PETROLEUM	299	231	62	6	169 R	77.3%	20.7%	78.8%	21.2%
4,253	PHILLIPS	2,213	1,475	652	86	823 R	66.7%	29.5%	69.3%	30.7%
6,153	PONDERA	2,721	1,439	1,192	90	247 R	52.9%	43.8%	54.7%	45.3%
1,743	POWDER RIVER	1,019	785	207	27	578 R	77.0%	20.3%	79.1%	20.9%
7,027	POWELL	2,797	1,545	1,146	106	399 R	55.2%	41.0%	57.4%	42.6%
1,179	PRAIRIE	708	470	216	22	254 R	66.4%	30.5%	68.5%	31.5%
40,212	RAVALLI	22,154	12,647	8,601	906	4,046 R	57.1%	38.8%	59.5%	40.5%
9,746	RICHLAND	4,643	3,247	1,206	190	2,041 R	69.9%	26.0%	72.9%	27.1%
10,425	ROOSEVELT	3,637	1,334	2,182	121	848 D	36.7%	60.0%	37.9%	62.1%
9,233	ROSEBUD	3,520	1,706	1,692	122	14 R	48.5%	48.1%	50.2%	49.8%
11,413	SANDERS	5,921	3,517	2,055	349	1,462 R	59.4%	34.7%	63.1%	36.9%
3,384	SHERIDAN	1,904	1,062	782	60	280 R	55.8%	41.1%	57.6%	42.4%
34,200	SILVER BOW	16,814	4,188	12,046	580	7,858 D	24.9%	71.6%	25.8%	74.2%
9,117	STILLWATER	4,691	2,894	1,634	163	1,260 R	61.7%	34.8%	63.9%	36.1%
3,651	SWEET GRASS	2,122	1,434	623	65	811 R	67.6%	29.4%	69.7%	30.3%
6,073	TETON	3,296	1,838	1,345	113	493 R	55.8%	40.8%	57.7%	42.3%
5,324	TOOLE	2,111	1,244	776	91	468 R	58.9%	36.8%	61.6%	38.4%
718	TREASURE	457	258	168	31	90 R	56.5%	36.8%	60.6%	39.4%
7,369	VALLEY	3,856	1,979	1,708	169	271 R	51.3%	44.3%	53.7%	46.3%
2,168	WHEATLAND	993	622	338	33	284 R	62.6%	34.0%	64.8%	35.2%
1,017	WIBAUX	536	370	142	24	228 R	69.0%	26.5%	72.3%	27.7%
147,972	YELLOWSTONE	68,836	33,606	32,802	2,428	804 R	48.8%	47.7%	50.6%	49.4%
989,415	TOTAL	483,489	228,879	236,450	18,160	7,571 D	47.3%	48.9%	49.2%	50.8%

MONTANA

SENATOR 2012

2010 Census Population	County	Total Vote	Republican (Rehberg)	Democratic (Tester)	Other	Rep.-Dem. Plurality	Percentage Total Vote Rep.	Dem.	Major Vote Rep.	Dem.
9,246	BEAVERHEAD	4,812	2,876	1,532	404	1,344 R	59.8%	31.8%	65.2%	34.8%
12,865	BIG HORN	4,661	1,309	3,141	211	1,832 D	28.1%	67.4%	29.4%	70.6%
6,491	BLAINE	2,871	897	1,834	140	937 D	31.2%	63.9%	32.8%	67.2%
5,612	BROADWATER	3,014	1,732	995	287	737 R	57.5%	33.0%	63.5%	36.5%
10,078	CARBON	5,863	2,788	2,691	384	97 R	47.6%	45.9%	50.9%	49.1%
1,160	CARTER	794	616	125	53	491 R	77.6%	15.7%	83.1%	16.9%
81,327	CASCADE	34,771	14,589	18,246	1,936	3,657 D	42.0%	52.5%	44.4%	55.6%
5,813	CHOUTEAU	2,851	1,321	1,374	156	53 D	46.3%	48.2%	49.0%	51.0%
11,699	CUSTER	5,396	2,661	2,283	452	378 R	49.3%	42.3%	53.8%	46.2%
1,751	DANIELS	1,003	607	327	69	280 R	60.5%	32.6%	65.0%	35.0%
8,966	DAWSON	4,430	2,504	1,571	355	933 R	56.5%	35.5%	61.4%	38.6%
9,298	DEER LODGE	4,489	1,049	3,122	318	2,073 D	23.4%	69.5%	25.1%	74.9%
2,890	FALLON	1,417	840	422	155	418 R	59.3%	29.8%	66.6%	33.4%
11,586	FERGUS	6,079	3,533	2,063	483	1,470 R	58.1%	33.9%	63.1%	36.9%
90,928	FLATHEAD	43,646	24,171	16,223	3,252	7,948 R	55.4%	37.2%	59.8%	40.2%
89,513	GALLATIN	48,001	20,386	24,781	2,834	4,395 D	42.5%	51.6%	45.1%	54.9%
1,206	GARFIELD	706	558	101	47	457 R	79.0%	14.3%	84.7%	15.3%
13,399	GLACIER	4,480	1,113	3,118	249	2,005 D	24.8%	69.6%	26.3%	73.7%
884	GOLDEN VALLEY	480	276	174	30	102 R	57.5%	36.2%	61.3%	38.7%
3,079	GRANITE	1,705	895	657	153	238 R	52.5%	38.5%	57.7%	42.3%
16,096	HILL	6,890	2,361	4,060	469	1,699 D	34.3%	58.9%	36.8%	63.2%
11,406	JEFFERSON	6,561	3,389	2,685	487	704 R	51.7%	40.9%	55.8%	44.2%
2,072	JUDITH BASIN	1,227	701	441	85	260 R	57.1%	35.9%	61.4%	38.6%
28,746	LAKE	13,321	5,717	6,561	1,043	844 D	42.9%	49.3%	46.6%	53.4%
63,395	LEWIS AND CLARK	33,474	13,446	18,189	1,839	4,743 D	40.2%	54.3%	42.5%	57.5%
2,339	LIBERTY	1,002	572	369	61	203 R	57.1%	36.8%	60.8%	39.2%
19,687	LINCOLN	8,928	5,080	3,091	757	1,989 R	56.9%	34.6%	62.2%	37.8%
7,691	MADISON	4,566	2,690	1,516	360	1,174 R	58.9%	33.2%	64.0%	36.0%
1,734	MCCONE	1,009	616	332	61	284 R	61.1%	32.9%	65.0%	35.0%
1,891	MEAGHER	979	544	342	93	202 R	55.6%	34.9%	61.4%	38.6%
4,223	MINERAL	2,030	963	866	201	97 R	47.4%	42.7%	52.7%	47.3%
109,299	MISSOULA	57,471	18,184	36,488	2,799	18,304 D	31.6%	63.5%	33.3%	66.7%
4,538	MUSSELSHELL	2,393	1,463	684	246	779 R	61.1%	28.6%	68.1%	31.9%
15,636	PARK	8,835	3,882	4,260	693	378 D	43.9%	48.2%	47.7%	52.3%
494	PETROLEUM	299	202	73	24	129 R	67.6%	24.4%	73.5%	26.5%
4,253	PHILLIPS	2,232	1,465	607	160	858 R	65.6%	27.2%	70.7%	29.3%
6,153	PONDERA	2,727	1,355	1,187	185	168 R	49.7%	43.5%	53.3%	46.7%
1,743	POWDER RIVER	1,025	719	239	67	480 R	70.1%	23.3%	75.1%	24.9%
7,027	POWELL	2,795	1,431	1,167	197	264 R	51.2%	41.8%	55.1%	44.9%
1,179	PRAIRIE	708	420	236	52	184 R	59.3%	33.3%	64.0%	36.0%
40,212	RAVALLI	22,258	11,990	8,602	1,666	3,388 R	53.9%	38.6%	58.2%	41.8%
9,746	RICHLAND	4,659	2,933	1,406	320	1,527 R	63.0%	30.2%	67.6%	32.4%
10,425	ROOSEVELT	3,695	1,235	2,269	191	1,034 D	33.4%	61.4%	35.2%	64.8%
9,233	ROSEBUD	3,550	1,578	1,704	268	126 D	44.5%	48.0%	48.1%	51.9%
11,413	SANDERS	5,957	3,219	2,044	694	1,175 R	54.0%	34.3%	61.2%	38.8%
3,384	SHERIDAN	1,923	995	812	116	183 R	51.7%	42.2%	55.1%	44.9%
34,200	SILVER BOW	16,847	4,148	11,673	1,026	7,525 D	24.6%	69.3%	26.2%	73.8%
9,117	STILLWATER	4,724	2,684	1,732	308	952 R	56.8%	36.7%	60.8%	39.2%
3,651	SWEET GRASS	2,119	1,328	661	130	667 R	62.7%	31.2%	66.8%	33.2%
6,073	TETON	3,313	1,760	1,341	212	419 R	53.1%	40.5%	56.8%	43.2%
5,324	TOOLE	2,120	1,209	721	190	488 R	57.0%	34.0%	62.6%	37.4%
718	TREASURE	462	252	157	53	95 R	54.5%	34.0%	61.6%	38.4%
7,369	VALLEY	3,888	1,824	1,749	315	75 R	46.9%	45.0%	51.0%	49.0%
2,168	WHEATLAND	992	559	365	68	194 R	56.4%	36.8%	60.5%	39.5%
1,017	WIBAUX	544	339	149	56	190 R	62.3%	27.4%	69.5%	30.5%
147,972	YELLOWSTONE	69,074	32,077	32,565	4,432	488 D	46.4%	47.1%	49.6%	50.4%
989,415	TOTAL	486,066	218,051	236,123	31,892	18,072 D	44.9%	48.6%	48.0%	52.0%

MONTANA

HOUSE OF REPRESENTATIVES

CD	Year	Total Vote	Republican Vote	Republican Candidate	Democratic Vote	Democratic Candidate	Other Vote	Rep.-Dem. Plurality	Total Vote Rep.	Total Vote Dem.	Major Vote Rep.	Major Vote Dem.
At Large	2012	479,740	255,468	DAINES, STEVE	204,939	GILLAN, KIM	19,333	50,529 R	53.3%	42.7%	55.5%	44.5%
At Large	2010	360,341	217,696	REHBERG, DENNIS "DENNY"*	121,954	MCDONALD, DENNIS	20,691	95,742 R	60.4%	33.8%	64.1%	35.9%
At Large	2008	480,900	308,470	REHBERG, DENNIS "DENNY"*	155,930	DRISCOLL, JOHN	16,500	152,540 R	64.1%	32.4%	66.4%	33.6%
At Large	2006	406,134	239,124	REHBERG, DENNIS "DENNY"*	158,916	LINDEEN, MONICA	8,094	80,208 R	58.9%	39.1%	60.1%	39.9%
At Large	2004	444,230	286,076	REHBERG, DENNIS "DENNY"*	145,606	VELAZQUEZ, TRACY E.	12,548	140,470 R	64.4%	32.8%	66.3%	33.7%
At Large	2002	331,321	214,100	REHBERG, DENNIS "DENNY"*	108,233	KELLY, STEVE	8,988	105,867 R	64.6%	32.7%	66.4%	33.6%
At Large	2000	410,523	211,418	REHBERG, DENNIS "DENNY"	189,971	KEENAN, NANCY	9,134	21,447 R	51.5%	46.3%	52.7%	47.3%
At Large	1998	331,551	175,748	HILL, RICK*	147,073	DESCHAMPS, DUSTY	8,730	28,675 R	53.0%	44.4%	54.4%	45.6%
At Large	1996	404,426	211,975	HILL, RICK	174,516	YELLOWTAIL, BILL	17,935	37,459 R	52.4%	43.2%	54.8%	45.2%
At Large	1994	352,133	148,715	JAMISON, CY	171,372	WILLIAMS, JOHN PATRICK "PAT"*	32,046	22,657 D	42.2%	48.7%	46.5%	53.5%
At Large	1992	403,735	189,570	MARLENEE, RON*	203,711	WILLIAMS, JOHN PATRICK "PAT"*	10,454	14,141 D	47.0%	50.5%	48.2%	51.8%

Note: An asterisk (*) denotes incumbent.

MONTANA

GENERAL AND PRIMARY ELECTIONS

GENERAL ELECTIONS: OTHER VOTE

President   Other vote was 14,165 Libertarian (Gary E. Johnson), 77 Write-in (Scattered Write-In), 39 Write-in (Virgil H. Goode)

Governor   Other vote was 18,160 Libertarian (Ron Vandevender)

Senator   Other vote was 31,892 Libertarian (Dan Cox)

House   Other vote was:

At Large   19,333 Libertarian (David Kaiser)

PRIMARY ELECTIONS: SUPPLEMENTARY INFORMATION

Primary   June 5, 2012   **Registration** (as of May 5, 2012)   642,308   No Party Registration

Primary Type   Open—Any registered voter could participate in the party primary of their choice.

MONTANA

GENERAL AND PRIMARY ELECTIONS

	REPUBLICAN PRIMARIES			DEMOCRATIC PRIMARIES		
President	Romney, W. Mitt	96,121	68.4%	Obama, Barack H.*	79,932	90.6%
	Paul, Ron	20,227	14.4%	No Preference	8,270	9.4%
	Santorum, Rick	12,546	8.9%	Wolfe, John	10	
	Gingrich, Newt	6,107	4.3%			
	No Preference	5,456	3.9%			
	TOTAL	140,457		TOTAL	88,212	
Senator	Rehberg, Dennis "Denny"	105,632	76.2%	Tester, Jon*	88,720	100.0%
	Teske, Dennis	33,079	23.8%			
	TOTAL	138,711		TOTAL	88,720	
Governor	Hill, Rick	46,802	49.4%	Bullock, Steve	76,738	86.6%
	Miller, Ken	24,496	25.9%	Margolis, Heather	11,823	13.4%
	Livingstone, Neil C.	12,038	12.7%			
	Lynch, Jim	8,323	8.8%			
	Fanning, Bob	3,087	3.3%			
	TOTAL	94,746		TOTAL	88,561	
House At Large	Daines, Steve	82,843	71.2%	Gillan, Kim	25,077	31.0%
	Brosten, Eric	21,012	18.1%	Wilmer, Franke	14,836	18.4%
	Melkus, Vincent	12,420	10.7%	Smith, Diane	12,618	15.6%
				Strohmaier, Dave	11,366	14.1%
				Rankin, Sam	9,382	11.6%
				Ward, Jason	4,959	6.1%
				Stutz, Robert	2,586	3.2%
	TOTAL	116,275		TOTAL	80,824	

Note: An asterisk (*) denotes incumbent.

NEBRASKA

Congressional districts first established for elections held in 2012

3 members

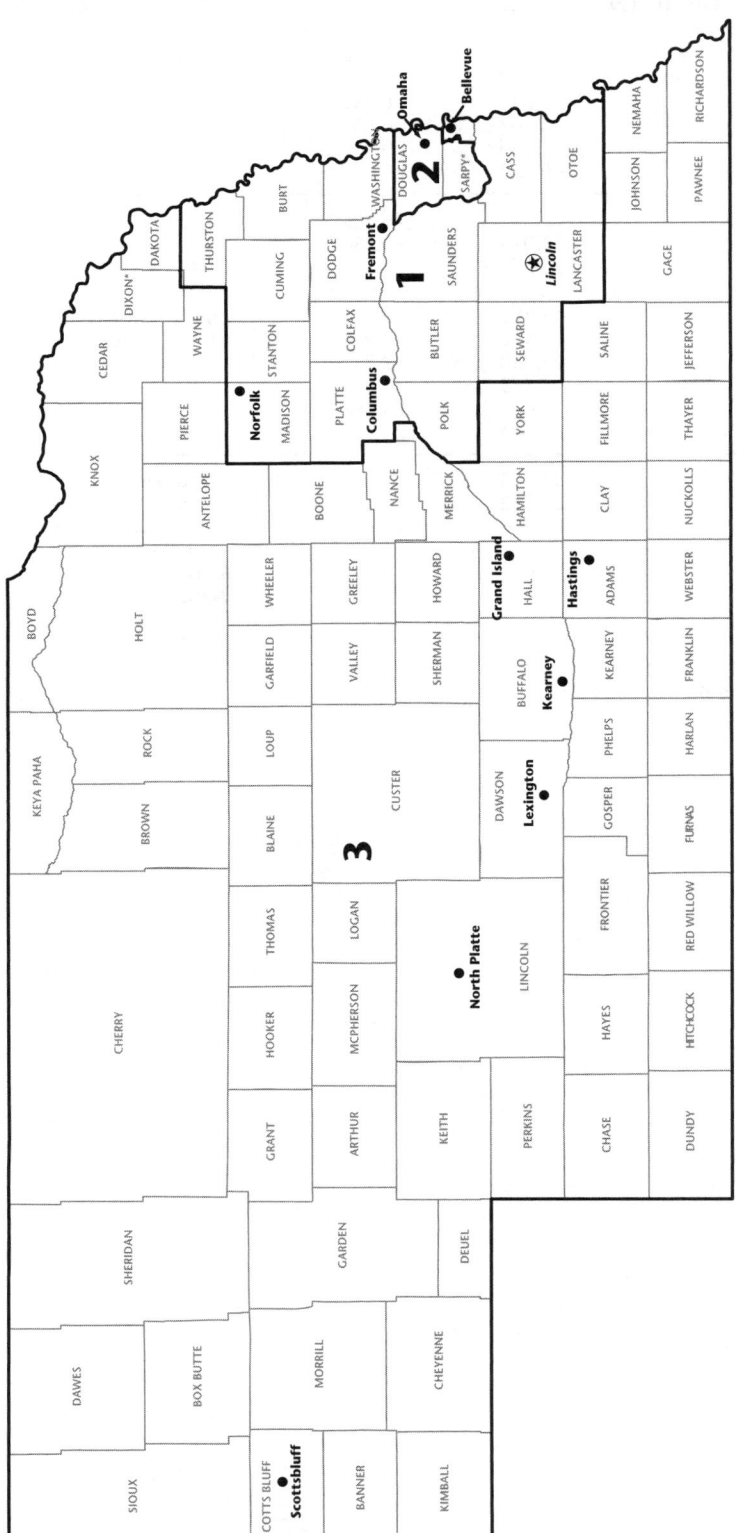

NEBRASKA

GOVERNOR
Dave Heineman (R). Reelected 2010 to a four-year term. Previously elected 2006. Became Governor January 21, 2005, upon the resignation of Mike Johanns (R) to become U.S. Secretary of Agriculture.

SENATORS (2 Republicans)
Mike Johanns (R). Elected 2008 to a six-year term.

Deb Fischer (R). Elected 2012 to a six-year term.

REPRESENTATIVES (3 Republicans)
1. Jeff Fortenberry (R)
2. Lee Terry (R)
3. Adrian Smith (R)

POSTWAR VOTE FOR PRESIDENT

		Republican		Democratic		Other	Rep.-Dem.	Total Vote		Major Vote	
Year	Total Vote	Vote	Candidate	Vote	Candidate	Vote	Plurality	Rep.	Dem.	Rep.	Dem.
2012	794,379	475,064	Romney, W. Mitt	302,081	Obama, Barack H.*	17,234	172,983 R	59.8%	38.0%	61.1%	38.9%
2008	801,281	452,979	McCain, John S. III	333,319	Obama, Barack H.	14,983	119,660 R	56.5%	41.6%	57.6%	42.4%
2004	778,186	512,814	Bush, George W.*	254,328	Kerry, John F.	11,044	258,486 R	65.9%	32.7%	66.8%	33.2%
2000**	697,019	433,862	Bush, George W.	231,780	Gore, Albert Jr.	31,377	202,082 R	62.2%	33.3%	65.2%	34.8%
1996**	677,415	363,467	Dole, Robert "Bob"	236,761	Clinton, Bill*	77,187	126,706 R	53.7%	35.0%	60.6%	39.4%
1992**	737,546	343,678	Bush, George H.*	216,864	Clinton, Bill	177,004	126,814 R	46.6%	29.4%	61.3%	38.7%
1988	661,465	397,956	Bush, George H.	259,235	Dukakis, Michael S.	4,274	138,721 R	60.2%	39.2%	60.6%	39.4%
1984	652,090	460,054	Reagan, Ronald*	187,866	Mondale, Walter F.	4,170	272,188 R	70.6%	28.8%	71.0%	29.0%
1980**	640,854	419,937	Reagan, Ronald	166,851	Carter, Jimmy*	54,066	253,086 R	65.5%	26.0%	71.6%	28.4%
1976	607,668	359,705	Ford, Gerald R.*	233,692	Carter, Jimmy	14,271	126,013 R	59.2%	38.5%	60.6%	39.4%
1972	576,289	406,298	Nixon, Richard M.*	169,991	McGovern, George S.		236,307 R	70.5%	29.5%	70.5%	29.5%
1968**	536,851	321,163	Nixon, Richard M.	170,784	Humphrey, Hubert H. Jr.	44,904	150,379 R	59.8%	31.8%	65.3%	34.7%
1964	584,154	276,847	Goldwater, Barry M. Sr.	307,307	Johnson, Lyndon B.*		30,460 D	47.4%	52.6%	47.4%	52.6%
1960	613,095	380,553	Nixon, Richard M.	232,542	Kennedy, John F.		148,011 R	62.1%	37.9%	62.1%	37.9%
1956	577,137	378,108	Eisenhower, Dwight D.*	199,029	Stevenson, Adlai E. II		179,079 R	65.5%	34.5%	65.5%	34.5%
1952	609,660	421,603	Eisenhower, Dwight D.	188,057	Stevenson, Adlai E. II		233,546 R	69.2%	30.8%	69.2%	30.8%
1948	488,940	264,774	Dewey, Thomas E.	224,165	Truman, Harry S.*	1	40,609 R	54.2%	45.8%	54.2%	45.8%

Note: An asterisk (*) denotes incumbent. **In past elections, the other vote included: 2000 - 24,540 Green (Ralph Nader); 1996 - 71,278 Reform (Ross Perot); 1992 - 174,104 Independent (Perot); 1980 - 44,993 Independent (John Anderson); 1968 - 44,904 American Independent (George Wallace).

NEBRASKA

POSTWAR VOTE FOR GOVERNOR

		Republican		Democratic		Other Vote	Rep.-Dem. Plurality	Percentage			
								Total Vote		Major Vote	
Year	Total Vote	Vote	Candidate	Vote	Candidate			Rep.	Dem.	Rep.	Dem.
2010	487,988	360,645	Heineman, Dave*	127,343	Meister, Mike		233,302 R	73.9%	26.1%	73.9%	26.1%
2006	593,357	435,507	Heineman, Dave*	145,115	Hahn, David	12,735	290,392 R	73.4%	24.5%	75.0%	25.0%
2002	480,991	330,349	Johanns, Mike*	132,348	Dean, Stormy	18,294	198,001 R	68.7%	27.5%	71.4%	28.6%
1998	545,238	293,910	Johanns, Mike	250,678	Hoppner, Bill	650	43,232 R	53.9%	46.0%	54.0%	46.0%
1994	579,561	148,230	Spence, Gene	423,270	Nelson, Earl "Ben"*	8,061	275,040 D	25.6%	73.0%	25.9%	74.1%
1990	586,542	288,741	Orr, Kay*	292,771	Nelson, Earl "Ben"	5,030	4,030 D	49.2%	49.9%	49.7%	50.3%
1986	564,422	298,325	Orr, Kay	265,156	Boosalis, Helen	941	33,169 R	52.9%	47.0%	52.9%	47.1%
1982	547,902	270,203	Thone, Charles*	277,436	Kerrey, Bob	263	7,233 D	49.3%	50.6%	49.3%	50.7%
1978	492,423	275,473	Thone, Charles	216,754	Whelan, Gerald T.	196	58,719 R	55.9%	44.0%	56.0%	44.0%
1974	451,306	159,780	Marvel, Richard D.	267,012	Exon, J. J.*	24,514	107,232 D	35.4%	59.2%	37.4%	62.6%
1970	461,619	201,994	Tiemann, Norbert T.*	248,552	Exon, J. J.	11,073	46,558 D	43.8%	53.8%	44.8%	55.2%
1966**	486,396	299,245	Tiemann, Norbert T.	186,985	Sorensen, Philip C.	166	112,260 R	61.5%	38.4%	61.5%	38.5%
1964	578,090	231,029	Burney, Dwight W.	347,026	Morrison, Frank B.*	35	115,997 D	40.0%	60.0%	40.0%	60.0%
1962	464,585	221,885	Seaton, Fred A.	242,669	Morrison, Frank B.*	31	20,784 D	47.8%	52.2%	47.8%	52.2%
1960	598,971	287,302	Cooper, John R.	311,344	Morrison, Frank B.	325	24,042 D	48.0%	52.0%	48.0%	52.0%
1958	421,067	209,705	Anderson, Victor E.*	211,345	Brooks, Ralph G.	17	1,640 D	49.8%	50.2%	49.8%	50.2%
1956	567,916	308,285	Anderson, Victor E.*	228,048	Sorrell, Frank	31,583	80,237 R	54.3%	40.2%	57.5%	42.5%
1954	414,841	250,080	Anderson, Victor E.	164,753	Ritchie, William	8	85,327 R	60.3%	39.7%	60.3%	39.7%
1952	594,814	365,409	Crosby, Robert B.	229,400	Raecke, Walter R.	5	136,009 R	61.4%	38.6%	61.4%	38.6%
1950	449,728	247,089	Peterson, Val*	202,638	Raecke, Walter R.	1	44,451 R	54.9%	45.1%	54.9%	45.1%
1948	476,352	286,119	Peterson, Val*	190,214	Sorrell, Frank	19	95,905 R	60.1%	39.9%	60.1%	39.9%
1946	380,835	249,468	Peterson, Val	131,367	Sorrell, Frank		118,101 R	65.5%	34.5%	65.5%	34.5%

Note: An asterisk (*) denotes incumbent. **The term of office of Nebraska's governor was increased from two to four years effective with the 1966 election.

POSTWAR VOTE FOR SENATOR

		Republican		Democratic		Other Vote	Rep.-Dem. Plurality	Percentage			
								Total Vote		Major Vote	
Year	Total Vote	Vote	Candidate	Vote	Candidate			Rep.	Dem.	Rep.	Dem.
2012	788,572	455,593	Fischer, Deb	332,979	Kerrey, Bob		122,614 R	57.8%	42.2%	57.8%	42.2%
2008	792,511	455,854	Johanns, Mike	317,456	Kleeb, Scott	19,201	138,398 R	57.5%	40.1%	58.9%	41.1%
2006	592,316	213,928	Ricketts, Pete	378,388	Nelson, Earl "Ben"*		164,460 D	36.1%	63.9%	36.1%	63.9%
2002	480,217	397,438	Hagel, Chuck*	70,290	Matulka, Charlie A.	12,489	327,148 R	82.8%	14.6%	85.0%	15.0%
2000	692,344	337,967	Stenberg, Don	353,097	Nelson, Earl "Ben"	1,280	15,130 D	48.8%	51.0%	48.9%	51.1%
1996	676,789	379,933	Hagel, Chuck	281,904	Nelson, Earl "Ben"	14,952	98,029 R	56.1%	41.7%	57.4%	42.6%
1994	579,205	260,668	Stoney, Jan	317,297	Kerrey, Bob*	1,240	56,629 D	45.0%	54.8%	45.1%	54.9%
1990	593,828	243,013	Daub, Harold J.	349,779	Exon, J. J.*	1,036	106,766 D	40.9%	58.9%	41.0%	59.0%
1988	667,860	278,250	Karnes, David	378,717	Kerrey, Bob	10,893	100,467 D	41.7%	56.7%	42.4%	57.6%
1984	639,668	307,147	Hoch, Nancy	332,217	Exon, J. J.*	304	25,070 D	48.0%	51.9%	48.0%	52.0%
1982	545,647	155,760	Keck, Jim	363,350	Zorinsky, Edward*	26,537	207,590 D	28.5%	66.6%	30.0%	70.0%
1978	494,368	159,806	Shasteen, Donald	334,276	Exon, J. J.	286	174,470 D	32.3%	67.6%	32.3%	67.7%
1976	598,314	284,284	McCollister, John Y.	313,809	Zorinsky, Edward	221	29,525 D	47.5%	52.4%	47.5%	52.5%
1972	568,580	301,841	Curtis, Carl T.*	265,922	Carpenter, Terry	817	35,919 R	53.1%	46.8%	53.2%	46.8%
1970	458,966	240,894	Hruska, Roman L.*	217,681	Morrison, Frank B.	391	23,213 R	52.5%	47.4%	52.5%	47.5%
1966	485,101	296,116	Curtis, Carl T.*	187,950	Morrison, Frank B.	1,035	108,166 R	61.0%	38.7%	61.2%	38.8%
1964	563,401	345,772	Hruska, Roman L.*	217,605	Arndt, Raymond W.	24	128,167 R	61.4%	38.6%	61.4%	38.6%
1960	598,743	352,748	Curtis, Carl T.*	245,837	Conrad, Robert B.	158	106,911 R	58.9%	41.1%	58.9%	41.1%
1958	417,385	232,227	Hruska, Roman L.*	185,152	Morrison, Frank B.	6	47,075 R	55.6%	44.4%	55.6%	44.4%
1954	418,691	255,695	Curtis, Carl T.	162,990	Neville, Keith	6	92,705 R	61.1%	38.9%	61.1%	38.9%
1954S	411,225	250,341	Hruska, Roman L.	160,881	Green, James F.	3	89,460 R	60.9%	39.1%	60.9%	39.1%
1952	591,749	408,971	Butler, Hugh*	164,660	Long, Stanley D.	18,118	244,311 R	69.1%	27.8%	71.3%	28.7%
1952S	581,750	369,841	Griswold, Dwight	211,898	Ritchie, William	11	157,943 R	63.6%	36.4%	63.6%	36.4%
1948	471,895	267,575	Wherry, Kenneth S.*	204,320	Carpenter, Terry		63,255 R	56.7%	43.3%	56.7%	43.3%
1946	382,959	271,208	Butler, Hugh*	111,751	Mekota, John E.		159,457 R	70.8%	29.2%	70.8%	29.2%

Note: An asterisk (*) denotes incumbent. **One each of the 1952 and 1954 elections was for a short term to fill a vacancy.

NEBRASKA

PRESIDENT 2012

2010 Census Population	County	Total Vote	Republican (Romney)	Democratic (Obama)	Other	Rep.-Dem. Plurality	Percentage			
							Total Vote		Major Vote	
							Rep.	Dem.	Rep.	Dem.
31,364	ADAMS	12,670	8,316	4,062	292	4,254 R	65.6%	32.1%	67.2%	32.8%
6,685	ANTELOPE	3,232	2,596	571	65	2,025 R	80.3%	17.7%	82.0%	18.0%
460	ARTHUR	262	227	30	5	197 R	86.6%	11.5%	88.3%	11.7%
690	BANNER	411	346	55	10	291 R	84.2%	13.4%	86.3%	13.7%
478	BLAINE	303	268	29	6	239 R	88.4%	9.6%	90.2%	9.8%
5,505	BOONE	2,806	2,138	615	53	1,523 R	76.2%	21.9%	77.7%	22.3%
11,308	BOX BUTTE	4,705	2,869	1,692	144	1,177 R	61.0%	36.0%	62.9%	37.1%
2,099	BOYD	1,071	873	188	10	685 R	81.5%	17.6%	82.3%	17.7%
3,145	BROWN	1,555	1,302	224	29	1,078 R	83.7%	14.4%	85.3%	14.7%
46,102	BUFFALO	19,453	13,570	5,365	518	8,205 R	69.8%	27.6%	71.7%	28.3%
6,858	BURT	3,375	2,029	1,291	55	738 R	60.1%	38.3%	61.1%	38.9%
8,395	BUTLER	3,859	2,738	1,045	76	1,693 R	71.0%	27.1%	72.4%	27.6%
25,241	CASS	12,180	7,556	4,367	257	3,189 R	62.0%	35.9%	63.4%	36.6%
8,852	CEDAR	4,334	3,278	958	98	2,320 R	75.6%	22.1%	77.4%	22.6%
3,966	CHASE	1,867	1,584	254	29	1,330 R	84.8%	13.6%	86.2%	13.8%
5,713	CHERRY	3,064	2,557	436	71	2,121 R	83.5%	14.2%	85.4%	14.6%
9,998	CHEYENNE	4,649	3,449	1,084	116	2,365 R	74.2%	23.3%	76.1%	23.9%
6,542	CLAY	2,947	2,232	667	48	1,565 R	75.7%	22.6%	77.0%	23.0%
10,515	COLFAX	3,069	2,051	969	49	1,082 R	66.8%	31.6%	67.9%	32.1%
9,139	CUMING	3,976	2,876	1,031	69	1,845 R	72.3%	25.9%	73.6%	26.4%
10,939	CUSTER	5,498	4,296	1,083	119	3,213 R	78.1%	19.7%	79.9%	20.1%
21,006	DAKOTA	6,136	3,094	2,922	120	172 R	50.4%	47.6%	51.4%	48.6%
9,182	DAWES	3,728	2,478	1,132	118	1,346 R	66.5%	30.4%	68.6%	31.4%
24,326	DAWSON	7,859	5,460	2,199	200	3,261 R	69.5%	28.0%	71.3%	28.7%
1,941	DEUEL	1,017	763	215	39	548 R	75.0%	21.1%	78.0%	22.0%
6,000	DIXON	2,686	1,745	870	71	875 R	65.0%	32.4%	66.7%	33.3%
36,691	DODGE	14,950	8,995	5,673	282	3,322 R	60.2%	37.9%	61.3%	38.7%
517,110	DOUGLAS	223,927	113,220	106,456	4,251	6,764 R	50.6%	47.5%	51.5%	48.5%
2,008	DUNDY	985	792	176	17	616 R	80.4%	17.9%	81.8%	18.2%
5,890	FILLMORE	2,879	2,007	807	65	1,200 R	69.7%	28.0%	71.3%	28.7%
3,225	FRANKLIN	1,536	1,112	384	40	728 R	72.4%	25.0%	74.3%	25.7%
2,756	FRONTIER	1,305	1,007	271	27	736 R	77.2%	20.8%	78.8%	21.2%
4,959	FURNAS	2,240	1,782	423	35	1,359 R	79.6%	18.9%	80.8%	19.2%
22,311	GAGE	9,661	5,513	3,903	245	1,610 R	57.1%	40.4%	58.5%	41.5%
2,057	GARDEN	1,091	829	242	20	587 R	76.0%	22.2%	77.4%	22.6%
2,049	GARFIELD	940	769	149	22	620 R	81.8%	15.9%	83.8%	16.2%
2,044	GOSPER	978	734	230	14	504 R	75.1%	23.5%	76.1%	23.9%
614	GRANT	363	322	30	11	292 R	88.7%	8.3%	91.5%	8.5%
2,538	GREELEY	1,185	820	340	25	480 R	69.2%	28.7%	70.7%	29.3%
58,607	HALL	20,229	12,646	7,161	422	5,485 R	62.5%	35.4%	63.8%	36.2%
9,124	HAMILTON	4,871	3,600	1,146	125	2,454 R	73.9%	23.5%	75.9%	24.1%
3,423	HARLAN	1,778	1,395	354	29	1,041 R	78.5%	19.9%	79.8%	20.2%
967	HAYES	539	476	51	12	425 R	88.3%	9.5%	90.3%	9.7%
2,908	HITCHCOCK	1,495	1,178	274	43	904 R	78.8%	18.3%	81.1%	18.9%
10,435	HOLT	4,939	3,922	882	135	3,040 R	79.4%	17.9%	81.6%	18.4%
736	HOOKER	395	330	59	6	271 R	83.5%	14.9%	84.8%	15.2%
6,274	HOWARD	2,870	1,890	914	66	976 R	65.9%	31.8%	67.4%	32.6%
7,547	JEFFERSON	3,446	2,166	1,195	85	971 R	62.9%	34.7%	64.4%	35.6%
5,217	JOHNSON	2,063	1,225	790	48	435 R	59.4%	38.3%	60.8%	39.2%
6,489	KEARNEY	3,180	2,349	773	58	1,576 R	73.9%	24.3%	75.2%	24.8%
8,368	KEITH	4,058	3,044	928	86	2,116 R	75.0%	22.9%	76.6%	23.4%
824	KEYA PAHA	484	393	80	11	313 R	81.2%	16.5%	83.1%	16.9%
3,821	KIMBALL	1,687	1,235	395	57	840 R	73.2%	23.4%	75.8%	24.2%
8,701	KNOX	4,036	2,885	1,059	92	1,826 R	71.5%	26.2%	73.1%	26.9%
285,407	LANCASTER	127,355	62,434	62,015	2,906	419 R	49.0%	48.7%	50.2%	49.8%
36,288	LINCOLN	15,655	10,728	4,450	477	6,278 R	68.5%	28.4%	70.7%	29.3%
763	LOGAN	431	356	68	7	288 R	82.6%	15.8%	84.0%	16.0%
632	LOUP	358	290	62	6	228 R	81.0%	17.3%	82.4%	17.6%
34,876	MADISON	13,885	10,062	3,485	338	6,577 R	72.5%	25.1%	74.3%	25.7%
539	MCPHERSON	291	237	41	13	196 R	81.4%	14.1%	85.3%	14.7%

NEBRASKA

PRESIDENT 2012

2010 Census Population	County	Total Vote	Republican (Romney)	Democratic (Obama)	Other	Rep.-Dem. Plurality	Percentage			
							Total Vote		Major Vote	
							Rep.	Dem.	Rep.	Dem.
7,845	MERRICK	3,489	2,490	925	74	1,565 R	71.4%	26.5%	72.9%	27.1%
5,042	MORRILL	2,190	1,681	455	54	1,226 R	76.8%	20.8%	78.7%	21.3%
3,735	NANCE	1,621	1,106	481	34	625 R	68.2%	29.7%	69.7%	30.3%
7,248	NEMAHA	3,214	2,012	1,128	74	884 R	62.6%	35.1%	64.1%	35.9%
4,500	NUCKOLLS	2,191	1,574	568	49	1,006 R	71.8%	25.9%	73.5%	26.5%
15,740	OTOE	6,982	4,258	2,561	163	1,697 R	61.0%	36.7%	62.4%	37.6%
2,773	PAWNEE	1,341	899	400	42	499 R	67.0%	29.8%	69.2%	30.8%
2,970	PERKINS	1,394	1,135	238	21	897 R	81.4%	17.1%	82.7%	17.3%
9,188	PHELPS	4,380	3,400	880	100	2,520 R	77.6%	20.1%	79.4%	20.6%
7,266	PIERCE	3,431	2,707	637	87	2,070 R	78.9%	18.6%	81.0%	19.0%
32,237	PLATTE	13,473	10,061	3,148	264	6,913 R	74.7%	23.4%	76.2%	23.8%
5,406	POLK	2,457	1,890	528	39	1,362 R	76.9%	21.5%	78.2%	21.8%
11,055	RED WILLOW	4,936	3,891	952	93	2,939 R	78.8%	19.3%	80.3%	19.7%
8,363	RICHARDSON	3,739	2,443	1,191	105	1,252 R	65.3%	31.9%	67.2%	32.8%
1,526	ROCK	789	672	103	14	569 R	85.2%	13.1%	86.7%	13.3%
14,200	SALINE	4,958	2,557	2,289	112	268 R	51.6%	46.2%	52.8%	47.2%
158,840	SARPY	71,490	43,213	26,671	1,606	16,542 R	60.4%	37.3%	61.8%	38.2%
20,780	SAUNDERS	10,312	6,770	3,307	235	3,463 R	65.7%	32.1%	67.2%	32.8%
36,970	SCOTTS BLUFF	14,287	9,648	4,327	312	5,321 R	67.5%	30.3%	69.0%	31.0%
16,750	SEWARD	7,573	5,003	2,386	184	2,617 R	66.1%	31.5%	67.7%	32.3%
5,469	SHERIDAN	2,472	2,021	390	61	1,631 R	81.8%	15.8%	83.8%	16.2%
3,152	SHERMAN	1,530	927	552	51	375 R	60.6%	36.1%	62.7%	37.3%
1,311	SIOUX	739	624	101	14	523 R	84.4%	13.7%	86.1%	13.9%
6,129	STANTON	2,644	1,949	614	81	1,335 R	73.7%	23.2%	76.0%	24.0%
5,228	THAYER	2,659	1,874	728	57	1,146 R	70.5%	27.4%	72.0%	28.0%
647	THOMAS	408	360	42	6	318 R	88.2%	10.3%	89.6%	10.4%
6,940	THURSTON	2,215	939	1,247	29	308 D	42.4%	56.3%	43.0%	57.0%
4,260	VALLEY	2,195	1,657	498	40	1,159 R	75.5%	22.7%	76.9%	23.1%
20,234	WASHINGTON	10,246	6,899	3,132	215	3,767 R	67.3%	30.6%	68.8%	31.2%
9,595	WAYNE	3,682	2,493	1,074	115	1,419 R	67.7%	29.2%	69.9%	30.1%
3,812	WEBSTER	1,742	1,258	442	42	816 R	72.2%	25.4%	74.0%	26.0%
818	WHEELER	448	345	93	10	252 R	77.0%	20.8%	78.8%	21.2%
13,665	YORK	6,355	4,874	1,373	108	3,501 R	76.7%	21.6%	78.0%	22.0%
1,826,341	TOTAL	794,379	475,064	302,081	17,234	172,983 R	59.8%	38.0%	61.1%	38.9%

NEBRASKA

SENATOR 2012

2010 Census Population	County	Total Vote	Republican (Fischer)	Democratic (Kerrey)	Other	Rep.-Dem. Plurality	Percentage			
							Total Vote		Major Vote	
							Rep.	Dem.	Rep.	Dem.
31,364	ADAMS	12,638	8,170	4,468		3,702 R	64.6%	35.4%	64.6%	35.4%
6,685	ANTELOPE	3,228	2,625	603		2,022 R	81.3%	18.7%	81.3%	18.7%
460	ARTHUR	264	229	35		194 R	86.7%	13.3%	86.7%	13.3%
690	BANNER	411	349	62		287 R	84.9%	15.1%	84.9%	15.1%
478	BLAINE	297	265	32		233 R	89.2%	10.8%	89.2%	10.8%
5,505	BOONE	2,803	2,139	664		1,475 R	76.3%	23.7%	76.3%	23.7%
11,308	BOX BUTTE	4,698	2,838	1,860		978 R	60.4%	39.6%	60.4%	39.6%
2,099	BOYD	1,059	851	208		643 R	80.4%	19.6%	80.4%	19.6%
3,145	BROWN	1,546	1,342	204		1,138 R	86.8%	13.2%	86.8%	13.2%
46,102	BUFFALO	19,270	13,491	5,779		7,712 R	70.0%	30.0%	70.0%	30.0%

NEBRASKA

SENATOR 2012

2010 Census Population	County	Total Vote	Republican (Fischer)	Democratic (Kerrey)	Other	Rep.-Dem. Plurality	Percentage			
							Total Vote		Major Vote	
							Rep.	Dem.	Rep.	Dem.
6,858	BURT	3,320	1,977	1,343		634 R	59.5%	40.5%	59.5%	40.5%
8,395	BUTLER	3,837	2,642	1,195		1,447 R	68.9%	31.1%	68.9%	31.1%
25,241	CASS	12,072	7,153	4,919		2,234 R	59.3%	40.7%	59.3%	40.7%
8,852	CEDAR	4,325	3,041	1,284		1,757 R	70.3%	29.7%	70.3%	29.7%
3,966	CHASE	1,850	1,546	304		1,242 R	83.6%	16.4%	83.6%	16.4%
5,713	CHERRY	2,988	2,328	660		1,668 R	77.9%	22.1%	77.9%	22.1%
9,998	CHEYENNE	4,610	3,344	1,266		2,078 R	72.5%	27.5%	72.5%	27.5%
6,542	CLAY	2,944	2,194	750		1,444 R	74.5%	25.5%	74.5%	25.5%
10,515	COLFAX	3,054	1,992	1,062		930 R	65.2%	34.8%	65.2%	34.8%
9,139	CUMING	3,963	2,893	1,070		1,823 R	73.0%	27.0%	73.0%	27.0%
10,939	CUSTER	5,495	4,439	1,056		3,383 R	80.8%	19.2%	80.8%	19.2%
21,006	DAKOTA	6,070	2,770	3,300		530 D	45.6%	54.4%	45.6%	54.4%
9,182	DAWES	3,708	2,405	1,303		1,102 R	64.9%	35.1%	64.9%	35.1%
24,326	DAWSON	7,797	5,422	2,375		3,047 R	69.5%	30.5%	69.5%	30.5%
1,941	DEUEL	1,016	762	254		508 R	75.0%	25.0%	75.0%	25.0%
6,000	DIXON	2,687	1,618	1,069		549 R	60.2%	39.8%	60.2%	39.8%
36,691	DODGE	14,879	8,823	6,056		2,767 R	59.3%	40.7%	59.3%	40.7%
517,110	DOUGLAS	221,651	106,951	114,700		7,749 D	48.3%	51.7%	48.3%	51.7%
2,008	DUNDY	979	767	212		555 R	78.3%	21.7%	78.3%	21.7%
5,890	FILLMORE	2,855	1,918	937		981 R	67.2%	32.8%	67.2%	32.8%
3,225	FRANKLIN	1,525	1,107	418		689 R	72.6%	27.4%	72.6%	27.4%
2,756	FRONTIER	1,307	1,008	299		709 R	77.1%	22.9%	77.1%	22.9%
4,959	FURNAS	2,233	1,729	504		1,225 R	77.4%	22.6%	77.4%	22.6%
22,311	GAGE	9,624	5,172	4,452		720 R	53.7%	46.3%	53.7%	46.3%
2,057	GARDEN	1,081	819	262		557 R	75.8%	24.2%	75.8%	24.2%
2,049	GARFIELD	944	774	170		604 R	82.0%	18.0%	82.0%	18.0%
2,044	GOSPER	980	738	242		496 R	75.3%	24.7%	75.3%	24.7%
614	GRANT	358	299	59		240 R	83.5%	16.5%	83.5%	16.5%
2,538	GREELEY	1,188	827	361		466 R	69.6%	30.4%	69.6%	30.4%
58,607	HALL	20,140	12,350	7,790		4,560 R	61.3%	38.7%	61.3%	38.7%
9,124	HAMILTON	4,840	3,498	1,342		2,156 R	72.3%	27.7%	72.3%	27.7%
3,423	HARLAN	1,757	1,329	428		901 R	75.6%	24.4%	75.6%	24.4%
967	HAYES	533	445	88		357 R	83.5%	16.5%	83.5%	16.5%
2,908	HITCHCOCK	1,483	1,112	371		741 R	75.0%	25.0%	75.0%	25.0%
10,435	HOLT	4,921	3,896	1,025		2,871 R	79.2%	20.8%	79.2%	20.8%
736	HOOKER	402	333	69		264 R	82.8%	17.2%	82.8%	17.2%
6,274	HOWARD	2,866	1,940	926		1,014 R	67.7%	32.3%	67.7%	32.3%
7,547	JEFFERSON	3,418	2,052	1,366		686 R	60.0%	40.0%	60.0%	40.0%
5,217	JOHNSON	2,057	1,147	910		237 R	55.8%	44.2%	55.8%	44.2%
6,489	KEARNEY	3,163	2,343	820		1,523 R	74.1%	25.9%	74.1%	25.9%
8,368	KEITH	4,051	2,988	1,063		1,925 R	73.8%	26.2%	73.8%	26.2%
824	KEYA PAHA	481	407	74		333 R	84.6%	15.4%	84.6%	15.4%
3,821	KIMBALL	1,680	1,233	447		786 R	73.4%	26.6%	73.4%	26.6%
8,701	KNOX	4,027	2,880	1,147		1,733 R	71.5%	28.5%	71.5%	28.5%
285,407	LANCASTER	126,352	58,306	68,046		9,740 D	46.1%	53.9%	46.1%	53.9%
36,288	LINCOLN	15,583	10,285	5,298		4,987 R	66.0%	34.0%	66.0%	34.0%
763	LOGAN	433	357	76		281 R	82.4%	17.6%	82.4%	17.6%
632	LOUP	357	281	76		205 R	78.7%	21.3%	78.7%	21.3%
34,876	MADISON	13,835	10,089	3,746		6,343 R	72.9%	27.1%	72.9%	27.1%
539	MCPHERSON	293	253	40		213 R	86.3%	13.7%	86.3%	13.7%
7,845	MERRICK	3,487	2,491	996		1,495 R	71.4%	28.6%	71.4%	28.6%
5,042	MORRILL	2,197	1,675	522		1,153 R	76.2%	23.8%	76.2%	23.8%
3,735	NANCE	1,608	1,068	540		528 R	66.4%	33.6%	66.4%	33.6%
7,248	NEMAHA	3,217	1,901	1,316		585 R	59.1%	40.9%	59.1%	40.9%
4,500	NUCKOLLS	2,182	1,532	650		882 R	70.2%	29.8%	70.2%	29.8%
15,740	OTOE	6,943	4,067	2,876		1,191 R	58.6%	41.4%	58.6%	41.4%
2,773	PAWNEE	1,343	861	482		379 R	64.1%	35.9%	64.1%	35.9%
2,970	PERKINS	1,388	1,091	297		794 R	78.6%	21.4%	78.6%	21.4%
9,188	PHELPS	4,374	3,368	1,006		2,362 R	77.0%	23.0%	77.0%	23.0%
7,266	PIERCE	3,414	2,716	698		2,018 R	79.6%	20.4%	79.6%	20.4%

NEBRASKA

SENATOR 2012

2010 Census Population	County	Total Vote	Republican (Fischer)	Democratic (Kerrey)	Other	Rep.-Dem. Plurality	Percentage			
							Total Vote		Major Vote	
							Rep.	Dem.	Rep.	Dem.
32,237	PLATTE	13,402	9,801	3,601		6,200 R	73.1%	26.9%	73.1%	26.9%
5,406	POLK	2,438	1,820	618		1,202 R	74.7%	25.3%	74.7%	25.3%
11,055	RED WILLOW	4,906	3,692	1,214		2,478 R	75.3%	24.7%	75.3%	24.7%
8,363	RICHARDSON	3,724	2,312	1,412		900 R	62.1%	37.9%	62.1%	37.9%
1,526	ROCK	786	683	103		580 R	86.9%	13.1%	86.9%	13.1%
14,200	SALINE	4,942	2,387	2,555		168 D	48.3%	51.7%	48.3%	51.7%
158,840	SARPY	70,678	40,682	29,996		10,686 R	57.6%	42.4%	57.6%	42.4%
20,780	SAUNDERS	10,275	6,547	3,728		2,819 R	63.7%	36.3%	63.7%	36.3%
36,970	SCOTTS BLUFF	14,316	9,299	5,017		4,282 R	65.0%	35.0%	65.0%	35.0%
16,750	SEWARD	7,540	4,764	2,776		1,988 R	63.2%	36.8%	63.2%	36.8%
5,469	SHERIDAN	2,475	1,986	489		1,497 R	80.2%	19.8%	80.2%	19.8%
3,152	SHERMAN	1,519	960	559		401 R	63.2%	36.8%	63.2%	36.8%
1,311	SIOUX	731	605	126		479 R	82.8%	17.2%	82.8%	17.2%
6,129	STANTON	2,639	1,979	660		1,319 R	75.0%	25.0%	75.0%	25.0%
5,228	THAYER	2,648	1,742	906		836 R	65.8%	34.2%	65.8%	34.2%
647	THOMAS	413	352	61		291 R	85.2%	14.8%	85.2%	14.8%
6,940	THURSTON	2,229	900	1,329		429 D	40.4%	59.6%	40.4%	59.6%
4,260	VALLEY	2,193	1,599	594		1,005 R	72.9%	27.1%	72.9%	27.1%
20,234	WASHINGTON	10,165	6,660	3,505		3,155 R	65.5%	34.5%	65.5%	34.5%
9,595	WAYNE	3,677	2,484	1,193		1,291 R	67.6%	32.4%	67.6%	32.4%
3,812	WEBSTER	1,727	1,203	524		679 R	69.7%	30.3%	69.7%	30.3%
818	WHEELER	450	359	91		268 R	79.8%	20.2%	79.8%	20.2%
13,665	YORK	6,320	4,726	1,594		3,132 R	74.8%	25.2%	74.8%	25.2%
1,826,341	TOTAL	788,572	455,593	332,979		122,614 R	57.8%	42.2%	57.8%	42.2%

NEBRASKA

HOUSE OF REPRESENTATIVES

CD	Year	Total Vote	Republican		Democratic		Other Vote	Rep.-Dem. Plurality	Percentage			
			Vote	Candidate	Vote	Candidate			Total Vote		Major Vote	
									Rep.	Dem.	Rep.	Dem.
1	2012	256,095	174,889	FORTENBERRY, JEFF*	81,206	REIMAN, KOREY L.		93,683 R	68.3%	31.7%	68.3%	31.7%
2	2012	263,731	133,964	TERRY, LEE*	129,767	EWING, JOHN W. JR.		4,197 R	50.8%	49.2%	50.8%	49.2%
3	2012	252,689	187,423	SMITH, ADRIAN*	65,266	SULLIVAN, MARK		122,157 R	74.2%	25.8%	74.2%	25.8%
TOTAL	2012	772,515	496,276		276,239			220,037 R	64.2%	35.8%	64.2%	35.8%

Note: An asterisk (*) denotes incumbent.

NEBRASKA

GENERAL AND PRIMARY ELECTIONS

GENERAL ELECTIONS: OTHER VOTE

President   Other vote was 11,109 Libertarian (Gary E. Johnson), 3,717 Write-in (Scattered Write-In), 2,408 Independent (Randall Terry)

PRIMARY ELECTIONS: SUPPLEMENTARY INFORMATION

Primary	May 15, 2012	**Registration** (as of May 15, 2012)	1,136,365	Republican	547,366
				Democratic	368,129
				Libertarian	2,054
				Americans Elect	12
				Nonpartisan	218,804

Primary Type   Semi-open—Registered Democrats and Republicans could vote only in their party's primary. Voters registered as Nonpartisan could participate in either party's primary for the Senate and House (but not for president).

	REPUBLICAN PRIMARIES			**DEMOCRATIC PRIMARIES**		
President	Romney, W. Mitt	131,436	70.9%	Obama, Barack H.*	63,881	100.0%
	Santorum, Rick	25,830	13.9%			
	Paul, Ron	18,508	10.0%			
	Gingrich, Newt	9,628	5.2%			
	TOTAL	*185,402*		*TOTAL*	*63,881*	
Senator	Fischer, Deb	79,941	41.0%	Kerrey, Bob	66,586	81.0%
	Bruning, Jon	70,067	35.9%	Hassebrook, Chuck	9,886	12.0%
	Stenberg, Don	36,727	18.8%	Lustgarten, Steven P.	2,177	2.6%
	Flynn, Pat	5,413	2.8%	Marvin, Larry	2,076	2.5%
	Zimmerman, Spencer	1,601	0.8%	Yates, Sherman	1,500	1.8%
	Elander, Sharyn	1,294	0.7%			
	TOTAL	*195,043*		*TOTAL*	*82,225*	
Congressional District 1	Fortenberry, Jeff*	55,658	86.4%	Reiman, Korey L.	14,804	62.9%
	Turek, Jessica Lynn	5,255	8.2%	Way, Robert	8,728	37.1%
	Parker, Dennis L.	3,511	5.4%			
	TOTAL	*64,424*		*TOTAL*	*23,532*	
Congressional District 2	Terry, Lee*	27,998	59.5%	Ewing, John W. Jr.	17,954	62.0%
	Lindstrom, Brett	10,753	22.8%	Howard, Gwen	11,009	38.0%
	Heidel, Jack	5,406	11.5%			
	Freeman, Glenn M.	1,885	4.0%			
	Anderson, Paul	1,051	2.2%			
	TOTAL	*47,093*		*TOTAL*	*28,963*	
Congressional District 3	Smith, Adrian*	62,645	81.4%	Sullivan, Mark	17,500	100.0%
	Lingenfelter, Bob	14,297	18.6%			
	TOTAL	*76,942*		*TOTAL*	*17,500*	

Notes: An asterisk (*) denotes incumbent. Ballots cast by Nonpartisan voters in party primaries for the House and Senate were tallied separately but were combined into an overall total for each candidate, which is listed here.

NEVADA

Congressional districts first established for elections held in 2012

4 members

The city of Carson City is an independent city that is treated as a county equivalent; the label is included only for the city.

* Asterisk indicates a county whose boundaries include parts of two or more Congressional districts.

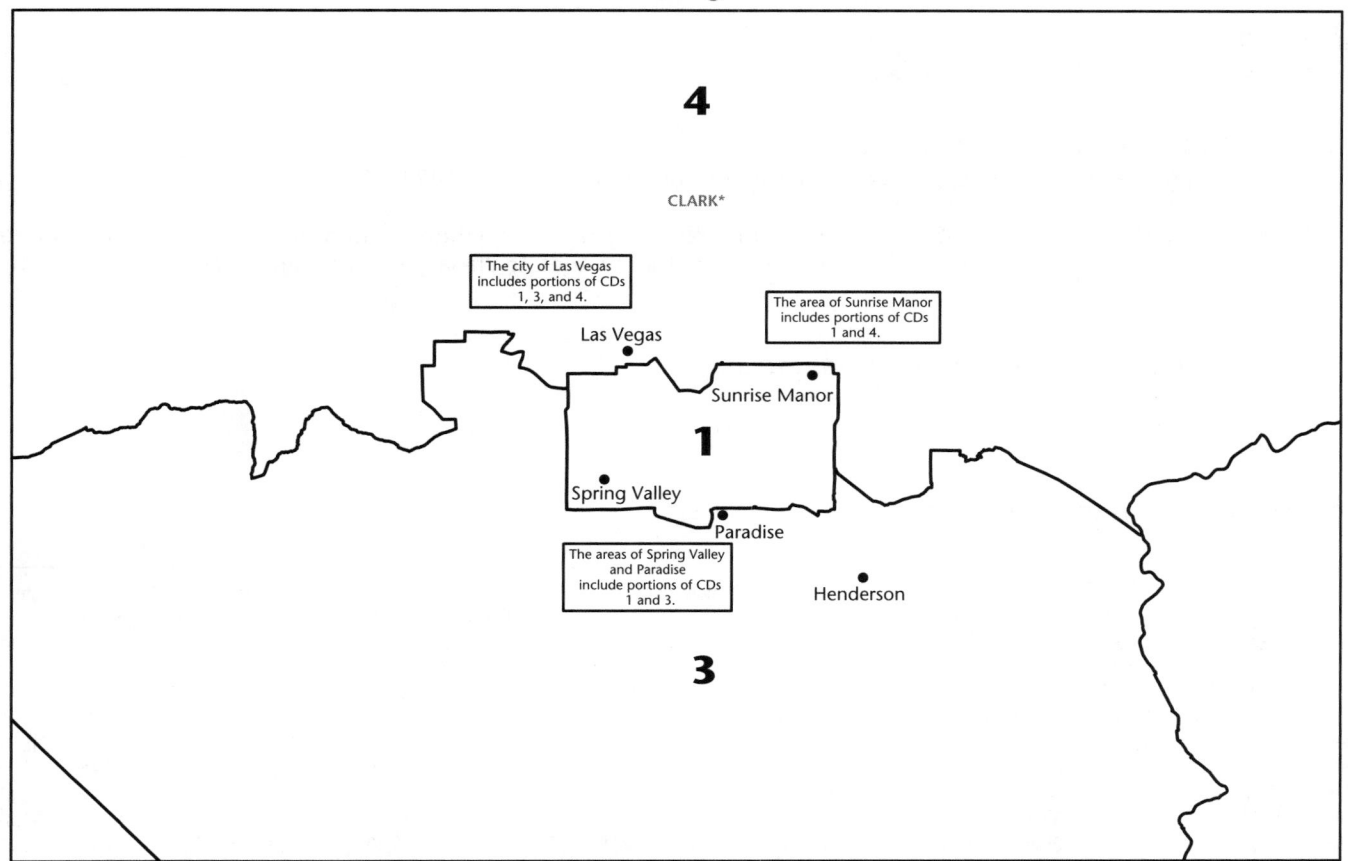

NEVADA
Greater Las Vegas Area

4

CLARK*

The city of Las Vegas
includes portions of CDs
1, 3, and 4.

The area of Sunrise Manor
includes portions of CDs
1 and 4.

Las Vegas

Sunrise Manor

1

Spring Valley

Paradise

The areas of Spring Valley
and Paradise
include portions of CDs
1 and 3.

Henderson

3

* Asterisk indicates a county whose boundaries include parts of two or more Congressional districts.

NEVADA

GOVERNOR
Brian Sandoval (R). Elected 2010 to a four-year term.

SENATORS (1 Republican, 1 Democrat)
Harry Reid (D). Reelected 2010 to a six-year term. Previously elected 2004, 1998, 1992, 1986.

Dean Heller (R). Sworn into office May 9, 2011, following the resignation of John Ensign (R), who was under investigation by the Senate Ethics Committee as to whether he tried to illegally cover up an extramarital affair with a former staff member.

REPRESENTATIVES (2 Republicans, 2 Democrats)
1. Dina Titus (D)
2. Mark Amodei (R)
3. Joe Heck (R)
4. Steven Horsford (D)

POSTWAR VOTE FOR PRESIDENT

		Republican		Democratic		Other	Rep.-Dem.	Total Vote		Major Vote	
Year	Total Vote	Vote	Candidate	Vote	Candidate	Vote	Plurality	Rep.	Dem.	Rep.	Dem.
2012	1,014,918	463,567	Romney, W. Mitt	531,373	Obama, Barack H.*	19,978	67,806 D	45.7%	52.4%	46.6%	53.4%
2008	967,848	412,827	McCain, John S. III	533,736	Obama, Barack H.	21,285	120,909 D	42.7%	55.1%	43.6%	56.4%
2004	829,587	418,690	Bush, George W.*	397,190	Kerry, John F.	13,707	21,500 R	50.5%	47.9%	51.3%	48.7%
2000**	608,970	301,575	Bush, George W.	279,978	Gore, Albert Jr.	27,417	21,597 R	49.5%	46.0%	51.9%	48.1%
1996**	464,279	199,244	Dole, Robert "Bob"	203,974	Clinton, Bill*	61,061	4,730 D	42.9%	43.9%	49.4%	50.6%
1992**	506,318	175,828	Bush, George H.*	189,148	Clinton, Bill	141,342	13,320 D	34.7%	37.4%	48.2%	51.8%
1988	350,067	206,040	Bush, George H.	132,738	Dukakis, Michael S.	11,289	73,302 R	58.9%	37.9%	60.8%	39.2%
1984	286,667	188,770	Reagan, Ronald*	91,655	Mondale, Walter F.	6,242	97,115 R	65.8%	32.0%	67.3%	32.7%
1980**	247,885	155,017	Reagan, Ronald	66,666	Carter, Jimmy*	26,202	88,351 R	62.5%	26.9%	69.9%	30.1%
1976	201,876	101,273	Ford, Gerald R.*	92,479	Carter, Jimmy	8,124	8,794 R	50.2%	45.8%	52.3%	47.7%
1972	181,766	115,750	Nixon, Richard M.*	66,016	McGovern, George S.		49,734 R	63.7%	36.3%	63.7%	36.3%
1968**	154,218	73,188	Nixon, Richard M.	60,598	Humphrey, Hubert H. Jr.	20,432	12,590 R	47.5%	39.3%	54.7%	45.3%
1964	135,433	56,094	Goldwater, Barry M. Sr.	79,339	Johnson, Lyndon B.*		23,245 D	41.4%	58.6%	41.4%	58.6%
1960	107,267	52,387	Nixon, Richard M.	54,880	Kennedy, John F.		2,493 D	48.8%	51.2%	48.8%	51.2%
1956	96,689	56,049	Eisenhower, Dwight D.*	40,640	Stevenson, Adlai E. II		15,409 R	58.0%	42.0%	58.0%	42.0%
1952	82,190	50,502	Eisenhower, Dwight D.	31,688	Stevenson, Adlai E. II		18,814 R	61.4%	38.6%	61.4%	38.6%
1948	62,117	29,357	Dewey, Thomas E.	31,291	Truman, Harry S.*	1,469	1,934 D	47.3%	50.4%	48.4%	51.6%

Note: An asterisk (*) denotes incumbent. **In past elections, the other vote included: 2000 - 15,008 Green (Ralph Nader); 1996 - 43,986 Reform (Ross Perot); 1992 - 132,580 Independent (Perot); 1980 - 17,651 Independent (John Anderson); 1968 - 20,432 American Independent (George Wallace).

NEVADA

POSTWAR VOTE FOR GOVERNOR

Year	Total Vote	Republican Vote	Candidate	Democratic Vote	Candidate	Other Vote	Rep.-Dem. Plurality	Total Vote Rep.	Dem.	Major Vote Rep.	Dem.
2010	716,529	382,350	Sandoval, Brian	298,171	Reid, Rory	36,008	84,179 R	53.4%	41.6%	56.2%	43.8%
2006	582,158	279,003	Gibbons, Jim	255,684	Titus, Dina	47,471	23,319 R	47.9%	43.9%	52.2%	47.8%
2002	504,079	344,001	Guinn, Kenny*	110,935	Neal, Joe	49,143	233,066 R	68.2%	22.0%	75.6%	24.4%
1998	433,630	223,892	Guinn, Kenny	182,281	Jones, Jan Laverty	27,457	41,611 R	51.6%	42.0%	55.1%	44.9%
1994	379,676	156,875	Gibbons, Jim	200,026	Miller, Robert J.*	22,775	43,151 D	41.3%	52.7%	44.0%	56.0%
1990	320,743	95,789	Gallaway, Jim	207,878	Miller, Robert J.*	17,076	112,089 D	29.9%	64.8%	31.5%	68.5%
1986	260,375	65,081	Cafferata, Patty	187,268	Bryan, Richard H.*	8,026	122,187 D	25.0%	71.9%	25.8%	74.2%
1982	239,751	100,104	List, Robert F.*	128,132	Bryan, Richard H.	11,515	28,028 D	41.8%	53.4%	43.9%	56.1%
1978	192,445	108,097	List, Robert F.	76,361	Rose, Robert E.	7,987	31,736 R	56.2%	39.7%	58.6%	41.4%
1974**	169,358	28,959	Crumpler, Shirley	114,114	O'Callaghan, Mike*	26,285	85,155 D	17.1%	67.4%	20.2%	79.8%
1970	146,991	64,400	Fike, Ed	70,697	O'Callaghan, Mike	11,894	6,297 D	43.8%	48.1%	47.7%	52.3%
1966	137,677	71,807	Laxalt, Paul	65,870	Sawyer, Grant*		5,937 R	52.2%	47.8%	52.2%	47.8%
1962	96,929	32,145	Gragson, Oran K.	64,784	Sawyer, Grant*		32,639 D	33.2%	66.8%	33.2%	66.8%
1958	84,889	34,025	Russell, Charles H.*	50,864	Sawyer, Grant		16,839 D	40.1%	59.9%	40.1%	59.9%
1954	78,462	41,665	Russell, Charles H.*	36,797	Pittman, Vail		4,868 R	53.1%	46.9%	53.1%	46.9%
1950	61,773	35,609	Russell, Charles H.	26,164	Pittman, Vail*		9,445 R	57.6%	42.4%	57.6%	42.4%
1946	49,902	21,247	Jepson, Melvin E.	28,655	Pittman, Vail		7,408 D	42.6%	57.4%	42.6%	57.4%

Note: An asterisk (*) denotes incumbent. **In past elections, the other vote included: 1974 - 26,285 Independent American (James Ray Houston).

POSTWAR VOTE FOR SENATOR

Year	Total Vote	Republican Vote	Candidate	Democratic Vote	Candidate	Other Vote	Rep.-Dem. Plurality	Total Vote Rep.	Dem.	Major Vote Rep.	Dem.
2012	997,805	457,656	Heller, Dean*	446,080	Berkley, Shelley	94,069	11,576 R	45.9%	44.7%	50.6%	49.4%
2010	721,404	321,361	Angle, Sharron E.	362,785	Reid, Harry*	37,258	41,424 D	44.5%	50.3%	47.0%	53.0%
2006	582,572	322,501	Ensign, John*	238,796	Carter, Jack	21,275	83,705 R	55.4%	41.0%	57.5%	42.5%
2004	810,068	284,640	Ziser, Richard	494,805	Reid, Harry*	30,623	210,165 D	35.1%	61.1%	36.5%	63.5%
2000	600,250	330,687	Ensign, John	238,260	Bernstein, Ed	31,303	92,427 R	55.1%	39.7%	58.1%	41.9%
1998	435,790	208,222	Ensign, John	208,650	Reid, Harry*	18,918	428 D	47.8%	47.9%	49.9%	50.1%
1994	380,530	156,020	Furman, Hal	193,804	Bryan, Richard H.*	30,706	37,784 D	41.0%	50.9%	44.6%	55.4%
1992	495,887	199,413	Dahl, Demar	253,150	Reid, Harry*	43,324	53,737 D	40.2%	51.0%	44.1%	55.9%
1988	349,649	161,336	Hecht, Chic*	175,548	Bryan, Richard H.	12,765	14,212 D	46.1%	50.2%	47.9%	52.1%
1986	261,932	116,606	Santini, James	130,955	Reid, Harry	14,371	14,349 D	44.5%	50.0%	47.1%	52.9%
1982	240,394	120,377	Hecht, Chic	114,720	Cannon, Howard W.*	5,297	5,657 R	50.1%	47.7%	51.2%	48.8%
1980	246,436	144,224	Laxalt, Paul*	92,129	Gojack, Mary	10,083	52,095 R	58.5%	37.4%	61.0%	39.0%
1976	201,980	63,471	Towell, David	127,295	Cannon, Howard W.*	11,214	63,824 D	31.4%	63.0%	33.3%	66.7%
1974	169,473	79,605	Laxalt, Paul	78,981	Reid, Harry	10,887	624 R	47.0%	46.6%	50.2%	49.8%
1970	147,768	60,838	Raggio, William J.	85,187	Cannon, Howard W.*	1,743	24,349 D	41.2%	57.6%	41.7%	58.3%
1968	152,690	69,068	Fike, Ed	83,622	Bible, Alan Harvey*		14,554 D	45.2%	54.8%	45.2%	54.8%
1964	134,624	67,288	Laxalt, Paul	67,336	Cannon, Howard W.*		48 D	50.0%	50.0%	50.0%	50.0%
1962	97,192	33,749	Wright, William B.	63,443	Bible, Alan Harvey*		29,694 D	34.7%	65.3%	34.7%	65.3%
1958	84,492	35,760	Malone, George W.*	48,732	Cannon, Howard W.		12,972 D	42.3%	57.7%	42.3%	57.7%
1956	96,389	45,712	Young, Cliff	50,677	Bible, Alan Harvey*		4,965 D	47.4%	52.6%	47.4%	52.6%
1954S	77,513	32,470	Brown, Ernest S.	45,043	Bible, Alan Harvey		12,573 D	41.9%	58.1%	41.9%	58.1%
1952	81,090	41,906	Malone, George W.*	39,184	Mechling, Thomas B.		2,722 R	51.7%	48.3%	51.7%	48.3%
1950	61,762	25,933	Marshall, George E.	35,829	McCarran, Patrick A.*		9,896 D	42.0%	58.0%	42.0%	58.0%
1946	50,354	27,801	Malone, George W.	22,553	Bunker, Berkeley L.		5,248 R	55.2%	44.8%	55.2%	44.8%

Note: An asterisk (*) denotes incumbent. **The 1954 election was for a short term to fill a vacancy.

NEVADA

PRESIDENT 2012

2010 Census Population	County	Total Vote	Republican (Romney)	Democratic (Obama)	Other	Rep.-Dem. Plurality	Percentage			
							Total Vote		Major Vote	
							Rep.	Dem.	Rep.	Dem.
55,274	CARSON CITY	23,319	12,394	10,291	634	2,103 R	53.1%	44.1%	54.6%	45.4%
24,877	CHURCHILL	10,265	7,061	2,961	243	4,100 R	68.8%	28.8%	70.5%	29.5%
1,951,269	CLARK	691,190	289,053	389,936	12,201	100,883 D	41.8%	56.4%	42.6%	57.4%
46,997	DOUGLAS	26,075	16,276	9,297	502	6,979 R	62.4%	35.7%	63.6%	36.4%
48,818	ELKO	15,986	12,014	3,511	461	8,503 R	75.2%	22.0%	77.4%	22.6%
783	ESMERALDA	435	317	92	26	225 R	72.9%	21.1%	77.5%	22.5%
1,987	EUREKA	808	663	107	38	556 R	82.1%	13.2%	86.1%	13.9%
16,528	HUMBOLDT	5,744	3,810	1,737	197	2,073 R	66.3%	30.2%	68.7%	31.3%
5,775	LANDER	2,165	1,580	534	51	1,046 R	73.0%	24.7%	74.7%	25.3%
5,345	LINCOLN	2,152	1,691	400	61	1,291 R	78.6%	18.6%	80.9%	19.1%
51,980	LYON	21,465	13,520	7,380	565	6,140 R	63.0%	34.4%	64.7%	35.3%
4,772	MINERAL	2,035	1,080	863	92	217 R	53.1%	42.4%	55.6%	44.4%
43,946	NYE	17,522	10,566	6,320	636	4,246 R	60.3%	36.1%	62.6%	37.4%
6,753	PERSHING	1,884	1,167	632	85	535 R	61.9%	33.5%	64.9%	35.1%
4,010	STOREY	2,314	1,321	920	73	401 R	57.1%	39.8%	58.9%	41.1%
421,407	WASHOE	187,855	88,453	95,409	3,993	6,956 D	47.1%	50.8%	48.1%	51.9%
10,030	WHITE PINE	3,704	2,601	983	120	1,618 R	70.2%	26.5%	72.6%	27.4%
2,700,551	TOTAL	1,014,918	463,567	531,373	19,978	67,806 D	45.7%	52.4%	46.6%	53.4%

NEVADA

SENATOR 2012

2010 Census Population	County	Total Vote	Republican (Heller)	Democratic (Berkley)	Other	Rep.-Dem. Plurality	Percentage			
							Total Vote		Major Vote	
							Rep.	Dem.	Rep.	Dem.
55,274	CARSON CITY	23,133	13,488	7,510	2,135	5,978 R	58.3%	32.5%	64.2%	35.8%
24,877	CHURCHILL	10,163	7,069	2,013	1,081	5,056 R	69.6%	19.8%	77.8%	22.2%
1,951,269	CLARK	677,692	277,459	338,629	61,604	61,170 D	40.9%	50.0%	45.0%	55.0%
46,997	DOUGLAS	25,790	16,644	6,952	2,194	9,692 R	64.5%	27.0%	70.5%	29.5%
48,818	ELKO	15,837	11,840	2,653	1,344	9,187 R	74.8%	16.8%	81.7%	18.3%
783	ESMERALDA	434	308	62	64	246 R	71.0%	14.3%	83.2%	16.8%
1,987	EUREKA	804	636	87	81	549 R	79.1%	10.8%	88.0%	12.0%
16,528	HUMBOLDT	5,691	3,876	1,124	691	2,752 R	68.1%	19.8%	77.5%	22.5%
5,775	LANDER	2,149	1,567	361	221	1,206 R	72.9%	16.8%	81.3%	18.7%
5,345	LINCOLN	2,130	1,532	347	251	1,185 R	71.9%	16.3%	81.5%	18.5%
51,980	LYON	21,273	13,703	5,404	2,166	8,299 R	64.4%	25.4%	71.7%	28.3%
4,772	MINERAL	2,020	1,059	612	349	447 R	52.4%	30.3%	63.4%	36.6%
43,946	NYE	17,266	9,561	5,267	2,438	4,294 R	55.4%	30.5%	64.5%	35.5%
6,753	PERSHING	1,858	1,194	396	268	798 R	64.3%	21.3%	75.1%	24.9%
4,010	STOREY	2,310	1,375	673	262	702 R	59.5%	29.1%	67.1%	32.9%
421,407	WASHOE	185,567	93,778	73,164	18,625	20,614 R	50.5%	39.4%	56.2%	43.8%
10,030	WHITE PINE	3,688	2,567	826	295	1,741 R	69.6%	22.4%	75.7%	24.3%
2,700,551	TOTAL	997,805	457,656	446,080	94,069	11,576 R	45.9%	44.7%	50.6%	49.4%

NEVADA

HOUSE OF REPRESENTATIVES

CD	Year	Total Vote	Republican Vote	Republican Candidate	Democratic Vote	Democratic Candidate	Other Vote	Rep.-Dem. Plurality	Total Vote Rep.	Total Vote Dem.	Major Vote Rep.	Major Vote Dem.
1	2012	179,278	56,521	EDWARDS, CHRIS	113,967	TITUS, DINA	8,790	57,446 D	31.5%	63.6%	33.2%	66.8%
2	2012	281,449	162,213	AMODEI, MARK*	102,019	KOEPNICK, SAMUEL	17,217	60,194 R	57.6%	36.2%	61.4%	38.6%
3	2012	272,523	137,244	HECK, JOE*	116,823	OCEGUERA, JOHN	18,456	20,421 R	50.4%	42.9%	54.0%	46.0%
4	2012	240,492	101,261	TARKANIAN, DANNY	120,501	HORSFORD, STEVEN	18,730	19,240 D	42.1%	50.1%	45.7%	54.3%
TOTAL	2012	973,742	457,239		453,310		63,193	3,929 R	47.0%	46.6%	50.2%	49.8%

Note: An asterisk (*) denotes incumbent.

NEVADA

GENERAL AND PRIMARY ELECTIONS

GENERAL ELECTIONS: OTHER VOTE

President Other vote was 10,968 Libertarian (Gary E. Johnson), 5,770 No Party Affiliation (None of these candidates), 3,240 Constitution (Virgil H. Goode)

Senator Other vote was 48,792 Independent American (David Lory VanderBeek), 45,277 No Party Affiliation (None of these candidates)

House Other vote was:

CD 1 4,645 Libertarian (William Bill Pojunis), 4,145 Independent American (Stan Vaughan)
CD 2 11,166 Independent (Michael L. Haines), 6,051 Independent American (Best Russell)
CD 3 12,856 Independent (Jim Murphy), 5,600 Independent American (Tom Jones)
CD 4 9,389 Independent American (Floyd Fitzgibbons), 9,341 Libertarian (Joseph Silvestri)

PRIMARY ELECTIONS: SUPPLEMENTARY INFORMATION

Primary	June 12, 2012	**Registration** (as of May 30, 2012 – includes 299,298 inactive registrants)	1,359,624	Democratic	572,866
				Republican	475,395
				Independent American	64,260
				Libertarian	8,796
				Green	4,121
				Other Parties	4,988
				Non-Partisan	229,198

Primary Type Closed—Only registered Democrats and Republicans could vote in their party's primary.

NEVADA

GENERAL AND PRIMARY ELECTIONS

	REPUBLICAN PRIMARIES			DEMOCRATIC PRIMARIES		
Senator	Heller, Dean*	88,958	86.3%	Berkley, Shelley	62,082	79.5%
	Brooks, Sherry	5,356	5.2%	Price, Nancy	4,210	5.4%
	None Of These Candidates	3,358	3.3%	Brown, Steve	3,998	5.1%
	Hamilton, Eddie ("In Liberty")	2,628	2.5%	None Of These Candidates	3,637	4.7%
	Charles, Richard	2,295	2.2%	Ellsworth, Barry	2,491	3.2%
	Poliak, Carlo	512	0.5%	Macias, Louis	1,714	2.2%
	TOTAL	*103,107*		*TOTAL*	*78,132*	
Congressional District 1	Edwards, Chris	4,786	48.2%	Titus, Dina	Unopposed	
	Landsberger, Brian	1,800	18.1%			
	Guss, Charmaine	1,534	15.5%			
	Rodrigues, Miguel "Mike"	1,163	11.7%			
	Peters, Herb	643	6.5%			
	TOTAL	*9,926*				
Congressional District 2	Amodei, Mark*	Unopposed		Koepnick, Samuel	8,865	40.5%
				Rodriguez, Xiomara "Xio"	7,405	33.9%
				Dehne, Denis "Sam"	5,604	25.6%
				TOTAL	*21,874*	
Congressional District 3	Heck, Joe*	20,798	90.1%	Oceguera, John	7,966	50.4%
	Dyer, Chris	2,298	9.9%	Frye, Stephen H.	2,659	16.8%
				Holder, Jesse Jake	2,099	13.3%
				Michaels, Barry	1,346	8.5%
				Sakura, Gerald "Jerry"	989	6.3%
				Haning, James Franklin II	736	4.7%
	TOTAL	*23,096*		*TOTAL*	*15,795*	
Congressional District 4	Tarkanian, Danny	7,605	31.5%	Horsford, Steven	Unopposed	
	Cegavske, Barbara K.	6,674	27.7%			
	Wegner, Kenneth	5,069	21.0%			
	Schwartz, Dan	2,728	11.3%			
	Hill, Kiran	666	2.8%			
	Anderson, Diana R.	607	2.5%			
	Delarosa, Mike	370	1.5%			
	Zeller, Sid	252	1.0%			
	Leeds, Robert X.	165	0.7%			
	TOTAL	*24,136*				

Notes: An asterisk (*) denotes incumbent. The names of unopposed candidates did not appear on the primary ballot; therefore, no votes were cast for these candidates.

NEW HAMPSHIRE

Congressional districts first established for elections held in 2012

2 members

* Asterisk indicates a county whose boundaries include parts of two or more Congressional districts.

NEW HAMPSHIRE

GOVERNOR
Maggie Hassan (D). Elected 2012 to a two-year term.

SENATORS (1 Republican, 1 Democrat)
Jeanne Shaheen (D). Elected 2008 to a six-year term.

Kelly Ayotte (R). Elected 2010 to a six-year term.

REPRESENTATIVES (2 Democrats)
1. Carol Shea-Porter (D)   2. Ann McLane Kuster (D)

POSTWAR VOTE FOR PRESIDENT

| | | Republican | | Democratic | | Other | Rep.-Dem. | Percentage | | | |
| | | | | | | | | Total Vote | | Major Vote | |
Year	Total Vote	Vote	Candidate	Vote	Candidate	Vote	Plurality	Rep.	Dem.	Rep.	Dem.
2012	710,972	329,918	Romney, W. Mitt	369,561	Obama, Barack H.*	11,493	39,643 D	46.4%	52.0%	47.2%	52.8%
2008	710,970	316,534	McCain, John S. III	384,826	Obama, Barack H.	9,610	68,292 D	44.5%	54.1%	45.1%	54.9%
2004	677,738	331,237	Bush, George W.*	340,511	Kerry, John F.	5,990	9,274 D	48.9%	50.2%	49.3%	50.7%
2000**	569,081	273,559	Bush, George W.	266,348	Gore, Albert Jr.	29,174	7,211 R	48.1%	46.8%	50.7%	49.3%
1996**	499,175	196,532	Dole, Robert "Bob"	246,214	Clinton, Bill*	56,429	49,682 D	39.4%	49.3%	44.4%	55.6%
1992**	537,943	202,484	Bush, George H.*	209,040	Clinton, Bill	126,419	6,556 D	37.6%	38.9%	49.2%	50.8%
1988	451,074	281,537	Bush, George H.	163,696	Dukakis, Michael S.	5,841	117,841 R	62.4%	36.3%	63.2%	36.8%
1984	389,066	267,051	Reagan, Ronald*	120,395	Mondale, Walter F.	1,620	146,656 R	68.6%	30.9%	68.9%	31.1%
1980**	383,990	221,705	Reagan, Ronald	108,864	Carter, Jimmy*	53,421	112,841 R	57.7%	28.4%	67.1%	32.9%
1976	339,618	185,935	Ford, Gerald R.*	147,635	Carter, Jimmy	6,048	38,300 R	54.7%	43.5%	55.7%	44.3%
1972	334,055	213,724	Nixon, Richard M.*	116,435	McGovern, George S.	3,896	97,289 R	64.0%	34.9%	64.7%	35.3%
1968**	297,298	154,903	Nixon, Richard M.	130,589	Humphrey, Hubert H. Jr.	11,806	24,314 R	52.1%	43.9%	54.3%	45.7%
1964	288,093	104,029	Goldwater, Barry M. Sr.	184,064	Johnson, Lyndon B.*		80,035 D	36.1%	63.9%	36.1%	63.9%
1960	295,761	157,989	Nixon, Richard M.	137,772	Kennedy, John F.		20,217 R	53.4%	46.6%	53.4%	46.6%
1956	266,994	176,519	Eisenhower, Dwight D.*	90,364	Stevenson, Adlai E. II	111	86,155 R	66.1%	33.8%	66.1%	33.9%
1952	272,950	166,287	Eisenhower, Dwight D.	106,663	Stevenson, Adlai E. II		59,624 R	60.9%	39.1%	60.9%	39.1%
1948	231,440	121,299	Dewey, Thomas E.	107,995	Truman, Harry S.*	2,146	13,304 R	52.4%	46.7%	52.9%	47.1%

Note: An asterisk (*) denotes incumbent. **In past elections, the other vote included: 2000 - 22,198 Green (Ralph Nader); 1996 - 48,390 Reform (Ross Perot); 1992 - 121,337 Independent (Perot); 1980 - 49,693 Independent (John Anderson); 1968 - 11,173 American Independent (George Wallace).

NEW HAMPSHIRE

POSTWAR VOTE FOR GOVERNOR

Year	Total Vote	Republican		Democratic		Other Vote	Rep.-Dem. Plurality	Percentage			
								Total Vote		Major Vote	
		Vote	Candidate	Vote	Candidate			Rep.	Dem.	Rep.	Dem.
2012	693,877	295,026	Lamontagne, Ovide M.	378,934	Hassan, Maggie	19,917	83,908 D	42.5%	54.6%	43.8%	56.2%
2010	456,588	205,616	Stephen, John A.	240,346	Lynch, John*	10,626	34,730 D	45.0%	52.6%	46.1%	53.9%
2008	682,910	188,555	Kenney, Joseph D.	479,042	Lynch, John*	15,313	290,487 D	27.6%	70.1%	28.2%	71.8%
2006	403,679	104,288	Coburn, Jim	298,760	Lynch, John*	631	194,472 D	25.8%	74.0%	25.9%	74.1%
2004	667,020	325,981	Benson, Craig*	340,299	Lynch, John	740	14,318 D	48.9%	51.0%	48.9%	51.1%
2002	442,976	259,663	Benson, Craig	169,277	Fernald, Mark D.	14,036	90,386 R	58.6%	38.2%	60.5%	39.5%
2000	564,953	246,952	Humphrey, Gordon J.	275,038	Shaheen, Jeanne*	42,963	28,086 D	43.7%	48.7%	47.3%	52.7%
1998	318,940	98,473	Lucas, Jay	210,769	Shaheen, Jeanne*	9,698	112,296 D	30.9%	66.1%	31.8%	68.2%
1996	497,040	196,321	Lamontagne, Ovide M.	284,175	Shaheen, Jeanne	16,544	87,854 D	39.5%	57.2%	40.9%	59.1%
1994	311,882	218,134	Merrill, Steve*	79,686	King, Wayne D.	14,062	138,448 R	69.9%	25.6%	73.2%	26.8%
1992	516,170	289,170	Merrill, Steve	206,232	Arnesen, Deborah A.	20,768	82,938 R	56.0%	40.0%	58.4%	41.6%
1990	295,018	177,773	Gregg, Judd*	101,923	Grandmaison, J. Joseph	15,322	75,850 R	60.3%	34.5%	63.6%	36.4%
1988	441,923	267,064	Gregg, Judd	172,543	McEachern, Paul*	2,316	94,521 R	60.4%	39.0%	60.8%	39.2%
1986	251,107	134,824	Sununu, John H.*	116,142	McEachern, Paul	141	18,682 R	53.7%	46.3%	53.7%	46.3%
1984	383,910	256,574	Sununu, John H.*	127,156	Spirou, Chris	180	129,418 R	66.8%	33.1%	66.9%	33.1%
1982	282,588	145,389	Sununu, John H.	132,317	Gallen, Hugh J.*	4,882	13,072 R	51.4%	46.8%	52.4%	47.6%
1980	384,031	156,178	Thomson, Meldrim	226,436	Gallen, Hugh J.*	1,417	70,258 D	40.7%	59.0%	40.8%	59.2%
1978	269,587	122,464	Thomson, Meldrim*	133,133	Gallen, Hugh J.	13,990	10,669 D	45.4%	49.4%	47.9%	52.1%
1976	342,669	197,589	Thomson, Meldrim*	145,015	Spanos, Harry V.	65	52,574 R	57.7%	42.3%	57.7%	42.3%
1974	226,665	115,933	Thomson, Meldrim*	110,591	Leonard, Richard W.	141	5,342 R	51.1%	48.8%	51.2%	48.8%
1972**	323,102	133,702	Thomson, Meldrim	126,107	Crowley, Roger J.	63,293	7,595 R	41.4%	39.0%	51.5%	48.5%
1970	222,441	102,298	Peterson, Walter R.*	98,098	Crowley, Roger J.	22,045	4,200 R	46.0%	44.1%	51.0%	49.0%
1968	285,342	149,902	Peterson, Walter R.	135,378	Bussiere, Emile R.	62	14,524 R	52.5%	47.4%	52.5%	47.5%
1966	233,642	107,259	Gregg, Hugh	125,882	King, John W.*	501	18,623 D	45.9%	53.9%	46.0%	54.0%
1964	285,863	94,824	Pillsbury, John	190,863	King, John W.*	176	96,039 D	33.2%	66.8%	33.2%	66.8%
1962	230,048	94,567	Pillsbury, John	135,481	King, John W.		40,914 D	41.1%	58.9%	41.1%	58.9%
1960	290,527	161,123	Powell, Wesley*	129,404	Boutin, Bernard L.		31,719 R	55.5%	44.5%	55.5%	44.5%
1958	206,745	106,790	Powell, Wesley	99,955	Boutin, Bernard L.		6,835 R	51.7%	48.3%	51.7%	48.3%
1956	258,695	141,578	Dwinell, Lane*	117,117	Shaw, John		24,461 R	54.7%	45.3%	54.7%	45.3%
1954	194,631	107,287	Dwinell, Lane	87,344	Shaw, John		19,943 R	55.1%	44.9%	55.1%	44.9%
1952	265,715	167,791	Gregg, Hugh	97,924	Craig, William H.		69,867 R	63.1%	36.9%	63.1%	36.9%
1950	191,239	108,907	Adams, Sherman*	82,258	Bingham, Robert P.	74	26,649 R	56.9%	43.0%	57.0%	43.0%
1948	222,571	116,212	Adams, Sherman	105,207	Hill, Herbert W.	1,152	11,005 R	52.2%	47.3%	52.5%	47.5%
1946	163,451	103,204	Dale, Charles M.	60,247	Keefe, F. Clyde		42,957 R	63.1%	36.9%	63.1%	36.9%

Note: An asterisk (*) denotes incumbent. **In past elections, the other vote included: 1972 - 63,199 Independent (Malcolm McLane).

NEW HAMPSHIRE

POSTWAR VOTE FOR SENATOR

Year	Total Vote	Republican Vote	Republican Candidate	Democratic Vote	Democratic Candidate	Other Vote	Rep.-Dem. Plurality	Total Vote Rep.	Total Vote Dem.	Major Vote Rep.	Major Vote Dem.
2010	455,149	273,218	Ayotte, Kelly	167,545	Hodes, Paul W.	14,386	105,673 R	60.0%	36.8%	62.0%	38.0%
2008	694,787	314,403	Sununu, John E.*	358,438	Shaheen, Jeanne	21,946	44,035 D	45.3%	51.6%	46.7%	53.3%
2004	657,086	434,847	Gregg, Judd*	221,549	Haddock, Dorris R. "Granny D"	690	213,298 R	66.2%	33.7%	66.2%	33.8%
2002	447,135	227,229	Sununu, John E.	207,478	Shaheen, Jeanne	12,428	19,751 R	50.8%	46.4%	52.3%	47.7%
1998	314,956	213,477	Gregg, Judd*	88,883	Condodemetraky, George	12,596	124,594 R	67.8%	28.2%	70.6%	29.4%
1996	491,966	242,304	Smith, Robert C.*	227,397	Swett, Dick	22,265	14,907 R	49.3%	46.2%	51.6%	48.4%
1992	518,416	249,591	Gregg, Judd	234,982	Rauh, John	33,843	14,609 R	48.1%	45.3%	51.5%	48.5%
1990	291,393	189,792	Smith, Robert C.	91,299	Durkin, John A.	10,302	98,493 R	65.1%	31.3%	67.5%	32.5%
1986	244,797	154,090	Rudman, Warren*	79,225	Peabody, Endicott	11,482	74,865 R	62.9%	32.4%	66.0%	34.0%
1984	384,406	225,828	Humphrey, Gordon J.*	157,447	D'Amours, Norman E.	1,131	68,381 R	58.7%	41.0%	58.9%	41.1%
1980	375,060	195,559	Rudman, Warren	179,455	Durkin, John A.*	46	16,104 R	52.1%	47.8%	52.1%	47.9%
1978	263,779	133,745	Humphrey, Gordon J.	127,945	McIntyre, Thomas J.*	2,089	5,800 R	50.7%	48.5%	51.1%	48.9%
1975S	262,682	113,007	Wyman, Louis C.	140,778	Durkin, John A.	8,897	27,771 D	43.0%	53.6%	44.5%	55.5%
1974**	223,363	110,926	Wyman, Louis C.	110,924	Durkin, John A.	1,513	2 R	49.7%	49.7%	50.0%	50.0%
1972	324,354	139,852	Powell, Wesley	184,495	McIntyre, Thomas J.*	7	44,643 D	43.1%	56.9%	43.1%	56.9%
1968	286,989	170,163	Cotton, Norris R.*	116,816	King, John W.	10	53,347 R	59.3%	40.7%	59.3%	40.7%
1966	229,305	105,241	Thyng, Harrison R.	123,888	McIntyre, Thomas J.*	176	18,647 D	45.9%	54.0%	45.9%	54.1%
1962	224,479	134,035	Cotton, Norris R.*	90,444	Catalfo, Alfred Jr.		43,591 R	59.7%	40.3%	59.7%	40.3%
1962S	224,811	107,199	Bass, Perkins	117,612	McIntyre, Thomas J.		10,413 D	47.7%	52.3%	47.7%	52.3%
1960	287,545	173,521	Bridges, Styles*	114,024	Hill, Herbert W.		59,497 R	60.3%	39.7%	60.3%	39.7%
1956	251,943	161,424	Cotton, Norris R.*	90,519	Pickett, Laurence M.		70,905 R	64.1%	35.9%	64.1%	35.9%
1954	194,536	117,150	Bridges, Styles*	77,386	Morin, Gerard L.		39,764 R	60.2%	39.8%	60.2%	39.8%
1954S	189,558	114,068	Cotton, Norris R.*	75,490	Betley, Stanley J.		38,578 R	60.2%	39.8%	60.2%	39.8%
1950	190,573	106,142	Tobey, Charles W.*	72,473	Kelley, Emmet J.	11,958	33,669 R	55.7%	38.0%	59.4%	40.6%
1948	222,898	129,600	Bridges, Styles*	91,760	Fortin, Alfred E.	1,538	37,840 R	58.1%	41.2%	58.5%	41.5%

Note: An asterisk (*) denotes incumbent. **Following the closely contested 1974 election, neither candidate was seated and the 1975 special election was held for the remaining years of that term. One each of the 1954 and 1962 elections was for a short term to fill a vacancy.

NEW HAMPSHIRE

PRESIDENT 2012

2010 Census Population	County	Total Vote	Republican (Romney)	Democratic (Obama)	Other	Rep.-Dem. Plurality	Total Vote Rep.	Total Vote Dem.	Major Vote Rep.	Major Vote Dem.
60,088	BELKNAP	33,887	17,571	15,890	426	1,681 R	51.9%	46.9%	52.5%	47.5%
47,818	CARROLL	28,602	14,207	13,977	418	230 R	49.7%	48.9%	50.4%	49.6%
77,117	CHESHIRE	41,360	15,156	25,380	824	10,224 D	36.6%	61.4%	37.4%	62.6%
33,055	COOS	15,699	6,342	9,095	262	2,753 D	40.4%	57.9%	41.1%	58.9%
89,118	GRAFTON	49,014	18,208	29,826	980	11,618 D	37.1%	60.9%	37.9%	62.1%
400,721	HILLSBOROUGH	205,667	99,991	102,303	3,373	2,312 D	48.6%	49.7%	49.4%	50.6%
146,445	MERRIMACK	80,514	34,524	44,756	1,234	10,232 D	42.9%	55.6%	43.5%	56.5%
295,223	ROCKINGHAM	170,423	87,921	80,142	2,360	7,779 R	51.6%	47.0%	52.3%	47.7%
123,143	STRAFFORD	63,969	26,729	36,026	1,214	9,297 D	41.8%	56.3%	42.6%	57.4%
43,742	SULLIVAN	21,837	9,269	12,166	402	2,897 D	42.4%	55.7%	43.2%	56.8%
1,316,470	TOTAL	710,972	329,918	369,561	11,493	39,643 D	46.4%	52.0%	47.2%	52.8%

NEW HAMPSHIRE

PRESIDENT 2012

2010 Census Population	City/Town	Total Vote	Republican (Romney)	Democratic (Obama)	Other	Rep.-Dem. Plurality	Percentage Total Vote Rep.	Dem.	Major Vote Rep.	Dem.
11,201	AMHERST	7,528	3,906	3,501	121	405 R	51.9%	46.5%	52.7%	47.3%
6,751	ATKINSON	4,359	2,691	1,630	38	1,061 R	61.7%	37.4%	62.3%	37.7%
8,576	BARRINGTON	4,945	2,271	2,577	97	306 D	45.9%	52.1%	46.8%	53.2%
21,203	BEDFORD	12,831	7,990	4,713	128	3,277 R	62.3%	36.7%	62.9%	37.1%
7,356	BELMONT	3,655	1,816	1,782	57	34 R	49.7%	48.8%	50.5%	49.5%
10,051	BERLIN	4,176	1,248	2,863	65	1,615 D	29.9%	68.6%	30.4%	69.6%
7,519	BOW	4,915	2,352	2,509	54	157 D	47.9%	51.0%	48.4%	51.6%
13,355	CLAREMONT	5,599	2,147	3,352	100	1,205 D	38.3%	59.9%	39.0%	61.0%
42,695	CONCORD	21,852	7,325	14,218	309	6,893 D	33.5%	65.1%	34.0%	66.0%
10,115	CONWAY	5,079	2,046	2,954	79	908 D	40.3%	58.2%	40.9%	59.1%
33,109	DERRY	16,239	8,350	7,612	277	738 R	51.4%	46.9%	52.3%	47.7%
29,987	DOVER	16,246	6,162	9,724	360	3,562 D	37.9%	59.9%	38.8%	61.2%
14,638	DURHAM	7,420	2,217	5,074	129	2,857 D	29.9%	68.4%	30.4%	69.6%
6,411	EPPING	3,565	1,697	1,793	75	96 D	47.6%	50.3%	48.6%	51.4%
14,306	EXETER	8,917	3,614	5,194	109	1,580 D	40.5%	58.2%	41.0%	59.0%
6,786	FARMINGTON	3,015	1,429	1,545	41	116 D	47.4%	51.2%	48.0%	52.0%
8,477	FRANKLIN	3,705	1,570	2,059	76	489 D	42.4%	55.6%	43.3%	56.7%
7,126	GILFORD	4,636	2,448	2,133	55	315 R	52.8%	46.0%	53.4%	46.6%
17,651	GOFFSTOWN	9,216	4,856	4,231	129	625 R	52.7%	45.9%	53.4%	46.6%
8,523	HAMPSTEAD	5,295	3,217	2,012	66	1,205 R	60.8%	38.0%	61.5%	38.5%
15,430	HAMPTON	9,702	4,742	4,843	117	101 D	48.9%	49.9%	49.5%	50.5%
11,260	HANOVER	7,295	1,727	5,469	99	3,742 D	23.7%	75.0%	24.0%	76.0%
7,684	HOLLIS	5,158	2,785	2,289	84	496 R	54.0%	44.4%	54.9%	45.1%
13,451	HOOKSETT	7,369	3,968	3,319	82	649 R	53.8%	45.0%	54.5%	45.5%
24,467	HUDSON	12,316	6,683	5,451	182	1,232 R	54.3%	44.3%	55.1%	44.9%
5,457	JAFFREY	2,834	1,235	1,538	61	303 D	43.6%	54.3%	44.5%	55.5%
23,409	KEENE	12,579	3,613	8,718	248	5,105 D	28.7%	69.3%	29.3%	70.7%
6,025	KINGSTON	3,427	1,854	1,518	55	336 R	54.1%	44.3%	55.0%	45.0%
15,951	LACONIA	7,884	3,859	3,938	87	79 D	48.9%	49.9%	49.5%	50.5%
13,151	LEBANON	6,924	2,060	4,772	92	2,712 D	29.8%	68.9%	30.2%	69.8%
8,271	LITCHFIELD	4,711	2,703	1,956	52	747 R	57.4%	41.5%	58.0%	42.0%
5,928	LITTLETON	2,913	1,293	1,566	54	273 D	44.4%	53.8%	45.2%	54.8%
24,129	LONDONDERRY	13,167	7,323	5,690	154	1,633 R	55.6%	43.2%	56.3%	43.7%
109,565	MANCHESTER	48,033	20,942	26,227	864	5,285 D	43.6%	54.6%	44.4%	55.6%
25,494	MERRIMACK TOWN	14,784	7,750	6,832	202	918 R	52.4%	46.2%	53.1%	46.9%
15,115	MILFORD	7,891	3,787	3,954	150	167 D	48.0%	50.1%	48.9%	51.1%
86,494	NASHUA	41,760	17,658	23,413	689	5,755 D	42.3%	56.1%	43.0%	57.0%
8,936	NEWMARKET	5,218	1,893	3,230	95	1,337 D	36.3%	61.9%	37.0%	63.0%
6,507	NEWPORT	2,816	1,310	1,448	58	138 D	46.5%	51.4%	47.5%	52.5%
12,897	PELHAM	7,133	4,184	2,870	79	1,314 R	58.7%	40.2%	59.3%	40.7%
7,115	PEMBROKE	3,889	1,729	2,102	58	373 D	44.5%	54.0%	45.1%	54.9%
6,284	PETERBOROUGH	3,836	1,309	2,479	48	1,170 D	34.1%	64.6%	34.6%	65.4%
7,609	PLAISTOW	4,149	2,387	1,709	53	678 R	57.5%	41.2%	58.3%	41.7%
6,990	PLYMOUTH	3,569	1,111	2,313	145	1,202 D	31.1%	64.8%	32.4%	67.6%
20,779	PORTSMOUTH	13,131	4,088	8,848	195	4,760 D	31.1%	67.4%	31.6%	68.4%
10,138	RAYMOND	5,013	2,632	2,289	92	343 R	52.5%	45.7%	53.5%	46.5%
29,752	ROCHESTER	14,559	6,816	7,493	250	677 D	46.8%	51.5%	47.6%	52.4%
28,776	SALEM	14,466	8,285	6,026	155	2,259 R	57.3%	41.7%	57.9%	42.1%
8,693	SEABROOK	4,303	2,211	2,030	62	181 R	51.4%	47.2%	52.1%	47.9%
11,766	SOMERSWORTH	5,227	2,101	3,028	98	927 D	40.2%	57.9%	41.0%	59.0%
7,230	SWANZEY	3,674	1,497	2,133	44	636 D	40.7%	58.1%	41.2%	58.8%
8,785	WEARE	4,787	2,592	2,105	90	487 R	54.1%	44.0%	55.2%	44.8%
13,592	WINDHAM	8,284	5,224	2,964	96	2,260 R	63.1%	35.8%	63.8%	36.2%
6,269	WOLFEBORO	4,311	2,400	1,854	57	546 R	55.7%	43.0%	56.4%	43.6%

NEW HAMPSHIRE

GOVERNOR 2012

2010 Census Population	County	Total Vote	Republican (Lamontagne)	Democratic (Hassan)	Other	Rep.-Dem. Plurality	Percentage Total Vote Rep.	Dem.	Major Vote Rep.	Dem.
60,088	BELKNAP	33,304	15,702	16,756	846	1,054 D	47.1%	50.3%	48.4%	51.6%
47,818	CARROLL	27,911	12,893	14,339	679	1,446 D	46.2%	51.4%	47.3%	52.7%
77,117	CHESHIRE	39,895	13,490	25,136	1,269	11,646 D	33.8%	63.0%	34.9%	65.1%
33,055	COOS	15,398	6,069	8,929	400	2,860 D	39.4%	58.0%	40.5%	59.5%
89,118	GRAFTON	47,522	16,476	29,412	1,634	12,936 D	34.7%	61.9%	35.9%	64.1%
400,721	HILLSBOROUGH	201,110	90,621	104,547	5,942	13,926 D	45.1%	52.0%	46.4%	53.6%
146,445	MERRIMACK	79,136	31,127	46,037	1,972	14,910 D	39.3%	58.2%	40.3%	59.7%
295,223	ROCKINGHAM	165,884	77,095	84,287	4,502	7,192 D	46.5%	50.8%	47.8%	52.2%
123,143	STRAFFORD	62,390	23,387	37,120	1,883	13,733 D	37.5%	59.5%	38.7%	61.3%
43,742	SULLIVAN	21,327	8,166	12,371	790	4,205 D	38.3%	58.0%	39.8%	60.2%
1,316,470	TOTAL	693,877	295,026	378,934	19,917	83,908 D	42.5%	54.6%	43.8%	56.2%

2010 Census Population	City/Town	Total Vote	Republican (Lamontagne)	Democratic (Hassan)	Other	Rep.-Dem. Plurality	Percentage Total Vote Rep.	Dem.	Major Vote Rep.	Dem.
11,201	AMHERST	7,337	3,532	3,610	195	78 D	48.1%	49.2%	49.5%	50.5%
6,751	ATKINSON	4,203	2,343	1,710	150	633 R	55.7%	40.7%	57.8%	42.2%
8,576	BARRINGTON	4,899	2,048	2,710	141	662 D	41.8%	55.3%	43.0%	57.0%
21,203	BEDFORD	12,676	7,471	5,017	188	2,454 R	58.9%	39.6%	59.8%	40.2%
7,356	BELMONT	3,601	1,606	1,888	107	282 D	44.6%	52.4%	46.0%	54.0%
10,051	BERLIN	4,178	1,248	2,824	106	1,576 D	29.9%	67.6%	30.6%	69.4%
7,519	BOW	4,858	2,135	2,643	80	508 D	43.9%	54.4%	44.7%	55.3%
13,355	CLAREMONT	5,458	1,913	3,350	195	1,437 D	35.0%	61.4%	36.3%	63.7%
42,695	CONCORD	21,505	6,497	14,507	501	8,010 D	30.2%	67.5%	30.9%	69.1%
10,115	CONWAY	4,926	1,893	2,914	119	1,021 D	38.4%	59.2%	39.4%	60.6%
33,109	DERRY	15,591	7,161	7,891	539	730 D	45.9%	50.6%	47.6%	52.4%
29,987	DOVER	15,831	5,343	10,006	482	4,663 D	33.8%	63.2%	34.8%	65.2%
14,638	DURHAM	6,951	1,862	4,815	274	2,953 D	26.8%	69.3%	27.9%	72.1%
6,411	EPPING	3,506	1,480	1,914	112	434 D	42.2%	54.6%	43.6%	56.4%
14,306	EXETER	8,768	3,123	5,479	166	2,356 D	35.6%	62.5%	36.3%	63.7%
6,786	FARMINGTON	2,955	1,293	1,556	106	263 D	43.8%	52.7%	45.4%	54.6%
8,477	FRANKLIN	3,640	1,360	2,147	133	787 D	37.4%	59.0%	38.8%	61.2%
7,126	GILFORD	4,522	2,162	2,257	103	95 D	47.8%	49.9%	48.9%	51.1%
17,651	GOFFSTOWN	9,028	4,536	4,257	235	279 R	50.2%	47.2%	51.6%	48.4%
8,523	HAMPSTEAD	5,170	2,819	2,198	153	621 R	54.5%	42.5%	56.2%	43.8%
15,430	HAMPTON	9,464	4,160	5,140	164	980 D	44.0%	54.3%	44.7%	55.3%
11,260	HANOVER	6,731	1,379	5,169	183	3,790 D	20.5%	76.8%	21.1%	78.9%
7,684	HOLLIS	5,029	2,441	2,450	138	9 D	48.5%	48.7%	49.9%	50.1%
13,451	HOOKSETT	7,253	3,703	3,389	161	314 R	51.1%	46.7%	52.2%	47.8%
24,467	HUDSON	11,943	5,675	5,812	456	137 D	47.5%	48.7%	49.4%	50.6%
5,457	JAFFREY	2,748	1,122	1,536	90	414 D	40.8%	55.9%	42.2%	57.8%
23,409	KEENE	11,902	3,130	8,317	455	5,187 D	26.3%	69.9%	27.3%	72.7%
6,025	KINGSTON	3,356	1,606	1,646	104	40 D	47.9%	49.0%	49.4%	50.6%
15,951	LACONIA	7,716	3,483	4,043	190	560 D	45.1%	52.4%	46.3%	53.7%
13,151	LEBANON	6,721	1,849	4,678	194	2,829 D	27.5%	69.6%	28.3%	71.7%
8,271	LITCHFIELD	4,600	2,344	2,089	167	255 R	51.0%	45.4%	52.9%	47.1%
5,928	LITTLETON	2,870	1,207	1,573	90	366 D	42.1%	54.8%	43.4%	56.6%
24,129	LONDONDERRY	12,850	6,516	6,022	312	494 R	50.7%	46.9%	52.0%	48.0%
109,565	MANCHESTER	47,179	19,997	25,778	1,404	5,781 D	42.4%	54.6%	43.7%	56.3%
25,494	MERRIMACK TOWN	14,439	6,900	7,180	359	280 D	47.8%	49.7%	49.0%	51.0%
15,115	MILFORD	7,745	3,350	4,160	235	810 D	43.3%	53.7%	44.6%	55.4%
86,494	NASHUA	40,500	15,442	23,852	1,206	8,410 D	38.1%	58.9%	39.3%	60.7%
8,936	NEWMARKET	5,079	1,612	3,333	134	1,721 D	31.7%	65.6%	32.6%	67.4%
6,507	NEWPORT	2,757	1,197	1,466	94	269 D	43.4%	53.2%	44.9%	55.1%
12,897	PELHAM	6,878	3,619	2,995	264	624 R	52.6%	43.5%	54.7%	45.3%

NEW HAMPSHIRE

GOVERNOR 2012

2010 Census Population	City/Town	Total Vote	Republican (Lamontagne)	Democratic (Hassan)	Other	Rep.-Dem. Plurality	Percentage			
							Total Vote		Major Vote	
							Rep.	Dem.	Rep.	Dem.
7,115	PEMBROKE	3,837	1,585	2,174	78	589 D	41.3%	56.7%	42.2%	57.8%
6,284	PETERBOROUGH	3,774	1,212	2,501	61	1,289 D	32.1%	66.3%	32.6%	67.4%
7,609	PLAISTOW	3,962	2,043	1,748	171	295 R	51.6%	44.1%	53.9%	46.1%
6,990	PLYMOUTH	3,357	1,019	2,154	184	1,135 D	30.4%	64.2%	32.1%	67.9%
20,779	PORTSMOUTH	12,773	3,473	8,951	349	5,478 D	27.2%	70.1%	28.0%	72.0%
10,138	RAYMOND	4,908	2,356	2,409	143	53 D	48.0%	49.1%	49.4%	50.6%
29,752	ROCHESTER	14,250	5,907	7,897	446	1,990 D	41.5%	55.4%	42.8%	57.2%
28,776	SALEM	13,935	7,239	6,219	477	1,020 R	51.9%	44.6%	53.8%	46.2%
8,693	SEABROOK	4,092	1,800	2,113	179	313 D	44.0%	51.6%	46.0%	54.0%
11,766	SOMERSWORTH	5,148	1,840	3,173	135	1,333 D	35.7%	61.6%	36.7%	63.3%
7,230	SWANZEY	3,599	1,354	2,155	90	801 D	37.6%	59.9%	38.6%	61.4%
8,785	WEARE	4,720	2,358	2,189	173	169 R	50.0%	46.4%	51.9%	48.1%
13,592	WINDHAM	8,015	4,664	3,160	191	1,504 R	58.2%	39.4%	59.6%	40.4%
6,269	WOLFEBORO	4,193	2,152	1,953	88	199 R	51.3%	46.6%	52.4%	47.6%

NEW HAMPSHIRE

HOUSE OF REPRESENTATIVES

CD	Year	Total Vote	Republican		Democratic		Other Vote	Rep.-Dem. Plurality	Percentage			
			Vote	Candidate	Vote	Candidate			Total Vote		Major Vote	
									Rep.	Dem.	Rep.	Dem.
1	2012	345,022	158,659	GUINTA, FRANK C.*	171,650	SHEA-PORTER, CAROL	14,713	12,991 D	46.0%	49.8%	48.0%	52.0%
2	2012	337,394	152,977	BASS, CHARLES*	169,275	KUSTER, ANN MCLANE	15,142	16,298 D	45.3%	50.2%	47.5%	52.5%
TOTAL	2012	682,416	311,636		340,925		29,855	29,289 D	45.7%	50.0%	47.8%	52.2%

Note: An asterisk (*) denotes incumbent.

NEW HAMPSHIRE

GENERAL AND PRIMARY ELECTIONS

GENERAL ELECTIONS: OTHER VOTE

President   Other vote was 8,212 Libertarian (Gary E. Johnson), 1,374 Write-in (Ron Paul), 875 Write-in (Scattered Write-In), 708 Constitution (Virgil H. Goode), 324 Write-in (Jill Stein)

Governor   Other vote was 19,251 Libertarian (John J. Babiarz), 666 Write-in (Scattered Write-In)

House   Other vote was:

CD 1   14,521 Libertarian (Brendan Kelly), 192 Write-in (Scattered Write-In)
CD 2   14,936 Libertarian (Hardy Macia), 206 Write-in (Scattered Write-In)

PRIMARY ELECTIONS: SUPPLEMENTARY INFORMATION

Primary   January 10, 2012 (President)   **Registration**   793,493   Republican   260,138
September 11, 2012 (Congress)   (as of September 11, 2012)   Democratic   224,814
Unenrolled   308,541

Primary Type   Semi-open—Registered Democrats and Republicans could vote only in their party's primary. "Undeclared" voters could participate in either party's primary.

NEW HAMPSHIRE

GENERAL AND PRIMARY ELECTIONS

	REPUBLICAN PRIMARIES			DEMOCRATIC PRIMARIES		
President	Romney, W. Mitt	97,591	39.3%	Obama, Barack H.*	49,080	80.9%
	Paul, Ron	56,872	22.9%	Scattered Write-In	6,778	11.2%
	Huntsman, Jon Jr.	41,964	16.9%	Cowan, Ed	945	1.6%
	Santorum, Rick	23,432	9.4%	Supreme, Vermin	833	1.4%
	Gingrich, Newt	23,421	9.4%	Terry, Randall	442	0.7%
	Perry, Rick	1,764	0.7%	Haywood, John	423	0.7%
	Roemer, Charles	950	0.4%	Freis, Craig "Tax Freeze"	400	0.7%
	Scattered Write-In	549	0.2%	Ely, Bob	287	0.5%
	Bachmann, Michele	350	0.1%	O'Connor, Cornelius E.	266	0.4%
	Karger, Fred	345	0.1%	Richardson, Darcy	264	0.4%
	Rubash, Kevin	250	0.1%	Wolfe, John	245	0.4%
	Johnson, Gary E.	181	0.1%	O'Donnell, Edward T. Jr.	222	0.4%
	Cain, Herman	161	0.1%	Greene, Bob	213	0.4%
	Lawman, Jeff	119		Jordan, Robert B.	155	0.3%
	Hill, Christopher	108		Tyler, Aldous C. Jr.	106	0.2%
	Linn, Benjamin	83				
	Meehan, Michael J.	54				
	Drummond, Keith	42				
	Story, Joe	42				
	Betzler, Bear	29				
	Robinson, Joe	25				
	Greenleaf, Stewart J.	24				
	Callahan, Mark	20				
	Martin, Andy	19				
	Swift, Linden	18				
	Brewer, Timothy	15				
	Wuensche, Vern	15				
	Davis, L. John Jr.	14				
	Crow, Randy	12				
	Cort, Hugh	3				
	Vestermark, James A.	3				
	TOTAL	*248,475*		*TOTAL*	*60,659*	
Governor	Lamontagne, Ovide M.	73,437	67.5%	Hassan, Maggie	45,120	53.0%
	Smith, Kevin H.	32,396	29.8%	Cilley, Jack	33,066	38.8%
	Tarr, Robert M.	1,725	1.6%	Kennedy, Bill Pearce	5,936	7.0%
	Scattered Write-In	1,170	1.1%	Scattered Write-In	991	1.2%
	TOTAL	*108,728*		*TOTAL*	*85,113*	
Congressional District 1	Guinta, Frank C.*	46,979	84.3%	Shea-Porter, Carol	38,623	99.1%
	Parent, Rick	6,923	12.4%	Guinta, Frank C.	204	0.5%
	Clough, Vern	1,639	2.9%	Scattered Write-In	142	0.4%
	Shea-Porter, Carol	130	0.2%	Parent, Rick	10	
	Scattered Write-In	74	0.1%	Clough, Vern	2	
	TOTAL	*55,745*		*TOTAL*	*38,981*	
Congressional District 2	Bass, Charles*	39,605	81.2%	Kuster, Ann McLane	40,627	99.2%
	Lamare, Dennis	4,263	8.7%	Scattered Write-In	170	0.4%
	Dean, Will	2,129	4.4%	Bass, Charles	157	0.4%
	Dziedzic, Miroslaw	1,310	2.7%	Dean, Will	4	
	Beloin, Gerard	1,127	2.3%	Dziedzic, Miroslaw	3	
	Kuster, Ann McLane	193	0.4%	Lamare, Dennis	3	
	Scattered Write-In	123	0.3%			
	TOTAL	*48,750*		*TOTAL*	*40,964*	

Note: An asterisk (*) denotes incumbent.

NEW JERSEY

Congressional districts first established for elections held in 2012

12 members

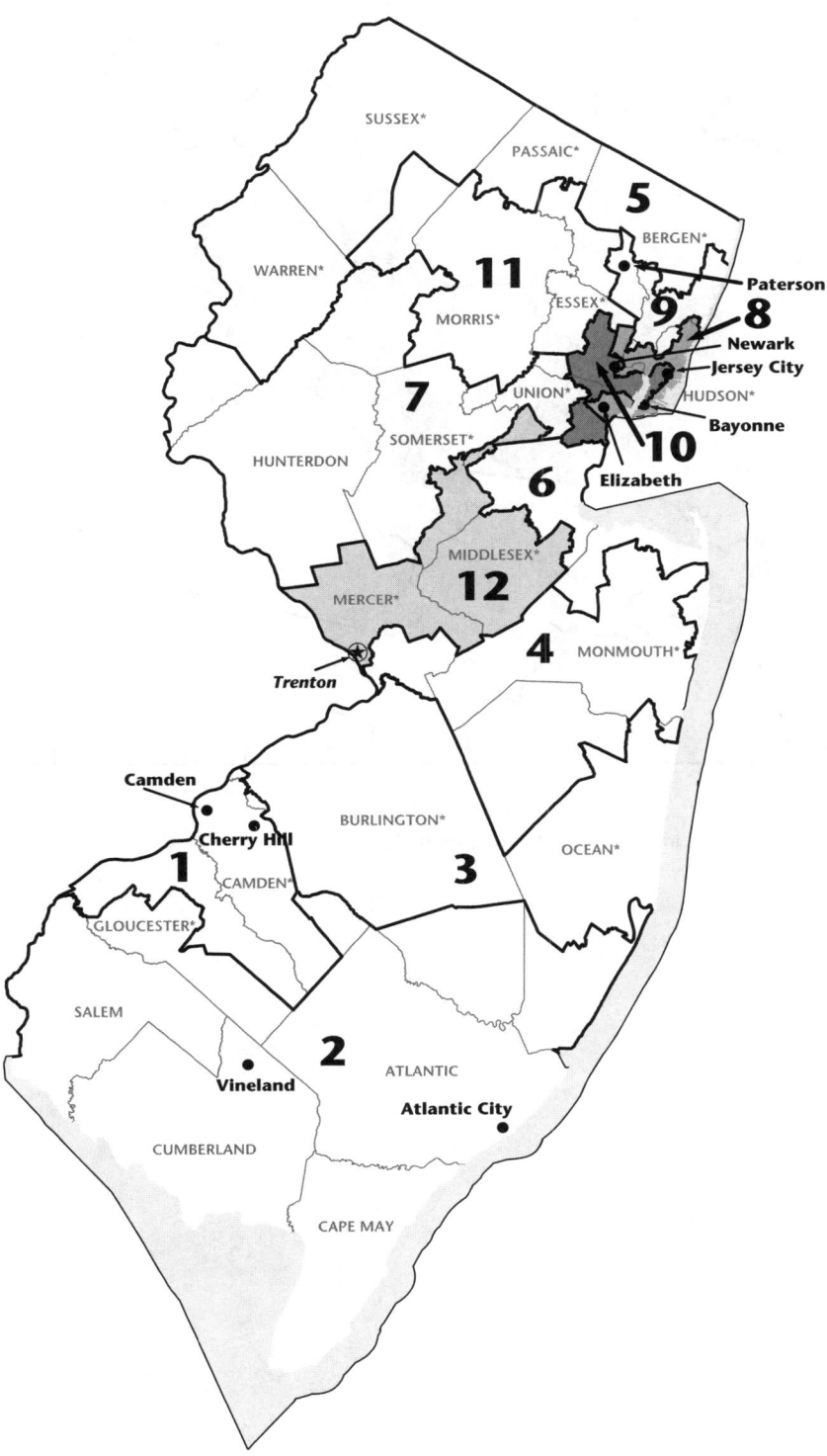

* Asterisk indicates a county whose boundaries include parts of two or more Congressional districts.

NEW JERSEY

Northern New Jersey Gateway Area

* Asterisk indicates a county whose boundaries include parts of two or more Congressional districts.

NEW JERSEY

GOVERNOR

Chris Christie (R). Elected 2009 to a four-year term.

SENATORS (1 Republican, 1 Democrat)

Robert Menendez (D). Reelected 2012 to a six-year term. Previously elected 2006.

Jeff Chiesa (R). Appointed June 6, 2013, to fill the vacancy left by the death of Frank R. Lautenberg (D) until an October 16, 2013, special election.

REPRESENTATIVES (6 Republicans, 6 Democrats)

1. Robert E. Andrews (D)
2. Frank A. LoBiondo (R)
3. Jon Runyan (R)
4. Chris Smith (R)
5. Scott Garrett (R)
6. Frank Pallone Jr. (D)
7. Leonard Lance (R)
8. Albio Sires (D)
9. Bill Pascrell Jr. (D)
10. Donald M. Payne Jr. (D)
11. Rodney Frelinghuysen (R)
12. Rush Holt (D)

POSTWAR VOTE FOR PRESIDENT

Year	Total Vote	Republican Vote	Republican Candidate	Democratic Vote	Democratic Candidate	Other Vote	Rep.-Dem. Plurality	Total Vote Rep.	Total Vote Dem.	Major Vote Rep.	Major Vote Dem.
2012	3,640,292	1,477,568	Romney, W. Mitt	2,125,101	Obama, Barack H.*	37,623	647,533 D	40.6%	58.4%	41.0%	59.0%
2008	3,868,237	1,613,207	McCain, John S. III	2,215,422	Obama, Barack H.	39,608	602,215 D	41.7%	57.3%	42.1%	57.9%
2004	3,611,691	1,670,003	Bush, George W.*	1,911,430	Kerry, John F.	30,258	241,427 D	46.2%	52.9%	46.6%	53.4%
2000**	3,187,226	1,284,173	Bush, George W.	1,788,850	Gore, Albert Jr.	114,203	504,677 D	40.3%	56.1%	41.8%	58.2%
1996**	3,075,807	1,103,078	Dole, Robert "Bob"	1,652,329	Clinton, Bill*	320,400	549,251 D	35.9%	53.7%	40.0%	60.0%
1992**	3,343,594	1,356,865	Bush, George H.*	1,436,206	Clinton, Bill	550,523	79,341 D	40.6%	43.0%	48.6%	51.4%
1988	3,099,553	1,743,192	Bush, George H.	1,320,352	Dukakis, Michael S.	36,009	422,840 R	56.2%	42.6%	56.9%	43.1%
1984	3,217,862	1,933,630	Reagan, Ronald*	1,261,323	Mondale, Walter F.	22,909	672,307 R	60.1%	39.2%	60.5%	39.5%
1980**	2,975,684	1,546,557	Reagan, Ronald	1,147,364	Carter, Jimmy*	281,763	399,193 R	52.0%	38.6%	57.4%	42.6%
1976	3,014,472	1,509,688	Ford, Gerald R.*	1,444,653	Carter, Jimmy	60,131	65,035 R	50.1%	47.9%	51.1%	48.9%
1972	2,997,229	1,845,502	Nixon, Richard M.*	1,102,211	McGovern, George S.	49,516	743,291 R	61.6%	36.8%	62.6%	37.4%
1968**	2,875,395	1,325,467	Nixon, Richard M.	1,264,206	Humphrey, Hubert H. Jr.	285,722	61,261 R	46.1%	44.0%	51.2%	48.8%
1964	2,847,663	964,174	Goldwater, Barry M. Sr.	1,868,231	Johnson, Lyndon B.*	15,258	904,057 D	33.9%	65.6%	34.0%	66.0%
1960	2,773,111	1,363,324	Nixon, Richard M.	1,385,415	Kennedy, John F.	24,372	22,091 D	49.2%	50.0%	49.6%	50.4%
1956	2,484,312	1,606,942	Eisenhower, Dwight D.*	850,337	Stevenson, Adlai E. II	27,033	756,605 R	64.7%	34.2%	65.4%	34.6%
1952	2,418,554	1,373,613	Eisenhower, Dwight D.	1,015,902	Stevenson, Adlai E. II	29,039	357,711 R	56.8%	42.0%	57.5%	42.5%
1948	1,949,555	981,124	Dewey, Thomas E.	895,455	Truman, Harry S.*	72,976	85,669 R	50.3%	45.9%	52.3%	47.7%

Note: An asterisk (*) denotes incumbent. **In past elections, the other vote included: 2000 - 94,554 Green (Ralph Nader); 1996 - 262,134 Reform (Ross Perot); 1992 - 521,829 Independent (Perot); 1980 - 234,632 Independent (John Anderson); 1968 - 262,187 American Independent (George Wallace).

NEW JERSEY

POSTWAR VOTE FOR GOVERNOR

Year	Total Vote	Republican		Democratic		Other Vote	Rep.-Dem. Plurality	Percentage			
		Vote	Candidate	Vote	Candidate			Total Vote		Major Vote	
								Rep.	Dem.	Rep.	Dem.
2009	2,423,792	1,174,445	Christie, Chris	1,087,731	Corzine, Jon S.*	161,616	86,714 R	48.5%	44.9%	51.9%	48.1%
2005	2,290,099	985,271	Forrester, Doug	1,224,551	Corzine, Jon S.	80,277	239,280 D	43.0%	53.5%	44.6%	55.4%
2001	2,227,165	928,174	Schundler, Bret	1,256,853	McGreevey, James	42,138	328,679 D	41.7%	56.4%	42.5%	57.5%
1997	2,418,344	1,133,394	Whitman, Christine T.*	1,107,968	McGreevey, James	176,982	25,426 R	46.9%	45.8%	50.6%	49.4%
1993	2,505,964	1,236,124	Whitman, Christine T.	1,210,031	Florio, James J.*	59,809	26,093 R	49.3%	48.3%	50.5%	49.5%
1989	2,253,800	838,553	Courter, James A.	1,379,973	Florio, James J.	35,274	541,420 D	37.2%	61.2%	37.8%	62.2%
1985	1,972,624	1,372,631	Kean, Thomas H.*	578,402	Shapiro, Peter	21,591	794,229 R	69.6%	29.3%	70.4%	29.6%
1981	2,317,239	1,145,999	Kean, Thomas H.	1,144,202	Florio, James J.	27,038	1,797 R	49.5%	49.4%	50.0%	50.0%
1977	2,126,264	888,880	Bateman, Raymond H.	1,184,564	Byrne, Brendan T.*	52,820	295,684 D	41.8%	55.7%	42.9%	57.1%
1973	2,122,010	676,235	Sandman, Charles W.	1,414,613	Byrne, Brendan T.	31,162	738,378 D	31.9%	66.7%	32.3%	67.7%
1969	2,366,606	1,411,905	Cahill, William T.	911,003	Meyner, Robert B.	43,698	500,902 R	59.7%	38.5%	60.8%	39.2%
1965	2,229,583	915,996	Dumont, Wayne Jr.	1,279,568	Hughes, Richard J.*	34,019	363,572 D	41.1%	57.4%	41.7%	58.3%
1961	2,152,662	1,049,274	Mitchell, James P.	1,084,194	Hughes, Richard J.	19,194	34,920 D	48.7%	50.4%	49.2%	50.8%
1957	2,018,488	897,321	Forbes, Malcolm S.	1,101,130	Meyner, Robert B.*	20,037	203,809 D	44.5%	54.6%	44.9%	55.1%
1953	1,810,812	809,068	Troast, Paul L.	962,710	Meyner, Robert B.	39,034	153,642 D	44.7%	53.2%	45.7%	54.3%
1949**	1,718,788	885,882	Driscoll, Alfred E.*	810,022	Wene, Elmer H.	22,884	75,860 R	51.5%	47.1%	52.2%	47.8%
1946	1,414,527	807,378	Driscoll, Alfred E.	585,960	Hansen, Lewis G.	21,189	221,418 R	57.1%	41.4%	57.9%	42.1%

Note: An asterisk (*) denotes incumbent. **The term of office of New Jersey's governor was increased from three to four years effective with the 1949 election.

POSTWAR VOTE FOR SENATOR

Year	Total Vote	Republican		Democratic		Other Vote	Rep.-Dem. Plurality	Percentage			
		Vote	Candidate	Vote	Candidate			Total Vote		Major Vote	
								Rep.	Dem.	Rep.	Dem.
2012	3,374,668	1,329,405	Kyrillos, Joe	1,985,783	Menendez, Robert*	59,480	656,378 D	39.4%	58.8%	40.1%	59.9%
2008	3,482,445	1,461,025	Zimmer, Dick	1,951,218	Lautenberg, Frank R.*	70,202	490,193 D	42.0%	56.0%	42.8%	57.2%
2006	2,250,070	997,775	Kean, Tom Jr.	1,200,843	Menendez, Robert*	51,452	203,068 D	44.3%	53.4%	45.4%	54.6%
2002	2,112,604	928,439	Forrester, Douglas R.	1,138,193	Lautenberg, Frank R.	45,972	209,754 D	43.9%	53.9%	44.9%	55.1%
2000	3,015,662	1,420,267	Franks, Bob	1,511,237	Corzine, Jon S.	84,158	90,970 D	47.1%	50.1%	48.4%	51.6%
1996	2,884,106	1,227,817	Zimmer, Dick	1,519,328	Torricelli, Robert G.	136,961	291,511 D	42.6%	52.7%	44.7%	55.3%
1994	2,054,887	966,244	Haytaian, Garabed	1,033,487	Lautenberg, Frank R.*	55,156	67,243 D	47.0%	50.3%	48.3%	51.7%
1990	1,938,454	918,874	Whitman, Christine T.	977,810	Bradley, Bill Warren*	41,770	58,936 D	47.4%	50.4%	48.4%	51.6%
1988	2,987,634	1,349,937	Dawkins, Peter M.	1,599,905	Lautenberg, Frank R.*	37,792	249,968 D	45.2%	53.6%	45.8%	54.2%
1984	3,096,456	1,080,100	Mochary, Mary V.	1,986,644	Bradley, Bill Warren*	29,712	906,544 D	34.9%	64.2%	35.2%	64.8%
1982	2,193,945	1,047,626	Fenwick, Millicent	1,117,549	Lautenberg, Frank R.	28,770	69,923 D	47.8%	50.9%	48.4%	51.6%
1978	1,957,515	844,200	Bell, Jeffrey	1,082,960	Bradley, Bill Warren	30,355	238,760 D	43.1%	55.3%	43.8%	56.2%
1976	2,771,387	1,054,505	Norcross, David F.	1,681,140	Williams, Harrison*	35,742	626,635 D	38.0%	60.7%	38.5%	61.5%
1972	2,791,907	1,743,854	Case, Clifford P.*	963,573	Kerbs, Paul J.	84,480	780,281 R	62.5%	34.5%	64.4%	35.6%
1970	2,142,105	903,026	Gross, Nelson G.	1,157,074	Williams, Harrison*	82,005	254,048 D	42.2%	54.0%	43.8%	56.2%
1966	2,130,688	1,278,843	Case, Clifford P.*	788,021	Wilentz, Warren W.	63,824	490,822 R	60.0%	37.0%	61.9%	38.1%
1964	2,709,575	1,011,280	Shanley, Bernard M.	1,677,515	Williams, Harrison*	20,780	666,235 D	37.3%	61.9%	37.6%	62.4%
1960	2,664,556	1,483,832	Case, Clifford P.*	1,151,385	Lord, Thorn	29,339	332,447 R	55.7%	43.2%	56.3%	43.7%
1958	1,881,329	882,287	Kean, Robert Winthrop	966,832	Williams, Harrison	32,210	84,545 D	46.9%	51.4%	47.7%	52.3%
1954	1,770,557	861,528	Case, Clifford P.	858,158	Howell, Charles R.	50,871	3,370 R	48.7%	48.5%	50.1%	49.9%
1952	2,318,232	1,286,782	Smith, H. Alexander*	1,011,187	Alexander, Archibald S.	20,263	275,595 R	55.5%	43.6%	56.0%	44.0%
1948	1,869,882	934,720	Hendrickson, Robert C.	884,414	Alexander, Archibald S.	50,748	50,306 R	50.0%	47.3%	51.4%	48.6%
1946	1,367,155	799,808	Smith, H. Alexander*	548,458	Brunner, George E.	18,889	251,350 R	58.5%	40.1%	59.3%	40.7%

Note: An asterisk (*) denotes incumbent.

NEW JERSEY

PRESIDENT 2012

2010 Census Population	County	Total Vote	Republican (Romney)	Democratic (Obama)	Other	Rep.-Dem. Plurality		Percentage			
								Total Vote		Major Vote	
								Rep.	Dem.	Rep.	Dem.
274,549	ATLANTIC	113,179	46,522	65,600	1,057	19,078	D	41.1%	58.0%	41.5%	58.5%
905,116	BERGEN	385,407	169,070	212,754	3,583	43,684	D	43.9%	55.2%	44.3%	55.7%
448,734	BURLINGTON	215,936	87,401	126,377	2,158	38,976	D	40.5%	58.5%	40.9%	59.1%
513,657	CAMDEN	225,428	69,476	153,682	2,270	84,206	D	30.8%	68.2%	31.1%	68.9%
97,265	CAPE MAY	47,931	25,781	21,657	493	4,124	R	53.8%	45.2%	54.3%	45.7%
156,898	CUMBERLAND	55,292	20,658	34,055	579	13,397	D	37.4%	61.6%	37.8%	62.2%
783,969	ESSEX	303,019	64,406	236,618	1,995	172,212	D	21.3%	78.1%	21.4%	78.6%
288,288	GLOUCESTER	135,186	59,456	74,013	1,717	14,557	D	44.0%	54.7%	44.5%	55.5%
634,266	HUDSON	197,504	42,369	153,108	2,027	110,739	D	21.5%	77.5%	21.7%	78.3%
128,349	HUNTERDON	66,494	38,687	26,876	931	11,811	R	58.2%	40.4%	59.0%	41.0%
366,513	MERCER	153,511	47,355	104,377	1,779	57,022	D	30.8%	68.0%	31.2%	68.8%
809,858	MIDDLESEX	301,315	107,310	190,555	3,450	83,245	D	35.6%	63.2%	36.0%	64.0%
630,380	MONMOUTH	283,978	147,513	133,145	3,320	14,368	R	51.9%	46.9%	52.6%	47.4%
492,276	MORRIS	227,392	124,947	100,146	2,299	24,801	R	54.9%	44.0%	55.5%	44.5%
576,567	OCEAN	251,275	146,474	102,300	2,501	44,174	R	58.3%	40.7%	58.9%	41.1%
501,226	PASSAIC	181,988	64,523	115,926	1,539	51,403	D	35.5%	63.7%	35.8%	64.2%
66,083	SALEM	29,501	14,334	14,719	448	385	D	48.6%	49.9%	49.3%	50.7%
323,444	SOMERSET	142,922	66,603	74,592	1,727	7,989	D	46.6%	52.2%	47.2%	52.8%
149,265	SUSSEX	67,933	40,625	26,104	1,204	14,521	R	59.8%	38.4%	60.9%	39.1%
536,499	UNION	209,831	68,314	139,752	1,765	71,438	D	32.6%	66.6%	32.8%	67.2%
108,692	WARREN	45,270	25,744	18,745	781	6,999	R	56.9%	41.4%	57.9%	42.1%
8,791,894	TOTAL	3,640,292	1,477,568	2,125,101	37,623	647,533	D	40.6%	58.4%	41.0%	59.0%

NEW JERSEY

SENATOR 2012

2010 Census Population	County	Total Vote	Republican (Kyrillos)	Democratic (Menendez)	Other	Rep.-Dem. Plurality		Percentage			
								Total Vote		Major Vote	
								Rep.	Dem.	Rep.	Dem.
274,549	ATLANTIC	105,634	42,378	61,464	1,792	19,086	D	40.1%	58.2%	40.8%	59.2%
905,116	BERGEN	352,137	144,709	201,870	5,558	57,161	D	41.1%	57.3%	41.8%	58.2%
448,734	BURLINGTON	205,255	82,374	121,211	1,670	38,837	D	40.1%	59.1%	40.5%	59.5%
513,657	CAMDEN	214,381	62,734	148,925	2,722	86,191	D	29.3%	69.5%	29.6%	70.4%
97,265	CAPE MAY	43,072	22,281	19,965	826	2,316	R	51.7%	46.4%	52.7%	47.3%
156,898	CUMBERLAND	49,213	16,795	31,367	1,051	14,572	D	34.1%	63.7%	34.9%	65.1%
783,969	ESSEX	270,724	53,009	213,404	4,311	160,395	D	19.6%	78.8%	19.9%	80.1%
288,288	GLOUCESTER	129,934	52,591	74,271	3,072	21,680	D	40.5%	57.2%	41.5%	58.5%
634,266	HUDSON	176,331	32,876	139,910	3,545	107,034	D	18.6%	79.3%	19.0%	81.0%
128,349	HUNTERDON	62,799	36,000	24,676	2,123	11,324	R	57.3%	39.3%	59.3%	40.7%
366,513	MERCER	144,647	43,793	97,964	2,890	54,171	D	30.3%	67.7%	30.9%	69.1%
809,858	MIDDLESEX	281,760	97,730	178,686	5,344	80,956	D	34.7%	63.4%	35.4%	64.6%
630,380	MONMOUTH	268,964	144,366	120,154	4,444	24,212	R	53.7%	44.7%	54.6%	45.4%
492,276	MORRIS	209,848	114,078	93,209	2,561	20,869	R	54.4%	44.4%	55.0%	45.0%
576,567	OCEAN	236,004	132,413	99,362	4,229	33,051	R	56.1%	42.1%	57.1%	42.9%
501,226	PASSAIC	162,215	54,149	105,286	2,780	51,137	D	33.4%	64.9%	34.0%	66.0%
66,083	SALEM	28,649	12,555	15,044	1,050	2,489	D	43.8%	52.5%	45.5%	54.5%
323,444	SOMERSET	136,258	63,349	70,264	2,645	6,915	D	46.5%	51.6%	47.4%	52.6%
149,265	SUSSEX	66,293	38,250	25,212	2,831	13,038	R	57.7%	38.0%	60.3%	39.7%
536,499	UNION	187,744	58,929	125,635	3,180	66,706	D	31.4%	66.9%	31.9%	68.1%
108,692	WARREN	42,806	24,046	17,904	856	6,142	R	56.2%	41.8%	57.3%	42.7%
8,791,894	TOTAL	3,374,668	1,329,405	1,985,783	59,480	656,378	D	39.4%	58.8%	40.1%	59.9%

NEW JERSEY

HOUSE OF REPRESENTATIVES

CD	Year	Total Vote	Republican		Democratic		Other Vote	Rep.-Dem. Plurality	Percentage			
									Total Vote		Major Vote	
			Vote	Candidate	Vote	Candidate			Rep.	Dem.	Rep.	Dem.
1	2012	308,519	92,459	HORTON, GREGORY W.	210,470	ANDREWS, ROBERT E.*	5,590	118,011 D	30.0%	68.2%	30.5%	69.5%
2	2012	289,072	166,679	LOBIONDO, FRANK A.*	116,463	SHOBER, CASSANDRA	5,930	50,216 R	57.7%	40.3%	58.9%	41.1%
3	2012	324,406	174,257	RUNYAN, JON*	145,509	ADLER, SHELLEY	4,640	28,748 R	53.7%	44.9%	54.5%	45.5%
4	2012	306,249	195,146	SMITH, CHRIS*	107,992	FROELICH, BRIAN P.	3,111	87,154 R	63.7%	35.3%	64.4%	35.6%
5	2012	304,377	167,503	GARRETT, SCOTT*	130,102	GUSSEN, ADAM	6,772	37,401 R	55.0%	42.7%	56.3%	43.7%
6	2012	239,638	84,360	LITTLE, ANNA C.	151,782	PALLONE, FRANK JR.*	3,496	67,422 D	35.2%	63.3%	35.7%	64.3%
7	2012	307,395	175,704	LANCE, LEONARD*	123,090	CHIVUKULA, UPENDRA J.	8,601	52,614 R	57.2%	40.0%	58.8%	41.2%
8	2012	167,800	31,767	KARCZEWSKI, MARIA	130,857	SIRES, ALBIO*	5,176	99,090 D	18.9%	78.0%	19.5%	80.5%
9	2012	220,148	55,094	BOTEACH, SHMULEY	162,834	PASCRELL, BILL JR.*	2,220	107,740 D	25.0%	74.0%	25.3%	74.7%
10	2012	230,060	24,271	KELEMEN, BRIAN C.	201,435	PAYNE, DONALD M. JR.	4,354	177,164 D	10.5%	87.6%	10.8%	89.2%
11	2012	309,899	182,239	FRELINGHUYSEN, RODNEY*	123,935	ARVANITES, JOHN	3,725	58,304 R	58.8%	40.0%	59.5%	40.5%
12	2012	274,391	80,907	BECK, ERIC A.	189,938	HOLT, RUSH*	3,546	109,031 D	29.5%	69.2%	29.9%	70.1%
TOTAL	2012	3,281,954	1,430,386		1,794,407		57,161	364,021 D	43.6%	54.7%	44.4%	55.6%

Note: An asterisk (*) denotes incumbent.

NEW JERSEY

GENERAL AND PRIMARY ELECTIONS

GENERAL ELECTIONS: OTHER VOTE

President Other vote was 21,045 Libertarian (Gary E. Johnson), 9,888 Green (Jill Stein), 2,064 Constitution (Virgil H. Goode), 1,724 Justice (Ross C. "Rocky" Anderson), 1,007 Other (Jeff Boss), 710 Socialist Workers Party (James Harris), 664 American Third Position (Merlin Miller), 521 Socialism and Liberation (Peta Lindsay)

Senator Other vote was 16,803 Libertarian (Kenneth R. Kaplan), 15,799 Green (Ken Wolski), 9,377 Independent (Gwen Diakos), 3,830 Independent (J. David Dranikoff), 3,595 America First (Inder "Andy" Soni), 3,544 Independent (Robert "Turk" Turkavage), 2,256 Socialist (Gregory J. Pason), 2,201 Independent (Eugene Martin Lavergne), 2,075 Independent (Daryl Mikell Brooks)

House Other vote was:

CD 1 4,413 Green (John William Reitter), 1,177 Reform (Margaret Chapman)

CD 2 2,699 Libertarian (John Ordille), 1,329 Constitutional Conservative (Charles Lukens), 1,010 The People's Agenda (David W. Bowen), 892 Conservative, Compassionate, Creative (Frank Jr. Faralli)

CD 3 1,956 Marijuana (R. Edward "Njweedman" Forchion), 1,104 Bob's for Jobs (Robert Shapiro), 770 No Slogan (Frederick John Lavergne), 530 None of Them (Robert Witterschein), 280 No Slogan Filed (Christopher G. Dennick)

CD 4 3,111 No Slogan (Leonard P. Marshall)

CD 5 6,772 Green (Patricia Alessandrini)

CD 6 1,392 Libertarian (Len Flynn), 868 Overthrow All Incumbents (Karen Anne Zaletel), 830 Independent (Mac Dara Francis X. Lyden), 406 Reform (Herbert L.Tarbous)

CD 7 4,520 Independent (Dennis A. Breen), 4,081 Libertarian (Patrick Mcknight)

CD 8 1,841 Politicans are Crooks (Herbert H. Shaw), 1,710 Restoring America's Promise (Stephen Deluca), 1,625 Unity Is Strength (Pablo Olivera)

CD 9 1,138 Abundant America (E. David Smith), 1,082 Constitution (Jeanette Woolsey)

CD 10 3,127 Change, Change, Change (Joanne Miller), 1,227 Libertarian (Mick Erickson)

CD 11 3,725 Opposing Congressional Gridlock (Barry Berlin)

CD 12 2,261 Independent (Jack Freudenheim), 1,285 Truth Vision Hope (Kenneth J. Cody)

NEW JERSEY

GENERAL AND PRIMARY ELECTIONS

PRIMARY ELECTIONS: SUPPLEMENTARY INFORMATION

Primary	June 5, 2012	**Registration** (as of June 5, 2012)	5,271,837	Democratic	1,719,729
				Republican	1,057,855
				Libertarian	1,472
				Green	1,076
				Conservative	396
				Constitution	144
				Reform	65
				Natural Law	36
				Unaffiliated	2,491,064

Primary Type   Semi-open—Registered Democrats and Republicans could vote only in their party's primary. "Unaffiliated" voters could participate in either party's primary if they were willing to become a member of that party.

	REPUBLICAN PRIMARIES			DEMOCRATIC PRIMARIES		
President	Romney, W. Mitt	188,121	81.3%	Obama, Barack H.*	283,673	100.0%
	Paul, Ron	24,017	10.4%			
	Santorum, Rick	12,115	5.2%			
	Gingrich, Newt	7,212	3.1%			
	TOTAL	*231,465*		*TOTAL*	*283,673*	
Senator	Kyrillos, Joe	163,817	76.9%	Menendez, Robert*	272,201	100.0%
	Brown, David Douglas	19,238	9.0%			
	Rullo, Joe Rudy	17,161	8.1%			
	Qarmout, Bader G.	12,823	6.0%			
	TOTAL	*213,039*		*TOTAL*	*272,201*	
Congressional District 1	Horton, Gregory W.	11,189	100.0%	Andrews, Robert E.*	21,318	88.4%
				Tenaglio, Francis X.	2,797	11.6%
	TOTAL	*11,189*		*TOTAL*	*24,115*	
Congressional District 2	LoBiondo, Frank A.*	20,551	87.6%	Shober, Cassandra	9,810	64.9%
	Assad, Mike	2,914	12.4%	Thomas-Hughes, Viola	3,971	26.3%
				Stein, Gary	1,327	8.8%
	TOTAL	*23,465*		*TOTAL*	*15,108*	
Congressional District 3	Runyan, Jon*	22,013	100.0%	Adler, Shelley	15,176	100.0%
	TOTAL	*22,013*		*TOTAL*	*15,176*	
Congressional District 4	Smith, Christopher H.*	21,520	83.6%	Froelich, Brian P.	12,110	100.0%
	McGowan, Terrence	4,209	16.4%			
	TOTAL	*25,729*		*TOTAL*	*12,110*	
Congressional District 5	Garrett, Scott*	24,709	87.2%	Gussen, Adam	10,208	54.9%
	Cino, Michael J.	2,107	7.4%	Castle, Jason	6,448	34.7%
	Somer, Bonnie	1,511	5.3%	Sare, Diane	1,925	10.4%
	TOTAL	*28,327*		*TOTAL*	*18,581*	
Congressional District 6	Little, Anna C.	7,692	70.1%	Pallone, Frank*	16,593	100.0%
	Cullari, Ernesto	3,277	29.9%			
	TOTAL	*10,969*		*TOTAL*	*16,593*	
Congressional District 7	Lance, Leonard*	23,432	60.6%	Chivukula, Upendra J.	11,506	100.0%
	Larsen, David	15,253	39.4%			
	TOTAL	*38,685*		*TOTAL*	*11,506*	

NEW JERSEY

GENERAL AND PRIMARY ELECTIONS

	REPUBLICAN PRIMARIES			DEMOCRATIC PRIMARIES		
Congressional District 8	Karczewski, Maria	2,981	100.0%	Sires, Albio*	30,840	89.0%
				Shurin, Michael J.	3,808	11.0%
	TOTAL	*2,981*		*TOTAL*	*34,648*	
Congressional District 9	Boteach, Shmuley	5,364	57.9%	Pascrell, Bill Jr.*	31,435	61.2%
	Castillo, Hector L.	2,623	28.3%	Rothman, Steven R.*	19,947	38.8%
	Billack, Blase	1,278	13.8%			
	TOTAL	*9,265*		*TOTAL*	*51,382*	
Congressional District 10	Kelemen, Brian C.	2,095	100.0%	Payne, Donald M. Jr.	36,576	59.6%
				Rice, Ronald C.	11,939	19.5%
				Gill, Nia H.	10,207	16.6%
				Smith, Wayne	1,356	2.2%
				Flynn, Dennis R.	779	1.3%
				Wright, Cathy	501	0.8%
	TOTAL	*2,095*		*TOTAL*	*61,358*	
Congressional District 11	Frelinghuysen, Rodney*	30,831	100.0%	Arvanites, John	13,387	100.0%
	TOTAL	*30,831*		*TOTAL*	*13,387*	
Congressional District 12	Beck, Eric A.	9,361	100.0%	Holt, Rush*	24,339	100.0%
	TOTAL	*9,361*		*TOTAL*	*24,339*	

Notes: An asterisk (*) denotes incumbent. Due to redistricting, the 9th district Democratic primary pitted two incumbents against each other (Pascrell, former 8th district, and Rothman, former 9th district).

NEW MEXICO

Congressional districts first established for elections held in 2012

3 members

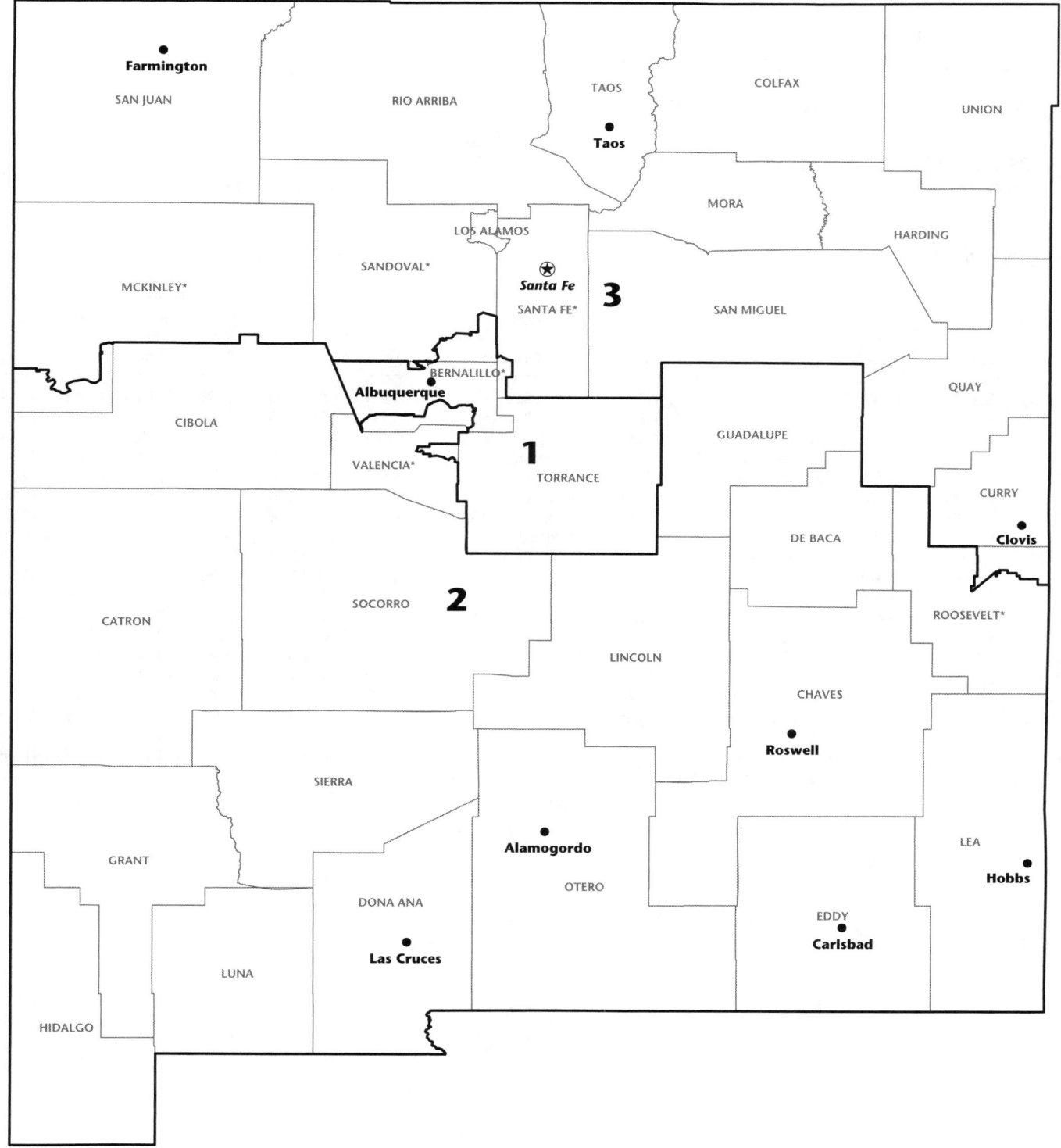

* Asterisk indicates a county whose boundaries include parts of two or more Congressional districts.

NEW MEXICO

GOVERNOR
Susana Martinez (R). Elected 2010 to a four-year term.

SENATORS (2 Democrats)
Tom Udall (D). Elected 2008 to a six-year term.

Martin Heinrich (D). Elected 2012 to a six-year term.

REPRESENTATIVES (1 Republican, 2 Democrats)
1. Michelle Lujan Grisham (D)   2. Steve Pearce (R)   3. Ben Ray Luján (D)

POSTWAR VOTE FOR PRESIDENT

Year	Total Vote	Republican Vote	Republican Candidate	Democratic Vote	Democratic Candidate	Other Vote	Rep.-Dem. Plurality	Total Vote Rep.	Total Vote Dem.	Major Vote Rep.	Major Vote Dem.
2012	783,757	335,788	Romney, W. Mitt	415,335	Obama, Barack H.*	32,634	79,547 D	42.8%	53.0%	44.7%	55.3%
2008	830,158	346,832	McCain, John S. III	472,422	Obama, Barack H.	10,904	125,590 D	41.8%	56.9%	42.3%	57.7%
2004	756,304	376,930	Bush, George W.*	370,942	Kerry, John F.	8,432	5,988 R	49.8%	49.0%	50.4%	49.6%
2000**	598,605	286,417	Bush, George W.	286,783	Gore, Albert Jr.	25,405	366 D	47.8%	47.9%	50.0%	50.0%
1996**	556,074	232,751	Dole, Robert "Bob"	273,495	Clinton, Bill*	49,828	40,744 D	41.9%	49.2%	46.0%	54.0%
1992**	569,986	212,824	Bush, George H.*	261,617	Clinton, Bill	95,545	48,793 D	37.3%	45.9%	44.9%	55.1%
1988	521,287	270,341	Bush, George H.	244,497	Dukakis, Michael S.	6,449	25,844 R	51.9%	46.9%	52.5%	47.5%
1984	514,370	307,101	Reagan, Ronald*	201,769	Mondale, Walter F.	5,500	105,332 R	59.7%	39.2%	60.3%	39.7%
1980**	456,971	250,779	Reagan, Ronald	167,826	Carter, Jimmy*	38,366	82,953 R	54.9%	36.7%	59.9%	40.1%
1976	418,409	211,419	Ford, Gerald R.*	201,148	Carter, Jimmy	5,842	10,271 R	50.5%	48.1%	51.2%	48.8%
1972	386,241	235,606	Nixon, Richard M.*	141,084	McGovern, George S.	9,551	94,522 R	61.0%	36.5%	62.5%	37.5%
1968**	327,350	169,692	Nixon, Richard M.	130,081	Humphrey, Hubert H. Jr.	27,577	39,611 R	51.8%	39.7%	56.6%	43.4%
1964	328,645	132,838	Goldwater, Barry M. Sr.	194,015	Johnson, Lyndon B.*	1,792	61,177 D	40.4%	59.0%	40.6%	59.4%
1960	311,107	153,733	Nixon, Richard M.	156,027	Kennedy, John F.	1,347	2,294 D	49.4%	50.2%	49.6%	50.4%
1956	253,926	146,788	Eisenhower, Dwight D.*	106,098	Stevenson, Adlai E. II	1,040	40,690 R	57.8%	41.8%	58.0%	42.0%
1952	238,608	132,170	Eisenhower, Dwight D.	105,661	Stevenson, Adlai E. II	777	26,509 R	55.4%	44.3%	55.6%	44.4%
1948	187,063	80,303	Dewey, Thomas E.	105,464	Truman, Harry S.*	1,296	25,161 D	42.9%	56.4%	43.2%	56.8%

Note: An asterisk (*) denotes incumbent. **In past elections, the other vote included: 2000 - 21,251 Green (Ralph Nader); 1996 - 32,257 Reform (Ross Perot); 1992 - 91,895 Independent (Perot); 1980 - 29,459 Independent (John Anderson); 1968 - 25,737 American Independent (George Wallace).

NEW MEXICO

POSTWAR VOTE FOR GOVERNOR

Year	Total Vote	Republican Vote	Republican Candidate	Democratic Vote	Democratic Candidate	Other Vote	Rep.-Dem. Plurality	Total Vote Rep.	Total Vote Dem.	Major Vote Rep.	Major Vote Dem.
2010	602,827	321,219	Martinez, Susana	280,614	Denish, Diane D.	994	40,605 R	53.3%	46.5%	53.4%	46.6%
2006	559,170	174,364	Dendahl, John	384,806	Richardson, Bill*		210,442 D	31.2%	68.8%	31.2%	68.8%
2002	484,233	189,074	Sanchez, John A.	268,693	Richardson, Bill	26,466	79,619 D	39.0%	55.5%	41.3%	58.7%
1998	498,703	271,948	Johnson, Gary E.*	226,755	Chavez, Martin J.		45,193 R	54.5%	45.5%	54.5%	45.5%
1994**	467,621	232,945	Johnson, Gary E.	186,686	King, Bruce*	47,990	46,259 R	49.8%	39.9%	55.5%	44.5%
1990	411,232	185,692	Bond, Frank	224,564	King, Bruce	976	38,872 D	45.2%	54.6%	45.3%	54.7%
1986	394,833	209,455	Carruthers, Garrey E.	185,378	Powell, Ray B.		24,077 R	53.0%	47.0%	53.0%	47.0%
1982	407,466	191,626	Irick, John B.	215,840	Anaya, Toney		24,214 D	47.0%	53.0%	47.0%	53.0%
1978	345,577	170,848	Skeen, Joseph R.	174,631	King, Bruce	98	3,783 D	49.4%	50.5%	49.5%	50.5%
1974	328,742	160,430	Skeen, Joseph R.	164,172	Apodaca, Jerry	4,140	3,742 D	48.8%	49.9%	49.4%	50.6%
1970**	290,375	134,640	Domenici, Peter V.	148,835	King, Bruce	6,900	14,195 D	46.4%	51.3%	47.5%	52.5%
1968	318,975	160,140	Cargo, David F.*	157,230	Chavez, Fabian	1,605	2,910 R	50.2%	49.3%	50.5%	49.5%
1966	260,232	134,625	Cargo, David F.	125,587	Lusk, T. E.	20	9,038 R	51.7%	48.3%	51.7%	48.3%
1964	318,042	126,540	Tucker, Merle H.	191,497	Campbell, Jack M.*	5	64,957 D	39.8%	60.2%	39.8%	60.2%
1962	247,135	116,184	Mechem, Edwin L.*	130,933	Campbell, Jack M.	18	14,749 D	47.0%	53.0%	47.0%	53.0%
1960	305,542	153,765	Mechem, Edwin L.	151,777	Burroughs, John*		1,988 R	50.3%	49.7%	50.3%	49.7%
1958	205,048	101,567	Mechem, Edwin L.*	103,481	Burroughs, John		1,914 D	49.5%	50.5%	49.5%	50.5%
1956	251,751	131,488	Mechem, Edwin L.	120,263	Simms, John F. Jr.*		11,225 R	52.2%	47.8%	52.2%	47.8%
1954	193,956	83,373	Stockton, Alvin	110,583	Simms, John F. Jr.		27,210 D	43.0%	57.0%	43.0%	57.0%
1952	240,150	129,116	Mechem, Edwin L.*	111,034	Grantham, Everett		18,082 R	53.8%	46.2%	53.8%	46.2%
1950	180,205	96,846	Mechem, Edwin L.	83,359	Miles, John E.		13,487 R	53.7%	46.3%	53.7%	46.3%
1948	189,992	86,023	Lujan, Manuel	103,969	Mabry, Thomas J.*		17,946 D	45.3%	54.7%	45.3%	54.7%
1946	132,630	62,575	Safford, Edward L.	70,055	Mabry, Thomas J.		7,480 D	47.2%	52.8%	47.2%	52.8%

Note: An asterisk (*) denotes incumbent. **In past elections, the other vote included: 1994 - 47,990 Green (Roberto Mondragon). The term of New Mexico's governor was increased from two to four years effective with the 1970 election.

POSTWAR VOTE FOR SENATOR

Year	Total Vote	Republican Vote	Republican Candidate	Democratic Vote	Democratic Candidate	Other Vote	Rep.-Dem. Plurality	Total Vote Rep.	Total Vote Dem.	Major Vote Rep.	Major Vote Dem.
2012	775,792	351,259	Wilson, Heather A.	395,717	Heinrich, Martin	28,816	44,458 D	45.3%	51.0%	47.0%	53.0%
2008	823,650	318,522	Pearce, Steve	505,128	Udall, Tom		186,606 D	38.7%	61.3%	38.7%	61.3%
2006	558,550	163,826	McCulloch, Allen	394,365	Bingaman, Jeff*	359	230,539 D	29.3%	70.6%	29.3%	70.7%
2002	483,340	314,301	Domenici, Peter V.*	169,039	Tristani, Gloria		145,262 R	65.0%	35.0%	65.0%	35.0%
2000	589,526	225,517	Redmond, Bill	363,744	Bingaman, Jeff*	265	138,227 D	38.3%	61.7%	38.3%	61.7%
1996	551,821	357,171	Domenici, Peter V.*	164,356	Trujillo, Art	30,294	192,815 R	64.7%	29.8%	68.5%	31.5%
1994	463,196	213,025	McMillan, Colin R.	249,989	Bingaman, Jeff*	182	36,964 D	46.0%	54.0%	46.0%	54.0%
1990	406,938	296,712	Domenici, Peter V.*	110,033	Benavides, Tom R.	193	186,679 R	72.9%	27.0%	72.9%	27.1%
1988	508,598	186,579	Valentine, William	321,983	Bingaman, Jeff*	36	135,404 D	36.7%	63.3%	36.7%	63.3%
1984	502,634	361,371	Domenici, Peter V.*	141,253	Pratt, Judith A.	10	220,118 R	71.9%	28.1%	71.9%	28.1%
1982	404,810	187,128	Schmitt, Harrison*	217,682	Bingaman, Jeff		30,554 D	46.2%	53.8%	46.2%	53.8%
1978	343,554	183,442	Domenici, Peter V.*	160,045	Anaya, Toney	67	23,397 R	53.4%	46.6%	53.4%	46.6%
1976	413,141	234,681	Schmitt, Harrison	176,382	Montoya, Joseph M.*	2,078	58,299 R	56.8%	42.7%	57.1%	42.9%
1972	378,330	204,253	Domenici, Peter V.	173,815	Daniels, Jack	262	30,438 R	54.0%	45.9%	54.0%	46.0%
1970	289,906	135,004	Carter, Anderson	151,486	Montoya, Joseph M.*	3,416	16,482 D	46.6%	52.3%	47.1%	52.9%
1966	258,203	120,988	Carter, Anderson	137,205	Anderson, Clinton P.*	10	16,217 D	46.9%	53.1%	46.9%	53.1%
1964	325,774	147,562	Mechem, Edwin L.	178,209	Montoya, Joseph M.	3	30,647 D	45.3%	54.7%	45.3%	54.7%
1960	300,551	109,897	Colwes, William	190,654	Anderson, Clinton P.*		80,757 D	36.6%	63.4%	36.6%	63.4%
1958	203,323	75,827	Atchley, Forrest S.	127,496	Chavez, Dennis*		51,669 D	37.3%	62.7%	37.3%	62.7%
1954	194,422	83,071	Mechem, Edwin L.	111,351	Anderson, Clinton P.*		28,280 D	42.7%	57.3%	42.7%	57.3%
1952	239,711	117,168	Hurley, Patrick J.	122,543	Chavez, Dennis*		5,375 D	48.9%	51.1%	48.9%	51.1%
1948	188,495	80,226	Hurley, Patrick J.	108,269	Anderson, Clinton P.		28,043 D	42.6%	57.4%	42.6%	57.4%
1946	133,282	64,632	Hurley, Patrick J.	68,650	Chavez, Dennis*		4,018 D	48.5%	51.5%	48.5%	51.5%

Note: An asterisk (*) denotes incumbent.

NEW MEXICO

PRESIDENT 2012

2010 Census Population	County	Total Vote	Republican (Romney)	Democratic (Obama)	Other	Rep.-Dem. Plurality	Total Vote Rep.	Total Vote Dem.	Major Vote Rep.	Major Vote Dem.
662,564	BERNALILLO	270,969	106,408	150,739	13,822	44,331 D	39.3%	55.6%	41.4%	58.6%
3,725	CATRON	2,123	1,494	560	69	934 R	70.4%	26.4%	72.7%	27.3%
65,645	CHAVES	20,292	13,088	6,604	600	6,484 R	64.5%	32.5%	66.5%	33.5%
27,213	CIBOLA	8,243	2,998	4,961	284	1,963 D	36.4%	60.2%	37.7%	62.3%
13,750	COLFAX	5,764	2,699	2,828	237	129 D	46.8%	49.1%	48.8%	51.2%
48,376	CURRY	13,625	9,251	4,022	352	5,229 R	67.9%	29.5%	69.7%	30.3%
2,022	DE BACA	902	586	287	29	299 R	65.0%	31.8%	67.1%	32.9%
209,233	DONA ANA	66,423	27,322	37,139	1,962	9,817 D	41.1%	55.9%	42.4%	57.6%
53,829	EDDY	19,269	12,583	6,142	544	6,441 R	65.3%	31.9%	67.2%	32.8%
29,514	GRANT	12,902	5,358	7,090	454	1,732 D	41.5%	55.0%	43.0%	57.0%
4,687	GUADALUPE	2,135	557	1,488	90	931 D	26.1%	69.7%	27.2%	72.8%
695	HARDING	601	327	260	14	67 R	54.4%	43.3%	55.7%	44.3%
4,894	HIDALGO	1,935	899	995	41	96 D	46.5%	51.4%	47.5%	52.5%
64,727	LEA	17,015	12,548	4,080	387	8,468 R	73.7%	24.0%	75.5%	24.5%
20,497	LINCOLN	9,242	5,961	2,942	339	3,019 R	64.5%	31.8%	67.0%	33.0%
17,950	LOS ALAMOS	10,654	4,796	5,191	667	395 D	45.0%	48.7%	48.0%	52.0%
25,095	LUNA	7,500	3,670	3,583	247	87 R	48.9%	47.8%	50.6%	49.4%
71,492	MCKINLEY	21,929	5,546	15,841	542	10,295 D	25.3%	72.2%	25.9%	74.1%
4,881	MORA	2,611	595	1,955	61	1,360 D	22.8%	74.9%	23.3%	76.7%
63,797	OTERO	20,012	12,451	6,829	732	5,622 R	62.2%	34.1%	64.6%	35.4%
9,041	QUAY	3,707	2,202	1,383	122	819 R	59.4%	37.3%	61.4%	38.6%
40,246	RIO ARRIBA	15,343	3,397	11,465	481	8,068 D	22.1%	74.7%	22.9%	77.1%
19,846	ROOSEVELT	5,969	4,043	1,727	199	2,316 R	67.7%	28.9%	70.1%	29.9%
130,044	SAN JUAN	46,237	28,849	15,855	1,533	12,994 R	62.4%	34.3%	64.5%	35.5%
29,393	SAN MIGUEL	11,509	2,303	8,850	356	6,547 D	20.0%	76.9%	20.6%	79.4%
131,561	SANDOVAL	54,078	24,387	27,236	2,455	2,849 D	45.1%	50.4%	47.2%	52.8%
144,170	SANTA FE	69,245	15,500	50,872	2,873	35,372 D	22.4%	73.5%	23.4%	76.6%
11,988	SIERRA	5,102	2,928	1,964	210	964 R	57.4%	38.5%	59.9%	40.1%
17,866	SOCORRO	7,193	2,722	4,058	413	1,336 D	37.8%	56.4%	40.1%	59.9%
32,937	TAOS	15,339	2,730	11,978	631	9,248 D	17.8%	78.1%	18.6%	81.4%
16,383	TORRANCE	6,402	3,529	2,428	445	1,101 R	55.1%	37.9%	59.2%	40.8%
4,549	UNION	1,759	1,236	472	51	764 R	70.3%	26.8%	72.4%	27.6%
76,569	VALENCIA	27,728	12,825	13,511	1,392	686 D	46.3%	48.7%	48.7%	51.3%
2,059,179	TOTAL	783,757	335,788	415,335	32,634	79,547 D	42.8%	53.0%	44.7%	55.3%

NEW MEXICO

SENATOR 2012

2010 Census Population	County	Total Vote	Republican (Wilson)	Democratic (Heinrich)	Other	Rep.-Dem. Plurality	Total Vote Rep.	Total Vote Dem.	Major Vote Rep.	Major Vote Dem.
662,564	BERNALILLO	268,978	115,514	144,659	8,805	29,145 D	42.9%	53.8%	44.4%	55.6%
3,725	CATRON	2,104	1,376	591	137	785 R	65.4%	28.1%	70.0%	30.0%
65,645	CHAVES	20,143	12,791	6,566	786	6,225 R	63.5%	32.6%	66.1%	33.9%
27,213	CIBOLA	8,157	3,256	4,493	408	1,237 D	39.9%	55.1%	42.0%	58.0%
13,750	COLFAX	5,717	2,732	2,737	248	5 D	47.8%	47.9%	50.0%	50.0%
48,376	CURRY	13,336	9,055	3,818	463	5,237 R	67.9%	28.6%	70.3%	29.7%
2,022	DE BACA	893	584	291	18	293 R	65.4%	32.6%	66.7%	33.3%
209,233	DONA ANA	65,115	25,145	36,579	3,391	11,434 D	38.6%	56.2%	40.7%	59.3%
53,829	EDDY	19,010	12,255	6,077	678	6,178 R	64.5%	32.0%	66.9%	33.1%
29,514	GRANT	12,829	5,255	7,049	525	1,794 D	41.0%	54.9%	42.7%	57.3%

NEW MEXICO

SENATOR 2012

2010 Census Population	County	Total Vote	Republican (Wilson)	Democratic (Heinrich)	Other	Rep.-Dem. Plurality	Percentage			
							Total Vote		Major Vote	
							Rep.	Dem.	Rep.	Dem.
4,687	GUADALUPE	2,125	656	1,396	73	740 D	30.9%	65.7%	32.0%	68.0%
695	HARDING	592	322	249	21	73 R	54.4%	42.1%	56.4%	43.6%
4,894	HIDALGO	1,890	909	892	89	17 R	48.1%	47.2%	50.5%	49.5%
64,727	LEA	16,767	12,200	4,006	561	8,194 R	72.8%	23.9%	75.3%	24.7%
20,497	LINCOLN	9,171	5,797	2,950	424	2,847 R	63.2%	32.2%	66.3%	33.7%
17,950	LOS ALAMOS	10,556	5,743	4,540	273	1,203 R	54.4%	43.0%	55.8%	44.2%
25,095	LUNA	7,383	3,471	3,494	418	23 D	47.0%	47.3%	49.8%	50.2%
71,492	MCKINLEY	21,504	7,647	13,004	853	5,357 D	35.6%	60.5%	37.0%	63.0%
4,881	MORA	2,580	705	1,803	72	1,098 D	27.3%	69.9%	28.1%	71.9%
63,797	OTERO	19,761	12,084	6,638	1,039	5,446 R	61.2%	33.6%	64.5%	35.5%
9,041	QUAY	3,639	2,104	1,385	150	719 R	57.8%	38.1%	60.3%	39.7%
40,246	RIO ARRIBA	15,191	4,654	10,071	466	5,417 D	30.6%	66.3%	31.6%	68.4%
19,846	ROOSEVELT	5,861	3,917	1,671	273	2,246 R	66.8%	28.5%	70.1%	29.9%
130,044	SAN JUAN	45,756	29,270	14,450	2,036	14,820 R	64.0%	31.6%	66.9%	33.1%
29,393	SAN MIGUEL	11,408	2,758	8,308	342	5,550 D	24.2%	72.8%	24.9%	75.1%
131,561	SANDOVAL	53,735	26,079	25,727	1,929	352 R	48.5%	47.9%	50.3%	49.7%
144,170	SANTA FE	68,575	17,456	49,291	1,828	31,835 D	25.5%	71.9%	26.2%	73.8%
11,988	SIERRA	5,047	2,790	1,984	273	806 R	55.3%	39.3%	58.4%	41.6%
17,866	SOCORRO	7,126	3,052	3,745	329	693 D	42.8%	52.6%	44.9%	55.1%
32,937	TAOS	15,156	3,326	11,373	457	8,047 D	21.9%	75.0%	22.6%	77.4%
16,383	TORRANCE	6,388	3,782	2,318	288	1,464 R	59.2%	36.3%	62.0%	38.0%
4,549	UNION	1,700	1,193	442	65	751 R	70.2%	26.0%	73.0%	27.0%
76,569	VALENCIA	27,599	13,381	13,120	1,098	261 R	48.5%	47.5%	50.5%	49.5%
2,059,179	TOTAL	775,792	351,259	395,717	28,816	44,458 D	45.3%	51.0%	47.0%	53.0%

NEW MEXICO

HOUSE OF REPRESENTATIVES

CD	Year	Total Vote	Republican		Democratic		Other Vote	Rep.-Dem. Plurality	Percentage			
			Vote	Candidate	Vote	Candidate			Total Vote		Major Vote	
									Rep.	Dem.	Rep.	Dem.
1	2012	275,856	112,473	ARNOLD-JONES, JANICE E.	162,924	GRISHAM, MICHELLE LUJAN	459	50,451 D	40.8%	59.1%	40.8%	59.2%
2	2012	225,515	133,180	PEARCE, STEVE*	92,162	ERHARD, EVELYN MADRID	173	41,018 R	59.1%	40.9%	59.1%	40.9%
3	2012	264,719	97,616	BYRD, JEFFERSON L.	167,103	LUJÁN, BEN RAY*		69,487 D	36.9%	63.1%	36.9%	63.1%
TOTAL	2012	766,090	343,269		422,189		632	78,920 D	44.8%	55.1%	44.8%	55.2%

Note: An asterisk (*) denotes incumbent.

NEW MEXICO

GENERAL AND PRIMARY ELECTIONS

GENERAL ELECTIONS: OTHER VOTE

President   Other vote was 27,787 Libertarian (Gary E. Johnson), 2,691 Green (Jill Stein), 1,174 Justice (Ross C. "Rocky" Anderson), 982 Constitution (Virgil H. Goode)

Senator   Other vote was 28,199 Independent American (Jon Barrie), 617 Write-in (Robert L. Anderson)

House   Other vote was:

CD 1   459 Write-in (Jeanne Pahls)
CD 2   173 Write-in (Jack McGrann)

PRIMARY ELECTIONS: SUPPLEMENTARY INFORMATION

Primary	June 5, 2012	**Registration** (as of May 24, 2012)	1,197,874	Republican	576,456
				Democratic	381,053
				Declined to State	205,351
				Other	35,014

Primary Type   Closed—Only registered Democrats and Republicans could vote in their party's primary.

	REPUBLICAN PRIMARIES			**DEMOCRATIC PRIMARIES**		
President	Romney, W. Mitt	65,935	73.2%	Obama, Barack H.*	122,958	100.0%
	Santorum, Rick	9,517	10.6%			
	Paul, Ron	9,363	10.4%			
	Gingrich, Newt	5,298	5.9%			
	TOTAL	*90,113*		*TOTAL*	*122,958*	
Senator	Wilson, Heather A.	63,631	70.0%	Heinrich, Martin	83,432	58.9%
	Sowards, Greg	27,214	30.0%	Balderas, Hector	58,128	41.1%
	TOTAL	*90,845*		*TOTAL*	*141,560*	
Congressional District 1	Arnold-Jones, Janice E.	26,198	100.0%	Grisham, Michelle Lujan	19,111	40.1%
				Griego, Eric J.	16,702	35.0%
				Chavez, Martin J.	11,895	24.9%
	TOTAL	*26,198*		*TOTAL*	*47,708*	
Congressional District 2	Pearce, Steve*	29,911	100.0%	Erhard, Evelyn Madrid	24,175	100.0%
	TOTAL	*29,911*		*TOTAL*	*24,175*	
Congressional District 3	Byrd, Jefferson L.	13,055	53.5%	Luján, Ben Ray*	53,908	100.0%
	Newton, Frederick L.	11,340	46.5%			
	TOTAL	*24,395*		*TOTAL*	*53,908*	

Note: An asterisk (*) denotes incumbent.

NEW YORK

Congressional districts first established for elections held in 2012
27 members

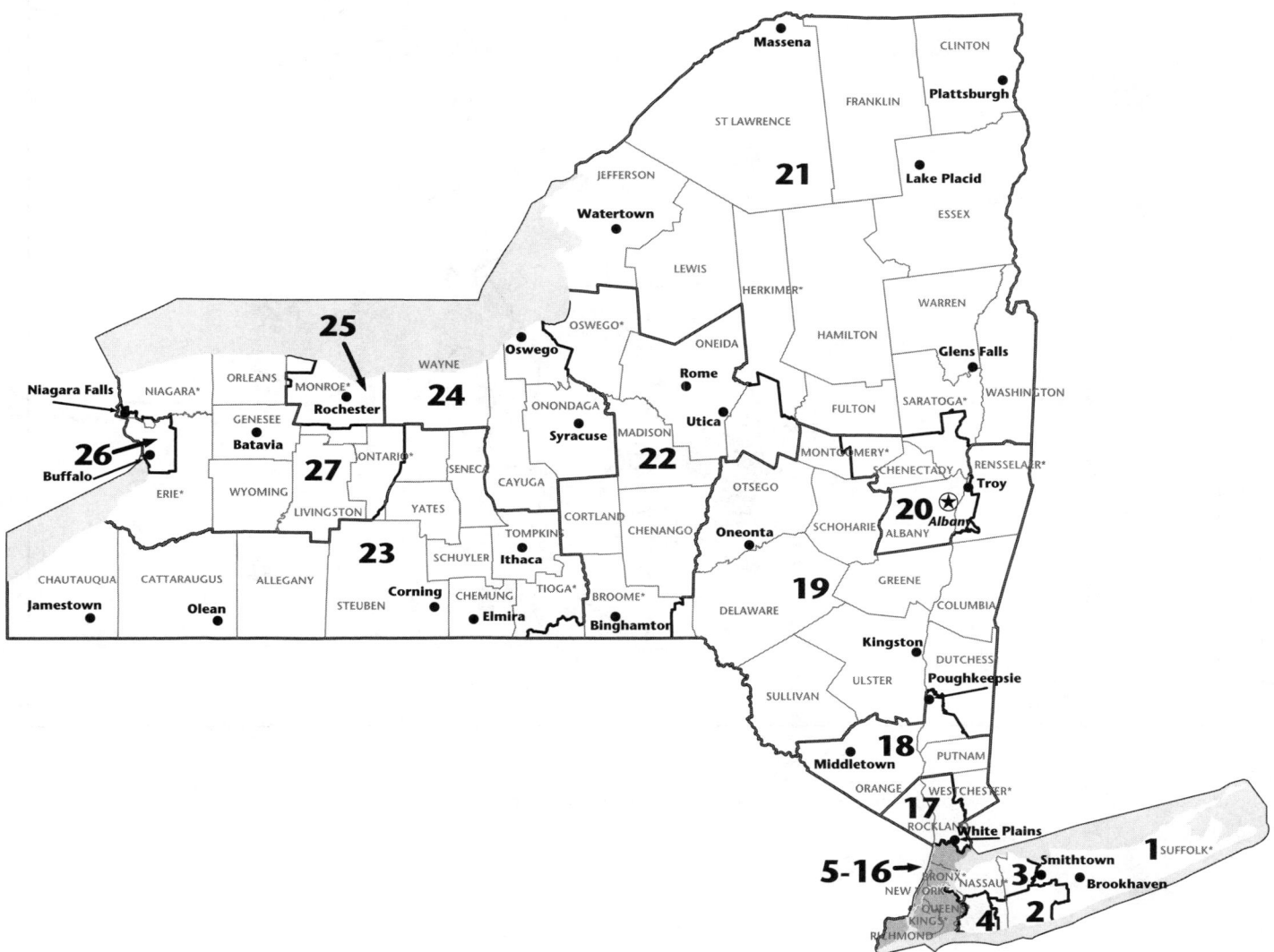

* Asterisk indicates a county whose boundaries include parts of two or more Congressional districts.

NEW YORK
New York City Area

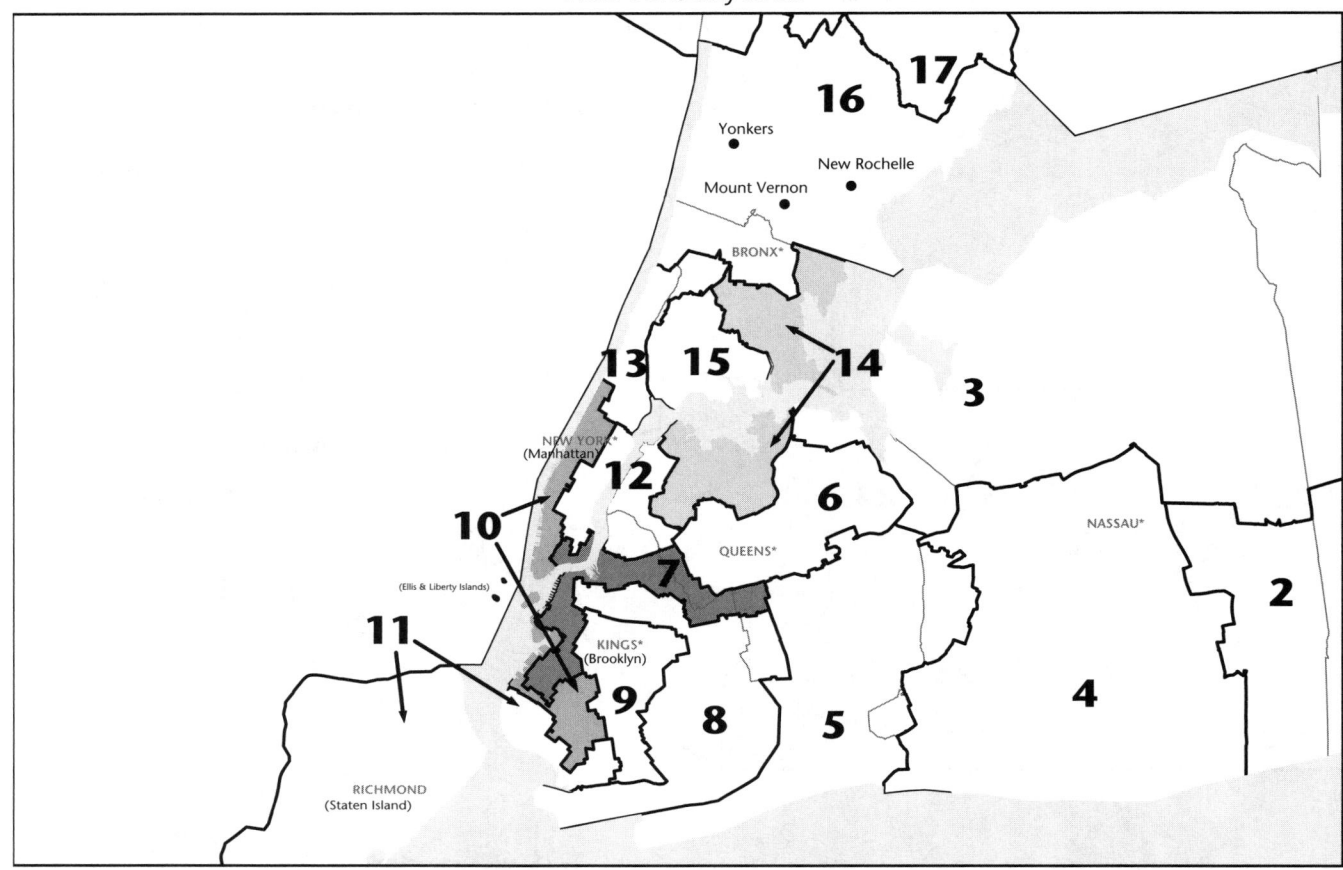

Yonkers

New Rochelle

Mount Vernon

BRONX*

13 15 14

3

NEW YORK*
(Manhattan)

12

10

6

NASSAU*

QUEENS*

(Ellis & Liberty Islands)

2

11

7

KINGS*
(Brooklyn)

9 8 5 4

RICHMOND
(Staten Island)

* Asterisk indicates a county whose boundaries include parts of two or more Congressional districts.

NEW YORK

GOVERNOR
Andrew M. Cuomo (D). Elected 2010 to a four-year term.

SENATORS (2 Democrats)
Charles E. Schumer (D). Reelected 2010 to a six-year term. Previously elected 2004, 1998.

Kirsten E. Gillibrand (D). Elected 2010 to fill the remaining two years of the term vacated by Hillary Rodham Clinton (D), who resigned to become U.S. Secretary of State. Gillibrand sworn in as senator January 27, 2009, shortly after the vacancy occurred.

REPRESENTATIVES (6 Republicans, 21 Democrats)

1. Tim Bishop (D)
2. Pete King (R)
3. Steve Israel (D)
4. Carolyn McCarthy (D)
5. Gregory W. Meeks (D)
6. Grace Meng (D)
7. Nydia M. Velázquez (D)
8. Hakeem Jeffries (D)
9. Yvette D. Clarke (D)
10. Jerrold Nadler (D)
11. Michael Grimm (R)
12. Carolyn B. Maloney (D)
13. Charles B. Rangel (D)
14. Joseph Crowley (D)
15. José E. Serrano (D)
16. Eliot L. Engel (D)
17. Nita Lowey (D)
18. Sean Patrick Maloney (D)
19. Chris Gibson (R)
20. Paul D. Tonko (D)
21. Bill Owens (D)
22. Richard Hanna (R)
23. Tom Reed (R)
24. Dan Maffei (D)
25. Louise M. Slaughter (D)
26. Brian Higgins (D)
27. Chris Collins (R)

POSTWAR VOTE FOR PRESIDENT

Year	Total Vote	Republican Vote	Republican Candidate	Democratic Vote	Democratic Candidate	Other Vote	Rep.-Dem. Plurality	Total Vote Rep.	Total Vote Dem.	Major Vote Rep.	Major Vote Dem.
2012	7,081,159	2,490,431	Romney, W. Mitt	4,485,741	Obama, Barack H.*	104,987	1,995,310 D	35.2%	63.3%	35.7%	64.3%
2008	7,640,931	2,752,771	McCain, John S. III	4,804,945	Obama, Barack H.	83,215	2,052,174 D	36.0%	62.9%	36.4%	63.6%
2004	7,391,036	2,962,567	Bush, George W.*	4,314,280	Kerry, John F.	114,189	1,351,713 D	40.1%	58.4%	40.7%	59.3%
2000**	6,821,999	2,403,374	Bush, George W.	4,107,697	Gore, Albert Jr.	310,928	1,704,323 D	35.2%	60.2%	36.9%	63.1%
1996**	6,316,129	1,933,492	Dole, Robert "Bob"	3,756,177	Clinton, Bill*	626,460	1,822,685 D	30.6%	59.5%	34.0%	66.0%
1992**	6,926,925	2,346,649	Bush, George H.*	3,444,450	Clinton, Bill	1,135,826	1,097,801 D	33.9%	49.7%	40.5%	59.5%
1988	6,485,683	3,081,871	Bush, George H.	3,347,882	Dukakis, Michael S.	55,930	266,011 D	47.5%	51.6%	47.9%	52.1%
1984	6,806,810	3,664,763	Reagan, Ronald*	3,119,609	Mondale, Walter F.	22,438	545,154 R	53.8%	45.8%	54.0%	46.0%
1980**	6,201,959	2,893,831	Reagan, Ronald	2,728,372	Carter, Jimmy*	579,756	165,459 R	46.7%	44.0%	51.5%	48.5%
1976	6,534,170	3,100,791	Ford, Gerald R.*	3,389,558	Carter, Jimmy	43,821	288,767 D	47.5%	51.9%	47.8%	52.2%
1972	7,165,919	4,192,778	Nixon, Richard M.*	2,951,084	McGovern, George S.	22,057	1,241,694 R	58.5%	41.2%	58.7%	41.3%
1968**	6,791,688	3,007,932	Nixon, Richard M.	3,378,470	Humphrey, Hubert H. Jr.	405,286	370,538 D	44.3%	49.7%	47.1%	52.9%
1964	7,166,275	2,243,559	Goldwater, Barry M. Sr.	4,913,102	Johnson, Lyndon B.*	9,614	2,669,543 D	31.3%	68.6%	31.3%	68.7%
1960	7,291,079	3,446,419	Nixon, Richard M.	3,830,085	Kennedy, John F.	14,575	383,666 D	47.3%	52.5%	47.4%	52.6%
1956	7,095,971	4,345,506	Eisenhower, Dwight D.*	2,747,944	Stevenson, Adlai E. II	2,521	1,597,562 R	61.2%	38.7%	61.3%	38.7%
1952	7,128,239	3,952,813	Eisenhower, Dwight D.	3,104,601	Stevenson, Adlai E. II	70,825	848,212 R	55.5%	43.6%	56.0%	44.0%
1948**	6,177,337	2,841,163	Dewey, Thomas E.	2,780,204	Truman, Harry S.*	555,970	60,959 R	46.0%	45.0%	50.5%	49.5%

Note: An asterisk (*) denotes incumbent. **In past elections, the other vote included: 2000 - 244,030 Green (Ralph Nader); 1996 - 503,458 Reform (Ross Perot); 1992 - 1,090,721 Independent (Perot); 1980 - 467,801 Independent (John Anderson); 1968 - 358,864 American Independent (George Wallace); 1948 - 509,559 Progressive (Henry Wallace).

NEW YORK

POSTWAR VOTE FOR GOVERNOR

Year	Total Vote	Republican		Democratic		Other Vote	Rep.-Dem. Plurality		Percentage			
		Vote	Candidate	Vote	Candidate				Total Vote		Major Vote	
									Rep.	Dem.	Rep.	Dem.
2010	4,658,825	1,548,184	Paladino, Carl	2,911,721	Cuomo, Andrew M.	198,920	1,363,537 D		33.2%	62.5%	34.7%	65.3%
2006	4,437,220	1,274,335	Faso, John	3,086,709	Spitzer, Eliot	76,176	1,812,374 D		28.7%	69.6%	29.2%	70.8%
2002**	4,579,078	2,262,255	Pataki, George E.*	1,534,064	McCall, H. Carl	782,759	728,191 R		49.4%	33.5%	59.6%	40.4%
1998	4,735,236	2,571,991	Pataki, George E.*	1,570,317	Vallone, Peter F.	592,928	1,001,674 R		54.3%	33.2%	62.1%	37.9%
1994	5,208,762	2,538,702	Pataki, George E.	2,364,904	Cuomo, Mario M.*	305,156	173,798 R		48.7%	45.4%	51.8%	48.2%
1990**	4,056,896	865,948	Rinfret, Pierre A.	2,157,087	Cuomo, Mario M.*	1,033,861	1,291,139 D		21.3%	53.2%	28.6%	71.4%
1986	4,294,124	1,363,810	O'Rourke, Andrew P.	2,775,229	Cuomo, Mario M.*	155,085	1,411,419 D		31.8%	64.6%	32.9%	67.1%
1982	5,254,891	2,494,827	Lehrman, Lew	2,675,213	Cuomo, Mario M.	84,851	180,386 D		47.5%	50.9%	48.3%	51.7%
1978	4,768,820	2,156,404	Duryea, Perry B.	2,429,272	Carey, Hugh L.*	183,144	272,868 D		45.2%	50.9%	47.0%	53.0%
1974	5,293,176	2,219,667	Wilson, Malcolm*	3,028,503	Carey, Hugh L.	45,006	808,836 D		41.9%	57.2%	42.3%	57.7%
1970	6,013,064	3,151,432	Rockefeller, Nelson A.*	2,421,426	Goldberg, Arthur	440,206	730,006 R		52.4%	40.3%	56.5%	43.5%
1966**	6,006,246	2,690,626	Rockefeller, Nelson A.*	2,298,363	O'Connor, Frank	1,017,257	392,263 R		44.8%	38.3%	53.9%	46.1%
1962	5,805,631	3,081,587	Rockefeller, Nelson A.*	2,552,418	Morgenthau, Robert M.	171,626	529,169 R		53.1%	44.0%	54.7%	45.3%
1958	5,712,665	3,126,929	Rockefeller, Nelson A.	2,553,895	Harriman, Averell*	31,841	573,034 R		54.7%	44.7%	55.0%	45.0%
1954	5,161,942	2,549,613	Ives, Irving M.	2,560,738	Harriman, Averell	51,591	11,125 D		49.4%	49.6%	49.9%	50.1%
1950	5,308,889	2,819,523	Dewey, Thomas E.*	2,246,855	Lynch, Walter A.	242,511	572,668 R		53.1%	42.3%	55.7%	44.3%
1946	4,964,552	2,825,633	Dewey, Thomas E.*	2,138,482	Mead, James M.	437	687,151 R		56.9%	43.1%	56.9%	43.1%

Note: An asterisk (*) denotes incumbent. **In past elections, the other vote included: 2002 - 654,016 Independence (B. Thomas Golisano); 1990 - 827,614 Conservative (Herbert I. London); 1966 - 510,023 Conservative (Paul L. Adams), 507,234 Liberal (Franklin Roosevelt Jr.).

POSTWAR VOTE FOR SENATOR

Year	Total Vote	Republican		Democratic		Other Vote	Rep.-Dem. Plurality		Percentage			
		Vote	Candidate	Vote	Candidate				Total Vote		Major Vote	
									Rep.	Dem.	Rep.	Dem.
2012	6,679,678	1,758,702	Long, Wendy	4,822,330	Gillibrand, Kirsten E.*	98,646	3,063,628 D		26.3%	72.2%	26.7%	73.3%
2010	4,596,796	1,480,423	Townsend, Jay	3,047,880	Schumer, Charles E.*	68,493	1,567,457 D		32.2%	66.3%	32.7%	67.3%
2010S	4,508,771	1,582,693	DioGuardi, Joseph J.	2,837,684	Gillibrand, Kirsten E.*	88,394	1,254,991 D		35.1%	62.9%	35.8%	64.2%
2006	4,490,053	1,392,189	Spencer, John	3,008,428	Clinton, Hillary Rodham*	89,436	1,616,239 D		31.0%	67.0%	31.6%	68.4%
2004	6,702,875	1,625,069	Mills, Howard D.	4,769,824	Schumer, Charles E.*	307,982	3,144,755 D		24.2%	71.2%	25.4%	74.6%
2000	6,779,839	2,915,730	Lazio, Rick A.	3,747,310	Clinton, Hillary Rodham	116,799	831,580 D		43.0%	55.3%	43.8%	56.2%
1998	4,670,805	2,058,988	D'Amato, Alfonse M.*	2,551,065	Schumer, Charles E.	60,752	492,077 D		44.1%	54.6%	44.7%	55.3%
1994	4,794,601	1,988,308	Castro, Bernadette	2,646,541	Moynihan, Daniel Patrick*	159,752	658,233 D		41.5%	55.2%	42.9%	57.1%
1992	6,458,826	3,166,994	D'Amato, Alfonse M.*	3,086,200	Abrams, Robert	205,632	80,794 R		49.0%	47.8%	50.6%	49.4%
1988	6,040,980	1,875,784	McMillan, Robert	4,048,649	Moynihan, Daniel Patrick*	116,547	2,172,865 D		31.1%	67.0%	31.7%	68.3%
1986	4,179,447	2,378,197	D'Amato, Alfonse M.*	1,723,216	Green, Mark J.	78,034	654,981 R		56.9%	41.2%	58.0%	42.0%
1982	4,967,729	1,696,766	Sullivan, Florence	3,232,146	Moynihan, Daniel Patrick*	38,817	1,535,380 D		34.2%	65.1%	34.4%	65.6%
1980**	6,014,914	2,699,652	D'Amato, Alfonse M.	2,618,661	Holtzman, Elizabeth	696,601	80,991 R		44.9%	43.5%	50.8%	49.2%
1976	6,319,755	2,836,633	Buckley, James L.*	3,422,594	Moynihan, Daniel Patrick	60,528	585,961 D		44.9%	54.2%	45.3%	54.7%
1974	5,163,600	2,340,188	Javits, Jacob K.*	1,973,781	Clark, Ramsey	849,631	366,407 R		45.3%	38.2%	54.2%	45.8%
1970**	5,904,782	1,434,472	Goodell, Charles*	2,171,232	Ottinger, Richard L.	2,299,078	736,760 D**		24.3%	36.8%	39.8%	60.2%
1968**	6,574,415	3,269,772	Javits, Jacob K.*	2,150,695	O'Dwyer, Paul	1,153,948	1,119,077 R		49.7%	32.7%	60.3%	39.7%
1964	7,151,686	3,104,056	Keating, Kenneth B.*	3,823,749	Kennedy, Robert F.	223,881	719,693 D		43.4%	53.5%	44.8%	55.2%
1962	5,703,168	3,272,417	Javits, Jacob K.*	2,289,323	Donovan, James B.	141,428	983,094 R		57.4%	40.1%	58.8%	41.2%
1958	5,602,088	2,842,942	Keating, Kenneth B.	2,709,950	Hogan, Frank S.	49,196	132,992 R		50.7%	48.4%	51.2%	48.8%
1956	6,991,136	3,723,933	Javits, Jacob K.	3,265,159	Wagner, Robert F. Jr.	2,044	458,774 R		53.3%	46.7%	53.3%	46.7%
1952	6,980,259	3,853,934	Ives, Irving M.*	2,521,736	Cashmore, John	604,589	1,332,198 R		55.2%	36.1%	60.4%	39.6%
1950	5,228,403	2,367,353	Hanley, Joe R.	2,632,313	Lehman, Herbert H.*	228,737	264,960 D		45.3%	50.3%	47.4%	52.6%
1949S	4,966,878	2,384,381	Dulles, John Foster	2,582,438	Lehman, Herbert H.	59	198,057 D		48.0%	52.0%	48.0%	52.0%
1946	4,867,564	2,559,365	Ives, Irving M.	2,308,112	Lehman, Herbert H.	87	251,253 R		52.6%	47.4%	52.6%	47.4%

Note: An asterisk (*) denotes incumbent. **In past elections, the other vote included: 1980 - 664,544 Liberal (Jacob K. Javits); 1970 - 2,288,190 Conservative (James L. Buckley); 1968 - 1,139,402 Conservative (Buckley). Buckley won the 1970 election with 38.8 percent of the total vote. The 1949 election and one of the 2010 elections were for short terms to fill a vacancy.

NEW YORK

PRESIDENT 2012

2010 Census Population	County	Total Vote	Republican (Romney)	Democratic (Obama)	Other	Rep.-Dem. Plurality	Percentage			
							Total Vote		Major Vote	
							Rep.	Dem.	Rep.	Dem.
304,204	ALBANY	135,767	45,064	87,556	3,147	42,492 D	33.2%	64.5%	34.0%	66.0%
48,946	ALLEGANY	16,953	10,390	6,139	424	4,251 R	61.3%	36.2%	62.9%	37.1%
1,385,108	BRONX	370,938	29,967	339,211	1,760	309,244 D	8.1%	91.4%	8.1%	91.9%
200,600	BROOME	81,565	37,641	41,970	1,954	4,329 D	46.1%	51.5%	47.3%	52.7%
80,317	CATTARAUGUS	29,767	16,569	12,649	549	3,920 R	55.7%	42.5%	56.7%	43.3%
80,026	CAYUGA	31,169	13,454	17,007	708	3,553 D	43.2%	54.6%	44.2%	55.8%
134,905	CHAUTAUQUA	52,852	27,971	23,812	1,069	4,159 R	52.9%	45.1%	54.0%	46.0%
88,830	CHEMUNG	35,010	17,612	16,797	601	815 R	50.3%	48.0%	51.2%	48.8%
50,477	CHENANGO	19,314	9,713	9,116	485	597 R	50.3%	47.2%	51.6%	48.4%
82,128	CLINTON	30,656	11,115	18,961	580	7,846 D	36.3%	61.9%	37.0%	63.0%
63,096	COLUMBIA	29,129	12,225	16,221	683	3,996 D	42.0%	55.7%	43.0%	57.0%
49,336	CORTLAND	19,624	8,695	10,482	447	1,787 D	44.3%	53.4%	45.3%	54.7%
47,980	DELAWARE	18,638	9,938	8,304	396	1,634 R	53.3%	44.6%	54.5%	45.5%
297,488	DUTCHESS	123,705	56,025	65,312	2,368	9,287 D	45.3%	52.8%	46.2%	53.8%
919,040	ERIE	414,195	169,675	237,356	7,164	67,681 D	41.0%	57.3%	41.7%	58.3%
39,370	ESSEX	16,717	6,647	9,784	286	3,137 D	39.8%	58.5%	40.5%	59.5%
51,599	FRANKLIN	15,934	5,740	9,894	300	4,154 D	36.0%	62.1%	36.7%	63.3%
55,531	FULTON	19,799	10,814	8,607	378	2,207 R	54.6%	43.5%	55.7%	44.3%
60,079	GENESEE	24,746	14,607	9,601	538	5,006 R	59.0%	38.8%	60.3%	39.7%
49,221	GREENE	20,668	11,174	9,030	464	2,144 R	54.1%	43.7%	55.3%	44.7%
4,836	HAMILTON	3,113	1,932	1,128	53	804 R	62.1%	36.2%	63.1%	36.9%
64,519	HERKIMER	25,040	13,282	11,273	485	2,009 R	53.0%	45.0%	54.1%	45.9%
116,229	JEFFERSON	35,708	18,122	17,099	487	1,023 R	50.8%	47.9%	51.5%	48.5%
2,504,700	KINGS	736,982	124,551	604,443	7,988	479,892 D	16.9%	82.0%	17.1%	82.9%
27,087	LEWIS	10,522	5,651	4,724	147	927 R	53.7%	44.9%	54.5%	45.5%
65,393	LIVINGSTON	26,770	14,448	11,705	617	2,743 R	54.0%	43.7%	55.2%	44.8%
73,442	MADISON	28,094	13,622	13,871	601	249 D	48.5%	49.4%	49.5%	50.5%
744,344	MONROE	333,813	133,362	193,501	6,950	60,139 D	40.0%	58.0%	40.8%	59.2%
50,219	MONTGOMERY	18,186	9,334	8,493	359	841 R	51.3%	46.7%	52.4%	47.6%
1,339,532	NASSAU	568,151	259,308	302,695	6,148	43,387 D	45.6%	53.3%	46.1%	53.9%
1,585,873	NEW YORK	600,291	89,559	502,674	8,058	413,115 D	14.9%	83.7%	15.1%	84.9%
216,469	NIAGARA	89,013	43,240	43,986	1,787	746 D	48.6%	49.4%	49.6%	50.4%
234,878	ONEIDA	86,700	44,530	40,468	1,702	4,062 R	51.4%	46.7%	52.4%	47.6%
467,026	ONONDAGA	204,717	78,831	122,254	3,632	43,423 D	38.5%	59.7%	39.2%	60.8%
107,931	ONTARIO	47,853	23,820	23,087	946	733 R	49.8%	48.2%	50.8%	49.2%
372,813	ORANGE	140,628	65,367	73,315	1,946	7,948 D	46.5%	52.1%	47.1%	52.9%
42,883	ORLEANS	14,706	8,594	5,787	325	2,807 R	58.4%	39.4%	59.8%	40.2%
122,109	OSWEGO	44,591	19,980	23,515	1,096	3,535 D	44.8%	52.7%	45.9%	54.1%
62,259	OTSEGO	24,139	11,461	12,117	561	656 D	47.5%	50.2%	48.6%	51.4%
99,710	PUTNAM	44,345	24,083	19,512	750	4,571 R	54.3%	44.0%	55.2%	44.8%
2,230,722	QUEENS	595,245	118,589	470,732	5,924	352,143 D	19.9%	79.1%	20.1%	79.9%
159,429	RENSSELAER	67,990	29,113	37,408	1,469	8,295 D	42.8%	55.0%	43.8%	56.2%
468,730	RICHMOND	154,180	74,223	78,181	1,776	3,958 D	48.1%	50.7%	48.7%	51.3%
311,687	ROCKLAND	124,442	57,363	65,657	1,422	8,294 D	46.1%	52.8%	46.6%	53.4%
219,607	SARATOGA	105,510	50,382	52,957	2,171	2,575 D	47.8%	50.2%	48.8%	51.2%
154,727	SCHENECTADY	64,933	26,568	36,844	1,521	10,276 D	40.9%	56.7%	41.9%	58.1%
32,749	SCHOHARIE	13,207	7,467	5,427	313	2,040 R	56.5%	41.1%	57.9%	42.1%
18,343	SCHUYLER	8,146	4,281	3,674	191	607 R	52.6%	45.1%	53.8%	46.2%
35,251	SENECA	13,266	5,889	7,094	283	1,205 D	44.4%	53.5%	45.4%	54.6%
111,944	ST. LAWRENCE	37,191	15,138	21,353	700	6,215 D	40.7%	57.4%	41.5%	58.5%
98,990	STEUBEN	38,531	21,954	15,787	790	6,167 R	57.0%	41.0%	58.2%	41.8%
1,493,350	SUFFOLK	594,266	282,131	304,079	8,056	21,948 D	47.5%	51.2%	48.1%	51.9%
77,547	SULLIVAN	28,415	12,705	15,268	442	2,563 D	44.7%	53.7%	45.4%	54.6%
51,125	TIOGA	21,589	12,117	8,930	542	3,187 R	56.1%	41.4%	57.6%	42.4%
101,564	TOMPKINS	39,670	11,107	27,244	1,319	16,137 D	28.0%	68.7%	29.0%	71.0%

NEW YORK

PRESIDENT 2012

2010 Census Population	County	Total Vote	Republican (Romney)	Democratic (Obama)	Other	Rep.-Dem. Plurality	Percentage			
							Total Vote		Major Vote	
							Rep.	Dem.	Rep.	Dem.
182,493	ULSTER	79,626	29,759	47,752	2,115	17,993 D	37.4%	60.0%	38.4%	61.6%
65,707	WARREN	29,578	14,119	14,806	653	687 D	47.7%	50.1%	48.8%	51.2%
63,216	WASHINGTON	23,095	11,085	11,523	487	438 D	48.0%	49.9%	49.0%	51.0%
93,772	WAYNE	37,547	20,060	16,635	852	3,425 R	53.4%	44.3%	54.7%	45.3%
949,113	WESTCHESTER	388,447	143,122	240,785	4,540	97,663 D	36.8%	62.0%	37.3%	62.7%
42,155	WYOMING	16,335	10,348	5,661	326	4,687 R	63.3%	34.7%	64.6%	35.4%
25,348	YATES	9,442	4,798	4,488	156	310 R	50.8%	47.5%	51.7%	48.3%
19,378,102	TOTAL	7,081,159	2,490,431	4,485,741	104,987	1,995,310 D	35.2%	63.3%	35.7%	64.3%

Note: Candidates in New York can appear on the ballot for more than one party: Barack Obama - 4,337,622 (Democrat), 148,119 (Working Families); Mitt Romney - 2,228,060 (Republican), 262,371 (Conservative).

NEW YORK

SENATOR 2012

2010 Census Population	County	Total Vote	Republican (Long)	Democratic (Gillibrand)	Other	Rep.-Dem. Plurality	Percentage			
							Total Vote		Major Vote	
							Rep.	Dem.	Rep.	Dem.
304,204	ALBANY	131,046	30,317	98,432	2,297	68,115 D	23.1%	75.1%	23.5%	76.5%
48,946	ALLEGANY	16,061	8,151	7,635	275	516 R	50.8%	47.5%	51.6%	48.4%
1,385,108	BRONX	345,227	21,618	321,378	2,231	299,760 D	6.3%	93.1%	6.3%	93.7%
200,600	BROOME	77,355	26,166	49,814	1,375	23,648 D	33.8%	64.4%	34.4%	65.6%
80,317	CATTARAUGUS	28,194	12,058	15,654	482	3,596 D	42.8%	55.5%	43.5%	56.5%
80,026	CAYUGA	29,120	10,265	18,067	788	7,802 D	35.3%	62.0%	36.2%	63.8%
134,905	CHAUTAUQUA	50,694	20,869	29,001	824	8,132 D	41.2%	57.2%	41.8%	58.2%
88,830	CHEMUNG	33,476	12,345	20,682	449	8,337 D	36.9%	61.8%	37.4%	62.6%
50,477	CHENANGO	18,111	6,956	10,672	483	3,716 D	38.4%	58.9%	39.5%	60.5%
82,128	CLINTON	28,366	8,373	19,439	554	11,066 D	29.5%	68.5%	30.1%	69.9%
63,096	COLUMBIA	28,490	8,154	19,905	431	11,751 D	28.6%	69.9%	29.1%	70.9%
49,336	CORTLAND	18,410	6,730	11,166	514	4,436 D	36.6%	60.7%	37.6%	62.4%
47,980	DELAWARE	18,066	6,606	11,172	288	4,566 D	36.6%	61.8%	37.2%	62.8%
297,488	DUTCHESS	118,256	38,607	77,809	1,840	39,202 D	32.6%	65.8%	33.2%	66.8%
919,040	ERIE	389,578	117,861	265,264	6,453	147,403 D	30.3%	68.1%	30.8%	69.2%
39,370	ESSEX	15,554	5,201	10,094	259	4,893 D	33.4%	64.9%	34.0%	66.0%
51,599	FRANKLIN	14,911	4,708	9,960	243	5,252 D	31.6%	66.8%	32.1%	67.9%
55,531	FULTON	18,783	7,401	11,122	260	3,721 D	39.4%	59.2%	40.0%	60.0%
60,079	GENESEE	23,048	10,745	11,845	458	1,100 D	46.6%	51.4%	47.6%	52.4%
49,221	GREENE	19,956	7,544	12,098	314	4,554 D	37.8%	60.6%	38.4%	61.6%
4,836	HAMILTON	2,975	1,449	1,487	39	38 D	48.7%	50.0%	49.4%	50.6%
64,519	HERKIMER	23,481	8,421	14,655	405	6,234 D	35.9%	62.4%	36.5%	63.5%
116,229	JEFFERSON	34,137	11,882	21,746	509	9,864 D	34.8%	63.7%	35.3%	64.7%
2,504,700	KINGS	687,587	79,504	598,834	9,249	519,330 D	11.6%	87.1%	11.7%	88.3%
27,087	LEWIS	9,697	3,662	5,886	149	2,224 D	37.8%	60.7%	38.4%	61.6%
65,393	LIVINGSTON	24,814	10,910	13,462	442	2,552 D	44.0%	54.3%	44.8%	55.2%
73,442	MADISON	26,588	10,101	15,732	755	5,631 D	38.0%	59.2%	39.1%	60.9%
744,344	MONROE	316,748	101,323	209,781	5,644	108,458 D	32.0%	66.2%	32.6%	67.4%
50,219	MONTGOMERY	17,186	5,938	10,957	291	5,019 D	34.6%	63.8%	35.1%	64.9%
1,339,532	NASSAU	536,658	188,430	342,644	5,584	154,214 D	35.1%	63.8%	35.5%	64.5%
1,585,873	NEW YORK	561,636	65,699	487,701	8,236	422,002 D	11.7%	86.8%	11.9%	88.1%
216,469	NIAGARA	83,728	30,645	51,592	1,491	20,947 D	36.6%	61.6%	37.3%	62.7%
234,878	ONEIDA	81,586	29,059	50,715	1,812	21,656 D	35.6%	62.2%	36.4%	63.6%
467,026	ONONDAGA	196,165	56,997	133,892	5,276	76,895 D	29.1%	68.3%	29.9%	70.1%
107,931	ONTARIO	45,726	18,838	25,987	901	7,149 D	41.2%	56.8%	42.0%	58.0%

NEW YORK

SENATOR 2012

2010 Census Population	County	Total Vote	Republican (Long)	Democratic (Gillibrand)	Other	Rep.-Dem. Plurality	Percentage			
							Total Vote		Major Vote	
							Rep.	Dem.	Rep.	Dem.
372,813	ORANGE	135,843	45,128	88,689	2,026	43,561 D	33.2%	65.3%	33.7%	66.3%
42,883	ORLEANS	13,739	6,556	6,884	299	328 D	47.7%	50.1%	48.8%	51.2%
122,109	OSWEGO	41,703	15,404	25,117	1,182	9,713 D	36.9%	60.2%	38.0%	62.0%
62,259	OTSEGO	23,259	7,767	15,114	378	7,347 D	33.4%	65.0%	33.9%	66.1%
99,710	PUTNAM	41,441	16,549	24,310	582	7,761 D	39.9%	58.7%	40.5%	59.5%
2,230,722	QUEENS	556,899	82,169	468,079	6,651	385,910 D	14.8%	84.1%	14.9%	85.1%
159,429	RENSSELAER	66,073	19,310	45,767	996	26,457 D	29.2%	69.3%	29.7%	70.3%
468,730	RICHMOND	148,316	51,782	94,843	1,691	43,061 D	34.9%	63.9%	35.3%	64.7%
311,687	ROCKLAND	117,220	37,955	77,915	1,350	39,960 D	32.4%	66.5%	32.8%	67.2%
219,607	SARATOGA	102,626	34,728	66,459	1,439	31,731 D	33.8%	64.8%	34.3%	65.7%
154,727	SCHENECTADY	62,462	18,273	43,030	1,159	24,757 D	29.3%	68.9%	29.8%	70.2%
32,749	SCHOHARIE	12,802	5,048	7,541	213	2,493 D	39.4%	58.9%	40.1%	59.9%
18,343	SCHUYLER	7,734	3,107	4,456	171	1,349 D	40.2%	57.6%	41.1%	58.9%
35,251	SENECA	12,444	4,815	7,345	284	2,530 D	38.7%	59.0%	39.6%	60.4%
111,944	ST. LAWRENCE	34,818	10,092	24,157	569	14,065 D	29.0%	69.4%	29.5%	70.5%
98,990	STEUBEN	36,882	16,240	20,044	598	3,804 D	44.0%	54.3%	44.8%	55.2%
1,493,350	SUFFOLK	560,740	198,683	354,929	7,128	156,246 D	35.4%	63.3%	35.9%	64.1%
77,547	SULLIVAN	26,432	8,551	17,427	454	8,876 D	32.4%	65.9%	32.9%	67.1%
51,125	TIOGA	20,624	8,995	11,206	423	2,211 D	43.6%	54.3%	44.5%	55.5%
101,564	TOMPKINS	38,034	9,059	27,764	1,211	18,705 D	23.8%	73.0%	24.6%	75.4%
182,493	ULSTER	77,016	20,908	54,455	1,653	33,547 D	27.1%	70.7%	27.7%	72.3%
65,707	WARREN	28,812	9,095	19,347	370	10,252 D	31.6%	67.1%	32.0%	68.0%
63,216	WASHINGTON	22,616	7,067	15,228	321	8,161 D	31.2%	67.3%	31.7%	68.3%
93,772	WAYNE	35,730	15,973	18,974	783	3,001 D	44.7%	53.1%	45.7%	54.3%
949,113	WESTCHESTER	359,652	100,279	254,723	4,650	154,444 D	27.9%	70.8%	28.2%	71.8%
42,155	WYOMING	15,314	7,556	7,475	283	81 R	49.3%	48.8%	50.3%	49.7%
25,348	YATES	9,033	4,080	4,772	181	692 D	45.2%	52.8%	46.1%	53.9%
19,378,102	TOTAL	6,679,678	1,758,702	4,822,330	98,646	3,063,628 D	26.3%	72.2%	26.7%	73.3%

Note: Candidates in New York can appear on the ballot line of more than one party. In the 2012 Senate election, the candidates received the following votes per party: Kirsten Gillibrand - 4,432,525 (Democrat), 251,292 (Working Families), 138,513 (Independence); Wendy Long - 1,517,578 (Republican), 241,124 (Conservative).

NEW YORK

HOUSE OF REPRESENTATIVES

CD	Year	Total Vote	Republican		Democratic		Other Vote	Rep.-Dem. Plurality	Percentage			
			Vote	Candidate	Vote	Candidate			Total Vote		Major Vote	
									Rep.	Dem.	Rep.	Dem.
1	2012	278,659	132,304	ALTSCHULER, RANDY	146,179	BISHOP, TIM*	176	13,875 D	47.5%	52.5%	47.5%	52.5%
2	2012	242,943	142,309	KING, PETE*	100,545	FALCONE, VIVIANNE	89	41,764 R	58.6%	41.4%	58.6%	41.4%
3	2012	273,171	113,203	LABATE, STEPHEN	157,880	ISRAEL, STEVE*	2,088	44,677 D	41.4%	57.8%	41.8%	58.2%
4	2012	265,300	85,693	BECKER, FRANCIS X. JR.	163,955	MCCARTHY, CAROLYN*	15,652	78,262 D	32.3%	61.8%	34.3%	65.7%
5	2012	187,141	17,875	JENNINGS, ALLAN JR.	167,836	MEEKS, GREGORY W.*	1,430	149,961 D	9.6%	89.7%	9.6%	90.4%
6	2012	164,374	50,846	HALLORAN, DANIEL	111,501	MENG, GRACE	2,027	60,655 D	30.9%	67.8%	31.3%	68.7%
7	2012	152,111			143,930	VELÁZQUEZ, NYDIA M.*	8,181	143,930 D		94.6%		100.0%
8	2012	204,207	17,650	BELLONE, ALAN	184,039	JEFFRIES, HAKEEM	2,518	166,389 D	8.6%	90.1%	8.8%	91.2%
9	2012	213,431	24,164	CAVANAGH, DANIEL	186,141	CLARKE, YVETTE D.*	3,126	161,977 D	11.3%	87.2%	11.5%	88.5%
10	2012	205,349	39,413	CHAN, MICHAEL	165,743	NADLER, JERROLD*	193	126,330 D	19.2%	80.7%	19.2%	80.8%
11	2012	197,635	103,118	GRIMM, MICHAEL*	92,430	MURPHY, MARK	2,087	10,688 R	52.2%	46.8%	52.7%	47.3%
12	2012	241,426	46,841	WIGHT, CHRISTOPHER	194,370	MALONEY, CAROLYN B.*	215	147,529 D	19.4%	80.5%	19.4%	80.6%
13	2012	192,913	12,147	SCHLEY, CRAIG	175,016	RANGEL, CHARLES B.*	5,750	162,869 D	6.3%	90.7%	6.5%	93.5%
14	2012	145,190	21,755	GIBBONS, WILLIAM JR.	120,761	CROWLEY, JOSEPH*	2,674	99,006 D	15.0%	83.2%	15.3%	84.7%
15	2012	157,115	4,427	DELLA VALLE, FRANK	152,661	SERRANO, JOSÉ E.*	27	148,234 D	2.8%	97.2%	2.8%	97.2%
16	2012	236,553	53,935	MCLAUGHLIN, JOSEPH	179,562	ENGEL, ELIOT L.*	3,056	125,627 D	22.8%	75.9%	23.1%	76.9%
17	2012	266,205	91,899	CARVIN, JOE	171,417	LOWEY, NITA*	2,889	79,518 D	34.5%	64.4%	34.9%	65.1%
18	2012	277,063	133,049	HAYWORTH, NAN*	143,845	MALONEY, SEAN PATRICK	169	10,796 D	48.0%	51.9%	48.1%	51.9%
19	2012	284,679	150,245	GIBSON, CHRIS*	134,295	SCHREIBMAN, JULIAN	139	15,950 R	52.8%	47.2%	52.8%	47.2%

NEW YORK

HOUSE OF REPRESENTATIVES

CD	Year	Total Vote	Republican		Democratic		Other Vote	Rep.-Dem. Plurality	Percentage			
			Vote	Candidate	Vote	Candidate			Total Vote		Major Vote	
									Rep.	Dem.	Rep.	Dem.
20	2012	297,314	93,778	DIETERICH, ROBERT	203,401	TONKO, PAUL D.*	135	109,623 D	31.5%	68.4%	31.6%	68.4%
21	2012	252,556	121,646	DOHENY, MATTHEW A.	126,631	OWENS, BILL*	4,279	4,985 D	48.2%	50.1%	49.0%	51.0%
22	2012	260,863	157,941	HANNA, RICHARD*	102,080	LAMB, DAN	842	55,861 R	60.5%	39.1%	60.7%	39.3%
23	2012	265,282	137,669	REED, TOM*	127,535	SHINAGAWA, NATE	78	10,134 R	51.9%	48.1%	51.9%	48.1%
24	2012	292,988	127,054	BUERKLE, ANN MARIE*	143,044	MAFFEI, DAN	22,890	15,990 D	43.4%	48.8%	47.0%	53.0%
25	2012	313,452	133,389	BROOKS, MAGGIE	179,810	SLAUGHTER, LOUISE M.*	253	46,421 D	42.6%	57.4%	42.6%	57.4%
26	2012	284,271	71,666	MADIGAN, MICHAEL H.	212,588	HIGGINS, BRIAN*	17	140,922 D	25.2%	74.8%	25.2%	74.8%
27	2012	317,534	161,220	COLLINS, CHRIS	156,219	HOCHUL, KATHY COURTNEY*	95	5,001 R	50.8%	49.2%	50.8%	49.2%
TOTAL	2012	6,469,725	2,245,236		4,143,414		81,075	1,898,178 D	34.7%	64.0%	35.1%	64.9%

Notes: An asterisk (*) denotes incumbent. Votes received by each Democratic and Republican candidate on the ballot lines of other parties (Working Families, Conservative, Independence) are included in their totals above. All major party candidates received votes on additional ballot lines except the following districts/candidates: 5 (both), 13 (Schley), 16 (McLaughlin), 17 (Carvin), and 22 (Lamb).

NEW YORK

GENERAL AND PRIMARY ELECTIONS

GENERAL ELECTIONS: OTHER VOTE

President   Other vote was 47,256 Libertarian (Gary E. Johnson), 39,982 Green (Jill Stein), 9,425 Write-in (Scattered Write-In), 6,274 Constitution (Virgil H. Goode), 2,050 Socialism and Liberation (Peta Lindsay)

Senator   Other vote was 42,591 Green (Colia Clark), 32,002 Libertarian (Chris Edes), 22,041 Common Sense (John Mangelli), 2,012 Write-in (Scattered Write-In)

House   Other vote was:

CD 1   176 Write-in (Scattered Write-In)

CD 2   89 Write-in (Scattered Write-In)

CD 3   1,644 Libertarian (Michael McDermott), 367 Constitution (Anthony Tolda), 77 Write-in (Scattered Write-In)

CD 4   15,603 Conservative (Frank Scaturro), 49 Write-in (Scattered Write-In)

CD 5   1,345 Libertarian (Catherine Wark), 85 Write-in (Scattered Write-In)

CD 6   1,913 Green (Evergreen Chou), 114 Write-in (Scattered Write-In)

CD 7   7,971 Conservative (James Murray), 210 Write-in (Scattered Write-In)

CD 8   2,441 Green (Colin Beavan), 77 Write-in (Scattered Write-In)

CD 9   2,991 Green (Vivia Morgan), 135 Write-in (Scattered Write-In)

CD 10   193 Write-in (Scattered Write-In)

CD 11   1,939 Green (Henry Bardel), 148 Write-in (Scattered Write-In)

CD 12   215 Write-in (Scattered Write-In)

CD 13   5,548 Socialist Workers (Deborah Liatos), 202 Write-in (Scattered Write-In)

CD 14   2,570 Green (Anthony Gronowicz), 104 Write-in (Scattered Write-In)

CD 15   27 Write-in (Scattered Write-In)

CD 16   2,974 Green (Joseph Diaferia), 82 Write-in (Scattered Write-In)

CD 17   2,771 We the People (Francis Morganthaler), 118 Write-in (Scattered Write-In)

CD 18   169 Write-in (Scattered Write-In)

CD 19   139 Write-in (Scattered Write-In)

CD 20   135 Write-in (Scattered Write-In)

CD 21   4,174 Green (Donald Hassig), 105 Write-in (Scattered Write-In)

CD 22   842 Write-in (Scattered Write-In)

CD 23   78 Write-in (Scattered Write-In)

CD 24   22,670 Green (Ursula E. Rozum), 220 Write-in (Scattered Write-In)

CD 25   253 Write-in (Scattered Write-In)

CD 26   17 Write-in (Scattered Write-In)

CD 27   95 Write-in (Scattered Write-In)

NEW YORK

GENERAL AND PRIMARY ELECTIONS

PRIMARY ELECTIONS: SUPPLEMENTARY INFORMATION

Primary	April 24, 2012 (President) June 26, 2012 (Congress)	**Registration** (as of April 1, 2012 – includes 960,834 inactive registrants)	11,477,613	Democratic Republican Independence Conservative Working Families Green Other Parties Unaffiliated	5,649,934 2,826,913 447,170 150,703 44,412 21,099 3,269 2,334,113

Primary Type   Closed—Only registered Democrats and Republicans could vote in their party's primary.

	REPUBLICAN PRIMARIES			DEMOCRATIC PRIMARIES		
President	Romney, W. Mitt	118,912	62.7%			
	Paul, Ron	27,699	14.6%			
	Gingrich, Newt	23,990	12.7%			
	Santorum, Rick	18,997	10.0%			
	Scattered Write-In	1				
	TOTAL	*189,599*				
Senator	Long, Wendy	75,924	50.2%	Gillibrand, Kirsten E.*	Unopposed	
	Turner, Bob	54,196	35.9%			
	Maragos, George	21,002	13.9%			
	TOTAL	*151,122*				
Congressional District 1	Altschuler, Randy	7,394	86.4%	Bishop, Tim*	Unopposed	
	Demos, George C.	1,166	13.6%			
	TOTAL	*8,560*				
Congressional District 2	King, Pete*	Unopposed		Falcone, Vivianne	Unopposed	
Congressional District 3	Labate, Stephen	Unopposed		Israel, Steve*	Unopposed	
Congressional District 4	Becker, Francis X. Jr.	6,357	55.1%	McCarthy, Carolyn*	Unopposed	
	Scaturro, Frank	5,175	44.9%			
	TOTAL	*11,532*				
Congressional District 5	Jennings, Allan Jr.	Unopposed		Meeks, Gregory W.*	9,920	66.5%
				Jennings, Allan Jr.	1,972	13.2%
				Scala, Mike	1,694	11.4%
				Marthone, Joseph R.	1,327	8.9%
				TOTAL	*14,913*	
Congressional District 6	Halloran, Daniel	Unopposed		Meng, Grace	14,825	53.0%
				Lancman, Rory I.	7,089	25.3%
				Crowley, Elizabeth S.	4,606	16.5%
				Mittman, Robert	1,462	5.2%
				TOTAL	*27,982*	
Congressional District 7				Velázquez, Nydia M.*	17,208	57.9%
				Dilan, Erik Martin	10,408	35.0%
				O'Connor, Daniel J.	1,351	4.5%
				Martinez, George	745	2.5%
				TOTAL	*29,712*	

NEW YORK

GENERAL AND PRIMARY ELECTIONS

	REPUBLICAN PRIMARIES			DEMOCRATIC PRIMARIES		
Congressional District 8	Bellone, Alan	Unopposed		Jeffries, Hakeem	28,271	71.8%
				Barron, Charles	11,130	28.2%
				TOTAL	39,401	
Congressional District 9	Cavanagh, Daniel	Unopposed		Clarke, Yvette D.*	15,069	88.3%
				Kinard, Sylvia G.	1,993	11.7%
				TOTAL	17,062	
Congressional District 10	Chan, Michael	Unopposed		Nadler, Jerrold*	Unopposed	
Congressional District 11	Grimm, Michael*	Unopposed		Murphy, Mark	Unopposed	
Congressional District 12	Wight, Christopher	Unopposed		Maloney, Carolyn B.*	Unopposed	
Congressional District 13	Schley, Craig	Unopposed		Rangel, Charles B.*	19,187	44.4%
				Espaillat, Adriano	18,101	41.9%
				Williams, Clyde Edward Jr.	4,266	9.9%
				Johnson, Joyce S.	1,018	2.4%
				Schley, Craig	598	1.4%
				TOTAL	43,170	
Congressional District 14	Gibbons, William Jr.	Unopposed		Crowley, Joseph*	Unopposed	
Congressional District 15	Della Valle, Frank	Unopposed		Serrano, José E.*	Unopposed	
Congressional District 16	McLaughlin, Joseph	Unopposed		Engel, Eliot L.*	12,856	87.3%
				Grimaldi, Aniello A.M.	1,864	12.7%
				TOTAL	14,720	
Congressional District 17	Carvin, Joe	4,225	64.7%	Lowey, Nita*	Unopposed	
	Russell, Jim	2,307	35.3%			
	TOTAL	6,532				
Congressional District 18	Hayworth, Nan*	Unopposed		Maloney, Sean Patrick	7,493	48.3%
				Becker, Richard H.	5,036	32.4%
				Alexander, Matthew C.	1,857	12.0%
				Jackson, Duane	780	5.0%
				Wilson, Thomas	356	2.3%
				TOTAL	15,522	
Congressional District 19	Gibson, Chris*	Unopposed		Schreibman, Julian	6,653	58.8%
				Tyner, Joel	4,657	41.2%
				TOTAL	11,310	
Congressional District 20	Dieterich, Robert	Unopposed		Tonko, Paul D.*	Unopposed	
Congressional District 21	Doheny, Matthew A.	9,331	70.8%	Owens, Bill*	Unopposed	
	Greene, Kellie A.	3,847	29.2%			
	TOTAL	13,178				
Congressional District 22	Hanna, Richard*	10,627	71.1%	Lamb, Dan	Unopposed	
	Kicinski, Michael J.	4,314	28.9%			
	TOTAL	14,941				
Congressional District 23	Reed, Tom*	Unopposed		Shinagawa, Nate	6,162	53.9%
				Burke, Leslie Danks	4,246	37.1%
				Dobson, Melissa K.	1,033	9.0%
				TOTAL	11,441	

NEW YORK

GENERAL AND PRIMARY ELECTIONS

	REPUBLICAN PRIMARIES			DEMOCRATIC PRIMARIES	
Congressional District 24	Buerkle, Ann Marie*	Unopposed		Maffei, Dan	Unopposed
Congressional District 25	Brooks, Maggie	Unopposed		Slaughter, Louise M.*	Unopposed
Congressional District 26	Madigan, Michael H.	Unopposed		Higgins, Brian*	Unopposed
Congressional District 27	Collins, Chris Bellavia, David G. TOTAL	11,677 7,830 19,507	59.9% 40.1%	Hochul, Kathy Courtney*	Unopposed

Note: An asterisk (*) denotes incumbent. Write-in votes for Senate and House primaries were listed in the official tally from New York City, but were not included in these results. Names of unopposed candidates did not appear on the primary ballot; therefore, no votes were cast for these candidates.

NORTH CAROLINA
Congressional districts first established for elections held in 2012
13 members

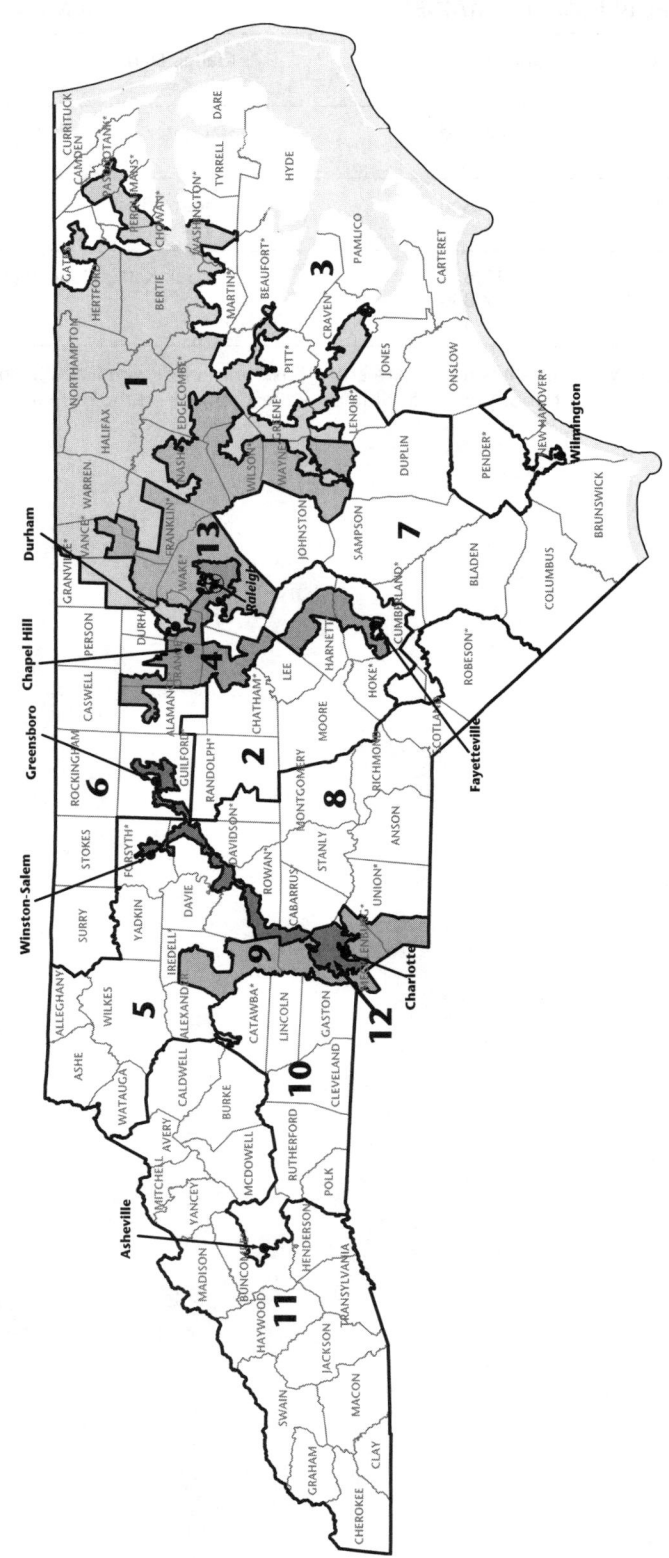

* Asterisk indicates a county whose boundaries include parts of two or more Congressional districts.

NORTH CAROLINA
Central North Carolina Area

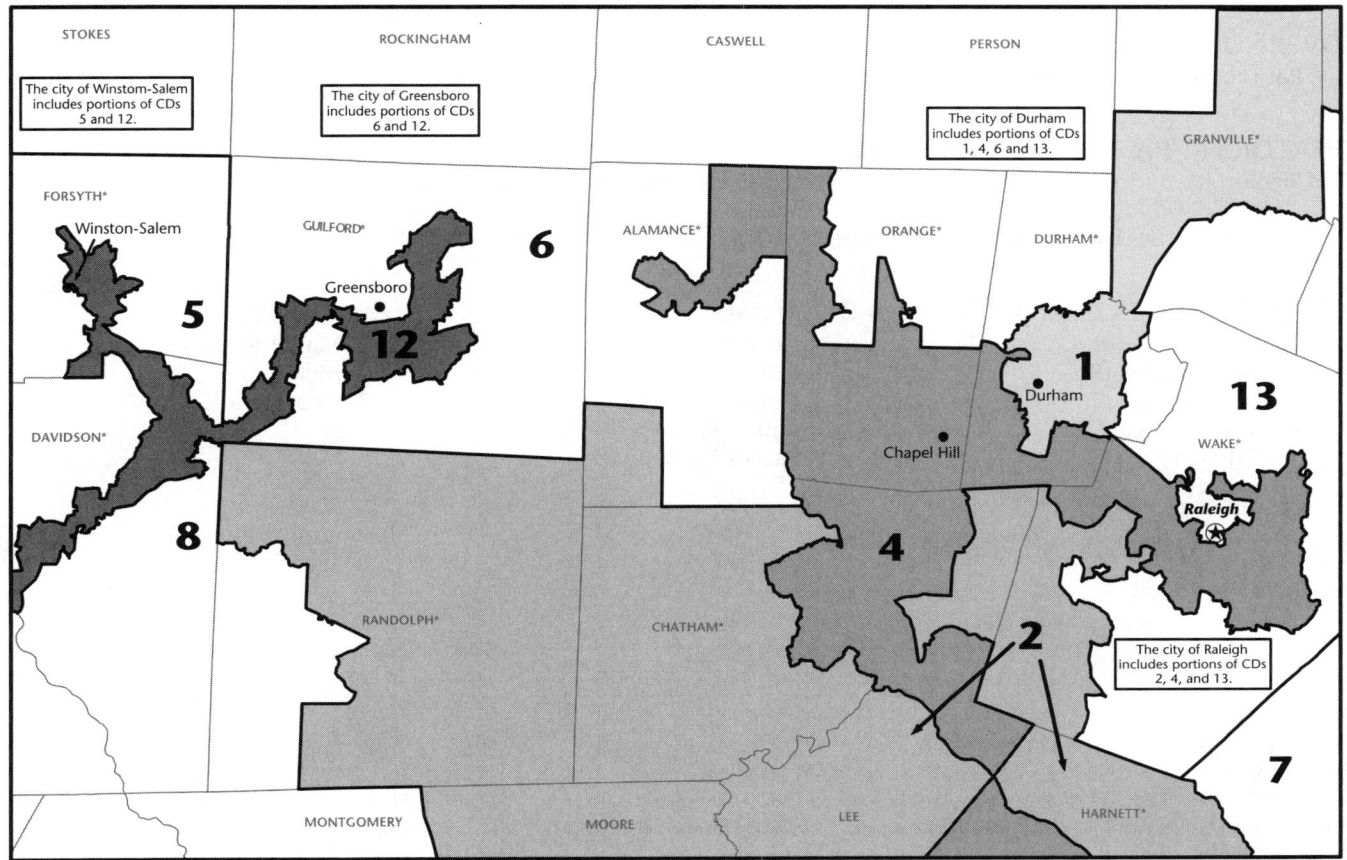

STOKES

The city of Winstom-Salem includes portions of CDs 5 and 12.

ROCKINGHAM

The city of Greensboro includes portions of CDs 6 and 12.

CASWELL

PERSON

The city of Durham includes portions of CDs 1, 4, 6 and 13.

GRANVILLE*

FORSYTH*

Winston-Salem

5

GUILFORD*

Greensboro

12

ALAMANCE*

6

ORANGE*

DURHAM*

1

Durham

13

WAKE*

DAVIDSON*

Chapel Hill

Raleigh

8

4

RANDOLPH*

CHATHAM*

2

The city of Raleigh includes portions of CDs 2, 4, and 13.

MONTGOMERY

MOORE

LEE

HARNETT*

7

* Asterisk indicates a county whose boundaries include parts of two or more Congressional districts.

NORTH CAROLINA

GOVERNOR

Pat McCrory (R). Elected 2012 to a four-year term.

SENATORS (1 Republican, 1 Democrat)

Richard M. Burr (R). Reelected 2010 to a six-year term. Previously elected 2004.

Kay Hagan (D). Elected 2008 to a six-year term.

REPRESENTATIVES (9 Republicans, 4 Democrats)

1. G. K. Butterfield (D)
2. Renee Ellmers (R)
3. Walter B. Jones Jr. (R)
4. David E. Price (D)
5. Virginia Foxx (R)
6. Howard Coble (R)
7. Mike McIntyre (D)
8. Richard Hudson (R)
9. Robert Pittenger (R)
10. Patrick McHenry (R)
11. Mark Meadows (R)
12. Mel Watt (D)
13. George Holding (R)

POSTWAR VOTE FOR PRESIDENT

		Republican		Democratic		Other	Rep.-Dem.	Total Vote		Major Vote	
Year	Total Vote	Vote	Candidate	Vote	Candidate	Vote	Plurality	Rep.	Dem.	Rep.	Dem.
2012	4,505,372	2,270,395	Romney, W. Mitt	2,178,391	Obama, Barack H.*	56,586	92,004 R	50.4%	48.4%	51.0%	49.0%
2008	4,310,789	2,128,474	McCain, John S. III	2,142,651	Obama, Barack H.	39,664	14,177 D	49.4%	49.7%	49.8%	50.2%
2004	3,501,007	1,961,166	Bush, George W.*	1,525,849	Kerry, John F.	13,992	435,317 R	56.0%	43.6%	56.2%	43.8%
2000	2,911,262	1,631,163	Bush, George W.	1,257,692	Gore, Albert Jr.	22,407	373,471 R	56.0%	43.2%	56.5%	43.5%
1996**	2,515,807	1,225,938	Dole, Robert "Bob"	1,107,849	Clinton, Bill*	182,020	118,089 R	48.7%	44.0%	52.5%	47.5%
1992**	2,611,850	1,134,661	Bush, George H.*	1,114,042	Clinton, Bill	363,147	20,619 R	43.4%	42.7%	50.5%	49.5%
1988	2,134,370	1,237,258	Bush, George H.	890,167	Dukakis, Michael S.	6,945	347,091 R	58.0%	41.7%	58.2%	41.8%
1984	2,175,361	1,346,481	Reagan, Ronald*	824,287	Mondale, Walter F.	4,593	522,194 R	61.9%	37.9%	62.0%	38.0%
1980**	1,855,833	915,018	Reagan, Ronald	875,635	Carter, Jimmy*	65,180	39,383 R	49.3%	47.2%	51.1%	48.9%
1976	1,677,914	741,960	Ford, Gerald R.*	926,365	Carter, Jimmy	9,589	184,405 D	44.2%	55.2%	44.5%	55.5%
1972	1,518,612	1,054,889	Nixon, Richard M.*	438,705	McGovern, George S.	25,018	616,184 R	69.5%	28.9%	70.6%	29.4%
1968**	1,587,493	627,192	Nixon, Richard M.	464,113	Humphrey, Hubert H. Jr.	496,188	163,079 R	39.5%	29.2%	57.5%	42.5%
1964	1,424,983	624,844	Goldwater, Barry M. Sr.	800,139	Johnson, Lyndon B.*		175,295 D	43.8%	56.2%	43.8%	56.2%
1960	1,368,556	655,420	Nixon, Richard M.	713,136	Kennedy, John F.		57,716 D	47.9%	52.1%	47.9%	52.1%
1956	1,165,592	575,062	Eisenhower, Dwight D.*	590,530	Stevenson, Adlai E. II		15,468 D	49.3%	50.7%	49.3%	50.7%
1952	1,210,910	558,107	Eisenhower, Dwight D.	652,803	Stevenson, Adlai E. II		94,696 D	46.1%	53.9%	46.1%	53.9%
1948**	791,209	258,572	Dewey, Thomas E.	459,070	Truman, Harry S.*	73,567	200,498 D	32.7%	58.0%	36.0%	64.0%

Note: An asterisk (*) denotes incumbent. **In past elections, the other vote included: 1996 - 168,059 Reform (Ross Perot); 1992 - 357,864 Independent (Perot); 1980 - 52,800 Independent (John Anderson); 1968 - 496,188 American Independent (George Wallace), who finished second; 1948 - 69,652 States' Rights (Strom Thurmond).

NORTH CAROLINA

POSTWAR VOTE FOR GOVERNOR

Year	Total Vote	Republican		Democratic		Other Vote	Rep.-Dem. Plurality	Percentage			
								Total Vote		Major Vote	
		Vote	Candidate	Vote	Candidate			Rep.	Dem.	Rep.	Dem.
2012	4,468,295	2,440,707	McCrory, Pat	1,931,580	Dalton, Walter H.	96,008	509,127 R	54.6%	43.2%	55.8%	44.2%
2008	4,268,941	2,001,168	McCrory, Pat	2,146,189	Perdue, Bev	121,584	145,021 D	46.9%	50.3%	48.3%	51.7%
2004	3,486,688	1,495,021	Ballantine, Patrick J.	1,939,154	Easley, Mike*	52,513	444,133 D	42.9%	55.6%	43.5%	56.5%
2000	2,942,062	1,360,960	Vinroot, Richard	1,530,324	Easley, Mike	50,778	169,364 D	46.3%	52.0%	47.1%	52.9%
1996	2,566,185	1,097,053	Hayes, Robert "Robin"	1,436,638	Hunt, James B. Jr.*	32,494	339,585 D	42.8%	56.0%	43.3%	56.7%
1992	2,595,184	1,121,955	Gardner, James C.	1,368,246	Hunt, James B. Jr.	104,983	246,291 D	43.2%	52.7%	45.1%	54.9%
1988	2,180,205	1,222,338	Martin, James G.*	957,867	Jordan, Robert B.		264,471 R	56.1%	43.9%	56.1%	43.9%
1984	2,226,727	1,208,167	Martin, James G.	1,011,209	Edmisten, Rufus	7,351	196,958 R	54.3%	45.4%	54.4%	45.6%
1980	1,847,432	691,449	Lake, Beverly	1,143,145	Hunt, James B. Jr.*	12,838	451,696 D	37.4%	61.9%	37.7%	62.3%
1976	1,663,814	564,092	Flaherty, David T.	1,081,293	Hunt, James B. Jr.	18,429	517,201 D	33.9%	65.0%	34.3%	65.7%
1972	1,504,785	767,470	Holshouser, James E.	729,104	Bowles, Hargrove	8,211	38,366 R	51.0%	48.5%	51.3%	48.7%
1968	1,558,308	737,075	Gardner, James C.	821,233	Scott, Robert W.		84,158 D	47.3%	52.7%	47.3%	52.7%
1964	1,396,508	606,165	Gavin, Robert L.	790,343	Moore, Dan K.		184,178 D	43.4%	56.6%	43.4%	56.6%
1960	1,350,360	613,975	Gavin, Robert L.	735,248	Sanford, Terry	1,137	121,273 D	45.5%	54.4%	45.5%	54.5%
1956	1,135,859	375,379	Hayes, Kyle	760,480	Hodges, Luther H.		385,101 D	33.0%	67.0%	33.0%	67.0%
1952	1,179,635	383,329	Seawell, Herbert F. Jr.	796,306	Umstead, William B.		412,977 D	32.5%	67.5%	32.5%	67.5%
1948	780,525	206,166	Pritchard, George M.	570,995	Scott, W. Kerr	3,364	364,829 D	26.4%	73.2%	26.5%	73.5%

Note: An asterisk (*) denotes incumbent.

POSTWAR VOTE FOR SENATOR

Year	Total Vote	Republican		Democratic		Other Vote	Rep.-Dem. Plurality	Percentage			
								Total Vote		Major Vote	
		Vote	Candidate	Vote	Candidate			Rep.	Dem.	Rep.	Dem.
2010	2,660,079	1,458,046	Burr, Richard M.*	1,145,074	Marshall, Elaine	56,959	312,972 R	54.8%	43.0%	56.0%	44.0%
2008	4,271,970	1,887,510	Dole, Elizabeth*	2,249,311	Hagan, Kay	135,149	361,801 D	44.2%	52.7%	45.6%	54.4%
2004	3,472,082	1,791,450	Burr, Richard M.	1,632,527	Bowles, Erskine B.	48,105	158,923 R	51.6%	47.0%	52.3%	47.7%
2002	2,331,181	1,248,664	Dole, Elizabeth	1,047,983	Bowles, Erskine B.	34,534	200,681 R	53.6%	45.0%	54.4%	45.6%
1998	2,012,143	945,943	Faircloth, Lauch*	1,029,237	Edwards, John	36,963	83,294 D	47.0%	51.2%	47.9%	52.1%
1996	2,556,456	1,345,833	Helms, Jesse*	1,173,875	Gantt, Harvey B.	36,748	171,958 R	52.6%	45.9%	53.4%	46.6%
1992	2,577,891	1,297,892	Faircloth, Lauch	1,194,015	Sanford, Terry*	85,984	103,877 R	50.3%	46.3%	52.1%	47.9%
1990	2,069,585	1,087,331	Helms, Jesse*	981,573	Gantt, Harvey B.	681	105,758 R	52.5%	47.4%	52.6%	47.4%
1986	1,591,330	767,668	Broyhill, James Thomas*	823,662	Sanford, Terry		55,994 D	48.2%	51.8%	48.2%	51.8%
1984	2,239,051	1,156,768	Helms, Jesse*	1,070,488	Hunt, James B. Jr.	11,795	86,280 R	51.7%	47.8%	51.9%	48.1%
1980	1,797,665	898,064	East, John P.	887,653	Morgan, Robert*	11,948	10,411 R	50.0%	49.4%	50.3%	49.7%
1978	1,135,814	619,151	Helms, Jesse*	516,663	Ingram, John		102,488 R	54.5%	45.5%	54.5%	45.5%
1974	1,020,367	377,618	Stevens, William E.	633,775	Morgan, Robert	8,974	256,157 D	37.0%	62.1%	37.3%	62.7%
1972	1,472,541	795,248	Helms, Jesse	677,293	Galifianakis, Nick		117,955 R	54.0%	46.0%	54.0%	46.0%
1968	1,437,340	566,934	Somers, Robert V.	870,406	Ervin, Sam J.*		303,472 D	39.4%	60.6%	39.4%	60.6%
1966	901,978	400,502	Shallcross, John S.	501,440	Jordan, B. Everett*	36	100,938 D	44.4%	55.6%	44.4%	55.6%
1962	813,155	321,635	Greene, Claude L. Jr.	491,520	Ervin, Sam J.*		169,885 D	39.6%	60.4%	39.6%	60.4%
1960	1,291,485	497,964	Hayes, Kyle	793,521	Jordan, B. Everett*		295,557 D	38.6%	61.4%	38.6%	61.4%
1958S	616,469	184,977	Clarke, Richard C. Jr.	431,492	Jordan, B. Everett*		246,515 D	30.0%	70.0%	30.0%	70.0%
1956	1,098,828	367,475	Johnson, Joel A.	731,353	Ervin, Sam J.*		363,878 D	33.4%	66.6%	33.4%	66.6%
1954	619,634	211,322	West, Paul C.	408,312	Scott, W. Kerr		196,990 D	34.1%	65.9%	34.1%	65.9%
1954S	410,574			410,574	Ervin, Sam J.*		410,574 D		100.0%		100.0%
1950	548,277	171,804	Leavitt, Halsey B.	376,473	Hoey, Clyde R.*		204,669 D	31.3%	68.7%	31.3%	68.7%
1950S	544,924	177,753	Gavin, E. L.	364,912	Smith, Willis	2,259	187,159 D	32.6%	67.0%	32.8%	67.2%
1948	764,559	220,307	Wilkinson, John A.	540,762	Broughton, J. Melville*	3,490	320,455 D	28.8%	70.7%	28.9%	71.1%

Note: An asterisk (*) denotes incumbent. **One each of the 1950 and 1954 elections as well as the 1958 election were for short terms to fill vacancies. The Republican Party did not run a Senate candidate in the 1954 election for the short term.

NORTH CAROLINA

PRESIDENT 2012

2010 Census Population	County	Total Vote	Republican (Romney)	Democratic (Obama)	Other	Rep.-Dem. Plurality	Percentage Total Vote Rep.	Dem.	Major Vote Rep.	Dem.
151,131	ALAMANCE	67,776	38,170	28,875	731	9,295 R	56.3%	42.6%	56.9%	43.1%
37,198	ALEXANDER	17,196	12,253	4,611	332	7,642 R	71.3%	26.8%	72.7%	27.3%
11,155	ALLEGHANY	5,067	3,390	1,583	94	1,807 R	66.9%	31.2%	68.2%	31.8%
26,948	ANSON	11,256	4,166	7,019	71	2,853 D	37.0%	62.4%	37.2%	62.8%
27,281	ASHE	12,610	8,242	4,116	252	4,126 R	65.4%	32.6%	66.7%	33.3%
17,797	AVERY	7,759	5,766	1,882	111	3,884 R	74.3%	24.3%	75.4%	24.6%
47,759	BEAUFORT	23,620	13,977	9,435	208	4,542 R	59.2%	39.9%	59.7%	40.3%
21,282	BERTIE	10,123	3,387	6,695	41	3,308 D	33.5%	66.1%	33.6%	66.4%
35,190	BLADEN	15,957	7,748	8,062	147	314 D	48.6%	50.5%	49.0%	51.0%
107,431	BRUNSWICK	57,362	34,743	22,038	581	12,705 R	60.6%	38.4%	61.2%	38.8%
238,318	BUNCOMBE	127,696	54,701	70,625	2,370	15,924 D	42.8%	55.3%	43.6%	56.4%
90,912	BURKE	36,544	22,267	13,701	576	8,566 R	60.9%	37.5%	61.9%	38.1%
178,011	CABARRUS	83,566	49,557	32,849	1,160	16,708 R	59.3%	39.3%	60.1%	39.9%
83,029	CALDWELL	34,732	23,229	10,898	605	12,331 R	66.9%	31.4%	68.1%	31.9%
9,980	CAMDEN	4,704	3,109	1,508	87	1,601 R	66.1%	32.1%	67.3%	32.7%
66,469	CARTERET	35,517	24,775	10,301	441	14,474 R	69.8%	29.0%	70.6%	29.4%
23,719	CASWELL	11,039	5,594	5,348	97	246 R	50.7%	48.4%	51.1%	48.9%
154,358	CATAWBA	69,601	44,538	24,069	994	20,469 R	64.0%	34.6%	64.9%	35.1%
63,505	CHATHAM	35,434	16,665	18,361	408	1,696 D	47.0%	51.8%	47.6%	52.4%
27,444	CHEROKEE	12,867	9,278	3,378	211	5,900 R	72.1%	26.3%	73.3%	26.7%
14,793	CHOWAN	7,505	3,891	3,556	58	335 R	51.8%	47.4%	52.2%	47.8%
10,587	CLAY	5,642	3,973	1,579	90	2,394 R	70.4%	28.0%	71.6%	28.4%
98,078	CLEVELAND	43,340	25,793	17,062	485	8,731 R	59.5%	39.4%	60.2%	39.8%
58,098	COLUMBUS	24,243	12,941	11,050	252	1,891 R	53.4%	45.6%	53.9%	46.1%
103,505	CRAVEN	46,170	26,928	18,763	479	8,165 R	58.3%	40.6%	58.9%	41.1%
319,431	CUMBERLAND	127,641	50,666	75,792	1,183	25,126 D	39.7%	59.4%	40.1%	59.9%
23,547	CURRITUCK	11,304	7,496	3,562	246	3,934 R	66.3%	31.5%	67.8%	32.2%
33,920	DARE	17,974	10,248	7,393	333	2,855 R	57.0%	41.1%	58.1%	41.9%
162,878	DAVIDSON	70,935	49,383	20,624	928	28,759 R	69.6%	29.1%	70.5%	29.5%
41,240	DAVIE	20,670	14,687	5,735	248	8,952 R	71.1%	27.7%	71.9%	28.1%
58,505	DUPLIN	20,592	11,416	9,033	143	2,383 R	55.4%	43.9%	55.8%	44.2%
267,587	DURHAM	146,735	33,769	111,224	1,742	77,455 D	23.0%	75.8%	23.3%	76.7%
56,552	EDGECOMBE	26,972	8,546	18,310	116	9,764 D	31.7%	67.9%	31.8%	68.2%
350,670	FORSYTH	174,069	79,768	92,323	1,978	12,555 D	45.8%	53.0%	46.4%	53.6%
60,619	FRANKLIN	28,389	14,603	13,436	350	1,167 R	51.4%	47.3%	52.1%	47.9%
206,086	GASTON	90,483	56,138	33,171	1,174	22,967 R	62.0%	36.7%	62.9%	37.1%
12,197	GATES	5,396	2,564	2,786	46	222 D	47.5%	51.6%	47.9%	52.1%
8,861	GRAHAM	3,947	2,750	1,119	78	1,631 R	69.7%	28.4%	71.1%	28.9%
59,916	GRANVILLE	26,275	12,405	13,598	272	1,193 D	47.2%	51.8%	47.7%	52.3%
21,362	GREENE	8,236	4,411	3,778	47	633 R	53.6%	45.9%	53.9%	46.1%
488,406	GUILFORD	253,852	104,789	146,365	2,698	41,576 D	41.3%	57.7%	41.7%	58.3%
54,691	HALIFAX	26,079	8,763	17,176	140	8,413 D	33.6%	65.9%	33.8%	66.2%
114,678	HARNETT	43,415	25,565	17,331	519	8,234 R	58.9%	39.9%	59.6%	40.4%
59,036	HAYWOOD	27,974	15,633	11,833	508	3,800 R	55.9%	42.3%	56.9%	43.1%
106,740	HENDERSON	52,392	32,994	18,642	756	14,352 R	63.0%	35.6%	63.9%	36.1%
24,669	HERTFORD	10,918	3,007	7,843	68	4,836 D	27.5%	71.8%	27.7%	72.3%
46,952	HOKE	17,089	6,819	10,076	194	3,257 D	39.9%	59.0%	40.4%	59.6%
5,810	HYDE	2,383	1,193	1,163	27	30 R	50.1%	48.8%	50.6%	49.4%
159,437	IREDELL	76,365	49,299	26,076	990	23,223 R	64.6%	34.1%	65.4%	34.6%
40,271	JACKSON	16,701	8,254	8,095	352	159 R	49.4%	48.5%	50.5%	49.5%
168,878	JOHNSTON	76,691	48,427	27,290	974	21,137 R	63.1%	35.6%	64.0%	36.0%
10,153	JONES	5,230	2,837	2,352	41	485 R	54.2%	45.0%	54.7%	45.3%
57,866	LEE	24,239	13,158	10,801	280	2,357 R	54.3%	44.6%	54.9%	45.1%
59,495	LENOIR	28,086	13,980	13,948	158	32 R	49.8%	49.7%	50.1%	49.9%
78,265	LINCOLN	36,775	25,267	11,024	484	14,243 R	68.7%	30.0%	69.6%	30.4%
33,922	MACON	16,861	10,835	5,712	314	5,123 R	64.3%	33.9%	65.5%	34.5%
20,764	MADISON	10,113	5,404	4,484	225	920 R	53.4%	44.3%	54.7%	45.3%
24,505	MARTIN	12,652	5,995	6,583	74	588 D	47.4%	52.0%	47.7%	52.3%
44,996	MCDOWELL	18,099	11,775	6,031	293	5,744 R	65.1%	33.3%	66.1%	33.9%
919,628	MECKLENBURG	448,900	171,668	272,262	4,970	100,594 D	38.2%	60.7%	38.7%	61.3%

NORTH CAROLINA

PRESIDENT 2012

2010 Census Population	County	Total Vote	Republican (Romney)	Democratic (Obama)	Other	Rep.-Dem. Plurality		Percentage Total Vote Rep.	Dem.	Major Vote Rep.	Dem.
15,579	MITCHELL	7,765	5,806	1,838	121	3,968	R	74.8%	23.7%	76.0%	24.0%
27,798	MONTGOMERY	11,231	6,404	4,706	121	1,698	R	57.0%	41.9%	57.6%	42.4%
88,247	MOORE	46,415	29,495	16,505	415	12,990	R	63.5%	35.6%	64.1%	35.9%
95,840	NASH	48,492	23,842	24,313	337	471	D	49.2%	50.1%	49.5%	50.5%
202,667	NEW HANOVER	103,628	53,385	48,668	1,575	4,717	R	51.5%	47.0%	52.3%	47.7%
22,099	NORTHAMPTON	10,756	3,483	7,232	41	3,749	D	32.4%	67.2%	32.5%	67.5%
177,772	ONSLOW	51,435	32,243	18,490	702	13,753	R	62.7%	35.9%	63.6%	36.4%
133,801	ORANGE	76,757	21,539	53,901	1,317	32,362	D	28.1%	70.2%	28.6%	71.4%
13,144	PAMLICO	6,762	4,051	2,647	64	1,404	R	59.9%	39.1%	60.5%	39.5%
40,661	PASQUOTANK	18,107	7,633	10,282	192	2,649	D	42.2%	56.8%	42.6%	57.4%
52,217	PENDER	24,527	14,617	9,632	278	4,985	R	59.6%	39.3%	60.3%	39.7%
13,453	PERQUIMANS	6,652	3,822	2,759	71	1,063	R	57.5%	41.5%	58.1%	41.9%
39,464	PERSON	19,106	10,496	8,418	192	2,078	R	54.9%	44.1%	55.5%	44.5%
168,148	PITT	78,856	36,214	41,843	799	5,629	D	45.9%	53.1%	46.4%	53.6%
20,510	POLK	10,389	6,236	4,013	140	2,223	R	60.0%	38.6%	60.8%	39.2%
141,752	RANDOLPH	60,715	45,160	14,773	782	30,387	R	74.4%	24.3%	75.4%	24.6%
46,639	RICHMOND	19,417	9,332	9,904	181	572	D	48.1%	51.0%	48.5%	51.5%
134,168	ROBESON	42,946	17,510	24,988	448	7,478	D	40.8%	58.2%	41.2%	58.8%
93,643	ROCKINGHAM	42,020	25,227	16,351	442	8,876	R	60.0%	38.9%	60.7%	39.3%
138,428	ROWAN	62,312	38,775	22,650	887	16,125	R	62.2%	36.3%	63.1%	36.9%
67,810	RUTHERFORD	28,702	18,954	9,374	374	9,580	R	66.0%	32.7%	66.9%	33.1%
63,431	SAMPSON	26,174	14,422	11,566	186	2,856	R	55.1%	44.2%	55.5%	44.5%
36,157	SCOTLAND	14,156	5,831	8,215	110	2,384	D	41.2%	58.0%	41.5%	58.5%
60,585	STANLY	28,717	19,904	8,431	382	11,473	R	69.3%	29.4%	70.2%	29.8%
47,401	STOKES	21,619	15,237	6,018	364	9,219	R	70.5%	27.8%	71.7%	28.3%
73,673	SURRY	29,470	19,923	9,112	435	10,811	R	67.6%	30.9%	68.6%	31.4%
13,981	SWAIN	5,728	2,976	2,618	134	358	R	52.0%	45.7%	53.2%	46.8%
33,090	TRANSYLVANIA	16,763	9,634	6,826	303	2,808	R	57.5%	40.7%	58.5%	41.5%
4,407	TYRRELL	1,783	930	837	16	93	R	52.2%	46.9%	52.6%	47.4%
201,292	UNION	94,728	61,107	32,473	1,148	28,634	R	64.5%	34.3%	65.3%	34.7%
45,422	VANCE	20,854	7,429	13,323	102	5,894	D	35.6%	63.9%	35.8%	64.2%
900,993	WAKE	486,427	211,596	267,262	7,569	55,666	D	43.5%	54.9%	44.2%	55.8%
20,972	WARREN	10,162	3,140	6,978	44	3,838	D	30.9%	68.7%	31.0%	69.0%
13,228	WASHINGTON	6,499	2,622	3,833	44	1,211	D	40.3%	59.0%	40.6%	59.4%
51,079	WATAUGA	27,674	13,861	13,002	811	859	R	50.1%	47.0%	51.6%	48.4%
122,623	WAYNE	51,352	27,641	23,314	397	4,327	R	53.8%	45.4%	54.2%	45.8%
69,340	WILKES	29,145	20,515	8,148	482	12,367	R	70.4%	28.0%	71.6%	28.4%
81,234	WILSON	39,109	17,954	20,875	280	2,921	D	45.9%	53.4%	46.2%	53.8%
38,406	YADKIN	16,813	12,578	3,957	278	8,621	R	74.8%	23.5%	76.1%	23.9%
17,818	YANCEY	9,451	5,278	3,981	192	1,297	R	55.8%	42.1%	57.0%	43.0%
9,535,483	TOTAL	4,505,372	2,270,395	2,178,391	56,586	92,004	R	50.4%	48.4%	51.0%	49.0%

NORTH CAROLINA
GOVERNOR 2012

2010 Census Population	County	Total Vote	Republican (McCrory)	Democratic (Dalton)	Other	Rep.-Dem. Plurality		Total Vote Rep.	Total Vote Dem.	Major Vote Rep.	Major Vote Dem.
151,131	ALAMANCE	67,113	40,044	25,624	1,445	14,420	R	59.7%	38.2%	61.0%	39.0%
37,198	ALEXANDER	17,227	13,216	3,768	243	9,448	R	76.7%	21.9%	77.8%	22.2%
11,155	ALLEGHANY	5,051	3,419	1,506	126	1,913	R	67.7%	29.8%	69.4%	30.6%
26,948	ANSON	11,257	4,561	6,591	105	2,030	D	40.5%	58.6%	40.9%	59.1%
27,281	ASHE	12,676	8,729	3,659	288	5,070	R	68.9%	28.9%	70.5%	29.5%
17,797	AVERY	7,653	6,010	1,456	187	4,554	R	78.5%	19.0%	80.5%	19.5%
47,759	BEAUFORT	23,507	14,124	8,992	391	5,132	R	60.1%	38.3%	61.1%	38.9%
21,282	BERTIE	10,037	3,365	6,587	85	3,222	D	33.5%	65.6%	33.8%	66.2%
35,190	BLADEN	15,852	7,545	8,118	189	573	D	47.6%	51.2%	48.2%	51.8%
107,431	BRUNSWICK	56,782	36,907	18,652	1,223	18,255	R	65.0%	32.8%	66.4%	33.6%
238,318	BUNCOMBE	126,187	57,541	64,389	4,257	6,848	D	45.6%	51.0%	47.2%	52.8%
90,912	BURKE	36,522	24,972	10,866	684	14,106	R	68.4%	29.8%	69.7%	30.3%
178,011	CABARRUS	83,278	56,888	24,827	1,563	32,061	R	68.3%	29.8%	69.6%	30.4%
83,029	CALDWELL	34,912	25,771	8,402	739	17,369	R	73.8%	24.1%	75.4%	24.6%
9,980	CAMDEN	4,604	2,831	1,587	186	1,244	R	61.5%	34.5%	64.1%	35.9%
66,469	CARTERET	35,388	25,584	9,141	663	16,443	R	72.3%	25.8%	73.7%	26.3%
23,719	CASWELL	10,898	5,536	5,168	194	368	R	50.8%	47.4%	51.7%	48.3%
154,358	CATAWBA	69,255	49,725	18,352	1,178	31,373	R	71.8%	26.5%	73.0%	27.0%
63,505	CHATHAM	35,224	17,517	16,920	787	597	R	49.7%	48.0%	50.9%	49.1%
27,444	CHEROKEE	12,460	8,193	3,683	584	4,510	R	65.8%	29.6%	69.0%	31.0%
14,793	CHOWAN	7,330	3,658	3,538	134	120	R	49.9%	48.3%	50.8%	49.2%
10,587	CLAY	5,524	3,680	1,641	203	2,039	R	66.6%	29.7%	69.2%	30.8%
98,078	CLEVELAND	43,121	26,368	16,193	560	10,175	R	61.1%	37.6%	62.0%	38.0%
58,098	COLUMBUS	23,969	11,857	11,737	375	120	R	49.5%	49.0%	50.3%	49.7%
103,505	CRAVEN	45,813	27,842	17,118	853	10,724	R	60.8%	37.4%	61.9%	38.1%
319,431	CUMBERLAND	125,741	52,310	70,680	2,751	18,370	D	41.6%	56.2%	42.5%	57.5%
23,547	CURRITUCK	10,983	7,073	3,329	581	3,744	R	64.4%	30.3%	68.0%	32.0%
33,920	DARE	17,543	9,905	6,941	697	2,964	R	56.5%	39.6%	58.8%	41.2%
162,878	DAVIDSON	70,741	51,500	17,758	1,483	33,742	R	72.8%	25.1%	74.4%	25.6%
41,240	DAVIE	20,648	15,466	4,792	390	10,674	R	74.9%	23.2%	76.3%	23.7%
58,505	DUPLIN	20,431	11,333	8,843	255	2,490	R	55.5%	43.3%	56.2%	43.8%
267,587	DURHAM	144,821	38,467	102,533	3,821	64,066	D	26.6%	70.8%	27.3%	72.7%
56,552	EDGECOMBE	26,860	8,695	17,948	217	9,253	D	32.4%	66.8%	32.6%	67.4%
350,670	FORSYTH	173,042	87,499	81,872	3,671	5,627	R	50.6%	47.3%	51.7%	48.3%
60,619	FRANKLIN	28,277	15,370	12,282	625	3,088	R	54.4%	43.4%	55.6%	44.4%
206,086	GASTON	90,133	61,844	26,877	1,412	34,967	R	68.6%	29.8%	69.7%	30.3%
12,197	GATES	5,322	2,334	2,862	126	528	D	43.9%	53.8%	44.9%	55.1%
8,861	GRAHAM	3,914	2,605	1,210	99	1,395	R	66.6%	30.9%	68.3%	31.7%
59,916	GRANVILLE	26,163	13,052	12,605	506	447	R	49.9%	48.2%	50.9%	49.1%
21,362	GREENE	8,213	4,388	3,745	80	643	R	53.4%	45.6%	54.0%	46.0%
488,406	GUILFORD	251,264	114,906	130,798	5,560	15,892	D	45.7%	52.1%	46.8%	53.2%
54,691	HALIFAX	26,144	8,951	16,973	220	8,022	D	34.2%	64.9%	34.5%	65.5%
114,678	HARNETT	43,235	26,289	16,033	913	10,256	R	60.8%	37.1%	62.1%	37.9%
59,036	HAYWOOD	27,665	16,016	10,907	742	5,109	R	57.9%	39.4%	59.5%	40.5%
106,740	HENDERSON	51,762	33,807	16,590	1,365	17,217	R	65.3%	32.1%	67.1%	32.9%
24,669	HERTFORD	10,752	2,840	7,793	119	4,953	D	26.4%	72.5%	26.7%	73.3%
46,952	HOKE	16,864	6,956	9,513	395	2,557	D	41.2%	56.4%	42.2%	57.8%
5,810	HYDE	2,371	1,240	1,080	51	160	R	52.3%	45.6%	53.4%	46.6%
159,437	IREDELL	75,957	54,587	20,043	1,327	34,544	R	71.9%	26.4%	73.1%	26.9%
40,271	JACKSON	16,655	8,517	7,554	584	963	R	51.1%	45.4%	53.0%	47.0%
168,878	JOHNSTON	76,420	50,225	24,691	1,504	25,534	R	65.7%	32.3%	67.0%	33.0%
10,153	JONES	5,215	2,927	2,224	64	703	R	56.1%	42.6%	56.8%	43.2%
57,866	LEE	24,092	13,528	10,083	481	3,445	R	56.2%	41.9%	57.3%	42.7%
59,495	LENOIR	27,831	14,020	13,498	313	522	R	50.4%	48.5%	50.9%	49.1%
78,265	LINCOLN	36,659	27,845	8,227	587	19,618	R	76.0%	22.4%	77.2%	22.8%
33,922	MACON	16,724	10,669	5,565	490	5,104	R	63.8%	33.3%	65.7%	34.3%
20,764	MADISON	10,161	5,586	4,272	303	1,314	R	55.0%	42.0%	56.7%	43.3%
24,505	MARTIN	12,596	5,851	6,611	134	760	D	46.5%	52.5%	47.0%	53.0%
44,996	MCDOWELL	17,996	11,905	5,624	467	6,281	R	66.2%	31.3%	67.9%	32.1%
919,628	MECKLENBURG	444,632	219,927	216,826	7,879	3,101	R	49.5%	48.8%	50.4%	49.6%

NORTH CAROLINA
GOVERNOR 2012

2010 Census Population	County	Total Vote	Republican (McCrory)	Democratic (Dalton)	Other	Rep.-Dem. Plurality		Percentage			
								Total Vote		Major Vote	
								Rep.	Dem.	Rep.	Dem.
15,579	MITCHELL	7,672	5,841	1,646	185	4,195	R	76.1%	21.5%	78.0%	22.0%
27,798	MONTGOMERY	11,229	6,730	4,320	179	2,410	R	59.9%	38.5%	60.9%	39.1%
88,247	MOORE	46,008	30,460	14,792	756	15,668	R	66.2%	32.2%	67.3%	32.7%
95,840	NASH	48,401	24,471	23,449	481	1,022	R	50.6%	48.4%	51.1%	48.9%
202,667	NEW HANOVER	101,911	57,108	41,633	3,170	15,475	R	56.0%	40.9%	57.8%	42.2%
22,099	NORTHAMPTON	10,709	3,477	7,115	117	3,638	D	32.5%	66.4%	32.8%	67.2%
177,772	ONSLOW	50,660	32,732	16,520	1,408	16,212	R	64.6%	32.6%	66.5%	33.5%
133,801	ORANGE	75,555	24,492	48,684	2,379	24,192	D	32.4%	64.4%	33.5%	66.5%
13,144	PAMLICO	6,703	4,122	2,450	131	1,672	R	61.5%	36.6%	62.7%	37.3%
40,661	PASQUOTANK	17,704	7,139	10,082	483	2,943	D	40.3%	56.9%	41.5%	58.5%
52,217	PENDER	24,360	15,113	8,726	521	6,387	R	62.0%	35.8%	63.4%	36.6%
13,453	PERQUIMANS	6,461	3,544	2,757	160	787	R	54.9%	42.7%	56.2%	43.8%
39,464	PERSON	18,817	10,672	7,784	361	2,888	R	56.7%	41.4%	57.8%	42.2%
168,148	PITT	78,277	37,999	38,877	1,401	878	D	48.5%	49.7%	49.4%	50.6%
20,510	POLK	10,267	6,065	3,954	248	2,111	R	59.1%	38.5%	60.5%	39.5%
141,752	RANDOLPH	60,684	46,583	12,939	1,162	33,644	R	76.8%	21.3%	78.3%	21.7%
46,639	RICHMOND	19,256	9,795	9,119	342	676	R	50.9%	47.4%	51.8%	48.2%
134,168	ROBESON	42,365	16,113	25,474	778	9,361	D	38.0%	60.1%	38.7%	61.3%
93,643	ROCKINGHAM	41,739	25,890	15,062	787	10,828	R	62.0%	36.1%	63.2%	36.8%
138,428	ROWAN	62,036	42,947	18,066	1,023	24,881	R	69.2%	29.1%	70.4%	29.6%
67,810	RUTHERFORD	28,697	16,005	12,203	489	3,802	R	55.8%	42.5%	56.7%	43.3%
63,431	SAMPSON	26,120	14,506	11,327	287	3,179	R	55.5%	43.4%	56.2%	43.8%
36,157	SCOTLAND	13,848	5,556	7,993	299	2,437	D	40.1%	57.7%	41.0%	59.0%
60,585	STANLY	28,649	21,523	6,725	401	14,798	R	75.1%	23.5%	76.2%	23.8%
47,401	STOKES	21,617	15,580	5,518	519	10,062	R	72.1%	25.5%	73.8%	26.2%
73,673	SURRY	29,351	20,757	7,982	612	12,775	R	70.7%	27.2%	72.2%	27.8%
13,981	SWAIN	5,690	2,952	2,532	206	420	R	51.9%	44.5%	53.8%	46.2%
33,090	TRANSYLVANIA	16,554	9,879	6,205	470	3,674	R	59.7%	37.5%	61.4%	38.6%
4,407	TYRRELL	1,760	919	811	30	108	R	52.2%	46.1%	53.1%	46.9%
201,292	UNION	94,075	68,095	24,407	1,573	43,688	R	72.4%	25.9%	73.6%	26.4%
45,422	VANCE	20,729	7,647	12,880	202	5,233	D	36.9%	62.1%	37.3%	62.7%
900,993	WAKE	482,102	234,584	233,822	13,696	762	R	48.7%	48.5%	50.1%	49.9%
20,972	WARREN	10,008	3,300	6,603	105	3,303	D	33.0%	66.0%	33.3%	66.7%
13,228	WASHINGTON	6,481	2,591	3,824	66	1,233	D	40.0%	59.0%	40.4%	59.6%
51,079	WATAUGA	27,075	14,887	10,930	1,258	3,957	R	55.0%	40.4%	57.7%	42.3%
122,623	WAYNE	51,064	28,259	22,106	699	6,153	R	55.3%	43.3%	56.1%	43.9%
69,340	WILKES	29,092	21,455	7,047	590	14,408	R	73.7%	24.2%	75.3%	24.7%
81,234	WILSON	38,790	18,288	20,058	444	1,770	D	47.1%	51.7%	47.7%	52.3%
38,406	YADKIN	16,764	13,070	3,339	355	9,731	R	78.0%	19.9%	79.7%	20.3%
17,818	YANCEY	9,548	5,245	4,122	181	1,123	R	54.9%	43.2%	56.0%	44.0%
9,535,483	TOTAL	4,468,295	2,440,707	1,931,580	96,008	509,127	R	54.6%	43.2%	55.8%	44.2%

NORTH CAROLINA

HOUSE OF REPRESENTATIVES

| | | | Republican | | Democratic | | Other | Rep.-Dem. | Percentage | | | |
| | | | | | | | | | Total Vote | | Major Vote | |
CD	Year	Total Vote	Vote	Candidate	Vote	Candidate	Vote	Plurality	Rep.	Dem.	Rep.	Dem.
1	2012	338,066	77,288	DILAURO, PETE	254,644	BUTTERFIELD, G. K.*	6,134	177,356 D	22.9%	75.3%	23.3%	76.7%
2	2012	311,397	174,066	ELLMERS, RENEE*	128,973	WILKINS, STEVE	8,358	45,093 R	55.9%	41.4%	57.4%	42.6%
3	2012	309,885	195,571	JONES, WALTER B. JR.*	114,314	ANDERSON, ERIK		81,257 R	63.1%	36.9%	63.1%	36.9%
4	2012	348,485	88,951	D'ANNUNZIO, TIM	259,534	PRICE, DAVID E.*		170,583 D	25.5%	74.5%	25.5%	74.5%
5	2012	349,197	200,945	FOXX, VIRGINIA*	148,252	MOTSINGER, ELISABETH		52,693 R	57.5%	42.5%	57.5%	42.5%
6	2012	364,583	222,116	COBLE, HOWARD*	142,467	FORIEST, TONY		79,649 R	60.9%	39.1%	60.9%	39.1%
7	2012	336,736	168,041	ROUZER, DAVID	168,695	MCINTYRE, MIKE*		654 D	49.9%	50.1%	49.9%	50.1%
8	2012	302,280	160,695	HUDSON, RICHARD	137,139	KISSELL, LARRY*	4,446	23,556 R	53.2%	45.4%	54.0%	46.0%
9	2012	375,690	194,537	PITTENGER, ROBERT	171,503	ROBERTS, JENNIFER	9,650	23,034 R	51.8%	45.7%	53.1%	46.9%
10	2012	334,849	190,826	MCHENRY, PATRICK*	144,023	KEEVER, PATRICIA R. "PATSY"		46,803 R	57.0%	43.0%	57.0%	43.0%
11	2012	331,426	190,319	MEADOWS, MARK	141,107	ROGERS, HAYDEN		49,212 R	57.4%	42.6%	57.4%	42.6%
12	2012	310,908	63,317	BROSCH, JACK	247,591	WATT, MEL*		184,274 D	20.4%	79.6%	20.4%	79.6%
13	2012	370,610	210,495	HOLDING, GEORGE	160,115	MALONE, CHARLES		50,380 R	56.8%	43.2%	56.8%	43.2%
TOTAL	2012	4,384,112	2,137,167		2,218,357		28,588	81,190 D	48.7%	50.6%	49.1%	50.9%

Note: An asterisk (*) denotes incumbent.

NORTH CAROLINA

GENERAL AND PRIMARY ELECTIONS

GENERAL ELECTIONS: OTHER VOTE

President   Other vote was 44,515 Libertarian (Gary E. Johnson), 11,537 Write-in (Scattered Write-In), 534 Write-in (Virgil H. Goode)

Governor   Other vote was 94,652 Libertarian (Barbara Howe), 1,297 Write-in (Scattered Write-In), 59 Write-in (Donald Kreamer)

House   Other vote was:

CD 1   6,134 Libertarian (Darryl Holloman)
CD 2   8,358 Libertarian (Brian Irving)
CD 8   3,990 Write-in (Antonio Blue), 456 Write-in (Scattered Write-In)
CD 9   9,650 Libertarian (Curtis Campbell)

PRIMARY ELECTIONS: SUPPLEMENTARY INFORMATION

Primary	May 8, 2012	**Registration** (as of May 8, 2012)	6,302,793	Democratic	2,738,924
				Republican	1,977,434
				Libertarian	13,833
				Unaffiliated	1,572,602

Primary Runoff July 17, 2012

Primary Type   Semi-open—Registered Democrats and Republicans could vote only in their party's primary. Unaffiliated voters could participate in the primary of either party. However, if a voter cast a ballot in one party's primary, they could not participate in the runoff of the other party.

NORTH CAROLINA

GENERAL AND PRIMARY ELECTIONS

	REPUBLICAN PRIMARIES			DEMOCRATIC PRIMARIES		
President	Romney, W. Mitt	638,601	65.6%	Obama, Barack H.*	766,077	79.2%
	Paul, Ron	108,217	11.1%	No Preference	200,810	20.8%
	Santorum, Rick	101,093	10.4%			
	Gingrich, Newt	74,367	7.6%			
	No Preference	50,928	5.2%			
	TOTAL	973,206		TOTAL	966,887	
Governor	McCrory, Pat	748,180	83.4%	Dalton, Walter H.	428,475	45.9%
	Wright, Paul	47,403	5.3%	Etheridge, Bob	354,923	38.0%
	Jones, Scott A.	31,191	3.5%	Faison, Bill	52,179	5.6%
	Mahan, Jim	30,056	3.4%	Henley, Gardenia M.	48,982	5.2%
	Harney, Jim	26,485	3.0%	Dunn, Gary M.	27,358	2.9%
	Moss, Charles Kenneth	13,822	1.5%	Blackmon, Bruce	22,370	2.4%
	TOTAL	897,137		TOTAL	934,287	
Congressional District 1	DiLauro, Pete	Unopposed		Butterfield, G. K.*	89,531	81.1%
				Whittacre, Dan	20,822	18.9%
				TOTAL	110,353	
Congressional District 2	Ellmers, Renee*	37,661	56.0%	Wilkins, Steve	24,327	50.7%
	Speer, Richard	20,099	29.9%	Morris, Toni	20,431	42.6%
	Holmes, Sonya	6,535	9.7%	Bibbs, Jim	3,238	6.7%
	Munno, Clement F.	2,982	4.4%			
	TOTAL	67,277		TOTAL	47,996	
Congressional District 3	Jones, Walter B. Jr.*	42,644	69.0%	Anderson, Erik	Unopposed	
	Palombo, Frank	19,166	31.0%			
	TOTAL	61,810				
Congressional District 4	D'Annunzio, Tim	14,065	46.4%	Price, David E.*	Unopposed	
	Allen, Jim	10,430	34.4%			
	Hutchins, George	5,811	19.2%			
	TOTAL	30,306				
Congressional District 5	Foxx, Virginia*	Unopposed		Motsinger, Elisabeth	38,512	69.7%
				Peller, Bruce G.	16,716	30.3%
				TOTAL	55,228	
Congressional District 6	Coble, Howard*	50,701	57.3%	Foriest, Tony	Unopposed	
	Flynn, Bill	19,741	22.3%			
	Yow, Billy	18,057	20.4%			
	TOTAL	88,499				
Congressional District 7	Rouzer, David	34,647	48.5%	McIntyre, Mike*	Unopposed	
	Pantano, Ilario Gregory	31,752	44.5%			
	Crow, Randy	5,012	7.0%			
	TOTAL	71,411				
Congressional District 8	Hudson, Richard	21,451	32.1%	Kissell, Larry*	45,987	72.6%
	Keadle, John "Scott"	14,687	22.0%	Williams, Marcus W.	17,393	27.4%
	Robinson, Vernon L.	12,181	18.2%			
	Steen, Fred F. II	9,670	14.5%			
	Whitley, John M.	8,894	13.3%			
	TOTAL	66,883		TOTAL	63,380	
	PRIMARY RUNOFF					
	Hudson, Richard	10,699	63.6%			
	Keadle, John "Scott"	6,118	36.4%			
	TOTAL	16,817				

NORTH CAROLINA

GENERAL AND PRIMARY ELECTIONS

	REPUBLICAN PRIMARIES			DEMOCRATIC PRIMARIES		
Congressional District 9	Pittenger, Robert	29,999	32.4%	Roberts, Jennifer	Unopposed	
	Pendergraph, Jim	23,401	25.3%			
	Peacock, Edwin B. III	11,336	12.3%			
	Killian, Ric	9,691	10.5%			
	Barry, Dan	5,515	6.0%			
	Dulin, Andy	4,526	4.9%			
	Steinberg, Mike	2,297	2.5%			
	Gauthier, Jon	2,056	2.2%			
	Leonczyk, Ken	2,047	2.2%			
	Lynch, Richard	1,000	1.1%			
	Shaffer, Michael	579	0.6%			
	TOTAL	*92,447*				
	PRIMARY RUNOFF					
	Pittenger, Robert	18,982	52.9%			
	Pendergraph, Jim	16,902	47.1%			
	TOTAL	*35,884*				
Congressional District 10	McHenry, Patrick*	58,844	72.5%	Keever, Patricia R. "Patsy"	36,791	57.9%
	Fortenberry, Ken H.	15,936	19.6%	Bellamy, Terry Michelle	16,865	26.5%
	Peterson, Don	6,337	7.8%	Murphy, Timothy	9,908	15.6%
	TOTAL	*81,117*		*TOTAL*	*63,564*	
Congressional District 11	Meadows, Mark	35,733	37.8%	Rogers, Hayden	35,518	55.7%
	Patterson, Vance	22,306	23.6%	Bothwell, Cecil	19,161	30.1%
	Hunt, Jeff	13,353	14.1%	Hill, Thomas	9,049	14.2%
	Wingfield, Ethan	10,697	11.3%			
	Harris, Susan	5,825	6.2%			
	West, Kenny	3,970	4.2%			
	Campbell, Spence	1,799	1.9%			
	Petrella, Chris	778	0.8%			
	TOTAL	*94,461*		*TOTAL*	*63,728*	
	PRIMARY RUNOFF					
	Meadows, Mark	17,520	76.2%			
	Patterson, Vance	5,471	23.8%			
	TOTAL	*22,991*				
Congressional District 12	Brosch, Jack	Unopposed		Watt, Mel*	52,968	80.9%
				Newton, Matt	12,495	19.1%
				TOTAL	*65,463*	
Congressional District 13	Holding, George	37,341	43.5%	Malone, Charles	45,865	66.9%
	Coble, Paul Y.	29,354	34.2%	Holliday, Bernard A.	22,703	33.1%
	Randall, William	19,119	22.3%			
	TOTAL	*85,814*		*TOTAL*	*68,568*	

Notes: An asterisk (*) denotes incumbent. The names of unopposed candidates did not appear on the primary ballot; therefore, no votes were cast for these candidates. A runoff was triggered if the leading candidate received less than a "substantial plurality" (40 percent) of the primary vote and the second-place candidate called for a runoff.

NORTH DAKOTA

One member At Large

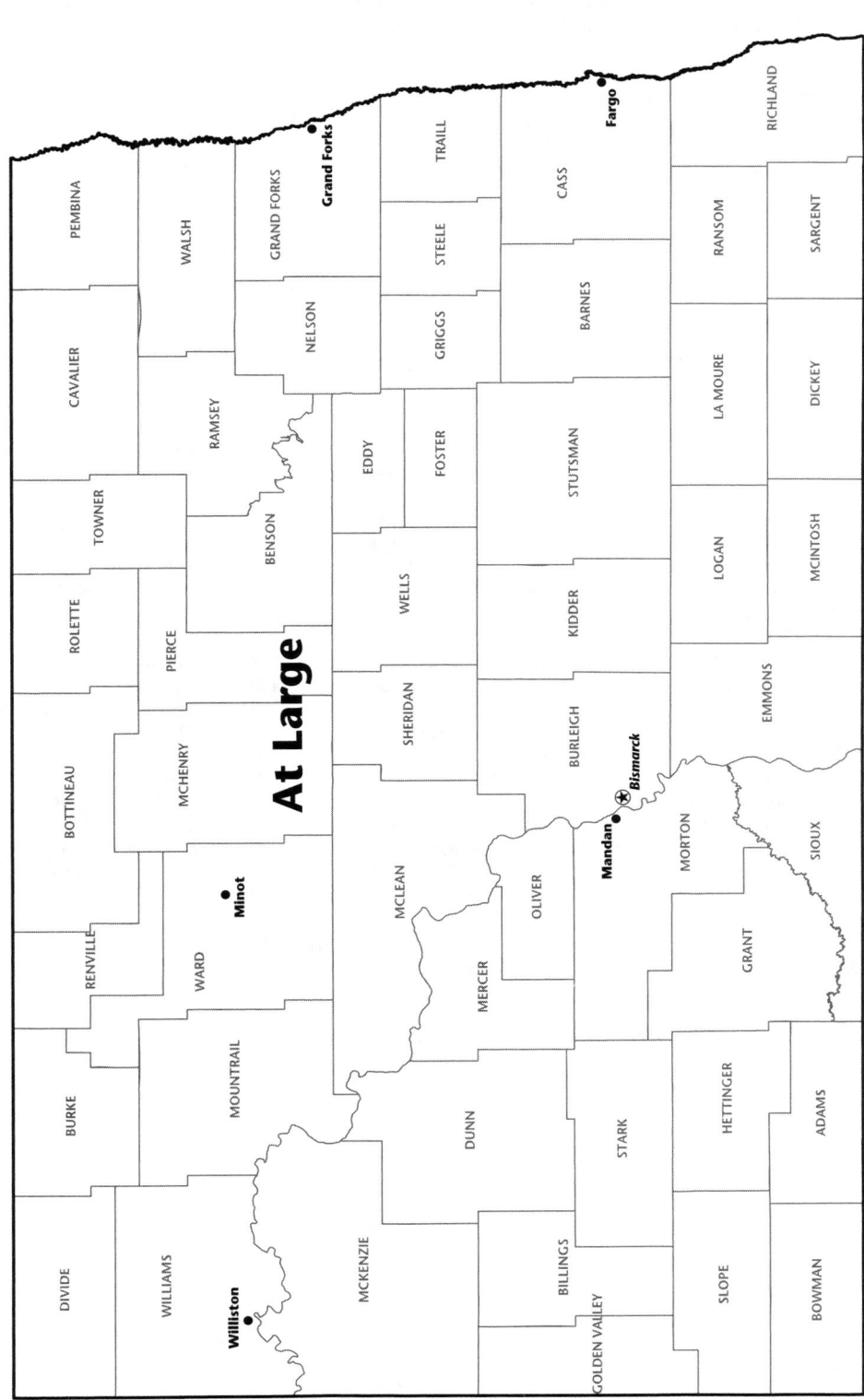

NORTH DAKOTA

GOVERNOR

Jack Dalrymple (R). Elected 2012 to a four-year term. Originally sworn in as governor December 7, 2010, to fill the vacancy created by the resignation of John Hoeven (R) following Hoeven's election to the Senate.

SENATORS (1 Republican, 1 Democrat)

John Hoeven (R). Elected 2010 to a six-year term.

Heidi Heitkamp (D). Elected 2012 to a six-year term.

REPRESENTATIVES (1 Republican)

At Large. Kevin Cramer (R)

POSTWAR VOTE FOR PRESIDENT

| | | Republican | | Democratic | | Other Vote | Rep.-Dem. Plurality | Percentage | | | |
| | | | | | | | | Total Vote | | Major Vote | |
Year	Total Vote	Vote	Candidate	Vote	Candidate			Rep.	Dem.	Rep.	Dem.
2012	322,627	188,163	Romney, W. Mitt	124,827	Obama, Barack H.*	9,637	63,336 R	58.3%	38.7%	60.1%	39.9%
2008	316,621	168,601	McCain, John S. III	141,278	Obama, Barack H.	6,742	27,323 R	53.3%	44.6%	54.4%	45.6%
2004	312,833	196,651	Bush, George W.*	111,052	Kerry, John F.	5,130	85,599 R	62.9%	35.5%	63.9%	36.1%
2000**	288,256	174,852	Bush, George W.	95,284	Gore, Albert Jr.	18,120	79,568 R	60.7%	33.1%	64.7%	35.3%
1996**	266,411	125,050	Dole, Robert "Bob"	106,905	Clinton, Bill*	34,456	18,145 R	46.9%	40.1%	53.9%	46.1%
1992**	308,133	136,244	Bush, George H.*	99,168	Clinton, Bill	72,721	37,076 R	44.2%	32.2%	57.9%	42.1%
1988	297,261	166,559	Bush, George H.	127,739	Dukakis, Michael S.	2,963	38,820 R	56.0%	43.0%	56.6%	43.4%
1984	308,971	200,336	Reagan, Ronald*	104,429	Mondale, Walter F.	4,206	95,907 R	64.8%	33.8%	65.7%	34.3%
1980**	301,545	193,695	Reagan, Ronald	79,189	Carter, Jimmy*	28,661	114,506 R	64.2%	26.3%	71.0%	29.0%
1976	297,188	153,470	Ford, Gerald R.*	136,078	Carter, Jimmy	7,640	17,392 R	51.6%	45.8%	53.0%	47.0%
1972	280,514	174,109	Nixon, Richard M.*	100,384	McGovern, George S.	6,021	73,725 R	62.1%	35.8%	63.4%	36.6%
1968**	247,882	138,669	Nixon, Richard M.	94,769	Humphrey, Hubert H. Jr.	14,444	43,900 R	55.9%	38.2%	59.4%	40.6%
1964	258,389	108,207	Goldwater, Barry M. Sr.	149,784	Johnson, Lyndon B.*	398	41,577 D	41.9%	58.0%	41.9%	58.1%
1960	278,431	154,310	Nixon, Richard M.	123,963	Kennedy, John F.	158	30,347 R	55.4%	44.5%	55.5%	44.5%
1956	253,991	156,766	Eisenhower, Dwight D.*	96,742	Stevenson, Adlai E. II	483	60,024 R	61.7%	38.1%	61.8%	38.2%
1952	270,127	191,712	Eisenhower, Dwight D.	76,694	Stevenson, Adlai E. II	1,721	115,018 R	71.0%	28.4%	71.4%	28.6%
1948	220,716	115,139	Dewey, Thomas E.	95,812	Truman, Harry S.*	9,765	19,327 R	52.2%	43.4%	54.6%	45.4%

Note: An asterisk (*) denotes incumbent. **In past elections, the other vote included: 2000 - 9,486 Green (Ralph Nader); 1996 - 32,515 Reform (Ross Perot); 1992 - 71,084 Independent (Perot); 1980 - 23,640 Independent (John Anderson); 1968 - 14,244 American Independent (George Wallace).

NORTH DAKOTA

POSTWAR VOTE FOR GOVERNOR

| Year | Total Vote | Republican | | Democratic | | Other Vote | Rep.-Dem. Plurality | Percentage | | | |
| | | Vote | Candidate | Vote | Candidate | | | Total Vote | | Major Vote | |
								Rep.	Dem.	Rep.	Dem.
2012	317,812	200,526	Dalrymple, Jack*	109,047	Taylor, Ryan M.	8,239	91,479 R	63.1%	34.3%	64.8%	35.2%
2008	315,692	235,009	Hoeven, John*	74,279	Mathern, Tim	6,404	160,730 R	74.4%	23.5%	76.0%	24.0%
2004	309,873	220,803	Hoeven, John*	84,877	Satrom, Joe	4,193	135,926 R	71.3%	27.4%	72.2%	27.8%
2000	289,412	159,255	Hoeven, John	130,144	Heitkamp, Heidi	13	29,111 R	55.0%	45.0%	55.0%	45.0%
1996	264,298	174,937	Schafer, Edward T.*	89,349	Kaldor, Lee	12	85,588 R	66.2%	33.8%	66.2%	33.8%
1992	304,861	176,398	Schafer, Edward T.	123,845	Spaeth, Nicholas	4,618	52,553 R	57.9%	40.6%	58.8%	41.2%
1988	299,080	119,986	Mallberg, Leon L.	179,094	Sinner, George*		59,108 D	40.1%	59.9%	40.1%	59.9%
1984	314,382	140,460	Olson, Allen I.	173,922	Sinner, George		33,462 D	44.7%	55.3%	44.7%	55.3%
1980	302,621	162,230	Olson, Allen I.	140,391	Link, Arthur A.*		21,839 R	53.6%	46.4%	53.6%	46.4%
1976	297,249	138,321	Elkin, Richard	153,309	Link, Arthur A.*	5,619	14,988 D	46.5%	51.6%	47.4%	52.6%
1972	281,931	138,032	Davis, John E.	143,899	Link, Arthur A.		5,867 D	49.0%	51.0%	49.0%	51.0%
1968	247,998	108,380	McCarney, Robert P.	135,955	Guy, William L.*	3,663	27,575 D	43.7%	54.8%	44.4%	55.6%
1964**	262,661	116,247	Halcrow, Don	146,414	Guy, William L.*		30,167 D	44.3%	55.7%	44.3%	55.7%
1962	228,509	113,251	Andrews, Mark	115,258	Guy, William L.*		2,007 D	49.6%	50.4%	49.6%	50.4%
1960	275,375	122,486	Dahl, C. P.	136,148	Guy, William L.	16,741	13,662 D	44.5%	49.4%	47.4%	52.6%
1958	210,599	111,836	Davis, John E.*	98,763	Lord, John F.		13,073 R	53.1%	46.9%	53.1%	46.9%
1956	252,435	147,566	Davis, John E.	104,869	Warner, Wallace E.		42,697 R	58.5%	41.5%	58.5%	41.5%
1954	193,501	124,253	Brunsdale, Norman*	69,248	Bymers, Cornelius		55,005 R	64.2%	35.8%	64.2%	35.8%
1952	253,934	199,944	Brunsdale, Norman*	53,990	Johnson, Ole S.		145,954 R	78.7%	21.3%	78.7%	21.3%
1950	183,772	121,822	Brunsdale, Norman	61,950	Byerly, Clyde G.		59,872 R	66.3%	33.7%	66.3%	33.7%
1948	214,958	131,764	Aandahl, Fred G.*	80,655	Henry, Howard	2,539	51,109 R	61.3%	37.5%	62.0%	38.0%
1946	169,391	116,672	Aandahl, Fred G.*	52,719	Burdick, Quentin N.		63,953 R	68.9%	31.1%	68.9%	31.1%

Note: An asterisk (*) denotes incumbent. **The term of office of North Dakota's governor was increased from two to four years effective with the 1964 election.

POSTWAR VOTE FOR SENATOR

| Year | Total Vote | Republican | | Democratic | | Other Vote | Rep.-Dem. Plurality | Percentage | | | |
| | | Vote | Candidate | Vote | Candidate | | | Total Vote | | Major Vote | |
								Rep.	Dem.	Rep.	Dem.
2012	320,851	158,282	Berg, Rick	161,163	Heitkamp, Heidi	1,406	2,881 D	49.3%	50.2%	49.5%	50.5%
2010	238,812	181,689	Hoeven, John	52,955	Potter, Tracy	4,168	128,734 R	76.1%	22.2%	77.4%	22.6%
2006	218,152	64,417	Grotberg, Dwight	150,146	Conrad, Kent*	3,589	85,729 D	29.5%	68.8%	30.0%	70.0%
2004	310,696	98,553	Liffrig, Mike G.	212,143	Dorgan, Byron L.*		113,590 D	31.7%	68.3%	31.7%	68.3%
2000	287,539	111,069	Sand, Duane	176,470	Conrad, Kent*		65,401 D	38.6%	61.4%	38.6%	61.4%
1998	213,358	75,013	Nalewaja, Donna	134,747	Dorgan, Byron L.*	3,598	59,734 D	35.2%	63.2%	35.8%	64.2%
1994	236,547	99,390	Clayburg, Ben	137,157	Conrad, Kent*		37,767 D	42.0%	58.0%	42.0%	58.0%
1992	303,957	118,162	Sydness, Steve	179,347	Dorgan, Byron L.	6,448	61,185 D	38.9%	59.0%	39.7%	60.3%
1992S	163,311	55,194	Dalrymple, Jack	103,246	Conrad, Kent*	4,871	48,052 D	33.8%	63.2%	34.8%	65.2%
1988	289,170	112,937	Striden, Earl	171,899	Burdick, Quentin N.*	4,334	58,962 D	39.1%	59.4%	39.6%	60.4%
1986	288,998	141,797	Andrews, Mark*	143,932	Conrad, Kent	3,269	2,135 D	49.1%	49.8%	49.6%	50.4%
1982	262,465	89,304	Knorr, Gene	164,873	Burdick, Quentin N.*	8,288	75,569 D	34.0%	62.8%	35.1%	64.9%
1980	299,272	210,347	Andrews, Mark	86,658	Johanneson, Kent	2,267	123,689 R	70.3%	29.0%	70.8%	29.2%
1976	283,062	103,466	Stroup, Richard	175,772	Burdick, Quentin N.*	3,824	72,306 D	36.6%	62.1%	37.1%	62.9%
1974	235,661	114,117	Young, Milton R.*	113,931	Guy, William L.	7,613	186 R	48.4%	48.3%	50.0%	50.0%
1970	219,560	82,996	Kleppe, Tom	134,519	Burdick, Quentin N.*	2,045	51,523 D	37.8%	61.3%	38.2%	61.8%
1968	239,776	154,968	Young, Milton R.*	80,815	Lashkowitz, Herschel	3,993	74,153 R	64.6%	33.7%	65.7%	34.3%
1964	258,945	109,681	Kleppe, Tom	149,264	Burdick, Quentin N.*		39,583 D	42.4%	57.6%	42.4%	57.6%
1962	223,737	135,705	Young, Milton R.*	88,032	Lanier, William		47,673 R	60.7%	39.3%	60.7%	39.3%
1960S	210,349	103,475	Davis, John E.	104,593	Burdick, Quentin N.	2,281	1,118 D	49.2%	49.7%	49.7%	50.3%
1958	204,635	117,070	Langer, William*	84,892	Vendsel, Raymond	2,673	32,178 R	57.2%	41.5%	58.0%	42.0%
1956	244,161	155,305	Young, Milton R.*	87,919	Burdick, Quentin N.	937	67,386 R	63.6%	36.0%	63.9%	36.1%
1952**	237,995	157,907	Langer, William*	55,347	Morrison, Harold A.	24,741	102,560 R	66.3%	23.3%	74.0%	26.0%
1950	186,716	126,209	Young, Milton R.*	60,507	O'Brien, Harry		65,702 R	67.6%	32.4%	67.6%	32.4%
1946**	165,382	88,210	Langer, William*	38,368	Larson, Abner B.	38,804	49,842 R	53.3%	23.2%	69.7%	30.3%
1946S**	136,852	75,998	Young, Milton R.*	37,507	Lanier, William	23,347	38,491 R	55.5%	27.4%	67.0%	33.0%

Note: An asterisk (*) denotes incumbent. **In past elections, the other vote included: 1952 - 24,741 Independent (Fred G. Aandahl); 1946 - 38,804 Independent (Arthur E. Thompson), who finished second; 1946 Special - 20,848 Independent (Gerald P. Nye). One of the 1992 elections was for a short term to fill a vacancy and the special election was held in December. The 1946 and 1960 special elections were held in June for short terms to fill vacancies.

NORTH DAKOTA

PRESIDENT 2012

2010 Census Population	County	Total Vote	Republican (Romney)	Democratic (Obama)	Other	Rep.-Dem. Plurality	Percentage Total Vote Rep.	Dem.	Major Vote Rep.	Dem.
2,343	ADAMS	1,286	918	328	40	590 R	71.4%	25.5%	73.7%	26.3%
11,066	BARNES	5,522	2,964	2,394	164	570 R	53.7%	43.4%	55.3%	44.7%
6,660	BENSON	2,157	868	1,235	54	367 D	40.2%	57.3%	41.3%	58.7%
783	BILLINGS	578	472	89	17	383 R	81.7%	15.4%	84.1%	15.9%
6,429	BOTTINEAU	3,555	2,280	1,183	92	1,097 R	64.1%	33.3%	65.8%	34.2%
3,151	BOWMAN	1,737	1,280	414	43	866 R	73.7%	23.8%	75.6%	24.4%
1,968	BURKE	1,023	769	230	24	539 R	75.2%	22.5%	77.0%	23.0%
81,308	BURLEIGH	43,387	27,951	14,122	1,314	13,829 R	64.4%	32.5%	66.4%	33.6%
149,778	CASS	73,855	36,855	34,712	2,288	2,143 R	49.9%	47.0%	51.5%	48.5%
3,993	CAVALIER	2,069	1,195	818	56	377 R	57.8%	39.5%	59.4%	40.6%
5,289	DICKEY	2,535	1,610	853	72	757 R	63.5%	33.6%	65.4%	34.6%
2,071	DIVIDE	1,162	733	385	44	348 R	63.1%	33.1%	65.6%	34.4%
3,536	DUNN	2,034	1,506	508	20	998 R	74.0%	25.0%	74.8%	25.2%
2,385	EDDY	1,157	634	486	37	148 R	54.8%	42.0%	56.6%	43.4%
3,550	EMMONS	1,884	1,435	383	66	1,052 R	76.2%	20.3%	78.9%	21.1%
3,343	FOSTER	1,682	1,030	607	45	423 R	61.2%	36.1%	62.9%	37.1%
1,680	GOLDEN VALLEY	928	742	162	24	580 R	80.0%	17.5%	82.1%	17.9%
66,861	GRAND FORKS	30,029	15,060	14,032	937	1,028 R	50.2%	46.7%	51.8%	48.2%
2,394	GRANT	1,413	1,025	334	54	691 R	72.5%	23.6%	75.4%	24.6%
2,420	GRIGGS	1,343	771	536	36	235 R	57.4%	39.9%	59.0%	41.0%
2,477	HETTINGER	1,362	1,000	313	49	687 R	73.4%	23.0%	76.2%	23.8%
2,435	KIDDER	1,328	870	393	65	477 R	65.5%	29.6%	68.9%	31.1%
4,139	LA MOURE	2,194	1,377	740	77	637 R	62.8%	33.7%	65.0%	35.0%
1,990	LOGAN	1,073	810	232	31	578 R	75.5%	21.6%	77.7%	22.3%
5,395	MCHENRY	2,712	1,678	943	91	735 R	61.9%	34.8%	64.0%	36.0%
2,809	MCINTOSH	1,530	1,035	459	36	576 R	67.6%	30.0%	69.3%	30.7%
6,360	MCKENZIE	3,451	2,458	927	66	1,531 R	71.2%	26.9%	72.6%	27.4%
8,962	MCLEAN	4,938	3,141	1,670	127	1,471 R	63.6%	33.8%	65.3%	34.7%
8,424	MERCER	4,455	3,152	1,166	137	1,986 R	70.8%	26.2%	73.0%	27.0%
27,471	MORTON	13,613	8,680	4,469	464	4,211 R	63.8%	32.8%	66.0%	34.0%
7,673	MOUNTRAIL	3,457	1,962	1,403	92	559 R	56.8%	40.6%	58.3%	41.7%
3,126	NELSON	1,678	865	767	46	98 R	51.5%	45.7%	53.0%	47.0%
1,846	OLIVER	1,013	693	281	39	412 R	68.4%	27.7%	71.1%	28.9%
7,413	PEMBINA	3,255	1,899	1,253	103	646 R	58.3%	38.5%	60.2%	39.8%
4,357	PIERCE	2,178	1,465	660	53	805 R	67.3%	30.3%	68.9%	31.1%
11,451	RAMSEY	4,999	2,665	2,164	170	501 R	53.3%	43.3%	55.2%	44.8%
5,457	RANSOM	2,425	1,009	1,343	73	334 D	41.6%	55.4%	42.9%	57.1%
2,470	RENVILLE	1,278	851	398	29	453 R	66.6%	31.1%	68.1%	31.9%
16,321	RICHLAND	7,613	4,229	3,198	186	1,031 R	55.5%	42.0%	56.9%	43.1%
13,937	ROLETTE	4,552	1,092	3,353	107	2,261 D	24.0%	73.7%	24.6%	75.4%
3,829	SARGENT	2,007	879	1,075	53	196 D	43.8%	53.6%	45.0%	55.0%
1,321	SHERIDAN	822	642	163	17	479 R	78.1%	19.8%	79.8%	20.2%
4,153	SIOUX	1,144	225	900	19	675 D	19.7%	78.7%	20.0%	80.0%
727	SLOPE	437	341	83	13	258 R	78.0%	19.0%	80.4%	19.6%
24,199	STARK	11,633	8,521	2,812	300	5,709 R	73.2%	24.2%	75.2%	24.8%
1,975	STEELE	1,042	498	518	26	20 D	47.8%	49.7%	49.0%	51.0%
21,100	STUTSMAN	9,558	5,685	3,585	288	2,100 R	59.5%	37.5%	61.3%	38.7%
2,246	TOWNER	1,182	623	516	43	107 R	52.7%	43.7%	54.7%	45.3%
8,121	TRAILL	3,921	1,996	1,811	114	185 R	50.9%	46.2%	52.4%	47.6%
11,119	WALSH	4,791	2,656	1,985	150	671 R	55.4%	41.4%	57.2%	42.8%
61,675	WARD	25,463	16,230	8,441	792	7,789 R	63.7%	33.2%	65.8%	34.2%
4,207	WELLS	2,379	1,654	673	52	981 R	69.5%	28.3%	71.1%	28.9%
22,398	WILLIAMS	9,808	7,184	2,322	302	4,862 R	73.2%	23.7%	75.6%	24.4%
672,591	TOTAL	322,627	188,163	124,827	9,637	63,336 R	58.3%	38.7%	60.1%	39.9%

Note: Democratic candidates appear on the ballot for the Democratic-Nonpartisan League Party.

NORTH DAKOTA

GOVERNOR 2012

2010 Census Population	County	Total Vote	Republican (Dalrymple)	Democratic (Taylor)	Other	Rep.-Dem. Plurality	Percentage Total Vote Rep.	Percentage Total Vote Dem.	Percentage Major Vote Rep.	Percentage Major Vote Dem.
2,343	ADAMS	1,288	916	349	23	567 R	71.1%	27.1%	72.4%	27.6%
11,066	BARNES	5,499	3,143	2,240	116	903 R	57.2%	40.7%	58.4%	41.6%
6,660	BENSON	2,151	765	1,319	67	554 D	35.6%	61.3%	36.7%	63.3%
783	BILLINGS	572	393	160	19	233 R	68.7%	28.0%	71.1%	28.9%
6,429	BOTTINEAU	3,522	2,212	1,246	64	966 R	62.8%	35.4%	64.0%	36.0%
3,151	BOWMAN	1,722	1,154	529	39	625 R	67.0%	30.7%	68.6%	31.4%
1,968	BURKE	1,023	719	287	17	432 R	70.3%	28.1%	71.5%	28.5%
81,308	BURLEIGH	42,958	29,997	12,152	809	17,845 R	69.8%	28.3%	71.2%	28.8%
149,778	CASS	72,015	44,690	25,142	2,183	19,548 R	62.1%	34.9%	64.0%	36.0%
3,993	CAVALIER	2,050	1,384	621	45	763 R	67.5%	30.3%	69.0%	31.0%
5,289	DICKEY	2,485	1,651	752	82	899 R	66.4%	30.3%	68.7%	31.3%
2,071	DIVIDE	1,159	680	447	32	233 R	58.7%	38.6%	60.3%	39.7%
3,536	DUNN	2,017	1,215	755	47	460 R	60.2%	37.4%	61.7%	38.3%
2,385	EDDY	1,163	586	549	28	37 R	50.4%	47.2%	51.6%	48.4%
3,550	EMMONS	1,878	1,292	537	49	755 R	68.8%	28.6%	70.6%	29.4%
3,343	FOSTER	1,677	942	699	36	243 R	56.2%	41.7%	57.4%	42.6%
1,680	GOLDEN VALLEY	924	659	250	15	409 R	71.3%	27.1%	72.5%	27.5%
66,861	GRAND FORKS	28,958	17,749	10,045	1,164	7,704 R	61.3%	34.7%	63.9%	36.1%
2,394	GRANT	1,423	924	473	26	451 R	64.9%	33.2%	66.1%	33.9%
2,420	GRIGGS	1,335	766	549	20	217 R	57.4%	41.1%	58.3%	41.7%
2,477	HETTINGER	1,363	913	416	34	497 R	67.0%	30.5%	68.7%	31.3%
2,435	KIDDER	1,330	788	511	31	277 R	59.2%	38.4%	60.7%	39.3%
4,139	LA MOURE	2,186	1,364	777	45	587 R	62.4%	35.5%	63.7%	36.3%
1,990	LOGAN	1,085	742	333	10	409 R	68.4%	30.7%	69.0%	31.0%
5,395	MCHENRY	2,748	1,257	1,459	32	202 D	45.7%	53.1%	46.3%	53.7%
2,809	MCINTOSH	1,538	1,079	424	35	655 R	70.2%	27.6%	71.8%	28.2%
6,360	MCKENZIE	3,379	2,174	1,107	98	1,067 R	64.3%	32.8%	66.3%	33.7%
8,962	MCLEAN	4,931	2,933	1,892	106	1,041 R	59.5%	38.4%	60.8%	39.2%
8,424	MERCER	4,461	3,047	1,347	67	1,700 R	68.3%	30.2%	69.3%	30.7%
27,471	MORTON	13,548	9,005	4,250	293	4,755 R	66.5%	31.4%	67.9%	32.1%
7,673	MOUNTRAIL	3,421	1,739	1,579	103	160 R	50.8%	46.2%	52.4%	47.6%
3,126	NELSON	1,676	906	733	37	173 R	54.1%	43.7%	55.3%	44.7%
1,846	OLIVER	1,019	658	342	19	316 R	64.6%	33.6%	65.8%	34.2%
7,413	PEMBINA	3,236	2,165	1,003	68	1,162 R	66.9%	31.0%	68.3%	31.7%
4,357	PIERCE	2,192	1,054	1,112	26	58 D	48.1%	50.7%	48.7%	51.3%
11,451	RAMSEY	4,976	2,732	2,129	115	603 R	54.9%	42.8%	56.2%	43.8%
5,457	RANSOM	2,409	1,082	1,276	51	194 D	44.9%	53.0%	45.9%	54.1%
2,470	RENVILLE	1,270	771	469	30	302 R	60.7%	36.9%	62.2%	37.8%
16,321	RICHLAND	7,520	4,713	2,589	218	2,124 R	62.7%	34.4%	64.5%	35.5%
13,937	ROLETTE	4,494	1,219	3,153	122	1,934 D	27.1%	70.2%	27.9%	72.1%
3,829	SARGENT	2,004	1,007	958	39	49 R	50.2%	47.8%	51.2%	48.8%
1,321	SHERIDAN	830	512	306	12	206 R	61.7%	36.9%	62.6%	37.4%
4,153	SIOUX	1,120	292	798	30	506 D	26.1%	71.2%	26.8%	73.2%
727	SLOPE	443	301	136	6	165 R	67.9%	30.7%	68.9%	31.1%
24,199	STARK	11,437	8,142	3,004	291	5,138 R	71.2%	26.3%	73.0%	27.0%
1,975	STEELE	1,036	549	463	24	86 R	53.0%	44.7%	54.2%	45.8%
21,100	STUTSMAN	9,322	5,984	3,063	275	2,921 R	64.2%	32.9%	66.1%	33.9%
2,246	TOWNER	1,176	630	529	17	101 R	53.6%	45.0%	54.4%	45.6%
8,121	TRAILL	3,885	2,200	1,585	100	615 R	56.6%	40.8%	58.1%	41.9%
11,119	WALSH	4,808	3,189	1,523	96	1,666 R	66.3%	31.7%	67.7%	32.3%
61,675	WARD	25,158	16,979	7,606	573	9,373 R	67.5%	30.2%	69.1%	30.9%
4,207	WELLS	2,373	1,445	886	42	559 R	60.9%	37.3%	62.0%	38.0%
22,398	WILLIAMS	9,619	7,118	2,188	313	4,930 R	74.0%	22.7%	76.5%	23.5%
672,591	TOTAL	317,812	200,526	109,047	8,239	91,479 R	63.1%	34.3%	64.8%	35.2%

Note: Democratic candidates appear on the ballot for the Democratic-Nonpartisan League Party.

NORTH DAKOTA

SENATOR 2012

2010 Census Population	County	Total Vote	Republican (Berg)	Democratic (Heitkamp)	Other	Rep.-Dem. Plurality	Percentage Total Vote Rep.	Dem.	Major Vote Rep.	Dem.
2,343	ADAMS	1,282	806	473	3	333 R	62.9%	36.9%	63.0%	37.0%
11,066	BARNES	5,531	2,329	3,181	21	852 D	42.1%	57.5%	42.3%	57.7%
6,660	BENSON	2,166	709	1,453	4	744 D	32.7%	67.1%	32.8%	67.2%
783	BILLINGS	573	412	160	1	252 R	71.9%	27.9%	72.0%	28.0%
6,429	BOTTINEAU	3,531	1,875	1,636	20	239 R	53.1%	46.3%	53.4%	46.6%
3,151	BOWMAN	1,711	1,086	621	4	465 R	63.5%	36.3%	63.6%	36.4%
1,968	BURKE	1,020	657	360	3	297 R	64.4%	35.3%	64.6%	35.4%
81,308	BURLEIGH	43,053	23,538	19,284	231	4,254 R	54.7%	44.8%	55.0%	45.0%
149,778	CASS	73,408	31,569	41,480	359	9,911 D	43.0%	56.5%	43.2%	56.8%
3,993	CAVALIER	2,071	977	1,087	7	110 D	47.2%	52.5%	47.3%	52.7%
5,289	DICKEY	2,532	1,399	1,125	8	274 R	55.3%	44.4%	55.4%	44.6%
2,071	DIVIDE	1,162	567	592	3	25 D	48.8%	50.9%	48.9%	51.1%
3,536	DUNN	2,032	1,283	746	3	537 R	63.1%	36.7%	63.2%	36.8%
2,385	EDDY	1,155	455	693	7	238 D	39.4%	60.0%	39.6%	60.4%
3,550	EMMONS	1,873	1,152	709	12	443 R	61.5%	37.9%	61.9%	38.1%
3,343	FOSTER	1,671	810	853	8	43 D	48.5%	51.0%	48.7%	51.3%
1,680	GOLDEN VALLEY	927	660	265	2	395 R	71.2%	28.6%	71.4%	28.6%
66,861	GRAND FORKS	29,750	13,101	16,542	107	3,441 D	44.0%	55.6%	44.2%	55.8%
2,394	GRANT	1,402	853	542	7	311 R	60.8%	38.7%	61.1%	38.9%
2,420	GRIGGS	1,332	628	704		76 D	47.1%	52.9%	47.1%	52.9%
2,477	HETTINGER	1,358	843	511	4	332 R	62.1%	37.6%	62.3%	37.7%
2,435	KIDDER	1,327	706	613	8	93 R	53.2%	46.2%	53.5%	46.5%
4,139	LA MOURE	2,203	1,125	1,065	13	60 R	51.1%	48.3%	51.4%	48.6%
1,990	LOGAN	1,062	610	446	6	164 R	57.4%	42.0%	57.8%	42.2%
5,395	MCHENRY	2,707	1,339	1,359	9	20 D	49.5%	50.2%	49.6%	50.4%
2,809	MCINTOSH	1,530	872	648	10	224 R	57.0%	42.4%	57.4%	42.6%
6,360	MCKENZIE	3,412	2,177	1,229	6	948 R	63.8%	36.0%	63.9%	36.1%
8,962	MCLEAN	4,915	2,544	2,357	14	187 R	51.8%	48.0%	51.9%	48.1%
8,424	MERCER	4,452	2,627	1,807	18	820 R	59.0%	40.6%	59.2%	40.8%
27,471	MORTON	13,550	7,135	6,325	90	810 R	52.7%	46.7%	53.0%	47.0%
7,673	MOUNTRAIL	3,427	1,673	1,745	9	72 D	48.8%	50.9%	48.9%	51.1%
3,126	NELSON	1,669	670	993	6	323 D	40.1%	59.5%	40.3%	59.7%
1,846	OLIVER	1,006	555	446	5	109 R	55.2%	44.3%	55.4%	44.6%
7,413	PEMBINA	3,259	1,579	1,672	8	93 D	48.5%	51.3%	48.6%	51.4%
4,357	PIERCE	2,175	1,136	1,027	12	109 R	52.2%	47.2%	52.5%	47.5%
11,451	RAMSEY	5,013	2,229	2,766	18	537 D	44.5%	55.2%	44.6%	55.4%
5,457	RANSOM	2,429	755	1,669	5	914 D	31.1%	68.7%	31.1%	68.9%
2,470	RENVILLE	1,261	676	580	5	96 R	53.6%	46.0%	53.8%	46.2%
16,321	RICHLAND	7,613	3,135	4,445	33	1,310 D	41.2%	58.4%	41.4%	58.6%
13,937	ROLETTE	4,573	902	3,662	9	2,760 D	19.7%	80.1%	19.8%	80.2%
3,829	SARGENT	2,012	679	1,321	12	642 D	33.7%	65.7%	34.0%	66.0%
1,321	SHERIDAN	824	521	299	4	222 R	63.2%	36.3%	63.5%	36.5%
4,153	SIOUX	1,153	185	963	5	778 D	16.0%	83.5%	16.1%	83.9%
727	SLOPE	445	294	149	2	145 R	66.1%	33.5%	66.4%	33.6%
24,199	STARK	11,535	7,393	4,110	32	3,283 R	64.1%	35.6%	64.3%	35.7%
1,975	STEELE	1,040	398	641	1	243 D	38.3%	61.6%	38.3%	61.7%
21,100	STUTSMAN	9,484	4,654	4,800	30	146 D	49.1%	50.6%	49.2%	50.8%
2,246	TOWNER	1,177	472	699	6	227 D	40.1%	59.4%	40.3%	59.7%
8,121	TRAILL	3,913	1,589	2,311	13	722 D	40.6%	59.1%	40.7%	59.3%
11,119	WALSH	4,814	2,151	2,645	18	494 D	44.7%	54.9%	44.8%	55.2%
61,675	WARD	25,263	13,888	11,230	145	2,658 R	55.0%	44.5%	55.3%	44.7%
4,207	WELLS	2,361	1,363	982	16	381 R	57.7%	41.6%	58.1%	41.9%
22,398	WILLIAMS	9,707	6,541	3,142	24	3,399 R	67.4%	32.4%	67.6%	32.4%
672,591	TOTAL	320,851	158,282	161,163	1,406	2,881 D	49.3%	50.2%	49.5%	50.5%

Note: Democratic candidates in North Dakota appear on the ballot for the Democratic-Nonpartisan League Party.

NORTH DAKOTA

HOUSE OF REPRESENTATIVES

			Republican		Democratic		Other Vote	Rep.-Dem. Plurality	Percentage			
									Total Vote		Major Vote	
CD	Year	Total Vote	Vote	Candidate	Vote	Candidate			Rep.	Dem.	Rep.	Dem.
At Large	2012	316,071	173,433	CRAMER, KEVIN	131,869	GULLESON, PAM	10,769	41,564 R	54.9%	41.7%	56.8%	43.2%
At Large	2010	237,137	129,802	BERG, RICK	106,542	POMEROY, EARL*	793	23,260 R	54.7%	44.9%	54.9%	45.1%
At Large	2008	313,965	119,388	SAND, DUANE	194,577	POMEROY, EARL*		75,189 D	38.0%	62.0%	38.0%	62.0%
At Large	2006	217,621	74,687	MECHTEL, MATT	142,934	POMEROY, EARL*		68,247 D	34.3%	65.7%	34.3%	65.7%
At Large	2004	310,814	125,684	SAND, DUANE	185,130	POMEROY, EARL*		59,446 D	40.4%	59.6%	40.4%	59.6%
At Large	2002	231,030	109,957	CLAYBURGH, RICK	121,073	POMEROY, EARL*		11,116 D	47.6%	52.4%	47.6%	52.4%
At Large	2000	285,658	127,251	DORSO, JOHN	151,173	POMEROY, EARL*	7,234	23,922 D	44.5%	52.9%	45.7%	54.3%
At Large	1998	212,888	87,511	CRAMER, KEVIN	119,668	POMEROY, EARL*	5,709	32,157 D	41.1%	56.2%	42.2%	57.8%
At Large	1996	263,010	113,684	CRAMER, KEVIN	144,833	POMEROY, EARL*	4,493	31,149 D	43.2%	55.1%	44.0%	56.0%
At Large	1994	235,389	105,988	PORTER, GARY	123,134	POMEROY, EARL*	6,267	17,146 D	45.0%	52.3%	46.3%	53.7%
At Large	1992	297,898	117,442	KORSMO, JOHN T.	169,273	POMEROY, EARL	11,183	51,831 D	39.4%	56.8%	41.0%	59.0%
At Large	1990	233,979	81,443	SCHAFER, EDWARD T.	152,530	DORGAN, BYRON L.*	6	71,087 D	34.8%	65.2%	34.8%	65.2%
At Large	1988	299,982	84,475	SYDNESS, STEVE	212,583	DORGAN, BYRON L.*	2,924	128,108 D	28.2%	70.9%	28.4%	71.6%
At Large	1986	286,361	66,989	VINJE, SYVER	216,258	DORGAN, BYRON L.*	3,114	149,269 D	23.4%	75.5%	23.7%	76.3%
At Large	1984	308,729	65,761	ALTENBURG, LOIS I.	242,968	DORGAN, BYRON L.*		177,207 D	21.3%	78.7%	21.3%	78.7%
At Large	1982	260,499	72,241	JONES, KENT	186,534	DORGAN, BYRON L.*	1,724	114,293 D	27.7%	71.6%	27.9%	72.1%
At Large	1980	293,076	124,707	SMYKOWSKI, JIM	166,437	DORGAN, BYRON L.	1,932	41,730 D	42.6%	56.8%	42.8%	57.2%
At Large	1978	220,348	147,746	ANDREWS, MARK*	68,016	HAGEN, BRUCE	4,586	79,730 R	67.1%	30.9%	68.5%	31.5%
At Large	1976	289,881	181,018	ANDREWS, MARK*	104,263	OMDAHL, LLOYD B.	4,600	76,755 R	62.4%	36.0%	63.5%	36.5%
At Large	1974	233,688	130,184	ANDREWS, MARK*	103,504	DORGAN, BYRON L.		26,680 R	55.7%	44.3%	55.7%	44.3%
At Large	1972	268,721	195,360	ANDREWS, MARK*	72,850	ISTA, RICHARD	511	122,510 R	72.7%	27.1%	72.8%	27.2%

Notes: An asterisk (*) denotes incumbent. Democratic candidates in North Dakota appear on the ballot for the Democratic-Nonpartisan League (NPL) party. North Dakota had two House seats prior to 1972.

NORTH DAKOTA

GENERAL AND PRIMARY ELECTIONS

GENERAL ELECTIONS: OTHER VOTE

President   Other vote was 5,231 Libertarian (Gary E. Johnson), 1,860 Write-in (Scattered Write-In), 1,361 Green (Jill Stein), 1,185 Constitution (Virgil H. Goode)

Governor   Other vote was 5,356 Independent (Paul Sorum), 2,616 Independent (Roland Riemers), 267 Write-in (Scattered Write-In)

Senator   Other vote was 1,406 Write-in (Scattered Write-In)

House   Other vote was:

At Large   10,261 Libertarian (Eric Olson), 508 Write-in (Scattered Write-In)

PRIMARY ELECTIONS: SUPPLEMENTARY INFORMATION

Primary   June 12, 2012   **Registration** (No Formal Registration)   No Party Registration

Primary Type   Open—Any person of voting age (18 years old at the time of the primary election) could participate in the primary of either party. As of June 8, 2010, North Dakota's estimated voting-age population was 502,873.

NORTH DAKOTA

GENERAL AND PRIMARY ELECTIONS

	REPUBLICAN PRIMARIES			DEMOCRATIC PRIMARIES		
Senator	Berg, Rick	67,860	66.4%	Heitkamp, Heidi	57,246	99.8%
	Sand, Duane	34,213	33.5%	Scattered Write-In	87	0.2%
	Scattered Write-In	111	0.1%			
	TOTAL	*102,184*		*TOTAL*	*57,333*	
Governor	Dalrymple, Jack*	94,866	99.4%	Taylor, Ryan M.	52,023	99.6%
	Scattered Write-In	617	0.6%	Scattered Write-In	215	0.4%
	TOTAL	*95,483*		*TOTAL*	*52,238*	
House At Large	Cramer, Kevin	54,405	54.4%	Gulleson, Pam	51,750	99.9%
	Kalk, Brian P.	45,415	45.4%	Scattered Write-In	74	0.1%
	Scattered Write-In	113	0.1%			
	TOTAL	*99,933*		*TOTAL*	*51,824*	

Note: An asterisk (*) denotes incumbent.

OHIO

Congressional districts first established for elections held in 2012

16 members

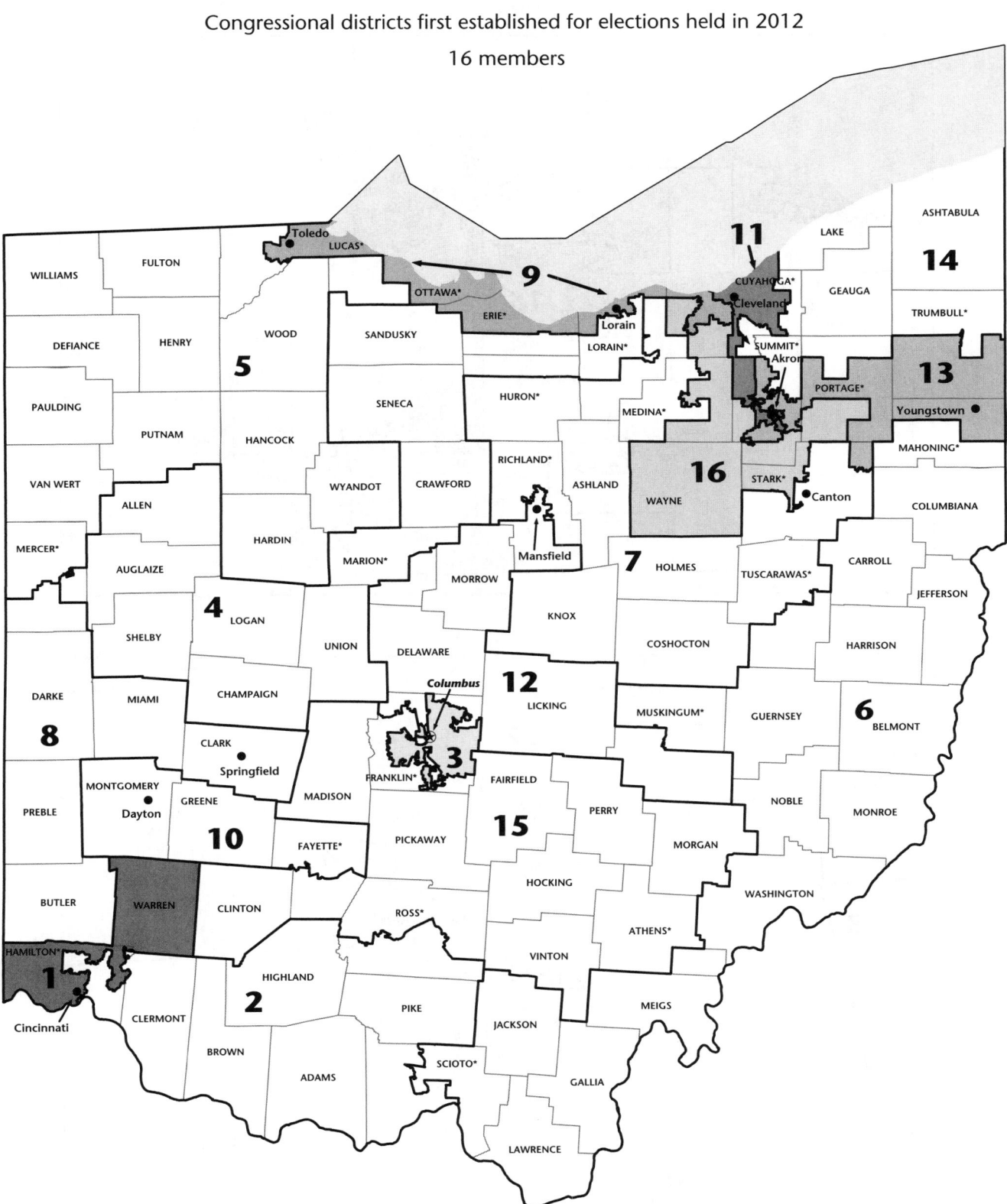

* Asterisk indicates a county whose boundaries include parts of two or more Congressional districts.

OHIO

Cleveland Area

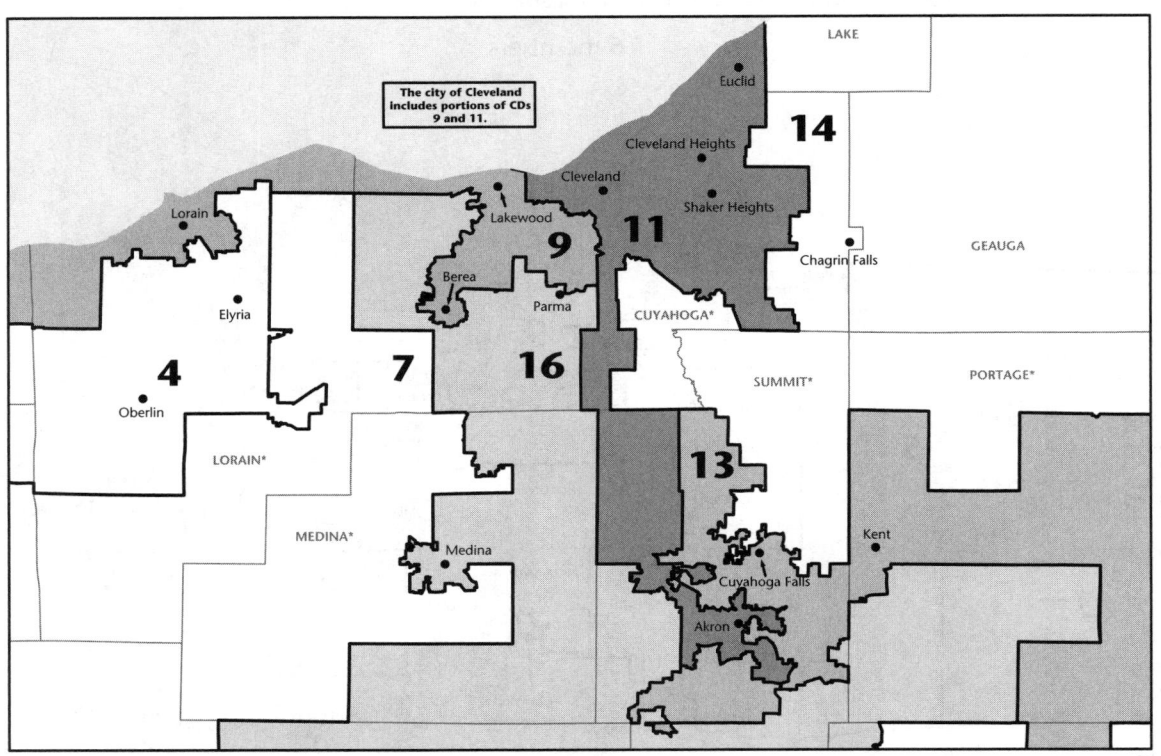

Columbus Area

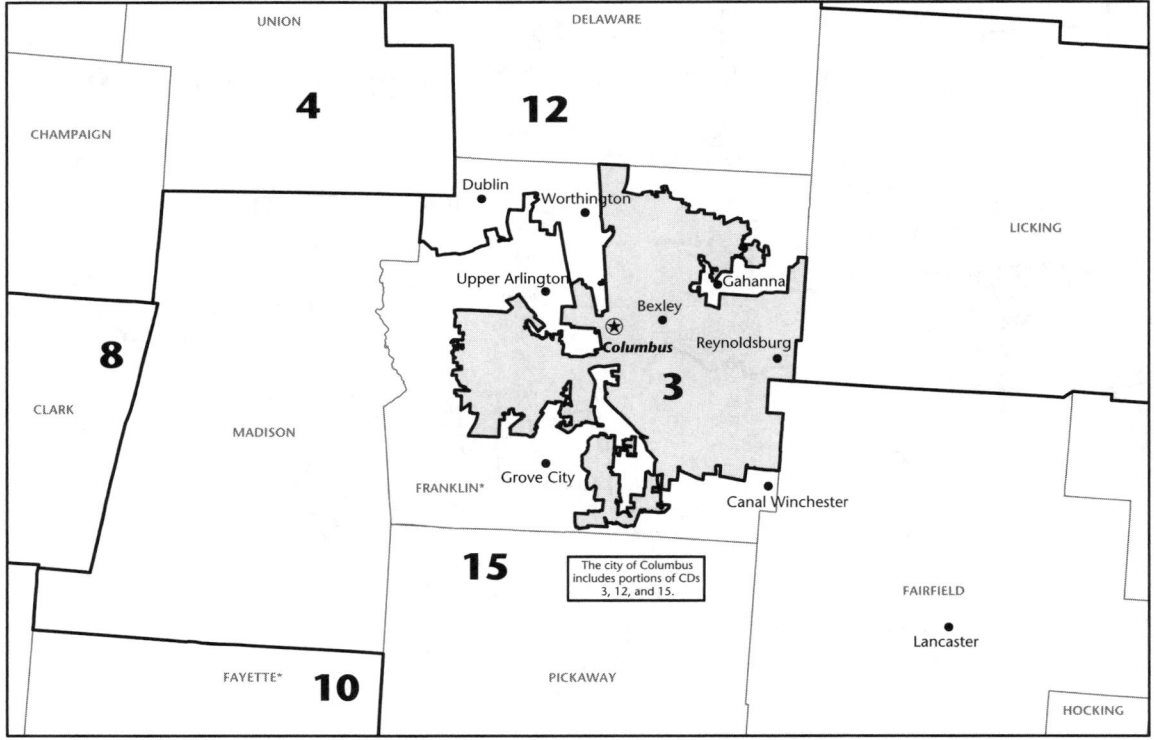

* Asterisk indicates a county whose boundaries include parts of two or more Congressional districts.

OHIO

GOVERNOR
John R. Kasich (R). Elected 2010 to a four-year term.

SENATORS (1 Republican, 1 Democrat)
Sherrod Brown (D). Reelected 2012 to a six-year term. Previously elected 2006.

Rob Portman (R). Elected 2010 to a six-year term.

REPRESENTATIVES (12 Republicans, 4 Democrats)
1. Steve Chabot (R)
2. Brad Wenstrup (R)
3. Joyce Beatty (D)
4. Jim Jordan (R)
5. Bob Latta (R)
6. Bill Johnson (R)
7. Bob Gibbs (R)
8. John Boehner (R)
9. Marcy Kaptur (D)
10. Michael Turner (R)
11. Marcia L. Fudge (D)
12. Pat Tiberi (R)
13. Tim Ryan (D)
14. David Joyce (R)
15. Steve Stivers (R)
16. Jim Renacci (R)

POSTWAR VOTE FOR PRESIDENT

| | | Republican | | Democratic | | | | Percentage | | | |
| | | | | | | Other | Rep.-Dem. | Total Vote | | Major Vote | |
Year	Total Vote	Vote	Candidate	Vote	Candidate	Vote	Plurality	Rep.	Dem.	Rep.	Dem.
2012	5,580,840	2,661,433	Romney, W. Mitt	2,827,710	Obama, Barack H.*	91,697	166,277 D	47.7%	50.7%	48.5%	51.5%
2008	5,708,350	2,677,820	McCain, John S. III	2,940,044	Obama, Barack H.	90,486	262,224 D	46.9%	51.5%	47.7%	52.3%
2004	5,627,908	2,859,768	Bush, George W.*	2,741,167	Kerry, John F.	26,973	118,601 R	50.8%	48.7%	51.1%	48.9%
2000**	4,701,998	2,350,363	Bush, George W.	2,183,628	Gore, Albert Jr.	168,007	166,735 R	50.0%	46.4%	51.8%	48.2%
1996**	4,534,434	1,859,883	Dole, Robert "Bob"	2,148,222	Clinton, Bill*	526,329	288,339 D	41.0%	47.4%	46.4%	53.6%
1992**	4,939,967	1,894,310	Bush, George H.*	1,984,942	Clinton, Bill	1,060,715	90,632 D	38.3%	40.2%	48.8%	51.2%
1988	4,393,699	2,416,549	Bush, George H.	1,939,629	Dukakis, Michael S.	37,521	476,920 R	55.0%	44.1%	55.5%	44.5%
1984	4,547,619	2,678,560	Reagan, Ronald*	1,825,440	Mondale, Walter F.	43,619	853,120 R	58.9%	40.1%	59.5%	40.5%
1980**	4,283,603	2,206,545	Reagan, Ronald	1,752,414	Carter, Jimmy*	324,644	454,131 R	51.5%	40.9%	55.7%	44.3%
1976	4,111,873	2,000,505	Ford, Gerald R.*	2,011,621	Carter, Jimmy	99,747	11,116 D	48.7%	48.9%	49.9%	50.1%
1972	4,094,787	2,441,827	Nixon, Richard M.*	1,558,889	McGovern, George S.	94,071	882,938 R	59.6%	38.1%	61.0%	39.0%
1968**	3,959,698	1,791,014	Nixon, Richard M.	1,700,586	Humphrey, Hubert H. Jr.	468,098	90,428 R	45.2%	42.9%	51.3%	48.7%
1964	3,969,196	1,470,865	Goldwater, Barry M. Sr.	2,498,331	Johnson, Lyndon B.*		1,027,466 D	37.1%	62.9%	37.1%	62.9%
1960	4,161,859	2,217,611	Nixon, Richard M.	1,944,248	Kennedy, John F.		273,363 R	53.3%	46.7%	53.3%	46.7%
1956	3,702,265	2,262,610	Eisenhower, Dwight D.*	1,439,655	Stevenson, Adlai E. II		822,955 R	61.1%	38.9%	61.1%	38.9%
1952	3,700,758	2,100,391	Eisenhower, Dwight D.	1,600,367	Stevenson, Adlai E. II		500,024 R	56.8%	43.2%	56.8%	43.2%
1948	2,936,071	1,445,684	Dewey, Thomas E.	1,452,791	Truman, Harry S.*	37,596	7,107 D	49.2%	49.5%	49.9%	50.1%

Note: An asterisk (*) denotes incumbent. **In past elections, the other vote included: 2000 - 117,799 Green (Ralph Nader); 1996 - 483,207 Reform (Ross Perot); 1992 - 1,036,426 Independent (Perot); 1980 - 254,472 Independent (John Anderson); 1968 - 467,495 American Independent (George Wallace).

OHIO

POSTWAR VOTE FOR GOVERNOR

Year	Total Vote	Republican Vote	Candidate	Democratic Vote	Candidate	Other Vote	Rep.-Dem. Plurality	Total Vote Rep.	Dem.	Major Vote Rep.	Dem.
2010	3,852,469	1,889,186	Kasich, John R.	1,812,059	Strickland, Ted*	151,224	77,127 R	49.0%	47.0%	51.0%	49.0%
2006	4,022,754	1,474,285	Blackwell, J. Kenneth	2,435,384	Strickland, Ted	113,085	961,099 D	36.6%	60.5%	37.7%	62.3%
2002	3,228,992	1,865,007	Taft, Robert A. Jr.*	1,236,924	Hagan, Timothy	127,061	628,083 R	57.8%	38.3%	60.1%	39.9%
1998	3,354,213	1,678,721	Taft, Robert A. Jr.	1,498,956	Fisher, Lee	176,536	179,765 R	50.0%	44.7%	52.8%	47.2%
1994	3,346,238	2,401,572	Voinovich, George*	835,849	Burch, Robert L.	108,817	1,565,723 R	71.8%	25.0%	74.2%	25.8%
1990	3,482,650	1,938,103	Voinovich, George	1,544,416	Celebrezze, Anthony J.	131	393,687 R	55.7%	44.3%	55.7%	44.3%
1986	3,066,611	1,207,264	Rhodes, James A.	1,858,372	Celeste, Richard F.*	975	651,108 D	39.4%	60.6%	39.4%	60.6%
1982	3,356,791	1,303,962	Brown, Clarence J. Jr.	1,981,952	Celeste, Richard F.	70,877	677,990 D	38.8%	59.0%	39.7%	60.3%
1978	2,843,351	1,402,167	Rhodes, James A.*	1,354,631	Celeste, Richard F.	86,553	47,536 R	49.3%	47.6%	50.9%	49.1%
1974	3,072,010	1,493,679	Rhodes, James A.	1,482,191	Gilligan, John J.*	96,140	11,488 R	48.6%	48.2%	50.2%	49.8%
1970	3,184,131	1,382,657	Cloud, Roger	1,725,560	Gilligan, John J.	75,914	342,903 D	43.4%	54.2%	44.5%	55.5%
1966	2,887,331	1,795,277	Rhodes, James A.*	1,092,054	Reams, Frazier Jr.		703,223 R	62.2%	37.8%	62.2%	37.8%
1962	3,116,953	1,836,432	Rhodes, James A.	1,280,521	Disalle, Michael V.*		555,911 R	58.9%	41.1%	58.9%	41.1%
1958**	3,284,134	1,414,874	O'Neill, C. William*	1,869,260	Disalle, Michael V.		454,386 D	43.1%	56.9%	43.1%	56.9%
1956	3,542,091	1,984,988	O'Neill, C. William	1,557,103	Disalle, Michael V.		427,885 R	56.0%	44.0%	56.0%	44.0%
1954	2,597,790	1,192,528	Rhodes, James A.	1,405,262	Lausche, Frank J.*		212,734 D	45.9%	54.1%	45.9%	54.1%
1952	3,605,168	1,590,058	Taft, Charles P.	2,015,110	Lausche, Frank J.*		425,052 D	44.1%	55.9%	44.1%	55.9%
1950	2,892,819	1,370,570	Ebright, Don H.	1,522,249	Lausche, Frank J.*		151,679 D	47.4%	52.6%	47.4%	52.6%
1948	3,018,289	1,398,514	Herbert, Thomas J.*	1,619,775	Lausche, Frank J.		221,261 D	46.3%	53.7%	46.3%	53.7%
1946	2,303,750	1,166,550	Herbert, Thomas J.	1,125,997	Lausche, Frank J.*	11,203	40,553 R	50.6%	48.9%	50.9%	49.1%

Note: An asterisk (*) denotes incumbent. **The term of office of Ohio's governor was increased from two to four years effective with the 1958 election.

POSTWAR VOTE FOR SENATOR

Year	Total Vote	Republican Vote	Candidate	Democratic Vote	Candidate	Other Vote	Rep.-Dem. Plurality	Total Vote Rep.	Dem.	Major Vote Rep.	Dem.
2012	5,449,114	2,435,740	Mandel, Josh	2,762,757	Brown, Sherrod*	250,617	327,017 D	44.7%	50.7%	46.9%	53.1%
2010	3,815,098	2,168,742	Portman, Rob	1,503,297	Fisher, Lee	143,059	665,445 R	56.8%	39.4%	59.1%	40.9%
2006	4,019,236	1,761,037	DeWine, Michael "Mike"*	2,257,369	Brown, Sherrod	830	496,332 D	43.8%	56.2%	43.8%	56.2%
2004	5,426,196	3,464,651	Voinovich, George*	1,961,249	Fingerhut, Eric D.	296	1,503,402 R	63.9%	36.1%	63.9%	36.1%
2000	4,448,801	2,665,512	DeWine, Michael "Mike"*	1,595,066	Celeste, Theodore S.	188,223	1,070,446 R	59.9%	35.9%	62.6%	37.4%
1998	3,404,351	1,922,087	Voinovich, George	1,482,054	Boyle, Mary O.	210	440,033 R	56.5%	43.5%	56.5%	43.5%
1994	3,436,884	1,836,556	DeWine, Michael "Mike"	1,348,213	Hyatt, Joel	252,115	488,343 R	53.4%	39.2%	57.7%	42.3%
1992	4,793,953	2,028,300	DeWine, Michael "Mike"	2,444,419	Glenn, John H.*	321,234	416,119 D	42.3%	51.0%	45.3%	54.7%
1988	4,352,905	1,872,716	Voinovich, George	2,480,038	Metzenbaum, Howard*	151	607,322 D	43.0%	57.0%	43.0%	57.0%
1986	3,121,188	1,171,893	Kindness, Thomas N.	1,949,208	Glenn, John H.*	87	777,315 D	37.5%	62.5%	37.5%	62.5%
1982	3,395,463	1,396,790	Pfeifer, Paul E.	1,923,767	Metzenbaum, Howard*	74,906	526,977 D	41.1%	56.7%	42.1%	57.9%
1980	4,027,303	1,137,695	Betts, James E.	2,770,786	Glenn, John H.*	118,822	1,633,091 D	28.2%	68.8%	29.1%	70.9%
1976	3,920,613	1,823,774	Taft, Robert A. Jr.*	1,941,113	Metzenbaum, Howard	155,726	117,339 D	46.5%	49.5%	48.4%	51.6%
1974	2,987,951	918,133	Perk, Ralph J.	1,930,670	Glenn, John H.	139,148	1,012,537 D	30.7%	64.6%	32.2%	67.8%
1970	3,151,274	1,565,682	Taft, Robert A. Jr.	1,495,262	Metzenbaum, Howard	90,330	70,420 R	49.7%	47.4%	51.2%	48.8%
1968	3,743,121	1,928,964	Saxbe, William B.	1,814,152	Gilligan, John J.	5	114,812 R	51.5%	48.5%	51.5%	48.5%
1964	3,830,389	1,906,781	Taft, Robert A. Jr.	1,923,608	Young, Stephen M.*		16,827 D	49.8%	50.2%	49.8%	50.2%
1962	2,995,105	1,151,292	Briley, John Marshall	1,843,813	Lausche, Frank J.*		692,521 D	38.4%	61.6%	38.4%	61.6%
1958	3,149,410	1,497,199	Bricker, John W.*	1,652,211	Young, Stephen M.		155,012 D	47.5%	52.5%	47.5%	52.5%
1956	3,525,499	1,660,910	Bender, George H.*	1,864,589	Lausche, Frank J.		203,679 D	47.1%	52.9%	47.1%	52.9%
1954S	2,512,773	1,257,874	Bender, George H.	1,254,899	Burke, Thomas A.		2,975 R	50.1%	49.9%	50.1%	49.9%
1952	3,442,291	1,878,961	Bricker, John W.*	1,563,330	Disalle, Michael V.		315,631 R	54.6%	45.4%	54.6%	45.4%
1950	2,860,102	1,645,643	Taft, Robert A.*	1,214,459	Ferguson, Joseph T.		431,184 R	57.5%	42.5%	57.5%	42.5%
1946	2,237,269	1,275,774	Bricker, John W.	947,610	Huffman, James W.	13,885	328,164 R	57.0%	42.4%	57.4%	42.6%
1946S	2,123,526	1,193,942	Taft, Kingsley A.	929,584	Webber, Henry P.		264,358 R	56.2%	43.8%	56.2%	43.8%

Note: An asterisk (*) denotes incumbent. **One of the 1946 elections and the 1954 election were for short terms to fill a vacancy.

OHIO
PRESIDENT 2012

2010 Census Population	County	Total Vote	Republican (Romney)	Democratic (Obama)	Other	Rep.-Dem. Plurality	Percentage			
							Total Vote		Major Vote	
							Rep.	Dem.	Rep.	Dem.
28,550	ADAMS	11,089	6,865	3,976	248	2,889 R	61.9%	35.9%	63.3%	36.7%
106,331	ALLEN	48,236	29,502	17,914	820	11,588 R	61.2%	37.1%	62.2%	37.8%
53,139	ASHLAND	24,330	15,519	8,281	530	7,238 R	63.8%	34.0%	65.2%	34.8%
101,497	ASHTABULA	43,064	18,298	23,803	963	5,505 D	42.5%	55.3%	43.5%	56.5%
64,757	ATHENS	27,638	8,543	18,307	788	9,764 D	30.9%	66.2%	31.8%	68.2%
45,949	AUGLAIZE	23,405	17,169	5,831	405	11,338 R	73.4%	24.9%	74.6%	25.4%
70,400	BELMONT	31,564	16,758	14,156	650	2,602 R	53.1%	44.8%	54.2%	45.8%
44,846	BROWN	19,392	11,916	7,107	369	4,809 R	61.4%	36.6%	62.6%	37.4%
368,130	BUTLER	170,191	105,176	62,388	2,627	42,788 R	61.8%	36.7%	62.8%	37.2%
28,836	CARROLL	13,262	7,315	5,543	404	1,772 R	55.2%	41.8%	56.9%	43.1%
40,097	CHAMPAIGN	18,421	11,045	7,044	332	4,001 R	60.0%	38.2%	61.1%	38.9%
138,333	CLARK	64,144	31,816	31,298	1,030	518 R	49.6%	48.8%	50.4%	49.6%
197,363	CLERMONT	96,271	64,208	30,458	1,605	33,750 R	66.7%	31.6%	67.8%	32.2%
42,040	CLINTON	18,143	12,009	5,791	343	6,218 R	66.2%	31.9%	67.5%	32.5%
107,841	COLUMBIANA	46,051	25,251	19,821	979	5,430 R	54.8%	43.0%	56.0%	44.0%
36,901	COSHOCTON	15,739	8,390	6,940	409	1,450 R	53.3%	44.1%	54.7%	45.3%
43,784	CRAWFORD	19,803	11,852	7,507	444	4,345 R	59.8%	37.9%	61.2%	38.8%
1,280,122	CUYAHOGA	644,331	190,660	447,273	6,398	256,613 D	29.6%	69.4%	29.9%	70.1%
52,959	DARKE	25,401	18,108	6,826	467	11,282 R	71.3%	26.9%	72.6%	27.4%
39,037	DEFIANCE	18,288	10,176	7,732	380	2,444 R	55.6%	42.3%	56.8%	43.2%
174,214	DELAWARE	98,759	60,194	37,292	1,273	22,902 R	61.0%	37.8%	61.7%	38.3%
77,079	ERIE	39,405	16,952	21,793	660	4,841 D	43.0%	55.3%	43.8%	56.2%
146,156	FAIRFIELD	72,068	41,034	29,890	1,144	11,144 R	56.9%	41.5%	57.9%	42.1%
29,030	FAYETTE	11,020	6,620	4,249	151	2,371 R	60.1%	38.6%	60.9%	39.1%
1,163,414	FRANKLIN	571,028	215,997	346,373	8,658	130,376 D	37.8%	60.7%	38.4%	61.6%
42,698	FULTON	21,268	11,738	9,073	457	2,665 R	55.2%	42.7%	56.4%	43.6%
30,934	GALLIA	12,595	7,750	4,557	288	3,193 R	61.5%	36.2%	63.0%	37.0%
93,389	GEAUGA	50,997	30,589	19,659	749	10,930 R	60.0%	38.5%	60.9%	39.1%
161,573	GREENE	83,489	49,819	32,256	1,414	17,563 R	59.7%	38.6%	60.7%	39.3%
40,087	GUERNSEY	16,814	8,993	7,450	371	1,543 R	53.5%	44.3%	54.7%	45.3%
802,374	HAMILTON	418,894	193,326	219,927	5,641	26,601 D	46.2%	52.5%	46.8%	53.2%
74,782	HANCOCK	35,694	22,443	12,564	687	9,879 R	62.9%	35.2%	64.1%	35.9%
32,058	HARDIN	12,449	7,489	4,619	341	2,870 R	60.2%	37.1%	61.9%	38.1%
15,864	HARRISON	7,141	4,019	2,950	172	1,069 R	56.3%	41.3%	57.7%	42.3%
28,215	HENRY	14,236	8,257	5,658	321	2,599 R	58.0%	39.7%	59.3%	40.7%
43,589	HIGHLAND	17,847	11,413	6,054	380	5,359 R	63.9%	33.9%	65.3%	34.7%
29,380	HOCKING	12,728	6,285	6,157	286	128 R	49.4%	48.4%	50.5%	49.5%
42,366	HOLMES	11,536	8,702	2,608	226	6,094 R	75.4%	22.6%	76.9%	23.1%
59,626	HURON	24,663	13,060	11,006	597	2,054 R	53.0%	44.6%	54.3%	45.7%
33,225	JACKSON	13,381	7,904	5,166	311	2,738 R	59.1%	38.6%	60.5%	39.5%
69,709	JEFFERSON	33,069	17,034	15,385	650	1,649 R	51.5%	46.5%	52.5%	47.5%
60,921	KNOX	28,345	17,266	10,470	609	6,796 R	60.9%	36.9%	62.3%	37.7%
230,041	LAKE	118,403	58,744	57,680	1,979	1,064 R	49.6%	48.7%	50.5%	49.5%
62,450	LAWRENCE	25,833	14,651	10,744	438	3,907 R	56.7%	41.6%	57.7%	42.3%
166,492	LICKING	81,387	45,503	34,201	1,683	11,302 R	55.9%	42.0%	57.1%	42.9%
45,858	LOGAN	21,137	13,633	7,062	442	6,571 R	64.5%	33.4%	65.9%	34.1%
301,356	LORAIN	143,252	59,405	81,464	2,383	22,059 D	41.5%	56.9%	42.2%	57.8%
441,815	LUCAS	210,218	69,940	136,616	3,662	66,676 D	33.3%	65.0%	33.9%	66.1%
43,435	MADISON	17,517	10,342	6,845	330	3,497 R	59.0%	39.1%	60.2%	39.8%
238,823	MAHONING	121,308	42,641	77,059	1,608	34,418 D	35.2%	63.5%	35.6%	64.4%
66,501	MARION	27,352	14,265	12,504	583	1,761 R	52.2%	45.7%	53.3%	46.7%
172,332	MEDINA	90,783	50,418	38,785	1,580	11,633 R	55.5%	42.7%	56.5%	43.5%
23,770	MEIGS	10,218	5,895	4,027	296	1,868 R	57.7%	39.4%	59.4%	40.6%
40,814	MERCER	21,661	16,561	4,745	355	11,816 R	76.5%	21.9%	77.7%	22.3%
102,506	MIAMI	51,936	34,606	16,383	947	18,223 R	66.6%	31.5%	67.9%	32.1%
14,642	MONROE	6,779	3,548	3,035	196	513 R	52.3%	44.8%	53.9%	46.1%
535,153	MONTGOMERY	266,278	124,841	137,139	4,298	12,298 D	46.9%	51.5%	47.7%	52.3%
15,054	MORGAN	6,129	3,179	2,814	136	365 R	51.9%	45.9%	53.0%	47.0%
34,827	MORROW	16,184	9,865	5,933	386	3,932 R	61.0%	36.7%	62.4%	37.6%
86,074	MUSKINGUM	37,086	19,264	17,002	820	2,262 R	51.9%	45.8%	53.1%	46.9%

OHIO

PRESIDENT 2012

2010 Census Population	County	Total Vote	Republican (Romney)	Democratic (Obama)	Other	Rep.-Dem. Plurality	Percentage Total Vote Rep.	Dem.	Major Vote Rep.	Dem.
14,645	NOBLE	5,872	3,563	2,131	178	1,432 R	60.7%	36.3%	62.6%	37.4%
41,428	OTTAWA	22,455	10,538	11,503	414	965 D	46.9%	51.2%	47.8%	52.2%
19,614	PAULDING	9,128	5,354	3,538	236	1,816 R	58.7%	38.8%	60.2%	39.8%
36,058	PERRY	14,983	7,627	7,033	323	594 R	50.9%	46.9%	52.0%	48.0%
55,698	PICKAWAY	24,123	14,037	9,684	402	4,353 R	58.2%	40.1%	59.2%	40.8%
28,709	PIKE	11,581	5,685	5,684	212	1 R	49.1%	49.1%	50.0%	50.0%
161,419	PORTAGE	76,239	35,242	39,453	1,544	4,211 D	46.2%	51.7%	47.2%	52.8%
42,270	PREBLE	20,167	13,535	6,211	421	7,324 R	67.1%	30.8%	68.5%	31.5%
34,499	PUTNAM	18,371	13,721	4,318	332	9,403 R	74.7%	23.5%	76.1%	23.9%
124,475	RICHLAND	57,715	33,867	22,687	1,161	11,180 R	58.7%	39.3%	59.9%	40.1%
78,064	ROSS	30,083	15,008	14,569	506	439 R	49.9%	48.4%	50.7%	49.3%
60,944	SANDUSKY	28,994	13,755	14,541	698	786 D	47.4%	50.2%	48.6%	51.4%
79,499	SCIOTO	31,161	15,492	15,077	592	415 R	49.7%	48.4%	50.7%	49.3%
56,745	SENECA	25,262	13,243	11,353	666	1,890 R	52.4%	44.9%	53.8%	46.2%
49,423	SHELBY	23,866	17,142	6,343	381	10,799 R	71.8%	26.6%	73.0%	27.0%
375,586	STARK	181,477	88,581	89,432	3,464	851 D	48.8%	49.3%	49.8%	50.2%
541,781	SUMMIT	267,709	111,001	153,041	3,667	42,040 D	41.5%	57.2%	42.0%	58.0%
210,312	TRUMBULL	101,718	38,279	61,672	1,767	23,393 D	37.6%	60.6%	38.3%	61.7%
92,582	TUSCARAWAS	41,613	22,242	18,407	964	3,835 R	53.4%	44.2%	54.7%	45.3%
52,300	UNION	25,567	16,289	8,805	473	7,484 R	63.7%	34.4%	64.9%	35.1%
28,744	VAN WERT	13,843	9,585	4,029	229	5,556 R	69.2%	29.1%	70.4%	29.6%
13,435	VINTON	5,467	2,856	2,436	175	420 R	52.2%	44.6%	54.0%	46.0%
212,693	WARREN	111,007	76,564	32,909	1,534	43,655 R	69.0%	29.6%	69.9%	30.1%
61,778	WASHINGTON	29,499	17,284	11,651	564	5,633 R	58.6%	39.5%	59.7%	40.3%
114,520	WAYNE	51,064	30,251	19,808	1,005	10,443 R	59.2%	38.8%	60.4%	39.6%
37,642	WILLIAMS	17,706	10,047	7,266	393	2,781 R	56.7%	41.0%	58.0%	42.0%
125,488	WOOD	63,948	29,704	32,802	1,442	3,098 D	46.5%	51.3%	47.5%	52.5%
22,615	WYANDOT	10,572	6,180	4,137	255	2,043 R	58.5%	39.1%	59.9%	40.1%
11,536,504	TOTAL	5,580,840	2,661,433	2,827,710	91,697	166,277 D	47.7%	50.7%	48.5%	51.5%

OHIO

SENATOR 2012

2010 Census Population	County	Total Vote	Republican (Mandel)	Democratic (Brown)	Other	Rep.-Dem. Plurality	Percentage Total Vote Rep.	Dem.	Major Vote Rep.	Dem.
28,550	ADAMS	10,943	6,410	3,924	609	2,486 R	58.6%	35.9%	62.0%	38.0%
106,331	ALLEN	47,808	28,817	17,456	1,535	11,361 R	60.3%	36.5%	62.3%	37.7%
53,139	ASHLAND	23,859	14,260	8,006	1,593	6,254 R	59.8%	33.6%	64.0%	36.0%
101,497	ASHTABULA	42,601	17,780	21,973	2,848	4,193 D	41.7%	51.6%	44.7%	55.3%
64,757	ATHENS	26,928	8,066	17,662	1,200	9,596 D	30.0%	65.6%	31.4%	68.6%
45,949	AUGLAIZE	22,840	16,481	5,417	942	11,064 R	72.2%	23.7%	75.3%	24.7%
70,400	BELMONT	30,776	14,370	15,021	1,385	651 D	46.7%	48.8%	48.9%	51.1%
44,846	BROWN	18,080	10,473	6,613	994	3,860 R	57.9%	36.6%	61.3%	38.7%
368,130	BUTLER	166,701	97,228	61,933	7,540	35,295 R	58.3%	37.2%	61.1%	38.9%
28,836	CARROLL	12,927	6,727	5,154	1,046	1,573 R	52.0%	39.9%	56.6%	43.4%
40,097	CHAMPAIGN	18,237	10,541	6,565	1,131	3,976 R	57.8%	36.0%	61.6%	38.4%
138,333	CLARK	63,757	30,216	30,590	2,951	374 D	47.4%	48.0%	49.7%	50.3%
197,363	CLERMONT	92,874	58,220	29,834	4,820	28,386 R	62.7%	32.1%	66.1%	33.9%
42,040	CLINTON	17,948	11,211	5,730	1,007	5,481 R	62.5%	31.9%	66.2%	33.8%
107,841	COLUMBIANA	45,467	21,884	20,382	3,201	1,502 R	48.1%	44.8%	51.8%	48.2%

OHIO

SENATOR 2012

2010 Census Population	County	Total Vote	Republican (Mandel)	Democratic (Brown)	Other	Rep.-Dem. Plurality	Percentage			
							Total Vote		Major Vote	
							Rep.	Dem.	Rep.	Dem.
36,901	COSHOCTON	15,582	8,037	6,457	1,088	1,580 R	51.6%	41.4%	55.5%	44.5%
43,784	CRAWFORD	19,571	11,168	7,197	1,206	3,971 R	57.1%	36.8%	60.8%	39.2%
1,280,122	CUYAHOGA	615,474	167,263	427,597	20,614	260,334 D	27.2%	69.5%	28.1%	71.9%
52,959	DARKE	25,114	17,204	6,649	1,261	10,555 R	68.5%	26.5%	72.1%	27.9%
39,037	DEFIANCE	17,927	9,566	7,314	1,047	2,252 R	53.4%	40.8%	56.7%	43.3%
174,214	DELAWARE	96,635	55,260	37,374	4,001	17,886 R	57.2%	38.7%	59.7%	40.3%
77,079	ERIE	38,874	15,653	21,035	2,186	5,382 D	40.3%	54.1%	42.7%	57.3%
146,156	FAIRFIELD	70,987	38,185	29,111	3,691	9,074 R	53.8%	41.0%	56.7%	43.3%
29,030	FAYETTE	10,658	6,121	4,000	537	2,121 R	57.4%	37.5%	60.5%	39.5%
1,163,414	FRANKLIN	560,594	199,293	339,260	22,041	139,967 D	35.6%	60.5%	37.0%	63.0%
42,698	FULTON	20,920	11,269	8,534	1,117	2,735 R	53.9%	40.8%	56.9%	43.1%
30,934	GALLIA	12,327	6,760	5,060	507	1,700 R	54.8%	41.0%	57.2%	42.8%
93,389	GEAUGA	50,052	27,533	20,264	2,255	7,269 R	55.0%	40.5%	57.6%	42.4%
161,573	GREENE	82,364	46,979	32,243	3,142	14,736 R	57.0%	39.1%	59.3%	40.7%
40,087	GUERNSEY	16,316	8,477	6,868	971	1,609 R	52.0%	42.1%	55.2%	44.8%
802,374	HAMILTON	409,745	176,058	219,299	14,388	43,241 D	43.0%	53.5%	44.5%	55.5%
74,782	HANCOCK	35,187	21,520	11,894	1,773	9,626 R	61.2%	33.8%	64.4%	35.6%
32,058	HARDIN	12,264	7,131	4,416	717	2,715 R	58.1%	36.0%	61.8%	38.2%
15,864	HARRISON	7,063	3,498	3,176	389	322 R	49.5%	45.0%	52.4%	47.6%
28,215	HENRY	14,015	7,738	5,448	829	2,290 R	55.2%	38.9%	58.7%	41.3%
43,589	HIGHLAND	17,629	10,683	5,982	964	4,701 R	60.6%	33.9%	64.1%	35.9%
29,380	HOCKING	12,576	6,057	5,717	802	340 R	48.2%	45.5%	51.4%	48.6%
42,366	HOLMES	11,391	8,252	2,506	633	5,746 R	72.4%	22.0%	76.7%	23.3%
59,626	HURON	24,277	12,443	10,083	1,751	2,360 R	51.3%	41.5%	55.2%	44.8%
33,225	JACKSON	13,184	7,268	5,258	658	2,010 R	55.1%	39.9%	58.0%	42.0%
69,709	JEFFERSON	32,313	14,786	16,031	1,496	1,245 D	45.8%	49.6%	48.0%	52.0%
60,921	KNOX	27,985	16,237	10,186	1,562	6,051 R	58.0%	36.4%	61.5%	38.5%
230,041	LAKE	113,904	52,795	54,981	6,128	2,186 D	46.4%	48.3%	49.0%	51.0%
62,450	LAWRENCE	24,568	12,407	11,085	1,076	1,322 R	50.5%	45.1%	52.8%	47.2%
166,492	LICKING	80,233	42,691	33,097	4,445	9,594 R	53.2%	41.3%	56.3%	43.7%
45,858	LOGAN	21,022	13,303	6,479	1,240	6,824 R	63.3%	30.8%	67.2%	32.8%
301,356	LORAIN	140,601	53,332	80,854	6,415	27,522 D	37.9%	57.5%	39.7%	60.3%
441,815	LUCAS	205,406	65,067	131,887	8,452	66,820 D	31.7%	64.2%	33.0%	67.0%
43,435	MADISON	16,902	9,379	6,518	1,005	2,861 R	55.5%	38.6%	59.0%	41.0%
238,823	MAHONING	114,766	33,480	76,182	5,104	42,702 D	29.2%	66.4%	30.5%	69.5%
66,501	MARION	27,017	13,656	11,376	1,985	2,280 R	50.5%	42.1%	54.6%	45.4%
172,332	MEDINA	88,746	45,176	39,008	4,562	6,168 R	50.9%	44.0%	53.7%	46.3%
23,770	MEIGS	9,891	5,175	4,132	584	1,043 R	52.3%	41.8%	55.6%	44.4%
40,814	MERCER	21,328	15,743	4,736	849	11,007 R	73.8%	22.2%	76.9%	23.1%
102,506	MIAMI	50,990	32,866	15,968	2,156	16,898 R	64.5%	31.3%	67.3%	32.7%
14,642	MONROE	6,680	3,114	3,274	292	160 D	46.6%	49.0%	48.7%	51.3%
535,153	MONTGOMERY	261,170	116,345	135,210	9,615	18,865 D	44.5%	51.8%	46.3%	53.7%
15,054	MORGAN	6,027	3,065	2,625	337	440 R	50.9%	43.6%	53.9%	46.1%
34,827	MORROW	16,036	9,414	5,511	1,111	3,903 R	58.7%	34.4%	63.1%	36.9%
86,074	MUSKINGUM	36,597	18,748	15,592	2,257	3,156 R	51.2%	42.6%	54.6%	45.4%
14,645	NOBLE	5,800	3,311	2,127	362	1,184 R	57.1%	36.7%	60.9%	39.1%
41,428	OTTAWA	22,278	9,872	11,291	1,115	1,419 D	44.3%	50.7%	46.6%	53.4%
19,614	PAULDING	8,952	5,147	3,277	528	1,870 R	57.5%	36.6%	61.1%	38.9%
36,058	PERRY	14,871	7,240	6,734	897	506 R	48.7%	45.3%	51.8%	48.2%
55,698	PICKAWAY	23,858	13,177	9,344	1,337	3,833 R	55.2%	39.2%	58.5%	41.5%
28,709	PIKE	11,429	5,117	5,751	561	634 D	44.8%	50.3%	47.1%	52.9%
161,419	PORTAGE	74,181	32,531	37,144	4,506	4,613 D	43.9%	50.1%	46.7%	53.3%
42,270	PREBLE	19,941	12,820	6,045	1,076	6,775 R	64.3%	30.3%	68.0%	32.0%
34,499	PUTNAM	18,205	12,899	4,584	722	8,315 R	70.9%	25.2%	73.8%	26.2%
124,475	RICHLAND	57,196	30,696	23,758	2,742	6,938 R	53.7%	41.5%	56.4%	43.6%
78,064	ROSS	29,835	14,059	14,147	1,629	88 D	47.1%	47.4%	49.8%	50.2%
60,944	SANDUSKY	28,656	13,280	13,606	1,770	326 D	46.3%	47.5%	49.4%	50.6%
79,499	SCIOTO	29,403	12,958	15,116	1,329	2,158 D	44.1%	51.4%	46.2%	53.8%
56,745	SENECA	25,030	12,802	10,525	1,703	2,277 R	51.1%	42.0%	54.9%	45.1%
49,423	SHELBY	23,239	16,087	6,045	1,107	10,042 R	69.2%	26.0%	72.7%	27.3%

OHIO

SENATOR 2012

2010 Census Population	County	Total Vote	Republican (Mandel)	Democratic (Brown)	Other	Rep.-Dem. Plurality	Percentage Total Vote Rep.	Dem.	Major Vote Rep.	Dem.
375,586	STARK	177,127	78,708	87,493	10,926	8,785 D	44.4%	49.4%	47.4%	52.6%
541,781	SUMMIT	262,181	98,442	151,198	12,541	52,756 D	37.5%	57.7%	39.4%	60.6%
210,312	TRUMBULL	99,647	32,066	62,386	5,195	30,320 D	32.2%	62.6%	33.9%	66.1%
92,582	TUSCARAWAS	40,484	19,946	17,940	2,598	2,006 R	49.3%	44.3%	52.6%	47.4%
52,300	UNION	25,066	15,553	8,144	1,369	7,409 R	62.0%	32.5%	65.6%	34.4%
28,744	VAN WERT	13,629	9,401	3,630	598	5,771 R	69.0%	26.6%	72.1%	27.9%
13,435	VINTON	5,397	2,679	2,414	304	265 R	49.6%	44.7%	52.6%	47.4%
212,693	WARREN	109,070	70,755	33,787	4,528	36,968 R	64.9%	31.0%	67.7%	32.3%
61,778	WASHINGTON	28,806	15,904	11,464	1,438	4,440 R	55.2%	39.8%	58.1%	41.9%
114,520	WAYNE	50,116	28,138	19,072	2,906	9,066 R	56.1%	38.1%	59.6%	40.4%
37,642	WILLIAMS	17,111	9,294	6,640	1,177	2,654 R	54.3%	38.8%	58.3%	41.7%
125,488	WOOD	62,523	27,905	31,633	2,985	3,728 D	44.6%	50.6%	46.9%	53.1%
22,615	WYANDOT	10,429	6,074	3,728	627	2,346 R	58.2%	35.7%	62.0%	38.0%
11,536,504	TOTAL	5,449,114	2,435,740	2,762,757	250,617	327,017 D	44.7%	50.7%	46.9%	53.1%

OHIO

HOUSE OF REPRESENTATIVES

CD	Year	Total Vote	Republican Vote	Candidate	Democratic Vote	Candidate	Other Vote	Rep.-Dem. Plurality	Total Vote Rep.	Dem.	Major Vote Rep.	Dem.
1	2012	349,716	201,907	CHABOT, STEVE*	131,490	SINNARD, JEFF	16,319	70,417 R	57.7%	37.6%	60.6%	39.4%
2	2012	331,381	194,299	WENSTRUP, BRAD	137,082	SMITH, WILLIAM		57,217 R	58.6%	41.4%	58.6%	41.4%
3	2012	295,938	77,903	LONG, CHRIS	201,921	BEATTY, JOYCE	16,114	124,018 D	26.3%	68.2%	27.8%	72.2%
4	2012	312,998	182,643	JORDAN, JIM*	114,214	SLONE, JIM	16,141	68,429 R	58.4%	36.5%	61.5%	38.5%
5	2012	351,878	201,514	LATTA, BOB*	137,806	ZIMMANN, ANGELA	12,558	63,708 R	57.3%	39.2%	59.4%	40.6%
6	2012	308,980	164,536	JOHNSON, BILL*	144,444	WILSON, CHARLES A. JR.		20,092 R	53.3%	46.7%	53.3%	46.7%
7	2012	315,812	178,104	GIBBS, BOB*	137,708	HEALY-ABRAMS, JOYCE		40,396 R	56.4%	43.6%	56.4%	43.6%
8	2012	246,442	246,380	BOEHNER, JOHN*			62	246,380 R	100.0%		100.0%	
9	2012	298,166	68,666	WURZELBACHER, SAMUEL	217,775	KAPTUR, MARCY*	11,725	149,109 D	23.0%	73.0%	24.0%	76.0%
10	2012	349,671	208,201	TURNER, MICHAEL*	131,097	NEUHARDT, SHAREN SWARTZ	10,373	77,104 R	59.5%	37.5%	61.4%	38.6%
11	2012	258,378			258,378	FUDGE, MARCIA L.*		258,378 D		100.0%		100.0%
12	2012	368,488	233,874	TIBERI, PAT*	134,614	REESE, JIM		99,260 R	63.5%	36.5%	63.5%	36.5%
13	2012	323,612	88,120	AGANA, MARISHA	235,492	RYAN, TIM*		147,372 D	27.2%	72.8%	27.2%	72.8%
14	2012	339,878	183,660	JOYCE, DAVID	131,638	BLANCHARD, DALE	24,580	52,022 R	54.0%	38.7%	58.2%	41.8%
15	2012	333,465	205,277	STIVERS, STEVE*	128,188	LANG, PAT		77,089 R	61.6%	38.4%	61.6%	38.4%
16	2012	355,771	185,167	RENACCI, JIM*	170,604	SUTTON, BETTY*		14,563 R	52.0%	48.0%	52.0%	48.0%
TOTAL	2012	5,140,574	2,620,251		2,412,451		107,872	207,800 R	51.0%	46.9%	52.1%	47.9%

Note: An asterisk (*) denotes incumbent. Due to redistricting, the 16th district general election pitted two incumbents against each other (Renacci, former 16th district, and Sutton, former 13th district).

OHIO

GENERAL AND PRIMARY ELECTIONS

GENERAL ELECTIONS: OTHER VOTE

President Other vote was 49,493 Libertarian (Gary E. Johnson), 18,574 Green (Jill Stein), 12,502 Independent (Richard Duncan), 8,151 Constitution (Virgil H. Goode), 2,944 Socialist (Stewart Alexander), 33 Write-in (Scattered Write-In)

Senator Other vote was 250,617 Independent (Scott Rupert)

House Other vote was:

CD 1 9,674 Libertarian (Jim Berns), 6,645 Green (Richard Lee Stevenson)
CD 3 9,462 Libertarian (Richard Ehrbar), 6,388 Green (Bob Fitrakis), 264 Write-in (Jeff Brown)
CD 4 16,141 Libertarian (Chris Kalla)
CD 5 12,558 Libertarian (Eric Eberly)
CD 8 62 Write-in (Jim Condit)
CD 9 11,725 Libertarian (Sean Stipe)
CD 10 10,373 Libertarian (David Harlow)
CD 14 13,038 Green (Elaine Mastromatteo), 11,536 Libertarian (David Macko), 6 Write-in (Aaron Zurbrugg), 5 Write-in (Steven Winfield), 1 Write-in (Erick Robinson)

PRIMARY ELECTIONS: SUPPLEMENTARY INFORMATION

Primary March 6, 2012 **Registration** (as of March 6, 2012) 7,722,180 No Party Registration

Primary Type Open—Any registered voter could participate in the primary of either party. However, records are kept of voter participation in recent primaries, and voters who recently cast a ballot in one party's primary could be challenged if they attempted to participate in the other party's primary. They could be asked to sign an affidavit affirming the fact that they were voting in the opposing party's primary and would become identified with that party because of their primary ballot cast.

		REPUBLICAN PRIMARIES		DEMOCRATIC PRIMARIES		
President	Romney, W. Mitt	460,831	38.0%	Obama, Barack H.*	542,086	100.0%
	Santorum, Rick	448,580	37.0%			
	Gingrich, Newt	177,183	14.6%			
	Paul, Ron	113,256	9.3%			
	Perry, Rick	7,539	0.6%			
	Huntsman, Jon Jr.	6,490	0.5%			
	TOTAL	1,213,879		TOTAL	542,086	
Senator	Mandel, Josh	586,556	63.0%	Brown, Sherrod*	522,827	100.0%
	Pryce, Michael	132,205	14.2%			
	Glisman, Donna	115,621	12.4%			
	Dodt, David	47,933	5.2%			
	Gregory, Eric	47,740	5.1%			
	Bliss, Russell	644	0.1%			
	TOTAL	930,699		TOTAL	522,827	
Congressional District 1	Chabot, Steve*	57,496	100.0%	Sinnard, Jeff	4,561	50.3%
				Kantzler, Malcolm	4,505	49.7%
	TOTAL	57,496		TOTAL	9,066	
Congressional District 2	Wenstrup, Brad	42,482	48.7%	Smith, William	10,175	50.2%
	Schmidt, Jean*	37,383	42.9%	Krikorian, David	10,114	49.8%
	Brush, Tony	4,275	4.9%			
	Kundrata, Fred	2,999	3.4%			
	Green, Joe	29				
	TOTAL	87,168		TOTAL	20,289	

OHIO

GENERAL AND PRIMARY ELECTIONS

	REPUBLICAN PRIMARIES			DEMOCRATIC PRIMARIES		
Congressional District 3	Long, Chris	16,711	57.5%	Beatty, Joyce	15,848	38.3%
	Adams, John	12,335	42.5%	Kilroy, Mary Jo	14,369	34.7%
				Tyson, Priscilla	6,244	15.1%
				Celeste, Theodore S.	4,895	11.8%
	TOTAL	29,046		TOTAL	41,356	
Congressional District 4	Jordan, Jim*	70,470	100.0%	Slone, Jim	23,341	100.0%
	TOTAL	70,470		TOTAL	23,341	
Congressional District 5	Latta, Bob*	76,477	82.6%	Zimmann, Angela	25,530	100.0%
	Wallis, Robert	16,135	17.4%			
	TOTAL	92,612		TOTAL	25,530	
Congressional District 6	Johnson, Bill*	56,905	83.9%	Wilson, Charles A. Jr.	37,374	82.2%
	Smith, Victor	10,888	16.1%	Adulewicz, Cas	8,117	17.8%
	TOTAL	67,793		TOTAL	45,491	
Congressional District 7	Gibbs, Bob*	54,067	79.9%	Healy-Abrams, Joyce	22,486	100.0%
	Liggett, Hombre	13,621	20.1%			
	TOTAL	67,688		TOTAL	22,486	
Congressional District 8	Boehner, John*	71,120	83.8%			
	Lewis, David	13,733	16.2%			
	TOTAL	84,853				
Congressional District 9	Wurzelbacher, Samuel	15,166	51.4%	Kaptur, Marcy*	42,902	56.2%
	Kraus, Steven	14,323	48.6%	Kucinich, Dennis J.*	30,564	40.0%
				Veysey, Graham	2,900	3.8%
	TOTAL	29,489		TOTAL	76,366	
Congressional District 10	Turner, Michael*	65,574	80.1%	Neuhardt, Sharen Swartz	7,705	35.7%
	Anderson, John	14,435	17.6%	Freeman, Olivia	5,530	25.6%
	Breen, Edward	1,839	2.2%	Esrati, David	2,952	13.7%
				McMasters, Thomas	2,212	10.3%
				Steele, Ryan	1,644	7.6%
				Van Allen, Mack	1,530	7.1%
	TOTAL	81,848		TOTAL	21,573	
Congressional District 11				Fudge, Marcia L.*	65,333	89.4%
				Henley, Gerald	4,570	6.3%
				Powell, Isaac	3,169	4.3%
				TOTAL	73,072	
Congressional District 12	Tiberi, Pat*	72,560	77.9%	Reese, Jim	14,312	69.9%
	Yarbrough, Bill	20,610	22.1%	Litt, Doug	6,165	30.1%
	TOTAL	93,170		TOTAL	20,477	
Congressional District 13	Agana, Marisha	27,754	100.0%	Ryan, Tim*	56,670	100.0%
	TOTAL	27,754		TOTAL	56,670	
Congressional District 14	LaTourette, Steven C.*	69,551	100.0%	Blanchard, Dale	29,508	100.0%
	Steven LaTourette withdrew after the primary election in 14th district and David Joyce was selected by the Republican Party to fill the vacancy on the general election ballot.					
	TOTAL	69,551		TOTAL	29,508	
Congressional District 15	Stivers, Steve*	70,191	89.3%	Lang, Pat	16,483	56.7%
	Chope, Charles	8,404	10.7%	Wharton, Scott	12,599	43.3%
	TOTAL	78,595		TOTAL	29,082	
Congressional District 16	Renacci, Jim*	66,487	100.0%	Sutton, Betty*	37,232	100.0%
	TOTAL	66,487		TOTAL	37,232	

Notes: An asterisk (*) denotes incumbent. Due to redistricting, the 9th district Democratic primary pitted two incumbents against each other (Kaptur, former 9th district, and Kucinich, former 10th district).

OKLAHOMA

Congressional districts first established for elections held in 2012

5 members

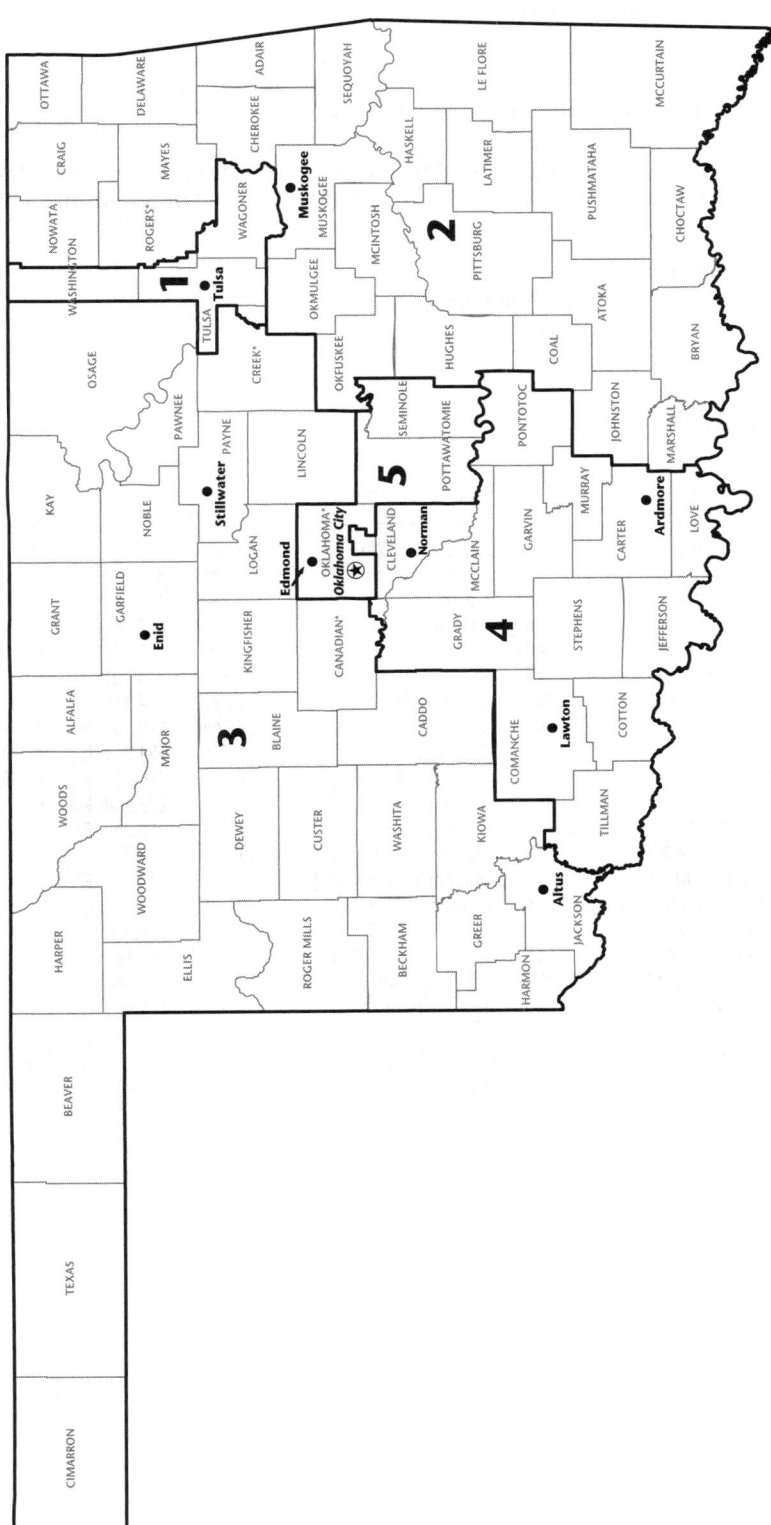

* Asterisk indicates a county whose boundaries include parts of two or more Congressional districts.

OKLAHOMA

GOVERNOR

Mary Fallin (R). Elected 2010 to a four-year term.

SENATORS (2 Republicans)

Tom Coburn (R). Reelected 2010 to a six-year term. Previously elected 2004.

James M. Inhofe (R). Reelected 2008 to a six-year term. Previously elected 2002, 1996, and 1994 to fill out the remaining two years of the term vacated when David L. Boren (D) resigned to become president of the University of Oklahoma.

REPRESENTATIVES (5 Republicans)

1. Jim Bridenstine (R)
2. Markwayne Mullin (R)
3. Frank Lucas (R)
4. Tom Cole (R)
5. James Lankford (R)

POSTWAR VOTE FOR PRESIDENT

| Year | Total Vote | Republican | | Democratic | | Other Vote | Rep.-Dem. Plurality | Percentage | | | |
| | | Vote | Candidate | Vote | Candidate | | | Total Vote | | Major Vote | |
								Rep.	Dem.	Rep.	Dem.
2012	1,334,872	891,325	Romney, W. Mitt	443,547	Obama, Barack H.*		447,778 R	66.8%	33.2%	66.8%	33.2%
2008	1,462,661	960,165	McCain, John S. III	502,496	Obama, Barack H.		457,669 R	65.6%	34.4%	65.6%	34.4%
2004	1,463,758	959,792	Bush, George W.*	503,966	Kerry, John F.		455,826 R	65.6%	34.4%	65.6%	34.4%
2000	1,234,229	744,337	Bush, George W.	474,276	Gore, Albert Jr.	15,616	270,061 R	60.3%	38.4%	61.1%	38.9%
1996**	1,206,713	582,315	Dole, Robert "Bob"	488,105	Clinton, Bill*	136,293	94,210 R	48.3%	40.4%	54.4%	45.6%
1992**	1,390,359	592,929	Bush, George H.*	473,066	Clinton, Bill	324,364	119,863 R	42.6%	34.0%	55.6%	44.4%
1988	1,171,036	678,367	Bush, George H.	483,423	Dukakis, Michael S.	9,246	194,944 R	57.9%	41.3%	58.4%	41.6%
1984	1,255,676	861,530	Reagan, Ronald*	385,080	Mondale, Walter F.	9,066	476,450 R	68.6%	30.7%	69.1%	30.9%
1980**	1,149,708	695,570	Reagan, Ronald	402,026	Carter, Jimmy*	52,112	293,544 R	60.5%	35.0%	63.4%	36.6%
1976	1,092,251	545,708	Ford, Gerald R.*	532,442	Carter, Jimmy	14,101	13,266 R	50.0%	48.7%	50.6%	49.4%
1972	1,029,900	759,025	Nixon, Richard M.*	247,147	McGovern, George S.	23,728	511,878 R	73.7%	24.0%	75.4%	24.6%
1968**	943,086	449,697	Nixon, Richard M.	301,658	Humphrey, Hubert H. Jr.	191,731	148,039 R	47.7%	32.0%	59.9%	40.1%
1964	932,499	412,665	Goldwater, Barry M. Sr.	519,834	Johnson, Lyndon B.*		107,169 D	44.3%	55.7%	44.3%	55.7%
1960	903,150	533,039	Nixon, Richard M.	370,111	Kennedy, John F.		162,928 R	59.0%	41.0%	59.0%	41.0%
1956	859,350	473,769	Eisenhower, Dwight D.*	385,581	Stevenson, Adlai E. II		88,188 R	55.1%	44.9%	55.1%	44.9%
1952	948,984	518,045	Eisenhower, Dwight D.	430,939	Stevenson, Adlai E. II		87,106 R	54.6%	45.4%	54.6%	45.4%
1948	721,599	268,817	Dewey, Thomas E.	452,782	Truman, Harry S.*		183,965 D	37.3%	62.7%	37.3%	62.7%

Note: An asterisk (*) denotes incumbent. **In past elections, the other vote included: 1996 - 130,788 Reform (Ross Perot); 1992 - 319,878 Independent (Perot); 1980 - 38,284 Independent (John Anderson); 1968 - 191,731 American Independent (George Wallace).

OKLAHOMA

POSTWAR VOTE FOR GOVERNOR

Year	Total Vote	Republican Vote	Republican Candidate	Democratic Vote	Democratic Candidate	Other Vote	Rep.-Dem. Plurality	Total Vote Rep.	Total Vote Dem.	Major Vote Rep.	Major Vote Dem.
2010	1,034,767	625,506	Fallin, Mary	409,261	Askins, Jari		216,245 R	60.4%	39.6%	60.4%	39.6%
2006	926,462	310,327	Istook, Ernest J.	616,135	Henry, Brad*		305,808 D	33.5%	66.5%	33.5%	66.5%
2002**	1,035,620	441,277	Largent, Steve	448,143	Henry, Brad	146,200	6,866 D	42.6%	43.3%	49.6%	50.4%
1998	873,585	505,498	Keating, Frank*	357,552	Boyd, Laura	10,535	147,946 R	57.9%	40.9%	58.6%	41.4%
1994**	995,012	466,740	Keating, Frank	294,936	Mildren, Jack	233,336	171,804 R	46.9%	29.6%	61.3%	38.7%
1990	911,314	297,584	Price, Bill	523,196	Walters, David	90,534	225,612 D	32.7%	57.4%	36.3%	63.7%
1986	909,925	431,762	Bellmon, Henry Louis	405,295	Walters, David	72,868	26,467 R	47.5%	44.5%	51.6%	48.4%
1982	883,130	332,207	Daxon, Tom	548,159	Nigh, George*	2,764	215,952 D	37.6%	62.1%	37.7%	62.3%
1978	777,414	367,055	Shotts, Ron	402,240	Nigh, George	8,119	35,185 D	47.2%	51.7%	47.7%	52.3%
1974	804,842	290,459	Inhofe, James M.	514,383	Boren, David L.		223,924 D	36.1%	63.9%	36.1%	63.9%
1970	698,790	336,157	Bartlett, Dewey F.*	338,338	Hall, David	24,295	2,181 D	48.1%	48.4%	49.8%	50.2%
1966	677,258	377,078	Bartlett, Dewey F.	296,328	Moore, Preston J.	3,852	80,750 R	55.7%	43.8%	56.0%	44.0%
1962	709,763	392,316	Bellmon, Henry Louis	315,357	Atkinson, W. P.	2,090	76,959 R	55.3%	44.4%	55.4%	44.6%
1958	538,839	107,495	Ferguson, Phil	399,504	Edmondson, J. Howard	31,840	292,009 D	19.9%	74.1%	21.2%	78.8%
1954	609,194	251,808	Sparks, Reuben K.	357,386	Gary, Raymond		105,578 D	41.3%	58.7%	41.3%	58.7%
1950	644,276	313,205	Ferguson, Jo O.	329,308	Murray, Johnston	1,763	16,103 D	48.6%	51.1%	48.7%	51.3%
1946	494,599	227,426	Flynn, Olney F.	259,491	Turner, Roy J.	7,682	32,065 D	46.0%	52.5%	46.7%	53.3%

Note: An asterisk (*) denotes incumbent. **In past elections, the other vote included: 2002 - 146,200 Independent (Gary L. Richardson); 1994 - 233,336 Independent (Wes Watkins).

POSTWAR VOTE FOR SENATOR

Year	Total Vote	Republican Vote	Republican Candidate	Democratic Vote	Democratic Candidate	Other Vote	Rep.-Dem. Plurality	Total Vote Rep.	Total Vote Dem.	Major Vote Rep.	Major Vote Dem.
2010	1,017,151	718,482	Coburn, Tom*	265,814	Rogers, Jim	32,855	452,668 R	70.6%	26.1%	73.0%	27.0%
2008	1,346,819	763,375	Inhofe, James M.*	527,736	Rice, Andrew	55,708	235,639 R	56.7%	39.2%	59.1%	40.9%
2004	1,446,846	763,433	Coburn, Tom	596,750	Carson, Brad	86,663	166,683 R	52.8%	41.2%	56.1%	43.9%
2002	1,018,424	583,579	Inhofe, James M.*	369,789	Walters, David	65,056	213,790 R	57.3%	36.3%	61.2%	38.8%
1998	859,713	570,682	Nickles, Don*	268,898	Carroll, Don E.	20,133	301,784 R	66.4%	31.3%	68.0%	32.0%
1996	1,183,150	670,610	Inhofe, James M.*	474,162	Boren, Jim	38,378	196,448 R	56.7%	40.1%	58.6%	41.4%
1994S	982,430	542,390	Inhofe, James M.	392,488	McCurdy, Dave	47,552	149,902 R	55.2%	40.0%	58.0%	42.0%
1992	1,294,423	757,876	Nickles, Don*	494,350	Lewis, Steve	42,197	263,526 R	58.5%	38.2%	60.5%	39.5%
1990	884,498	148,814	Jones, Stephen	735,684	Boren, David L.*		586,870 D	16.8%	83.2%	16.8%	83.2%
1986	893,666	493,436	Nickles, Don*	400,230	Jones, James R.		93,206 R	55.2%	44.8%	55.2%	44.8%
1984	1,197,937	280,638	Crozier, Will E.	906,131	Boren, David L.*	11,168	625,493 D	23.4%	75.6%	23.6%	76.4%
1980	1,098,294	587,252	Nickles, Don	478,283	Coats, Andrew	32,759	108,969 R	53.5%	43.5%	55.1%	44.9%
1978	754,264	247,857	Kamm, Robert B.	493,953	Boren, David L.	12,454	246,096 D	32.9%	65.5%	33.4%	66.6%
1974	791,809	390,997	Bellmon, Henry Louis*	387,162	Edmondson, Ed	13,650	3,835 R	49.4%	48.9%	50.2%	49.8%
1972	1,005,148	516,934	Bartlett, Dewey F.	478,212	Edmondson, Ed	10,002	38,722 R	51.4%	47.6%	51.9%	48.1%
1968	909,119	470,120	Bellmon, Henry Louis	419,658	Monroney, A. S. Mike*	19,341	50,462 R	51.7%	46.2%	52.8%	47.2%
1966	638,742	295,585	Patterson, Pat J.	343,157	Harris, Fred R.*		47,572 D	46.3%	53.7%	46.3%	53.7%
1964S	912,174	445,392	Wilkinson, Bud	466,782	Harris, Fred R.		21,390 D	48.8%	51.2%	48.8%	51.2%
1962	664,712	307,966	Crawford, B. Hayden	353,890	Monroney, A. S. Mike*	2,856	45,924 D	46.3%	53.2%	46.5%	53.5%
1960	864,475	385,646	Crawford, B. Hayden	474,116	Kerr, Robert S. Sr.*	4,713	88,470 D	44.6%	54.8%	44.9%	55.1%
1956	831,142	371,146	McKeever, Douglas	459,996	Monroney, A. S. Mike*		88,850 D	44.7%	55.3%	44.7%	55.3%
1954	600,120	262,013	Mock, Fred M.	335,127	Kerr, Robert S. Sr.*	2,980	73,114 D	43.7%	55.8%	43.9%	56.1%
1950	631,177	285,224	Alexander, W. H.	345,953	Monroney, A. S. Mike		60,729 D	45.2%	54.8%	45.2%	54.8%
1948	708,931	265,169	Rizley, Ross	441,654	Kerr, Robert S. Sr.	2,108	176,485 D	37.4%	62.3%	37.5%	62.5%

Note: An asterisk (*) denotes incumbent. **The 1964 and 1994 elections were for short terms to fill vacancies.

OKLAHOMA

PRESIDENT 2012

2010 Census Population	County	Total Vote	Republican (Romney)	Democratic (Obama)	Other	Rep.-Dem. Plurality	Percentage			
							Total Vote		Major Vote	
							Rep.	Dem.	Rep.	Dem.
22,683	ADAIR	6,508	4,381	2,127		2,254 R	67.3%	32.7%	67.3%	32.7%
5,642	ALFALFA	2,083	1,761	322		1,439 R	84.5%	15.5%	84.5%	15.5%
14,182	ATOKA	4,781	3,538	1,243		2,295 R	74.0%	26.0%	74.0%	26.0%
5,636	BEAVER	2,306	2,062	244		1,818 R	89.4%	10.6%	89.4%	10.6%
22,119	BECKHAM	6,925	5,508	1,417		4,091 R	79.5%	20.5%	79.5%	20.5%
11,943	BLAINE	3,816	2,824	992		1,832 R	74.0%	26.0%	74.0%	26.0%
42,416	BRYAN	13,201	9,520	3,681		5,839 R	72.1%	27.9%	72.1%	27.9%
29,600	CADDO	8,851	5,687	3,164		2,523 R	64.3%	35.7%	64.3%	35.7%
115,541	CANADIAN	46,162	35,625	10,537		25,088 R	77.2%	22.8%	77.2%	22.8%
47,557	CARTER	17,122	12,214	4,908		7,306 R	71.3%	28.7%	71.3%	28.7%
46,987	CHEROKEE	14,306	8,162	6,144		2,018 R	57.1%	42.9%	57.1%	42.9%
15,205	CHOCTAW	5,066	3,572	1,494		2,078 R	70.5%	29.5%	70.5%	29.5%
2,475	CIMARRON	1,197	1,082	115		967 R	90.4%	9.6%	90.4%	9.6%
255,755	CLEVELAND	93,887	59,116	34,771		24,345 R	63.0%	37.0%	63.0%	37.0%
5,925	COAL	2,359	1,710	649		1,061 R	72.5%	27.5%	72.5%	27.5%
124,098	COMANCHE	30,185	17,664	12,521		5,143 R	58.5%	41.5%	58.5%	41.5%
6,193	COTTON	2,453	1,796	657		1,139 R	73.2%	26.8%	73.2%	26.8%
15,029	CRAIG	5,306	3,559	1,747		1,812 R	67.1%	32.9%	67.1%	32.9%
69,967	CREEK	26,114	18,986	7,128		11,858 R	72.7%	27.3%	72.7%	27.3%
27,469	CUSTER	9,805	7,446	2,359		5,087 R	75.9%	24.1%	75.9%	24.1%
41,487	DELAWARE	14,276	10,080	4,196		5,884 R	70.6%	29.4%	70.6%	29.4%
4,810	DEWEY	2,093	1,792	301		1,491 R	85.6%	14.4%	85.6%	14.4%
4,151	ELLIS	1,801	1,575	226		1,349 R	87.5%	12.5%	87.5%	12.5%
60,580	GARFIELD	19,910	15,177	4,733		10,444 R	76.2%	23.8%	76.2%	23.8%
27,576	GARVIN	9,484	6,925	2,559		4,366 R	73.0%	27.0%	73.0%	27.0%
52,431	GRADY	19,619	14,833	4,786		10,047 R	75.6%	24.4%	75.6%	24.4%
4,527	GRANT	2,068	1,675	393		1,282 R	81.0%	19.0%	81.0%	19.0%
6,239	GREER	1,832	1,344	488		856 R	73.4%	26.6%	73.4%	26.6%
2,922	HARMON	923	659	264		395 R	71.4%	28.6%	71.4%	28.6%
3,685	HARPER	1,434	1,261	173		1,088 R	87.9%	12.1%	87.9%	12.1%
12,769	HASKELL	4,244	3,069	1,175		1,894 R	72.3%	27.7%	72.3%	27.7%
14,003	HUGHES	4,208	2,838	1,370		1,468 R	67.4%	32.6%	67.4%	32.6%
26,446	JACKSON	7,919	5,965	1,954		4,011 R	75.3%	24.7%	75.3%	24.7%
6,472	JEFFERSON	2,239	1,634	605		1,029 R	73.0%	27.0%	73.0%	27.0%
10,957	JOHNSTON	3,786	2,649	1,137		1,512 R	70.0%	30.0%	70.0%	30.0%
46,562	KAY	16,126	11,499	4,627		6,872 R	71.3%	28.7%	71.3%	28.7%
15,034	KINGFISHER	5,768	4,870	898		3,972 R	84.4%	15.6%	84.4%	15.6%
9,446	KIOWA	3,422	2,316	1,106		1,210 R	67.7%	32.3%	67.7%	32.3%
11,154	LATIMER	3,798	2,628	1,170		1,458 R	69.2%	30.8%	69.2%	30.8%
50,384	LE FLORE	15,839	11,177	4,662		6,515 R	70.6%	29.4%	70.6%	29.4%
34,273	LINCOLN	12,826	9,553	3,273		6,280 R	74.5%	25.5%	74.5%	25.5%
41,848	LOGAN	17,038	12,314	4,724		7,590 R	72.3%	27.7%	72.3%	27.7%
9,423	LOVE	3,470	2,436	1,034		1,402 R	70.2%	29.8%	70.2%	29.8%
7,527	MAJOR	3,146	2,700	446		2,254 R	85.8%	14.2%	85.8%	14.2%
15,840	MARSHALL	5,140	3,744	1,396		2,348 R	72.8%	27.2%	72.8%	27.2%
41,259	MAYES	14,460	9,637	4,823		4,814 R	66.6%	33.4%	66.6%	33.4%
34,506	MCCLAIN	14,306	11,112	3,194		7,918 R	77.7%	22.3%	77.7%	22.3%
33,151	MCCURTAIN	10,075	7,635	2,440		5,195 R	75.8%	24.2%	75.8%	24.2%
20,252	MCINTOSH	7,288	4,509	2,779		1,730 R	61.9%	38.1%	61.9%	38.1%
13,488	MURRAY	5,146	3,606	1,540		2,066 R	70.1%	29.9%	70.1%	29.9%
70,990	MUSKOGEE	23,356	13,404	9,952		3,452 R	57.4%	42.6%	57.4%	42.6%
11,561	NOBLE	4,631	3,488	1,143		2,345 R	75.3%	24.7%	75.3%	24.7%
10,536	NOWATA	4,076	2,832	1,244		1,588 R	69.5%	30.5%	69.5%	30.5%
12,191	OKFUSKEE	3,591	2,335	1,256		1,079 R	65.0%	35.0%	65.0%	35.0%
718,633	OKLAHOMA	256,710	149,728	106,982		42,746 R	58.3%	41.7%	58.3%	41.7%
40,069	OKMULGEE	13,163	7,731	5,432		2,299 R	58.7%	41.3%	58.7%	41.3%
47,472	OSAGE	17,946	11,242	6,704		4,538 R	62.6%	37.4%	62.6%	37.4%
31,848	OTTAWA	9,975	6,466	3,509		2,957 R	64.8%	35.2%	64.8%	35.2%
16,577	PAWNEE	6,045	4,232	1,813		2,419 R	70.0%	30.0%	70.0%	30.0%
77,350	PAYNE	25,679	16,481	9,198		7,283 R	64.2%	35.8%	64.2%	35.8%

OKLAHOMA

PRESIDENT 2012

2010 Census Population	County	Total Vote	Republican (Romney)	Democratic (Obama)	Other	Rep.-Dem. Plurality	Percentage			
							Total Vote		Major Vote	
							Rep.	Dem.	Rep.	Dem.
45,837	PITTSBURG	15,672	10,841	4,831		6,010 R	69.2%	30.8%	69.2%	30.8%
37,492	PONTOTOC	12,892	8,945	3,947		4,998 R	69.4%	30.6%	69.4%	30.6%
69,442	POTTAWATOMIE	23,438	16,250	7,188		9,062 R	69.3%	30.7%	69.3%	30.7%
11,572	PUSHMATAHA	4,130	3,087	1,043		2,044 R	74.7%	25.3%	74.7%	25.3%
3,647	ROGER MILLS	1,674	1,402	272		1,130 R	83.8%	16.2%	83.8%	16.2%
86,905	ROGERS	36,701	27,553	9,148		18,405 R	75.1%	24.9%	75.1%	24.9%
25,482	SEMINOLE	7,456	4,856	2,600		2,256 R	65.1%	34.9%	65.1%	34.9%
42,391	SEQUOYAH	13,771	9,578	4,193		5,385 R	69.6%	30.4%	69.6%	30.4%
45,048	STEPHENS	16,847	12,908	3,939		8,969 R	76.6%	23.4%	76.6%	23.4%
20,640	TEXAS	5,792	4,930	862		4,068 R	85.1%	14.9%	85.1%	14.9%
7,992	TILLMAN	2,721	1,815	906		909 R	66.7%	33.3%	66.7%	33.3%
603,403	TULSA	227,806	145,062	82,744		62,318 R	63.7%	36.3%	63.7%	36.3%
73,085	WAGONER	28,691	20,900	7,791		13,109 R	72.8%	27.2%	72.8%	27.2%
50,976	WASHINGTON	21,200	15,668	5,532		10,136 R	73.9%	26.1%	73.9%	26.1%
11,629	WASHITA	4,316	3,494	822		2,672 R	81.0%	19.0%	81.0%	19.0%
8,878	WOODS	3,398	2,727	671		2,056 R	80.3%	19.7%	80.3%	19.7%
20,081	WOODWARD	7,078	5,945	1,133		4,812 R	84.0%	16.0%	84.0%	16.0%
3,751,351	TOTAL	1,334,872	891,325	443,547		447,778 R	66.8%	33.2%	66.8%	33.2%

OKLAHOMA

HOUSE OF REPRESENTATIVES

CD	Year	Total Vote	Republican		Democratic		Other Vote	Rep.-Dem. Plurality	Percentage			
			Vote	Candidate	Vote	Candidate			Total Vote		Major Vote	
									Rep.	Dem.	Rep.	Dem.
1	2012	285,312	181,084	BRIDENSTINE, JIM	91,421	OLSON, JOHN	12,807	89,663 R	63.5%	32.0%	66.5%	33.5%
2	2012	250,612	143,701	MULLIN, MARKWAYNE	96,081	WALLACE, ROB	10,830	47,620 R	57.3%	38.3%	59.9%	40.1%
3	2012	268,003	201,744	LUCAS, FRANK*	53,472	MURRAY, TIMOTHY RAY	12,787	148,272 R	75.3%	20.0%	79.0%	21.0%
4	2012	260,331	176,740	COLE, TOM*	71,846	BEBO, DONNA MARIE	11,745	104,894 R	67.9%	27.6%	71.1%	28.9%
5	2012	261,677	153,603	LANKFORD, JAMES*	97,504	GUILD, TOM	10,570	56,099 R	58.7%	37.3%	61.2%	38.8%
TOTAL	2012	1,325,935	856,872		410,324		58,739	446,548 R	64.6%	30.9%	67.6%	32.4%

Notes: An asterisk (*) denotes incumbent.

OKLAHOMA

GENERAL AND PRIMARY ELECTIONS

GENERAL ELECTIONS: OTHER VOTE

President

House	Other vote was:
CD 1	12,807 Independent (Craig Allen)
CD 2	10,830 Independent (Michael G. Fulks)
CD 3	12,787 Independent (William M. Sanders)
CD 4	11,745 Independent (RJ Harris)
CD 5	5,394 Independent (Pat Martin), 5,176 Independent (Robert T. Murphy)

PRIMARY ELECTIONS: SUPPLEMENTARY INFORMATION

Primary	March 6, 2012 (President)	**Registration**	2,000,610	Democratic	943,283
	June 26, 2012 (Congress)	(as of January 15, 2012)		Republican	828,257
				Independent	229,070
Primary Runoff	August 28, 2012				
Primary Type	Closed—Only registered Democrats and Republicans could vote in their party's primary.				

	REPUBLICAN PRIMARIES			DEMOCRATIC PRIMARIES		
President	Santorum, Rick	96,849	33.8%	Obama, Barack H.*	64,389	57.1%
	Romney, W. Mitt	80,356	28.0%	Terry, Randall	20,312	18.0%
	Gingrich, Newt	78,730	27.5%	Rogers, Jim	15,546	13.8%
	Paul, Ron	27,596	9.6%	Richardson, Darcy	7,201	6.4%
	Perry, Rick	1,291	0.5%	Ely, Bob	5,323	4.7%
	Bachmann, Michele	951	0.3%			
	Huntsman, Jon Jr.	750	0.3%			
	TOTAL	*286,523*		*TOTAL*	*112,771*	
Congressional District 1	Bridenstine, Jim	28,055	53.8%	Olson, John	Unopposed	
	Sullivan, John*	24,058	46.2%			
	TOTAL	*52,113*				
Congressional District 2	Mullin, Markwayne	12,008	42.4%	Wallace, Rob	31,793	46.1%
	Faught, George	6,582	23.2%	Herriman, Wayne	28,632	41.6%
	Wood, Dakota	3,479	12.3%	Everett, Earl E.	8,484	12.3%
	Rowe, Dustin	2,871	10.1%			
	Pettigrew, Wayne	2,479	8.8%			
	Thompson, Dwayne	901	3.2%			
	TOTAL	*28,320*		*TOTAL*	*68,909*	
	PRIMARY RUNOFF			**PRIMARY RUNOFF**		
	Mullin, Markwayne	12,059	56.8%	Wallace, Rob	25,105	57.0%
	Faught, George	9,167	43.2%	Herriman, Wayne	18,926	43.0%
	TOTAL	*21,226*		*TOTAL*	*44,031*	
Congressional District 3	Lucas, Frank*	33,454	88.2%	Murray, Timothy Ray	9,252	52.3%
	Stump, William Craig	4,492	11.8%	Robbins, Frankie	8,429	47.7%
	TOTAL	*37,946*		*TOTAL*	*17,681*	
Congressional District 4	Cole, Tom*	22,840	87.7%	Bebo, Donna Marie	11,935	58.3%
	Caissie, Gary D.	3,195	12.3%	Smith, Bert	8,532	41.7%
	TOTAL	*26,035*		*TOTAL*	*20,467*	
Congressional District 5	Lankford, James*	Unopposed		Guild, Tom	Unopposed	

Notes: An asterisk (*) denotes incumbent. The names of unopposed candidates did not appear on the primary ballot; therefore, no votes were cast for these candidates. A runoff was triggered if the leading candidate received less than 50 percent of the primary vote.

OREGON

Congressional districts first established for elections held in 2012
5 members

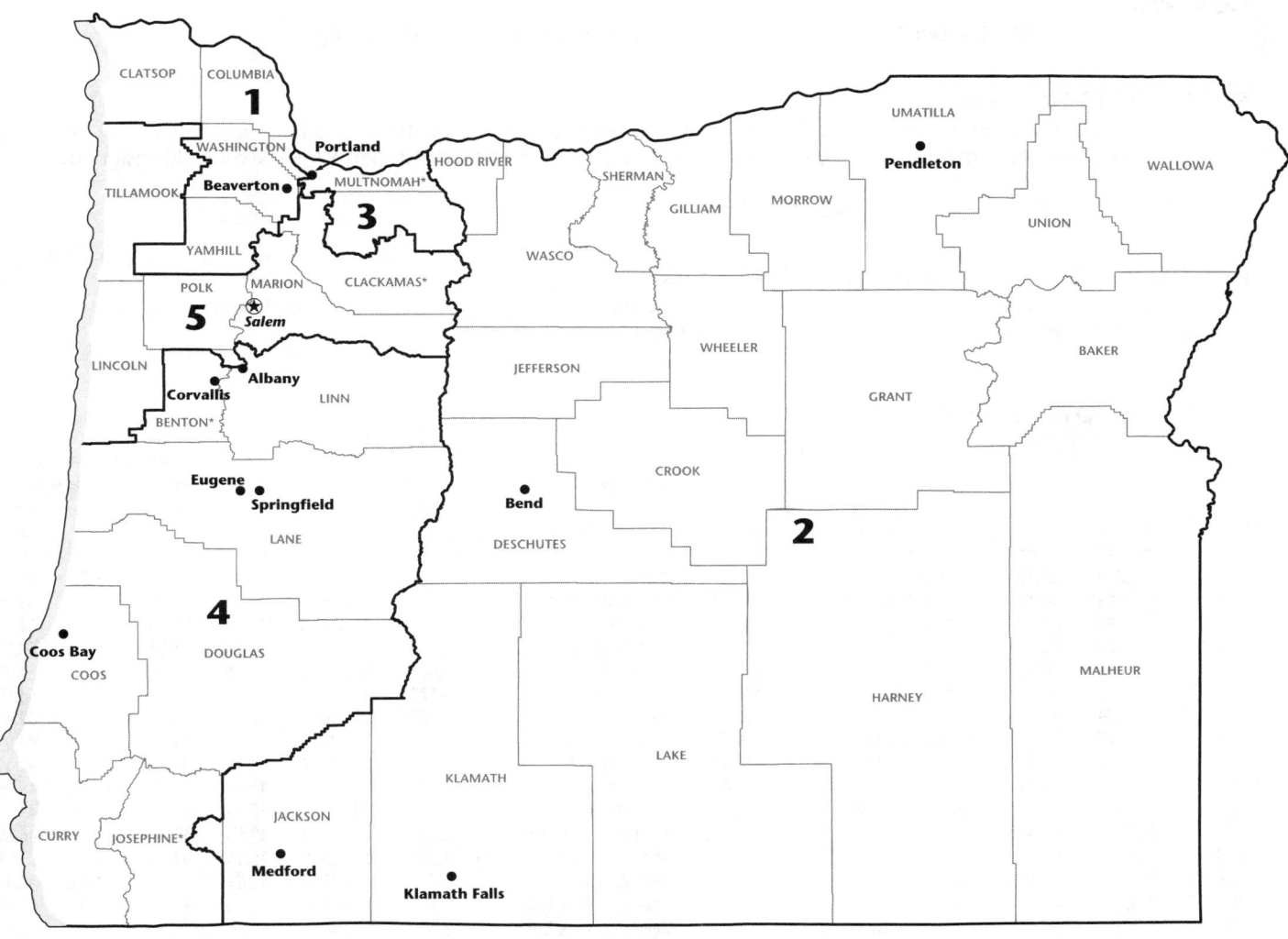

* Asterisk indicates a county whose boundaries include parts of two or more Congressional districts.

OREGON

GOVERNOR
John Kitzhaber (D). Elected 2010 to a four-year term. Previously elected 1998, 1994.

SENATORS (2 Democrats)
Ron Wyden (D). Reelected 2010 to a six-year term. Previously elected 2004, 1998, and in a special election January 30, 1996, to serve the remaining three years of the term vacated when Senator Robert W. Packwood (R) resigned.

Jeff Merkley (D). Elected 2008 to a six-year term.

REPRESENTATIVES (1 Republican, 4 Democrats)
1. Suzanne Bonamici (D)
2. Greg Walden (R)
3. Earl Blumenauer (D)
4. Peter DeFazio (D)
5. Kurt Schrader (D)

POSTWAR VOTE FOR PRESIDENT

Year	Total Vote	Republican Vote	Republican Candidate	Democratic Vote	Democratic Candidate	Other Vote	Rep.-Dem. Plurality	Total Vote Rep.	Total Vote Dem.	Major Vote Rep.	Major Vote Dem.
2012	1,789,270	754,175	Romney, W. Mitt	970,488	Obama, Barack H.*	64,607	216,313 D	42.1%	54.2%	43.7%	56.3%
2008	1,827,864	738,475	McCain, John S. III	1,037,291	Obama, Barack H.	52,098	298,816 D	40.4%	56.7%	41.6%	58.4%
2004	1,836,782	866,831	Bush, George W.*	943,163	Kerry, John F.	26,788	76,332 D	47.2%	51.3%	47.9%	52.1%
2000**	1,533,968	713,577	Bush, George W.	720,342	Gore, Albert Jr.	100,049	6,765 D	46.5%	47.0%	49.8%	50.2%
1996**	1,377,760	538,152	Dole, Robert "Bob"	649,641	Clinton, Bill*	189,967	111,489 D	39.1%	47.2%	45.3%	54.7%
1992**	1,462,643	475,757	Bush, George H.*	621,314	Clinton, Bill	365,572	145,557 D	32.5%	42.5%	43.4%	56.6%
1988	1,201,694	560,126	Bush, George H.	616,206	Dukakis, Michael S.	25,362	56,080 D	46.6%	51.3%	47.6%	52.4%
1984	1,226,527	685,700	Reagan, Ronald*	536,479	Mondale, Walter F.	4,348	149,221 R	55.9%	43.7%	56.1%	43.9%
1980**	1,181,516	571,044	Reagan, Ronald	456,890	Carter, Jimmy*	153,582	114,154 R	48.3%	38.7%	55.6%	44.4%
1976	1,029,876	492,120	Ford, Gerald R.*	490,407	Carter, Jimmy	47,349	1,713 R	47.8%	47.6%	50.1%	49.9%
1972	927,946	486,686	Nixon, Richard M.*	392,760	McGovern, George S.	48,500	93,926 R	52.4%	42.3%	55.3%	44.7%
1968**	819,622	408,433	Nixon, Richard M.	358,866	Humphrey, Hubert H. Jr.	52,323	49,567 R	49.8%	43.8%	53.2%	46.8%
1964	786,305	282,779	Goldwater, Barry M. Sr.	501,017	Johnson, Lyndon B.*	2,509	218,238 D	36.0%	63.7%	36.1%	63.9%
1960	776,421	408,060	Nixon, Richard M.	367,402	Kennedy, John F.	959	40,658 R	52.6%	47.3%	52.6%	47.4%
1956	736,132	406,393	Eisenhower, Dwight D.*	329,204	Stevenson, Adlai E. II	535	77,189 R	55.2%	44.7%	55.2%	44.8%
1952	695,059	420,815	Eisenhower, Dwight D.	270,579	Stevenson, Adlai E. II	3,665	150,236 R	60.5%	38.9%	60.9%	39.1%
1948	524,080	260,904	Dewey, Thomas E.	243,147	Truman, Harry S.*	20,029	17,757 R	49.8%	46.4%	51.8%	48.2%

Note: An asterisk (*) denotes incumbent. **In past elections, the other vote included: 2000 - 77,357 Green (Ralph Nader); 1996 - 121,221 Reform (Ross Perot); 1992 - 354,091 Independent (Perot); 1980 - 112,389 Independent (John Anderson); 1968 - 49,683 American Independent (George Wallace).

OREGON

POSTWAR VOTE FOR GOVERNOR

Year	Total Vote	Republican Vote	Candidate	Democratic Vote	Candidate	Other Vote	Rep.-Dem. Plurality	Percentage Total Vote Rep.	Dem.	Major Vote Rep.	Dem.
2010	1,453,548	694,287	Dudley, Chris	716,525	Kitzhaber, John	42,736	22,238 D	47.8%	49.3%	49.2%	50.8%
2006	1,379,475	589,748	Saxton, Ron	699,786	Kulongoski, Ted*	89,941	110,038 D	42.8%	50.7%	45.7%	54.3%
2002	1,260,497	581,785	Mannix, Kevin L.	618,004	Kulongoski, Ted	60,708	36,219 D	46.2%	49.0%	48.5%	51.5%
1998	1,113,098	334,001	Sizemore, Bill	717,061	Kitzhaber, John*	62,036	383,060 D	30.0%	64.4%	31.8%	68.2%
1994	1,221,010	517,874	Smith, Denny	622,083	Kitzhaber, John	81,053	104,209 D	42.4%	50.9%	45.4%	54.6%
1990**	1,112,847	444,646	Frohnmayer, Dave	508,749	Roberts, Barbara	159,452	64,103 D	40.0%	45.7%	46.6%	53.4%
1986	1,059,630	506,986	Paulus, Norma	549,456	Goldschmidt, Neil	3,188	42,470 D	47.8%	51.9%	48.0%	52.0%
1982	1,042,009	639,841	Atiyeh, Victor*	374,316	Kulongoski, Ted	27,852	265,525 R	61.4%	35.9%	63.1%	36.9%
1978	911,143	498,452	Atiyeh, Victor	409,411	Straub, Robert W.*	3,280	89,041 R	54.7%	44.9%	54.9%	45.1%
1974	770,574	324,751	Atiyeh, Victor	444,812	Straub, Robert W.	1,011	120,061 D	42.1%	57.7%	42.2%	57.8%
1970	666,394	369,964	McCall, Tom*	293,892	Straub, Robert W.	2,538	76,072 R	55.5%	44.1%	55.7%	44.3%
1966	682,862	377,346	McCall, Tom	305,008	Straub, Robert W.	508	72,338 R	55.3%	44.7%	55.3%	44.7%
1962	637,407	345,497	Hatfield, Mark O.*	265,359	Thornton, Robert Y.	26,551	80,138 R	54.2%	41.6%	56.6%	43.4%
1958	599,994	331,900	Hatfield, Mark O.	267,934	Holmes, Robert D.*	160	63,966 R	55.3%	44.7%	55.3%	44.7%
1956S	731,279	361,840	Smith, Elmo E.	369,439	Holmes, Robert D.		7,599 D	49.5%	50.5%	49.5%	50.5%
1954	566,701	322,522	Patterson, Paul	244,179	Carson, Joseph K. Jr.		78,343 R	56.9%	43.1%	56.9%	43.1%
1950	505,910	334,160	McKay, Douglas*	171,750	Flegal, Austin F.		162,410 R	66.1%	33.9%	66.1%	33.9%
1948S	509,624	271,295	McKay, Douglas	226,949	Wallace, Lew	11,380	44,346 R	53.2%	44.5%	54.5%	45.5%
1946	344,155	237,681	Snell, Earl*	106,474	Donaugh, Carl C.		131,207 R	69.1%	30.9%	69.1%	30.9%

Note: An asterisk (*) denotes incumbent. **In past elections, the other vote included: 1990 - 144,062 Independent (Al Mobley). The 1948 and 1956 elections were for short terms to fill a vacany.

POSTWAR VOTE FOR SENATOR

Year	Total Vote	Republican Vote	Candidate	Democratic Vote	Candidate	Other Vote	Rep.-Dem. Plurality	Percentage Total Vote Rep.	Dem.	Major Vote Rep.	Dem.
2010	1,442,588	566,199	Huffman, Jim	825,507	Wyden, Ron*	50,882	259,308 D	39.2%	57.2%	40.7%	59.3%
2008	1,767,504	805,159	Smith, Gordon H.*	864,392	Merkley, Jeff	97,953	59,233 D	45.6%	48.9%	48.2%	51.8%
2004	1,780,550	565,254	King, Al	1,128,728	Wyden, Ron*	86,568	563,474 D	31.7%	63.4%	33.4%	66.6%
2002	1,267,221	712,287	Smith, Gordon H.*	501,898	Bradbury, Bill	53,036	210,389 R	56.2%	39.6%	58.7%	41.3%
1998	1,117,747	377,739	Lim, John	682,425	Wyden, Ron*	57,583	304,686 D	33.8%	61.1%	35.6%	64.4%
1996	1,360,230	677,336	Smith, Gordon H.*	624,370	Bruggere, Tom	58,524	52,966 R	49.8%	45.9%	52.0%	48.0%
1996S	1,196,608	553,519	Smith, Gordon H.*	571,739	Wyden, Ron	71,350	18,220 D	46.3%	47.8%	49.2%	50.8%
1992	1,376,033	717,455	Packwood, Robert W.*	639,851	Aucoin, Les	18,727	77,604 R	52.1%	46.5%	52.9%	47.1%
1990	1,099,255	590,095	Hatfield, Mark*	507,743	Lonsdale, Harry	1,417	82,352 R	53.7%	46.2%	53.8%	46.2%
1986	1,042,555	656,317	Packwood, Robert W.*	375,735	Bauman, Rick	10,503	280,582 R	63.0%	36.0%	63.6%	36.4%
1984	1,214,735	808,152	Hatfield, Mark*	406,122	Hendriksen, Margie	461	402,030 R	66.5%	33.4%	66.6%	33.4%
1980	1,140,494	594,290	Packwood, Robert W.*	501,963	Kulongoski, Ted	44,241	92,327 R	52.1%	44.0%	54.2%	45.8%
1978	892,518	550,165	Hatfield, Mark*	341,616	Cook, Vernon	737	208,549 R	61.6%	38.3%	61.7%	38.3%
1974	766,414	420,984	Packwood, Robert W.*	338,591	Roberts, Betty	6,839	82,393 R	54.9%	44.2%	55.4%	44.6%
1972	920,833	494,671	Hatfield, Mark*	425,036	Morse, Wayne L.	1,126	69,635 R	53.7%	46.2%	53.8%	46.2%
1968	814,176	408,646	Packwood, Robert W.	405,353	Morse, Wayne L.*	177	3,293 R	50.2%	49.8%	50.2%	49.8%
1966	685,067	354,391	Hatfield, Mark	330,374	Duncan, Robert B.	302	24,017 R	51.7%	48.2%	51.8%	48.2%
1962	636,558	291,587	Unander, Sig	344,716	Morse, Wayne L.*	255	53,129 D	45.8%	54.2%	45.8%	54.2%
1960	755,875	343,009	Smith, Elmo E.	412,757	Neuberger, Maurine B.	109	69,748 D	45.4%	54.6%	45.4%	54.6%
1956	732,254	335,405	McKay, Douglas	396,849	Morse, Wayne L.*		61,444 D	45.8%	54.2%	45.8%	54.2%
1954	569,088	283,313	Cordon, Guy*	285,775	Neuberger, Richard L.		2,462 D	49.8%	50.2%	49.8%	50.2%
1950	503,455	376,510	Morse, Wayne L.*	116,780	Latourette, Howard	10,165	259,730 R	74.8%	23.2%	76.3%	23.7%
1948	498,570	299,295	Cordon, Guy*	199,275	Wilson, Manley J.		100,020 R	60.0%	40.0%	60.0%	40.0%

Note: An asterisk (*) denotes incumbent. **The January 1996 election was for a short term to fill a vacancy.

OREGON

PRESIDENT 2012

2010 Census Population	County	Total Vote	Republican (Romney)	Democratic (Obama)	Other	Rep.-Dem. Plurality	Percentage Total Vote Rep.	Dem.	Major Vote Rep.	Dem.
16,134	BAKER	8,448	5,702	2,369	377	3,333 R	67.5%	28.0%	70.6%	29.4%
85,579	BENTON	44,802	14,991	27,776	2,035	12,785 D	33.5%	62.0%	35.1%	64.9%
375,992	CLACKAMAS	189,332	88,592	95,493	5,247	6,901 D	46.8%	50.4%	48.1%	51.9%
37,039	CLATSOP	17,818	7,249	9,861	708	2,612 D	40.7%	55.3%	42.4%	57.6%
49,351	COLUMBIA	23,875	10,772	12,004	1,099	1,232 D	45.1%	50.3%	47.3%	52.7%
63,043	COOS	28,686	14,673	12,845	1,168	1,828 R	51.2%	44.8%	53.3%	46.7%
20,978	CROOK	10,230	6,790	3,104	336	3,686 R	66.4%	30.3%	68.6%	31.4%
22,364	CURRY	11,678	6,598	4,625	455	1,973 R	56.5%	39.6%	58.8%	41.2%
157,733	DESCHUTES	81,900	42,463	36,961	2,476	5,502 R	51.8%	45.1%	53.5%	46.5%
107,667	DOUGLAS	49,803	30,776	17,145	1,882	13,631 R	61.8%	34.4%	64.2%	35.8%
1,871	GILLIAM	1,061	639	371	51	268 R	60.2%	35.0%	63.3%	36.7%
7,445	GRANT	3,911	2,926	853	132	2,073 R	74.8%	21.8%	77.4%	22.6%
7,422	HARNEY	3,583	2,607	832	144	1,775 R	72.8%	23.2%	75.8%	24.2%
22,346	HOOD RIVER	9,838	3,429	6,058	351	2,629 D	34.9%	61.6%	36.1%	63.9%
203,206	JACKSON	97,127	49,020	44,468	3,639	4,552 R	50.5%	45.8%	52.4%	47.6%
21,720	JEFFERSON	8,175	4,642	3,301	232	1,341 R	56.8%	40.4%	58.4%	41.6%
82,713	JOSEPHINE	40,238	23,673	14,953	1,612	8,720 R	58.8%	37.2%	61.3%	38.7%
66,380	KLAMATH	28,152	18,898	8,302	952	10,596 R	67.1%	29.5%	69.5%	30.5%
7,895	LAKE	3,710	2,808	770	132	2,038 R	75.7%	20.8%	78.5%	21.5%
351,715	LANE	171,850	62,509	102,652	6,689	40,143 D	36.4%	59.7%	37.8%	62.2%
46,034	LINCOLN	22,984	8,686	13,401	897	4,715 D	37.8%	58.3%	39.3%	60.7%
116,672	LINN	51,426	28,944	20,378	2,104	8,566 R	56.3%	39.6%	58.7%	41.3%
31,313	MALHEUR	9,956	6,851	2,759	346	4,092 R	68.8%	27.7%	71.3%	28.7%
315,335	MARION	120,376	60,190	56,376	3,810	3,814 R	50.0%	46.8%	51.6%	48.4%
11,173	MORROW	3,882	2,532	1,202	148	1,330 R	65.2%	31.0%	67.8%	32.2%
735,334	MULTNOMAH	364,722	75,302	274,887	14,533	199,585 D	20.6%	75.4%	21.5%	78.5%
75,403	POLK	35,257	17,819	16,292	1,146	1,527 R	50.5%	46.2%	52.2%	47.8%
1,765	SHERMAN	1,026	678	319	29	359 R	66.1%	31.1%	68.0%	32.0%
25,250	TILLAMOOK	12,519	5,684	6,293	542	609 D	45.4%	50.3%	47.5%	52.5%
75,889	UMATILLA	24,969	15,499	8,584	886	6,915 R	62.1%	34.4%	64.4%	35.6%
25,748	UNION	12,070	7,636	3,973	461	3,663 R	63.3%	32.9%	65.8%	34.2%
7,008	WALLOWA	4,205	2,804	1,253	148	1,551 R	66.7%	29.8%	69.1%	30.9%
25,213	WASCO	10,873	5,229	5,211	433	18 R	48.1%	47.9%	50.1%	49.9%
529,710	WASHINGTON	237,023	93,974	135,291	7,758	41,317 D	39.6%	57.1%	41.0%	59.0%
1,441	WHEELER	858	545	266	47	279 R	63.5%	31.0%	67.2%	32.8%
99,193	YAMHILL	42,907	22,045	19,260	1,602	2,785 R	51.4%	44.9%	53.4%	46.6%
3,831,074	TOTAL	1,789,270	754,175	970,488	64,607	216,313 D	42.1%	54.2%	43.7%	56.3%

OREGON

HOUSE OF REPRESENTATIVES

CD	Year	Total Vote	Republican Vote	Candidate	Democratic Vote	Candidate	Other Vote	Rep.-Dem. Plurality	Percentage Total Vote Rep.	Dem.	Major Vote Rep.	Dem.
1	2012	331,980	109,699	MORGAN, DELINDA	197,845	BONAMICI, SUZANNE*	24,436	88,146 D	33.0%	59.6%	35.7%	64.3%
2	2012	332,255	228,043	WALDEN, GREG*	96,741	SEGERS, JOYCE B.	7,471	131,302 R	68.6%	29.1%	70.2%	29.8%
3	2012	355,875	70,325	GREEN, RONALD	264,979	BLUMENAUER, EARL*	20,571	194,654 D	19.8%	74.5%	21.0%	79.0%
4	2012	360,088	140,549	ROBINSON, ART	212,866	DEFAZIO, PETER*	6,673	72,317 D	39.0%	59.1%	39.8%	60.2%
5	2012	327,970	139,223	THOMPSON, FRED	177,229	SCHRADER, KURT*	11,518	38,006 D	42.4%	54.0%	44.0%	56.0%
TOTAL	2012	1,708,168	687,839		949,660		70,669	261,821 D	40.3%	55.6%	42.0%	58.0%

Note: An asterisk (*) denotes incumbent.

OREGON

GENERAL AND PRIMARY ELECTIONS

GENERAL ELECTIONS: OTHER VOTE

President   Other vote was 24,089 Libertarian (Gary E. Johnson), 19,427 Green (Jill Stein), 13,275 Write-in (Scattered Write-In), 4,432 Constitution (Will Christensen), 3,384 Justice (Ross C. "Rocky" Anderson)

House   Other vote was:

CD 1   15,009 Progressive (Steve Reynolds), 8,918 Constitution (Bob Ekstrom), 509 Write-in (Scattered Write-In)
CD 2   7,025 Libertarian (Joe Tabor), 446 Write-in (Scattered Write-In)
CD 3   13,159 Pacific Green (Woodrow Broadnax), 6,640 Libertarian (Michael Cline), 772 Write-in (Scattered Write-In)
CD 4   6,205 Libertarian (Chuck Huntting), 468 Write-in (Scattered Write-In)
CD 5   7,516 Pacific Green (Christina Jean Lugo), 3,600 Constitution (Raymond Baldwin), 402 Write-in (Scattered Write-In)

PRIMARY ELECTIONS: SUPPLEMENTARY INFORMATION

Primary	May 15, 2012	**Registration** (as of May 15, 2012)	2,021,263	Democratic	816,943
				Republican	663,949
				Non-Affiliated	415,838
				Other	124,533

Primary Type   Closed—Only registered Democrats and Republicans could vote in their party's primary for federal offices.

	REPUBLICAN PRIMARIES			**DEMOCRATIC PRIMARIES**		
President	Romney, W. Mitt	204,176	70.9%	Obama, Barack H.*	309,358	94.8%
	Paul, Ron	36,810	12.8%	Scattered Write-In	16,998	5.2%
	Santorum, Rick	27,042	9.4%			
	Gingrich, Newt	15,451	5.4%			
	Scattered Write-In	4,476	1.6%			
	TOTAL	287,955		TOTAL	326,356	
Congressional District 1	Morgan, Delinda	18,996	56.3%	Bonamici, Suzanne*	57,146	98.9%
	Michaels, Lisa	14,274	42.3%	Scattered Write-In	608	1.1%
	Scattered Write-In	447	1.3%			
	TOTAL	33,717		TOTAL	57,754	
Congressional District 2	Walden, Greg*	77,498	99.3%	Segers, Joyce B.	31,157	76.5%
	Scattered Write-In	581	0.7%	Sweeney, John	8,825	21.7%
				Scattered Write-In	751	1.8%
	TOTAL	78,079		TOTAL	40,733	
Congressional District 3	Green, Ronald	14,844	63.2%	Blumenauer, Earl*	84,628	98.9%
	Delia, Lopez	8,237	35.0%	Scattered Write-In	969	1.1%
	Scattered Write-In	424	1.8%			
	TOTAL	23,505		TOTAL	85,597	
Congressional District 4	Robinson, Art	50,090	97.3%	DeFazio, Peter*	69,864	89.9%
	Scattered Write-In	1,414	2.7%	Robinson, Matthew L.	7,665	9.9%
				Scattered Write-In	212	0.3%
	TOTAL	51,504		TOTAL	77,741	
Congressional District 5	Thompson, Fred	33,448	67.0%	Schrader, Kurt*	51,652	98.5%
	Bowerman, Karen	16,174	32.4%	Scattered Write-In	805	1.5%
	Scattered Write-In	320	0.6%			
	TOTAL	49,942		TOTAL	52,457	

Notes: An asterisk (*) denotes incumbent. The primary and general elections were conducted entirely by mail.

PENNSYLVANIA

Congressional districts first established for elections held in 2012

18 members

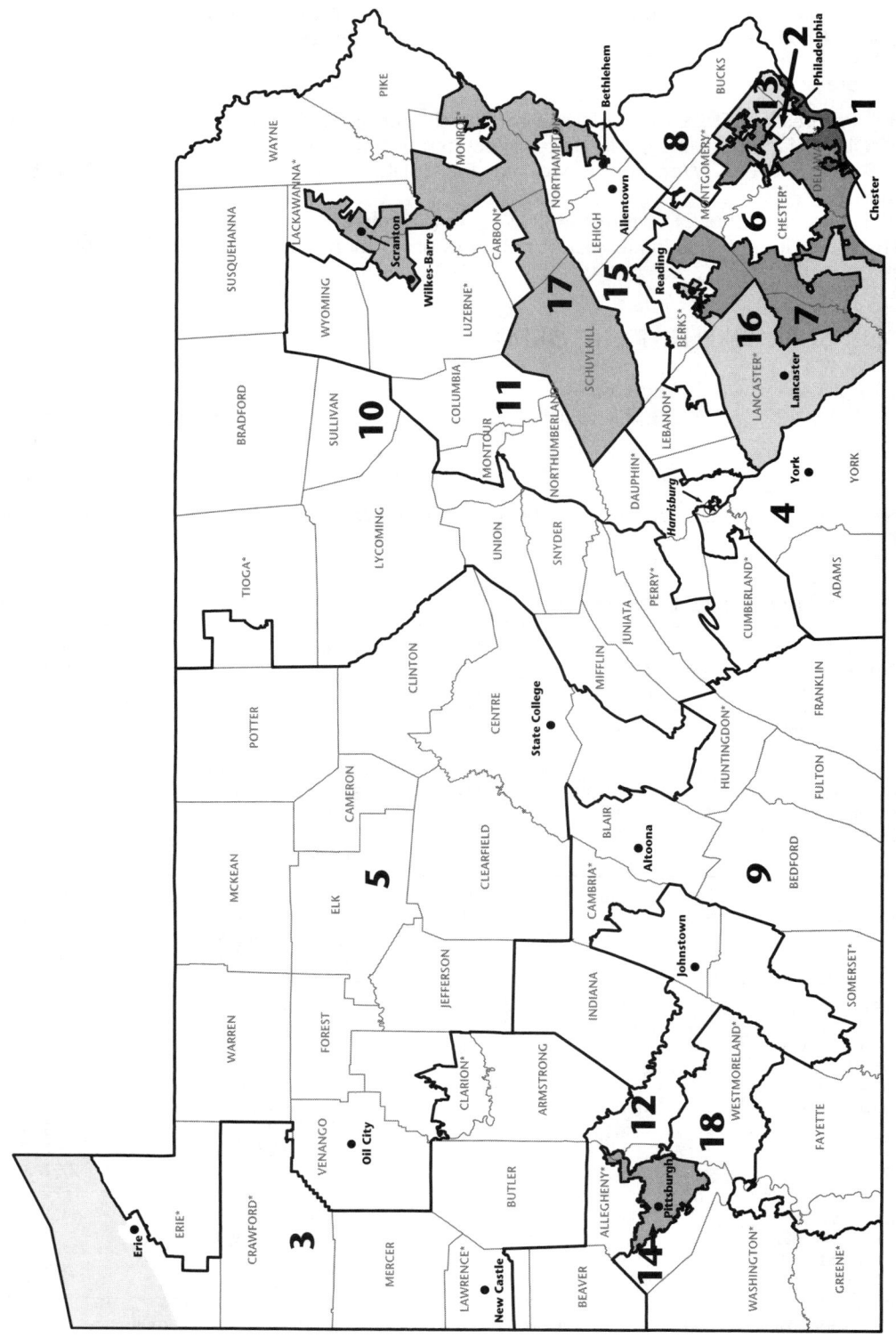

The city of Philadelphia is coextensive with the county of Philadelphia.

* Asterisk indicates a county whose boundaries include parts of two or more Congressional districts.

PENNSYLVANIA
Greater Pittsburgh Area

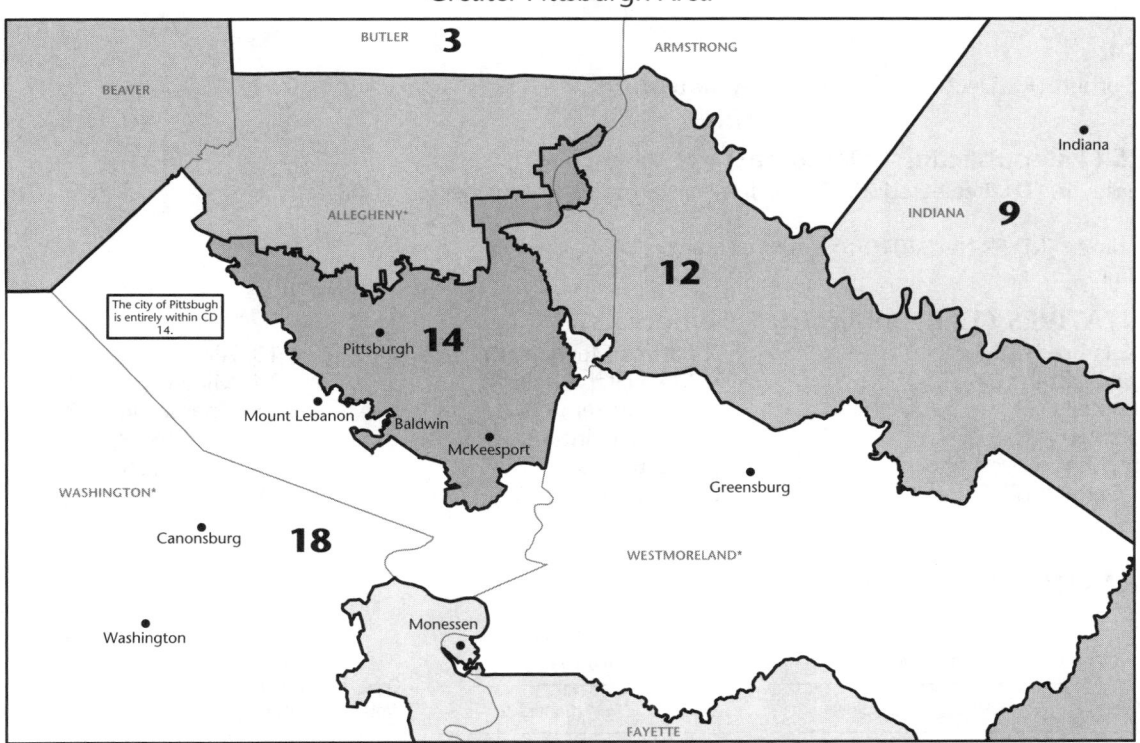

Greater Philadelphia Area

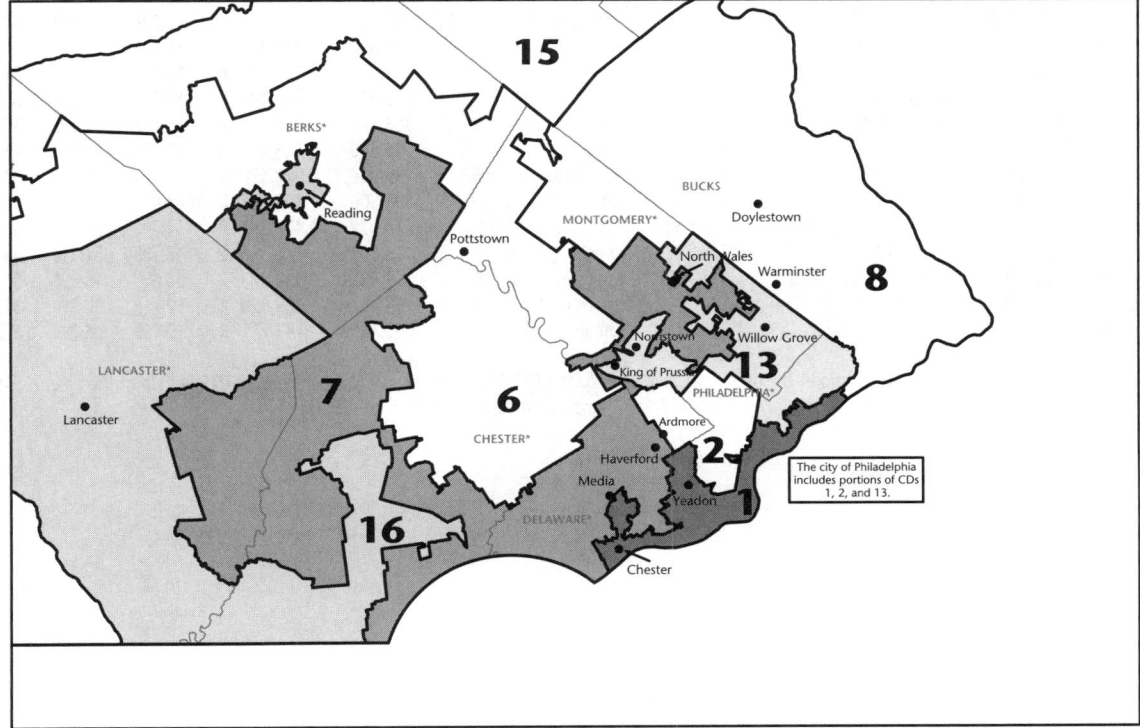

* Asterisk indicates a county whose boundaries include parts of two or more Congressional districts.

PENNSYLVANIA

GOVERNOR

Tom Corbett (R). Elected 2010 to a four-year term.

SENATORS (1 Republican, 1 Democrat)

Bob Casey Jr. (D). Reelected 2012 to a six-year term. Previously elected 2006.

Pat Toomey (R). Elected 2010 to a six-year term.

REPRESENTATIVES (13 Republicans, 5 Democrats)

1. Robert Brady (D)	7. Patrick Meehan (R)	13. Allyson Y. Schwartz (D)
2. Chaka Fattah (D)	8. Mike Fitzpatrick (R)	14. Mike Doyle (D)
3. Mike Kelly (R)	9. Bill Shuster (R)	15. Charlie Dent (R)
4. Scott Perry (R)	10. Tom Marino (R)	16. Joe Pitts (R)
5. Glenn Thompson (R)	11. Lou Barletta (R)	17. Matt Cartwright (D)
6. Jim Gerlach (R)	12. Keith Rothfus (R)	18. Tim Murphy (R)

POSTWAR VOTE FOR PRESIDENT

Year	Total Vote	Republican		Democratic		Other Vote	Rep.-Dem. Plurality	Percentage			
								Total Vote		Major Vote	
		Vote	Candidate	Vote	Candidate			Rep.	Dem.	Rep.	Dem.
2012	5,753,670	2,680,434	Romney, W. Mitt	2,990,274	Obama, Barack H.*	82,962	309,840 D	46.6%	52.0%	47.3%	52.7%
2008	6,013,272	2,655,885	McCain, John S. III	3,276,363	Obama, Barack H.	81,024	620,478 D	44.2%	54.5%	44.8%	55.2%
2004	5,769,590	2,793,847	Bush, George W.*	2,938,095	Kerry, John F.	37,648	144,248 D	48.4%	50.9%	48.7%	51.3%
2000**	4,913,119	2,281,127	Bush, George W.	2,485,967	Gore, Albert Jr.	146,025	204,840 D	46.4%	50.6%	47.9%	52.1%
1996**	4,506,118	1,801,169	Dole, Robert "Bob"	2,215,819	Clinton, Bill*	489,130	414,650 D	40.0%	49.2%	44.8%	55.2%
1992**	4,959,810	1,791,841	Bush, George H.*	2,239,164	Clinton, Bill	928,805	447,323 D	36.1%	45.1%	44.5%	55.5%
1988	4,536,251	2,300,087	Bush, George H.	2,194,944	Dukakis, Michael S.	41,220	105,143 R	50.7%	48.4%	51.2%	48.8%
1984	4,844,903	2,584,323	Reagan, Ronald*	2,228,131	Mondale, Walter F.	32,449	356,192 R	53.3%	46.0%	53.7%	46.3%
1980**	4,561,501	2,261,872	Reagan, Ronald	1,937,540	Carter, Jimmy*	362,089	324,332 R	49.6%	42.5%	53.9%	46.1%
1976	4,620,787	2,205,604	Ford, Gerald R.*	2,328,677	Carter, Jimmy	86,506	123,073 D	47.7%	50.4%	48.6%	51.4%
1972	4,592,106	2,714,521	Nixon, Richard M.*	1,796,951	McGovern, George S.	80,634	917,570 R	59.1%	39.1%	60.2%	39.8%
1968**	4,747,928	2,090,017	Nixon, Richard M.	2,259,405	Humphrey, Hubert H. Jr.	398,506	169,388 D	44.0%	47.6%	48.1%	51.9%
1964	4,822,690	1,673,657	Goldwater, Barry M. Sr.	3,130,954	Johnson, Lyndon B.*	18,079	1,457,297 D	34.7%	64.9%	34.8%	65.2%
1960	5,006,541	2,439,956	Nixon, Richard M.	2,556,282	Kennedy, John F.	10,303	116,326 D	48.7%	51.1%	48.8%	51.2%
1956	4,576,503	2,585,252	Eisenhower, Dwight D.*	1,981,769	Stevenson, Adlai E. II	9,482	603,483 R	56.5%	43.3%	56.6%	43.4%
1952	4,580,969	2,415,789	Eisenhower, Dwight D.	2,146,269	Stevenson, Adlai E. II	18,911	269,520 R	52.7%	46.9%	53.0%	47.0%
1948	3,735,348	1,902,197	Dewey, Thomas E.	1,752,426	Truman, Harry S.*	80,725	149,771 R	50.9%	46.9%	52.0%	48.0%

Note: An asterisk (*) denotes incumbent. **In past elections, the other vote included: 2000 - 103,392 Green (Ralph Nader); 1996 - 430,984 Reform (Ross Perot); 1992 - 902,667 Independent (Perot); 1980 - 292,921 Independent (John Anderson); 1968 - 378,582 American Independent (George Wallace).

PENNSYLVANIA

POSTWAR VOTE FOR GOVERNOR

Year	Total Vote	Republican Vote	Candidate	Democratic Vote	Candidate	Other Vote	Rep.-Dem. Plurality	Percentage Total Vote Rep.	Dem.	Major Vote Rep.	Dem.
2010	3,989,102	2,172,763	Corbett, Tom	1,814,788	Onorato, Dan	1,551	357,975 R	54.5%	45.5%	54.5%	45.5%
2006	4,096,077	1,622,135	Swann, Lynn	2,470,517	Rendell, Edward G.*	3,425	848,382 D	39.6%	60.3%	39.6%	60.4%
2002	3,583,179	1,589,408	Fisher, Mike	1,913,235	Rendell, Edward G.	80,536	323,827 D	44.4%	53.4%	45.4%	54.6%
1998**	3,025,152	1,736,844	Ridge, Thomas J.*	938,745	Itkin, Ivan	349,563	798,099 R	57.4%	31.0%	64.9%	35.1%
1994**	3,588,526	1,627,976	Ridge, Thomas J.	1,433,099	Singel, Mark S.	527,451	194,877 R	45.4%	39.9%	53.2%	46.8%
1990	3,052,760	987,516	Hafer, Barbara	2,065,244	Casey, Robert*		1,077,728 D	32.3%	67.7%	32.3%	67.7%
1986	3,388,275	1,638,268	Scranton, William W.	1,717,484	Casey, Robert	32,523	79,216 D	48.4%	50.7%	48.8%	51.2%
1982	3,683,985	1,872,784	Thornburgh, Richard*	1,772,353	Ertel, Allen E.	38,848	100,431 R	50.8%	48.1%	51.4%	48.6%
1978	3,741,969	1,966,042	Thornburgh, Richard	1,737,888	Flaherty, Peter	38,039	228,154 R	52.5%	46.4%	53.1%	46.9%
1974	3,491,234	1,578,917	Lewis, Andrew L.	1,878,252	Shapp, Milton*	34,065	299,335 D	45.2%	53.8%	45.7%	54.3%
1970	3,700,060	1,542,854	Broderick, Raymond	2,043,029	Shapp, Milton*	114,177	500,175 D	41.7%	55.2%	43.0%	57.0%
1966	4,050,668	2,110,349	Shafer, Raymond P.	1,868,719	Shapp, Milton	71,600	241,630 R	52.1%	46.1%	53.0%	47.0%
1962	4,378,042	2,424,918	Scranton, William W.	1,938,627	Dilworth, Richardson	14,497	486,291 R	55.4%	44.3%	55.6%	44.4%
1958	3,986,918	1,948,769	McGonigle, Arthur T.	2,024,852	Lawrence, David L.	13,297	76,083 D	48.9%	50.8%	49.0%	51.0%
1954	3,720,457	1,717,070	Wood, Lloyd H.	1,996,266	Leader, George M.	7,121	279,196 D	46.2%	53.7%	46.2%	53.8%
1950	3,540,059	1,796,119	Fine, John S.	1,710,355	Dilworth, Richardson	33,585	85,764 R	50.7%	48.3%	51.2%	48.8%
1946	3,123,994	1,828,462	Duff, James H.	1,270,947	Rice, John S.	24,585	557,515 R	58.5%	40.7%	59.0%	41.0%

Note: An asterisk (*) denotes incumbent. **In past elections, the other vote included: 1998 - 315,761 Constitutional (Peg Luksik); 1994 - 460,269 Constitutional (Luksik).

POSTWAR VOTE FOR SENATOR

Year	Total Vote	Republican Vote	Candidate	Democratic Vote	Candidate	Other Vote	Rep.-Dem. Plurality	Percentage Total Vote Rep.	Dem.	Major Vote Rep.	Dem.
2012	5,629,491	2,509,132	Smith, Tom	3,021,364	Casey, Bob Jr.*	98,995	512,232 D	44.6%	53.7%	45.4%	54.6%
2010	3,977,661	2,028,945	Toomey, Pat	1,948,716	Sestak, Joe		80,229 R	51.0%	49.0%	51.0%	49.0%
2006	4,081,043	1,684,778	Santorum, Rick*	2,392,984	Casey, Bob Jr.	3,281	708,206 D	41.3%	58.6%	41.3%	58.7%
2004	5,559,105	2,925,080	Specter, Arlen*	2,334,126	Hoeffel, Joseph M.	299,899	590,954 R	52.6%	42.0%	55.6%	44.4%
2000	4,735,504	2,481,962	Santorum, Rick*	2,154,908	Klink, Ron	98,634	327,054 R	52.4%	45.5%	53.5%	46.5%
1998	2,957,772	1,814,180	Specter, Arlen*	1,028,839	Lloyd, Bill	114,753	785,341 R	61.3%	34.8%	63.8%	36.2%
1994	3,513,361	1,735,691	Santorum, Rick	1,648,481	Wofford, Harris*	129,189	87,210 R	49.4%	46.9%	51.3%	48.7%
1992	4,802,410	2,358,125	Specter, Arlen*	2,224,966	Yeakel, Lynn	219,319	133,159 R	49.1%	46.3%	51.5%	48.5%
1991S	3,382,746	1,521,986	Thornburgh, Richard	1,860,760	Wofford, Harris*		338,774 D	45.0%	55.0%	45.0%	55.0%
1988	4,366,598	2,901,715	Heinz, H. John*	1,416,764	Vignola, Joseph C.	48,119	1,484,951 R	66.5%	32.4%	67.2%	32.8%
1986	3,378,226	1,906,537	Specter, Arlen*	1,448,219	Edgar, Robert W.	23,470	458,318 R	56.4%	42.9%	56.8%	43.2%
1982	3,604,108	2,136,418	Heinz, H. John*	1,412,965	Wecht, Cyril H.	54,725	723,453 R	59.3%	39.2%	60.2%	39.8%
1980	4,418,042	2,230,404	Specter, Arlen	2,122,391	Flaherty, Peter	65,247	108,013 R	50.5%	48.0%	51.2%	48.8%
1976	4,546,353	2,381,891	Heinz, H. John	2,126,977	Green, William J.	37,485	254,914 R	52.4%	46.8%	52.8%	47.2%
1974	3,477,812	1,843,317	Schweiker, Richard S.*	1,596,121	Flaherty, Peter	38,374	247,196 R	53.0%	45.9%	53.6%	46.4%
1970	3,644,305	1,874,106	Scott, Hugh*	1,653,774	Sesler, William G.	116,425	220,332 R	51.4%	45.4%	53.1%	46.9%
1968	4,624,218	2,399,762	Schweiker, Richard S.	2,117,662	Clark, Joseph S.*	106,794	282,100 R	51.9%	45.8%	53.1%	46.9%
1964	4,803,835	2,429,858	Scott, Hugh*	2,359,223	Blatt, Genevieve	14,754	70,635 R	50.6%	49.1%	50.7%	49.3%
1962	4,383,475	2,134,649	Van Zandt, James E.	2,238,383	Clark, Joseph S.*	10,443	103,734 D	48.7%	51.1%	48.8%	51.2%
1958	3,988,622	2,042,586	Scott, Hugh	1,929,821	Leader, George M.	16,215	112,765 R	51.2%	48.4%	51.4%	48.6%
1956	4,529,874	2,250,671	Duff, James H.*	2,268,641	Clark, Joseph S.	10,562	17,970 D	49.7%	50.1%	49.8%	50.2%
1952	4,519,761	2,331,034	Martin, Edward*	2,168,546	Bard, Guy Kurtz	20,181	162,488 R	51.6%	48.0%	51.8%	48.2%
1950	3,548,703	1,820,400	Duff, James H.	1,694,076	Myers, Francis J.*	34,227	126,324 R	51.3%	47.7%	51.8%	48.2%
1946	3,127,860	1,853,458	Martin, Edward	1,245,338	Guffey, Joseph F.*	29,064	608,120 R	59.3%	39.8%	59.8%	40.2%

Note: An asterisk (*) denotes incumbent. **The 1991 election was for a short term to fill a vacancy.

PENNSYLVANIA

PRESIDENT 2012

2010 Census Population	County	Total Vote	Republican (Romney)	Democratic (Obama)	Other	Rep.-Dem. Plurality	Total Vote Rep.	Total Vote Dem.	Major Vote Rep.	Major Vote Dem.
101,407	ADAMS	42,457	26,767	15,091	599	11,676 R	63.0%	35.5%	63.9%	36.1%
1,223,348	ALLEGHENY	622,081	262,039	352,687	7,355	90,648 D	42.1%	56.7%	42.6%	57.4%
68,941	ARMSTRONG	29,602	20,142	9,045	415	11,097 R	68.0%	30.6%	69.0%	31.0%
170,539	BEAVER	80,474	42,344	37,055	1,075	5,289 R	52.6%	46.0%	53.3%	46.7%
49,762	BEDFORD	21,697	16,702	4,788	207	11,914 R	77.0%	22.1%	77.7%	22.3%
411,442	BERKS	170,320	84,702	83,011	2,607	1,691 R	49.7%	48.7%	50.5%	49.5%
127,089	BLAIR	50,241	33,319	16,276	646	17,043 R	66.3%	32.4%	67.2%	32.8%
62,622	BRADFORD	23,426	14,410	8,624	392	5,786 R	61.5%	36.8%	62.6%	37.4%
625,249	BUCKS	321,016	156,579	160,521	3,916	3,942 D	48.8%	50.0%	49.4%	50.6%
183,862	BUTLER	89,445	59,761	28,550	1,134	31,211 R	66.8%	31.9%	67.7%	32.3%
143,679	CAMBRIA	60,526	35,163	24,249	1,114	10,914 R	58.1%	40.1%	59.2%	40.8%
5,085	CAMERON	2,111	1,359	724	28	635 R	64.4%	34.3%	65.2%	34.8%
65,249	CARBON	25,581	13,504	11,580	497	1,924 R	52.8%	45.3%	53.8%	46.2%
153,990	CENTRE	69,626	34,001	34,176	1,449	175 D	48.8%	49.1%	49.9%	50.1%
498,886	CHESTER	251,973	124,840	124,311	2,822	529 R	49.5%	49.3%	50.1%	49.9%
39,988	CLARION	16,186	10,828	5,056	302	5,772 R	66.9%	31.2%	68.2%	31.8%
81,642	CLEARFIELD	31,967	20,347	11,121	499	9,226 R	63.7%	34.8%	64.7%	35.3%
39,238	CLINTON	13,265	7,303	5,734	228	1,569 R	55.1%	43.2%	56.0%	44.0%
67,295	COLUMBIA	25,623	14,236	10,937	450	3,299 R	55.6%	42.7%	56.6%	43.4%
88,765	CRAWFORD	35,388	20,901	13,883	604	7,018 R	59.1%	39.2%	60.1%	39.9%
235,406	CUMBERLAND	110,814	64,809	44,367	1,638	20,442 R	58.5%	40.0%	59.4%	40.6%
268,100	DAUPHIN	124,008	57,450	64,965	1,593	7,515 D	46.3%	52.4%	46.9%	53.1%
558,979	DELAWARE	285,564	110,853	171,792	2,919	60,939 D	38.8%	60.2%	39.2%	60.8%
31,946	ELK	13,238	7,579	5,463	196	2,116 R	57.3%	41.3%	58.1%	41.9%
280,566	ERIE	118,619	49,025	68,036	1,558	19,011 D	41.3%	57.4%	41.9%	58.1%
136,606	FAYETTE	48,505	26,018	21,971	516	4,047 R	53.6%	45.3%	54.2%	45.8%
7,716	FOREST	2,312	1,383	896	33	487 R	59.8%	38.8%	60.7%	39.3%
149,618	FRANKLIN	63,078	43,260	18,995	823	24,265 R	68.6%	30.1%	69.5%	30.5%
14,845	FULTON	6,195	4,814	1,310	71	3,504 R	77.7%	21.1%	78.6%	21.4%
38,686	GREENE	14,464	8,428	5,852	184	2,576 R	58.3%	40.5%	59.0%	41.0%
45,913	HUNTINGDON	17,639	11,979	5,409	251	6,570 R	67.9%	30.7%	68.9%	31.1%
88,880	INDIANA	36,321	21,257	14,473	591	6,784 R	58.5%	39.8%	59.5%	40.5%
45,200	JEFFERSON	18,097	13,048	4,787	262	8,261 R	72.1%	26.5%	73.2%	26.8%
24,636	JUNIATA	9,535	6,862	2,547	126	4,315 R	72.0%	26.7%	72.9%	27.1%
214,437	LACKAWANNA	98,015	35,085	61,838	1,092	26,753 D	35.8%	63.1%	36.2%	63.8%
519,445	LANCASTER	222,436	130,669	88,481	3,286	42,188 R	58.7%	39.8%	59.6%	40.4%
91,108	LAWRENCE	39,036	21,047	17,513	476	3,534 R	53.9%	44.9%	54.6%	45.4%
133,568	LEBANON	56,580	35,872	19,900	808	15,972 R	63.4%	35.2%	64.3%	35.7%
349,497	LEHIGH	147,002	66,874	78,283	1,845	11,409 D	45.5%	53.3%	46.1%	53.9%
320,918	LUZERNE	124,439	58,325	64,307	1,807	5,982 D	46.9%	51.7%	47.6%	52.4%
116,111	LYCOMING	46,493	30,658	15,203	632	15,455 R	65.9%	32.7%	66.8%	33.2%
43,450	MCKEAN	15,108	9,545	5,297	266	4,248 R	63.2%	35.1%	64.3%	35.7%
116,638	MERCER	50,863	25,925	24,232	706	1,693 R	51.0%	47.6%	51.7%	48.3%
46,682	MIFFLIN	16,371	11,939	4,273	159	7,666 R	72.9%	26.1%	73.6%	26.4%
169,842	MONROE	62,917	26,867	35,221	829	8,354 D	42.7%	56.0%	43.3%	56.7%
799,874	MONTGOMERY	412,200	174,381	233,356	4,463	58,975 D	42.3%	56.6%	42.8%	57.2%
18,267	MONTOUR	7,831	4,652	3,053	126	1,599 R	59.4%	39.0%	60.4%	39.6%
297,735	NORTHAMPTON	130,735	61,446	67,606	1,683	6,160 D	47.0%	51.7%	47.6%	52.4%
94,528	NORTHUMBERLAND	33,212	19,518	13,072	622	6,446 R	58.8%	39.4%	59.9%	40.1%
45,969	PERRY	19,128	13,120	5,685	323	7,435 R	68.6%	29.7%	69.8%	30.2%
1,526,006	PHILADELPHIA	690,327	96,467	588,806	5,054	492,339 D	14.0%	85.3%	14.1%	85.9%
57,369	PIKE	23,279	12,786	10,210	283	2,576 R	54.9%	43.9%	55.6%	44.4%
17,457	POTTER	7,242	5,231	1,897	114	3,334 R	72.2%	26.2%	73.4%	26.6%
148,289	SCHUYLKILL	57,727	32,278	24,546	903	7,732 R	55.9%	42.5%	56.8%	43.2%
39,702	SNYDER	15,002	10,073	4,687	242	5,386 R	67.1%	31.2%	68.2%	31.8%
77,742	SOMERSET	33,942	23,984	9,436	522	14,548 R	70.7%	27.8%	71.8%	28.2%
6,428	SULLIVAN	2,949	1,868	1,034	47	834 R	63.3%	35.1%	64.4%	35.6%
43,356	SUSQUEHANNA	18,044	10,800	6,935	309	3,865 R	59.9%	38.4%	60.9%	39.1%
41,981	TIOGA	17,004	11,342	5,357	305	5,985 R	66.7%	31.5%	67.9%	32.1%
44,947	UNION	16,268	9,896	6,109	263	3,787 R	60.8%	37.6%	61.8%	38.2%

PENNSYLVANIA

PRESIDENT 2012

2010 Census Population	County	Total Vote	Republican (Romney)	Democratic (Obama)	Other	Rep.-Dem. Plurality	Percentage			
							Total Vote		Major Vote	
							Rep.	Dem.	Rep.	Dem.
54,984	VENANGO	22,167	13,815	7,945	407	5,870 R	62.3%	35.8%	63.5%	36.5%
41,815	WARREN	17,299	10,010	6,995	294	3,015 R	57.9%	40.4%	58.9%	41.1%
207,820	WASHINGTON	94,750	53,230	40,345	1,175	12,885 R	56.2%	42.6%	56.9%	43.1%
52,822	WAYNE	21,607	12,896	8,396	315	4,500 R	59.7%	38.9%	60.6%	39.4%
365,169	WESTMORELAND	169,572	103,932	63,722	1,918	40,210 R	61.3%	37.6%	62.0%	38.0%
28,276	WYOMING	11,872	6,587	5,061	224	1,526 R	55.5%	42.6%	56.6%	43.4%
434,972	YORK	189,229	113,304	73,191	2,734	40,113 R	59.9%	38.7%	60.8%	39.2%
	Votes Not Reported by County	11,630			11,630					
12,702,379	TOTAL	5,753,670	2,680,434	2,990,274	82,962	309,840 D	46.6%	52.0%	47.3%	52.7%

PENNSYLVANIA

SENATOR 2012

2010 Census Population	County	Total Vote	Republican (Smith)	Democratic (Casey)	Other	Rep.-Dem. Plurality	Percentage			
							Total Vote		Major Vote	
							Rep.	Dem.	Rep.	Dem.
101,407	ADAMS	42,232	25,467	15,763	1,002	9,704 R	60.3%	37.3%	61.8%	38.2%
1,223,348	ALLEGHENY	611,111	236,546	362,459	12,106	125,913 D	38.7%	59.3%	39.5%	60.5%
68,941	ARMSTRONG	29,512	19,442	9,496	574	9,946 R	65.9%	32.2%	67.2%	32.8%
170,539	BEAVER	79,763	38,092	39,970	1,701	1,878 D	47.8%	50.1%	48.8%	51.2%
49,762	BEDFORD	21,573	15,673	5,553	347	10,120 R	72.7%	25.7%	73.8%	26.2%
411,442	BERKS	165,991	78,679	84,403	2,909	5,724 D	47.4%	50.8%	48.2%	51.8%
127,089	BLAIR	50,187	31,666	17,424	1,097	14,242 R	63.1%	34.7%	64.5%	35.5%
62,622	BRADFORD	23,238	14,423	8,234	581	6,189 R	62.1%	35.4%	63.7%	36.3%
625,249	BUCKS	314,156	147,595	162,258	4,303	14,663 D	47.0%	51.6%	47.6%	52.4%
183,862	BUTLER	88,691	56,320	30,620	1,751	25,700 R	63.5%	34.5%	64.8%	35.2%
143,679	CAMBRIA	60,311	30,202	28,779	1,330	1,423 R	50.1%	47.7%	51.2%	48.8%
5,085	CAMERON	2,113	1,277	767	69	510 R	60.4%	36.3%	62.5%	37.5%
65,249	CARBON	25,271	12,758	11,924	589	834 R	50.5%	47.2%	51.7%	48.3%
153,990	CENTRE	68,480	32,112	34,156	2,212	2,044 D	46.9%	49.9%	48.5%	51.5%
498,886	CHESTER	249,565	119,296	125,671	4,598	6,375 D	47.8%	50.4%	48.7%	51.3%
39,988	CLARION	16,141	10,451	5,105	585	5,346 R	64.7%	31.6%	67.2%	32.8%
81,642	CLEARFIELD	31,844	19,845	11,286	713	8,559 R	62.3%	35.4%	63.7%	36.3%
39,238	CLINTON	13,172	7,020	5,857	295	1,163 R	53.3%	44.5%	54.5%	45.5%
67,295	COLUMBIA	25,437	13,509	11,336	592	2,173 R	53.1%	44.6%	54.4%	45.6%
88,765	CRAWFORD	35,213	21,140	13,146	927	7,994 R	60.0%	37.3%	61.7%	38.3%
235,406	CUMBERLAND	110,035	61,296	46,294	2,445	15,002 R	55.7%	42.1%	57.0%	43.0%
268,100	DAUPHIN	120,610	53,649	65,235	1,726	11,586 D	44.5%	54.1%	45.1%	54.9%
558,979	DELAWARE	276,942	103,719	170,477	2,746	66,758 D	37.5%	61.6%	37.8%	62.2%
31,946	ELK	13,179	7,182	5,611	386	1,571 R	54.5%	42.6%	56.1%	43.9%
280,566	ERIE	116,951	48,708	65,406	2,837	16,698 D	41.6%	55.9%	42.7%	57.3%
136,606	FAYETTE	48,094	22,950	24,298	846	1,348 D	47.7%	50.5%	48.6%	51.4%
7,716	FOREST	2,301	1,356	884	61	472 R	58.9%	38.4%	60.5%	39.5%
149,618	FRANKLIN	62,709	41,697	19,726	1,286	21,971 R	66.5%	31.5%	67.9%	32.1%
14,845	FULTON	6,137	4,407	1,605	125	2,802 R	71.8%	26.2%	73.3%	26.7%
38,686	GREENE	14,299	7,262	6,768	269	494 R	50.8%	47.3%	51.8%	48.2%
45,913	HUNTINGDON	17,539	11,285	5,820	434	5,465 R	64.3%	33.2%	66.0%	34.0%
88,880	INDIANA	36,203	20,452	14,908	843	5,544 R	56.5%	41.2%	57.8%	42.2%
45,200	JEFFERSON	18,086	12,780	4,878	428	7,902 R	70.7%	27.0%	72.4%	27.6%
24,636	JUNIATA	9,551	6,337	3,010	204	3,327 R	66.3%	31.5%	67.8%	32.2%
214,437	LACKAWANNA	97,411	30,928	64,940	1,543	34,012 D	31.8%	66.7%	32.3%	67.7%

PENNSYLVANIA

SENATOR 2012

2010 Census Population	County	Total Vote	Republican (Smith)	Democratic (Casey)	Other	Rep.-Dem. Plurality	Percentage			
							Total Vote		Major Vote	
							Rep.	Dem.	Rep.	Dem.
519,445	LANCASTER	220,300	127,135	88,778	4,387	38,357 R	57.7%	40.3%	58.9%	41.1%
91,108	LAWRENCE	38,645	19,353	18,603	689	750 R	50.1%	48.1%	51.0%	49.0%
133,568	LEBANON	55,960	33,843	21,007	1,110	12,836 R	60.5%	37.5%	61.7%	38.3%
349,497	LEHIGH	144,310	62,071	79,527	2,712	17,456 D	43.0%	55.1%	43.8%	56.2%
320,918	LUZERNE	122,857	53,168	66,951	2,738	13,783 D	43.3%	54.5%	44.3%	55.7%
116,111	LYCOMING	46,154	29,024	16,179	951	12,845 R	62.9%	35.1%	64.2%	35.8%
43,450	MCKEAN	14,921	9,250	5,355	316	3,895 R	62.0%	35.9%	63.3%	36.7%
116,638	MERCER	50,187	24,772	24,314	1,101	458 R	49.4%	48.4%	50.5%	49.5%
46,682	MIFFLIN	16,304	11,099	4,937	268	6,162 R	68.1%	30.3%	69.2%	30.8%
169,842	MONROE	59,999	25,579	33,502	918	7,923 D	42.6%	55.8%	43.3%	56.7%
799,874	MONTGOMERY	402,791	163,882	235,197	3,712	71,315 D	40.7%	58.4%	41.1%	58.9%
18,267	MONTOUR	7,746	4,435	3,121	190	1,314 R	57.3%	40.3%	58.7%	41.3%
297,735	NORTHAMPTON	126,292	56,268	68,203	1,821	11,935 D	44.6%	54.0%	45.2%	54.8%
94,528	NORTHUMBERLAND	32,681	19,057	12,904	720	6,153 R	58.3%	39.5%	59.6%	40.4%
45,969	PERRY	19,092	12,420	6,168	504	6,252 R	65.1%	32.3%	66.8%	33.2%
1,526,006	PHILADELPHIA	653,850	84,461	564,886	4,503	480,425 D	12.9%	86.4%	13.0%	87.0%
57,369	PIKE	22,798	12,267	10,081	450	2,186 R	53.8%	44.2%	54.9%	45.1%
17,457	POTTER	7,154	5,035	1,950	169	3,085 R	70.4%	27.3%	72.1%	27.9%
148,289	SCHUYLKILL	57,468	31,625	24,639	1,204	6,986 R	55.0%	42.9%	56.2%	43.8%
39,702	SNYDER	14,868	9,851	4,651	366	5,200 R	66.3%	31.3%	67.9%	32.1%
77,742	SOMERSET	33,800	22,190	10,866	744	11,324 R	65.7%	32.1%	67.1%	32.9%
6,428	SULLIVAN	2,925	1,803	1,050	72	753 R	61.6%	35.9%	63.2%	36.8%
43,356	SUSQUEHANNA	18,022	10,555	7,082	385	3,473 R	58.6%	39.3%	59.8%	40.2%
41,981	TIOGA	16,815	11,179	5,255	381	5,924 R	66.5%	31.3%	68.0%	32.0%
44,947	UNION	16,074	9,592	6,112	370	3,480 R	59.7%	38.0%	61.1%	38.9%
54,984	VENANGO	22,032	13,608	7,816	608	5,792 R	61.8%	35.5%	63.5%	36.5%
41,815	WARREN	17,051	10,136	6,432	483	3,704 R	59.4%	37.7%	61.2%	38.8%
207,820	WASHINGTON	93,608	48,047	43,711	1,850	4,336 R	51.3%	46.7%	52.4%	47.6%
52,822	WAYNE	21,500	12,276	8,791	433	3,485 R	57.1%	40.9%	58.3%	41.7%
365,169	WESTMORELAND	167,709	95,218	69,431	3,060	25,787 R	56.8%	41.4%	57.8%	42.2%
28,276	WYOMING	11,818	6,391	5,117	310	1,274 R	54.1%	43.3%	55.5%	44.5%
434,972	YORK	187,643	108,021	74,681	4,941	33,340 R	57.6%	39.8%	59.1%	40.9%
	Votes Not Reported by County	2,069			2,069					
12,702,379	TOTAL	5,629,491	2,509,132	3,021,364	98,995	512,232 D	44.6%	53.7%	45.4%	54.6%

PENNSYLVANIA

HOUSE OF REPRESENTATIVES

			Republican		Democratic		Other Vote	Rep.-Dem. Plurality	Percentage			
									Total Vote		Major Vote	
CD	Year	Total Vote	Vote	Candidate	Vote	Candidate			Rep.	Dem.	Rep.	Dem.
1	2012	277,102	41,708	FEATHERMAN, JOHN J.	235,394	BRADY, ROBERT*		193,686 D	15.1%	84.9%	15.1%	84.9%
2	2012	356,386	33,381	MANSFIELD, ROBERT	318,176	FATTAH, CHAKA*	4,829	284,795 D	9.4%	89.3%	9.5%	90.5%
3	2012	302,514	165,826	KELLY, MIKE*	123,933	EATON, MISSA	12,755	41,893 R	54.8%	41.0%	57.2%	42.8%
4	2012	303,980	181,603	PERRY, SCOTT	104,643	PERKINSON, HARRY	17,734	76,960 R	59.7%	34.4%	63.4%	36.6%
5	2012	282,465	177,740	THOMPSON, GLENN*	104,725	DUMAS, CHARLES		73,015 R	62.9%	37.1%	62.9%	37.1%
6	2012	335,528	191,725	GERLACH, JIM*	143,803	TRIVEDI, MANAN		47,922 R	57.1%	42.9%	57.1%	42.9%
7	2012	353,451	209,942	MEEHAN, PATRICK*	143,509	BADEY, GEORGE		66,433 R	59.4%	40.6%	59.4%	40.6%
8	2012	352,238	199,379	FITZPATRICK, MIKE*	152,859	BOOCKVAR, KATHY		46,520 R	56.6%	43.4%	56.6%	43.4%
9	2012	274,305	169,177	SHUSTER, BILL*	105,128	RAMSBURG, KAREN		64,049 R	61.7%	38.3%	61.7%	38.3%
10	2012	273,790	179,563	MARINO, TOM*	94,227	SCOLLO, PHILLIP		85,336 R	65.6%	34.4%	65.6%	34.4%
11	2012	285,198	166,967	BARLETTA, LOU*	118,231	STILP, GENE		48,736 R	58.5%	41.5%	58.5%	41.5%
12	2012	338,941	175,352	ROTHFUS, KEITH	163,589	CRITZ, MARK S.*		11,763 R	51.7%	48.3%	51.7%	48.3%
13	2012	303,819	93,918	ROONEY, JOE	209,901	SCHWARTZ, ALLYSON Y.*		115,983 D	30.9%	69.1%	30.9%	69.1%
14	2012	327,634	75,702	LESSMANN, HANS	251,932	DOYLE, MIKE*		176,230 D	23.1%	76.9%	23.1%	76.9%
15	2012	297,724	168,960	DENT, CHARLIE*	128,764	DAUGHERTY, RICK		40,196 R	56.8%	43.2%	56.8%	43.2%
16	2012	284,781	156,192	PITTS, JOE*	111,185	STRADER, ARYANNA	17,404	45,007 R	54.8%	39.0%	58.4%	41.6%
17	2012	267,601	106,208	CUMMINGS, LAUREEN	161,393	CARTWRIGHT, MATT		55,185 D	39.7%	60.3%	39.7%	60.3%
18	2012	338,873	216,727	MURPHY, TIM*	122,146	MAGGI, LARRY		94,581 R	64.0%	36.0%	64.0%	36.0%
TOTAL	2012	5,556,330	2,710,070		2,793,538		52,722	83,468 D	48.8%	50.3%	49.2%	50.8%

Notes: An asterisk (*) denotes incumbent. Pennsylvania tallied the total number of write-in votes for all districts as 4,265. It does not provide a district-by-district count of write-in votes for the general election.

PENNSYLVANIA

GENERAL AND PRIMARY ELECTIONS

GENERAL ELECTIONS: OTHER VOTE

President   Other vote was 49,991 Libertarian (Gary E. Johnson), 21,341 Green (Jill Stein), 11,247 Write-in (Scattered Write-In), 383 Write-in (Virgil H. Goode)

Senator   Other vote was 96,926 Libertarian (Ray Burn Smith), 2,069 Write-in (Scattered Write-In)

House   Other vote was:

CD 2   4,829 Independent (James Foster)
CD 3   12,755 Independent (Steven C. Porter)
CD 4   11,524 Independent (Wayne Wolff), 6,210 Libertarian (Mike Koffenberger)
CD 16   12,250 Independent (John Murphy), 5,154 Independent (James Bednarksi)

Statewide   4,265 scattered write-ins were not enumerated by district.

PRIMARY ELECTIONS: SUPPLEMENTARY INFORMATION

Primary	April 24, 2012	**Registration** (as of April 24, 2012)	8,207,355	Democratic	4,131,280
				Republican	3,061,125
				Other	1,014,950

Primary Type   Closed—Only registered Democrats and Republicans could vote in their party's primary.

PENNSYLVANIA

GENERAL AND PRIMARY ELECTIONS

	REPUBLICAN PRIMARIES			DEMOCRATIC PRIMARIES		
President	Romney, W. Mitt	468,374	57.8%	Obama, Barack H.*	616,102	97.0%
	Santorum, Rick	149,056	18.4%	Scattered Write-In	19,082	3.0%
	Paul, Ron	106,148	13.1%			
	Gingrich, Newt	84,537	10.4%			
	Scattered Write-In	2,819	0.3%			
	TOTAL	810,934		TOTAL	635,184	
Senator	Smith, Tom	299,726	39.4%	Casey, Bob Jr.*	565,488	80.6%
	Rohrer, Samuel E.	169,118	22.2%	Vodvarka, Joseph John	133,683	19.1%
	Welch, Steven D.	158,181	20.8%	Scattered Write-In	2,441	0.3%
	Christian, David A.	79,581	10.5%			
	Scaringi, Marc A.	51,908	6.8%			
	Scattered Write-In	2,044	0.3%			
	TOTAL	760,558		TOTAL	701,612	
Congressional District 1	Featherman, John J.	10,288	99.9%	Brady, Robert*	42,744	99.9%
	Scattered Write-In	11	0.1%	Scattered Write-In	39	0.1%
	TOTAL	10,299		TOTAL	42,783	
Congressional District 2	Mansfield, Robert	5,562	99.8%	Fattah, Chaka*	87,620	99.9%
	Scattered Write-In	12	0.2%	Scattered Write-In	66	0.1%
	TOTAL	5,574		TOTAL	87,686	
Congressional District 3	Kelly, Mike*	46,382	99.5%	Eaton, Missa	28,355	99.3%
	Scattered Write-In	215	0.5%	Scattered Write-In	188	0.7%
	TOTAL	46,597		TOTAL	28,543	
Congressional District 4	Perry, Scott	34,881	53.4%	Perkinson, Harry	14,188	55.6%
	Reilly, Christopher B.	12,143	18.6%	Lee, Ken	11,134	43.6%
	Summers, Sean	9,316	14.3%	Scattered Write-In	203	0.8%
	Waga, Theodore	3,086	4.7%			
	Martin, Eric Robert	2,159	3.3%			
	Swomley, Mark M.	2,150	3.3%			
	Downs, Kevin E	1,451	2.2%			
	Scattered Write-In	111	0.2%			
	TOTAL	65,297		TOTAL	25,525	
Congressional District 5	Thompson, Glenn*	49,941	99.5%	Dumas, Charles	25,252	98.9%
	Scattered Write-In	263	0.5%	Scattered Write-In	278	1.1%
	TOTAL	50,204		TOTAL	25,530	
Congressional District 6	Gerlach, Jim*	45,206	99.4%	Trivedi, Manan	20,037	99.5%
	Scattered Write-In	274	0.6%	Scattered Write-In	94	0.5%
	TOTAL	45,480		TOTAL	20,131	
Congressional District 7	Meehan, Patrick*	55,387	99.9%	Badey, George	20,075	99.9%
	Scattered Write-In	67	0.1%	Scattered Write-In	26	0.1%
	TOTAL	55,454		TOTAL	20,101	
Congressional District 8	Fitzpatrick, Mike*	42,935	100.0%	Boockvar, Kathy	25,595	100.0%
	TOTAL	42,935		TOTAL	25,595	
Congressional District 9	Shuster, Bill*	41,735	100.0%	Ramsburg, Karen	1,581	76.5%
				Scattered Write-In	485	23.5%
	TOTAL	41,735		TOTAL	2,066	
Congressional District 10	Marino, Tom*	51,373	99.7%	Scollo, Phillip	19,291	99.1%
	Scattered Write-In	161	0.3%	Scattered Write-In	182	0.9%
	TOTAL	51,534		TOTAL	19,473	

PENNSYLVANIA

GENERAL AND PRIMARY ELECTIONS

	REPUBLICAN PRIMARIES			DEMOCRATIC PRIMARIES		
Congressional District 11	Barletta, Lou*	49,511	99.4%	Stilp, Gene	18,716	54.1%
	Scattered Write-In	286	0.6%	Vinsko, Bill	15,609	45.1%
				Scattered Write-In	276	0.8%
	TOTAL	49,797		TOTAL	34,601	
Congressional District 12	Rothfus, Keith	44,360	99.2%	Critz, Mark S.*	32,384	51.0%
	Scattered Write-In	362	0.8%	Altmire, Jason*	30,895	48.7%
				Scattered Write-In	176	0.3%
	TOTAL	44,722		TOTAL	63,455	
Congressional District 13	Rooney, Joe	21,644	100.0%	Schwartz, Allyson Y.*	36,756	99.9%
	Scattered Write-In	5		Scattered Write-In	35	0.1%
	TOTAL	21,649		TOTAL	36,791	
Congressional District 14	Lessmann, Hans	15,936	98.6%	Doyle, Mike*	50,323	79.9%
	Scattered Write-In	225	1.4%	Brooks, Janis C.	12,484	19.8%
				Scattered Write-In	149	0.2%
	TOTAL	16,161		TOTAL	62,956	
Congressional District 15	Dent, Charlie*	38,651	99.8%	Daugherty, Rick	14,623	58.7%
	Scattered Write-In	74	0.2%	Eaton, Jackson	10,265	41.2%
				Scattered Write-In	29	0.1%
	TOTAL	38,725		TOTAL	24,917	
Congressional District 16	Pitts, Joe*	44,110	99.2%	Strader, Aryanna	15,839	99.5%
	Scattered Write-In	374	0.8%	Scattered Write-In	82	0.5%
	TOTAL	44,484		TOTAL	15,921	
Congressional District 17	Cummings, Laureen	26,953	98.1%	Cartwright, Matt	33,255	57.1%
	Scattered Write-In	524	1.9%	Holden, Tim*	24,953	42.8%
				Scattered Write-In	60	0.1%
	TOTAL	27,477		TOTAL	58,268	
Congressional District 18	Murphy, Tim*	32,854	63.4%	Maggi, Larry	39,096	99.3%
	Feinberg, Evan	18,937	36.5%	Scattered Write-In	279	0.7%
	Scattered Write-In	67	0.1%			
	TOTAL	51,858		TOTAL	39,375	

Notes: An asterisk (*) denotes incumbent. Due to redistricting, the 12th district Democratic primary pitted two incumbents against each other (Critz, former 12th district, and Altmire, former 4th district).

RHODE ISLAND

Congressional districts first established for elections held in 2012

2 members

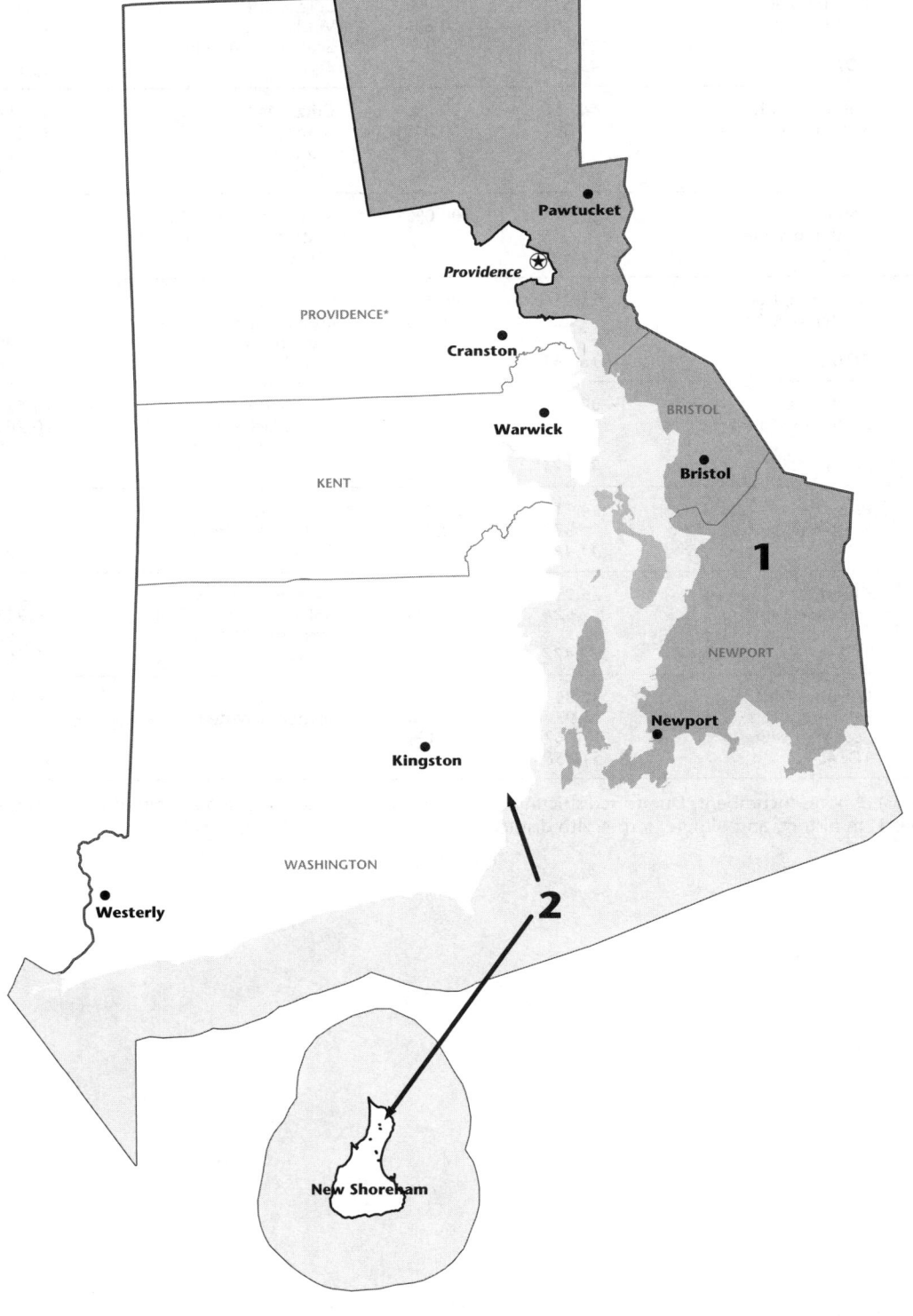

* Asterisk indicates a county whose boundaries include parts of two or more Congressional districts.

RHODE ISLAND

GOVERNOR

Lincoln D. Chafee (D). Elected 2010 to a four-year term. Registered as an independent until May 30, 2013 when he became a Democrat.

SENATORS (2 Democrats)

Jack Reed (D). Reelected 2008 to a six-year term. Previously elected 2002, 1996.

Sheldon Whitehouse (D). Reelected 2012 to a six-year term. Previously elected 2006.

REPRESENTATIVES (2 Democrats)

1. David Cicilline (D)   2. Jim Langevin (D)

POSTWAR VOTE FOR PRESIDENT

		Republican		Democratic		Other	Rep.-Dem.	Percentage			
								Total Vote		Major Vote	
Year	Total Vote	Vote	Candidate	Vote	Candidate	Vote	Plurality	Rep.	Dem.	Rep.	Dem.
2012	446,049	157,204	Romney, W. Mitt	279,677	Obama, Barack H.*	9,168	122,473 D	35.2%	62.7%	36.0%	64.0%
2008	471,766	165,391	McCain, John S. III	296,571	Obama, Barack H.	9,804	131,180 D	35.1%	62.9%	35.8%	64.2%
2004	437,134	169,046	Bush, George W.*	259,760	Kerry, John F.	8,328	90,714 D	38.7%	59.4%	39.4%	60.6%
2000**	409,047	130,555	Bush, George W.	249,508	Gore, Albert Jr.	28,984	118,953 D	31.9%	61.0%	34.4%	65.6%
1996**	390,284	104,683	Dole, Robert "Bob"	233,050	Clinton, Bill*	52,551	128,367 D	26.8%	59.7%	31.0%	69.0%
1992**	453,477	131,601	Bush, George H.*	213,299	Clinton, Bill	108,577	81,698 D	29.0%	47.0%	38.2%	61.8%
1988	404,620	177,761	Bush, George H.	225,123	Dukakis, Michael S.	1,736	47,362 D	43.9%	55.6%	44.1%	55.9%
1984	410,492	212,080	Reagan, Ronald*	197,106	Mondale, Walter F.	1,306	14,974 R	51.7%	48.0%	51.8%	48.2%
1980**	416,072	154,793	Reagan, Ronald	198,342	Carter, Jimmy*	62,937	43,549 D	37.2%	47.7%	43.8%	56.2%
1976	411,170	181,249	Ford, Gerald R.*	227,636	Carter, Jimmy	2,285	46,387 D	44.1%	55.4%	44.3%	55.7%
1972	415,808	220,383	Nixon, Richard M.*	194,645	McGovern, George S.	780	25,738 R	53.0%	46.8%	53.1%	46.9%
1968**	385,000	122,359	Nixon, Richard M.	246,518	Humphrey, Hubert H. Jr.	16,123	124,159 D	31.8%	64.0%	33.2%	66.8%
1964	390,091	74,615	Goldwater, Barry M. Sr.	315,463	Johnson, Lyndon B.*	13	240,848 D	19.1%	80.9%	19.1%	80.9%
1960	405,535	147,502	Nixon, Richard M.	258,032	Kennedy, John F.	1	110,530 D	36.4%	63.6%	36.4%	63.6%
1956	387,609	225,819	Eisenhower, Dwight D.*	161,790	Stevenson, Adlai E. II		64,029 R	58.3%	41.7%	58.3%	41.7%
1952	414,498	210,935	Eisenhower, Dwight D.	203,293	Stevenson, Adlai E. II	270	7,642 R	50.9%	49.0%	50.9%	49.1%
1948	327,702	135,787	Dewey, Thomas E.	188,736	Truman, Harry S.*	3,179	52,949 D	41.4%	57.6%	41.8%	58.2%

Note: An asterisk (*) denotes incumbent. **In past elections, the other vote included: 2000 - 25,052 Green (Ralph Nader); 1996 - 43,723 Reform (Ross Perot); 1992 - 105,045 Independent (Perot); 1980 - 59,819 Independent (John Anderson); 1968 - 15,678 American Independent (George Wallace).

RHODE ISLAND

POSTWAR VOTE FOR GOVERNOR

Year	Total Vote	Republican		Democratic		Other Vote	Rep.-Dem. Plurality	Percentage			
								Total Vote		Major Vote	
		Vote	Candidate	Vote	Candidate			Rep.	Dem.	Rep.	Dem.
2010**	342,545	114,911	Robitaille, John F.	78,896	Caprio, Frank T.	148,738	36,015 R**	33.5%	23.0%	59.3%	40.7%
2006	387,010	197,366	Carcieri, Donald L.*	189,562	Fogarty, Charles J.	82	7,804 R	51.0%	49.0%	51.0%	49.0%
2002	332,655	181,827	Carcieri, Donald L.	150,229	York, Myrth	599	31,598 R	54.7%	45.2%	54.8%	45.2%
1998	306,383	156,180	Almond, Lincoln C.*	129,105	York, Myrth	21,098	27,075 R	51.0%	42.1%	54.7%	45.3%
1994**	361,377	171,194	Almond, Lincoln C.	157,361	York, Myrth	32,822	13,833 R	47.4%	43.5%	52.1%	47.9%
1992	424,818	145,590	Leonard, Elizabeth Ann	261,484	Sundlun, Bruce G.*	17,744	115,894 D	34.3%	61.6%	35.8%	64.2%
1990	356,672	92,177	Diprete, Edward*	264,411	Sundlun, Bruce G.	84	172,234 D	25.8%	74.1%	25.8%	74.2%
1988	400,516	203,550	Diprete, Edward*	196,936	Sundlun, Bruce G.	30	6,614 R	50.8%	49.2%	50.8%	49.2%
1986	322,724	208,822	Diprete, Edward*	104,508	Sundlun, Bruce G.	9,394	104,314 R	64.7%	32.4%	66.6%	33.4%
1984	408,375	245,059	Diprete, Edward	163,311	Solomon, Anthony J.	5	81,748 R	60.0%	40.0%	60.0%	40.0%
1982	337,259	79,602	Marzullo, Vincent	247,208	Garrahy, J. Joseph*	10,449	167,606 D	23.6%	73.3%	24.4%	75.6%
1980	405,916	106,729	Cianci, Vincent A.	299,174	Garrahy, J. Joseph*	13	192,445 D	26.3%	73.7%	26.3%	73.7%
1978	314,363	96,596	Almond, Lincoln C.	197,386	Garrahy, J. Joseph*	20,381	100,790 D	30.7%	62.8%	32.9%	67.1%
1976	398,683	178,254	Taft, James L.	218,561	Garrahy, J. Joseph	1,868	40,307 D	44.7%	54.8%	44.9%	55.1%
1974	321,660	69,224	Nugent, James W.	252,436	Noel, Philip W.*		183,212 D	21.5%	78.5%	21.5%	78.5%
1972	412,866	194,315	DeSimone, Herbert F.	216,953	Noel, Philip W.	1,598	22,638 D	47.1%	52.5%	47.2%	52.8%
1970	346,342	171,549	DeSimone, Herbert F.	173,420	Licht, Frank*	1,373	1,871 D	49.5%	50.1%	49.7%	50.3%
1968	383,725	187,958	Chafee, John H.*	195,766	Licht, Frank	1	7,808 D	49.0%	51.0%	49.0%	51.0%
1966	332,064	210,202	Chafee, John H.*	121,862	Hobbs, Horace E.		88,340 R	63.3%	36.7%	63.3%	36.7%
1964	391,668	239,501	Chafee, John H.*	152,165	Gallogly, Edward P.	2	87,336 R	61.1%	38.9%	61.1%	38.9%
1962	327,506	163,952	Chafee, John H.	163,554	Notte, John A. Jr.*		398 R	50.1%	49.9%	50.1%	49.9%
1960	401,362	174,044	Del Sesto, Christopher*	227,318	Notte, John A. Jr.		53,274 D	43.4%	56.6%	43.4%	56.6%
1958	346,780	176,505	Del Sesto, Christopher	170,275	Roberts, Dennis J.*		6,230 R	50.9%	49.1%	50.9%	49.1%
1956	383,919	191,604	Del Sesto, Christopher	192,315	Roberts, Dennis J.*		711 D	49.9%	50.1%	49.9%	50.1%
1954	328,670	137,131	Lewis, Dean J.	189,595	Roberts, Dennis J.*	1,944	52,464 D	41.7%	57.7%	42.0%	58.0%
1952	409,689	194,102	Archambault, Raoul Jr.	215,587	Roberts, Dennis J.*		21,485 D	47.4%	52.6%	47.4%	52.6%
1950	296,808	120,683	Lachapelle, Eugene J.	176,125	Roberts, Dennis J.		55,442 D	40.7%	59.3%	40.7%	59.3%
1948	323,863	124,441	Ruerat, Albert P.	198,056	Pastore, John O.*	1,366	73,615 D	38.4%	61.2%	38.6%	61.4%
1946	275,341	126,456	Murphy, John G.	148,885	Pastore, John O.*		22,429 D	45.9%	54.1%	45.9%	54.1%

Note: An asterisk (*) denotes incumbent. **In past elections, the other vote included: 2010 - 123,571 Independent (Lincoln Chafee), who was elected with 36.1 percent of the total vote. The term of office of Rhode Island's governor was increased from two to four years effective with the 1994 election.

POSTWAR VOTE FOR SENATOR

Year	Total Vote	Republican		Democratic		Other Vote	Rep.-Dem. Plurality	Percentage			
								Total Vote		Major Vote	
		Vote	Candidate	Vote	Candidate			Rep.	Dem.	Rep.	Dem.
2012	418,189	146,222	Hinckley, Barry	271,034	Whitehouse, Sheldon*	933	124,812 D	35.0%	64.8%	35.0%	65.0%
2008	438,812	116,174	Tingle, Robert G.	320,644	Reed, Jack*	1,994	204,470 D	26.5%	73.1%	26.6%	73.4%
2006	385,451	179,001	Chafee, Lincoln D.*	206,110	Whitehouse, Sheldon	340	27,109 D	46.4%	53.5%	46.5%	53.5%
2002	323,912	69,881	Tingle, Robert G.	253,922	Reed, Jack*	109	184,041 D	21.6%	78.4%	21.6%	78.4%
2000	391,537	222,588	Chafee, Lincoln D.*	161,023	Weygand, Robert A.	7,926	61,565 R	56.8%	41.1%	58.0%	42.0%
1996	363,371	127,368	Mayer, Nancy	230,676	Reed, Jack	5,327	103,308 D	35.1%	63.5%	35.6%	64.4%
1994	345,388	222,856	Chafee, John H.*	122,532	Kushner, Linda J.		100,324 R	64.5%	35.5%	64.5%	35.5%
1990	364,062	138,947	Schneider, Claudine	225,105	Pell, Claiborne*	10	86,158 D	38.2%	61.8%	38.2%	61.8%
1988	397,996	217,273	Chafee, John H.*	180,717	Licht, Richard A.	6	36,556 R	54.6%	45.4%	54.6%	45.4%
1984	395,285	108,492	Leonard, Barbara	286,780	Pell, Claiborne*	13	178,288 D	27.4%	72.6%	27.4%	72.6%
1982	342,779	175,495	Chafee, John H.*	167,283	Michaelson, Julius C.	1	8,212 R	51.2%	48.8%	51.2%	48.8%
1978	305,618	76,061	Reynolds, James G.	229,557	Pell, Claiborne*		153,496 D	24.9%	75.1%	24.9%	75.1%
1976	398,906	230,329	Chafee, John H.*	167,665	Lorber, Richard P.	912	62,664 R	57.7%	42.0%	57.9%	42.1%
1972	413,432	188,990	Chafee, John H.	221,942	Pell, Claiborne*	2,500	32,952 D	45.7%	53.7%	46.0%	54.0%
1970	341,222	107,351	McLaughlin, John	230,469	Pastore, John O.*	3,402	123,118 D	31.5%	67.5%	31.8%	68.2%
1966	324,173	104,838	Briggs, Ruth M.	219,331	Pell, Claiborne*	4	114,493 D	32.3%	67.7%	32.3%	67.7%
1964	386,322	66,715	Lagueux, Ronald R.	319,607	Pastore, John O.*		252,892 D	17.3%	82.7%	17.3%	82.7%
1960	399,983	124,408	Archambault, Raoul	275,575	Pell, Claiborne		151,167 D	31.1%	68.9%	31.1%	68.9%
1958	344,519	122,353	Ewing, Bayard	222,166	Pastore, John O.*		99,813 D	35.5%	64.5%	35.5%	64.5%
1954	326,624	132,970	Sundlun, Walter I.	193,654	Green, Theodore F.*		60,684 D	40.7%	59.3%	40.7%	59.3%
1952	410,978	185,850	Ewing, Bayard	225,128	Pastore, John O.*		39,278 D	45.2%	54.8%	45.2%	54.8%
1950S	299,410	114,890	Levy, Austin T.	184,520	Pastore, John O.		69,630 D	38.4%	61.6%	38.4%	61.6%
1948	320,952	130,668	Hazard, Thomas P.	190,284	Green, Theodore F.*		59,616 D	40.7%	59.3%	40.7%	59.3%
1946	273,528	122,780	Dyer, W. Gurnee	150,748	McGrath, J. Howard		27,968 D	44.9%	55.1%	44.9%	55.1%

Note: An asterisk (*) denotes incumbent. **The 1950 election was for a short term to fill a vacancy.

RHODE ISLAND

PRESIDENT 2012

2010 Census Population	County	Total Vote	Republican (Romney)	Democratic (Obama)	Other	Rep.-Dem. Plurality	Total Vote Rep.	Total Vote Dem.	Major Vote Rep.	Major Vote Dem.
49,875	BRISTOL	24,676	9,231	14,974	471	5,743 D	37.4%	60.7%	38.1%	61.9%
166,158	KENT	78,923	31,567	45,564	1,792	13,997 D	40.0%	57.7%	40.9%	59.1%
82,888	NEWPORT	39,452	15,202	23,463	787	8,261 D	38.5%	59.5%	39.3%	60.7%
626,667	PROVIDENCE	239,786	75,785	159,520	4,481	83,735 D	31.6%	66.5%	32.2%	67.8%
126,979	WASHINGTON	62,879	25,366	35,888	1,625	10,522 D	40.3%	57.1%	41.4%	58.6%
	Votes Not Reported by County	333	53	268	12	215 D	15.9%	80.5%	16.5%	83.5%
1,052,567	TOTAL	446,049	157,204	279,677	9,168	122,473 D	35.2%	62.7%	36.0%	64.0%

2010 Census Population	City/Town	Total Vote	Republican (Romney)	Democratic (Obama)	Other	Rep.-Dem. Plurality	Total Vote Rep.	Total Vote Dem.	Major Vote Rep.	Major Vote Dem.
16,310	BARRINGTON	9,556	3,836	5,557	163	1,721 D	40.1%	58.2%	40.8%	59.2%
22,954	BRISTOL TOWN	10,267	3,707	6,359	201	2,652 D	36.1%	61.9%	36.8%	63.2%
15,955	BURRILLVILLE	6,889	3,044	3,666	179	622 D	44.2%	53.2%	45.4%	54.6%
19,376	CENTRAL FALLS	3,971	512	3,410	49	2,898 D	12.9%	85.9%	13.1%	86.9%
7,827	CHARLESTOWN	4,177	1,616	2,445	116	829 D	38.7%	58.5%	39.8%	60.2%
35,014	COVENTRY	16,506	6,969	9,122	415	2,153 D	42.2%	55.3%	43.3%	56.7%
80,387	CRANSTON	34,970	13,008	21,388	574	8,380 D	37.2%	61.2%	37.8%	62.2%
33,506	CUMBERLAND	16,676	7,106	9,291	279	2,185 D	42.6%	55.7%	43.3%	56.7%
13,146	EAST GREENWICH	7,308	3,649	3,535	124	114 R	49.9%	48.4%	50.8%	49.2%
47,037	EAST PROVIDENCE	20,253	5,752	14,095	406	8,343 D	28.4%	69.6%	29.0%	71.0%
6,425	EXETER	3,381	1,541	1,743	97	202 D	45.6%	51.6%	46.9%	53.1%
4,606	FOSTER	2,443	1,091	1,280	72	189 D	44.7%	52.4%	46.0%	54.0%
9,746	GLOCESTER	5,047	2,410	2,539	98	129 D	47.8%	50.3%	48.7%	51.3%
8,188	HOPKINTON	3,888	1,602	2,164	122	562 D	41.2%	55.7%	42.5%	57.5%
5,405	JAMESTOWN	3,603	1,329	2,181	93	852 D	36.9%	60.5%	37.9%	62.1%
28,769	JOHNSTON	13,125	5,417	7,503	205	2,086 D	41.3%	57.2%	41.9%	58.1%
21,105	LINCOLN	11,064	4,866	6,028	170	1,162 D	44.0%	54.5%	44.7%	55.3%
3,492	LITTLE COMPTON	2,172	908	1,214	50	306 D	41.8%	55.9%	42.8%	57.2%
16,150	MIDDLETOWN	7,223	2,785	4,304	134	1,519 D	38.6%	59.6%	39.3%	60.7%
15,868	NARRAGANSETT	7,756	3,223	4,339	194	1,116 D	41.6%	55.9%	42.6%	57.4%
1,051	NEW SHOREHAM	972	276	666	30	390 D	28.4%	68.5%	29.3%	70.7%
24,672	NEWPORT CITY	9,313	2,959	6,174	180	3,215 D	31.8%	66.3%	32.4%	67.6%
26,486	NORTH KINGSTOWN	14,681	6,451	7,847	383	1,396 D	43.9%	53.5%	45.1%	54.9%
32,078	NORTH PROVIDENCE	15,298	5,404	9,613	281	4,209 D	35.3%	62.8%	36.0%	64.0%
11,967	NORTH SMITHFIELD	6,037	2,852	3,050	135	198 D	47.2%	50.5%	48.3%	51.7%
71,148	PAWTUCKET	23,784	5,228	18,155	401	12,927 D	22.0%	76.3%	22.4%	77.6%
17,389	PORTSMOUTH	9,363	4,165	5,017	181	852 D	44.5%	53.6%	45.4%	54.6%
178,042	PROVIDENCE CITY	51,937	7,282	43,617	1,038	36,335 D	14.0%	84.0%	14.3%	85.7%
7,708	RICHMOND	3,686	1,555	2,002	129	447 D	42.2%	54.3%	43.7%	56.3%
10,329	SCITUATE	5,760	3,018	2,607	135	411 R	52.4%	45.3%	53.7%	46.3%
21,430	SMITHFIELD	10,163	4,681	5,293	189	612 D	46.1%	52.1%	46.9%	53.1%
30,639	SOUTH KINGSTOWN	13,698	4,720	8,611	367	3,891 D	34.5%	62.9%	35.4%	64.6%
15,780	TIVERTON	7,778	3,056	4,573	149	1,517 D	39.3%	58.8%	40.1%	59.9%
10,611	WARREN	4,853	1,688	3,058	107	1,370 D	34.8%	63.0%	35.6%	64.4%
82,672	WARWICK	40,380	15,027	24,448	905	9,421 D	37.2%	60.5%	38.1%	61.9%
6,135	WEST GREENWICH	3,162	1,590	1,503	69	87 R	50.3%	47.5%	51.4%	48.6%
29,191	WEST WARWICK	11,567	4,332	6,956	279	2,624 D	37.5%	60.1%	38.4%	61.6%
22,787	WESTERLY	10,640	4,382	6,071	187	1,689 D	41.2%	57.1%	41.9%	58.1%
41,186	WOONSOCKET	12,369	4,114	7,985	270	3,871 D	33.3%	64.6%	34.0%	66.0%

RHODE ISLAND

SENATOR 2012

2010 Census Population	County	Total Vote	Republican (Hinckley)	Democratic (Whitehouse)	Other	Rep.-Dem. Plurality	Percentage Total Vote Rep.	Dem.	Major Vote Rep.	Dem.
49,875	BRISTOL	22,978	8,390	14,556	32	6,166 D	36.5%	63.3%	36.6%	63.4%
166,158	KENT	74,719	30,217	44,332	170	14,115 D	40.4%	59.3%	40.5%	59.5%
82,888	NEWPORT	37,048	14,224	22,774	50	8,550 D	38.4%	61.5%	38.4%	61.6%
626,667	PROVIDENCE	223,808	69,136	154,123	549	84,987 D	30.9%	68.9%	31.0%	69.0%
126,979	WASHINGTON	59,346	24,209	35,006	131	10,797 D	40.8%	59.0%	40.9%	59.1%
	Votes Not Reported	290	46	243	1	197 D	15.9%	83.8%	15.9%	84.1%
1,052,567	TOTAL	418,189	146,222	271,034	933	124,812 D	35.0%	64.8%	64.8%	65.0%

2010 Census Population	City/Town	Total Vote	Republican (Hinckley)	Democratic (Whitehouse)	Other	Rep.-Dem. Plurality	Percentage Total Vote Rep.	Dem.	Major Vote Rep.	Dem.
16,310	BARRINGTON	9,030	3,534	5,482	14	1,948 D	39.1%	60.7%	39.2%	60.8%
22,954	BRISTOL TOWN	9,379	3,256	6,109	14	2,853 D	34.7%	65.1%	34.8%	65.2%
15,955	BURRILLVILLE	6,560	2,741	3,805	14	1,064 D	41.8%	58.0%	41.9%	58.1%
19,376	CENTRAL FALLS	3,544	484	3,046	14	2,562 D	13.7%	85.9%	13.7%	86.3%
7,827	CHARLESTOWN	3,939	1,611	2,320	8	709 D	40.9%	58.9%	41.0%	59.0%
35,014	COVENTRY	15,620	6,548	9,032	40	2,484 D	41.9%	57.8%	42.0%	58.0%
80,387	CRANSTON	32,572	11,818	20,660	94	8,842 D	36.3%	63.4%	36.4%	63.6%
33,506	CUMBERLAND	15,704	6,282	9,388	34	3,106 D	40.0%	59.8%	40.1%	59.9%
13,146	EAST GREENWICH	6,900	3,504	3,382	14	122 R	50.8%	49.0%	50.9%	49.1%
47,037	EAST PROVIDENCE	18,875	5,325	13,507	43	8,182 D	28.2%	71.6%	28.3%	71.7%
6,425	EXETER	3,198	1,509	1,687	2	178 D	47.2%	52.8%	47.2%	52.8%
4,606	FOSTER	2,353	1,080	1,272	1	192 D	45.9%	54.1%	45.9%	54.1%
9,746	GLOCESTER	4,860	2,307	2,549	4	242 D	47.5%	52.4%	47.5%	52.5%
8,188	HOPKINTON	3,647	1,509	2,132	6	623 D	41.4%	58.5%	41.4%	58.6%
5,405	JAMESTOWN	3,376	1,277	2,094	5	817 D	37.8%	62.0%	37.9%	62.1%
28,769	JOHNSTON	12,363	4,787	7,538	38	2,751 D	38.7%	61.0%	38.8%	61.2%
21,105	LINCOLN	10,409	4,334	6,052	23	1,718 D	41.6%	58.1%	41.7%	58.3%
3,492	LITTLE COMPTON	2,073	946	1,126	1	180 D	45.6%	54.3%	45.7%	54.3%
16,150	MIDDLETOWN	6,754	2,546	4,204	4	1,658 D	37.7%	62.2%	37.7%	62.3%
15,868	NARRAGANSETT	7,282	3,064	4,196	22	1,132 D	42.1%	57.6%	42.2%	57.8%
1,051	NEW SHOREHAM	924	255	668	1	413 D	27.6%	72.3%	27.6%	72.4%
24,672	NEWPORT CITY	8,639	2,747	5,879	13	3,132 D	31.8%	68.1%	31.8%	68.2%
26,486	NORTH KINGSTOWN	14,000	6,249	7,708	43	1,459 D	44.6%	55.1%	44.8%	55.2%
32,078	NORTH PROVIDENCE	14,244	4,837	9,381	26	4,544 D	34.0%	65.9%	34.0%	66.0%
11,967	NORTH SMITHFIELD	5,695	2,462	3,228	5	766 D	43.2%	56.7%	43.3%	56.7%
71,148	PAWTUCKET	22,627	4,951	17,628	48	12,677 D	21.9%	77.9%	21.9%	78.1%
17,389	PORTSMOUTH	8,858	3,844	5,000	14	1,156 D	43.4%	56.4%	43.5%	56.5%
178,042	PROVIDENCE CITY	47,265	6,924	40,213	128	33,289 D	14.6%	85.1%	14.7%	85.3%
7,708	RICHMOND	3,549	1,531	2,009	9	478 D	43.1%	56.6%	43.2%	56.8%
10,329	SCITUATE	5,522	2,867	2,640	15	227 R	51.9%	47.8%	52.1%	47.9%
21,430	SMITHFIELD	9,641	4,294	5,332	15	1,038 D	44.5%	55.3%	44.6%	55.4%
30,639	SOUTH KINGSTOWN	12,890	4,696	8,168	26	3,472 D	36.4%	63.4%	36.5%	63.5%
15,780	TIVERTON	7,348	2,864	4,471	13	1,607 D	39.0%	60.8%	39.0%	61.0%
10,611	WARREN	4,569	1,600	2,965	4	1,365 D	35.0%	64.9%	35.0%	65.0%
82,672	WARWICK	38,243	14,497	23,656	90	9,159 D	37.9%	61.9%	38.0%	62.0%
6,135	WEST GREENWICH	3,008	1,542	1,460	6	82 R	51.3%	48.5%	51.4%	48.6%
29,191	WEST WARWICK	10,948	4,126	6,802	20	2,676 D	37.7%	62.1%	37.8%	62.2%
22,787	WESTERLY	9,917	3,785	6,118	14	2,333 D	38.2%	61.7%	38.2%	61.8%
41,186	WOONSOCKET	11,574	3,643	7,884	47	4,241 D	31.5%	68.1%	31.6%	68.4%

RHODE ISLAND
HOUSE OF REPRESENTATIVES

			Republican		Democratic		Other Vote	Rep.-Dem. Plurality	Percentage			
									Total Vote		Major Vote	
CD	Year	Total Vote	Vote	Candidate	Vote	Candidate			Rep.	Dem.	Rep.	Dem.
1	2012	205,115	83,737	DOHERTY, BRENDAN P.	108,612	CICILLINE, DAVID*	12,766	24,875 D	40.8%	53.0%	43.5%	56.5%
2	2012	222,660	78,189	RILEY, MICHAEL G.	124,067	LANGEVIN, Jim*	20,404	45,878 D	35.1%	55.7%	38.7%	61.3%
TOTAL	2012	427,775	161,926		232,679		33,170	70,753 D	37.9%	54.4%	41.0%	59.0%

Note: An asterisk (*) denotes incumbent.

RHODE ISLAND

GENERAL AND PRIMARY ELECTIONS

GENERAL ELECTIONS: OTHER VOTE

President — Other vote was 4,388 Libertarian (Gary E. Johnson), 2,421 Green (Jill Stein), 1,381 Write-in (Scattered Write-In), 430 Constitution (Virgil H. Goode), 416 Justice (Ross C. "Rocky" Anderson), 132 Socialism and Liberation (Peta Lindsay)

Senator — Other vote was 933 Write-in (Scattered Write-In)

House — Other vote was:

CD 1 — 12,504 Independent (David S. Vogel), 262 Write-in (Scattered Write-In)
CD 2 — 20,212 Independent (Abel G. Collins), 192 Write-in (Scattered Write-In)

PRIMARY ELECTIONS: SUPPLEMENTARY INFORMATION

Primary — April 24, 2012 (President) / September 11, 2012 (Congress)

Registration (as of September 11, 2012) — 720,603

Democratic	283,723
Republican	41,952
Non-Partisan	15,607
Unaffiliated	379,321

Primary Type — Semi-open—Registered Democrats and Republicans could vote only in their party's primary. Unaffiliated voters could participate in either party's primary if they were willing to remain a member of that party for a period of at least 90 days.

REPUBLICAN PRIMARIES			DEMOCRATIC PRIMARIES		
President					
Romney, W. Mitt	9,178	63.0%	Obama, Barack H.*	6,759	83.4%
Paul, Ron	3,473	23.8%	Uncommitted	1,133	14.0%
Gingrich, Newt	880	6.0%	Scattered Write-In	214	2.6%
Santorum, Rick	825	5.7%			
Uncommitted	131	0.9%			
Roemer, Charles	40	0.3%			
Scattered Write-In	37	0.3%			
TOTAL	14,564		TOTAL	8,106	
Senator					
Hinckley, Barry	6,934	100.0%	Whitehouse, Sheldon*	60,754	100.0%
Congressional District 1					
Doherty, Brendan P.	Unopposed		Cicilline, David*	30,203	62.1%
			Gemma, Anthony P.	14,702	30.2%
			Young, Christopher F.	3,701	7.6%
			TOTAL	48,606	
Congressional District 2					
Riley, Michael G.	5,283	65.6%	Langevin, Jim*	22,161	74.1%
Russo, Kara D.	1,488	18.5%	Matson, John O.	7,748	25.9%
Gardiner, Michael J.	825	10.2%			
Robbio, Donald F.	454	5.6%			
TOTAL	8,050		TOTAL	29,909	

Note: An asterisk (*) denotes incumbent.

SOUTH CAROLINA

Congressional districts first established for elections held in 2012

7 members

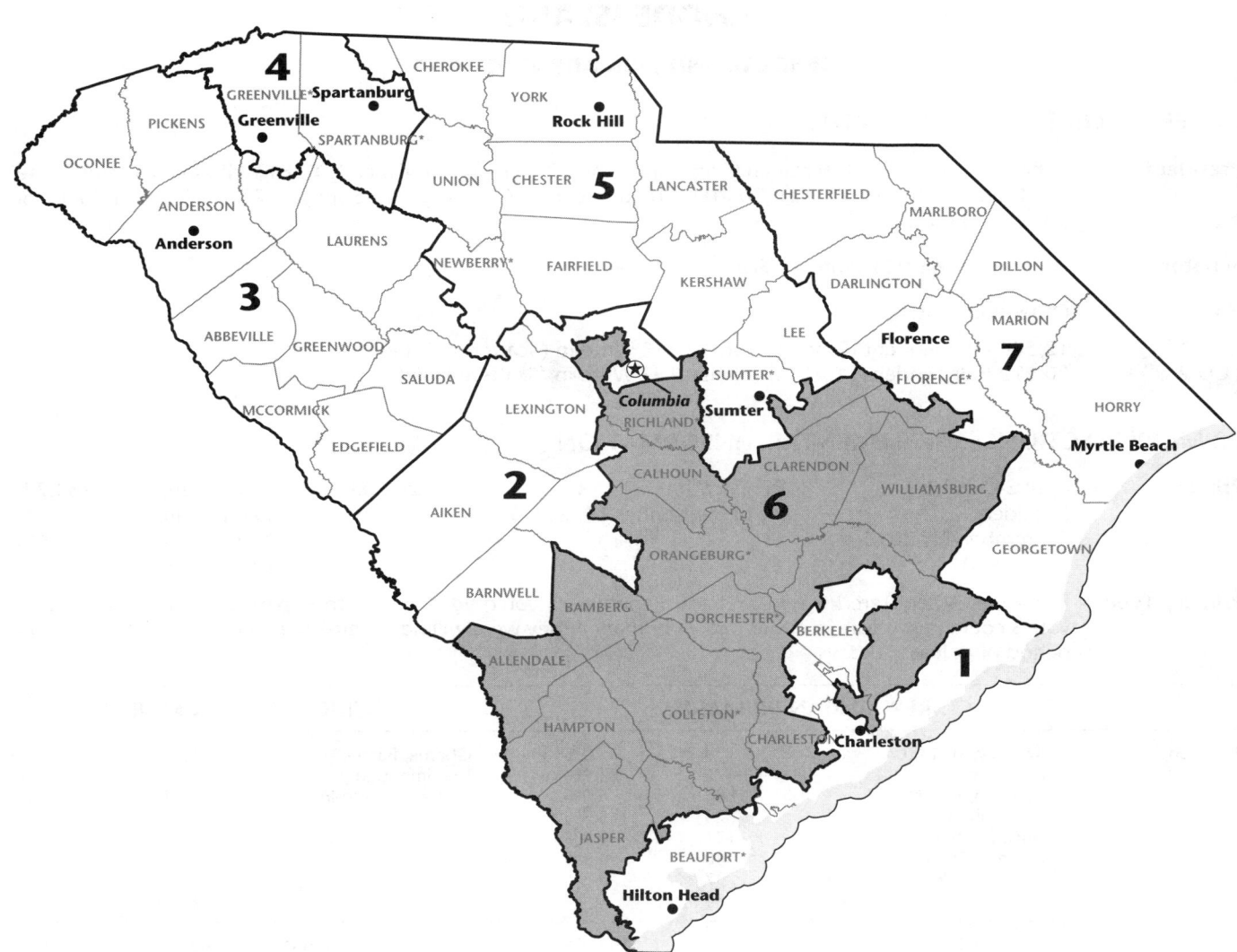

* Asterisk indicates a county whose boundaries include parts of two or more Congressional districts.

SOUTH CAROLINA

GOVERNOR

Nikki R. Haley (R). Elected 2010 to a four-year term.

SENATORS (2 Republicans)

Lindsey Graham (R). Reelected 2008 to a six-year term. Previously elected 2002.

Tim Scott (R). Sworn in on January 3, 2013, having been appointed to fill the vacancy left by Jim DeMint (R), who resigned to serve as president of the Heritage Foundation, until a 2014 special election.

REPRESENTATIVES (6 Republicans, 1 Democrat)

1. Mark Sanford (R)
2. Joe Wilson (R)
3. Jeff Duncan (R)
4. Trey Gowdy (R)
5. Mick Mulvaney (R)
6. James E. Clyburn (D)
7. Tom Rice (R)

POSTWAR VOTE FOR PRESIDENT

		Republican		Democratic		Other Vote	Rep.-Dem. Plurality	Percentage			
								Total Vote		Major Vote	
Year	Total Vote	Vote	Candidate	Vote	Candidate			Rep.	Dem.	Rep.	Dem.
2012	1,964,118	1,071,645	Romney, W. Mitt	865,941	Obama, Barack H.*	26,532	205,704 R	54.6%	44.1%	55.3%	44.7%
2008	1,920,969	1,034,896	McCain, John S. III	862,449	Obama, Barack H.	23,624	172,447 R	53.9%	44.9%	54.5%	45.5%
2004	1,617,730	937,974	Bush, George W.*	661,699	Kerry, John F.	18,057	276,275 R	58.0%	40.9%	58.6%	41.4%
2000**	1,382,717	785,937	Bush, George W.	565,561	Gore, Albert Jr.	31,219	220,376 R	56.8%	40.9%	58.2%	41.8%
1996**	1,151,689	573,458	Dole, Robert "Bob"	506,283	Clinton, Bill*	71,948	67,175 R	49.8%	44.0%	53.1%	46.9%
1992**	1,202,527	577,507	Bush, George H.*	479,514	Clinton, Bill	145,506	97,993 R	48.0%	39.9%	54.6%	45.4%
1988	986,009	606,443	Bush, George H.	370,554	Dukakis, Michael S.	9,012	235,889 R	61.5%	37.6%	62.1%	37.9%
1984	968,529	615,539	Reagan, Ronald*	344,459	Mondale, Walter F.	8,531	271,080 R	63.6%	35.6%	64.1%	35.9%
1980**	894,071	441,841	Reagan, Ronald	430,385	Carter, Jimmy*	21,845	11,456 R	49.4%	48.1%	50.7%	49.3%
1976	802,583	346,149	Ford, Gerald R.*	450,807	Carter, Jimmy	5,627	104,658 D	43.1%	56.2%	43.4%	56.6%
1972	673,960	477,044	Nixon, Richard M.*	186,824	McGovern, George S.	10,092	290,220 R	70.8%	27.7%	71.9%	28.1%
1968**	666,978	254,062	Nixon, Richard M.	197,486	Humphrey, Hubert H. Jr.	215,430	56,576 R	38.1%	29.6%	56.3%	43.7%
1964	524,779	309,048	Goldwater, Barry M. Sr.	215,723	Johnson, Lyndon B.*	8	93,325 R	58.9%	41.1%	58.9%	41.1%
1960	386,688	188,558	Nixon, Richard M.	198,129	Kennedy, John F.	1	9,571 D	48.8%	51.2%	48.8%	51.2%
1956**	300,583	75,700	Eisenhower, Dwight D.*	136,372	Stevenson, Adlai E. II	88,511	60,672 D	25.2%	45.4%	35.7%	64.3%
1952	341,087	168,082	Eisenhower, Dwight D.	173,004	Stevenson, Adlai E. II	1	4,922 D	49.3%	50.7%	49.3%	50.7%
1948**	142,571	5,386	Dewey, Thomas E.	34,423	Truman, Harry S.*	102,762	29,037 D**	3.8%	24.1%	13.5%	86.5%

Note: An asterisk (*) denotes incumbent. **In past elections, the other vote included: 2000 - 20,200 Green (Ralph Nader); 1996 - 64,386 Reform (Ross Perot); 1992 - 138,872 Independent (Perot); 1980 - 14,153 Independent (John Anderson); 1968 - 215,430 American Independent (George Wallace), who finished second; 1956 - 88,509 Uncommitted States' Rights electors, which placed second; 1948 - 102,607 States' Rights (Strom Thurmond), who won South Carolina with 72.0 percent of the total vote.

SOUTH CAROLINA

POSTWAR VOTE FOR GOVERNOR

Year	Total Vote	Republican		Democratic		Other Vote	Rep.-Dem. Plurality	Percentage			
								Total Vote		Major Vote	
		Vote	Candidate	Vote	Candidate			Rep.	Dem.	Rep.	Dem.
2010	1,344,198	690,525	Haley, Nikki R.	630,534	Sheheen, Vincent A.	23,139	59,991 R	51.4%	46.9%	52.3%	47.7%
2006	1,091,952	601,868	Sanford, Mark*	489,076	Moore, Tommy	1,008	112,792 R	55.1%	44.8%	55.2%	44.8%
2002	1,107,725	585,422	Sanford, Mark	521,140	Hodges, James H.*	1,163	64,282 R	52.8%	47.0%	52.9%	47.1%
1998	1,070,869	484,088	Beasley, David*	570,070	Hodges, James H.	16,711	85,982 D	45.2%	53.2%	45.9%	54.1%
1994	933,850	470,756	Beasley, David	447,002	Theodore, Nick A.	16,092	23,754 R	50.4%	47.9%	51.3%	48.7%
1990	760,965	528,831	Campbell, Carroll*	212,034	Mitchell, Theo	20,100	316,797 R	69.5%	27.9%	71.4%	28.6%
1986	753,751	384,565	Campbell, Carroll	361,325	Daniel, Mike	7,861	23,240 R	51.0%	47.9%	51.6%	48.4%
1982	671,625	202,806	Workman, W. D. III	468,819	Riley, Richard W.*		266,013 D	30.2%	69.8%	30.2%	69.8%
1978	627,182	236,946	Young, Edward L.	384,898	Riley, Richard W.	5,338	147,952 D	37.8%	61.4%	38.1%	61.9%
1974	523,199	266,109	Edwards, James B.	248,938	Dorn, W.J. Bryan	8,152	17,171 R	50.9%	47.6%	51.7%	48.3%
1970	484,257	221,233	Watson, Albert W.	249,951	West, John C.	13,073	28,718 D	45.7%	51.6%	47.0%	53.0%
1966	439,942	184,088	Rogers, Joseph O. Jr.	255,854	McNair, Robert E.*		71,766 D	41.8%	58.2%	41.8%	58.2%
1962	253,721			253,704	Russell, Donald	17	253,704 D		100.0%		100.0%
1958	77,740			77,714	Hollings, Ernest F.	26	77,714 D		100.0%		100.0%
1954	214,212			214,204	Timmerman, George Bell	8	214,204 D		100.0%		100.0%
1950	50,642			50,633	Byrnes, James F.	9	50,633 D		100.0%		100.0%
1946	26,520			26,520	Thurmond, James Strom		26,520 D		100.0%		100.0%

Note: An asterisk (*) denotes incumbent. **The Republican Party did not run a candidate in the gubernatorial elections of 1946, 1950, 1954, 1958, and 1962.

POSTWAR VOTE FOR SENATOR

Year	Total Vote	Republican		Democratic		Other Vote	Rep.-Dem. Plurality	Percentage			
								Total Vote		Major Vote	
		Vote	Candidate	Vote	Candidate			Rep.	Dem.	Rep.	Dem.
2010	1,318,794	810,771	DeMint, Jim*	364,598	Greene, Alvin M.	143,425	446,173 R	61.5%	27.6%	69.0%	31.0%
2008	1,871,431	1,076,534	Graham, Lindsey*	790,621	Conley, Bob	4,276	285,913 R	57.5%	42.2%	57.7%	42.3%
2004	1,597,221	857,167	DeMint, Jim	704,384	Tenenbaum, Inez M.	35,670	152,783 R	53.7%	44.1%	54.9%	45.1%
2002	1,102,948	600,010	Graham, Lindsey	487,359	Sanders, Alex	15,579	112,651 R	54.4%	44.2%	55.2%	44.8%
1998	1,068,367	488,132	Inglis, Robert D.	562,791	Hollings, Ernest F.*	17,444	74,659 D	45.7%	52.7%	46.4%	53.6%
1996	1,161,372	619,859	Thurmond, James Strom*	510,951	Close, Elliott	30,562	108,908 R	53.4%	44.0%	54.8%	45.2%
1992	1,180,438	554,175	Hartnett, Thomas F.	591,030	Hollings, Ernest F.*	35,233	36,855 D	46.9%	50.1%	48.4%	51.6%
1990	750,716	482,032	Thurmond, James Strom*	244,112	Cunningham, Bob	24,572	237,920 R	64.2%	32.5%	66.4%	33.6%
1986	737,962	262,886	McMaster, Henry D.	465,500	Hollings, Ernest F.*	9,576	202,614 D	35.6%	63.1%	36.1%	63.9%
1984	965,130	644,815	Thurmond, James Strom*	306,982	Purvis, Melvin	13,333	337,833 R	66.8%	31.8%	67.7%	32.3%
1980	870,594	257,946	Mays, Marshall T.	612,554	Hollings, Ernest F.*	94	354,608 D	29.6%	70.4%	29.6%	70.4%
1978	632,852	351,733	Thurmond, James Strom*	281,119	Ravenel, Charles D.		70,614 R	55.6%	44.4%	55.6%	44.4%
1974	512,397	146,645	Bush, Gwenfred	356,126	Hollings, Ernest F.*	9,626	209,481 D	28.6%	69.5%	29.2%	70.8%
1972	672,246	426,601	Thurmond, James Strom*	245,457	Zeigler, Eugene N.	188	181,144 R	63.5%	36.5%	63.5%	36.5%
1968	652,855	248,780	Parker, Marshall	404,060	Hollings, Ernest F.*	15	155,280 D	38.1%	61.9%	38.1%	61.9%
1966	436,252	271,297	Thurmond, James Strom*	164,955	Morrah, Bradley		106,342 R	62.2%	37.8%	62.2%	37.8%
1966S	435,822	212,032	Parker, Marshall	223,790	Hollings, Ernest F.		11,758 D	48.7%	51.3%	48.7%	51.3%
1962	312,647	133,930	Workman, W. D. Jr.	178,712	Johnston, Olin D.*	5	44,782 D	42.8%	57.2%	42.8%	57.2%
1960	330,266			330,164	Thurmond, James Strom*	102	330,164 D		100.0%		100.0%
1956	279,845	49,695	Crawford, L. P.	230,150	Johnston, Olin D.*		180,455 D	17.8%	82.2%	17.8%	82.2%
1956S	245,371			245,371	Thurmond, James Strom		245,371 D		100.0%		100.0%
1954**	226,967			83,525	Brown, Edgar A.	143,442	83,525 D**		36.8%		100.0%
1950	50,277			50,240	Johnston, Olin D.*	37	50,240 D		99.9%		100.0%
1948	141,006	5,008	Gerald, J. Bates	135,998	Maybank, Burnet R.*		130,990 D	3.6%	96.4%	3.6%	96.4%

Note: An asterisk (*) denotes incumbent. **In past elections, the other vote included: 1954 - 143,442 Independent Democratic (Strom Thurmond). Thurmond ran as a write-in candidate and won with 63.1 percent of the total vote. One each of the 1956 and 1966 elections was for a short term to fill a vacancy. The Republican Party did not run a Senate candidate in 1950, 1954, 1956 (for the short term), and 1960.

SOUTH CAROLINA

PRESIDENT 2012

2010 Census Population	County	Total Vote	Republican (Romney)	Democratic (Obama)	Other	Rep.-Dem. Plurality		Percentage			
								Total Vote		Major Vote	
								Rep.	Dem.	Rep.	Dem.
25,417	ABBEVILLE	10,671	5,981	4,543	147	1,438	R	56.0%	42.6%	56.8%	43.2%
160,099	AIKEN	70,363	44,042	25,322	999	18,720	R	62.6%	36.0%	63.5%	36.5%
10,419	ALLENDALE	4,163	838	3,297	28	2,459	D	20.1%	79.2%	20.3%	79.7%
187,126	ANDERSON	72,212	48,709	22,405	1,098	26,304	R	67.5%	31.0%	68.5%	31.5%
15,987	BAMBERG	6,882	2,194	4,624	64	2,430	D	31.9%	67.2%	32.2%	67.8%
22,621	BARNWELL	9,923	4,659	5,188	76	529	D	47.0%	52.3%	47.3%	52.7%
162,233	BEAUFORT	73,297	42,687	29,848	762	12,839	R	58.2%	40.7%	58.9%	41.1%
177,843	BERKELEY	68,195	38,475	28,542	1,178	9,933	R	56.4%	41.9%	57.4%	42.6%
15,175	CALHOUN	7,834	3,707	4,045	82	338	D	47.3%	51.6%	47.8%	52.2%
350,209	CHARLESTON	161,707	77,629	81,487	2,591	3,858	D	48.0%	50.4%	48.8%	51.2%
55,342	CHEROKEE	20,773	13,314	7,231	228	6,083	R	64.1%	34.8%	64.8%	35.2%
33,140	CHESTER	14,407	6,367	7,891	149	1,524	D	44.2%	54.8%	44.7%	55.3%
46,734	CHESTERFIELD	16,594	8,490	7,958	146	532	R	51.2%	48.0%	51.6%	48.4%
34,971	CLARENDON	16,292	7,071	9,091	130	2,020	D	43.4%	55.8%	43.8%	56.2%
38,892	COLLETON	17,086	8,443	8,475	168	32	D	49.4%	49.6%	49.9%	50.1%
68,681	DARLINGTON	30,150	14,434	15,457	259	1,023	D	47.9%	51.3%	48.3%	51.7%
32,062	DILLON	13,035	5,427	7,523	85	2,096	D	41.6%	57.7%	41.9%	58.1%
136,555	DORCHESTER	56,855	32,531	23,445	879	9,086	R	57.2%	41.2%	58.1%	41.9%
26,985	EDGEFIELD	11,586	6,512	4,967	107	1,545	R	56.2%	42.9%	56.7%	43.3%
23,956	FAIRFIELD	11,895	3,999	7,777	119	3,778	D	33.6%	65.4%	34.0%	66.0%
136,885	FLORENCE	58,122	28,961	28,614	547	347	R	49.8%	49.2%	50.3%	49.7%
60,158	GEORGETOWN	30,965	16,526	14,163	276	2,363	R	53.4%	45.7%	53.8%	46.2%
451,225	GREENVILLE	193,189	121,685	68,070	3,434	53,615	R	63.0%	35.2%	64.1%	35.9%
69,661	GREENWOOD	28,672	16,348	11,972	352	4,376	R	57.0%	41.8%	57.7%	42.3%
21,090	HAMPTON	9,206	3,312	5,834	60	2,522	D	36.0%	63.4%	36.2%	63.8%
269,291	HORRY	112,393	72,127	38,885	1,381	33,242	R	64.2%	34.6%	65.0%	35.0%
24,777	JASPER	10,021	4,169	5,757	95	1,588	D	41.6%	57.4%	42.0%	58.0%
61,697	KERSHAW	27,946	16,324	11,259	363	5,065	R	58.4%	40.3%	59.2%	40.8%
76,652	LANCASTER	33,144	19,333	13,419	392	5,914	R	58.3%	40.5%	59.0%	41.0%
66,537	LAURENS	25,416	14,746	10,318	352	4,428	R	58.0%	40.6%	58.8%	41.2%
19,220	LEE	8,907	2,832	5,977	98	3,145	D	31.8%	67.1%	32.1%	67.9%
262,391	LEXINGTON	112,623	76,662	34,148	1,813	42,514	R	68.1%	30.3%	69.2%	30.8%
33,062	MARION	14,986	5,164	9,688	134	4,524	D	34.5%	64.6%	34.8%	65.2%
28,933	MARLBORO	9,853	3,676	6,100	77	2,424	D	37.3%	61.9%	37.6%	62.4%
10,233	MCCORMICK	5,160	2,467	2,653	40	186	D	47.8%	51.4%	48.2%	51.8%
37,508	NEWBERRY	16,351	9,260	6,913	178	2,347	R	56.6%	42.3%	57.3%	42.7%
74,273	OCONEE	30,666	21,611	8,550	505	13,061	R	70.5%	27.9%	71.7%	28.3%
92,501	ORANGEBURG	43,041	12,022	30,720	299	18,698	D	27.9%	71.4%	28.1%	71.9%
119,224	PICKENS	45,549	33,474	11,156	919	22,318	R	73.5%	24.5%	75.0%	25.0%
384,504	RICHLAND	159,154	53,105	103,989	2,060	50,884	D	33.4%	65.3%	33.8%	66.2%
19,875	SALUDA	8,564	5,135	3,328	101	1,807	R	60.0%	38.9%	60.7%	39.3%
284,307	SPARTANBURG	109,906	66,969	41,461	1,476	25,508	R	60.9%	37.7%	61.8%	38.2%
107,456	SUMTER	47,309	19,274	27,589	446	8,315	D	40.7%	58.3%	41.1%	58.9%
28,961	UNION	12,541	6,584	5,796	161	788	R	52.5%	46.2%	53.2%	46.8%
34,423	WILLIAMSBURG	16,304	4,824	11,335	145	6,511	D	29.6%	69.5%	29.9%	70.1%
226,073	YORK	100,210	59,546	39,131	1,533	20,415	R	59.4%	39.0%	60.3%	39.7%
4,625,364	TOTAL	1,964,118	1,071,645	865,941	26,532	205,704	R	54.6%	44.1%	55.3%	44.7%

SOUTH CAROLINA

HOUSE OF REPRESENTATIVES

| | | | Republican | | Democratic | | | | Percentage | | | |
| | | | | | | | Other | Rep.-Dem. | Total Vote | | Major Vote | |
CD	Year	Total Vote	Vote	Candidate	Vote	Candidate	Vote	Plurality	Rep.	Dem.	Rep.	Dem.
1	2012	290,013	179,908	SCOTT, TIM*	103,557	ROSE, BOBBIE G.	6,548	76,351 R	62.0%	35.7%	63.5%	36.5%
2	2012	203,718	196,116	WILSON, JOE*			7,602	196,116 R	96.3%		100.0%	
3	2012	254,763	169,512	DUNCAN, JEFF*	84,735	DOYLE, BRIAN RYAN B.	516	84,777 R	66.5%	33.3%	66.7%	33.3%
4	2012	266,884	173,201	GOWDY, TREY*	89,964	MORROW, DEB	3,719	83,237 R	64.9%	33.7%	65.8%	34.2%
5	2012	278,003	154,324	MULVANEY, MICK*	123,443	KNOTT, JOYCE	236	30,881 R	55.5%	44.4%	55.6%	44.4%
6	2012	233,615			218,717	CLYBURN, JAMES E.*	14,898	218,717 D		93.6%		100.0%
7	2012	275,738	153,068	RICE, TOM	122,389	TINUBU, GLORIA BROMELL	281	30,679 R	55.5%	44.4%	55.6%	44.4%
TOTAL	2012	1,802,734	1,026,129		742,805		33,800	283,324 R	56.9%	41.2%	58.0%	42.0%

Note: An asterisk (*) denotes incumbent. Some Democratic candidates received votes on an additional ballot line for the Working Families Party as well: District 1: Rose, Bobbie G.; District 4: Morrow, Deb; District 5: Knott, Joyce; District 7: Tinubu, Gloria Bromel. These votes are included in their totals above.

SOUTH CAROLINA

GENERAL AND PRIMARY ELECTIONS

GENERAL ELECTIONS: OTHER VOTE

President Other vote was 16,321 Libertarian (Gary E. Johnson), 5,446 Green (Jill Stein), 4,765 Constitution (Virgil H. Goode)

House Other vote was:

CD 1 6,334 Libertarian (Keith Blandford), 214 Write-in (Scattered Write-In)
CD 2 7,602 Write-in (Scattered Write-In)
CD 3 516 Write-in (Scattered Write-In)
CD 4 3,390 Green (Jeff Sumerel), 329 Write-in (Scattered Write-In)
CD 5 236 Write-in (Scattered Write-In)
CD 6 12,920 Green (Nammu Y. Muhammad), 1,978 Write-in (Scattered Write-In)
CD 7 281 Write-in (Scattered Write-In)

PRIMARY ELECTIONS: SUPPLEMENTARY INFORMATION

Primary Republican: January 21, 2012; Democratic: January 28, 2012 (President) June 12, 2012 (Congress) **Registration** (as of June 12, 2012) 2,448,757 No Party Registration

Primary Runoff June 26, 2012

Primary Type Open—Any registered voter could participate in either the Democratic or Republican primary, although any voter who participated in one party's primary could not vote in a primary runoff of the other party.

SOUTH CAROLINA

GENERAL AND PRIMARY ELECTIONS

	REPUBLICAN PRIMARIES			DEMOCRATIC PRIMARIES		
President	Gingrich, Newt	244,065	40.4%			
	Romney, W. Mitt	168,123	27.8%			
	Santorum, Rick	102,475	17.0%			
	Paul, Ron	78,360	13.0%			
	Cain, Herman	6,338	1.0%			
	Perry, Rick	2,534	0.4%			
	Huntsman, Jon Jr.	1,173	0.2%			
	Bachmann, Michele	491	0.1%			
	Johnson, Gary E.	211				
	TOTAL	603,770				
Congressional District 1	Scott, Tim*	Unopposed		Rose, Bobbie G.	Unopposed	
Congressional District 2	Wilson, Joe*	23,062	80.6%			
	Black, Phil	5,557	19.4%			
	TOTAL	28,619				
Congressional District 3	Duncan, Jeff*	Unopposed		Doyle, Brian Ryan B.	4,782	66.0%
				Gaither, Cason	2,464	34.0%
				TOTAL	7,246	
Congressional District 4	Gowdy, Trey*	Unopposed		Morrow, Deb	3,678	70.6%
				Tobias, Jimmy	1,528	29.4%
				TOTAL	5,206	
Congressional District 5	Mulvaney, Mick*	Unopposed		Knott, Joyce	Unopposed	
Congressional District 6				Clyburn, James E.*	Unopposed	
Congressional District 7	Bauer, Andre	12,037	32.1%	Tinubu, Gloria Bromell	16,404	48.7%
	Rice, Tom	10,252	27.4%	Brittain, Preston	12,347	36.7%
	Jordan, Jay	8,107	21.6%	Vick, Ted	2,375	7.1%
	Prosser, Chad	3,824	10.2%	Diggs, Parnell	1,408	4.2%
	Jenerette, Katherine	1,457	3.9%	Pavilack, Harry	1,132	3.4%
	Wallace, Randal	691	1.8%			
	Withington, Dick	641	1.7%			
	Culler, Renee	279	0.7%			
	Mader, Jim	180	0.5%			
	TOTAL	37,468		TOTAL	33,666	
	PRIMARY RUNOFF			**PRIMARY RUNOFF**		
	Rice, Tom	16,844	56.1%	Tinubu, Gloria Bromell	17,930	72.7%
	Bauer, Andre	13,173	43.9%	Brittain, Preston	6,733	27.3%
	TOTAL	30,017		TOTAL	24,663	

Notes: An asterisk (*) denotes incumbent. The names of unopposed candidates did not appear on the primary ballot; therefore, no votes were cast for these candidates. A runoff was triggered if the leading candidate received less than a majority of the primary vote.

SOUTH DAKOTA

One member At Large

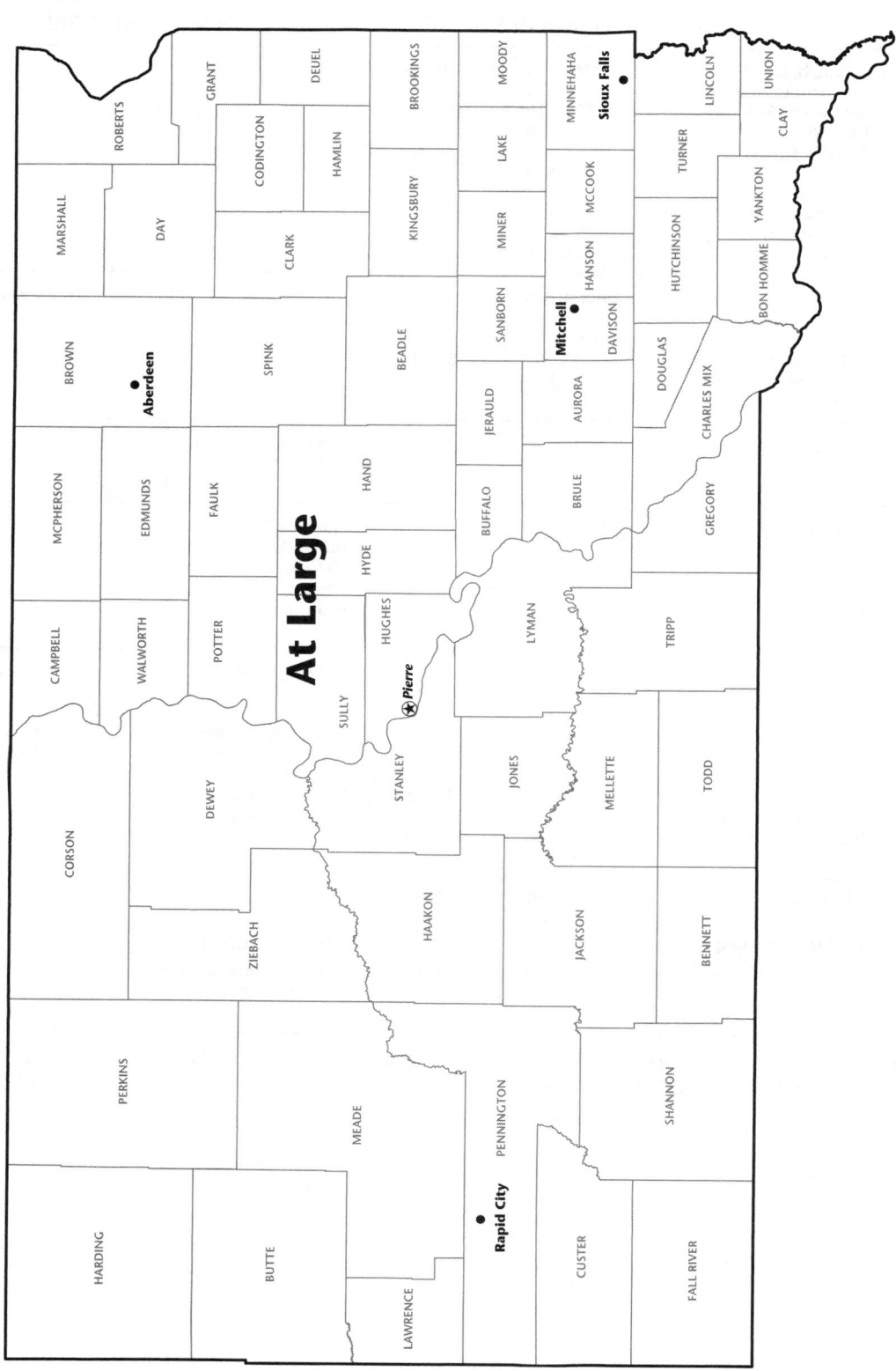

SOUTH DAKOTA

GOVERNOR
Dennis Daugaard (R). Elected 2010 to a four-year term.

SENATORS (1 Republican, 1 Democrat)
Tim Johnson (D). Reelected 2008 to a six-year term. Previously elected 2002, 1996.

John Thune (R). Reelected 2010 to a six-year term. Previously elected 2004.

REPRESENTATIVE (1 Republican)
At Large. Kristi Noem (R)

POSTWAR VOTE FOR PRESIDENT

| | | Republican | | Democratic | | | | Percentage | | | |
| | | | | | | | | Total Vote | | Major Vote | |
Year	Total Vote	Vote	Candidate	Vote	Candidate	Other Vote	Rep.-Dem. Plurality	Rep.	Dem.	Rep.	Dem.
2012	363,815	210,610	Romney, W. Mitt	145,039	Obama, Barack H.*	8,166	65,571 R	57.9%	39.9%	59.2%	40.8%
2008	381,975	203,054	McCain, John S. III	170,924	Obama, Barack H.	7,997	32,130 R	53.2%	44.7%	54.3%	45.7%
2004	388,215	232,584	Bush, George W.*	149,244	Kerry, John F.	6,387	83,340 R	59.9%	38.4%	60.9%	39.1%
2000	316,269	190,700	Bush, George W.	118,804	Gore, Albert Jr.	6,765	71,896 R	60.3%	37.6%	61.6%	38.4%
1996**	323,826	150,543	Dole, Robert "Bob"	139,333	Clinton, Bill*	33,950	11,210 R	46.5%	43.0%	51.9%	48.1%
1992**	336,254	136,718	Bush, George H.*	124,888	Clinton, Bill	74,648	11,830 R	40.7%	37.1%	52.3%	47.7%
1988	312,991	165,415	Bush, George H.	145,560	Dukakis, Michael S.	2,016	19,855 R	52.8%	46.5%	53.2%	46.8%
1984	317,867	200,267	Reagan, Ronald*	116,113	Mondale, Walter F.	1,487	84,154 R	63.0%	36.5%	63.3%	36.7%
1980**	327,703	198,343	Reagan, Ronald	103,855	Carter, Jimmy*	25,505	94,488 R	60.5%	31.7%	65.6%	34.4%
1976	300,678	151,505	Ford, Gerald R.*	147,068	Carter, Jimmy	2,105	4,437 R	50.4%	48.9%	50.7%	49.3%
1972	307,415	166,476	Nixon, Richard M.*	139,945	McGovern, George S.	994	26,531 R	54.2%	45.5%	54.3%	45.7%
1968**	281,264	149,841	Nixon, Richard M.	118,023	Humphrey, Hubert H. Jr.	13,400	31,818 R	53.3%	42.0%	55.9%	44.1%
1964	293,118	130,108	Goldwater, Barry M. Sr.	163,010	Johnson, Lyndon B.*		32,902 D	44.4%	55.6%	44.4%	55.6%
1960	306,487	178,417	Nixon, Richard M.	128,070	Kennedy, John F.		50,347 R	58.2%	41.8%	58.2%	41.8%
1956	293,857	171,569	Eisenhower, Dwight D.*	122,288	Stevenson, Adlai E. II		49,281 R	58.4%	41.6%	58.4%	41.6%
1952	294,283	203,857	Eisenhower, Dwight D.	90,426	Stevenson, Adlai E. II		113,431 R	69.3%	30.7%	69.3%	30.7%
1948	250,105	129,651	Dewey, Thomas E.	117,653	Truman, Harry S.*	2,801	11,998 R	51.8%	47.0%	52.4%	47.6%

Note: An asterisk (*) denotes incumbent. **In past elections, the other vote included: 1996 - 31,250 Reform (Ross Perot); 1992 - 73,295 Independent (Perot); 1980 - 21,431 Independent (John Anderson); 1968 - 13,400 American Independent (George Wallace).

SOUTH DAKOTA

POSTWAR VOTE FOR GOVERNOR

Year	Total Vote	Republican Vote	Republican Candidate	Democratic Vote	Democratic Candidate	Other Vote	Rep.-Dem. Plurality	Total Vote Rep.	Total Vote Dem.	Major Vote Rep.	Major Vote Dem.
2010	317,083	195,046	Daugaard, Dennis	122,037	Heidepriem, Scott		73,009 R	61.5%	38.5%	61.5%	38.5%
2006	335,508	206,990	Rounds, Mike*	121,226	Billion, Jack	7,292	85,764 R	61.7%	36.1%	63.1%	36.9%
2002	334,559	189,920	Rounds, Mike	140,263	Abbott, Jim	4,376	49,657 R	56.8%	41.9%	57.5%	42.5%
1998	260,187	166,621	Janklow, William J.*	85,473	Hunhoff, Bernie	8,093	81,148 R	64.0%	32.9%	66.1%	33.9%
1994	311,613	172,515	Janklow, William J.	126,273	Beddow, Jim	12,825	46,242 R	55.4%	40.5%	57.7%	42.3%
1990	256,723	151,198	Mickelson, George S.*	105,525	Samuelson, Bob L.		45,673 R	58.9%	41.1%	58.9%	41.1%
1986	294,441	152,543	Mickelson, George S.	141,898	Herseth, R. Lars		10,645 R	51.8%	48.2%	51.8%	48.2%
1982	278,565	197,429	Janklow, William J.*	81,136	O'Connor, Michael J.		116,293 R	70.9%	29.1%	70.9%	29.1%
1978	259,795	147,116	Janklow, William J.	112,679	McKellips, Roger		34,437 R	56.6%	43.4%	56.6%	43.4%
1974**	278,228	129,077	Olson, John E.	149,151	Kneip, Richard F.*		20,074 D	46.4%	53.6%	46.4%	53.6%
1972	308,177	123,165	Thompson, Carveth	185,012	Kneip, Richard F.*		61,847 D	40.0%	60.0%	40.0%	60.0%
1970	239,963	108,347	Farrar, Frank*	131,616	Kneip, Richard F.		23,269 D	45.2%	54.8%	45.2%	54.8%
1968	276,906	159,646	Farrar, Frank	117,260	Chamerlin, Robert		42,386 R	57.7%	42.3%	57.7%	42.3%
1966	228,214	131,710	Boe, Nils A.*	96,504	Chamerlin, Robert		35,206 R	57.7%	42.3%	57.7%	42.3%
1964	290,570	150,151	Boe, Nils A.	140,419	Lindley, John F.		9,732 R	51.7%	48.3%	51.7%	48.3%
1962	256,120	143,682	Gubbrud, Archie M.*	112,438	Herseth, Ralph		31,244 R	56.1%	43.9%	56.1%	43.9%
1960	304,625	154,530	Gubbrud, Archie M.	150,095	Herseth, Ralph*		4,435 R	50.7%	49.3%	50.7%	49.3%
1958	258,281	125,520	Saunders, Phil	132,761	Herseth, Ralph		7,241 D	48.6%	51.4%	48.6%	51.4%
1956	292,017	158,819	Foss, Joe*	133,198	Herseth, Ralph		25,621 R	54.4%	45.6%	54.4%	45.6%
1954	236,255	133,878	Foss, Joe	102,377	Martin, Ed C.		31,501 R	56.7%	43.3%	56.7%	43.3%
1952	289,514	203,102	Anderson, Sigurd*	86,412	Iverson, Sherman A.		116,690 R	70.2%	29.8%	70.2%	29.8%
1950	253,316	154,254	Anderson, Sigurd	99,062	Robbie, Joe		55,192 R	60.9%	39.1%	60.9%	39.1%
1948	245,372	149,883	Mickelson, George T.*	95,489	Volz, Harold J.		54,394 R	61.1%	38.9%	61.1%	38.9%
1946	162,292	108,998	Mickelson, George T.	53,294	Haeder, Richard		55,704 R	67.2%	32.8%	67.2%	32.8%

Note: An asterisk (*) denotes incumbent. **The term of office of South Dakota's governor was increased from two to four years effective with the 1974 election.

POSTWAR VOTE FOR SENATOR

Year	Total Vote	Republican Vote	Republican Candidate	Democratic Vote	Democratic Candidate	Other Vote	Rep.-Dem. Plurality	Total Vote Rep.	Total Vote Dem.	Major Vote Rep.	Major Vote Dem.
2010	227,947	227,947	Thune, John*				227,947 R	100.0%		100.0%	
2008	380,673	142,784	Dykstra, Joel	237,889	Johnson, Tim*		95,105 D	37.5%	62.5%	37.5%	62.5%
2004	391,188	197,848	Thune, John	193,340	Daschle, Thomas A.*		4,508 R	50.6%	49.4%	50.6%	49.4%
2002	337,508	166,957	Thune, John	167,481	Johnson, Tim*	3,070	524 D	49.5%	49.6%	49.9%	50.1%
1998	262,111	95,431	Schmidt, Ron	162,884	Daschle, Thomas A.*	3,796	67,453 D	36.4%	62.1%	36.9%	63.1%
1996	324,487	157,954	Pressler, Larry*	166,533	Johnson, Tim		8,579 D	48.7%	51.3%	48.7%	51.3%
1992	334,495	108,733	Haar, Charlene	217,095	Daschle, Thomas A.*	8,667	108,362 D	32.5%	64.9%	33.4%	66.6%
1990	258,976	135,682	Pressler, Larry*	116,727	Muenster, Ted	6,567	18,955 R	52.4%	45.1%	53.8%	46.2%
1986	295,830	143,173	Abdnor, James*	152,657	Daschle, Thomas A.		9,484 D	48.4%	51.6%	48.4%	51.6%
1984	315,713	235,176	Pressler, Larry*	80,537	Cunningham, George V.		154,639 R	74.5%	25.5%	74.5%	25.5%
1980	327,478	190,594	Abdnor, James	129,018	McGovern, George S.*	7,866	61,576 R	58.2%	39.4%	59.6%	40.4%
1978	255,599	170,832	Pressler, Larry	84,767	Barnett, Don		86,065 R	66.8%	33.2%	66.8%	33.2%
1974	278,884	130,955	Thorsness, Leo K.	147,929	McGovern, George S.*		16,974 D	47.0%	53.0%	47.0%	53.0%
1972	306,386	131,613	Hirsch, Robert W.	174,773	Abourezk, James George*		43,160 D	43.0%	57.0%	43.0%	57.0%
1968	279,912	120,951	Gubbrud, Archie M.	158,961	McGovern, George S.*		38,010 D	43.2%	56.8%	43.2%	56.8%
1966	227,080	150,517	Mundt, Karl E.*	76,563	Wright, Donn H.		73,954 R	66.3%	33.7%	66.3%	33.7%
1962	254,319	126,861	Bottum, Joe*	127,458	McGovern, George S.		597 D	49.9%	50.1%	49.9%	50.1%
1960	305,442	160,181	Mundt, Karl E.*	145,261	McGovern, George S.		14,920 R	52.4%	47.6%	52.4%	47.6%
1956	290,622	147,621	Case, Francis*	143,001	Holum, Kenneth		4,620 R	50.8%	49.2%	50.8%	49.2%
1954	235,745	135,071	Mundt, Karl E.*	100,674	Holum, Kenneth		34,397 R	57.3%	42.7%	57.3%	42.7%
1950	251,362	160,670	Case, Francis	90,692	Engel, John A.		69,978 R	63.9%	36.1%	63.9%	36.1%
1948	242,833	144,084	Mundt, Karl E.	98,749	Engel, John A.		45,335 R	59.3%	40.7%	59.3%	40.7%

Note: An asterisk (*) denotes incumbent. **The Democratic Party did not run a Senate candidate in the 2010 election.

SOUTH DAKOTA

PRESIDENT 2012

2010 Census Population	County	Total Vote	Republican (Romney)	Democratic (Obama)	Other	Rep.-Dem. Plurality	Percentage Total Vote Rep.	Percentage Total Vote Dem.	Percentage Major Vote Rep.	Percentage Major Vote Dem.
2,710	AURORA	1,400	804	556	40	248 R	57.4%	39.7%	59.1%	40.9%
17,398	BEADLE	7,263	4,230	2,881	152	1,349 R	58.2%	39.7%	59.5%	40.5%
3,431	BENNETT	1,203	626	548	29	78 R	52.0%	45.6%	53.3%	46.7%
7,070	BON HOMME	3,074	1,830	1,167	77	663 R	59.5%	38.0%	61.1%	38.9%
31,965	BROOKINGS	12,400	6,220	5,827	353	393 R	50.2%	47.0%	51.6%	48.4%
36,531	BROWN	16,068	8,321	7,250	497	1,071 R	51.8%	45.1%	53.4%	46.6%
5,255	BRULE	2,379	1,499	824	56	675 R	63.0%	34.6%	64.5%	35.5%
1,912	BUFFALO	641	166	472	3	306 D	25.9%	73.6%	26.0%	74.0%
10,110	BUTTE	4,208	3,073	1,002	133	2,071 R	73.0%	23.8%	75.4%	24.6%
1,466	CAMPBELL	787	616	153	18	463 R	78.3%	19.4%	80.1%	19.9%
9,129	CHARLES MIX	3,764	2,230	1,483	51	747 R	59.2%	39.4%	60.1%	39.9%
3,691	CLARK	1,821	1,067	713	41	354 R	58.6%	39.2%	59.9%	40.1%
13,864	CLAY	5,234	2,147	2,955	132	808 D	41.0%	56.5%	42.1%	57.9%
27,227	CODINGTON	11,524	6,696	4,588	240	2,108 R	58.1%	39.8%	59.3%	40.7%
4,050	CORSON	1,200	515	648	37	133 D	42.9%	54.0%	44.3%	55.7%
8,216	CUSTER	4,520	3,062	1,335	123	1,727 R	67.7%	29.5%	69.6%	30.4%
19,504	DAVISON	7,971	4,757	3,042	172	1,715 R	59.7%	38.2%	61.0%	39.0%
5,710	DAY	2,873	1,320	1,497	56	177 D	45.9%	52.1%	46.9%	53.1%
4,364	DEUEL	2,171	1,175	941	55	234 R	54.1%	43.3%	55.5%	44.5%
5,301	DEWEY	1,895	663	1,207	25	544 D	35.0%	63.7%	35.5%	64.5%
3,002	DOUGLAS	1,690	1,334	332	24	1,002 R	78.9%	19.6%	80.1%	19.9%
4,071	EDMUNDS	1,936	1,264	622	50	642 R	65.3%	32.1%	67.0%	33.0%
7,094	FALL RIVER	3,516	2,258	1,140	118	1,118 R	64.2%	32.4%	66.5%	33.5%
2,364	FAULK	1,127	765	331	31	434 R	67.9%	29.4%	69.8%	30.2%
7,356	GRANT	3,606	2,034	1,493	79	541 R	56.4%	41.4%	57.7%	42.3%
4,271	GREGORY	2,151	1,507	599	45	908 R	70.1%	27.8%	71.6%	28.4%
1,937	HAAKON	1,092	940	138	14	802 R	86.1%	12.6%	87.2%	12.8%
5,903	HAMLIN	2,793	1,803	921	69	882 R	64.6%	33.0%	66.2%	33.8%
3,431	HAND	1,848	1,242	575	31	667 R	67.2%	31.1%	68.4%	31.6%
3,331	HANSON	2,416	1,627	760	29	867 R	67.3%	31.5%	68.2%	31.8%
1,255	HARDING	739	638	82	19	556 R	86.3%	11.1%	88.6%	11.4%
17,022	HUGHES	8,155	5,219	2,786	150	2,433 R	64.0%	34.2%	65.2%	34.8%
7,343	HUTCHINSON	3,425	2,451	923	51	1,528 R	71.6%	26.9%	72.6%	27.4%
1,420	HYDE	733	531	189	13	342 R	72.4%	25.8%	73.8%	26.2%
3,031	JACKSON	1,106	661	426	19	235 R	59.8%	38.5%	60.8%	39.2%
2,071	JERAULD	1,006	538	452	16	86 R	53.5%	44.9%	54.3%	45.7%
1,006	JONES	609	490	108	11	382 R	80.5%	17.7%	81.9%	18.1%
5,148	KINGSBURY	2,608	1,451	1,092	65	359 R	55.6%	41.9%	57.1%	42.9%
11,200	LAKE	6,285	3,419	2,724	142	695 R	54.4%	43.3%	55.7%	44.3%
24,097	LAWRENCE	11,359	7,025	3,973	361	3,052 R	61.8%	35.0%	63.9%	36.1%
44,828	LINCOLN	21,952	13,611	7,982	359	5,629 R	62.0%	36.4%	63.0%	37.0%
3,755	LYMAN	1,569	933	605	31	328 R	59.5%	38.6%	60.7%	39.3%
4,656	MARSHALL	1,987	889	1,061	37	172 D	44.7%	53.4%	45.6%	54.4%
5,618	MCCOOK	2,613	1,655	905	53	750 R	63.3%	34.6%	64.6%	35.4%
2,459	MCPHERSON	1,215	921	272	22	649 R	75.8%	22.4%	77.2%	22.8%
25,434	MEADE	10,817	7,566	2,928	323	4,638 R	69.9%	27.1%	72.1%	27.9%
2,048	MELLETTE	769	381	375	13	6 R	49.5%	48.8%	50.4%	49.6%
2,389	MINER	1,140	636	479	25	157 R	55.8%	42.0%	57.0%	43.0%
169,468	MINNEHAHA	76,583	40,342	34,674	1,567	5,668 R	52.7%	45.3%	53.8%	46.2%
6,486	MOODY	3,033	1,535	1,429	69	106 R	50.6%	47.1%	51.8%	48.2%
100,948	PENNINGTON	44,464	28,232	15,125	1,107	13,107 R	63.5%	34.0%	65.1%	34.9%
2,982	PERKINS	1,590	1,205	319	66	886 R	75.8%	20.1%	79.1%	20.9%
2,329	POTTER	1,381	1,029	339	13	690 R	74.5%	24.5%	75.2%	24.8%
10,149	ROBERTS	4,256	1,883	2,302	71	419 D	44.2%	54.1%	45.0%	55.0%
2,355	SANBORN	1,115	688	389	38	299 R	61.7%	34.9%	63.9%	36.1%
13,586	SHANNON	3,145	188	2,937	20	2,749 D	6.0%	93.4%	6.0%	94.0%
6,415	SPINK	3,041	1,670	1,300	71	370 R	54.9%	42.7%	56.2%	43.8%
2,966	STANLEY	1,540	1,063	435	42	628 R	69.0%	28.2%	71.0%	29.0%
1,373	SULLY	818	613	186	19	427 R	74.9%	22.7%	76.7%	23.3%
9,612	TODD	2,497	498	1,976	23	1,478 D	19.9%	79.1%	20.1%	79.9%

SOUTH DAKOTA

PRESIDENT 2012

2010 Census Population	County	Total Vote	Republican (Romney)	Democratic (Obama)	Other	Rep.-Dem. Plurality	Percentage			
							Total Vote		Major Vote	
							Rep.	Dem.	Rep.	Dem.
5,644	TRIPP	2,691	1,905	737	49	1,168 R	70.8%	27.4%	72.1%	27.9%
8,347	TURNER	4,210	2,715	1,411	84	1,304 R	64.5%	33.5%	65.8%	34.2%
14,399	UNION	7,596	4,698	2,782	116	1,916 R	61.8%	36.6%	62.8%	37.2%
5,438	WALWORTH	2,462	1,731	671	60	1,060 R	70.3%	27.3%	72.1%	27.9%
22,438	YANKTON	9,974	5,495	4,226	253	1,269 R	55.1%	42.4%	56.5%	43.5%
2,801	ZIEBACH	761	314	439	8	125 D	41.3%	57.7%	41.7%	58.3%
814,180	TOTAL	363,815	210,610	145,039	8,166	65,571 R	57.9%	39.9%	59.2%	40.8%

SOUTH DAKOTA

HOUSE OF REPRESENTATIVES

CD	Year	Total Vote	Republican		Democratic		Other Vote	Rep.-Dem. Plurality	Percentage			
			Vote	Candidate	Vote	Candidate			Total Vote		Major Vote	
									Rep.	Dem.	Rep.	Dem.
At Large	2012	361,429	207,640	NOEM, KRISTI*	153,789	VARILEK, MATT		53,851 R	57.4%	42.6%	57.4%	42.6%
At Large	2010	319,426	153,703	NOEM, KRISTI	146,589	SANDLIN, STEPHANIE HERSETH*	19,134	7,114 R	48.1%	45.9%	51.2%	48.8%
At Large	2008	379,007	122,966	LIEN, CHRIS	256,041	SANDLIN, STEPHANIE HERSETH*		133,075 D	32.4%	67.6%	32.4%	67.6%
At Large	2006	333,562	97,864	WHALEN, BRUCE W.	230,468	SANDLIN, STEPHANIE HERSETH*	5,230	132,604 D	29.3%	69.1%	29.8%	70.2%
At Large	2004	389,468	178,823	DIEDRICH, LARRY W.	207,837	SANDLIN, STEPHANIE HERSETH*	2,808	29,014 D	45.9%	53.4%	46.2%	53.8%
At Large	2002	336,807	180,023	JANKLOW, WILLIAM J.	153,656	SANDLIN, STEPHANIE HERSETH	3,128	26,367 R	53.4%	45.6%	54.0%	46.0%
At Large	2000	314,761	231,083	THUNE, JOHN*	78,321	HOHN, CURT	5,357	152,762 R	73.4%	24.9%	74.7%	25.3%
At Large	1998	258,590	194,157	THUNE, JOHN*	64,433	MOSER, JEFF		129,724 R	75.1%	24.9%	75.1%	24.9%
At Large	1996	323,203	186,393	THUNE, JOHN	119,547	WEILAND, RICK	17,263	66,846 R	57.7%	37.0%	60.9%	39.1%
At Large	1994	305,922	112,054	BERKHOUT, JAN	183,036	JOHNSON, TIM*	10,832	70,982 D	36.6%	59.8%	38.0%	62.0%
At Large	1992	332,902	89,375	TIMMER, JOHN	230,070	JOHNSON, TIM*	13,457	140,695 D	26.8%	69.1%	28.0%	72.0%
At Large	1990	257,298	83,484	FRANKENFELD, DON	173,814	JOHNSON, TIM*		90,330 D	32.4%	67.6%	32.4%	67.6%
At Large	1988	311,916	88,157	VOLK, DAVID	223,759	JOHNSON, TIM*		135,602 D	28.3%	71.7%	28.3%	71.7%
At Large	1986	289,723	118,261	BELL, DALE	171,462	JOHNSON, TIM		53,201 D	40.8%	59.2%	40.8%	59.2%
At Large	1984	316,222	134,821	BELL, DALE	181,401	DASCHLE, THOMAS A.*		46,580 D	42.6%	57.4%	42.6%	57.4%
At Large	1982	275,652	133,530	ROBERTS, CLINT*	142,122	DASCHLE, THOMAS A.*		8,592 D	48.4%	51.6%	48.4%	51.6%

Notes: An asterisk (*) denotes incumbent. South Dakota had two House seats before 1982.

SOUTH DAKOTA

GENERAL AND PRIMARY ELECTIONS

GENERAL ELECTIONS: OTHER VOTE

President   Other vote was 5,795 Libertarian (Gary E. Johnson), 2,371 Constitution (Virgil H. Goode)

PRIMARY ELECTIONS: SUPPLEMENTARY INFORMATION

Primary   June 5, 2012   **Registration** (as of June 5, 2012 – active registrants only)   441,385   Republican   234,515
Democratic/Independent   183,377
Other   23,493

Primary Type   Republicans held a "closed" primary, with only registered Republicans allowed to vote in it. Democrats held a "semi-open" primary, with both registered Democrats and Independents eligible to cast a Democratic primary ballot.

SOUTH DAKOTA

GENERAL AND PRIMARY ELECTIONS

	REPUBLICAN PRIMARIES			DEMOCRATIC PRIMARIES		
President	Romney, W. Mitt	33,872	66.2%			
	Paul, Ron	6,657	13.0%			
	Santorum, Rick	5,844	11.4%			
	Uncommitted	2,771	5.4%			
	Gingrich, Newt	2,001	3.9%			
	TOTAL	51,145				
House At Large	Noem, Kristi*	Unopposed		Varilek, Matt	21,759	71.9%
				Barth, Jeff	8,494	28.1%
				TOTAL	30,253	

Notes: An asterisk (*) denotes incumbent. The names of unopposed candidates did not appear on the primary ballot; therefore, no votes were cast for these candidates. A runoff would be triggered if the leading candidate received less than 35 percent of the primary vote.

TENNESSEE
Congressional districts first established for elections held in 2012
9 members

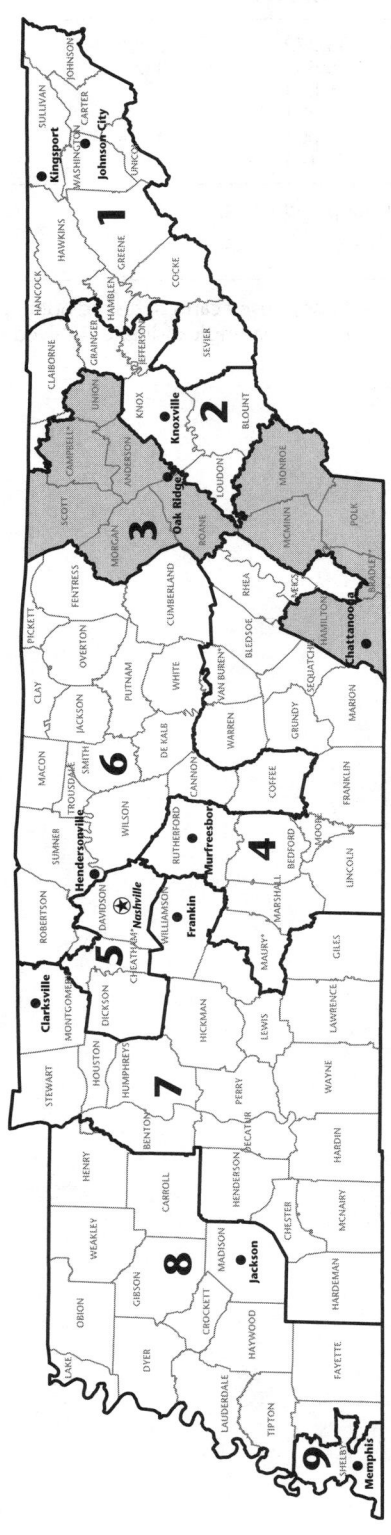

* Asterisk indicates a county whose boundaries include parts of two or more Congressional districts.

TENNESSEE

GOVERNOR
Bill Haslam (R). Elected 2010 to a four-year term.

SENATORS (2 Republicans)
Lamar Alexander (R). Reelected 2008 to a six-year term. Previously elected 2002.

Bob Corker (R). Reelected 2012 to a six-year term. Previously elected 2006.

REPRESENTATIVES (7 Republicans, 2 Democrats)
1. Phil Roe (R)
2. John J. Duncan Jr. (R)
3. Chuck Fleischmann (R)
4. Scott DesJarlais (R)
5. Jim Cooper (D)
6. Diane Black (R)
7. Marsha Blackburn (R)
8. Stephen Fincher (R)
9. Steve Cohen (D)

POSTWAR VOTE FOR PRESIDENT

| | | Republican | | Democratic | | | | Percentage | | | |
| | | | | | | | | Total Vote | | Major Vote | |
Year	Total Vote	Vote	Candidate	Vote	Candidate	Other Vote	Rep.-Dem. Plurality	Rep.	Dem.	Rep.	Dem.
2012	2,458,577	1,462,330	Romney, W. Mitt	960,709	Obama, Barack H.*	35,538	501,621 R	59.5%	39.1%	60.4%	39.6%
2008	2,599,749	1,479,178	McCain, John S. III	1,087,437	Obama, Barack H.	33,134	391,741 R	56.9%	41.8%	57.6%	42.4%
2004	2,437,319	1,384,375	Bush, George W.*	1,036,477	Kerry, John F.	16,467	347,898 R	56.8%	42.5%	57.2%	42.8%
2000**	2,076,181	1,061,949	Bush, George W.	981,720	Gore, Albert Jr.	32,512	80,229 R	51.1%	47.3%	52.0%	48.0%
1996**	1,894,105	863,530	Dole, Robert "Bob"	909,146	Clinton, Bill*	121,429	45,616 D	45.6%	48.0%	48.7%	51.3%
1992**	1,982,638	841,300	Bush, George H.*	933,521	Clinton, Bill	207,817	92,221 D	42.4%	47.1%	47.4%	52.6%
1988	1,636,250	947,233	Bush, George H.	679,794	Dukakis, Michael S.	9,223	267,439 R	57.9%	41.5%	58.2%	41.8%
1984	1,711,994	990,212	Reagan, Ronald*	711,714	Mondale, Walter F.	10,068	278,498 R	57.8%	41.6%	58.2%	41.8%
1980**	1,617,616	787,761	Reagan, Ronald	783,051	Carter, Jimmy*	46,804	4,710 R	48.7%	48.4%	50.1%	49.9%
1976	1,476,345	633,969	Ford, Gerald R.*	825,879	Carter, Jimmy	16,497	191,910 D	42.9%	55.9%	43.4%	56.6%
1972	1,201,182	813,147	Nixon, Richard M.*	357,293	McGovern, George S.	30,742	455,854 R	67.7%	29.7%	69.5%	30.5%
1968**	1,248,617	472,592	Nixon, Richard M.	351,233	Humphrey, Hubert H. Jr.	424,792	121,359 R	37.8%	28.1%	57.4%	42.6%
1964	1,143,946	508,965	Goldwater, Barry M. Sr.	634,947	Johnson, Lyndon B.*	34	125,982 D	44.5%	55.5%	44.5%	55.5%
1960	1,051,792	556,577	Nixon, Richard M.	481,453	Kennedy, John F.	13,762	75,124 R	52.9%	45.8%	53.6%	46.4%
1956	939,404	462,288	Eisenhower, Dwight D.*	456,507	Stevenson, Adlai E. II	20,609	5,781 R	49.2%	48.6%	50.3%	49.7%
1952	892,553	446,147	Eisenhower, Dwight D.	443,710	Stevenson, Adlai E. II	2,696	2,437 R	50.0%	49.7%	50.1%	49.9%
1948**	550,283	202,914	Dewey, Thomas E.	270,402	Truman, Harry S.*	76,967	67,488 D	36.9%	49.1%	42.9%	57.1%

Note: An asterisk (*) denotes incumbent. **In past elections, the other vote included: 2000 - 19,781 Green (Ralph Nader); 1996 - 105,918 Reform (Ross Perot); 1992 - 199,968 Independent (Perot); 1980 - 35,991 Independent (John Anderson); 1968 - 424,792 American Independent (George Wallace), who finished second; 1948 - 73,815 States' Rights (Strom Thurmond).

TENNESSEE

POSTWAR VOTE FOR GOVERNOR

| | | Republican | | Democratic | | Other | Rep.-Dem. | Percentage | | | |
| | | | | | | | | Total Vote | | Major Vote | |
Year	Total Vote	Vote	Candidate	Vote	Candidate	Vote	Plurality	Rep.	Dem.	Rep.	Dem.
2010	1,601,549	1,041,545	Haslam, Bill	529,851	McWherter, Mike	30,153	511,694 R	65.0%	33.1%	66.3%	33.7%
2006	1,818,549	540,853	Bryson, Jim	1,247,491	Bredesen, Phil*	30,205	706,638 D	29.7%	68.6%	30.2%	69.8%
2002	1,653,167	786,803	Hilleary, Van	837,284	Bredesen, Phil	29,080	50,481 D	47.6%	50.6%	48.4%	51.6%
1998	976,236	669,973	Sundquist, Don*	287,750	Hooker, John Jay	18,513	382,223 R	68.6%	29.5%	70.0%	30.0%
1994	1,487,124	807,107	Sundquist, Don	664,243	Bredesen, Phil	15,774	142,864 R	54.3%	44.7%	54.9%	45.1%
1990	790,441	289,348	Henry, Dwight	480,885	McWherter, Ned*	20,208	191,537 D	36.6%	60.8%	37.6%	62.4%
1986	1,210,339	553,449	Dunn, Winfield	656,602	McWherter, Ned	288	103,153 D	45.7%	54.2%	45.7%	54.3%
1982	1,238,927	737,963	Alexander, Lamar*	500,937	Tyree, Randy	27	237,026 R	59.6%	40.4%	59.6%	40.4%
1978	1,189,695	661,959	Alexander, Lamar	523,495	Butcher, Jake	4,241	138,464 R	55.6%	44.0%	55.8%	44.2%
1974	1,040,714	455,467	Alexander, Lamar	576,833	Blanton, L. Ray	8,414	121,366 D	43.8%	55.4%	44.1%	55.9%
1970	1,108,247	575,777	Dunn, Winfield	509,521	Hooker, John Jay	22,949	66,256 R	52.0%	46.0%	53.1%	46.9%
1966	656,566			532,998	Ellington, Buford	123,568	532,998 D		81.2%		100.0%
1962**	620,758	99,884	Patty, Hubert D.	315,648	Clement, Frank G.	205,226	215,764 D	16.1%	50.8%	24.0%	76.0%
1958**	432,545	35,938	Wall, Thomas P.	248,874	Ellington, Buford	147,733	212,936 D	8.3%	57.5%	12.6%	87.4%
1954**	322,586			281,291	Clement, Frank G.*	41,295	281,291 D		87.2%		100.0%
1952	806,771	166,377	Witt, R. Beecher	640,290	Clement, Frank G.	104	473,913 D	20.6%	79.4%	20.6%	79.4%
1950**	236,194			184,437	Browning, Gordon*	51,757	184,437 D		78.1%		100.0%
1948	543,881	179,957	Acuff, Roy	363,903	Browning, Gordon	21	183,946 D	33.1%	66.9%	33.1%	66.9%
1946	229,456	73,222	Lowe, W. O.	149,937	McCord, James N.*	6,297	76,715 D	31.9%	65.3%	32.8%	67.2%

Note: An asterisk (*) denotes incumbent. **In past elections, the other vote included: 1962 - 203,765 Independent (William R. Anderson), who finished second; 1958 - 136,399 Independent (Jim Nance McCord), who finished second; 1954 - 39,574 Independent (John R. Neal), who finished second; 1950 - 51,757 Independent (Neal), who finished second. The Republican Party did not run a gubernatorial candidate in 1950, 1954, and 1966. The term of office of Tennessee's governor was increased from two to four years effective with the 1954 election.

POSTWAR VOTE FOR SENATOR

| | | Republican | | Democratic | | Other | Rep.-Dem. | Percentage | | | |
| | | | | | | | | Total Vote | | Major Vote | |
Year	Total Vote	Vote	Candidate	Vote	Candidate	Vote	Plurality	Rep.	Dem.	Rep.	Dem.
2012	2,321,477	1,506,443	Corker, Bob*	705,882	Clayton, Mark E.	109,152	800,561 R	64.9%	30.4%	68.1%	31.9%
2008	2,424,585	1,579,477	Alexander, Lamar*	767,236	Tuke, Robert D.	77,872	812,241 R	65.1%	31.6%	67.3%	32.7%
2006	1,833,695	929,911	Corker, Bob	879,976	Ford, Harold E. Jr.	23,808	49,935 R	50.7%	48.0%	51.4%	48.6%
2002	1,642,421	891,420	Alexander, Lamar	728,295	Clement, Robert Nelson	22,706	163,125 R	54.3%	44.3%	55.0%	45.0%
2000	1,928,613	1,255,444	Frist, William H.*	621,152	Clark, Jeff	52,017	634,292 R	65.1%	32.2%	66.9%	33.1%
1996	1,778,664	1,091,554	Thompson, Fred*	654,937	Houston, Gordon J.	32,173	436,617 R	61.4%	36.8%	62.5%	37.5%
1994	1,480,391	834,226	Frist, William H.	623,164	Sasser, James R.*	23,001	211,062 R	56.4%	42.1%	57.2%	42.8%
1994S	1,465,862	885,998	Thompson, Fred	565,930	Cooper, Jim	13,934	320,068 R	60.4%	38.6%	61.0%	39.0%
1990	783,922	233,703	Hawkins, William R.	530,898	Gore, Albert Jr.*	19,321	297,195 D	29.8%	67.7%	30.6%	69.4%
1988	1,567,181	541,033	Anderson, Bill	1,020,061	Sasser, James R.*	6,087	479,028 D	34.5%	65.1%	34.7%	65.3%
1984	1,648,036	557,016	Ashe, Victor	1,000,607	Gore, Albert Jr.	90,413	443,591 D	33.8%	60.7%	35.8%	64.2%
1982	1,259,785	479,642	Beard, Robin L.	780,113	Sasser, James R.*	30	300,471 D	38.1%	61.9%	38.1%	61.9%
1978	1,157,094	642,644	Baker, Howard H. Jr.*	466,228	Eskind, Jane	48,222	176,416 R	55.5%	40.3%	58.0%	42.0%
1976	1,432,046	673,231	Brock, William E.*	751,180	Sasser, James R.	7,635	77,949 D	47.0%	52.5%	47.3%	52.7%
1972	1,164,195	716,539	Baker, Howard H. Jr.*	440,599	Blanton, L. Ray	7,057	275,940 R	61.5%	37.8%	61.9%	38.1%
1970	1,097,041	562,645	Brock, William E.	519,858	Gore, Albert Sr.*	14,538	42,787 R	51.3%	47.4%	52.0%	48.0%
1966	866,961	483,063	Baker, Howard H. Jr.	383,843	Clement, Frank G.	55	99,220 R	55.7%	44.3%	55.7%	44.3%
1964	1,064,018	493,475	Kuykendall, Daniel H.	570,542	Gore, Albert Sr.*	1	77,067 D	46.4%	53.6%	46.4%	53.6%
1964S	1,091,093	517,330	Baker, Howard H. Jr.	568,905	Bass, Ross	4,858	51,575 D	47.4%	52.1%	47.6%	52.4%
1960	828,519	234,053	Frazier, A. Bradley	594,460	Kefauver, Estes*	6	360,407 D	28.2%	71.7%	28.2%	71.8%
1958	401,666	76,371	Atkins, Hobart F.	317,324	Gore, Albert Sr.*	7,971	240,953 D	19.0%	79.0%	19.4%	80.6%
1954	356,094	106,971	Wall, Tom	249,121	Kefauver, Estes*	2	142,150 D	30.0%	70.0%	30.0%	70.0%
1952	735,219	153,479	Atkins, Hobart F.	545,432	Gore, Albert Sr.	36,308	391,953 D	20.9%	74.2%	22.0%	78.0%
1948	499,138	166,947	Reece, B. Carroll	326,062	Kefauver, Estes	6,129	159,115 D	33.4%	65.3%	33.9%	66.1%
1946	218,713	57,237	Ladd, W. B.	145,654	McKellar, Kenneth D.*	15,822	88,417 D	26.2%	66.6%	28.2%	71.8%

Note: An asterisk (*) denotes incumbent. **One each of the 1964 and 1994 elections was for a short term to fill a vacancy.

TENNESSEE

PRESIDENT 2012

2010 Census Population	County	Total Vote	Republican (Romney)	Democratic (Obama)	Other	Rep.-Dem. Plurality	Percentage Total Vote		Percentage Major Vote	
							Rep.	Dem.	Rep.	Dem.
75,129	ANDERSON	29,659	18,968	10,122	569	8,846 R	64.0%	34.1%	65.2%	34.8%
45,058	BEDFORD	14,445	10,034	4,211	200	5,823 R	69.5%	29.2%	70.4%	29.6%
16,489	BENTON	6,226	3,850	2,258	118	1,592 R	61.8%	36.3%	63.0%	37.0%
12,876	BLEDSOE	4,359	3,022	1,267	70	1,755 R	69.3%	29.1%	70.5%	29.5%
123,010	BLOUNT	49,234	35,441	12,934	859	22,507 R	72.0%	26.3%	73.3%	26.7%
98,963	BRADLEY	35,963	27,422	8,037	504	19,385 R	76.3%	22.3%	77.3%	22.7%
40,716	CAMPBELL	12,101	8,604	3,328	169	5,276 R	71.1%	27.5%	72.1%	27.9%
13,801	CANNON	4,973	3,309	1,564	100	1,745 R	66.5%	31.4%	67.9%	32.1%
28,522	CARROLL	10,851	7,225	3,475	151	3,750 R	66.6%	32.0%	67.5%	32.5%
57,424	CARTER	20,617	15,503	4,789	325	10,714 R	75.2%	23.2%	76.4%	23.6%
39,105	CHEATHAM	15,182	10,268	4,659	255	5,609 R	67.6%	30.7%	68.8%	31.2%
17,131	CHESTER	6,410	4,684	1,624	102	3,060 R	73.1%	25.3%	74.3%	25.7%
32,213	CLAIBORNE	10,178	7,617	2,433	128	5,184 R	74.8%	23.9%	75.8%	24.2%
7,861	CLAY	2,820	1,747	1,037	36	710 R	62.0%	36.8%	62.8%	37.2%
35,662	COCKE	11,454	8,459	2,804	191	5,655 R	73.9%	24.5%	75.1%	24.9%
52,796	COFFEE	19,259	13,023	5,870	366	7,153 R	67.6%	30.5%	68.9%	31.1%
14,586	CROCKETT	5,498	3,783	1,669	46	2,114 R	68.8%	30.4%	69.4%	30.6%
56,053	CUMBERLAND	25,247	18,653	6,261	333	12,392 R	73.9%	24.8%	74.9%	25.1%
626,681	DAVIDSON	244,873	97,622	143,120	4,131	45,498 D	39.9%	58.4%	40.6%	59.4%
11,757	DECATUR	4,251	2,874	1,303	74	1,571 R	67.6%	30.7%	68.8%	31.2%
18,723	DEKALB	6,422	4,143	2,174	105	1,969 R	64.5%	33.9%	65.6%	34.4%
49,666	DICKSON	17,835	11,296	6,233	306	5,063 R	63.3%	34.9%	64.4%	35.6%
38,335	DYER	13,800	9,921	3,757	122	6,164 R	71.9%	27.2%	72.5%	27.5%
38,413	FAYETTE	19,574	12,689	6,688	197	6,001 R	64.8%	34.2%	65.5%	34.5%
17,959	FENTRESS	6,895	5,243	1,561	91	3,682 R	76.0%	22.6%	77.1%	22.9%
41,052	FRANKLIN	16,119	10,262	5,603	254	4,659 R	63.7%	34.8%	64.7%	35.3%
49,683	GIBSON	19,667	12,883	6,564	220	6,319 R	65.5%	33.4%	66.2%	33.8%
29,485	GILES	10,799	6,915	3,760	124	3,155 R	64.0%	34.8%	64.8%	35.2%
22,657	GRAINGER	7,252	5,470	1,668	114	3,802 R	75.4%	23.0%	76.6%	23.4%
68,831	GREENE	23,887	17,245	6,225	417	11,020 R	72.2%	26.1%	73.5%	26.5%
13,703	GRUNDY	4,237	2,516	1,643	78	873 R	59.4%	38.8%	60.5%	39.5%
62,544	HAMBLEN	20,032	14,522	5,234	276	9,288 R	72.5%	26.1%	73.5%	26.5%
336,463	HAMILTON	141,181	79,933	58,836	2,412	21,097 R	56.6%	41.7%	57.6%	42.4%
6,819	HANCOCK	2,046	1,527	475	44	1,052 R	74.6%	23.2%	76.3%	23.7%
27,253	HARDEMAN	10,439	4,865	5,482	92	617 D	46.6%	52.5%	47.0%	53.0%
26,026	HARDIN	10,495	7,886	2,467	142	5,419 R	75.1%	23.5%	76.2%	23.8%
56,833	HAWKINS	19,797	14,382	5,088	327	9,294 R	72.6%	25.7%	73.9%	26.1%
18,787	HAYWOOD	7,569	2,960	4,569	40	1,609 D	39.1%	60.4%	39.3%	60.7%
27,769	HENDERSON	10,055	7,421	2,517	117	4,904 R	73.8%	25.0%	74.7%	25.3%
32,330	HENRY	12,739	8,193	4,339	207	3,854 R	64.3%	34.1%	65.4%	34.6%
24,690	HICKMAN	7,602	4,758	2,698	146	2,060 R	62.6%	35.5%	63.8%	36.2%
8,426	HOUSTON	3,027	1,579	1,400	48	179 R	52.2%	46.3%	53.0%	47.0%
18,538	HUMPHREYS	6,863	3,833	2,905	125	928 R	55.9%	42.3%	56.9%	43.1%
11,638	JACKSON	4,184	2,383	1,739	62	644 R	57.0%	41.6%	57.8%	42.2%
51,407	JEFFERSON	17,559	13,038	4,232	289	8,806 R	74.3%	24.1%	75.5%	24.5%
18,244	JOHNSON	6,194	4,611	1,483	100	3,128 R	74.4%	23.9%	75.7%	24.3%
432,226	KNOX	172,507	109,707	59,399	3,401	50,308 R	63.6%	34.4%	64.9%	35.1%
7,832	LAKE	2,087	1,163	884	40	279 R	55.7%	42.4%	56.8%	43.2%
27,815	LAUDERDALE	8,689	4,616	4,011	62	605 R	53.1%	46.2%	53.5%	46.5%
41,869	LAWRENCE	15,219	10,770	4,237	212	6,533 R	70.8%	27.8%	71.8%	28.2%
12,161	LEWIS	4,694	3,117	1,447	130	1,670 R	66.4%	30.8%	68.3%	31.7%
33,361	LINCOLN	13,268	9,803	3,290	175	6,513 R	73.9%	24.8%	74.9%	25.1%
48,556	LOUDON	22,073	16,707	5,058	308	11,649 R	75.7%	22.9%	76.8%	23.2%
22,248	MACON	6,905	5,260	1,552	93	3,708 R	76.2%	22.5%	77.2%	22.8%
98,294	MADISON	40,702	21,993	18,367	342	3,626 R	54.0%	45.1%	54.5%	45.5%
28,237	MARION	10,409	6,272	3,953	184	2,319 R	60.3%	38.0%	61.3%	38.7%
30,617	MARSHALL	10,741	6,832	3,725	184	3,107 R	63.6%	34.7%	64.7%	35.3%
80,956	MAURY	33,006	20,708	11,825	473	8,883 R	62.7%	35.8%	63.7%	36.3%
52,266	MCMINN	17,834	12,967	4,609	258	8,358 R	72.7%	25.8%	73.8%	26.2%
26,075	MCNAIRY	9,802	7,015	2,645	142	4,370 R	71.6%	27.0%	72.6%	27.4%

TENNESSEE

PRESIDENT 2012

2010 Census Population	County	Total Vote	Republican (Romney)	Democratic (Obama)	Other	Rep.-Dem. Plurality	Percentage			
							Total Vote		Major Vote	
							Rep.	Dem.	Rep.	Dem.
11,753	MEIGS	3,964	2,734	1,163	67	1,571 R	69.0%	29.3%	70.2%	29.8%
44,519	MONROE	16,338	11,731	4,372	235	7,359 R	71.8%	26.8%	72.8%	27.2%
172,331	MONTGOMERY	55,584	30,245	24,499	840	5,746 R	54.4%	44.1%	55.2%	44.8%
6,362	MOORE	2,799	2,053	705	41	1,348 R	73.3%	25.2%	74.4%	25.6%
21,987	MORGAN	6,504	4,669	1,725	110	2,944 R	71.8%	26.5%	73.0%	27.0%
31,807	OBION	12,297	8,814	3,321	162	5,493 R	71.7%	27.0%	72.6%	27.4%
22,083	OVERTON	7,664	4,775	2,805	84	1,970 R	62.3%	36.6%	63.0%	37.0%
7,915	PERRY	2,621	1,578	992	51	586 R	60.2%	37.8%	61.4%	38.6%
5,077	PICKETT	2,453	1,712	712	29	1,000 R	69.8%	29.0%	70.6%	29.4%
16,825	POLK	6,059	4,108	1,856	95	2,252 R	67.8%	30.6%	68.9%	31.1%
72,321	PUTNAM	25,500	17,254	7,802	444	9,452 R	67.7%	30.6%	68.9%	31.1%
31,809	RHEA	10,590	7,802	2,628	160	5,174 R	73.7%	24.8%	74.8%	25.2%
54,181	ROANE	21,090	14,724	6,018	348	8,706 R	69.8%	28.5%	71.0%	29.0%
66,283	ROBERTSON	26,289	17,643	8,290	356	9,353 R	67.1%	31.5%	68.0%	32.0%
262,604	RUTHERFORD	98,848	60,846	36,414	1,588	24,432 R	61.6%	36.8%	62.6%	37.4%
22,228	SCOTT	6,668	5,117	1,452	99	3,665 R	76.7%	21.8%	77.9%	22.1%
14,112	SEQUATCHIE	5,142	3,541	1,489	112	2,052 R	68.9%	29.0%	70.4%	29.6%
89,889	SEVIER	33,864	25,984	7,418	462	18,566 R	76.7%	21.9%	77.8%	22.2%
927,644	SHELBY	371,109	135,649	232,443	3,017	96,794 D	36.6%	62.6%	36.9%	63.1%
19,166	SMITH	7,087	4,495	2,470	122	2,025 R	63.4%	34.9%	64.5%	35.5%
13,324	STEWART	5,115	2,963	2,069	83	894 R	57.9%	40.4%	58.9%	41.1%
156,823	SULLIVAN	59,887	43,562	15,321	1,004	28,241 R	72.7%	25.6%	74.0%	26.0%
160,645	SUMNER	65,366	46,003	18,579	784	27,424 R	70.4%	28.4%	71.2%	28.8%
61,081	TIPTON	24,081	16,672	7,133	276	9,539 R	69.2%	29.6%	70.0%	30.0%
7,870	TROUSDALE	2,905	1,612	1,240	53	372 R	55.5%	42.7%	56.5%	43.5%
18,313	UNICOI	7,086	5,032	1,913	141	3,119 R	71.0%	27.0%	72.5%	27.5%
19,109	UNION	5,828	4,282	1,478	68	2,804 R	73.5%	25.4%	74.3%	25.7%
5,548	VAN BUREN	2,300	1,386	875	39	511 R	60.3%	38.0%	61.3%	38.7%
39,839	WARREN	13,015	8,010	4,752	253	3,258 R	61.5%	36.5%	62.8%	37.2%
122,979	WASHINGTON	48,032	32,808	14,325	899	18,483 R	68.3%	29.8%	69.6%	30.4%
17,021	WAYNE	5,486	4,253	1,163	70	3,090 R	77.5%	21.2%	78.5%	21.5%
35,021	WEAKLEY	12,337	8,605	3,548	184	5,057 R	69.7%	28.8%	70.8%	29.2%
25,841	WHITE	9,140	6,197	2,795	148	3,402 R	67.8%	30.6%	68.9%	31.1%
183,182	WILLIAMSON	96,225	69,850	25,142	1,233	44,708 R	72.6%	26.1%	73.5%	26.5%
113,993	WILSON	51,499	36,109	14,695	695	21,414 R	70.1%	28.5%	71.1%	28.9%
6,346,105	TOTAL	2,458,577	1,462,330	960,709	35,538	501,621 R	59.5%	39.1%	60.4%	39.6%

TENNESSEE

SENATOR 2012

2010 Census Population	County	Total Vote	Republican (Corker)	Democratic (Clayton)	Other	Rep.-Dem. Plurality	Percentage			
							Total Vote		Major Vote	
							Rep.	Dem.	Rep.	Dem.
75,129	ANDERSON	27,962	19,604	6,698	1,660	12,906 R	70.1%	24.0%	74.5%	25.5%
45,058	BEDFORD	13,207	9,671	3,050	486	6,621 R	73.2%	23.1%	76.0%	24.0%
16,489	BENTON	5,977	3,746	1,944	287	1,802 R	62.7%	32.5%	65.8%	34.2%
12,876	BLEDSOE	4,170	3,069	961	140	2,108 R	73.6%	23.0%	76.2%	23.8%
123,010	BLOUNT	46,677	35,846	8,295	2,536	27,551 R	76.8%	17.8%	81.2%	18.8%
98,963	BRADLEY	34,557	28,186	5,299	1,072	22,887 R	81.6%	15.3%	84.2%	15.8%
40,716	CAMPBELL	11,255	8,336	2,411	508	5,925 R	74.1%	21.4%	77.6%	22.4%
13,801	CANNON	4,553	3,199	1,091	263	2,108 R	70.3%	24.0%	74.6%	25.4%
28,522	CARROLL	10,130	6,910	2,796	424	4,114 R	68.2%	27.6%	71.2%	28.8%
57,424	CARTER	18,788	14,874	3,107	807	11,767 R	79.2%	16.5%	82.7%	17.3%

TENNESSEE
SENATOR 2012

2010 Census Population	County	Total Vote	Republican (Corker)	Democratic (Clayton)	Other	Rep.-Dem. Plurality	Percentage Total Vote Rep.	Dem.	Major Vote Rep.	Dem.
39,105	CHEATHAM	14,481	10,544	3,132	805	7,412 R	72.8%	21.6%	77.1%	22.9%
17,131	CHESTER	6,061	4,572	1,266	223	3,306 R	75.4%	20.9%	78.3%	21.7%
32,213	CLAIBORNE	9,443	7,219	1,808	416	5,411 R	76.4%	19.1%	80.0%	20.0%
7,861	CLAY	2,493	1,676	714	103	962 R	67.2%	28.6%	70.1%	29.9%
35,662	COCKE	10,505	8,396	1,706	403	6,690 R	79.9%	16.2%	83.1%	16.9%
52,796	COFFEE	18,530	13,227	4,488	815	8,739 R	71.4%	24.2%	74.7%	25.3%
14,586	CROCKETT	4,900	3,623	1,148	129	2,475 R	73.9%	23.4%	75.9%	24.1%
56,053	CUMBERLAND	23,571	17,900	4,483	1,188	13,417 R	75.9%	19.0%	80.0%	20.0%
626,681	DAVIDSON	232,585	111,176	105,631	15,778	5,545 R	47.8%	45.4%	51.3%	48.7%
11,757	DECATUR	4,032	2,735	1,137	160	1,598 R	67.8%	28.2%	70.6%	29.4%
18,723	DEKALB	5,648	3,836	1,523	289	2,313 R	67.9%	27.0%	71.6%	28.4%
49,666	DICKSON	16,666	11,471	4,264	931	7,207 R	68.8%	25.6%	72.9%	27.1%
38,335	DYER	12,862	9,570	2,919	373	6,651 R	74.4%	22.7%	76.6%	23.4%
38,413	FAYETTE	17,831	12,828	4,407	596	8,421 R	71.9%	24.7%	74.4%	25.6%
17,959	FENTRESS	6,320	4,996	1,119	205	3,877 R	79.1%	17.7%	81.7%	18.3%
41,052	FRANKLIN	14,962	10,312	4,092	558	6,220 R	68.9%	27.3%	71.6%	28.4%
49,683	GIBSON	18,069	12,473	4,996	600	7,477 R	69.0%	27.6%	71.4%	28.6%
29,485	GILES	9,839	6,494	2,923	422	3,571 R	66.0%	29.7%	69.0%	31.0%
22,657	GRAINGER	6,785	5,318	1,187	280	4,131 R	78.4%	17.5%	81.8%	18.2%
68,831	GREENE	22,852	17,614	4,185	1,053	13,429 R	77.1%	18.3%	80.8%	19.2%
13,703	GRUNDY	3,856	2,453	1,264	139	1,189 R	63.6%	32.8%	66.0%	34.0%
62,544	HAMBLEN	18,789	14,547	3,612	630	10,935 R	77.4%	19.2%	80.1%	19.9%
336,463	HAMILTON	137,539	91,497	41,570	4,472	49,927 R	66.5%	30.2%	68.8%	31.2%
6,819	HANCOCK	1,822	1,456	291	75	1,165 R	79.9%	16.0%	83.3%	16.7%
27,253	HARDEMAN	8,945	4,785	3,712	448	1,073 R	53.5%	41.5%	56.3%	43.7%
26,026	HARDIN	9,997	7,534	2,146	317	5,388 R	75.4%	21.5%	77.8%	22.2%
56,833	HAWKINS	19,068	14,344	4,042	682	10,302 R	75.2%	21.2%	78.0%	22.0%
18,787	HAYWOOD	6,973	3,180	3,617	176	437 D	45.6%	51.9%	46.8%	53.2%
27,769	HENDERSON	9,405	7,103	1,981	321	5,122 R	75.5%	21.1%	78.2%	21.8%
32,330	HENRY	11,692	7,934	3,271	487	4,663 R	67.9%	28.0%	70.8%	29.2%
24,690	HICKMAN	7,098	4,675	1,965	458	2,710 R	65.9%	27.7%	70.4%	29.6%
8,426	HOUSTON	2,821	1,558	1,125	138	433 R	55.2%	39.9%	58.1%	41.9%
18,538	HUMPHREYS	6,493	3,786	2,300	407	1,486 R	58.3%	35.4%	62.2%	37.8%
11,638	JACKSON	3,624	2,282	1,127	215	1,155 R	63.0%	31.1%	66.9%	33.1%
51,407	JEFFERSON	16,535	12,811	2,991	733	9,820 R	77.5%	18.1%	81.1%	18.9%
18,244	JOHNSON	5,733	4,456	1,009	268	3,447 R	77.7%	17.6%	81.5%	18.5%
432,226	KNOX	164,470	114,940	38,459	11,071	76,481 R	69.9%	23.4%	74.9%	25.1%
7,832	LAKE	1,912	1,062	762	88	300 R	55.5%	39.9%	58.2%	41.8%
27,815	LAUDERDALE	7,859	4,671	2,869	319	1,802 R	59.4%	36.5%	61.9%	38.1%
41,869	LAWRENCE	13,433	9,867	3,120	446	6,747 R	73.5%	23.2%	76.0%	24.0%
12,161	LEWIS	4,438	3,036	1,124	278	1,912 R	68.4%	25.3%	73.0%	27.0%
33,361	LINCOLN	12,489	9,155	2,816	518	6,339 R	73.3%	22.5%	76.5%	23.5%
48,556	LOUDON	21,248	17,015	3,274	959	13,741 R	80.1%	15.4%	83.9%	16.1%
22,248	MACON	6,171	4,854	1,050	267	3,804 R	78.7%	17.0%	82.2%	17.8%
98,294	MADISON	38,276	22,629	14,439	1,208	8,190 R	59.1%	37.7%	61.0%	39.0%
28,237	MARION	9,923	6,608	2,995	320	3,613 R	66.6%	30.2%	68.8%	31.2%
30,617	MARSHALL	10,043	6,696	2,856	491	3,840 R	66.7%	28.4%	70.1%	29.9%
80,956	MAURY	31,889	19,992	10,243	1,654	9,749 R	62.7%	32.1%	66.1%	33.9%
52,266	MCMINN	17,188	13,422	3,139	627	10,283 R	78.1%	18.3%	81.0%	19.0%
26,075	MCNAIRY	9,504	6,812	2,409	283	4,403 R	71.7%	25.3%	73.9%	26.1%
11,753	MEIGS	3,705	2,799	799	107	2,000 R	75.5%	21.6%	77.8%	22.2%
44,519	MONROE	15,881	11,845	3,186	850	8,659 R	74.6%	20.1%	78.8%	21.2%
172,331	MONTGOMERY	51,434	30,923	17,893	2,618	13,030 R	60.1%	34.8%	63.3%	36.7%
6,362	MOORE	2,677	2,036	544	97	1,492 R	76.1%	20.3%	78.9%	21.1%
21,987	MORGAN	6,139	4,626	1,253	260	3,373 R	75.4%	20.4%	78.7%	21.3%
31,807	OBION	11,514	7,710	3,100	704	4,610 R	67.0%	26.9%	71.3%	28.7%
22,083	OVERTON	6,450	4,372	1,797	281	2,575 R	67.8%	27.9%	70.9%	29.1%
7,915	PERRY	2,299	1,529	655	115	874 R	66.5%	28.5%	70.0%	30.0%
5,077	PICKETT	2,308	1,740	492	76	1,248 R	75.4%	21.3%	78.0%	22.0%
16,825	POLK	5,865	4,143	1,513	209	2,630 R	70.6%	25.8%	73.2%	26.8%

TENNESSEE

SENATOR 2012

2010 Census Population	County	Total Vote	Republican (Corker)	Democratic (Clayton)	Other	Rep.-Dem. Plurality	Percentage			
							Total Vote		Major Vote	
							Rep.	Dem.	Rep.	Dem.
72,321	PUTNAM	23,486	16,703	5,406	1,377	11,297 R	71.1%	23.0%	75.5%	24.5%
31,809	RHEA	10,014	7,989	1,705	320	6,284 R	79.8%	17.0%	82.4%	17.6%
54,181	ROANE	20,192	15,075	4,218	899	10,857 R	74.7%	20.9%	78.1%	21.9%
66,283	ROBERTSON	24,416	17,722	5,584	1,110	12,138 R	72.6%	22.9%	76.0%	24.0%
262,604	RUTHERFORD	94,597	61,962	27,731	4,904	34,231 R	65.5%	29.3%	69.1%	30.9%
22,228	SCOTT	5,942	4,768	974	200	3,794 R	80.2%	16.4%	83.0%	17.0%
14,112	SEQUATCHIE	4,793	3,652	963	178	2,689 R	76.2%	20.1%	79.1%	20.9%
89,889	SEVIER	32,915	26,266	5,296	1,353	20,970 R	79.8%	16.1%	83.2%	16.8%
927,644	SHELBY	347,641	152,612	181,253	13,776	28,641 D	43.9%	52.1%	45.7%	54.3%
19,166	SMITH	6,390	4,403	1,717	270	2,686 R	68.9%	26.9%	71.9%	28.1%
13,324	STEWART	4,801	3,011	1,556	234	1,455 R	62.7%	32.4%	65.9%	34.1%
156,823	SULLIVAN	57,249	43,329	11,725	2,195	31,604 R	75.7%	20.5%	78.7%	21.3%
160,645	SUMNER	61,583	46,321	12,616	2,646	33,705 R	75.2%	20.5%	78.6%	21.4%
61,081	TIPTON	22,530	16,480	5,264	786	11,216 R	73.1%	23.4%	75.8%	24.2%
7,870	TROUSDALE	2,532	1,615	798	119	817 R	63.8%	31.5%	66.9%	33.1%
18,313	UNICOI	6,506	4,939	1,247	320	3,692 R	75.9%	19.2%	79.8%	20.2%
19,109	UNION	5,295	4,093	989	213	3,104 R	77.3%	18.7%	80.5%	19.5%
5,548	VAN BUREN	2,016	1,321	624	71	697 R	65.5%	31.0%	67.9%	32.1%
39,839	WARREN	11,690	7,905	3,210	575	4,695 R	67.6%	27.5%	71.1%	28.9%
122,979	WASHINGTON	44,721	32,637	9,869	2,215	22,768 R	73.0%	22.1%	76.8%	23.2%
17,021	WAYNE	4,934	3,891	872	171	3,019 R	78.9%	17.7%	81.7%	18.3%
35,021	WEAKLEY	11,851	8,011	3,276	564	4,735 R	67.6%	27.6%	71.0%	29.0%
25,841	WHITE	8,622	6,039	2,113	470	3,926 R	70.0%	24.5%	74.1%	25.9%
183,182	WILLIAMSON	93,761	72,402	16,789	4,570	55,613 R	77.2%	17.9%	81.2%	18.8%
113,993	WILSON	49,784	36,993	10,497	2,294	26,496 R	74.3%	21.1%	77.9%	22.1%
6,346,105	TOTAL	2,321,477	1,506,443	705,882	109,152	800,561 R	64.9%	30.4%	68.1%	31.9%

TENNESSEE

HOUSE OF REPRESENTATIVES

CD	Year	Total Vote	Republican		Democratic		Other Vote	Rep.-Dem. Plurality	Percentage			
			Vote	Candidate	Vote	Candidate			Total Vote		Major Vote	
									Rep.	Dem.	Rep.	Dem.
1	2012	239,672	182,252	ROE, PHIL*	47,663	WOODRUFF, ALAN	9,757	134,589 R	76.0%	19.9%	79.3%	20.7%
2	2012	264,505	196,894	DUNCAN, JOHN J. JR.*	54,522	GOODALE, TROY	13,089	142,372 R	74.4%	20.6%	78.3%	21.7%
3	2012	256,909	157,830	FLEISCHMANN, CHUCK*	91,094	HEADRICK, MARY M.	7,985	66,736 R	61.4%	35.5%	63.4%	36.6%
4	2012	230,590	128,568	DESJARLAIS, SCOTT*	102,022	STEWART, ERIC	26,546 R	55.8%	44.2%	55.8%	44.2%
5	2012	263,095	86,240	STAATS, BRAD	171,621	COOPER, JIM*	5,234	85,381 D	32.8%	65.2%	33.4%	66.6%
6	2012	241,241	184,383	BLACK, DIANE*			56,858	184,383 R	76.4%		100.0%	
7	2012	257,306	182,730	BLACKBURN, MARSHA*	61,679	AMOUZOUVIK, CREDO	12,897	121,051 R	71.0%	24.0%	74.8%	25.2%
8	2012	279,422	190,923	FINCHER, STEPHEN*	79,490	DIXON, TIMOTHY	9,009	111,433 R	68.3%	28.4%	70.6%	29.4%
9	2012	250,987	59,742	FLINN, GEORGE S. "JR."	188,422	COHEN, STEVE*	2,823	128,680 D	23.8%	75.1%	24.1%	75.9%
TOTAL	2012	2,283,727	1,369,562		796,513		117,652	573,049 R	60.0%	34.9%	63.2%	36.8%

Note: An asterisk (*) denotes incumbent.

TENNESSEE

GENERAL AND PRIMARY ELECTIONS

GENERAL ELECTIONS: OTHER VOTE

President	Other vote was 18,623 Libertarian (Gary E. Johnson), 6,515 Green (Jill Stein), 6,022 Constitution (Virgil H. Goode), 2,639 Justice (Ross C. "Rocky" Anderson), 1,739 American Third Position (Merlin Miller)
Senator	Other vote was 38,472 Green (Martin Pleasant), 20,936 Independent (Shaun Crowell), 18,620 Constitution (Kermit Steck), 8,085 Independent (James Higdon), 8,080 Independent (Michael Joseph Long), 7,148 Independent (Troy Stephen Scoggin), 6,523 Independent (David Gatchell), 1,288 Write-in (Scattered Write-In)
House	Other vote was:
CD 1	4,837 Independent (Karen Sherry Brackett), 2,872 Green (Robert N. Smith), 2,048 Independent (Michael D. Salyer)
CD 2	5,733 Green (Norris Dryer), 4,382 Independent (Greg Samples), 2,974 Independent (Brandon Stewart)
CD 3	7,905 Independent (Matthew Deniston), 62 Write-in (Jean Howard-Hill), 18 Write-in (Richard Hall)
CD 5	5,222 Green (John Miglietta), 12 Write-in (Sean Puckett)
CD 6	34,766 Independent (Scott Beasley), 21,633 Green (Pat Riley), 455 Write-in (Rachel Robinson), 4 Write-in (Michael Thompson)
CD 7	4,640 Green (Howard K. Switzer), 4,256 Independent (Jack Arnold), 2,740 Independent (William Ryan Akin), 1,261 Independent (Leonard D. Ladner)
CD 8	6,139 Independent (James Hart), 2,870 Independent (Mark J. Rawles)
CD 9	1,448 Independent (Brian L. Saulsberry), 1,372 Independent (Gregory M. Joiner), 2 Write-in (Kimberlee E. Smith), 1 Write-in (Herbert A. Bass)

PRIMARY ELECTIONS: SUPPLEMENTARY INFORMATION

Primary	March 6, 2012 (President) August 2, 2012 (Congress)	**Registration** (as of June 1, 2012)	3,370,094 No Party Registration
Primary Type	Open—Any registered voter could participate in either the Democratic or Republican primary, although state party rules can spell out the grounds for a challenge to primary voters who were not party "members."		

	REPUBLICAN PRIMARIES			DEMOCRATIC PRIMARIES		
President	Santorum, Rick	205,809	37.1%	Obama, Barack H.*	80,705	88.5%
	Romney, W. Mitt	155,630	28.1%	Uncommitted	10,497	11.5%
	Gingrich, Newt	132,889	24.0%	Wolfe, John	7	
	Paul, Ron	50,156	9.0%			
	Uncommitted	3,536	0.6%			
	Perry, Rick	1,966	0.4%			
	Bachmann, Michele	1,895	0.3%			
	Huntsman, Jon Jr.	1,239	0.2%			
	Roemer, Charles	881	0.2%			
	Johnson, Gary E.	572	0.1%			
	TOTAL	*554,573*		*TOTAL*	*91,209*	
Senator	Corker, Bob*	389,613	85.2%	Clayton, Mark E.	48,196	29.9%
	Poskevich, Zach	28,311	6.2%	Davis, Gary G.	24,814	15.4%
	Anderson, Fred R.	15,951	3.5%	Overall, Park	24,289	15.1%
	Clemens, Mark Twain	11,795	2.6%	Crim, Larry	17,744	11.0%
	Lenard, Brenda S.	11,384	2.5%	Roberts, Benjamin	16,387	10.2%
				Hancock, Dave	16,194	10.1%
				Owens, T. K.	13,392	8.3%
	TOTAL	*457,054*		*TOTAL*	*161,016*	

TENNESSEE

GENERAL AND PRIMARY ELECTIONS

	REPUBLICAN PRIMARIES			DEMOCRATIC PRIMARIES		
Congressional District 1	Roe, Phil*	53,490	100.0%	Woodruff, Alan	5,687	100.0%
	TOTAL	53,490		TOTAL	5,687	
Congressional District 2	Duncan, John J. Jr.*	36,335	83.4%	Goodale, Troy	5,617	100.0%
	Leinweber, Joseph Jr.	3,919	9.0%			
	Ciparro, Nick	3,317	7.6%			
	TOTAL	43,571		TOTAL	5,617	
Congressional District 3	Fleischmann, Chuck*	29,947	39.1%	Headrick, Mary M.	14,925	67.0%
	Mayfield, Scottie	23,779	31.0%	Taylor, Bill	7,342	33.0%
	Wamp, Weston	21,997	28.7%			
	Bhalla, Ron	926	1.2%			
	TOTAL	76,649		TOTAL	22,267	
Congressional District 4	DesJarlais, Scott*	36,088	76.8%	Stewart, Eric	17,378	100.0%
	Kelley, Shannon	10,927	23.2%			
	TOTAL	47,015		TOTAL	17,378	
Congressional District 5	Staats, Brad	5,462	26.4%	Cooper, Jim*	28,110	100.0%
	Ries, Bob	5,422	26.2%			
	Smith, John "Big John"	4,200	20.3%			
	Jones, Justin	3,381	16.4%			
	Tarum, Tracey C.	2,212	10.7%			
	TOTAL	20,677		TOTAL	28,110	
Congressional District 6	Black, Diane*	44,949	69.4%			
	Zelenik, Lou Ann	19,836	30.6%			
	TOTAL	64,785				
Congressional District 7	Blackburn, Marsha*	41,524	100.0%	Amouzouvik, Credo	10,436	100.0%
	TOTAL	41,524		TOTAL	10,436	
Congressional District 8	Fincher, Stephen*	60,355	86.7%	Dixon, Timothy	6,951	37.9%
	Justice, Annette	9,288	13.3%	Bradley, Wes	6,771	36.9%
				Stoscheck, Christa	4,621	25.2%
	TOTAL	69,643		TOTAL	18,343	
Congressional District 9	Flinn, George S. "Jr."	11,748	63.9%	Cohen, Steve*	49,585	89.3%
	Bergmann, Charlotte	4,398	23.9%	Hart, Tomeka	5,944	10.7%
	Stooksberry, Rollin Wilson	1,858	10.1%			
	Lunati, Ernest	368	2.0%			
	TOTAL	18,372		TOTAL	55,529	

Note: An asterisk (*) denotes incumbent.

TEXAS

Congressional districts first established for elections held in 2012
36 members

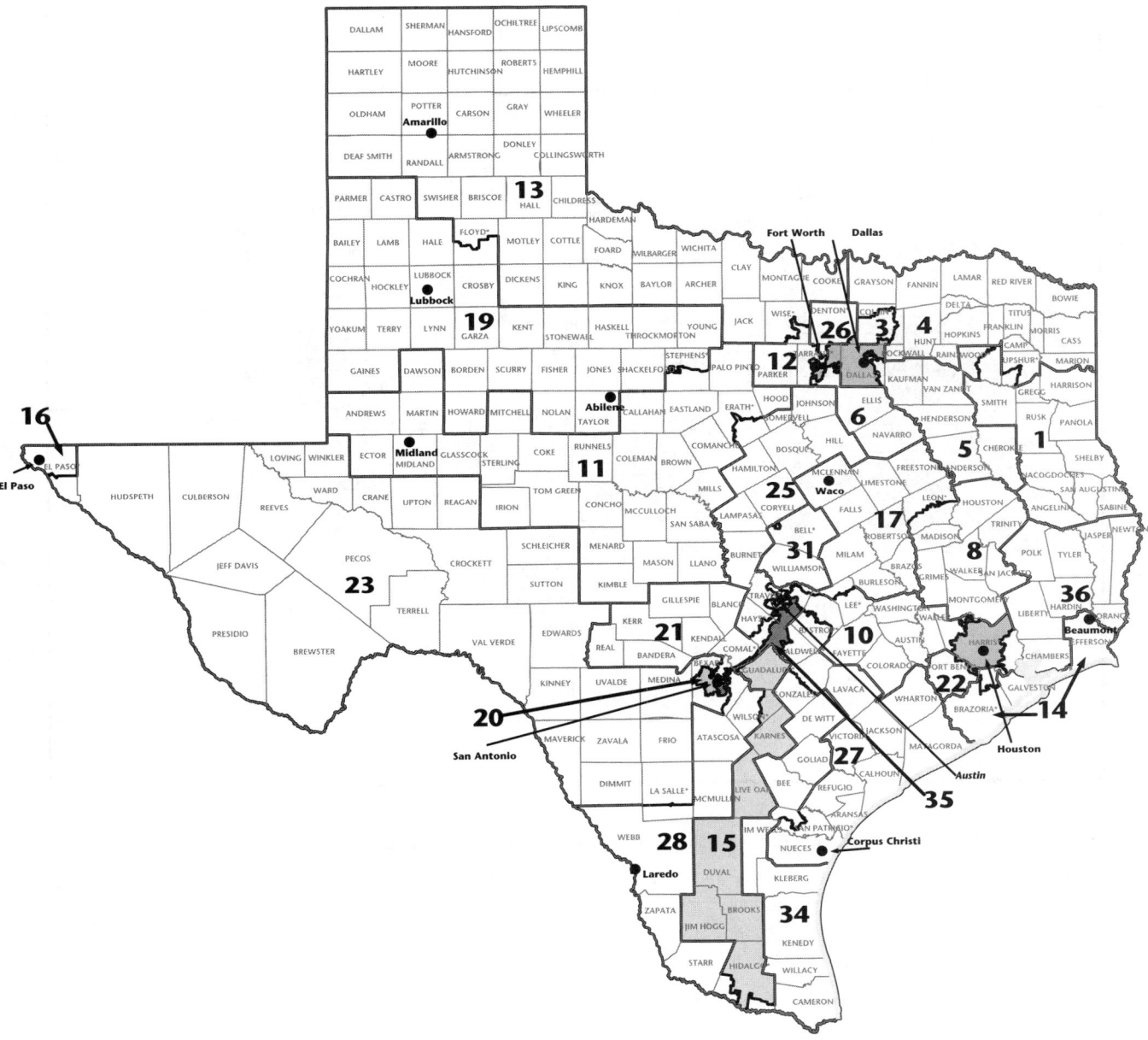

* Asterisk indicates a county whose boundaries include parts of two or more Congressional districts.

TEXAS

Greater Dallas-Fort Worth Area

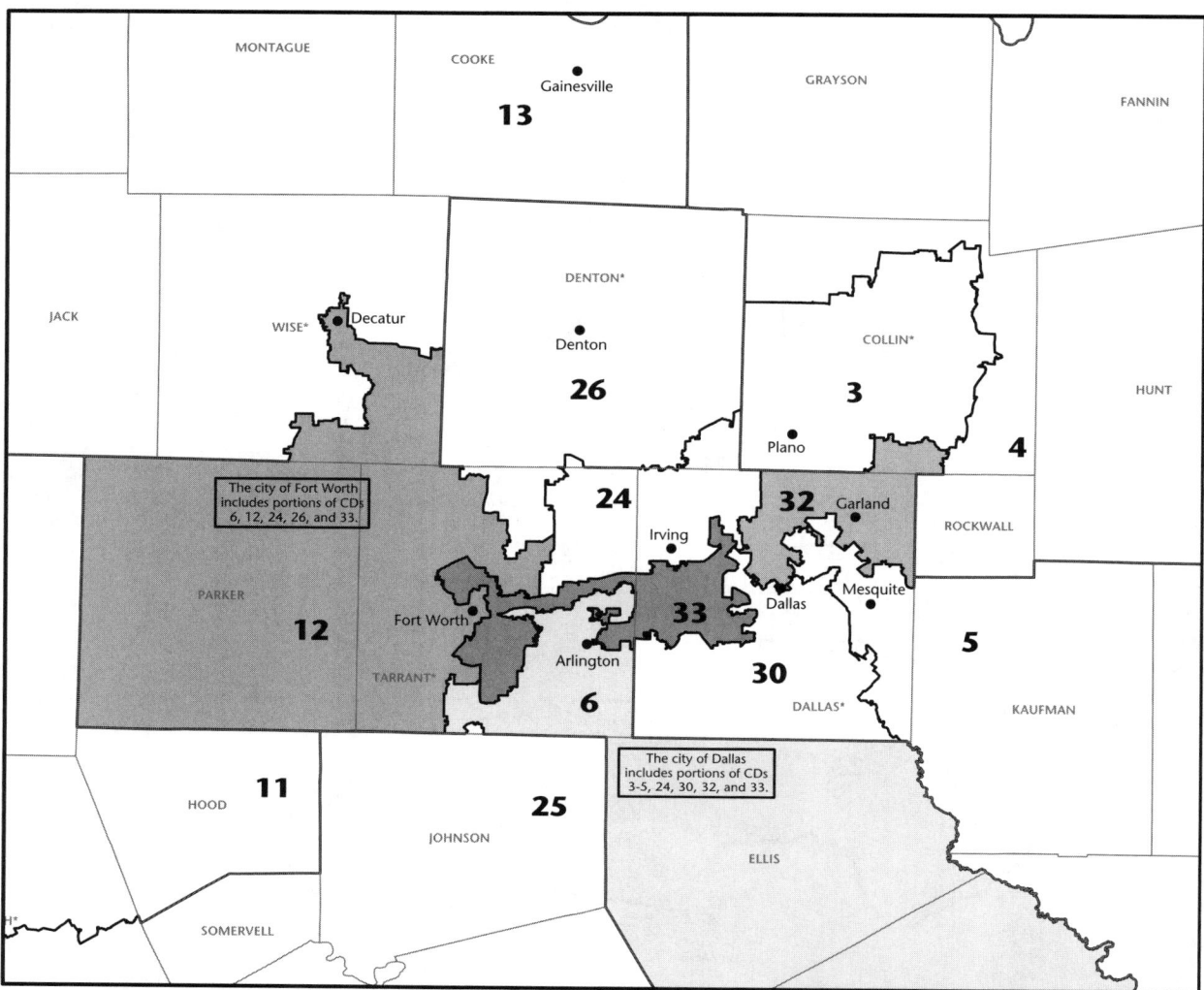

* Asterisk indicates a county whose boundaries include parts of two or more Congressional districts.

TEXAS

Greater Houston Area

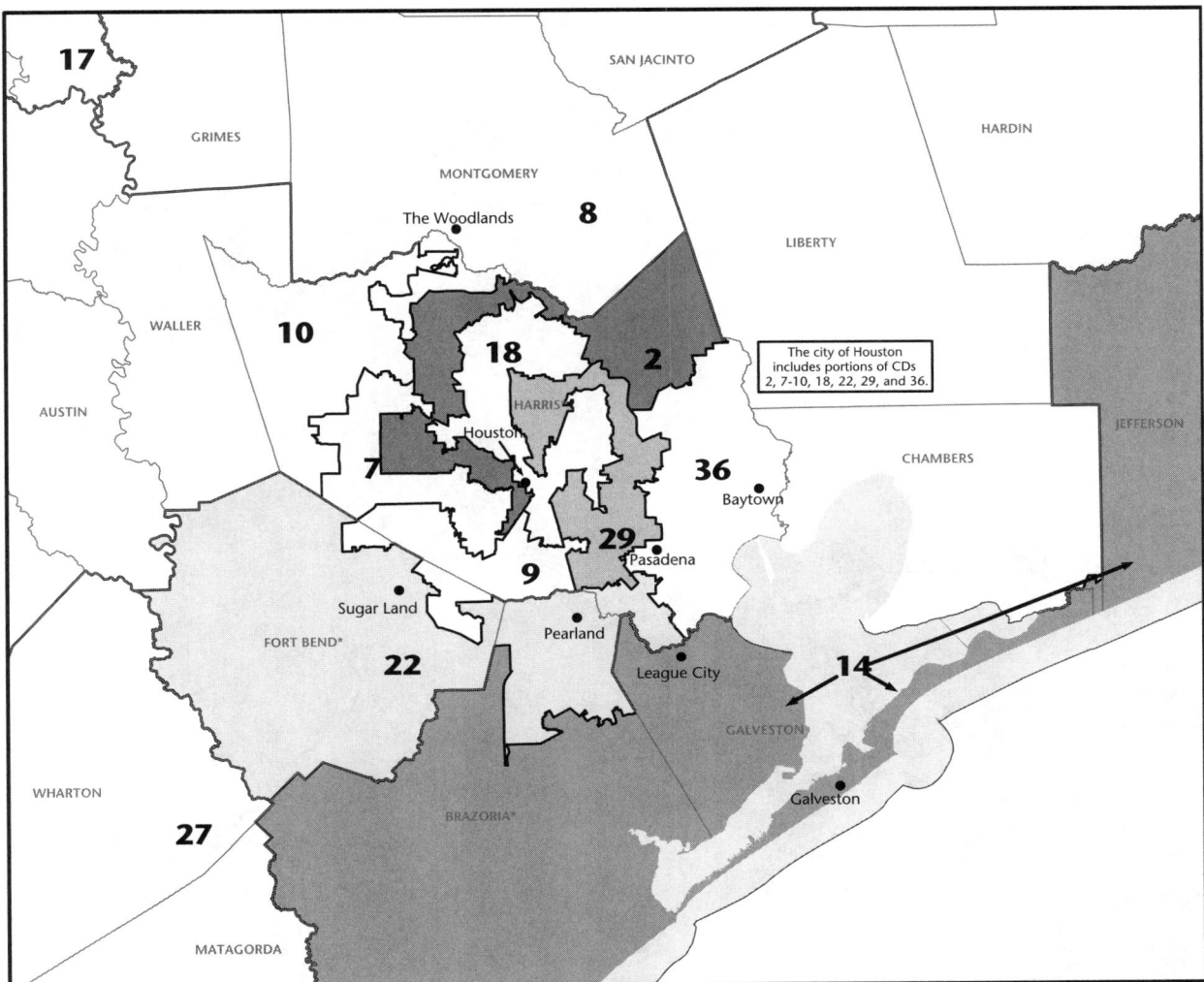

The city of Houston includes portions of CDs 2, 7-10, 18, 22, 29, and 36.

* Asterisk indicates a county whose boundaries include parts of two or more Congressional districts.

TEXAS

Greater San Antonio, Austin Areas

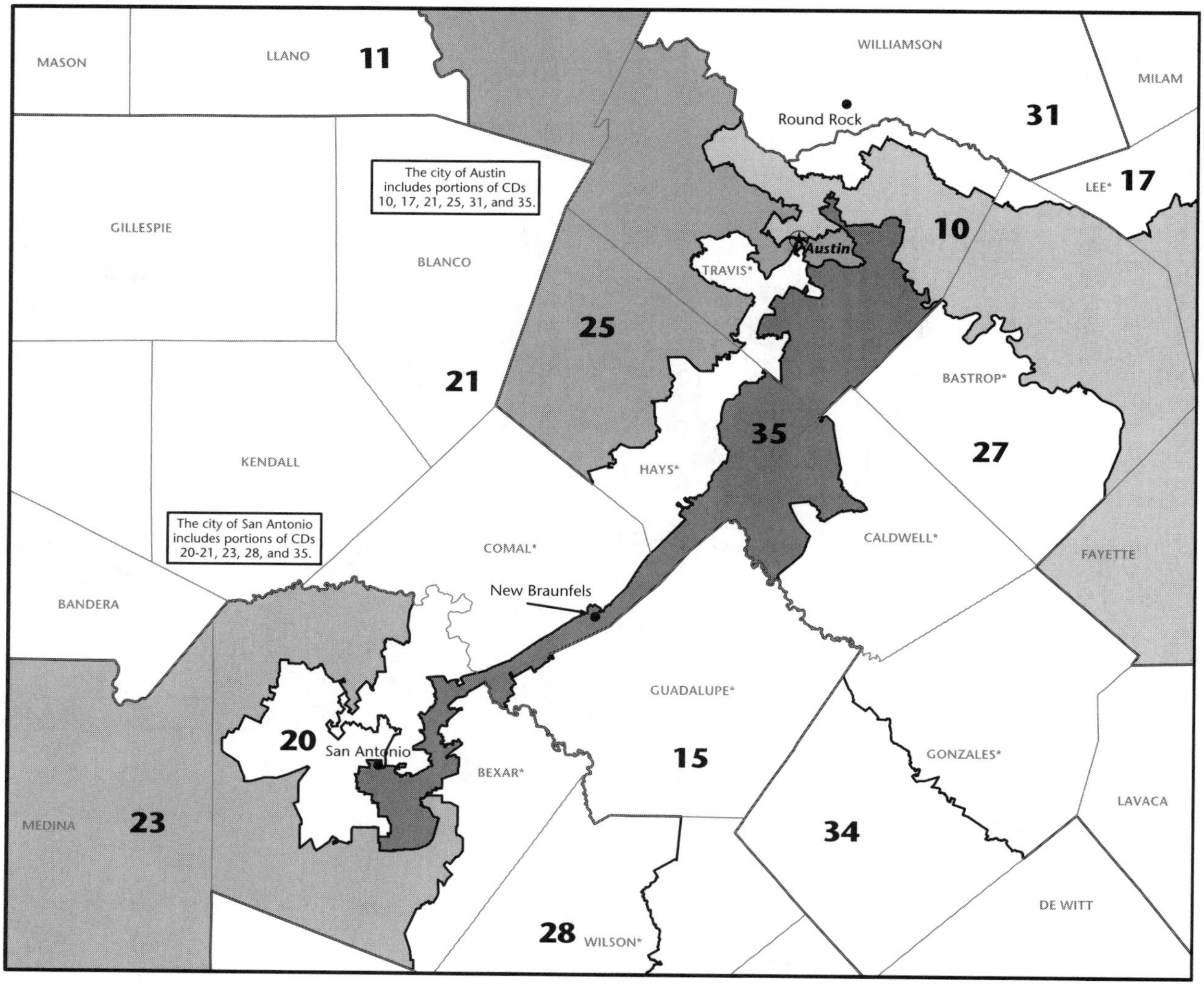

MASON   LLANO   **11**

WILLIAMSON

MILAM

Round Rock

31

GILLESPIE

LEE*   **17**

The city of Austin
includes portions of CDs
10, 17, 21, 25, 31, and 35.

10

BLANCO

TRAVIS*   Austin

25

BASTROP*

21

35

KENDALL

HAYS*

27

The city of San Antonio
includes portions of CDs
20-21, 23, 28, and 35.

CALDWELL*

FAYETTE

COMAL*

BANDERA

New Braunfels

GUADALUPE*

20   San Antonio

15

GONZALES*

BEXAR*

LAVACA

MEDINA   **23**

34

DE WITT

28   WILSON*

* Asterisk indicates a county whose boundaries include parts of two or more Congressional districts.

TEXAS

GOVERNOR

Rick Perry (R). Reelected 2010 to a four-year term. Previously elected 2006, 2002. Assumed office December 21, 2000, following the resignation of president-elect George W. Bush.

SENATORS (2 Republicans)

John Cornyn (R). Reelected 2008 to a six-year term. Previously elected 2002.

Ted Cruz (R). Elected 2012 to a six-year term.

REPRESENTATIVES (24 Republicans, 12 Democrats)

1. Louis Gohmert (R)
2. Ted Poe (R)
3. Sam Johnson (R)
4. Ralph Hall (R)
5. Jeb Hensarling (R)
6. Joe Barton (R)
7. John Culberson (R)
8. Kevin Brady (R)
9. Al Green (D)
10. Michael McCaul (R)
11. Mike Conaway (R)
12. Kay Granger (R)
13. Mac Thornberry (R)
14. Randy Weber (R)
15. Rubén Hinojosa (D)
16. Beto O'Rourke (D)
17. Bill Flores (R)
18. Sheila Jackson Lee (D)
19. Randy Neugebauer (R)
20. Joaquin Castro (D)
21. Lamar Smith (R)
22. Pete Olson (R)
23. Pete Gallego (D)
24. Kenny Marchant (R)
25. Roger Williams (R)
26. Michael C. Burgess (R)
27. Blake Farenthold (R)
28. Henry Cuellar (D)
29. Gene Green (D)
30. Eddie Bernice Johnson (D)
31. John Carter (R)
32. Pete Sessions (R)
33. Marc Veasey (D)
34. Filemon Vela (D)
35. Lloyd Doggett (D)
36. Steve Stockman (R)

POSTWAR VOTE FOR PRESIDENT

Year	Total Vote	Republican		Democratic		Other Vote	Rep.-Dem. Plurality	Percentage			
								Total Vote		Major Vote	
		Vote	Candidate	Vote	Candidate			Rep.	Dem.	Rep.	Dem.
2012	7,993,851	4,569,843	Romney, W. Mitt	3,308,124	Obama, Barack H.*	115,884	1,261,719 R	57.2%	41.4%	58.0%	42.0%
2008	8,077,795	4,479,328	McCain, John S. III	3,528,633	Obama, Barack H.	69,834	950,695 R	55.5%	43.7%	55.9%	44.1%
2004	7,410,765	4,526,917	Bush, George W.*	2,832,704	Kerry, John F.	51,144	1,694,213 R	61.1%	38.2%	61.5%	38.5%
2000**	6,407,637	3,799,639	Bush, George W.	2,433,746	Gore, Albert Jr.	174,252	1,365,893 R	59.3%	38.0%	61.0%	39.0%
1996**	5,611,644	2,736,167	Dole, Robert "Bob"	2,459,683	Clinton, Bill*	415,794	276,484 R	48.8%	43.8%	52.7%	47.3%
1992**	6,154,018	2,496,071	Bush, George H.*	2,281,815	Clinton, Bill	1,376,132	214,256 R	40.6%	37.1%	52.2%	47.8%
1988	5,427,410	3,036,829	Bush, George H.	2,352,748	Dukakis, Michael S.	37,833	684,081 R	56.0%	43.3%	56.3%	43.7%
1984	5,397,571	3,433,428	Reagan, Ronald*	1,949,276	Mondale, Walter F.	14,867	1,484,152 R	63.6%	36.1%	63.8%	36.2%
1980**	4,541,636	2,510,705	Reagan, Ronald	1,881,147	Carter, Jimmy*	149,784	629,558 R	55.3%	41.4%	57.2%	42.8%
1976	4,071,884	1,953,300	Ford, Gerald R.*	2,082,319	Carter, Jimmy	36,265	129,019 D	48.0%	51.1%	48.4%	51.6%
1972	3,471,285	2,298,896	Nixon, Richard M.*	1,154,293	McGovern, George S.	18,096	1,144,603 R	66.2%	33.3%	66.6%	33.4%
1968**	3,079,216	1,227,844	Nixon, Richard M.	1,266,804	Humphrey, Hubert H. Jr.	584,568	38,960 D	39.9%	41.1%	49.2%	50.8%
1964	2,626,811	958,566	Goldwater, Barry M. Sr.	1,663,185	Johnson, Lyndon B.*	5,060	704,619 D	36.5%	63.3%	36.6%	63.4%
1960	2,311,084	1,121,310	Nixon, Richard M.	1,167,567	Kennedy, John F.	22,207	46,257 D	48.5%	50.5%	49.0%	51.0%
1956	1,955,168	1,080,619	Eisenhower, Dwight D.*	859,958	Stevenson, Adlai E. II	14,591	220,661 R	55.3%	44.0%	55.7%	44.3%
1952	2,075,946	1,102,878	Eisenhower, Dwight D.	969,228	Stevenson, Adlai E. II	3,840	133,650 R	53.1%	46.7%	53.2%	46.8%
1948**	1,249,577	303,467	Dewey, Thomas E.	824,235	Truman, Harry S.*	121,875	520,768 D	24.3%	66.0%	26.9%	73.1%

Note: An asterisk (*) denotes incumbent. **In past elections, the other vote included: 2000 - 137,994 Green (Ralph Nader); 1996 - 378,537 Reform (Ross Perot); 1992 - 1,354,781 Independent (Perot); 1980 - 111,613 Independent (John Anderson); 1968 - 584,269 American Independent (George Wallace); 1948 - 113,920 States' Rights (Strom Thurmond).

TEXAS

POSTWAR VOTE FOR GOVERNOR

Year	Total Vote	Republican		Democratic		Other Vote	Rep.-Dem. Plurality	Percentage			
								Total Vote		Major Vote	
		Vote	Candidate	Vote	Candidate			Rep.	Dem.	Rep.	Dem.
2010	4,979,870	2,737,481	Perry, Rick*	2,106,395	White, Bill	135,994	631,086 R	55.0%	42.3%	56.5%	43.5%
2006**	4,399,116	1,716,792	Perry, Rick*	1,310,337	Bell, Chris	1,371,987	406,455 R	39.0%	29.8%	56.7%	43.3%
2002	4,553,987	2,632,591	Perry, Rick*	1,819,798	Sanchez, Tony	101,598	812,793 R	57.8%	40.0%	59.1%	40.9%
1998	3,738,483	2,551,454	Bush, George W.*	1,165,444	Mauro, Garry	21,585	1,386,010 R	68.2%	31.2%	68.6%	31.4%
1994	4,396,242	2,350,994	Bush, George W.	2,016,928	Richards, Ann*	28,320	334,066 R	53.5%	45.9%	53.8%	46.2%
1990	3,892,487	1,826,231	Williams, Clayton	1,925,670	Richards, Ann	140,586	99,439 D	46.9%	49.5%	48.7%	51.3%
1986	3,441,460	1,813,779	Clements, William P.	1,584,515	White, Mark*	43,166	229,264 R	52.7%	46.0%	53.4%	46.6%
1982	3,191,091	1,465,937	Clements, William P.*	1,697,870	White, Mark	27,284	231,933 D	45.9%	53.2%	46.3%	53.7%
1978	2,369,764	1,183,839	Clements, William P.	1,166,979	Hill, John	18,946	16,860 R	50.0%	49.2%	50.4%	49.6%
1974**	1,654,957	514,725	Granberry, Jim	1,016,334	Briscoe, Dolph*	123,898	501,609 D	31.1%	61.4%	33.6%	66.4%
1972	3,410,071	1,534,060	Grover, Henry C.	1,633,913	Briscoe, Dolph	242,098	99,853 D	45.0%	47.9%	48.4%	51.6%
1970	2,235,855	1,037,723	Eggers, Paul W.	1,197,736	Smith, Preston*	396	160,013 D	46.4%	53.6%	46.4%	53.6%
1968	2,916,508	1,254,331	Eggers, Paul W.	1,662,019	Smith, Preston	158	407,688 D	43.0%	57.0%	43.0%	57.0%
1966	1,425,861	368,025	Kennerly, T. E.	1,037,517	Connally, John B.*	20,319	669,492 D	25.8%	72.8%	26.2%	73.8%
1964	2,544,753	661,675	Crichton, Jack	1,877,793	Connally, John B.*	5,285	1,216,118 D	26.0%	73.8%	26.1%	73.9%
1962	1,569,181	715,025	Cox, Jack	847,036	Connally, John B.	7,120	132,011 D	45.6%	54.0%	45.8%	54.2%
1960	2,250,718	612,963	Steger, William M.	1,637,755	Daniel, Price*		1,024,792 D	27.2%	72.8%	27.2%	72.8%
1958	789,133	94,098	Mayer, Edwin S.	695,035	Daniel, Price*		600,937 D	11.9%	88.1%	11.9%	88.1%
1956	1,826,242	271,088	Bryant, William R.	1,433,051	Daniel, Price	122,103	1,161,963 D	14.8%	78.5%	15.9%	84.1%
1954	636,892	66,154	Adams, Tod R.	569,533	Shivers, Allan*	1,205	503,379 D	10.4%	89.4%	10.4%	89.6%
1952	1,890,535			1,853,863	Shivers, Allan*	36,672	1,853,863 D		98.1%		100.0%
1950	407,138	39,793	Currie, Ralph W.	367,345	Shivers, Allan*		327,552 D	9.8%	90.2%	9.8%	90.2%
1948	1,208,860	177,399	Lane, Alvin H.	1,024,160	Jester, Beauford H.*	7,301	846,761 D	14.7%	84.7%	14.8%	85.2%
1946	378,784	33,277	Nolte, Eugene Jr.	345,507	Jester, Beauford H.		312,230 D	8.8%	91.2%	8.8%	91.2%

Note: An asterisk (*) denotes incumbent. **In past elections, the other vote included: 2006 - 796,851 Independent (Carole Keeton Strayhorn); 547,674 Independent (Richard "Kinky" Friedman). The term of office of Texas's governor was increased from two to four years effective with the 1974 election. The Republican Party did not run a candidate in the 1952 gubernatorial election.

TEXAS

POSTWAR VOTE FOR SENATOR

Year	Total Vote	Republican Vote	Republican Candidate	Democratic Vote	Democratic Candidate	Other Vote	Rep.-Dem. Plurality		Total Vote Rep.	Total Vote Dem.	Major Vote Rep.	Major Vote Dem.
2012	7,864,822	4,440,137	Cruz, Ted	3,194,927	Sadler, Paul	229,758	1,245,210	R	56.5%	40.6%	58.2%	41.8%
2008	7,912,075	4,337,469	Cornyn, John*	3,389,365	Noriega, Richard J. "Rick"	185,241	948,104	R	54.8%	42.8%	56.1%	43.9%
2006	4,314,663	2,661,789	Hutchison, Kay Bailey*	1,555,202	Radnofsky, Barbara Ann	97,672	1,106,587	R	61.7%	36.0%	63.1%	36.9%
2002	4,514,012	2,496,243	Cornyn, John	1,955,758	Kirk, Ron	62,011	540,485	R	55.3%	43.3%	56.1%	43.9%
2000	6,276,652	4,082,091	Hutchison, Kay Bailey*	2,030,315	Kelly, Gene	164,246	2,051,776	R	65.0%	32.3%	66.8%	33.2%
1996	5,527,441	3,027,680	Gramm, W. Phil*	2,428,776	Morales, Victor M.	70,985	598,904	R	54.8%	43.9%	55.5%	44.5%
1994	4,279,940	2,604,218	Hutchison, Kay Bailey*	1,639,615	Mattox, Jim	36,107	964,603	R	60.8%	38.3%	61.4%	38.6%
1993S	1,765,254	1,188,716	Hutchison, Kay Bailey	576,538	Krueger, Robert*		612,178	R	67.3%	32.7%	67.3%	32.7%
1990	3,822,157	2,302,357	Gramm, W. Phil*	1,429,986	Parmer, Hugh	89,814	872,371	R	60.2%	37.4%	61.7%	38.3%
1988	5,323,606	2,129,228	Boulter, E. Beau	3,149,806	Bentsen, Lloyd*	44,572	1,020,578	D	40.0%	59.2%	40.3%	59.7%
1984	5,319,178	3,116,348	Gramm, W. Phil	2,202,557	Doggett, Lloyd	273	913,791	R	58.6%	41.4%	58.6%	41.4%
1982	3,103,167	1,256,759	Collins, James M.	1,818,223	Bentsen, Lloyd*	28,185	561,464	D	40.5%	58.6%	40.9%	59.1%
1978	2,312,540	1,151,376	Tower, John G.*	1,139,149	Krueger, Robert	22,015	12,227	R	49.8%	49.3%	50.3%	49.7%
1976	3,874,516	1,636,370	Steelman, Alan	2,199,956	Bentsen, Lloyd*	38,190	563,586	D	42.2%	56.8%	42.7%	57.3%
1972	3,413,918	1,822,877	Tower, John G.*	1,511,985	Sanders, Barefoot	79,056	310,892	R	53.4%	44.3%	54.7%	45.3%
1970	2,231,671	1,035,794	Bush, George H.	1,194,069	Bentsen, Lloyd	1,808	158,275	D	46.4%	53.5%	46.5%	53.5%
1966	1,493,182	842,501	Tower, John G.*	643,855	Carr, Waggoner	6,826	198,646	R	56.4%	43.1%	56.7%	43.3%
1964	2,603,856	1,134,337	Bush, George H.	1,463,958	Yarborough, Ralph*	5,561	329,621	D	43.6%	56.2%	43.7%	56.3%
1961S	886,091	448,217	Tower, John G.	437,874	Blakley, William A.*		10,343	R	50.6%	49.4%	50.6%	49.4%
1960	2,253,764	926,653	Tower, John G.	1,306,605	Johnson, Lyndon B.*	20,506	379,952	D	41.1%	58.0%	41.5%	58.5%
1958	787,128	185,926	Whittenburg, Roy	587,030	Yarborough, Ralph*	14,172	401,104	D	23.6%	74.6%	24.1%	75.9%
1957S	957,298				Yarborough, Ralph							
1954	636,475	94,131	Watson, Carlos G.	539,319	Johnson, Lyndon B.*	3,025	445,188	D	14.8%	84.7%	14.9%	85.1%
1952	1,894,671			1,894,671	Daniel, Price		1,894,671	D		100.0%		100.0%
1948	1,061,363	349,665	Porter, Jack	702,785	Johnson, Lyndon B.	8,913	353,120	D	32.9%	66.2%	33.2%	66.8%
1946	380,550	43,619	Sells, Murray C.	336,931	Connally, Tom T.*		293,312	D	11.5%	88.5%	11.5%	88.5%

Note: An asterisk (*) denotes incumbent. **The June 1993 election was for a short term to fill a vacancy; the vote above was for the special election runoff. The April 1957 and May 1961 elections were also for short terms to fill vacancies. Although neither vote was held with official party designations, the 1961 vote above reflected the result of a runoff between unofficial party candidates. In 1957 there was a single ballot without a runoff and Democrat Ralph Yarborough polled 364,605 votes (38.1 percent of the total vote) and won the election with a 73,802-vote plurality over Democrat Martin Dies. The Republican Party did not run a candidate in the 1952 Senate election.

TEXAS

PRESIDENT 2012

2010 Census Population	County	Total Vote	Republican (Romney)	Democratic (Obama)	Other	Rep.-Dem. Plurality	Percentage Total Vote Rep.	Dem.	Major Vote Rep.	Dem.
58,458	ANDERSON	16,212	12,262	3,813	137	8,449 R	75.6%	23.5%	76.3%	23.7%
14,786	ANDREWS	4,482	3,639	795	48	2,844 R	81.2%	17.7%	82.1%	17.9%
86,771	ANGELINA	28,406	20,303	7,834	269	12,469 R	71.5%	27.6%	72.2%	27.8%
23,158	ARANSAS	9,648	6,830	2,704	114	4,126 R	70.8%	28.0%	71.6%	28.4%
9,054	ARCHER	4,164	3,600	525	39	3,075 R	86.5%	12.6%	87.3%	12.7%
1,901	ARMSTRONG	935	828	98	9	730 R	88.6%	10.5%	89.4%	10.6%
44,911	ATASCOSA	12,721	7,461	5,133	127	2,328 R	58.7%	40.4%	59.2%	40.8%
28,417	AUSTIN	11,649	9,265	2,252	132	7,013 R	79.5%	19.3%	80.4%	19.6%
7,165	BAILEY	1,816	1,339	466	11	873 R	73.7%	25.7%	74.2%	25.8%
20,485	BANDERA	9,448	7,426	1,864	158	5,562 R	78.6%	19.7%	79.9%	20.1%
74,171	BASTROP	24,481	14,033	9,864	584	4,169 R	57.3%	40.3%	58.7%	41.3%
3,726	BAYLOR	1,592	1,297	267	28	1,030 R	81.5%	16.8%	82.9%	17.1%
31,861	BEE	7,879	4,356	3,452	71	904 R	55.3%	43.8%	55.8%	44.2%
310,235	BELL	86,206	49,574	35,512	1,120	14,062 R	57.5%	41.2%	58.3%	41.7%
1,714,773	BEXAR	513,681	241,617	264,856	7,208	23,239 D	47.0%	51.6%	47.7%	52.3%
10,497	BLANCO	4,973	3,638	1,220	115	2,418 R	73.2%	24.5%	74.9%	25.1%
641	BORDEN	363	324	32	7	292 R	89.3%	8.8%	91.0%	9.0%
18,212	BOSQUE	7,356	5,885	1,367	104	4,518 R	80.0%	18.6%	81.2%	18.8%
92,565	BOWIE	35,404	24,869	10,196	339	14,673 R	70.2%	28.8%	70.9%	29.1%
313,166	BRAZORIA	106,739	70,862	34,421	1,456	36,441 R	66.4%	32.2%	67.3%	32.7%
194,851	BRAZOS	55,962	37,209	17,477	1,276	19,732 R	66.5%	31.2%	68.0%	32.0%
9,232	BREWSTER	3,867	1,976	1,765	126	211 R	51.1%	45.6%	52.8%	47.2%
1,637	BRISCOE	702	578	117	7	461 R	82.3%	16.7%	83.2%	16.8%
7,223	BROOKS	2,403	507	1,886	10	1,379 D	21.1%	78.5%	21.2%	78.8%
38,106	BROWN	13,947	11,895	1,904	148	9,991 R	85.3%	13.7%	86.2%	13.8%
17,187	BURLESON	6,456	4,671	1,705	80	2,966 R	72.4%	26.4%	73.3%	26.7%
42,750	BURNET	16,796	12,843	3,674	279	9,169 R	76.5%	21.9%	77.8%	22.2%
38,066	CALDWELL	11,068	6,021	4,791	256	1,230 R	54.4%	43.3%	55.7%	44.3%
21,381	CALHOUN	6,648	4,144	2,410	94	1,734 R	62.3%	36.3%	63.2%	36.8%
13,544	CALLAHAN	5,197	4,378	751	68	3,627 R	84.2%	14.5%	85.4%	14.6%
406,220	CAMERON	76,895	26,099	49,975	821	23,876 D	33.9%	65.0%	34.3%	65.7%
12,401	CAMP	4,335	2,881	1,428	26	1,453 R	66.5%	32.9%	66.9%	33.1%
6,182	CARSON	2,778	2,451	292	35	2,159 R	88.2%	10.5%	89.4%	10.6%
30,464	CASS	11,788	8,763	2,924	101	5,839 R	74.3%	24.8%	75.0%	25.0%
8,062	CASTRO	2,119	1,470	630	19	840 R	69.4%	29.7%	70.0%	30.0%
35,096	CHAMBERS	14,735	11,787	2,790	158	8,997 R	80.0%	18.9%	80.9%	19.1%
50,845	CHEROKEE	16,126	12,094	3,875	157	8,219 R	75.0%	24.0%	75.7%	24.3%
7,041	CHILDRESS	1,996	1,665	320	11	1,345 R	83.4%	16.0%	83.9%	16.1%
10,752	CLAY	5,057	4,266	740	51	3,526 R	84.4%	14.6%	85.2%	14.8%
3,127	COCHRAN	917	649	256	12	393 R	70.8%	27.9%	71.7%	28.3%
3,320	COKE	1,408	1,218	179	11	1,039 R	86.5%	12.7%	87.2%	12.8%
8,895	COLEMAN	3,492	3,012	442	38	2,570 R	86.3%	12.7%	87.2%	12.8%
782,341	COLLIN	302,821	196,888	101,415	4,518	95,473 R	65.0%	33.5%	66.0%	34.0%
3,057	COLLINGSWORTH	1,150	962	177	11	785 R	83.7%	15.4%	84.5%	15.5%
20,874	COLORADO	8,117	6,026	2,029	62	3,997 R	74.2%	25.0%	74.8%	25.2%
108,472	COMAL	51,529	39,318	11,450	761	27,868 R	76.3%	22.2%	77.4%	22.6%
13,974	COMANCHE	4,906	3,944	890	72	3,054 R	80.4%	18.1%	81.6%	18.4%
4,087	CONCHO	1,001	793	194	14	599 R	79.2%	19.4%	80.3%	19.7%
38,437	COOKE	14,351	11,951	2,246	154	9,705 R	83.3%	15.7%	84.2%	15.8%
75,388	CORYELL	16,604	11,220	5,158	226	6,062 R	67.6%	31.1%	68.5%	31.5%
1,505	COTTLE	741	555	180	6	375 R	74.9%	24.3%	75.5%	24.5%
4,375	CRANE	1,283	985	275	23	710 R	76.8%	21.4%	78.2%	21.8%
3,719	CROCKETT	1,457	957	480	20	477 R	65.7%	32.9%	66.6%	33.4%
6,059	CROSBY	1,787	1,132	639	16	493 R	63.3%	35.8%	63.9%	36.1%
2,398	CULBERSON	879	295	568	16	273 D	33.6%	64.6%	34.2%	65.8%
6,703	DALLAM	1,534	1,248	253	33	995 R	81.4%	16.5%	83.1%	16.9%
2,368,139	DALLAS	710,117	295,813	405,571	8,733	109,758 D	41.7%	57.1%	42.2%	57.8%
13,833	DAWSON	3,642	2,591	1,019	32	1,572 R	71.1%	28.0%	71.8%	28.2%
20,097	DE WITT	6,638	5,122	1,467	49	3,655 R	77.2%	22.1%	77.7%	22.3%
19,372	DEAF SMITH	4,309	3,042	1,239	28	1,803 R	70.6%	28.8%	71.1%	28.9%

TEXAS

PRESIDENT 2012

2010 Census Population	County	Total Vote	Republican (Romney)	Democratic (Obama)	Other	Rep.-Dem. Plurality	Percentage Total Vote Rep.	Dem.	Major Vote Rep.	Dem.
5,231	DELTA	2,018	1,524	454	40	1,070 R	75.5%	22.5%	77.0%	23.0%
662,614	DENTON	242,781	157,579	80,978	4,224	76,601 R	64.9%	33.4%	66.1%	33.9%
2,444	DICKENS	1,019	793	216	10	577 R	77.8%	21.2%	78.6%	21.4%
9,996	DIMMIT	2,917	762	2,141	14	1,379 D	26.1%	73.4%	26.2%	73.8%
3,677	DONLEY	1,535	1,287	226	22	1,061 R	83.8%	14.7%	85.1%	14.9%
11,782	DUVAL	4,344	980	3,331	33	2,351 D	22.6%	76.7%	22.7%	77.3%
18,583	EASTLAND	6,495	5,444	970	81	4,474 R	83.8%	14.9%	84.9%	15.1%
137,130	ECTOR	32,513	24,010	8,118	385	15,892 R	73.8%	25.0%	74.7%	25.3%
2,002	EDWARDS	884	642	232	10	410 R	72.6%	26.2%	73.5%	26.5%
800,647	EL PASO	172,412	57,150	112,952	2,310	55,802 D	33.1%	65.5%	33.6%	66.4%
149,610	ELLIS	54,151	39,574	13,881	696	25,693 R	73.1%	25.6%	74.0%	26.0%
37,890	ERATH	12,473	10,329	1,965	179	8,364 R	82.8%	15.8%	84.0%	16.0%
17,866	FALLS	5,434	3,356	2,033	45	1,323 R	61.8%	37.4%	62.3%	37.7%
33,915	FANNIN	10,804	8,161	2,486	157	5,675 R	75.5%	23.0%	76.7%	23.3%
24,554	FAYETTE	10,551	8,106	2,315	130	5,791 R	76.8%	21.9%	77.8%	22.2%
3,974	FISHER	1,629	1,094	512	23	582 R	67.2%	31.4%	68.1%	31.9%
6,446	FLOYD	2,085	1,523	551	11	972 R	73.0%	26.4%	73.4%	26.6%
1,336	FOARD	495	348	140	7	208 R	70.3%	28.3%	71.3%	28.7%
585,375	FORT BEND	219,489	116,126	101,144	2,219	14,982 R	52.9%	46.1%	53.4%	46.6%
10,605	FRANKLIN	4,257	3,446	751	60	2,695 R	80.9%	17.6%	82.1%	17.9%
19,816	FREESTONE	7,570	5,646	1,850	74	3,796 R	74.6%	24.4%	75.3%	24.7%
17,217	FRIO	3,968	1,559	2,376	33	817 D	39.3%	59.9%	39.6%	60.4%
17,526	GAINES	4,066	3,484	535	47	2,949 R	85.7%	13.2%	86.7%	13.3%
291,309	GALVESTON	110,078	69,059	39,511	1,508	29,548 R	62.7%	35.9%	63.6%	36.4%
6,461	GARZA	1,560	1,263	279	18	984 R	81.0%	17.9%	81.9%	18.1%
24,837	GILLESPIE	12,550	10,306	2,055	189	8,251 R	82.1%	16.4%	83.4%	16.6%
1,226	GLASSCOCK	578	526	44	8	482 R	91.0%	7.6%	92.3%	7.7%
7,210	GOLIAD	3,458	2,294	1,127	37	1,167 R	66.3%	32.6%	67.1%	32.9%
19,807	GONZALES	6,057	4,216	1,777	64	2,439 R	69.6%	29.3%	70.3%	29.7%
22,535	GRAY	7,389	6,443	886	60	5,557 R	87.2%	12.0%	87.9%	12.1%
120,877	GRAYSON	42,264	30,936	10,670	658	20,266 R	73.2%	25.2%	74.4%	25.6%
121,730	GREGG	41,507	28,742	12,398	367	16,344 R	69.2%	29.9%	69.9%	30.1%
26,604	GRIMES	8,601	6,141	2,339	121	3,802 R	71.4%	27.2%	72.4%	27.6%
131,533	GUADALUPE	49,514	33,117	15,744	653	17,373 R	66.9%	31.8%	67.8%	32.2%
36,273	HALE	8,854	6,490	2,243	121	4,247 R	73.3%	25.3%	74.3%	25.7%
3,353	HALL	1,109	832	265	12	567 R	75.0%	23.9%	75.8%	24.2%
8,517	HAMILTON	3,552	2,918	591	43	2,327 R	82.2%	16.6%	83.2%	16.8%
5,613	HANSFORD	1,962	1,788	159	15	1,629 R	91.1%	8.1%	91.8%	8.2%
4,139	HARDEMAN	1,495	1,176	302	17	874 R	78.7%	20.2%	79.6%	20.4%
54,635	HARDIN	21,297	17,746	3,359	192	14,387 R	83.3%	15.8%	84.1%	15.9%
4,092,459	HARRIS	1,188,585	586,073	587,044	15,468	971 D	49.3%	49.4%	50.0%	50.0%
65,631	HARRISON	26,170	17,512	8,456	202	9,056 R	66.9%	32.3%	67.4%	32.6%
6,062	HARTLEY	1,913	1,708	184	21	1,524 R	89.3%	9.6%	90.3%	9.7%
5,899	HASKELL	2,013	1,424	553	36	871 R	70.7%	27.5%	72.0%	28.0%
157,107	HAYS	59,011	31,661	25,537	1,813	6,124 R	53.7%	43.3%	55.4%	44.6%
3,807	HEMPHILL	1,509	1,298	192	19	1,106 R	86.0%	12.7%	87.1%	12.9%
78,532	HENDERSON	27,627	21,231	6,106	290	15,125 R	76.8%	22.1%	77.7%	22.3%
774,769	HIDALGO	139,159	39,865	97,969	1,325	58,104 D	28.6%	70.4%	28.9%	71.1%
35,089	HILL	12,045	9,132	2,752	161	6,380 R	75.8%	22.8%	76.8%	23.2%
22,935	HOCKLEY	7,134	5,546	1,486	102	4,060 R	77.7%	20.8%	78.9%	21.1%
51,182	HOOD	22,535	18,409	3,843	283	14,566 R	81.7%	17.1%	82.7%	17.3%
35,161	HOPKINS	12,753	9,836	2,777	140	7,059 R	77.1%	21.8%	78.0%	22.0%
23,732	HOUSTON	8,214	5,880	2,265	69	3,615 R	71.6%	27.6%	72.2%	27.8%
35,012	HOWARD	8,695	6,453	2,110	132	4,343 R	74.2%	24.3%	75.4%	24.6%
3,476	HUDSPETH	863	471	379	13	92 R	54.6%	43.9%	55.4%	44.6%
86,129	HUNT	28,049	21,011	6,671	367	14,340 R	74.9%	23.8%	75.9%	24.1%
22,150	HUTCHINSON	7,928	6,804	1,045	79	5,759 R	85.8%	13.2%	86.7%	13.3%
1,599	IRION	788	668	112	8	556 R	84.8%	14.2%	85.6%	14.4%
9,044	JACK	2,908	2,580	303	25	2,277 R	88.7%	10.4%	89.5%	10.5%
14,075	JACKSON	5,025	3,906	1,070	49	2,836 R	77.7%	21.3%	78.5%	21.5%

TEXAS

PRESIDENT 2012

2010 Census Population	County	Total Vote	Republican (Romney)	Democratic (Obama)	Other	Rep.-Dem. Plurality	Percentage Total Vote Rep.	Dem.	Major Vote Rep.	Dem.
35,710	JASPER	13,517	9,957	3,423	137	6,534 R	73.7%	25.3%	74.4%	25.6%
2,342	JEFF DAVIS	1,192	719	440	33	279 R	60.3%	36.9%	62.0%	38.0%
252,273	JEFFERSON	88,627	43,242	44,668	717	1,426 D	48.8%	50.4%	49.2%	50.8%
5,300	JIM HOGG	1,667	356	1,301	10	945 D	21.4%	78.0%	21.5%	78.5%
40,838	JIM WELLS	11,166	4,598	6,492	76	1,894 D	41.2%	58.1%	41.5%	58.5%
150,934	JOHNSON	48,838	37,661	10,496	681	27,165 R	77.1%	21.5%	78.2%	21.8%
20,202	JONES	5,567	4,262	1,226	79	3,036 R	76.6%	22.0%	77.7%	22.3%
14,824	KARNES	4,185	2,825	1,325	35	1,500 R	67.5%	31.7%	68.1%	31.9%
103,350	KAUFMAN	34,670	24,846	9,472	352	15,374 R	71.7%	27.3%	72.4%	27.6%
33,410	KENDALL	17,783	14,508	3,043	232	11,465 R	81.6%	17.1%	82.7%	17.3%
416	KENEDY	167	84	82	1	2 R	50.3%	49.1%	50.6%	49.4%
808	KENT	405	335	66	4	269 R	82.7%	16.3%	83.5%	16.5%
49,625	KERR	21,879	17,274	4,338	267	12,936 R	79.0%	19.8%	79.9%	20.1%
4,607	KIMBLE	1,892	1,667	217	8	1,450 R	88.1%	11.5%	88.5%	11.5%
286	KING	145	139	5	1	134 R	95.9%	3.4%	96.5%	3.5%
3,598	KINNEY	1,425	880	522	23	358 R	61.8%	36.6%	62.8%	37.2%
32,061	KLEBERG	8,907	4,058	4,754	95	696 D	45.6%	53.4%	46.1%	53.9%
3,719	KNOX	1,510	1,160	332	18	828 R	76.8%	22.0%	77.7%	22.3%
6,886	LA SALLE	1,646	669	965	12	296 D	40.6%	58.6%	40.9%	59.1%
49,793	LAMAR	17,197	12,826	4,181	190	8,645 R	74.6%	24.3%	75.4%	24.6%
13,977	LAMB	4,091	3,058	998	35	2,060 R	74.7%	24.4%	75.4%	24.6%
19,677	LAMPASAS	7,204	5,621	1,479	104	4,142 R	78.0%	20.5%	79.2%	20.8%
19,263	LAVACA	8,294	6,796	1,428	70	5,368 R	81.9%	17.2%	82.6%	17.4%
16,612	LEE	6,221	4,507	1,632	82	2,875 R	72.4%	26.2%	73.4%	26.6%
16,801	LEON	6,945	5,814	1,062	69	4,752 R	83.7%	15.3%	84.6%	15.4%
75,643	LIBERTY	22,746	17,323	5,202	221	12,121 R	76.2%	22.9%	76.9%	23.1%
23,384	LIMESTONE	7,563	5,288	2,208	67	3,080 R	69.9%	29.2%	70.5%	29.5%
3,302	LIPSCOMB	1,168	1,044	119	5	925 R	89.4%	10.2%	89.8%	10.2%
11,531	LIVE OAK	4,113	3,154	919	40	2,235 R	76.7%	22.3%	77.4%	22.6%
19,301	LLANO	9,558	7,610	1,822	126	5,788 R	79.6%	19.1%	80.7%	19.3%
82	LOVING	64	54	9	1	45 R	84.4%	14.1%	85.7%	14.3%
278,831	LUBBOCK	91,184	63,469	26,271	1,444	37,198 R	69.6%	28.8%	70.7%	29.3%
5,915	LYNN	1,959	1,439	506	14	933 R	73.5%	25.8%	74.0%	26.0%
13,664	MADISON	4,028	3,028	967	33	2,061 R	75.2%	24.0%	75.8%	24.2%
10,546	MARION	4,282	2,733	1,495	54	1,238 R	63.8%	34.9%	64.6%	35.4%
4,799	MARTIN	1,624	1,368	248	8	1,120 R	84.2%	15.3%	84.7%	15.3%
4,012	MASON	1,968	1,565	380	23	1,185 R	79.5%	19.3%	80.5%	19.5%
36,702	MATAGORDA	12,133	8,040	3,980	113	4,060 R	66.3%	32.8%	66.9%	33.1%
54,258	MAVERICK	10,563	2,171	8,303	89	6,132 D	20.6%	78.6%	20.7%	79.3%
8,283	MCCULLOCH	2,993	2,419	537	37	1,882 R	80.8%	17.9%	81.8%	18.2%
234,906	MCLENNAN	74,541	47,903	25,694	944	22,209 R	64.3%	34.5%	65.1%	34.9%
707	MCMULLEN	503	431	67	5	364 R	85.7%	13.3%	86.5%	13.5%
46,006	MEDINA	16,049	11,079	4,784	186	6,295 R	69.0%	29.8%	69.8%	30.2%
2,242	MENARD	849	665	171	13	494 R	78.3%	20.1%	79.5%	20.5%
136,872	MIDLAND	44,597	35,689	8,286	622	27,403 R	80.0%	18.6%	81.2%	18.8%
24,757	MILAM	8,230	5,481	2,636	113	2,845 R	66.6%	32.0%	67.5%	32.5%
4,936	MILLS	2,201	1,882	279	40	1,603 R	85.5%	12.7%	87.1%	12.9%
9,403	MITCHELL	2,316	1,756	538	22	1,218 R	75.8%	23.2%	76.5%	23.5%
19,719	MONTAGUE	7,751	6,549	1,116	86	5,433 R	84.5%	14.4%	85.4%	14.6%
455,746	MONTGOMERY	173,113	137,969	32,920	2,224	105,049 R	79.7%	19.0%	80.7%	19.3%
21,904	MOORE	4,985	3,968	964	53	3,004 R	79.6%	19.3%	80.5%	19.5%
12,934	MORRIS	5,139	3,232	1,858	49	1,374 R	62.9%	36.2%	63.5%	36.5%
1,210	MOTLEY	600	538	55	7	483 R	89.7%	9.2%	90.7%	9.3%
64,524	NACOGDOCHES	20,653	13,925	6,465	263	7,460 R	67.4%	31.3%	68.3%	31.7%
47,735	NAVARRO	15,364	10,847	4,350	167	6,497 R	70.6%	28.3%	71.4%	28.6%
14,445	NEWTON	5,869	4,112	1,677	80	2,435 R	70.1%	28.6%	71.0%	29.0%
15,216	NOLAN	4,575	3,282	1,216	77	2,066 R	71.7%	26.6%	73.0%	27.0%
340,223	NUECES	96,104	48,966	45,772	1,366	3,194 R	51.0%	47.6%	51.7%	48.3%
10,223	OCHILTREE	2,993	2,719	253	21	2,466 R	90.8%	8.5%	91.5%	8.5%
2,052	OLDHAM	869	790	71	8	719 R	90.9%	8.2%	91.8%	8.2%

TEXAS

PRESIDENT 2012

2010 Census Population	County	Total Vote	Republican (Romney)	Democratic (Obama)	Other	Rep.-Dem. Plurality	Percentage			
							Total Vote		Major Vote	
							Rep.	Dem.	Rep.	Dem.
81,837	ORANGE	30,518	23,366	6,800	352	16,566 R	76.6%	22.3%	77.5%	22.5%
28,111	PALO PINTO	9,337	7,393	1,811	133	5,582 R	79.2%	19.4%	80.3%	19.7%
23,796	PANOLA	10,230	7,950	2,211	69	5,739 R	77.7%	21.6%	78.2%	21.8%
116,927	PARKER	47,694	39,243	7,853	598	31,390 R	82.3%	16.5%	83.3%	16.7%
10,269	PARMER	2,554	2,011	529	14	1,482 R	78.7%	20.7%	79.2%	20.8%
15,507	PECOS	4,150	2,512	1,591	47	921 R	60.5%	38.3%	61.2%	38.8%
45,413	POLK	19,134	14,071	4,859	204	9,212 R	73.5%	25.4%	74.3%	25.7%
121,073	POTTER	26,450	18,918	7,126	406	11,792 R	71.5%	26.9%	72.6%	27.4%
7,818	PRESIDIO	1,817	504	1,282	31	778 D	27.7%	70.6%	28.2%	71.8%
10,914	RAINS	4,087	3,279	761	47	2,518 R	80.2%	18.6%	81.2%	18.8%
120,725	RANDALL	49,696	41,447	7,574	675	33,873 R	83.4%	15.2%	84.5%	15.5%
3,367	REAGAN	843	676	158	9	518 R	80.2%	18.7%	81.1%	18.9%
3,309	REAL	1,535	1,236	277	22	959 R	80.5%	18.0%	81.7%	18.3%
12,860	RED RIVER	5,074	3,549	1,482	43	2,067 R	69.9%	29.2%	70.5%	29.5%
13,783	REEVES	2,877	1,188	1,655	34	467 D	41.3%	57.5%	41.8%	58.2%
7,383	REFUGIO	2,677	1,663	998	16	665 R	62.1%	37.3%	62.5%	37.5%
929	ROBERTS	508	468	33	7	435 R	92.1%	6.5%	93.4%	6.6%
16,622	ROBERTSON	7,287	4,419	2,798	70	1,621 R	60.6%	38.4%	61.2%	38.8%
78,337	ROCKWALL	35,678	27,113	8,120	445	18,993 R	76.0%	22.8%	77.0%	23.0%
10,501	RUNNELS	3,668	3,104	519	45	2,585 R	84.6%	14.1%	85.7%	14.3%
53,330	RUSK	18,546	13,924	4,451	171	9,473 R	75.1%	24.0%	75.8%	24.2%
10,834	SABINE	4,578	3,727	807	44	2,920 R	81.4%	17.6%	82.2%	17.8%
8,865	SAN AUGUSTINE	3,690	2,469	1,193	28	1,276 R	66.9%	32.3%	67.4%	32.6%
26,384	SAN JACINTO	9,616	7,107	2,410	99	4,697 R	73.9%	25.1%	74.7%	25.3%
64,804	SAN PATRICIO	20,078	12,005	7,856	217	4,149 R	59.8%	39.1%	60.4%	39.6%
6,131	SAN SABA	2,259	1,905	323	31	1,582 R	84.3%	14.3%	85.5%	14.5%
3,461	SCHLEICHER	1,017	787	221	9	566 R	77.4%	21.7%	78.1%	21.9%
16,921	SCURRY	5,027	4,124	838	65	3,286 R	82.0%	16.7%	83.1%	16.9%
3,378	SHACKELFORD	1,363	1,218	131	14	1,087 R	89.4%	9.6%	90.3%	9.7%
25,448	SHELBY	9,284	6,879	2,322	83	4,557 R	74.1%	25.0%	74.8%	25.2%
3,034	SHERMAN	1,038	908	121	9	787 R	87.5%	11.7%	88.2%	11.8%
209,714	SMITH	79,601	57,331	21,456	814	35,875 R	72.0%	27.0%	72.8%	27.2%
8,490	SOMERVELL	3,538	2,871	613	54	2,258 R	81.1%	17.3%	82.4%	17.6%
60,968	STARR	11,883	1,547	10,260	76	8,713 D	13.0%	86.3%	13.1%	86.9%
9,630	STEPHENS	3,412	2,892	475	45	2,417 R	84.8%	13.9%	85.9%	14.1%
1,143	STERLING	494	459	31	4	428 R	92.9%	6.3%	93.7%	6.3%
1,490	STONEWALL	675	507	160	8	347 R	75.1%	23.7%	76.0%	24.0%
4,128	SUTTON	1,489	1,110	369	10	741 R	74.5%	24.8%	75.1%	24.9%
7,854	SWISHER	2,270	1,655	579	36	1,076 R	72.9%	25.5%	74.1%	25.9%
1,809,034	TARRANT	610,890	348,920	253,071	8,899	95,849 R	57.1%	41.4%	58.0%	42.0%
131,506	TAYLOR	43,263	32,904	9,750	609	23,154 R	76.1%	22.5%	77.1%	22.9%
984	TERRELL	555	358	184	13	174 R	64.5%	33.2%	66.1%	33.9%
12,651	TERRY	3,709	2,602	1,059	48	1,543 R	70.2%	28.6%	71.1%	28.9%
1,641	THROCKMORTON	813	700	109	4	591 R	86.1%	13.4%	86.5%	13.5%
32,334	TITUS	8,854	6,084	2,648	122	3,436 R	68.7%	29.9%	69.7%	30.3%
110,224	TOM GREEN	36,720	26,878	9,294	548	17,584 R	73.2%	25.3%	74.3%	25.7%
1,024,266	TRAVIS	387,057	140,152	232,788	14,117	92,636 D	36.2%	60.1%	37.6%	62.4%
14,585	TRINITY	6,235	4,537	1,614	84	2,923 R	72.8%	25.9%	73.8%	26.2%
21,766	TYLER	7,654	5,910	1,668	76	4,242 R	77.2%	21.8%	78.0%	22.0%
39,309	UPSHUR	15,138	12,015	2,971	152	9,044 R	79.4%	19.6%	80.2%	19.8%
3,355	UPTON	1,300	953	333	14	620 R	73.3%	25.6%	74.1%	25.9%
26,405	UVALDE	8,435	4,529	3,825	81	704 R	53.7%	45.3%	54.2%	45.8%
48,879	VAL VERDE	12,081	5,635	6,285	161	650 D	46.6%	52.0%	47.3%	52.7%
52,579	VAN ZANDT	19,100	15,794	3,084	222	12,710 R	82.7%	16.1%	83.7%	16.3%
86,793	VICTORIA	28,853	19,692	8,802	359	10,890 R	68.2%	30.5%	69.1%	30.9%
67,861	WALKER	18,685	12,140	6,252	293	5,888 R	65.0%	33.5%	66.0%	34.0%
43,205	WALLER	15,902	9,244	6,514	144	2,730 R	58.1%	41.0%	58.7%	41.3%
10,658	WARD	3,245	2,366	841	38	1,525 R	72.9%	25.9%	73.8%	26.2%
33,718	WASHINGTON	14,397	10,857	3,381	159	7,476 R	75.4%	23.5%	76.3%	23.7%
250,304	WEBB	49,110	11,078	37,597	435	26,519 D	22.6%	76.6%	22.8%	77.2%

TEXAS

PRESIDENT 2012

2010 Census Population	County	Total Vote	Republican (Romney)	Democratic (Obama)	Other	Rep.-Dem. Plurality	Percentage			
							Total Vote		Major Vote	
							Rep.	Dem.	Rep.	Dem.
41,280	WHARTON	14,087	9,750	4,235	102	5,515 R	69.2%	30.1%	69.7%	30.3%
5,410	WHEELER	2,128	1,878	232	18	1,646 R	88.3%	10.9%	89.0%	11.0%
131,500	WICHITA	41,018	29,812	10,525	681	19,287 R	72.7%	25.7%	73.9%	26.1%
13,535	WILBARGER	3,980	2,956	971	53	1,985 R	74.3%	24.4%	75.3%	24.7%
22,134	WILLACY	5,064	1,416	3,600	48	2,184 D	28.0%	71.1%	28.2%	71.8%
422,679	WILLIAMSON	163,271	97,006	61,875	4,390	35,131 R	59.4%	37.9%	61.1%	38.9%
42,918	WILSON	17,205	12,218	4,821	166	7,397 R	71.0%	28.0%	71.7%	28.3%
7,110	WINKLER	1,725	1,311	398	16	913 R	76.0%	23.1%	76.7%	23.3%
59,127	WISE	20,745	17,207	3,221	317	13,986 R	82.9%	15.5%	84.2%	15.8%
41,964	WOOD	17,581	14,351	3,056	174	11,295 R	81.6%	17.4%	82.4%	17.6%
7,879	YOAKUM	2,128	1,698	409	21	1,289 R	79.8%	19.2%	80.6%	19.4%
18,550	YOUNG	7,316	6,225	992	99	5,233 R	85.1%	13.6%	86.3%	13.7%
14,018	ZAPATA	3,543	997	2,527	19	1,530 D	28.1%	71.3%	28.3%	71.7%
11,677	ZAVALA	3,653	574	3,042	37	2,468 D	15.7%	83.3%	15.9%	84.1%
25,145,561	TOTAL	7,993,851	4,569,843	3,308,124	115,884	1,261,719 R	57.2%	41.4%	58.0%	42.0%

TEXAS

SENATOR 2012

2010 Census Population	County	Total Vote	Republican (Cruz)	Democratic (Sadler)	Other	Rep.-Dem. Plurality	Percentage			
							Total Vote		Major Vote	
							Rep.	Dem.	Rep.	Dem.
58,458	ANDERSON	16,009	11,487	4,154	368	7,333 R	71.8%	25.9%	73.4%	26.6%
14,786	ANDREWS	4,387	3,495	758	134	2,737 R	79.7%	17.3%	82.2%	17.8%
86,771	ANGELINA	27,909	19,296	8,121	492	11,175 R	69.1%	29.1%	70.4%	29.6%
23,158	ARANSAS	9,485	6,640	2,592	253	4,048 R	70.0%	27.3%	71.9%	28.1%
9,054	ARCHER	4,066	3,380	598	88	2,782 R	83.1%	14.7%	85.0%	15.0%
1,901	ARMSTRONG	919	786	109	24	677 R	85.5%	11.9%	87.8%	12.2%
44,911	ATASCOSA	12,391	7,149	4,883	359	2,266 R	57.7%	39.4%	59.4%	40.6%
28,417	AUSTIN	11,508	9,001	2,305	202	6,696 R	78.2%	20.0%	79.6%	20.4%
7,165	BAILEY	1,779	1,328	421	30	907 R	74.6%	23.7%	75.9%	24.1%
20,485	BANDERA	9,378	7,189	1,833	356	5,356 R	76.7%	19.5%	79.7%	20.3%
74,171	BASTROP	24,136	12,720	10,244	1,172	2,476 R	52.7%	42.4%	55.4%	44.6%
3,726	BAYLOR	1,485	1,090	332	63	758 R	73.4%	22.4%	76.7%	23.3%
31,861	BEE	7,583	4,158	3,235	190	923 R	54.8%	42.7%	56.2%	43.8%
310,235	BELL	84,756	48,913	33,427	2,416	15,486 R	57.7%	39.4%	59.4%	40.6%
1,714,773	BEXAR	508,610	236,161	256,629	15,820	20,468 D	46.4%	50.5%	47.9%	52.1%
10,497	BLANCO	4,912	3,408	1,281	223	2,127 R	69.4%	26.1%	72.7%	27.3%
641	BORDEN	343	297	39	7	258 R	86.6%	11.4%	88.4%	11.6%
18,212	BOSQUE	7,245	5,560	1,478	207	4,082 R	76.7%	20.4%	79.0%	21.0%
92,565	BOWIE	34,365	21,825	11,760	780	10,065 R	63.5%	34.2%	65.0%	35.0%
313,166	BRAZORIA	106,056	69,497	33,744	2,815	35,753 R	65.5%	31.8%	67.3%	32.7%
194,851	BRAZOS	55,299	36,837	16,404	2,058	20,433 R	66.6%	29.7%	69.2%	30.8%
9,232	BREWSTER	3,742	1,875	1,624	243	251 R	50.1%	43.4%	53.6%	46.4%
1,637	BRISCOE	669	513	142	14	371 R	76.7%	21.2%	78.3%	21.7%
7,223	BROOKS	2,353	583	1,737	33	1,154 D	24.8%	73.8%	25.1%	74.9%
38,106	BROWN	13,721	11,267	2,069	385	9,198 R	82.1%	15.1%	84.5%	15.5%
17,187	BURLESON	6,418	4,549	1,758	111	2,791 R	70.9%	27.4%	72.1%	27.9%
42,750	BURNET	16,628	12,110	3,888	630	8,222 R	72.8%	23.4%	75.7%	24.3%
38,066	CALDWELL	10,898	5,552	4,965	381	587 R	50.9%	45.6%	52.8%	47.2%
21,381	CALHOUN	6,463	3,809	2,446	208	1,363 R	58.9%	37.8%	60.9%	39.1%
13,544	CALLAHAN	5,106	4,156	797	153	3,359 R	81.4%	15.6%	83.9%	16.1%

TEXAS

SENATOR 2012

2010 Census Population	County	Total Vote	Republican (Cruz)	Democratic (Sadler)	Other	Rep.-Dem. Plurality	Percentage Total Vote Rep.	Dem.	Major Vote Rep.	Dem.
406,220	CAMERON	74,366	28,997	42,683	2,686	13,686 D	39.0%	57.4%	40.5%	59.5%
12,401	CAMP	4,284	2,643	1,567	74	1,076 R	61.7%	36.6%	62.8%	37.2%
6,182	CARSON	2,740	2,334	336	70	1,998 R	85.2%	12.3%	87.4%	12.6%
30,464	CASS	11,505	7,863	3,427	215	4,436 R	68.3%	29.8%	69.6%	30.4%
8,062	CASTRO	2,002	1,379	582	41	797 R	68.9%	29.1%	70.3%	29.7%
35,096	CHAMBERS	14,378	11,324	2,749	305	8,575 R	78.8%	19.1%	80.5%	19.5%
50,845	CHEROKEE	15,895	11,270	4,334	291	6,936 R	70.9%	27.3%	72.2%	27.8%
7,041	CHILDRESS	1,940	1,567	334	39	1,233 R	80.8%	17.2%	82.4%	17.6%
10,752	CLAY	4,855	3,820	910	125	2,910 R	78.7%	18.7%	80.8%	19.2%
3,127	COCHRAN	893	648	224	21	424 R	72.6%	25.1%	74.3%	25.7%
3,320	COKE	1,387	1,145	204	38	941 R	82.6%	14.7%	84.9%	15.1%
8,895	COLEMAN	3,385	2,804	508	73	2,296 R	82.8%	15.0%	84.7%	15.3%
782,341	COLLIN	294,627	189,142	96,726	8,759	92,416 R	64.2%	32.8%	66.2%	33.8%
3,057	COLLINGSWORTH	1,099	845	221	33	624 R	76.9%	20.1%	79.3%	20.7%
20,874	COLORADO	7,964	5,761	2,063	140	3,698 R	72.3%	25.9%	73.6%	26.4%
108,472	COMAL	50,327	37,696	10,972	1,659	26,724 R	74.9%	21.8%	77.5%	22.5%
13,974	COMANCHE	4,813	3,680	1,015	118	2,665 R	76.5%	21.1%	78.4%	21.6%
4,087	CONCHO	973	760	187	26	573 R	78.1%	19.2%	80.3%	19.7%
38,437	COOKE	14,109	11,270	2,467	372	8,803 R	79.9%	17.5%	82.0%	18.0%
75,388	CORYELL	16,316	10,766	4,978	572	5,788 R	66.0%	30.5%	68.4%	31.6%
1,505	COTTLE	666	465	166	35	299 R	69.8%	24.9%	73.7%	26.3%
4,375	CRANE	1,227	940	253	34	687 R	76.6%	20.6%	78.8%	21.2%
3,719	CROCKETT	1,337	883	404	50	479 R	66.0%	30.2%	68.6%	31.4%
6,059	CROSBY	1,707	1,053	611	43	442 R	61.7%	35.8%	63.3%	36.7%
2,398	CULBERSON	705	313	355	37	42 D	44.4%	50.4%	46.9%	53.1%
6,703	DALLAM	1,519	1,237	235	47	1,002 R	81.4%	15.5%	84.0%	16.0%
2,368,139	DALLAS	698,669	291,263	389,398	18,008	98,135 D	41.7%	55.7%	42.8%	57.2%
13,833	DAWSON	3,522	2,509	939	74	1,570 R	71.2%	26.7%	72.8%	27.2%
20,097	DE WITT	6,442	4,785	1,487	170	3,298 R	74.3%	23.1%	76.3%	23.7%
19,372	DEAF SMITH	4,214	3,032	1,084	98	1,948 R	72.0%	25.7%	73.7%	26.3%
5,231	DELTA	1,972	1,414	513	45	901 R	71.7%	26.0%	73.4%	26.6%
662,614	DENTON	240,327	154,208	77,314	8,805	76,894 R	64.2%	32.2%	66.6%	33.4%
2,444	DICKENS	969	715	236	18	479 R	73.8%	24.4%	75.2%	24.8%
9,996	DIMMIT	2,773	842	1,839	92	997 D	30.4%	66.3%	31.4%	68.6%
3,677	DONLEY	1,502	1,212	251	39	961 R	80.7%	16.7%	82.8%	17.2%
11,782	DUVAL	4,123	946	3,078	99	2,132 D	22.9%	74.7%	23.5%	76.5%
18,583	EASTLAND	6,447	5,187	1,065	195	4,122 R	80.5%	16.5%	83.0%	17.0%
137,130	ECTOR	32,238	23,629	7,770	839	15,859 R	73.3%	24.1%	75.3%	24.7%
2,002	EDWARDS	820	624	172	24	452 R	76.1%	21.0%	78.4%	21.6%
800,647	EL PASO	167,514	59,876	102,046	5,592	42,170 D	35.7%	60.9%	37.0%	63.0%
149,610	ELLIS	53,488	37,865	14,045	1,578	23,820 R	70.8%	26.3%	72.9%	27.1%
37,890	ERATH	12,385	9,973	2,066	346	7,907 R	80.5%	16.7%	82.8%	17.2%
17,866	FALLS	5,277	3,139	2,032	106	1,107 R	59.5%	38.5%	60.7%	39.3%
33,915	FANNIN	10,645	7,606	2,699	340	4,907 R	71.5%	25.4%	73.8%	26.2%
24,554	FAYETTE	10,341	7,334	2,776	231	4,558 R	70.9%	26.8%	72.5%	27.5%
3,974	FISHER	1,574	975	559	40	416 R	61.9%	35.5%	63.6%	36.4%
6,446	FLOYD	2,044	1,468	545	31	923 R	71.8%	26.7%	72.9%	27.1%
1,336	FOARD	464	287	162	15	125 R	61.9%	34.9%	63.9%	36.1%
585,375	FORT BEND	218,051	115,580	98,345	4,126	17,235 R	53.0%	45.1%	54.0%	46.0%
10,605	FRANKLIN	4,153	3,139	902	112	2,237 R	75.6%	21.7%	77.7%	22.3%
19,816	FREESTONE	7,323	5,235	1,930	158	3,305 R	71.5%	26.4%	73.1%	26.9%
17,217	FRIO	3,772	1,583	2,083	106	500 D	42.0%	55.2%	43.2%	56.8%
17,526	GAINES	3,940	3,312	546	82	2,766 R	84.1%	13.9%	85.8%	14.2%
291,309	GALVESTON	109,232	66,912	39,443	2,877	27,469 R	61.3%	36.1%	62.9%	37.1%
6,461	GARZA	1,494	1,209	252	33	957 R	80.9%	16.9%	82.8%	17.2%
24,837	GILLESPIE	12,409	9,791	2,227	391	7,564 R	78.9%	17.9%	81.5%	18.5%
1,226	GLASSCOCK	548	493	52	3	441 R	90.0%	9.5%	90.5%	9.5%
7,210	GOLIAD	3,243	2,101	1,035	107	1,066 R	64.8%	31.9%	67.0%	33.0%
19,807	GONZALES	5,843	3,938	1,760	145	2,178 R	67.4%	30.1%	69.1%	30.9%
22,535	GRAY	7,342	6,251	943	148	5,308 R	85.1%	12.8%	86.9%	13.1%

TEXAS

SENATOR 2012

2010 Census Population	County	Total Vote	Republican (Cruz)	Democratic (Sadler)	Other	Rep.-Dem. Plurality	Percentage			
							Total Vote		Major Vote	
							Rep.	Dem.	Rep.	Dem.
120,877	GRAYSON	41,242	29,112	10,831	1,299	18,281 R	70.6%	26.3%	72.9%	27.1%
121,730	GREGG	41,169	27,272	13,303	594	13,969 R	66.2%	32.3%	67.2%	32.8%
26,604	GRIMES	8,473	5,894	2,372	207	3,522 R	69.6%	28.0%	71.3%	28.7%
131,533	GUADALUPE	48,268	31,654	14,892	1,722	16,762 R	65.6%	30.9%	68.0%	32.0%
36,273	HALE	8,713	6,231	2,266	216	3,965 R	71.5%	26.0%	73.3%	26.7%
3,353	HALL	1,041	754	262	25	492 R	72.4%	25.2%	74.2%	25.8%
8,517	HAMILTON	3,481	2,714	697	70	2,017 R	78.0%	20.0%	79.6%	20.4%
5,613	HANSFORD	1,912	1,722	157	33	1,565 R	90.1%	8.2%	91.6%	8.4%
4,139	HARDEMAN	1,412	1,013	352	47	661 R	71.7%	24.9%	74.2%	25.8%
54,635	HARDIN	20,987	17,025	3,558	404	13,467 R	81.1%	17.0%	82.7%	17.3%
4,092,459	HARRIS	1,174,884	582,328	564,355	28,201	17,973 R	49.6%	48.0%	50.8%	49.2%
65,631	HARRISON	25,713	15,689	9,607	417	6,082 R	61.0%	37.4%	62.0%	38.0%
6,062	HARTLEY	1,891	1,647	215	29	1,432 R	87.1%	11.4%	88.5%	11.5%
5,899	HASKELL	1,934	1,242	631	61	611 R	64.2%	32.6%	66.3%	33.7%
157,107	HAYS	58,277	30,217	24,795	3,265	5,422 R	51.9%	42.5%	54.9%	45.1%
3,807	HEMPHILL	1,461	1,256	179	26	1,077 R	86.0%	12.3%	87.5%	12.5%
78,532	HENDERSON	27,377	20,119	6,616	642	13,503 R	73.5%	24.2%	75.3%	24.7%
774,769	HIDALGO	133,165	41,671	88,391	3,103	46,720 D	31.3%	66.4%	32.0%	68.0%
35,089	HILL	11,889	8,700	2,898	291	5,802 R	73.2%	24.4%	75.0%	25.0%
22,935	HOCKLEY	6,984	5,356	1,384	244	3,972 R	76.7%	19.8%	79.5%	20.5%
51,182	HOOD	22,263	17,695	3,963	605	13,732 R	79.5%	17.8%	81.7%	18.3%
35,161	HOPKINS	12,373	8,815	3,288	270	5,527 R	71.2%	26.6%	72.8%	27.2%
23,732	HOUSTON	8,029	5,578	2,320	131	3,258 R	69.5%	28.9%	70.6%	29.4%
35,012	HOWARD	8,477	6,169	2,039	269	4,130 R	72.8%	24.1%	75.2%	24.8%
3,476	HUDSPETH	784	458	287	39	171 R	58.4%	36.6%	61.5%	38.5%
86,129	HUNT	27,497	19,782	6,897	818	12,885 R	71.9%	25.1%	74.1%	25.9%
22,150	HUTCHINSON	7,842	6,583	1,056	203	5,527 R	83.9%	13.5%	86.2%	13.8%
1,599	IRION	770	622	119	29	503 R	80.8%	15.5%	83.9%	16.1%
9,044	JACK	2,847	2,382	391	74	1,991 R	83.7%	13.7%	85.9%	14.1%
14,075	JACKSON	4,814	3,610	1,104	100	2,506 R	75.0%	22.9%	76.6%	23.4%
35,710	JASPER	13,070	9,012	3,755	303	5,257 R	69.0%	28.7%	70.6%	29.4%
2,342	JEFF DAVIS	1,132	659	417	56	242 R	58.2%	36.8%	61.2%	38.8%
252,273	JEFFERSON	86,968	41,337	44,463	1,168	3,126 D	47.5%	51.1%	48.2%	51.8%
5,300	JIM HOGG	1,596	433	1,139	24	706 D	27.1%	71.4%	27.5%	72.5%
40,838	JIM WELLS	10,876	4,674	5,994	208	1,320 D	43.0%	55.1%	43.8%	56.2%
150,934	JOHNSON	48,397	36,161	10,747	1,489	25,414 R	74.7%	22.2%	77.1%	22.9%
20,202	JONES	5,415	3,983	1,286	146	2,697 R	73.6%	23.7%	75.6%	24.4%
14,824	KARNES	3,992	2,435	1,443	114	992 R	61.0%	36.1%	62.8%	37.2%
103,350	KAUFMAN	34,320	23,935	9,589	796	14,346 R	69.7%	27.9%	71.4%	28.6%
33,410	KENDALL	17,576	14,114	2,952	510	11,162 R	80.3%	16.8%	82.7%	17.3%
416	KENEDY	153	80	67	6	13 R	52.3%	43.8%	54.4%	45.6%
808	KENT	382	287	85	10	202 R	75.1%	22.3%	77.2%	22.8%
49,625	KERR	21,483	16,493	4,309	681	12,184 R	76.8%	20.1%	79.3%	20.7%
4,607	KIMBLE	1,827	1,535	242	50	1,293 R	84.0%	13.2%	86.4%	13.6%
286	KING	122	117	4	1	113 R	95.9%	3.3%	96.7%	3.3%
3,598	KINNEY	1,349	852	451	46	401 R	63.2%	33.4%	65.4%	34.6%
32,061	KLEBERG	8,676	4,136	4,310	230	174 D	47.7%	49.7%	49.0%	51.0%
3,719	KNOX	1,462	1,046	372	44	674 R	71.5%	25.4%	73.8%	26.2%
6,886	LA SALLE	1,529	645	853	31	208 D	42.2%	55.8%	43.1%	56.9%
49,793	LAMAR	16,924	11,726	4,798	400	6,928 R	69.3%	28.4%	71.0%	29.0%
13,977	LAMB	3,987	2,979	912	96	2,067 R	74.7%	22.9%	76.6%	23.4%
19,677	LAMPASAS	7,160	5,509	1,440	211	4,069 R	76.9%	20.1%	79.3%	20.7%
19,263	LAVACA	8,002	6,141	1,680	181	4,461 R	76.7%	21.0%	78.5%	21.5%
16,612	LEE	5,937	3,936	1,830	171	2,106 R	66.3%	30.8%	68.3%	31.7%
16,801	LEON	6,847	5,610	1,124	113	4,486 R	81.9%	16.4%	83.3%	16.7%
75,643	LIBERTY	22,383	16,486	5,401	496	11,085 R	73.7%	24.1%	75.3%	24.7%
23,384	LIMESTONE	7,434	4,992	2,302	140	2,690 R	67.2%	31.0%	68.4%	31.6%
3,302	LIPSCOMB	1,139	986	135	18	851 R	86.6%	11.9%	88.0%	12.0%
11,531	LIVE OAK	3,999	2,917	959	123	1,958 R	72.9%	24.0%	75.3%	24.7%
19,301	LLANO	9,502	7,222	2,000	280	5,222 R	76.0%	21.0%	78.3%	21.7%

TEXAS

SENATOR 2012

2010 Census Population	County	Total Vote	Republican (Cruz)	Democratic (Sadler)	Other	Rep.-Dem. Plurality	Percentage			
							Total Vote		Major Vote	
							Rep.	Dem.	Rep.	Dem.
82	LOVING	61	43	15	3	28 R	70.5%	24.6%	74.1%	25.9%
278,831	LUBBOCK	89,929	62,650	24,299	2,980	38,351 R	69.7%	27.0%	72.1%	27.9%
5,915	LYNN	1,909	1,365	510	34	855 R	71.5%	26.7%	72.8%	27.2%
13,664	MADISON	4,013	2,909	1,043	61	1,866 R	72.5%	26.0%	73.6%	26.4%
10,546	MARION	4,186	2,429	1,670	87	759 R	58.0%	39.9%	59.3%	40.7%
4,799	MARTIN	1,581	1,333	230	18	1,103 R	84.3%	14.5%	85.3%	14.7%
4,012	MASON	1,933	1,447	435	51	1,012 R	74.9%	22.5%	76.9%	23.1%
36,702	MATAGORDA	11,811	7,530	3,995	286	3,535 R	63.8%	33.8%	65.3%	34.7%
54,258	MAVERICK	9,646	2,674	6,551	421	3,877 D	27.7%	67.9%	29.0%	71.0%
8,283	MCCULLOCH	2,897	2,282	535	80	1,747 R	78.8%	18.5%	81.0%	19.0%
234,906	MCLENNAN	73,899	47,075	25,102	1,722	21,973 R	63.7%	34.0%	65.2%	34.8%
707	MCMULLEN	439	363	64	12	299 R	82.7%	14.6%	85.0%	15.0%
46,006	MEDINA	15,818	10,765	4,608	445	6,157 R	68.1%	29.1%	70.0%	30.0%
2,242	MENARD	848	645	181	22	464 R	76.1%	21.3%	78.1%	21.9%
136,872	MIDLAND	44,080	35,202	7,826	1,052	27,376 R	79.9%	17.8%	81.8%	18.2%
24,757	MILAM	8,026	5,063	2,759	204	2,304 R	63.1%	34.4%	64.7%	35.3%
4,936	MILLS	2,131	1,732	344	55	1,388 R	81.3%	16.1%	83.4%	16.6%
9,403	MITCHELL	2,235	1,598	569	68	1,029 R	71.5%	25.5%	73.7%	26.3%
19,719	MONTAGUE	7,527	6,104	1,225	198	4,879 R	81.1%	16.3%	83.3%	16.7%
455,746	MONTGOMERY	172,084	135,276	32,608	4,200	102,668 R	78.6%	18.9%	80.6%	19.4%
21,904	MOORE	4,867	3,872	872	123	3,000 R	79.6%	17.9%	81.6%	18.4%
12,934	MORRIS	4,955	2,687	2,156	112	531 R	54.2%	43.5%	55.5%	44.5%
1,210	MOTLEY	551	473	65	13	408 R	85.8%	11.8%	87.9%	12.1%
64,524	NACOGDOCHES	20,263	13,479	6,324	460	7,155 R	66.5%	31.2%	68.1%	31.9%
47,735	NAVARRO	14,950	10,201	4,381	368	5,820 R	68.2%	29.3%	70.0%	30.0%
14,445	NEWTON	5,591	3,473	1,941	177	1,532 R	62.1%	34.7%	64.1%	35.9%
15,216	NOLAN	4,478	3,001	1,309	168	1,692 R	67.0%	29.2%	69.6%	30.4%
340,223	NUECES	94,226	48,008	43,526	2,692	4,482 R	50.9%	46.2%	52.4%	47.6%
10,223	OCHILTREE	2,948	2,670	230	48	2,440 R	90.6%	7.8%	92.1%	7.9%
2,052	OLDHAM	852	748	80	24	668 R	87.8%	9.4%	90.3%	9.7%
81,837	ORANGE	30,132	21,870	7,567	695	14,303 R	72.6%	25.1%	74.3%	25.7%
28,111	PALO PINTO	9,194	6,953	1,963	278	4,990 R	75.6%	21.4%	78.0%	22.0%
23,796	PANOLA	10,037	6,835	3,045	157	3,790 R	68.1%	30.3%	69.2%	30.8%
116,927	PARKER	47,495	38,127	8,117	1,251	30,010 R	80.3%	17.1%	82.4%	17.6%
10,269	PARMER	2,512	1,968	498	46	1,470 R	78.3%	19.8%	79.8%	20.2%
15,507	PECOS	3,977	2,472	1,399	106	1,073 R	62.2%	35.2%	63.9%	36.1%
45,413	POLK	18,637	13,258	4,905	474	8,353 R	71.1%	26.3%	73.0%	27.0%
121,073	POTTER	26,070	18,557	6,724	789	11,833 R	71.2%	25.8%	73.4%	26.6%
7,818	PRESIDIO	1,339	478	795	66	317 D	35.7%	59.4%	37.5%	62.5%
10,914	RAINS	4,026	3,070	845	111	2,225 R	76.3%	21.0%	78.4%	21.6%
120,725	RANDALL	49,378	40,815	7,256	1,307	33,559 R	82.7%	14.7%	84.9%	15.1%
3,367	REAGAN	805	666	119	20	547 R	82.7%	14.8%	84.8%	15.2%
3,309	REAL	1,484	1,159	278	47	881 R	78.1%	18.7%	80.7%	19.3%
12,860	RED RIVER	4,874	3,069	1,685	120	1,384 R	63.0%	34.6%	64.6%	35.4%
13,783	REEVES	2,657	1,141	1,439	77	298 D	42.9%	54.2%	44.2%	55.8%
7,383	REFUGIO	2,629	1,554	1,015	60	539 R	59.1%	38.6%	60.5%	39.5%
929	ROBERTS	496	452	32	12	420 R	91.1%	6.5%	93.4%	6.6%
16,622	ROBERTSON	7,124	4,077	2,890	157	1,187 R	57.2%	40.6%	58.5%	41.5%
78,337	ROCKWALL	35,188	26,179	8,006	1,003	18,173 R	74.4%	22.8%	76.6%	23.4%
10,501	RUNNELS	3,597	2,935	577	85	2,358 R	81.6%	16.0%	83.6%	16.4%
53,330	RUSK	18,304	11,548	6,526	230	5,022 R	63.1%	35.7%	63.9%	36.1%
10,834	SABINE	4,441	3,407	917	117	2,490 R	76.7%	20.6%	78.8%	21.2%
8,865	SAN AUGUSTINE	3,548	2,196	1,256	96	940 R	61.9%	35.4%	63.6%	36.4%
26,384	SAN JACINTO	9,378	6,545	2,597	236	3,948 R	69.8%	27.7%	71.6%	28.4%
64,804	SAN PATRICIO	19,643	11,552	7,576	515	3,976 R	58.8%	38.6%	60.4%	39.6%
6,131	SAN SABA	2,200	1,833	326	41	1,507 R	83.3%	14.8%	84.9%	15.1%
3,461	SCHLEICHER	988	748	217	23	531 R	75.7%	22.0%	77.5%	22.5%
16,921	SCURRY	4,875	3,881	851	143	3,030 R	79.6%	17.5%	82.0%	18.0%
3,378	SHACKELFORD	1,337	1,162	152	23	1,010 R	86.9%	11.4%	88.4%	11.6%
25,448	SHELBY	8,921	6,027	2,733	161	3,294 R	67.6%	30.6%	68.8%	31.2%

TEXAS

SENATOR 2012

2010 Census Population	County	Total Vote	Republican (Cruz)	Democratic (Sadler)	Other	Rep.-Dem. Plurality	Percentage Total Vote Rep.	Dem.	Major Vote Rep.	Dem.
3,034	SHERMAN	996	855	117	24	738 R	85.8%	11.7%	88.0%	12.0%
209,714	SMITH	78,582	55,204	22,037	1,341	33,167 R	70.3%	28.0%	71.5%	28.5%
8,490	SOMERVELL	3,447	2,693	652	102	2,041 R	78.1%	18.9%	80.5%	19.5%
60,968	STARR	11,179	1,886	9,075	218	7,189 D	16.9%	81.2%	17.2%	82.8%
9,630	STEPHENS	3,276	2,599	564	113	2,035 R	79.3%	17.2%	82.2%	17.8%
1,143	STERLING	482	425	50	7	375 R	88.2%	10.4%	89.5%	10.5%
1,490	STONEWALL	643	409	213	21	196 R	63.6%	33.1%	65.8%	34.2%
4,128	SUTTON	1,426	1,081	329	16	752 R	75.8%	23.1%	76.7%	23.3%
7,854	SWISHER	2,223	1,539	625	59	914 R	69.2%	28.1%	71.1%	28.9%
1,809,034	TARRANT	603,610	342,386	243,914	17,310	98,472 R	56.7%	40.4%	58.4%	41.6%
131,506	TAYLOR	42,787	32,168	9,392	1,227	22,776 R	75.2%	22.0%	77.4%	22.6%
984	TERRELL	507	309	175	23	134 R	60.9%	34.5%	63.8%	36.2%
12,651	TERRY	3,539	2,530	915	94	1,615 R	71.5%	25.9%	73.4%	26.6%
1,641	THROCKMORTON	756	603	130	23	473 R	79.8%	17.2%	82.3%	17.7%
32,334	TITUS	8,668	5,401	3,091	176	2,310 R	62.3%	35.7%	63.6%	36.4%
110,224	TOM GREEN	36,200	25,920	9,039	1,241	16,881 R	71.6%	25.0%	74.1%	25.9%
1,024,266	TRAVIS	381,517	133,984	225,209	22,324	91,225 D	35.1%	59.0%	37.3%	62.7%
14,585	TRINITY	5,984	4,057	1,746	181	2,311 R	67.8%	29.2%	69.9%	30.1%
21,766	TYLER	7,447	5,463	1,824	160	3,639 R	73.4%	24.5%	75.0%	25.0%
39,309	UPSHUR	14,979	11,111	3,541	327	7,570 R	74.2%	23.6%	75.8%	24.2%
3,355	UPTON	1,164	845	280	39	565 R	72.6%	24.1%	75.1%	24.9%
26,405	UVALDE	8,197	4,349	3,622	226	727 R	53.1%	44.2%	54.6%	45.4%
48,879	VAL VERDE	11,728	5,568	5,732	428	164 D	47.5%	48.9%	49.3%	50.7%
52,579	VAN ZANDT	18,818	14,762	3,597	459	11,165 R	78.4%	19.1%	80.4%	19.6%
86,793	VICTORIA	28,013	18,727	8,526	760	10,201 R	66.9%	30.4%	68.7%	31.3%
67,861	WALKER	18,464	11,653	6,186	625	5,467 R	63.1%	33.5%	65.3%	34.7%
43,205	WALLER	15,857	9,220	6,390	247	2,830 R	58.1%	40.3%	59.1%	40.9%
10,658	WARD	3,164	2,263	804	97	1,459 R	71.5%	25.4%	73.8%	26.2%
33,718	WASHINGTON	14,201	10,513	3,410	278	7,103 R	74.0%	24.0%	75.5%	24.5%
250,304	WEBB	47,531	14,949	30,434	2,148	15,485 D	31.5%	64.0%	32.9%	67.1%
41,280	WHARTON	13,831	9,348	4,245	238	5,103 R	67.6%	30.7%	68.8%	31.2%
5,410	WHEELER	2,041	1,744	266	31	1,478 R	85.4%	13.0%	86.8%	13.2%
131,500	WICHITA	39,739	27,926	10,566	1,247	17,360 R	70.3%	26.6%	72.6%	27.4%
13,535	WILBARGER	3,862	2,708	1,047	107	1,661 R	70.1%	27.1%	72.1%	27.9%
22,134	WILLACY	4,683	1,781	2,717	185	936 D	38.0%	58.0%	39.6%	60.4%
422,679	WILLIAMSON	160,632	92,034	60,279	8,319	31,755 R	57.3%	37.5%	60.4%	39.6%
42,918	WILSON	16,776	11,436	4,804	536	6,632 R	68.2%	28.6%	70.4%	29.6%
7,110	WINKLER	1,695	1,270	383	42	887 R	74.9%	22.6%	76.8%	23.2%
59,127	WISE	20,574	16,475	3,474	625	13,001 R	80.1%	16.9%	82.6%	17.4%
41,964	WOOD	17,378	13,576	3,503	299	10,073 R	78.1%	20.2%	79.5%	20.5%
7,879	YOAKUM	2,071	1,653	376	42	1,277 R	79.8%	18.2%	81.5%	18.5%
18,550	YOUNG	7,200	5,900	1,126	174	4,774 R	81.9%	15.6%	84.0%	16.0%
14,018	ZAPATA	3,218	1,107	1,989	122	882 D	34.4%	61.8%	35.8%	64.2%
11,677	ZAVALA	3,371	659	2,612	100	1,953 D	19.5%	77.5%	20.1%	79.9%
25,145,561	TOTAL	7,864,822	4,440,137	3,194,927	229,758	1,245,210 R	56.5%	40.6%	58.2%	41.8%

TEXAS

HOUSE OF REPRESENTATIVES

			Republican		Democratic		Other Vote	Rep.-Dem. Plurality	Percentage			
									Total Vote		Major Vote	
CD	Year	Total Vote	Vote	Candidate	Vote	Candidate			Rep.	Dem.	Rep.	Dem.
1	2012	249,658	178,322	GOHMERT, LOUIS*	67,222	MCKELLAR, SHIRLEY J.	4,114	111,100 R	71.4%	26.9%	72.6%	27.4%
2	2012	246,328	159,664	POE, TED*	80,512	DOUGHERTY, JIM	6,152	79,152 R	64.8%	32.7%	66.5%	33.5%
3	2012	187,180	187,180	JOHNSON, SAM*				187,180 R	100.0%		100.0%	
4	2012	250,343	182,679	HALL, RALPH*	60,214	HATHCOX, VALINDA	7,450	122,465 R	73.0%	24.1%	75.2%	24.8%
5	2012	208,230	134,091	HENSARLING, JEB*	69,178	MROSKO, LINDA S.	4,961	64,913 R	64.4%	33.2%	66.0%	34.0%
6	2012	249,936	145,019	BARTON, JOE*	98,053	SANDERS, KENNETH	6,864	46,966 R	58.0%	39.2%	59.7%	40.3%
7	2012	234,837	142,793	CULBERSON, JOHN*	85,553	CARGAS, JAMES	6,491	57,240 R	60.8%	36.4%	62.5%	37.5%
8	2012	251,052	194,043	BRADY, KEVIN*	51,051	BURNS, NEIL	5,958	142,992 R	77.3%	20.3%	79.2%	20.8%
9	2012	183,566	36,139	MUELLER, STEVE	144,075	GREEN, AL*	3,352	107,936 D	19.7%	78.5%	20.1%	79.9%
10	2012	264,019	159,783	MCCAUL, MICHAEL*	95,710	CADIEN, TAWANA W.	8,526	64,073 R	60.5%	36.3%	62.5%	37.5%
11	2012	226,023	177,742	CONAWAY, MIKE*	41,970	RILEY, JIM	6,311	135,772 R	78.6%	18.6%	80.9%	19.1%
12	2012	247,712	175,649	GRANGER, KAY*	66,080	ROBINSON, DAVE	5,983	109,569 R	70.9%	26.7%	72.7%	27.3%
13	2012	206,388	187,775	THORNBERRY, MAC*			18,613	187,775 R	91.0%		100.0%	
14	2012	245,839	131,460	WEBER, RANDY	109,697	LAMPSON, NICK	4,682	21,763 R	53.5%	44.6%	54.5%	45.5%
15	2012	146,661	54,056	BRUEGGEMANN, DALE A.	89,296	HINOJOSA, RUBEN*	3,309	35,240 D	36.9%	60.9%	37.7%	62.3%
16	2012	155,005	51,043	CARRASCO, BARBARA	101,403	O'ROURKE, BETO	2,559	50,360 D	32.9%	65.4%	33.5%	66.5%
17	2012	179,262	143,284	FLORES, BILL*			35,978	143,284 R	79.9%		100.0%	
18	2012	194,932	44,015	SEIBERT, SEAN	146,223	JACKSON LEE, SHEILA*	4,694	102,208 D	22.6%	75.0%	23.1%	76.9%
19	2012	192,063	163,239	NEUGEBAUER, RANDY*			28,824	163,239 R	85.0%		100.0%	
20	2012	186,177	62,376	ROSA, DAVID	119,032	CASTRO, JOAQUIN	4,769	56,656 D	33.5%	63.9%	34.4%	65.6%
21	2012	308,865	187,015	SMITH, LAMAR*	109,326	DUVAL, CANDACE E.	12,524	77,689 R	60.5%	35.4%	63.1%	36.9%
22	2012	250,911	160,668	OLSON, PETE*	80,203	ROGERS, KESHA	10,040	80,465 R	64.0%	32.0%	66.7%	33.3%
23	2012	192,169	87,547	CANSECO, FRANCISCO "QUICO"*	96,676	GALLEGO, PETE	7,946	9,129 D	45.6%	50.3%	47.5%	52.5%
24	2012	243,489	148,586	MARCHANT, KENNY*	87,645	RUSK, TIM	7,258	60,941 R	61.0%	36.0%	62.9%	37.1%
25	2012	263,932	154,245	WILLIAMS, ROGER	98,827	HENDERSON, ELAINE M.	10,860	55,418 R	58.4%	37.4%	60.9%	39.1%
26	2012	258,723	176,642	BURGESS, MICHAEL C.*	74,237	SANCHEZ, DAVID	7,844	102,405 R	68.3%	28.7%	70.4%	29.6%
27	2012	212,651	120,684	FARENTHOLD, BLAKE*	83,395	HARRISON, ROSE MEZA	8,572	37,289 R	56.8%	39.2%	59.1%	40.9%
28	2012	165,645	49,309	HAYWARD, WILLIAM R.	112,456	CUELLAR, HENRY*	3,880	63,147 D	29.8%	67.9%	30.5%	69.5%
29	2012	95,611			86,053	GREEN, GENE*	9,558	86,053 D		90.0%		100.0%
30	2012	217,014	41,222	WASHINGTON, TRAVIS	171,059	JOHNSON, EDDIE Bernice*	4,733	129,837 D	19.0%	78.8%	19.4%	80.6%
31	2012	237,187	145,348	CARTER, JOHN*	82,977	WYMAN, STEPHEN M.	8,862	62,371 R	61.3%	35.0%	63.7%	36.3%
32	2012	251,636	146,653	SESSIONS, PETE*	99,288	MCGOVERN, KATHERINE SAVERS	5,695	47,365 R	58.3%	39.5%	59.6%	40.4%
33	2012	117,375	30,252	BRADLEY, CHUCK	85,114	VEASEY, MARC	2,009	54,862 D	25.8%	72.5%	26.2%	73.8%
34	2012	144,778	52,448	BRADSHAW, JESSICA PUENTE	89,606	VELA, FILEMON	2,724	37,158 D	36.2%	61.9%	36.9%	63.1%
35	2012	165,179	52,894	NARVAIZ, SUSAN	105,626	DOGGETT, LLOYD*	6,659	52,732 D	32.0%	63.9%	33.4%	66.6%
36	2012	233,832	165,405	STOCKMAN, STEVE	62,143	MARTIN, MAX	6,284	103,262 R	70.7%	26.6%	72.7%	27.3%
TOTAL	2012	7,664,208	4,429,270		2,949,900		285,038	1,479,370 R	57.8%	38.5%	60.0%	40.0%

Note: An asterisk (*) denotes incumbent.

TEXAS

GENERAL AND PRIMARY ELECTIONS

GENERAL ELECTIONS: OTHER VOTE

President Other vote was 88,580 Libertarian (Gary E. Johnson), 24,657 Green (Jill Stein), 1,360 Write-in (Scattered Write-In), 1,287 Write-in (Virgil H. Goode)

Senator Other vote was 162,354 Libertarian (John Jay Myers), 67,404 Green (David Collins)

House Other vote was:

CD 1 4,114 Libertarian (Clark Patterson)

CD 2 4,140 Libertarian (Kenneth Duncan), 2,012 Green (Mark A.Roberts)

CD 4 7,262 Libertarian (Thomas Griffing), 188 Write-in (Fred Rostek)

CD 5 4,961 Libertarian (Ken Ashby)

CD 6 4,847 Libertarian (Hugh Chauvin), 2,017 Green (Brandon Parmer)

CD 7 4,669 Libertarian (Drew P. Parks), 1,822 Green (Lance Findley)

CD 8 5,958 Libertarian (Roy Hall)

CD 9 1,743 Green (Vanessa Foster), 1,609 Libertarian (John Wieder)

TEXAS

GENERAL AND PRIMARY ELECTIONS

GENERAL ELECTIONS: OTHER VOTE

House	Other vote was:
CD 10	8,526 Libertarian (Richard Priest)
CD 11	6,311 Libertarian (Scott J. Ballard)
CD 12	5,983 Libertarian (Matthew Solodow)
CD 13	12,701 Libertarian (John Robert Deek), 5,912 Green (Keith F. Houston)
CD 14	3,619 Libertarian (Zach Grady), 1,063 Green (Rhett R. Smith)
CD 15	3,309 Libertarian (Ron Finch)
CD 16	2,559 Libertarian (Junart Sodoy)
CD 17	35,978 Libertarian (Ben Easton)
CD 18	4,694 Libertarian (Christopher Barber)
CD 19	28,824 Libertarian (Richard "Chip" Peterson)
CD 20	3,143 Libertarian (A.E. "Tracy" Potts), 1,626 Green (Antonio Diaz)
CD 21	12,524 Libertarian (John-Henry Liberty)
CD 22	5,986 Libertarian (Steven Susman), 4,054 Green (Don Cook)
CD 23	5,841 Libertarian (Jeffrey C. Blunt), 2,105 Green (Ed Scharf)
CD 24	7,258 Libertarian (John Stathas)
CD 25	10,860 Libertarian (Betsy Dewey)
CD 26	7,844 Libertarian (Mark Boler)
CD 27	5,354 Independent (Bret Baldwin), 3,218 Libertarian (Corrie Byrd)
CD 28	2,473 Libertarian (Patrick Hisel), 1,407 Green (Michael D. Cary)
CD 29	4,996 Libertarian (James Stanczak), 4,562 Green (Maria Selva)
CD 30	4,733 Libertarian (Ed Rankin)
CD 31	8,862 Libertarian (Ethan Garofolo)
CD 32	5,695 Libertarian (Seth Hollist)
CD 33	2,009 Green (Ed Lindsay)
CD 34	2,724 Libertarian (Steven "Ziggy" Shanklin)
CD 35	4,082 Libertarian (Ross Lynn Leone), 2,540 Green (Meghan Owen), 37 Write-in (Simon Alvarado)
CD 36	6,284 Libertarian (Michael K. Cole)

PRIMARY ELECTIONS: SUPPLEMENTARY INFORMATION

Primary	May 29, 2012	**Registration** (as of May 29, 2012)	13,065,425	No Party Registration

Primary Runoff July 31, 2012

Primary Type Open—Any registered voter could participate in the Democratic or Republican primary, although if they voted in the primary of one party they could not vote in the runoff of the other party.

TEXAS

GENERAL AND PRIMARY ELECTIONS

	REPUBLICAN PRIMARIES			DEMOCRATIC PRIMARIES		
President	Romney, W. Mitt	1,001,387	69.1%	Obama, Barack H.*	520,410	88.2%
	Paul, Ron	174,207	12.0%	Wolfe, John	29,879	5.1%
	Santorum, Rick	115,584	8.0%	Richardson, Darcy	25,430	4.3%
	Gingrich, Newt	68,247	4.7%	Ely, Bob	14,445	2.4%
	Uncommitted	60,659	4.2%			
	Bachmann, Michele	12,097	0.8%			
	Huntsman, Jon Jr.	8,695	0.6%			
	Roemer, Charles	4,714	0.3%			
	Davis, John	3,887	0.3%			
	TOTAL	1,449,477		TOTAL	590,164	
Senator	Dewhurst, David	627,731	44.6%	Sadler, Paul	174,772	35.1%
	Cruz, Ted	480,558	34.2%	Yarbrough, Grady	128,746	25.9%
	Leppert, Tom	187,900	13.4%	Allen, Addie Dainell	113,935	22.9%
	James, Craig	50,569	3.6%	Hubbard, Sean	80,034	16.1%
	Addison, Glenn	23,177	1.6%			
	Pittenger, Lela	18,143	1.3%			
	Gambini, Ben	7,225	0.5%			
	Cleaver, Curt	6,671	0.5%			
	Agris, Joe	4,674	0.3%			
	TOTAL	1,406,648		TOTAL	497,487	
	PRIMARY RUNOFF			**PRIMARY RUNOFF**		
	Cruz, Ted	631,812	56.8%	Sadler, Paul	148,940	63.0%
	Dewhurst, David	480,126	43.2%	Yarbrough, Grady	87,365	37.0%
	TOTAL	1,111,938		TOTAL	236,305	
Congressional District 1	Gohmert, Louis*	67,705	100.0%	McKellar, Shirley J.	8,207	100.0%
	TOTAL	67,705		TOTAL	8,207	
Congressional District 2	Poe, Ted*	39,336	100.0%	Dougherty, Jim	6,676	100.0%
	TOTAL	39,336		TOTAL	6,676	
Congressional District 3	Johnson, Sam*	33,592	83.1%			
	Pierce, Harry	4,848	12.0%			
	Caesar, Josh	2,002	5.0%			
	TOTAL	40,442				
Congressional District 4	Hall, Ralph*	38,202	58.4%	Hathcox, Valinda	7,389	100.0%
	Clark, Steve	13,719	21.0%			
	Gigliotti, Lou	13,532	20.7%			
	TOTAL	65,453		TOTAL	7,389	
Congressional District 5	Hensarling, Jeb*	41,348	100.0%	Mrosko, Linda S.	2,778	39.2%
				Berry, Tom	2,219	31.3%
				Wallace, Pat	2,097	29.6%
	TOTAL	41,348		TOTAL	7,094	
				PRIMARY RUNOFF		
				Mrosko, Linda S.	1,848	60.8%
				Berry, Tom	1,190	39.2%
				TOTAL	3,038	
Congressional District 6	Barton, Joe*	26,192	63.2%	Sanders, Kenneth	6,609	61.3%
	Chow, Joe	8,154	19.7%	Hinojosa-Flores, Brianna	3,483	32.3%
	Kuchar, Frank C.	4,725	11.4%	Jaquess, Don	698	6.5%
	Gelbman, Itamar	2,356	5.7%			
	TOTAL	41,427		TOTAL	10,790	

TEXAS

GENERAL AND PRIMARY ELECTIONS

	REPUBLICAN PRIMARIES			DEMOCRATIC PRIMARIES		
Congressional District 7	Culberson, John*	37,590	86.3%	Squiers, Lissa	2,848	39.9%
	Tofte, Bill	5,971	13.7%	Cargas, James	2,410	33.8%
				Andrews, Phillip	1,876	26.3%
	TOTAL	43,561		TOTAL	7,134	
				PRIMARY RUNOFF		
				Cargas, James	2,121	57.9%
				Squiers, Lissa	1,545	42.1%
				TOTAL	3,666	
Congressional District 8	Brady, Kevin*	48,366	76.1%	Burns, Neil	5,789	100.0%
	Youngblood, Larry	15,181	23.9%			
	TOTAL	63,547		TOTAL	5,789	
Congressional District 9	Mueller, Steve	7,255	100.0%	Green, Al*	20,917	100.0%
	TOTAL	7,255		TOTAL	20,917	
Congressional District 10	McCaul, Michael*	39,543	83.8%	Cadien, Tawana W.	8,061	56.6%
	Traylor, Eddie	7,664	16.2%	Miller, William E. Jr.	6,169	43.4%
	TOTAL	47,207		TOTAL	14,230	
Congressional District 11	Conaway, Mike*	48,581	70.4%	Riley, Jim	4,322	100.0%
	Younts, Chris	12,917	18.7%			
	Brown, Wade	7,547	10.9%			
	TOTAL	69,045		TOTAL	4,322	
Congressional District 12	Granger, Kay*	34,828	80.2%	Robinson, Dave	6,530	100.0%
	Lawrence, Bill	8,611	19.8%			
	TOTAL	43,439		TOTAL	6,530	
Congressional District 13	Thornberry, Mac*	47,051	77.5%			
	Barlow, Pamela Lee	13,637	22.5%			
	TOTAL	60,688				
Congressional District 14	Weber, Randy	12,088	27.6%	Lampson, Nick	18,500	83.2%
	Harris, Felicia	8,287	18.9%	Dailey, Linda	3,724	16.8%
	Truncale, Michael	6,212	14.2%			
	Old, Jay	6,143	14.0%			
	Gonzalez, Robert	4,302	9.8%			
	Sargent, Bill	3,328	7.6%			
	Gay, John	2,075	4.7%			
	Harper, George	813	1.9%			
	Mansius, Mark A.	554	1.3%			
	TOTAL	43,802		TOTAL	22,224	
	PRIMARY RUNOFF					
	Weber, Randy	23,295	62.8%			
	Harris, Felicia	13,792	37.2%			
	TOTAL	37,087				
Congressional District 15	Zamora, Eddie	4,749	33.1%	Hinojosa, Rubén*	29,397	71.2%
	Brueggemann, Dale A.	4,551	31.7%	Cantu, David	5,008	12.1%
	Cervera, Rebecca	2,942	20.5%	Cross, Jane	4,208	10.2%
	Kuiken, Jim	2,124	14.8%	Ramirez, Ruben Ramon	2,012	4.9%
				Partain, Johnny "JP"	687	1.7%
	TOTAL	14,366		TOTAL	41,312	
	PRIMARY RUNOFF					
	Brueggemann, Dale A.	6,403	57.3%			
	Zamora, Eddie	4,771	42.7%			
	TOTAL	11,174				

TEXAS

GENERAL AND PRIMARY ELECTIONS

REPUBLICAN PRIMARIES			DEMOCRATIC PRIMARIES		
Congressional District 16	Carrasco, Barbara	5,268	58.9%	O'Rourke, Beto	23,261	50.5%
	Roen, Corey Dean	3,681	41.1%	Reyes, Silvestre*	20,440	44.3%
				Tilghman, Jerome	1,270	2.8%
				Mendoza, Ben E. "Buddy"	701	1.5%
				Johnson, Paul Jr.	419	0.9%
	TOTAL	8,949		TOTAL	46,091	
Congressional District 17	Flores, Bill*	41,449	82.5%			
	Hindman, George W.	8,790	17.5%			
	TOTAL	50,239				
Congressional District 18	Seibert, Sean	7,493	100.0%	Jackson Lee, Sheila*	21,171	100.0%
	TOTAL	7,493		TOTAL	21,171	
Congressional District 19	Neugebauer, Randy*	45,444	74.3%			
	Winn, Chris	15,707	25.7%			
	TOTAL	61,151				
Congressional District 20	Rosa, David	9,582	100.0%	Castro, Joaquin	16,562	100.0%
	TOTAL	9,582		TOTAL	16,562	
Congressional District 21	Smith, Lamar*	52,404	76.6%	Duval, Candace E.	9,522	61.1%
	Mack, Richard	10,111	14.8%	Boone, Daniel	6,070	38.9%
	Morgan, Richard	5,868	8.6%			
	TOTAL	68,383		TOTAL	15,592	
Congressional District 22	Olson, Pete*	35,838	76.5%	Rogers, Kesha	3,666	50.7%
	Carlson, Barbara J.	11,019	23.5%	George, KP	3,563	49.3%
	TOTAL	46,857		TOTAL	7,229	
Congressional District 23	Canseco, Francisco "Quico"*	17,438	100.0%	Rodriguez, Ciro D.	18,237	46.0%
				Gallego, Pete	16,202	40.8%
				Bustamante, John M.	5,240	13.2%
	TOTAL	17,438		TOTAL	39,679	
				PRIMARY RUNOFF		
				Gallego, Pete	15,815	54.8%
				Rodriguez, Ciro D.	13,038	45.2%
				TOTAL	28,853	
Congressional District 24	Marchant, Kenny*	27,926	67.9%	Rusk, Tim	5,267	100.0%
	Stinchfield, Grant	13,184	32.1%			
	TOTAL	41,110		TOTAL	5,267	
Congressional District 25	Williams, Roger	12,894	25.1%	Henderson, Elaine M.	13,465	100.0%
	Riddle, Wes	7,481	14.6%			
	Hewlett, Justin	6,178	12.0%			
	Garrison, Dave	6,133	11.9%			
	Williams, Michael	5,392	10.5%			
	Costa, Dianne	4,810	9.4%			
	Matthews, Brian	1,824	3.6%			
	Holcomb, Charlie	1,690	3.3%			
	Wilbanks, Chad	1,593	3.1%			
	Burch, Bill	1,575	3.1%			
	Dillon, James "Patriot"	1,174	2.3%			
	Beltz, Ernie Jr.	596	1.2%			
	TOTAL	51,340		TOTAL	13,465	
	PRIMARY RUNOFF					
	Williams, Roger	26,495	58.0%			
	Riddle, Wes	19,210	42.0%			
	TOTAL	45,705				

TEXAS

GENERAL AND PRIMARY ELECTIONS

REPUBLICAN PRIMARIES				DEMOCRATIC PRIMARIES		
Congressional District 26	Burgess, Michael C.*	33,605	100.0%	Sanchez, David	3,682	100.0%
	TOTAL	33,605		TOTAL	3,682	
Congressional District 27	Farenthold, Blake*	28,058	70.8%	Trevino, Jerry J.	8,231	39.8%
	Roberts, Trey	4,653	11.7%	Harrison, Rose Meza	6,354	30.7%
	Middlebrook, Don Al	3,676	9.3%	McDonald, Ronnie C.	5,682	27.5%
	Grunwald, John	3,256	8.2%	Junaid, Murphy Alade	432	2.1%
	TOTAL	39,643		TOTAL	20,699	
				PRIMARY RUNOFF		
				Harrison, Rose Meza	7,024	60.6%
				Trevino, Jerry J.	4,565	39.4%
				TOTAL	11,589	
Congressional District 28	Hayward, William R.	9,710	100.0%	Cuellar, Henry*	35,350	100.0%
	TOTAL	9,710		TOTAL	35,350	
Congressional District 29				Green, Gene*	10,667	100.0%
				TOTAL	10,667	
Congressional District 30	Washington, Travis	6,260	100.0%	Johnson, Eddie Bernice*	23,346	70.1%
				Caraway, Barbara Mallory	5,996	18.0%
				Clayton, Taj	3,981	11.9%
	TOTAL	6,260		TOTAL	33,323	
Congressional District 31	Carter, John*	32,917	76.0%	Wyman, Stephen M.	5,864	100.0%
	Klingemann, Eric	10,400	24.0%			
	TOTAL	43,317		TOTAL	5,864	
Congressional District 32	Sessions, Pete*	29,523	100.0%	McGovern, Katherine Savers	7,301	84.2%
				Hofheinz, Walter W.	1,370	15.8%
	TOTAL	29,523		TOTAL	8,671	
Congressional District 33	Bradley, Chuck	3,706	63.8%	Veasey, Marc	6,938	36.8%
	King, Charles	2,104	36.2%	Garcia, Domingo	4,715	25.0%
				Hicks, Kathleen	2,372	12.6%
				Alameel, David	2,064	10.9%
				Valdez, Manuel	884	4.7%
				Salazar, Steve	482	2.6%
				Castañeda, Chrysta	395	2.1%
				Roberts, Jason E.	342	1.8%
				Quintanilla, Carlos	286	1.5%
				Tatum, Kyev P. Sr.	201	1.1%
				Molina, J.R.	189	1.0%
	TOTAL	5,810		TOTAL	18,868	
				PRIMARY RUNOFF		
				Veasey, Marc	10,766	52.7%
				Garcia, Domingo	9,653	47.3%
				TOTAL	20,419	

TEXAS

GENERAL AND PRIMARY ELECTIONS

	REPUBLICAN PRIMARIES			DEMOCRATIC PRIMARIES		
Congressional District 34	Garza, Adela	4,632	36.3%	Vela, Filemon	18,233	40.5%
	Bradshaw, Jessica Puente	4,409	34.6%	Blanchard, Denise Saenz	5,810	12.9%
	Haring, Paul B.	3,710	29.1%	Garza, Ramiro Jr.	5,575	12.4%
				Torres, Salomon	4,745	10.5%
				Villalobos, Armando	3,926	8.7%
				Troiani, Anthony P.	3,638	8.1%
				Guerra, Juan Angel	2,200	4.9%
				Aycock, Elmo M.	935	2.1%
	TOTAL	12,751		TOTAL	45,062	
	PRIMARY RUNOFF			**PRIMARY RUNOFF**		
	Bradshaw, Jessica Puente	5,309	55.3%	Vela, Filemon	15,628	66.6%
	Garza, Adela	4,287	44.7%	Blanchard, Denise Saenz	7,824	33.4%
	TOTAL	9,596		TOTAL	23,452	
Congressional District 35	Narvaiz, Susan	6,040	51.8%	Doggett, Lloyd*	14,559	73.2%
	Roark, Rob	3,454	29.6%	Romo, Sylvia	4,212	21.2%
	Yoggerst, John	2,171	18.6%	Alvarado, Maria Luisa	1,105	5.6%
	TOTAL	11,665		TOTAL	19,876	
Congressional District 36	Takach, Stephen	12,208	22.4%	Martin, Max	9,869	100.0%
	Stockman, Steve	11,858	21.8%			
	Jackson, Mike	10,786	19.8%			
	Engstrand, Jim	5,114	9.4%			
	Griffin, Ky D.	4,025	7.4%			
	Meyer, Charles B. "Chuck"	2,156	4.0%			
	Morrel, Kim	1,930	3.5%			
	Myers, Lois Dickson	1,558	2.9%			
	Doyle, Jerry L.	1,479	2.7%			
	Casey, Keith	1,225	2.3%			
	Whitton, Daniel	1,110	2.0%			
	Wintill, Tim	984	1.8%			
	TOTAL	54,433		TOTAL	9,869	
	PRIMARY RUNOFF					
	Stockman, Steve	21,472	55.3%			
	Takach, Stephen	17,378	44.7%			
	TOTAL	38,850				

Notes: An asterisk (*) denotes incumbent. A runoff was triggered if the leading vote-getter in the primary received less than a majority of the primary vote.

UTAH

Congressional districts first established for elections held in 2012

4 members

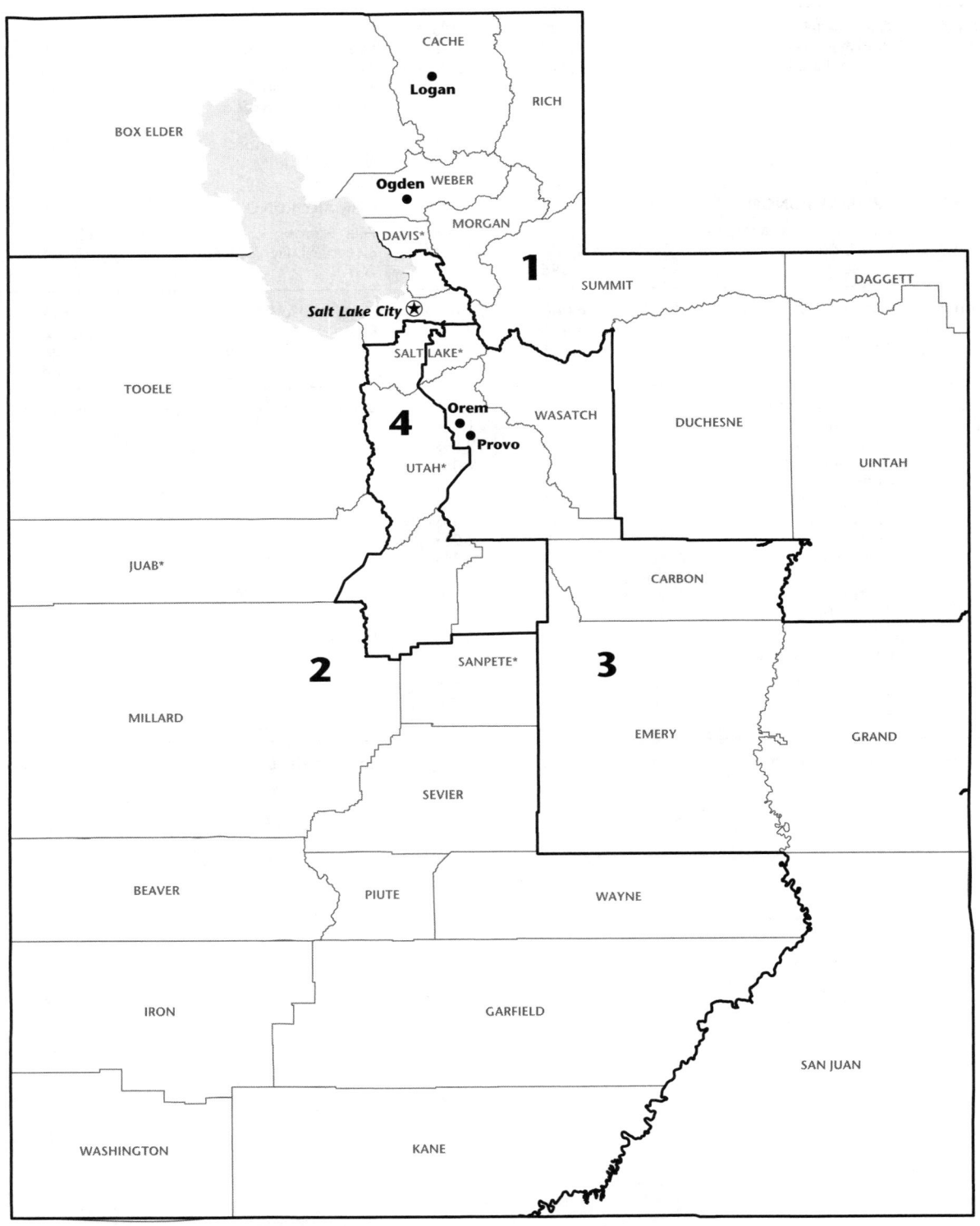

* Asterisk indicates a county whose boundaries include parts of two or more Congressional districts.

UTAH

GOVERNOR
Gary R. Herbert (R). Reelected 2012 to a four-year term. Previously elected 2010 to remaining two years of term vacated by resignation of Jon Huntsman Jr. (R) to become ambassador to China. Herbert sworn in as governor August 11, 2009.

SENATORS (2 Republicans)
Orrin G. Hatch (R). Reelected 2012 to a six-year term. Previously elected 2006, 2000, 1994, 1988, 1982, 1976.

Mike Lee (R). Elected 2010 to a six-year term.

REPRESENTATIVES (3 Republicans, 1 Democrat)
1. Rob Bishop (R)
2. Chris Stewart (R)
3. Jason Chaffetz (R)
4. Jim Matheson (D)

POSTWAR VOTE FOR PRESIDENT

| | | Republican | | Democratic | | Other | Rep.-Dem. | Percentage | | | |
| | | | | | | | | Total Vote | | Major Vote | |
Year	Total Vote	Vote	Candidate	Vote	Candidate	Vote	Plurality	Rep.	Dem.	Rep.	Dem.
2012	1,017,440	740,600	Romney, W. Mitt	251,813	Obama, Barack H.*	25,027	488,787 R	72.8%	24.7%	74.6%	25.4%
2008	952,370	596,030	McCain, John S. III	327,670	Obama, Barack H.	28,670	268,360 R	62.6%	34.4%	64.5%	35.5%
2004	927,844	663,742	Bush, George W.*	241,199	Kerry, John F.	22,903	422,543 R	71.5%	26.0%	73.3%	26.7%
2000**	770,754	515,096	Bush, George W.	203,053	Gore, Albert Jr.	52,605	312,043 R	66.8%	26.3%	71.7%	28.3%
1996**	665,629	361,911	Dole, Robert "Bob"	221,633	Clinton, Bill*	82,085	140,278 R	54.4%	33.3%	62.0%	38.0%
1992**	743,999	322,632	Bush, George H.*	183,429	Clinton, Bill	237,938	139,203 R	43.4%	24.7%	63.8%	36.2%
1988	647,008	428,442	Bush, George H.	207,343	Dukakis, Michael S.	11,223	221,099 R	66.2%	32.0%	67.4%	32.6%
1984	629,656	469,105	Reagan, Ronald*	155,369	Mondale, Walter F.	5,182	313,736 R	74.5%	24.7%	75.1%	24.9%
1980**	604,222	439,687	Reagan, Ronald	124,266	Carter, Jimmy*	40,269	315,421 R	72.8%	20.6%	78.0%	22.0%
1976	541,198	337,908	Ford, Gerald R.*	182,110	Carter, Jimmy	21,180	155,798 R	62.4%	33.6%	65.0%	35.0%
1972	478,476	323,643	Nixon, Richard M.*	126,284	McGovern, George S.	28,549	197,359 R	67.6%	26.4%	71.9%	28.1%
1968**	422,568	238,728	Nixon, Richard M.	156,665	Humphrey, Hubert H. Jr.	27,175	82,063 R	56.5%	37.1%	60.4%	39.6%
1964	401,413	181,785	Goldwater, Barry M. Sr.	219,628	Johnson, Lyndon B.*		37,843 D	45.3%	54.7%	45.3%	54.7%
1960	374,709	205,361	Nixon, Richard M.	169,248	Kennedy, John F.	100	36,113 R	54.8%	45.2%	54.8%	45.2%
1956	333,995	215,631	Eisenhower, Dwight D.*	118,364	Stevenson, Adlai E. II		97,267 R	64.6%	35.4%	64.6%	35.4%
1952	329,554	194,190	Eisenhower, Dwight D.	135,364	Stevenson, Adlai E. II		58,826 R	58.9%	41.1%	58.9%	41.1%
1948	276,306	124,402	Dewey, Thomas E.	149,151	Truman, Harry S.*	2,753	24,749 D	45.0%	54.0%	45.5%	54.5%

Note: An asterisk (*) denotes incumbent. **In past elections, the other vote included: 2000 - 35,850 Green (Ralph Nader); 1996 - 66,461 Reform (Ross Perot); 1992 - 203,400 Independent (Perot), who finished second; 1980 - 30,284 Independent (John Anderson); 1968 - 26,906 American Independent (George Wallace).

UTAH

POSTWAR VOTE FOR GOVERNOR

| Year | Total Vote | Republican | | Democratic | | Other Vote | Rep.-Dem. Plurality | Percentage | | | |
| | | Vote | Candidate | Vote | Candidate | | | Total Vote | | Major Vote | |
								Rep.	Dem.	Rep.	Dem.
2012	1,006,524	688,592	Herbert, Gary R.*	277,622	Cooke, Peter S.	40,310	410,970 R	68.4%	27.6%	71.3%	28.7%
2010S	643,307	412,151	Herbert, Gary R.*	205,246	Corroon, Peter	25,910	206,905 R	64.1%	31.9%	66.8%	33.2%
2008	945,525	734,049	Huntsman, Jon Jr.*	186,503	Springmeyer, Bob	24,973	547,546 R	77.6%	19.7%	79.7%	20.3%
2004	919,960	531,190	Huntsman, Jon Jr.	380,359	Matheson, Scot Jr.	8,411	150,831 R	57.7%	41.3%	58.3%	41.7%
2000	761,806	424,837	Leavitt, Mike O.*	321,979	Orton, Bill	14,990	102,858 R	55.8%	42.3%	56.9%	43.1%
1996	671,879	503,693	Leavitt, Mike O.*	156,616	Bradley, Jim	11,570	347,077 R	75.0%	23.3%	76.3%	23.7%
1992**	762,549	321,713	Leavitt, Mike O.	177,181	Hanson, Stewart	263,655	144,532 R	42.2%	23.2%	64.5%	35.5%
1988**	649,114	260,462	Bangerter, Norman H.*	249,321	Wilson, Ted	139,331	11,141 R	40.1%	38.4%	51.1%	48.9%
1984	629,619	351,792	Bangerter, Norman H.	275,669	Owens, Wayne	2,158	76,123 R	55.9%	43.8%	56.1%	43.9%
1980	600,019	266,578	Wright, Bob	330,974	Matheson, Scott M.*	2,467	64,396 D	44.4%	55.2%	44.6%	55.4%
1976	539,649	248,027	Romney, Vernon B.	280,706	Matheson, Scott M.	10,916	32,679 D	46.0%	52.0%	46.9%	53.1%
1972	476,447	144,449	Strike, Nicholas L.	331,998	Rampton, Calvin L.*		187,549 D	30.3%	69.7%	30.3%	69.7%
1968	421,012	131,729	Buehner, Carl W.	289,283	Rampton, Calvin L.*		157,554 D	31.3%	68.7%	31.3%	68.7%
1964	398,256	171,300	Melich, Mitchell	226,956	Rampton, Calvin L.		55,656 D	43.0%	57.0%	43.0%	57.0%
1960	371,489	195,634	Clyde, George Dewey*	175,855	Barlocker, William A.		19,779 R	52.7%	47.3%	52.7%	47.3%
1956**	332,889	127,164	Clyde, George Dewey	111,297	Romney, L. C.	94,428	15,867 R	38.2%	33.4%	53.3%	46.7%
1952	327,704	180,516	Lee, J. Bracken*	147,188	Glade, Earl J.		33,328 R	55.1%	44.9%	55.1%	44.9%
1948	275,067	151,253	Lee, J. Bracken	123,814	Maw, Herbert B.*		27,439 R	55.0%	45.0%	55.0%	45.0%

Note: An asterisk (*) denotes incumbent. **In past elections, the other vote included: 1992 - 255,753 Independent (Merrill Cook), who finished second; 1988 - 136,651 Independent (Cook); 1956 - 94,428 Independent (J. Bracken Lee). The 2010 election was for a short term to fill a vacancy.

POSTWAR VOTE FOR SENATOR

| Year | Total Vote | Republican | | Democratic | | Other Vote | Rep.-Dem. Plurality | Percentage | | | |
| | | Vote | Candidate | Vote | Candidate | | | Total Vote | | Major Vote | |
								Rep.	Dem.	Rep.	Dem.
2012	1,006,901	657,608	Hatch, Orrin G.*	301,873	Howell, Scott N.	47,420	355,735 R	65.3%	30.0%	68.5%	31.5%
2010	633,829	390,179	Lee, Mike	207,685	Granato, Sam	35,965	182,494 R	61.6%	32.8%	65.3%	34.7%
2006	571,252	356,238	Hatch, Orrin G.*	177,459	Ashdown, Pete	37,555	178,779 R	62.4%	31.1%	66.7%	33.3%
2004	911,726	626,640	Bennett, Robert F.*	258,955	Van Dam, R. Paul	26,131	367,685 R	68.7%	28.4%	70.8%	29.2%
2000	769,704	504,803	Hatch, Orrin G.*	242,569	Howell, Scott N.	22,332	262,234 R	65.6%	31.5%	67.5%	32.5%
1998	494,909	316,652	Bennett, Robert F.*	163,172	Leckman, Scott	15,085	153,480 R	64.0%	33.0%	66.0%	34.0%
1994	519,323	357,297	Hatch, Orrin G.*	146,938	Shea, Patrick A.	15,088	210,359 R	68.8%	28.3%	70.9%	29.1%
1992	758,479	420,069	Bennett, Robert F.	301,228	Owens, Wayne	37,182	118,841 R	55.4%	39.7%	58.2%	41.8%
1988	640,702	430,089	Hatch, Orrin G.*	203,364	Moss, Brian	7,249	226,725 R	67.1%	31.7%	67.9%	32.1%
1986	435,111	314,608	Garn, E. J.*	115,523	Oliver, Craig	4,980	199,085 R	72.3%	26.6%	73.1%	26.9%
1982	530,802	309,332	Hatch, Orrin G.*	219,482	Wilson, Ted	1,988	89,850 R	58.3%	41.3%	58.5%	41.5%
1980	594,298	437,675	Garn, E. J.*	151,454	Berman, Dan	5,169	286,221 R	73.6%	25.5%	74.3%	25.7%
1976	540,108	290,221	Hatch, Orrin G.	241,948	Moss, Frank E.*	7,939	48,273 R	53.7%	44.8%	54.5%	45.5%
1974	420,642	210,299	Garn, E. J.	185,377	Owens, Wayne	24,966	24,922 R	50.0%	44.1%	53.1%	46.9%
1970	374,303	159,004	Burton, Laurence J.	210,207	Moss, Frank E.*	5,092	51,203 D	42.5%	56.2%	43.1%	56.9%
1968	419,262	225,075	Bennett, Wallace F.*	192,168	Weilenmann, Milton	2,019	32,907 R	53.7%	45.8%	53.9%	46.1%
1964	397,384	169,562	Wilkinson, Ernest L.	227,822	Moss, Frank E.*		58,260 D	42.7%	57.3%	42.7%	57.3%
1962	318,411	166,755	Bennett, Wallace F.*	151,656	King, David S.		15,099 R	52.4%	47.6%	52.4%	47.6%
1958**	291,311	101,471	Watkins, Arthur V.*	112,827	Moss, Frank E.	77,013	11,356 D	34.8%	38.7%	47.4%	52.6%
1956	330,381	178,261	Bennett, Wallace F.*	152,120	Hopkin, Alonzo F.		26,141 R	54.0%	46.0%	54.0%	46.0%
1952	327,033	177,435	Watkins, Arthur V.*	149,598	Granger, Walter K.		27,837 R	54.3%	45.7%	54.3%	45.7%
1950	264,440	142,427	Bennett, Wallace F.	121,198	Thomas, Elbert D.*	815	21,229 R	53.9%	45.8%	54.0%	46.0%
1946	197,399	101,142	Watkins, Arthur V.	96,257	Murdock, Abe*		4,885 R	51.2%	48.8%	51.2%	48.8%

Note: An asterisk (*) denotes incumbent. **In past elections, the other vote included: 1958 - 77,013 Independent (J. Bracken Lee).

UTAH

PRESIDENT 2012

| | | | | | | | Percentage | | | |
| | | | | | | | Total Vote | | Major Vote | |
2010 Census Population	County	Total Vote	Republican (Romney)	Democratic (Obama)	Other	Rep.-Dem. Plurality	Rep.	Dem.	Rep.	Dem.
6,629	BEAVER	2,560	2,174	346	40	1,828 R	84.9%	13.5%	86.3%	13.7%
49,975	BOX ELDER	19,408	17,101	1,984	323	15,117 R	88.1%	10.2%	89.6%	10.4%
112,656	CACHE	42,293	35,039	6,244	1,010	28,795 R	82.8%	14.8%	84.9%	15.1%
21,403	CARBON	7,567	5,090	2,275	202	2,815 R	67.3%	30.1%	69.1%	30.9%
1,059	DAGGETT	520	406	94	20	312 R	78.1%	18.1%	81.2%	18.8%
306,479	DAVIS	121,069	96,861	21,889	2,319	74,972 R	80.0%	18.1%	81.6%	18.4%
18,607	DUCHESNE	6,379	5,698	581	100	5,117 R	89.3%	9.1%	90.7%	9.3%
10,976	EMERY	4,449	3,777	569	103	3,208 R	84.9%	12.8%	86.9%	13.1%
5,172	GARFIELD	2,182	1,832	308	42	1,524 R	84.0%	14.1%	85.6%	14.4%
9,225	GRAND	3,950	1,996	1,727	227	269 R	50.5%	43.7%	53.6%	46.4%
46,163	IRON	16,701	14,200	2,148	353	12,052 R	85.0%	12.9%	86.9%	13.1%
10,246	JUAB	3,972	3,448	451	73	2,997 R	86.8%	11.4%	88.4%	11.6%
7,125	KANE	3,371	2,522	744	105	1,778 R	74.8%	22.1%	77.2%	22.8%
12,503	MILLARD	5,026	4,478	431	117	4,047 R	89.1%	8.6%	91.2%	8.8%
9,469	MORGAN	4,597	4,114	403	80	3,711 R	89.5%	8.8%	91.1%	8.9%
1,556	PIUTE	782	697	74	11	623 R	89.1%	9.5%	90.4%	9.6%
2,264	RICH	1,007	915	83	9	832 R	90.9%	8.2%	91.7%	8.3%
1,029,655	SALT LAKE	381,799	223,811	146,147	11,841	77,664 R	58.6%	38.3%	60.5%	39.5%
14,746	SAN JUAN	5,307	3,074	2,139	94	935 R	57.9%	40.3%	59.0%	41.0%
27,822	SANPETE	9,547	8,406	980	161	7,426 R	88.0%	10.3%	89.6%	10.4%
20,802	SEVIER	8,069	7,207	738	124	6,469 R	89.3%	9.1%	90.7%	9.3%
36,324	SUMMIT	17,488	8,884	8,072	532	812 R	50.8%	46.2%	52.4%	47.6%
58,218	TOOELE	19,261	14,268	4,524	469	9,744 R	74.1%	23.5%	75.9%	24.1%
32,588	UINTAH	11,583	10,421	997	165	9,424 R	90.0%	8.6%	91.3%	8.7%
516,564	UTAH	177,713	156,950	17,281	3,482	139,669 R	88.3%	9.7%	90.1%	9.9%
23,530	WASATCH	9,589	7,220	2,191	178	5,029 R	75.3%	22.8%	76.7%	23.3%
138,115	WASHINGTON	54,012	44,698	8,337	977	36,361 R	82.8%	15.4%	84.3%	15.7%
2,778	WAYNE	1,327	1,089	215	23	874 R	82.1%	16.2%	83.5%	16.5%
231,236	WEBER	75,912	54,224	19,841	1,847	34,383 R	71.4%	26.1%	73.2%	26.8%
2,763,885	TOTAL	1,017,440	740,600	251,813	25,027	488,787 R	72.8%	24.7%	74.6%	25.4%

UTAH

GOVERNOR 2012

| | | | | | | | Percentage | | | |
| | | | | | | | Total Vote | | Major Vote | |
2010 Census Population	County	Total Vote	Republican (Herbert)	Democratic (Cooke)	Other	Rep.-Dem. Plurality	Rep.	Dem.	Rep.	Dem.
6,629	BEAVER	2,522	2,040	390	92	1,650 R	80.9%	15.5%	84.0%	16.0%
49,975	BOX ELDER	19,265	15,802	2,767	696	13,035 R	82.0%	14.4%	85.1%	14.9%
112,656	CACHE	41,721	32,173	7,595	1,953	24,578 R	77.1%	18.2%	80.9%	19.1%
21,403	CARBON	7,546	4,787	2,494	265	2,293 R	63.4%	33.1%	65.7%	34.3%
1,059	DAGGETT	509	390	96	23	294 R	76.6%	18.9%	80.2%	19.8%
306,479	DAVIS	119,939	89,002	26,794	4,143	62,208 R	74.2%	22.3%	76.9%	23.1%
18,607	DUCHESNE	6,319	5,388	688	243	4,700 R	85.3%	10.9%	88.7%	11.3%
10,976	EMERY	4,436	3,532	728	176	2,804 R	79.6%	16.4%	82.9%	17.1%
5,172	GARFIELD	2,148	1,753	333	62	1,420 R	81.6%	15.5%	84.0%	16.0%
9,225	GRAND	3,862	1,968	1,689	205	279 R	51.0%	43.7%	53.8%	46.2%
46,163	IRON	16,504	13,094	2,464	946	10,630 R	79.3%	14.9%	84.2%	15.8%
10,246	JUAB	3,937	3,182	588	167	2,594 R	80.8%	14.9%	84.4%	15.6%
7,125	KANE	3,307	2,455	708	144	1,747 R	74.2%	21.4%	77.6%	22.4%
12,503	MILLARD	5,018	4,049	704	265	3,345 R	80.7%	14.0%	85.2%	14.8%
9,469	MORGAN	4,556	3,697	699	160	2,998 R	81.1%	15.3%	84.1%	15.9%

UTAH

GOVERNOR 2012

2010 Census Population	County	Total Vote	Republican (Herbert)	Democratic (Cooke)	Other	Rep.-Dem. Plurality	Percentage			
							Total Vote		Major Vote	
							Rep.	Dem.	Rep.	Dem.
1,556	PIUTE	765	658	82	25	576 R	86.0%	10.7%	88.9%	11.1%
2,264	RICH	987	841	122	24	719 R	85.2%	12.4%	87.3%	12.7%
1,029,655	SALT LAKE	378,107	209,310	154,361	14,436	54,949 R	55.4%	40.8%	57.6%	42.4%
14,746	SAN JUAN	5,245	3,095	1,941	209	1,154 R	59.0%	37.0%	61.5%	38.5%
27,822	SANPETE	9,487	7,676	1,384	427	6,292 R	80.9%	14.6%	84.7%	15.3%
20,802	SEVIER	8,004	6,632	1,044	328	5,588 R	82.9%	13.0%	86.4%	13.6%
36,324	SUMMIT	17,195	8,541	8,045	609	496 R	49.7%	46.8%	51.5%	48.5%
58,218	TOOELE	19,076	13,072	4,969	1,035	8,103 R	68.5%	26.0%	72.5%	27.5%
32,588	UINTAH	11,467	9,950	1,103	414	8,847 R	86.8%	9.6%	90.0%	10.0%
516,564	UTAH	175,123	144,942	22,630	7,551	122,312 R	82.8%	12.9%	86.5%	13.5%
23,530	WASATCH	9,505	6,824	2,344	337	4,480 R	71.8%	24.7%	74.4%	25.6%
138,115	WASHINGTON	53,435	41,915	9,244	2,276	32,671 R	78.4%	17.3%	81.9%	18.1%
2,778	WAYNE	1,318	1,050	239	29	811 R	79.7%	18.1%	81.5%	18.5%
231,236	WEBER	75,221	50,774	21,377	3,070	29,397 R	67.5%	28.4%	70.4%	29.6%
2,763,885	TOTAL	1,006,524	688,592	277,622	40,310	410,970 R	68.4%	27.6%	71.3%	28.7%

UTAH

SENATOR 2012

2010 Census Population	County	Total Vote	Republican (Hatch)	Democratic (Howell)	Other	Rep.-Dem. Plurality	Percentage			
							Total Vote		Major Vote	
							Rep.	Dem.	Rep.	Dem.
6,629	BEAVER	2,510	1,953	437	120	1,516 R	77.8%	17.4%	81.7%	18.3%
49,975	BOX ELDER	19,190	14,971	3,379	840	11,592 R	78.0%	17.6%	81.6%	18.4%
112,656	CACHE	41,814	31,347	8,446	2,021	22,901 R	75.0%	20.2%	78.8%	21.2%
21,403	CARBON	7,504	4,429	2,774	301	1,655 R	59.0%	37.0%	61.5%	38.5%
1,059	DAGGETT	502	352	132	18	220 R	70.1%	26.3%	72.7%	27.3%
306,479	DAVIS	120,008	86,244	28,877	4,887	57,367 R	71.9%	24.1%	74.9%	25.1%
18,607	DUCHESNE	6,319	5,123	831	365	4,292 R	81.1%	13.2%	86.0%	14.0%
10,976	EMERY	4,421	3,379	884	158	2,495 R	76.4%	20.0%	79.3%	20.7%
5,172	GARFIELD	2,143	1,672	366	105	1,306 R	78.0%	17.1%	82.0%	18.0%
9,225	GRAND	3,877	1,938	1,717	222	221 R	50.0%	44.3%	53.0%	47.0%
46,163	IRON	16,518	12,399	2,821	1,298	9,578 R	75.1%	17.1%	81.5%	18.5%
10,246	JUAB	3,946	2,925	780	241	2,145 R	74.1%	19.8%	78.9%	21.1%
7,125	KANE	3,308	2,234	853	221	1,381 R	67.5%	25.8%	72.4%	27.6%
12,503	MILLARD	5,018	3,771	857	390	2,914 R	75.1%	17.1%	81.5%	18.5%
9,469	MORGAN	4,547	3,491	866	190	2,625 R	76.8%	19.0%	80.1%	19.9%
1,556	PIUTE	764	636	95	33	541 R	83.2%	12.4%	87.0%	13.0%
2,264	RICH	996	821	148	27	673 R	82.4%	14.9%	84.7%	15.3%
1,029,655	SALT LAKE	378,749	199,824	162,904	16,021	36,920 R	52.8%	43.0%	55.1%	44.9%
14,746	SAN JUAN	5,188	3,130	1,805	253	1,325 R	60.3%	34.8%	63.4%	36.6%
27,822	SANPETE	9,435	7,273	1,650	512	5,623 R	77.1%	17.5%	81.5%	18.5%
20,802	SEVIER	8,003	6,380	1,207	416	5,173 R	79.7%	15.1%	84.1%	15.9%
36,324	SUMMIT	17,196	7,980	8,524	692	544 D	46.4%	49.6%	48.4%	51.6%
58,218	TOOELE	19,056	12,593	5,475	988	7,118 R	66.1%	28.7%	69.7%	30.3%
32,588	UINTAH	11,454	9,708	1,255	491	8,453 R	84.8%	11.0%	88.6%	11.4%
516,564	UTAH	175,414	138,589	27,483	9,342	111,106 R	79.0%	15.7%	83.5%	16.5%
23,530	WASATCH	9,505	6,432	2,735	338	3,697 R	67.7%	28.8%	70.2%	29.8%
138,115	WASHINGTON	53,074	38,863	10,850	3,361	28,013 R	73.2%	20.4%	78.2%	21.8%
2,778	WAYNE	1,314	1,009	259	46	750 R	76.8%	19.7%	79.6%	20.4%
231,236	WEBER	75,128	48,142	23,463	3,523	24,679 R	64.1%	31.2%	67.2%	32.8%
2,763,885	TOTAL	1,006,901	657,608	301,873	47,420	355,735 R	65.3%	30.0%	68.5%	31.5%

UTAH
HOUSE OF REPRESENTATIVES

CD	Year	Total Vote	Republican		Democratic		Other Vote	Rep.-Dem. Plurality	Percentage			
									Total Vote		Major Vote	
			Vote	Candidate	Vote	Candidate			Rep.	Dem.	Rep.	Dem.
1	2012	245,528	175,487	BISHOP, ROB*	60,611	MCALEER, DONNA M.	9,430	114,876 R	71.5%	24.7%	74.3%	25.7%
2	2012	248,545	154,523	STEWART, CHRIS	83,176	SEEGMILLER, JAY	10,846	71,347 R	62.2%	33.5%	65.0%	35.0%
3	2012	259,547	198,828	CHAFFETZ, JASON*	60,719	SIMONSEN, SOREN D.		138,109 R	76.6%	23.4%	76.6%	23.4%
4	2012	245,277	119,035	LOVE, MIA B.	119,803	MATHESON, JIM*	6,439	768 D	48.5%	48.8%	49.8%	50.2%
TOTAL	2012	998,897	647,873		324,309		26,715	323,564 R	64.9%	32.5%	66.6%	33.4%

Note: An asterisk (*) denotes incumbent.

UTAH
GENERAL AND PRIMARY ELECTIONS

GENERAL ELECTIONS: OTHER VOTE

President   Other vote was 12,572 Libertarian (Gary E. Johnson), 5,335 Justice (Ross C. "Rocky" Anderson), 3,817 Green (Jill Stein), 2,871 Constitution (Virgil H. Goode), 393 Socialism and Liberation (Gloria La Riva), 39 Write-in (Scattered Write-In)

Governor   Other vote was 22,611 Libertarian (Ken Larsen), 17,696 Constitution (Kirk D. Pearson), 3 Write-in (Scattered Write-In)

Senator   Other vote was 31,905 Constitution (Shaun McCausland), 8,342 Justice (Daniel Geery), 7,172 Unaffiliated (Bill Barron), 1 Write-in (Scattered Write-In)

House   Other vote was:

CD 1   9,430 Constitution (Sherry Phipps)

CD 2   5,051 Constitution (Jonathan D. Garrard), 2,971 No Party (Joseph Andrade), 2,824 No Party (Charles E. Kimball)

CD 4   6,439 Libertarian (Jim L. Vein)

PRIMARY ELECTIONS: SUPPLEMENTARY INFORMATION

Primary   June 26, 2012   **Registration** (as of June 26, 2012)   1,287,892   Party Registration Not Published

Primary Type   Registered Democrats and unaffiliated voters could participate in the Democratic primary. Registered Republicans and unaffiliated voters who chose to change their registration to Republican on primary day could vote in the Republican primary.

UTAH

GENERAL AND PRIMARY ELECTIONS

	REPUBLICAN PRIMARIES			DEMOCRATIC PRIMARIES		
President	Romney, W. Mitt	225,428	93.0%			
	Paul, Ron	11,520	4.8%			
	Santorum, Rick	3,594	1.5%			
	Gingrich, Newt	1,146	0.5%			
	Karger, Fred	584	0.2%			
	TOTAL	242,272				
Senator	Hatch, Orrin G.*	160,359	66.5%	Howell, Scott N.	Unopposed	
	Liljenquist, Dan	80,915	33.5%			
	TOTAL	241,274				
Governor	Herbert, Gary R.*	Unopposed		Cooke, Peter S.	Unopposed	
Congressional District 1	Bishop, Rob*	Unopposed		McAleer, Donna M.	3,881	66.6%
				Combe, Ryan	1,944	33.4%
				TOTAL	5,825	
Congressional District 2	Stewart, Chris	Unopposed		Seegmiller, Jay	Unopposed	
Congressional District 3	Chaffetz, Jason*	Unopposed		Simonsen, Soren D.	Unopposed	
Congressional District 4	Love, Mia B.	Unopposed		Matheson, Jim*	Unopposed	

Notes: An asterisk (*) denotes incumbent. Candidates in Utah are usually nominated by convention. It is up to each party to determine the percentage of the convention vote that is needed to force a primary. All House candidates were nominated by convention in 2012 except the Democrat in the 1st district (McAleer). Both gubernatorial candidates were nominated by convention. The Democratic candidate for U.S. Senate (Howell) was nominated by convention.

VERMONT

One member At Large

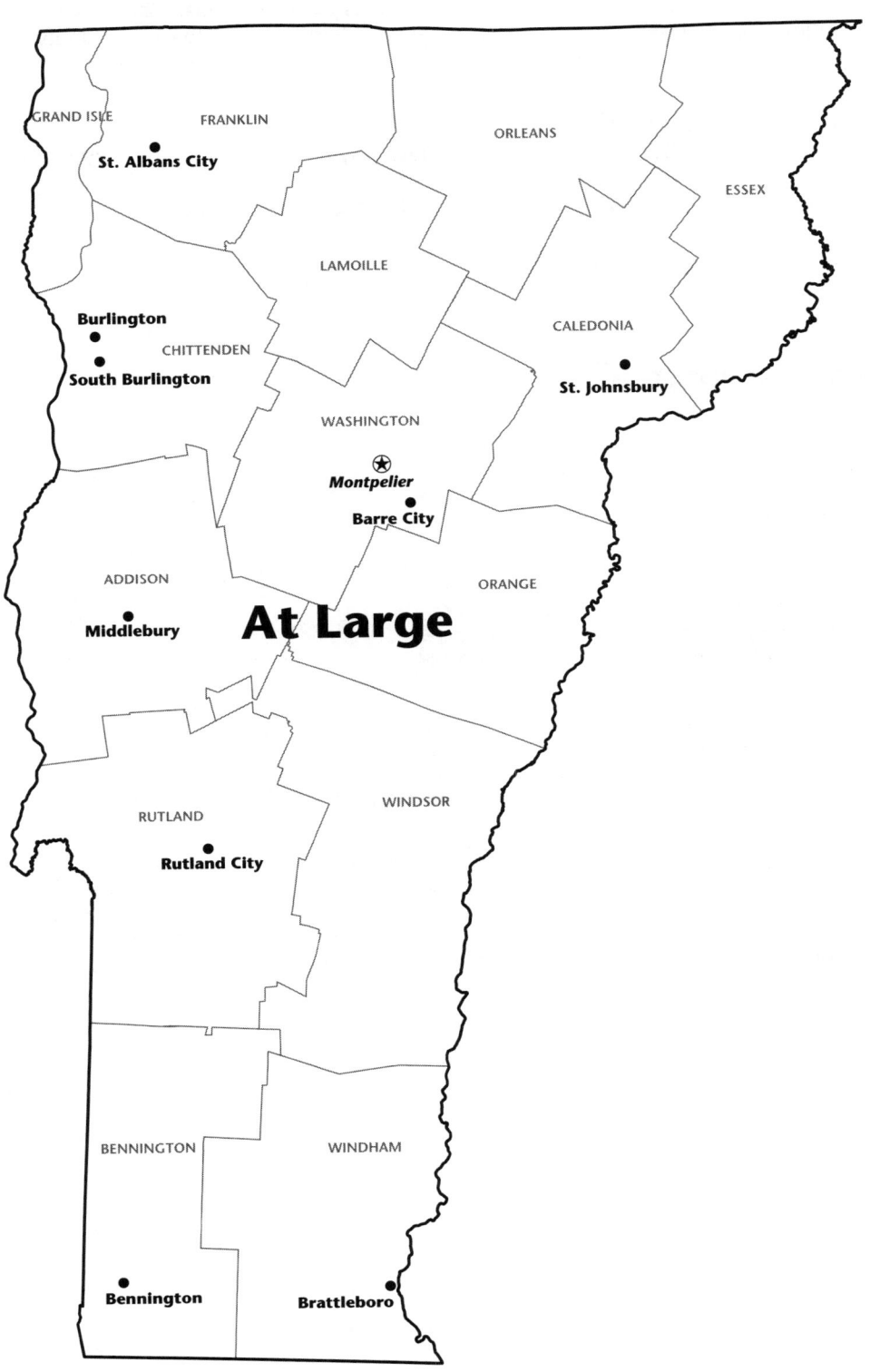

VERMONT

GOVERNOR

Peter Shumlin (D). Reelected 2012 to a two-year term. Previously elected January 2011 by the State Legislature to a two-year term. Shumlin had finished first in the 2010 general election but failed to win a majority of the vote as required by Vermont law.

SENATORS (1 Democrat, 1 Independent)

Patrick J. Leahy (D). Reelected 2010 to a six-year term. Previously elected 2004, 1998, 1992, 1986, 1980, 1974.

Bernard Sanders (Ind.). Reelected 2012 to a six-year term. Previously elected 2006.

REPRESENTATIVE (1 Democrat)

At Large. Peter Welch (D)

POSTWAR VOTE FOR PRESIDENT

| | | Republican | | Democratic | | | | Percentage | | | |
| | | | | | | | | Total Vote | | Major Vote | |
Year	Total Vote	Vote	Candidate	Vote	Candidate	Other Vote	Rep.-Dem. Plurality	Rep.	Dem.	Rep.	Dem.
2012	299,290	92,698	Romney, W. Mitt	199,239	Obama, Barack H.*	7,353	106,541 D	31.0%	66.6%	31.8%	68.2%
2008	325,046	98,974	McCain, John S. III	219,262	Obama, Barack H.	6,810	120,288 D	30.4%	67.5%	31.1%	68.9%
2004	312,309	121,180	Bush, George W.*	184,067	Kerry, John F.	7,062	62,887 D	38.8%	58.9%	39.7%	60.3%
2000**	294,308	119,775	Bush, George W.	149,022	Gore, Albert Jr.	25,511	29,247 D	40.7%	50.6%	44.6%	55.4%
1996**	258,449	80,352	Dole, Robert "Bob"	137,894	Clinton, Bill*	40,203	57,542 D	31.1%	53.4%	36.8%	63.2%
1992**	289,701	88,122	Bush, George H.*	133,592	Clinton, Bill	67,987	45,470 D	30.4%	46.1%	39.7%	60.3%
1988	243,328	124,331	Bush, George H.	115,776	Dukakis, Michael S.	3,221	8,555 R	51.1%	47.6%	51.8%	48.2%
1984	234,561	135,865	Reagan, Ronald*	95,730	Mondale, Walter F.	2,966	40,135 R	57.9%	40.8%	58.7%	41.3%
1980**	213,299	94,628	Reagan, Ronald	81,952	Carter, Jimmy*	36,719	12,676 R	44.4%	38.4%	53.6%	46.4%
1976	187,765	102,085	Ford, Gerald R.*	80,954	Carter, Jimmy	4,726	21,131 R	54.4%	43.1%	55.8%	44.2%
1972	186,947	117,149	Nixon, Richard M.*	68,174	McGovern, George S.	1,624	48,975 R	62.7%	36.5%	63.2%	36.8%
1968**	161,404	85,142	Nixon, Richard M.	70,255	Humphrey, Hubert H. Jr.	6,007	14,887 R	52.8%	43.5%	54.8%	45.2%
1964	163,089	54,942	Goldwater, Barry M. Sr.	108,127	Johnson, Lyndon B.*	20	53,185 D	33.7%	66.3%	33.7%	66.3%
1960	167,324	98,131	Nixon, Richard M.	69,186	Kennedy, John F.	7	28,945 R	58.6%	41.3%	58.6%	41.4%
1956	152,978	110,390	Eisenhower, Dwight D.*	42,549	Stevenson, Adlai E. II	39	67,841 R	72.2%	27.8%	72.2%	27.8%
1952	153,557	109,717	Eisenhower, Dwight D.	43,355	Stevenson, Adlai E. II	485	66,362 R	71.5%	28.2%	71.7%	28.3%
1948	123,382	75,926	Dewey, Thomas E.	45,557	Truman, Harry S.*	1,899	30,369 R	61.5%	36.9%	62.5%	37.5%

Note: An asterisk (*) denotes incumbent. **In past elections, the other vote included: 2000 - 20,374 Green (Ralph Nader); 1996 - 31,024 Reform (Ross Perot); 1992 - 65,991 Independent (Perot); 1980 - 31,761 Independent (John Anderson); 1968 - 5,104 American Independent (George Wallace).

VERMONT

POSTWAR VOTE FOR GOVERNOR

Year	Total Vote	Republican		Democratic		Other Vote	Rep.-Dem. Plurality	Percentage			
								Total Vote		Major Vote	
		Vote	Candidate	Vote	Candidate			Rep.	Dem.	Rep.	Dem.
2012	295,261	110,940	Brock, Randy	170,598	Shumlin, Peter*	13,723	59,658 D	37.6%	57.8%	39.4%	60.6%
2010**	241,605	115,212	Dubie, Brian E.	119,543	Shumlin, Peter	6,850	4,331 D	47.7%	49.5%	49.1%	50.9%
2008**	319,085	170,492	Douglas, Jim*	69,534	Symington, Gaye	79,059	100,958 R	53.4%	21.8%	71.0%	29.0%
2006	262,524	148,014	Douglas, Jim*	108,090	Parker, Scudder	6,420	39,924 R	56.4%	41.2%	57.8%	42.2%
2004	309,285	181,540	Douglas, Jim*	117,327	Clavell, Peter	10,418	64,213 R	58.7%	37.9%	60.7%	39.3%
2002**	230,161	103,436	Douglas, Jim	97,565	Racine, Doug	29,160	5,871 R	44.9%	42.4%	51.5%	48.5%
2000	293,473	111,359	Dwyer, Ruth	148,059	Dean, Howard B.*	34,055	36,700 D	37.9%	50.5%	42.9%	57.1%
1998	218,120	89,726	Dwyer, Ruth	121,425	Dean, Howard B.*	6,969	31,699 D	41.1%	55.7%	42.5%	57.5%
1996	254,648	57,161	Gropper, John L.	179,544	Dean, Howard B.*	17,943	122,383 D	22.4%	70.5%	24.1%	75.9%
1994	212,046	40,292	Kelley, David F.	145,661	Dean, Howard B.*	26,093	105,369 D	19.0%	68.7%	21.7%	78.3%
1992	285,728	65,837	McClaughry, John	213,523	Dean, Howard B.*	6,368	147,686 D	23.0%	74.7%	23.6%	76.4%
1990	211,422	109,540	Snelling, Richard A.	97,321	Welch, Peter	4,561	12,219 R	51.8%	46.0%	53.0%	47.0%
1988	242,879	105,191	Bernhardt, Michael	134,438	Kunin, Madeline*	3,250	29,247 D	43.3%	55.4%	43.9%	56.1%
1986**	196,716	75,162	Smith, Peter	92,379	Kunin, Madeline*	29,175	17,217 D	38.2%	47.0%	44.9%	55.1%
1984	233,753	113,264	Easton, John J.	116,938	Kunin, Madeline	3,551	3,674 D	48.5%	50.0%	49.2%	50.8%
1982	169,251	93,111	Snelling, Richard A.*	74,394	Kunin, Madeline	1,746	18,717 R	55.0%	44.0%	55.6%	44.4%
1980	210,381	123,229	Snelling, Richard A.*	77,363	Diamond, M. Jerome	9,789	45,866 R	58.6%	36.8%	61.4%	38.6%
1978	124,482	78,181	Snelling, Richard A.*	42,482	Granai, Edwin C.	3,819	35,699 R	62.8%	34.1%	64.8%	35.2%
1976	185,929	99,268	Snelling, Richard A.	75,262	Hackel, Stella B.	11,399	24,006 R	53.4%	40.5%	56.9%	43.1%
1974	141,156	53,672	Kennedy, Walter L.	79,842	Salmon, Thomas P.*	7,642	26,170 D	38.0%	56.6%	40.2%	59.8%
1972	189,237	82,491	Hackett, Luther F.	104,533	Salmon, Thomas P.	2,213	22,042 D	43.6%	55.2%	44.1%	55.9%
1970	153,528	87,458	Davis, Deane C.*	66,028	O'Brien, Leo	42	21,430 R	57.0%	43.0%	57.0%	43.0%
1968	161,089	89,387	Davis, Deane C.	71,656	Daley, John J.	46	17,731 R	55.5%	44.5%	55.5%	44.5%
1966	136,262	57,577	Snelling, Richard A.	78,669	Hoff, Philip H.*	16	21,092 D	42.3%	57.7%	42.3%	57.7%
1964	164,199	57,576	Foote, Ralph A.	106,611	Hoff, Philip H.*	12	49,035 D	35.1%	64.9%	35.1%	64.9%
1962	121,422	60,035	Keyser, F. Ray Jr.*	61,383	Hoff, Philip H.	4	1,348 D	49.4%	50.6%	49.4%	50.6%
1960	164,632	92,861	Keyser, F. Ray Jr.	71,755	Niquette, Russell F.	16	21,106 R	56.4%	43.6%	56.4%	43.6%
1958	123,728	62,222	Stafford, Robert T.	61,503	Leddy, Bernard J.	3	719 R	50.3%	49.7%	50.3%	49.7%
1956	153,809	88,379	Johnson, Joseph B.*	65,420	Branon, E. Frank	10	22,959 R	57.5%	42.5%	57.5%	42.5%
1954	114,360	59,778	Johnson, Joseph B.	54,554	Branon, E. Frank	28	5,224 R	52.3%	47.7%	52.3%	47.7%
1952	150,836	78,338	Emerson, Lee E.*	60,051	Larrow, Robert W.	12,447	18,287 R	51.9%	39.8%	56.6%	43.4%
1950	87,155	64,915	Emerson, Lee E.	22,227	Moran, J. Edward	13	42,688 R	74.5%	25.5%	74.5%	25.5%
1948	120,183	86,394	Gibson, Ernest W.*	33,588	Ryan, Charles F.	201	52,806 R	71.9%	27.9%	72.0%	28.0%
1946	72,044	57,849	Gibson, Ernest W.	14,096	Coburn, Berthold C.	99	43,753 R	80.3%	19.6%	80.4%	19.6%

Note: An asterisk (*) denotes incumbent. **In past elections, the other vote included: 2008 - 69,791 Independent (Anthony Pollina), who finished second; 1986 - 28,430 Independent (Bernard Sanders). In 1986, 2002, and 2010, in the absence of a majority of the total vote for any candidate, the State Legislature elected the governor — Democrat Madeleine M. Kunin in January 1987, Republican Jim Douglas in January 2003, and Democrat Peter Shumlin in January 2011.

VERMONT

POSTWAR VOTE FOR SENATOR

Year	Total Vote	Republican Vote	Republican Candidate	Democratic Vote	Democratic Candidate	Other Vote	Rep.-Dem. Plurality	Total Vote Rep.	Total Vote Dem.	Major Vote Rep.	Major Vote Dem.
2012**	294,267	73,198	MacGovern, John			221,069	73,198 R**	24.9%		100.0%	
2010	235,178	72,699	Britton, Len	151,281	Leahy, Patrick J.*	11,198	78,582 D	30.9%	64.3%	32.5%	67.5%
2006**	262,419	84,924	Tarrant, Richard			177,495	84,924 R**	32.4%		100.0%	
2004	307,208	75,398	McMullen, Jack	216,972	Leahy, Patrick J.*	14,838	141,574 D	24.5%	70.6%	25.8%	74.2%
2000	288,500	189,133	Jeffords, James M.*	73,352	Flanagan, Ed	26,015	115,781 R	65.6%	25.4%	72.1%	27.9%
1998	214,036	48,051	Tuttle, Fred	154,567	Leahy, Patrick J.*	11,418	106,516 D	22.4%	72.2%	23.7%	76.3%
1994	211,672	106,505	Jeffords, James M.*	85,868	Backus, Jan	19,299	20,637 R	50.3%	40.6%	55.4%	44.6%
1992	285,739	123,854	Douglas, Jim	154,762	Leahy, Patrick J.*	7,123	30,908 D	43.3%	54.2%	44.5%	55.5%
1988	240,108	163,183	Jeffords, James M.	71,460	Gray, William H.	5,465	91,723 R	68.0%	29.8%	69.5%	30.5%
1986	196,532	67,798	Snelling, Richard A.	124,123	Leahy, Patrick J.*	4,611	56,325 D	34.5%	63.2%	35.3%	64.7%
1982	168,003	84,450	Stafford, Robert T.*	79,340	Guest, James A.	4,213	5,110 R	50.3%	47.2%	51.6%	48.4%
1980	209,124	101,421	Ledbetter, Stewart M.	104,176	Leahy, Patrick J.*	3,527	2,755 D	48.5%	49.8%	49.3%	50.7%
1976	189,046	94,481	Stafford, Robert T.*	85,682	Salmon, Thomas P.	8,883	8,799 R	50.0%	45.3%	52.4%	47.6%
1974	142,772	66,223	Mallary, Richard W.	70,629	Leahy, Patrick J.	5,920	4,406 D	46.4%	49.5%	48.4%	51.6%
1972S	71,348	45,888	Stafford, Robert T.*	23,842	Major, Randolph T.	1,618	22,046 R	64.3%	33.4%	65.8%	34.2%
1970	154,899	91,198	Prouty, Winston L.*	62,271	Hoff, Philip H.	1,430	28,927 R	58.9%	40.2%	59.4%	40.6%
1968**	157,375	157,154	Aiken, George David*			221	157,154 R	99.9%		100.0%	
1964	164,350	87,879	Prouty, Winston L.*	76,457	Fayette, Frederick J.	14	11,422 R	53.5%	46.5%	53.5%	46.5%
1962	121,571	81,241	Aiken, George David*	40,134	Johnson, W. Robert	196	41,107 R	66.8%	33.0%	66.9%	33.1%
1958	124,442	64,900	Prouty, Winston L.	59,536	Fayette, Frederick J.	6	5,364 R	52.2%	47.8%	52.2%	47.8%
1956	155,289	103,101	Aiken, George David*	52,184	O'Shea, Bernard G.	4	50,917 R	66.4%	33.6%	66.4%	33.6%
1952	154,052	111,406	Flanders, Ralph E.*	42,630	Johnston, Allan R.	16	68,776 R	72.3%	27.7%	72.3%	27.7%
1950	89,171	69,543	Aiken, George David*	19,608	Bigelow, James E.	20	49,935 R	78.0%	22.0%	78.0%	22.0%
1946	73,340	54,729	Flanders, Ralph E.*	18,594	McDevitt, Charles P.	17	36,135 R	74.6%	25.4%	74.6%	25.4%

Note: An asterisk (*) denotes incumbent. **In past elections, the other vote included: 2012 - 209,053 Independent (Bernard Sanders), who received 71.0 percent of the total vote and was re-elected; 2006 - 171,638 Independent (Bernard Sanders), who received 65.4 percent of the total vote and was elected. Sanders also won the Democratic primary in 2006 and 2012, but declined the nomination each time in order to run as an independent. The Democratic Party did not run a candidate in the 2006 or 2012 Senate election. The January 1972 election was for a short term to fill a vacancy. In 1968 the Republican candidate (George D. Aiken) won both major party nominations.

VERMONT

PRESIDENT 2012

2010 Census Population	County	Total Vote	Republican (Romney)	Democratic (Obama)	Other	Rep.-Dem. Plurality	Percentage			
							Total Vote		Major Vote	
							Rep.	Dem.	Rep.	Dem.
36,821	ADDISON	17,910	5,203	12,257	450	7,054 D	29.1%	68.4%	29.8%	70.2%
37,125	BENNINGTON	17,593	5,687	11,514	392	5,827 D	32.3%	65.4%	33.1%	66.9%
31,227	CALEDONIA	13,661	5,088	8,192	381	3,104 D	37.2%	60.0%	38.3%	61.7%
156,545	CHITTENDEN	77,080	21,571	53,626	1,883	32,055 D	28.0%	69.6%	28.7%	71.3%
6,306	ESSEX	2,798	1,164	1,539	95	375 D	41.6%	55.0%	43.1%	56.9%
47,746	FRANKLIN	19,888	7,405	12,057	426	4,652 D	37.2%	60.6%	38.0%	62.0%
6,970	GRAND ISLE	4,075	1,471	2,531	73	1,060 D	36.1%	62.1%	36.8%	63.2%
24,475	LAMOILLE	11,988	3,342	8,371	275	5,029 D	27.9%	69.8%	28.5%	71.5%
28,936	ORANGE	14,053	4,588	9,076	389	4,488 D	32.6%	64.6%	33.6%	66.4%
27,231	ORLEANS	11,692	4,306	7,117	269	2,811 D	36.8%	60.9%	37.7%	62.3%
61,642	RUTLAND	28,609	10,835	17,088	686	6,253 D	37.9%	59.7%	38.8%	61.2%
59,534	WASHINGTON	29,307	8,093	20,351	863	12,258 D	27.6%	69.4%	28.5%	71.5%
44,513	WINDHAM	21,937	5,347	16,026	564	10,679 D	24.4%	73.1%	25.0%	75.0%
56,670	WINDSOR	28,699	8,598	19,494	607	10,896 D	30.0%	67.9%	30.6%	69.4%
625,741	TOTAL	299,290	92,698	199,239	7,353	106,541 D	31.0%	66.6%	31.8%	68.2%

2010 Census Population	City/Town	Total Vote	Republican (Romney)	Democratic (Obama)	Other	Rep.-Dem. Plurality	Percentage			
							Total Vote		Major Vote	
							Rep.	Dem.	Rep.	Dem.
9,052	BARRE CITY	3,081	1,048	1,946	87	898 D	34.0%	63.2%	35.0%	65.0%
7,924	BARRE TOWN	3,924	1,734	2,127	63	393 D	44.2%	54.2%	44.9%	55.1%
15,764	BENNINGTON	6,415	1,753	4,503	159	2,750 D	27.3%	70.2%	28.0%	72.0%
12,046	BRATTLEBORO	5,699	915	4,621	163	3,706 D	16.1%	81.1%	16.5%	83.5%
42,417	BURLINGTON	17,616	2,592	14,326	698	11,734 D	14.7%	81.3%	15.3%	84.7%
17,067	COLCHESTER	7,331	2,551	4,618	162	2,067 D	34.8%	63.0%	35.6%	64.4%
4,621	DERBY	2,120	848	1,234	38	386 D	40.0%	58.2%	40.7%	59.3%
19,587	ESSEX	10,441	3,640	6,630	171	2,990 D	34.9%	63.5%	35.4%	64.6%
9,952	HARTFORD	4,849	1,417	3,356	76	1,939 D	29.2%	69.2%	29.7%	70.3%
5,009	JERICHO	3,067	1,026	1,990	51	964 D	33.5%	64.9%	34.0%	66.0%
5,981	LYNDON	2,079	866	1,140	73	274 D	41.7%	54.8%	43.2%	56.8%
4,391	MANCHESTER	2,327	850	1,439	38	589 D	36.5%	61.8%	37.1%	62.9%
8,496	MIDDLEBURY	3,370	661	2,635	74	1,974 D	19.6%	78.2%	20.1%	79.9%
10,352	MILTON	4,650	1,966	2,589	95	623 D	42.3%	55.7%	43.2%	56.8%
7,855	MONTPELIER	4,522	700	3,694	128	2,994 D	15.5%	81.7%	15.9%	84.1%
5,227	MORRISTOWN	2,499	668	1,780	51	1,112 D	26.7%	71.2%	27.3%	72.7%
6,207	NORTHFIELD	2,113	685	1,378	50	693 D	32.4%	65.2%	33.2%	66.8%
4,778	RANDOLPH	2,132	663	1,409	60	746 D	31.1%	66.1%	32.0%	68.0%
4,081	RICHMOND	2,419	650	1,722	47	1,072 D	26.9%	71.2%	27.4%	72.6%
5,282	ROCKINGHAM	2,119	497	1,562	60	1,065 D	23.5%	73.7%	24.1%	75.9%
16,495	RUTLAND CITY	6,848	2,430	4,252	166	1,822 D	35.5%	62.1%	36.4%	63.6%
4,054	RUTLAND TOWN	2,283	1,029	1,211	43	182 D	45.1%	53.0%	45.9%	54.1%
7,144	SHELBURNE	4,538	1,403	3,076	59	1,673 D	30.9%	67.8%	31.3%	68.7%
17,904	SOUTH BURLINGTON	9,459	2,748	6,513	198	3,765 D	29.1%	68.9%	29.7%	70.3%
9,373	SPRINGFIELD	3,782	1,342	2,344	96	1,002 D	35.5%	62.0%	36.4%	63.6%
6,918	ST. ALBANS CITY	2,434	752	1,593	89	841 D	30.9%	65.4%	32.1%	67.9%
5,999	ST. ALBANS TOWN	2,782	1,147	1,592	43	445 D	41.2%	57.2%	41.9%	58.1%
7,603	ST. JOHNSBURY	2,937	1,081	1,789	67	708 D	36.8%	60.9%	37.7%	62.3%
4,314	STOWE	2,660	800	1,805	55	1,005 D	30.1%	67.9%	30.7%	69.3%
6,427	SWANTON	2,452	947	1,461	44	514 D	38.6%	59.6%	39.3%	60.7%
5,064	WATERBURY	2,714	654	1,978	82	1,324 D	24.1%	72.9%	24.8%	75.2%
8,698	WILLISTON	5,123	1,697	3,329	97	1,632 D	33.1%	65.0%	33.8%	66.2%
7,267	WINOOSKI	2,576	552	1,941	83	1,389 D	21.4%	75.3%	22.1%	77.9%
3,048	WOODSTOCK	1,899	508	1,361	30	853 D	26.8%	71.7%	27.2%	72.8%

VERMONT
GOVERNOR 2012

2010 Census Population	County	Total Vote	Republican (Brock)	Democratic (Shumlin)	Other	Rep.-Dem. Plurality	Percentage Total Vote Rep.	Dem.	Major Vote Rep.	Dem.
36,821	ADDISON	17,730	6,664	10,442	624	3,778 D	37.6%	58.9%	39.0%	61.0%
37,125	BENNINGTON	17,192	5,109	10,855	1,228	5,746 D	29.7%	63.1%	32.0%	68.0%
31,227	CALEDONIA	13,531	6,479	6,373	679	106 R	47.9%	47.1%	50.4%	49.6%
156,545	CHITTENDEN	75,752	25,609	47,115	3,028	21,506 D	33.8%	62.2%	35.2%	64.8%
6,306	ESSEX	2,755	1,377	1,207	171	170 R	50.0%	43.8%	53.3%	46.7%
47,746	FRANKLIN	19,808	10,265	8,937	606	1,328 R	51.8%	45.1%	53.5%	46.5%
6,970	GRAND ISLE	4,043	1,811	2,089	143	278 D	44.8%	51.7%	46.4%	53.6%
24,475	LAMOILLE	11,835	4,686	6,539	610	1,853 D	39.6%	55.3%	41.7%	58.3%
28,936	ORANGE	13,881	5,387	7,918	576	2,531 D	38.8%	57.0%	40.5%	59.5%
27,231	ORLEANS	11,583	5,737	5,186	660	551 R	49.5%	44.8%	52.5%	47.5%
61,642	RUTLAND	28,314	13,005	13,954	1,355	949 D	45.9%	49.3%	48.2%	51.8%
59,534	WASHINGTON	28,996	10,540	17,216	1,240	6,676 D	36.3%	59.4%	38.0%	62.0%
44,513	WINDHAM	21,567	5,364	14,747	1,456	9,383 D	24.9%	68.4%	26.7%	73.3%
56,670	WINDSOR	28,274	8,907	18,020	1,347	9,113 D	31.5%	63.7%	33.1%	66.9%
625,741	TOTAL	295,261	110,940	170,598	13,723	59,658 D	37.6%	57.8%	39.4%	60.6%

2010 Census Population	City/Town	Total Vote	Republican (Brock)	Democratic (Shumlin)	Other	Rep.-Dem. Plurality	Percentage Total Vote Rep.	Dem.	Major Vote Rep.	Dem.
9,052	BARRE CITY	3,062	1,287	1,657	118	370 D	42.0%	54.1%	43.7%	56.3%
7,924	BARRE TOWN	3,903	2,094	1,697	112	397 R	53.7%	43.5%	55.2%	44.8%
15,764	BENNINGTON	6,255	1,423	4,339	493	2,916 D	22.7%	69.4%	24.7%	75.3%
12,046	BRATTLEBORO	5,588	965	4,239	384	3,274 D	17.3%	75.9%	18.5%	81.5%
42,417	BURLINGTON	17,087	3,039	12,948	1,100	9,909 D	17.8%	75.8%	19.0%	81.0%
17,067	COLCHESTER	7,235	3,028	3,979	228	951 D	41.9%	55.0%	43.2%	56.8%
4,621	DERBY	2,109	1,095	936	78	159 R	51.9%	44.4%	53.9%	46.1%
19,587	ESSEX	10,326	4,485	5,530	311	1,045 D	43.4%	53.6%	44.8%	55.2%
9,952	HARTFORD	4,766	1,320	3,217	229	1,897 D	27.7%	67.5%	29.1%	70.9%
5,009	JERICHO	3,024	1,192	1,742	90	550 D	39.4%	57.6%	40.6%	59.4%
5,981	LYNDON	2,060	1,071	875	114	196 R	52.0%	42.5%	55.0%	45.0%
4,391	MANCHESTER	2,262	924	1,214	124	290 D	40.8%	53.7%	43.2%	56.8%
8,496	MIDDLEBURY	3,313	880	2,287	146	1,407 D	26.6%	69.0%	27.8%	72.2%
10,352	MILTON	4,607	2,272	2,181	154	91 R	49.3%	47.3%	51.0%	49.0%
7,855	MONTPELIER	4,456	923	3,340	193	2,417 D	20.7%	75.0%	21.7%	78.3%
5,227	MORRISTOWN	2,462	984	1,355	123	371 D	40.0%	55.0%	42.1%	57.9%
6,207	NORTHFIELD	2,085	893	1,101	91	208 D	42.8%	52.8%	44.8%	55.2%
4,778	RANDOLPH	2,101	797	1,210	94	413 D	37.9%	57.6%	39.7%	60.3%
4,081	RICHMOND	2,379	805	1,499	75	694 D	33.8%	63.0%	34.9%	65.1%
5,282	ROCKINGHAM	2,069	474	1,433	162	959 D	22.9%	69.3%	24.9%	75.1%
16,495	RUTLAND CITY	6,757	2,898	3,530	329	632 D	42.9%	52.2%	45.1%	54.9%
4,054	RUTLAND TOWN	2,266	1,206	994	66	212 R	53.2%	43.9%	54.8%	45.2%
7,144	SHELBURNE	4,463	1,589	2,745	129	1,156 D	35.6%	61.5%	36.7%	63.3%
17,904	SOUTH BURLINGTON	9,309	3,182	5,806	321	2,624 D	34.2%	62.4%	35.4%	64.6%
9,373	SPRINGFIELD	3,731	1,326	2,167	238	841 D	35.5%	58.1%	38.0%	62.0%
6,918	ST. ALBANS CITY	2,421	1,075	1,238	108	163 D	44.4%	51.1%	46.5%	53.5%
5,999	ST. ALBANS TOWN	2,772	1,539	1,180	53	359 R	55.5%	42.6%	56.6%	43.4%
7,603	ST. JOHNSBURY	2,933	1,405	1,384	144	21 R	47.9%	47.2%	50.4%	49.6%
4,314	STOWE	2,616	1,074	1,428	114	354 D	41.1%	54.6%	42.9%	57.1%
6,427	SWANTON	2,448	1,412	978	58	434 R	57.7%	40.0%	59.1%	40.9%
5,064	WATERBURY	2,678	1,023	1,545	110	522 D	38.2%	57.7%	39.8%	60.2%
8,698	WILLISTON	5,054	2,060	2,862	132	802 D	40.8%	56.6%	41.9%	58.1%
7,267	WINOOSKI	2,522	690	1,671	161	981 D	27.4%	66.3%	29.2%	70.8%
3,048	WOODSTOCK	1,865	543	1,258	64	715 D	29.1%	67.5%	30.1%	69.9%

VERMONT

SENATOR 2012

2010 Census Population	County	Total Vote	Republican (MacGovern)	Democratic	Independent (Sanders)	Other	Rep.-Dem. Plurality	Percentage of Total Vote		
								Rep.	Dem.	Ind.
36,821	ADDISON	17,741	4,324		12,845	572	8,521 I	24.4%		72.4%
37,125	BENNINGTON	17,130	4,437		11,525	1,168	7,088 I	25.9%		67.3%
31,227	CALEDONIA	13,466	4,158		8,763	545	4,605 I	30.9%		65.1%
156,545	CHITTENDEN	75,475	17,369		55,615	2,491	38,246 I	23.0%		73.7%
6,306	ESSEX	2,736	848		1,746	142	898 I	31.0%		63.8%
47,746	FRANKLIN	19,730	5,336		13,607	787	8,271 I	27.0%		69.0%
6,970	GRAND ISLE	4,032	1,119		2,769	144	1,650 I	27.8%		68.7%
24,475	LAMOILLE	11,811	2,672		8,701	438	6,029 I	22.6%		73.7%
28,936	ORANGE	13,853	3,533		9,750	570	6,217 I	25.5%		70.4%
27,231	ORLEANS	11,553	3,106		8,033	414	4,927 I	26.9%		69.5%
61,642	RUTLAND	28,077	8,577		18,286	1,214	9,709 I	30.5%		65.1%
59,534	WASHINGTON	28,967	6,448		21,502	1,017	15,054 I	22.3%		74.2%
44,513	WINDHAM	21,487	4,143		16,050	1,294	11,907 I	19.3%		74.7%
56,670	WINDSOR	28,209	7,128		19,861	1,220	12,733 I	25.3%		70.4%
625,741	TOTAL	294,267	73,198		209,053	12,016	135,855 I	24.9%		71.0%

Note: In each county, as well as statewide, the plurality is based on the winner's margin over the second-place finisher. In all fourteen counties, Independent Bernard "Bernie" Sanders finished first ahead of the Republican candidate, John MacGovern. There was no Democratic candidate.

2010 Census Population	City/Town	Total Vote	Republican (MacGovern)	Democratic	Independent (Sanders)	Other	Rep.-Dem. Plurality	Percentage of Total Vote		
								Rep.	Dem.	Ind.
9,052	BARRE CITY	3,051	765		2,140	146	1,375 I	25.1%		70.1%
7,924	BARRE TOWN	3,895	1,377		2,397	121	1,020 I	35.4%		61.5%
15,764	BENNINGTON	6,198	1,266		4,471	461	3,205 I	20.4%		72.1%
12,046	BRATTLEBORO	5,594	692		4,556	346	3,864 I	12.4%		81.4%
42,417	BURLINGTON	17,113	2,036		14,306	771	12,270 I	11.9%		83.6%
17,067	COLCHESTER	7,194	1,917		5,036	241	3,119 I	26.6%		70.0%
4,621	DERBY	2,102	591		1,436	75	845 I	28.1%		68.3%
19,587	ESSEX	10,273	2,965		7,048	260	4,083 I	28.9%		68.6%
9,952	HARTFORD	4,753	1,145		3,426	182	2,281 I	24.1%		72.1%
5,009	JERICHO	3,015	835		2,106	74	1,271 I	27.7%		69.9%
5,981	LYNDON	2,046	708		1,253	85	545 I	34.6%		61.2%
4,391	MANCHESTER	2,289	758		1,391	140	633 I	33.1%		60.8%
8,496	MIDDLEBURY	3,324	579		2,625	120	2,046 I	17.4%		79.0%
10,352	MILTON	4,579	1,429		2,997	153	1,568 I	31.2%		65.5%
7,855	MONTPELIER	4,461	573		3,754	134	3,181 I	12.8%		84.2%
5,227	MORRISTOWN	2,459	508		1,877	74	1,369 I	20.7%		76.3%
6,207	NORTHFIELD	2,080	514		1,472	94	958 I	24.7%		70.8%
4,778	RANDOLPH	2,123	510		1,533	80	1,023 I	24.0%		72.2%
4,081	RICHMOND	2,381	486		1,822	73	1,336 I	20.4%		76.5%
5,282	ROCKINGHAM	2,070	331		1,592	147	1,261 I	16.0%		76.9%
16,495	RUTLAND CITY	6,677	1,869		4,507	301	2,638 I	28.0%		67.5%
4,054	RUTLAND TOWN	2,234	846		1,310	78	464 I	37.9%		58.6%
7,144	SHELBURNE	4,425	1,203		3,110	112	1,907 I	27.2%		70.3%
17,904	SOUTH BURLINGTON	9,223	2,336		6,604	283	4,268 I	25.3%		71.6%
9,373	SPRINGFIELD	3,742	1,090		2,422	230	1,332 I	29.1%		64.7%
6,918	ST. ALBANS CITY	2,403	565		1,743	95	1,178 I	23.5%		72.5%
5,999	ST. ALBANS TOWN	2,754	820		1,826	108	1,006 I	29.8%		66.3%
7,603	ST. JOHNSBURY	2,905	883		1,909	113	1,026 I	30.4%		65.7%
4,314	STOWE	2,594	722		1,771	101	1,049 I	27.8%		68.3%
6,427	SWANTON	3,199	878		2,196	125	1,318 I	27.4%		68.6%
5,064	WATERBURY	2,677	541		2,051	85	1,510 I	20.2%		76.6%
8,698	WILLISTON	5,030	1,476		3,446	108	1,970 I	29.3%		68.5%
7,267	WINOOSKI	2,504	429		1,938	137	1,509 I	17.1%		77.4%
3,048	WOODSTOCK	1,861	477		1,330	54	853 I	25.6%		71.5%

Note: In each city/town, as well as statewide, the plurality is based on the winner's margin over the second-place finisher. In all cities/towns listed here, Independent Bernard "Bernie" Sanders finished first ahead of the Republican candidate, John MacGovern. There was no Democratic candidate.

VERMONT

HOUSE OF REPRESENTATIVES

CD	Year	Total Vote	Republican		Democratic		Other Vote	Rep.-Dem. Plurality	Percentage			
									Total Vote		Major Vote	
			Vote	Candidate	Vote	Candidate			Rep.	Dem.	Rep.	Dem.
At Large	2012	289,931	67,543	DONKA, MARK	208,600	WELCH, PETER*	13,788	141,057 D	23.3%	71.9%	24.5%	75.5%
At Large	2010	238,521	76,403	BEAUDRY, PAUL D.	154,006	WELCH, PETER*	8,112	77,603 D	32.0%	64.6%	33.2%	66.8%
At Large	2008	298,151			248,203	WELCH, PETER*	49,948	248,203 D		83.2%		100.0%
At Large	2006	262,726	117,023	RAINVILLE, MARTHA	139,815	WELCH, PETER	5,888	22,792 D	44.5%	53.2%	45.6%	54.4%
At Large	2004	305,008	74,271	PARKE, GREG	21,684	DROWN, LARRY	209,053	52,587 R	24.4%	7.1%	77.4%	22.6%
At Large	2002	225,476	72,813	MEUB, WILLIAM			152,663	72,813 R	32.3%		100.0%	
At Large	2000	283,366	51,977	KERIN, KAREN ANN	14,918	DIAMONDSTONE, PETE	216,471	37,059 R	18.3%	5.3%	77.7%	22.3%
At Large	1998	215,133	70,740	CANDON, MARK			144,393	70,740 R	32.9%		100.0%	
At Large	1996	254,706	83,021	SWEETSER, SUSAN W.	23,830	LONG, JACK	147,855	59,191 R	32.6%	9.4%	77.7%	22.3%
At Large	1994	211,449	98,523	CARROLL, JOHN			112,926	98,523 R	46.6%		100.0%	
At Large	1992	281,626	86,901	PHILBIN, TIMOTHY	22,279	YOUNG, LEWIS E.	172,446	64,622 R	30.9%	7.9%	79.6%	20.4%
At Large	1990	209,856	82,938	SMITH, PETER*	6,315	SANDOVAL, DOLORES	120,603	76,623 R	39.5%	3.0%	92.9%	7.1%
At Large	1988	240,131	98,937	SMITH, PETER	45,330	POIRIER, PAUL N.	95,864	53,607 R	41.2%	18.9%	68.6%	31.4%
At Large	1986	188,954	168,403	JEFFORDS, JAMES M.*			20,551	168,403 R	89.1%		100.0%	
At Large	1984	226,297	148,025	JEFFORDS, JAMES M.*	60,360	POLLINA, ANTHONY	17,912	87,665 R	65.4%	26.7%	71.0%	29.0%
At Large	1982	164,951	114,191	JEFFORDS, JAMES M.*	38,296	KAPLAN, MARK A.	12,464	75,895 R	69.2%	23.2%	74.9%	25.1%
At Large	1980	194,697	154,274	JEFFORDS, JAMES M.*			40,423	154,274 R	79.2%		100.0%	
At Large	1978	120,502	90,688	JEFFORDS, JAMES M.*	23,228	DIETZ, S. MARIE	6,586	67,460 R	75.3%	19.3%	79.6%	20.4%
At Large	1976	184,783	124,458	JEFFORDS, JAMES M.*	60,202	BURGESS, JOHN A.	123	64,256 R	67.4%	32.6%	67.4%	32.6%
At Large	1974	140,899	74,561	JEFFORDS, JAMES M.	56,342	CAIN, FRANCIS J.	9,996	18,219 R	52.9%	40.0%	57.0%	43.0%
At Large	1972	186,028	120,924	MALLARY, RICHARD W.	65,062	MEYER, WILLIAM H.	42	55,862 R	65.0%	35.0%	65.0%	35.0%
At Large	1970	152,557	103,806	STAFFORD, ROBERT T.*	44,415	O'SHEA, BERNARD G.	4,336	59,391 R	68.0%	29.1%	70.0%	30.0%
At Large	1968	157,133	156,956	STAFFORD, ROBERT T.*			177	156,956 R	99.9%		100.0%	
At Large	1966	135,748	89,097	STAFFORD, ROBERT T.*	46,643	RYAN, WILLIAM J.	8	42,454 R	65.6%	34.4%	65.6%	34.4%
At Large	1964	163,452	92,252	STAFFORD, ROBERT T.*	71,193	O'SHEA, BERNARD G.	7	21,059 R	56.4%	43.6%	56.4%	43.6%
At Large	1962	121,381	68,822	STAFFORD, ROBERT T.*	52,535	REYNOLDS, HAROLD	24	16,287 R	56.7%	43.3%	56.7%	43.3%
At Large	1960	166,035	94,905	STAFFORD, ROBERT T.	71,111	MEYER, WILLIAM H.*	19	23,794 R	57.2%	42.8%	57.2%	42.8%
At Large	1958	122,702	59,536	ARTHUR, HAROLD J.	63,131	MEYER, WILLIAM H.	35	3,595 D	48.5%	51.5%	48.5%	51.5%
At Large	1956	154,536	103,736	PROUTY, WINSTON L.*	50,797	ST. AMOUR, CAMILLE	3	52,939 R	67.1%	32.9%	67.1%	32.9%
At Large	1954	114,289	70,143	PROUTY, WINSTON L.*	44,141	BOYLAN, JOHN J.	5	26,002 R	61.4%	38.6%	61.4%	38.6%
At Large	1952	153,060	109,871	PROUTY, WINSTON L.*	43,187	COMINGS, HERBERT B.	2	66,684 R	71.8%	28.2%	71.8%	28.2%
At Large	1950	88,851	65,248	PROUTY, WINSTON L.	22,709	COMINGS, HERBERT B.	894	42,539 R	73.4%	25.6%	74.2%	25.8%
At Large	1948	121,968	74,076	PLUMLEY, CHARLES A.*	47,767	READY, ROBERT W.	125	26,309 R	60.7%	39.2%	60.8%	39.2%
At Large	1946	73,066	46,985	PLUMLEY, CHARLES A.*	26,056	CALDBECK, MATTHEW J.	25	20,929 R	64.3%	35.7%	64.3%	35.7%

Note: An asterisk (*) denotes incumbent. Seat was won in 1990, 1992, 1994, 1996, 1998, 2000, 2002, and 2004 by Bernard "Bernie" Sanders, an Independent. His vote totals and percentages in those years were: 1992–162,724 (57.8%); 1994–105,502 (49.9%); 1996–140,678 (55.2%); 1998–136,403 (63.4%); 2000–196,118 (69.2%); 2002–144,880 (64.3%); 2004–205,774 (67.5%). "Other Vote" for those years includes the total for Sanders and for other Independent and third party candidates. Sanders also finished second in 1988. The plurality in those years, if listed, shows only the difference between the Republican and Democratic candidates, as in all other years.

VERMONT

GENERAL AND PRIMARY ELECTIONS

GENERAL ELECTIONS: OTHER VOTE

President Other vote was 3,487 Libertarian (Gary E. Johnson), 1,449 Write-in (Scattered Write-In), 1,128 Justice (Ross C. "Rocky" Anderson), 695 Socialism and Liberation (Peta Lindsay), 594 Green (Jill Stein)

Governor Other vote was 5,868 Independent (Emily Peyton), 5,583 U.S. Marijuana (Cris Ericson), 1,303 Liberty Union (Dave Eagle), 969 Write-in (Scattered Write-In)

Senator Other vote was 209,053 Independent (Bernard Sanders), 5,924 U.S. Marijuana (Cris Ericson), 2,511 Liberty Union (Pete Diamondstone), 2,452 Peace and Prosperity (Peter Moss), 877 VoteKISS (Laurel LaFramboise), 252 Write-in (Scattered Write-In)

House Other vote was:

At Large 8,302 Independent (James "Sam" Desrochers), 4,065 Liberty Union (Jane E. Newton), 1,153 VoteKISS (Andre LaFramboise), 268 Write-in (Scattered Write-In)

VERMONT

GENERAL AND PRIMARY ELECTIONS

PRIMARY ELECTIONS: SUPPLEMENTARY INFORMATION

Primary	March 6, 2012 (President) August 28, 2012 (Congress)	**Registration** (as of August 28, 2012)	448,173	No Party Registration

Primary Type   Open—Any registered voter could participate in the primary of any recognized party for most offices. In presidential primaries, voters must specify which one party ballot they choose at the time of voting.

	REPUBLICAN PRIMARIES			DEMOCRATIC PRIMARIES		
President	Romney, W. Mitt	24,008	39.5%	Obama, Barack H.*	40,247	98.4%
	Paul, Ron	15,391	25.3%	Scattered Write-In	675	1.6%
	Santorum, Rick	14,368	23.6%			
	Gingrich, Newt	4,949	8.1%			
	Huntsman, Jon Jr.	1,198	2.0%			
	Perry, Rick	544	0.9%			
	Scattered Write-In	392	0.6%			
	TOTAL	*60,850*		*TOTAL*	*40,922*	
Senator	MacGovern, John	6,358	72.5%	Sanders, Bernard*	36,902	98.7%
	Paige, H. Brooke	2,084	23.8%	Scattered Write-In	498	1.3%
	Scattered Write-In	331	3.8%			
	TOTAL	*8,773*		*TOTAL*	*37,400*	
Governor	Brock, Randy	9,083	97.4%	Shumlin, Peter*	34,423	96.4%
	Scattered Write-In	239	2.6%	Scattered Write-In	1,289	3.6%
	TOTAL	*9,322*		*TOTAL*	*35,712*	
House At Large	Donka, Mark	7,623	95.8%	Welch, Peter*	36,863	99.0%
	Scattered Write-In	334	4.2%	Scattered Write-In	359	1.0%
	TOTAL	*7,957*		*TOTAL*	*37,222*	

Note: An asterisk (*) denotes incumbent.

VIRGINIA

Congressional districts first established for elections held in 2012

11 members

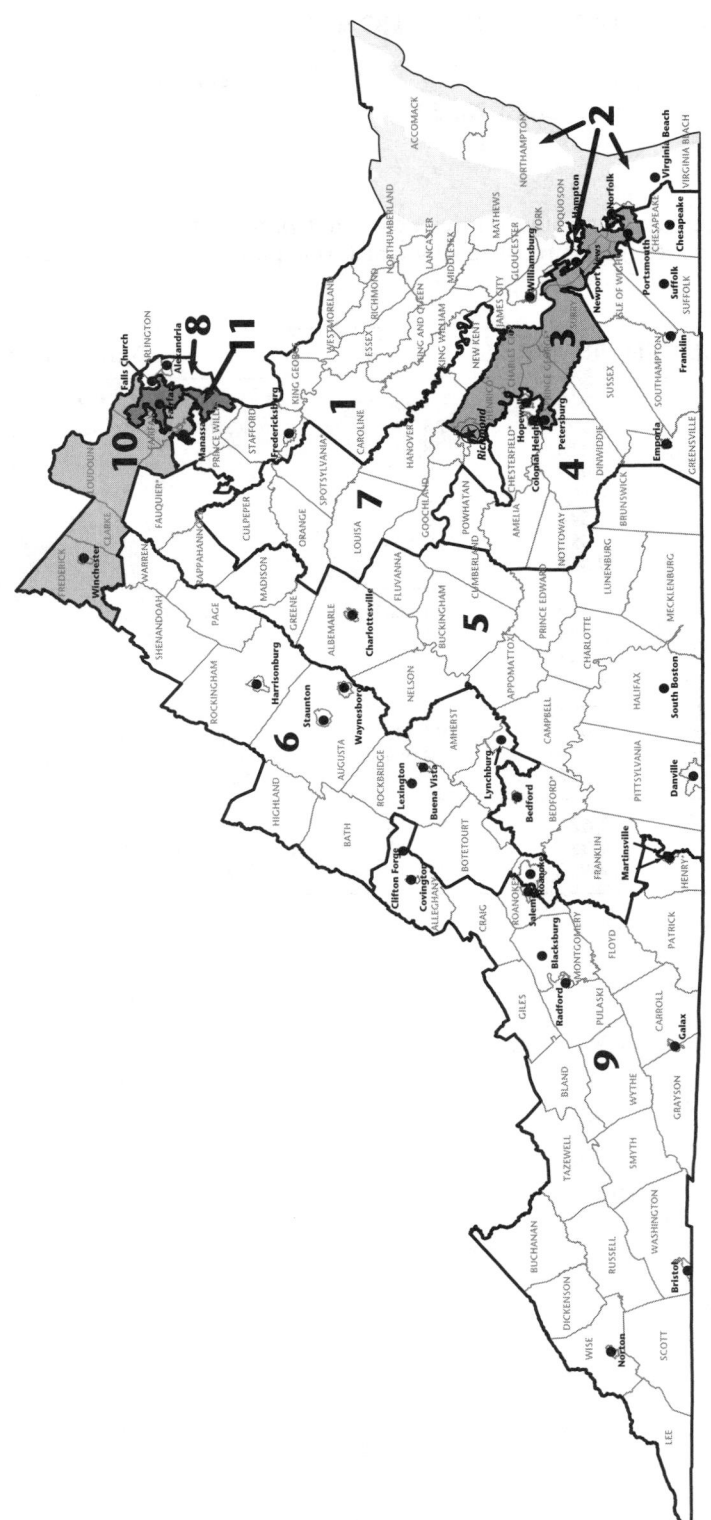

Independent cities are treated as county equivalents; in most cases labels are included only for the city.

* Asterisk indicates a county whose boundaries include parts of two or more Congressional districts.

VIRGINIA

Northern Virginia Area

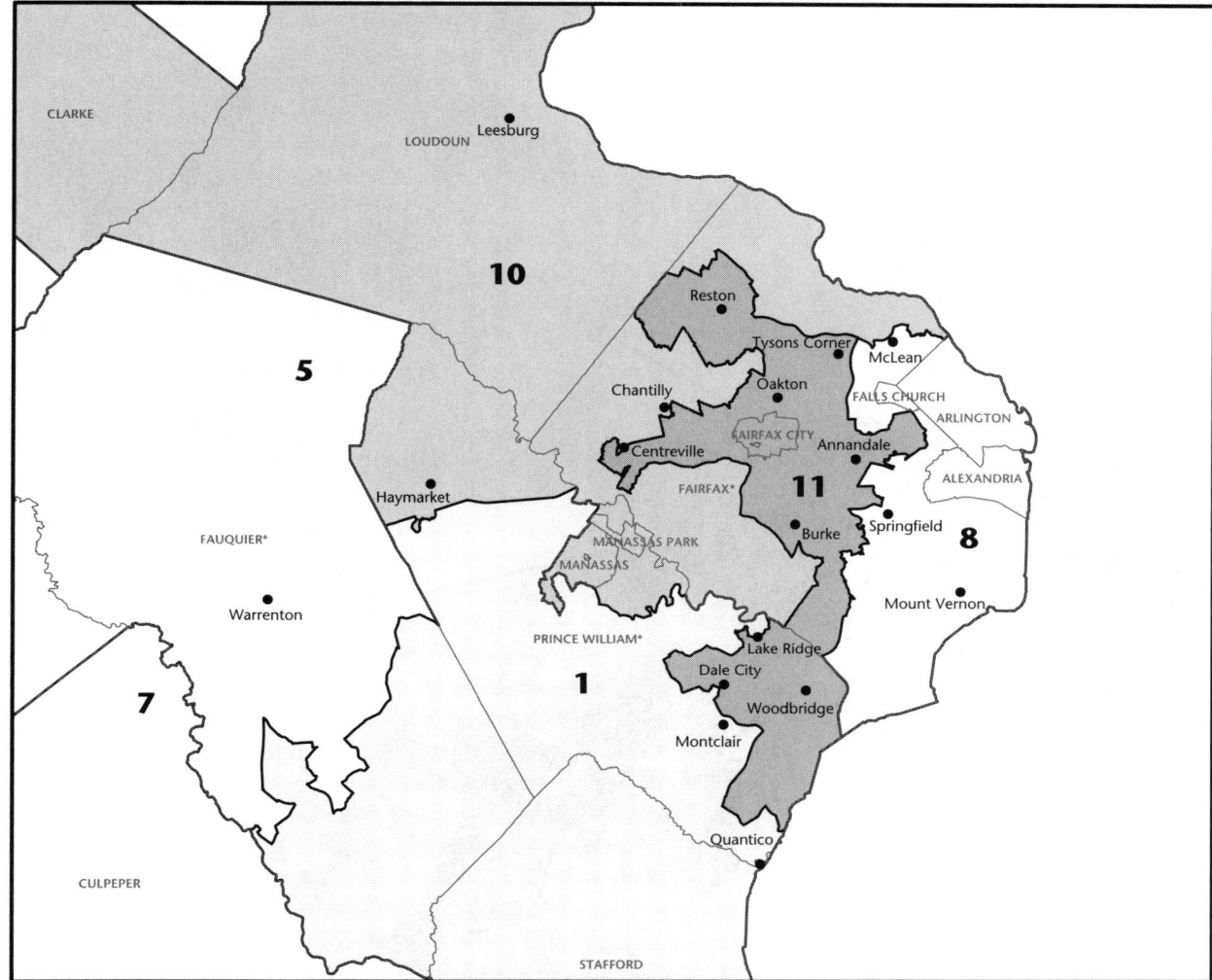

CLARKE

LOUDOUN Leesburg

10

5

Reston

Tysons Corner

McLean

Chantilly Oakton

FALLS CHURCH

ARLINGTON

FAIRFAX CITY

Centreville Annandale

ALEXANDRIA

Haymarket FAIRFAX*

11

FAUQUIER* MANASSAS PARK

MANASSAS Burke Springfield

8

Warrenton Mount Vernon

PRINCE WILLIAM* Lake Ridge

1 Dale City

Woodbridge

7 Montclair

CULPEPER Quantico

STAFFORD

* Asterisk indicates a county whose boundaries include parts of two or more Congressional districts.

VIRGINIA

Hampton Roads, Virginia Beach Areas

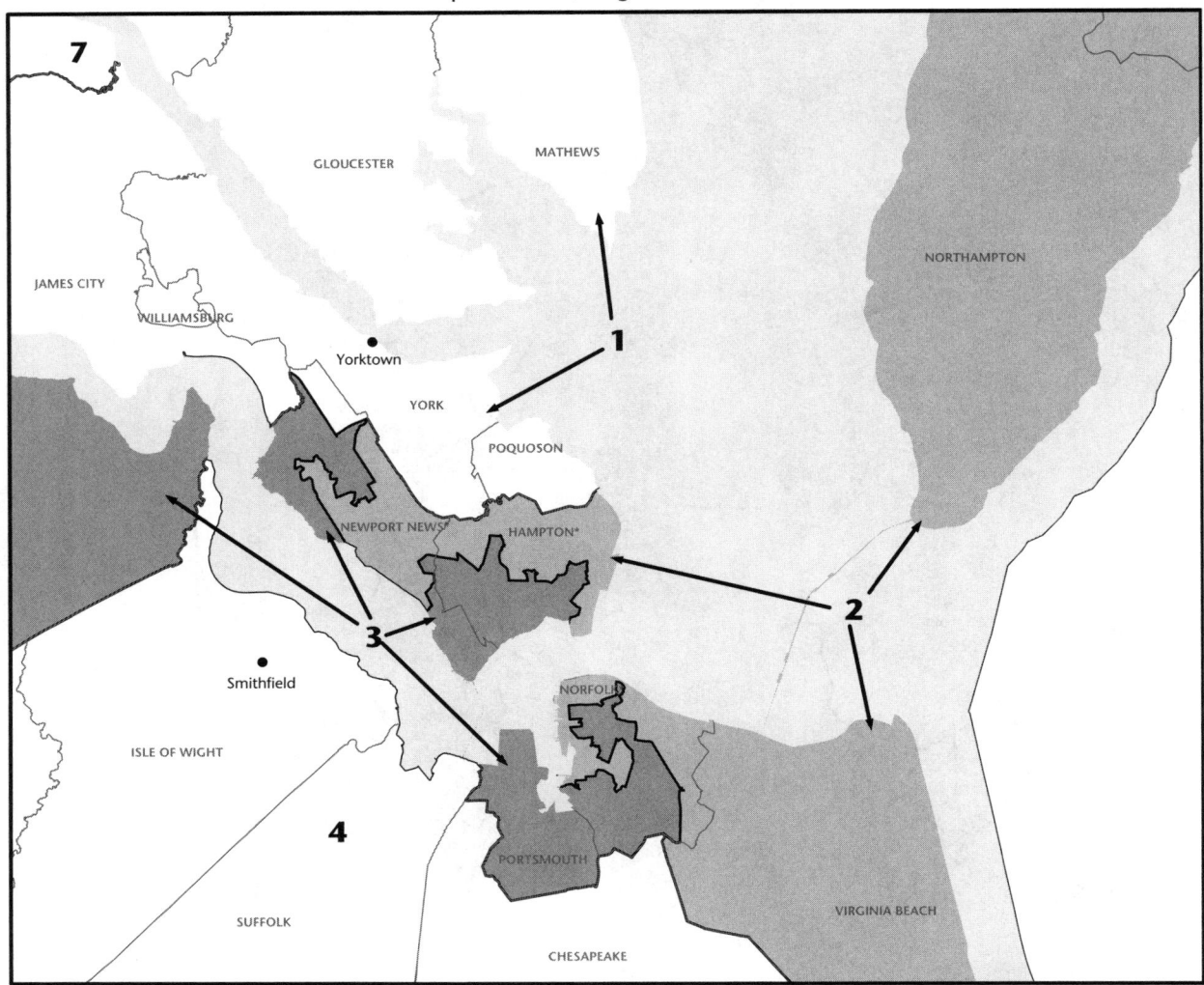

* Asterisk indicates a county whose boundaries include parts of two or more Congressional districts.

VIRGINIA

GOVERNOR

Robert F. McDonnell (R). Elected 2009 to a four-year term.

SENATORS (2 Democrats)

Mark R. Warner (D). Elected 2008 to a six-year term.

Tim Kaine (D). Elected 2012 to a six-year term.

REPRESENTATIVES (8 Republicans, 3 Democrats)

1. Rob Wittman (R)
2. Scott Rigell (R)
3. Bobby Scott (D)
4. J. Randy Forbes (R)
5. Robert Hurt (R)
6. Bob Goodlatte (R)
7. Eric Cantor (R)
8. Jim Moran (D)
9. H. Morgan Griffith (R)
10. Frank R. Wolf (R)
11. Gerald E. "Gerry" Connolly (D)

POSTWAR VOTE FOR PRESIDENT

| | | Republican | | Democratic | | Other Vote | Rep.-Dem. Plurality | Percentage | | | |
| | | | | | | | | Total Vote | | Major Vote | |
Year	Total Vote	Vote	Candidate	Vote	Candidate			Rep.	Dem.	Rep.	Dem.
2012	3,854,489	1,822,522	Romney, W. Mitt	1,971,820	Obama, Barack H.*	60,147	149,298 D	47.3%	51.2%	48.0%	52.0%
2008	3,723,260	1,725,005	McCain, John S. III	1,959,532	Obama, Barack H.	38,723	234,527 D	46.3%	52.6%	46.8%	53.2%
2004	3,198,367	1,716,959	Bush, George W.*	1,454,742	Kerry, John F.	26,666	262,217 R	53.7%	45.5%	54.1%	45.9%
2000**	2,739,447	1,437,490	Bush, George W.	1,217,290	Gore, Albert Jr.	84,667	220,200 R	52.5%	44.4%	54.1%	45.9%
1996**	2,416,642	1,138,350	Dole, Robert "Bob"	1,091,060	Clinton, Bill*	187,232	47,290 R	47.1%	45.1%	51.1%	48.9%
1992**	2,558,665	1,150,517	Bush, George H.*	1,038,650	Clinton, Bill	369,498	111,867 R	45.0%	40.6%	52.6%	47.4%
1988	2,191,609	1,309,162	Bush, George H.	859,799	Dukakis, Michael S.	22,648	449,363 R	59.7%	39.2%	60.4%	39.6%
1984	2,146,635	1,337,078	Reagan, Ronald*	796,250	Mondale, Walter F.	13,307	540,828 R	62.3%	37.1%	62.7%	37.3%
1980**	1,866,032	989,609	Reagan, Ronald	752,174	Carter, Jimmy*	124,249	237,435 R	53.0%	40.3%	56.8%	43.2%
1976	1,697,094	836,554	Ford, Gerald R.*	813,896	Carter, Jimmy	46,644	22,658 R	49.3%	48.0%	50.7%	49.3%
1972	1,457,019	988,493	Nixon, Richard M.*	438,887	McGovern, George S.	29,639	549,606 R	67.8%	30.1%	69.3%	30.7%
1968**	1,361,491	590,319	Nixon, Richard M.	442,387	Humphrey, Hubert H. Jr.	328,785	147,932 R	43.4%	32.5%	57.2%	42.8%
1964	1,042,267	481,334	Goldwater, Barry M. Sr.	558,038	Johnson, Lyndon B.*	2,895	76,704 D	46.2%	53.5%	46.3%	53.7%
1960	771,449	404,521	Nixon, Richard M.	362,327	Kennedy, John F.	4,601	42,194 R	52.4%	47.0%	52.8%	47.2%
1956	697,978	386,459	Eisenhower, Dwight D.*	267,760	Stevenson, Adlai E. II	43,759	118,699 R	55.4%	38.4%	59.1%	40.9%
1952	619,689	349,037	Eisenhower, Dwight D.	268,677	Stevenson, Adlai E. II	1,975	80,360 R	56.3%	43.4%	56.5%	43.5%
1948**	419,256	172,070	Dewey, Thomas E.	200,786	Truman, Harry S.*	46,400	28,716 D	41.0%	47.9%	46.1%	53.9%

Note: An asterisk (*) denotes incumbent. **In past elections, the other vote included: 2000 - 59,398 Green (Ralph Nader); 1996 - 159,861 Reform (Ross Perot); 1992 - 348,639 Independent (Perot); 1980 - 95,418 Independent (John Anderson); 1968 - 321,833 American Independent (George Wallace); 1948 - 43,393 States' Rights (Strom Thurmond).

VIRGINIA

POSTWAR VOTE FOR GOVERNOR

Year	Total Vote	Republican		Democratic		Other Vote	Rep.-Dem. Plurality	Percentage			
								Total Vote		Major Vote	
		Vote	Candidate	Vote	Candidate			Rep.	Dem.	Rep.	Dem.
2009	1,985,103	1,163,651	McDonnell, Robert F.	818,950	Deeds, R. Creigh	2,502	344,701 R	58.6%	41.3%	58.7%	41.3%
2005	1,983,778	912,327	Kilgore, Jerry W.	1,025,942	Kaine, Tim	45,509	113,615 D	46.0%	51.7%	47.1%	52.9%
2001	1,886,721	887,234	Earley, Mark	984,177	Warner, Mark R.	15,310	96,943 D	47.0%	52.2%	47.4%	52.6%
1997	1,736,314	969,062	Gilmore, James S. III	738,971	Beyer, Donald S. Jr.	28,281	230,091 R	55.8%	42.6%	56.7%	43.3%
1993	1,793,916	1,045,319	Allen, George F.	733,527	Terry, Mary Sue	15,070	311,792 R	58.3%	40.9%	58.8%	41.2%
1989	1,789,078	890,195	Coleman, J. Marshall	896,936	Wilder, L. Douglas	1,947	6,741 D	49.8%	50.1%	49.8%	50.2%
1985	1,343,240	601,649	Durrette, Wyatt B.	741,438	Baliles, Gerald L.	153	139,789 D	44.8%	55.2%	44.8%	55.2%
1981	1,420,638	659,398	Coleman, J. Marshall	760,384	Robb, Charles S.	856	100,986 D	46.4%	53.5%	46.4%	53.6%
1977	1,250,940	699,302	Dalton, John M.	541,319	Howell, Henry	10,319	157,983 R	55.9%	43.3%	56.4%	43.6%
1973**	1,035,495	525,075	Godwin, Mills E.			510,420	525,075 R	50.7%		100.0%	
1969	915,764	480,869	Holton, Linwood	415,695	Battle, William C.	19,200	65,174 R	52.5%	45.4%	53.6%	46.4%
1965**	562,789	212,207	Holton, Linwood	269,526	Godwin, Mills E. Jr.	81,056	57,319 D	37.7%	47.9%	44.1%	55.9%
1961	394,490	142,567	Pearson, H. Clyde	251,861	Harrison, Albertis S. Jr.	62	109,294 D	36.1%	63.8%	36.1%	63.9%
1957	517,655	188,628	Dalton, Ted	326,921	Almond, J. Lindsay Jr.	2,106	138,293 D	36.4%	63.2%	36.6%	63.4%
1953	414,025	183,328	Dalton, Ted	226,998	Stanley, Thomas B.	3,699	43,670 D	44.3%	54.8%	44.7%	55.3%
1949	262,350	71,991	Johnson, Walter	184,772	Battle, John S.	5,587	112,781 D	27.4%	70.4%	28.0%	72.0%
1945	164,741	52,386	Landreth, S. Lloyd	112,355	Tuck, William M.		59,969 D	31.8%	68.2%	31.8%	68.2%

Note: An asterisk (*) denotes incumbent. **In past elections, the other vote included: 1973 - 510,103 Independent (Henry Howell), who finished second; 1965 - 75,307 Conservative (William J. Story Jr.). The Democratic Party did not run a candidate in the 1973 gubernatorial election.

POSTWAR VOTE FOR SENATOR

Year	Total Vote	Republican		Democratic		Other Vote	Rep.-Dem. Plurality	Percentage			
								Total Vote		Major Vote	
		Vote	Candidate	Vote	Candidate			Rep.	Dem.	Rep.	Dem.
2012	3,802,196	1,785,542	Allen, George F.	2,010,067	Kaine, Tim	6,587	224,525 D	47.0%	52.9%	47.0%	53.0%
2008	3,643,294	1,228,830	Gilmore, James S.	2,369,327	Warner, Mark R.	45,137	1,140,497 D	33.7%	65.0%	34.2%	65.8%
2006	2,370,445	1,166,277	Allen, George F.*	1,175,606	Webb, Jim H. Jr.	28,562	9,329 D	49.2%	49.6%	49.8%	50.2%
2002	1,489,422	1,229,894	Warner, John W.*			259,528	1,229,894 R	82.6%		100.0%	
2000	2,718,301	1,420,460	Allen, George F.	1,296,093	Robb, Charles S.*	1,748	124,367 R	52.3%	47.7%	52.3%	47.7%
1996	2,354,715	1,235,744	Warner, John W.*	1,115,982	Warner, Mark R.	2,989	119,762 R	52.5%	47.4%	52.5%	47.5%
1994**	2,057,463	882,213	North, Oliver L.	938,376	Robb, Charles S.*	236,874	56,163 D	42.9%	45.6%	48.5%	51.5%
1990**	1,083,660	876,782	Warner, John W.*			206,878	876,782 R	80.9%		100.0%	
1988	2,068,897	593,652	Dawkins, Maurice A.	1,474,086	Robb, Charles S.	1,159	880,434 D	28.7%	71.2%	28.7%	71.3%
1984	2,007,487	1,406,194	Warner, John W.*	601,142	Harrison, Edythe C.	151	805,052 R	70.0%	29.9%	70.1%	29.9%
1982	1,415,622	724,571	Trible, Paul	690,839	Davis, Richard	212	33,732 R	51.2%	48.8%	51.2%	48.8%
1978	1,222,256	613,232	Warner, John W.	608,511	Miller, Andrew P.	513	4,721 R	50.2%	49.8%	50.2%	49.8%
1976**	1,557,500			596,009	Zumwalt, Elmo R.	961,491	596,009 D**		38.3%		100.0%
1972	1,396,268	718,337	Scott, William L.	643,963	Spong, William B.*	33,968	74,374 R	51.4%	46.1%	52.7%	47.3%
1970**	946,751	145,031	Garland, Ray L.	295,057	Rawlings, George C.	506,663	150,026 D**	15.3%	31.2%	33.0%	67.0%
1966	733,879	245,681	Ould, James P. Jr.	429,855	Spong, William B.	58,343	184,174 D	33.5%	58.6%	36.4%	63.6%
1966S	729,839	272,804	Traylor, Lawrence M.	389,028	Byrd, Harry Flood Jr.*	68,007	116,224 D	37.4%	53.3%	41.2%	58.8%
1964**	928,363	176,624	May, Richard A.	592,260	Byrd, Harry F.*	159,479	415,636 D	19.0%	63.8%	23.0%	77.0%
1960**	622,820			506,169	Robertson, A. Willis*	116,651	506,169 D		81.3%		100.0%
1958**	457,640			317,221	Byrd, Harry F.*	140,419	317,221 D		69.3%		100.0%
1954**	306,447			244,844	Robertson, A. Willis*	61,603	244,844 D		79.9%		100.0%
1952**	543,516			398,677	Byrd, Harry F.*	144,839	398,677 D		73.4%		100.0%
1948	386,998	119,366	Woods, Robert H.	253,865	Robertson, A. Willis*	13,767	134,499 D	30.8%	65.6%	32.0%	68.0%
1946	252,863	77,005	Parsons, Lester S.	163,960	Byrd, Harry F.*	11,898	86,955 D	30.5%	64.8%	32.0%	68.0%
1946S	248,962	72,253	Woods, Robert H.	169,680	Robertson, A. Willis	7,029	97,427 D	29.0%	68.2%	29.9%	70.1%

Note: An asterisk (*) denotes incumbent. **In past elections, the other vote included: 1994 - 235,324 Independent (J. Marshall Coleman); 1990 - 196,755 Independent (Nancy Spannaus), who finished second; 1976 - 890,778 Independent (Harry Flood Byrd Jr.), who won the election with 57.2 percent of the total vote; 1970 - 506,633 Independent (Harry Flood Byrd Jr.), who won the election with 53.5 percent of the total vote; 1964 - 95,526 Independent (James W. Respess); 1960 - 88,718 Independent Democrat (Stuart D. Baker), who finished second; 1958 - 120,224 Independent (Louis Wensel), who finished second; 1954 - 32,681 Independent Democrat (Charles William Lewis Jr.), who finished second; 1952 - 69,133 Independent Democrat (H. M. Vise Sr.), who finished second; 67,281 Social Democrat (Clarke T. Robb). One each of the 1946 and 1966 elections was for a short term to fill a vacancy. The Democratic Party did not run a candidate in the Senate elections of 1990 and 2002. The Republican Party did not run a candidate in the Senate elections of 1952, 1954, 1958, 1960, and 1976.

VIRGINIA

PRESIDENT 2012

2010 Census Population	County/City	Total Vote	Republican (Romney)	Democratic (Obama)	Other	Rep.-Dem. Plurality	Percentage Total Vote Rep.	Percentage Total Vote Dem.	Percentage Major Vote Rep.	Percentage Major Vote Dem.
33,164	ACCOMACK	16,051	8,213	7,655	183	558 R	51.2%	47.7%	51.8%	48.2%
98,970	ALBEMARLE	53,907	23,297	29,757	853	6,460 D	43.2%	55.2%	43.9%	56.1%
16,250	ALLEGHANY	7,173	3,595	3,403	175	192 R	50.1%	47.4%	51.4%	48.6%
12,690	AMELIA	6,915	4,331	2,490	94	1,841 R	62.6%	36.0%	63.5%	36.5%
32,353	AMHERST	14,970	8,876	5,900	194	2,976 R	59.3%	39.4%	60.1%	39.9%
14,973	APPOMATTOX	7,935	5,340	2,453	142	2,887 R	67.3%	30.9%	68.5%	31.5%
207,627	ARLINGTON	117,608	34,474	81,269	1,865	46,795 D	29.3%	69.1%	29.8%	70.2%
73,750	AUGUSTA	33,672	23,624	9,451	597	14,173 R	70.2%	28.1%	71.4%	28.6%
4,731	BATH	2,223	1,274	894	55	380 R	57.3%	40.2%	58.8%	41.2%
68,676	BEDFORD COUNTY	37,425	26,679	10,209	537	16,470 R	71.3%	27.3%	72.3%	27.7%
6,824	BLAND	2,948	2,144	735	69	1,409 R	72.7%	24.9%	74.5%	25.5%
33,148	BOTETOURT	18,241	12,479	5,452	310	7,027 R	68.4%	29.9%	69.6%	30.4%
17,434	BRUNSWICK	8,037	2,968	4,994	75	2,026 D	36.9%	62.1%	37.3%	62.7%
24,098	BUCHANAN	9,646	6,436	3,094	116	3,342 R	66.7%	32.1%	67.5%	32.5%
17,146	BUCKINGHAM	7,457	3,569	3,750	138	181 D	47.9%	50.3%	48.8%	51.2%
54,842	CAMPBELL	25,696	17,695	7,595	406	10,100 R	68.9%	29.6%	70.0%	30.0%
28,545	CAROLINE	13,652	6,151	7,276	225	1,125 D	45.1%	53.3%	45.8%	54.2%
30,042	CARROLL	12,918	8,736	3,685	497	5,051 R	67.6%	28.5%	70.3%	29.7%
7,256	CHARLES CITY	4,232	1,396	2,772	64	1,376 D	33.0%	65.5%	33.5%	66.5%
12,586	CHARLOTTE	5,898	3,311	2,503	84	808 R	56.1%	42.4%	56.9%	43.1%
316,236	CHESTERFIELD	170,988	90,934	77,694	2,360	13,240 R	53.2%	45.4%	53.9%	46.1%
14,034	CLARKE	7,762	4,296	3,239	227	1,057 R	55.3%	41.7%	57.0%	43.0%
5,190	CRAIG	2,667	1,757	830	80	927 R	65.9%	31.1%	67.9%	32.1%
46,689	CULPEPER	20,211	11,580	8,285	346	3,295 R	57.3%	41.0%	58.3%	41.7%
10,052	CUMBERLAND	5,048	2,538	2,422	88	116 R	50.3%	48.0%	51.2%	48.8%
15,903	DICKENSON	6,904	4,274	2,473	157	1,801 R	61.9%	35.8%	63.3%	36.7%
28,001	DINWIDDIE	13,589	6,875	6,550	164	325 R	50.6%	48.2%	51.2%	48.8%
11,151	ESSEX	5,675	2,602	3,016	57	414 D	45.9%	53.1%	46.3%	53.7%
1,081,726	FAIRFAX COUNTY	529,287	206,773	315,273	7,241	108,500 D	39.1%	59.6%	39.6%	60.4%
65,203	FAUQUIER	35,555	21,034	13,965	556	7,069 R	59.2%	39.3%	60.1%	39.9%
15,279	FLOYD	7,644	4,673	2,732	239	1,941 R	61.1%	35.7%	63.1%	36.9%
25,691	FLUVANNA	12,749	6,678	5,893	178	785 R	52.4%	46.2%	53.1%	46.9%
56,159	FRANKLIN COUNTY	26,707	16,718	9,090	899	7,628 R	62.6%	34.0%	64.8%	35.2%
78,305	FREDERICK	36,394	22,858	12,690	846	10,168 R	62.8%	34.9%	64.3%	35.7%
17,286	GILES	7,558	4,660	2,730	168	1,930 R	61.7%	36.1%	63.1%	36.9%
36,858	GLOUCESTER	19,283	12,137	6,764	382	5,373 R	62.9%	35.1%	64.2%	35.8%
21,717	GOOCHLAND	13,315	8,448	4,676	191	3,772 R	63.4%	35.1%	64.4%	35.6%
15,533	GRAYSON	7,121	4,801	2,068	252	2,733 R	67.4%	29.0%	69.9%	30.1%
18,403	GREENE	9,023	5,569	3,290	164	2,279 R	61.7%	36.5%	62.9%	37.1%
12,243	GREENSVILLE	4,926	1,766	3,135	25	1,369 D	35.9%	63.6%	36.0%	64.0%
36,241	HALIFAX	16,692	8,694	7,766	232	928 R	52.1%	46.5%	52.8%	47.2%
99,863	HANOVER	59,058	39,940	18,294	824	21,646 R	67.6%	31.0%	68.6%	31.4%
306,935	HENRICO	162,241	70,449	89,594	2,198	19,145 D	43.4%	55.2%	44.0%	56.0%
54,151	HENRY	24,963	13,984	10,317	662	3,667 R	56.0%	41.3%	57.5%	42.5%
2,321	HIGHLAND	1,413	924	459	30	465 R	65.4%	32.5%	66.8%	33.2%
35,270	ISLE OF WIGHT	20,827	11,802	8,761	264	3,041 R	56.7%	42.1%	57.4%	42.6%
67,009	JAMES CITY	41,240	22,843	17,879	518	4,964 R	55.4%	43.4%	56.1%	43.9%
6,945	KING AND QUEEN	3,655	1,865	1,745	45	120 R	51.0%	47.7%	51.7%	48.3%
23,584	KING GEORGE	11,325	6,604	4,477	244	2,127 R	58.3%	39.5%	59.6%	40.4%
15,935	KING WILLIAM	8,923	5,466	3,344	113	2,122 R	61.3%	37.5%	62.0%	38.0%
11,391	LANCASTER	6,961	3,753	3,149	59	604 R	53.9%	45.2%	54.4%	45.6%
25,587	LEE	9,598	6,847	2,583	168	4,264 R	71.3%	26.9%	72.6%	27.4%
312,311	LOUDOUN	160,060	75,292	82,479	2,289	7,187 D	47.0%	51.5%	47.7%	52.3%
33,153	LOUISA	16,452	9,215	6,953	284	2,262 R	56.0%	42.3%	57.0%	43.0%
12,914	LUNENBURG	5,734	2,969	2,684	81	285 R	51.8%	46.8%	52.5%	47.5%
13,308	MADISON	6,614	3,869	2,639	106	1,230 R	58.5%	39.9%	59.4%	40.6%
8,978	MATHEWS	5,374	3,488	1,807	79	1,681 R	64.9%	33.6%	65.9%	34.1%
32,727	MECKLENBURG	15,077	7,973	6,921	183	1,052 R	52.9%	45.9%	53.5%	46.5%
10,959	MIDDLESEX	6,080	3,619	2,370	91	1,249 R	59.5%	39.0%	60.4%	39.6%
94,392	MONTGOMERY	41,009	20,006	19,903	1,100	103 R	48.8%	48.5%	50.1%	49.9%

VIRGINIA
PRESIDENT 2012

2010 Census Population	County/City	Total Vote	Republican (Romney)	Democratic (Obama)	Other	Rep.-Dem. Plurality	Percentage Total Vote Rep.	Dem.	Major Vote Rep.	Dem.
15,020	NELSON	8,250	3,947	4,171	132	224 D	47.8%	50.6%	48.6%	51.4%
18,429	NEW KENT	10,953	7,246	3,555	152	3,691 R	66.2%	32.5%	67.1%	32.9%
12,389	NORTHAMPTON	6,491	2,676	3,741	74	1,065 D	41.2%	57.6%	41.7%	58.3%
12,330	NORTHUMBERLAND	7,558	4,310	3,191	57	1,119 R	57.0%	42.2%	57.5%	42.5%
15,853	NOTTOWAY	6,846	3,409	3,344	93	65 R	49.8%	48.8%	50.5%	49.5%
33,481	ORANGE	16,354	9,244	6,870	240	2,374 R	56.5%	42.0%	57.4%	42.6%
24,042	PAGE	10,228	6,344	3,724	160	2,620 R	62.0%	36.4%	63.0%	37.0%
18,490	PATRICK	8,259	5,622	2,417	220	3,205 R	68.1%	29.3%	69.9%	30.1%
63,506	PITTSYLVANIA	30,681	19,263	10,858	560	8,405 R	62.8%	35.4%	64.0%	36.0%
28,046	POWHATAN	15,525	11,200	4,088	237	7,112 R	72.1%	26.3%	73.3%	26.7%
23,368	PRINCE EDWARD	9,239	3,952	5,132	155	1,180 D	42.8%	55.5%	43.5%	56.5%
35,725	PRINCE GEORGE	16,046	8,879	6,991	176	1,888 R	55.3%	43.6%	55.9%	44.1%
402,002	PRINCE WILLIAM	180,195	74,458	103,331	2,406	28,873 D	41.3%	57.3%	41.9%	58.1%
34,872	PULASKI	14,680	8,920	5,292	468	3,628 R	60.8%	36.0%	62.8%	37.2%
7,373	RAPPAHANNOCK	4,357	2,311	1,980	66	331 R	53.0%	45.4%	53.9%	46.1%
9,254	RICHMOND COUNTY	3,770	2,160	1,574	36	586 R	57.3%	41.8%	57.8%	42.2%
92,376	ROANOKE COUNTY	51,217	31,624	18,711	882	12,913 R	61.7%	36.5%	62.8%	37.2%
22,307	ROCKBRIDGE	10,177	5,898	4,088	191	1,810 R	58.0%	40.2%	59.1%	40.9%
76,314	ROCKINGHAM	34,866	24,186	10,065	615	14,121 R	69.4%	28.9%	70.6%	29.4%
28,897	RUSSELL	12,088	8,180	3,718	190	4,462 R	67.7%	30.8%	68.8%	31.2%
23,177	SCOTT	9,992	7,439	2,395	158	5,044 R	74.4%	24.0%	75.6%	24.4%
41,993	SHENANDOAH	19,373	12,538	6,469	366	6,069 R	64.7%	33.4%	66.0%	34.0%
32,208	SMYTH	12,777	8,379	4,171	227	4,208 R	65.6%	32.6%	66.8%	33.2%
18,570	SOUTHAMPTON	9,264	4,733	4,437	94	296 R	51.1%	47.9%	51.6%	48.4%
122,397	SPOTSYLVANIA	57,974	31,844	25,165	965	6,679 R	54.9%	43.4%	55.9%	44.1%
128,961	STAFFORD	60,583	32,480	27,182	921	5,298 R	53.6%	44.9%	54.4%	45.6%
7,058	SURRY	4,308	1,671	2,576	61	905 D	38.8%	59.8%	39.3%	60.7%
12,087	SUSSEX	5,440	2,021	3,358	61	1,337 D	37.2%	61.7%	37.6%	62.4%
45,078	TAZEWELL	17,732	13,843	3,661	228	10,182 R	78.1%	20.6%	79.1%	20.9%
37,575	WARREN	16,698	9,869	6,452	377	3,417 R	59.1%	38.6%	60.5%	39.5%
54,876	WASHINGTON	25,632	18,141	7,076	415	11,065 R	70.8%	27.6%	71.9%	28.1%
17,454	WESTMORELAND	8,120	3,731	4,295	94	564 D	45.9%	52.9%	46.5%	53.5%
41,452	WISE	15,018	11,076	3,760	182	7,316 R	73.8%	25.0%	74.7%	25.3%
29,235	WYTHE	12,358	8,324	3,783	251	4,541 R	67.4%	30.6%	68.8%	31.2%
65,464	YORK	33,953	20,204	13,183	566	7,021 R	59.5%	38.8%	60.5%	39.5%

Independent Cities

2010 Census Population	County/City	Total Vote	Republican (Romney)	Democratic (Obama)	Other	Rep.-Dem. Plurality	Rep.	Dem.	Rep.	Dem.
139,966	ALEXANDRIA	73,411	20,249	52,199	963	31,950 D	27.6%	71.1%	27.9%	72.1%
6,222	BEDFORD CITY	2,805	1,527	1,225	53	302 R	54.4%	43.7%	55.5%	44.5%
17,835	BRISTOL	7,387	4,780	2,492	115	2,288 R	64.7%	33.7%	65.7%	34.3%
6,650	BUENA VISTA	2,526	1,564	919	43	645 R	61.9%	36.4%	63.0%	37.0%
43,475	CHARLOTTESVILLE	21,797	4,844	16,510	443	11,666 D	22.2%	75.7%	22.7%	77.3%
222,209	CHESAPEAKE	110,425	53,900	55,052	1,473	1,152 D	48.8%	49.9%	49.5%	50.5%
17,411	COLONIAL HEIGHTS	8,624	5,941	2,544	139	3,397 R	68.9%	29.5%	70.0%	30.0%
5,961	COVINGTON	2,330	975	1,319	36	344 D	41.8%	56.6%	42.5%	57.5%
43,055	DANVILLE	20,204	7,763	12,218	223	4,455 D	38.4%	60.5%	38.9%	61.1%
5,927	EMPORIA	2,696	886	1,793	17	907 D	32.9%	66.5%	33.1%	66.9%
22,565	FAIRFAX CITY	11,629	4,775	6,651	203	1,876 D	41.1%	57.2%	41.8%	58.2%
12,332	FALLS CHURCH	7,276	2,147	5,015	114	2,868 D	29.5%	68.9%	30.0%	70.0%
8,582	FRANKLIN CITY	4,360	1,496	2,833	31	1,337 D	34.3%	65.0%	34.6%	65.4%
24,286	FREDERICKSBURG	11,437	4,060	7,131	246	3,071 D	35.5%	62.4%	36.3%	63.7%
7,042	GALAX	2,277	1,332	900	45	432 R	58.5%	39.5%	59.7%	40.3%
137,436	HAMPTON	66,490	18,640	46,966	884	28,326 D	28.0%	70.6%	28.4%	71.6%
48,914	HARRISONBURG	15,593	6,565	8,654	374	2,089 D	42.1%	55.5%	43.1%	56.9%
22,591	HOPEWELL	9,031	3,739	5,179	113	1,440 D	41.4%	57.3%	41.9%	58.1%
7,042	LEXINGTON	2,687	1,146	1,486	55	340 D	42.6%	55.3%	43.5%	56.5%
75,568	LYNCHBURG	36,448	19,806	15,948	694	3,858 R	54.3%	43.8%	55.4%	44.6%
37,821	MANASSAS	15,200	6,463	8,478	259	2,015 D	42.5%	55.8%	43.3%	56.7%
14,273	MANASSAS PARK	4,656	1,699	2,879	78	1,180 D	36.5%	61.8%	37.1%	62.9%
13,821	MARTINSVILLE	6,284	2,312	3,855	117	1,543 D	36.8%	61.3%	37.5%	62.5%
180,719	NEWPORT NEWS	79,444	27,230	51,100	1,114	23,870 D	34.3%	64.3%	34.8%	65.2%
242,803	NORFOLK	87,043	23,147	62,687	1,209	39,540 D	26.6%	72.0%	27.0%	73.0%

VIRGINIA

PRESIDENT 2012

2010 Census Population	County/City	Total Vote	Republican (Romney)	Democratic (Obama)	Other	Rep.-Dem. Plurality	Percentage: Total Vote Rep.	Total Vote Dem.	Major Vote Rep.	Major Vote Dem.
3,958	NORTON	1,492	895	566	31	329 R	60.0%	37.9%	61.3%	38.7%
32,420	PETERSBURG	15,908	1,527	14,283	98	12,756 D	9.6%	89.8%	9.7%	90.3%
12,150	POQUOSON	7,106	5,312	1,679	115	3,633 R	74.8%	23.6%	76.0%	24.0%
95,535	PORTSMOUTH	45,922	12,858	32,501	563	19,643 D	28.0%	70.8%	28.3%	71.7%
16,408	RADFORD	5,399	2,520	2,732	147	212 D	46.7%	50.6%	48.0%	52.0%
204,214	RICHMOND CITY	97,569	20,050	75,921	1,598	55,871 D	20.5%	77.8%	20.9%	79.1%
97,032	ROANOKE CITY	40,155	14,991	24,134	1,030	9,143 D	37.3%	60.1%	38.3%	61.7%
24,802	SALEM	12,318	7,299	4,760	259	2,539 R	59.3%	38.6%	60.5%	39.5%
23,746	STAUNTON	11,210	5,272	5,728	210	456 D	47.0%	51.1%	47.9%	52.1%
84,585	SUFFOLK	42,566	17,820	24,267	479	6,447 D	41.9%	57.0%	42.3%	57.7%
437,994	VIRGINIA BEACH	196,641	99,291	94,299	3,051	4,992 R	50.5%	48.0%	51.3%	48.7%
21,006	WAYNESBORO	8,791	4,790	3,840	161	950 R	54.5%	43.7%	55.5%	44.5%
14,068	WILLIAMSBURG	7,748	2,682	4,903	163	2,221 D	34.6%	63.3%	35.4%	64.6%
26,203	WINCHESTER	10,296	4,946	5,094	256	148 D	48.0%	49.5%	49.3%	50.7%
8,001,024	*TOTAL*	*3,854,489*	*1,822,522*	*1,971,820*	*60,147*	*149,298 D*	*47.3%*	*51.2%*	*48.0%*	*52.0%*

VIRGINIA

SENATOR 2012

2010 Census Population	County/City	Total Vote	Republican (Allen)	Democratic (Kaine)	Other	Rep.-Dem. Plurality	Percentage: Total Vote Rep.	Total Vote Dem.	Major Vote Rep.	Major Vote Dem.
33,164	ACCOMACK	15,574	8,041	7,521	12	520 R	51.6%	48.3%	51.7%	48.3%
98,970	ALBEMARLE	53,369	22,342	30,973	54	8,631 D	41.9%	58.0%	41.9%	58.1%
16,250	ALLEGHANY	7,309	3,798	3,507	4	291 R	52.0%	48.0%	52.0%	48.0%
12,690	AMELIA	6,762	4,276	2,481	5	1,795 R	63.2%	36.7%	63.3%	36.7%
32,353	AMHERST	14,998	8,905	6,073	20	2,832 R	59.4%	40.5%	59.5%	40.5%
14,973	APPOMATTOX	7,823	5,244	2,568	11	2,676 R	67.0%	32.8%	67.1%	32.9%
207,627	ARLINGTON	115,775	32,807	82,689	279	49,882 D	28.3%	71.4%	28.4%	71.6%
73,750	AUGUSTA	34,068	24,153	9,879	36	14,274 R	70.9%	29.0%	71.0%	29.0%
4,731	BATH	2,272	1,374	890	8	484 R	60.5%	39.2%	60.7%	39.3%
68,676	BEDFORD COUNTY	36,866	26,160	10,669	37	15,491 R	71.0%	28.9%	71.0%	29.0%
6,824	BLAND	2,982	2,132	850		1,282 R	71.5%	28.5%	71.5%	28.5%
33,148	BOTETOURT	18,182	12,253	5,898	31	6,355 R	67.4%	32.4%	67.5%	32.5%
17,434	BRUNSWICK	7,809	3,071	4,736	2	1,665 D	39.3%	60.6%	39.3%	60.7%
24,098	BUCHANAN	9,542	6,132	3,408	2	2,724 R	64.3%	35.7%	64.3%	35.7%
17,146	BUCKINGHAM	7,267	3,610	3,654	3	44 D	49.7%	50.3%	49.7%	50.3%
54,842	CAMPBELL	25,833	17,904	7,900	29	10,004 R	69.3%	30.6%	69.4%	30.6%
28,545	CAROLINE	13,445	6,057	7,329	59	1,272 D	45.1%	54.5%	45.2%	54.8%
30,042	CARROLL	12,689	8,596	4,075	18	4,521 R	67.7%	32.1%	67.8%	32.2%
7,256	CHARLES CITY	4,126	1,413	2,706	7	1,293 D	34.2%	65.6%	34.3%	65.7%
12,586	CHARLOTTE	5,880	3,364	2,516		848 R	57.2%	42.8%	57.2%	42.8%
316,236	CHESTERFIELD	169,744	88,142	81,239	363	6,903 R	51.9%	47.9%	52.0%	48.0%
14,034	CLARKE	7,659	4,224	3,419	16	805 R	55.2%	44.6%	55.3%	44.7%
5,190	CRAIG	2,641	1,755	883	3	872 R	66.5%	33.4%	66.5%	33.5%
46,689	CULPEPER	20,221	11,743	8,457	21	3,286 R	58.1%	41.8%	58.1%	41.9%
10,052	CUMBERLAND	4,964	2,544	2,411	9	133 R	51.2%	48.6%	51.3%	48.7%
15,903	DICKENSON	6,833	4,064	2,768	1	1,296 R	59.5%	40.5%	59.5%	40.5%
28,001	DINWIDDIE	13,381	6,880	6,489	12	391 R	51.4%	48.5%	51.5%	48.5%
11,151	ESSEX	5,529	2,562	2,964	3	402 D	46.3%	53.6%	46.4%	53.6%
1,081,726	FAIRFAX COUNTY	522,307	201,414	319,748	1,145	118,334 D	38.6%	61.2%	38.6%	61.4%
65,203	FAUQUIER	35,164	20,745	14,351	68	6,394 R	59.0%	40.8%	59.1%	40.9%

VIRGINIA

SENATOR 2012

2010 Census Population	County/City	Total Vote	Republican (Allen)	Democratic (Kaine)	Other	Rep.-Dem. Plurality	Percentage Total Vote Rep.	Dem.	Major Vote Rep.	Dem.
15,279	FLOYD	7,531	4,551	2,968	12	1,583 R	60.4%	39.4%	60.5%	39.5%
25,691	FLUVANNA	12,582	6,618	5,945	19	673 R	52.6%	47.3%	52.7%	47.3%
56,159	FRANKLIN COUNTY	26,388	16,478	9,870	40	6,608 R	62.4%	37.4%	62.5%	37.5%
78,305	FREDERICK	35,871	22,464	13,342	65	9,122 R	62.6%	37.2%	62.7%	37.3%
17,286	GILES	7,732	4,640	3,082	10	1,558 R	60.0%	39.9%	60.1%	39.9%
36,858	GLOUCESTER	19,268	12,044	7,195	29	4,849 R	62.5%	37.3%	62.6%	37.4%
21,717	GOOCHLAND	13,156	8,082	5,050	24	3,032 R	61.4%	38.4%	61.5%	38.5%
15,533	GRAYSON	7,055	4,657	2,398		2,259 R	66.0%	34.0%	66.0%	34.0%
18,403	GREENE	8,932	5,552	3,374	6	2,178 R	62.2%	37.8%	62.2%	37.8%
12,243	GREENSVILLE	4,810	1,794	3,014	2	1,220 D	37.3%	62.7%	37.3%	62.7%
36,241	HALIFAX	16,553	8,878	7,649	26	1,229 R	53.6%	46.2%	53.7%	46.3%
99,863	HANOVER	58,554	38,432	20,003	119	18,429 R	65.6%	34.2%	65.8%	34.2%
306,935	HENRICO	160,401	67,015	93,124	262	26,109 D	41.8%	58.1%	41.8%	58.2%
54,151	HENRY	24,215	13,831	10,365	19	3,466 R	57.1%	42.8%	57.2%	42.8%
2,321	HIGHLAND	1,434	957	477		480 R	66.7%	33.3%	66.7%	33.3%
35,270	ISLE OF WIGHT	20,530	11,645	8,860	25	2,785 R	56.7%	43.2%	56.8%	43.2%
67,009	JAMES CITY	40,900	21,957	18,878	65	3,079 R	53.7%	46.2%	53.8%	46.2%
6,945	KING AND QUEEN	3,690	1,877	1,806	7	71 R	50.9%	48.9%	51.0%	49.0%
23,584	KING GEORGE	11,211	6,565	4,625	21	1,940 R	58.6%	41.3%	58.7%	41.3%
15,935	KING WILLIAM	8,862	5,371	3,470	21	1,901 R	60.6%	39.2%	60.8%	39.2%
11,391	LANCASTER	6,872	3,622	3,241	9	381 R	52.7%	47.2%	52.8%	47.2%
25,587	LEE	9,479	6,588	2,883	8	3,705 R	69.5%	30.4%	69.6%	30.4%
312,311	LOUDOUN	157,978	74,325	83,383	270	9,058 D	47.0%	52.8%	47.1%	52.9%
33,153	LOUISA	16,292	9,036	7,232	24	1,804 R	55.5%	44.4%	55.5%	44.5%
12,914	LUNENBURG	5,610	2,985	2,616	9	369 R	53.2%	46.6%	53.3%	46.7%
13,308	MADISON	6,661	3,978	2,678	5	1,300 R	59.7%	40.2%	59.8%	40.2%
8,978	MATHEWS	5,295	3,383	1,907	5	1,476 R	63.9%	36.0%	64.0%	36.0%
32,727	MECKLENBURG	14,381	8,037	6,344		1,693 R	55.9%	44.1%	55.9%	44.1%
10,959	MIDDLESEX	5,949	3,489	2,455	5	1,034 R	58.6%	41.3%	58.7%	41.3%
94,392	MONTGOMERY	40,293	19,335	20,875	83	1,540 D	48.0%	51.8%	48.1%	51.9%
15,020	NELSON	8,169	3,946	4,215	8	269 D	48.3%	51.6%	48.4%	51.6%
18,429	NEW KENT	10,898	7,070	3,815	13	3,255 R	64.9%	35.0%	65.0%	35.0%
12,389	NORTHAMPTON	6,347	2,606	3,735	6	1,129 D	41.1%	58.8%	41.1%	58.9%
12,330	NORTHUMBERLAND	7,478	4,220	3,253	5	967 R	56.4%	43.5%	56.5%	43.5%
15,853	NOTTOWAY	6,623	3,327	3,294	2	33 R	50.2%	49.7%	50.2%	49.8%
33,481	ORANGE	16,148	9,114	6,972	62	2,142 R	56.4%	43.2%	56.7%	43.3%
24,042	PAGE	10,204	6,376	3,806	22	2,570 R	62.5%	37.3%	62.6%	37.4%
18,490	PATRICK	8,223	5,537	2,679	7	2,858 R	67.3%	32.6%	67.4%	32.6%
63,506	PITTSYLVANIA	30,564	19,520	11,027	17	8,493 R	63.9%	36.1%	63.9%	36.1%
28,046	POWHATAN	15,386	10,887	4,470	29	6,417 R	70.8%	29.1%	70.9%	29.1%
23,368	PRINCE EDWARD	9,225	4,100	5,118	7	1,018 D	44.4%	55.5%	44.5%	55.5%
35,725	PRINCE GEORGE	15,842	8,778	7,052	12	1,726 R	55.4%	44.5%	55.5%	44.5%
402,002	PRINCE WILLIAM	177,988	74,809	102,859	320	28,050 D	42.0%	57.8%	42.1%	57.9%
34,872	PULASKI	14,468	8,717	5,732	19	2,985 R	60.3%	39.6%	60.3%	39.7%
7,373	RAPPAHANNOCK	4,316	2,272	2,036	8	236 R	52.6%	47.2%	52.7%	47.3%
9,254	RICHMOND COUNTY	3,680	2,122	1,550	8	572 R	57.7%	42.1%	57.8%	42.2%
92,376	ROANOKE COUNTY	50,611	30,530	20,008	73	10,522 R	60.3%	39.5%	60.4%	39.6%
22,307	ROCKBRIDGE	10,269	6,063	4,195	11	1,868 R	59.0%	40.9%	59.1%	40.9%
76,314	ROCKINGHAM	34,402	24,340	10,015	47	14,325 R	70.8%	29.1%	70.8%	29.2%
28,897	RUSSELL	11,964	7,714	4,243	7	3,471 R	64.5%	35.5%	64.5%	35.5%
23,177	SCOTT	9,908	7,122	2,776	10	4,346 R	71.9%	28.0%	72.0%	28.0%
41,993	SHENANDOAH	19,083	12,411	6,630	42	5,781 R	65.0%	34.7%	65.2%	34.8%
32,208	SMYTH	12,592	8,022	4,562	8	3,460 R	63.7%	36.2%	63.7%	36.3%
18,570	SOUTHAMPTON	9,077	4,627	4,440	10	187 R	51.0%	48.9%	51.0%	49.0%
122,397	SPOTSYLVANIA	57,211	31,265	25,833	113	5,432 R	54.6%	45.2%	54.8%	45.2%
128,961	STAFFORD	59,982	31,997	27,820	165	4,177 R	53.3%	46.4%	53.5%	46.5%
7,058	SURRY	4,221	1,658	2,553	10	895 D	39.3%	60.5%	39.4%	60.6%
12,087	SUSSEX	5,342	2,057	3,278	7	1,221 D	38.5%	61.4%	38.6%	61.4%
45,078	TAZEWELL	17,810	13,477	4,318	15	9,159 R	75.7%	24.2%	75.7%	24.3%
37,575	WARREN	16,404	9,747	6,616	41	3,131 R	59.4%	40.3%	59.6%	40.4%

VIRGINIA

SENATOR 2012

2010 Census Population	County/City	Total Vote	Republican (Allen)	Democratic (Kaine)	Other	Rep.-Dem. Plurality	Percentage Total Vote Rep.	Dem.	Major Vote Rep.	Dem.
54,876	WASHINGTON	25,362	17,417	7,916	29	9,501 R	68.7%	31.2%	68.8%	31.2%
17,454	WESTMORELAND	8,048	3,703	4,331	14	628 D	46.0%	53.8%	46.1%	53.9%
41,452	WISE	14,768	10,520	4,236	12	6,284 R	71.2%	28.7%	71.3%	28.7%
29,235	WYTHE	12,171	8,080	4,031	60	4,049 R	66.4%	33.1%	66.7%	33.3%
65,464	YORK	33,653	19,745	13,849	59	5,896 R	58.7%	41.2%	58.8%	41.2%
	Independent Cities									
139,966	ALEXANDRIA	72,138	19,498	52,502	138	33,004 D	27.0%	72.8%	27.1%	72.9%
6,222	BEDFORD CITY	2,703	1,520	1,180	3	340 R	56.2%	43.7%	56.3%	43.7%
17,835	BRISTOL	7,288	4,594	2,682	12	1,912 R	63.0%	36.8%	63.1%	36.9%
6,650	BUENA VISTA	2,450	1,478	964	8	514 R	60.3%	39.3%	60.5%	39.5%
43,475	CHARLOTTESVILLE	21,427	4,589	16,800	38	12,211 D	21.4%	78.4%	21.5%	78.5%
222,209	CHESAPEAKE	108,509	52,182	56,109	218	3,927 D	48.1%	51.7%	48.2%	51.8%
17,411	COLONIAL HEIGHTS	8,448	5,772	2,662	14	3,110 R	68.3%	31.5%	68.4%	31.6%
5,961	COVINGTON	2,379	1,071	1,306	2	235 D	45.0%	54.9%	45.1%	54.9%
43,055	DANVILLE	19,761	7,902	11,840	19	3,938 D	40.0%	59.9%	40.0%	60.0%
5,927	EMPORIA	2,642	957	1,685		728 D	36.2%	63.8%	36.2%	63.8%
22,565	FAIRFAX CITY	11,436	4,682	6,728	26	2,046 D	40.9%	58.8%	41.0%	59.0%
12,332	FALLS CHURCH	7,211	2,051	5,147	13	3,096 D	28.4%	71.4%	28.5%	71.5%
8,582	FRANKLIN CITY	4,119	1,464	2,651	4	1,187 D	35.5%	64.4%	35.6%	64.4%
24,286	FREDERICKSBURG	11,226	3,957	7,233	36	3,276 D	35.2%	64.4%	35.4%	64.6%
7,042	GALAX	2,291	1,309	981	1	328 R	57.1%	42.8%	57.2%	42.8%
137,436	HAMPTON	65,307	18,732	46,432	143	27,700 D	28.7%	71.1%	28.7%	71.3%
48,914	HARRISONBURG	15,219	6,681	8,507	31	1,826 D	43.9%	55.9%	44.0%	56.0%
22,591	HOPEWELL	8,905	3,809	5,087	9	1,278 D	42.8%	57.1%	42.8%	57.2%
7,042	LEXINGTON	2,682	1,102	1,573	7	471 D	41.1%	58.7%	41.2%	58.8%
75,568	LYNCHBURG	35,813	19,601	16,129	83	3,472 R	54.7%	45.0%	54.9%	45.1%
37,821	MANASSAS	14,899	6,550	8,322	27	1,772 D	44.0%	55.9%	44.0%	56.0%
14,273	MANASSAS PARK	4,596	1,752	2,829	15	1,077 D	38.1%	61.6%	38.2%	61.8%
13,821	MARTINSVILLE	6,120	2,300	3,811	9	1,511 D	37.6%	62.3%	37.6%	62.4%
180,719	NEWPORT NEWS	78,275	27,332	50,800	143	23,468 D	34.9%	64.9%	35.0%	65.0%
242,803	NORFOLK	84,977	22,953	61,887	137	38,934 D	27.0%	72.8%	27.1%	72.9%
3,958	NORTON	1,480	859	620	1	239 R	58.0%	41.9%	58.1%	41.9%
32,420	PETERSBURG	15,486	1,569	13,882	35	12,313 D	10.1%	89.6%	10.2%	89.8%
12,150	POQUOSON	7,053	5,194	1,844	15	3,350 R	73.6%	26.1%	73.8%	26.2%
95,535	PORTSMOUTH	45,168	12,818	32,281	69	19,463 D	28.4%	71.5%	28.4%	71.6%
16,408	RADFORD	5,305	2,453	2,839	13	386 D	46.2%	53.5%	46.4%	53.6%
204,214	RICHMOND CITY	96,048	19,081	76,783	184	57,702 D	19.9%	79.9%	19.9%	80.1%
97,032	ROANOKE CITY	39,533	14,601	24,871	61	10,270 D	36.9%	62.9%	37.0%	63.0%
24,802	SALEM	12,188	7,032	5,138	18	1,894 R	57.7%	42.2%	57.8%	42.2%
23,746	STAUNTON	10,877	5,239	5,625	13	386 D	48.2%	51.7%	48.2%	51.8%
84,585	SUFFOLK	41,828	17,544	24,247	37	6,703 D	41.9%	58.0%	42.0%	58.0%
437,994	VIRGINIA BEACH	192,080	95,390	96,465	225	1,075 D	49.7%	50.2%	49.7%	50.3%
21,006	WAYNESBORO	8,662	4,775	3,873	14	902 R	55.1%	44.7%	55.2%	44.8%
14,068	WILLIAMSBURG	7,594	2,546	5,037	11	2,491 D	33.5%	66.3%	33.6%	66.4%
26,203	WINCHESTER	10,137	4,816	5,292	29	476 D	47.5%	52.2%	47.6%	52.4%
8,001,024	*TOTAL*	*3,802,196*	*1,785,542*	*2,010,067*	*6,587*	*224,525 D*	*47.0%*	*52.9%*	*47.0%*	*53.0%*

VIRGINIA

HOUSE OF REPRESENTATIVES

			Republican		Democratic		Other	Rep.-Dem.	Total Vote		Major Vote	
									Percentage			
CD	Year	Total Vote	Vote	Candidate	Vote	Candidate	Vote	Plurality	Rep.	Dem.	Rep.	Dem.
1	2012	356,806	200,845	WITTMAN, ROB*	147,036	COOK, ADAM M.	8,925	53,809 R	56.3%	41.2%	57.7%	42.3%
2	2012	309,222	166,231	RIGELL, SCOTT*	142,548	HIRSCHBIEL, PAUL O. JR.	443	23,683 R	53.8%	46.1%	53.8%	46.2%
3	2012	318,936	58,931	LONGO, DEAN J.	259,199	SCOTT, BOBBY*	806	200,268 D	18.5%	81.3%	18.5%	81.5%
4	2012	350,046	199,292	FORBES, J. RANDY*	150,190	WARD, ELLA P.	564	49,102 R	56.9%	42.9%	57.0%	43.0%
5	2012	348,111	193,009	HURT, ROBERT*	149,214	DOUGLASS, JOHN WADE	5,888	43,795 R	55.4%	42.9%	56.4%	43.6%
6	2012	323,893	211,278	GOODLATTE, BOB*	111,949	SCHMOOKLER, ANDY	666	99,329 R	65.2%	34.6%	65.4%	34.6%
7	2012	381,909	222,983	CANTOR, ERIC*	158,012	POWELL, E. WAYNE	914	64,971 R	58.4%	41.4%	58.5%	41.5%
8	2012	351,187	107,370	MURRAY, J. PATRICK	226,847	MORAN, JIM*	16,970	119,477 D	30.6%	64.6%	32.1%	67.9%
9	2012	301,658	184,882	GRIFFITH, H. MORGAN*	116,400	FLACCAVENTO, ANTHONY J.	376	68,482 R	61.3%	38.6%	61.4%	38.6%
10	2012	366,444	214,038	WOLF, FRANK R.*	142,024	CABRAL, KRISTIN A.	10,382	72,014 R	58.4%	38.8%	60.1%	39.9%
11	2012	332,243	117,902	PERKINS, CHRIS S.	202,606	CONNOLLY, GERALD E. "Gerry"*	11,735	84,704 D	35.5%	61.0%	36.8%	63.2%
TOTAL	2012	3,740,455	1,876,761		1,806,025		57,669	70,736 R	50.2%	48.3%	51.0%	49.0%

Note: An asterisk (*) denotes incumbent.

VIRGINIA

GENERAL AND PRIMARY ELECTIONS

GENERAL ELECTIONS: OTHER VOTE

President Other vote was 31,216 Libertarian (Gary E. Johnson), 13,058 Constitution (Virgil H. Goode), 8,627 Green (Jill Stein), 7,246 Write-in (Scattered Write-In)

Senator Other vote was 6,587 Write-in (Scattered Write-In)

House Other vote was:

CD 1 8,308 Independent Green (G. Gail Parker), 617 Write-in (Scattered Write-In)

CD 2 443 Write-in (Scattered Write-In)

CD 3 806 Write-in (Scattered Write-In)

CD 4 564 Write-in (Scattered Write-In)

CD 5 5,500 Independent Green (Kenneth J. Hildebrandt), 388 Write-in (Scattered Write-In)

CD 6 666 Write-in (Scattered Write-In)

CD 7 914 Write-in (Scattered Write-In)

CD 8 10,180 Independent (Jason J. Howell), 5,985 Independent Green (Janet Murphy), 805 Write-in (Scattered Write-In)

CD 9 376 Write-in (Scattered Write-In)

CD 10 9,855 Independent (J. Kevin Chisholm), 527 Write-in (Scattered Write-In)

CD 11 3,806 Independent (Mark T. Gibson), 3,027 Independent (Christopher F. Decarlo), 2,195 Green (Joe F. Galdo), 1,919 Independent Green (Peter M. Marchetti), 788 Write-in (Scattered Write-In)

PRIMARY ELECTIONS: SUPPLEMENTARY INFORMATION

Primary March 6, 2012 (President) **Registration** 5,216,248 No Party Registration
June 12, 2012 (Congress) (as of June 7, 2012
– includes 473,397
inactive registrants)

Primary Type Open—Any registered voter could participate in the primary of either party.

VIRGINIA

GENERAL AND PRIMARY ELECTIONS

	REPUBLICAN PRIMARIES			DEMOCRATIC PRIMARIES		
President	Romney, W. Mitt	158,119	59.5%			
	Paul, Ron	107,451	40.5%			
	TOTAL	265,570				
Senator	Allen, George W.	167,452	65.5%	Kaine, Tim	Unopposed	
	Radtke, Jamie L.	58,980	23.1%			
	Marshall, R. G. "Bob"	17,308	6.8%			
	Jackson, E. W.	12,086	4.7%			
	TOTAL	255,826				
Congressional District 1	Wittman, Rob*	Unopposed		Cook, Adam M.	Unopposed	
Congressional District 2	Rigell, Scott*	Unopposed		Hirschbiel, Paul O. Jr.	Unopposed	
Congressional District 3	Longo, Dean J.	Unopposed		Scott, Bobby*	Unopposed	
Congressional District 4	Forbes, J. Randy*	26,879	89.7%	Ward, Ella P.	5,830	85.3%
	Girard, R.M. "Bonnie"	3,081	10.3%	Elliott, Joe T. Jr.	1,005	14.7%
	TOTAL	29,960		TOTAL	6,835	
Congressional District 5	Hurt, Robert*	Unopposed		Douglass, John Wade	Unopposed	
Congressional District 6	Goodlatte, Bob*	21,808	66.5%	Schmookler, Andy	Unopposed	
	Kwiatkowski, Karen U.	10,991	33.5%			
	TOTAL	32,799				
Congressional District 7	Cantor, Eric*	37,369	79.4%	Powell, E. Wayne	Unopposed	
	Bayne, Floyd C.	9,668	20.6%			
	TOTAL	47,037				
Congressional District 8	Murray, J. Patrick	Unopposed		Moran, Jim*	23,018	74.2%
				Shuttleworth, Bruce B.	8,006	25.8%
				TOTAL	31,024	
Congressional District 9	Griffith, H. Morgan*	Unopposed		Flaccavento, Anthony J.	Unopposed	
Congressional District 10	Wolf, Frank R.*	Unopposed		Cabral, Kristin A.	Unopposed	
Congressional District 11	Perkins, Chris S.	11,600	62.8%	Connolly, Gerald E. "Gerry"*	Unopposed	
	Vaughn, Ken L.	6,866	37.2%			
	TOTAL	18,466				

Note: An asterisk (*) denotes incumbent. The state parties and local party committees traditionally have the option of holding a primary or nominating candidates by convention or committee. If a primary was called and only one candidate filed to run in it, then no primary was held. Candidates nominated by convention in 2012 for U.S. House were all Democrats: 1st district, Cook; 5th district, Douglass; 7th district, Powell; 9th district, Flaccavento; 10th district, Cabral.

WASHINGTON

Congressional districts first established for elections held in 2012
10 members

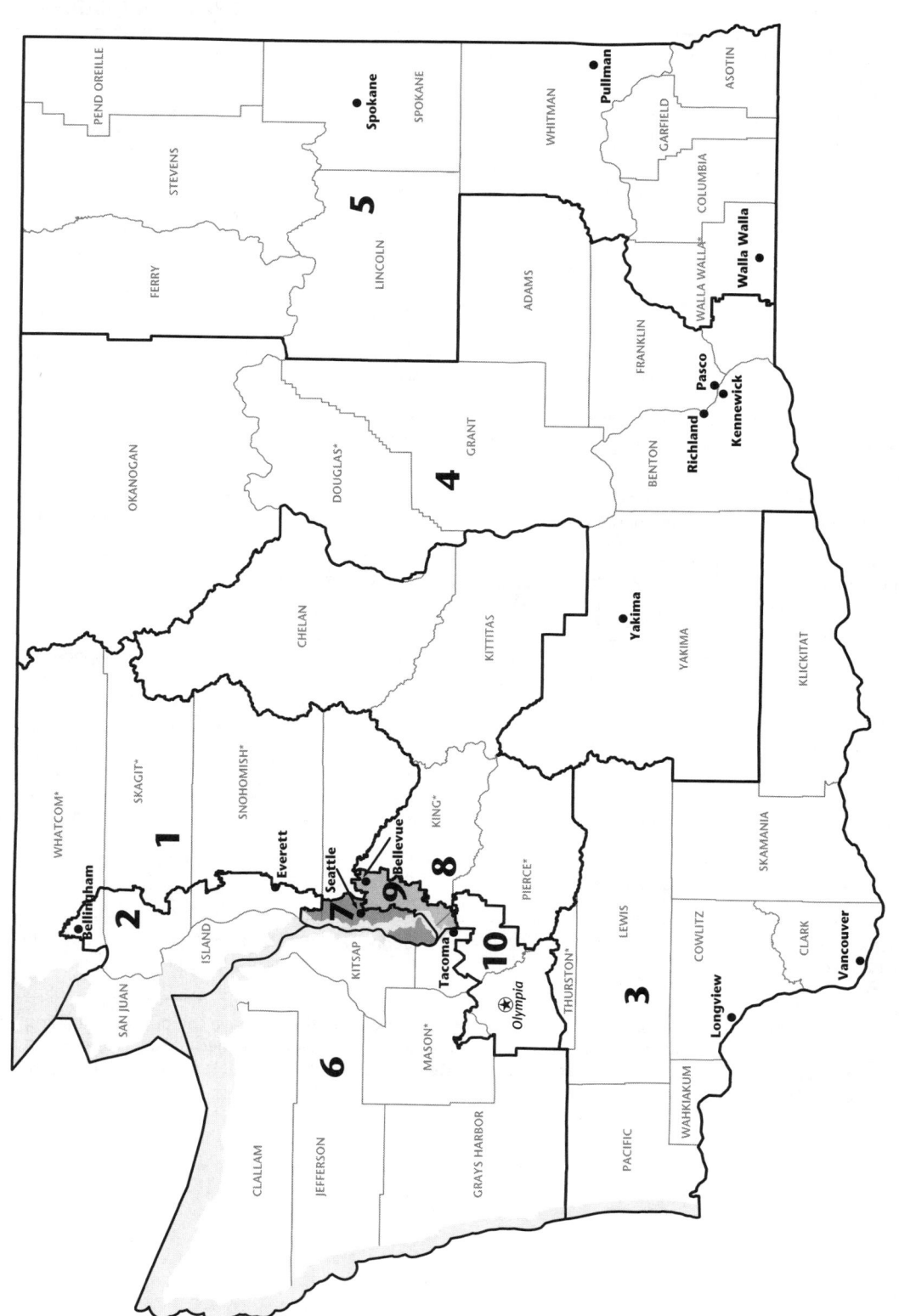

* Asterisk indicates a county whose boundaries include parts of two or more Congressional districts.

WASHINGTON
Seattle Area

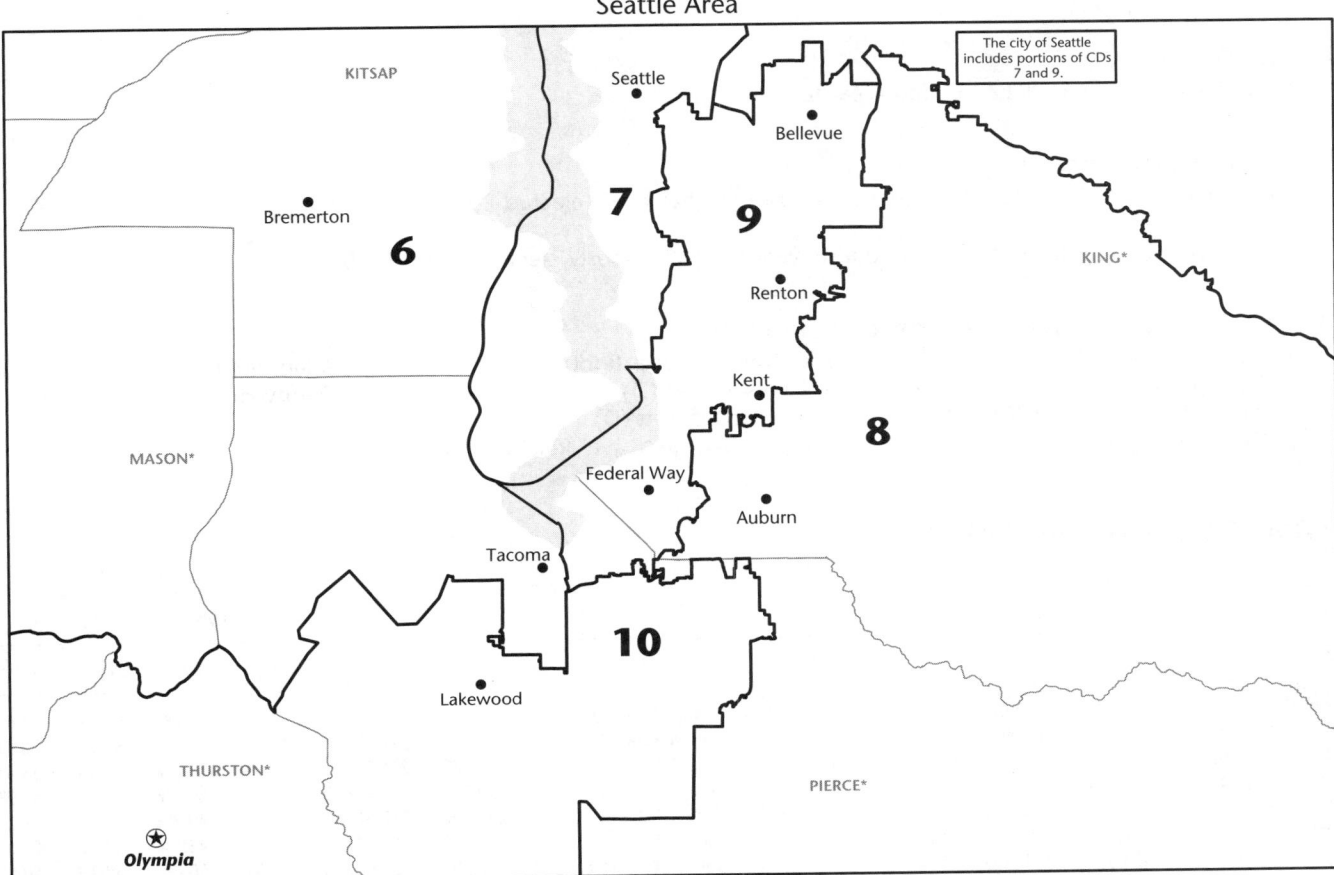

The city of Seattle includes portions of CDs 7 and 9.

* Asterisk indicates a county whose boundaries include parts of two or more Congressional districts.

WASHINGTON

GOVERNOR
Jay Inslee (D). Elected 2012 to a four-year term.

SENATORS (2 Democrats)
Patty Murray (D). Reelected 2010 to a six-year term. Previously elected 2004, 1998, 1992.

Maria Cantwell (D). Reelected 2012 to a six-year term. Previously elected 2006, 2000.

REPRESENTATIVES (4 Republicans, 6 Democrats)
1. Suzan DelBene (D)
2. Rick Larsen (D)
3. Jaime Herrera Beutler (R)
4. Doc Hastings (R)
5. Cathy McMorris Rodgers (R)
6. Derek Kilmer (D)
7. Jim McDermott (D)
8. David George "Dave" Reichert (R)
9. Adam Smith (D)
10. Denny Heck (D)

POSTWAR VOTE FOR PRESIDENT

| | | Republican | | Democratic | | Other Vote | Rep.-Dem. Plurality | Percentage | | | |
| | | | | | | | | Total Vote | | Major Vote | |
Year	Total Vote	Vote	Candidate	Vote	Candidate			Rep.	Dem.	Rep.	Dem.
2012	3,125,516	1,290,670	Romney, W. Mitt	1,755,396	Obama, Barack H.*	79,450	464,726 D	41.3%	56.2%	42.4%	57.6%
2008	3,036,878	1,229,216	McCain, John S. III	1,750,848	Obama, Barack H.	56,814	521,632 D	40.5%	57.7%	41.2%	58.8%
2004	2,859,084	1,304,894	Bush, George W.*	1,510,201	Kerry, John F.	43,989	205,307 D	45.6%	52.8%	46.4%	53.6%
2000**	2,487,433	1,108,864	Bush, George W.	1,247,652	Gore, Albert Jr.	130,917	138,788 D	44.6%	50.2%	47.1%	52.9%
1996**	2,253,837	840,712	Dole, Robert "Bob"	1,123,323	Clinton, Bill*	289,802	282,611 D	37.3%	49.8%	42.8%	57.2%
1992**	2,288,230	731,234	Bush, George H.*	993,037	Clinton, Bill	563,959	261,803 D	32.0%	43.4%	42.4%	57.6%
1988	1,865,253	903,835	Bush, George H.	933,516	Dukakis, Michael S.	27,902	29,681 D	48.5%	50.0%	49.2%	50.8%
1984	1,883,910	1,051,670	Reagan, Ronald*	807,352	Mondale, Walter F.	24,888	244,318 R	55.8%	42.9%	56.6%	43.4%
1980**	1,742,394	865,244	Reagan, Ronald	650,193	Carter, Jimmy*	226,957	215,051 R	49.7%	37.3%	57.1%	42.9%
1976	1,555,534	777,732	Ford, Gerald R.*	717,323	Carter, Jimmy	60,479	60,409 R	50.0%	46.1%	52.0%	48.0%
1972	1,470,847	837,135	Nixon, Richard M.*	568,334	McGovern, George S.	65,378	268,801 R	56.9%	38.6%	59.6%	40.4%
1968**	1,304,281	588,510	Nixon, Richard M.	616,037	Humphrey, Hubert H. Jr.	99,734	27,527 D	45.1%	47.2%	48.9%	51.1%
1964	1,258,556	470,366	Goldwater, Barry M. Sr.	779,881	Johnson, Lyndon B.*	8,309	309,515 D	37.4%	62.0%	37.6%	62.4%
1960	1,241,572	629,273	Nixon, Richard M.	599,298	Kennedy, John F.	13,001	29,975 R	50.7%	48.3%	51.2%	48.8%
1956	1,150,889	620,430	Eisenhower, Dwight D.*	523,002	Stevenson, Adlai E. II	7,457	97,428 R	53.9%	45.4%	54.3%	45.7%
1952	1,102,708	599,107	Eisenhower, Dwight D.	492,845	Stevenson, Adlai E. II	10,756	106,262 R	54.3%	44.7%	54.9%	45.1%
1948	905,058	386,314	Dewey, Thomas E.	476,165	Truman, Harry S.*	42,579	89,851 D	42.7%	52.6%	44.8%	55.2%

Note: An asterisk (*) denotes incumbent. **In past elections, the other vote included: 2000 - 103,002 Green (Ralph Nader); 1996 - 201,003 Reform (Ross Perot); 1992 - 541,780 Independent (Perot); 1980 - 185,073 Independent (John Anderson); 1968 - 96,990 American Independent (George Wallace).

WASHINGTON

POSTWAR VOTE FOR GOVERNOR

Year	Total Vote	Republican		Democratic		Other Vote	Rep.-Dem. Plurality	Percentage			
								Total Vote		Major Vote	
		Vote	Candidate	Vote	Candidate			Rep.	Dem.	Rep.	Dem.
2012	3,071,047	1,488,245	McKenna, Rob	1,582,802	Inslee, Jay		94,557 D	48.5%	51.5%	48.5%	51.5%
2008	3,002,862	1,404,124	Rossi, Dino	1,598,738	Gregoire, Christine*		194,614 D	46.8%	53.2%	46.8%	53.2%
2004**	2,810,058	1,373,232	Rossi, Dino	1,373,361	Gregoire, Christine	63,465	129 D	48.9%	48.9%	50.0%	50.0%
2000	2,469,852	980,060	Carlson, John	1,441,973	Locke, Gary*	47,819	461,913 D	39.7%	58.4%	40.5%	59.5%
1996	2,237,030	940,538	Craswell, Ellen	1,296,492	Locke, Gary		355,954 D	42.0%	58.0%	42.0%	58.0%
1992	2,270,826	1,086,216	Eikenberry, Ken	1,184,315	Lowry, Mike	295	98,099 D	47.8%	52.2%	47.8%	52.2%
1988	1,874,929	708,481	Williams, Bob	1,166,448	Gardner, Booth*		457,967 D	37.8%	62.2%	37.8%	62.2%
1984	1,888,987	881,994	Spellman, John D.*	1,006,993	Gardner, Booth		124,999 D	46.7%	53.3%	46.7%	53.3%
1980	1,730,896	981,083	Spellman, John D.	749,813	McDermott, Jim		231,270 R	56.7%	43.3%	56.7%	43.3%
1976	1,546,380	687,039	Spellman, John D.	821,797	Ray, Dixy Lee	37,544	134,758 D	44.4%	53.1%	45.5%	54.5%
1972	1,472,542	747,825	Evans, Daniel J.*	630,613	Rosellini, Albert D.	94,104	117,212 R	50.8%	42.8%	54.3%	45.7%
1968	1,265,354	692,377	Evans, Daniel J.*	560,262	O'Connell, John J.	12,715	132,115 R	54.7%	44.3%	55.3%	44.7%
1964	1,250,274	697,256	Evans, Daniel J.	548,692	Rosellini, Albert D.*	4,326	148,564 R	55.8%	43.9%	56.0%	44.0%
1960	1,215,748	594,122	Andrews, Lloyd	611,987	Rosellini, Albert D.*	9,639	17,865 D	48.9%	50.3%	49.3%	50.7%
1956	1,128,977	508,041	Anderson, Emmett T.	616,773	Rosellini, Albert D.	4,163	108,732 D	45.0%	54.6%	45.2%	54.8%
1952	1,078,497	567,822	Langlie, Arthur B.*	510,675	Mitchell, Hugh B.		57,147 R	52.6%	47.4%	52.6%	47.4%
1948	883,141	445,958	Langlie, Arthur B.	417,035	Wallgren, Monrad C.*	20,148	28,923 R	50.5%	47.2%	51.7%	48.3%

Note: An asterisk (*) denotes incumbent. **In 2004, the initial official vote count put Republican Dino Rossi ahead by 261 votes. A machine recount reduced Rossi's margin to 42 votes. A subsequent manual recount gave Democrat Christine Gregoire the election by a margin of 129 votes (see above), and she was inaugurated governor.

POSTWAR VOTE FOR SENATOR

Year	Total Vote	Republican		Democratic		Other Vote	Rep.-Dem. Plurality	Percentage			
								Total Vote		Major Vote	
		Vote	Candidate	Vote	Candidate			Rep.	Dem.	Rep.	Dem.
2012	3,069,417	1,213,924	Baumgartner, Michael	1,855,493	Cantwell, Maria*		641,569 D	39.5%	60.5%	39.5%	60.5%
2010	2,511,094	1,196,164	Rossi, Dino	1,314,930	Murray, Patty*		118,766 D	47.6%	52.4%	47.6%	52.4%
2006	2,083,734	832,106	McGavick, Mike	1,184,659	Cantwell, Maria*	66,969	352,553 D	39.9%	56.9%	41.3%	58.7%
2004	2,818,651	1,204,584	Nethercutt, George R.	1,549,708	Murray, Patty*	64,359	345,124 D	42.7%	55.0%	43.7%	56.3%
2000	2,461,379	1,197,208	Gorton, Slade*	1,199,437	Cantwell, Maria	64,734	2,229 D	48.6%	48.7%	50.0%	50.0%
1998	1,888,561	785,377	Smith, Linda	1,103,184	Murray, Patty*		317,807 D	41.6%	58.4%	41.6%	58.4%
1994	1,700,173	947,821	Gorton, Slade*	752,352	Sims, Ron		195,469 R	55.7%	44.3%	55.7%	44.3%
1992	2,219,162	1,020,829	Chandler, Rod	1,197,973	Murray, Patty	360	177,144 D	46.0%	54.0%	46.0%	54.0%
1988	1,848,542	944,359	Gorton, Slade	904,183	Lowry, Mike		40,176 R	51.1%	48.9%	51.1%	48.9%
1986	1,337,367	650,931	Gorton, Slade*	677,471	Adams, Brock	8,965	26,540 D	48.7%	50.7%	49.0%	51.0%
1983S	1,213,307	672,326	Evans, Daniel J.*	540,981	Lowry, Mike		131,345 R	55.4%	44.6%	55.4%	44.6%
1982	1,368,476	332,273	Jewett, Doug	943,655	Jackson, Henry M.*	92,548	611,382 D	24.3%	69.0%	26.0%	74.0%
1980	1,728,369	936,317	Gorton, Slade	792,052	Magnuson, Warren G.*		144,265 R	54.2%	45.8%	54.2%	45.8%
1976	1,491,111	361,546	Brown, George M.	1,071,219	Jackson, Henry M.*	58,346	709,673 D	24.2%	71.8%	25.2%	74.8%
1974	1,007,847	363,626	Metcalf, Jack	611,811	Magnuson, Warren G.*	32,410	248,185 D	36.1%	60.7%	37.3%	62.7%
1970	1,066,807	170,790	Elicker, Charles W.	879,385	Jackson, Henry M.*	16,632	708,595 D	16.0%	82.4%	16.3%	83.7%
1968	1,236,063	435,894	Metcalf, Jack	796,183	Magnuson, Warren G.*	3,986	360,289 D	35.3%	64.4%	35.4%	64.6%
1964	1,213,088	337,138	Andrews, Lloyd J.	875,950	Jackson, Henry M.*		538,812 D	27.8%	72.2%	27.8%	72.2%
1962	943,229	446,204	Christensen, Richard G.	491,365	Magnuson, Warren G.*	5,660	45,161 D	47.3%	52.1%	47.6%	52.4%
1958	886,822	278,271	Bantz, William B.	597,040	Jackson, Henry M.*	11,511	318,769 D	31.4%	67.3%	31.8%	68.2%
1956	1,122,217	436,652	Langlie, Arthur B.	685,565	Magnuson, Warren G.*		248,913 D	38.9%	61.1%	38.9%	61.1%
1952	1,058,735	460,884	Cain, Harry P.*	595,288	Jackson, Henry M.	2,563	134,404 D	43.5%	56.2%	43.6%	56.4%
1950	744,783	342,464	Williams, Walter	397,719	Magnuson, Warren G.*	4,600	55,255 D	46.0%	53.4%	46.3%	53.7%
1946	660,342	358,847	Cain, Harry P.	298,683	Mitchell, Hugh B.	2,812	60,164 R	54.3%	45.2%	54.6%	45.4%

Note: An asterisk (*) denotes incumbent. **The 1983 election was for a short term to fill a vacancy.

WASHINGTON

PRESIDENT 2012

2010 Census Population	County	Total Vote	Republican (Romney)	Democratic (Obama)	Other	Rep.-Dem. Plurality		Percentage			
								Total Vote		Major Vote	
								Rep.	Dem.	Rep.	Dem.
18,728	ADAMS	4,793	3,171	1,540	82	1,631	R	66.2%	32.1%	67.3%	32.7%
21,623	ASOTIN	9,901	5,654	4,003	244	1,651	R	57.1%	40.4%	58.5%	41.5%
175,177	BENTON	79,559	49,461	28,145	1,953	21,316	R	62.2%	35.4%	63.7%	36.3%
72,453	CHELAN	32,250	18,402	13,112	736	5,290	R	57.1%	40.7%	58.4%	41.6%
71,404	CLALLAM	38,066	18,437	18,580	1,049	143	D	48.4%	48.8%	49.8%	50.2%
425,363	CLARK	190,805	92,951	93,382	4,472	431	D	48.7%	48.9%	49.9%	50.1%
4,078	COLUMBIA	2,259	1,568	645	46	923	R	69.4%	28.6%	70.9%	29.1%
102,410	COWLITZ	44,620	20,746	22,726	1,148	1,980	D	46.5%	50.9%	47.7%	52.3%
38,431	DOUGLAS	14,942	9,425	5,166	351	4,259	R	63.1%	34.6%	64.6%	35.4%
7,551	FERRY	3,440	1,995	1,294	151	701	R	58.0%	37.6%	60.7%	39.3%
78,163	FRANKLIN	22,643	13,748	8,398	497	5,350	R	60.7%	37.1%	62.1%	37.9%
2,266	GARFIELD	1,278	913	336	29	577	R	71.4%	26.3%	73.1%	26.9%
89,120	GRANT	27,558	17,852	8,950	756	8,902	R	64.8%	32.5%	66.6%	33.4%
72,797	GRAYS HARBOR	28,684	11,914	15,960	810	4,046	D	41.5%	55.6%	42.7%	57.3%
78,506	ISLAND	42,099	19,605	21,478	1,016	1,873	D	46.6%	51.0%	47.7%	52.3%
29,872	JEFFERSON	19,829	6,405	12,739	685	6,334	D	32.3%	64.2%	33.5%	66.5%
1,931,249	KING	967,154	275,700	668,004	23,450	392,304	D	28.5%	69.1%	29.2%	70.8%
251,133	KITSAP	123,367	52,846	67,277	3,244	14,431	D	42.8%	54.5%	44.0%	56.0%
40,915	KITTITAS	18,171	9,782	7,949	440	1,833	R	53.8%	43.7%	55.2%	44.8%
20,318	KLICKITAT	10,274	5,316	4,598	360	718	R	51.7%	44.8%	53.6%	46.4%
75,455	LEWIS	34,044	20,452	12,664	928	7,788	R	60.1%	37.2%	61.8%	38.2%
10,570	LINCOLN	5,872	4,063	1,673	136	2,390	R	69.2%	28.5%	70.8%	29.2%
60,699	MASON	28,235	12,761	14,764	710	2,003	D	45.2%	52.3%	46.4%	53.6%
41,120	OKANOGAN	16,846	9,221	7,108	517	2,113	R	54.7%	42.2%	56.5%	43.5%
20,920	PACIFIC	10,524	4,499	5,711	314	1,212	D	42.7%	54.3%	44.1%	55.9%
13,001	PEND OREILLE	6,668	3,952	2,508	208	1,444	R	59.3%	37.6%	61.2%	38.8%
795,225	PIERCE	342,910	148,467	186,430	8,013	37,963	D	43.3%	54.4%	44.3%	55.7%
15,769	SAN JUAN	10,594	3,111	7,125	358	4,014	D	29.4%	67.3%	30.4%	69.6%
116,901	SKAGIT	55,269	25,071	28,688	1,510	3,617	D	45.4%	51.9%	46.6%	53.4%
11,066	SKAMANIA	5,466	2,687	2,628	151	59	R	49.2%	48.1%	50.6%	49.4%
713,335	SNOHOMISH	329,817	133,016	188,516	8,285	55,500	D	40.3%	57.2%	41.4%	58.6%
471,221	SPOKANE	223,830	115,285	102,295	6,250	12,990	R	51.5%	45.7%	53.0%	47.0%
43,531	STEVENS	22,161	13,691	7,762	708	5,929	R	61.8%	35.0%	63.8%	36.2%
252,264	THURSTON	127,063	49,287	74,037	3,739	24,750	D	38.8%	58.3%	40.0%	60.0%
3,978	WAHKIAKUM	2,294	1,119	1,094	81	25	R	48.8%	47.7%	50.6%	49.4%
58,781	WALLA WALLA	25,108	14,648	9,768	692	4,880	R	58.3%	38.9%	60.0%	40.0%
201,140	WHATCOM	103,029	42,703	57,089	3,237	14,386	D	41.4%	55.4%	42.8%	57.2%
44,776	WHITMAN	17,121	8,507	8,037	577	470	R	49.7%	46.9%	51.4%	48.6%
243,231	YAKIMA	76,973	42,239	33,217	1,517	9,022	R	54.9%	43.2%	56.0%	44.0%
6,724,540	TOTAL	3,125,516	1,290,670	1,755,396	79,450	464,726	D	41.3%	56.2%	42.4%	57.6%

WASHINGTON

GOVERNOR 2012

2010 Census Population	County	Total Vote	Republican (McKenna)	Democratic (Inslee)	Other	Rep.-Dem. Plurality	Total Vote Rep.	Total Vote Dem.	Major Vote Rep.	Major Vote Dem.
18,728	ADAMS	4,728	3,320	1,408		1,912 R	70.2%	29.8%	70.2%	29.8%
21,623	ASOTIN	9,704	5,677	4,027		1,650 R	58.5%	41.5%	58.5%	41.5%
175,177	BENTON	78,048	50,757	27,291		23,466 R	65.0%	35.0%	65.0%	35.0%
72,453	CHELAN	31,907	20,291	11,616		8,675 R	63.6%	36.4%	63.6%	36.4%
71,404	CLALLAM	37,537	20,021	17,516		2,505 R	53.3%	46.7%	53.3%	46.7%
425,363	CLARK	184,863	98,131	86,732		11,399 R	53.1%	46.9%	53.1%	46.9%
4,078	COLUMBIA	2,221	1,565	656		909 R	70.5%	29.5%	70.5%	29.5%
102,410	COWLITZ	43,663	22,612	21,051		1,561 R	51.8%	48.2%	51.8%	48.2%
38,431	DOUGLAS	14,885	10,139	4,746		5,393 R	68.1%	31.9%	68.1%	31.9%
7,551	FERRY	3,420	2,121	1,299		822 R	62.0%	38.0%	62.0%	38.0%
78,163	FRANKLIN	22,413	14,232	8,181		6,051 R	63.5%	36.5%	63.5%	36.5%
2,266	GARFIELD	1,253	920	333		587 R	73.4%	26.6%	73.4%	26.6%
89,120	GRANT	27,396	18,742	8,654		10,088 R	68.4%	31.6%	68.4%	31.6%
72,797	GRAYS HARBOR	28,469	13,978	14,491		513 D	49.1%	50.9%	49.1%	50.9%
78,506	ISLAND	41,406	22,082	19,324		2,758 R	53.3%	46.7%	53.3%	46.7%
29,872	JEFFERSON	19,546	7,370	12,176		4,806 D	37.7%	62.3%	37.7%	62.3%
1,931,249	KING	947,592	356,713	590,879		234,166 D	37.6%	62.4%	37.6%	62.4%
251,133	KITSAP	121,839	61,261	60,578		683 R	50.3%	49.7%	50.3%	49.7%
40,915	KITTITAS	17,889	10,752	7,137		3,615 R	60.1%	39.9%	60.1%	39.9%
20,318	KLICKITAT	10,080	5,638	4,442		1,196 R	55.9%	44.1%	55.9%	44.1%
75,455	LEWIS	33,867	22,002	11,865		10,137 R	65.0%	35.0%	65.0%	35.0%
10,570	LINCOLN	5,804	4,088	1,716		2,372 R	70.4%	29.6%	70.4%	29.6%
60,699	MASON	27,883	14,708	13,175		1,533 R	52.7%	47.3%	52.7%	47.3%
41,120	OKANOGAN	16,668	9,909	6,759		3,150 R	59.4%	40.6%	59.4%	40.6%
20,920	PACIFIC	10,399	5,020	5,379		359 D	48.3%	51.7%	48.3%	51.7%
13,001	PEND OREILLE	6,590	4,148	2,442		1,706 R	62.9%	37.1%	62.9%	37.1%
795,225	PIERCE	338,289	174,078	164,211		9,867 R	51.5%	48.5%	51.5%	48.5%
15,769	SAN JUAN	10,434	3,671	6,763		3,092 D	35.2%	64.8%	35.2%	64.8%
116,901	SKAGIT	54,681	28,803	25,878		2,925 R	52.7%	47.3%	52.7%	47.3%
11,066	SKAMANIA	5,301	2,867	2,434		433 R	54.1%	45.9%	54.1%	45.9%
713,335	SNOHOMISH	324,892	158,440	166,452		8,012 D	48.8%	51.2%	48.8%	51.2%
471,221	SPOKANE	219,248	123,894	95,354		28,540 R	56.5%	43.5%	56.5%	43.5%
43,531	STEVENS	21,980	14,554	7,426		7,128 R	66.2%	33.8%	66.2%	33.8%
252,264	THURSTON	125,301	57,948	67,353		9,405 D	46.2%	53.8%	46.2%	53.8%
3,978	WAHKIAKUM	2,251	1,287	964		323 R	57.2%	42.8%	57.2%	42.8%
58,781	WALLA WALLA	24,591	15,238	9,353		5,885 R	62.0%	38.0%	62.0%	38.0%
201,140	WHATCOM	100,939	47,340	53,599		6,259 D	46.9%	53.1%	46.9%	53.1%
44,776	WHITMAN	16,772	9,421	7,351		2,070 R	56.2%	43.8%	56.2%	43.8%
243,231	YAKIMA	76,298	44,507	31,791		12,716 R	58.3%	41.7%	58.3%	41.7%
6,724,540	TOTAL	3,071,047	1,488,245	1,582,802		94,557 D	48.5%	51.5%	48.5%	51.5%

WASHINGTON

SENATOR 2012

2010 Census Population	County	Total Vote	Republican (Baumgartner)	Democratic (Cantwell)	Other	Rep.-Dem. Plurality	Percentage			
							Total Vote		Major Vote	
							Rep.	Dem.	Rep.	Dem.
18,728	ADAMS	4,731	2,872	1,859		1,013 R	60.7%	39.3%	60.7%	39.3%
21,623	ASOTIN	9,756	5,193	4,563		630 R	53.2%	46.8%	53.2%	46.8%
175,177	BENTON	78,219	44,828	33,391		11,437 R	57.3%	42.7%	57.3%	42.7%
72,453	CHELAN	31,700	16,808	14,892		1,916 R	53.0%	47.0%	53.0%	47.0%
71,404	CLALLAM	37,583	17,331	20,252		2,921 D	46.1%	53.9%	46.1%	53.9%
425,363	CLARK	185,607	87,150	98,457		11,307 D	47.0%	53.0%	47.0%	53.0%
4,078	COLUMBIA	2,237	1,410	827		583 R	63.0%	37.0%	63.0%	37.0%
102,410	COWLITZ	43,990	19,170	24,820		5,650 D	43.6%	56.4%	43.6%	56.4%
38,431	DOUGLAS	14,798	8,570	6,228		2,342 R	57.9%	42.1%	57.9%	42.1%
7,551	FERRY	3,421	1,927	1,494		433 R	56.3%	43.7%	56.3%	43.7%
78,163	FRANKLIN	22,475	12,786	9,689		3,097 R	56.9%	43.1%	56.9%	43.1%
2,266	GARFIELD	1,245	792	453		339 R	63.6%	36.4%	63.6%	36.4%
89,120	GRANT	27,432	16,811	10,621		6,190 R	61.3%	38.7%	61.3%	38.7%
72,797	GRAYS HARBOR	28,462	10,971	17,491		6,520 D	38.5%	61.5%	38.5%	61.5%
78,506	ISLAND	41,499	18,475	23,024		4,549 D	44.5%	55.5%	44.5%	55.5%
29,872	JEFFERSON	19,585	6,114	13,471		7,357 D	31.2%	68.8%	31.2%	68.8%
1,931,249	KING	945,101	262,034	683,067		421,033 D	27.7%	72.3%	27.7%	72.3%
251,133	KITSAP	121,546	49,890	71,656		21,766 D	41.0%	59.0%	41.0%	59.0%
40,915	KITTITAS	17,769	9,023	8,746		277 R	50.8%	49.2%	50.8%	49.2%
20,318	KLICKITAT	10,105	4,990	5,115		125 D	49.4%	50.6%	49.4%	50.6%
75,455	LEWIS	33,584	19,139	14,445		4,694 R	57.0%	43.0%	57.0%	43.0%
10,570	LINCOLN	5,811	3,654	2,157		1,497 R	62.9%	37.1%	62.9%	37.1%
60,699	MASON	27,942	11,885	16,057		4,172 D	42.5%	57.5%	42.5%	57.5%
41,120	OKANOGAN	16,646	8,683	7,963		720 R	52.2%	47.8%	52.2%	47.8%
20,920	PACIFIC	10,390	4,067	6,323		2,256 D	39.1%	60.9%	39.1%	60.9%
13,001	PEND OREILLE	6,636	3,769	2,867		902 R	56.8%	43.2%	56.8%	43.2%
795,225	PIERCE	337,715	135,888	201,827		65,939 D	40.2%	59.8%	40.2%	59.8%
15,769	SAN JUAN	10,446	3,095	7,351		4,256 D	29.6%	70.4%	29.6%	70.4%
116,901	SKAGIT	54,535	23,900	30,635		6,735 D	43.8%	56.2%	43.8%	56.2%
11,066	SKAMANIA	5,313	2,490	2,823		333 D	46.9%	53.1%	46.9%	53.1%
713,335	SNOHOMISH	324,856	128,322	196,534		68,212 D	39.5%	60.5%	39.5%	60.5%
471,221	SPOKANE	220,405	110,372	110,033		339 R	50.1%	49.9%	50.1%	49.9%
43,531	STEVENS	22,112	13,441	8,671		4,770 R	60.8%	39.2%	60.8%	39.2%
252,264	THURSTON	124,917	46,449	78,468		32,019 D	37.2%	62.8%	37.2%	62.8%
3,978	WAHKIAKUM	2,265	1,012	1,253		241 D	44.7%	55.3%	44.7%	55.3%
58,781	WALLA WALLA	24,681	13,217	11,464		1,753 R	53.6%	46.4%	53.6%	46.4%
201,140	WHATCOM	100,756	40,818	59,938		19,120 D	40.5%	59.5%	40.5%	59.5%
44,776	WHITMAN	16,847	8,463	8,384		79 R	50.2%	49.8%	50.2%	49.8%
243,231	YAKIMA	76,299	38,115	38,184		69 D	50.0%	50.0%	50.0%	50.0%
6,724,540	TOTAL	3,069,417	1,213,924	1,855,493		641,569 D	39.5%	60.5%	39.5%	60.5%

WASHINGTON

HOUSE OF REPRESENTATIVES

			Republican		Democratic		Other Vote	Rep.-Dem. Plurality	Percentage			
									Total Vote		Major Vote	
CD	Year	Total Vote	Vote	Candidate	Vote	Candidate			Rep.	Dem.	Rep.	Dem.
1	2012	328,212	151,187	KOSTER, JOHN	177,025	DELBENE, SUZAN		25,838 D	46.1%	53.9%	46.1%	53.9%
2	2012	302,291	117,465	MATTHEWS, DAN	184,826	LARSEN, RICK*		67,361 D	38.9%	61.1%	38.9%	61.1%
3	2012	293,884	177,446	BEUTLER, JAIME HERRERA*	116,438	HAUGEN, JON T.		61,008 R	60.4%	39.6%	60.4%	39.6%
4	2012	233,689	154,749	HASTINGS, DOC*	78,940	BAECHLER, MARY		75,809 R	66.2%	33.8%	66.2%	33.8%
5	2012	308,578	191,066	RODGERS, CATHY MCMORRIS*	117,512	COWAN, RICH		73,554 R	61.9%	38.1%	61.9%	38.1%
6	2012	316,386	129,725	DRISCOLL, BILL	186,661	KILMER, DEREK		56,936 D	41.0%	59.0%	41.0%	59.0%
7	2012	374,580	76,212	BEMIS, RON	298,368	MCDERMOTT, JIM*		222,156 D	20.3%	79.7%	20.3%	79.7%
8	2012	302,090	180,204	REICHERT, DAVID GEORGE "DAVE"*	121,886	PORTERFIELD, KAREN		58,318 R	59.7%	40.3%	59.7%	40.3%
9	2012	268,139	76,105	POSTMA, JAMES	192,034	SMITH, ADAM*		115,929 D	28.4%	71.6%	28.4%	71.6%
10	2012	278,417	115,381	MURI, RICHARD	163,036	HECK, DENNY		47,655 D	41.4%	58.6%	41.4%	58.6%
TOTAL	2012	3,006,266	1,369,540		1,636,726			267,186 D	45.6%	54.4%	45.6%	54.4%

Note: An asterisk (*) denotes incumbent.

WASHINGTON

GENERAL AND PRIMARY ELECTIONS

GENERAL ELECTIONS: OTHER VOTE

President — Other vote was 42,202 Libertarian (Gary E. Johnson), 20,928 Green (Jill Stein), 8,851 Constitution (Virgil H. Goode), 4,946 Justice (Ross C. "Rocky" Anderson), 1,318 Socialism and Liberation (Peta Lindsay), 1,205 Socialist Workers Party (James Harris)

Senator — Due to Washington's primary system, there were only two candidates in the general election.

PRIMARY ELECTIONS: SUPPLEMENTARY INFORMATION

Primary August 7, 2012   **Registration** (as of August 7, 2012)   3,731,657   No Party Registration

Primary Type Open—Any registered voter could participate in the primary.

ALL-PARTY PRIMARIES

Senator	Cantwell, Maria* (Democrat)	772,058	55.7%
	Baumgartner, Michael (Republican)	417,141	30.1%
	Coday, Art (Republican)	79,727	5.7%
	Wilson, Timmy "Doc" (Democrat)	31,817	2.3%
	Jackson, Chuck (Republican)	25,983	1.9%
	Stockwell, Glen R. "Stocky" (Republican)	25,793	1.9%
	Mike The Mover (Republican)	19,535	1.4%
	Baker, Will (Reform)	15,005	1.1%
	TOTAL	1,387,059	
Governor	Inslee, Jay (Democrat)	664,534	47.1%
	McKenna, Rob (Republican)	604,872	42.9%
	Hadian, Shahram (Republican)	46,169	3.3%
	Hill, Rob (Democrat)	45,453	3.2%
	White, James (Independent Party)	13,764	1.0%
	Joubert, Christian Pierre (No Party Affiliation)	10,457	0.7%
	Sorgen, L. Dale (Independent Party)	9,734	0.7%
	Sampson, Max (Republican)	8,753	0.6%
	Lopez, Javier O. (Republican)	6,131	0.4%
	TOTAL	1,409,867	

WASHINGTON

GENERAL AND PRIMARY ELECTIONS

ALL-PARTY PRIMARIES

Congressional District 1			
	Koster, John (Republican)	67,185	44.9%
	DelBene, Suzan (Democrat)	33,670	22.5%
	Burner, Darcy (Democrat)	20,844	13.9%
	Ruderman, Laura (Democrat)	10,582	7.1%
	Hobbs, Steve (Democrat)	10,279	6.9%
	Rauniyar, Darshan (Democrat)	4,134	2.8%
	Ishmael, Larry W. (Independent)	3,062	2.0%
	TOTAL	149,756	

Congressional District 2			
	Larsen, Rick* (Democrat)	79,632	57.2%
	Matthews, Dan (Republican)	39,956	28.7%
	Shoop, John C.W. (Republican)	8,130	5.8%
	Lapointe, Mike (Other)	5,806	4.2%
	Olson, Eli (Republican)	3,373	2.4%
	Johnson, Glen S. (No Party Affiliation)	2,289	1.6%
	TOTAL	139,186	

Congressional District 3			
	Beutler, Jaime Herrera* (Republican)	68,603	56.5%
	Haugen, Jon T. (Democrat)	45,693	37.6%
	Stevens, Norma Jean (No Party)	7,108	5.9%
	TOTAL	121,404	

Congressional District 4			
	Hastings, Doc* (Republican)	60,774	59.3%
	Baechler, Mary (Democrat)	27,130	26.5%
	Wheeler, Jamie (Republican)	11,581	11.3%
	Said, Mohammad (Democrat)	2,958	2.9%
	TOTAL	102,443	

Congressional District 5			
	Rodgers, Cathy McMorris* (Republican)	83,186	55.8%
	Cowan, Rich (Democrat)	49,406	33.1%
	Yearout, Randall (Republican)	11,894	8.0%
	Moody, Ian (No Party)	4,693	3.1%
	TOTAL	149,179	

Congressional District 6			
	Kilmer, Derek (Democrat)	86,436	53.4%
	Driscoll, Bill (Republican)	29,602	18.3%
	Young, Jesse (Republican)	18,075	11.2%
	Cloud, Doug (Republican)	14,267	8.8%
	Eichner, David "Ike" (Republican)	7,966	4.9%
	Arentz, Eric G. Jr. (Independent)	4,101	2.5%
	Brodhead, Stephan Andrew (Republican)	1,387	0.9%
	TOTAL	161,834	

Congressional District 7			
	McDermott, Jim* (Democrat)	124,692	70.9%
	Bemis, Ron (Republican)	26,791	15.2%
	Hughes, Andrew (Democrat)	10,340	5.9%
	Sutherland, S. (GOP)	5,573	3.2%
	Allen, Charles (Democrat)	4,367	2.5%
	Rivers, Donovan (Democrat)	2,688	1.5%
	Goodspaceguy (Other)	1,387	0.8%
	TOTAL	175,838	

Congressional District 8			
	Reichert, David George "Dave"* (Republican)	66,220	50.6%
	Porterfield, Karen (Democrat)	37,083	28.3%
	Swank, Keith (Republican)	10,942	8.4%
	Arnold, Keith (Democrat)	7,144	5.5%
	Windle, James (No Party)	5,269	4.0%
	Huber, Ernest (Republican)	4,165	3.2%
	TOTAL	130,823	

WASHINGTON

GENERAL AND PRIMARY ELECTIONS

ALL-PARTY PRIMARIES

Congressional District 9	Smith, Adam* (Democrat)	72,868	61.2%
	Postma, James (Republican)	27,616	23.2%
	Cramer, Tom (Democrat)	8,376	7.0%
	Orlinski, John (Republican)	6,624	5.6%
	Christie, Dave (Other)	3,659	3.1%
	TOTAL	119,143	
Congressional District 10	Heck, Denny (Democrat)	51,047	39.7%
	Muri, Richard (Republican)	36,173	28.2%
	Flemming, Stan (Republican)	19,934	15.5%
	Ferguson, Jennifer (Democrat)	14,026	10.9%
	Gunn, Sue (Progressive Independent)	4,292	3.3%
	Hannon, Steve (Democrat)	3,025	2.4%
	TOTAL	128,497	

Notes: An asterisk (*) denotes incumbent. For offices besides president, Washington held an all-party primary, in which candidates of all parties ran together on a single ballot. The top two vote-getters, regardless of party, advanced to the November general election. Candidates identified themselves on the ballot as "preferring" a particular party (or independent, non-party status), whether or not they were a member of that party or were supported by that party. Virtually all counties in Washington in 2012 voted by mail.

WEST VIRGINIA

Congressional districts first established for elections held in 2012

3 members

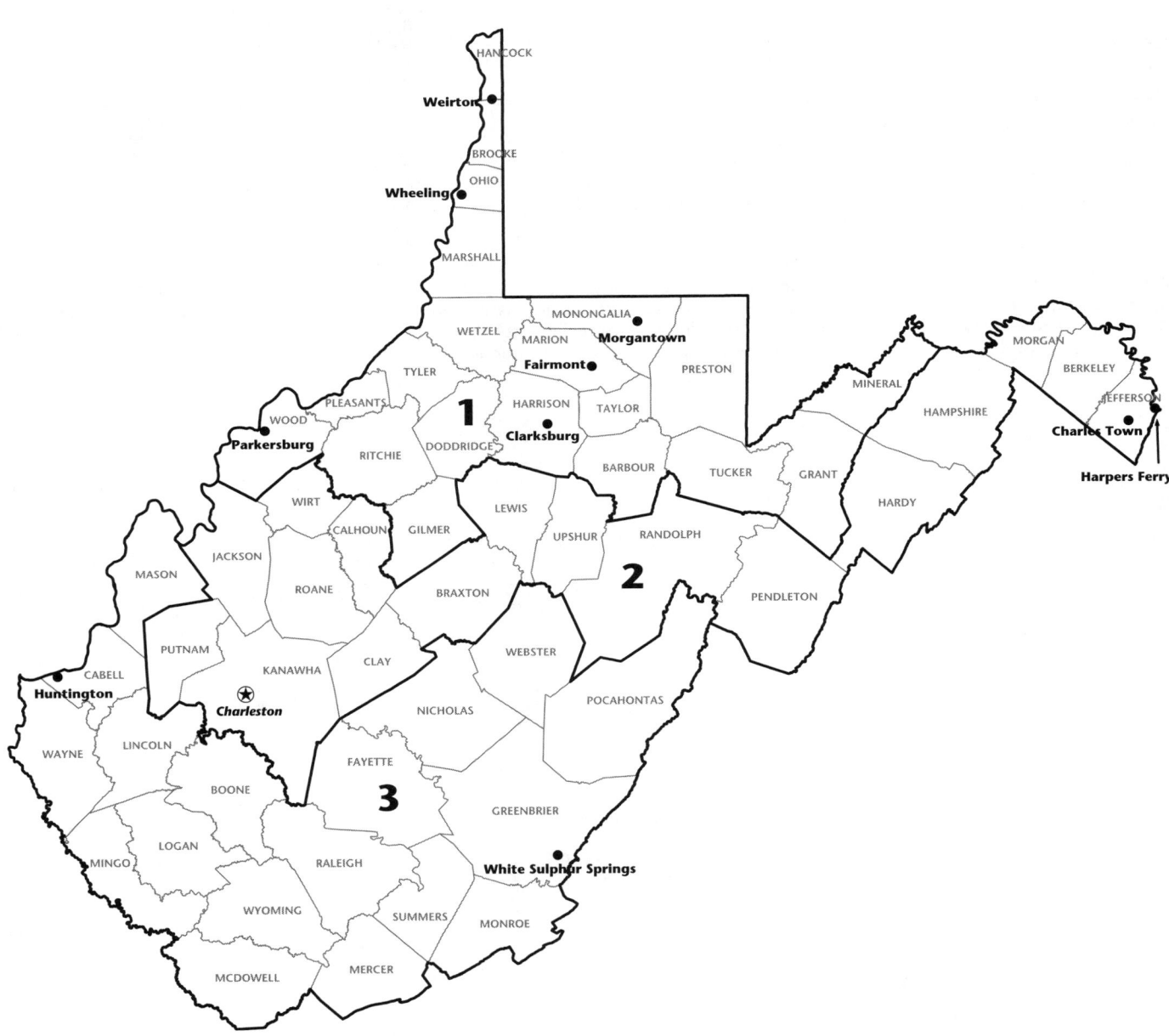

WEST VIRGINIA

GOVERNOR

Earl Ray Tomblin (D). Reelected 2012 to a four-year term. Sworn in as acting governor November 15, 2010, to fill the vacancy created by the resignation of Joe Manchin III (D) following his election to the U.S. Senate.

SENATORS (2 Democrats)

John D. Rockefeller IV (D). Reelected 2008 to a six-year term. Previously elected 2002, 1996, 1990, 1984.

Joe Manchin III (D). Reelected 2012 to a six-year term. Previously elected 2010 to fill the remaining two years of the term vacated by the death of Robert C. Byrd (D) in June 2010. Carte Goodwin (D) was appointed to fill the vacancy until the special election could be held in November 2010.

REPRESENTATIVES (2 Republicans, 1 Democrat)

1. David McKinley (R)　　　2. Shelley Moore Capito (R)　　　3. Nick J. Rahall II (D)

POSTWAR VOTE FOR PRESIDENT

| | | Republican | | Democratic | | | | Percentage | | | |
| | | | | | | | | Total Vote | | Major Vote | |
Year	Total Vote	Vote	Candidate	Vote	Candidate	Other Vote	Rep.-Dem. Plurality	Rep.	Dem.	Rep.	Dem.
2012	670,438	417,655	Romney, W. Mitt	238,269	Obama, Barack H.*	14,514	179,386 R	62.3%	35.5%	63.7%	36.3%
2008	713,451	397,466	McCain, John S. III	303,857	Obama, Barack H.	12,128	93,609 R	55.7%	42.6%	56.7%	43.3%
2004	755,887	423,778	Bush, George W.*	326,541	Kerry, John F.	5,568	97,237 R	56.1%	43.2%	56.5%	43.5%
2000**	648,124	336,475	Bush, George W.	295,497	Gore, Albert Jr.	16,152	40,978 R	51.9%	45.6%	53.2%	46.8%
1996**	636,459	233,946	Dole, Robert "Bob"	327,812	Clinton, Bill*	74,701	93,866 D	36.8%	51.5%	41.6%	58.4%
1992**	683,762	241,974	Bush, George H.*	331,001	Clinton, Bill	110,787	89,027 D	35.4%	48.4%	42.2%	57.8%
1988	653,311	310,065	Bush, George H.	341,016	Dukakis, Michael S.	2,230	30,951 D	47.5%	52.2%	47.6%	52.4%
1984	735,742	405,483	Reagan, Ronald*	328,125	Mondale, Walter F.	2,134	77,358 R	55.1%	44.6%	55.3%	44.7%
1980**	737,715	334,206	Reagan, Ronald	367,462	Carter, Jimmy*	36,047	33,256 D	45.3%	49.8%	47.6%	52.4%
1976	750,964	314,760	Ford, Gerald R.*	435,914	Carter, Jimmy	290	121,154 D	41.9%	58.0%	41.9%	58.1%
1972	762,399	484,964	Nixon, Richard M.*	277,435	McGovern, George S.		207,529 R	63.6%	36.4%	63.6%	36.4%
1968**	754,206	307,555	Nixon, Richard M.	374,091	Humphrey, Hubert H. Jr.	72,560	66,536 D	40.8%	49.6%	45.1%	54.9%
1964	792,040	253,953	Goldwater, Barry M. Sr.	538,087	Johnson, Lyndon B.*		284,134 D	32.1%	67.9%	32.1%	67.9%
1960	837,781	395,995	Nixon, Richard M.	441,786	Kennedy, John F.		45,791 D	47.3%	52.7%	47.3%	52.7%
1956	830,831	449,297	Eisenhower, Dwight D.*	381,534	Stevenson, Adlai E. II		67,763 R	54.1%	45.9%	54.1%	45.9%
1952	873,548	419,970	Eisenhower, Dwight D.	453,578	Stevenson, Adlai E. II		33,608 D	48.1%	51.9%	48.1%	51.9%
1948	748,750	316,251	Dewey, Thomas E.	429,188	Truman, Harry S.*	3,311	112,937 D	42.2%	57.3%	42.4%	57.6%

Note: An asterisk (*) denotes incumbent. **In past elections, the other vote included: 2000 - 10,680 Green (Ralph Nader); 1996 - 71,639 Reform (Ross Perot); 1992 - 108,829 Independent (Perot); 1980 - 31,691 Independent (John Anderson); 1968 - 72,560 American Independent (George Wallace).

WEST VIRGINIA

POSTWAR VOTE FOR GOVERNOR

Year	Total Vote	Republican		Democratic		Other Vote	Rep.-Dem. Plurality	Percentage			
								Total Vote		Major Vote	
		Vote	Candidate	Vote	Candidate			Rep.	Dem.	Rep.	Dem.
2012	664,455	303,291	Maloney, Bill	335,468	Tomblin, Earl Ray*	25,696	32,177 D	45.6%	50.5%	47.5%	52.5%
2011S**	301,084	141,656	Maloney, Bill	149,202	Tomblin, Earl Ray*	10,226	7,546 D	47.0%	49.6%	48.7%	51.3%
2008	706,046	181,612	Weeks, Russ	492,697	Manchin, Joe III*	31,737	311,085 D	25.7%	69.8%	26.9%	73.1%
2004	744,433	253,131	Warner, Monty	472,758	Manchin, Joe III	18,544	219,627 D	34.0%	63.5%	34.9%	65.1%
2000	648,047	305,926	Underwood, Cecil H.*	324,822	Wise, Robert Ellsworth	17,299	18,896 D	47.2%	50.1%	48.5%	51.5%
1996	628,559	324,518	Underwood, Cecil H.	287,870	Pritt, Charlotte	16,171	36,648 R	51.6%	45.8%	53.0%	47.0%
1992	657,193	240,390	Benedict, Cleveland K.	368,302	Caperton, Gaston*	48,501	127,912 D	36.6%	56.0%	39.5%	60.5%
1988	649,593	267,172	Moore, Arch A.*	382,421	Caperton, Gaston		115,249 D	41.1%	58.9%	41.1%	58.9%
1984	741,502	394,937	Moore, Arch A.	346,565	See, Clyde M.		48,372 R	53.3%	46.7%	53.3%	46.7%
1980	742,150	337,240	Moore, Arch A.	401,863	Rockefeller, John D. IV*	3,047	64,623 D	45.4%	54.1%	45.6%	54.4%
1976	749,270	253,420	Underwood, Cecil H.	495,661	Rockefeller, John D. IV	189	242,241 D	33.8%	66.2%	33.8%	66.2%
1972	774,279	423,817	Moore, Arch A.*	350,462	Rockefeller, John D. IV		73,355 R	54.7%	45.3%	54.7%	45.3%
1968	743,845	378,315	Moore, Arch A.	365,530	Sprouse, James M.		12,785 R	50.9%	49.1%	50.9%	49.1%
1964	788,582	355,559	Underwood, Cecil H.	433,023	Smith, Hulett		77,464 D	45.1%	54.9%	45.1%	54.9%
1960	827,420	380,665	Neely, Harold E.	446,755	Barron, William W.		66,090 D	46.0%	54.0%	46.0%	54.0%
1956	817,623	440,502	Underwood, Cecil H.	377,121	Mollohan, Robert H.		63,381 R	53.9%	46.1%	53.9%	46.1%
1952	882,527	427,629	Holt, Rush D.	454,898	Marland, William C.		27,269 D	48.5%	51.5%	48.5%	51.5%
1948	768,061	329,309	Boreman, Herbert S.	438,752	Patteson, Okey L.		109,443 D	42.9%	57.1%	42.9%	57.1%

Note: An asterisk (*) denotes incumbent. **The 2011 election was for a short term to fill a vacancy.

POSTWAR VOTE FOR SENATOR

Year	Total Vote	Republican		Democratic		Other Vote	Rep.-Dem. Plurality	Percentage			
								Total Vote		Major Vote	
		Vote	Candidate	Vote	Candidate			Rep.	Dem.	Rep.	Dem.
2012	660,212	240,787	Raese, John R.	399,908	Manchin, Joe III*	19,517	159,121 D	36.5%	60.6%	37.6%	62.4%
2010S	529,948	230,013	Raese, John R.	283,358	Manchin, Joe III	16,577	53,345 D	43.4%	53.5%	44.8%	55.2%
2008	702,308	254,629	Wolfe, Jay	447,560	Rockefeller, John D. IV*	119	192,931 D	36.3%	63.7%	36.3%	63.7%
2006	459,884	155,043	Raese, John R.	296,276	Byrd, Robert C.*	8,565	141,233 D	33.7%	64.4%	34.4%	65.6%
2002	436,183	160,902	Wolfe, M. Jay	275,281	Rockefeller, John D. IV*		114,379 D	36.9%	63.1%	36.9%	63.1%
2000	603,477	121,635	Gallaher, David T.	469,215	Byrd, Robert C.*	12,627	347,580 D	20.2%	77.8%	20.6%	79.4%
1996	595,614	139,088	Burks, Betty A.	456,526	Rockefeller, John D. IV*		317,438 D	23.4%	76.6%	23.4%	76.6%
1994	420,936	130,441	Klos, Stan	290,495	Byrd, Robert C.*		160,054 D	31.0%	69.0%	31.0%	69.0%
1990	404,305	128,071	Yoder, John	276,234	Rockefeller, John D. IV*		148,163 D	31.7%	68.3%	31.7%	68.3%
1988	634,547	223,564	Wolfe, M. Jay	410,983	Byrd, Robert C.*		187,419 D	35.2%	64.8%	35.2%	64.8%
1984	722,212	344,680	Raese, John R.	374,233	Rockefeller, John D. IV	3,299	29,553 D	47.7%	51.8%	47.9%	52.1%
1982	565,314	173,910	Benedict, Cleveland K.	387,170	Byrd, Robert C.*	4,234	213,260 D	30.8%	68.5%	31.0%	69.0%
1978	493,351	244,317	Moore, Arch A.	249,034	Randolph, Jennings*		4,717 D	49.5%	50.5%	49.5%	50.5%
1976	566,790			566,423	Byrd, Robert C.*	367	566,423 D		99.9%		100.0%
1972	731,841	245,531	Leonard, Louise	486,310	Randolph, Jennings*		240,779 D	33.5%	66.5%	33.5%	66.5%
1970	445,623	99,658	Dodson, Elmer H.	345,965	Byrd, Robert C.*		246,307 D	22.4%	77.6%	22.4%	77.6%
1966	491,216	198,891	Love, Francis J.	292,325	Randolph, Jennings*		93,434 D	40.5%	59.5%	40.5%	59.5%
1964	761,087	246,072	Benedict, Cooper P.	515,015	Byrd, Robert C.*		268,943 D	32.3%	67.7%	32.3%	67.7%
1960	828,292	369,935	Underwood, Cecil H.	458,355	Randolph, Jennings*	2	88,420 D	44.7%	55.3%	44.7%	55.3%
1958	644,917	263,172	Revercomb, Chapman*	381,745	Byrd, Robert C.		118,573 D	40.8%	59.2%	40.8%	59.2%
1958S	630,677	256,510	Hoblitzell, John D. Jr.*	374,167	Randolph, Jennings		117,657 D	40.7%	59.3%	40.7%	59.3%
1956S	805,174	432,123	Revercomb, Chapman	373,051	Marland, William C.		59,072 R	53.7%	46.3%	53.7%	46.3%
1954	593,329	268,066	Sweeney, Thomas	325,263	Neely, Matthew M.*		57,197 D	45.2%	54.8%	45.2%	54.8%
1952	876,573	406,554	Revercomb, Chapman	470,019	Kilgore, Harley M.*		63,465 D	46.4%	53.6%	46.4%	53.6%
1948	763,888	328,534	Revercomb, Chapman*	435,354	Neely, Matthew M.		106,820 D	43.0%	57.0%	43.0%	57.0%
1946	542,768	269,617	Sweeney, Thomas	273,151	Kilgore, Harley M.*		3,534 D	49.7%	50.3%	49.7%	50.3%

Note: An asterisk (*) denotes incumbent. **The 1956 election, one of the 1958 elections, and the 2010 election were for short terms to fill a vacancy. The Republican Party did not run a candidate in the 1976 Senate election.

WEST VIRGINIA

PRESIDENT 2012

2010 Census Population	County	Total Vote	Republican (Romney)	Democratic (Obama)	Other	Rep.-Dem. Plurality	Percentage			
							Total Vote		Major Vote	
							Rep.	Dem.	Rep.	Dem.
16,589	BARBOUR	5,761	3,824	1,768	169	2,056 R	66.4%	30.7%	68.4%	31.6%
104,169	BERKELEY	37,172	22,156	14,275	741	7,881 R	59.6%	38.4%	60.8%	39.2%
24,629	BOONE	8,500	5,467	2,790	243	2,677 R	64.3%	32.8%	66.2%	33.8%
14,523	BRAXTON	4,804	2,725	1,998	81	727 R	56.7%	41.6%	57.7%	42.3%
24,069	BROOKE	9,294	5,060	4,005	229	1,055 R	54.4%	43.1%	55.8%	44.2%
96,319	CABELL	32,144	17,985	13,568	591	4,417 R	56.0%	42.2%	57.0%	43.0%
7,627	CALHOUN	2,207	1,319	818	70	501 R	59.8%	37.1%	61.7%	38.3%
9,386	CLAY	3,012	1,971	931	110	1,040 R	65.4%	30.9%	67.9%	32.1%
8,202	DODDRIDGE	2,769	2,130	575	64	1,555 R	76.9%	20.8%	78.7%	21.3%
46,039	FAYETTE	14,070	8,350	5,419	301	2,931 R	59.3%	38.5%	60.6%	39.4%
8,693	GILMER	2,509	1,595	840	74	755 R	63.6%	33.5%	65.5%	34.5%
11,937	GRANT	4,586	3,783	718	85	3,065 R	82.5%	15.7%	84.0%	16.0%
35,480	GREENBRIER	12,963	7,930	4,710	323	3,220 R	61.2%	36.3%	62.7%	37.3%
23,964	HAMPSHIRE	7,986	5,523	2,299	164	3,224 R	69.2%	28.8%	70.6%	29.4%
30,676	HANCOCK	12,118	7,226	4,627	265	2,599 R	59.6%	38.2%	61.0%	39.0%
14,025	HARDY	5,168	3,536	1,482	150	2,054 R	68.4%	28.7%	70.5%	29.5%
69,099	HARRISON	26,147	15,876	9,732	539	6,144 R	60.7%	37.2%	62.0%	38.0%
29,211	JACKSON	11,544	7,408	3,854	282	3,554 R	64.2%	33.4%	65.8%	34.2%
53,498	JEFFERSON	22,138	11,258	10,398	482	860 R	50.9%	47.0%	52.0%	48.0%
193,063	KANAWHA	75,077	41,364	32,480	1,233	8,884 R	55.1%	43.3%	56.0%	44.0%
16,372	LEWIS	6,287	4,375	1,736	176	2,639 R	69.6%	27.6%	71.6%	28.4%
21,720	LINCOLN	6,818	4,383	2,227	208	2,156 R	64.3%	32.7%	66.3%	33.7%
36,743	LOGAN	11,946	8,222	3,469	255	4,753 R	68.8%	29.0%	70.3%	29.7%
56,418	MARION	21,542	12,054	8,959	529	3,095 R	56.0%	41.6%	57.4%	42.6%
33,107	MARSHALL	12,916	8,135	4,484	297	3,651 R	63.0%	34.7%	64.5%	35.5%
27,324	MASON	9,789	5,741	3,778	270	1,963 R	58.6%	38.6%	60.3%	39.7%
22,113	MCDOWELL	6,188	3,959	2,109	120	1,850 R	64.0%	34.1%	65.2%	34.8%
62,264	MERCER	21,276	15,450	5,432	394	10,018 R	72.6%	25.5%	74.0%	26.0%
28,212	MINERAL	10,979	7,833	2,885	261	4,948 R	71.3%	26.3%	73.1%	26.9%
26,839	MINGO	8,830	6,191	2,428	211	3,763 R	70.1%	27.5%	71.8%	28.2%
96,189	MONONGALIA	31,475	16,831	13,826	818	3,005 R	53.5%	43.9%	54.9%	45.1%
13,502	MONROE	5,212	3,616	1,455	141	2,161 R	69.4%	27.9%	71.3%	28.7%
17,541	MORGAN	7,044	4,513	2,363	168	2,150 R	64.1%	33.5%	65.6%	34.4%
26,233	NICHOLAS	8,785	5,898	2,664	223	3,234 R	67.1%	30.3%	68.9%	31.1%
44,443	OHIO	17,911	10,768	6,786	357	3,982 R	60.1%	37.9%	61.3%	38.7%
7,695	PENDLETON	3,239	2,095	1,074	70	1,021 R	64.7%	33.2%	66.1%	33.9%
7,605	PLEASANTS	2,840	1,825	955	60	870 R	64.3%	33.6%	65.6%	34.4%
8,719	POCAHONTAS	3,576	2,182	1,303	91	879 R	61.0%	36.4%	62.6%	37.4%
33,520	PRESTON	11,155	7,889	2,931	335	4,958 R	70.7%	26.3%	72.9%	27.1%
55,486	PUTNAM	23,673	16,032	7,256	385	8,776 R	67.7%	30.7%	68.8%	31.2%
78,859	RALEIGH	28,829	20,614	7,739	476	12,875 R	71.5%	26.8%	72.7%	27.3%
29,405	RANDOLPH	9,754	6,160	3,342	252	2,818 R	63.2%	34.3%	64.8%	35.2%
10,449	RITCHIE	3,788	2,921	768	99	2,153 R	77.1%	20.3%	79.2%	20.8%
14,926	ROANE	5,047	2,982	1,939	126	1,043 R	59.1%	38.4%	60.6%	39.4%
13,927	SUMMERS	4,735	2,981	1,621	133	1,360 R	63.0%	34.2%	64.8%	35.2%
16,895	TAYLOR	5,908	3,840	1,941	127	1,899 R	65.0%	32.9%	66.4%	33.6%
7,141	TUCKER	3,138	2,176	880	82	1,296 R	69.3%	28.0%	71.2%	28.8%
9,208	TYLER	3,279	2,314	890	75	1,424 R	70.6%	27.1%	72.2%	27.8%
24,254	UPSHUR	8,273	5,939	2,158	176	3,781 R	71.8%	26.1%	73.3%	26.7%
42,481	WAYNE	13,955	8,688	4,931	336	3,757 R	62.3%	35.3%	63.8%	36.2%
9,154	WEBSTER	2,755	1,710	947	98	763 R	62.1%	34.4%	64.4%	35.6%
16,583	WETZEL	5,856	3,473	2,217	166	1,256 R	59.3%	37.9%	61.0%	39.0%
5,717	WIRT	2,171	1,427	676	68	751 R	65.7%	31.1%	67.9%	32.1%
86,956	WOOD	33,977	22,183	11,230	564	10,953 R	65.3%	33.1%	66.4%	33.6%
23,796	WYOMING	7,523	5,769	1,583	171	4,186 R	76.7%	21.0%	78.5%	21.5%
1,852,994	TOTAL	670,438	417,655	238,269	14,514	179,386 R	62.3%	35.5%	63.7%	36.3%

WEST VIRGINIA

GOVERNOR 2011 (SPECIAL)

2010 Census Population	County	Total Vote	Republican (Maloney)	Democratic (Tomblin)	Other	Rep.-Dem. Plurality	Percentage			
							Total Vote		Major Vote	
							Rep.	Dem.	Rep.	Dem.
16,589	BARBOUR	3,821	1,762	1,922	137	160 D	46.1%	50.3%	47.8%	52.2%
104,169	BERKELEY	11,494	6,678	4,501	315	2,177 R	58.1%	39.2%	59.7%	40.3%
24,629	BOONE	4,569	1,085	3,391	93	2,306 D	23.7%	74.2%	24.2%	75.8%
14,523	BRAXTON	2,588	1,007	1,476	105	469 D	38.9%	57.0%	40.6%	59.4%
24,069	BROOKE	3,946	1,700	2,102	144	402 D	43.1%	53.3%	44.7%	55.3%
96,319	CABELL	14,246	6,414	7,482	350	1,068 D	45.0%	52.5%	46.2%	53.8%
7,627	CALHOUN	1,117	536	515	66	21 R	48.0%	46.1%	51.0%	49.0%
9,386	CLAY	1,503	632	813	58	181 D	42.0%	54.1%	43.7%	56.3%
8,202	DODDRIDGE	1,674	1,116	476	82	640 R	66.7%	28.4%	70.1%	29.9%
46,039	FAYETTE	6,007	2,149	3,568	290	1,419 D	35.8%	59.4%	37.6%	62.4%
8,693	GILMER	1,351	698	539	114	159 R	51.7%	39.9%	56.4%	43.6%
11,937	GRANT	1,818	1,374	408	36	966 R	75.6%	22.4%	77.1%	22.9%
35,480	GREENBRIER	5,303	2,350	2,633	320	283 D	44.3%	49.7%	47.2%	52.8%
23,964	HAMPSHIRE	3,065	1,997	959	109	1,038 R	65.2%	31.3%	67.6%	32.4%
30,676	HANCOCK	5,394	2,422	2,753	219	331 D	44.9%	51.0%	46.8%	53.2%
14,025	HARDY	2,078	1,146	812	120	334 R	55.1%	39.1%	58.5%	41.5%
69,099	HARRISON	12,585	6,038	6,165	382	127 D	48.0%	49.0%	49.5%	50.5%
29,211	JACKSON	6,018	3,114	2,717	187	397 R	51.7%	45.1%	53.4%	46.6%
53,498	JEFFERSON	6,847	3,363	3,237	247	126 R	49.1%	47.3%	51.0%	49.0%
193,063	KANAWHA	37,129	17,780	18,376	973	596 D	47.9%	49.5%	49.2%	50.8%
16,372	LEWIS	3,341	1,650	1,545	146	105 R	49.4%	46.2%	51.6%	48.4%
21,720	LINCOLN	3,401	1,065	2,270	66	1,205 D	31.3%	66.7%	31.9%	68.1%
36,743	LOGAN	7,351	567	6,734	50	6,167 D	7.7%	91.6%	7.8%	92.2%
56,418	MARION	10,208	4,240	5,624	344	1,384 D	41.5%	55.1%	43.0%	57.0%
33,107	MARSHALL	6,611	3,123	3,246	242	123 D	47.2%	49.1%	49.0%	51.0%
27,324	MASON	4,506	2,057	2,221	228	164 D	45.7%	49.3%	48.1%	51.9%
22,113	MCDOWELL	2,290	504	1,747	39	1,243 D	22.0%	76.3%	22.4%	77.6%
62,264	MERCER	7,958	3,817	3,930	211	113 D	48.0%	49.4%	49.3%	50.7%
28,212	MINERAL	3,661	2,245	1,306	110	939 R	61.3%	35.7%	63.2%	36.8%
26,839	MINGO	4,593	629	3,912	52	3,283 D	13.7%	85.2%	13.9%	86.1%
96,189	MONONGALIA	14,459	8,011	5,580	868	2,431 R	55.4%	38.6%	58.9%	41.1%
13,502	MONROE	2,050	988	954	108	34 R	48.2%	46.5%	50.9%	49.1%
17,541	MORGAN	2,656	1,644	886	126	758 R	61.9%	33.4%	65.0%	35.0%
26,233	NICHOLAS	4,225	1,896	2,137	192	241 D	44.9%	50.6%	47.0%	53.0%
44,443	OHIO	8,520	4,491	3,775	254	716 R	52.7%	44.3%	54.3%	45.7%
7,695	PENDLETON	1,286	735	490	61	245 R	57.2%	38.1%	60.0%	40.0%
7,605	PLEASANTS	1,301	590	669	42	79 D	45.3%	51.4%	46.9%	53.1%
8,719	POCAHONTAS	1,359	649	568	142	81 R	47.8%	41.8%	53.3%	46.7%
33,520	PRESTON	4,865	3,003	1,656	206	1,347 R	61.7%	34.0%	64.5%	35.5%
55,486	PUTNAM	11,411	6,790	4,376	245	2,414 R	59.5%	38.3%	60.8%	39.2%
78,859	RALEIGH	10,540	5,024	5,192	324	168 D	47.7%	49.3%	49.2%	50.8%
29,405	RANDOLPH	4,818	1,991	2,604	223	613 D	41.3%	54.0%	43.3%	56.7%
10,449	RITCHIE	1,724	1,108	556	60	552 R	64.3%	32.3%	66.6%	33.4%
14,926	ROANE	2,635	1,289	1,228	118	61 R	48.9%	46.6%	51.2%	48.8%
13,927	SUMMERS	2,066	808	1,170	88	362 D	39.1%	56.6%	40.8%	59.2%
16,895	TAYLOR	2,830	1,436	1,300	94	136 R	50.7%	45.9%	52.5%	47.5%
7,141	TUCKER	1,509	682	763	64	81 D	45.2%	50.6%	47.2%	52.8%
9,208	TYLER	1,653	922	652	79	270 R	55.8%	39.4%	58.6%	41.4%
24,254	UPSHUR	4,429	2,566	1,673	190	893 R	57.9%	37.8%	60.5%	39.5%
42,481	WAYNE	6,872	2,767	3,960	145	1,193 D	40.3%	57.6%	41.1%	58.9%
9,154	WEBSTER	1,382	437	879	66	442 D	31.6%	63.6%	33.2%	66.8%
16,583	WETZEL	3,362	1,385	1,816	161	431 D	41.2%	54.0%	43.3%	56.7%
5,717	WIRT	1,058	541	488	29	53 R	51.1%	46.1%	52.6%	47.4%
86,956	WOOD	14,721	7,888	6,396	437	1,492 R	53.6%	43.4%	55.2%	44.8%
23,796	WYOMING	2,880	757	2,054	69	1,297 D	26.3%	71.3%	26.9%	73.1%
1,852,994	TOTAL	301,084	141,656	149,202	10,226	7,546 D	47.0%	49.6%	48.7%	51.3%

Note: Earl Ray Tomblin had become acting governor in November 2010, to fill the vacancy created by the resignation of Joe Manchin (D), who was elected to the U.S. Senate in 2010. The special election to fill the remainder of Manchin's term was held on October 4, 2011.

WEST VIRGINIA

GOVERNOR 2012

2010 Census Population	County	Total Vote	Republican (Maloney)	Democratic (Tomblin)	Other	Rep.-Dem. Plurality	Percentage			
							Total Vote		Major Vote	
							Rep.	Dem.	Rep.	Dem.
16,589	BARBOUR	5,746	2,789	2,757	200	32 R	48.5%	48.0%	50.3%	49.7%
104,169	BERKELEY	36,487	17,999	17,195	1,293	804 R	49.3%	47.1%	51.1%	48.9%
24,629	BOONE	8,658	2,624	5,800	234	3,176 D	30.3%	67.0%	31.1%	68.9%
14,523	BRAXTON	4,731	1,784	2,796	151	1,012 D	37.7%	59.1%	39.0%	61.0%
24,069	BROOKE	9,132	3,797	5,067	268	1,270 D	41.6%	55.5%	42.8%	57.2%
96,319	CABELL	32,001	13,357	17,447	1,197	4,090 D	41.7%	54.5%	43.4%	56.6%
7,627	CALHOUN	2,167	986	1,051	130	65 D	45.5%	48.5%	48.4%	51.6%
9,386	CLAY	3,029	1,278	1,605	146	327 D	42.2%	53.0%	44.3%	55.7%
8,202	DODDRIDGE	2,725	1,721	872	132	849 R	63.2%	32.0%	66.4%	33.6%
46,039	FAYETTE	13,960	5,932	7,353	675	1,421 D	42.5%	52.7%	44.7%	55.3%
8,693	GILMER	2,504	1,033	1,345	126	312 D	41.3%	53.7%	43.4%	56.6%
11,937	GRANT	4,492	2,919	1,453	120	1,466 R	65.0%	32.3%	66.8%	33.2%
35,480	GREENBRIER	12,837	5,821	6,357	659	536 D	45.3%	49.5%	47.8%	52.2%
23,964	HAMPSHIRE	7,884	3,944	3,610	330	334 R	50.0%	45.8%	52.2%	47.8%
30,676	HANCOCK	11,901	5,454	6,077	370	623 D	45.8%	51.1%	47.3%	52.7%
14,025	HARDY	5,133	2,074	2,868	191	794 D	40.4%	55.9%	42.0%	58.0%
69,099	HARRISON	26,065	12,460	12,818	787	358 D	47.8%	49.2%	49.3%	50.7%
29,211	JACKSON	11,600	5,711	5,508	381	203 R	49.2%	47.5%	50.9%	49.1%
53,498	JEFFERSON	21,761	9,514	11,091	1,156	1,577 D	43.7%	51.0%	46.2%	53.8%
193,063	KANAWHA	74,284	31,584	38,785	3,915	7,201 D	42.5%	52.2%	44.9%	55.1%
16,372	LEWIS	6,343	3,192	2,920	231	272 R	50.3%	46.0%	52.2%	47.8%
21,720	LINCOLN	6,916	2,476	4,241	199	1,765 D	35.8%	61.3%	36.9%	63.1%
36,743	LOGAN	12,026	2,393	9,480	153	7,087 D	19.9%	78.8%	20.2%	79.8%
56,418	MARION	21,410	9,236	11,358	816	2,122 D	43.1%	53.0%	44.8%	55.2%
33,107	MARSHALL	12,795	5,807	6,593	395	786 D	45.4%	51.5%	46.8%	53.2%
27,324	MASON	9,756	4,229	5,212	315	983 D	43.3%	53.4%	44.8%	55.2%
22,113	MCDOWELL	6,077	1,919	4,007	151	2,088 D	31.6%	65.9%	32.4%	67.6%
62,264	MERCER	20,867	10,974	9,257	636	1,717 R	52.6%	44.4%	54.2%	45.8%
28,212	MINERAL	10,899	5,708	4,874	317	834 R	52.4%	44.7%	53.9%	46.1%
26,839	MINGO	8,881	2,656	6,078	147	3,422 D	29.9%	68.4%	30.4%	69.6%
96,189	MONONGALIA	30,964	15,034	14,160	1,770	874 R	48.6%	45.7%	51.5%	48.5%
13,502	MONROE	5,151	2,592	2,320	239	272 R	50.3%	45.0%	52.8%	47.2%
17,541	MORGAN	6,856	3,439	3,075	342	364 R	50.2%	44.9%	52.8%	47.2%
26,233	NICHOLAS	8,829	4,173	4,367	289	194 D	47.3%	49.5%	48.9%	51.1%
44,443	OHIO	17,677	8,519	8,603	555	84 D	48.2%	48.7%	49.8%	50.2%
7,695	PENDLETON	3,221	1,391	1,720	110	329 D	43.2%	53.4%	44.7%	55.3%
7,605	PLEASANTS	2,820	1,306	1,452	62	146 D	46.3%	51.5%	47.4%	52.6%
8,719	POCAHONTAS	3,489	1,384	1,863	242	479 D	39.7%	53.4%	42.6%	57.4%
33,520	PRESTON	10,981	6,020	4,096	865	1,924 R	54.8%	37.3%	59.5%	40.5%
55,486	PUTNAM	23,593	12,534	10,303	756	2,231 R	53.1%	43.7%	54.9%	45.1%
78,859	RALEIGH	28,363	14,900	12,602	861	2,298 R	52.5%	44.4%	54.2%	45.8%
29,405	RANDOLPH	9,653	4,115	5,070	468	955 D	42.6%	52.5%	44.8%	55.2%
10,449	RITCHIE	3,737	2,171	1,438	128	733 R	58.1%	38.5%	60.2%	39.8%
14,926	ROANE	5,041	2,191	2,609	241	418 D	43.5%	51.8%	45.6%	54.4%
13,927	SUMMERS	4,687	1,969	2,511	207	542 D	42.0%	53.6%	44.0%	56.0%
16,895	TAYLOR	5,910	2,969	2,755	186	214 R	50.2%	46.6%	51.9%	48.1%
7,141	TUCKER	3,141	1,420	1,527	194	107 D	45.2%	48.6%	48.2%	51.8%
9,208	TYLER	3,244	1,711	1,424	109	287 R	52.7%	43.9%	54.6%	45.4%
24,254	UPSHUR	8,222	4,464	3,425	333	1,039 R	54.3%	41.7%	56.6%	43.4%
42,481	WAYNE	14,004	5,928	7,713	363	1,785 D	42.3%	55.1%	43.5%	56.5%
9,154	WEBSTER	2,791	1,019	1,635	137	616 D	36.5%	58.6%	38.4%	61.6%
16,583	WETZEL	5,841	2,367	3,282	192	915 D	40.5%	56.2%	41.9%	58.1%
5,717	WIRT	2,166	1,030	1,071	65	41 D	47.6%	49.4%	49.0%	51.0%
86,956	WOOD	33,538	16,272	16,284	982	12 D	48.5%	48.6%	50.0%	50.0%
23,796	WYOMING	7,469	3,002	4,288	179	1,286 D	40.2%	57.4%	41.2%	58.8%
1,852,994	TOTAL	664,455	303,291	335,468	25,696	32,177 D	45.6%	50.5%	47.5%	52.5%

WEST VIRGINIA
SENATOR 2012

2010 Census Population	County	Total Vote	Republican (Raese)	Democratic (Manchin)	Other	Rep.-Dem. Plurality	Percentage Total Vote Rep.	Dem.	Major Vote Rep.	Dem.
16,589	BARBOUR	5,708	2,199	3,358	151	1,159 D	38.5%	58.8%	39.6%	60.4%
104,169	BERKELEY	36,206	16,046	19,306	854	3,260 D	44.3%	53.3%	45.4%	54.6%
24,629	BOONE	8,514	2,318	5,955	241	3,637 D	27.2%	69.9%	28.0%	72.0%
14,523	BRAXTON	4,589	1,297	3,160	132	1,863 D	28.3%	68.9%	29.1%	70.9%
24,069	BROOKE	9,074	2,479	6,441	154	3,962 D	27.3%	71.0%	27.8%	72.2%
96,319	CABELL	32,021	9,133	22,007	881	12,874 D	28.5%	68.7%	29.3%	70.7%
7,627	CALHOUN	2,172	695	1,360	117	665 D	32.0%	62.6%	33.8%	66.2%
9,386	CLAY	3,018	993	1,893	132	900 D	32.9%	62.7%	34.4%	65.6%
8,202	DODDRIDGE	2,726	1,489	1,142	95	347 R	54.6%	41.9%	56.6%	43.4%
46,039	FAYETTE	13,897	4,524	8,764	609	4,240 D	32.6%	63.1%	34.0%	66.0%
8,693	GILMER	2,528	881	1,409	238	528 D	34.8%	55.7%	38.5%	61.5%
11,937	GRANT	4,507	2,955	1,473	79	1,482 R	65.6%	32.7%	66.7%	33.3%
35,480	GREENBRIER	12,646	4,112	7,952	582	3,840 D	32.5%	62.9%	34.1%	65.9%
23,964	HAMPSHIRE	7,918	3,761	3,955	202	194 D	47.5%	49.9%	48.7%	51.3%
30,676	HANCOCK	11,734	3,628	7,920	186	4,292 D	30.9%	67.5%	31.4%	68.6%
14,025	HARDY	5,057	2,170	2,763	124	593 D	42.9%	54.6%	44.0%	56.0%
69,099	HARRISON	26,204	10,452	15,009	743	4,557 D	39.9%	57.3%	41.1%	58.9%
29,211	JACKSON	11,377	4,092	7,039	246	2,947 D	36.0%	61.9%	36.8%	63.2%
53,498	JEFFERSON	21,798	8,619	12,338	841	3,719 D	39.5%	56.6%	41.1%	58.9%
193,063	KANAWHA	74,219	24,837	46,255	3,127	21,418 D	33.5%	62.3%	34.9%	65.1%
16,372	LEWIS	6,360	2,673	3,455	232	782 D	42.0%	54.3%	43.6%	56.4%
21,720	LINCOLN	6,738	2,059	4,504	175	2,445 D	30.6%	66.8%	31.4%	68.6%
36,743	LOGAN	11,579	2,768	8,642	169	5,874 D	23.9%	74.6%	24.3%	75.7%
56,418	MARION	21,314	7,101	13,606	607	6,505 D	33.3%	63.8%	34.3%	65.7%
33,107	MARSHALL	12,722	4,167	8,270	285	4,103 D	32.8%	65.0%	33.5%	66.5%
27,324	MASON	9,616	2,669	6,771	176	4,102 D	27.8%	70.4%	28.3%	71.7%
22,113	MCDOWELL	6,064	1,550	4,385	129	2,835 D	25.6%	72.3%	26.1%	73.9%
62,264	MERCER	20,555	7,898	12,243	414	4,345 D	38.4%	59.6%	39.2%	60.8%
28,212	MINERAL	10,948	5,142	5,623	183	481 D	47.0%	51.4%	47.8%	52.2%
26,839	MINGO	8,700	2,216	6,336	148	4,120 D	25.5%	72.8%	25.9%	74.1%
96,189	MONONGALIA	30,883	13,563	15,896	1,424	2,333 D	43.9%	51.5%	46.0%	54.0%
13,502	MONROE	5,104	1,958	2,997	149	1,039 D	38.4%	58.7%	39.5%	60.5%
17,541	MORGAN	6,698	3,071	3,417	210	346 D	45.8%	51.0%	47.3%	52.7%
26,233	NICHOLAS	8,848	3,036	5,440	372	2,404 D	34.3%	61.5%	35.8%	64.2%
44,443	OHIO	17,601	5,976	11,210	415	5,234 D	34.0%	63.7%	34.8%	65.2%
7,695	PENDLETON	3,249	1,500	1,670	79	170 D	46.2%	51.4%	47.3%	52.7%
7,605	PLEASANTS	2,796	961	1,779	56	818 D	34.4%	63.6%	35.1%	64.9%
8,719	POCAHONTAS	3,474	1,141	2,092	241	951 D	32.8%	60.2%	35.3%	64.7%
33,520	PRESTON	10,876	6,325	4,159	392	2,166 R	58.2%	38.2%	60.3%	39.7%
55,486	PUTNAM	23,471	9,379	13,509	583	4,130 D	40.0%	57.6%	41.0%	59.0%
78,859	RALEIGH	28,177	10,791	16,748	638	5,957 D	38.3%	59.4%	39.2%	60.8%
29,405	RANDOLPH	9,612	3,310	5,979	323	2,669 D	34.4%	62.2%	35.6%	64.4%
10,449	RITCHIE	3,763	1,696	1,969	98	273 D	45.1%	52.3%	46.3%	53.7%
14,926	ROANE	4,989	1,595	3,205	189	1,610 D	32.0%	64.2%	33.2%	66.8%
13,927	SUMMERS	4,638	1,452	3,028	158	1,576 D	31.3%	65.3%	32.4%	67.6%
16,895	TAYLOR	5,917	2,422	3,353	142	931 D	40.9%	56.7%	41.9%	58.1%
7,141	TUCKER	3,166	1,302	1,780	84	478 D	41.1%	56.2%	42.2%	57.8%
9,208	TYLER	3,221	1,342	1,803	76	461 D	41.7%	56.0%	42.7%	57.3%
24,254	UPSHUR	8,170	3,531	4,403	236	872 D	43.2%	53.9%	44.5%	55.5%
42,481	WAYNE	13,833	4,023	9,580	230	5,557 D	29.1%	69.3%	29.6%	70.4%
9,154	WEBSTER	2,792	888	1,750	154	862 D	31.8%	62.7%	33.7%	66.3%
16,583	WETZEL	5,785	1,784	3,866	135	2,082 D	30.8%	66.8%	31.6%	68.4%
5,717	WIRT	2,144	683	1,401	60	718 D	31.9%	65.3%	32.8%	67.2%
86,956	WOOD	33,112	11,583	20,891	638	9,308 D	35.0%	63.1%	35.7%	64.3%
23,796	WYOMING	7,384	2,552	4,649	183	2,097 D	34.6%	63.0%	35.4%	64.6%
1,852,994	TOTAL	660,212	240,787	399,908	19,517	159,121 D	36.5%	60.6%	37.6%	62.4%

WEST VIRGINIA

HOUSE OF REPRESENTATIVES

| | | | Republican | | Democratic | | Other Vote | Rep.-Dem. Plurality | Percentage | | | |
| | | | | | | | | | Total Vote | | Major Vote | |
CD	Year	Total Vote	Vote	Candidate	Vote	Candidate			Rep.	Dem.	Rep.	Dem.
1	2012	214,151	133,809	MCKINLEY, DAVID*	80,342	THORN, SUE		53,467 R	62.5%	37.5%	62.5%	37.5%
2	2012	226,766	158,206	CAPITO, SHELLEY MOORE*	68,560	SWINT, HOWARD		89,646 R	69.8%	30.2%	69.8%	30.2%
3	2012	200,437	92,238	SNUFFER, RICK	108,199	RAHALL, NICK J. II*		15,961 D	46.0%	54.0%	46.0%	54.0%
TOTAL	2012	641,354	384,253		257,101			127,152 R	59.9%	40.1%	59.9%	40.1%

Note: An asterisk (*) denotes incumbent.

WEST VIRGINIA

GENERAL AND PRIMARY ELECTIONS

GENERAL ELECTIONS: OTHER VOTE

President   Other vote was 6,302 Libertarian (Gary E. Johnson), 4,406 Green (Jill Stein), 3,806 No Party Affiliation (Randall Terry)

Governor   Other vote was 16,787 Mountain (Jesse Johnson), 8,909 Libertarian (David Moran)

Senator   Other vote was 19,517 Mountain (Bob Henry Baber)

Primary	May 8, 2012	**Registration** (as of April 2012)	1,226,545	Democratic	640,888
				Republican	352,304
				Mountain	1,286
				No Party	210,562
				Other	21,505

Primary Type   Semi-Open—Registered Democrats and registered Republicans could vote only in their party's primary. Those voters registered with no party could participate in either the Democratic or Republican primary.

	REPUBLICAN PRIMARIES			**DEMOCRATIC PRIMARIES**		
President	Romney, W. Mitt	78,197	69.6%	Obama, Barack H.*	106,770	59.3%
	Santorum, Rick	13,590	12.1%	Judd, Keith	73,138	40.7%
	Paul, Ron	12,412	11.0%			
	Gingrich, Newt	7,076	6.3%			
	Roemer, Charles	1,141	1.0%			
	TOTAL	112,416		TOTAL	179,908	
Senator	Raese, John R.	88,510	100.0%	Manchin, Joe III*	163,891	79.9%
				Fletcher, Sheirl L.	41,118	20.1%
	TOTAL	88,510		TOTAL	205,009	
Governor	Maloney, Bill	86,925	83.5%	Tomblin, Earl Ray*	170,481	84.4%
	Clark, Ralph William	17,165	16.5%	Moltis, Arne	31,587	15.6%
	TOTAL	104,090		TOTAL	202,068	
Congressional District 1	McKinley, David*	36,107	100.0%	Thorn, Sue	49,203	100.0%
	TOTAL	36,107		TOTAL	49,203	

WEST VIRGINIA

GENERAL AND PRIMARY ELECTIONS

	REPUBLICAN PRIMARIES			DEMOCRATIC PRIMARIES		
Congressional District 2	Capito, Shelley Moore*	35,088	83.0%	Swint, Howard	22,563	48.3%
	Miller, Jonathan	4,711	11.1%	McCann, William	13,668	29.2%
	Davis, Michael	2,495	5.9%	Brown, Dugald	10,514	22.5%
	TOTAL	*42,294*		*TOTAL*	*46,745*	
Congressional District 3	Snuffer, Rick	12,359	53.4%	Rahall, Nick J. II*	66,745	100.0%
	Bias, Lee Allen	6,671	28.8%			
	Lester, Bill	4,104	17.7%			
	TOTAL	*23,134*		*TOTAL*	*66,745*	

Note: An asterisk (*) denotes incumbent. For the nomination to the 2011 special gubernatorial election for a short term, the results for the Republican primary were: Bill Maloney 27,871 (45.0%); Betty Ireland 19,027 (30.8%); Clark Barnes 5,891 (9.5%); Mark A. Sorsaia 3,177 (5.1%); Larry V. Faircloth 2,400 (3.9%); Mitch B. Carmichael 2,073 (3.4%); Ralph William Clark 1,164 (1.9%); Cliff Ellis 283 (0.5%); total votes were 61,886. The results for the Democratic primary were: Earl Ray Tomblin 51,348 (40.4%); Rick Thompson 30,631 (24.1%); Natalie E. Tennant 22,106 (17.4%); John D. Perdue 15,995 (12.6%); Jeffrey V. Kessler 6,550 (5.2%); Arne Moltis 481 (0.4%); total votes were 127,111.

WISCONSIN

Congressional districts first established for elections held in 2012

8 members

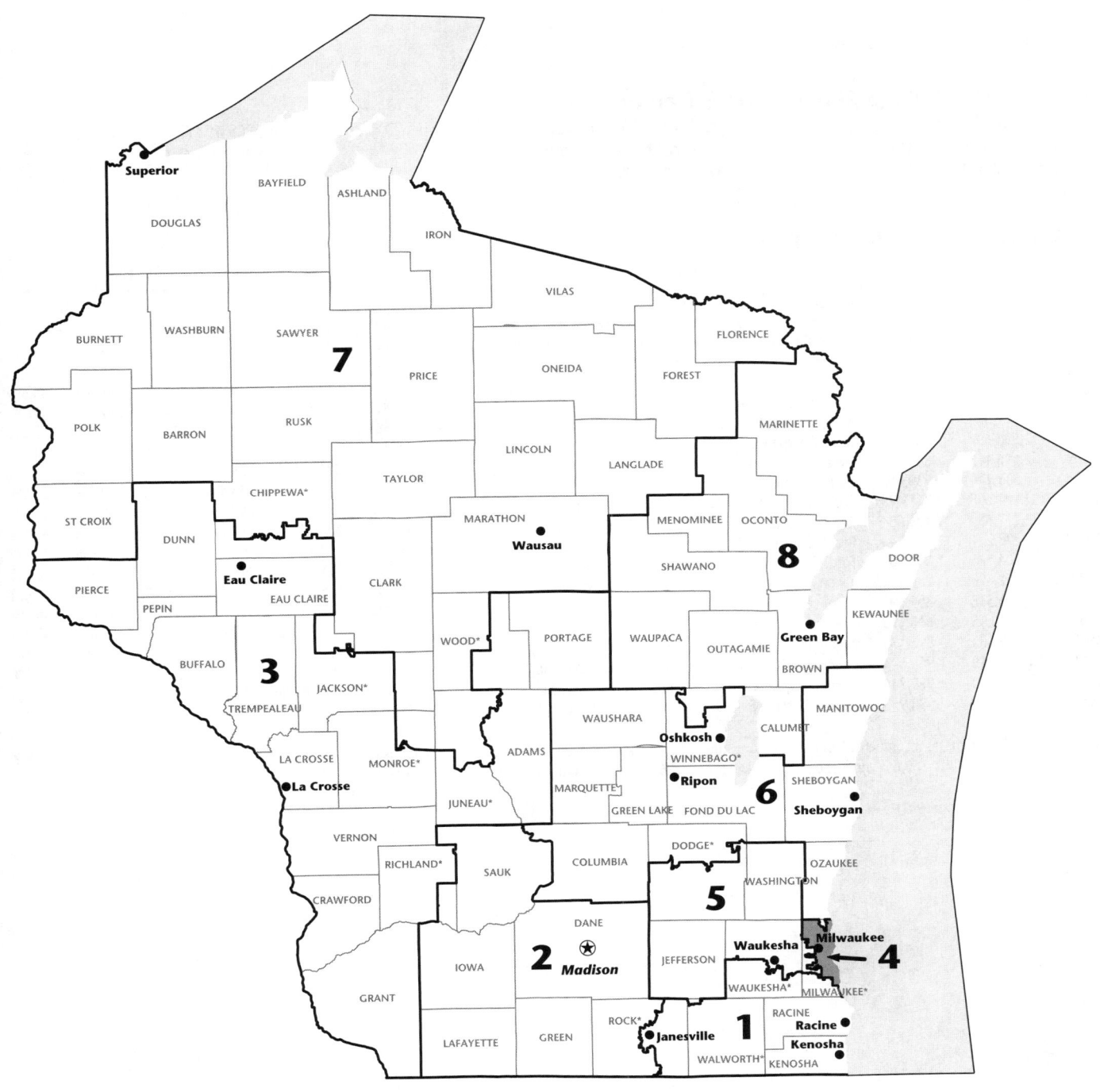

* Asterisk indicates a county whose boundaries include parts of two or more Congressional districts.

WISCONSIN

GOVERNOR
Scott Walker (R). Elected 2010 to a four-year term. Won special recall election June 5, 2012, to remain in office.

SENATORS (1 Republican, 1 Democrat)
Ron Johnson (R). Elected 2010 to a six-year term.

Tammy Baldwin (D). Elected 2012 to a six-year term.

REPRESENTATIVES (5 Republicans, 3 Democrats)
1. Paul Ryan (R)
2. Mark Pocan (D)
3. Ron Kind (D)
4. Gwendolynne S. "Gwen" Moore (D)
5. Jim Sensenbrenner (R)
6. Tom Petri (R)
7. Sean Duffy (R)
8. Reid Ribble (R)

POSTWAR VOTE FOR PRESIDENT

		Republican		Democratic		Other Vote	Rep.-Dem. Plurality	Percentage			
								Total Vote		Major Vote	
Year	Total Vote	Vote	Candidate	Vote	Candidate			Rep.	Dem.	Rep.	Dem.
2012	3,068,434	1,407,966	Romney, W. Mitt	1,620,985	Obama, Barack H.*	39,483	213,019 D	45.9%	52.8%	46.5%	53.5%
2008	2,983,417	1,262,393	McCain, John S. III	1,677,211	Obama, Barack H.	43,813	414,818 D	42.3%	56.2%	42.9%	57.1%
2004	2,997,007	1,478,120	Bush, George W.*	1,489,504	Kerry, John F.	29,383	11,384 D	49.3%	49.7%	49.8%	50.2%
2000**	2,598,607	1,237,279	Bush, George W.	1,242,987	Gore, Albert Jr.	118,341	5,708 D	47.6%	47.8%	49.9%	50.1%
1996**	2,196,169	845,029	Dole, Robert "Bob"	1,071,971	Clinton, Bill*	279,169	226,942 D	38.5%	48.8%	44.1%	55.9%
1992**	2,531,114	930,855	Bush, George H.*	1,041,066	Clinton, Bill	559,193	110,211 D	36.8%	41.1%	47.2%	52.8%
1988	2,191,608	1,047,499	Bush, George H.	1,126,794	Dukakis, Michael S.	17,315	79,295 D	47.8%	51.4%	48.2%	51.8%
1984	2,211,689	1,198,584	Reagan, Ronald*	995,740	Mondale, Walter F.	17,365	202,844 R	54.2%	45.0%	54.6%	45.4%
1980**	2,273,221	1,088,845	Reagan, Ronald	981,584	Carter, Jimmy*	202,792	107,261 R	47.9%	43.2%	52.6%	47.4%
1976	2,104,175	1,004,987	Ford, Gerald R.*	1,040,232	Carter, Jimmy	58,956	35,245 D	47.8%	49.4%	49.1%	50.9%
1972	1,852,890	989,430	Nixon, Richard M.*	810,174	McGovern, George S.	53,286	179,256 R	53.4%	43.7%	55.0%	45.0%
1968**	1,691,538	809,997	Nixon, Richard M.	748,804	Humphrey, Hubert H. Jr.	132,737	61,193 R	47.9%	44.3%	52.0%	48.0%
1964	1,691,815	638,495	Goldwater, Barry M. Sr.	1,050,424	Johnson, Lyndon B.*	2,896	411,929 D	37.7%	62.1%	37.8%	62.2%
1960	1,729,082	895,175	Nixon, Richard M.	830,805	Kennedy, John F.	3,102	64,370 R	51.8%	48.0%	51.9%	48.1%
1956	1,550,558	954,844	Eisenhower, Dwight D.*	586,768	Stevenson, Adlai E. II	8,946	368,076 R	61.6%	37.8%	61.9%	38.1%
1952	1,607,370	979,744	Eisenhower, Dwight D.	622,175	Stevenson, Adlai E. II	5,451	357,569 R	61.0%	38.7%	61.2%	38.8%
1948	1,276,800	590,959	Dewey, Thomas E.	647,310	Truman, Harry S.*	38,531	56,351 D	46.3%	50.7%	47.7%	52.3%

Note: An asterisk (*) denotes incumbent. **In past elections, the other vote included: 2000 - 94,070 Green (Ralph Nader); 1996 - 227,339 Reform (Ross Perot); 1992 - 544,479 Independent (Perot); 1980 - 160,657 Independent (John Anderson); 1968 - 127,835 American Independent (George Wallace).

WISCONSIN

POSTWAR VOTE FOR GOVERNOR

Year	Total Vote	Republican Vote	Republican Candidate	Democratic Vote	Democratic Candidate	Other Vote	Rep.-Dem. Plurality	Total Vote Rep.	Total Vote Dem.	Major Vote Rep.	Major Vote Dem.
2012S**	2,516,065	1,335,585	Walker, Scott*	1,164,480	Barrett, Thomas M.	16,000	171,105 R	53.1%	46.3%	53.4%	46.6%
2010	2,160,832	1,128,941	Walker, Scott	1,004,303	Barrett, Thomas M.	27,588	124,638 R	52.2%	46.5%	52.9%	47.1%
2006	2,161,700	979,427	Green, Mark	1,139,115	Doyle, James E.*	43,158	159,688 D	45.3%	52.7%	46.2%	53.8%
2002**	1,775,349	734,779	McCallum, Scott*	800,515	Doyle, James E.	240,055	65,736 D	41.4%	45.1%	47.9%	52.1%
1998	1,756,014	1,047,716	Thompson, Tommy G.*	679,553	Garvey, Ed	28,745	368,163 R	59.7%	38.7%	60.7%	39.3%
1994	1,563,835	1,051,326	Thompson, Tommy G.*	482,850	Chvala, Chuck	29,659	568,476 R	67.2%	30.9%	68.5%	31.5%
1990	1,379,727	802,321	Thompson, Tommy G.*	576,280	Loftus, Thomas	1,126	226,041 R	58.2%	41.8%	58.2%	41.8%
1986	1,526,960	805,090	Thompson, Tommy G.	705,578	Earl, Anthony S.*	16,292	99,512 R	52.7%	46.2%	53.3%	46.7%
1982	1,580,344	662,838	Kohler, Terry J.	896,812	Earl, Anthony S.	20,694	233,974 D	41.9%	56.7%	42.5%	57.5%
1978	1,500,996	816,056	Dreyfus, Lee S.	673,813	Schreiber, Martin J.*	11,127	142,243 R	54.4%	44.9%	54.8%	45.2%
1974	1,181,976	497,195	Dyke, William D.	628,639	Lucey, Patrick J.*	56,142	131,444 D	42.1%	53.2%	44.2%	55.8%
1970**	1,343,160	602,617	Olson, Jack B.	728,403	Lucey, Patrick J.	12,140	125,786 D	44.9%	54.2%	45.3%	54.7%
1968	1,689,738	893,463	Knowles, Warren P.*	791,100	Lafollette, Bronson C.	5,175	102,363 R	52.9%	46.8%	53.0%	47.0%
1966	1,170,173	626,041	Knowles, Warren P.*	539,258	Lucey, Patrick J.	4,874	86,783 R	53.5%	46.1%	53.7%	46.3%
1964	1,694,887	856,779	Knowles, Warren P.	837,901	Reynolds, John W.*	207	18,878 R	50.6%	49.4%	50.6%	49.4%
1962	1,265,900	625,536	Kuehn, Philip G.	637,491	Reynolds, John W.	2,873	11,955 D	49.4%	50.4%	49.5%	50.5%
1960	1,728,009	837,123	Kuehn, Philip G.	890,868	Nelson, Gaylord A.*	18	53,745 D	48.4%	51.6%	48.4%	51.6%
1958	1,202,219	556,391	Thomson, Vernon W.*	644,296	Nelson, Gaylord A.	1,532	87,905 D	46.3%	53.6%	46.3%	53.7%
1956	1,557,788	808,273	Thomson, Vernon W.	749,421	Proxmire, William	94	58,852 R	51.9%	48.1%	51.9%	48.1%
1954	1,158,666	596,158	Kohler, Walter J. Jr.*	560,747	Proxmire, William	1,761	35,411 R	51.5%	48.4%	51.5%	48.5%
1952	1,615,214	1,009,171	Kohler, Walter J. Jr.*	601,844	Proxmire, William	4,199	407,327 R	62.5%	37.3%	62.6%	37.4%
1950	1,138,148	605,649	Kohler, Walter J. Jr.	525,319	Thompson, Carl W.	7,180	80,330 R	53.2%	46.2%	53.6%	46.4%
1948	1,266,139	684,839	Rennebohm, Oscar*	558,497	Thompson, Carl W.	22,803	126,342 R	54.1%	44.1%	55.1%	44.9%
1946	1,040,444	621,970	Goodland, Walter S.*	406,499	Hoan, Daniel W.	11,975	215,471 R	59.8%	39.1%	60.5%	39.5%

Note: An asterisk (*) denotes incumbent. **The 2012 Wisconsin gubernatorial contest was a special recall election held in June 2012. Governor Scott Walker retained his office. In past elections, the other vote included: 2002 - 185,455 Libertarian (Ed Thompson). The term of office of Wisconsin's governor was increased from two to four years effective with the 1970 election.

POSTWAR VOTE FOR SENATOR

Year	Total Vote	Republican Vote	Republican Candidate	Democratic Vote	Democratic Candidate	Other Vote	Rep.-Dem. Plurality	Total Vote Rep.	Total Vote Dem.	Major Vote Rep.	Major Vote Dem.
2012	3,009,411	1,380,126	Thompson, Tommy G.	1,547,104	Baldwin, Tammy	82,181	166,978 D	45.9%	51.4%	47.1%	52.9%
2010	2,171,331	1,125,999	Johnson, Ron	1,020,958	Feingold, Russell D.*	24,374	105,041 R	51.9%	47.0%	52.4%	47.6%
2006	2,138,297	630,299	Lorge, Robert Gerald	1,439,214	Kohl, Herbert H.*	68,784	808,915 D	29.5%	67.3%	30.5%	69.5%
2004	2,949,743	1,301,183	Michels, Tim	1,632,697	Feingold, Russell D.*	15,863	331,514 D	44.1%	55.4%	44.4%	55.6%
2000	2,540,083	940,744	Gillespie, John	1,563,238	Kohl, Herbert H.*	36,101	622,494 D	37.0%	61.5%	37.6%	62.4%
1998	1,760,836	852,272	Neumann, Mark W.	890,059	Feingold, Russell D.*	18,505	37,787 D	48.4%	50.5%	48.9%	51.1%
1994	1,565,628	636,989	Welch, Robert T.	912,662	Kohl, Herbert H.*	15,977	275,673 D	40.7%	58.3%	41.1%	58.9%
1992	2,455,124	1,129,599	Kasten, Robert W.*	1,290,662	Feingold, Russell D.	34,863	161,063 D	46.0%	52.6%	46.7%	53.3%
1988	2,168,190	1,030,440	Engeleiter, Susan	1,128,625	Kohl, Herbert H.	9,125	98,185 D	47.5%	52.1%	47.7%	52.3%
1986	1,483,174	754,573	Kasten, Robert W.*	702,963	Garvey, Ed	25,638	51,610 R	50.9%	47.4%	51.8%	48.2%
1982	1,544,981	527,355	McCallum, Scott	983,311	Proxmire, William*	34,315	455,956 D	34.1%	63.6%	34.9%	65.1%
1980	2,204,202	1,106,311	Kasten, Robert W.	1,065,487	Nelson, Gaylord A.*	32,404	40,824 R	50.2%	48.3%	50.9%	49.1%
1976	1,935,183	521,902	York, Stanley	1,396,970	Proxmire, William*	16,311	875,068 D	27.0%	72.2%	27.2%	72.8%
1974	1,199,495	429,327	Petri, Tom	740,700	Nelson, Gaylord A.*	29,468	311,373 D	35.8%	61.8%	36.7%	63.3%
1970	1,338,967	381,297	Erickson, John E.	948,445	Proxmire, William*	9,225	567,148 D	28.5%	70.8%	28.7%	71.3%
1968	1,654,861	633,910	Leonard, Jerris	1,020,931	Nelson, Gaylord A.*	20	387,021 D	38.3%	61.7%	38.3%	61.7%
1964	1,673,776	780,116	Renk, Wilbur N.	892,013	Proxmire, William*	1,647	111,897 D	46.6%	53.3%	46.7%	53.3%
1962	1,260,168	594,846	Wiley, Alexander*	662,342	Nelson, Gaylord A.	2,980	67,496 D	47.2%	52.6%	47.3%	52.7%
1958	1,194,678	510,398	Steinle, Roland J.	682,440	Proxmire, William*	1,840	172,042 D	42.7%	57.1%	42.8%	57.2%
1957S	772,620	312,931	Kohler, Walter J. Jr.	435,985	Proxmire, William	23,704	123,054 D	40.5%	56.4%	41.8%	58.2%
1956	1,523,356	892,473	Wiley, Alexander*	627,903	Maier, Henry W.	2,980	264,570 R	58.6%	41.2%	58.7%	41.3%
1952	1,605,228	870,444	McCarthy, Joseph R.*	731,402	Fairchild, Thomas E.	3,382	139,042 R	54.2%	45.6%	54.3%	45.7%
1950	1,116,135	595,283	Wiley, Alexander*	515,539	Fairchild, Thomas E.	5,313	79,744 R	53.3%	46.2%	53.6%	46.4%
1946	1,014,594	620,430	McCarthy, Joseph R.	378,772	McMurray, Howard J.	15,392	241,658 R	61.2%	37.3%	62.1%	37.9%

Note: An asterisk (*) denotes incumbent. **The August 1957 election was for a short term to fill a vacancy.

WISCONSIN

PRESIDENT 2012

2010 Census Population	County	Total Vote	Republican (Romney)	Democratic (Obama)	Other	Rep.-Dem. Plurality		Percentage			
								Total Vote		Major Vote	
								Rep.	Dem.	Rep.	Dem.
20,875	ADAMS	10,287	4,644	5,542	101	898	D	45.1%	53.9%	45.6%	54.4%
16,157	ASHLAND	8,372	2,820	5,399	153	2,579	D	33.7%	64.5%	34.3%	65.7%
45,870	BARRON	22,692	11,443	10,890	359	553	R	50.4%	48.0%	51.2%	48.8%
15,014	BAYFIELD	9,788	3,603	6,033	152	2,430	D	36.8%	61.6%	37.4%	62.6%
248,007	BROWN	128,928	64,836	62,526	1,566	2,310	R	50.3%	48.5%	50.9%	49.1%
13,587	BUFFALO	7,039	3,364	3,570	105	206	D	47.8%	50.7%	48.5%	51.5%
15,457	BURNETT	8,677	4,550	3,986	141	564	R	52.4%	45.9%	53.3%	46.7%
48,971	CALUMET	26,420	14,539	11,489	392	3,050	R	55.0%	43.5%	55.9%	44.1%
62,415	CHIPPEWA	30,932	15,322	15,237	373	85	R	49.5%	49.3%	50.1%	49.9%
34,690	CLARK	13,801	7,412	6,172	217	1,240	R	53.7%	44.7%	54.6%	45.4%
56,833	COLUMBIA	30,546	13,026	17,175	345	4,149	D	42.6%	56.2%	43.1%	56.9%
16,644	CRAWFORD	7,817	3,067	4,629	121	1,562	D	39.2%	59.2%	39.9%	60.1%
488,073	DANE	304,181	83,644	216,071	4,466	132,427	D	27.5%	71.0%	27.9%	72.1%
88,759	DODGE	44,488	25,211	18,762	515	6,449	R	56.7%	42.2%	57.3%	42.7%
27,785	DOOR	17,671	8,121	9,357	193	1,236	D	46.0%	53.0%	46.5%	53.5%
44,159	DOUGLAS	22,894	7,705	14,863	326	7,158	D	33.7%	64.9%	34.1%	65.9%
43,857	DUNN	21,992	10,224	11,316	452	1,092	D	46.5%	51.5%	47.5%	52.5%
98,736	EAU CLAIRE	54,806	23,256	30,666	884	7,410	D	42.4%	56.0%	43.1%	56.9%
4,423	FLORENCE	2,625	1,645	953	27	692	R	62.7%	36.3%	63.3%	36.7%
101,633	FOND DU LAC	53,402	30,355	22,379	668	7,976	R	56.8%	41.9%	57.6%	42.4%
9,304	FOREST	4,648	2,172	2,425	51	253	D	46.7%	52.2%	47.2%	52.8%
51,208	GRANT	24,248	10,255	13,594	399	3,339	D	42.3%	56.1%	43.0%	57.0%
36,842	GREEN	19,322	7,857	11,206	259	3,349	D	40.7%	58.0%	41.2%	58.8%
19,051	GREEN LAKE	9,675	5,782	3,793	100	1,989	R	59.8%	39.2%	60.4%	39.6%
23,687	IOWA	12,534	4,287	8,105	142	3,818	D	34.2%	64.7%	34.6%	65.4%
5,916	IRON	3,632	1,790	1,784	58	6	R	49.3%	49.1%	50.1%	49.9%
20,449	JACKSON	9,313	3,900	5,298	115	1,398	D	41.9%	56.9%	42.4%	57.6%
83,686	JEFFERSON	44,281	23,517	20,158	606	3,359	R	53.1%	45.5%	53.8%	46.2%
26,664	JUNEAU	11,827	5,411	6,242	174	831	D	45.8%	52.8%	46.4%	53.6%
166,426	KENOSHA	80,897	34,977	44,867	1,053	9,890	D	43.2%	55.5%	43.8%	56.2%
20,574	KEWAUNEE	11,037	5,747	5,153	137	594	R	52.1%	46.7%	52.7%	47.3%
114,638	LA CROSSE	63,462	25,751	36,693	1,018	10,942	D	40.6%	57.8%	41.2%	58.8%
16,836	LAFAYETTE	7,952	3,314	4,536	102	1,222	D	41.7%	57.0%	42.2%	57.8%
19,977	LANGLADE	10,519	5,816	4,573	130	1,243	R	55.3%	43.5%	56.0%	44.0%
28,743	LINCOLN	15,216	7,455	7,563	198	108	D	49.0%	49.7%	49.6%	50.4%
81,442	MANITOWOC	42,617	21,604	20,403	610	1,201	R	50.7%	47.9%	51.4%	48.6%
134,063	MARATHON	69,862	36,617	32,363	882	4,254	R	52.4%	46.3%	53.1%	46.9%
41,749	MARINETTE	20,777	10,619	9,882	276	737	R	51.1%	47.6%	51.8%	48.2%
15,404	MARQUETTE	8,105	3,992	4,014	99	22	D	49.3%	49.5%	49.9%	50.1%
4,232	MENOMINEE	1,377	179	1,191	7	1,012	D	13.0%	86.5%	13.1%	86.9%
947,735	MILWAUKEE	492,576	154,924	332,438	5,214	177,514	D	31.5%	67.5%	31.8%	68.2%
44,673	MONROE	19,485	9,675	9,515	295	160	R	49.7%	48.8%	50.4%	49.6%
37,660	OCONTO	19,859	10,741	8,865	253	1,876	R	54.1%	44.6%	54.8%	45.2%
35,998	ONEIDA	21,652	10,917	10,452	283	465	R	50.4%	48.3%	51.1%	48.9%
176,695	OUTAGAMIE	94,596	47,372	45,659	1,565	1,713	R	50.1%	48.3%	50.9%	49.1%
86,395	OZAUKEE	55,817	36,077	19,159	581	16,918	R	64.6%	34.3%	65.3%	34.7%
7,469	PEPIN	3,699	1,794	1,876	29	82	D	48.5%	50.7%	48.9%	51.1%
41,019	PIERCE	21,020	10,397	10,235	388	162	R	49.5%	48.7%	50.4%	49.6%
44,205	POLK	22,573	12,094	10,073	406	2,021	R	53.6%	44.6%	54.6%	45.4%
70,019	PORTAGE	39,337	16,615	22,075	647	5,460	D	42.2%	56.1%	42.9%	57.1%
14,159	PRICE	7,901	3,884	3,887	130	3	D	49.2%	49.2%	50.0%	50.0%
195,408	RACINE	103,364	49,347	53,008	1,009	3,661	D	47.7%	51.3%	48.2%	51.8%
18,021	RICHLAND	8,655	3,573	4,969	113	1,396	D	41.3%	57.4%	41.8%	58.2%
160,331	ROCK	80,690	30,517	49,219	954	18,702	D	37.8%	61.0%	38.3%	61.7%
14,755	RUSK	7,191	3,676	3,397	118	279	R	51.1%	47.2%	52.0%	48.0%
61,976	SAUK	31,927	12,838	18,736	353	5,898	D	40.2%	58.7%	40.7%	59.3%
16,557	SAWYER	9,025	4,442	4,486	97	44	D	49.2%	49.7%	49.8%	50.2%
41,949	SHAWANO	20,279	11,022	9,000	257	2,022	R	54.4%	44.4%	55.0%	45.0%
115,507	SHEBOYGAN	62,651	34,072	27,918	661	6,154	R	54.4%	44.6%	55.0%	45.0%
84,345	ST. CROIX	46,225	25,503	19,910	812	5,593	R	55.2%	43.1%	56.2%	43.8%

WISCONSIN

PRESIDENT 2012

2010 Census Population	County	Total Vote	Republican (Romney)	Democratic (Obama)	Other	Rep.-Dem. Plurality	Percentage Total Vote Rep.	Dem.	Major Vote Rep.	Dem.
20,689	TAYLOR	9,512	5,601	3,763	148	1,838 R	58.9%	39.6%	59.8%	40.2%
28,816	TREMPEALEAU	13,481	5,707	7,605	169	1,898 D	42.3%	56.4%	42.9%	57.1%
29,773	VERNON	14,269	5,942	8,044	283	2,102 D	41.6%	56.4%	42.5%	57.5%
21,430	VILAS	13,842	7,749	5,951	142	1,798 R	56.0%	43.0%	56.6%	43.4%
102,228	WALWORTH	52,303	29,006	22,552	745	6,454 R	55.5%	43.1%	56.3%	43.7%
15,911	WASHBURN	9,287	4,699	4,447	141	252 R	50.6%	47.9%	51.4%	48.6%
131,887	WASHINGTON	78,742	54,765	23,166	811	31,599 R	69.5%	29.4%	70.3%	29.7%
389,891	WAUKESHA	243,856	162,798	78,779	2,279	84,019 R	66.8%	32.3%	67.4%	32.6%
52,410	WAUPACA	25,840	14,002	11,578	260	2,424 R	54.2%	44.8%	54.7%	45.3%
24,496	WAUSHARA	12,048	6,562	5,335	151	1,227 R	54.5%	44.3%	55.2%	44.8%
166,994	WINNEBAGO	89,173	42,122	45,449	1,602	3,327 D	47.2%	51.0%	48.1%	51.9%
74,749	WOOD	38,900	19,704	18,581	615	1,123 R	50.7%	47.8%	51.5%	48.5%
5,686,986	TOTAL	3,068,434	1,407,966	1,620,985	39,483	213,019 D	45.9%	52.8%	46.5%	53.5%

WISCONSIN

GOVERNOR (RECALL ELECTION) 2012

2010 Census Population	County	Total Vote	Republican (Walker)	Democratic (Barrett)	Other	Rep.-Dem. Plurality	Percentage Total Vote Rep.	Dem.	Major Vote Rep.	Dem.
20,875	ADAMS	8,260	4,497	3,658	105	839 R	54.4%	44.3%	55.1%	44.9%
16,157	ASHLAND	6,827	2,598	4,174	55	1,576 D	38.1%	61.1%	38.4%	61.6%
45,870	BARRON	17,584	10,420	7,015	149	3,405 R	59.3%	39.9%	59.8%	40.2%
15,014	BAYFIELD	8,216	3,269	4,889	58	1,620 D	39.8%	59.5%	40.1%	59.9%
248,007	BROWN	103,893	61,969	41,238	686	20,731 R	59.6%	39.7%	60.0%	40.0%
13,587	BUFFALO	5,599	3,403	2,148	48	1,255 R	60.8%	38.4%	61.3%	38.7%
15,457	BURNETT	6,576	3,998	2,536	42	1,462 R	60.8%	38.6%	61.2%	38.8%
48,971	CALUMET	22,638	15,004	7,515	119	7,489 R	66.3%	33.2%	66.6%	33.4%
62,415	CHIPPEWA	25,556	14,877	10,419	260	4,458 R	58.2%	40.8%	58.8%	41.2%
34,690	CLARK	11,851	8,133	3,618	100	4,515 R	68.6%	30.5%	69.2%	30.8%
56,833	COLUMBIA	26,172	12,912	13,070	190	158 D	49.3%	49.9%	49.7%	50.3%
16,644	CRAWFORD	6,582	3,357	3,160	65	197 R	51.0%	48.0%	51.5%	48.5%
488,073	DANE	255,416	77,595	176,407	1,414	98,812 D	30.4%	69.1%	30.5%	69.5%
88,759	DODGE	39,071	24,851	13,958	262	10,893 R	63.6%	35.7%	64.0%	36.0%
27,785	DOOR	14,791	8,401	6,308	82	2,093 R	56.8%	42.6%	57.1%	42.9%
44,159	DOUGLAS	18,199	6,374	11,711	114	5,337 D	35.0%	64.3%	35.2%	64.8%
43,857	DUNN	15,633	8,417	7,099	117	1,318 R	53.8%	45.4%	54.2%	45.8%
98,736	EAU CLAIRE	41,685	20,740	20,595	350	145 R	49.8%	49.4%	50.2%	49.8%
4,423	FLORENCE	2,066	1,338	717	11	621 R	64.8%	34.7%	65.1%	34.9%
101,633	FOND DU LAC	45,483	29,060	16,105	318	12,955 R	63.9%	35.4%	64.3%	35.7%
9,304	FOREST	3,710	2,180	1,485	45	695 R	58.8%	40.0%	59.5%	40.5%
51,208	GRANT	18,275	9,498	8,623	154	875 R	52.0%	47.2%	52.4%	47.6%
36,842	GREEN	16,478	8,407	7,981	90	426 R	51.0%	48.4%	51.3%	48.7%
19,051	GREEN LAKE	8,425	5,800	2,564	61	3,236 R	68.8%	30.4%	69.3%	30.7%
23,687	IOWA	10,699	4,957	5,660	82	703 D	46.3%	52.9%	46.7%	53.3%
5,916	IRON	2,895	1,613	1,267	15	346 R	55.7%	43.8%	56.0%	44.0%
20,449	JACKSON	7,608	4,074	3,466	68	608 R	53.5%	45.6%	54.0%	46.0%
83,686	JEFFERSON	37,478	22,475	14,698	305	7,777 R	60.0%	39.2%	60.5%	39.5%
26,664	JUNEAU	9,753	5,429	4,225	99	1,204 R	55.7%	43.3%	56.2%	43.8%
166,426	KENOSHA	58,961	28,935	29,638	388	703 D	49.1%	50.3%	49.4%	50.6%

WISCONSIN

GOVERNOR (RECALL ELECTION) 2012

2010 Census Population	County	Total Vote	Republican (Walker)	Democratic (Barrett)	Other	Rep.-Dem. Plurality		Percentage			
								Total Vote		Major Vote	
								Rep.	Dem.	Rep.	Dem.
20,574	KEWAUNEE	9,542	6,108	3,388	46	2,720	R	64.0%	35.5%	64.3%	35.7%
114,638	LA CROSSE	47,663	22,608	24,651	404	2,043	D	47.4%	51.7%	47.8%	52.2%
16,836	LAFAYETTE	6,858	3,887	2,923	48	964	R	56.7%	42.6%	57.1%	42.9%
19,977	LANGLADE	8,591	5,621	2,898	72	2,723	R	65.4%	33.7%	66.0%	34.0%
28,743	LINCOLN	12,664	7,201	5,351	112	1,850	R	56.9%	42.3%	57.4%	42.6%
81,442	MANITOWOC	36,061	23,085	12,682	294	10,403	R	64.0%	35.2%	64.5%	35.5%
134,063	MARATHON	58,601	36,352	21,809	440	14,543	R	62.0%	37.2%	62.5%	37.5%
41,749	MARINETTE	16,603	10,267	6,242	94	4,025	R	61.8%	37.6%	62.2%	37.8%
15,404	MARQUETTE	6,926	4,102	2,764	60	1,338	R	59.2%	39.9%	59.7%	40.3%
4,232	MENOMINEE	786	208	575	3	367	D	26.5%	73.2%	26.6%	73.4%
947,735	MILWAUKEE	396,183	143,455	250,476	2,252	107,021	D	36.2%	63.2%	36.4%	63.6%
44,673	MONROE	15,326	9,064	6,093	169	2,971	R	59.1%	39.8%	59.8%	40.2%
37,660	OCONTO	16,937	11,049	5,782	106	5,267	R	65.2%	34.1%	65.6%	34.4%
35,998	ONEIDA	17,962	10,433	7,365	164	3,068	R	58.1%	41.0%	58.6%	41.4%
176,695	OUTAGAMIE	78,062	47,840	29,714	508	18,126	R	61.3%	38.1%	61.7%	38.3%
86,395	OZAUKEE	48,560	34,303	14,095	162	20,208	R	70.6%	29.0%	70.9%	29.1%
7,469	PEPIN	3,082	1,849	1,216	17	633	R	60.0%	39.5%	60.3%	39.7%
41,019	PIERCE	15,124	8,317	6,744	63	1,573	R	55.0%	44.6%	55.2%	44.8%
44,205	POLK	16,839	10,133	6,593	113	3,540	R	60.2%	39.2%	60.6%	39.4%
70,019	PORTAGE	30,782	14,846	15,672	264	826	D	48.2%	50.9%	48.6%	51.4%
14,159	PRICE	6,811	4,083	2,651	77	1,432	R	59.9%	38.9%	60.6%	39.4%
195,408	RACINE	86,351	45,526	40,287	538	5,239	R	52.7%	46.7%	53.1%	46.9%
18,021	RICHLAND	7,248	3,895	3,296	57	599	R	53.7%	45.5%	54.2%	45.8%
160,331	ROCK	63,358	27,498	35,316	544	7,818	D	43.4%	55.7%	43.8%	56.2%
14,755	RUSK	5,954	3,722	2,167	65	1,555	R	62.5%	36.4%	63.2%	36.8%
61,976	SAUK	26,649	13,648	12,815	186	833	R	51.2%	48.1%	51.6%	48.4%
16,557	SAWYER	7,085	3,999	3,038	48	961	R	56.4%	42.9%	56.8%	43.2%
41,949	SHAWANO	16,942	11,201	5,646	95	5,555	R	66.1%	33.3%	66.5%	33.5%
115,507	SHEBOYGAN	52,953	34,047	18,612	294	15,435	R	64.3%	35.1%	64.7%	35.3%
84,345	ST. CROIX	34,207	20,894	13,177	136	7,717	R	61.1%	38.5%	61.3%	38.7%
20,689	TAYLOR	8,032	5,751	2,201	80	3,550	R	71.6%	27.4%	72.3%	27.7%
28,816	TREMPEALEAU	10,992	6,266	4,634	92	1,632	R	57.0%	42.2%	57.5%	42.5%
29,773	VERNON	12,223	6,352	5,762	109	590	R	52.0%	47.1%	52.4%	47.6%
21,430	VILAS	11,534	7,300	4,154	80	3,146	R	63.3%	36.0%	63.7%	36.3%
102,228	WALWORTH	40,790	26,221	14,346	223	11,875	R	64.3%	35.2%	64.6%	35.4%
15,911	WASHBURN	7,493	4,278	3,156	59	1,122	R	57.1%	42.1%	57.5%	42.5%
131,887	WASHINGTON	69,203	52,306	16,634	263	35,672	R	75.6%	24.0%	75.9%	24.1%
389,891	WAUKESHA	213,332	154,316	58,234	782	96,082	R	72.3%	27.3%	72.6%	27.4%
52,410	WAUPACA	21,799	14,094	7,564	141	6,530	R	64.7%	34.7%	65.1%	34.9%
24,496	WAUSHARA	10,292	6,463	3,754	75	2,709	R	62.8%	36.5%	63.3%	36.7%
166,994	WINNEBAGO	71,272	39,881	30,885	506	8,996	R	56.0%	43.3%	56.4%	43.6%
74,749	WOOD	32,013	18,535	13,171	307	5,364	R	57.9%	41.1%	58.5%	41.5%
5,686,986	*TOTAL*	*2,516,065*	*1,335,585*	*1,164,480*	*16,000*	*171,105*	*R*	*53.1%*	*46.3%*	*53.4%*	*46.6%*

Note: Special recall election held June 5, 2012, after a petition to recall Governor Scott Walker, elected in 2010, received well more than the required 540,208 signatures to trigger the special election.

WISCONSIN

SENATOR 2012

2010 Census Population	County	Total Vote	Republican (Thompson)	Democratic (Baldwin)	Other	Rep.-Dem. Plurality	Percentage			
							Total Vote		Major Vote	
							Rep.	Dem.	Rep.	Dem.
20,875	ADAMS	9,810	4,404	5,161	245	757 D	44.9%	52.6%	46.0%	54.0%
16,157	ASHLAND	8,388	2,912	5,306	170	2,394 D	34.7%	63.3%	35.4%	64.6%
45,870	BARRON	22,285	10,805	10,644	836	161 R	48.5%	47.8%	50.4%	49.6%
15,014	BAYFIELD	9,630	3,476	6,017	137	2,541 D	36.1%	62.5%	36.6%	63.4%
248,007	BROWN	125,976	61,838	60,409	3,729	1,429 R	49.1%	48.0%	50.6%	49.4%
13,587	BUFFALO	6,877	3,284	3,366	227	82 D	47.8%	48.9%	49.4%	50.6%
15,457	BURNETT	8,438	4,288	3,996	154	292 R	50.8%	47.4%	51.8%	48.2%
48,971	CALUMET	25,972	14,053	10,989	930	3,064 R	54.1%	42.3%	56.1%	43.9%
62,415	CHIPPEWA	30,500	14,677	14,774	1,049	97 D	48.1%	48.4%	49.8%	50.2%
34,690	CLARK	13,547	6,875	6,159	513	716 R	50.7%	45.5%	52.7%	47.3%
56,833	COLUMBIA	30,203	13,413	16,028	762	2,615 D	44.4%	53.1%	45.6%	54.4%
16,644	CRAWFORD	7,635	3,117	4,321	197	1,204 D	40.8%	56.6%	41.9%	58.1%
488,073	DANE	300,587	88,395	206,917	5,275	118,522 D	29.4%	68.8%	29.9%	70.1%
88,759	DODGE	43,899	24,646	17,867	1,386	6,779 R	56.1%	40.7%	58.0%	42.0%
27,785	DOOR	17,432	7,996	8,966	470	970 D	45.9%	51.4%	47.1%	52.9%
44,159	DOUGLAS	22,464	7,478	14,599	387	7,121 D	33.3%	65.0%	33.9%	66.1%
43,857	DUNN	21,509	10,038	10,671	800	633 D	46.7%	49.6%	48.5%	51.5%
98,736	EAU CLAIRE	53,833	23,036	29,057	1,740	6,021 D	42.8%	54.0%	44.2%	55.8%
4,423	FLORENCE	2,550	1,586	908	56	678 R	62.2%	35.6%	63.6%	36.4%
101,633	FOND DU LAC	52,294	29,539	21,273	1,482	8,266 R	56.5%	40.7%	58.1%	41.9%
9,304	FOREST	4,455	2,028	2,288	139	260 D	45.5%	51.4%	47.0%	53.0%
51,208	GRANT	23,628	10,902	12,027	699	1,125 D	46.1%	50.9%	47.5%	52.5%
36,842	GREEN	19,153	7,954	10,721	478	2,767 D	41.5%	56.0%	42.6%	57.4%
19,051	GREEN LAKE	9,530	5,600	3,637	293	1,963 R	58.8%	38.2%	60.6%	39.4%
23,687	IOWA	12,382	4,631	7,454	297	2,823 D	37.4%	60.2%	38.3%	61.7%
5,916	IRON	3,478	1,785	1,656	37	129 R	51.3%	47.6%	51.9%	48.1%
20,449	JACKSON	9,156	3,894	4,979	283	1,085 D	42.5%	54.4%	43.9%	56.1%
83,686	JEFFERSON	43,514	23,393	19,081	1,040	4,312 R	53.8%	43.9%	55.1%	44.9%
26,664	JUNEAU	11,609	5,805	5,474	330	331 R	50.0%	47.2%	51.5%	48.5%
166,426	KENOSHA	79,111	33,273	42,825	3,013	9,552 D	42.1%	54.1%	43.7%	56.3%
20,574	KEWAUNEE	10,918	5,419	5,149	350	270 R	49.6%	47.2%	51.3%	48.7%
114,638	LA CROSSE	62,351	26,271	34,203	1,877	7,932 D	42.1%	54.9%	43.4%	56.6%
16,836	LAFAYETTE	7,824	3,549	4,110	165	561 D	45.4%	52.5%	46.3%	53.7%
19,977	LANGLADE	10,175	5,255	4,580	340	675 R	51.6%	45.0%	53.4%	46.6%
28,743	LINCOLN	14,935	6,911	7,379	645	468 D	46.3%	49.4%	48.4%	51.6%
81,442	MANITOWOC	41,862	20,646	19,616	1,600	1,030 R	49.3%	46.9%	51.3%	48.7%
134,063	MARATHON	68,787	34,688	31,751	2,348	2,937 R	50.4%	46.2%	52.2%	47.8%
41,749	MARINETTE	20,263	9,989	9,685	589	304 R	49.3%	47.8%	50.8%	49.2%
15,404	MARQUETTE	8,005	4,032	3,744	229	288 R	50.4%	46.8%	51.9%	48.1%
4,232	MENOMINEE	1,273	213	1,015	45	802 D	16.7%	79.7%	17.3%	82.7%
947,735	MILWAUKEE	477,884	155,410	312,618	9,856	157,208 D	32.5%	65.4%	33.2%	66.8%
44,673	MONROE	19,157	9,899	8,629	629	1,270 R	51.7%	45.0%	53.4%	46.6%
37,660	OCONTO	19,535	10,032	8,792	711	1,240 R	51.4%	45.0%	53.3%	46.7%
35,998	ONEIDA	21,199	10,183	10,047	969	136 R	48.0%	47.4%	50.3%	49.7%
176,695	OUTAGAMIE	92,928	46,212	43,297	3,419	2,915 R	49.7%	46.6%	51.6%	48.4%
86,395	OZAUKEE	55,050	35,463	18,285	1,302	17,178 R	64.4%	33.2%	66.0%	34.0%
7,469	PEPIN	3,592	1,702	1,812	78	110 D	47.4%	50.4%	48.4%	51.6%
41,019	PIERCE	20,606	9,850	10,254	502	404 D	47.8%	49.8%	49.0%	51.0%
44,205	POLK	22,144	11,310	10,192	642	1,118 R	51.1%	46.0%	52.6%	47.4%
70,019	PORTAGE	38,274	15,710	21,469	1,095	5,759 D	41.0%	56.1%	42.3%	57.7%
14,159	PRICE	7,730	3,623	3,832	275	209 D	46.9%	49.6%	48.6%	51.4%
195,408	RACINE	101,462	47,030	51,630	2,802	4,600 D	46.4%	50.9%	47.7%	52.3%
18,021	RICHLAND	8,437	3,786	4,504	147	718 D	44.9%	53.4%	45.7%	54.3%
160,331	ROCK	79,243	30,010	46,892	2,341	16,882 D	37.9%	59.2%	39.0%	61.0%
14,755	RUSK	7,043	3,393	3,298	352	95 R	48.2%	46.8%	50.7%	49.3%
61,976	SAUK	31,599	13,565	17,247	787	3,682 D	42.9%	54.6%	44.0%	56.0%
16,557	SAWYER	8,739	4,163	4,445	131	282 D	47.6%	50.9%	48.4%	51.6%
41,949	SHAWANO	19,852	10,417	8,755	680	1,662 R	52.5%	44.1%	54.3%	45.7%
115,507	SHEBOYGAN	61,766	33,472	26,284	2,010	7,188 R	54.2%	42.6%	56.0%	44.0%
84,345	ST. CROIX	45,572	24,347	20,053	1,172	4,294 R	53.4%	44.0%	54.8%	45.2%

WISCONSIN

SENATOR 2012

2010 Census Population	County	Total Vote	Republican (Thompson)	Democratic (Baldwin)	Other	Rep.-Dem. Plurality	Percentage			
							Total Vote		Major Vote	
							Rep.	Dem.	Rep.	Dem.
20,689	TAYLOR	9,280	5,049	3,859	372	1,190 R	54.4%	41.6%	56.7%	43.3%
28,816	TREMPEALEAU	13,223	5,699	7,144	380	1,445 D	43.1%	54.0%	44.4%	55.6%
29,773	VERNON	14,022	6,051	7,543	428	1,492 D	43.2%	53.8%	44.5%	55.5%
21,430	VILAS	13,526	7,308	5,762	456	1,546 R	54.0%	42.6%	55.9%	44.1%
102,228	WALWORTH	51,376	28,069	21,390	1,917	6,679 R	54.6%	41.6%	56.8%	43.2%
15,911	WASHBURN	9,037	4,442	4,405	190	37 R	49.2%	48.7%	50.2%	49.8%
131,887	WASHINGTON	77,787	52,950	22,702	2,135	30,248 R	68.1%	29.2%	70.0%	30.0%
389,891	WAUKESHA	240,142	159,450	75,408	5,284	84,042 R	66.4%	31.4%	67.9%	32.1%
52,410	WAUPACA	25,473	13,601	11,011	861	2,590 R	53.4%	43.2%	55.3%	44.7%
24,496	WAUSHARA	11,822	6,239	5,213	370	1,026 R	52.8%	44.1%	54.5%	45.5%
166,994	WINNEBAGO	87,541	41,545	42,782	3,214	1,237 D	47.5%	48.9%	49.3%	50.7%
74,749	WOOD	38,132	18,052	18,748	1,332	696 D	47.3%	49.2%	49.1%	50.9%
5,686,986	TOTAL	3,009,411	1,380,126	1,547,104	82,181	166,978 D	45.9%	51.4%	47.1%	52.9%

WISCONSIN

HOUSE OF REPRESENTATIVES

CD	Year	Total Vote	Republican		Democratic		Other Vote	Rep.-Dem. Plurality	Percentage			
			Vote	Candidate	Vote	Candidate			Total Vote		Major Vote	
									Rep.	Dem.	Rep.	Dem.
1	2012	365,058	200,423	RYAN, PAUL*	158,414	ZEBRAN, ROB	6,221	42,009 R	54.9%	43.4%	55.9%	44.1%
2	2012	390,898	124,683	LEE, CHAD	265,422	POCAN, MARK	793	140,739 D	31.9%	67.9%	32.0%	68.0%
3	2012	339,764	121,713	BOLAND, RAY	217,712	KIND, RON*	339	95,999 D	35.8%	64.1%	35.9%	64.1%
4	2012	325,788	80,787	SEBRING, DAN	235,257	MOORE, GWENDOLYNNE S. "GWEN"	9,744	154,470 D	24.8%	72.2%	25.6%	74.4%
5	2012	369,664	250,335	SENSENBRENNER, JIM*	118,478	HEASTER, DAVE	851	131,857 R	67.7%	32.1%	67.9%	32.1%
6	2012	359,745	223,460	PETRI, TOM*	135,921	KALLAS, JOSEPH C.	364	87,539 R	62.1%	37.8%	62.2%	37.8%
7	2012	359,669	201,720	DUFFY, SEAN*	157,524	KREITLOW, PAT	425	44,196 R	56.1%	43.8%	56.2%	43.8%
8	2012	355,464	198,874	RIBBLE, REID*	156,287	WALL, JAMIE	303	42,587 R	55.9%	44.0%	56.0%	44.0%
TOTAL	2012	2,866,050	1,401,995		1,445,015		19,040	43,020 D	48.9%	50.4%	49.2%	50.8%

Note: An asterisk (*) denotes incumbent.

WISCONSIN

GENERAL AND PRIMARY ELECTIONS

GENERAL ELECTIONS: OTHER VOTE

President   Other vote was 20,439 Libertarian (Gary E. Johnson), 7,665 Green (Jill Stein), 5,370 Write-in (Scattered Write-In), 4,930 Constitution (Virgil H. Goode), 553 Socialist Equality (Jerry White), 526 Socialism and Liberation (Gloria La Riva)

Senator   Other vote was 62,240 Independent (Joseph Kexel), 16,455 Independent (Nimrod Allen), 3,486 Write-in (Scattered Write-In)

WISCONSIN

GENERAL AND PRIMARY ELECTIONS

GENERAL ELECTIONS: OTHER VOTE

House   Other vote was:

CD 1   6,054 Libertarian (Keith Deschler), 167 Write-in (Scattered Write-In)
CD 2   787 Write-in (Scattered Write-In), 6 Write-in (Joe Kopsick)
CD 3   339 Write-in (Scattered Write-In)
CD 4   9,277 Independent (Robert R. Raymond), 467 Write-in (Scattered Write-In)
CD 5   851 Write-in (Scattered Write-In)
CD 6   364 Write-in (Scattered Write-In)
CD 7   405 Write-in (Scattered Write-In), 20 Independent (Dale C. Lehner)
CD 8   303 Write-in (Scattered Write-In)

PRIMARY ELECTIONS: SUPPLEMENTARY INFORMATION

Primary   April 3, 2012 (President)   **Registration**   3,453,794   No Party Registration
                August 14, 2012 (Congress)   (as of August 9, 2012)

Primary Type   Open—Any registered voter could participate in the party primary of their choice.

	REPUBLICAN PRIMARIES			DEMOCRATIC PRIMARIES		
President	Romney, W. Mitt	346,876	44.0%	Obama, Barack H.*	293,914	97.9%
	Santorum, Rick	290,139	36.8%	Uninstructed Delegation	5,492	1.8%
	Paul, Ron	87,858	11.2%	Scattered Write-In	849	0.3%
	Gingrich, Newt	45,978	5.8%			
	Bachmann, Michele	6,045	0.8%			
	Huntsman, Jon Jr.	5,083	0.6%			
	Uninstructed Delegation	4,200	0.5%			
	Scattered Write-In	1,668	0.2%			
	TOTAL	*787,847*		*TOTAL*	*300,255*	
Senator	Thompson, Tommy G.	197,928	34.0%	Baldwin, Tammy	185,265	99.8%
	Hovde, Eric	179,557	30.8%	Scattered Write-In	424	0.2%
	Neumann, Mark W.	132,786	22.8%			
	Fitzgerald, Jeff	71,871	12.3%			
	Scattered Write-In	244				
	TOTAL	*582,386*		*TOTAL*	*185,689*	
Governor	Walker, Scott*	626,962	96.9%	Barrett, Thomas M.	390,191	58.1%
	Kohl-Riggs, Arthur	19,939	3.1%	Falk, Kathleen	229,236	34.1%
	Scattered Write-In	204		Vinehout, Kathleen	26,967	4.0%
	O'Brien, Patrick J.	17		La Follette, Doug	19,497	2.9%
				Huber, Gladys R.	4,847	0.7%
				Scattered Write-In	864	0.1%
	TOTAL	*647,122*		*TOTAL*	*671,602*	
Congressional District 1	Ryan, Paul*	65,700	99.6%	Zebran, Rob	16,265	99.8%
	Scattered Write-In	278	0.4%	Scattered Write-In	27	0.2%
	TOTAL	*65,978*		*TOTAL*	*16,292*	
Congressional District 2	Lee, Chad	32,813	99.5%	Pocan, Mark	43,171	72.2%
	Scattered Write-In	158	0.5%	Roys, Kelda Helen	13,081	21.9%
				Silverman, Matt	2,365	4.0%
				Hall, Dennis	1,163	1.9%
				Scattered Write-In	46	0.1%
	TOTAL	*32,971*		*TOTAL*	*59,826*	

WISCONSIN

GENERAL AND PRIMARY ELECTIONS

	REPUBLICAN PRIMARIES			DEMOCRATIC PRIMARIES		
Congressional District 3	Boland, Ray	35,668	99.6%	Kind, Ron*	19,755	99.9%
	Scattered Write-In	148	0.4%	Scattered Write-In	27	0.1%
	TOTAL	35,816		TOTAL	19,782	
Congressional District 4	Sebring, Dan	19,144	99.0%	Moore, Gwendolynne S. "Gwen"*	34,525	99.7%
	Scattered Write-In	200	1.0%	Scattered Write-In	115	0.3%
	TOTAL	19,344		TOTAL	34,640	
Congressional District 5	Sensenbrenner, Jim*	89,370	99.4%	Heaster, Dave	9,266	99.9%
	Scattered Write-In	535	0.6%	Scattered Write-In	13	0.1%
	TOTAL	89,905		TOTAL	9,279	
Congressional District 6	Petri, Tom*	73,376	82.2%	Kallas, Joseph C.	11,285	99.8%
	Stephens, Lauren	15,821	17.7%	Scattered Write-In	18	0.2%
	Scattered Write-In	75	0.1%			
	TOTAL	89,272		TOTAL	11,303	
Congressional District 7	Duffy, Sean*	46,987	99.5%	Kreitlow, Pat	16,053	99.9%
	Scattered Write-In	252	0.5%	Scattered Write-In	19	0.1%
	TOTAL	47,239		TOTAL	16,072	
Congressional District 8	Ribble, Reid*	64,689	99.6%	Wall, Jamie	11,513	99.8%
	Scattered Write-In	251	0.4%	Scattered Write-In	19	0.2%
	TOTAL	64,940		TOTAL	11,532	

Notes: An asterisk (*) denotes incumbent. Gubernatorial primary is for special recall election.

WYOMING

One member At Large

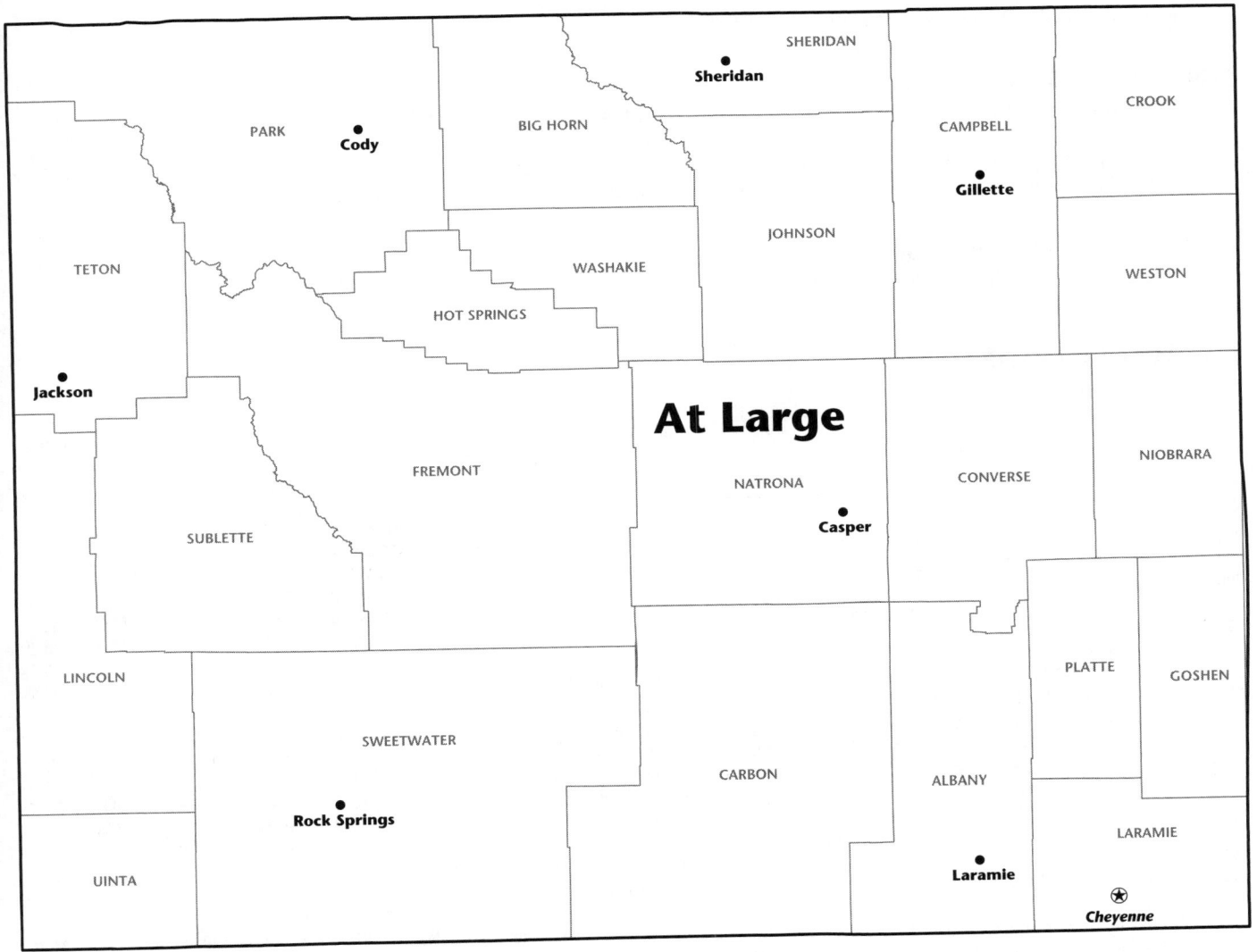

WYOMING

GOVERNOR

Matt Mead (R). Elected 2010 to a four-year term.

SENATORS (2 Republicans)

Michael B. Enzi (R). Reelected 2008 to a six-year term. Previously elected 2002, 1996.

John Barrasso (R). Reelected 2012. Previously elected 2008 to fill out the remaining four years of the term vacated by the June 2007 death of Senator Craig Thomas (R); sworn in as Thomas's successor June 25, 2007.

REPRESENTATIVE (1 Republican)

At Large. Cynthia M. Lummis (R)

POSTWAR VOTE FOR PRESIDENT

		Republican		Democratic				Percentage			
								Total Vote		Major Vote	
Year	Total Vote	Vote	Candidate	Vote	Candidate	Other Vote	Rep.-Dem. Plurality	Rep.	Dem.	Rep.	Dem.
2012	249,061	170,962	Romney, W. Mitt	69,286	Obama, Barack H.*	8,813	101,676 R	68.6%	27.8%	71.2%	28.8%
2008	254,658	164,958	McCain, John S. III	82,868	Obama, Barack H.	6,832	82,090 R	64.8%	32.5%	66.6%	33.4%
2004	243,428	167,629	Bush, George W.*	70,776	Kerry, John F.	5,023	96,853 R	68.9%	29.1%	70.3%	29.7%
2000**	218,351	147,947	Bush, George W.	60,481	Gore, Albert Jr.	9,923	87,466 R	67.8%	27.7%	71.0%	29.0%
1996**	211,571	105,388	Dole, Robert "Bob"	77,934	Clinton, Bill*	28,249	27,454 R	49.8%	36.8%	57.5%	42.5%
1992**	200,598	79,347	Bush, George H.*	68,160	Clinton, Bill	53,091	11,187 R	39.6%	34.0%	53.8%	46.2%
1988	176,551	106,867	Bush, George H.	67,113	Dukakis, Michael S.	2,571	39,754 R	60.5%	38.0%	61.4%	38.6%
1984	188,968	133,241	Reagan, Ronald*	53,370	Mondale, Walter F.	2,357	79,871 R	70.5%	28.2%	71.4%	28.6%
1980**	176,713	110,700	Reagan, Ronald	49,427	Carter, Jimmy*	16,586	61,273 R	62.6%	28.0%	69.1%	30.9%
1976	156,343	92,717	Ford, Gerald R.*	62,239	Carter, Jimmy	1,387	30,478 R	59.3%	39.8%	59.8%	40.2%
1972	145,570	100,464	Nixon, Richard M.*	44,358	McGovern, George S.	748	56,106 R	69.0%	30.5%	69.4%	30.6%
1968**	127,205	70,927	Nixon, Richard M.	45,173	Humphrey, Hubert H. Jr.	11,105	25,754 R	55.8%	35.5%	61.1%	38.9%
1964	142,716	61,998	Goldwater, Barry M. Sr.	80,718	Johnson, Lyndon B.*		18,720 D	43.4%	56.6%	43.4%	56.6%
1960	140,782	77,451	Nixon, Richard M.	63,331	Kennedy, John F.		14,120 R	55.0%	45.0%	55.0%	45.0%
1956	124,127	74,573	Eisenhower, Dwight D.*	49,554	Stevenson, Adlai E. II		25,019 R	60.1%	39.9%	60.1%	39.9%
1952	129,253	81,049	Eisenhower, Dwight D.	47,934	Stevenson, Adlai E. II	270	33,115 R	62.7%	37.1%	62.8%	37.2%
1948	101,425	47,947	Dewey, Thomas E.	52,354	Truman, Harry S.*	1,124	4,407 D	47.3%	51.6%	47.8%	52.2%

Note: An asterisk (*) denotes incumbent. **In past elections, the other vote included: 2000 - 4,625 Green (Ralph Nader); 1996 - 25,928 Reform (Ross Perot); 1992 - 51,263 Independent (Perot); 1980 - 12,072 Independent (John Anderson); 1968 - 11,105 American Independent (George Wallace).

WYOMING

POSTWAR VOTE FOR GOVERNOR

Year	Total Vote	Republican		Democratic		Other Vote	Rep.-Dem. Plurality	Percentage			
		Vote	Candidate	Vote	Candidate			Total Vote		Major Vote	
								Rep.	Dem.	Rep.	Dem.
2010	188,463	123,780	Mead, Matt	43,240	Petersen, Leslie	21,443	80,540 R	65.7%	22.9%	74.1%	25.9%
2006	193,892	58,100	Hunkins, Ray	135,516	Freudenthal, Dave*	276	77,416 D	30.0%	69.9%	30.0%	70.0%
2002	185,459	88,873	Bebout, Eli	92,662	Freudenthal, Dave	3,924	3,789 D	47.9%	50.0%	49.0%	51.0%
1998	174,888	97,235	Geringer, Jim*	70,754	Vinich, John P.	6,899	26,481 R	55.6%	40.5%	57.9%	42.1%
1994	200,990	118,016	Geringer, Jim	80,747	Karpan, Kathy	2,227	37,269 R	58.7%	40.2%	59.4%	40.6%
1990	160,109	55,471	Mead, Mary	104,638	Sullivan, Mike*		49,167 D	34.6%	65.4%	34.6%	65.4%
1986	164,720	75,841	Simpson, Peter	88,879	Sullivan, Mike		13,038 D	46.0%	54.0%	46.0%	54.0%
1982	168,555	62,128	Morton, Warren A.	106,427	Herschler, Ed*		44,299 D	36.9%	63.1%	36.9%	63.1%
1978	137,567	67,595	Ostlund, John C.	69,972	Herschler, Ed*		2,377 D	49.1%	50.9%	49.1%	50.9%
1974	128,386	56,645	Jones, Dick	71,741	Herschler, Ed		15,096 D	44.1%	55.9%	44.1%	55.9%
1970	118,257	74,249	Hathaway, Stanley K.*	44,008	Rooney, John J.		30,241 R	62.8%	37.2%	62.8%	37.2%
1966	120,873	65,624	Hathaway, Stanley K.	55,249	Wilkerson, Ernest		10,375 R	54.3%	45.7%	54.3%	45.7%
1962	119,268	64,970	Hansen, Clifford P.	54,298	Gage, Jack R.*		10,672 R	54.5%	45.5%	54.5%	45.5%
1958	112,537	52,488	Simpson, Milward L.*	55,070	Hickey, John J.	4,979	2,582 D	46.6%	48.9%	48.8%	51.2%
1954	111,438	56,275	Simpson, Milward L.	55,163	Jack, William		1,112 R	50.5%	49.5%	50.5%	49.5%
1950	96,959	54,441	Barrett, Frank A.	42,518	McIntyre, John J.		11,923 R	56.1%	43.9%	56.1%	43.9%
1946	81,353	38,333	Wright, Earl	43,020	Hunt, Lester C.*		4,687 D	47.1%	52.9%	47.1%	52.9%

Note: An asterisk (*) denotes incumbent.

POSTWAR VOTE FOR SENATOR

Year	Total Vote	Republican		Democratic		Other Vote	Rep.-Dem. Plurality	Percentage			
		Vote	Candidate	Vote	Candidate			Total Vote		Major Vote	
								Rep.	Dem.	Rep.	Dem.
2012	244,862	185,250	Barrasso, John*	53,019	Chestnut, Tim	6,593	132,231 R	75.7%	21.7%	77.7%	22.3%
2008	249,946	189,046	Enzi, Michael B.*	60,631	Rothfuss, Chris	269	128,415 R	75.6%	24.3%	75.7%	24.3%
2008S	249,558	183,063	Barrasso, John*	66,202	Carter, Nick	293	116,861 R	73.4%	26.5%	73.4%	26.6%
2006	193,136	135,174	Thomas, Craig*	57,671	Groutage, Dale	291	77,503 R	70.0%	29.9%	70.1%	29.9%
2002	183,280	133,710	Enzi, Michael B.*	49,570	Corcoran, Joyce Jansa		84,140 R	73.0%	27.0%	73.0%	27.0%
2000	213,659	157,622	Thomas, Craig*	47,087	Logan, Mel	8,950	110,535 R	73.8%	22.0%	77.0%	23.0%
1996	211,077	114,116	Enzi, Michael B.	89,103	Karpan, Kathy	7,858	25,013 R	54.1%	42.2%	56.2%	43.8%
1994	201,710	118,754	Thomas, Craig	79,287	Sullivan, Mike	3,669	39,467 R	58.9%	39.3%	60.0%	40.0%
1990	157,632	100,784	Simpson, Alan K.*	56,848	Helling, Kathy		43,936 R	63.9%	36.1%	63.9%	36.1%
1988	180,964	91,143	Wallop, Malcolm*	89,821	Vinich, John P.		1,322 R	50.4%	49.6%	50.4%	49.6%
1984	186,898	146,373	Simpson, Alan K.*	40,525	Ryan, Victor A.		105,848 R	78.3%	21.7%	78.3%	21.7%
1982	167,191	94,725	Wallop, Malcolm*	72,466	McDaniel, Rodger		22,259 R	56.7%	43.3%	56.7%	43.3%
1978	133,364	82,908	Simpson, Alan K.	50,456	Whitaker, Raymond B.		32,452 R	62.2%	37.8%	62.2%	37.8%
1976	155,368	84,810	Wallop, Malcolm	70,558	McGee, Gale*		14,252 R	54.6%	45.4%	54.6%	45.4%
1972	142,067	101,314	Hansen, Clifford P.*	40,753	Vinich, Mike		60,561 R	71.3%	28.7%	71.3%	28.7%
1970	120,486	53,279	Wold, John S.	67,207	McGee, Gale*		13,928 D	44.2%	55.8%	44.2%	55.8%
1966	122,689	63,548	Hansen, Clifford P.	59,141	Roncalio, Teno		4,407 R	51.8%	48.2%	51.8%	48.2%
1964	141,670	65,185	Wold, John S.	76,485	McGee, Gale*		11,300 D	46.0%	54.0%	46.0%	54.0%
1962S	119,372	69,043	Simpson, Milward L.	50,329	Hickey, John J.*		18,714 R	57.8%	42.2%	57.8%	42.2%
1960	138,550	78,103	Thomson, E. Keith	60,447	Whitaker, Raymond B.		17,656 R	56.4%	43.6%	56.4%	43.6%
1958	114,157	56,122	Barrett, Frank A.*	58,035	McGee, Gale		1,913 D	49.2%	50.8%	49.2%	50.8%
1954	112,252	54,407	Harrison, William Henry	57,845	O'Mahoney, Joseph C.*		3,438 D	48.5%	51.5%	48.5%	51.5%
1952	130,097	67,176	Barrett, Frank A.	62,921	O'Mahoney, Joseph C.*		4,255 R	51.6%	48.4%	51.6%	48.4%
1948	101,480	43,527	Robertson, Edward V.*	57,953	Hunt, Lester C.		14,426 D	42.9%	57.1%	42.9%	57.1%
1946	81,557	35,714	Henderson, Harry B.	45,843	O'Mahoney, Joseph C.*		10,129 D	43.8%	56.2%	43.8%	56.2%

Note: An asterisk (*) denotes incumbent. **The 1962 election and one of the 2008 elections were for short terms to fill a vacancy.

WYOMING

PRESIDENT 2012

2010 Census Population	County	Total Vote	Republican (Romney)	Democratic (Obama)	Other	Rep.-Dem. Plurality	Percentage Total Vote Rep.	Dem.	Major Vote Rep.	Dem.
36,299	ALBANY	16,300	7,866	7,458	976	408 R	48.3%	45.8%	51.3%	48.7%
11,668	BIG HORN	5,324	4,285	868	171	3,417 R	80.5%	16.3%	83.2%	16.8%
46,133	CAMPBELL	17,571	14,953	2,163	455	12,790 R	85.1%	12.3%	87.4%	12.6%
15,885	CARBON	6,509	4,148	2,110	251	2,038 R	63.7%	32.4%	66.3%	33.7%
13,833	CONVERSE	6,343	5,043	1,089	211	3,954 R	79.5%	17.2%	82.2%	17.8%
7,083	CROOK	3,685	3,109	426	150	2,683 R	84.4%	11.6%	87.9%	12.1%
40,123	FREMONT	16,939	11,075	5,333	531	5,742 R	65.4%	31.5%	67.5%	32.5%
13,249	GOSHEN	5,806	4,178	1,458	170	2,720 R	72.0%	25.1%	74.1%	25.9%
4,812	HOT SPRINGS	2,515	1,895	523	97	1,372 R	75.3%	20.8%	78.4%	21.6%
8,569	JOHNSON	4,259	3,363	749	147	2,614 R	79.0%	17.6%	81.8%	18.2%
91,738	LARAMIE	39,505	23,904	14,295	1,306	9,609 R	60.5%	36.2%	62.6%	37.4%
18,106	LINCOLN	8,618	7,144	1,287	187	5,857 R	82.9%	14.9%	84.7%	15.3%
75,450	NATRONA	32,373	22,132	8,961	1,280	13,171 R	68.4%	27.7%	71.2%	28.8%
2,484	NIOBRARA	1,276	1,022	200	54	822 R	80.1%	15.7%	83.6%	16.4%
28,205	PARK	14,608	11,234	2,927	447	8,307 R	76.9%	20.0%	79.3%	20.7%
8,667	PLATTE	4,531	3,136	1,223	172	1,913 R	69.2%	27.0%	71.9%	28.1%
29,116	SHERIDAN	14,322	10,267	3,618	437	6,649 R	71.7%	25.3%	73.9%	26.1%
10,247	SUBLETTE	4,376	3,472	767	137	2,705 R	79.3%	17.5%	81.9%	18.1%
43,806	SWEETWATER	16,895	11,428	4,774	693	6,654 R	67.6%	28.3%	70.5%	29.5%
21,294	TETON	11,464	4,858	6,213	393	1,355 D	42.4%	54.2%	43.9%	56.1%
21,118	UINTA	8,539	6,615	1,628	296	4,987 R	77.5%	19.1%	80.2%	19.8%
8,533	WASHAKIE	3,944	3,014	794	136	2,220 R	76.4%	20.1%	79.1%	20.9%
7,208	WESTON	3,359	2,821	422	116	2,399 R	84.0%	12.6%	87.0%	13.0%
563,626	TOTAL	249,061	170,962	69,286	8,813	101,676 R	68.6%	27.8%	71.2%	28.8%

WYOMING

SENATOR 2012

2010 Census Population	County	Total Vote	Republican (Barrasso)	Democratic (Chestnut)	Other	Rep.-Dem. Plurality	Percentage Total Vote Rep.	Dem.	Major Vote Rep.	Dem.
36,299	ALBANY	15,971	9,096	6,469	406	2,627 R	57.0%	40.5%	58.4%	41.6%
11,668	BIG HORN	5,268	4,560	554	154	4,006 R	86.6%	10.5%	89.2%	10.8%
46,133	CAMPBELL	17,268	15,028	1,668	572	13,360 R	87.0%	9.7%	90.0%	10.0%
15,885	CARBON	6,400	4,864	1,405	131	3,459 R	76.0%	22.0%	77.6%	22.4%
13,833	CONVERSE	6,288	5,365	772	151	4,593 R	85.3%	12.3%	87.4%	12.6%
7,083	CROOK	3,641	3,177	348	116	2,829 R	87.3%	9.6%	90.1%	9.9%
40,123	FREMONT	16,674	12,369	3,767	538	8,602 R	74.2%	22.6%	76.7%	23.3%
13,249	GOSHEN	5,739	4,633	944	162	3,689 R	80.7%	16.4%	83.1%	16.9%
4,812	HOT SPRINGS	2,499	2,078	354	67	1,724 R	83.2%	14.2%	85.4%	14.6%
8,569	JOHNSON	4,217	3,634	492	91	3,142 R	86.2%	11.7%	88.1%	11.9%
91,738	LARAMIE	38,688	26,712	10,950	1,026	15,762 R	69.0%	28.3%	70.9%	29.1%
18,106	LINCOLN	8,488	7,230	1,070	188	6,160 R	85.2%	12.6%	87.1%	12.9%
75,450	NATRONA	31,888	24,431	6,533	924	17,898 R	76.6%	20.5%	78.9%	21.1%
2,484	NIOBRARA	1,264	1,110	124	30	986 R	87.8%	9.8%	90.0%	10.0%
28,205	PARK	14,357	11,789	2,183	385	9,606 R	82.1%	15.2%	84.4%	15.6%
8,667	PLATTE	4,490	3,420	905	165	2,515 R	76.2%	20.2%	79.1%	20.9%
29,116	SHERIDAN	14,161	11,174	2,757	230	8,417 R	78.9%	19.5%	80.2%	19.8%
10,247	SUBLETTE	4,310	3,631	576	103	3,055 R	84.2%	13.4%	86.3%	13.7%
43,806	SWEETWATER	16,629	12,399	3,778	452	8,621 R	74.6%	22.7%	76.6%	23.4%
21,294	TETON	10,969	5,562	5,140	267	422 R	50.7%	46.9%	52.0%	48.0%
21,118	UINTA	8,383	6,780	1,365	238	5,415 R	80.9%	16.3%	83.2%	16.8%
8,533	WASHAKIE	3,924	3,321	529	74	2,792 R	84.6%	13.5%	86.3%	13.7%
7,208	WESTON	3,346	2,887	336	123	2,551 R	86.3%	10.0%	89.6%	10.4%
563,626	TOTAL	244,862	185,250	53,019	6,593	132,231 R	75.7%	21.7%	77.7%	22.3%

WYOMING

HOUSE OF REPRESENTATIVES

CD	Year	Total Vote	Republican Vote	Republican Candidate	Democratic Vote	Democratic Candidate	Other Vote	Rep.-Dem. Plurality	Total Vote Rep.	Total Vote Dem.	Major Vote Rep.	Major Vote Dem.
At Large	2012	241,621	166,452	LUMMIS, CYNTHIA M.*	57,573	HENRICHSEN, CHRIS	17,596	108,879 R	68.9%	23.8%	74.3%	25.7%
At Large	2010	186,969	131,661	LUMMIS, CYNTHIA M.*	45,768	WENDT, DAVID	9,540	85,893 R	70.4%	24.5%	74.2%	25.8%
At Large	2008	249,395	131,244	LUMMIS, CYNTHIA M.	106,758	TRAUNER, GARY	11,393	24,486 R	52.6%	42.8%	55.1%	44.9%
At Large	2006	193,369	93,336	CUBIN, BARBARA*	92,324	TRAUNER, GARY	7,709	1,012 R	48.3%	47.7%	50.3%	49.7%
At Large	2004	239,034	132,107	CUBIN, BARBARA*	99,989	LADD, TED	6,938	32,118 R	55.3%	41.8%	56.9%	43.1%
At Large	2002	182,152	110,229	CUBIN, BARBARA*	65,961	AKIN, RON	5,962	44,268 R	60.5%	36.2%	62.6%	37.4%
At Large	2000	212,312	141,848	CUBIN, BARBARA*	60,638	GREEN, MICHAEL ALLEN	9,826	81,210 R	66.8%	28.6%	70.1%	29.9%
At Large	1998	174,219	100,687	CUBIN, BARBARA*	67,399	FARRIS, SCOTT	6,133	33,288 R	57.8%	38.7%	59.9%	40.1%
At Large	1996	209,983	116,004	CUBIN, BARBARA*	85,724	MAXFIELD, PETE	8,255	30,280 R	55.2%	40.8%	57.5%	42.5%
At Large	1994	196,197	104,426	CUBIN, BARBARA	81,022	SCHUSTER, BOB	10,749	23,404 R	53.2%	41.3%	56.3%	43.7%
At Large	1992	196,977	113,882	THOMAS, CRAIG*	77,418	HERSCHLER, JON	5,677	36,464 R	57.8%	39.3%	59.5%	40.5%
At Large	1990	158,055	87,078	THOMAS, CRAIG	70,977	MAXFIELD, PETE		16,101 R	55.1%	44.9%	55.1%	44.9%
At Large	1988	177,651	118,350	CHENEY, RICHARD*	56,527	SHARRATT, BRYAN	2,774	61,823 R	66.6%	31.8%	67.7%	32.3%
At Large	1986	159,787	111,007	CHENEY, RICHARD*	48,780	GILMORE, RICK		62,227 R	69.5%	30.5%	69.5%	30.5%
At Large	1984	187,904	138,234	CHENEY, RICHARD*	45,857	MCFADDEN, HUGH B.	3,813	92,377 R	73.6%	24.4%	75.1%	24.9%
At Large	1982	159,277	113,236	CHENEY, RICHARD*	46,041	HOMMEL, THEODORE H.		67,195 R	71.1%	28.9%	71.1%	28.9%
At Large	1980	169,699	116,361	CHENEY, RICHARD*	53,338	ROGERS, JIM		63,023 R	68.6%	31.4%	68.6%	31.4%
At Large	1978	129,377	75,855	CHENEY, RICHARD	53,522	BAGLEY, BILL		22,333 R	58.6%	41.4%	58.6%	41.4%
At Large	1976	151,868	66,147	HART, LARRY	85,721	RONCALIO, TENO*		19,574 D	43.6%	56.4%	43.6%	56.4%
At Large	1974	126,933	57,499	STROOCK, TOM	69,434	RONCALIO, TENO*		11,935 D	45.3%	54.7%	45.3%	54.7%
At Large	1972	146,299	70,667	KIDD, WILLIAM	75,632	RONCALIO, TENO*		4,965 D	48.3%	51.7%	48.3%	51.7%
At Large	1970	116,304	57,848	ROBERTS, HARRY	58,456	RONCALIO, TENO		608 D	49.7%	50.3%	49.7%	50.3%
At Large	1968	123,313	77,363	WOLD, JOHN S.	45,950	LINFORD, VELMA		31,413 R	62.7%	37.3%	62.7%	37.3%
At Large	1966	120,426	62,984	HARRISON, WILLIAM HENRY	57,442	CHRISTIAN, AL		5,542 R	52.3%	47.7%	52.3%	47.7%
At Large	1964	139,175	68,482	HARRISON, WILLIAM HENRY	70,693	RONCALIO, TENO		2,211 D	49.2%	50.8%	49.2%	50.8%
At Large	1962	116,474	71,489	HARRISON, WILLIAM HENRY*	44,985	MANKUS, LOUIS A.		26,504 R	61.4%	38.6%	61.4%	38.6%
At Large	1960	134,331	70,241	HARRISON, WILLIAM HENRY	64,090	ARMSTRONG, HEPBURN T.		6,151 R	52.3%	47.7%	52.3%	47.7%
At Large	1958	111,780	59,894	THOMSON, E. KEITH*	51,886	WHITAKER, RAYMOND B.		8,008 R	53.6%	46.4%	53.6%	46.4%
At Large	1956	120,128	69,903	THOMSON, E. KEITH*	50,225	O'CALLAGHAN, JERRY A.		19,678 R	58.2%	41.8%	58.2%	41.8%
At Large	1954	108,771	61,111	THOMSON, E. KEITH	47,660	TULLY, SAM		13,451 R	56.2%	43.8%	56.2%	43.8%
At Large	1952	126,720	76,161	HARRISON, WILLIAM HENRY*	50,559	ROSS, ROBERT R. JR.		25,602 R	60.1%	39.9%	60.1%	39.9%
At Large	1950	93,348	50,865	HARRISON, WILLIAM HENRY	42,483	CLARK, JOHN B.		8,382 R	54.5%	45.5%	54.5%	45.5%
At Large	1948	97,464	50,218	BARRETT, FRANK A.*	47,246	FLANNERY, L. G.		2,972 R	51.5%	48.5%	51.5%	48.5%
At Large	1946	79,438	44,482	BARRETT, FRANK A.*	34,956	MCINTYRE, JOHN J.		9,526 R	56.0%	44.0%	56.0%	44.0%

Note: An asterisk (*) denotes incumbent.

WYOMING

GENERAL AND PRIMARY ELECTIONS

GENERAL ELECTIONS: OTHER VOTE

President   Other vote was 5,326 Libertarian (Gary E. Johnson), 2,035 Write-in (Scattered Write-In), 1,452 Constitution (Virgil H. Goode)

Senator   Other vote was 6,176 Wyoming Country (Joel Otto), 417 Write-in (Scattered Write-In)

House   Other vote was:

At Large   8,442 Libertarian (Richard Brubaker), 4,963 Constitution (Daniel Clyde Cummings), 3,775 Country (Don Wills), 416 Write-in (Scattered Write-In)

WYOMING

GENERAL AND PRIMARY ELECTIONS

PRIMARY ELECTIONS: SUPPLEMENTARY INFORMATION

Primary	August 21, 2012	**Registration** (as of August 1, 2012)		216,552	Republican	145,269
					Democratic	47,117
					Libertatian	887
					Unaffiliated	23,235
					Other	15

Primary Type Semi-Open—Only registered Democrats and Republicans could vote in their party's primary, although on primary day any new voter could register with the party of their choice and any previously registered voter could participate in another party's primary by changing their registration to that party.

	REPUBLICAN PRIMARIES			DEMOCRATIC PRIMARIES		
Senator	Barrasso, John*	73,516	89.9%	Chestnut, Tim	9,173	53.7%
	Bleming, Thomas	5,080	6.2%	Hamburg, Al	4,630	27.1%
	Mavy, Emmett A.	2,873	3.5%	Bryk, William	3,047	17.8%
	Scattered Write-In	279	0.3%	Scattered Write-In	222	1.3%
	TOTAL	*81,748*		*TOTAL*	*17,072*	
House At Large	Lummis, Cynthia M.*	73,153	98.1%	Henrichsen, Chris	16,259	98.9%
	Scattered Write-In	1,393	1.9%	Scattered Write-In	177	1.1%
	TOTAL	*74,546*		*TOTAL*	*16,436*	

Note: An asterisk (*) denotes incumbent.

DISTRICT OF COLUMBIA

DISTRICT OF COLUMBIA

DELEGATE

Elaine Holmes Norton (D). Reelected 2012 to a two-year term. Previously elected 2010, 2008, 2006, 2004, 2002, 2000, 1998, 1996, 1994, 1992, 1990.

POSTWAR VOTE FOR PRESIDENT

| | | Republican | | Democratic | | | | Percentage | | | |
| | | | | | | | | Total Vote | | Major Vote | |
Year	Total Vote	Vote	Candidate	Vote	Candidate	Other Vote	Rep.-Dem. Plurality	Rep.	Dem.	Rep.	Dem.
2012	293,764	21,381	Romney, W. Mitt	267,070	Obama, Barack H.*	5,313	245,689 D	7.3%	90.9%	7.4%	92.6%
2008	265,853	17,367	McCain, John S. III	245,800	Obama, Barack H.	2,686	228,433 D	6.5%	92.5%	6.6%	93.4%
2004	227,586	21,256	Bush, George W.*	202,970	Kerry, John F.	3,360	181,714 D	9.3%	89.2%	9.5%	90.5%
2000**	201,894	18,073	Bush, George W.	171,923	Gore, Albert Jr.	11,898	153,850 D	9.0%	85.2%	9.5%	90.5%
1996**	185,726	17,339	Dole, Robert "Bob"	158,220	Clinton, Bill*	10,167	140,881 D	9.3%	85.2%	9.9%	90.1%
1992**	227,572	20,698	Bush, George H.*	192,619	Clinton, Bill	14,255	171,921 D	9.1%	84.6%	9.7%	90.3%
1988	192,877	27,590	Bush, George H.	159,407	Dukakis, Michael S.	5,880	131,817 D	14.3%	82.6%	14.8%	85.2%
1984	211,288	29,009	Reagan, Ronald*	180,408	Mondale, Walter F.	1,871	151,399 D	13.7%	85.4%	13.9%	86.1%
1980**	175,237	23,545	Reagan, Ronald	131,113	Carter, Jimmy*	20,579	107,568 D	13.4%	74.8%	15.2%	84.8%
1976	168,830	27,873	Ford, Gerald R.*	137,818	Carter, Jimmy	3,139	109,945 D	16.5%	81.6%	16.8%	83.2%
1972	163,421	35,226	Nixon, Richard M.*	127,627	McGovern, George S.	568	92,401 D	21.6%	78.1%	21.6%	78.4%
1968	170,578	31,012	Nixon, Richard M.	139,566	Humphrey, Hubert H. Jr.		108,554 D	18.2%	81.8%	18.2%	81.8%
1964**	198,597	28,801	Goldwater, Barry M. Sr.	169,796	Johnson, Lyndon B.*		140,995 D	14.5%	85.5%	14.5%	85.5%

Note: An asterisk (*) denotes incumbent. **In past elections, the other vote included: 2000 - 10,576 Green (Ralph Nader); 1996 - 3,611 Reform (Ross Perot); 1992 - 9,681 Independent (Perot); 1980 - 16,337 Independent (John Anderson). Under the Twenty-third Amendment to the Constitution, the District of Columbia could choose presidential electors beginning with the 1964 election.

POSTWAR VOTE FOR DELEGATE

| | | Republican | | Democratic | | | | Percentage | | | |
| | | | | | | | | Total Vote | | Major Vote | |
Year	Total Vote	Vote	Candidate	Vote	Candidate	Other Vote	Rep.-Dem. Plurality	Rep.	Dem.	Rep.	Dem.
2012	278,563			246,664	Norton, Eleanor Holmes*	31,899	246,664 D		88.5%		100.0%
2010	132,656	8,109	Smith, Missy Reilly	117,990	Norton, Eleanor Holmes*	6,557	109,881 D	6.1%	88.9%	6.4%	93.6%
2008	247,741			228,376	Norton, Eleanor Holmes*	19,095	228,376 D		92.3%		100.0%
2006	114,777			111,726	Norton, Eleanor Holmes*	3,051	111,726 D		97.3%		100.0%
2004	221,213	18,296	Monroe, Michael Andrew	202,027	Norton, Eleanor Holmes*	890	183,731 D	8.3%	91.3%	8.3%	91.7%
2002	128,233			119,268	Norton, Eleanor Holmes*	8,965	119,628 D		93.0%		100.0%
2000	175,631	10,258	Wolterbeek, Edward	158,824	Norton, Eleanor Holmes*	6,549	148,566 D	5.8%	90.4%	6.1%	93.9%
1998	136,359	8,610	Wolterbeek, Edward	122,228	Norton, Eleanor Holmes*	5,221	113,618 D	6.3%	89.6%	6.6%	93.4%
1996	149,998	11,306	Simonds, Sprague	134,996	Norton, Eleanor Holmes*	3,696	123,690 D	7.5%	90.0%	7.7%	92.3%
1994	173,664	13,828	Saltz, Donald	154,988	Norton, Eleanor Holmes*	4,848	141,160 D	8.0%	89.2%	8.2%	91.8%
1992	196,574	20,108	Emerson, Susan	166,808	Norton, Eleanor Holmes*	9,838	146,700 D	10.2%	84.8%	10.8%	89.2%
1990	159,627	41,999	Singleton, Harry M.	98,442	Norton, Eleanor Holmes	19,186	56,443 D	26.3%	61.7%	29.9%	70.1%
1988	170,933	22,936	Reed, William	121,817	Fauntroy, Walter E.*	26,180	98,881 D	13.4%	71.3%	15.8%	84.2%
1986	126,855	17,643	King, Mary L.H.	101,604	Fauntroy, Walter E.*	7,608	83,961 D	13.9%	80.1%	14.8%	85.2%
1984	161,771			154,583	Fauntroy, Walter E.*	7,188	154,583 D		95.6%		100.0%
1982	112,543	17,242	West, John	93,422	Fauntroy, Walter E.*	1,879	76,180 D	15.3%	83.0%	15.6%	84.4%
1980	151,046	21,245	Roehr, Robert J.	112,339	Fauntroy, Walter E.*	17,462	91,094 D	14.1%	74.4%	15.9%	84.1%
1978	96,306	11,677	Champion, Jackson R.	76,557	Fauntroy, Walter E.*	8,072	64,880 D	12.1%	79.5%	13.2%	86.8%
1976	159,790	21,699	Hall, Daniel L.	123,464	Fauntroy, Walter E.*	14,627	101,765 D	13.6%	77.3%	14.9%	85.1%
1974	104,014	9,166	Phillips, William R.	66,337	Fauntroy, Walter E.*	28,511	57,171 D	8.8%	63.8%	12.1%	87.9%
1972	159,612	39,487	Chin-Lee, William	95,300	Fauntroy, Walter E.*	24,825	55,813 D	24.7%	59.7%	29.3%	70.7%
1971S	116,635	29,249	Nevius, John A.	68,166	Fauntroy, Walter E.	19,220	38,917 D	25.1%	58.4%	30.0%	70.0%

Note: An asterisk (*) denotes incumbent. **The 1971 election was held in March for a short term until the end of the 92nd Congress.

DISTRICT OF COLUMBIA

PRESIDENT 2012

2010 Census Population	Ward	Total Vote	Republican (Romney)	Democratic (Obama)	Other	Rep.-Dem. Plurality	Percentage			
							Total Vote		Major Vote	
							Rep.	Dem.	Rep.	Dem.
76,197	Ward 1	34,945	1,782	32,131	1,032	30,349 D	5.1%	91.9%	5.3%	94.7%
79,915	Ward 2	29,801	4,876	24,096	829	19,220 D	16.4%	80.9%	16.8%	83.2%
77,152	Ward 3	38,978	6,771	31,202	1,005	24,431 D	17.4%	80.1%	17.8%	82.2%
75,773	Ward 4	39,139	1,674	36,864	601	35,190 D	4.3%	94.2%	4.3%	95.7%
74,308	Ward 5	38,001	1,097	36,436	468	35,339 D	2.9%	95.9%	2.9%	97.1%
76,598	Ward 6	44,469	4,620	38,825	1,024	34,205 D	10.4%	87.3%	10.6%	89.4%
71,068	Ward 7	36,069	324	35,536	209	35,212 D	0.9%	98.5%	0.9%	99.1%
70,712	Ward 8	32,362	237	31,980	145	31,743 D	0.7%	98.8%	0.7%	99.3%
601,723	TOTAL	293,764	21,381	267,070	5,313	245,689 D	7.3%	90.9%	7.4%	92.6%

DISTRICT OF COLUMBIA

GENERAL AND PRIMARY ELECTIONS 2012

GENERAL ELECTIONS: OTHER VOTE

President   Other vote was 2,458 Statehood Green (Jill Stein), 2,083 Libertarian (Gary E. Johnson), 772 Write-in (Scattered Write-In)

Delegate   Other vote was 16,524 Libertarian (Bruce Majors), 13,243 Statehood Green (Natale Lino Stracuzzi), 2,132 Write-in (Scattered Write-in)

PRIMARY ELECTIONS: SUPPLEMENTARY INFORMATION

Primary	April 3, 2012	**Registration** (as of March 31, 2012)	460,134	Democratic	344,555
				Republican	30,286
				Statehood Green	4,155
				Other	1,441
				No Party Affiliation	79,697

Primary Type   Closed—Only registered Democrats and Republicans could vote in their party's primary.

	REPUBLICAN PRIMARIES			DEMOCRATIC PRIMARIES		
President	Romney, W. Mitt	3,577	70.1%	Obama, Barack H.*	56,503	97.4%
	Paul, Ron	621	12.2%	Uncommitted	1,100	1.9%
	Gingrich, Newt	558	10.9%	Scattered Write-In	386	0.7%
	Huntsman, Jon Jr.	348	6.8%			
	TOTAL	5,104		TOTAL	57,989	
Delegate	Scattered Write-in	769		Norton, Eleanor Holmes*	52,881	97.2%
				Scattered Write-In	1,474	2.8%
	TOTAL	769		TOTAL	54,355	

Note: An asterisk (*) denotes incumbent.